# STARGAZER

The
VideoHound
&
All-Movie Guide

# STARGAZER

DETROIT
NEW YORK
TORONTO
WASHINGTON, D.C.

# THE VIDEOHOUND & ALL-MOVIE GUIDE STARGAZER

ISBN 0-7876-0698-7

# Credits

## VideoHound

**Editors**
Martin Connors
Beth A. Fhaner
Kelly M. Cross

**Contributing Editors**
Terri Kessler Schell
Julia Furtaw

**Copywriter**
Sue Stefani

**Product Design Manager**
Cindy Baldwin

**Production**
Dorothy Maki
Evi Seoud

**Photo Editors**
Barbara Yarrow
Pam Hayes
Christine Tomassini

**Typesetter**
Judy Hartman, General Graphic Services

**And the VideoHound Staff**

## All-Movie Guide

**Editor**
Michael Erlewine

**Database Design**
Vladimir Bogdanov

**Assistant Editor**
Chris Woodstra

**Film Historians**
Hal Erikson
Bruce Eder

**And the All-Movie Guide Staff**

**Photos**
courtesy of The Kobal Collection

**A Cunning Canine Production**

# Contents

# Introduction

"Every now and then some elder statesman of the theater or cinema assures the public that actors and actresses are just plain folks, ignoring the fact that their greatest attraction to the public is their complete lack of resemblance to normal human beings." Theater critic Addison DeWitt (George Sanders) in *All About Eve* (1950).

"I am big! It's the pictures that got small." Norma Desmond (Gloria Swanson), in *Sunset Boulevard* (1950).

Arguably the most fascinating aspect of the movie industry is its human element. For nearly a century the personalities and players have held our gaze both on and off the screen—the starlets and studio moguls, the clowns and creative geniuses, the visionaries and victims. Our appetite for details on the range of celebrity triumph and scandal is both voracious and fickle. We love them and loathe them, applaud them and scathe them, admire them and judge them—and we don't even know them. The white-hot flash of fame distorts our view of film talent, and very often their view of themselves as well, leading everyone involved to forget that behind the glamour, power, money, and ego, they are, indeed, human beings.

From industry trailblazers and classic screen performers to today's hottest talent, *The VideoHound and All-Movie Guide StarGazer* represents a collection of biographical sketches on over 1,600 human beings who make the movies great. *StarGazer* covers Hollywood mainstream as well as influential independent and foreign film personalities—actors, directors, producers, screenwriters, special effects and make-up artists, cinematographers, choreographers, and composers lauded worldwide for their contributions to cinematic art. *StarGazer* pays tribute to the roots of film by featuring pioneers of vaudeville and the silent era such as D. W. Griffith, Lillian Gish, Rudolph Valentino, and Ernst Lubitsch; honors film's Golden Age with the inclusion of Frank Capra, Marlene Dietrich, Busby Berkeley, Samuel Goldwyn, and many others; and examines modern legends such as Woody Allen, Henry Mancini, Sophia Loren, and Audrey Hepburn. *StarGazer* maintains a contemporary edge with up-to-date information on current screen phenoms, including Brad Pitt, Quentin Tarantino, Demi Moore, and Sandra Bullock.

No book on movie people would be complete without a survey of who's who in foreign movies, and *StarGazer* includes profiles of personalities such as Pedro Almodovar, Klaus-Maria Brandauer, Gong Li, Akira Kurosawa, Krzysztof Kieslowski, and Satyajit Ray.

The selection of names was based on a variety of criteria, including the person's overall contribution to the film arts, current standing, and celebrity status (hot, not, up and coming). Like all books of this nature, events conspire to date the information; new movies are released, people die, and fresh personalities arrive. Additionally, the print medium imposes a space limitation; we very easily could have included another thousand biographies, but not in a single volume. We welcome suggestions on additional coverage and improvements, as well as corrections and criticisms.

Arranged alphabetically by last name, profiles begin with the listee's name, followed in parentheses by birth name (if different), birth and death dates, and biographical text. Each profile also contains a graph that prominently depicts the listee's active years in the industry by decade, and ends with a list of selected films (including recent releases) that are not previously noted in the text. More than 500 photos are included. To help you find information quickly, two indexes are provided. The Genre Index categorizes the artists by some 20 types of films in which they gained success or prominence, including action, adventure, drama, children, comedy, crime, action adventure, sex and sexuality, and thriller. On the lighter side, the Birthdate and Astrological Index invites the question, What's your sign?, classifying listees chronologically by date of birth, a unique dimension that provides insight into how the stars relate to the stars.

Read as individual entities, each *StarGazer* biography gives a concise summary of the person's life and work. Childhood events, big breaks, major accomplishments, trademark characteristics, awards, personal milestones, recent activities, and other pertinent details flesh out the image of a person whose talent, drive, looks, or simply good fortune earned him or her prominence in an industry where thousands remain faceless. Read as a collection, *StarGazer* reflects through the experiences of individuals the trends and themes that shaped filmmaking today—vaudeville as a showcase for talent; the advent of talkies adding a new dimension to star potential; the motives and tactics of a studio system that shaped images and controlled destinies; careers halted by the Communist scare, blacklists, and House Un-American Activities Committee; the rise of television as both a career launcher and an industry competitor. In range, diversity, and number, *StarGazer* represents the lore, grit, and delight that is filmmaking.

    *StarGazer* is the end result of a collaboration between Video-Hound and the All-Movie Guide. The basis of the partnership is a shared love of movies and the desire to create an informative and entertaining book for film fans, scholars, and critics alike. AMG, located in Big Rapids, Michigan, is run by a group of music and film enthusiasts, who, in addition to the *All-Movie Guide*, are responsible for the *All-Music Guide,* a definitive series on music recordings available on CD-ROM, online, and in print. Out of Detroit, Video-Hound is a collection of film buffs responsible for the best-selling annual, *VideoHound's Golden Movie Retriever*, and a large litter of other books and CD-ROMs on the topic of popular video. Both AMG and VideoHound appreciate hearing from you—comments, suggestions, criticisms, additions, and other topics near and dear.

Contact us at:

The All-Movie Guide
315 Marion Avenue
Big Rapids, MI 49307
Ph: (616) 796-3437
Fax: (616) 796-3060

VideoHound
c/o Visible Ink Press
835 Penobscot
Detroit, MI 48226
Ph: (313) 961-2242
Fax: (313) 961-6814

We hope you enjoy *StarGazer!*

Ann-Margret

Bud Abbott

Tim Allen
Sir Richard Attenborough

Charles Aznavour

# A

## Bud Abbott (William A. Abbott)

**Born:** October 2, 1895; Asbury Park, NJ
**Died:** April 24, 1974; Woodland Hills, CA

**Years Active in the Industry:** by decade

| 10ˢ | 20ˢ | 30ˢ | 40ˢ | 50ˢ | 60ˢ | 70ˢ | 80ˢ | 90ˢ |
|-----|-----|-----|-----|-----|-----|-----|-----|-----|
|     |     | ███ |     |     |     |     |     |     |

American comedian Bud Abbott was the tall, bullying member of the popular comedy team Abbott and Costello. The son of circus employees, Abbott entered show business as a burlesque show producer, then took to the stage himself as straight man for a number of comedians, finally teaming with fledgling comic Lou Costello in 1936. After working in burlesque, in radio and on Broadway, Abbott and Costello made their movie debut in *One Night in the Tropics* (1940). Their first starring picture was *Buck Privates* (1941), a box office bonanza which catapulted the team to "top moneymaker" status for the next fifteen years; in all, Abbott and Costello made 36 feature films. In 1951, Bud and Lou made their TV debut on *Colgate Comedy Hour,* and later that year starred in a widely distributed 52-week, half hour situation comedy series, *The Abbott and Costello Show.* After the team broke up in 1957, Abbott retired, but was compelled to revive his career due to income tax problems. He appeared solo in a supporting role on a 1961 *GE Theatre* TV drama, then made an unsuccessful comeback attempt as straight man for comedian Candy Candido. Abbott's last performing job was providing the voice of "himself" in a series of 156 *Abbott and Costello* animated cartoons produced for television by Hanna-Barbera in 1966.

## Walter Abel

**Born:** June 6, 1898; St. Paul, MN
**Died:** April 24, 1987; Essex, CT

**Years Active in the Industry:** by decade

| 10ˢ | 20ˢ | 30ˢ | 40ˢ | 50ˢ | 60ˢ | 70ˢ | 80ˢ | 90ˢ |
|-----|-----|-----|-----|-----|-----|-----|-----|-----|
|     |     | ███ |     |     |     |     |     |     |

A graduate of the American Academy of Dramatic Arts, American actor Walter Abel began his stage career in 1919, and made his first film in 1920. Tall and quietly dignified, Abel was well cast in several of the plays of Eugene O'Neill. His first talking picture role was as the industrious young bridegroom Wolf in *Liliom* (1930). Abel had a go at a romantic lead when he replaced Francis Lederer as D'Artagnan in the 1935 filmization of *The Three Musketeers;* but the film was dull and Abel's performance mannered, so thereafter he was more effectively cast in top supporting roles. With his performance as the prosecuting attorney in *Fury,* Abel established his standard screen image: The well-groomed, mustachioed professional man, within whom lurks a streak of barely controlled hysteria. In this guise, Abel was excellent as the dyspeptic newspaper editor in *Arise My Love* (1941) and as Bing Crosby and Fred Astaire's long-suffering agent in *Holiday Inn* (1942). Busier on stage and television than in films during the 1950s, Abel received extensive critical and public attention for his role as a doomed industrialist in the 1965 melodrama *Mirage.* Sent out by Universal to promote the film, Abel regaled talk-show hosts with the story of how his fatal plunge from a skyscraper was actually filmed. Also during this period, Abel was appointed president of the American National Theatre and Academy. Walter Abel's last screen performance was opposite Katharine Hepburn in *The Ultimate Solution of Grace Quigley* (1985). **Selected Works:** *Mr. Skeffington* (1944), *Hold Back the Dawn* (1941), *So Proudly We Hail* (1943)

## F. Murray Abraham

**Born:** October 24, 1939; Pittsburgh, PA

**Years Active in the Industry:** by decade

| 10ˢ | 20ˢ | 30ˢ | 40ˢ | 50ˢ | 60ˢ | 70ˢ | 80ˢ | 90ˢ |
|-----|-----|-----|-----|-----|-----|-----|-----|-----|
|     |     |     |     |     |     | ███ |     |     |

F. Murray Abraham is a gaunt, character actor. Born to Syrian and Italian parents and raised in Texas, he has worked in TV commercials and in Central Park productions of Shakespeare in

New York. He debuted off-Broadway in the musical *The Fantasticks* in 1967; he made his Broadway debut in 1968 in *The Man in the Glass Booth*. Abraham has done much additional work onstage. He made his onscreen debut in *They Might Be Giants* (1971), but appeared in films only sporadically until the mid-1980s. For his portrayal of the jealous composer Salieri in *Amadeus* (1983) he won the Best Actor Oscar and the Golden Globe Award, leading to much more film work later in the decade. **Selected Works:** *All the President's Men* (1976), *Last Action Hero* (1993), *Serpico* (1973), *Sunshine Boys* (1975), *Season of Giants* (1991)

# Jim Abrahams

**Born:** May 10, 1944; Milwaukee, WI

**Years Active in the Industry:** by decade

| 10s | 20s | 30s | 40s | 50s | 60s | 70s | 80s | 90s |
|-----|-----|-----|-----|-----|-----|-----|-----|-----|
|     |     |     |     |     |     | ■ | ■ | ■ |

Jim Abrahams grew up in Milwaukee, where his father was a partner in a real estate business with the father of Jerry and David Zucker; Abrahams and the Zuckers grew up together and influenced each other's tastes in film and TV. When Abrahams was 26 he hooked up again with the Zuckers, and they founded the comedic Kentucky Fried Theater in Madison, Wisconsin, the site of a large, progressive university; the show was a multimedia work combining live improvisational sketches with filmed satirical pieces. They moved to Los Angeles and entered movies when filmmaker John Landis spotlighted them in *Kentucky Fried Movie* (1977), a hit on the college and late-night cinema circuit. Having learned the rudiments of filmmaking while watching Landis, three years later they produced, directed, and wrote the disaster movie send-up *Airplane!* (1980); with only a $3.5 million budget, the film grossed almost $80 million. They went on from there to make other films in the vein of *Airplane!,* including the *Top Gun* parody *Hot Shots* (1991) and *Hot Shots! Part Deux* (1993). Each also did independent work. Abrahams first solo directing effort was *Big Business* (1988).

# Isabelle Adjani

**Born:** June 27, 1955; Paris, France

**Years Active in the Industry:** by decade

| 10s | 20s | 30s | 40s | 50s | 60s | 70s | 80s | 90s |
|-----|-----|-----|-----|-----|-----|-----|-----|-----|
|     |     |     |     |     |     | ■ | ■ | ■ |

Of Algerian/German parentage, Paris-born Isabelle Adjani was first seen in films when she was 14, after two seasons in amateur and semi-professional stage productions. At age 17, she was permitted to join the prestigious Comedie Francaise, where she drew excellent audience and critical response performing the Classics. In 1975, director Francois Truffault cast her as the tormented daughter of Victor Hugo in *The Story of Adele H*, which earned her an Oscar nomination and worldwide acclaim. Adjani has continued racking up excellent screen portrayals and industry awards ever since; one of her best performances in recent years was the title role in *Camille Claudel*, directed by Adjani's former longtime companion (and father of her son) Bruno Nuytten. In her private life, she is currently involved with the actor Daniel Day-Lewis and recently gave birth to their child. **Selected Works:** *Nosferatu the Vampyre* (1979), *Queen Margot* (1994)

# Percy Adlon

**Born:** June 1, 1935; Munich, Germany

**Years Active in the Industry:** by decade

| 10s | 20s | 30s | 40s | 50s | 60s | 70s | 80s | 90s |
|-----|-----|-----|-----|-----|-----|-----|-----|-----|
|     |     |     |     |     |     |     | ■ | ■ |

German director Percy Adlon was a product of state-run theatre, radio and television. It was in TV that he made a name for himself as an award-winning documentary filmmaker. His first non-documentary feature was *Celeste* (1981), an elegiac study of the relationship between Marcel Proust and his faithful housekeeper. Adlon continued in this same bittersweet nostalgic vein until his first international hit, *Sugarbaby* (1985), the unorthodox saga of the romance between overweight morgue attendant Marianne Sagebrecht and subway driver Eisi Gulp. He utilized the apparently limitless talents of actress Sagebrecht in two subsequent films, *Bagdad Cafe* (1988) and *Rosalie Goes Shopping* (1990). Adlon's style is sharp and incisive, but untainted by anger; he loves his characters no matter how offbeat, and conveys this love to the audience. **Selected Works:** *Five Last Days* (1982), *Salmonberries* (1994)

# Danny Aiello (Danny Louis Aiello, Jr)

**Born:** June 20, 1933; New York, NY

**Years Active in the Industry:** by decade

| 10s | 20s | 30s | 40s | 50s | 60s | 70s | 80s | 90s |
|-----|-----|-----|-----|-----|-----|-----|-----|-----|
|     |     |     |     |     |     | ■ | ■ | ■ |

An Italian-American character actor with a beefy physique, no-nonsense expression, and intimidating presence, Danny Aiello came to acting late in life, having been a bus driver, a transport labor official, night-club bouncer and (he claims) an occasional thief. He began performing at an improvisational night spot. As he was approaching middle age, he appeared in a regional theater production of Jason Miller's *That Championship Season,* for which he won a Most Outstanding Newcomer award. Aiello made his screen debut in *Bang the Drum Slowly* (1973), and went on over the next 15 years to play a succession of tough guys, cops, brutes, slobs, and "ordinary guys" in a wide variety of movies, but broke out of that mold when he portrayed Cher's suitor in *Moonstruck*

(1987). His first lead role came in the title part of *Ruby* (1992). He has also appeared frequently on Broadway, and in 1976 won a Theater World Award for his Broadway debut in *Lampost Reunion*. His work in TV movies includes *Family of Strangers* (1981), for which he won an Emmy. For his portrayal of a pizza parlor owner in Spike Lee's *Do the Right Thing* (1989) he received a Best Supporting Actor Oscar nomination. **Selected Works:** *Cemetery Club* (1993), *Mistress* (1991), *Once Around* (1991), *Pickle* (1993), *Professional* (1994)

## Anouk Aimée (Françoise Sorya Dreyfus)

**Born:** April 27, 1932; Paris, France

**Years Active in the Industry:** by decade

| 10s | 20s | 30s | 40s | 50s | 60s | 70s | 80s | 90s |
|-----|-----|-----|-----|-----|-----|-----|-----|-----|
|     |     |     |     |     |     |     |     |     |

The daughter of actors, actress Anouk Aimée, born Francoise Sorya (Dreyfus), began studying acting and dancing in childhood then debuted onscreen at age 14. Poet-screenwriter Jacques Prevert created a Juliet-like role for her in *The Lovers of Verona* (1949), in which she attracted much attention. Her feline, enigmatic screen presence was eventually utilized to good effect by such directors as Fellini and Lelouch; for her work in Lelouch's *A Man and a Woman* (1966) she won the British Academy Award as Best Foreign Actress and received an Oscar nomination. For *Leap Into Void* (1980) she won the Cannes Film Festival Best Actress award. From 1952-54 she was married to director Nico Papatakis. From 1970-78 she was married to actor Albert Finney, her fourth husband. **Selected Works:** *8 1/2* (1963), *Dolce Vita* (1960), *Leap into the Void* (1982)

## Chantal Akerman

**Born:** June 1950; Brussels, Belgium

**Years Active in the Industry:** by decade

| 10s | 20s | 30s | 40s | 50s | 60s | 70s | 80s | 90s |
|-----|-----|-----|-----|-----|-----|-----|-----|-----|
|     |     |     |     |     |     |     |     |     |

Unless you're a wine-and-cheese film critic or habitue of the arthouse circuit, you might not be familiar with Belgian filmmaker Chantal Akerman. A disciple of Jean Luc Godard, Akerman attended Brussels' INSAS film school and Paris Universite Internationale du Paris. She demonstrated her devotion to Godard with her first amateur short subject, 1968's *Saute Ma Ville* (*Blow Up My City*), which three years after its completion was entered in the Oberhausen festival. Working on the fringes of show business in New York in the early 1970s, Akerman became an enthusiastic participant in the avante garde film movement, putting her theories to good use in such European movie projects as *Jeanne Dielman 23 Quai de Commerce 1080 Bruxelles* (1975) (Ms. Dielman is Akerman's mother), *Tout la Nuit* (1982) and *Seven Women Seven Sins* (1986). Plot and continuity are unknown quantities in the films of Akerman, most of whose efforts concentrate on mundane everyday activities (the 1972 short *Hotel Monterey* consists entirely of shots of people walking in and out of a rundown New York hotel) or experimental compositions of light and architectural design, with detached, non-sequitur soundtracks underscoring the "action". **Selected Works:** *Akermania, Vol. 1* (1992), *Night and Day* (1992), *Portrait of a Young Girl at the End of The 1960's in Brussels* (1994)

## Eddie Albert (Edward Albert Heimberger)

**Born:** April 22, 1908; Rock Island, IL

**Years Active in the Industry:** by decade

| 10s | 20s | 30s | 40s | 50s | 60s | 70s | 80s | 90s |
|-----|-----|-----|-----|-----|-----|-----|-----|-----|
|     |     |     |     |     |     |     |     |     |

Born Edward Albert Heimberger, actor Eddie Albert has sustained a fifty-year career with numerous roles as a back-slapping good guy and best-friend-next-door, never getting the girl but on occasion landing a major role. Albert began as a circus performer, then switched to stage and radio work before his film debut in *Brother Rat* (1938), in which he excelled as the star pitcher for the baseball team of a small military college. He received Oscar nominations for *Roman Holiday* (1953) and *The Heartbreak Kid* (1972). Albert is perhaps best known to modern viewers as the co-star (with Eva Gabor) of the TV series *Green Acres*. He is the father of actor Edward Albert and is married to the Mexican-American actress Margo. **Selected Works:** *Body Language* (1992), *Butterflies Are Free* (1972), *Girl From Mars* (1991), *Guarding Tess* (1994)

## Alan Alda

**Born:** January 28, 1936; New York, NY

**Years Active in the Industry:** by decade

| 10s | 20s | 30s | 40s | 50s | 60s | 70s | 80s | 90s |
|-----|-----|-----|-----|-----|-----|-----|-----|-----|
|     |     |     |     |     |     |     |     |     |

The son of actor Robert Alda, Alan Alda grew up around vaudeville and burlesque comedians, soaking up as many jokes and routines as traffic would allow. The elder Alda had hoped that Alan would become a doctor, but the boy's inbred urge to perform won

out. A graduate of Fordham University, Alda first acted at the Cleveland Playhouse, then put his computerlike retention of comedy bits to good use as an improv performer with Chicago's Second City and an ensemble player on the satirical TV weekly *That Was the Week That Was.* His first film was *Gone Are the Days* (1963), adapted from the Ossie Davis play in which Alda had appeared on Broadway. Among Alda's many subsequent stage credits were the original productions of *The Apple Tree* and *The Owl and the Pussycat.* Most of Alda's films were critical successes but financial disappointments: he portrayed George Plimpton in the 1968 filmization of Plimpton's bestseller *Paper Lion* and was a crazed Vietnam vet (a role he'd undoubtedly turn down in later years) in the 1972 movie *To Kill a Clown.* Alda's "signature" performance was as wisecracking Army surgeon Benjamin Franklin "Hawkeye" Pierce in the TV series *M\*A\*S\*H,* which ran from 1972 through 1983. Intensely pacifistic, the series adhered to Alda's own attitudes towards warfare (he'd once been an ROTC member in college, but became physically ill at the notion of learning how to kill). During his *M\*A\*S\*H* hitch, Alda began auxilliary careers as a director and scriptwriter, winning numerous Emmy Awards in the process. He also developed a separate sitcom in which he did not star, 1974's *We'll Get By.* While still with *M\*A\*S\*H* in 1978, Alda took advantage of an unusually lengthy production break to star back-to-back in three films: *California Suite, Same Time Next Year* and *The Seduction of Joe Tynan.* In 1981, Alda made his theatrical-movie directorial bow with *The Four Seasons* (1981), a semiserious exploration of modern romantic gamesmanship; it would prove to be his most successful film as director, with subsequent efforts like *Sweet Liberty* (1986) and *Betsy's Wedding* (1989) running very distant seconds. Long associated with major political and social causes and well established both off-screen and on as a man of heightened sensitivity, Alda has occasionally delighted in going against the grain of his carefully cultivated image with nasty, spiteful characterizations in such films as *Crimes and Misdemeanors* (1989). **Selected Works:** *And the Band Played On* (1993), *Manhattan Murder Mystery* (1993)

# Robert Aldrich

**Born:** August 9, 1918; Cranston, RI
**Died:** December 5, 1983; Los Angeles, CA

**Years Active in the Industry:** by decade

| 10ˢ | 20ˢ | 30ˢ | 40ˢ | 50ˢ | 60ˢ | 70ˢ | 80ˢ | 90ˢ |
|-----|-----|-----|-----|-----|-----|-----|-----|-----|

Beginning in 1941 as a production clerk at RKO, Aldrich advanced to script clerk and assistant to various directors, including Renoir (*The Southerner*), Chaplin (*Limelight*), and Abraham Polonsky (*Force of Evil*), and to the position of associate producer. It was in early television that Aldrich became a screenwriter and director, and he made his debut in feature films in 1953. His television work, with its requirement to make the most of shots on very little time and budget, helped shape his subsequent movie work, which was characterized by a strong emphasis on violence. His pictures were honored at the Venice Film Festival (*The Big Knife*), earned the Italian Critics' Award (*Attack*), and the Best Director honors at the West Berlin Festival (*Autumn Leaves*). During the 1960s, Aldrich came into his own as a respected "money" director in Hollywood with *Whatever Happened To Baby Jane* and *Hush, Hush, Sweet Charlotte* (which he also produced), and *The Dirty Dozen.* The seventies saw a decline in his fortunes, but not his style, which was very much in evidence in *Emperor Of the North* and *Twilight's Last Gleaming.* He saw a return to commercial success in the early 1980s, and a sequel to his last film, *All The Marbles,* was under discussion at the time of his death in 1983.

# Jane Alexander (Jane Quigley)

**Born:** October 28, 1939; Boston, MA

**Years Active in the Industry:** by decade

| 10ˢ | 20ˢ | 30ˢ | 40ˢ | 50ˢ | 60ˢ | 70ˢ | 80ˢ | 90ˢ |
|-----|-----|-----|-----|-----|-----|-----|-----|-----|

A graduate of Sarah Lawrence University and the University of Edinburgh, American actress Jane Alexander first gained national fame for her Tony-winning performance in the 1965 Broadway play *The Great White Hope.* She repeated her portrayal of the white mistress of a turn-of-century black heavyweight boxing champ (played by James Earl Jones) for the 1969 film version of *Hope,* which served as her film debut and earned her an Oscar nomination. The actress' subsequent theatrical-feature appearances have often been short in duration, but long on dramatic impact: most memorable was her single scene as a terrified Republican party bookkeeper ("If you can get Mitchell, that would be *great!*") in *All the President's Men* (1976). Alexander made the first of two TV-special appearances as Eleanor Roosevelt in *Eleanor and Franklin,* telecast in two parts on January 11 and 12, 1976; this was followed by *Eleanor and Franklin: The White House Years* (March 13,1977). While she surprisingly did not win an Emmy for either of these superlative performances, she finally attained the award for her supporting appearance in 1981's *Playing for Time.* Her best-remembered television appearance was as the California housewife faced with the enormity of a nearby nuclear attack in *Testament* (1983), which was slated for PBS' *American Playhouse,* then redirected for a theatrical premiere—a move that enabled Alexander to receive her third Oscar nomination (the second was for 1979's *Kramer vs. Kramer*). On a lighter note, the actress was hilariously *outre* as Hollywood gossip columnist Hedda Hopper in the TV biopic *Malice in Wonderland* (1989). Well known for her diplomacy and her espousal of liberal causes, Alexander found herself in the position to exercise both of these traits when, in 1993, she was appointed chairperson of the beleaguered National Endowment for the Arts.

# Jason Alexander (Jay Scott Greenspan)

**Born:** September 23, 1959; Newark, NJ

**Years Active in the Industry:** by decade

| 10s | 20s | 30s | 40s | 50s | 60s | 70s | 80s | 90s |
|-----|-----|-----|-----|-----|-----|-----|-----|-----|
|     |     |     |     |     |     |     |     | ■ |

Most everyone who went to high school in Livingston, New Jersey with Newark-born Jason Alexander knew that the lad was destined to become a major actor. Though inclined to stoutness—and baldness—from age 16 onward, Alexander had such a commanding stage presence that he was invariably cast as the star in school plays, in roles ranging from romantic leads to elderly character parts. While attending Boston University, the 20-year-old Alexander was cast in the lead of the Stephen Sondheim Broadway musical *Merrily We Roll Along*, which might have made him an overnight star had it not closed almost as soon as it opened. Alexander's first film role was in 1981's *The Burning*; that same year he made his TV-movie bow in *Senior Trip*. By 1989, Alexander had two major industry awards to his credit: the Tony and Grammy, both for his participation in *Jerome Robbins' Broadway*. In 1990, he was cast as not-a-clue loser George Coztanza in the popular sitcom *Seinfeld* (the character was allegedly based on series co-creator Larry David). And in 1994, his voice could be heard each week on the USA cable network as the webfooted, sex-obsessed private eye hero of the animated cartoon series *Duckman*. **Selected Works:** *Coneheads* (1993), *I Don't Buy Kisses Anymore* (1992), *Pretty Woman* (1990), *White Palace* (1990), *Paper* (1994)

# Gracie Allen (Grace Ethel Cecile Rosalie Allen)

**Born:** July 26, 1902; San Francisco, CA
**Died:** August 28, 1964

**Years Active in the Industry:** by decade

| 10s | 20s | 30s | 40s | 50s | 60s | 70s | 80s | 90s |
|-----|-----|-----|-----|-----|-----|-----|-----|-----|
|     | ■ | ■ | ■ | ■ |     |     |     |     |

The daughter of a musical comedy performer, Frisco-born comedienne Gracie Allen joined her sisters on the vaudeville stage at the age of 3 1/2. After convent school, Allen returned to the family act, then at age 18 joined the Larry Reilly Stock Company. Quitting the Reilly troupe over a dispute about billing, Allen left show business to become a secretary. In 1922, she was introduced by her showbiz friends to struggling vaudevillian George Burns. After striking out professionally with several male partners, Burns was anxious to launch a boy-girl act. He and Allen toured small-time vaude-

ville with a routine largely borrowed from other performers. At the time, it was customary in boy-girl routines for the girl to play "straight" while the boy told the jokes, but as Burns would later claim, "They laughed at all of her questions but none of my answers." Burns wisely switched roles, allowing Allen to be the "funny one." Allen's stage character would ever after be the dumb-dora chatterbox who confounded Burns with her convoluted logic. Burns would react in exasperation to double the laugh, but learned early on that he couldn't indulge in any slapstick with Allen; the audience was firmly on her side, and wouldn't stand for any rough stuff. After three years of courtship, Burns finally convinced Allen to marry him in 1926 (it was her first marriage, his second). That same year the team graduated to the prestigious Palace Theatre with an act called "Dizzy"; later on they would score a bigger success with the Al Boasberg-written routine "Lambchops." While touring the British Isles in 1929, Burns and Allen made their radio debut with a 26-week BBC series. Back in New York, they began appearing in one-reel movie comedy shorts, first for Vitaphone, then Paramount. Rudy Vallee "discovered" the team for American radio in 1931; the next year, they costarred with Guy Lombardo on a weekly CBS program, quickly entering the realm of folklore with an extended running gag about Allen's "missing brother." With *The Big Broadcast* (1932), Burns and Allen inaugurated their feature-film career, first as guest stars and supporting players, and finally as leads in such programmers as *Many Happy Returns* (1934), *Love in Bloom* (1935) and *Here Comes Cookie* (1936). Though their film career had begun to peter out by the late 1930s, Burns and Allen were selected to costar with Fred Astaire in his first film without Ginger Rogers, *A Damsel in Distress* (1937). Here for the first time, the moviegoing public was treated to the terpsichorean skill of Burns and Allen, who not only kept up with Astaire, but at times matched him step for step. In 1939, mystery writer S. S. Van Dyne came up with a "Philo Vance" story idea titled *The Gracie Allen Murder Case.* While both Burns and Allen "appear" in the published version of the story, Allen alone starred in the 1939 film version, driving erudite detective Vance (Warren William) to distraction by referring to him as Fido Vance. Allen could get a bit trying without Burns around to rein in her insanity, but audiences were pleased with *The Gracie Allen Murder Case,* prompting MGM to concoct another Gracie Allen solo vehicle, *Mr. and Mrs. North* (1941). With the exception of a guest appearance in *Two Girls and a Sailor* (1944), the *North* film closed out Allen's movie career. She stayed busy in radio, and made headlines in 1940 when Burns concocted a nonsensical presidential campaign for Allen on the Surprise Party ticket. When their radio ratings began dropping in the 1940s, Burns changed their radio characterizations from young sweethearts to middle-aged parents (the couple had adopted two children in the 1930s); this transition was successful, and was carried over into the popular *Burns and Allen* TV series, which ran from 1950 through 1958. Plagued by illness and increasing stage fright, Allen decided to retire in 1958, a move that warranted a cover story in *Life* magazine. Burns continued performing without her, working with several partners (including Carol Channing) until he felt secure enough to go it alone. Comfortably retired for many years, Gracie Allen died in her sleep of a heart attack in August of 1964.

# Irwin Allen

**Born:** June 12, 1916; New York, NY
**Died:** November 2, 1991; Santa Monica, CA

**Years Active in the Industry:** by decade

| 10s | 20s | 30s | 40s | 50s | 60s | 70s | 80s | 90s |
|-----|-----|-----|-----|-----|-----|-----|-----|-----|
|     |     |     |     |     |     |     |     |     |

A one-time journalism student from New York, Irwin Allen went on to carve out a unique niche for himself in Hollywood as a maker of big-budget exploitation movies, which often made use of middle-level character stars and major actors in their declining years in vital supporting roles. After breaking into features with serious nature films such as *The Sea Around Us* and *The Animal World,* Allen turned to exploitation movies. Most of these were either relatively low budget titles that capitalized on bigger, better mega-hits (his *Big Circus* followed in the wake of DeMille's *The Greatest Show On Earth,* and Allen capitalized on both Disney's *20,000 Leagues Under The Sea* and Mike Todd's *Around The World In Eighty Days* with *Five Weeks In a Balloon* and *Voyage To The Bottom Of The Sea* respectively). Allen spent most of the 1960's producing a quartet of science-fiction television series (*Lost In Space, Voyage To The Bottom of the Sea, Time Tunnel, Land of the Giants*) and some lesser, failed pilots that primarily appealed to children, but in the 1970's re-emerged as the most prominent and flamboyant maker of disaster movies, including *The Poseidon Adventure, The Towering Inferno,* and *The Swarm,* all made on huge budgets and featuring all-star casts.

# Karen Allen

**Born:** October 5, 1951; Carrollton, IL

**Years Active in the Industry:** by decade

| 10s | 20s | 30s | 40s | 50s | 60s | 70s | 80s | 90s |
|-----|-----|-----|-----|-----|-----|-----|-----|-----|
|     |     |     |     |     |     |     |     |     |

Sweet, babyfaced American actress with a lopsided grin, Karen Allen trained for the theater in Washington, DC, and New York, then spent several years with an experimental theater company; she also worked in student films. Allen debuted onscreen in the hugely successful comedy *Animal House* (1977). Her breakthrough role was in her seventh film, Steven Spielberg's blockbuster *Raiders of the Lost Ark* (1981), in which she played Harrison Ford's sidekick and love interest. Her screen career since then has been uneven. Besides her film work, she has also appeared frequently onstage; for her Broadway debut in 1982 as Helen Keller in *Monday After the Miracle* she won a Theater World Award. **Selected Works:** *King of the Hill* (1993), *Malcolm X* (1992), *Sandlot* (1993), *Sweet Talker* (1991), *Wanderers* (1979)

# Nancy Allen

**Born:** June 24, 1950; Yonkers, NY

**Years Active in the Industry:** by decade

| 10s | 20s | 30s | 40s | 50s | 60s | 70s | 80s | 90s |
|-----|-----|-----|-----|-----|-----|-----|-----|-----|
|     |     |     |     |     |     |     |     |     |

Pretty, wholesome lead actress, with energy, freshness, and positivity, actress Nancy Allen took dancing classes from age four and attended New York's High School of Performing Arts. She became a model at age 15 and appeared in over 100 TV commercials. After playing a bit part in *The Last Detail* (1973) she got an agent and moved to Los Angeles to pursue a screen career. Her break came in her second movie, Brian De Palma's *Carrie* (1976), in which she played a bitchy high school student who torments the title character. She and De Palma married shortly thereafter, and she went on to appear in two more of his films, *Dressed to Kill* (1980) and *Blow Out* (1981). They were divorced in 1984, after which she remarried. **Selected Works:** *Robocop* (1987), *Robocop 2* (1990)

# Tim Allen

**Born:** June 13, 1953

**Years Active in the Industry:** by decade

| 10s | 20s | 30s | 40s | 50s | 60s | 70s | 80s | 90s |
|-----|-----|-----|-----|-----|-----|-----|-----|-----|
|     |     |     |     |     |     |     |     |     |

An alumnus of Western Michigan University, Tim Allen worked in an ad agency before giving standup comedy a try. His career momentum was interrupted by the 28 months he spent in jail after being arrested for attempted drug dealing in 1978. Allen came to prominence on the comedy club and talk-show circuit in the mid-1980s. His occasional appearances in the "Mr. Goodwrench" TV ads indirectly led to his starring role as Tim Taylor, a Bob Vila-type handyman, on the top-rated ABC sitcom *Home Improvement* in 1991. Allen has a reputation for courtesy and consideration on his set, though these qualities must have been sorely tested when his staff forgot to submit his name to the Emmy Award committee in 1994. Later that same year, Allen became a money-spinning movie star with his film debut in the runaway hit *The Santa Clause.*

# Woody Allen (Allen Stewart Konigsberg)

**Born:** December 1, 1935; Brooklyn, NY

**Years Active in the Industry:** by decade

| 10s | 20s | 30s | 40s | 50s | 60s | 70s | 80s | 90s |
|-----|-----|-----|-----|-----|-----|-----|-----|-----|
|     |     |     |     |     |     |     |     |     |

The quintessential New York filmmaker, Woody Allen began as a gag writer in newspapers, and first came to prominence when he began performing as a night club comedian in the early 1960s, where his understated humor and cynicism, coupled with his unique perspective as a misfit New Yorker brought him to the attention of talk-show bookers and record companies. After an initial

screen appearance in *What's New, Pussycat* in 1966, which he also wrote, Allen's penchant for absurd humor burst on the film world in 1966 with *What's Up, Tiger Lily?* in which he redubbed a Japanese spy-thriller with ridiculous dialogue and created a hit. His first full-fledged outing as director, *Take The Money And Run,* made use of many gags that Allen had worked out in his stand-up routines and various other venues. During the early 1970s, Allen found success as a maker of parodies of established film and literary genres, as well as conventions of the popular (*Bananas, Love And Death, Sleeper*). But it was with *Annie Hall* in 1977 that he struck cinematic gold, mining a wealth of material loosely based on his own personal life and his relationship with longtime co-star Diane Keaton, and ended up not only with a hit film but a brace of Oscar nominations, and Academy Awards for Best Picture, Best Director, and Best Screenplay. *Manhattan* (1979) was an attempt to repeat the earlier film in a more serious vein, and it was successful, but also revealed a darker side to Allen's work every bit as strong as his sense of humor, which audiences found off-putting. In between the two films, he had done the very serious drama *Interiors,* which owed much to Ingmar Bergman, whom Allen acknowledges as a major influence. Allen had a number of modestly proportioned comic successes in the 1980s, including *Broadway Danny Rose, Hannah and Her Sisters,* and *Zelig,* which proved especially popular with urban audiences if not universally accepted. His career progressed despite the absence of any film remotely as popular as Annie Hall—helped principally by the existence of a large cult audience for Allen's work and his ability to work within very strictly controlled budgets, a rare virtue in Hollywood of the 1980's—but the 1990s saw his career momentarily interrupted when his personal problems entered the public arena, amid a child custody battle between Allen and his longtime lover and leading lady Mia Farrow. He re-emerged with a lighthearted, release in 1993, *Manhattan Murder Mystery*, which in many respects took its lead from Annie Hall, even presenting Allen re-teamed with Diane Keaton. **Selected Works:** *Alice* (1990), *Crimes and Misdemeanors* (1989), *Husbands and Wives* (1992), *Radio Days* (1987), *Bullets over Broadway* (1994)

## Kirstie Alley

**Born:** Janurary 12, 1955; Wichita, KS

**Years Active in the Industry:** by decade

| 10s | 20s | 30s | 40s | 50s | 60s | 70s | 80s | 90s |
|-----|-----|-----|-----|-----|-----|-----|-----|-----|
|     |     |     |     |     |     |     | ■   |     |

Actress Kirstie Alley studied drama in her native Kansas, but then became an interior decorator. After some time living the wild life as a "biker chick" and cocaine abuser, she moved to California where she got her life back together in a rehabilitation clinic and embraced Scientology, which she still espouses. She debuted onscreen as Mr. Spock's Vulcan protegee in *Star Trek II: The Wrath of Khan* (1982), then gained much exposure in the epic TV miniseries *North and South.* The role which made her famous, however, was that of bar manager Rebecca Howe in the highly successful, long-running TV sitcom *Cheers.* She has displayed comedic talent in films, as well, particularly in the hit *Look Who's Talking* (1989); for a while in 1989, *Cheers* was the highest-rated TV show and *Look Who's Talking* was the top film. She is married to actor Parker Stevenson. **Selected Works:** *Sibling Rivalry* (1990)

## Nestor Almendros

**Born:** October 30, 1930; Barcelona, Spain
**Died:** March 4, 1992; Manhattan, NY

**Years Active in the Industry:** by decade

| 10s | 20s | 30s | 40s | 50s | 60s | 70s | 80s | 90s |
|-----|-----|-----|-----|-----|-----|-----|-----|-----|
|     |     |     |     | ■   | ■   | ■   | ■   |     |

After studying cinematography at Rome's Centro Sperimentale di Cinematografia, Almendros shot and directed documentaries in Cuba. Meeting with disfavor from the communist regime, he went to France in the mid-1960s and was director of photography for a series of major films by Eric Rohmer (*La Collectioneuse, My Night At Maud's, Claire's Knee, Chloe In The Afternoon*) and François Truffaut (*The Wild Child, Two English Girls, The Story Of Adele H., The Last Metro*). He has also lensed notable films for directors Monte Hellman (*Cockfighter*), Barbet Schroeder (*Ma"tresse, General Idi Amin Dada*), Terence Malick (*Days Of Heaven*), Robert Benton (*Kramer Vs. Kramer, Places In The Heart, Nadine, Billy Bathgate*), and Mike Nichols (*Heartburn*). In the 1980s Almendros also co-directed two provocative documentaries of repression in Castro's Cuba, *Improper Conduct* (with Orlando Jiminez-Leal) and *Nobody Listened* (with Jorge Ulla).

## Pedro Almodóvar

**Born:** September 25, 1951; Calzada de Clatrava, La Mancha, Spain

**Years Active in the Industry:** by decade

| 10s | 20s | 30s | 40s | 50s | 60s | 70s | 80s | 90s |
|-----|-----|-----|-----|-----|-----|-----|-----|-----|
|     |     |     |     |     |     |     | ■   |     |

In the mid 1970s Almodovar joined the theater group Los Goliardos and made numerous underground Super-8 shorts with them, starting in 1974 with *Dos Futas, Or Historia De Amor Que Termina En Boda* and *La Caida De Sodoma;* by the end of the decade he also wrote and directed the Super-8 feature *Folle, Folle,*

*Folleme, Tim* and the 16-mm *Salome*. In the early '80s, he made his first theatrical features, *Pepi, Luci, Bom Y Otras Chicas De Mont·n* (*Pepi, Luci, Bom And The Other Girls*) and *Laberinto De Pasiones* (*Labyrinth Of Passion*). He followed these outrageous sex farces with a series of provocative comedies starring Carmen Maura, which made him internationally famous: *Entre Tinieblas* (*Dark Habits*), *Qué Me Hacho Yo Para Merecer Esto?* (*What Have I Done To Deserve This?*), *Matador, La Ley Del Deseo* (*Law Of Desire),* and *Mujeres Al Borde De Un Ataque De Nervios* (*Women On The Verge Of A Nervous Breakdown*). His '90s films *Atame! (Tie Me Up! Tie Me Down!)* and *High Heels* have met with less favor, but Almodovar's wit and ferocity show no signs of mellowing. **Selected Works:** *Kika* (1994)

# Maria Conchita Alonso

**Born:** 1957; Cuba

**Years Active in the Industry:** by decade

| 10ˢ | 20ˢ | 30ˢ | 40ˢ | 50ˢ | 60ˢ | 70ˢ | 80ˢ | 90ˢ |
|-----|-----|-----|-----|-----|-----|-----|-----|-----|
|     |     |     |     |     |     |     | ■ | ■ |

Stunningly beautiful Cuban-born actress Maria Conchita Alonso emigrated with her family to Caracas, Venezuela when she was five years old; there she appeared in films and commercials while still a child. At age 14 she won the title of Miss Teenager of the World. Four years later, she became Miss Venezuela, going on to combine a successful modeling career with acting and making TV commercials; eventually, she starred in four Venezuelan films and appeared in ten Spanish-language soap operas. She moved to the United States in 1982, going on to make her English-speaking film debut in Abel Ferrara's *Fear City* (1984); though only a small part in a large cast, this led to a supporting role as Robin Williams's girl friend in *Moscow Hudson* (1986), which moved her up in the film world to the status of a co-star. **Selected Works:** *Teamster Boss: The Jackie Presser Story* (1992)

# John A. Alonzo

**Born:** June 12, 1934; Dallas, TX

**Years Active in the Industry:** by decade

| 10ˢ | 20ˢ | 30ˢ | 40ˢ | 50ˢ | 60ˢ | 70ˢ | 80ˢ | 90ˢ |
|-----|-----|-----|-----|-----|-----|-----|-----|-----|
|     |     |     |     |     |     | ■ | ■ | ■ |

A graduate of the Roger Corman school of fast-n-furious filmmaking, American cinematographer John A. Alonzo has been fortunate enough to be associated with some of the most significant films of the 1970s. He oversaw the photography of such classics as *Harold and Maude* (1971), *Sounder* (1972), *Lady Sings the Blues* (1972), and *Norma Rae*, and was co-photographer for *Close Encounters of the Third Kind* (1978). The ever-inventive Alonzo was the man whose 1974 *Chinatown* set the industry standard for the use of soft focus and saturated color to convey the "look" of the

1930s. He remained in demand into the 1980s and 1990s, shooting films as varied as the airborne actioner *Blue Thunder* (1981) and the cartoon/live action hybrid *Cool World* (1992). Thus far, Alonzo's only foray into film directing has been the engaging rock-n-roll comedy *FM* (1978). **Selected Works:** *Housesitter* (1992), *Innocent Victim* (1990), *Star Trek Generations* (1994)

# Robert Altman

**Born:** February 20, 1925; Kansas City, MO

**Years Active in the Industry:** by decade

| 10ˢ | 20ˢ | 30ˢ | 40ˢ | 50ˢ | 60ˢ | 70ˢ | 80ˢ | 90ˢ |
|-----|-----|-----|-----|-----|-----|-----|-----|-----|
|     |     |     |     |     |     | ■ | ■ | ■ |

Altman started out in the late 1950s with industrial films and low-budget teen-oriented features. After making numerous television shows, he returned to films in the late '60s. He won international attention in 1970 with his Army comedy *M*A*S*H*, a film which still sums up his strengths and weaknesses. On the plus side are his quirky casting sense and a gift for bringing out spontaneous revelations of character; a nuanced, detailed feeling for composition and atmosphere; a savage wit focused on the American experience. The minuses include knee-jerk liberalism rank with sexism and homophobia; overstated arguments and obvious symbolism; a fondness for cheap shots and easy laughs. The best and worst of Altman can be found in his sprawling tapestries of America: *Nashville, A Wedding, Short Cuts.* He's also a stern genre revisionist and has done brilliant work with the western (*McCabe And Mrs. Miller*), detective (*The Long Goodbye*), and crime films (*Thieves Like Us*). A prolific filmmaker who can resourcefully use a low budget, Altman filmed several plays with varying degrees of theatricality in the '80s, most notably *Come Back To The 5 & Dime, Jimmy Dean, Jimmy Dean* and *Secret Honor.* He is an invaluable presence in American film and has brought his special gifts and provocative slant to all his projects, big or small. **Selected Works:** *The Player* (1992), *Vincent and Theo* (1990), *Three Women* (1977)

# John Alton

**Born:** October 5, 1901; Hungary

**Years Active in the Industry:** by decade

| 10ˢ | 20ˢ | 30ˢ | 40ˢ | 50ˢ | 60ˢ | 70ˢ | 80ˢ | 90ˢ |
|-----|-----|-----|-----|-----|-----|-----|-----|-----|

Starting at MGM in 1924 as a lab technician, Hungarian-born John Alton became a cameraman within four years. For reasons of his own, Alton decided that better opportunities awaited him in South America rather than Hollywood. He was right: In 1937, he won the Argentine film industry prize for best photography. Back in Hollywood in 1940, Alton found that he couldn't rely upon his foreign reputation to secure a big-studio assignment. Setting his sights a bit lower, he wisely chose to work at Republic, a B-picture factory which prided itself on the excellence of its photography. Alton's subsequent work on Republic programmers and musicals did not go unnoticed; he signed on with MGM in 1949, and two years later won an Academy Award for his first Technicolor film, *An American in Paris.* Alton retired in 1960 after wrapping up work on *12 to the Moon,* to devote himself to writing books about photography.

# Don Ameche (Dominic Felix Amici)

**Born:** May 31, 1908; Kenosha, WI
**Died:** December 6, 1993; Scottsdale, AZ

**Years Active in the Industry:** by decade

| 10ˢ | 20ˢ | 30ˢ | 40ˢ | 50ˢ | 60ˢ | 70ˢ | 80ˢ | 90ˢ |
|-----|-----|-----|-----|-----|-----|-----|-----|-----|

Though his popularity rose and fell during his long career, American actor Don Ameche, born Dominic Amici in Kenosha, WI, was one of Hollywood's most enduring stars. He began his acting

career in college where he had been studying law. He had a natural gift for acting and got his first professional opportunity when he filled in for a missing lead in the stock theater production of *Excess Baggage.* After that, he forewent his law career and became a full time theatrical actor. He also worked briefly in vaudeville beside Texas Guinan. Following that he spent five years as a radio announcer. He made his screen debut in a feature short, *Beauty at the World's Fair* (1933). Following this, Ameche moved to Hollywood where he screen tested with MGM; they rejected him. In 1935, he managed to obtain a small role in *Clive of India* and this resulted in his signing a seven-year contract with 20th Century Fox. Ameche, with his trim figure, pencil-thin mustache, and rich baritone voice was neither a conventionally handsome leading man nor the dashing hero type. Instead he embodied a wholesomeness and bland honesty that made him the ideal co-lead and foil for the more complex heroes. He played supporting roles for many years before he came into his own playing the leads in light romances and musicals such as *Alexander's Rag Time Band* (1938), where he demonstrated a real flair for romantic comedy. In 1939, Ameche played the title role in the classic biopic *The Story of Alexander Graham Bell* (1939). The film was a tremendous success and for years afterwards, fans quipped that it was he, not Bell who invented the telephone; for a time the telephone was even called an "ameche." He continued working steadily through the mid-'40s and then his film career ground to an abrupt halt. He returned to radio to play opposite Frances Langford in the long-running and popular series "The Bickersons." During the 1950s, he worked occasionally on television. He began appearing infrequently in low-budget films during the '60s and '70s, but did not really make his comeback until 1983, when he was cast as a replacement for the ailing Ray Milland in the comedy *Trading Places.* The success of this film, brought Ameche back in demand. In 1985, the aging actor received a Best Supporting Actor Oscar for his work in *Cocoon.* He continued appearing in films until 1988. **Selected Works:** *Heaven Can Wait* (1943), *Alexander's Ragtime Band* (1938), *In Old Chicago* (1938)

# Dame Judith Anderson (Francis Margaret Anderson)

**Born:** February 10, 1898; Adelaide, Australia
**Died:** January 3, 1992; Santa Barbara, CA

**Years Active in the Industry:** by decade

| 10ˢ | 20ˢ | 30ˢ | 40ˢ | 50ˢ | 60ˢ | 70ˢ | 80ˢ | 90ˢ |
|-----|-----|-----|-----|-----|-----|-----|-----|-----|

Australian-born Dame Judith Anderson (she was knighted in 1960) was for nearly seventy years one of the foremost Shakespearian actresses of the stage, playing everything from Lady MacBeth to Portia to Hamlet (yes, Hamlet). In films, she was Cruella DeVil—over and over again. Perhaps this is an oversimplification, but it is true that movies seldom took full advantage of Anderson's versatility and rich speaking voice, opting instead to confine her to unsympathetic roles on the basis of her hard, cruel facial features. She made her first film appearance as an incongrously sexy temptress in 1933's *Blood Money;* seven years later, she essayed her most famous screen role, the obsessed housekeeper Mrs. Danvers in *Rebecca* (1940). For the rest of her career, she was apparently regarded by Hollywood as an alternate for Gale Sondergaard in roles calling for refined bitchiness. She played the New York society dragon who "keeps" weak-willed Vincent Price in *Laura* (1944), the sinister wife of tormented farmer Edward G. Robinson in *The Red House* (1948), the imperious Queen Herodias in *Salome* (1953) and the wicked stepmother of Jerry Lewis in *Cinderfella* (1960). Some of Judith Anderson's later film roles allowed her a modicum of audience empathy, notably the aged Sioux Indian matriarch in *A Man Called Horse*

(1970) and the High Priestess of the Vulcans in *Star Trek IV: The Search for Spock* (1984). **Selected Works:** *Cat on a Hot Tin Roof* (1958), *Ten Commandments* (1956), *King's Row* (1942)

# Lindsay Anderson

**Born:** April 17, 1923; Bangalore, India

**Years Active in the Industry:** by decade

| 10s | 20s | 30s | 40s | 50s | 60s | 70s | 80s | 90s |
|-----|-----|-----|-----|-----|-----|-----|-----|-----|
|     |     |     |     |     |     |     |     |     |

Born in India, and the son of a military officer, Lindsay Anderson emerged as a critic and journalist in the late 1940s and early 1950s, and became a major force in the reshaping of British cinema. With his calls for greater topicality and social awareness in British films, he—along with such figures as Tony Richardson—helped transform the image of British pictures from their post-World War II stodginess into a vital force in international films during the 1960s. Anderson began as a filmmaker in the field of documentaries during the late 1940s, and earned an Academy award in 1954 for his short *Thursday's Children,* and he subsequently worked as a director on television. He became a theatrical director in the late 1950s, and moved into feature film work in 1963 with *This Sporting Life.* This and his subsequent movies, including *If. . . , O Lucky Man!,* and *Britannia Hospital* (all of which starred Malcolm McDowell) are characterized by a grim view of English society, government, and their institutions, and a generally nihilist view of the world, coupled with disconcerting elements of realism. **Selected Works:** *Blame It on the Bellboy* (1992), *Chariots of Fire* (1981), *Glory! Glory!* (1990), *Prisoner of Honor* (1991)

# Dana Andrews (Carver Dana Andrews)

**Born:** January 1, 1909; Collinsville, MA
**Died:** December 17, 1992

**Years Active in the Industry:** by decade

| 10s | 20s | 30s | 40s | 50s | 60s | 70s | 80s | 90s |
|-----|-----|-----|-----|-----|-----|-----|-----|-----|
|     |     |     |     |     |     |     |     |     |

After hitching to Hollywood and spending several years working at a gas station, aspiring actor Dana Andrews was finally signed to a contract by Sam Goldwyn in 1940, debuting in *Lucky Cisco Kid* and going on to do much work in secondary roles for Goldwyn and Fox. Gradually, he received roles of greater importance, culminating in his work in *The Ox-Bow Incident* (1943) in which he played the target of a lynch mob. His career peaked in the mid-40s, after which his hard features and taciturn demeanor limited the roles he received. However, his reliability and versatility kept him in movies straight through the '90s. He also appeared on TV, including a stint on the soap opera *Bright Promise* (1969-72). **Selected Works:** *Ball of Fire* (1941), *Best Years of Our Lives* (1946), *Laura* (1944), *Walk in the Sun* (1946), *Crash Dive* (1943)

# Julie Andrews (Julie Elizabeth Wells)

**Born:** October 1, 1935; Walton-on-Thames, England

**Years Active in the Industry:** by decade

| 10s | 20s | 30s | 40s | 50s | 60s | 70s | 80s | 90s |
|-----|-----|-----|-----|-----|-----|-----|-----|-----|
|     |     |     |     |     |     |     |     |     |

A music-hall favorite since childhood, British entertainer Julie Andrews spent the war years dodging Nazi bombs and bowing to the plaudits of her fans. Thanks to her own talents and the

persistence of her performer parents, Andrews maintained her career momentum with appearances in such extravaganzas as 1947's *Starlight Roof Revue.* It was in the role of a 1920's flapper in Sandy Wilson's satirical *The Boy Friend* (1953) that brought Andrews to Broadway; who could resist this attractively angular young miss warbling such deliberately sappy lyrics as "I Could be Happy With You/If You Could Be Happy With Me"? Following a live-TV performance of *High Tor,* Andrews regaled American audiences in the starmaking role of cockney flower girl Eliza Doolittle in the 1956 Broadway blockbuster *My Fair Lady.* The oft-told backstage story of this musical classic, wherein producer Moss Hart mercilessly drilled Andrews for 48 hours in order for her to get her lines, her songs and her dialect in proper working order, is enough to dissuade anyone from thinking that Andrews was an Overnight Success. In 1957, Andrews again enchanted TV audiences in the title role of Rodgers and Hammerstein's musical adaptation of *Cinderella.* Lerner and Loewe, the composers of *My Fair Lady,* developed the role of Guinevere in their 1960 musical *Camelot* with Andrews in mind, and the result was another Broadway triumph, albeit never as profitable as *Fair Lady.* Though a proven favorite with American audiences thanks to her frequent TV variety show appearances (notably a memorable 1962 teaming with Carol Burnett), Andrews did not make a motion picture until 1964. As *Mary Poppins,* Andrews not only headlined one of Walt Disney's biggest moneymakers ever, but also won the Academy Award—a sweet compensation for having lost the Eliza role to Audrey Hepburn for the filmization of *My Fair Lady.* Andrews hoped that *Poppins* would not type her in goody-goody parts, and to that end accepted a decidedly mature role as James Garner's love interest in *The Americanization of Emily* (1964). However, Andrews' next film, *The Sound of Music* (1965) effectively locked her into "sweetness and light" parts in the minds of moviegoers. On the strength of the *Music* success, Andrews was signed to numerous Hollywood projects, but her stardom had peaked, and by the time she made the much-maligned *Darling Lili* (1970) for her director/husband Blake Edwards, she was perceived to be a has-been. Not that her talent had diminished, as witness her 1970s appearances in nightclubs and on her own weekly TV series, where she was better than ever. But Andrews was the victim of changing Hollywood tastes and mores; so far as the producers and the public was concerned, she was sentimental, sugary and old-hat. A strong comeback in 1978's *10* confounded these ney-sayers, as did Andrews' portrayals of such complex characters as the bitchy movie prima donna in *SOB* (1981), the female/male/female impersonator in *Victor Victoria* (1982), the frustrated multiple sclerosis victim in *Duet for One* (1986), and the grieving mother of an AIDs victim in *Our Sons* (1991). Working in recent years almost exclusively for husband Blake Edwards, Andrews may never be the world's biggest box office attraction again, but has definitely secured her reputation as an actress of unbounded versatility.

# Ann-Margret (Ann-Margaret Olson)

**Born:** April 28, 1941; Valsjobyn, Jamtland, Sweden

**Years Active in the Industry:** by decade

| 10s | 20s | 30s | 40s | 50s | 60s | 70s | 80s | 90s |
|-----|-----|-----|-----|-----|-----|-----|-----|-----|
|     |     |     |     |     |     |     |     |     |

Swedish-born actress Ann-Margret came to the US with her family at age 7, settling in a suburb of Chicago and later attending the drama department at Northwestern University. Despite an in-

nate shyness, Ann-Margret set out to become a musical entertainer, making her professional debut as a singer at age 17. Fortunately she was spotted by comedian George Burns, who hired her for his Las Vegas Show and arranged for several professional doors to be opened for his protegee. Ann-Margret's first film was *Pocketful of Miracles* (1961), in which she played Bette Davis' daughter; this was followed by a lead in *State Fair* (1962). The actress tended to be withdrawn when interviewed, which earned her the press corps' "Sour Apple" award as least cooperative newcomer. Luckily she was able to overcome this initial bad press via a show-stopping appearance at the 1962 Academy Awards telecast, which turned her into an "overnight" national favorite and encouraged the producers of *Bye Bye Birdie* (1963) to build up her role. Perhaps the best indication of Ann-Margret's total public acceptance was her appearance - as a cartoon! - on a 1963 episode of *The Flintstones* (she was "Ann Margrock." Re-

member?) Ann-Margret's career faltered in the mid-1960s thanks to a string of forgettable pictures like *Made in Paris* (1966) and *Kitten With a Whip* (1966); one of the few highlights of this period in her career was her appearance in Elvis Presley's *Viva Las Vegas,* which led to a very pleasant offscreen relation with The King. Her career in doldrums, Ann-Margret began marshaling a comeback in the early 1970s thanks to the tireless efforts of her husband and manager, former actor Roger Smith. Sold-out Las Vegas and concert performances were one aspect of Ann-Margret's career turnabout; the most crucial was her Oscar nomination for a difficult role in 1971's *Carnal Knowledge.* The comeback nearly ended before it began in 1972 when Ann-Margret was seriously injured in a fall during her Vegas act. With the help of physical rehabilitation and plastic surgery, not to mention the loving ministrations and encouragement of Roger Moore, the actress made a complete recovery and went on to even greater career heights. She won her second Oscar nomination for her bravura performance in the rock-opera film *Tommy* (1975), where in one of the high points of 1970s cinema erotica she sang a number while being drenched in chocolate sauce! Ann-Margret was equally impressive (though in a less messy manner) in such powerhouse TV movies as *Who Will Love My Children?* (1983) and *A Streetcar Named Desire* (1984). As vibrant as ever in the 1990s (and not set back too seriously by such disappointing projects as the 1992 film *Newsies*), Ann-Margret took a little time out of her packed schedule to write her 1993 autobiography, which managed to be quite revelatory about herself and her own personal demons while still maintaining courtesy and respect towards her show-business mentors and coworkers. **Selected Works:** *Twice in a Lifetime* (1985), *Grumpy Old Men* (1993), *Our Sons* (1991)

# Jean-Jacques Annaud

**Born:** October 1, 1943; Draveil, France

**Years Active in the Industry:** by decade

| 10s | 20s | 30s | 40s | 50s | 60s | 70s | 80s | 90s |
|-----|-----|-----|-----|-----|-----|-----|-----|-----|
|     |     |     |     |     |     |     |     |     |

French director Jean-Jacques Annaud received his training in the nuts-and-bolts aspects of filmmaking through his many army training films and TV commercials. Annaud's feature film debut, *Black and White in Color* (1976), an amusing but affectionate look at French national chauvinism which won an Oscar for Best Foreign Picture. Annaud's tastes have run to "long ago and far away" story material, though unlike his Hollywood contemporaries, he refuses to "pretty up" historical films with modern facial makeup and attractive clothing. We fully believe that his *Quest for Fire* (1981) took place 80,000 years ago amongst hirsute human beings just one step above primates; and we accept such big-name stars as Sean Connery and F. Murray Abraham as pasty-faced, gargoylish 14th century monks in Annaud's *The Name of the Rose* (1986). The director was honored with the French Cesar award for both of these productions, and would win a third Cesar for his outdoors adventure *The Bear* (1989). More recently, Annaud turned to stylish soft-core sexual matters with *The Lovers*, a 1992 adaptation of Marguerite Dura's novel concerning interracial romance in 1929 Indochina.

# Michelangelo Antonioni

**Born:** September 29, 1912; Ferrara, Italy

**Years Active in the Industry:** by decade

| 10ˢ | 20ˢ | 30ˢ | 40ˢ | 50ˢ | 60ˢ | 70ˢ | 80ˢ | 90ˢ |
|-----|-----|-----|-----|-----|-----|-----|-----|-----|
|     |     |     |     |     |     |     |     |     |

Antonioni entered motion pictures in 1942, contributing to the writing of Roberto Rossellini's *Una Pilota Ritorna*. He also wrote and assistant directed other films, and in 1947 completed *Gente Del Po,* his first film and the first in a series of short documentaries. With his first feature, *Cronaca Di Un Amore* ( *Story Of A Love Story*), he explored the loss of emotional connectedness between people and the displacement of human beings in the environment—themes that would dominate his entire career. His dramatic films of the '50s, usually focusing on women, gradually refined his technique. His breakthrough came in 1960 with the classic *L'Avventura,* in which a woman disappears while on a holiday and her friends search for her in vain. The film was tremendously influential both for its narrative freedom—the slow-paced story simply dissolves into irresolution—and for Antonioni's unsettling camera eye, which brought a stark unreality to landscapes both urban and natural. His approach to tempo, composition, and story became increasingly austere with *La Notte and L'Eclisse* (*The Eclipse*) —the latter, perhaps his greatest film, climaxes with a stunning montage of ordinary objects at a street corner. Antonioni's first color film, *Deserto Rosso* (*Red Desert*), brought a new expressive dimension to his work (even if he had to paint the trees to get the right look). *Blow-Up,* an open-ended mystery set in then-trendy London, was his first English-language film and an international success. But his American film *Zabriskie Point* failed in the States, and since the 1970s his career has been slowed by bouts of ill health and a paucity of financial backers. Yet all Antonioni's subsequent work, from the China documentary *Chung Kuo* to the dramas *The Passenger* and *Identification Of A Woman,* are distinguished by the clarity and purity of his vision.

# Michael Apted

**Born:** February 10, 1941; Aylesbury, Buckinghamshire, England

**Years Active in the Industry:** by decade

| 10ˢ | 20ˢ | 30ˢ | 40ˢ | 50ˢ | 60ˢ | 70ˢ | 80ˢ | 90ˢ |
|-----|-----|-----|-----|-----|-----|-----|-----|-----|
|     |     |     |     |     |     |     |     |     |

After directing British television in the late 1960's, Apted began helming theatrical features in 1973 with the transvestite drama *The Triple Echo,* adapted from H.E. Bates' novel. An eclectic director, Apted has done impressive work in comedy (*Continental Divide, Kipperbang*), mystery (*Agatha*), biopic (*Coal Miner's Daughter, Gorillas In The Mist*), thriller (*Gorky Park, Thunderheart*), and documentaries (*Bring On The Night, Incident At Oglala*). Apted is especially admired for his ongoing series of documentaries, which began in the mid 1960s when he assisted on a television documentary that interviewed fourteen seven-year-old children from a range of social classes. Apted has returned to look in on their lives at ages 14, 21, and 28, cutting his footage together for the 1984 theatrical feature *28 Up;* in 1991 he released *35 Up.* **Selected Works:** *Class Action* (1991), *Incident at Oglala: The Leonard Peltier Story* (1992), *Nell* (1994)

# Gregg Araki

**Born:** Not Available

**Years Active in the Industry:** by decade

| 10ˢ | 20ˢ | 30ˢ | 40ˢ | 50ˢ | 60ˢ | 70ˢ | 80ˢ | 90ˢ |
|-----|-----|-----|-----|-----|-----|-----|-----|-----|
|     |     |     |     |     |     |     |     |     |

Manhattan-based independent filmmaker Greg Araki appeared almost literally out of nowhere in 1991. That was the year that his first feature, *Long Weekend (o' Despair),* began making the festival rounds. Produced, directed, written, photographed and edited by Araki (for his own whimsically yclept Desperate Pictures Company), this very small-scale *Big Chill* derivation involved a group of recent college graduates, brooding over their futures during a woozy, boozy evening. Araki followed this modest effort with *The Living End* (1992), a freewheeling comedy/drama/road movie in which two young HIV-positive males embark on a "nothing to lose" fantasy binge. **Selected Works:** *Living End* (1992), *Doom Generation* (1995)

# Alfonso Arau

**Born:** January 11, 1932; Mexico City, Mexico

**Years Active in the Industry:** by decade

| 10ˢ | 20ˢ | 30ˢ | 40ˢ | 50ˢ | 60ˢ | 70ˢ | 80ˢ | 90ˢ |
|-----|-----|-----|-----|-----|-----|-----|-----|-----|
|     |     |     |     |     |     |     |     |     |

Mexican actor Alfonso Arau's first American film role was as bloodthirsty bandit Herrera in Sam Peckinpah's *The Wild Bunch* (1969), a role he would later parody (albeit with a straight face) in the 1985 comedy *Three Amigos*. U.S. filmgoers were by and large unaware that Arau had long been a popular vaudeville, theater and TV performer, and built his Mexican film reputation as an independent producer/director, beginning with 1967's *The Barefoot Eagle*. Arau reached the plateau of art-house idolatry when he decided to adapt a novel about the mystical aspects of gourmet cooking, written by his wife Laura Esquivel. The subsequent film, *Like Water for Chocolate* (1992), ended up as one of the most profitable foreign movies ever exhibited in America. **Selected Works:** *Posse* (1975), *Romancing the Stone* (1984), *A Walk in the Clouds* (1995)

# Denys Arcand

**Born:** June 25, 1941; Deschambault, Quebec, Canada

**Years Active in the Industry:** by decade

| 10s | 20s | 30s | 40s | 50s | 60s | 70s | 80s | 90s |
|-----|-----|-----|-----|-----|-----|-----|-----|-----|

Director-screenwriter Denys Arcand has not earned his place as one of Canada's premiere screenwriter-directors by sidestepping controversy. Arcand spent 9 years in Jesuit school before attending the University of Montreal where he studied history and made one film. He then began working for the National Film Board of Canada; his first feature documentary *On est au coton* (1970), a chronicle of the wretched conditions in the textile industry, was officially banned. His next political documentary *Gina* (1975) —also considered quite controversial—was based on his experiences making *On est au coton* and told a violent story of revenge concerning a stripper and a film crew attempting to film a documentary about the textile industry. Arcand's films did not gain renown until his internationally acclaimed *The Decline of the American Empire* (1986), a film chronicling the relationships and life views of a group of Quebec artists preparing to eat a gourmet meal together. The film won 9 Genies (the Canadian Academy Award), the 'Fipresci' at Cannes, and an Oscar nomination for best foreign language film. In one of his latest films *Jesus of Montreal* (1989), Arcand uses his trademark cynical humor to create a scathing portrait of a struggling group of Montreal actors who piously play Biblical figures at night in passion plays, and work in beer commercials and porno films during the day. Based

on a real actor's story, Arcand uses the tale to air his personal feelings about religious hypocrisy.

# Anne Archer

**Born:** August 25, 1947; Los Angeles, CA

**Years Active in the Industry:** by decade

| 10s | 20s | 30s | 40s | 50s | 60s | 70s | 80s | 90s |
|-----|-----|-----|-----|-----|-----|-----|-----|-----|

American lead and supporting actress Anne Archer is the daughter of B-movie actor John Archer, and actress Marjorie Lord, a former co-star on the sitcom *Make Room for Daddy*. Archer launched her own screen career in 1972's *Honkers* after studying theater arts at Claremont College and subsequently touring the nation with the production *Glad Tidings*. Though she has gone on to appear in a number of feature films, television shows and mini-series, Archer is best known for her portrayal of the perfect suburban housewife opposite Michael Douglas in the 1987 smash hit *Fatal Attraction*. During the early '80s, the actress temporarily retired from film to spend time raising her children. Following *Fatal Attraction* her career began to pick up speed and she has played a variety of roles in mainstream films. Most recently she appeared in *Clear and Present Danger* (1994). **Selected Works:** *Family Prayers* (1991), *Narrow Margin* (1990), *Question of Faith* (1993), *Short Cuts* (1993)

# Eve Arden (Eunice Quedens)

**Born:** April 30, 1912; Mill Valley, CA
**Died:** November 12, 1990; Beverly Hills, CA

**Years Active in the Industry:** by decade

| 10s | 20s | 30s | 40s | 50s | 60s | 70s | 80s | 90s |
|-----|-----|-----|-----|-----|-----|-----|-----|-----|

Actress Eve Arden made her stage debut in stock at 16. Her first New York appearance came in *The Ziegfeld Follies* in 1934. She appeared in two films billed under her real name, then began her screen career in earnest as Eve Arden in 1937. She specialized in comedic character and supporting roles, often playing the heroine's wisecracking but warmhearted buddy. She remained very busy onscreen through the early '50s. She was best known for her portrayal of the title character in the *Our Miss Brooks* series on radio and TV in the late '40s and '50s; in 1953 she won an Emmy for her work on the show. She later starred in the TV series *The Eve Arden Show* and *The Mothers-in-Law*. For her work in *Mildred Pierce* (1945) she received a Best Supporting Actress Oscar nomination. Her film work after 1960 was infrequent, though she appeared in five movies between 1975-82. She married actor Brooks West. She authored an autobiography, *The Three Phases of Eve* (1985). **Selected Works:** *Anatomy of a Murder* (1959), *Stage Door* (1937), *Dark at the Top of the Stairs* (1960)

# Alan Arkin

**Born:** March 26, 1934; New York, NY

**Years Active in the Industry:** by decade

| 10ˢ | 20ˢ | 30ˢ | 40ˢ | 50ˢ | 60ˢ | 70ˢ | 80ˢ | 90ˢ |
|-----|-----|-----|-----|-----|-----|-----|-----|-----|
|     |     |     |     |     |     |     |     |     |

Actor and director Alan Arkin began his entertainment career as a member of The Terriers, a folk music group. Later he joined Chicago's celebrated Second City improvisational comedy group where he attracted some attention. He debuted on Broadway in Carl Reiner's *Enter Laughing* in 1963, quickly earning critical raves. He went on to a number of Hollywood shows, both as an actor and as a director; he directed both the stage and screen version of Jules Feiffer's *Little Murders* (screen version, 1971), and later directed the film *Fire Sale* (1977). He debuted onscreen in the comedy *The Russians Are Coming, the Russians Are Coming* (1966), going on to play primarily comic roles in films, in which he is often cast as a loud, bumbling type; however, he has also played straight dramatic parts. He has written several children's books; he is also a songwriter as well as a photographer whose work has been exhibited. He has twice been nominated for Oscars, and won a New York Critics Award for his portrayal of an early Hollywood film director in *Hearts of the West* (1975). He is married to actress Barbara Luna, who appeared with him in *Fire Sale* and who wrote the screenplay for his film *Chu Chu and the Philly Flash* (1981). His son is actor Adam Arkin, who co-wrote the script for the elder Arkin's film *Improper Channels* (1981) and appeared with him in *Full Moon High* (1982). **Selected Works:** *Catch-22* (1970), *Heart Is a Lonely Hunter* (1968), *Indian Summer* (1993), *Rocketeer* (1991)

# Pedro Armendariz, Sr.

**Born:** May 9, 1912; Churubusco, Mexico
**Died:** June 18, 1963; Los Angeles, CA

**Years Active in the Industry:** by decade

| 10ˢ | 20ˢ | 30ˢ | 40ˢ | 50ˢ | 60ˢ | 70ˢ | 80ˢ | 90ˢ |
|-----|-----|-----|-----|-----|-----|-----|-----|-----|
|     |     |     |     |     |     |     |     |     |

A major star in his native Mexico since 1935, actor Pedro Armendariz came to the attention of North American audiences with his sensitive portrayal of a man ruined by greed in the film adaptation of John Steinbeck's *The Pearl* (1947). Thereafter, Armendariz was active on both sides of the border: several of his best-known Hollywood films, such as *The Fugitive* (1947) and *Three Godfathers* (1948), were directed by John Ford. It is difficult to assess which of the actor's film was his best, less difficult to pinpoint his worst. That would have to be *The Conqueror* (1956), a moron's-eye-view of the life of Genghis Khan starring John Wayne. While modern-day viewings of *The Conqueror* evoke loud laughter at its idiotic dialogue and overblown performances, the film's risibility is clouded by tragedy. The film was shot on location in Utah

not far from where the U.S. government was testing its atomic bombs. In the three decades following *Conqueror,* many of the people involved in the making of the film developed cancer, including John Wayne, Susan Hayward, Agnes Moorehead, Richard Boone, director Dick Powell...and Armendariz. Viewers who enjoyed Armendariz's final performance as witty Turkish spy Karim Bey in the James Bond picture *From Russia With Love* (1963) could not help but notice that the usually corpulent actor was far thinner than he'd been in such earlier films as *Captain Sinbad* (1963); the fact was that Armendariz was suffering from lymph cancer. Unwilling to suffer the lingering death that would be the fate of many of the *Conqueror* participants, Armendariz shot himself in his room at the UCLA Medical Center.

# Gilliam Armstrong

**Born:** December 18, 1950; Melbourne, Australia

**Years Active in the Industry:** by decade

| 10ˢ | 20ˢ | 30ˢ | 40ˢ | 50ˢ | 60ˢ | 70ˢ | 80ˢ | 90ˢ |
|-----|-----|-----|-----|-----|-----|-----|-----|-----|
|     |     |     |     |     |     |     |     |     |

Director Gillian Armstrong, considered one of Australia's five most important filmmakers, is notable for her depiction of Aussie culture during the '70s. She began her career at Swineb-

urne, the Melbourne film school where, in 1974, she graduated to the interim program of the Australian Film and Television school. Between 1973 and 1976 she directed a number of shorts and a documentary series. Her first feature film, *My Brilliant Career,* came out in 1979—it was the first Australian narrative film in 46 years to be made by a female director. Like much of Armstrong's work, the story is drawn from the experiences of women living in the bush, a once popular subject for Australian silent films. **Selected Works:** *Last Days of Chez Nous* (1992), *Little Women* (1994)

# Robert Armstrong

**Born:** November 20, 1890; Saginaw, MI
**Died:** April 20, 1973; Santa Monica, CA

**Years Active in the Industry:** by decade

| 10ˢ | 20ˢ | 30ˢ | 40ˢ | 50ˢ | 60ˢ | 70ˢ | 80ˢ | 90ˢ |
|-----|-----|-----|-----|-----|-----|-----|-----|-----|
|     |     |     |     |     |     |     |     |     |

Forever remembered by film buffs as the man who brought King Kong to New York, American actor Robert Armstrong was a law student at the University of Washington in Seattle when he dropped out in favor of a vaudeville tour. Learning by doing, Armstrong worked his way up to "leading man" roles in a New York stock company run by veteran character man Jimmy Gleason. Gleason's play *Iz Zat So?* led to a film contract for Armstrong, whose first picture was *The Main Event* (1927). The actor's stage training served him well during Hollywood's switchover to sound, and he appeared with frequency in the early talkie years, at one point costarring with Broadway legend Fanny Brice in *My Man* (1930). An expert at playing sports and showbiz promoters, Armstrong was a natural for the role of the enthusiastic but foolhardy Carl Denham in *King Kong* (1933). Armstrong enjoyed some of the best dialogue of his career as he coerced erstwhile actress Fay Wray to go with him to Skull Island to seek out "money, adventure, the thrill of a lifetime", and as he egged on his crew to explore the domain of 50-foot ape Kong. And of course, Armstrong was allowed to speak the final lines of this imperishable classic: "It wasn't the planes...It was beauty killed the beast." Armstrong played Carl Denham again in a sequel, *Son of Kong* (1933), and later played Denham in everything but name as a shoestring theatrical promoter in *Mighty Joe Young* (1949), wherein he brought a *nice* giant gorilla into civilization. Always in demand as a character actor, Armstrong continued to make films in the 1940s; he had the rare distinction of playing an American military officer in *Around the World* (1943), a Nazi agent in *My Favorite Spy* (1942), and a Japanese general in *Blood on the Sun* (1945)! In the 1950s and 1960s, Armstrong was a fixture on TV cop and adventure programs. Perhaps the most characteristic moment in Armstrong's TV career was during a sketch on *The Red Skelton Show*, in which Red took one look at Armstrong and ad-libbed "Say, did you ever get that monkey off that building?" **Selected Works:** *Fugitive* (1948)

# Edward Arnold (Guenther Schneider)

**Born:** February 18, 1890; New York, NY
**Died:** April 26, 1956; Encino, CA

**Years Active in the Industry:** by decade

| 10ˢ | 20ˢ | 30ˢ | 40ˢ | 50ˢ | 60ˢ | 70ˢ | 80ˢ | 90ˢ |
|-----|-----|-----|-----|-----|-----|-----|-----|-----|

Edward Arnold was a well known character actor in films. Arnold started acting on the New York stage and had a stint as a cowboy star in films from 1915-1919 for the Essanay Company. He returned to the screen in 1932 and worked steadily for almost 25 years. He was a versatile actor with a strong deep voice and wonderful jovial laugh who could portray portly authoritative types of either virtuous or vile bent. Some of his most memorable performances include Diamond Jim Brady in *Diamond Jim* (1935), twisted politician Jim Taylor in Frank Capra's classic, *Mr. Smith Goes to Washington* (1939) and his resplendent portrayal of Daniel

Webster in *All that Money Can Buy* (1941) which is arguably his most beloved. The much seen actor appeared in films right up until his death on April 26, 1956. **Selected Works:** *Devil and Daniel Webster* (1941), *Meet John Doe* (1941), *Mrs. Parkington* (1944), *You Can't Take It with You* (1938), *Ziegfeld Follies* (1946)

# Patricia Arquette

**Born:** April 8, 1968; Los Angeles, CA

**Years Active in the Industry:** by decade

| 10ˢ | 20ˢ | 30ˢ | 40ˢ | 50ˢ | 60ˢ | 70ˢ | 80ˢ | 90ˢ |
|-----|-----|-----|-----|-----|-----|-----|-----|-----|

Actress Patricia Arquette is the granddaughter of Cliff "Charley Weaver" Arquette, the daughter of character actor Lewis Arquette, and the sister of movie leading lady Rosanna Arquette. Inaugurating her own film career in the mid-1980s, Arquette came into her own with a gallery of fine portrayals in the 1990s. In 1993 alone, the blonde, willowy actress was seen as the hero's cousin/inamorta in *Ethan Frome*, the strung-out "heroine" of the road film/murder spree *True Romance*, and a faux college girl on the lam from the mafia in *Trouble Bound*. Patricia Arquette closed out 1994 with her sympathetic portrayal of Kathy O'Hara, the second wife of Hollywood's "world's worst director," in Tim Burton's *Ed Wood*. She married actor Nicolas Cage in 1995. **Selected Works:** *Indian Runner* (1991), *Wildflower* (1991), *Dillinger* (1991)

# Rosanna Arquette

**Born:** August 10, 1959; New York, NY

**Years Active in the Industry:** by decade

| 10ˢ | 20ˢ | 30ˢ | 40ˢ | 50ˢ | 60ˢ | 70ˢ | 80ˢ | 90ˢ |
|-----|-----|-----|-----|-----|-----|-----|-----|-----|

Actress Rosanna Arquette, the granddaughter of actor Cliff Arquette (aka "Charley Weaver"), was born into a theatrical family; her father was a founding member of the Committee, an improvisational theater troupe. As a youth she moved often with her family. At age 17 she appeared on the Los Angeles stage in *Metamorphosis*. Her family settled in Virginia, where she worked in local theater where she was spotted by a casting director. She soon had much work in TV movies in the late '70s. She debuted onscreen in *More American Graffitti* (1979). Her breakthrough came with her portrayal of condemned murderer Gary Gilmore's girlfriend in the TV movie *The Executioner's Song* (1982), which earned her much praise. That success led to a lead role in John Sayles's *Baby, It's You* (1983). She gained her greatest fame in the hit film *Desperately Seeking Susan* (1985), co-starring Madonna. From there she has maintained a steady screen career, usually playing kooky, offbeat, spacey, slightly eccentric women. She is the sister of actress Patricia Arquette. **Selected Works:** *After Hours* (1985), *Black Rainbow* (1991), *Wrong Man* (1993), *Pulp Fiction* (1994)

# Jean Arthur (Gladys Georgianna Greene)

**Born:** October 17, 1905; Plattsburg, NY
**Died:** June 19, 1991; Carmel, CA

**Years Active in the Industry:** by decade

| 10s | 20s | 30s | 40s | 50s | 60s | 70s | 80s | 90s |
|-----|-----|-----|-----|-----|-----|-----|-----|-----|
|     |     |     |     |     |     |     |     |     |

It is one of the great Hollywood paradoxes that American actress Jean Arthur, whose film specialty was glib, carefree, relaxed comic performances, was in real life taciturn, temperamental and as tense as a coiled spring. The daughter of a commercial artist, Jean became a model early in life, then went on to work in films. Whatever self-confidence she may have built up was dashed when she was removed from the starring role of *Temple of Venus* (1923) after a few days' shooting; according to some reports, the event left her close to suicide. It was the first of many disappointments for the young actress, who nevertheless persevered and by 1928 was being given costarring roles at Paramount Pictures. Jean's curious voice, best described as possessing a lilting crack, ensured her work in talkies, but she was seldom used to full advantage in the early 1930s. Dissatisfied with the vapid ingenue, society debutante and damsel-in-distress parts she was getting (though she was chillingly effective as a murderess in 1930's *The Greene Murder Case*), Arthur left films for Broadway in 1932 for the play *Foreign Affairs*. In 1934, she signed with Columbia Pictures, where at long last her gift for combining fast-paced verbal comedy with truly moving pathos was utilized to the fullest. She was fortunate enough to work with some of the most accomplished directors in Hollywood: Frank Capra (*Mr. Deeds Goes to Town* [1936], *You Can't Take It With You* [1938] *Mr. Smith Goes to Washington* [1939]), John Ford (*The Whole Town's Talking* [1935]) and Howard Hawks (*Only Angels Have Wings* [1937]). Equally fortunate was the willingness of her coworkers to be patient and understanding with Arthur, for she was mercurial in her attitudes, terribly nervous both before and after filming a scene—she often threw up after her scene was finished—and so painfully shy that it was a chore to get her to show up. Jean could become hysterical when besieged by fans, and aloof and nonresponsive to reporters. Many of her coworkers of this period, notably director Frank Capra and comedian Phil Silvers, were willing to forgive Arthur for her chaotic behavior, chalking it up to her crippling inferiority complex. In 1943, Arthur received her only Oscar nomination for *The More the Merrier* (1943), the second of her two great films of the '40s directed by George Stevens (*Talk of the Town* [1942] was the first). After her contract with Columbia ended, she tried and failed to become her own producer, then was signed to star in the 1946 Broadway play *Born Yesterday*—only to succumb to a debilitating case of stage fright, forcing the producers to replace her at virtually the last moment with Judy Holliday. Arthur only made two more films after that: Billy Wilder's *A Foreign Affair* (1948), and George Stevens' *Shane* (1952). She also played the lead in Leonard Bernstein's 1950 musical version of *Peter Pan,* which costarred Boris Karloff as Captain Hook. In the early 1960s, the extremely reclusive Arthur tentatively returned to show business with a few stage appearances and an ill-advised TV situation comedy, *The Jean Arthur Show* (she played an attorney), which was mercifully canceled before the 1966-67 season was half over. Surprisingly, the ultra-introverted Arthur decided to tackle the extroverted profession of teaching drama, first at Vassar College and then at North Carolina School of the Arts; one of her students at North Carolina remembered Arthur as "odd" and her lectures as somewhat whimsical and rambling. Retiring for good in 1972, she retreated to her ocean home in Carmel California, steadfastly refusing interviews until her resistance was broken down (but only a bit) by the author of a book on her onetime director Frank Capra. In the end, Arthur was totally alone and withdrawn from the world—perhaps as she'd always wanted to be. **Selected Works:** *Devil and Miss Jones* (1941), *Arizona* (1940)

# Dorothy Arzner

**Born:** January 3, 1900; San Francisco, CA
**Died:** October 1, 1979; La Quinta, CA

**Years Active in the Industry:** by decade

| 10s | 20s | 30s | 40s | 50s | 60s | 70s | 80s | 90s |
|-----|-----|-----|-----|-----|-----|-----|-----|-----|
|     |     |     |     |     |     |     |     |     |

Though not the first woman director, California-born Dorothy Arzner was for many years the best known, as well as the only female member of the Director's Guild of America. Publicity releases of the 1930s and 1940s tended to emphasize the so-called "masculine" traits in Arzner's background—she was a pre-med student at the University of Southern California and an ambulance driver during World War I. Her film career began with a clerical job for director William C. deMille. Arzner then became a film editor for Paramount Pictures' subsidiary Realart Films, working on many of the Bebe Daniels comedies. Director James Cruze was so impressed by Arzner's editing of the Rudolph Valentino picture *Blood and Sand* (1922) that he immediately engaged her to work on his *The Covered Wagon* (1923); one of Arzner's first screenplay credits was for Cruze's *Old Ironsides* (1926). In 1927, Arzner directed her first film, *Fashions for Women*. Two years later, she helmed her first talkie, the Clara Bow vehicle *The Wild Party* (1929). At the height of her fame in the 1930s, Arzner adopted "mannish" clothing and kept her hair cut short possibly as a defense mechanism against chauvinism. Despite her efforts to fit in with Hollywood's all-male hierarchy, latter-day historians insist upon imposing all sorts of feminist elements and subthemes upon Arzner's work. Certainly *Christopher Strong* (1933) and *Dance Girl Dance* (1940) contain a great deal of pro-female proselytizing. On the other hand, the leading character in Arzner's *Craig's Wife* is hardly a shining example of womanhood (or humanity, for that matter). Arzner left Hollywood in 1943 to direct training films for the Womens Army Corps. She retired from active filmmaking after the war due to ill health. During the 1950s and 1960s, she taught filmmaking at the Pasadena Playhouse. Among the festivals and organizations to bestow awards upon Dorothy Arzner were the First International Festival of Women's Films in 1972 and the Directors Guild of America in 1975.

# Hal Ashby

**Born:** 1936; Ogden, UT
**Died:** December 27, 1988; Malibu, CA

**Years Active in the Industry:** by decade

| 10ˢ | 20ˢ | 30ˢ | 40ˢ | 50ˢ | 60ˢ | 70ˢ | 80ˢ | 90ˢ |
|-----|-----|-----|-----|-----|-----|-----|-----|-----|
|     |     |     |     |     |  ■  |  ■  |  ■  |     |

As an editor in the 1960s, Ashby's credits include *The Loved One* and several of Norman Jewison's films, among them *The Cincinnati Kid* and *The Russians Are Coming, The Russians Are Coming* After associate producing Jewison's *The Thomas Crown Affair* and *Gaily, Gaily*, he directed his first film, the Jewison-produced *The Landlord*, in 1970. He made a series of provocative and original films throughout the '70s: the cult romantic comedy *Harold And Maude;* the Navy comedy/drama *The Last Detail;* the Beverly Hills satire *Shampoo;* the Woody Guthrie biopic *Bound For Glory;* the romantic-triangle drama of Vietnam veterans, *Coming Home;* and *Being There,* an adaptation of Jerzy Kosinski's allegorical satire. His '80s work was uneven; it includes television work and the Rolling Stones concert documentary *Let's Spend The Night Together.* **Selected Works:** *In the Heat of the Night* (1967)

# Dame Peggy Ashcroft

**Born:** December 22, 1907; Croydon, England
**Died:** June 14, 1991; London, England

**Years Active in the Industry:** by decade

| 10ˢ | 20ˢ | 30ˢ | 40ˢ | 50ˢ | 60ˢ | 70ˢ | 80ˢ | 90ˢ |
|-----|-----|-----|-----|-----|-----|-----|-----|-----|
|     |  ■  |  ■  |  ■  |  ■  |  ■  |  ■  |  ■  |     |

Educated at London's Central School of Speech and Drama, British actress Peggy Ashcroft made her West End theatrical debut in 1927. Within three years, she achieved fame with her performance of Desdemona opposite African American actor Paul Robeson's Othello. Thereafter, she appeared in the company of London's theatrical elite, most often costarring with Sir John Gielgud. Ashcroft made her film bow in 1933's *The Wandering Jew*, four years before her first Broadway appearance. In honor of her innumerable Shakespearean performances, Ashcroft was made a Dame Commander of the British Empire in 1956. Appearing very infrequently in films throughout most of her career, Ashcroft is best remembered for her movie roles in Hitchcock's *The Thirty Nine Steps* (1935) and the Audrey Hepburn vehicle *The Nun's Story* (1959). In 1984, the 77-year-old actress received the Academy Award for her portrayal of Mrs. Moore in David Lean's *A Passage to India.* When she did not appear at the Oscar ceremony, rumors began circulating that Ashcroft was terminally ill. In fact, Dame Peggy Ashcroft had six more years' worth of performances in her, culminating with her magnificent portrayal of a lifelong mental institution resident in the made-for-TV *She's Been Away* (1990). **Selected Works:** *Jewel in the Crown* (1984), *Madame Sousatzka* (1988), *Sunday, Bloody Sunday* (1971)

# Armand Assante

**Born:** October 4, 1949; New York, NY

**Years Active in the Industry:** by decade

| 10ˢ | 20ˢ | 30ˢ | 40ˢ | 50ˢ | 60ˢ | 70ˢ | 80ˢ | 90ˢ |
|-----|-----|-----|-----|-----|-----|-----|-----|-----|
|     |     |     |     |     |     |  ■  |  ■  |  ■  |

American supporting and occasional lead actor Armand Assante has been working in films, on stage and television since the mid-1970's but has yet to become a major star. The New York City born actor first studied at the American Academy of Dramatic Arts and then went on to a stage career. In 1974 he made his screen debut with a bit part in *The Lords of Flatbush*. Another unknown actor, Sylvester Stallone, was also in that picture; later Stallone would hire Assante to appear as his brother in his 1978 film *Paradise Alley*. Following that, Assante began to appear more frequently in a variety of films ranging from detective dramas, *I, the Jury* (1992) to light comedies *Private Benjamin* (1980) to sci-fi thrillers *Judge Dredd* (1995), in the latter, Assante again worked with Stallone. **Selected Works:** *Hoffa* (1992), *Mambo Kings* (1992), *Q & A* (1990), *Passion in Paradise* (1994), *Trial by Jury* (1994)

# Fred Astaire (Frederick Austerlitz)

**Born:** May 10, 1899; Omaha, NE
**Died:** June 22, 1987; Los Angeles, CA

**Years Active in the Industry:** by decade

| 10ˢ | 20ˢ | 30ˢ | 40ˢ | 50ˢ | 60ˢ | 70ˢ | 80ˢ | 90ˢ |
|-----|-----|-----|-----|-----|-----|-----|-----|-----|
|     |  ■  |  ■  |  ■  |  ■  |  ■  |  ■  |     |     |

Few will argue with the opinion that American entertainer Fred Astaire was the greatest dancer ever seen on film. Born to a wealthy Omaha family, young Astaire was trained at the Alvienne School of Dance and the Ned Wayburn School of Dancing. In a double act with his sister Adele, Fred danced in cabarets, vaudeville houses and music halls all over the world before he was twenty. The Astaires reportedly made their film bow in a 1917 Mary Pickford vehicle, and it's a matter of record that their first major Broadway success was *Over the Top* that same year. Fred and Adele Astaire headlined one New York stage hit after another in the 1920s, their grace and sophistication spilling into their social life, wherein they hobnobbed with literary and theatrical giants as well as millionaires and European royalty. When Adele married the British Lord Charles Cavendish in 1931, Fred found himself soloing for the first time in his life. As with many other Broadway luminaries, Astaire was beckoned to Hollywood, where legend has it his first screen test was dismissed with "Can't act. Slightly bald. Can dance a little." He danced more than a little in his first film, *Dancing Lady* (1933), though he didn't actually play a role and was confined to the production numbers. Later in 1933, Fred was cast as comic/dancing relief in the RKO musical *Flying Down to Rio*, which top-billed Dolores Del Rio and Gene Raymond. Astaire was billed fifth, just below the film's *female* comedy relief Ginger Rogers. Spending most of the picture trading wisecracks while the "real" stars pitched woo, Fred and Ginger did a very brief dance during a production number called "The Carioca." As it turned out, *Flying Down to Rio* was an enormous moneymaker—in fact, it was the film that saved RKO from receivership. Fans of the film besieged the studio with demands to see more of those two funny people who danced in the middle of the picture. RKO complied with 1934's *Gay Divorcee*, based on one of Astaire's Broadway hits. Supporting no one this time, Fred and Ginger were the whole show as they sang and danced their way through such Cole Porter hits as "Night and Day" and the Oscar-winning "The Continental." "She gave him sex and he gave her class" was the statement allegedly made by Katharine Hepburn in assessing the Astaire-Rogers appeal. Fred and Ginger were fast friends, but both yearned to be appreciated as individuals rather than a part of a team. After six films with Rogers, Astaire finally got a chance to work as a single in *Damsel in Distress* (1937) —which, despite a superb Gershwin score and topnotch supporting cast, was a box-office disappointment, leading RKO to reteam him with Rogers in *Carefree* (1938). After *The Story of Vernon and Irene Castle* (1939), Astaire decided to go solo again, and after a few secondary films he found the person he would later insist was his favorite female costar, Rita Hayworth, with whom he appeared in *You'll Never Get Rich* (1942) and *You Were Never Lovelier* (1946). Other partners followed, including Lucille Bremer, Judy Garland, Betty Hutton, Jane Powell, Cyd Charisse and Barrie Chase, but in the minds of moviegoers Fred Astaire would forever be linked with Ginger Rogers—even though a reteaming in *The Barkeleys of Broadway* (1949) seemed to prove how much they *didn't* need each other. Astaire set himself apart from other musical performers by insisting that he be photographed full-figure, rather than have his numbers "improved" by tricky camera techniques or unnecessary close-ups. And unlike certain venerable performers who find a specialty early in life and never vary from it, Astaire's dancing matured with him. He is in his fifties in such films as *The Band Wagon* (1953) and *Funny Face* (1957), but he has adapted his style so that he neither draws attention to his age nor tries to pretend to be any younger than he is. Perhaps his most distinctive characteristic was making it look so easy. We seldom get the impression that Astaire has worked like a trooper to get his effects—though of course he has. To the audience, it's as though he's doing it for the first time and making it up as he goes along. With the exceptions of his multi-Emmy award winning TV specials of the late 1950s and early 1960s, Astaire cut down on his dancing in the latter stages of his career to concentrate on straight acting. While he was superb as a troubled, suicidal scientist in *On the Beach* (1959) and was nominated for an

Oscar for his work in *The Towering Inferno* (1974) few of his later films took full advantage of his acting abilities (by 1976, he was appearing in *The Amazing Dobermans*!) In 1981, over a decade since he last danced in public, Astaire was honored with a Lifetime Achievement Award from the AFI. While this award usually was bestowed upon personalities who had no work left in them, Fred Astaire remained busy as an actor almost until his death. The same year as his AFI prize, Astaire joined fellow show business veterans Melvyn Douglas, Douglas Fairbanks Jr. and John Houseman in the movie thriller *Ghost Story*. **Selected Works:** *Easter Parade* (1948), *Holiday Inn* (1942), *Swing Time* (1936), *Top Hat* (1935), *Ziegfeld Follies* (1946)

# Mary Astor (Lucille Vasconsellos Langhanke)

**Born:** May 3, 1906; Quincy, IL
**Died:** September 25, 1987; Woodland Hills, CA

**Years Active in the Industry:** by decade

| 10s | 20s | 30s | 40s | 50s | 60s | 70s | 80s | 90s |
|-----|-----|-----|-----|-----|-----|-----|-----|-----|
|     | ■   | ■   | ■   | ■   | ■   |     |     |     |

Pressured into an acting career by her ambitious parents, Mary Astor was a silent film star before she was 17—a tribute more to her dazzling good looks than any discernible talent. Debuting in *The Beggar Maid* (1921), Astor was appearing opposite John Barrymore in 1923's *Beau Brummell* when she inaugurated another hallmark of her career—falling desperately in love seemingly at the drop of a hat. True, Barrymore did teach the actress valuable lessons about the art of acting and introduce her to such intellectual pursuits as art, literature, and poetry, but he also stole her heart. The affair had cooled by the time they starred together in *Don Juan* (1926), but if nothing else Astor came away with a better appreciation of her chosen profession, and matured into an intelligent and skillful actress. Anxious not to be a victim of the talking-picture revolution, the actress perfected her vocal technique in several stage productions for Edward Everett Horton's Los Angeles-based Majestic Theatre, and the result was a most successful talkie career. Things nearly fell to pieces in 1936 when, in the midst of a divorce suit, Astor's ex-husband tried to gain custody of the couple's daughter by making public a diary she had kept. In this volume, Astor lovingly detailed her torrid affair with playwright George S. Kaufman; portions of the diary made it to the newspapers, causing despair for Astor and no end of embarrassment for Kaufman. But Astor's then-current employer, producer Sam Goldwyn, stood by his star and permitted her to complete her role in his production of *Dodsworth* (1936). Goldwyn was touched by Astor's fight for the custody of her child, and was willing to overlook her carnal carelessness. Some of Astor's best films were made after the scandal subsided, including *The Maltese Falcon* (1941), in which she played the gloriously untrustworthy Brigid O'Shaughnessy opposite Humphrey Bogart's Sam Spade, and *The Great Lie* (1941), in which she played a supremely bitchy concert pianist (and won an Academy Award in the bargain). Seemingly getting better as she got older, Astor spent the final phase of her career playing spiteful or snobbish mothers, with one atypical role as murderer Robert Wagner's slow-on-the-uptake mom in *A Kiss Before Dying* (1956). A lifelong aspiring writer, Astor wrote two entertaining and insightful books on her career, *My Story* and *A Life on Film*. Retiring after the film *Hush Hush Sweet Charlotte* (1966), Astor fell victim to health complications and financial tangles, compelling her to spend her last years in a small but comfortable bungalow on the grounds of the Motion Picture Country House and Hospital. **Selected Works:** *Hurricane* (1937), *Meet Me in St. Louis* (1944), *Prisoner of Zenda* (1937), *Holiday* (1930)

## Sir Richard Attenborough

**Born:** August 29, 1923; Cambridge, England

**Years Active in the Industry:** by decade

| 10s | 20s | 30s | 40s | 50s | 60s | 70s | 80s | 90s |
|-----|-----|-----|-----|-----|-----|-----|-----|-----|
|     |     |     |     |     |     |     |     |     |

Actor, director, and producer Richard Attenborough, made his professional stage debut in 1941 at age 18. Early in his career, he tended to be typecast as a nervous, ineffectual men and low-ranking, cowardly soldiers (as the result of his appearance as that type in Noel Coward's film *In Which We Serve*), but soon broadened his range of characterizations to an impressive degree. Forming a partnership in the late '50s with actor-director-screenwriter Brian Forbes, he turned to producing; his directorial debut, *Oh What a Lovely War!*, appeared in 1969. He won the British Film Academy Award for Best Actor for his work in *Guns at Batasi* (1964), then went on to win the Best Director Oscar for *Ghandi* (1982). He was knighted in 1976. Since 1944, he has been married to actress Sheila Sim. **Selected Works:** *Gandhi* (1982), *Jurassic Park* (1993), *Shadowlands* (1993), *Miracle on 34th Street* (1994)

## Lionel Atwill (Lionel Alfred William Atwill)

**Born:** March 1, 1885; Croydon, England
**Died:** November 20, 1946; Santa Monica, CA

**Years Active in the Industry:** by decade

| 10s | 20s | 30s | 40s | 50s | 60s | 70s | 80s | 90s |
|-----|-----|-----|-----|-----|-----|-----|-----|-----|
|     |     |     |     |     |     |     |     |     |

British actor Lionel Atwill was born into wealth and educated at London's prestigious Mercer School, where he planned to pursue a career as an architect; instead, he became a stage actor, working steadily from his debut at age 20, most often in the plays of Ibsen and Shaw. Establishing himself in America, Atwill continued his stage work, supplementing his income with silent film appearances, the first being *Eve's Daughter* (1918). Atwill's rich rolling voice made him a natural for talking pictures. Following a pair of Vitaphone short subjects in 1928, the actor made his talkie bow in *The Verdict* (1932). Most effective in roles as an aristocratic villain, Atwill found himself appearing in numerous melodramas and horror films, including the classic *Mystery of the Wax Museum* (1933). Atwill's career was threatened in 1940, when it was revealed that he'd thrown an "orgy" at his home, complete with naked guests and pornographic films. Atwill "lied like a gentleman" to protect his party guests at the subsequent trial, and was convicted of perjury. The ensuing scandal made Atwill virtually unemployable at most studios, but he found a semi-permanent home at Universal Pictures, which at the time was grinding out low budget horror films. Lionel Atwill died in harness in the middle of production of the 1946 Universal serial *Lost City of the Jungle*; viewers watching this serial today will no doubt notice how often Lionel's character turns his back to the camera, allowing the producers to cover his absence with a stand-in. **Selected Works:** *Captain Blood* (1935), *Three Comrades* (1938), *To Be or Not to Be* (1942)

## René Auberjonois

**Born:** July 1, 1940; New York, NY

**Years Active in the Industry:** by decade

| 10s | 20s | 30s | 40s | 50s | 60s | 70s | 80s | 90s |
|-----|-----|-----|-----|-----|-----|-----|-----|-----|
|     |     |     |     |     |     |     |     |     |

While his name might suggest a birthplace somewhere in France—or at the very least Quebec—actor Rene Auberjonois was born in New York City. However, his well-to-do parents were of noble European blood, thus French was the language of choice in his household. Despite his first-born-American status, Auberjonois was shunned by many of his schoolmates as a foreigner, and teased for having a "girl's" name. As a defense mechanism, Auberjonois became the class clown, which somehow led naturally to amateur theatricals. The influence of such neighborhood family friends as Burgess Meredith and Lotte Lenya solidified Auberjonois' determination to make performing his life's work. He was cast in a production at Stratford (Ontario's) Shakespeare company by John Houseman—another neighbor of his parents'—and after moving with his family to England, Auberjonois returned to complete his acting training at Carnegie-Mellon University. There he decided to specialize in character parts rather than leads—a wise decision, in that he's still at it while some of his handsomer and more charismatic Carnegie-Mellon classmates have fallen by the wayside. Three years with the Arena Stage in Washington DC led Auberjonois to San Francisco's American Conservatory Theatre, of which he was a founding member. Movie and TV work was not as easy to come by, so the actor returned to New York, where he won a Tony for his Broadway role in the musical *Coco*. An introduction to director Robert Altman led Auberjonois to his first film, *M\*A\*S\*H* (1970), in which he introduced the character that would later be fleshed out on TV as Father Mulcahy (with William Christopher in the role). He worked in two more Altman films before he and the director began to grow in opposite directions. More stage work and films followed, then TV assignments; Auberjonois' characters ranged from arrogant dress designers to snooty aristocrats to schizophrenic killers on film, while the stage afforded him more richly textured roles in such plays as *King Lear* and *The Good Doctor*. In 1981, Auberjonois was cast as Clayton Endicott III, the terminally fussy chief of staff to Governor Gatling on *Benson*. Like so many other professional twits in so many other films, Auberjonois' job was to make life miserable for the more down-to-earth hero, in this case Robert "Benson" Guillaume. Blessed with one of the most flexible voiceboxes in show business, Auberjonois has spent much of the last two decades providing voice-overs for cartoon characters, notably Chef Louie in the Disney animated feature *Beauty and the Beast*. In 1993, Rene Auberjonois assured himself a permanent place in the hearts of "Trekkies" everywhere when he was cast as Odo (complete with understated but distinctive "alien" makeup) on the weekly syndicated TV show *Star Trek: Deep Space Nine*. **Selected Works:** *Petulia* (1968), *Player* (1992), *McCabe and Mrs. Miller* (1971), *Ballad of Little Jo* (1993).

# Mischa Auer (Mischa Ounskowski)

**Born:** 1905; St. Petersburg, Russia
**Died:** 1967

**Years Active in the Industry:** by decade

| 10s | 20s | 30s | 40s | 50s | 60s | 70s | 80s | 90s |
|-----|-----|-----|-----|-----|-----|-----|-----|-----|

Actor Mischa Auer was brought to America in 1920 by his grandfather, the violinist Leopold Auer, from whom he adopted his pseudonym. Auer began his career onstage, and was appearing in the Broadway play *Magda* when film director Frank Tuttle spotted him and offered a role in the silent *Something Always Happens* (1928). At first he only got minor roles as villains, then broke through comedically in *My Man Godfrey* (1936), after which he became known as a hyperactive, emaciated, goggle-eyed, English-language-fracturing Russian; he subsequently lit up the '30s and '40s comedies in which he appeared. Nominated for a Best Supporting Actor Oscar for his work in *My Man Godfrey*, he appeared in over sixty American films before moving to Europe and accepting many more roles there. **Selected Works:** *You Can't Take It with You* (1938), *Gay Desperado* (1936), *Hellzapoppin'* (1941), *Three Smart Girls* (1937), *One Hundred Men and a Girl* (1937)

# Jean-Pierre Aumont (Jean-Pierre Salomons)

**Born:** January 5, 1909; Paris, France

**Years Active in the Industry:** by decade

| 10s | 20s | 30s | 40s | 50s | 60s | 70s | 80s | 90s |
|-----|-----|-----|-----|-----|-----|-----|-----|-----|

Jean-Pierre Aumont was a tall, charming, blond and blue-eyed leading man, who became the archetype of the "continental" gentleman. Born into the French upper class (his father owned a chain of department stores, while his mother was a former actress), he leaped into theater at age 16, studying at the Paris Conservatory. He made his stage debut at 21 and his first film appearance a year later in *Jean de la Lune* (1931); his career really took off after he appeared in Cocteau's play *La Machine Infernal* in 1934, establishing his attractiveness as a leading man and prompting film-makers to demand his services. Following his appearance in Carne's classic film *Hotel du Nord* (1938), he put his career on the back burner in order to serve with the Free French forces in Tunisia, Italy, and France; a brave soldier, he was ultimately awarded the Legion of Honor and the Croix de Guerre. With France under Hitler's occupation, he moved to California in 1942, where his role in a stage production led to a contract with MGM. Cleverly utilizing his background, the studio assigned him the leads in *Cross of Lorraine* (1942) and *Assignment in Brittany* (1943), a film about the French resistance. His Hollywood career was fairly routine, and he returned to France after the war. However, he had become popular in the states, and continued to make occasional American TV, stage, and movie appearances into the '80s. The author of several plays, he also penned the autobiography *Sun and Shadow* (1976). A complex love-life produced marriages to French film actress Blanche Montel, whom he divorced, and Hollywood vixen Maria Montez, who died in 1951. He and Montez had a daughter, Tina (Maria-Christina) Aumont, who went on to become a film actress. An engagement to star Hedy Lamarr was broken off and followed by a marriage, divorce, and re-marriage to actress Marisa Pavan. His brother is French film director Francoise Villiers. **Selected Works:** *Day for Night* (1973), *Lili* (1953)

# Gene Autry

**Born:** September 29, 1907; Tioga, TX

**Years Active in the Industry:** by decade

| 10s | 20s | 30s | 40s | 50s | 60s | 70s | 80s | 90s |
|-----|-----|-----|-----|-----|-----|-----|-----|-----|

Gene Autry, the archetype of the guitar strumming, singing Hollywood cowboy, is one of American cinema's most beloved figures. Born Orvon Autry, his entry to showbiz has a story book quality. During the 1920s he was working as a telegraph operator when American folk hero Will Rogers overheard him singing and convinced him to give show business a try. By 1928 he was singing regularly on a small radio station. Three years later, he was starring in his own national radio show (*The National Barn Dance*) and making records for Columbia. He first made his mark in films starring roles in the 13-part Republic serial *Phantom Empire* (1935) and the movie *Tumblin' Tumbleweeds* (1935). Then he went on to make dozens of Westerns, usually with his famed horse Champion and his comic sidekick Smiley Burnette. He was the top Western star at the box office from 1937-42, and is the only Western actor ever to make the list of Hollywood's top ten attractions, an achievement attained in 1940, '41, and '42. His career was interrupted by service in World War II (he served as a flight officer), during which his place was supplanted at Republic by singing cowboy Roy Rogers. Between 1947 and 1954, now working for Columbia Pictures, Autry trailed behind Rogers as the second most popular western star. His films focus exclusively on action, with little romantic interest. Autry's special twist, though, was to pause from time to time for an easy-going song, creating a new genre of action films that is considered by film historians to constitute a revolution in B-movies (one that went on to have many imitators). As a recording artist, he had nine million-sellers; and as a songwriter, he penned 200 popular songs including the holiday classic "Here Comes Santa Claus." After 20 years as a singing cowboy, Autry retired from movies in 1954 to further his career as a highly successful businessman (among many other investments, he eventually bought the California Angels, a major league baseball team). However, he continued performing on television until the '60s. In 1978 he published his autobiography *Back in the Saddle Again*, titled after his signature song.

# John G. Avildsen

**Born:** December 21, 1935; Oak Park, IL

**Years Active in the Industry:** by decade

| 10s | 20s | 30s | 40s | 50s | 60s | 70s | 80s | 90s |
|-----|-----|-----|-----|-----|-----|-----|-----|-----|

Director John G. Avildsen's career has endured many ups and downs over the past thirty years. Not only has he produced a string of bombs, and low-budget films, the self-described dreamer has also produced some of the most popular films of our time— most notably the triple Oscar winning *Rocky* (1976) and the thematically similar *The Karate Kid* (1984). The son of a Chicago tool manufacturer, Avildsen worked as a copywriter at an ad agency; he then served as a chaplain's assistant in the military before coming to Hollywood in the early 60s where he first worked as a production manager, assistant director, and cinematographer before directing his first films—best forgotten according to some critics—in the late '60s. His first hit was the low-budget (he filmed it himself) sleeper *Joe* (1970), which told the tale of a bigoted construction worker and made a star of Peter Boyle. After the smashing success of *Rocky* the director did not have another major commercial hit until *The Karate Kid*, even though some of his films featured popular stars such as Burt Reynolds in *W.W. and the Dixie Dancekings*, Marlon Brando in *The Formula*, and John Belushi in his last film, *Neighbors*. He followed *The Karate Kid* with three sequels. In 1989 he created the fine drama *Lean on Me*, which showcased the talents of the charismatic Morgan Freeman. **Selected Works:** *Power of One* (1992), *Eight Seconds to Glory* (1994), *8 Seconds* (1994)

# George Axelrod

**Born:** June 9, 1922; New York, NY

**Years Active in the Industry:** by decade

| 10s | 20s | 30s | 40s | 50s | 60s | 70s | 80s | 90s |
|-----|-----|-----|-----|-----|-----|-----|-----|-----|

American writer/producer/director George Axelrod cut his teeth on scores of radio and TV scripts during the postwar era. He also penned a well-received 1947 novel titled *Beggar's Choice*. Axelrod's specialty was the packaging of sex farce together with social satire; he thrived both on stage and on films, though for many years the film versions of his works had to be watered down to accommodate the censors. A case in point was his 1954 stage play *The Seven Year Itch*, in which a middle-class husband has a brief affair while his wife and children are on vacation. In the 1955 film version, starring Tom Ewell and Marilyn Monroe, the husband merely fantasizes about the affair, which gets no farther than a clumsy pass and a pratfall. Axelrod was represented throughout the 1950s with such stage-to-screen hits as *Will Success Spoil Rock Hunter?* and such movie originals as *Phffft*. Oddly, when the old censorial walls began to crumble in the 1960s, Axelrod seemed to lose his touch, and his later works seem quaintly anachronistic. The best of Axelrod's 1960s output was *Lord Love a Duck* (1965), a quirky lampoon of Southern California lifestyles which he wrote, produced and directed. Axelrod also had success adapting the works of other writers for the movies, as witness *Bus Stop* (1956), *Breakfast at Tiffany's* (1961) and *The Manchurian Candidate* (1962). In 1971, George Axelrod composed his wry memoirs, *Where am I Now When I Need Me?*, then spent the next decade or so writing screenplays in England.

# Dan Aykroyd (Daniel Edward Aykroyd)

**Born:** July 1, 1950; Ottawa, Ontario, Canada

**Years Active in the Industry:** by decade

| 10s | 20s | 30s | 40s | 50s | 60s | 70s | 80s | 90s |
|-----|-----|-----|-----|-----|-----|-----|-----|-----|

Actor and screenwriter Dan Aykroyd got his professional start in his native Canada. Before working as a stand-up comedian in various Canadian nightclubs, Aykroyd studied at a Catholic seminary from which he was later expelled; he then worked as a train brakeman, a surveyor, and studied sociology at Carleton University in Ottawa where he began writing and performing comedy sketches. His success in school lead him to work with the Toronto branch of the Second City Comedy improvisational troupe. At the same time, he was also managing the hot nightspot Club 505. At this time, he met comedian and writer John Belushi who had come to Toronto to scout new talent for "The National Lampoon Radio Hour." Both Aykroyd and Belushi were chosen to appear in the first season of Canadian producer Lorne Michael's innovative comedy television series *Saturday Night Live* in 1975. It was there

that Aykroyd gained notoriety for his dead on impersonations of presidents Nixon and Carter. The show also allowed him to develop other popular characters such as Beldar, the patriarch of the Conehead clan of suburban aliens, and Elwood Blues, the second half of the Blues Brothers (Jake Blues was played by Belushi). He made his feature film debut in 1977 in the Canadian comedy *Love at First Sight,* but neither it nor his subsequent film *Mr. Mike's Mondo Video* were successful. His first major Hollywood screen venture was a co-lead in Spielberg's *1941* (1979). Aykroyd still did not earn much recognition until 1980 when he and Belushi reprised their popular SNL characters in *The Blues Brothers.* Following that success, he and Belushi teamed up one more time for *Neighbor's* (1981)—the next year Belushi died. As an actor, Aykroyd himself believes that he works best as part of a team and his subsequent films, such as *Ghostbusters* (1984), bear this out. During the 1980s he has appeared with some of Hollywood's foremost comedians, including fellow SNL alumni Chevy Chase, Bill Murray, and Eddie Murphy. He has also teamed up with the late John Candy, and Tom Hanks. In such pairings, Aykroyd usually plays the straight man, typically an uptight intellectual, or latent psycho. He tried his hand at drama in 1989 as Jessica Tandy's son in *Driving Miss Daisy* and for his efforts won an Academy Award nomination for Best Supporting Actor. As a screenwriter he has co-written many of his films, including *Blues Brothers* and *Dragnet* (1987). **Selected Works:** *Coneheads* (1993), *My Girl* (1991), *Sneakers* (1992), *This Is My Life* (1992)

# Lew Ayres

**Born:** December 28, 1908; Minneapolis, MN

**Years Active in the Industry:** by decade

| 10s | 20s | 30s | 40s | 50s | 60s | 70s | 80s | 90s |
|-----|-----|-----|-----|-----|-----|-----|-----|-----|
|     |     |     |     |     |     |     |     |     |

The son of a court reporter, actor Lew Ayres began his performing career upon high school graduation when he attempted to make a living as a banjo player. Ayres' college-boy good looks led to extra work in the movies, and before he was 21 the young actor

was starring opposite Greta Garbo in *The Kiss* (1929). Director Lewis Milestone, recognizing Ayres' natural talent and precocious self-confidence, cast Lew in the demanding role of disillusioned German soldier Paul Baumer in Milestone's *All Quiet on the Western Front* (1930), an intensely powerful anti-war film which went on to win an Academy Award. Ayres was superb, but his gentle demeanor and callow handsomeness resulted in his being stereotyped in film roles as a spoiled rich boy (though one of these roles, as Katharine Hepburn's perennially drunken younger brother in *Holiday* [1938], was among Lew's best work). The actor's star status was boosted in 1938 when he was hired to play Dr. Kildare in MGM's long-running series of Kildare "B" pictures. After appearing in nine *Kildare* films, Ayres declared himself a conscientious objector and refused to bear weapons when called upon to serve in World War II; the actor was publicly perceived to be a coward, and MGM dropped his contract. After the war, the public learned of Ayres' bravery under fire as a non-combatant medical corpsman, and he was permitted to resume his career. Ayres continued to work in character roles throughout the 1950s, 1960s, 1970s and 1980s; he even portrayed one of Mary Richards' dates (!) on a 1976 episode of *The Mary Tyler Moore Show.* As active socially as he was professionally, Ayres has been married three times; his second wife was none other than Ginger Rogers. **Selected Works:** *Johnny Belinda* (1948), *State Fair* (1933)

# Charles Aznavour

**Born:** May 21, 1924; Paris, France

**Years Active in the Industry:** by decade

| 10s | 20s | 30s | 40s | 50s | 60s | 70s | 80s | 90s |
|-----|-----|-----|-----|-----|-----|-----|-----|-----|
|     |     |     |     |     |     |     |     |     |

Born in Paris to an Armenian family, sad-eyed, sinewy singer/composer Charles Aznavour started performing as a dancer at age nine. During the 1950s, Aznavour rose to stardom as a soulful interpreter of melancholy romance ballads. Many filmgoers assume that his film debut was as the gangster-obsessed musician in Truffault's *Shoot the Piano Player* (1962), but in fact Aznavour made his first film, *Le Tete Contre les Murs,* in 1959. Many of his movie roles have been in the same noirish vein as his *Piano Player* performance; in the 1975 remake of *Ten Little Indians,* he was on screen only long enough to brood over his miserable past and sing a sad refrain before he is poisoned. Busy in films as both performer and composer into the late 1980s, Aznavour is the sort of wordly, hard-shelled performer who'd seem naked without a cigarette dangling from his lips and a half-consumed drink on the top of the piano. **Selected Works:** *Tin Drum* (1979)

## Lauren Bacall (Betty Jean Perske)

**Born:** September 16, 1924; Bronx, NY

**Years Active in the Industry:** by decade

| 10s | 20s | 30s | 40s | 50s | 60s | 70s | 80s | 90s |
|-----|-----|-----|-----|-----|-----|-----|-----|-----|

Following study at the American Academy of Dramatic Art and subsequent stage and modeling experience, American actress Lauren Bacall gained nationwide attention by posing for a 1943 cover of *Look* magazine.

This photo prompted film director Howard Hawks to put her under personal contract; it was his wish to "create" a movie star from fresh, raw material. For her screen debut Hawks cast Bacall opposite Humphrey Bogart in *To Have and Have Not* (1944). The young actress was so nervous that she walked around with her chin pressed against her collarbone to keep from shaking. As a result, she had to glance upward every time she spoke, an affectation which came across as sexy and alluring, earning Bacall the nickname "The Look." She also spoke in a deep, throaty manner, effectively obscuring the fact that she was only 19 years old. Thanks to the diligence of Hawks and his crew, and the actress' unique delivery of such lines as "If you want anything, just whistle...", Bacall found herself lauded as the most sensational newcomer of 1944. She also found herself in love with Humphrey Bogart, whom she subsequently married. Bogart, a legendary drinker and carouser whose previous three marriages had fallen apart in full view of the public, smoothed out many of his worst characteristics out of respect for his young wife; he still partied into the night, but his alcoholic intake diminished, and he even submitted to hormone shots in order to become a father (and a good one). Bogie and Bacall costarred in three more films, which increased her popularity but also led critics to suggest that she was incapable of carrying a picture on her own. Bacall's disappointing solo turn in *Confidential Agent* (1945) seemed to confirm this, but the actress was a quick study and good listener, and before long she was turning in first-rate performances in such films as *Young Man with a Horn* (1950) and *How to Marry a Millionaire* (1953). Bogart's death in 1957 after a long and painful bout with cancer left Bacall personally devastated, though in the tradition of her show-must-go-on husband she continued to give of her best in films like *Designing Woman* (1957) and *The Gift of Love* (1958). Bacall's second marriage to another hardcase actor, Jason Robards Jr., wasn't anywhere near as happy as her first, and this domestic dilemma coupled with a handful of negligible film roles led to the actress' dropping out of moviemaking in the late 1960s. In 1970, Bacall made a triumphant comeback in the stage production *Applause*, a musical adaptation of *All About Eve* in which she played the Bette Davis part. Her sultry-vixen persona long in the past, Bacall spent the 1970s playing variations on her worldly, resourceful *Applause* role, sometimes merely being decorative (*Murder on the Orient Express* [1974]) but most often delivering class-A work (*The Shootist* [1976]). After playing the quasi-autobiographical part of a legendary, outspoken Broadway actress in 1981's *The Fan*, she spent the next ten years portraying Lauren Bacall - and no one did it better. In 1993, Bacall proved once more that she was a superb actress and not merely a "professional personality" in the made-for-cable film *The Portrait*, in which she and her *Designing Woman* costar Gregory Peck played a still-amorous elderly couple. **Selected Works:** *Key Largo* (1948), *Misery* (1990), *Written on the Wind* (1956)

## Jim Backus (James Gilmore Backus)

**Born:** February 25, 1913; Cleveland, OH
**Died:** July 3, 1989

**Years Active in the Industry:** by decade

| 10ˢ | 20ˢ | 30ˢ | 40ˢ | 50ˢ | 60ˢ | 70ˢ | 80ˢ | 90ˢ |
|-----|-----|-----|-----|-----|-----|-----|-----|-----|

Jowly, heavily-browed character actor in both serious and comic roles, Jim Backus began his career in vaudeville, radio, and theater after graduating from the American Academy of Dramatic Arts in 1933. Other than a 1942 appearance (in *The Pied Piper*), he did not begin his film career until 1949 when he made three pictures including Bob Hope's *The Great Lover*. Backus then went on to scores of roles, most memorably as James Dean's weakling father in *Rebel Without a Cause* (1955). He is best known for his character of snobby east coast millionaire Thurston Howell III ("world's richest man") in the mid-60s TV sitcom *Gilligan's Island*, and for providing the voice for the animated Mr. Magoo, a myopic innocent, in UPA cartoons of the '50s. In addition to acting, Backus also penned several books (some co-written with his wife), beginning with the autobiography *Rocks on the Roof* (1958). A victim of Parkinson's disease, Backus nevertheless lived to be 76. **Selected Works:** *Man of a Thousand Faces* (1957)

# Kevin Bacon

**Born:** July 8, 1958; Philadelphia, PA

**Years Active in the Industry:** by decade

| 10ˢ | 20ˢ | 30ˢ | 40ˢ | 50ˢ | 60ˢ | 70ˢ | 80ˢ | 90ˢ |
|-----|-----|-----|-----|-----|-----|-----|-----|-----|

Kevin Bacon's training began with the Manning Street Actor's Theatre in Philadelphia. His first film, at age 20, was *National Lampoon's Animal House*, while his first regular TV work was on the soap opera *The Guiding Light*. Bacon entered the teen-idol category with his leading role in 1984's *Footloose*. He periodically returned to the stage, winning an Obie Award for the off-Broadway play *Forty Deuce*. After several iffy movie vehicles, Bacon discovered that his weight as an actor more effectively fell in colorful secondary roles: among his more recent supporting-cast assignments are Willie O'Keefe *JFK* (1991), the prosecuting attorney in *A Few Good Men* (1993), a cold-blooded villain in *The River Wild* (1994), Alcatraz lifer Henri Young in *Murder in the First* (1994), and astronaut Swigert in *Apollo 13* (1995). Kevin Bacon has long been married to actress Kyra Sedgwick. **Selected Works:** *Diner* (1982), *Flatliners* (1990), *He Said, She Said* (1991), *Queens Logic* (1991)

# John Badham

**Born:** August 25, 1939; Luton, England

**Years Active in the Industry:** by decade

| 10ˢ | 20ˢ | 30ˢ | 40ˢ | 50ˢ | 60ˢ | 70ˢ | 80ˢ | 90ˢ |
|-----|-----|-----|-----|-----|-----|-----|-----|-----|

A casting director and associate producer by the early 1970s, Badham began directing for television, most notably the murder mystery *Isn't It Shocking?*. He helmed his first theatrical feature in 1976: *The Bingo Long Travelling All-Stars And Motor Kings*, a comedy of the Negro National League in 1939. The following year he scored a major success with *Saturday Night Fever*. Badham has gone on to specialize in actioners, including *Blue Thunder*, *Stakeout*, *The Hard Way*, *Point Of No Return*, and *Another Stakeout*; he is also highly regarded for his version of *Dracula* with Frank Langella, the right-to-die drama *Whose Life Is It Anyway?*, and the doomsday thriller *WarGames*. **Selected Works:** *Drop Zone* (1994)

# John Bailey

**Born:** August 10, 1942; Moberly, MO

**Years Active in the Industry:** by decade

| 10ˢ | 20ˢ | 30ˢ | 40ˢ | 50ˢ | 60ˢ | 70ˢ | 80ˢ | 90ˢ |
|-----|-----|-----|-----|-----|-----|-----|-----|-----|

American cinematographer John Bailey's academic credits range from Loyola University to the University of Vienna. He received his most practical training at USC's film school, then moved on to inexpensive, independent productions. Bailey received critical praise for his work on the cult film *Boulevard Nights* (1979), which led to higher-budgeted projects. Though he has made a respectable emergence as a director with *The Search for Signs of Intelligent Life in the Universe* (1990) and *China Moon* (1991), Bailey has remained busy as a photographer; in 1993 he successfully made Illinois look like Pennsylvania (no mean feat) in director Harold Ramis' *Ground Hog Day* (1993) **Selected Works:** *Accidental Tourist* (1988), *Brief History of Time* (1992), *In the Line of Fire* (1993), *Ordinary People* (1980), *Nobody's Fool* (1994)

# Fay Bainter

**Born:** December 7, 1891; Los Angeles, CA
**Died:** April 16, 1968; Beverly Hills, CA

**Years Active in the Industry:** by decade

| 10ˢ | 20ˢ | 30ˢ | 40ˢ | 50ˢ | 60ˢ | 70ˢ | 80ˢ | 90ˢ |
|-----|-----|-----|-----|-----|-----|-----|-----|-----|

American actress Fay Bainter was working in stock at age 5, and by the time she was 19 was one of the privileged members of theatrical impresario David Belasco's company. First starring on Broadway in 1912, Bainter was cast in ingenue or romantic parts for the first portion of her career. When she finally decided to give movies a try, it was as a mature, somewhat plump character actress. Her first film was *This Side of Heaven* (1934), after which, according to many historians she was established in kindly, motherly roles - except for those in which she wasn't so kind and motherly, which constituted the more interesting moments of her film career. In 1938, Bainter made cinema history by being nominated for two Academy Awards in two different categories: As best actress for *White Banners*, a second-string Warners drama in which she played a "Mrs. Fixit", and as best supporting actress in *Jezebel*, where she had the somewhat harsher role of southern belle Bette Davis' remonstrative Aunt Belle. Academy members were confused by Bainter's dual nomination, the result being that the Academy was compelled to change its nominating and voting rules (P.S.: She won for *Jezebel*). Occasionally a star (*The War Against Mrs. Hadley* [1943]) and always near the top of the supporting-cast list, Bainter worked steadily in films until the early 1950s, shifting her attention at that time to television. In 1958, she appeared in the touring company of the Eugene O'Neill play *Long Day's Journey Into Night* in the role of Mary Tyrone - a difficult and demanding assignment even for a woman half her age, but one that she pulled off brilliantly. Bainter returned to films as an unsympathetic wealthy dowager in *The Children's Hour* (1961), which earned her another Oscar nomination - this time in one category only. **Selected Works:** *Human Comedy* (1943), *Our Town* (1940), *Woman of the Year* (1942)

# Carroll Baker

**Born:** May 28, 1935; Johnstown, PA

**Years Active in the Industry:** by decade

| 10ˢ | 20ˢ | 30ˢ | 40ˢ | 50ˢ | 60ˢ | 70ˢ | 80ˢ | 90ˢ |
|-----|-----|-----|-----|-----|-----|-----|-----|-----|

The daughter of a traveling salesman, actress Carroll Baker joined a dance company after one year of college, then worked as a magician's assistant. After a brief marriage to a furrier, she went to Hollywood to act, but was unable to get anything more than a bit role (in 1953's *Easy to Love*) and so left for New York. At first finding work only in commercials (plus a walk-on in the Broadway play *Escapade*), in 1954 she enrolled at the Actors Studio; there she met director Jack Garfein, whom she married the following year (they were divorced in 1969). After her appearance in a few TV dramas and Robert Anderson's play *All Summer Long* (1955), she was noticed by Warner scouts and subsequently cast in James Dean's vehicle *Giant* (1956). Her success continued that same year when her role as the thumb-sucking wife in *Baby Doll* earned her an Academy Award nomination for Best Actress. With the success of Marilyn Monroe, Hollywood started looking for other Monroe "types" and producers began grooming Baker for the role, as is evident from her work in such films as *The Carpetbaggers* (1964); in 1965, she played the doomed title role in the film *Harlow*, another attempt to cast her in the Monroe mold. However, she never caught on with American audiences; in the late '60s, she moved to Italy and began appearing in Italian productions. In 1977 she made her London stage debut in W. Somerset Maugham's *Rain*, then made a few Hollywood and UK pictures in the late 70s and 80s, as well as putting in a "camp" appearance in *Andy Warhol's Bad* (1977). **Selected Works:** *Big Country* (1958), *How the West Was Won* (1963), *Kindergarten Cop* (1990)

# Kathy Baker (Kathy Whitton Baker)

**Born:** June 8, 1950; Midland, TX

**Years Active in the Industry:** by decade

| 10ˢ | 20ˢ | 30ˢ | 40ˢ | 50ˢ | 60ˢ | 70ˢ | 80ˢ | 90ˢ |
|-----|-----|-----|-----|-----|-----|-----|-----|-----|

American supporting actress Kathy Baker is known for her exceptional talent and versatility. Born in Midland, Texas, Baker was raised as a Quaker by her French mother and her American father, a prominent academic who has taught at Princeton and the Sorbonne. She has been acting since she was ten, but did not formally study until she entered the theater department of the California Institute of the Arts. She later transferred to the University of California, Berkley where she earned a Bachelor's degree in French. By this time, she'd abandoned acting in favor of marriage. Following her divorce, Baker trained to be a Cordon Bleu chef in Paris. Back in the States, she worked as a pastry chef and a chocolate vendor. Eventually Baker returned to acting and in 1983 won an Obie award for her work in Sam Shephard's play *Fool for Love*. That same year she made her big screen debut in the astronaut epic *The Right Stuff*. Though not all of the films in which Baker has appeared have been critical and box office successes, her ability to bring her diverse characters to life has won her consistently favorable notice. In 1987, Baker was named Best Supporting Actress by the National Society of Film Critics for her work in *Street Smart*. Though she still occasionally works in film, she has most recently appeared as a main character on the popular CBS television series *Picket Fences*. **Selected Works:** *Article 99* (1992), *Clean & Sober* (1988), *Edward Scissorhands* (1990), *Jennifer 8* (1992), *Mad Dog and Glory* (1993)

# Rick Baker

**Born:** December 8, 1950; Binghamton, NY

**Years Active in the Industry:** by decade

| 10s | 20s | 30s | 40s | 50s | 60s | 70s | 80s | 90s |
|-----|-----|-----|-----|-----|-----|-----|-----|-----|
|     |     |     |     |     |     |     |     |     |

American movie-makeup specialist Rick Baker began his career in his teens as an assistant to cosmetic artist Dick Smith. Working independently from 1972 onward, Baker has been responsible for several landmark accomplishments in the field of character makeup, such as Cicely Tyson's makeover into a 110-year-old woman for the 1974 TV movie *The Autobiography of Miss Jane Pittman*. Baker is particularly adept at man-to-beast "transformation" effects (*An American Werewolf in London* [1981]) and at creating extraterrestrial makeup and models for such films as *Starman* (1984), *Gremlins* (1984) and *Cocoon* (1986). An inveterate ham, Baker has frequently appeared on screen decked out in a gorilla suit; his first such assignment was in John Landis' *Schlock* (1974), and he continued "going ape" in films even after his behind-the-screen fame was established. Baker was the first-ever recipient of a "best makeup" Academy Award for *An American Werewolf in London*; he has subsequently won Oscars for *Harry and the Hendersons* (1987) and *Ed Wood* (1994). **Selected Works:** *Gremlins 2: The New Batch* (1990)

# Alec Baldwin

**Born:** April 3, 1958; Massapequa, NY

**Years Active in the Industry:** by decade

| 10s | 20s | 30s | 40s | 50s | 60s | 70s | 80s | 90s |
|-----|-----|-----|-----|-----|-----|-----|-----|-----|
|     |     |     |     |     |     |     |     |     |

Contemporary American actor Alec Baldwin is equally at home playing leads and character roles. He was born in Amityville, New York, the second in a family of six children. Before becoming an actor he studied political science with the intention of becoming a lawyer and politician at George Washington University. He later studied drama at NYU and at the Lee Strasberg Theater Institute in New York. Early in his career Baldwin was a busy man, simultaneously playing a role on  the television daily serial *The Doctors* and playing in Shakespeare's *Midsummer Night Dream* onstage in the evening. He made his Broadway debut in 1980 and later moved to Los Angeles where he landed a role in the television series *Knots Landing*. In 1986, Baldwin made his feature film debut with *Forever Lulu*, which led to several supporting roles in major films. In one year, 1988-89, Baldwin appeared in seven films. In 1989, he played ace CIA agent Jack Ryan in the undersea thriller, *The Hunt for Red October*. The film was popular and won him much acclaim, so it was surprising when he forewent the opportunity to reprise Jack Ryan in the sequel *Patriot Games* (he was replaced by Harrison Ford, and like the first, it was a major hit) so he could return to Broadway to play Stanley Kowalski in the Broadway revival of *A Streetcar Named Desire*; for this role he received a Tony nomination. In addition to playing in action films and thrillers, Baldwin has shown that he can also handle himself well in comedies, straight dramas, and fantasy films. Three of his other brothers, William, Daniel and Stephen, are also actors. **Selected Works:** *Glengarry Glen Ross* (1992), *Miami Blues* (1990), *Prelude to a Kiss* (1992), *The Juror* (1995), *Heaven's Prisoners* (1995)

# Stephen Baldwin

**Born:** 1966; Massapequa, NY

**Years Active in the Industry:** by decade

| 10s | 20s | 30s | 40s | 50s | 60s | 70s | 80s | 90s |
|-----|-----|-----|-----|-----|-----|-----|-----|-----|
|     |     |     |     |     |     |     |     |     |

Like his older brother William Baldwin, actor Stephen Baldwin attended the State University of New York at Binghamton and briefly modeled for Calvin Klein. While working in a New York City pizza parlor, Stephen was spotted by an agent, making his TV bow shortly afterward in the 1987 PBS *American Playhouse* presentation *The Prodigious Hickey*, in which he played an inveterate turn-of-the-century practical joker. One year later he was seen in his first film, *Homeboy*. From 1989 through 1992, he costarred as a pre-Buffalo Bill William Cody in the weekly TV series *The Young Riders*. In addition to William Baldwin, Stephen Baldwin has two other acting brothers, Alec and Daniel—the result, according to quipster Jay Leno, of a lab cloning experiment. **Selected Works:** *Born on the Fourth of July* (1989), *Last Exit to Brooklyn* (1990), *Threesome* (1994), *The Usual Suspects* (1995)

# William Baldwin

**Born:** 1963

**Years Active in the Industry:** by decade

| 10s | 20s | 30s | 40s | 50s | 60s | 70s | 80s | 90s |
|-----|-----|-----|-----|-----|-----|-----|-----|-----|
|     |     |     |     |     |     |     |     |     |

William Baldwin is the second oldest of the acting Baldwin brothers, a brood which includes Alec, Stephen, and Daniel. There

are a few Baldwin sisters as well, but they aren't in show business; as the brothers have jokingly commented on several occasions, the girls have all the brains in the family. A graduate of the political science department of SUNY at Binghamton, Baldwin wanted to be a baseball player, but he ultimately followed Alec's lead into acting. After briefly modeling for Calvin Klein, he made his first film, *Born on the Fourth of July* (1989). Baldwin established his stardom with his performance as a courageous Chicago firefighter in *Backdraft* (1991). **Selected Works:** *Fair Game* (1995), *Sliver* (1993), *Three of Hearts* (1993)

# Lucille Ball (Lucille Desiree Ball)

**Born:** August 6, 1911; Jamestown, NY
**Died:** April 26, 1989; Beverly Hills, CA

**Years Active in the Industry:** by decade

| 10ˢ | 20ˢ | 30ˢ | 40ˢ | 50ˢ | 60ˢ | 70ˢ | 80ˢ | 90ˢ |
|-----|-----|-----|-----|-----|-----|-----|-----|-----|

Left fatherless at age four, American actress Lucille Ball developed a strong work ethic in childhood; among her more unusual assignments was as a "seeing eye kid" for a blind soap peddler. Ball's mother sent the girl to the Chautauqua Institution for piano lessons, but she was determined to pursue an acting career after watching the positive audience reaction given to vaudeville monologist Julius Tannen. Young Ball did amateur plays for the Elks club and her high school, at one point starring, staging and publicizing a production of *Charley's Aunt*. In 1926, Ball enrolled in the John Murray Anderson dramatic school in Manhattan (where Bette Davis was the "star" pupil), but was discouraged by her teachers to continue due to her shyness. Her reticence notwithstanding, Ball plugged away until she got chorus-girl work and modeling jobs, but even here she received little encouragement from her peers, and the combination of a serious auto accident and recurring stomach ailments seemed to bode ill for Ball's theatrical future. Still, she was no quitter, and in 1933 managed to become one of the singing/dancing "Goldwyn Girls" for movie producer Sam Goldwyn; her first picture was Eddie Cantor's *Roman Scandals* (1933). Working her way up from bit roles at both Columbia Pictures (where one of her assignments was a "Three Stooges" short) and RKO Radio, Ball finally attained featured billing in 1935, and stardom—albeit mostly in B pictures—in 1938. Throughout the late 1930s and 1940s, Lucille Ball's movie career moved steadily if not spectacularly; even when she got a good role like the nasty-tempered night-

club star in *The Big Star* (1942), it was usually because the "bigger" RKO contract actresses had turned it down. By the time she finished an MGM contract (she was dubbed "Technicolor Tessie" at the studio because of her photogenic red hair and bright smile) and returned to Columbia in 1947, she was considered washed up. Ball's home life was none too secure, either. She'd married Cuban bandleader Desi Arnaz in 1940, but despite an obvious strong affection for one another, they had separated and considered divorce numerous times during the war years. Hoping to keep her household together, Ball sought out professional work in which she could work with Desi; offered her own starring TV series in 1950, she refused unless Arnaz would costar. Television was a godsend for the Arnazes; Desi discovered he had a natural executive ability, and soon he was calling all the shots for what would become *I Love Lucy*. From 1951 through 1957, *I Love Lucy* was the most popular sitcom on television, and Ball, after years of career stops and starts, was firmly established as a megastar in her role of zany, disaster-prone Lucy Ricardo; when her much-publicized baby was born in January 1952, the story received bigger press coverage than President Eisenhower's inauguration. With their new Hollywood prestige, Ball and Arnaz were able to set up the powerful Desilu Studios production complex, ultimately purchasing the facilities of RKO, where both performers had once been contract players. But professional pressures and personal problems began eroding the marriage, and in 1960 Ball and Arnaz were divorced, though both continued to operate Desilu. Ball gave Broadway a try in the 1960 musical *Wildcat*, which was successful but no hit, and in 1962 returned to TV to solo as Lucy Carmichael on *The Lucy Show*. She'd already bought out Desi's interest in Desilu, and before selling the studio to Gulf and Western in 1969, Ball had become a powerful executive in her own right, determinedly guiding the destinies of such fondly remembered TV series as *Star Trek* and *Mission, Impossible*. *The Lucy Show* ended in the spring of 1968, but that fall Ball was back in *Here's Lucy*, in which she played "odd job" specialist Lucy Carter and was costarred with her real-life children, Desi Jr. and Lucie. *Here's Lucy* lasted until 1974, at which time her career took some odd directions. She poured a lot of her own money in a filmization of the Broadway musical *Mame* (1974), which can charitably be labeled an embarrassment. Her later attempts to resume TV production, and her benighted TV comeback in the 1986 sitcom *Life with Lucy*, were unsuccessful, even though Lucy herself continued to be lionized as the First Lady of Television, accumulating numerous awards and honorariums. Despite her many latter-day attempts to change her image—and despite her blunt, commandeering offstage personality—Lucille Ball would forever remain the wacky "Lucy" that all Americans had loved intensely in the 1950s. **Selected Works:** *Broadway Bill* (1934), *Stage Door* (1937), *Ziegfeld Follies* (1946), *Facts of Life* (1960)

# Michael Ballhaus

**Born:** August 5, 1935; Berlin, Germany

**Years Active in the Industry:** by decade

| 10ˢ | 20ˢ | 30ˢ | 40ˢ | 50ˢ | 60ˢ | 70ˢ | 80ˢ | 90ˢ |
|---|---|---|---|---|---|---|---|---|
|  |  |  |  |  |  | ■ | ■ |  |

"Who?" wondered many American filmgoers when cinematographer Michael Ballhaus picked up his Academy Award for 1989's *The Fabulous Baker Boys*. German movie buffs would have known better; the Berlin-born Ballhaus had been active in the German film industry since 1970. Ballhaus was best known for his collaborations with the hyperkinetic director Rainer Werner Fassbinder, notably *Mother Kusters Goes to Heaven* (1974) and *The Marriage of Maria Braun* (1979). The editors of *TV Guide* thought enough of Ballhaus to make special mention of his photography for the 1985 TV movie *Death of a Salesman*, directed by another highly regarded European talent, Volker Schlondorff. American directors who have benefited from the expertise of Ballhaus have included Francis Ford Coppola (*Bram Stoker's Dracula* [1993]) and Martin Scorsese (*The Age of Innocence* [1993]). **Selected Works:** *Broadcast News* (1987), *Goodfellas* (1990), *Mambo Kings* (1992), *Sheer Madness* (1984), *Quiz Show* (1994)

# Martin Balsam

**Born:** November 4, 1919; Bronx, NY

**Years Active in the Industry:** by decade

| 10ˢ | 20ˢ | 30ˢ | 40ˢ | 50ˢ | 60ˢ | 70ˢ | 80ˢ | 90ˢ |
|---|---|---|---|---|---|---|---|---|
|  |  |  | ■ | ■ | ■ | ■ | ■ |  |

Bronx-raised actor Martin Balsam was the oldest of three children of a ladies' sportwear salesman. "Actors are bums" was dad's reaction when Balsam announced his intention of going into show business; still, young Martin took full advantage of lunch breaks from his "real" jobs to rehearse for amateur theatricals. After World War II, Balsam joined New York's Actors Studio, supporting himself by waiting on tables and ushering at Radio City Music Hall. During his formative years he was briefly married to actress Joyce Van Patten; their daughter Talia Balsam would later become a successful film and TV performer. Working steadily if not profitably in nightclubs and TV, Balsam made his first film, the Actors Studio-dominated *On the Waterfront*, in 1954. Averaging a movie and/or a play a year starting in 1957 (among his best-known film roles were Juror #1 in *Twelve Angry Men* [1957] and the unfortunate detective Arbogast in *Psycho* [1960]), Balsam went on to win a Tony for the Broadway play *I Know You Can't Hear Me When the Water's Running*, an Obie for the off-Broadway production *Cold Storage*, and an Academy Award for his performance as Jason Robards' older brother in the 1965 film version of *A Thousand Clowns*. Not unexpectedly, the Oscar was as much a curse as a blessing on his career, and soon he was playing little more than variations on his *Thousand Clowns* role. In 1979, he was engaged by Norman Lear to play "loveable bigot" Archie Bunker's acerbic Jewish business partner Murray Klein on the CBS sitcom *Archie Bunker's Place*; he remained with the series until 1981. Recently, Balsam appeared in Martin Scorsese's *Cape Fear*, the 1991 remake

of a film in which Balsam had costarred (in an entirely different role) in 1962. **Selected Works:** *All the President's Men* (1976), *Catch-22* (1970), *Little Big Man* (1970), *Murder on the Orient Express* (1974), *Seven Days in May* (1964)

# Anne Bancroft

**Born:** September 17, 1931; Bronx, NY

**Years Active in the Industry:** by decade

| 10ˢ | 20ˢ | 30ˢ | 40ˢ | 50ˢ | 60ˢ | 70ˢ | 80ˢ | 90ˢ |
|---|---|---|---|---|---|---|---|---|
|  |  |  |  | ■ | ■ | ■ | ■ | ■ |

Born Anna Maria Louisa Italiano, the daughter of Italian immigrants, actress Anne Bancroft began studying dancing and acting at age four. After studying theater at the American Academy of Dramatic Arts and the Actors' Studio, she began working professionally on TV in 1950, using the name Anne Marno. Signed by Fox in 1952, she debuted onscreen in *Don't Bother to Knock* (1952); for the next six years she was busily employed in a series of B gangster movies and Westerns. Discouraged, in 1958 she returned to New York and soon established herself as a serious actress in the Broadway play *Two for the Seesaw*, opposite Henry Fonda; she won a Tony for her performance and went on to star as Annie Sullivan, Helen Keller's partially blind mentor, in *The Miracle Worker*, for which she won another Tony as well as the New York Drama Critics Award for Best Actress. She returned to films in the screen version of *The Miracle Worker* (1962), for which she won the Best Actress Oscar; this began a new phase in her screen career in which she got much better roles in superior films, notably *The Graduate* (1967) in which she went against type in the semi-comedic role of Mrs. Robinson, the older woman who seduces Dustin Hoffman's character. While appearing steadily in films, she continued her work on the stage. She is married to comedian-actor-filmmaker Mel Brooks, with whom she appeared in *To Be Or Not To Be* (1983). **Selected Works:** *Agnes of God* (1985), *Point of No Return* (1993), *Turning Point* (1977), *Pumpkin Eater* (1964), *Oldest Living Confederate Widow Tells All* (1994)

# George Bancroft

**Born:** September 30, 1882; Philadelphia, PA
**Died:** 1956

**Years Active in the Industry:** by decade

| 10ˢ | 20ˢ | 30ˢ | 40ˢ | 50ˢ | 60ˢ | 70ˢ | 80ˢ | 90ˢ |
|---|---|---|---|---|---|---|---|---|
|  | ■ | ■ |  |  |  |  |  |  |

After a stint in the navy, George Bancroft became a blackface performer in minstrel shows; this performing experience led to work on Broadway, both in musicals and straight shows. In 1921 he made his screen debut in *The Journey's End*, but his big break came in his first film for Paramount, *Code of the West* (1925), which brought him to the attention of director James Cruze; that same year, he appeared in Cruze's *The Pony Express*, beginning a string of films in which his burly looks, large frame, and menacing air made him the ideal screen "heavy," albeit one with a disarmingly smooth style. After 1927's *Underworld* he became the number one box office attraction, an internationally known and recognized movie king. His superstardom lasted until the mid-'30s, and included occasional roles as tough "good guys" as well as supporting parts. By the mid-'30s, however, he had been supplanted as the premiere screen gangster by Jimmy Cagney, Edgar G. Robinson, and Paul Muni, and so he changed his focus and went on to become one of Hollywood's most accomplished character actors. He was nominated for a Best Actor Oscar for his work in *Thunderbolt* (1929), and was married to actress Octavia Brooke. In 1942 he retired from the screen to his ranch. **Selected Works:** *Angels with Dirty Faces* (1938), *Mr. Deeds Goes to Town* (1936), *Stagecoach* (1939)

# Antonio Banderas

**Born:** 1960; Malaga, Spain

**Years Active in the Industry:** by decade

| 10s | 20s | 30s | 40s | 50s | 60s | 70s | 80s | 90s |
|-----|-----|-----|-----|-----|-----|-----|-----|-----|
|     |     |     |     |     |     |     |     |     |

Spanish actor Antonio Banderas studied at the School of Dramatic Art in his home town of Malaga. He supported himself as

a waiter and advertising model before making his stage debut in 1981. He made his film bow in director Pedro Almodovar's *Labyrinth of Passion* (1982), rapidly becoming a member in good standing of Almodovar's "stock company". When Banderas appeared as a homosexual in Almodovar's *Law of Desire*, his first male-to-male screen kiss made headlines in the Spanish press. International acclaim came to Banderas by way of such Almodovar films as *Woman on the Verge of a Nervous Breakdown* (1988) and *Tie Me Up! Tie Me Down!* (1989), and his roles in *The Mambo Kings* (1992) and *Philadelphia* (1993) as the lover of Tom Hanks' leading character solidified his reputation with American audiences. He continues to work in American films (*Interview with the Vampire* [1994], *Miami Rhapsody* [1995]) and makes an interesting turn in the actioner *Desperado* (1995). Banderas has made off-screen news as well for his affair with actress Melanie Griffith. Banderas has recently expressed a

desire to play such character roles as Quasimodo in *The Hunchback of Notre Dame*, though he has also expressed concern that his good looks may work against such casting. **Selected Works:** *Desperado* (1995), *Four Rooms* (1995)

# Tallulah Bankhead

**Born:** Janurary 31, 1902; Birmingham, AL
**Died:** 1968

**Years Active in the Industry:** by decade

| 10s | 20s | 30s | 40s | 50s | 60s | 70s | 80s | 90s |
|-----|-----|-----|-----|-----|-----|-----|-----|-----|
|     |     |     |     |     |     |     |     |     |

Seductive, whiskey-voiced, one-of-a-kind American leading lady Tallulah Bankhead, the daughter of the Speaker of the House of Representatives William Brockman Bankhead, began her stage career at age 15 after being educated in a convent. She did more stage work plus two silent films, then went to London in 1923 where she became a celebrity while performing brilliantly in a string of plays. The hot-blooded Bankhead preferred to live dangerously and became notorious for her uninhibited behavior (such as taking off her clothes in public), a tendency many have seen as detrimental to the use of her considerable talents. She appeared in two British silents before coming to America in 1930; signed by Paramount, she began her movie career in earnest but remained more a fixture of Broadway, where she shone in plays such as *The Little Foxes* (for which she won the New York Drama Critics' Circle Award in 1939, an award she won again in 1942 for *The Skin of Our Teeth*). Her movie career was spotty and included several box office disasters, perhaps because her extravagant, larger-than-life personality was not done justice on the screen; her more memorable appearances include a celebrated performance in Hitchcock's *Lifeboat* (1944), for which she was cited by New York Film Critics. Bankhead made only three more films after *Lifeboat*. She is divorced from actor John Emery. In 1952, she wrote her autobiography, *Tallulah*.

# Theda Bara (Theodosia Goodman)

**Born:** July 20, 1890; Cincinnati, OH
**Died:** April 7, 1955; Los Angeles, CA

**Years Active in the Industry:** by decade

| 10s | 20s | 30s | 40s | 50s | 60s | 70s | 80s | 90s |
|-----|-----|-----|-----|-----|-----|-----|-----|-----|
|     |     |     |     |     |     |     |     |     |

Although publicized as an Egyptian of royal lineage, silent film actress Theda Bara was actually born in Cincinnati, Ohio. Her exotic good looks brought her to the attention of Fox studios in 1914; reasoning that there were too many sweet little ingenues in films of that period, Fox decided to create a worldly "vamp" character, a woman who could destroy men with little more than a sexy glance. The studio changed Theodosia's name to Theda Bara (which coincidentally was an anagram for "Arab Death"), casting her in a liberal adaptation of Rudyard Kipling's *A Fool There Was*(1914). She became Fox's biggest star, appearing in as many as ten feature films per year, including *Salome* (1918) and *Cleopatra* (1918). Her somewhat overripe histrionics became out of fashion by 1920, so she retired from acting to married life; Bara resurfaced in a "so bad it's good" Broadway play *The Blue Flame*, then made an unsuccessful film comeback attempt in 1925. Her last screen work was in a two-reel lampoon of her vamp character, *Madame Mystery* (1926), directed by, of all people, Stan Laurel. Though happily married and fabulously wealthy, Bara never gave up the dream that she might someday return to screen glory; at the time of her death in 1955, Hollywood's casting service directories still listed the actress as "at liberty."

# Joseph Barbera

**Born:** 1911; New York, NY

**Years Active in the Industry:** by decade

| 10s | 20s | 30s | 40s | 50s | 60s | 70s | 80s | 90s |
|-----|-----|-----|-----|-----|-----|-----|-----|-----|
|     |     |     |     |     |     |     |     |     |

A writer at MGM by the late 1930s, Barbera teamed up with Joseph Hanna, with whom he made a series of "Tom & Jerry" cartoons between 1940 and 1958, most notably *Mouse Trouble*, *The Cat Concerto*, *Kitty Foiled*, *The Two Mouseketeers*, and *Johann Mouse*. They also made animated sequences for the MGM musicals *Anchors Aweigh*, *Holiday In Mexico*, *Dangerous When Wet*, and *Invitation To The Dance*. Hanna and Barbera turned to television in the 1960s and created several beloved animated series, including "The Flintstones," "Huckleberry Hound," "Yogi Bear," "Top Cat," "The Jetsons," and "Johnny Quest." Their shows led to their '60s theatrical animated features *Hey There, It's Yogi Bear* and *A Man Called Flintstone*, as well as their recent *Jetsons: The Movie*.

# Brigitte Bardot (Camille Javal)

**Born:** September 28, 1934; Paris, France

**Years Active in the Industry:** by decade

| 10s | 20s | 30s | 40s | 50s | 60s | 70s | 80s | 90s |
|-----|-----|-----|-----|-----|-----|-----|-----|-----|
|     |     |     |     |     |     |     |     |     |

French actress Brigitte Bardot, born Camille Javal, was the archetypal "sex kitten" of the late 50s and 60s. A student of ballet from early childhood; she appeared on the cover of French fashion magazine *Elle* at age 16. Her pouty, sensuous beauty brought her to the attention of director Marc Allegret's assistant, Roger Vadim, to whom she was married from 1952-57. Between 1952-56 she

performed in several films (beginning with Jean Boyer's *Crazy For Love*), at first in secondary roles and then in leads. A massive breakthrough occurred after her appearance in Vadim's *And God Created Woman* (1956), in which she and Vadim created the sensuous "woman-child" she would play in most of her subsequent films. Bardot became an international celebrity upon the film's extraordinary success, and soon was the subject of gossip, adulation, and imitation. Like Madonna, she set the style for a generation of young women while quickening the heartbeats of men of all ages. Also like Madonna, she became a symbol of scandal for those who saw her as the representative of an out-of-control sexual revolution. In 1959 she married French actor Jacques Charrier after co-starring with him in *Babette Goes to War*, but the marriage was short-lived and marked by Charrier's nervous breakdowns and attempted suicides. Bardot is credited with single-handedly bringing French film out of the specialty theaters and into the mainstream. Her subsequent roles tended to be more of the same, featuring her in bathing suits and other scant attire; however, she did gain considerable critical respect for her performance in *The Truth* (1961). She retired from film after 1973, but continued to make occasional TV appearances. Attempting (as she put it) "to erase the Bardot legend," in her later years she devoted herself to charitable causes, most notably the preservation of endangered animal species. **Selected Works:** *Masculine Feminine* (1966), *Viva Maria* (1965)

# Ellen Barkin

**Born:** 1954; Bronx, NY

**Years Active in the Industry:** by decade

| 10s | 20s | 30s | 40s | 50s | 60s | 70s | 80s | 90s |
|-----|-----|-----|-----|-----|-----|-----|-----|-----|
|     |     |     |     |     |     |     |     |     |

Actress Ellen Barkin is one of the most respected, versatile actresses on the screen; she is equally at home playing supporting roles, character roles and leads—yet true stardom has eluded her. Prior to becoming an actress, Barkin attended the renowned High School for the Performing Arts in New York, studied history and drama at Hunter College, and took workshops at the Actors Studio. She made her critically acclaimed film debut as the neglected wife of an obsessive record collector in Barry Levinson's feature *Diner* (1982) and subsequently went on to play supporting roles ranging from unhappy wives to white-hot sexpots. Following her appearance in the romantic thriller *The Big Easy* in 1987, Barkin gained a small but devoted following. While filming the experimental super-

natural thriller *Siesta* in 1987, Barkin met her estranged husband, Irish actor Gabriel Byrne with whom she has had a son. She is perhaps best known for her role in the 1989 film *Sea of Love*. **Selected Works:** *Mac* (1993), *Switch* (1991), *Tender Mercies* (1983), *This Boy's Life* (1993), *Wild Bill* (1995)

## Binnie Barnes (Gitelle Gertrude Maude Barnes)

**Born:** March 25, 1905; London, England
**Died:** 1983

**Years Active in the Industry:** by decade

| 10s | 20s | 30s | 40s | 50s | 60s | 70s | 80s | 90s |
|-----|-----|-----|-----|-----|-----|-----|-----|-----|
|     |     |     |     |     |     |     |     |     |

British actress Binnie Barnes took several performing and nonperforming jobs, not the least of which was as a milkmaid, before making her screen bow in a 1929 sound short. She was leading lady to British comic Stanley Lupino in a long series of two-reelers (she later appeared in Lupino's starring feature *Love Lies* [1931], directed by the star's brother, Lupino Lane). Signed by Alexander Korda in 1931, Barnes worked as a nominal leading lady in budget features for a staggering 35 pounds per week (approximately 180 dollars). Her first important role was as Catherine Howard in Korda's *Private Life of Henry VIII* (1933), which didn't bring her any more money but enabled her to receive better roles. After acting in the London stage production of *Cavalcade*, Barnes was brought to Hollywood for the film version, but she didn't like America and headed right back to England, where after some legal unpleasantries over breaking her contract she costarred with Douglas Fairbanks Sr. in Korda's *The Private Life of Don Juan* (1934) (Korda's title department must have been in a rut). Contractually obligated to return to the US, she made her first Hollywood film, *There's Always Tomorrow*, in 1934. Toning down her English accent, the actress made her mark in secondary "wiseacre" roles, usually as the heroine's worldly best friend. She would later claim to have taken everything offered her because she liked to eat; that would explain her casting as Milady DeWinter in the Ritz Brothers' version of *The Three Musketeers* (1939) (in truth, it was one of her favorite roles, even though the Ritzes turned her upside down and shook her at one point in the film). In the early 1950s, Barnes tried her hand at producing films. The results were several middling European productions, including *Decameron Nights* (1953) - in which, to cut down costs, she played eight roles! She retired in 1955 to devote her time to her marriage to Columbia production chief Mike Frankovich. Barnes re-entered films only at the insis-

tence of Frankovich, who cast her in *The Trouble With Angels* (1968), *Where Angels Go - Trouble Follows* (1968) and *Forty Carats* (1972). **Selected Works:** *Holiday* (1938), *Three Smart Girls* (1937)

## John Barry (John B. Prendergast)

**Born:** November 3, 1933; York, England

**Years Active in the Industry:** by decade

| 10s | 20s | 30s | 40s | 50s | 60s | 70s | 80s | 90s |
|-----|-----|-----|-----|-----|-----|-----|-----|-----|
|     |     |     |     |     |     |     |     |     |

British composer John Barry's formal training came by way of a correspondence course and experience with a military band. After serving his country, Barry, his trumpet, and six other guys formed a popular rock'n'roll/ rhythm'n'blues aggregation, the John Barry Seven. His first movie score was the lively British programmer *Beat Girl* (1959), but worldwide fame would elude Barry until he arranged the music for the first James Bond film, *Dr. No* (1962) (he did not, as is commonly assumed, compose the steel-guitar James Bond theme; that was the handiwork of Monty Norman). Barry stayed with the Bond series for nearly three decades, scoring virtually every entry until *The Living Daylights* (1987). During this period he was Oscar-nominated for his work on *Born Free* (1966), *The Lion in Winter* (1968) and *Out of Africa* (1985). American films that have benefited from the Barry touch have included *Midnight Cowboy* (1969), *Body Heat* (1984), *Dances with Wolves* (1990) and *Indecent Proposal* (1993). **Selected Works:** *Empire Strikes Back* (1980), *Mary, Queen of Scots* (1971), *My Life* (1993), *Specialist* (1994)

## Drew Barrymore

**Born:** February 22, 1975; Los Angeles, CA

**Years Active in the Industry:** by decade

| 10s | 20s | 30s | 40s | 50s | 60s | 70s | 80s | 90s |
|-----|-----|-----|-----|-----|-----|-----|-----|-----|
|     |     |     |     |     |     |     |     |     |

As a member of America's most illustrious family of actors, one might think that a successful future for actress Drew Barrymore, the daughter of John Drew Barrymore, Jr., would be a given. But though she is still a young woman, Barrymore has already had more than her share of personal and professional ups and downs, and any success she has found is due to her own hard work and developing talent. Perhaps part of the problems she has endured have come from spending her entire life in the industry; she made a television commercial at nine months, debuted in a television movie, *Suddenly Love* at age two, and made her feature film debut in Ken Russell's *Altered States* (1980) at age four. She became a star at age seven for her precocious performance in the enormous 1982 hit *E.T. The Extra-Terrestrial*. She appeared in three more big budget films by 1985 before she dropped out of films for four

years. Her sudden rise into stardom took a terrible toll for like many child actors, she found herself thrust into a world where she was supposed to be a child on screen and a professional young adult at other times. By the time Barrymore was nine she had begun drinking; she continued abusing alcohol and drugs through her early teens, and was also heavily involved in the nightclub scene. It all culminated with a suicide attempt and she ended up spending several years in rehabilitation (her troubled life and tendency towards chemical excess seem to be a Barrymore family legacy). In 1989, she chronicled her youthful struggles in her autobiography *Little Girl Lost*. As a young adult actress, Barrymore has begun to cultivate the image of the contemporary siren, seductive, independent, and tough as nails. She most recently won critical acclaim for her portrayal of a manic-depressive teen in *Mad Love* (1995). **Selected Works:** *Guncrazy* (1992), *Poison Ivy* (1992), *Sketch Artist* (1992), *Boys on the Side* (1995)

# Ethel Barrymore (Edith Blythe)

**Born:** August 15, 1879; Philadelphia, PA
**Died:** June 18, 1959; Hollywood, CA

**Years Active in the Industry:** by decade

| 10ˢ | 20ˢ | 30ˢ | 40ˢ | 50ˢ | 60ˢ | 70ˢ | 80ˢ | 90ˢ |
|-----|-----|-----|-----|-----|-----|-----|-----|-----|
|     |     |     |     |     |     |     |     |     |

Born into a long-established American theatrical family, Ethel Barrymore dreamed of being a concert pianist, but found that acting was virtually the only profession for which she was truly qualified - and which ensured a livable income. Like all her forebears, she worked her way up the theatrical ladder from bits to full leads. Though she was quite popular on the road and in Europe, her first full fledged Broadway hit was Clyde Fitch's 1901 play *Captain Jinks of the Horse Marines*, in the virtuoso role of a supercilious woman of wealth. Her later attempts to excel in the Classics were to no avail; from *Captain Jinks* on, she was confined to glamorous roles, usually comic in nature, specially written for her. Disdaining movies for the most part (several silent films notwithstanding) Ethel was intrigued at the notion of working with her celebrated brothers John and Lionel Barrymore, but the film vehicle chosen by MGM, *Rasputin and the Empress* (1932), showed only Lionel to advantage; besides, Ethel managed to alienate Hollywood (and her brothers) with her imperious attitude towards film people. After ten years of unsuccessful plays - excepting a "come-

back" in the 1940 hit *The Corn is Green* - and a brief retirement, she was more open to films, accepting Cary Grant's personal invitation to play Grant's mother in *None But the Lonely Heart* (1944), for which she won an Oscar. A few encore stage appearances later, Ethel "went Hollywood" full force with strong character roles in such films as *The Spiral Staircase* (1946), *The Farmer's Daughter* (1947) and *Pinky* (1949), her trademarked aristocratic features and crisp enunciation becoming even more pronounced with the advancing years. Though she shared the Barrymore "family curse" of alcoholic overindulgence, she was more successful handling her liquor than her brothers, and was able to keep her wits and talent long enough to headline on television; one of her last efforts was a syndicated anthology, *Ethel Barrymore Theatre*, in which she hosted and occasionally acted. Even so, Ethel Barrymore was as uncompromising in her assessment of TV as she was of other persons and things that displeased her: Her two-word assessment of The Tube was "It's hell." **Selected Works:** *Portrait of Jennie* (1948)

# John Barrymore (John Blythe)

**Born:** February 14, 1882; Philadelphia, PA
**Died:** May 19, 1942; Hollywood, CA

**Years Active in the Industry:** by decade

| 10ˢ | 20ˢ | 30ˢ | 40ˢ | 50ˢ | 60ˢ | 70ˢ | 80ˢ | 90ˢ |
|-----|-----|-----|-----|-----|-----|-----|-----|-----|
|     |     |     |     |     |     |     |     |     |

Like his brother Lionel and his sister Ethel, American actor John Barrymore had early intentions to break away from the family theatrical tradition and become an artist, in the "demonic" style of Gustav Dore. But acting won out; thanks to his natural flair and good looks, Barrymore was a matinee idol within a few seasons after his 1903 stage debut. His best known Broadway role for many years was as an inebriated wireless operator in the Dick Davis farce *The Dictator*; the play was prescient in presenting John as a comedian and a drunkard. On stage and in silent films (including a 1915 version of *The Dictator*), John was most at home in comedies; offstage, he was most at home in a saloon. Throughout his life, Barrymore was plagued by two Demons: His own self-hatred (he never felt as talented as his brother Lionel or sister Ethel) and his taste for alcohol. His one chance for greatness occurred in 1922, when he played Hamlet; even British audiences hailed Barrymore's performance as one of the best, if not *the* best, interpretations of the melancholy Dane. But his sorry financial state led him to abandon the theatre altogether for the movies, where he was often cast more for his looks than his talent. Perhaps in revenge against Hollywood "flesh peddlers," Barrymore loved to play roles that required physical distortion, grotesque makeup, or all-out "mad" scenes; to him, his *Dr. Jekyll and Mr. Hyde* (1920) was infinitely more satisfying than *Don Juan* (1926). When talkies came in, Barrymore's days as a romantic lead had passed, but his exquisite voice and superb bearing guaranteed him stronger film roles than he'd had in silents; still, for every *Grand Hotel* (1932), there were the gloriously hammy excesses of *Moby Dick* (1930) and *Svengali* (1931) which enabled the insecure Barrymore to hide behind false noses and accents. His alcoholic intake, indiscriminate womanizing and tabloid-press lifestyle began catching up with him in the mid-1930s. From *Romeo and Juliet* (1936) onward, the actor's memory had become so befuddled that he had to recite his lines from cue cards, and from *The Great Profile* (1940) onward, virtually the only parts he'd get were those in which he lampooned his screen image and his offstage shenanigans. In 1939, at the behest of his latest wife Elaine Barrie, Barrymore returned to the stage in *My Dear Children*, a second-rate play that evolved into a freak show as Barrymore's performance deteriorated and he began profanely ad-libbing, behaving outrageously and drinking profusely during the play's run. Sadly, the more Barrymore debased himself in public, the more the public ate it up, and *My Dear Children* was a hit, as were his humiliatingly hilarious appearances on Rudy Vallee's radio show. With the alcoholic's knack of being charming one moment and terrifying the next, Barrymore had lost most of his friends and all of his money by the time of his death. To paraphrase his old friend and drinking companion Gene Fowler, Barrymore had gone over Niagara Falls in a barrel; we are lucky indeed that he left a gallery of brilliant film portrayals before the fall. **Selected Works:** *Twentieth Century* (1934)

# Lionel Barrymore (Lionel Blythe)

**Born:** April 28, 1878; Philadelphia, PA
**Died:** November 15, 1954; Van Nuys, CA

**Years Active in the Industry:** by decade

| 10s | 20s | 30s | 40s | 50s | 60s | 70s | 80s | 90s |
|-----|-----|-----|-----|-----|-----|-----|-----|-----|

Like his younger brother John, American actor Lionel Barrymore wanted more than anything to be an artist. But a member of the celebrated Barrymore family was expected to enter the family trade, so Lionel reluctantly launched an acting career. Not as attractive as John or sister Ethel, he was most effectively cast in character roles - villains, military officers, fathers - even in his youth. Unable to save what he earned, Barrymore was "reduced" to appearing in films for the Biograph Company in 1911, where he was directed by the great D.W. Griffith and where he was permitted to write a few film stories himself, which to Lionel was far more satisfying than playacting. His stage career was boosted when cast in 1917 as Colonel Ibbetson in *Peter Ibbetson*, which led to his most celebrated role, Milt Shanks in *The Copperhead*; even late in life, he could always count on being asked to recite his climactic *Copperhead* soliloquy, which never failed to bring down the house. Money problems and an increasing dependence on cocaine stymied his stage career in the early 1920s, and he was obliged to revitalize his film career, which moved in spurts of success and failure until talkies arrived in 1929. Signed to what would be a 25-year hitch with MGM, Barrymore begged the MGM heads to be allowed to direct; he showed only moderate talent in this field, and was most often hired to guide those films in which MGM wanted to

"punish" its more rebellious talent. Resigning himself to acting again in 1931, he managed to cop an Academy Award for his bravura performance as a drunken defense attorney in *A Free Soul* (1931), the first in an increasingly prestigious series of movie character parts. In 1937, Barrymore was crippled by arthritis, and for the rest of his career was confined to a wheelchair. The actor became more popular than ever as he reached his sixtieth birthday, principally as a result of his annual radio appearance as Scrooge in *A Christmas Carol* and his continuing role as Dr. Gillespie in MGM's *Dr. Kildare* film series. Barrymore was aware that venerability and talent are not often the same thing, but he'd become somewhat lazy (if one can call a sixtyish wheelchair-bound man who showed up on time and appeared in at least three films per year "lazy") and settled into repeating his "old curmudgeon with a heart of gold" performance, save for the occasional topnotch part in such films as *It's a Wonderful Life* (1946) and *Down to the Sea in Ships* (1949). Denied access to television work by his MGM contract, Barrymore nonetheless remained active in radio (he'd starred in the long-running series *Mayor of the Town*), and at one point conducted a talk program from his own home; additionally, the actor continued pursuing his hobbies of writing, composing music, painting and engraving until arthritis overcame him. On the day of his death, he was preparing for his weekly performance on radio's *Hallmark Playhouse*; that evening, the program offered a glowing tribute to Barrymore, never once alluding to the fact that he'd spent a lifetime in a profession he openly despised. **Selected Works:** *Camille* (1936), *Duel in the Sun* (1946), *Grand Hotel* (1932), *Key Largo* (1948), *Madame X* (1929)

# Paul Bartel

**Born:** August 6, 1938; New York, NY

**Years Active in the Industry:** by decade

| 10s | 20s | 30s | 40s | 50s | 60s | 70s | 80s | 90s |
|-----|-----|-----|-----|-----|-----|-----|-----|-----|

American actor, screenwriter and filmmaker Paul Bartel is perhaps best known as the director and star of the quirky sleeper *Eating Raoul* (1982). Bartel has been a film aficionado since childhood and entered the industry at age 13 working as an assistant animator for UPA. He later studied film at UCLA and while there made several short animated films and documentaries; for his work as a student actor and playwright, Bartel won several awards. Later he studied at Rome's prestigious Centro Sperimental di Cinematografica on a Fulbright Scholarship; there his graduation film, *Progetti*, was shown at the Venice Film Festival. Soon after coming back to the U.S., Bartel began working as an assistant director for military films; he then went on to make films for the U.S. government. As a feature filmmaker, Bartel is consistently drawn to the darkly funny, more perverse aspects of life. His provocative directorial debut was *Private Parts* (1972) which centered on a runaway teenage girl who encounters several residents involved with bizarre sexual practices in her aunt's ramshackle San Francisco hotel. Though it was a box office flop, the film earned Bartel decent notice from critics. He next involved himself with B movie king Roger Corman and worked for him as both an actor and a second unit photographer. In 1974, he again tried directing with *Big Bad Mama*. He directed one more film before coming up with *Raoul* which he also co-wrote. Bartel continued directing a variety of films through the 1980s, but most recently can be seen as a B movie actor in films such as *Pucker up and Bark Like a Dog* (1992) and *The Jerky Boys* (1994). **Selected Works:** *Liquid Dreams* (1992), *Living End* (1992), *Posse* (1993)

# Richard Barthelmess

**Born:** May 9, 1895; New York, NY
**Died:** 1963

**Years Active in the Industry:** by decade

| 10ˢ | 20ˢ | 30ˢ | 40ˢ | 50ˢ | 60ˢ | 70ˢ | 80ˢ | 90ˢ |
|-----|-----|-----|-----|-----|-----|-----|-----|-----|
|     |     |     |     |     |     |     |     |     |

Most notably an actor in silent films, Barthelmess studied dramatics at Trinity College in Hartford, CT and was discovered by screen idol, Alla Nazimova. His honest, handsome looks and strong yet gentle performances made him a leading star, landing him much envied roles in several of D. W. Griffith's films, most notably as a kindly Chinaman in *Broken Blossoms* (1919) and in *Way Down East* (1920) where he performed an incredible stunt, requiring him to run across an ice floe to save Lillian Gish from an icy death. In 1920, Barthelmess left Griffith to begin a collaboration with director Henry King, which resulted in his signature piece, *Tol'able David* (1921). Later, he received Oscar nominations for his roles in *The Patent Leather Kid* (1927) and *The Noose* (1928). He continued into the sound era, eventually playing character roles. He retired from films in 1942 and served in the Naval Reserve. He eventually died of cancer in 1963. **Selected Works:** *Only Angels Have Wings* (1939)

# Freddie Bartholomew (Frederick Llewellyn)

**Born:** March 28, 1924; London, England
**Died:** January 23, 1992; Sarasota, FL

**Years Active in the Industry:** by decade

| 10ˢ | 20ˢ | 30ˢ | 40ˢ | 50ˢ | 60ˢ | 70ˢ | 80ˢ | 90ˢ |
|-----|-----|-----|-----|-----|-----|-----|-----|-----|
|     |     |     |     |     |     |     |     |     |

British actor Freddie Bartholomew was plying his trade at the age of three, and had already made two British films - *Fascination* (1930) and *Lily Christine* (1932) - when he was brought to the States by MGM. The studio was mounting an elaborate film version of *David Copperfield*, and wanted to have as many British actors as possible in the cast; impressed by ten-year-old Freddie, producer David O. Selznick decided to "introduce" the boy in this lavish production. Though critics of the time tended to dismiss young Bartholomew as a simpering "professional kid", his performances hold up fairly well today. Certainly the public of 1935 was impressed, and before long Bartholomew was the second most popular child star in the movies (Shirley Temple, of course, was first). He worked with ease with some of the most imposing adult talents in the business, from W.C. Fields to Greta Garbo, until the 1940s. Bartholomew's natural charm evaporated when he reached his teens; though still a competent actor, he lost the quality that had once made him special. His assignments deteriorated in quality, and his last film, *St. Benny the Dip* (1951), was downright amateurish at times. Bartholomew quit the business cold in the 1950s, concentrating instead on a lucrative career in advertising. Viewers of a 1992 cable special on the history of MGM studios were somewhat surprised to see Bartholomew as one of the narrators. Affable, down to earth, prosperous looking and speaking without a trace of British accent, this Freddie Bartholomew was miles removed from the unctuous young star of *David Copperfield*, *Little Lord Fauntleroy* (1936) and *Captains Courageous* (1938). **Selected Works:** *Anna Karenina* (1935), *Swiss Family Robinson* (1940)

# Billy Barty

**Born:** October 15, 1924; Hillsboro, PA

**Years Active in the Industry:** by decade

| 10ˢ | 20ˢ | 30ˢ | 40ˢ | 50ˢ | 60ˢ | 70ˢ | 80ˢ | 90ˢ |
|-----|-----|-----|-----|-----|-----|-----|-----|-----|
|     |     |     |     |     |     |     |     |     |

American dwarf actor Billy Barty has always claimed to have been born in the early 1920s, but the evidence of his somewhat wizened, all-knowing countenance in his film appearances of the 1930s would suggest that he was at least ten years shy of the whole truth. At any rate, Barty made several films appearances from at least 1931 onward, most often cast due to his height as bratty children. He was a peripheral member of an "Our Gang" rip-off in the Mickey McGuire comedy shorts, portrayed the infant-turned-pig in *Alice in Wonderland* (1932), did a turn in blackface as a "shrunken" Eddie Cantor in *Roman Scandals* (1933) and frequently popped up as a lasciviously leering baby in the risqué musical highlights of Busby Berkeley's Warner Bros. films. One of Barty's most celebrated cinema moments occurred in 1937's *Nothing Sacred*, in which, playing a small boy, he pops up out of nowhere to bite Fredric March in the leg. Barty was busy but virtually anonymous in films, since he seldom received screen credit. TV audiences began to connect his name with his face in the 1950s when Barty was featured on various variety series hosted by bandleader Spike Jones. Disdainful of certain professional "little people" who rely on size alone to get laughs, Barty was seen at his very best on the Jones programs, dancing, singing, and delivering dead-on impressions: the diminutive actor's takeoff on Liberace was almost unbearably funny. Though he was willing to poke fun at himself on camera, Barty was fiercely opposed to TV and film producers who exploited midgets and dwarves, and as he continued his career into the 1970s and 1980s, Barty saw to it that his own roles were devoid of patronization - in fact, he often secured parts that could have been portrayed by so-called "normal" actors, proof that one's stature has little to do with one's talent. A two-fisted advocate of equitable treatment of short actors, Billy Barty has taken time away from his many roles in movies (*Foul Play* [1978], *Willow* [1986]) and TV to maintain his support organization, The Little People of America. **Selected Works:** *Life Stinks* (1991), *Wishful Thinking* (1992)

# Mikhail Baryshnikov

**Born:** January 27, 1948; Riga, Latvia

**Years Active in the Industry:** by decade

| 10ˢ | 20ˢ | 30ˢ | 40ˢ | 50ˢ | 60ˢ | 70ˢ | 80ˢ | 90ˢ |
|-----|-----|-----|-----|-----|-----|-----|-----|-----|
|     |     |     |     |     |     |     |     |     |

Born in the former Soviet Union, dancer/actor Mikhail Baryshnikov came to ballet at the advanced age of 15. Because of his extraordinary leg-muscle strength, Baryshnikov was permitted to join Leningrad's Kirov Company, in which he worked his way up to featured soloist. During the Kirov's Canadian tour in 1974, Baryshnikov disappeared for several days, and when he resurfaced it was in the United States and he was asking for political asylum. The decision had as much to do with aesthetics as ideology; in Russia, even a ballet star could only go so far socially and financially. Baryshnikov joined the American Ballet, but later in what was considered a controversial move he switched to George Balanchine's New York City Ballet. The reason was simple: Balanchine had strong links to musical comedy, and Baryshnikov was a lifelong fan of such American musicals as *Oklahoma*, *West Side Story*, and even *Where's Charley?*. This devotion would later be manifested in a well-received 1980 ABC television special, *Baryshnikov on Broadway*. In 1977, Baryshnikov made his American film debut in *The Turning Point* (1977), the most successful ballet-themed motion picture since *The Red Shoes* (1948). For his down-to-earth acting as much as for his unquestioned dance skill, Baryshnikov received an Oscar nomination. That he quickly adapted himself to the Hollywood lifestyle was evident in his private life; he fathered a child by actress Jessica Lange, who ultimately left him for a longer liaison with actor/playwright Sam Shepard. Baryshnikov did not spare himself in his work as he grew older, and magazines frequently featured close-up photos of his battered knees and ankles. By the very nature of his reputation, Baryshnikov does not lend himself to being cast in "normal" film roles. His best movie showing outside of *Turning Point* was in *White Knights* (1985) in which he played a ballet star who'd defected from the Soviet Union (deja vu) only to be kidnapped back into his homeland. The film wasn't exactly like Real Life, but it did allow Mikhail Baryshnikov to trade steps with famed American dancer Gregory Hines - and even permitted Baryshnikov to dabble in Errol Flynn-style acrobatics in his efforts to elude the Soviets. **Selected Works:** *Company Business* (1991)

# Richard Basehart

**Born:** August 31, 1914; Zanesville, OH
**Died:** September 17, 1984; Los Angeles, CA

**Years Active in the Industry:** by decade

| 10ˢ | 20ˢ | 30ˢ | 40ˢ | 50ˢ | 60ˢ | 70ˢ | 80ˢ | 90ˢ |
|-----|-----|-----|-----|-----|-----|-----|-----|-----|
|     |     |     |     |     |     |     |     |     |

Richard Basehart was a thoughtful American leading man who never achieved major stardom. He was the son of a newspaper editor and began his career as a reporter and radio announcer. He began his Broadway career in 1938; in 1945, he won the New York Drama Critics Award for his lead in *The Hasty Heart*. This brought him to the attention of Hollywood, and in 1947 he made his film debut in *Cry Wolf*. That began a successful and varied screen career of almost four decades' duration. He selected his roles carefully and with discrimination to avoid typecasting. During his career he has played heroes, villains, the mentally disturbed, and many other types, often in a rugged and forceful manner. Besides making the occasional stage appearance, he further stretched his talents by performing in many European films, notably Fellini's *La Strada* (1954) in which he gave a sensitive performance as the Fool. Other roles include Ishmael in *Moby Dick* (1956) and the title role in the peculiar black-and-white film *Hitler* (1962). He also appeared frequently on television including a long stint on *Voyage to the Bottom of the Sea*. He was married to actress Valentina Cortese. **Selected Works:** *Being There* (1979), *Decision Before Dawn* (1951), *Titanic* (1953)

# Kim Basinger

**Born:** December 8, 1953; Athens, GA

**Years Active in the Industry:** by decade

| 10ˢ | 20ˢ | 30ˢ | 40ˢ | 50ˢ | 60ˢ | 70ˢ | 80ˢ | 90ˢ |
|-----|-----|-----|-----|-----|-----|-----|-----|-----|
|     |     |     |     |     |     |     |     |     |

Georgia-born Kim Basinger studied dancing and singing from childhood, intending to make her professional bow as a musical comedy performer. While still a high schooler, Kim left for

New York to pursue a career as a model; her blonde hair and beautiful, pliable features were equally suited to the demureness of Breck's home-permanent ads and the more revelatory requirements of *Playboy* magazine. After studying acting at the Neighborhood Playhouse, she made her starring debut in the 1978 TV-movie *Katie: Portrait of a Cen-*

*terfold*. The reviews were kind but condescending, noting that as an actress, Kim was very pretty. She countered her critics with an excellent performance as prostitute Lorene Rogers in the 1980 TV miniseries *From Here to Eternity*, which led to plum acting assignments in theatrical features. Successfully dissipating the standard "dumb blonde" onus often attached to models-turned-actresses of the 1980s, Basinger was an active environmentalist offscreen, and in 1989 she endeared herself to the Georgia chamber of commerce by purchasing a small village not far from her home town of Athens and attempting to pump up the local economy. Much of the laudatory press enjoyed by Basinger and her actor husband Alec Baldwin was scuttled during the troubled filming of 1991's *The Marrying Man*, wherein the couple allegedly comported themselves in as unprofessional a manner as possible. This storm subsided, but within a year she made headlines again due to a costly lawsuit. Determining that Basinger's verbal agreement to appear in the film *Boxing Helena* was legal and binding, a judge ordered the actress, who'd pulled out of the project, to pay eight million dollars in damages to the film's producers. Recast with Sherilyn Fenn, *Boxing Helena* proved to be just as disastrous as Basinger feared. Despite the fact that the film's production company went bankrupt, Basinger has since been compelled to take on as many film assignments as possible to pay off her crippling legal fees. **Selected Works:** *Final Analysis* (1992), *Wayne's World, Part 2* (1993)

# Angela Bassett

**Born:** 1958; St. Petersburg, FL

**Years Active in the Industry:** by decade

| 10s | 20s | 30s | 40s | 50s | 60s | 70s | 80s | 90s |
|-----|-----|-----|-----|-----|-----|-----|-----|-----|
|     |     |     |     |     |     |     | ■   | ■   |

Angela Bassett is a prominent, versatile actress who has found success on stage, television, and in film. In 1985, she made her screen debut on the television series *Spenser: For Hire* (1985); she then went on to do the miniseries *Doubletake* (1985). She made her feature film debut in the action thriller *F/X* in 1986. At this point, Bassett, seems to have made a career out of playing wives but what wives she has played! In films, she has played the wife of Malcolm X, the Jackson Family mother (in a 1992 TV miniseries, *The Jacksons: An American Dream*, and Tina Turner. She also played a wife in *Boyz N the Hood* (1991) and *City of Hope* (1991). For her role as Tina Turner in 1993's *What's Love Got to Do with It*—her first leading role—Bassett was praised by critics and nominated for Best Actress. **Selected Works:** *Kindergarten Cop* (1990), *Passion Fish* (1992), *Strange Days* (1995), *Waiting to Exhale* (1995)

# Alan Bates (Alan Arthur Bates)

**Born:** February 19, 1934; Allestree, Derbyshire, England

**Years Active in the Industry:** by decade

| 10s | 20s | 30s | 40s | 50s | 60s | 70s | 80s | 90s |
|-----|-----|-----|-----|-----|-----|-----|-----|-----|
|     |     |     |     | ■   | ■   | ■   | ■   | ■   |

British actor Alan Bates, one of the foremost participants of the early-1960s "angry young man" school of English drama, made his acting debut, possibly as an angry young boy, in 1945. Bates' career went into high gear after his graduation from the Royal Academy of Dramatic Art; from 1955 through 1960, the actor etched several searing portraits of disenfranchised young working-class Britons in such plays as *Look Back in Anger* and *The Caretaker*. After his first film appearance in *The Entertainer* (1960), Bates helped bring the insolent new-wave acting style into such international successes as *Nothing But the Best* (1964) *Georgy Girl* (1966) and *From the Madding Crowd* (1967); the actor won a BFA award for *The Fixer* (1968), no financial success but later to emerge as a cult film. It was for another cult item, *King of Hearts* (1966), that Bates became the darling of college coeds everywhere; from 1967 onward, hardly a campus-cinema season has gone by in the U.S. without at least one glimpse of Bates standing naked before the lunatic asylum gates at the end of the whimsical anti-establishment *King of Hearts*. While Bates has mellowed and matured, his incisive acting style has gotten sharper and more fascinating in the last few decades, as witness his performances in *An Unmarried Woman* (1978) and *The Rose* (1980). Easing effortlessly into character roles, Bates could be seen breathing fire into the role of Claudius in the 1991 Mel Gibson filmization of Hamlet - a unique experience in that virtually the entire male supporting cast, including Bates, Paul Scofield and Ian Holm, had previously excelled as Hamlet onstage. **Selected Works:** *Englishman Abroad* (1983), *Go-Between* (1971), *Women in Love* (1970), *Zorba the Greek* (1964), *Pack of Lies* (1987)

# Kathy Bates (Kathleen Doyle Bates)

**Born:** June 28, 1948; Memphis, TN

**Years Active in the Industry:** by decade

| 10s | 20s | 30s | 40s | 50s | 60s | 70s | 80s | 90s |
|-----|-----|-----|-----|-----|-----|-----|-----|-----|
|     |     |     |     |     |     | ■   | ■   | ■   |

American actress Kathy Bates has been involved in the arts in one way or another since graduating from Southern Methodist University. Among her earliest jobs were a stint as a singing waitress in a Catskill resort and a sojourn as a gift-shop cashier in New York's Museum of Modern Art. Short and pleasantly plump, Kathy was typed in character roles early on, which assured her a lot more work than the thousands of faceless ingenues in the business. Her film debut occurred with 1971's *Taking Off*, and her off-Broadway debut five years later in *Vanities*. In 1983, she was nominated for a Tony award for her stage appearance as a garrulous would-be suicide in *'night, Mother*, a role played on screen by Sissy Spacek. She also appeared as Lenny McGrath in Beth Henley's Pulitzer Prize-winning play *Crimes of the Heart*...a role played on screen by Diane Keaton. And in 1987, playwright Terence McNally wrote a part specifically tailored to her talents: the much-abused waitress Frankie in *Frankie and Johnny at the Clair de Lune*, a role which won her an Obie award...... and a role played on screen by Michelle Pfeiffer. Did Kathy *ever* get to star in a movie herself? Of course she did: In 1990's *Misery*, she starred as the psychotic "Number One Fan" of writer James Caan, a searing performance which earned the actress an Academy Award and a Golden Globe. Bates has taken her subsequent film stardom in stride, remaining the same outgoing, gregarious and cheerfully scatological person she'd been throughout her stage career. In addition to her stage, movie and TV work, Bates has for many years owned and operated a successful "talking books" audiocassette company. **Selected Works:** *Dick Tracy* (1990), *Fried Green Tomatoes* (1991), *Hostages* (1993), *Prelude to a Kiss* (1992), *White Palace* (1990)

# Anne Baxter

**Born:** May 7, 1923; Michigan City, IN
**Died:** December 12, 1985; New York, NY

**Years Active in the Industry:** by decade

| 10s | 20s | 30s | 40s | 50s | 60s | 70s | 80s | 90s |
|-----|-----|-----|-----|-----|-----|-----|-----|-----|
|     |     |     |     |     |     |     |     |     |

Raised in Bronxville, N.Y., the granddaughter of renowned architect Frank Lloyd Wright, Anne Baxter took up acting at the age of 11 with Maria Ouspenskaya, debuting on Broadway two years later (in *Seen but Not Heard*); she continued working on Broadway until her screen debut at age 17 in *Twenty-Mule Team* (1940), a minor Western featuring Wallace Beery and Marjorie Rambeau. Charming if not beautiful, she tended to play shy and innocent types and gave a few outstanding performances, such as that with Bette Davis in *All About Eve* (1950); she and Davis were both nominated for the Best Actress Oscar, but it went to Judy Holliday. Her "breakthrough" film was Orson Welles's *The Magnificent Ambersons* (1942), leading to many more roles in the next few years. At home in a variety of parts, she won the Best Supporting Actress Oscar in 1946 for her work in *The Razor's Edge*. Although she has worked with many of Hollywood's most celebrated and accomplished directors (Welles, Hitchcock, Lang, Mankiewicz, Wilder, Wellman), after the mid-'50s she tended to get poor roles in mediocre movies. Baxter left Hollywood in 1961 for an isolated cattle station in Australia, an experience she described in her critically-acclaimed book *Intermission: A True Story*. She made a few more films, but her major work was as Lauren Bacall's replacement as Margo Channing in *Applause*, the musical version of *All About Eve*; having played Eve in the film, she now assumed the role earlier held by Davis. Baxter also did some TV work, including a part in the early '80s series *Hotel*. She was married from 1946-53 to actor John Hodiak, whom she met while filming *Sunday Dinner for a Soldier* (1944). **Selected Works:** *Ten Commandments* (1956), *Crash Dive* (1943), *Luck of the Irish* (1948), *Pied Piper* (1942), *Sullivans* (1944)

# Jennifer Beals

**Born:** December 19, 1963; Chicago, IL

**Years Active in the Industry:** by decade

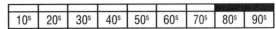

| 10s | 20s | 30s | 40s | 50s | 60s | 70s | 80s | 90s |
|-----|-----|-----|-----|-----|-----|-----|-----|-----|
|     |     |     |     |     |     |     |     |     |

Remember Jennifer Beals? She was the onetime model who ignited the screen as the welder-cum-dancer in 1983's *Flashdance*. Her performance was impressive indeed on first glance, but became less so when it was revealed that several of her more athletic dance scenes had been performed by doubles. Not even the Jennifer Beals Fan Club was interested in her follow-up film, a misguided "remake" of *The Bride of Frankenstein* starring rock singer Sting and titled *The Bride* (1989). The last time we looked, Beals was heading the cast of the direct-to-video *Terror Stalks the Class Reunion* (1992), and essaying a creditable supporting role in the independently produced theatrical film *In the Soup* (1992). **Selected Works:** *Blood & Concrete: A Love Story* (1990), *Indecency* (1992), *Four Rooms* (1995), *Devil in a Blue Dress* (1995)

# Ned Beatty

**Born:** July 6, 1937; Louisville, KY

**Years Active in the Industry:** by decade

| 10s | 20s | 30s | 40s | 50s | 60s | 70s | 80s | 90s |
|-----|-----|-----|-----|-----|-----|-----|-----|-----|
|     |     |     |     |     |     |     |     |     |

Portly American character actor Ned Beatty originally planned to enter the clergy, but after appearing in a single high school play, changed his mind and decided to become a thespian instead. By his early 20s, Beatty was playing Broadway and it was his work in the play *The Great White Hope* that attracted the interest of film director John Boorman, who cast him as one of the four main stars (Beatty played the one who got raped by a brutal woodsman) in his gripping backwoods thriller, *Deliverance* (1972). He has since gone on to become one of the more prolific supporting actors, frequently appearing in up to four films per year. Most recently, he appeared in *Radioland Murders* (1994). **Selected Works:** *Big Easy* (1987), *Hear My Song* (1991), *Prelude to a Kiss* (1992), *Tragedy of Flight 103: The Inside Story* (1991), *Rudy* (1993)

# Warren Beatty (Warren Beaty)

**Born:** March 30, 1938; Richmond, VA

**Years Active in the Industry:** by decade

| 10s | 20s | 30s | 40s | 50s | 60s | 70s | 80s | 90s |
|-----|-----|-----|-----|-----|-----|-----|-----|-----|
|     |     |     |     |     |     |     |     |     |

It might have been easy to write off American actor Warren Beatty as merely the younger brother of film star Shirley MacLaine,

were it not for the fact that Beatty was a profoundly gifted performer whose creative range extended beyond mere acting. After studying at Northwestern University and with acting coach Stella Adler, Beatty was being groomed for stardom almost before he was of voting age, cast in prominent supporting roles in TV dramas and attaining the recurring part of the insufferable Milton Armitage on the TV sitcom *Dobie Gillis*. Beatty left *Dobie* after a handful of episodes, writing off his part as "ridiculous", and headed for the stage, where he appeared in a stock production of *Compulsion* and in William Inge's Broadway play *A Loss of Roses*. The actor's auspicious film debut occurred in *Splendor in the Grass* (1961), after which he spent a number of years being written off by the more narrow-minded movie critics as a would-be Brando. Both Beatty and his fans knew that there was more to his skill than that, and in 1965 Beatty sank a lot of his energy and money into a quirky, impressionistic crime drama, *Mickey One* (1965). The film was a critical success but failed to secure top bookings, though its teaming of Beatty with director Arthur Penn proved crucial to the shape of moviemaking in the 1960s. With Penn again in the director's chair, Beatty took on his first film as producer/star, *Bonnie and Clyde* (1967). Once more, critics were hostile - at first. But an onrush of praise from fellow filmmakers and the word-of-mouth buzz from film fans turned *Bonnie and Clyde* into the most significant film of 1967 - and compelled many critics to reverse their initial opinions and issue apologies. This isn't the place to analyze the value and influence *Bonnie and Clyde* had; suffice it to say that this one film propelled Warren Beatty from a handsome, talented film star into a powerful film *maker*. Picking and choosing his next projects very carefully, Beatty was off screen as much as on from 1970 through 1975, though several of his projects - most prominently *McCabe and Mrs. Miller* (1971) and *The Parallax View* (1974) - would be greeted with effusion by film critics and historians. In 1975, Beatty wrote his first screenplay, and the result was *Shampoo* (1975), a trenchant satire on the misguided mores of the late 1960s. Beatty turned director for 1978's *Heaven Can Wait*, a delightful remake of *Here Comes Mr. Jordan* which was successful enough to encourage future Hollywood bankrolling of Beatty's directorial efforts. In 1981, Beatty produced, directed, coscripted and acted in *Reds*, a spectacular recounting of the Russian Revolution as seen through the eyes of American Communist John Reed. It was a pet project of Beatty's, one he'd been trying to finance since the 1970s (at that time, he'd intended to have Sergei Bondarchuk, of *War and Peace* fame, as director). Perhaps because it was somewhat ideologically muddled and, by fade-out time, a bit too sentimentalized, *Reds* failed to win a Best Picture Academy Award, though Beatty did pick up an Oscar as Best Director. Nothing Beatty has done since *Reds* has been without interest; refusing to turn out mere vehicles, he has taken on a benighted attempt to respark the spirit of the old Hope-Crosby "Road" movies (*Ishtar* [1984]); brought a popular comic strip to the screen, complete with primary colors and artistic hyperbole (*Dick Tracy* [1991]); and managed to make the ruthless gangster Bugsy Siegel a sympathetic visionary (*Bugsy* [1992]). Fiercely protective of his private life, and so much an advocate of total control that he will dictate the type of film stock and lighting to be used when being interviewed for television, Beatty has nonetheless had no luck at all in keeping his many *amours* out of the tabloids. However, Beatty's long and well-documented history of high-profile romances with such actresses as Leslie Caron, Julie Christie and Diane Keaton came to an abrupt end upon his marriage to *Bugsy* costar Annette Bening.

# Bonnie Bedelia

**Born:** March 25, 1952; Yorkville, NY

**Years Active in the Industry:** by decade

| 10s | 20s | 30s | 40s | 50s | 60s | 70s | 80s | 90s |
|-----|-----|-----|-----|-----|-----|-----|-----|-----|
|     |     |     |     |     |     |     |     |     |

    American actress Bonnie Bedelia began performing as a child. She studied ballet at age four; by age eight she was studying at the School of American Ballet on a scholarship, and by nine was playing in a stage production of *Tom Sawyer*. Over the next four years, young Bedelia began dancing professionally with the New York City Ballet and appearing in summer stock and off-Broadway productions. She made her television debut at age 13 playing a regular on the daytime serial *Love of Life*. While working on the show, busy Bedelia continued attending high school and studying at the Quintano School of acting; later she studied briefly with Uta Hagen. She also appeared in four Broadway shows, and in 1967 won a Theater World Award for her work in the play *My Sweet Charlie*. Bedelia made her feature film debut in *The Gypsy Moths* (1969) and later that year was elected The Most Promising Personality. She appeared in three more distinguished films through the early 1970s, and then went on to appear only infrequently in films as she was quite choosy about the roles she would accept. She did, however, appear frequently on television. In 1983, Bedelia made an astounding big screen comeback playing auto racer Shirley Muldowney in *Heart Like a Wheel*. In the late 1980s she began appearing in more mainstream films such as *Die Hard* (1988) and *Presumed Innocent* (1990). Most recently she appeared in *Speechless* (1994). **Selected Works:** *Die Hard* (1988), *Die Hard 2: Die Harder* (1990), *Presumed Innocent* (1990), *Switched at Birth* (1991), *They Shoot Horses, Don't They?* (1969)

# Noah Beery, Sr.

**Born:** 1884; Kansas City, MO
**Died:** 1946

**Years Active in the Industry:** by decade

| 10ˢ | 20ˢ | 30ˢ | 40ˢ | 50ˢ | 60ˢ | 70ˢ | 80ˢ | 90ˢ |
|-----|-----|-----|-----|-----|-----|-----|-----|-----|

Supporting actor in over 100 silents and talkies, usually in villainous roles, Noah Beery was one of the silent era's best-"loved" villains and scoundrels. The half-brother of actor Wallace Beery and the father of actor Noah Beery, Jr., he started his stage career around 1900. He debuted in silent films with *The Mormon Maid* (1917), then went on to establish himself as the heaviest of heavies, particularly in the series of Zane Grey Westerns. Perhaps best known for his portrayal of the cruel, ruthless Sergeant Lejaune in the classic silent *Beau Geste* (1926). His speaking voice was low and resonant, and he was able to continue as a character actor during the sound era. **Selected Works:** *She Done Him Wrong* (1933)

## Ed Begley, Sr. (Edward James Begley)

**Born:** March 25, 1901; Hartford, CT
**Died:** 1970

**Years Active in the Industry:** by decade

| 10ˢ | 20ˢ | 30ˢ | 40ˢ | 50ˢ | 60ˢ | 70ˢ | 80ˢ | 90ˢ |
|-----|-----|-----|-----|-----|-----|-----|-----|-----|

American character actor Ed Begley, the son of Irish immigrants, ran away from home at age 11 and joined a traveling carnival; later he signed up with the navy. Begley became a radio announcer in 1931, leading to dramatic roles in radio (ultimately appearing in over 12,000 shows) and on stage. Made his Broadway debut in 1943; in 1947, he created the Joe Keller role on Broadway in Arthur Miller's *All My Sons*, directed by Elia Kazan. His film career then began when Kazan enlisted him to appear in his production *Boomerang*. Eventually he made 35 films, often playing corrupt politicians or businessmen, such as Boss Finley in *Sweet Bird of Youth* (1962), for which he won the Best Supporting Actor Oscar; however, he also took lighter roles, including some in which he sang and danced. He is the father of actor Ed Begley, Jr. **Selected Works:** *Sorry, Wrong Number* (1948), *Twelve Angry Men* (1957), *It Happens Every Spring* (1949), *Sitting Pretty* (1948)

## Ralph Bellamy

**Born:** June 17, 1904; Chicago, IL
**Died:** November 29, 1991; Santa Monica, CA

**Years Active in the Industry:** by decade

| 10ˢ | 20ˢ | 30ˢ | 40ˢ | 50ˢ | 60ˢ | 70ˢ | 80ˢ | 90ˢ |
|-----|-----|-----|-----|-----|-----|-----|-----|-----|

From his late teens to his late '20s, Ralph Bellamy worked with 15 different traveling stock companies, not just as an actor but also as a director, producer, set designer, and prop handler. In 1927 he started his own company, the Ralph Bellamy Players. He debuted on Broadway in 1929, then broke into films in 1931. He went on to play leads in dozens of B-movies; he also played the title role in the "Ellery Queen" series. For his work in *The Awful Truth* (1937) he received an Oscar nomination, playing the "other man" who loses the girl to the hero; he was soon typecast in this sort of role in sophisticated comedies. After 1945 his film work was highly sporadic as he changed his focus to the stage, going on to play leads in many Broadway productions; for his portrayal of FDR in *Sunrise at Campobello* (1958) he won a Tony Award and the New York Drama Critics Award. From 1940-60 he served on the State of California Arts Commission. From 1952-64 he was the president of Actors' Equity. In 1986 he was awarded an honorary Oscar "for his unique artistry and his distinguished service to the profession of acting." He authored an autobiography, *When the Smoke Hits the Fan* (1979). **Selected Works:** *Pretty Woman* (1990), *Professionals* (1966), *Rosemary's Baby* (1968), *Trading Places* (1983)

## Jean-Paul Belmondo

**Born:** April 9, 1933; Neuilly-sur-Seine, France

**Years Active in the Industry:** by decade

| 10ˢ | 20ˢ | 30ˢ | 40ˢ | 50ˢ | 60ˢ | 70ˢ | 80ˢ | 90ˢ |
|-----|-----|-----|-----|-----|-----|-----|-----|-----|

Charming but homely French leading man, Jean-Paul Belmondo, the son of a sculptor, studied drama at the Paris Conservatory then appeared in stage productions, first in the provinces and  then (after several years) in Paris. He won supporting roles in nearly a dozen films, beginning in 1958; his breakthrough came with his lead role in Godard's first feature, *Breathless*, which skyrocketed him to fame and made him the archetype of the French New Wave anti-hero and rebellious youth. Soon he was France's leading male star, and his ambivalent character made him popular internationally. At age thirty he published an autobiography (*Thirty Years and Twenty-five Films*) and was elected President of the French actors' union. Since then—although he has made both good and mediocre films—he has remained a prominent star, and has worked with nearly every major French director, including Truffaut, Resnais, and Malle. He is the head of his own production company, Cerito films. **Selected Works:** *Pierrot Le Fou* (1965), *Stavisky* (1974), *Two Women* (1961), *A Woman Is a Woman* (1960)

# James Belushi

**Born:** May 15, 1954; Chicago, IL

**Years Active in the Industry:** by decade

| 10ˢ | 20ˢ | 30ˢ | 40ˢ | 50ˢ | 60ˢ | 70ˢ | 80ˢ | 90ˢ |
|-----|-----|-----|-----|-----|-----|-----|-----|-----|
|     |     |     |     |     |     |     | ▓ | ▓ |

Versatile actor James Belushi is slowly coming into his own, but it has not been an easy task as he has had to follow in the fiery footsteps of his flamboyant, self-destructive brother the late John Belushi. Despite that obstacle, the easy going actor with the crooked smile has still managed to forge a respectable career playing co-leads in a variety of film genres including comedy, action, and drama in roles ranging from a sleazeball thief to a cop to a party animal in a go-rilla suit. Prior to his first television appearances, the Chicago born actor earned a degree in speech and theater. He has worked on stage in *The Pirates of Penzance* and *True West*. Like John, James then joined the notorious Second City improvisational group. He also be-gan making regular guest appearances on *Saturday Night Live* where his brother became famous. In 1981, he made his feature film debut playing James Cann's calm partner in *Thief*. He began acting under John Landis, who also directed his brother, in *Trading Places* (1983). He continued playing supporting roles and some leads, but his big break came when he played a bad cop in 1988's *Red Heat* with Arnold Schwarzenegger. He was equally popular in 1989's *K-9*. Though his subsequent films have not been as successful, Belushi continues to grow as a dramatic actor. **Selected Works:** *Diary of a Hitman* (1991), *Little Shop of Horrors* (1986), *Mr. Destiny* (1990), *Only the Lonely* (1991), *Salvador* (1986), *About Last Night* (1986)

# John Belushi

**Born:** January 25, 1949; Chicago, IL
**Died:** March 5, 1982; West Hollywood, CA

**Years Active in the Industry:** by decade

| 10ˢ | 20ˢ | 30ˢ | 40ˢ | 50ˢ | 60ˢ | 70ˢ | 80ˢ | 90ˢ |
|-----|-----|-----|-----|-----|-----|-----|-----|-----|
|     |     |     |     |     |     | ▓ | ▓ |     |

Son of a Chicago restauranteur, American comic actor John Belushi played drums in a high school band and excelled in foot-ball. But acting was his first love, a love requited by college produc-tions and summer stock. Belushi and several old pals auditioned for Chicago's Second City comedy troupe; only Belushi was selected, and he became the youngest-ever performer to appear in Second City's "mainstage" productions. Belushi's improvisational style sometimes had a nasty, dangerous, "politically incorrect" edge, but these were the early 1970s, when such traits were prized rather than discouraged. John's guerrilla comic techniques were reportedly in-spired by the 1968 Democratic convention riots in Chicago; he was among the few performers who could *successfully* exploit violence and social upheaval as a source of humor. Belushi was hired in 1973 for the off-Broadway *National Lampoon's Lemmings*; he then participated in future National Lampoon projects like the syndicated

*Radio Hour.* From here he was cast (along with several Second City alumni) in NBC's new "gonzo" satirical revue program *Saturday Night Live* in 1975. Frustrated by the media's concen-tration on costar Chevy Chase during *SNL*'s maiden season, Belushi fully came into his own once Chase left in 1976; among Belushi's cele-brated comic creations were the fish-out-of-water Samurai Warrior, the "chizzburger chizzburger" short-order cook, and - in tandem with close friend Dan Aykroyd - the ultra-hip Blues Brothers. Belushi's first film appearance was a disappointingly small role in the Jack Nicholson western *Goin' South* (1978), but with his next movie he truly hit his stride. As Bluto, the beer-besotted fraternity goof in *National Lampoon's Animal House* (1978), Belushi was grossly uproarious, almost single-handedly launching a nationwide collegiate craze for toga parties. The actor was a full-fledged movie star, but audiences were generally permitted to see only the "Bluto" side of Belushi. The actor fought for better and more varied film roles, sometimes succeeding (1982's *Blues Broth-ers*), often failing (1981's *Continental Divide*). Never an advocate of "moderation in everything", Belushi tended to emulate "Bluto" in real life with his excessive eating and drinking; his drug intake, already formidable in his *Lemmings* days, increased as his star ascended, ter-rifying even those friends who were themselves cocaine users. On March 5, 1982, comedian Robin Williams and writer Nelson Ryan came to visit Belushi in his temporary living quarters at West Holly-wood's Chateau Marmont Hotel; they were the last of his friends to see him alive. Belushi was dead before the day was over, the victim of a cocaine and heroin overdose. With him at the time was erstwhile singer Cathy Smith, who would later be charged with involuntary manslaughter for her alleged role in administering the fatal drug jolt. The meteoric rise and fall of Belushi was the stuff that legends are made of, overshadowing his brilliant comic gifts in favor of the sordid details. Two books have been written about Belushi: Robert Wood-ward's *Wired*, and John's widow Jackie Belushi's "answer" to Wood-ward, *Samurai Widow.*

# William Bendix

**Born:** January 4, 1906; New York, NY
**Died:** 1964

**Years Active in the Industry:** by decade

| 10ˢ | 20ˢ | 30ˢ | 40ˢ | 50ˢ | 60ˢ | 70ˢ | 80ˢ | 90ˢ |
|-----|-----|-----|-----|-----|-----|-----|-----|-----|
|     |     |     | ▓ |     |     |     |     |     |

Although he went on to play a variety of street-wise work-ing-class louts, William Bendix was the son of the conductor of the

New York Metropolitan Orchestra. He appeared in one film as a child, then went on to a variety of jobs (including time spent as a minor league baseball player) before joining the New York Theater Guild. His first Broadway appearance was as a cop in William Saroyan's *The Time of Your Life* (1939); he then began a healthy film career in 1942 with *Woman of the Year*, the same year, he appeared in *Wake Island*, for which he was nominated for Best Supporting Actor. With his thick features, broken nose and affected Brooklyn accent, Bendix often played the time-weathered meanie with a heart of gold; eventually he was typecast as dumb and brutish characters. He is best known for his role on the radio show *The Life of Riley*, which he reprised in the film of the same name (1949). He played Babe Ruth in *The Babe Ruth Story* (1948), and generally worked for Paramount. **Selected Works:** *Detective Story* (1951), *Lifeboat* (1944), *Star Spangled Rhythm* (1942)

# Roberto Benigni

**Born:** October 27, 1952; Vergaio, Italy

**Years Active in the Industry:** by decade

| 10s | 20s | 30s | 40s | 50s | 60s | 70s | 80s | 90s |
|-----|-----|-----|-----|-----|-----|-----|-----|-----|
|     |     |     |     |     |     |     | ■   |     |

Arguably the most popular Italian screen comedian since the immortal Toto, Roberto Benigni mastered early on the exacting art of improvisational humor. In his native country, Benigni starred in his own must-see TV series, sustaining his vast following with several hilarious movie appearances. One of his best-known monologues, "Cioni Mario", was expanded into the feature film *I Love You Berlinger*. American filmgoers became aware of the Benigni brand of comedy with the 1988 Walter Matthau vehicle *Little Devils*, which Benigni wrote, directed, and costarred in. Thus, when Blake Edwards chose Benigni to play the pratfalling offspring of Inspector Clouseau in 1992's *Son of the Pink Panther*, the choice seemed inspired. That it was, save for one small matter: though funny, inventive and eager to please, Benigni was simply not Peter Sellers. **Selected Works:** *Johnny Stecchino* (1992), *Night on Earth* (1991), *Monster* (1994)

# Annette Bening

**Born:** May 5, 1958; Topeka, KS

**Years Active in the Industry:** by decade

| 10s | 20s | 30s | 40s | 50s | 60s | 70s | 80s | 90s |
|-----|-----|-----|-----|-----|-----|-----|-----|-----|
|     |     |     |     |     |     |     | ■   |     |

Contemporary American actress Annette Bening is an up-and-coming star noted for her versatility. She began training as an actress and singer while still a child. As a young woman, Bening had extensive experience in repertory theater and has appeared with such major troupes as Washington's Arena Stage company. She then moved to New York where she had a brief, distinguished

career on Broadway. In 1988, Bening made her film debut playing a small part in John Hughes's *The Great Outdoors*. Two years later, she played the lead in *Valmont*, but did not really begin making a name for herself until she won an Academy Award for Best Supporting Actress in the 1990 film *The Grifters*. In 1991, Bening married actor, filmmaker Warren Beatty and took a two year break to bear and raise his child. She recently appeared opposite Beatty in a remake of the classic romantic comedy *Love Affair* (1994). **Selected Works:** *Guilty by Suspicion* (1991), *Postcards from the Edge* (1990), *The American President* (1995)

# Richard Benjamin

**Born:** May 22, 1938; New York, NY

**Years Active in the Industry:** by decade

| 10s | 20s | 30s | 40s | 50s | 60s | 70s | 80s | 90s |
|-----|-----|-----|-----|-----|-----|-----|-----|-----|
|     |     |     |     |     |     | ■   |     |     |

American leading man and filmmaker Richard Benjamin began his career on the stage after studying at the prestigious New York High School of Performing Arts. He became a Broadway star in 1966 after appearing in Neil Simon's *The Star Spangled Girl*. Benjamin and his wife Paula Prentiss then began working on a television series *He and She*. Benjamin established himself as a major film talent with his feature film debut in *Goodbye Columbus* (1969). Unfortunately, he played his role as a comical neurotic with intellectual affectations so well that he became typecast. In 1975, Benjamin was awarded a Golden Globe for his role in *The Sunshine Boys*. He continued acting until the early 1980s when he made his directorial debut with the acclaimed comedy *My Favorite Year* (1982). As a director, Benjamin has continued to work with popular but rather mainstream comedies, such as *Mermaids* (1990). **Selected Works:** *Catch-22* (1970), *Diary of a Mad Housewife* (1970), *Made in America* (1993)

# Constance Bennett

**Born:** October 22, 1905; New York, NY
**Died:** 1965

**Years Active in the Industry:** by decade

| 10ˢ | 20ˢ | 30ˢ | 40ˢ | 50ˢ | 60ˢ | 70ˢ | 80ˢ | 90ˢ |
|-----|-----|-----|-----|-----|-----|-----|-----|-----|
|     |     |     |     |     |     |     |     |     |

Actress Constance Bennett is the sister of actresses Barbara and Joan Bennett and the daughter of matinee idol Richard Bennett. Educated in New York and Paris, she appeared in a bit role at age 12, married at age 16 (annulled), and made her real screen debut at 17 in *Reckless Youth* (1922). She went on to become, briefly, Hollywood's highest paid star in the silents, but she abandoned stardom from 1926-29 in order to live a glamorous, jet-set life. She re-entered films in time for the talkies; with her husky, sardonic voice, she made the transition easily, and specialized as wise-cracking, brittle sophisticates in parlor-room comedies; she also made tearjerkers. At first dark-haired, her sleek blonde pageboy hair style became her trademark. In the 1950s, she left films for the stage appearing in only three films after 1948. Bennett was married five times, once to actor Gilbert Roland (1941-44). While shooting *Madame X* she died of a cerebral hemorrhage. The film was released posthumously in 1966. **Selected Works:** *Topper* (1937), *Affairs of Cellini* (1934), *Merrily We Live* (1938)

# Joan Sterndale Bennett

**Born:** February 27, 1910; Palisades, NJ
**Died:** December 7, 1990; Scarsdale, NY

**Years Active in the Industry:** by decade

| 10ˢ | 20ˢ | 30ˢ | 40ˢ | 50ˢ | 60ˢ | 70ˢ | 80ˢ | 90ˢ |
|-----|-----|-----|-----|-----|-----|-----|-----|-----|
|     |     |     |     |     |     |     |     |     |

The daughter of actors Richard Bennett and Adrienne Morrison, Joan Bennett debuted onstage in *Jarnegan* (1928), which featured her father. That same year she went to Hollywood, and a year later became a star after she appeared in *Bulldog Drummond* (1929) opposite Ronald Colman. She went on to a very busy screen career in leading roles, playing everything from mothers to femme fatales to mercenary types. She got most of her best roles after she married producer Walter Wanger in 1940. In 1952 Wanger was jailed for several months for allegedly shooting Bennett's agent in a jealous rage. She divorced Wanger in 1965 and later married critic David Wilde. Previously she had been married to producer and writer Gene Markey. Her film work slowed down after 1951. She appeared in a number of stage shows in the '50s and early '60s. She was also a regular on the TV series *Dark Shadows*. She was the sister of actresses Barbara and Constance Bennett. **Selected Works:** *Disraeli* (1929), *Father of the Bride* (1950), *Little Women* (1933), *Scarlet Street* (1945), *Woman in the Window* (1945)

# Jack Benny (Benjamin Kubelsky)

**Born:** February 14, 1894; Waukegan, IL
**Died:** December 26, 1974; Beverly Hills, CA

**Years Active in the Industry:** by decade

| 10ˢ | 20ˢ | 30ˢ | 40ˢ | 50ˢ | 60ˢ | 70ˢ | 80ˢ | 90ˢ |
|-----|-----|-----|-----|-----|-----|-----|-----|-----|
|     |     |     |     |     |     |     |     |     |

Though born in a Chicago hospital, entertainer Jack Benny was a Waukegan boy through and through. The son of a Polish immigrant haberdasher, Benny studied the violin from an early age (he really *could* play, though he was certainly no virtuoso), and managed to find work in local theatre orchestras. As a teenager, Benny gave vaudeville a try with a musical act in partnership with pianist Cora Salisbury, but this first fling at show business was only fitfully successful. During World War I, Benny was assigned to the Great Lakes Naval Training Center, where, while appearing in camp shows, he first began telling jokes in between violin selections. Benny returned to vaudeville with a comedy act, slowly building himself up into a headliner. He made his first radio appearance on Ed Sullivan's interview show on March 29, 1932; within a year he had his own show, which would evolve over the next two decades into one of radio's most popular programs. He met with equal success when he moved into television in 1950. There are few comedy fans in existence who aren't familiar with the character Benny played on the air: The vain, tone-deaf, penny-pinching, eternal 39-year-old who spent his life being flustered and humiliated by his supporting cast (Mary Livingstone, Eddie "Rochester" Anderson, Dennis Day, Frank Nelson, Mel Blanc, Don Wilson et. al.); nor need his fans be reminded that this character developed *gradually*, rather than springing full-blown upon the world way back in 1932. What is usually de-emphasized in the many accounts of Benny's life and career is his sizeable body of movie work. Benny himself insisted that most of his films were no good, and many casual viewers have been willing to accept his word on this. Actually, Benny's films, while not all classics, were by and large moneymakers, and never anything to be truly ashamed of. Jack's first feature appearance was as the wisecracking emcee of MGM's *The Hollywood Revue of 1929*. He followed this with a comic-relief role in *Chasing Rainbows* (1930) and an uncharacteristic straight part in the low-budget *The Medicine Man* (1930). He was a perfectly acceptable semicomic romantic lead in *It's in the Air* (1935), *Artists and Models* (1936), *Artists and Models Abroad* (1936), and in his appearances in Paramount's *College* and *Big Broadcast* series. Whenever Benny expressed displeasure over his film career, he was usually alluding to those pictures that insisted upon casting him as Benny the Famous Radio Comedian rather than a wholly different screen character. *Transatlantic Merry-Go-Round* (1934), *Man About Town* (1939) and *Buck Benny Rides Again* (1940), though enjoyable, are totally reliant upon Benny's pre-established radio character and "schtick" for their laughs, and as such aren't nearly as effective as his actual radio appearances. His most disappointing movie vehicle was *Love Thy Neighbor* (1940), designed to cash in on his phony feud with fellow radio humorist Fred Allen. Not only was the film uninspired, but also outdated, since the feud's full comic value had pretty much peaked by 1937. Many of Benny's best films were made during his last four years in Hollywood. 1941's *Charley's Aunt* was a lively adaptation of the old Brandon Thomas theatrical chestnut (though it did have to work overtime in explaining why a man in his forties was still an Oxford undergraduate!); 1942's *George Washington Slept Here*, likewise adapted from a stage play (by George S. Kaufman and Moss Hart), was a reasonably funny comedy of frustration; and yet another stage derivation, 1943's *The Meanest Man in the World* (based on a George M. Cohan farce), allowed Benny to go far afield from his truculent radio persona by playing a man who is too *nice* for his own good. Benny's finest film, bar none, was the Ernst Lubitsch-directed *To Be or Not to Be* (1942), in which the comedian was superbly cast as "that great, great Polish actor" Joseph Tura. Benny's final starring feature, the much maligned *Horn Blows at Midnight* (1945), was an enjoyable effort, and not by any means the unmitigated disaster he used to joke about on radio. The film's problem at the box-office was that it was a comedy fantasy, and audiences in 1945 had had their fill of comedy fantasies. After *Horn Blows at Midnight*, Benny's theatrical film appearances were confined to guest spots and unbilled gag bits (e.g. *The Great Lover* and *Beau James*). In 1949, Benny produced a Dorothy Lamour movie vehicle, *The Lucky Stiff*; in addition, his J&M Productions, which produced his weekly television series from 1950 through 1965, was also responsible for the moderately popular TV adventure series *Checkmate* (1960-62). In 1974, Benny was primed to restart his long-dormant movie career by appearing opposite his lifelong friend George Burns in the film adaptation of Neil Simon's *The Sunshine Boys*; unfortunately, he died of cancer before filming could begin, and his role was eventually played by Walter Matthau. **Selected Works:** *Broadway Melody of 1936* (1935)

# Robby Benson (Robert Segal)

**Born:** January 21, 1956; Dallas, TX

**Years Active in the Industry:** by decade

| 10s | 20s | 30s | 40s | 50s | 60s | 70s | 80s | 90s |
|-----|-----|-----|-----|-----|-----|-----|-----|-----|
|     |     |     |     |     |     |     |     |     |

When 13-year-old Robby Benson appeared with "Josephine the Plumber" (Jane Withers) in a well-circulated TV commercial of the late 1960s, he was already a ten-year veteran of show business. The son of a writer and a stage actress, Benson went from the straw-hat theater circuit to the leading role of *Oliver* in a 1964 Japanese touring production. At fourteen he made his Broadway debut, and at that same time became the first of five actors to play the role of Bruce Carson on the TV daytime drama *Search for Tomorrow*. In films from 1972, Benson specialized in playing sensitive teenagers with severe emotional and/or physical problems. He also was frequently costarred in romantic roles with young actress Glynnis O'Connor, notably in the 1973 film *Jeremy* and the 1977 TV production of *Our Town*. While his early theatrical films were generally okay, Benson was better served in made-for-TV movies: he was excellent as the dying son of author John Gunther in *Death Be Not Proud* (1975) and as George Burns' retarded grandson in *Two of a Kind* (1983). Benson endured an awkward period in the 1980s when, except for such career highlights as *The*

*Chosen* (1981), he seemed to be pulling out the same bag of acting tricks in role after role. An effort to establish himself as a producer resulted in the risible bomb *Die Laughing* (1979). He backed away from show business in 1984 when he underwent delicate open-heart surgery; the ordeal seemed to strengthen his resolve to broaden his performing skills. He starred as a tough Chicago cop in brief TV series *Tough Cookies* (1986), and in 1988 directed his first film, *Crack in the Mirror*. Benson's most successful film project of recent years was one in which his face was never seen: as the growling, deep-voiced Beast in the Disney cartoon feature *Beauty and the Beast* (though touted in some articles as his voiceover debut, Benson had actually been dubbing TV cartoons for several years, notably the 1991 series *Pirates of Dark Water*). **Selected Works:** *Betrayal of the Dove* (1992), *Invasion of Privacy* (1992)

# Robert R. Benton

**Born:** September 29, 1932; Waxahachie, TX

**Years Active in the Industry:** by decade

| 10s | 20s | 30s | 40s | 50s | 60s | 70s | 80s | 90s |
|-----|-----|-----|-----|-----|-----|-----|-----|-----|
|     |     |     |     |     |     |     |     |     |

Director and screenwriter Robert Benton may not have achieved the legendary mainstream status as his peers Scorsese, Spielberg, and Coppola, but this idiosyncratic filmmaker and screenwriter has had more than his share of major successes on the silver screen. His best known film as director is the 1979 winner of five Academy Awards—including best direction and best screenplay—*Kramer vs. Kramer*. Benton has also achieved considerable fame for his screenwriting partnership with David Newman. Together they have written such cinema favorites as *Bonnie and Clyde* (1967), and *What's Up Doc?* (1972). By himself he wrote *Bad Company*; he wrote *Superman* (1978) with Mario Puzo. In 1956, he was hired by *Esquire* magazine in New York where he met David Newman who would become his writing partner with whom he worked for 10 years before writing *Bonnie and Clyde*, a film that was rejected by 20 directors before it was turned into a movie classic by director Arthur Penn. He tried directing with his *Bad Company*, but the film was not a commercial success. He then directed the detective spoof *The Late Show* (1977). During the 1980s, Benton began directing a series of well-made, but small scale films such as 1982's Hitchcockian thriller *Still of the Night*. In 1984, he again scored big with the autobiographical *Places of the Heart* based on a true story that happened to his great-grandmother. The film won an Oscar for lead actress Sally Field and was also nominated for best screenplay. **Selected Works:** *Billy Bathgate* (1991), *Places in the Heart* (1984), *Nobody's Fool* (1994)

# Tom Berenger

**Born:** May 31, 1950; Chicago, IL

**Years Active in the Industry:** by decade

| 10s | 20s | 30s | 40s | 50s | 60s | 70s | 80s | 90s |
|-----|-----|-----|-----|-----|-----|-----|-----|-----|
|     |     |     |     |     |     |  ■  |  ■  |  ■  |

University of Missouri graduate Tom Berenger began his theatre work in regional repertory. Once he hit New York, Berenger was employed by several TV soap operas, most prominently as the ill-fated Timmy Siegel on *One Life to Live*. His first film assignments ranged from the cavalier heroics of *Butch and Sundance: The Early Years* (1979) to the grittier urban demands of *Looking for Mr. Goodbar* (1977). After such relatively sympathetic assignments as *The Big Chill* (1983), Berenger shocked his following in the role of the sociopathic, battle-scarred Sergeant Barnes in *Platoon* (1986), a performance that earned him an Oscar nomination. Not that this stopped the versatile Berenger from essaying future good-guy roles like the irresponsible baseball player in *Major League* (1988). Berenger continues to successfully fluctuate between heroes and villains into the 1990s, with a few sidetrips into TV, notably an amusing, unheralded guest stint in the waning days of the sitcom *Cheers*. **Selected Works:** *At Play in the Fields of the Lord* (1991), *Gettysburg* (1992), *Shattered* (1991), *Avenging Angel* (1995)

# Bruce Beresford

**Born:** August 16, 1940; Sydney, Australia

**Years Active in the Industry:** by decade

| 10s | 20s | 30s | 40s | 50s | 60s | 70s | 80s | 90s |
|-----|-----|-----|-----|-----|-----|-----|-----|-----|
|     |     |     |     |     |     |  ■  |  ■  |  ■  |

Beresford produced short documentaries as head of the British Film Institute Production Board from 1966 to 1970. He returned to Australia in 1971 and directed his first features, the rowdy Barry Crocker and Barry Humphries comedies *The Adventures Of Barry McKenzie* and *Barry McKenzie Holds His Own*, which he also co-scripted. He began attracting international attention in the late 1970s and early '80s with the satire *Don's Party*, the period drama *The Getting Of Wisdom*, and *Breaker Morant*, a bitter drama of the Boer War. Beresford began making films in the States with the admired drama of a country singer, *Tender Mercies*; his track record here has been erratic, from the silliness of *King David*

to the popular drama *Driving Miss Daisy*. Working in the Australian film industry, Beresford's notable recent work includes *The Fringe Dwellers* and *Black Robe*. **Selected Works:** *Indian Summer* (1993), *Mister Johnson* (1991), *Rich in Love* (1993), *Silent Fall* (1994)

# Candice Bergen

**Born:** May 9, 1946; Beverly Hills, CA

**Years Active in the Industry:** by decade

| 10s | 20s | 30s | 40s | 50s | 60s | 70s | 80s | 90s |
|-----|-----|-----|-----|-----|-----|-----|-----|-----|
|     |     |     |     |     |     |  ■  |  ■  |  ■  |

American actress Candice Bergen was a celebrity even before she was born. As the first child of popular radio ventriloquist Edgar Bergen and his young wife Frances, Candice was a hot news item months before her birth, and headline material upon that blessed event (her coming into the world even prompted magazine cartoons which suggested that Edgar would try to confound the nurses by "giving" his new daughter a voice.) Candice made her first public appearance as an infant, featured with her parents in a magazine advertisement. Before she was ten, Candice was appearing sporadically on dad's radio program, demonstrating a precocious ability to throw her own voice (a skill she hasn't been called upon to repeat in recent years); at 11 she and Groucho Marx's daughter Melinda were guest contestants on Groucho's TV quiz show *You Bet Your Life*. Candice loved her parents and luxuriated in her posh lifestyle, though she was set apart from other children in that her "brothers" were the wooden dummies Charlie McCarthy and Mortimer Snerd - and Charlie had a bigger bedroom than she did! Like most 1960s teens, however, she rebelled against the conservatism of her parents and adopted a well-publicized, freewheeling lifestyle - and a movie career. In her first film, *The Group* (1965), Candice played a wealthy young lesbian - a character light years away from the sensibilities of her old-guard father. She next appeared with Steve McQueen in the big budget *The Sand Pebbles* (1966), simultaneously running smack dab into the unkind cuts of critics, who made the expected (given her parentage) comments concerning her "wooden" performance. Truth to tell, Candice did look far better than she acted, and this status quo remained throughout most of her film appearances of the late 1960s; even Candice admitted she wasn't much of an actress, though she allowed (in another moment that must have given papa Edgar pause) that she was terrific when required in a film to simulate an orgasm. Several films later, Candice decided to take her career more seriously than did her critics, and began emerging into a talented and reliable actress in such films as *Carnal Knowledge* (1971) and *The Wind and the Lion* (1975). Most observers agree that Candice's true turnaround was her touching but hilarious performance as a divorced woman pursuing a singing career - with little in the way of talent - in the Burt Reynolds comedy *Starting Over* (1979). Candice's roller-coaster offscreen life settled into relative normality when she married French film director Louis Malle; meanwhile, her acting career gained momentum as she sought out and received ever-improving movie and TV roles. In 1988, Candice began a still-thriving run in the title role of the television sitcom *Murphy Brown*, in which she was brilliant as a mercurial, high-strung TV newsmagazine reporter, a role that won Ms. Bergen several Emmy Awards. While *Murphy Brown* capped Candice Bergen's full acceptance by audiences and critics as an actress of stature, it also restored her to "headline" status in 1992 - when, in direct response to the fictional Murphy Brown's decision to become a single mother, Vice President Dan Quayle delivered his notorious "family values" speech. **Selected Works:** *Bite the Bullet* (1975), *Gandhi* (1982)

# Patrick Bergin

**Born:** 1953; Dublin, Ireland

**Years Active in the Industry:** by decade

| 10ˢ | 20ˢ | 30ˢ | 40ˢ | 50ˢ | 60ˢ | 70ˢ | 80ˢ | 90ˢ |
|-----|-----|-----|-----|-----|-----|-----|-----|-----|
|     |     |     |     |     |     |     |     |     |

Patrick Bergin is a versatile actor who has yet to make it big in Hollywood. The son of a trade union activist and founder of a political theater, Bergin was born and raised in Dublin, Ireland, but left for London when he was only 17. There he worked at different jobs and eventually set up an experimental theater group. Originally a high school drop out, Bergin returned to night school and by his early 20s had become a school teacher. He worked as an educator for five years and then quit to go on an extensive tour of Europe. Upon his return to Britain, he began working in repertory theater, and occasionally on television before appearing in a short British Film School production. Bergin made his feature film debut in 1988 with *The Courier*, that year he also won acclaim for his role as an IRA informer in the TV movie *Act of Betrayal*. His success with the latter film lead director Bob Rafelson to cast him as Sir Richard Burton in his epic *Mountains of the Moon* (1990). While in Britain Bergin typically played heroes, but in Hollywood he is usually cast as a villainous lowlife. He was particularly nasty as the obsessed, abusive husband in *Sleeping with the Enemy* (1991). **Selected Works:** *Highway to Hell* (1992), *Map of the Human Heart* (1993), *Patriot Games* (1992), *Robin Hood* (1991)

# Andrew Bergman

**Born:** 1945; Queens, NY

**Years Active in the Industry:** by decade

| 10ˢ | 20ˢ | 30ˢ | 40ˢ | 50ˢ | 60ˢ | 70ˢ | 80ˢ | 90ˢ |
|-----|-----|-----|-----|-----|-----|-----|-----|-----|
|     |     |     |     |     |     |     |     |     |

The son of a *New York Daily News* columnist, director/writer Andrew Bergman attended Harper College and the University of Wisconsin-Madison. After receiving his doctorate in teaching in 1970, Bergman established his reputation as a "progressive" film historian/sociologist with his 1971 overview of 1930s films, *We're In the Money*. Bergman was hired as a "youth contact" p.r. man for United Artists; it was his job to clue the studio in as to what was "hot" amongst the young. Following his Broadway playwriting bow with *Social Security*, Bergman received his first screenwriting credit for Mel Brooks' blockbuster western parody *Blazing Saddles* (a later attempt by Bergman to write a genre spoof on his own, *Rhapsody of Crime*, died on the vine). After the success of his screenplay and story for 1979's *The In-Laws*, Bergman was given an opportunity to direct the Madison Avenue satire *So Fine* (1981). Forming his own production company with Michael Lobell, Bergman has written and/or directed such moneymakers as *Fletch* (1985), *The Freshman* (1990), *Honeymoon in Vegas* and *It Could Happen to You* (1994). Keeping Andrew Bergman "honest" have been such occasional non-hits as the 1991 soap-opera lampoon *Soapdish* and the weekly TV fiasco *The Dictator* (1992). **Selected Works:** *Enemies, a Love Story* (1989), *Scout* (1994)

# Ingmar Bergman (Ernst Ingmar Bergman)

**Born:** July 14, 1918; Uppsala, Sweden

**Years Active in the Industry:** by decade

| 10ˢ | 20ˢ | 30ˢ | 40ˢ | 50ˢ | 60ˢ | 70ˢ | 80ˢ | 90ˢ |
|-----|-----|-----|-----|-----|-----|-----|-----|-----|
|     |     |     |     |     |     |     |     |     |

The most famous filmmaker ever to come out of Sweden, Ingmar Bergman was, for a time, one of the most influential of all European directors. After a traumatic childhood in a rigidly religious household, Bergman gravitated toward theater and film, and directed plays while still a boy. A literary major in college, he began writing fiction as well as plays, and entered the film industry in Sweden as a script writer in the early 1940s. He wrote his first screenplay in 1944 (*Torment*) and graduated to the director's chair soon after. Bergman began emerging as an important filmmaker in the early 1950s with films such as *Secrets of Women*, *Summer With Monika*, and *Smiles of a Summer Night*. The latter comedy subsequently became the basis for the Stephen Sondheim musical *A Little Night Music*, as well as the movie *A Midsummer Night's Sex Comedy* by Woody Allen, who is a dedicated Bergman fan and disciple. By the end of the 1950s, with movies like *The Seventh Seal*, a grim symbolic costume drama, and *Wild Strawberries*, Bergman had developed a wide international following, especially among college students, who took easily to his serious psychological delvings into the inner workings of his characters. The 1960s saw a further progression of Bergman's work, and his arrival in the 1970s on American television with the series *Scenes From A Marriage* made him a household name of sorts. His work in the 1970s and 1980s was less well received, despite the acclaim that greeted *Cries and Whispers*, and his tax difficulties with the Swedish government in the middle of the 1970s interrupted his career, although he had returned to form in the beginning of the 1980s with *Fanny and Alexander*. **Selected Works:** *Autumn Sonata* (1978), *Face to Face* (1976), *Passion of Anna* (1970), *Shame* (1968), *Virgin Spring* (1959)

# Ingrid Bergman

**Born:** August 29, 1915; Stockholm, Sweden
**Died:** August 29, 1982

**Years Active in the Industry:** by decade

| 10s | 20s | 30s | 40s | 50s | 60s | 70s | 80s | 90s |
|-----|-----|-----|-----|-----|-----|-----|-----|-----|

At 18, Ingrid Bergman enrolled in Stockholm's Royal Dramatic Theater School. The following year, 1934, she debuted on-screen and almost immediately became the foremost young actress in Swedish cinema. Hollywood moguls decided to remake her film *Intermezzo* (1936), and she was invited to star in the 1939 version, after which she spent a decade in American and British films. She debuted on Broadway in *Liliom* in 1940. For her work in *Gaslight* (1944) she won the Best Actress Oscar; by 1946 she was the highest-paid actress in Hollywood. For her portrayal of Joan of Arc in the Broadway play *Joan of Lorraine* (1946) she won a Tony Award. Strikingly beautiful and exuding a wholesome, almost saintly aura, she suffered a major backlash of public resentment when she left her husband to live with director Roberto Rossellini, bearing him a child two months before they were married in 1950. She became demonized as a wanton woman and never regained her full popularity; Hollywood blackballed her for seven years, during which she appeared in Rossellini's European films. Her career was resurrected when she won a Best Actress Oscar for *Anastasia* (1956), her first Hollywood film (filmed in England) since the scandal. Her marriage to Rossellini was annulled in 1958; she later married Swedish stage producer Lars Schmidt, divorcing him in 1975. Suffering from cancer the last eight years of her life, she continued acting in films and on TV. For her work in *Murder on the Orient Ex-*

*press* (1974) she won a Best Supporting Actress Oscar. She was nominated for another Best Actress Oscar for her last film, Ingmar Bergman's *Autumn Sonata* (1978). Her final performance was as Golda Meir in the TV movie *A Woman Called Golda* (1981). She was the mother of actress Isabella Rossellini. She authored an autobiography, *Ingrid Bergman: My Story* (1980). **Selected Works:** *Bells of St. Mary's* (1945), *Casablanca* (1942), *Intermezzo: A Love Story* (1939), *Notorious* (1946), *For Whom the Bell Tolls* (1943)

# Busby Berkeley (William Berkeley Enos)

**Born:** November 29, 1895; Los Angeles, CA
**Died:** March 14, 1976; Palm Desert, CA

**Years Active in the Industry:** by decade

| 10s | 20s | 30s | 40s | 50s | 60s | 70s | 80s | 90s |
|-----|-----|-----|-----|-----|-----|-----|-----|-----|

American director/choreographer Busby Berkeley made his stage debut at five, acting in the company of his performing family. During World War I, Berkeley served as a field artillery lieutenant, where he learned the intricacies of drilling and disciplining large groups of people. During the 1920s, Berkeley was a dance director for nearly two dozen Broadway musicals, including such hits as *A Connecticut Yankee*. As a choreographer, Berkeley was less concerned with the terpsichorean skill of his chorus girls as he was with their ability to form themselves into attractive geometric patterns. His musical numbers were among the largest and best-regimented on Broadway. The only way they'd get any larger was if Berkeley moved to films, which he did the moment films learned to talk. His earliest movie gigs were on Sam Goldwyn's Eddie Cantor musicals, where he began developing such techniques as "individualizing" each chorus girl with a loving close-up, and moving his dancers all over the stage (and often beyond) in as many kaleidoscopic patterns as possible. Berkeley's legendary "top shot" technique (the kaleidoscope again, this time shot from overhead) first appeared seminally in the Cantor films, and also the 1932 Universal programmer *Night World*. Berkeley's popularity with an entertainment-hungry Depression audience was secured in 1933, when he choreographed three musicals back-to-back for Warner Bros.: *42nd Street*, *Footlight Parade* and *The Gold Diggers of 1933*. Berkeley's innovative and often times splendidly vulgar dance numbers have been analyzed at length by cinema scholars who insist upon reading "meaning" and "subtext" in each dancer's movement. Berkeley always pooh-poohed any deep significance to his work, arguing that his main professional goals were to constantly top himself and to never repeat his past accomplishments. As the outsized musicals in which Berkeley specialized became passé, he turned to straight directing, begging Warners to give him a chance at drama; the result was 1939's *They Made Me a Criminal*, one of John Garfield's best films. Berkeley moved to MGM in 1940, where his Field Marshal tactics sparked a great deal of resentment with the studio's pampered personnel. He was fired in the middle of *Girl Crazy* (1941), reportedly at the insistence of Judy Garland. His next stop was at 20th Century-Fox for 1943's *The Gang's All Here*. Berkeley entered the Valhalla of Kitsch with Carmen Miranda's outrageous "Lady in the Tutti-Frutti Hat" number. The film made money, but Berkeley and the Fox brass didn't see eye to eye over budget matters. Berkeley returned to MGM in the late 1940s, where among many other accomplishments he conceived the gloriously garish Technicolor finales for the studio's Esther Williams films. Berkeley's final film as choreographer was MGM's *Billy Rose's Jumbo* (1962). In private life, Berkeley was as flamboyant as his work, though not as much fun. He went through six wives, an alienation-of-affections suit involving a prominent movie queen, and a fatal car accident which resulted in his being tried (and acquitted) for second degree murder. In the late 1960s, the "camp" craze brought the Berkeley musicals back into the forefront. He hit the college and lecture circuit, and even directed a 1930s-style cold tablet commercial, complete with a top shot of a "dancing clock". In his 75th year, Busby Berkeley returned to Broadway to direct a success revival of *No, No Nanette*, starring his old Warner Bros. colleague and *42nd Street* star Ruby Keeler.

# Milton Berle (Milton Berlinger)

**Born:** July 12, 1908; New York, NY

**Years Active in the Industry:** by decade

| 10s | 20s | 30s | 40s | 50s | 60s | 70s | 80s | 90s |
|-----|-----|-----|-----|-----|-----|-----|-----|-----|

Few American comedians have had so aggressive a "stage mother" as did Milton Berle. Berle's mother Sarah dragged her son to New Jersey's Edison movie studios in 1914 to do extra work, then finessed the lad into supporting roles, including the part of a newsboy in the first-ever feature length comedy, *Tillie's Punctured Romance* (1914), which starred Charlie Chaplin. Under Sarah's powerhouse tutelage, Berle moved into vaudeville, making his debut at the prestigious Palace Theatre in 1921. Berle continued as a vaudeville headliner, with occasional stopovers on Broadway and in Hollywood, into the World War II years. His lengthy starring stint in the 1943 edition of Broadway's *Ziegfeld Follies* established Berle as a brash, broad, wisecracking comedian *par excellence*, whose carefully publicized propensity for "lifting" other comedians' material earned him the nickname "The Thief of Bad Gags." After only moderate success on radio and in films, Berle made a spectacular television debut as star of NBC's *Texaco Star Theatre* in 1948, which was the single most popular comedy/variety series of TV's earliest years and earned the comedian one of the industry's first Emmy Awards. So valuable was Berle to NBC that the network signed him to a thirty-year "lifetime contract" in 1951, which paid him $100,000 annually whether he performed or not (Berle managed to outlive the contract). Though his TV stardom waned in the late 1950s, Berle is still very much in demand as an emcee, lecturer, author, TV guest star, motion picture character actor, and nightclub comedian - still using essentially the same material and delivery which made him a star over sixty years ago. **Selected Works:** *Broadway Danny Rose* (1984)

# Sandra Bernhard

**Born:** June 6, 1955; Flint, MI

**Years Active in the Industry:** by decade

| 10s | 20s | 30s | 40s | 50s | 60s | 70s | 80s | 90s |
|-----|-----|-----|-----|-----|-----|-----|-----|-----|

It might be stretching things to suggest that American comedienne Sandra Bernhard's off-kilter spin on life was caused by her family's moving from the cozy confines of Michigan to the rough-and-tumble expanses of Arizona. One gets the feeling that Bernhard would have been on the outside looking in wherever she went. Utilizing her outsized lips and jutting chin for comic effect, Sandra became a standup comedian at age 19, and two years later got her first big break as a regular on the short-lived *Richard Pryor Show* (where the press release misspelled her name as Bernhart). Her act, which like all good comedy acts was better seen than described, consisted of cutting-edge commentary about sexual stereotyping and survival; one felt compelled to laugh lest Bernhard bolt from the stage and physically assault the audience. This dangerous quality carried over into her star-making film role in *King of Comedy*, as a psychotic fan of talk show host Jerry Lewis. While Bernhard's funkiness worked in this film's favor, it was detrimental to her villainous turn in the 1990 fiasco *Hudson Hawk*, though she was no worse than any other element of this notorious bomb. A tireless creator of comedy, Bernhard has scored with her 1985 best-selling record album *I'm Your Woman*, her 1988 solo off-Broadway show *Without You I'm Nothing* (made into a film in 1990), and her autobiography *Confessions of a Pretty Lady*. While she spent much of her early career skirting around the subject of her own sexual preferences, in recent years Bernhard has "outed" herself, which has added an extra layer of public fascination to her onetime close friendship with Madonna, as well as her recurring appearances on the TV sitcom *Roseanne*. **Selected Works:** *Truth or Dare* (1991), *Inside Monkey Zetterland* (1993)

# Corbin Bernsen

**Born:** September 7, 1954; North Hollywood, CA

**Years Active in the Industry:** by decade

| 10s | 20s | 30s | 40s | 50s | 60s | 70s | 80s | 90s |
|-----|-----|-----|-----|-----|-----|-----|-----|-----|

The son of actress Jeanne Cooper, Corbin Bernsen graduated from UCLA, boasting a BA degree in theatre arts and an MFA in playwrighting. From age 20 onward, Bernsen managed to find work in LA-based movies and TV productions. Things didn't immediately break for him when he moved to New York in the 1980s, so he took carpentry and modelling jobs until landing the part of Kenny Graham in the ABC daytime drama *Ryan's Hope*. Bernsen achieved celebrity status with his regular role as Arnie Becker in the TV series *LA Law* (1987-94). The best of his most recent films has been *Major League* (1990), in which he plays an investment-conscious baseball player. Corbin Bernsen remained more or less in this line of work with his role as an athlete-turned-sportcaster in the 1995 sitcom *Whole New Ballgame*. **Selected Works:** *Dead on the Money* (1991), *Shattered* (1991)

# Elmer Bernstein

**Born:** April 4, 1922; New York, NY

**Years Active in the Industry:** by decade

| 10ˢ | 20ˢ | 30ˢ | 40ˢ | 50ˢ | 60ˢ | 70ˢ | 80ˢ | 90ˢ |
|-----|-----|-----|-----|-----|-----|-----|-----|-----|
|     |     |     |     |     |     |     |     |     |

No relation to Leonard Bernstein, American film composer Elmer Bernstein was a graduate of the prestigious Julliard school of music. He dabbled in all aspects of the arts (including dance) before devoting himself to composing; his first major stint was for United Nations radio. In the early 1950s, Bernstein was willing to take any job available just to establish himself—which explains why his name is on the credits of that "golden turkey" *Robot Monster*. The big breakthrough came with Bernstein's progressive jazz score for *Man with the Golden Arm*, after which he switched artistic gears with his Wagnerian orchestrations for DeMille's *Ten Commandments* (1956). Bernstein's pulsating score for *The Magnificent Seven* (1960) has since become a classic—so much so that Bernstein is often mistakenly credited for Jerome Moross' similar theme music for *The Big Country* [1959]). As film tastes changed in the late 1960s and early 1970s, Bernstein's overarranged compositions seemed a bit anachronistic, a fact that Bernstein himself apparently realized, as witness his semi-satirical score for *National Lampoon's Animal House* (1978). The composer has remained active into the 1990s, rearranging Bernard Herrmann's original score for the remake of *Cape Fear* (1991) and underlining the innate romanticism of such films as *Rambling Rose* (1992) and *A River Runs Through It* (1992). In 1967, Elmer Bernstein won his only Academy Award for *Thoroughly Modern Millie*, for which he wrote only the background music and none of the individual songs. **Selected Works:** *To Kill a Mockingbird* (1962), *Trading Places* (1983), *True Grit* (1969), *Age of Innocence* (1993)

# Halle Berry

**Born:** August 14, 1968; Cleveland, OH

**Years Active in the Industry:** by decade

| 10ˢ | 20ˢ | 30ˢ | 40ˢ | 50ˢ | 60ˢ | 70ˢ | 80ˢ | 90ˢ |
|-----|-----|-----|-----|-----|-----|-----|-----|-----|
|     |     |     |     |     |     |     |     |     |

African American actress Halle Berry has been raising eyebrows even since she was elected prom queen in high school (she nearly lost the crown upon being accused of ballot-box stuffing). After participating in the Miss USA pageant, Berry became a model, which led to her first weekly TV series, 1989's *Living Dolls*. Rapidly gaining a reputation for on-set tenacity, Berry preferred to

"live" her roles, remaining in character even when the cameras stopped turning. This technique was not universally condoned by her fellow workers, especially when she refused to bathe for several days before starting work on her role as a crack addict in Spike Lee's *Jungle Fever*. In 1992, Berry was cast as Eddie Murphy's vis-a-vis in *Boomerang*, one of the few times that the explosive Murphy was evenly matched on screen. Usually appearing in adult-oriented films, Berry gained a youthful following for her performance as sexy secretary Sharon Stone in *The Flintstones* (1993). Berry's highly publicized costarring stint with Jessica Lange in *Losing Isiah* (1995) made some observers feel that her scenes with Lange merely amplify Berry's artistic shortcomings, while others believe that she has never given a more dynamic performance. **Selected Works:** *Last Boy Scout* (1991)

# Bernardo Bertolucci

**Born:** March 16, 1940; Parma, Italy

**Years Active in the Industry:** by decade

| 10ˢ | 20ˢ | 30ˢ | 40ˢ | 50ˢ | 60ˢ | 70ˢ | 80ˢ | 90ˢ |
|-----|-----|-----|-----|-----|-----|-----|-----|-----|
|     |     |     |     |     |     |     |     |     |

The son of film critic and poet Attilio Bertolucci, Bernardo Bertolucci began making 16-mm films as a teenager. In 1961 he left college to assistant direct Pier Paolo Pasolini's *Accatone*. He

made his directing debut the next year with *La Commare Secca* (*The Grim Reaper*) based on a script by Pasolini. After working out a severe Godard fixation with *Prima Della Revoluzione* (*Before The Revolution*) and *Partner*, Bertolucci emerged into a more personal, peculiarly Italian vision of guilt and decadence with *La Strategia Del Ragno* (*The Spider's Stratagem*) and *The Conformist*. Spectacularly shot by his regular cinematographer Vittorio Storaro, they brought

Bertolucci international fame. His first English-language film, the sexually explicit *Last Tango In Paris*, provoked a worldwide scandal; it also gave Marlon Brando one of the transcendent roles of his acting career. Bertolucci's subsequent films of the '70s generated less publicity and box office—*1900* and *Luna* are handsome, stylish films but have little sense of story or characterization. Sticking with English, Bertolucci scored a new commercial and critical success with his award-winning epic of China's Pu Yi in *The Last Emperor*, the first Western film shot in the Forbidden City. He has kept to long tales shot in exotic locations with *The Sheltering Sky* and *Little Buddha*.

# Luc Besson

**Born:** March 18, 1959; Paris, France

**Years Active in the Industry:** by decade

| 10s | 20s | 30s | 40s | 50s | 60s | 70s | 80s | 90s |
|-----|-----|-----|-----|-----|-----|-----|-----|-----|

French director Luc Besson briefly became the darling of the Sci-Fi convention circuit with his first film, the highly imaginative post-apocalyptic yarn *Le Derniere Combat* (1984). At this early stage of the game, Besson hadn't quite learned to tell a story, but he made up for this minor shortcoming with his most popular film, the densely cross-plotted assasination caper *La Femme Nikita* (1991). In between these two career milestones, Besson turned out the MTV-inspired comedy *Subway* (1985) and a fairly straightforward biopic of free-diver Jacques Mayol titled *The Big Blue* (1988). With the possible exception of the last-named film, Luc Besson's directorial style can adequately be summed up as "Stylish Chaos." **Selected Works:** *Point of No Return* (1993), *The Professional* (1994)

# Charles Bickford

**Born:** January 1, 1889; Cambridge, MA
**Died:** 1967

**Years Active in the Industry:** by decade

| 10s | 20s | 30s | 40s | 50s | 60s | 70s | 80s | 90s |
|-----|-----|-----|-----|-----|-----|-----|-----|-----|

Hard-fighting, strong, durable redhead Charles Bickford graduated from MIT before he began appearing in burlesque in 1914. After serving in World War I, he started a career on Broadway in 1919. He didn't come to Hollywood until the birth of the Sound Era in 1929. His first film was Cecil B. DeMille's *Dynamite*, during the production of which, he punched out DeMille. He became a star after playing Greta Garbo's lover in *Anna Christie* (1930), but didn't develop into a romantic lead, instead becoming a powerful character actor whose screen appearances commanded attention throughout a career spanning almost four decades. His craggy, intense features lent themselves to roles as likable fathers, businessmen, captains, etc. He sometimes played stubborn or unethical

roles, but more often projected honesty or warmth. He co-authored a play, *The Cyclone Lover* (1928) and wrote an autobiography, *Bulls, Balls, Bicycles, and Actors* (1965). He was Oscar-nominated three times but never won the award. Late in his life he starred in the TV show *The Virginian*. **Selected Works:** *Big Country* (1958), *Duel in the Sun* (1946), *Farmer's Daughter* (1947), *Johnny Belinda* (1948), *Song of Bernadette* (1943)

# Michael Biehn

**Born:** July 31, 1956; Anniston, AL

**Years Active in the Industry:** by decade

| 10s | 20s | 30s | 40s | 50s | 60s | 70s | 80s | 90s |
|-----|-----|-----|-----|-----|-----|-----|-----|-----|

At age 18, Michael Biehn made the big move from his Alabama hometown to LA. After two years of intensive training, he made his professional stage bow. In 1978, Biehn was cast as Mark Johnson, the hard-veneered but vulnerable ward of psychiatrist Robert Reed, in the TV series *Operation Runaway*. For the next few years, malevolence was Biehn's on-screen strong suit, first as the psycho title character in 1981's *The Fan*, then as the neofascist military-school upperclassman in *The Lords of Discipline* (1982). After switching gears with the sympathetic role of futuristic android-hunter Kyle Reese in director James Cameron's *The Terminator*, Michael Biehn became a member of Cameron's informal stock company, playing colorful leading roles in *Aliens* (1986) and *The Abyss* (1988). **Selected Works:** *K2: The Ultimate High* (1992), *Taste for Killing* (1992), *Tombstone* (1993), *Strapped* (1993)

# Kathryn Bigelow

**Born:** 1952

**Years Active in the Industry:** by decade

| 10s | 20s | 30s | 40s | 50s | 60s | 70s | 80s | 90s |
|-----|-----|-----|-----|-----|-----|-----|-----|-----|

Kathryn Bigelow was a talented and recognized painter when she entered Columbia University, where she decided to rechannel her talents into filmmaking. Bigelow was an unabashed devotee of Hollywood's B pictures, even going so far as to teach a course on the subject at the California Institute of the Arts. Her first directing assignment was the student short subject *Set-Up*, after which she entered the mainstream as script supervisor of director Mark Reichart's *Union City* (1980). Two years later, she acted in *Born in Flames* (1982); the following year, she received her first feature film directing credit for *The Loveless* (co-directed by Monty Montgomery), in which she harked back to her painting days by deliberately recreating the look and texture of Edward Hopper's 1930s portraits. With the release of *Near Dark* (1987), a bizarre amalgam of the biker, horror and western genres, Bigelow was considered deserving of a Museum of Modern Art retrospective. Since 1989, Bigelow has been the wife of another director of note, James (*The Terminator*) Cameron. **Selected Works:** *Blue Steel* (1990), *Point Break* (1991), *Wild Palms* (1993), *Strange Days* (1995)

# Theodore Bikel

**Born:** May 2, 1924; Vienna, Austria

**Years Active in the Industry:** by decade

| 10s | 20s | 30s | 40s | 50s | 60s | 70s | 80s | 90s |
|-----|-----|-----|-----|-----|-----|-----|-----|-----|

Though he has logged many impressive credits as an actor, Vienna-born Theodore Bikel prefers to think of himself—and bill himself—as a folksinger. Emigrating to Palestine in the 1930s, Bikel supported himself with his music, and also acted with Tel Aviv's Habimah Theatre in Sholem Alecheim's *Tevye the Milkman*. A quick study in several languages, Bikel honed his acting skills with Britain's Royal Academy of Dramatic Art. Three years after his London stage debut, Bikel made his first film, playing a German naval officer (the first of many villainous roles) in *The African Queen* (1951). In 1958, he was nominated for an Oscar for his supporting appearance in *The Defiant Ones*. One year later, he costarred with Mary Martin on Broadway, originating the role of Captain Von Trapp in Rodgers and Hammerstein's *The Sound of Music*. Active in many political causes ranging from Jewish relief to the Democratic Party, Bikel served as president of Actor's Equity from 1973 until 1982. In a mid-1980s interview, Theodore Bikel noted with amusement that, in spite of his many stage and screen appearances, many fans remembered him best for his brief unsympathetic appearance as a Russian officer in the otherwise forgettable 1957 film *Fraulein*. **Selected Works:** *I Want to Live!* (1958), *My Fair Lady* (1964)

# Jacqueline Bisset (Jacqueline Fraser)

**Born:** September 13, 1944; Weybridge, Surrey, England

**Years Active in the Industry:** by decade

| 10s | 20s | 30s | 40s | 50s | 60s | 70s | 80s | 90s |
|-----|-----|-----|-----|-----|-----|-----|-----|-----|

Actress Jacqueline Bisset appeared most frequently in American and international films of the 1970s. Her exceptional beauty led her to become a model at age 18, and this in turn, led to her playing a bit part in the feature film *The Knack, and How to Get It* (1965). She then moved to Hollywood where she began playing small supporting roles. She gained notoriety when her bikini top came off while she was cavorting in the waves in *The Sweet Ride* (1968). She continued playing lightweight roles in mainstream films of varying popularity until 1973 when she played a mentally exhausted actress in Truffaut's distinguished *Day for Night*. Later

she returned to standard sex-symbol roles as in *The Deep* (1977) where her wet T-shirt seemed to make more of an impact in the film than her acting skills. That year, *Newsweek* magazine voted her "the most beautiful film actress of all time." She has continued to act, but after the 1980s, she began appearing in low-budget films, and her career has suffered. She last appeared in the 1990 exploitational film *Wild Orchid*. **Selected Works:** *Airport* (1970), *Bullitt* (1968), *Maid* (1990), *Murder on the Orient Express* (1974), *Under the Volcano* (1984)

# Karen Black (Karen Blanche Ziegler)

**Born:** June 1, 1942; Park Ridge, IL

**Years Active in the Industry:** by decade

| 10s | 20s | 30s | 40s | 50s | 60s | 70s | 80s | 90s |
|-----|-----|-----|-----|-----|-----|-----|-----|-----|

Karen Black began acting shortly after college, appearing in off-Broadway satirical revues. She trained with Lee Strasberg at the Actors' Studio. Her Broadway debut was in a play that closed within a month, *The Playroom* (1965), but she was acclaimed for her performance and nominated for a Critics Circle award. A year later, 26-year-old filmmaker Francis Ford Coppola cast her in his first professional film, *You're a Big Boy Now* (1967), a comedy in which she co-starred as one of three women involved with a young man learning about sex. After another film she landed her first important role, as an LSD-taking prostitute in the surprise hit *Easy Rider* (1969), which featured Jack Nicholson; she went on to appear again with Nicholson in her next two films: *Five Easy Pieces* (1970), for which she won the New York Critics Award for Best Supporting Actress and an Oscar nomination; and *Drive He Said* (1971), Nicholson's directorial debut. She went on from there to be one of the screen's busiest actresses, though the quality of her films has been wildly uneven. **Selected Works:** *Auntie Lee's Meat Pies* (1992), *Day of the Locust* (1975), *Mirror, Mirror* (1990), *Nashville* (1975), *Overexposed* (1990)

# Rubén Blades

**Born:** July 16, 1948; Panama City, Panama

**Years Active in the Industry:** by decade

| 10s | 20s | 30s | 40s | 50s | 60s | 70s | 80s | 90s |
|-----|-----|-----|-----|-----|-----|-----|-----|-----|

The son of a musician and an actress, Latin-American actor, writer, and singer songwriter Ruben Blades studied political sceience and law, then worked as a legal aide before returning to school to get his Master's in Law at Harvard. Having done that much, he gave it all up to become a musician and actor, basing himself in Miami. He debuted onscreen in *The Last Fight* (1983), going on to appear in three more low-budget films before his first mainstream Hollywood production, *Critical Condition* (1987) with Richard Pryor. Meanwhile, in the mid-'80s he released the album "Buscando Americana" ("Searching for America"), which became an international hit and increased the popularity of salsa music. He went on to make several more hit records with his band, Seis del Solar, and gave concerts in Europe, Central America, and the U.S. (at Carnegie Hall and the Kennedy Center, among other places). As a screen actor, he has had bad luck in almost all of his films, which have tended to be unsuccessful. **Selected Works:** *Crazy from the Heart* (1991), *Josephine Baker Story* (1990), *Mo' Better Blues* (1990), *One Man's War* (1990), *Two Jakes* (1990)

# Linda Blair

**Born:** January 22, 1959; Westport, CT

**Years Active in the Industry:** by decade

| 10s | 20s | 30s | 40s | 50s | 60s | 70s | 80s | 90s |
|-----|-----|-----|-----|-----|-----|-----|-----|-----|

Although many people assume that *The Exorcist* (1974) was American actress Linda Blair's film debut, she had actually been working in commercials since age six. Blair was chosen from a field of 500 hopefuls for *Exorcist* because of her resemblance to the film's star, Ellen Burstyn. To the casual viewer, the film, which dealt with the Devil's possession of an innocent preteen girl, was hardly the sort of fare that any responsible parent would allow their child to appear in. But the *Exorcist*'s director, William Friedkin, was careful to prearrange the special effects (head turning around, bloody body wounds, vomiting green bile) with the least amount of danger or trauma for Blair. From all reports, she handled the assignment like a trouper, though she balked at having her hair messed up for the purposes of the plot. Blair was up for an Academy Award for her *Exorcist* work, but this campaign was scuttled when it was learned that, not only had the girl been extensively doubled by a dummy, but her horrendous "Satan" voice, explicit obscenities and all, had been dubbed by adult actress Mercedes McCambridge. A major celebrity at 15, Blair was able for a while to parlay her *Exorcist* work into a series of demanding film and TV roles, most of which cast her as a much-abused victim. Her rape scene in the TV movie *Born Innocent* was so graphic that the network was forced to cut the scene when the film was rerun. In other appearances, Blair played a teen alcoholic, a kidnap victim, a heart-transplant patient on an endangered airliner, and her *Exorcist* role again in *Exorcist II* (1977). Blair's private life rapidly became a maelstrom of unfortunate romantic liaisons and drug arrests. She was unable to maintain the equilibrium of her career, which degenerated into exploitative crime or girls-in-prison films. Blair was recently seen in *Repossessed* (1990), a ham-handed spoof of the film that made her famous. **Selected Works:** *Bail Out* (1990), *Dead Sleep* (1991)

# Robert Blake

**Born:** September 18, 1933; Nutley, NJ

**Years Active in the Industry:** by decade

| 10s | 20s | 30s | 40s | 50s | 60s | 70s | 80s | 90s |
|-----|-----|-----|-----|-----|-----|-----|-----|-----|

American actor, born Michael Gubitosi, began his long, acting career as a very young child appearing under the names "Mickey Gubitosi" and "Bobby Blake" in 40 *Our Gang* comedies during the 1930s and early '40s. Blake then went on to play "Little Beaver" in the *Red Ryder* Westerns. He also appeared in other films, notably as a Mexican boy in John Huston's *The Treasure of the Sierra Madre* (1948). He took a few years off, then returned as "Robert Blake" to play a variety of unusual adult roles; he is perhaps best known as one of the murderers in the screen version of Truman Capote's *In Cold Blood* (1968). He also starred in the mid-70s TV series *Baretta*. Blake overcame a drug problem, something he frequently mentioned in his many appearances on Johnny Carson's *Tonight Show* during the '70s, where he was a clownish semi-regular always to be seen with an unlit cigarette dangling from his lips. **Selected Works:** *Tell Them Willie Boy Is Here* (1969)

# Mel Blanc (Melvin Jerome Blanc)

**Born:** May 30, 1908; San Francisco, CA
**Died:** July 10, 1989; Los Angeles, CA

**Years Active in the Industry:** by decade

| 10s | 20s | 30s | 40s | 50s | 60s | 70s | 80s | 90s |
|-----|-----|-----|-----|-----|-----|-----|-----|-----|

American entertainer Mel Blanc, who would make his name and fortune by way of his muscular vocal chords, started out in the comparatively non-verbal world of band music. He entered radio in 1927, and within six years was costarring with his wife on a largely adlibbed weekly program emanating from Portland, Oregon, titled *Cobwebs and Nuts*. Denied a huge budget, Blanc was compelled to provide most of the character voices himself, and in so doing cultivated the skills that would bring him fame. He made the Los Angeles radio rounds in the mid-1930s, then was hired to provide the voice for a drunken bull in the 1937 Warner Bros. "Looney Tune" *Picador Porky*. Taking over the voice of Porky ("Th-th-th-that's all, Folks") Pig from a genuine stammerer who knew nothing about comic timing, Blanc became a valuable member of the "Termite Terrace" cartoon staff. Before long, he created the voice of Daffy Duck, whose lisping cadence was inspired by Warner Bros. cartoon boss Leon Schlesinger. In 1940, Blanc introduced his most enduring Warners voice—the insouciant, carrot-chopping Bugs Bunny (ironically, Blanc was allergic to carrots). He freelanced with the MGM and Walter Lantz animation firms (creating the laugh for Woody Woodpecker at the latter studio) before signing exclusively with Warners in the early 1940s. Reasoning that his limitless character repertoire—including Sylvester, Foghorn Leghorn, Speedy Gonzales, Tweety Pie, Pepe Le Pew, Yosemite Sam and so many others—had made him a valuable commodity to the studio, Blanc asked for a raise. Denied this, he demanded and got screen credit —a rarity for a cartoon voice artist of the 1940s. Though his salary at Warners never went above $20,000 per year, Blanc was very well compensated for his prolific work on radio. He was a regular on such series as *The Abbott and Costello Show* and *The Burns and Allen Show*, and in 1946 headlined his own weekly radio sitcom. For nearly three decades, Blanc was closely associated with the radio and TV output of comedian Jack Benny, essaying such roles as the "Si-Sy-Si" Mexican, harried violin teacher Professor LeBlanc, Polly the parrot, and the sputtering Maxwell automobile. While his voice was heard in dozens of live-action films, Blanc appeared *on* screen in only two pictures: *Neptune's Daughter* (1949) and *Kiss Me Stupid* (1964). Extremely busy in the world of made-for-TV cartoons during the 1950s and 1960s, Blanc added such new characterizations to his resume as Barney Rubble on *The Flintstones* (1960-66) and Cosmo Spacely on *The Jetsons* (1962). In early 1961, Blanc was seriously injured in an auto accident. For weeks, the doctor was unable to communicate with the comatose Blanc, until, in desperation, he addressed the actor with "How are you today, Bugs Bunny?" "Eh...just fine, Doc," Blanc replied weakly in his Bugs voice. At that miraculous moment, Blanc made the first step towards his eventual full recovery (this story sounds apocryphical, and even Blanc himself can't confirm that it took place, but those who witnessed the event swear that it really happened). In the 1970s, Blanc and his actor/producer son Noel—whom Mel was grooming to take over the roles of Bugs, Daffy and the rest— an their own school for voice actors. Mel Blanc continued performing right up to his death in July of 1989; earlier that same year, he published his autobiography, *That's Not All, Folks*. **Selected Works:** *Who Framed Roger Rabbit?* (1988)

# Joan Blondell

**Born:** August 30, 1906; New York, NY
**Died:** 1979

**Years Active in the Industry:** by decade

| 10s | 20s | 30s | 40s | 50s | 60s | 70s | 80s | 90s |
|-----|-----|-----|-----|-----|-----|-----|-----|-----|
|     |     |     |     |     |     |     |     |     |

A lovable star with a vivacious personality, mesmerizing smile, and big blue eyes, Joan Blondell, the daughter of stage comic Eddie Blondell (one of the original Katzenjammer Kids), spent her childhood touring the world with her vaudevillian parents and appearing with them in shows. She joined a stock company at age 17, then came to New York after winning a Miss Dallas beauty contest. She then appeared in several Broadway productions and in the Ziegfeld Follies before being paired with another unknown, actor James Cagney, in the stage musical *Penny Arcade*; a year later this became the film *Sinners Holiday*, propelling her to stardom. Blondell spent eight years under contract with Warner Bros., where she was cast as dizzy blondes and wisecracking gold-diggers. She generally appeared in comedies and musicals and was paired ten times on the screen with actor Dick Powell, to whom she

was married from 1936-45. Through the '30s and '40s she continued to play cynical, wisecracking girls with hearts of gold appearing in as many as ten films a year during the '30s. In the '50s she left films for the stage, but then came back to do more mature character parts. Blondell is the author of a *roman a clef* novel titled *Center Door Fancy* (1972) and was also married to producer Mike Todd (1947-50). **Selected Works:** *Gold Diggers of 1933* (1933), *Public Enemy* (1931), *Tree Grows in Brooklyn* (1945)

# Claire Bloom

**Born:** February 15, 1931; London, England

**Years Active in the Industry:** by decade

| 10s | 20s | 30s | 40s | 50s | 60s | 70s | 80s | 90s |
|-----|-----|-----|-----|-----|-----|-----|-----|-----|
|     |     |     |     |     |     |     |     |     |

Graceful and dignified British actress Claire Bloom came to the U.S. at age nine as a war evacuee during the London blitz; she returned to England in 1943 and enrolled in a drama school. As a young teen she appeared in a BBC radio play, then at age 15 joined the Oxford Repertory Theater. Two years later, after appearing in several Stratford-on-Avon productions, she debuted onscreen in *The Blind Goddess* (1948). She became internationally known after Chaplin cast her as the female lead in his film *Limelight* (1952). She also joined the Old Vic, going on to tour Canada and the U.S. with that company. Since then she has appeared in many films and stage plays, and has done much work on TV. She was married to actor Rod Steiger, with whom she appeared in *The Illustrated Man* (1969). **Selected Works:** *Crimes and Misdemeanors* (1989), *Richard III* (1955), *Spy Who Came in from the Cold* (1965)

# Eric Blore

**Born:** December 23, 1887; London, England
**Died:** March 2, 1959; Hollywood, CA

**Years Active in the Industry:** by decade

| 10s | 20s | 30s | 40s | 50s | 60s | 70s | 80s | 90s |
|-----|-----|-----|-----|-----|-----|-----|-----|-----|
|     |     |     |     |     |     |     |     |     |

Most often cast as a snide gentleman's gentleman or dissipated nobleman, British actor Eric Blore abandoned the business world for the theatre when he was in his mid-twenties. Established in both London and New York, Blore began adding movies to his acting achievements with 1920's *A Night Out and a Day In* (1920); he also appeared in the 1926 silent version of F. Scott Fitzgerald's *The Great Gatsby*. A scene-stealing role in RKO's Fred Astaire-Ginger Rogers musical *Flying Down to Rio* (1933) led to Blore's becoming a fixture in such subsequent Astaire-Rogers projects as *Gay Divorcee* (1934), *Top Hat* (1935) and *Shall We Dance?* (1937). The actor also became a "regular" in the unorthodox film comedies of Preston Sturges, notably *The Lady Eve* (1941) and *Sullivan's Travels* (1942). In addition, Blore found himself in support of several "star" comedians, from Laurel and Hardy to Bob Hope to The Marx Brothers. When pickings became lean for "veddy" British character actors in the mid 1950s, Blore was reduced to co-starring with the bargain-counter Bowery Boys in *Bowery to Baghdad* (1955); he played an inebriated genie in this, his last film. On a more artistically rewarding note, cartoon fans will recall the pixilated voice of Blore as the automobile-happy Mr. Toad in the 1949 Disney animated feature *Ichabod and Mr. Toad*. **Selected Works:** *Swing Time* (1936)

# Ann Blyth (Ann Marie Blyth)

**Born:** August 16, 1928; Mt. Kisco, NY

**Years Active in the Industry:** by decade

| 10s | 20s | 30s | 40s | 50s | 60s | 70s | 80s | 90s |
|-----|-----|-----|-----|-----|-----|-----|-----|-----|

A radio singer at age 5, American actress Ann Blyth studied for an operatic career, making her debut in this endeavor with the San Carlo Opera Company. In 1943, at age 15, Ann was playing Paul Lukas' daughter in the Broadway production *Watch on the Rhine*; two years later she was under contract to Universal studios as the latest in that company's "threats" against their recalcitrant resident soprano Deanna Durbin. Blyth wasn't given anything close to a chance to show her talents until she was cast as Joan Crawford's hateful daughter Veda in *Mildred Pierce* (1945). For this performance, which ran the gamut from thinly veiled insults addressed at Crawford to the murder of her mother's paramour (Zachary Scott), she was nominated for an Academy Award. After recovering from a back injury, Blyth worked ceaselessly in films, alternating between sappily sweet parts in such fluff as *Free for All* (1949) and *Sally and St. Anne* (1951) and tougher assignments like the white-hot bitchery expended in her portrayal of Regina Hubbard in *Another Part of the Forest* (1948). Perhaps the most off-kilter of her starring roles was in *Mr. Peabody and the Mermaid* (1948) wherein she played the female half of the title, spending much of the film in a state of (implied) toplessness. In 1954, she was finally permitted to display her beautifully trained voice in such musicals as *The Student Prince* (1954), *Rose Marie* (1955) and *Kismet* (1956). But when called upon to play a real-life songstress in *The Helen Morgan Story* (1957), she was dubbed by Gogi Grant! *Helen Morgan Story* was Blyth's final film role; she spent the rest of her career on stage, TV and in concert - and, in the late 1970s, she showed up as the surprisingly domesticated spokesperson for Hostess Cupcakes.

# Ralf D. Bode

**Born:** Berlin, Germany

**Years Active in the Industry:** by decade

| 10s | 20s | 30s | 40s | 50s | 60s | 70s | 80s | 90s |
|-----|-----|-----|-----|-----|-----|-----|-----|-----|

Born in Germany and educated in New England, cinematographer Ralf Bode attended the film and drama departments of Yale University. While in the American army, Bode received the practical camera training that would serve him well in the movie industry. After working as a lighting designer for director John Avildsen, Bode received his first film credit on the minor feature *Foreplay*, followed by a 2nd unit photography assignment on Avildsen's *Rocky* (1976). His next assignment, *Saturday Night Fever* (1977), secured Bode's reputation as a master of evocative lighting and color schemes. Bode has since brought to cinematic life the Southeastern coal fields of *Coal Miner's Daughter* (1981), the bleakness of wintertime Moscow in *Gorky Park* (1983), the sleaziness of the blue-collar barhopping scene in *The Accused* (1988), and the melting-pot ambience of Chicago and its suburbs in *Uncle Buck* (1989). **Selected Works:** *Leaving Normal* (1992), *Love Field* (1991), *Made in America* (1993), *One Good Cop* (1991), *Safe Passage* (1994)

# Dirk Bogarde

**Born:** March 28, 1921; Hampstead, London, England

**Years Active in the Industry:** by decade

| 10s | 20s | 30s | 40s | 50s | 60s | 70s | 80s | 90s |
|-----|-----|-----|-----|-----|-----|-----|-----|-----|

Handsome actor Dirk Bogarde, born Derek Van Den Bogaerd, the son of a Dutch-born art editor for the London *Times*, first appeared onstage in 1939, but his career was interrupted by service in World War II. When he returned, his appearance in the play *Power Without Glory* landed him a movie contract with Rank Studios, for whom he made a string of mostly weak pictures (though one, *The Blue Lamp*, was the most successful British film of 1950). Gradually he was given better and better roles; critics praised him in *Hunted* (1952). Finally came his first big hit, *Doctor in the House* (1953), the first of a series of "doctor" comedies. As his popularity increased (he was Britain's top box office draw in the mid- to late '50s) so did the range and depth of the roles he was offered; by the 1960s he could pick and choose from many different and complex parts, showing his subtlety and sensitivity as an actor to its best advantage. In *Victim* (1961) he took the risk of playing a gay character, while his performance as a decadent valet in *The Servant* won him a British Film Academy Award as Best Actor; later he won the same award again, this time for his work in *Darling* (1965). In the late 60s and 70s he moved to Italy and then France, in search of meatier roles in international productions. Notably, his work in *Death In Venice* (1971) was considered by many to be a tour de force. **Selected Works:** *Quartet* (1948), *Fixer* (1968), *King and Country* (1964), *Oh! What a Lovely War* (1969), *Daddy Nostalgia* (1992)

# Humphrey Bogart (Humphrey DeForest Bogart)

**Born:** January 23, 1899; New York, NY
**Died:** 1957

**Years Active in the Industry:** by decade

| 10s | 20s | 30s | 40s | 50s | 60s | 70s | 80s | 90s |
|-----|-----|-----|-----|-----|-----|-----|-----|-----|
|     |     |     |     |     |     |     |     |     |

One of the screen's all-time greatest stars and a cult figure to film buffs the world over, Humphrey Bogart, born to a Manhattan surgeon and a magazine illustrator, was expelled from Phillips Academy in Andover, Mass. where he'd been prepping for med school. He joined the Navy during World War I; during a shelling on the ship *Leviathan* his lip was scarred and partly paralyzed, leading to the tight-set mouth and lisp that became his trademarks. After the war, he found work with a theater company, at first behind the scenes, but after 1920, as an actor. Throughout the 20s, he performed in a string of mediocre plays, attracting little attention. After 1930 he found work in Hollywood, usually in bland secondary roles. Thanks to actor Leslie Howard's insistence, Bogart was given the biggest gangster role in the film *The Petrified Forest* (1935), which was a huge success and made Bogart a popular actor. He went on to appear in 28 features between 1936-40, usually as a gangster or villain. He broke out of this mold once he started working with director John Huston, who cast him as a more soulful gangster in *High Sierra* (1941) (Huston wrote the script but did not direct), and then as the ruthless private eye Sam Spade in *The Maltese Falcon* (1941). Bogart began to establish his character: world-weary, cynical, an amiable, unflappable tough guy in a trench coat. 1942 produced *Casablanca*, the classic World War II film with Ingrid Bergman. While filming *To Have and Have Not* he met and fell in love with co-star Lauren Bacall, who became his fourth and last wife; they were married and remained so until his death in 1957. In 1947, Bogart formed his own company, Santana Pictures. In 1948 he landed one of his most memorable roles, as the greedy prospector in Huston's *The Treasure of the Sierra Madre.* Following that he went on to extend his range and depth as an actor through the rest of his career. He was nominated three times for the Best Actor Academy Award, winning for his work in *The African Queen* (1952) with Katherine Hepburn. In March, 1956, he underwent an operation for cancer of the esophagus, then died in his sleep on January 14, 1957. **Selected Works:** *Caine Mutiny* (1954), *Dark Victory* (1939), *Harder They Fall* (1956), *Key Largo* (1948), *Sabrina* (1954)

# Peter Bogdanovich

**Born:** July 30, 1939; Kingston, NY

**Years Active in the Industry:** by decade

| 10s | 20s | 30s | 40s | 50s | 60s | 70s | 80s | 90s |
|-----|-----|-----|-----|-----|-----|-----|-----|-----|
|     |     |     |     |     |     |     |     |     |

Although born in the year regarded as the greatest in the history of Hollywood films, director Peter Bogdanovich was more interested in radio than in movies while growing up. By the time he was 15, however, Bogdanovich had aspirations of becoming a movie star. Lying about his age, he was accepted for training by acting coach Stella Adler, which led to several seasons of Summer Stock, and ultimately (at age 19) an off-Broadway staging of Clifford Odets' *The Big Knife*, which Bogdanovich produced. The son of a prominent artist, Bogdanovich had early access to the museums and retrospective societies that ran the classic films; he was content to believe that the actors were the "auteurs" of these films until introduced to the work of Orson Welles, after which Bogdanovich was determined to be the new Welles (it was an affection that lasted all his life, culminating in a long-awaited book of Welles interviews in 1992). By the age of 21, Bogdanovich was writing monographs on films for the Museum of Modern Art - his first piece being on Orson Welles. Perhaps Bogdanovich's best-known monograph was on director John Ford, in which Ford's hostility towards the nosy young interviewer is deliciously obvious. Edging toward the production end of movies, Bogdanovich became an assistant to low-budget king Roger Corman, receiving his first on-screen credit on Corman's *The Wild Angels* (1966) (he managed to get drawn into a fight with a motorcycle gang, footage of which reportedly wound up in the picture). After acting in *The Trip* (1967) and adapting a ponderous Russian sci-fier into *Voyage to the Planet of the Prehistoric Women* (1968), Bogdanovich was finally able to bankroll his directorial debut, a still-frightening study of the American violence ethic titled *Targets* (1968). The director was able to secure the services of star Boris Karloff only because Karloff owed two days' work to Roger Corman, but so enthusiastic was the actor on this project that he worked an additional three days for scale salary. *Targets* was poorly distributed by Paramount, but built up such a word-of-mouth reputation that Bogdanovich was permitted a main-stream directorial job in 1971. *The Last Picture Show* turned out to be one of the landmark films of the 1970s, and for the next few years Bogdanovich seemingly had the golden touch. *What's Up Doc?* (1972) and *Paper Moon* (1973), like *Picture Show*, bore the influence of such Bogdanovich icons as John Ford and Howard Hawks, but audiences forgave the director's "liftings" and lined up at the box-office. Bogdanovich's luck changed when he suddenly became determined to make a major star of lady friend Cybill Shepherd; the results were the tepid *Daisy Miller* (1974) and the atrocious *At Long Last Love* (1975). Bogdanovich's projects became fewer and farther between, and by the time he made *Saint Jack* (1979) the director was both personally and professionally bankrupt. He endured profound tragedy in private life as well when his then-current lover Dorothy Stratten was murdered. By the mid-1980s, Bogdanovich had made too many bad films and far too many industry enemies to work as an independent; he did an excellent directorial job on *Mask* (1985), but he was a hired hand rather than the final arbiter. Bogdanovich has had several comeback opportunities since, ranging from okay (*Noises Off* [1972]) to dreadful (*Texasville* [1990]), but like his idol Orson Welles, Bogdanovich has seldom scaled the heights of his Boy Wonder days. **Selected Works:** *Thing Called Love* (1993)

# Eric Bogosian

**Born:** April 24, 1953; Woburn, MA

**Years Active in the Industry:** by decade

| 10ˢ | 20ˢ | 30ˢ | 40ˢ | 50ˢ | 60ˢ | 70ˢ | 80ˢ | 90ˢ |
|-----|-----|-----|-----|-----|-----|-----|-----|-----|

Together with Spalding Gray, Eric Bogosian is one of the best-known practitioners of that curious performance-art skill known as the "dramatic monologue". Bogosian has written and performed in such compelling one-man stage shows as *Talk Radio* and *Sex, Drugs and Rock 'N' Roll*. In 1988, he starred in Oliver Stone's film version of *Talk Radio*, which was rather unnecessarily "cinematized" with additional characters and a wider range of backgrounds. Bogosian has noted that he knew he'd "arrived" when he and Spalding Gray were spoofed on *Saturday Night Live*, though he expressed slight dismay as being considered the punch line to a joke. Most often appearing in "alternative" films, Bogosian has been willing to accept the occasional mainstream character part: in 1994 he was seen in the HBO presentation *Witchhunt*, a McCarthy-era parody in which he played a Nixon-like senator on a vendetta against *genuine* witches. **Selected Works:** *Last Flight Out* (1990), *Sex, Drugs and Rock-N-Roll* (1991)

# Ray Bolger (Raymond Wallace Bolger)

**Born:** January 10, 1904; Boston, MA
**Died:** January 15, 1988; Los Angeles, CA

**Years Active in the Industry:** by decade

| 10ˢ | 20ˢ | 30ˢ | 40ˢ | 50ˢ | 60ˢ | 70ˢ | 80ˢ | 90ˢ |
|-----|-----|-----|-----|-----|-----|-----|-----|-----|

The son of a house painter, American actor/dancer Ray Bolger grew up in a middle-class Boston neighborhood called Dorchester. Bolger knew what he wanted to do in life the moment he saw Broadway entertainer Fred Stone literally bounce on stage in a Boston production of *Jack O'Lantern*. "That moment opened up a whole new world for me" Bolger would remember; after a relatively aimless childhood, he determined to become a performer himself. Starting out in vaudeville as a dancer, Bolger developed a loose-limbed ad lib style that would win him starring spots in such 1930s Broadway musicals as *Life Begins at 8:40* and *On Your Toes*; in the latter, Bolger introduced Richard Rodgers' "Slaughter on Tenth Avenue". Signed by MGM in 1936 for a featured solo in *The Great Ziegfeld*, Bolger was given a $3,000 per week contract and was expected to take whatever part was assigned him. But Bolger balked when he was cast as the Tin Man in the studio's *Wizard of Oz*. He

felt the role was too confining for his talents, so Bolger convinced the film's Scarecrow, Buddy Ebsen, to switch parts with him. This move, of course, assured film immortality for Bolger, but wasn't so beneficial for Ebsen, whose allergic reaction to the Tin Man's silver makeup forced him to drop out of the film and be replaced by Jack Haley. Bolger's movie career pretty much took second place to his Broadway work in the 1940s. In 1948, Bolger was awarded the lead in a musical version of *Charley's Aunt* titled *Where's Charley?* It was when the daughter of one of the production people began singing his lyrics back to him during out-of-town tryouts that Bolger, in league with composer Frank Loesser, developed the "everybody sing" chorus for the song "Once in Love With Amy". Bolger repeated his role in the 1952 filmization of *Where's Charley* (1952), then continued his Broadway career with intermittent film appearances into the 1960s. He also starred in a 1953 TV series, alternately titled *The Ray Bolger Show* and *Where's Raymond?*, which was so bad that even he was uncharacteristically putting himself down before the inevitable cancellation. Bolger suffered a few career setbacks on stage in the early 1960s, and his villain role in Disney's *Babes in Toyland* (1961) hardly showed him to best advantage, but the performer prospered as a nightclub performer during the rest of the decade in a nostalgic (if slightly lachrymose) act which recalled his past song hits. While accused by some fellow performers of being a bit too self-involved and spotlight-conscious to be totally lovable, Bolger nonetheless charmed live audiences with his still-athletic hoofing skills into the 1970s. In the twilight of his career, Bolger was allowed to sparkle in guest spots on such TV programs as *The Partridge Family*, *The Love Boat*, *Baretta*, and even PBS's *Evening at the Pops*.

# Ward Bond

**Born:** April 9, 1903; Denver, CO
**Died:** November 5, 1960; Dallas, TX

**Years Active in the Industry:** by decade

| 10ˢ | 20ˢ | 30ˢ | 40ˢ | 50ˢ | 60ˢ | 70ˢ | 80ˢ | 90ˢ |
|-----|-----|-----|-----|-----|-----|-----|-----|-----|

American actor Ward Bond was a football player at the University of Southern California when, together with teammate and lifelong chum John Wayne, he was hired for extra work in the silent film *Salute* (1928), directed by John Ford. Both Bond and Wayne continued in films, but it was Wayne who ascended to stardom, while Bond would have to be content with bit roles and character parts throughout the 1930s. Mostly playing traffic cops, bus drivers and western heavies, Bond began getting better breaks after a showy role as the murderous Cass in John Ford's *Young Mr. Lincoln* (1939). Ford cast Bond in important roles all through the 1940s, usually contriving to include at least one scene per picture in which the camera would favor Bond's rather sizable posterior; it was an "inside" joke which delighted everyone on the set but Bond. A starring role in Ford's *Wagonmaster* (1950) led, somewhat indirectly, to Bond's most lasting professional achievement: His continuing part as trailmaster Seth Adams on the extremely popular NBC TV western, *Wagon Train*. No longer supporting anyone, Bond exerted considerable creative control over the series from its 1957 debut onward, even seeing to it that his old mentor John Ford would direct one episode in which John Wayne had a bit role, billed under his real name, Marion Michael Morrison. Finally achieving the wide popularity that had eluded him during his screen career, Bond stayed with *Wagon Train* for three years, during which time he became as famous for his offscreen clashes with his supporting cast and his ultra-conservative politics as he was for his acting. *Wagon Train* was still NBC's Number One series when, in November of 1960, Bond unexpectedly suffered a heart attack and died while taking a shower. **Selected Works:** *Fugitive* (1948), *Long Voyage Home* (1940), *Quiet Man* (1952), *They Were Expendable* (1945), *Hondo* (1953)

## Beulah Bondi (Beulah Bondy)

**Born:** May 3, 1892; Chicago, IL
**Died:** January 11, 1981; Woodland Hills, CA

**Years Active in the Industry:** by decade

| 10s | 20s | 30s | 40s | 50s | 60s | 70s | 80s | 90s |
|-----|-----|-----|-----|-----|-----|-----|-----|-----|
|     |     |     |     |     |     |     |     |     |

American actress Beulah Bondi entered the theatre at age 7, playing the male role of Little Lord Fauntleroy; it would be her last role "in drag" and one of the very few times that she'd play a character her own age. Upon graduation from Valparaiso University, she joined a stock company, working throughout the US until her 1925 Broadway debut in *Wild Birds*. Even in her late twenties and early thirties, Bondi specialized in playing mothers, grandmothers and society dowagers. She made her first film, *Street Scene*, in 1931, concentrating on movies thereafter. She is best known to modern film fans for her role as James Stewart's mother in the Christmastime favorite *It's a Wonderful Life* (1946). It was but one of several occasions (among them *Vivacious Lady* [1938] and *Mr. Smith Goes to Washington* [1939]) that the actress played Stewart's mother; as late as 1971, Bondi was essaying the same role in the short-lived sitcom *The Jimmy Stewart Show*. Even after her "official" screen retirement - her last film was *Tammy and the Doctor* (1963), in which, not surprisingly, she played a wealthy old invalid - Bondi kept herself open for television roles, including an Emmy-winning 1977 performance on the dramatic TV series *The Waltons*.

**Selected Works:** *Our Town* (1940), *Snake Pit* (1948), *Southerner* (1945), *Watch on the Rhine* (1943), *Of Human Hearts* (1938)

## Helena Bonham-Carter

**Born:** May 26, 1966; London, England

**Years Active in the Industry:** by decade

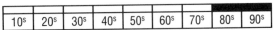

| 10s | 20s | 30s | 40s | 50s | 60s | 70s | 80s | 90s |
|-----|-----|-----|-----|-----|-----|-----|-----|-----|
|     |     |     |     |     |     |     |     |     |

Befitting her double-barrelled family name, sylphlike actress Helena Bonham-Carter was born to British artistocracy — both social and cinematic. She is the great-granddaughter of P.M.

Lord Herbert Asquith and the grandniece of famed director Anthony Asquith. Raised in wealth, she brought an inbred grace and serenity to her first stage and film roles, and along the way learned to act in the bargain. She has appeared as Jane Grey in *Lady Jane* (1986) and as Ophelia in the Mel Gibson version of *Hamlet* (1990). Not content with simply interpreting the classics, she amazed her fans with her marvelously erotic portrayal of a mixed-up socialite in 1989's *Getting It Right*. Had she done no other screen work, Bonham-Carter's fame would have been justified on the basis of two Merchant/Ivory productions: *A Room with a View* (1985) and *Howard's End* (1992). **Selected Works:** *Where Angels Fear to Tread* (1991), *Mary Shelley's Frankenstein* (1994)

## John Boorman

**Born:** January 18, 1933; Shepperton, Middlesex, England

**Years Active in the Industry:** by decade

| 10s | 20s | 30s | 40s | 50s | 60s | 70s | 80s | 90s |
|-----|-----|-----|-----|-----|-----|-----|-----|-----|
|     |     |     |     |     |     |     |     |     |

British director John Boorman held down a few "joe jobs" before he began writing film reviews and working as a BBC film editor; by 1962, he was head of the Bristol BBC documentary unit. Boorman directed his first fictional film in 1965, the whimsically free-form *Having A Wild Weekend*, starring the Dave Clark Five. What could have been just another *Hard Day's Night* ripoff was original enough for Boorman to be recognized as an distinctive stylist by the classier film publications of the period. More BBC

work followed, and then Boorman made his Hollywood directing bow with the Lee Marvin vehicle *Point Blank* (1967). Here as in such subsequent essays in graphic violence as *Hell in the Pacific* (1968), *Deliverance* (1972) and *Excalibur* (1981), Boorman expected everyone on his casts and crews to share his own macho outlook on life and its confrontations - and woe betide the weakling who didn't want to go along for the ride. In *The Emerald Forest* (1985), Boorman cast his own son Charley as an Anglo-Saxon boy raised as an Amazonian Indian, and demanded no less from Charley than he did from the rest of his harried coworkers (Perhaps significantly, Charley Boorman has acted very little since *Forest*). Since that time, John Boorman's most critically acclaimed production has been *Hope and Glory* (1987) an autobiographical study of a small London neighborhood during the World War II "blitz years", as seen through the eyes of an adventure-craving young boy. **Selected Works:** *I Dreamt I Woke Up* (1991)

## Ernest Borgnine (Ermes Effron Borgnine)

**Born:** January 24, 1917; Hamden, CT

**Years Active in the Industry:** by decade

| 10s | 20s | 30s | 40s | 50s | 60s | 70s | 80s | 90s |
|-----|-----|-----|-----|-----|-----|-----|-----|-----|
|     |     |     | ██  | ██  | ██  | ██  | ██  |     |

Born Ermes Borgnino to Italian parents, actor Ernest Borgnine lived in Milan as a child, then moved back to Connecticut, his birth place. He joined the Navy in 1935; after his discharge at the end of WW II, Borgnine began studying acting at the Randall School of Dramatic Arts in Hartford. He then went on to join a theatrical group in Virginia from 1946-50. After making some TV appearances, he debuted in films with *China Corsair* (1951). With his broad, pug-dog face, beady eyes and gapped teeth he made a natural villain, and so was typecast as tough guys during his early career. A change of pace came with the title role in *Marty* (1955), in which he played a kind, lonely, sensitive Bronx butcher; for his performance he was awarded the Best Actor Oscar, the British Film Academy Award, the Cannes Film Festival Best Actor Award, the New York Film Critics Award, and the National Board of Review Award. After *Marty* his range of roles broadened, rarely leaning toward the villainous but usually retaining a Bronx "regular guy" flavor. He also starred as the hero of the popular *McHale's Navy* TV sitcom (1962-65). He was married briefly to actress-singer Ethel Merman. **Selected Works:** *Dirty Dozen* (1967), *Flight of the Phoenix* (1965), *From Here to Eternity* (1953), *Poseidon Adventure* (1972), *Wild Bunch* (1969)

## Frank Borzage

**Born:** April 23, 1893; Salt Lake City, UT
**Died:** 1962

**Years Active in the Industry:** by decade

| 10s | 20s | 30s | 40s | 50s | 60s | 70s | 80s | 90s |
|-----|-----|-----|-----|-----|-----|-----|-----|-----|
|     |     |     |     |     |     |     |     |     |

Filmmaker Frank Borzage began his film career as a handsome, curly-haired lead in a number of silent films. He found work in a silver mine at age 13, then got into a touring stage company as a stagehand and later actor. At age 19, he went to Hollywood and moved from playing bit parts to leads and heavies in dozens of Ince Westerns and Mutual comedies. In 1916, he began directing for Universal, at first making melodramas and Westerns in which he also starred. As a director, his first significant film was *Humoresque* (1920). He is known as a great romanticist and sentimentalist as a director, telling love stories with lyrical tenderness, and frequently used soft focus and gauzed photography. He won Academy Awards for the silent *Seventh Heaven* (1927) and the talkie *Bad Girl* (1931), at which point his reputation reached its peak. His films of the '40s and '50s were much less interesting than his earlier work.

## Philip Bosco

**Born:** September 26, 1930; Jersey City, NJ

**Years Active in the Industry:** by decade

| 10s | 20s | 30s | 40s | 50s | 60s | 70s | 80s | 90s |
|-----|-----|-----|-----|-----|-----|-----|-----|-----|
|     |     |     |     |     |     |     | ██  |     |

Catholic University was the alma mater of American actor Philip Bosco—or would have been if he hadn't been expelled. Bosco would not collect a college degree until age 27, after a long stint as an Army cryptographer. Most comfortable in classical stage roles, Bosco has found it expedient to don modern garb for most of his movie work. After a one-shot screen appearance in 1968's *A Lovely Way to Die*, Bosco didn't step before the movie cameras again until 1983, making up for the lost years with supporting appearances in such films as *Trading Places* (1983), *The Pope of Greenwich Village* (1984), *Three Men and a Baby* (1987), *Working Girl* (1988) and *Shadows and Fog* (1992). Philip Bosco won a Tony Award for his performance in the popular door-slamming farce *Lend Me a Tenor*. **Selected Works:** *Children of a Lesser God* (1986), *Quick Change* (1990), *Return of Eliot Ness* (1991), *Angie* (1994), *Nobody's Fool* (1994)

## Clara Bow

**Born:** August 25, 1905; Brooklyn, NY
**Died:** 1965

**Years Active in the Industry:** by decade

| 10s | 20s | 30s | 40s | 50s | 60s | 70s | 80s | 90s |
|-----|-----|-----|-----|-----|-----|-----|-----|-----|

Famous as the "It" girl of the Roaring 20s; Clara Bow was the flapper to end all flappers. The daughter of a Coney Island waiter and a mentally unstable mother, she spent her youth in poverty. At 16 she won a movie magazine beauty contest; part of the prize was a trip to visit the New York studios and a bit part in a silent, soon leading to other roles mostly in low-budget films. Under contract to producer B.P. Schulberg, she went with Schulberg from New York to Hollywood's Paramount, where the studio's publicity machine helped mold her into a star, particularly after *Mantrap* (1926), her first smash hit. Soon she became a symbol of the emancipated woman during the flapper age: vibrant, liberated, energetic. Her bobbed hair, bow lips, and sparkling eyes came to represent the era, and her bangled, beaded "look" soon became imitated by women throughout America. After appearing in the film *It* (1927) she became known as the "It" girl, a woman with "something extra" which set her apart from the common herd. While living the life of the Roaring 20s, however, she became the victim of scandals, was involved in alleged affairs involving sex and gambling, and quickly fell from grace with the public (which in a 1928 poll had named her America's favorite actress). Her mental fragility increased; and with the advent of sound her career ground to a halt. In 1931 she eloped with cowboy star Rex Bell, who eventually became lieutenant governor of Nevada. After retiring from the screen in 1933, Bow spent the rest of her life in and out of mental institutions. **Selected Works:** *Wings* (1927)

# David Bowie (David Robert Jones)

**Born:** January 8, 1947; Brixton, South London, England

**Years Active in the Industry:** by decade

| 10s | 20s | 30s | 40s | 50s | 60s | 70s | 80s | 90s |
|-----|-----|-----|-----|-----|-----|-----|-----|-----|

British actor/singer David Bowie had what one can expansively call a show-biz background: His father was a wrestling promoter, and his mother was a moviehouse usherette. Leaving school at 16, Bowie worked as a commercial designer until turning to rock music. When he started out in this endeavor in 1972, it was not as David Bowie but as an androgynous alter ego named Ziggy Stardust - the talented prototype of many future less-than-talented punk rockers. His 1976 film appearance (as good old David Bowie again) in the zesty fantasy *The Man Who Fell to Earth* was auspicious, but not the auspicious debut some supposed it to be, since the performer had been playing movie bits since 1967. Most of Bowie's films have been as kinky as the performer himself, notably *Merry Christmas Mr. Lawrence* (1983), a near-hallucinatory drama set in a POW camp. He has also introduced unsuspected filmgoers to old standby Ziggy Stardust in *Ziggy Stardust and the Spiders From Mars*, which despite its title was a concert film, and which despite its 1982 release was filmed nine years earlier. In addition to his acting, Bowie has composed the music for several films, including *Cat People* (1982) and *When the Wind Blows* (1989). Bowie's participation in the equally enigmatic director David Lynch's 1992 film *Twin Peaks: Fire Walk With Me* was a prime example of two gusts of weirdness canceling one another out. Best to forget it and enjoy Bowie's restrained (for him!) interpretation of Pontius Pilate in *The Last Temptation of Christ* (1989). **Selected Works:** *Buddha of Suburbia* (1994)

# William "Stage" Boyd

**Born:** June 5, 1895; Cambridge, OH
**Died:** 1972

**Years Active in the Industry:** by decade

| 10s | 20s | 30s | 40s | 50s | 60s | 70s | 80s | 90s |
|-----|-----|-----|-----|-----|-----|-----|-----|-----|

An "Okie" whose parents died when he was a child, Boyd became a manual laborer before breaking into the movies in 1919 as an extra in Cecil B. De Mille's *Why Change Your Wife?* He soon became one of De Mille's favorite actors and was cast as an unassuming leading man in comedies and swashbuckling adventure films. A hard-drinking, fast-living gambling man, he continued his success in the sound era, but was hurt when a scandal hit another actor named "William Boyd" and the public confused the two. His career took off in 1935 when he began to appear in "Hopalong Cassidy" films (based on the Clarence E. Mulford stories of the Old West), beginning with *Hop-A-Long Cassidy* and eventually amounting to 66 episodes, the final twelve of which Boyd produced. Cassidy, dressed in black and mounted on his famous horse Topper, was a clean-living good guy who didn't smoke, drink, or swear, and hardly ever kissed the heroine; the character became an enormous hero to millions of American boys, and Boyd bought the rights to it. With the breakthrough of TV in the early 50s, Boyd began to reap huge profits from the character as the old shows found a new audience and by-products began to be produced and sold; he played Cassidy the rest of his life, even into genial, gray-haired old age. Ultimately, William Boyd Enterprises was sold for $8 million. Boyd was married four times and divorced three, each time to an actress: Ruth Miller, Elinor Fair, Dorothy Sebastion, and Grace Bradley.

# Charles Boyer

**Born:** August 28, 1899; Figeac, France
**Died:** 1978

**Years Active in the Industry:** by decade

| 10s | 20s | 30s | 40s | 50s | 60s | 70s | 80s | 90s |
|-----|-----|-----|-----|-----|-----|-----|-----|-----|

With his passionate, deep-set eyes, classical features, and ultra-suave manner, it is small wonder that French actor Charles Boyer was known as one of the great cinematic lovers. During the 20s, Boyer made a few nondescript silent films but was primarily a theatrical actor. From 1929-31 he made an unsuccessful attempt to make it in Hollywood before returning to Europe until 1934 when his films began to win public favor. He became a true star with *Garden of Allah* (1936), and went on to play opposite the most alluring actresses of the 30s and 40s, including Lamarr, Bergman, and Garbo. During World War II he became active in encouraging French-American relations and established the French Research Foundation, for which he was awarded a special Academy Award in 1942 for "progressive cultural achievement" (he was nominated as an actor four times but never won). Later Boyer became an American citizen and went on to play more mature roles, including the occasional stage appearance (notably in Shaw's *Don Juan in Hell*). With actors Dick Powell and David Niven, Boyer co-founded Four Star Television in 1951, starring in many of the company's TV productions during the 50s and 60s. His career tapered off after the suicide of his 21-year-old son in 1965, after which he mostly made European films, though he returned to America to appear as the ancient High Lama in the musical remake of *Lost Horizon* (1973). He won the New York Film Critics Circle Award for his work in *Stavisky*, his final performance. Two days after his wife of forty-plus years, actress Patricia Peterson, died of cancer in 1978, he took his own life with an overdose of Seconal. **Selected Works:** *Algiers* (1938), *Barefoot in the Park* (1967), *Fanny* (1961), *Gaslight* (1944)

# Lara Flynn Boyle

**Born:** March 24, 1970; Davenport, IA

**Years Active in the Industry:** by decade

| 10s | 20s | 30s | 40s | 50s | 60s | 70s | 80s | 90s |
|-----|-----|-----|-----|-----|-----|-----|-----|-----|

Actress Lara Flynn Boyle has David Lynch to thank for becoming so famous at so young an age. She was barely twenty when she made her series TV bow on *Twin Peaks* in the role of Donna Hayward, best friend of the ill-fated Laura Palmer. Since the debut of *Twin Peaks* in 1990, she has seldom had an unbusy day in her profession of choice. The showiest (and to date the best) of her film roles has been as the "secretary from Hell" in 1993's *The Temp*. **Selected Works:** *Equinox* (1993), *Wayne's World* (1992), *Where the Day Takes You* (1992), *Red Rock West* (1993), *Threesome* (1994)

# Peter Boyle

**Born:** October 18, 1933; Philadelphia, PA

**Years Active in the Industry:** by decade

| 10s | 20s | 30s | 40s | 50s | 60s | 70s | 80s | 90s |
|-----|-----|-----|-----|-----|-----|-----|-----|-----|

Balding, burly, character actor with intense eyes and manic smile, Peter Boyle became an off-Broadway actor during the early '60s, after putting in time as a monk in the order of the Christian

Brothers. Later, he moved to Chicago to join the celebrated Second City satirical improvisation troupe, and finally found some work in TV and movies in the late '60s, beginning his film career with an appearance in *The Virgin President* (1968). Big success came with his true-to-life portrayal of a redneck bigot in *Joe* (1970), after which he found steady work (in both lead and supporting roles) in a stream of mostly off-beat pictures; these included his hilarious turn as the singing and dancing monster in Mel Brooks's comedy classic *Young Frankenstein* (1974), as well as his role as Robert DeNiro's buddy in Martin Scorsese's *Taxi Driver* (1976). On TV he portrayed Senator Joseph McCarthy in a 1977 special. **Selected Works:** *Honeymoon in Vegas* (1992), *Malcolm X* (1992), *Tragedy of Flight 103: The Inside Story* (1991), *Shadow* (1994)

# Lorraine Bracco

**Born:** 1955; Brooklyn, NY

**Years Active in the Industry:** by decade

| 10s | 20s | 30s | 40s | 50s | 60s | 70s | 80s | 90s |
|-----|-----|-----|-----|-----|-----|-----|-----|-----|

Contemporary American actress Lorraine Bracco began her career as an internationally recognized high fashion model. While working as a disc jockey for Radio Luxembourg in Paris, she made her feature film debut in the French film *Duos sur Canape* (1979). She made a couple of other European films before returning to the US and winning a small part in *The Pick-Up Artist* (1987). That same year, she made her breakthrough playing the wife of Tom Berenger in *Someone to Watch over Me*. In 1990, she earned an Oscar nomination for Best Supporting Actress for her role in Scorsese's *GoodFellas*. Bracco has since continued to star in many mainstream features of varying quality. Most recently, she appeared in *Basketball Diaries* (1995). **Selected Works:** *Medicine Man* (1992), *Scam* (1993), *Switch* (1991), *Being Human* (1994)

# Eddie Bracken (Edward Vincent Bracken)

**Born:** February 7, 1920; Astoria, NY

**Years Active in the Industry:** by decade

| 10s | 20s | 30s | 40s | 50s | 60s | 70s | 80s | 90s |
|-----|-----|-----|-----|-----|-----|-----|-----|-----|
|     |     |     |     |     |     |     |     |     |

Character actor Eddie Bracken is best known for his roles as lovable, befuddled losers and nervous hayseeds. As a child, he acted and sang on stage and in vaudeville and nightclubs; he also appeared in four "Our Gang" comedy shorts and in six episodes of the "New York Kiddie Troopers" series. As a juvenile, he worked on Broadway and with touring shows, then made his film debut with *Too Many Girls* (1940). Bracken is best known for his work as a shy bumbler in two light Preston Sturges comedies, *The Miracle of Morgan's Creek* and *Hail the Conquering Hero* (both 1944); in the latter he appeared as Norval Jones, the character that established his "type" and which (he would later complain) ruined his film career by restricting the sorts of roles he was offered. In the early '50s his career ground to a halt and he quit making movies in 1953, going on to do much touring stage work with his wife, the former Connie Nickerson. During the early 70s he lost $2 million in a failed scheme to create a chain of stock theaters. He returned briefly to Hollywood in 1983 to appear as a Walt Disney send-up in *National Lampoon's Vacation*. **Selected Works:** *Rookie of the Year* (1993)

# Alice Brady

**Born:** November 2, 1892; New York, NY
**Died:** October 28, 1939; New York, NY

**Years Active in the Industry:** by decade

| 10s | 20s | 30s | 40s | 50s | 60s | 70s | 80s | 90s |
|-----|-----|-----|-----|-----|-----|-----|-----|-----|
|     |     |     |     |     |     |     |     |     |

American actress Alice Brady first came to prominence in the silent films produced by World Studios, which was owned and operated by Alice's father, the influential theatrical producer William H. Brady. A star from her first film, *As Ye Sow* (1914), onward, she was applauded for her acting skills, though critics at the time noted that her somewhat offbeat facial features would be better suited to character roles than to ingenues. Brady devoted the 1920s to motherly and matronly portrayals on stage - which, as it turned out, were far more rewarding professionally than the heroines she'd played at World. Making her talking-picture debut in 1933's *When Ladies Meet*, Brady rapidly became one of Hollywood's most prolific portrayers of addlebrained society matrons and world-weary matriarchs. Her comic skills won her roles in such classics as *My Man Godfrey* (1936) and *Three Smart Girls*, but it was for her dramatic portrayal of the resilient, much-maligned Mrs. O'Leary in *In Old Chicago* (1938) that she won an Academy Award. Shortly after completing her work on John Ford's *Young Mr. Lincoln* (1939), Brady passed away at the age of 47. **Selected Works:** *Gay Divorcee* (1934), *One Hundred Men and a Girl* (1937)

# Sonia Braga

**Born:** 1951; Maringa, Parana, Brazil

**Years Active in the Industry:** by decade

| 10s | 20s | 30s | 40s | 50s | 60s | 70s | 80s | 90s |
|-----|-----|-----|-----|-----|-----|-----|-----|-----|
|     |     |     |     |     |     |     |     |     |

Born to mixed-race Brazilian parents, Sonia Braga went to work at age fourteen to help support her widowed mother and six siblings. Personable and photogenic, she had little trouble securing acting assignments on TV and later on stage. By her early twenties, Braga was a major soap opera star, a status comparable to goddess in Brazil. She began making films domestically in 1969, but it was not until 1977's *Dona Flor and Her Two Husbands* that she gained international screen stardom. Her most famous movie appearance was her performance as the enigmatic "dream heroine" in *Kiss of the Spider Woman* (1985). Braga's later films have tended to cash in on her sultry, "dangerous" beauty rather than her talent, as witness her S-and-M turn in Clint Eastwood's *The Rookie* (1990). **Selected Works:** *Last Prostitute* (1991)

# Kenneth Branagh

**Born:** December 10, 1960; Belfast, Northern Ireland

**Years Active in the Industry:** by decade

| 10s | 20s | 30s | 40s | 50s | 60s | 70s | 80s | 90s |
|-----|-----|-----|-----|-----|-----|-----|-----|-----|
|     |     |     |     |     |     |     |     |     |

At age 10, Irish-born Kenneth Branagh moved with his family to London. Frankly determined to be a star, Branagh scored his first stage hit in *Another Country* when barely out of his teens. He joined the Royal Shakespearean Company, where he quickly built up a reputation for brilliance—and for being imperious, arrogant and argumentative. Unhappy with the perceived conservatism of

the RSC, Branagh bolted to form his own Renaissance Theatre Company. Hailed as the brightest young talent since Laurence Olivier, Branagh had the marvelous audacity to follow precisely in Olivier's footsteps by directing and starring in a lavish film version of Shakespeare's *Henry V* in 1989. While he'd already appeared in two films, as well as the 1987 *Masterpiece Theatre* serial *Fortunes of War*, Branagh was lauded as 1989's most stellar newcomer. Branagh switched from the classics to a contemporary original for his next acting/directing film effort, *Dead Again* (1991), a nail-biting murder mystery in which he played a dual role as a 1940s Briton and his 1990s American forebear; likewise essaying two roles was Branagh's wife, actress Emma Thompson, who has appeared in virtually all of her husband's projects. Branagh's box-office magic faltered slightly with *Peter's Friends* (1992), a romantic comedy which he directed from a screenplay by comedienne Rita Rudner, but he regained his lost footing with a lusty 1993 filmization of Shakespeare's *Much Ado About Nothing*. Unfortunately, Kenneth Branagh's next directorial effort, 1994's *Frankenstein*, was a conspicuous failure despite its spectacular special effects and its horrendously effective makeup work. **Selected Works:** *Othello* (1995), *In the Bleak Midwinter* (1995)

# Klaus-Maria Brandauer

**Born:** June 22, 1944; Alt Aussee, Austria

**Years Active in the Industry:** by decade

| 10ˢ | 20ˢ | 30ˢ | 40ˢ | 50ˢ | 60ˢ | 70ˢ | 80ˢ | 90ˢ |
|---|---|---|---|---|---|---|---|---|
| | | | | | | | | |

Acclaimed actor Klaus-Maria Brandauer is quite well-known in Germany and in his native Austria for his work in theater and films such as *Mephisto* (1981). For his leading role in that film, he won the Best Actor award at Cannes. In the United States, Brandauer is best known for his memorable role as Meryl Streep's neer-do-well husband in *Out of Africa* for which he was given an Oscar nomination for Best Supporting Actor. Born Klaus Maria Stenji, he was educated at the Stuttgart Academy of Music and Dramatic Arts in Germany. Upon graduation, he began working in repertory theater in well-known companies such as Tubingen and Dusseldorf until he was hired into the troupe at Burgtheater in Vienna, one of Austria's best known theaters. By 1970, Brandauer had become one of the most famous stage actors in the German-speaking world, known for his range and charisma on stage. He

made his film debut in the French TV mini-series *Jean Christophe*. He later debuted in cinema playing a villain in *The Salzburg Connection* (1982), which bombed critically, but lead him to play a series of villains including the deliciously evil Largo in the 1983 Bond thriller *Never Say Never Again*. His best films have been made with Hungarian director Istvan Sazbo including *Colonel Redl* (1985). **Selected Works:** *Hanussen* (1988), *White Fang* (1991), *Mario and the Magician* (1994)

# Marlon Brando (Marlon Brando, Jr.)

**Born:** April 3, 1924; Omaha, NE

**Years Active in the Industry:** by decade

| 10ˢ | 20ˢ | 30ˢ | 40ˢ | 50ˢ | 60ˢ | 70ˢ | 80ˢ | 90ˢ |
|---|---|---|---|---|---|---|---|---|
| | | | | | | | | |

Marlon Brando is among an elite handful of the most celebrated American actors in film history. Brando is also noted for his stage performances. Although a versatile actor, he is best known

for his portrayals of brooding, brutal, (almost Neanderthal-like) men. The son of a salesman and an amateur actress, Brando was sent to military school during his rebellious youth; after being expelled he went to New York where he studied acting under Stella Adler at the Actors' Studio. A "Method" actor of the Stanislavski school, he brought his skills to Broadway in 1944 and appeared in several plays in subsequent years. With his explosive performance as the violent Stanley Kowalski in Tennessee Williams's *A Streetcar Named Desire* (1947) he became a major American star. In 1950 he made his film debut as a paraplegic in Stanley Kramer's *The Men*; in preparation for the role he spent a month in a paraplegic's rehabilitation ward, typical behavior for a "Method" actor. In 1951 he appeared in the screen version of *A Streetcar Named Desire*, for which he received a Best Actor Academy Award nomination; he received the same nomination in each of the next three successive years, finally winning in 1954 for his work in Elia Kazan's *On the Waterfront*. Brando's charismatic rebelliousness and non-conformity in a decade of conformity made him an artistic and social force; he is considered the most influential actor of his generation. Young audiences saw him as the prototype of the Beat generation; older viewers saw him as something to be feared, an unrestrained, unkempt, animalistic, anti-social menace. He formed his own production company in 1959, Pennebraker Productions, and produced, directed, and starred in *One-Eyed Jacks* (1959). In the '60s, during a period of upheaval in his personal life (including three broken marriages), he received lesser parts and began to be thought of as a temperamental artist who was difficult to work with. He made a remarkable comeback, however, in the title role of Francis Ford Coppola's *The Godfather* (1972); the same year he made the impressive erotic film *Last Tango in Paris*. Many of his later roles were done mostly for the money, as Brando preferred a life of ease in Tahiti, but he continued to take the occasional major part, such as that of the evil Kurtz in Coppola's *Apocalypse Now* (1979). His first two marriages were to actresses Anna Kashfi and Movita (Castenada). He is the brother of actress Jocelyn Brando. **Selected Works:** *Don Juan DeMarco* (1994), *Dry White Season* (1989), *Freshman* (1990), *Sayonara* (1957), *Viva Zapata!* (1952)

# Eileen Brennan

**Born:** September 3, 1935; Los Angeles, CA

**Years Active in the Industry:** by decade

| 10ˢ | 20ˢ | 30ˢ | 40ˢ | 50ˢ | 60ˢ | 70ˢ | 80ˢ | 90ˢ |
|----|----|----|----|----|----|----|----|----|
|    |    |    |    |    | ▓ | ▓ | ▓ | ▓ |

American actress Eileen Brennan was the daughter of Jean Manahan, a moderately successful silent screen actress. Brennan studied at both Georgetown University and the American Academy of Dramatic Art before making her mark as star of the 1959 off-Broadway musical *Little Mary Sunshine*. On the surface, it would seem that this production was out of character for the earthy, sardonic Brennan most familiar to filmgoers. Not so. A lampoon of insipid 1920s operettas, *Little Mary Sunshine* was in its own lah-dee-dah way one of the dirtiest musicals ever written (something that doesn't seem to dawn on the many high schools that have since produced it). Brennan was among the first-season stars of TV's *Rowan and Martin's Laugh-In*, essentially doing hilarious variations of her simpering "Mary Sunshine" persona. With her 1970s film appearances in *The Last Picture Show* (1971), *The Sting* (1972) and *Hustle* (1974) came the world-weary, hard-bitten characterizations with which she built her movie following. She was nominated for an Oscar for her expert interpretation of an army sergeant in Goldie Hawn's *Private Benjamin* (1980), then recreated the role for the 1981 TV sitcom version of this film (which won her an Emmy). While filming the TV *Benjamin*, Brennan was seriously injured in a car accident. The recovery was long and painful, but by 1985 she was back at work, as caustic as ever in recent films as *White Palace* (1991) and the *Last Picture Show* sequel *Texasville* (1990).

# Walter Brennan

**Born:** July 25, 1894; Lynn, MA
**Died:** September 23, 1974; Oxnard, CA

**Years Active in the Industry:** by decade

| 10ˢ | 20ˢ | 30ˢ | 40ˢ | 50ˢ | 60ˢ | 70ˢ | 80ˢ | 90ˢ |
|----|----|----|----|----|----|----|----|----|
|    | ▓ | ▓ | ▓ | ▓ | ▓ | ▓ |    |    |

American actor Walter Brennan had plans early in life to be an engineer, but the lure of amateur theatricals changed his destiny. The story goes that while serving his country during World War I, Brennan fell victim to a poison gas attack which permanently affected his vocal chords, resulting in the reedy, codger-like tones which would earn him "old" character parts even when he was a young man. After several years in vaudeville, Brennan entered films in the mid-1920s as an extra and bit player. He supplemented his acting income as a real estate speculator until a meaty supporting role in *The Wedding Night* (1935) assured him a full-time movie career. In 1936, Brennan won the first "best supporting actor" Academy Award for his work in *Come and Get It* (1936) - the first of three such awards for the actor. Brennan's other Oscars were for his role as a septuagenarian horse breeder in *Kentucky* (1938), and for *The Westerner* (1940), in which the actor played legendary rapscallion Judge Roy Bean. In 1957, Brennan extended his talents to television as star of the long-running sitcom *The Real McCoys*; the actor's portrayal of Grandpa Amos McCoy not only endeared him to millions, but provided limitless material for nightclub impressionists ("Hey, Little Luke! Hey, Pepino!"). Brennan's career flourished into the 1960s, embracing two more weekly TV series, *The Tycoon* (1964) and *Guns of Will Sonnett* (1967-69). In addition to his television and movie work, Brennan was very active in Right Wing political causes, even when prevailing Hollywood sentiments veered to the Left. **Selected Works:** *Bad Day at Black Rock* (1954), *How the West Was Won* (1963), *Meet John Doe* (1941), *Red River* (1948), *Sergeant York* (1941)

# George Brent (George Brendan Nolan)

**Born:** March 15, 1904; Shannonsbridge, Ireland
**Died:** 1979

**Years Active in the Industry:** by decade

| 10ˢ | 20ˢ | 30ˢ | 40ˢ | 50ˢ | 60ˢ | 70ˢ | 80ˢ | 90ˢ |
|----|----|----|----|----|----|----|----|----|
|    |    | ▓ | ▓ | ▓ |    |    |    |    |

With his pencil-thin mustache, the suave, gallant George Brent was one of Hollywood's most dependable leading men. A handsome, but never very exciting or dynamic lead, he played opposite all of Warner's greatest actresses, including Barbara Stanwyck and Olivia de Havilland; he is best known for his work with Bette Davis, with whom (according to some sources) he had a lasting but secret off-screen romance. He began his career playing small roles as a child in Abbey Theater (Ireland) plays. During the Irish Rebellion he participated in subversive activities and had to be smuggled out of the country to Canada where he eventually toured with a stock company for two years, before moving on to New York. There he continued to appear with several stock companies, three of which he formed on his own. Brent then found work on Broadway in the late '20s, before heading for Hollywood to begin a career that spanned two decades. Brent was typically cast as a gentlemanly, romantic leading man (after briefly being cast in tough hero roles). He debuted in *Under Suspicion* (1930). He retired from the big screen in 1953, going on to star in the TV series

*Wire Service* (1956-59). He made his final screen appearance in 1978, playing a judge in *Born Again*. His six wives included actresses Ruth Chatterton (with whom he co-starred in *The Rich Are Always With Us*, [1932]), Constance Worth, and Ann Sheridan (with whom he appeared in *Honeymoon for Three*, [1941]). **Selected Works:** *42nd Street* (1933), *Dark Victory* (1939), *Great Lie* (1941), *Spiral Staircase* (1946), *Rains Came* (1939)

# Robert Bresson

**Born:** September 25, 1907; Bromont-Lamothe, Puy-de-Dome, France

**Years Active in the Industry:** by decade

| 10ˢ | 20ˢ | 30ˢ | 40ˢ | 50ˢ | 60ˢ | 70ˢ | 80ˢ | 90ˢ |
|-----|-----|-----|-----|-----|-----|-----|-----|-----|

French director Robert Bresson studied philosophy and the classics before writing his first screenplay in 1933. His earliest directing assignments were a handful of mid-1930s short subjects; he graduated to features with 1943's *Les Anges du Peche*, released shortly before his incarceration by the Germans as a POW. After the international attention heaped upon him for his *Diary of a Country Priest* (1950), Bresson gained fame as a major exponent of the cinema of personal expression. Unlike many so-called "auteurs", Bresson has resisted falling in step with such trends as neorealism and the New Wave. He has frequently been described as a "painter" of film; he would more accurately be designated a puppeteer. Using non-professional actors, Bresson manipulates the movements and facial expressions of his cast members to the smallest detail. What might end up looking stilted and over-rehearsed in anyone else's work comes across as warmly human in Bresson's films. Advocating the philosophy of "less is more", Bresson is most comfortable with limited subject matter, small casts and minimal plots. One of his best cinematic "miniatures" is *Au Hasard Balthasar* (1966), which concentrates on the life of a rural donkey—and reduces even the most jaded filmgoer to tears when the donkey dies after several human-inflicted indignities. Bresson has written several essays on filmmaking, and won numerous international awards, most recently for 1983's *L'Argent*. **Selected Works:** *Man Escaped* (1957), *Mouchette* (1967), *Pickpocket* (1959), *Lancelot of the Lake* (1975)

# Martin Brest

**Born:** August 8, 1951; Bronx, NY

**Years Active in the Industry:** by decade

| 10ˢ | 20ˢ | 30ˢ | 40ˢ | 50ˢ | 60ˢ | 70ˢ | 80ˢ | 90ˢ |
|-----|-----|-----|-----|-----|-----|-----|-----|-----|

While attending New York University, Martin Brest directed the award-winning student project *Hot Dogs for Gaugin*, starring a then-unknown Danny DeVito. Brest went on to produce, direct, write and edit *Hot Tomorrows* (1977) for the American Film Institute. These formative efforts caught the eye of Warner Bros.; the studio hired the 27-year-old Brest to direct the venerable George Burns, Art Carney and Lee Strasberg in the melancholy comedy *Going In Style* (1979). The handling of this film evinced a maturity well beyond Brest's physical age, and it looked for awhile as though Hollywood had another *wunderkind* on its hands. Brest developed the teenage-oriented suspense film *Wargames* (1983), but the project was wrested from his control after an on-set tiff with the producers. For nearly two years, Brest was virtually blacklisted, surfacing only for an acting assignment in *Fast Times at Ridgemont High* (1982). The director made a successful comeback with the mega-hit *Beverly Hills Cop* (1984); he has continued to prosper professionally (his early dismissal from *Rain Man* (1988) was only a minor irritation), winning an Oscar nomination for *Scent of a Woman* (1992), which he produced as well as directed. Brest is married to producer Lisa Weinstein.

# Marshall Brickman

**Born:** August 25, 1941; Rio de Janeiro, Brazil

**Years Active in the Industry:** by decade

| 10ˢ | 20ˢ | 30ˢ | 40ˢ | 50ˢ | 60ˢ | 70ˢ | 80ˢ | 90ˢ |
|-----|-----|-----|-----|-----|-----|-----|-----|-----|

Born in Brazil to American parents, Marshall Brickman paid his way through college as a folksinger. While still in his teens, Brickman was a member of the Tarriers, a group which also included future actor Alan Arkin. Turning to writing, Brickman penned special material for *Candid Camera*, then hit the talk show circuit, winning an Emmy for his work on *The Dick Cavett Show*. Through Cavett, Brickman became acquainted with Woody Allen; he would collaborate on the scripts of some of Allen's best films of the 1970s. In 1977, Brickman and Allen shared an Oscar for the screenplay of *Annie Hall* (both men should have gotten Purple Hearts, considering the numerous torturous rewrites the script underwent before emerging on the screen). As a solo director, Brickman has displayed an acute gift for timing and a delightful sense of the ridiculous, though the quality of his films lacks the consistency of his Woody Allen collaborations. Brickman's best directorial effort was 1980's *Simon*, an identity-crisis science fiction satire starring Brickman's onetime fellow "Tarrier" Alan Arkin; his weakest effort was the teen-oriented flick *The Manhattan Project* (1985). **Selected Works:** *Manhattan Murder Mystery* (1993)

# Beau Bridges (Lloyd Vernet Bridges III)

**Born:** December 9, 1941; Los Angeles, CA

**Years Active in the Industry:** by decade

| 10ˢ | 20ˢ | 30ˢ | 40ˢ | 50ˢ | 60ˢ | 70ˢ | 80ˢ | 90ˢ |
|-----|-----|-----|-----|-----|-----|-----|-----|-----|

Born Lloyd Vernet Bridges III, Beau Bridges is the son of actor Llloyd Bridges and elder brother of populuar leading man Jeff Bridges. He made his film debut at age seven in *Force of Evil* (1948). This led to several more appearances in features. Later, while studying at UCLA, Bridges made an attempt at becoming a basketball player. He failed and returned to acting. Bridges made his adult debut in *The Explosive Generation* (1961), a film centered on basketball. As an actor, he has worked steadily since then; he is typically cast as an amiable regular joe. In 1989, he and his more popular little brother Jeff played co-leads in *The Fabulous Baker Boys* where Beau won good reviews. Bridges made his directorial debut with the television movie *The Thanksgiving Promise* (1986), in which he starred with his father Lloyd and his son. During the late '80s, he also directed and starred in two violent action films. Bridges continues to act and work behind the screen. **Selected Works:** *Daddy's Dyin'... Who's Got the Will?* (1990), *Sidekicks* (1993), *Without Warning: The James Brady Story* (1991), *Positively True Adventures of the Alleged Texas Cheerleader-Murdering Mom* (1993), *Secret Sins of the Father* (1994)

# James Bridges

**Born:** February 3, 1936; Paris, AR
**Died:** June 6, 1993; Los Angeles, CA

**Years Active in the Industry:** by decade

| 10s | 20s | 30s | 40s | 50s | 60s | 70s | 80s | 90s |
|-----|-----|-----|-----|-----|-----|-----|-----|-----|
|     |     |     |     |     |     |     |     |     |

Like his contemporaries Paul Mazursky and Sidney Pollack, James Bridges started his show-business career playing insouciant teenagers in various movies and TV programs of the 1950s, then decided to concentrate on the production end of the business. He wrote the screenplays for such films as *The Appaloosa* (1966) and *Colossus: The Forbin Project* (1970) before finessing one of his scripts into his first directorial assignment, *The Baby Maker* (1970). The most successful of his earliest directing gigs was *The Paper Chase* (1973), an entertaining glance at academic gamesmanship which Bridges later spun off into a *succes d'estime* TV series. Bridges' most prescient production was *The China Syndrome* (1978), a nuclear-meltdown melodrama which had the great good fortune to be released shortly after Three Mile Island. The director's *Mike's Murder* (1984) became a cause celebre among film fans because it was shelved by its distributors for several years; alas, it was not worth the wait. Bridges' last film, made five years before his death of kidney failure at age 56, was the unsuccessful "absolute success corrupts absolutely" effort *Bright Lights, Big City* (1988). **Selected Works:** *White Hunter, Black Heart* (1990)

# Jeff Bridges

**Born:** December 4, 1949; Los Angeles, CA

**Years Active in the Industry:** by decade

| 10s | 20s | 30s | 40s | 50s | 60s | 70s | 80s | 90s |
|-----|-----|-----|-----|-----|-----|-----|-----|-----|
|     |     |     |     |     |     |     |     |     |

Rangy, blonde and handsome Jeff Bridges, the son of actor Lloyd Bridges and brother of actor Beau Bridges, is considered one of Hollywood's most versatile, and most amiable actors, noted for playing off-beat roles with unusual intelligence and depth. He began his profession appearing in his father's 1950s TV series *Sea Hunt* when he was only eight. Though he made his adult film debut in *Halls of Anger* (1970), Bridges didn't become a star until he appeared in Bogdanovich's *The Last Picture Show* (1971), for which he received his first Best Supporting Actor Oscar nomination. He has also been nominated for his supporting role in *Thunderbolt and Lightfoot* (1974) and was nominated for best actor in *Starman* (1984). He co-starred with his brother Beau in *The Fabulous Baker Boys* (1989). As the nineties progress, Bridges continues to put out consistently excellent performances in a variety of roles. **Selected Works:** *Hearts of the West* (1975), *Tucker: The Man & His Dream* (1988), *Fisher King* (1991), *American Heart* (1993), *Fearless* (1993)

# Lloyd Bridges (Lloyd Vernet Bridges)

**Born:** January 15, 1913; San Leandro, CA

**Years Active in the Industry:** by decade

| 10s | 20s | 30s | 40s | 50s | 60s | 70s | 80s | 90s |
|-----|-----|-----|-----|-----|-----|-----|-----|-----|
|     |     |     |     |     |     |     |     |     |

Tall, blond actor Lloyd Bridges is best known for his starring role in the long-running TV drama *Sea Hunt*, but he has also appeared in many films. Prior to coming to Hollywood, Bridges worked in stock theater and then, in the late '30s debuted on Broadway in a modern-dress production of *Othello*. Signed by Columbia in 1941, he went on to appear in 25 low-budget films over the next four years; he often appeared in Westerns and action pictures, occasionally playing a heavy. He left Columbia in 1945 and started free-lancing, landing lead roles in B movies and important supporting parts in A-movies (e.g., his portrayal of the hotheaded, cowardly deputy sheriff in the classic *High Noon*, 1952). During the McCarthy-era "witch hunts" of the early '50s, he admitted to the House Un-American Activities Commission that he'd formerly been a member of the Communist party; in the hearings he became a key witness for the government. He is the father of actors Beau and Jeff Bridges. **Selected Works:** *Hot Shots* (1991), *Hot Shots! Part Deux* (1993), *Tucker: The Man & His Dream* (1988), *Leona Helmsley - The Queen of Mean* (1990)

# Matthew Broderick

**Born:** March 21, 1962; New York, NY

**Years Active in the Industry:** by decade

| 10ˢ | 20ˢ | 30ˢ | 40ˢ | 50ˢ | 60ˢ | 70ˢ | 80ˢ | 90ˢ |
|-----|-----|-----|-----|-----|-----|-----|-----|-----|
|     |     |     |     |     |     |     |  ■  |  ■  |

American actor Matthew Broderick has found success on both stage and screen. Having developed a working relationship as a teenager with playwrights Horton Foote and Neil Simon, he appeared

in Foote's plays *On Valentine's Day* (Broderick's professional stage debut) and *The Widow Clare*, Foote's movie *1918* (1982), Simon's play *Broadway Beach Memoirs* (on Broadway), and Simon's film *Max Dugan Returns* (1982), all before his 21st birthday. He won a Tony for his work in *Brighton Beach Memoirs*; he also appeared in the stage and screen versions of

that play's sequel, *Biloxi Blues* (film, 1987). For his performance in Harvey Fierstein's play *Torch Song Trilogy* he won an Outer Critics Circle Award for Best Supporting Actor and a Villager Award; he also appeared in the screen version of that play. Onscreen he first made an impact portraying a teenage computer genius in John Badham's *WarGames* (1983). His greatest popularity came with the title role in John Hughes' *Ferris Bueller's Day Off* (1986), in which he (at the age of 24) played a 16-year-old. As the 1990s progress, Broderick has moved away from playing adolescents and has begun playing characters closer to his own age. **Selected Works:** *Freshman* (1990), *Glory* (1989), *The Road to Wellville* (1994)

# Charles Bronson

**Born:** November 3, 1920; Ehrenfield, PA

**Years Active in the Industry:** by decade

| 10ˢ | 20ˢ | 30ˢ | 40ˢ | 50ˢ | 60ˢ | 70ˢ | 80ˢ | 90ˢ |
|-----|-----|-----|-----|-----|-----|-----|-----|-----|
|     |     |     |  ■  |  ■  |  ■  |  ■  |  ■  |  ■  |

The son of a Lithuanian coal miner, American actor Charles Bronson has claimed to have spoken no English at home during his childhood in Pennsylvania. Though he managed to complete

high school, it was expected of Bronson that he'd go into the mines like his father and many brothers. Experiencing the world outside Pennsylvania during World War II service, Bronson came back to America determined to pursue an art career. While working as a set designer for a Philadelphia theatre troupe, Bronson played a few small roles and almost immediately switched his allegiance from the production end of theatre to the acting end. After a few scattered acting jobs in New York, he enrolled in the Pasadena Playhouse in 1949. By 1951 he was in films, playing uncredited bits in such pictures as *You're In the Navy Now* (1952) (which also featured a young bit actor named Lee Marvin), *The People Against O'Hara* (1951), *Diplomatic Courier* (1952), *Bloodhounds of Broadway* (1952) (as a waiter!) and *The Clown* (1953). When he finally achieved billing, it was under his own name, Charles Buchinsky (sometimes spelled Buchinski). His first role of importance was as Igor, the mute granite-faced henchman of deranged sculptor Vincent Price in *House of Wax* (1953). The actor was billed as Charles Bronson for the first time in *Drum Beat* (1954), though he was still consigned to character roles as slavics, American Indians, hoodlums and convicts. Most sources claim that Bronson's first starring role was in *Machine Gun Kelly* (1958), but in fact he had the lead in 1957's *Gang War*, playing an embryonic version of his later *Death Wish* persona as a mild-mannered man who turned vengeful after the death of his wife. Bronson achieved his first fan following with the TV series *Man with a Camera* (1959), where he played adventurous photojournalist Mike Kovac (and did double duty promoting the sponsor's camera products in the commercials!) His best film role up to 1960 was as one of *The Magnificent Seven* (1960), dominating several scenes despite the costar competition of Yul Brynner, Steve McQueen, Eli Wallach et. al. Most of Bronson's film assignments after *Seven* remained in the supporting-villainy category, however, so in 1968 the actor packed himself off to Europe, where American action players like Clint Eastwood and Lee Van Cleef were given bigger and better opportunities. Multiplying his international box office appeal tenfold with such films as *Guns for San Sebastian* (1967), *Once Upon a Time in the West* (1968), *Cold Sweat* (1970) and *The Valachi Papers* (1971), Bronson returned to Hollywood a full-fledged star at last. His most successful films of the 1970s were *Death Wish* (1974) and its sequels, a series of brutal "vigilante" pictures which suggested not so subliminally that honest people would ultimately have to dole out their own terminal justice to criminals. In many of his 1970s films, Bronson costarred with second wife Jill Ireland, with whom he remained married until she lost her valiant fight against cancer in 1990. In the last few years, Bronson's bankability has fallen off, due in part to younger action stars doing what he used to do twice as vigorously, and also because of his truculent attitude towards fans. *Death Wish 5: The Face of Death* (1994), Bronson's most recent film, was unfortunately his all-time worst. **Selected Works:** *Dirty Dozen* (1967), *Great Escape* (1963), *Indian Runner* (1991), *Rider on the Rain* (1970), *Sea Wolf* (1993)

# Sir Peter Brook

**Born:** March 21, 1925; London, England

**Years Active in the Industry:** by decade

| 10s | 20s | 30s | 40s | 50s | 60s | 70s | 80s | 90s |
|-----|-----|-----|-----|-----|-----|-----|-----|-----|

A pioneer of the British experimental theatre movement, Peter Brook was "in the movies" before ever directing his first play. As an Oxford undergrad, Brook directed the amateur short subject *Sentimental Journey* (1943), and a few months later staged his first theatrical production, *Dr. Faustus.* His first mainstream film was *The Beggar's Opera*, a 1953 version of John Gay's 18th century satirical musical extravaganza, starring Laurence Olivier in his singing debut as MacHeath. It would be the director's last "normal" film production; his next was the Renais-like 1960 French film *Moderato Canabile*, which can be described as an interior monologue come to life. Brook's 1963 movie version of *Lord of the Flies* used William Goldman's allegorical novel as a springboard for a largely improvised and intensely brutal skewering of the British social structure, enacted by a group of nonprofessional children and filmed with two handheld cameras to create the illusion of complete spontaneity. The director followed up this innovational effort with 1967's *Marat/Sade*, an in-your-face filmization of his own Royal Shakespeare Company production, featuring Glenda Jackson in her first film. Three years later, Brook founded Paris' International Centre for Theatre Research, now known as the Centre for International Creation. Many of Brook's techniques — outrageous settings, mixed media, the elimination of the "fourth wall", distinguished actors making bizarre entrances in even more bizarre costumes — have since been adopted by far less talented college and regional-theatre directors. Seldom concerned with the commercial viability of his efforts, Brook's more recent films include two dreamlike excursions into Eastern mysticism, *Meetings with Remarkable Men* (1979) and *The Mahabharata* (1990).

# Albert Brooks (Albert Einstein)

**Born:** July 22, 1947; Los Angeles, CA

**Years Active in the Industry:** by decade

| 10s | 20s | 30s | 40s | 50s | 60s | 70s | 80s | 90s |
|-----|-----|-----|-----|-----|-----|-----|-----|-----|

Filmmaker, screenwriter, and actor Albert Brooks, born Albert Einstein and the son of comedian Harry Einstein, briefly at-

tended college before trying his luck as a stand-up comic. By 1969 he was a regular on Dean Martin's weekly TV variety show, and was a frequent guest on a number of another shows. For his second comedy album, *A Star is Bought* (1975), he received an Emmy nomination; also in 1975, he began making short comedy films for the sketch-comedy TV series *Saturday Night Live.* He debuted on-screen in a supporting role in Martin Scorsese's classic *Taxi Driver* (1976). Three years later, he co-wrote and directed his next film, *Real Life* (1979), going on to direct and co-write three more films between 1981-1991. For his performance in the comedy *Broadcast News* (1987) he received a Best Supporting Actor nomination. **Selected Works:** *Defending Your Life* (1991)

# James L. Brooks

**Born:** May 9, 1940; North Bergen, NJ

**Years Active in the Industry:** by decade

| 10s | 20s | 30s | 40s | 50s | 60s | 70s | 80s | 90s |
|-----|-----|-----|-----|-----|-----|-----|-----|-----|

One of the few producer/director/writers to handle both movie and TV assignments with equal success, James L. Brooks was born in New Jersey and spent his college years in New York City. Following an apprenticeship with CBS news, Brooks went to work for documentary producer David L. Wolper. In 1969, Brooks broke into the nondocumentary end of the business with his TV sit-com *Room 222*, which though dated and obvious when seen today was an important stepping-stone in improving the racial balance on prime time television. *Room 222* was a "soft" program (it didn't even have a laugh track), thus Hollywood insiders were surprised when Brooks formed a partnership with writer Allan Burns, formerly of such raucous projects as *The Bullwinkle Show* and *My Mother the Car.* Brooks and Burns knew what sort of programs they wanted to do, but were forced to fight tooth and nail with the CBS higher-ups to get what they wanted to do on the air. Nobody, they were told, wanted to see a show about a single woman working at a television station. Further, nobody wanted to see anyone on TV who was Jewish, had a mustache, or came from New York City. All these "unwanted" elements would be present in the Brooks/Burns project *The Mary Tyler Moore Show;* the show that nobody wanted ran from 1970 through 1977, earning its production team a multitude of awards. Brooks would later be on the ground floor of such TV hits as *Cheers* and *Taxi*, which more than compensated for such relative failures as *The Associates.* Moving into films as producer/scripter (*Starting Over* [1979]) and even an occasional actor (Albert Brooks' *Real Life* [1979]), Brooks would end up director/producer/writer of *Terms of Endearment*, the Academy Award winner of 1983. Brooks went on to *Broadcast News* (1987), a truer but no less hilarious glance at the cutthroat network news business than *Mary Tyler Moore Show* had been. In recent years, Brooks has had equal parts success and failure. Among the winning projects was *The Simpsons*, the first successful prime time cartoon series since *The Flintstones* (successful because, it was rumored, Brooks took *Simpsons* creator Matt Groening in hand to teach him all about story structure and character development). Brooks' failures have included *I'll Do Anything* (1994) which was conceived and filmed as a return to the Big-Budget Musical genre, but which tested so badly that it was released with all the songs cut out!

# Louise Brooks

**Born:** November 14, 1906; Cherryvale, KS
**Died:** August 8, 1985; Rochester, NY

**Years Active in the Industry:** by decade

| 10ˢ | 20ˢ | 30ˢ | 40ˢ | 50ˢ | 60ˢ | 70ˢ | 80ˢ | 90ˢ |
|-----|-----|-----|-----|-----|-----|-----|-----|-----|

American leading lady Louise Brooks was considered one of the screen's most enigmatic stars of the '20s, and has become a figure of cult adoration. Her sleek, bobbed, helmet-like hairdo, emphasizing her eyes, became one of the most widely imitated "looks" of the '20s, and to this day remains a fashionable option. She began her career as a dancer at age 15 ; she was discovered by Hollywood after her appearances in *George White's Scandals* and the *Ziegfield Follies*, and she debuted as a flapper in Paramount's *The American Venus*. Brooks went on to appear in a number of films, working with major directors such as Hawks and Wellman, but her critical reputation rests on two films she made with director G.W. Pabst in Germany, *Pandora's Box* and *Diary of a Lost Girl* (both 1929). Brooks is said to have possessed a charismatic, strongly erotic screen presence, and some have referred to her as a genius. Back in Hollywood, however, she was offered only minor roles, so she retired from the screen for a few years then made a very weak comeback in a couple of B-movies in the late '30s. She made a stab at radio in the '40s, then gave up show business altogether. Afterwards she became a recluse, but began to write essays about her Hollywood experiences and about films generally; her autobiography, *Lulu in Hollywood* (1982), was critically acclaimed. It is said that no actress has ever become a more accomplished writer.

# Mel Brooks (Melvin Kaminsky)

**Born:** June 28, 1926; Brooklyn, NY

**Years Active in the Industry:** by decade

| 10ˢ | 20ˢ | 30ˢ | 40ˢ | 50ˢ | 60ˢ | 70ˢ | 80ˢ | 90ˢ |
|-----|-----|-----|-----|-----|-----|-----|-----|-----|

American comedian Mel Brooks overcame a childhood of abuse from his peers (he was small and sickly) by taking on the comically aggressive job of "toomler" in various Catskills resorts. For very little money but a great deal of personal satisfaction Brooks kept the resort clientele happy by performing quickie monologues and routines, pretending to insult both the help and the customers, and when all else failed, jumping fully clothed into the swimming pool. Applying for the writing staff of TV comedian Sid Caesar, Brooks literally fell to his knees and sang a song about himself. Before he was thirty, Brooks was earning $2500 per show writing for Caesar, in collaboration with such formidable wits as Neil Simon, Woody Allen and Carl Reiner. Though the work was grueling and at times dangerous (Caesar had a Hellenic temper, and at one point beat up Brooks while arguing over a joke), it was the best formal education that any comedian could have. Brooks left Caesar in the mid-1950s, and the sudden severe drop in his income fed Brooks' longtime phobia that success would invariably lead to crushing defeat. In the early 1960s, Brooks teamed with Carl Reiner for their celebrated "2000 Year Old Man" routines, which graduated into a hit record and numerous TV appearances. With Buck Henry, Brooks developed a satirical spy sitcom for comedian Don Adams titled *Get Smart*, which ran successfully from 1965 through 1970. Itching to make movies, Brooks directed a very low budget comedy about a conniving shoestring impresario titled *The Producers* (1968). He clashed violently with star Zero Mostel, behaved like a lunatic on the set, and (according to one observer) appeared ready to commit suicide at a moment's notice: Somehow *The Producers* came together, and though it died at the box office it has since gained a reputation as one of the most screamingly funny comedies of all time. Brooks wasn't laughing in the late 1960s, however; his average yearly income was around $8000 per year, forcing his wife, actress Anne Bancroft, to be the family breadwinner. After five or six years of disappointment, Brooks convinced Warner Bros. to finance an uproariously tasteless comedy about a black western sheriff. Directed, co-written and costarring Brooks, *Blazing Saddles* was one of the biggest moneyspinners of 1974, and for several years thereafter the world was Brook's oyster (even though he continually believed that the oyster would spoil). *Young Frankenstein* (1974) followed, and once again Brooks had a hit on his hands. Then he decided to star in as well as direct his films. *Silent Movie* (1976) and *High Anxiety* (1977) both had their moments, but might have even been funnier if someone other than Brooks had played the leads (it wasn't that he was unfunny; it was simply that he was a bit too much). By the time of *History of the World Part One* (1981), audiences were growing weary of Brooks' recycled gags and repetitious style. Still neurotic but a bit more willing to take advice than in earlier years, Brooks starred and produced in *To Be Or Not to Be* (1983), but did not direct, allowing director Alan Johnson to tone down Brooks' thespic excesses and deliver a well-balanced performance. While this and subsequent projects would suggest that Brooks has nothing more than wild slapstick and raunchy verbal humor on the brain, he is more than capable of turning out a project of restraint and taste. He bought the rights for *The Elephant Man*, the melancholy true story of a hideously deformed 19th century Londoner, and with his partner Michael Gruskopf produced an exquisite film version of the story in 1980. However, the self-flagellating Brooks rose again, here as elsewhere: Worried that filmgoers might think that *Elephant Man* would be just another gross-out comedy, Brooks had his own name removed from all publicity pertaining to the film. **Selected Works:** *Life Stinks* (1991), *Robin Hood: Men in Tights* (1993)

# Edward S. Brophy

**Born:** March 27, 1895; New York, NY
**Died:** May 30, 1960; Los Angeles, CA

**Years Active in the Industry:** by decade

| 10s | 20s | 30s | 40s | 50s | 60s | 70s | 80s | 90s |
|-----|-----|-----|-----|-----|-----|-----|-----|-----|
|     |     |     |     |     |     |     |     |     |

Born in New York City and educated at the University of Virginia, comic actor Edward Brophy entered films as a small part player in 1919. After a few years, he opted for the more financially secure production end of the business, though he never abandoned acting altogether. While working as property master for the Buster Keaton unit at MGM, Brophy was lured before the cameras for a memorable sequence in *The Cameraman* (1928) in which he and Buster both try to undress in a tiny wardrobe closet. Keaton saw to it that Brophy was prominently cast in two of the famed comedian's talking pictures, and by 1934 Brophy was once again acting full-time. Using his popping eyes, high pitched voiced and balding head to his best advantage, Brophy scored in role after role as funny gangsters and dyspeptic fight managers (he was less effective in such serious parts as the crazed killer in the 1935 horror film *Mad Love*). In 1940, Brophy entered the realm of screen immortality as the voice of Timothy Mouse in Walt Disney's feature-length cartoon *Dumbo* (1940). Curtailing his activities in the 1950s, he did his last work for director John Ford. Brophy died during production of Ford's *Two Rode Together* (1961); according to some sources, the actor's few completed scenes remain in the final release version of that popular western. **Selected Works:** *Last Hurrah* (1958), *Thin Man* (1934), *Champ* (1931), *It Happened Tomorrow* (1944)

# Pierce Brosnan

**Born:** May 16, 1952; County Meath, Ireland

**Years Active in the Industry:** by decade

| 10s | 20s | 30s | 40s | 50s | 60s | 70s | 80s | 90s |
|-----|-----|-----|-----|-----|-----|-----|-----|-----|
|     |     |     |     |     |     |     |     |     |

Moving to London with his family at an early age, Irish-born actor Pierce Brosnan made ends meet as a commercial illustrator and cab driver before turning to acting full-time. After training at the London Drama Centre, Brosnan made his West End stage bow in 1976, and appeared in his first film, *The Long Good Friday*, four years later. American audiences got their first glimpse of the charismatic, muscular young actor in the 1981 network miniseries *The Manions of America*. The following year, Brosnan was cast as the suave adventurer hero of the weekly TV series *Remington Steele*. The actor's casual panache and his gift for quippery led the producers of the James Bond movies to select Brosnan as the new Bond upon the departure of Roger Moore in 1986. At the last moment, the canceled *Remington Steele* was renewed, and Brosnan was contractually obligated to remain with the program, forcing him to relinquish the James Bond role to the less suitable Timothy

Dalton. It later became evident that the renewal of *Steele* was something of a subterfuge by its producers to keep Brosnan on their leash. This professional setback was compounded by personal tragedy seven years later when Brosnan's actress wife Cassandra Harris died after a long illness. Cast in a choice secondary role in the megahit 1993 comedy *Mrs. Doubtfire*, Brosnan regained his motion picture bankability, and at last report the actor was preparing to make his long-awaited debut in the role of James Bond. **Selected Works:** *Live Wire* (1992), *Mister Johnson* (1991), *Murder 101* (1991), *Victim of Love* (1991), *Goldeneye* (1995)

# Bryan Brown

**Born:** June 23, 1947; Sydney, Australia

**Years Active in the Industry:** by decade

| 10s | 20s | 30s | 40s | 50s | 60s | 70s | 80s | 90s |
|-----|-----|-----|-----|-----|-----|-----|-----|-----|
|     |     |     |     |     |     |     |     |     |

After cutting his acting teeth in his native Australia, Bryan Brown headed to London at age 27, where he joined the National Theatre. Upon his return to Australia three years later, Brown began

appearing in films, gaining international attention as one of two idealistic Aussie World War I soldiers (the other was Mel Gibson) in *Breaker Morant* (1979). Thereafter, the sexy, dynamic young actor divided his time between British and American films, scoring a hit with his portrayal of a movie special effects wizard in the Hollywood actioner *F/X* (1988). TV miniseries fans will remember Brown for his portrayal of Luke O'Neill in the Australian-based *The Thorn Birds* (1983) and for his starring stint on the multi-part 1980 British adaptation of *A Town Like Alice*, which ran in America on PBS and the Arts & Entertainment cable service. **Selected Works:** *Devlin* (1992), *F/X2: The Deadly Art of Illusion* (1991), *Gorillas in the Mist* (1988), *Last Hit* (1993), *Sweet Talker* (1991)

# Johnny Mack Brown

**Born:** September 1, 1904; Dothan, AL
**Died:** 1974

**Years Active in the Industry:** by decade

| 10s | 20s | 30s | 40s | 50s | 60s | 70s | 80s | 90s |
|-----|-----|-----|-----|-----|-----|-----|-----|-----|

Former All-American halfback Johnny Mack Brown was a popular screen cowboy during the 1930s. Already in the public eye for his athletic prowess, Brown was persuaded by a friend to give Hollywood a try after graduating from the University of Alabama. In 1927, the muscular macho man was signed by MGM where he played in a number of leading roles opposite popular actresses such as Garbo, Pickford, and Crawford for several years. But Brown never really found his acting niche until he starred in King Vidor's *Billy the Kid* (1930). From then on he was happily typecast as a cowboy actor, and became a hero to millions of American boys, appearing in over 200 B-grade Westerns over the next two decades. From 1942-50 he was consistently among the screen's ten most popular Western actors. Brown formally retired from movies in 1953 but made occasional return appearances as a "nostalgia" act.

# Tod Browning (Charles Albert Browning)

**Born:** July 12, 1882; Louisville, Kentucky
**Died:** October 6, 1962; Malibu, CA

**Years Active in the Industry:** by decade

| 10s | 20s | 30s | 40s | 50s | 60s | 70s | 80s | 90s |
|-----|-----|-----|-----|-----|-----|-----|-----|-----|

Browning joined a traveling circus while still a teenager, performing as a clown and contortionist. In 1915 he began acting at the Biograph studio and appeared in the modern sequence of D.W. Griffith's classic *Intolerance*; he also served as one of Griffith's assistants on that monumental project. Browning began directing in 1917, frequently co-writing his films. His first film with actor Lon Chaney, *The Unholy Three*, was a hit and led to several memorable silent melodramas with the great character actor, including *The Unknown*, *London After Midnight* (which Browning remade in 1935 as *Mark Of The Vampire*), and *West Of Zanzibar*. By the 1930s Browning was specializing in horror, and directed two classics of the era: *Dracula* with Bela Lugosi, and the astounding *Freaks*. The latter, a shocker set among the freaks of a traveling sideshow, was far too disturbing for its time and was quickly yanked from theaters; only in the 1960s did the film come to be hailed as a masterpiece.

# Nigel Bruce (William Nigel Bruce)

**Born:** February 4, 1895; Ensenada, Mexico
**Died:** October 8, 1953; Los Angeles, CA

**Years Active in the Industry:** by decade

| 10s | 20s | 30s | 40s | 50s | 60s | 70s | 80s | 90s |
|-----|-----|-----|-----|-----|-----|-----|-----|-----|

Though a British subject through and through, actor Nigel Bruce was born in Mexico while his parents were on vacation there. His education was interrupted by service in World War I, during which he suffered a leg injury and was confined to a wheelchair for the duration. At the end of the war, Bruce pursued an acting career, making his stage debut in *The Creaking Door* (1920). A stint in British silent pictures began in 1928, after which Bruce divided his time between stage and screen, finally settling in Hollywood in 1934 (though he continued to make sporadic appearances in such British films as *The Scarlet Pimpernel*). Nigel's first Hollywood picture was *Springtime for Henry* (1934), and soon he'd carved a niche for himself in roles as bumbling, befuddled middle-aged English gentlemen. It was this quality which led Bruce to being cast as Sherlock Holmes' companion Dr. Watson in *The Hound of the Baskervilles* (1939), a pleasurable assignment in that the film's Holmes, Basil Rathbone, was one of Bruce's oldest and closest friends. While Bruce's interpretation of Watson is out of favor with some Holmes purists (who prefer the more intelligent Watson of the original Conan Doyle stories), the actor played the role in 14 feature films, successfully cementing the cinema image of Sherlock's somewhat slower, older compatriot - even though he was in fact three years younger than Rathbone. Bruce continued to play Dr. Watson on a popular Sherlock Holmes radio series, even after Rathbone had deserted the role of Holmes in 1946. Bruce's last film role was in the pioneering 3-D feature, *Bwana Devil* (1952). He fell ill and died in 1953, missing the opportunity to be reunited with Basil Rathbone in a Sherlock Holmes theatrical production. **Selected Works:** *Charge of the Light Brigade* (1936), *Lassie Come Home* (1943), *Limelight* (1952), *Rebecca* (1940), *Suspicion* (1941)

# Yul Brynner

**Born:** July 11, 1920; Vladivostock, Russia
**Died:** October 10, 1985; New York, NY

**Years Active in the Industry:** by decade

| 10s | 20s | 30s | 40s | 50s | 60s | 70s | 80s | 90s |
|-----|-----|-----|-----|-----|-----|-----|-----|-----|

It was hard during his lifetime to determine when and where actor Yul Brynner was born, simply because he changed the story in every interview; confronted with these discrepancies late in life, he replied "Ordinary mortals need but one birthday." At any rate, it appears that Brynner's mother was part Russian, his father part Swiss, and that he lived in Russia until his mother moved the family to Manchuria and then to Paris in the early 1930s. He worked as a trapeze artist with the touring Cirque D'Hiver, then joined a repertory theatre company in Paris in 1934. Brynner's fluency in Russian and French enabled him to build up a following with the Czarist expatriates in Paris, and his talents as a singer-guitarist increased his popularity. When Michael Chekhov hired Brynner for his Amer-

ican theatre company, he added a third language - English - to his repertoire. After several years of regional acting, Brynner was hired by the Office of War Information as announcer for their French radio service. In 1945, Brynner was cast as Tsai-Yong in the musical play *Lute Song*, which starred Mary Martin; the play opened on Broadway in 1946, and though its run was short, Brynner won the "most promising actor" Donaldson Award. He went on to do theatre in London and to direct early live TV programs in the States, including a kid's puppet show, *Life with Snarky Parker*. His impatience and bad temper nearly cost Brynner his job with CBS, but while on brief suspension the actor made his movie debut as a two-bit smuggler in a Manhattan-filmed quickie *Port of New York* (1949), which has taken on a video-store life of its own since lapsing into Public Domain. On the strength of his *Lute Song* work of several years earlier, Brynner was cast as the King of Siam in Rodgers and Hammerstein's 1951 musical *The King and I*. The play was supposed to be a vehicle for Gertrude Lawrence, with the King an important but secondary role; but so powerful was Brynner's work that the role was beefed up in rehearsal, causing supporting actor Murvyn Vye to quit the show when Vye's only song was cut to give more stage time to Brynner. *The King and I* was an enormous hit, supplying Brynner with the role of a lifetime, one which he'd repeat brilliantly in the 1955 film version - and win an Oscar in the bargain. Cecil B. DeMille, impressed by Brynner's *King* performance, cast the actor as the King of Egypt in DeMille's multi-million dollar blockbuster *The Ten Commandments* (1956). After this, it was difficult for Brynner to play a "normal" character, so he seldom tried, though he came close to subtle believability in *Anastasia* (1956) and *The Journey* (1959). The first baldheaded movie idol, Brynner occasionally donned a wig or, as in *Taras Bulba* (1962), a Russian pigtail, but his fans (particularly the ladies) preferred him "scalped", as it were. Outside of his film work, Brynner was an accomplished photographer, and many of his photos appeared in major magazine spreads or were used as official studio production stills. Hollywood changed radically in the 1970s and the sort of larger-than-life fare in which Brynner thrived thinned out, so in 1972 the actor agreed to recreate his *King and I* role in an expensive weekly TV series, *Anna and the King*. It lasted all of eight weeks. Brynner's last major film role was in the sci-fi thriller *Westworld* (1973) as a murderously malfunctioning robot, dressed in Western garb reminiscent of Brynner's wardrobe in *The Magnificent Seven* (1960). What could have been campy or ludicrous became a chilling characterization in Brynner's hands; his steady, steely-eyed automaton glare as he approached his

human victims was one of the more enjoyably frightening filmgoing benefits of the 1970s. In 1977, Brynner embarked upon a stage revival of *The King and I*, and though he was dogged by tales of his outrageous temperament and seemingly petty demands during the tour, audiences in New York and all over the country loved the show. The actor inaugurated a second *King* tour in 1985; this time, however, he knew he was dying of cancer, but kept the news from both his fans and his coworkers. Unable to perform the "Shall We Dance" waltz or to get all the words out for the song "A Puzzlement", Brynner nonetheless played to packed audiences willing to shell out $75 a ticket. Two months after the play closed, Brynner died in a New York hospital - still insisting that his public not know the severity of his condition until after his death.

# Edgar Buchanan

**Born:** March 20, 1903; Humansville, MO
**Died:** April 4, 1979; Palm Desert, CA

**Years Active in the Industry:** by decade

| 10ˢ | 20ˢ | 30ˢ | 40ˢ | 50ˢ | 60ˢ | 70ˢ | 80ˢ | 90ˢ |
|-----|-----|-----|-----|-----|-----|-----|-----|-----|

Intending to become a dentist like his father, American actor Edgar Buchanan wound up with grades so bad in college that he was compelled to take an "easy" course to improve his average. Buchanan chose a course in play interpretation, and after listening to a few recitations of Shakespeare he was stagestruck. After completing dental school, Buchanan plied his oral surgery skills in the summertime, devoting the fall, winter and spring months to acting in stock companies and at the Pasadena Playhouse in California. He was given a screen test by Warner Bros. studios in 1940, received several bit roles, then worked himself up to supporting parts upon transferring to Columbia Pictures. Though still comparatively youthful, Buchanan specialized in grizzled old westerners, with a propensity towards villainy or at least larceny. The actor worked at every major studio (and not a few minor ones) over the next few years, still holding onto his dentist's license just in case he needed something to fall back on. Though he preferred movie work to the hurried pace of TV filming, Buchanan was quite busy in television's first decade, costarring with William Boyd on the immensely popular *Hopalong Cassidy* series, then receiving a starring series of his own, *Judge Roy Bean*, in 1954. Buchanan became an international success in 1963 thanks to his regular role as the lovably lazy Uncle Joe Bradley on the classic sitcom *Petticoat Junction*, which ran until 1970. After that, the actor experienced a considerably shorter run on the adventure series *Cade's County*, which starred Buchanan's close friend Glenn Ford. Buchanan's last movie role was in *Benji* (1974), which reunited him with the titular doggie star, who had first appeared as the family mutt on *Petticoat Junction*. **Selected Works:** *Shane* (1953), *Talk of the Town* (1942), *Sheepman* (1958)

# Jack Buchanan

**Born:** April 2, 1890; Helensborough Scotland
**Died:** October 20, 1957; London, England

**Years Active in the Industry:** by decade

| 10s | 20s | 30s | 40s | 50s | 60s | 70s | 80s | 90s |
|-----|-----|-----|-----|-----|-----|-----|-----|-----|
|     |     |     |     |     |     |     |     |     |

Scottish-born entertainer Jack Buchanan became caught up in amateur theatricals while he was a London office worker. He made his stage bow in 1911, and his London theatre debut in 1912, but full stardom would have to wait until his long run (beginning in 1915) in the play *Tonight's the Night*. He entered films with 1917's *Auld Lang Syne*, playing the sort of sticklike hero that any lesser actor could have portrayed. Buchanan's true celebrity rested on his stage work, notably 1921's *Charlot A-Z Revue*. The early-talkie hunger for cultured British voices brought Buchanan to Hollywood in 1929, where he appeared opposite Irene Bordoni in *Paris* (1929), Jeanette MacDonald in *Monte Carlo* (1930), and just about the entire Warner Bros. contract roster in *The Show of Shows* (1929). These early films reveal Buchanan to be a dry, debonair tie-and-tail type not far removed from the stage persona of Clifton Webb or Fred Astaire - except that Buchanan's charm did not transfer as well to the screen. Back in England, Buchanan tackled his first directing job with *Yes Mr. Brown* (1931) and in 1933 he built the Leicester Square Theatre. Relaxing sufficiently before the cameras to become an agreeable screen personality, Buchanan starred in the 1934 British production of *Brewster's Millions*, and costarred with Maurice Chevalier, whose style was similar to Buchanan's, in *Break the News* (1937). American film audiences did not see Buchanan again until 1953, when he was cast as the impresario Cordova in the Fred Astaire vehicle *The Band Wagon* (1953). Among the treasured musical moments in this delightful film was *Triplets*, wherein the Astaire, Buchanan and Nanette Fabray were decked out in baby bonnets. It would be nice to record *Band Wagon* as Buchanan's final appearance before his death in 1957; alas, Buchanan was subsequently and unhappily cast in the misfire farce *Le Carnets Du Major Thompson*, a.k.a. *The French They Are a Funny Race* (1957) - also the swan song of once-great director Preston Sturges.

# Horst Buchholz

**Born:** December 4, 1933; Berlin, Germany

**Years Active in the Industry:** by decade

| 10s | 20s | 30s | 40s | 50s | 60s | 70s | 80s | 90s |
|-----|-----|-----|-----|-----|-----|-----|-----|-----|
|     |     |     |     |     |     |     |     |     |

Wiry and intense German leading man Horst Buchholz appeared in many British and Hollywood films where he was usually cast as a romantic lead. During his youth he frequently appeared on radio and stage; he entered films as a voice-over actor in the dubbing of foreign pictures. After appearing at Berlin's Schiller

Theater, he was discovered by director Julien Duvivier, who gave him his debut screen role in *Marianne de ma Jeunesse* (1955). That same year he appeared in Helmut Kautner's *Sky Without Stars*, for which he won the Cannes Film Festival Best Actor award. Buchholz broke through as a major star after playing the title role in the internationally successful *The Confessions of Felix Krull* (based on the 1957 Thomas Mann novel), leading him to Hollywood. Although he had a slight German accent, he made his American debut as a cowboy in *The Magnificent Seven* (1960). He is married to French actress Myriam Bru. **Selected Works:** *Fanny* (1961), *One, Two, Three* (1961), *Faraway, So Close* (1993)

# Geneviéve Bujold

**Born:** July 1, 1942; Montreal, Quebec, Canada

**Years Active in the Industry:** by decade

| 10s | 20s | 30s | 40s | 50s | 60s | 70s | 80s | 90s |
|-----|-----|-----|-----|-----|-----|-----|-----|-----|
|     |     |     |     |     |     |     |     |     |

French-Canadian leading lady Genevieve Bujold was educated in a convent before she went on to study at the Quebec Conservatory of Drama. Born to working class parents, she worked as an usherette in a Montreal cinema to pay for drama school. She debuted on the Canadian stage in *The Barber of Seville*, then landed a film role in the internationally-produced *The Adolescents* (1964). While visiting Europe she was given her big break when she was chosen by director Alan Resnais to appear opposite celebrated French actor Yves Montand (as a woman he sleeps with in a "one-night stand") in *La Guerre est finie* (1966). She then went on to appear in several French and Canadian productions, including a role as the gently demented girl in *King of Hearts* (1966). However, she really came into her own as Anne Boleyn in the U.S./U.K. film *Anne of a Thousand Days* (1969) for which she was nominated for a Best Actress Academy Award. After that she expanded her range of roles considerably, going on to play a variety of roles in international productions . **Selected Works:** *Dance Goes on* (1992), *Dead Ringers* (1988), *False Identity* (1990)

# Sandra Bullock

**Born:** 1967; Washington, DC

**Years Active in the Industry:** by decade

| 10s | 20s | 30s | 40s | 50s | 60s | 70s | 80s | 90s |
|-----|-----|-----|-----|-----|-----|-----|-----|-----|
|     |     |     |     |     |     |     |     |     |

The daughter of a vocal coach and an opera singer, American actress Sandra Bullock was raised in Washington, D.C. and Europe, then attended East Carolina University. After making the rounds in New York, Bullock landed a leading role in the short-lived 1990 TV series *Working Girl*. Supporting roles in such films as Sylvester Stallone's *Demolition Man* (1992) and Robert De Niro's *Wrestling Ernest Hemingway* (1992) gained Bullock a mod-

icum of attention, but her big breakthrough came by way of a film assignment in which she wore one outfit throughout the picture and played 90 percent of her scenes sitting down. The film was the moneyspinning *Speed* (1994), wherein Sandra portrayed the reluctant but plucky "substitute driver" on a booby-trapped bus. On the strength of *Speed*, Sandra Bullock attained full celebrity status—not to mention top billing in her next film, the profitable romantic comedy *While You Were Sleeping* (1995). **Selected Works:** *Thing Called Love* (1993), *Vanishing [USA]* (1993), *Who Shot Patakango?* (1992), *When the Party's Over* (1993)

# Luis Buñuel

**Born:** February 22, 1900; Calanda, Aragon, Spain
**Died:** July 29, 1983; Mexico City, Mexico

**Years Active in the Industry:** by decade

| 10s | 20s | 30s | 40s | 50s | 60s | 70s | 80s | 90s |
|-----|-----|-----|-----|-----|-----|-----|-----|-----|
|     |     |     |     |     |     |     |     |     |

Bundled off to a Jesuit education by his prosperous Spanish parents, Luis Bunuel went on to attend the University of Madrid, where he first became interested in the burgeoning European film industry. His earliest movie job upon graduating from Paris' Academie du Cinema was as an assistant to French-based directors Jean Epstein and Mario Nalpas. In partnership with an old friend, Spanish painter/sculptor Salvadore Dali, Bunuel put together the three-reel surrealist masterpiece *Un Chien Andalou* (1928); this is the one which features the dead donkeys on the pianos, the razor-slashed eyeball, and all the other deliberately shocking images that cineastes have either praised or damned for the past seven decades. Bunuel's first feature film, *L'Age D'Or*, was banned from public exhibition almost immediately from the moment of its 1930 premiere: its principal opponents were high-ranking members of the Catholic Church, who condemned the film as savagely sacrilegous. After 1932's *Land Without Bread*, an uncompromising look at the squalor, poverty and ignorance inherent in Spain's peasant villages, Bunuel signed on at Paramount Paris in 1933, overseeing the dubbing of Hollywood pictures. He moved on to an executive producer's post at Madrid's Filmfono Studios, where, during the Spanish Civil War, he began work on a Hollywood-financed pro-Loyalist film that was abandoned when Franco emerged victorious. Broke and *persona non grata* in his own country, Bunuel came to New York, where from 1939 through 1942 he

worked at the Museum of Modern Art. His plans to assemble an epic anti-Nazi documentary from the museum's reserve of newsreel footage never came to fruition, though he did manage to complete a 1940 *March of Time* piece on the Vatican. In 1946 he moved to Mexico, where his first directorial effort was *Gran Casino* (aka *Tampico*). Bunuel regained the international attention that he'd lost back in 1930 with *Los Olivados*, a purely "commercial" film which nonetheless contained elements of his old anti-Catholicism. With 1952's *El*, Bunuel was able to fulfill his long-held ambition to make a film about utter, irredeemable madness, something he'd been denied back in 1946 when he was removed from the production staff of Warner Bros.' *Beast With Five Fingers* (1946). One of the few Bunuel films of the 1950s to be marketed to the Hollywood mainstream was *Robinson Crusoe* (1954), which would remain the most iconoclastic version of DeFoe's novel until director Jack Gold's *Man Friday* (1976). After several years in Mexico, Bunuel returned to Spain in 1961 to make *Viridiana*. When the Spanish government censors took a good long look at the film's parody "Last Supper" scene (with beggars, thieves and morons in place of the disciples), Bunuel once more found his works banned in his native land. Apparently unfazed, the director went on to make such remarkable works as *Exterminating Angel* (1962), *Belle de Jour* (1966) and *The Discreet Charm of the Bourgeoisie* (1972), each film distinguished by Bunuel's elegant decadence, his ceaseless search for beauty within ugliness and vice versa, and his utter hatred for all things religious and "Establishment". The censorial climate in the US had relaxed enough by 1972 to allow *Discreet Charm of the Bourgeoisie* to win the "best foreign language film" Academy Award. Bunuel's final film was *That Obscure Object of Desire* (1984), a loose remake of 1935's *The Devil is A Woman* (a film directed by another stylish maverick, Joseph Von Sternberg). In 1995, a long-deceased Luis Bunuel became center of attention once more with the reissue of his 1966 exercise in sexual obsession, *Belle De Jour*. **Selected Works:** *Adventures of Robinson Crusoe* (1954), *El (This Strange Passion)* (1952)

# Billie Burke (Mary William Ethelbert Appleton Burke)

**Born:** August 6, 1885; Washington, DC
**Died:** May 14, 1970; Los Angeles, CA

**Years Active in the Industry:** by decade

| 10s | 20s | 30s | 40s | 50s | 60s | 70s | 80s | 90s |
|-----|-----|-----|-----|-----|-----|-----|-----|-----|
|     |     |     |     |     |     |     |     |     |

The daughter of a circus clown, American actress Billie Burke became a musical comedy star in the early 1900s under the aegis of two powerful Broadway producers: Charles K. Frohman and Florenz Ziegfeld. Burke's career soared after her marriage to Ziegfeld, which was both a blessing and a curse in that some newspaper critics, assuming she wouldn't have reached the heights without her husband's patronage, gave her some pretty rough reviews. Actually, she had a very pleasant singing voice and ingratiating personality, not to mention natural comic gift that transferred well to the screen for her film debut in *Peggy* (1915). She had no qualms about adjusting to characters roles upon reaching 40, but she was devoted to the stage and didn't intend to revive her film career - until the crippling debts left behind by Ziegfeld after his death in 1932 forced her to return full-time to Hollywood. At first concentrating on drama, Burke found that her true strength lay in comedy, particularly in portraying fey, bird-brained society ladies. She worked most often at MGM during the sound era, with rewarding side trips to Hal Roach studios, where she appeared as Mrs. Topper in the three *Topper* fantasy films, played Oliver Hardy's wife in *Zenobia* (1939) and earned an academy award nomination for her performance in *Merrily We Live* (1938). A tireless trouper, Burke appeared in virtually every sort of film, from rugged westerns like *Sgt. Rutledge* (1960) to a pair of surprisingly good two-reel comedies for Columbia Pictures in the late 1940s. If she had done nothing else worthwhile in her seven-decade career, Burke would forever be remembered for her light-hearted portrayal of Glinda the Good Witch in the matchless *The Wizard of Oz* (1939). In addition to her many film portrayals, Burke was herself portrayed in two filmed biographies of Flo Ziegfeld: Myrna Loy played her in *The Great Ziegfeld* (1936), while Samantha Eggar took the role in the TV-movie *Ziegfeld: The Man and His Women* (1978). **Selected Works:** *Father of the Bride* (1950), *Man Who Came to Dinner* (1941), *Young in Heart* (1938)

# George Burns

**Born:** January 20, 1896; New York, NY

**Years Active in the Industry:** by decade

| 10s | 20s | 30s | 40s | 50s | 60s | 70s | 80s | 90s |
|-----|-----|-----|-----|-----|-----|-----|-----|-----|

American comedian George Burns had a taste for show business from his youth on New York's Lower East Side, and by the time he was seven he and his buddies had formed a singing group called the Pee Wee Quartet. Amateur shows led to small-time vaudeville, where Burns faced rejection time and again, often gaining jobs from people who'd fired him earlier through the simple expedient of constantly changing his professional name. Usually working as part of a song-and-snappy-patter team, he was in the process of breaking up with his latest partner Billy Lorraine in 1922 when he met a pretty young singer/dancer named Gracie Allen. The game plan for this new team was to have Gracie play the "straight man" and George the comic, but so ingenuous and light-headed was Gracie's delivery that the audience laughed at her questions and not at George's answers. Burns realized he'd have to reverse the roles and become the straight man for the act to succeed, and within a few years Burns and Allen was one of the hottest acts in vaudeville, with George writing the material and Gracie garnering the laughs. George and Gracie married in 1926; thereafter the team worked on stage, in radio, in movies (first in a series of one-reel comedies, then making their feature debut in 1932's *The Big Broadcast*) and ultimately in television, seldom failing to bring down the house with their basic "dizzy lady, long-suffering man"

routine. Though the public at large believed that Gracie had all the talent, show business insiders knew that the act would have been nothing without George's brilliant comic input; indeed, George was often referred to by his peers as "The Comedian's Comedian". Gracie decided to retire in 1958, after which George went out on his own in television and in nightclubs, to less than spectacular success. After Gracie's death in 1964, George concentrated on television production (he had vested interests in several series, among them *Mr. Ed*) and for a nervous few years tried using other comic actresses in the "Gracie" role for his club appearances. But it wasn't the same; George Burns would be first to admit there was only one Gracie Allen. Though he never retired, Burns was more or less out of the consciousness of moviegoers until he was hired at the last minute to replace his late friend Jack Benny in the film version of Neil Simon's *The Sunshine Boys* (1975). His performance as a cantankerous old vaudeville comic won him an Oscar, and launched a whole new career for the octogenarian entertainer as a solo movie star. Perhaps his most conspicuous achievement in the late 1970s was his portrayal of the Almighty Spirit - with distinct Palace Theatre undertones - in *Oh, God!* (1977). As sharp-witted as ever at this writing, Burns has gone beyond the realm of Show Business Legend; he is practically an immortal. With cigar in hand and jokes and songs at the ready, Burns is currently going full speed ahead with his well publicized plans to headline a Las Vegas show on his 100th Birthday. **Selected Works:** *Going in Style* (1979)

# Raymond Burr

**Born:** May 21, 1917; New Westminster, BC, Canada
**Died:** September 12, 1993; Dry Creek Valley, CA

**Years Active in the Industry:** by decade

| 10s | 20s | 30s | 40s | 50s | 60s | 70s | 80s | 90s |
|-----|-----|-----|-----|-----|-----|-----|-----|-----|

Heavily-built American lead and supporting actor Raymond Burr began in theater and radio, during which time he developed his distinctive, commanding voice. He made his film debut in 1946, then went on to be cast in a number of films as a smooth villain, largely due to his ominous, rasping voice, large frame, sad face, and intense, brooding eyes; one notable role was as the wife-murderer discovered by Jimmy Stewart in Hitchcock's *Rear Window* (1954) in which Burr managed to humanize his character and make him almost pitiable. He is best known for his role on TV as the good-guy attorney Perry Mason in the series of the same name, which ran from 1957-66 and then again in the late 80s and early 90s; he also played the title role as the wheelchair-bound detective in the TV series *Ironside* (1967-74). With his success on TV, he went on to do little additional film work. **Selected Works:** *Place in the Sun* (1951), *Showdown at Williams Creek* (1991)

# Ellen Burstyn (Edna Gillooly)

**Born:** December 7, 1932; Detroit, MI

**Years Active in the Industry:** by decade

| 10ˢ | 20ˢ | 30ˢ | 40ˢ | 50ˢ | 60ˢ | 70ˢ | 80ˢ | 90ˢ |
|-----|-----|-----|-----|-----|-----|-----|-----|-----|
|     |     |     |     |     |     |     |     |     |

American actress of stage and screen Ellen Burstyn has had almost as many stage names as she has had roles. She left home at age 18 to be a model in Texas and New York under the name "Edna Rae." While appearing as a Montreal nightclub dancer, she went by "Keri Flynn." For her screen test during the mid-50's she became "Erica Dean." In her 1957, Broadway debut, the play *Fair Game*, she was billed as "Ellen McRae," the name she stuck with until her marriage in 1970. She went on to act in a couple of films, notably *Goodbye Charlie* (1964), and to do much TV work including a stint on the series *The Doctors*. She took time off to study acting with Lee Strasberg at the Actors Studio, then got her big break when Peter Bogdanovich cast her as the female lead in *The Last Picture Show* (1971), for which she received an Oscar nomination and both the New York Film Critics Award and National Film Critics Award as Best Actress. She went on to be nominated for another Oscar as the mother of the demon-possessed child in *The Exorcist* (1973), then finally won the Best Actress Oscar for her work (the title role) in Martin Scorsese's *Alice Doesn't Live Here Anymore* (1975), a film she packaged and produced herself. She went on that same year to win a Tony Award for her work in the Broadway play *Same Time Next Year*, reprising her role in the film version (1978), she was again nominated for a Best Actress Oscar. **Selected Works:** *Cemetery Club* (1993), *Grand Isle* (1992), *Harry and Tonto* (1974), *Roommates* (1995)

# Richard Burton (Richard Walter Jenkins, Jr.)

**Born:** November 10, 1925; Pontrhyfenigaid, S. Wales
**Died:** August 5, 1984; Geneva, Switzerland

**Years Active in the Industry:** by decade

| 10ˢ | 20ˢ | 30ˢ | 40ˢ | 50ˢ | 60ˢ | 70ˢ | 80ˢ | 90ˢ |
|-----|-----|-----|-----|-----|-----|-----|-----|-----|
|     |     |     |     |     |     |     |     |     |

The youngest of 12 children of a Welsh miner, actor Richard Burton escaped his humble environs by winning a scholarship to Oxford. Blessed with a thrillingly theatrical voice, Burton took to the stage, and by 1949 had been tagged as one of Britain's most promising newcomers. Director Phillip Dunne, who later helmed several of Burton's Hollywood films, would recall viewing a 1949 London staging of *The Lady's Not For Burning* and watching in awe as star John Gielgud was eclipsed by juvenile lead Richard Burton: "He 'took' the stage and kept a firm grip on it during every one of his brief appearances." Burton was not quite able to grip the films as well as he did the stage; a few years after his film bow in *The Last Days of Dolwyn* (1949) the actor was signed by 20th Century-Fox, which had hopes of turning Burton into the new Olivier. *The Robe* (1953) aside, most of Burton's Fox films were disappointments, and the actor was unable to shake his to-the-rafters theatricality for the smaller scope of the camera lens. Still, he was handsome and self-assured, so Burton was permitted a standard-issue

1950s spectacle, *Alexander the Great* (1956). Burton's own film greatness would not manifest itself until he played the dirt-under-the-nails role of Jimmy Porter in *Look Back in Anger* (1959). In this, he spoke the vernacular of Human Beings—rather than that of high-priced, affected Hollywood screenwriters—and delivered a jolting performance as a working-class man trapped by the System and his own personal demons. One of those demons was Drink, something with which Burton was intimately familiar; those close to him would note that while Burton was the soul of sweetness and generosity when sober, it was best to steer clear from him when drunk. Following a well-received Broadway run in the musical *Camelot*, Burton was signed in 1961 to replace Stephen Boyd on the benighted film spectacular *Cleopatra* (1963). It probably isn't necessary to elaborate on what happened next, but the result was that Burton suddenly found himself an international celebrity, not for his acting but for his tempestuous romance with *Cleopatra* star Elizabeth Taylor. A hot property at last, Burton apparently signed every long-term contract thrust in front of him, while television networks found themselves besieged with requests for screenings of such earlier Burton film "triumphs" as *Prince of Players* (1955) and *The Rains of Ranchipur* (1956). In the midst of the initial wave of notoriety, Burton appeared in a Broadway modern-dress version of *Hamlet* directed by John Gielgud, which played to SRO crowds who were less interested in the Melancholy Dane than in possibly catching a glimpse of The Lovely Liz. Amidst choice film work like *Becket* (1964) and *The Spy Who Came In From the Cold* (1966), Burton was contractually obligated to costar with Taylor in such high-priced kitsch as *The VIPS* (1963) *The Sandpiper* (1965) and *Boom!* (1968). A few of the Burton-Taylor vehicles were excellent, notably *Who's Afraid of Virginia Woolf? in 1966* (she won an Oscar; he didn't but should have), but the circus of publicity began to erode the public's ability to take Burton seriously. It became even harder when the Burtons broke up, remarried, and broke up again. Moreover, Burton was bound by contract to appear in some of the foulest dreck ever served up by the movie industry: *Camdy* (1968), *Villain* (1971), *The Assassination of Trotsky* (1977), *The Klansman* (1974), and that rancid masterpiece *Exorcist II: The Heretic* (1977). So low had Burton's reputation sunk that when he delivered an Oscar-caliber performance in *Equus* (1977), it was hailed as a "comeback", even though the actor had never left (Once again he lost the Oscar, this time to Richard Dreyfuss). Though his physical constitution had been eroded by years of alcohol abuse, Burton managed to recapture his old performing fire in his last moviemaking years, offering up one of his best performances in his final picture, *1984* (1984) **Selected Works:** *Anne of the Thousand Days* (1969),

*Longest Day* (1962), *Night of the Iguana* (1964), *Taming of the Shrew* (1967), *My Cousin Rachel* (1952)

# Tim Burton

**Born:** 1959; Burbank, CA

**Years Active in the Industry:** by decade

| 10s | 20s | 30s | 40s | 50s | 60s | 70s | 80s | 90s |
|-----|-----|-----|-----|-----|-----|-----|-----|-----|
|     |     |     |     |     |     |     | ■   | ■   |

It should come as no shock to the fans of American director Tim Burton that he spent his formative years glued to the Tube, watching old cartoons and horror flicks. Winning a scholarship in 1980 to the Disney-created California Institute of the Arts, Burton went to work as an apprentice animator at Disney. It was an aesthetically and financially dead period for Disney animation (megahits like *The Little Mermaid* were years in the future), and Burton's most vivid memories of his time at the studio were of constant firings, ill-will, indecisiveness and paranoia. The Disney higher-ups weren't interested in any of Burton's independent ideas, and the one they were *least* interested in was a stop-motion animation project about a Halloweenish wraith who kidnaps Santa Claus. After leaving Disney, Burton gained prestige on his own with the 1982 short subject *Vincent*, which was about Burton's lifelong idol Vincent Price, who narrated the film. As an independent contractor Burton put together a half hour cartoon for Disney called *Frankenweenie* (1983) which was considered too frightening for a young audience (the same audience then being enthralled by the *Friday the 13th* and *Halloween* pictures) and was shelved by the studio. But Warner Bros. studios, impressed by *Frankenweenie* and looking for someone to direct a film starring "human cartoon" Pee-wee Herman, hired Burton to helm *Pee-wee's Big Adventure* (1984). The director wisely treated the whole project like a live-action Looney Tune, and the film, originally intended for limited release as a kid's picture, became one of Warners' biggest hits of the early 1980s. *Pee-wee's Big Adventure* (1984) led to Burton's next project, *Beetlejuice* (1985), a comic twist on all the "Shock Theatre" pictures that had kept Burton up late as a child. *Edward Scissorshands* (1989) had a lot in common with Burton's earlier *Frankenweenie*; it was the tale of an artificial boy put together by a benign scientist (Vincent Price again, in his penultimate performances), who unfortunately dies before he can complete the boy; as a result, the fabricated youth has hedge clipper-like scissors for hands. Alternately frightening, funny and touching, *Edward Scissorhands* proved that Burton could inject humanity and audience empathy into an otherwise unbelievable yarn. An A-list director thanks to his two blockbusting *Batman* films, Burton was able to write his own Hollywood ticket by the early 1990s, which resulted in a lucrative contractual arrangement with his one-time employer, Disney studios. The company that once turned down Burton's "Halloween" concept now practically tripped over itself giving him carte blanche to produce the project, which came to fruition as 1993's *The Nightmare Before Christmas*. It wasn't the hit everyone hoped it would be, but *Nightmare* was irrevocably Burton's film and his film alone,

from drawing board to final release. Disney also put *Frankenweenie* into mass-market distribution at long last, running the onetime "untouchable" film over and over again on cable's Disney Channel. There have been a few missteps in Burton's career, notably the lackluster *Family Dog* (1993), a TV cartoon series coproduced by Steven Spielberg which gave new meaning to the phrase "too many cooks"; there was also the middling *Cabin Boy* (1994), a film vehicle for Chris Elliot which Burton co-produced. As of this writing, Burton is riding high in film-critic circles thanks to his long-awaited *Ed Wood* (1994), the biopic of another visionary filmmaker, Edward D. Wood Jr. - celebrated as the worst director in movie history. But Burton knows how it feels to be unappreciated for one's enthusiasms, and *Ed Wood*, deliberately filmed to emulate Wood's seedy visual style, has emerged as one of the most affectionate film biographies ever made.

# Stephen H. Burum

**Born:** 1940; Visalia, CA

**Years Active in the Industry:** by decade

| 10s | 20s | 30s | 40s | 50s | 60s | 70s | 80s | 90s |
|-----|-----|-----|-----|-----|-----|-----|-----|-----|
|     |     |     |     |     |     | ■   | ■   | ■   |

California-born cinematographer Stephen Burum matriculated from student to instructor at the UCLA film school in the 1960s. He applied his skills first to government films, then to public television, where he won an Emmy for his other-worldly special effects on the 1978 series *Cosmos*. On behalf of his onetime UCLA classmate Francis Ford Coppola, Burum wielded his camera on the second units of *The Black Stallion* (1978) and *Apocalypse Now* (1979). Since 1980, Burum has worked with directors ranging from Brian De Palma (*The Untouchables* [1987]) to Danny De Vito (*War of the Roses* [1989]). **Selected Works:** *He Said, She Said* (1991), *Hoffa* (1992), *Raising Cain* (1992), *Carlito's Way* (1993), *Shadow* (1994)

# Steve Buscemi

**Born:** 1958; Brooklyn, NY

**Years Active in the Industry:** by decade

| 10s | 20s | 30s | 40s | 50s | 60s | 70s | 80s | 90s |
|-----|-----|-----|-----|-----|-----|-----|-----|-----|
|     |     |     |     |     |     |     | ■   | ■   |

American actor/performance artist Steve Buscemi has made movies whenever the spirit has moved him, or whenever he hasn't been busy working on stage with his regular partner/ collaborators Mark Boone Jr. and Jo Andres (Mrs. Buscemi). In films since 1984, Buscemi gained his widest attention as the acerbic, AIDs-stricken Nick in *Parting Glances* (1986). While most of his films were made for deliberately limited and specialized audiences, Buscemi has broken into the mainstream on occasion, notably in

*New York Stories* (1988)—in which he was characteristically cast as a performance artist—and *Tales From the Darkside: The Movie* (1992). Buscemi was on the ground floor of the Quentin Tarantino Explosion when he was cast as the quirky Mr. Pink in Tarantino's debut feature *Reservoir Dogs.* **Selected Works:** *In the Soup* (1992), *Rising Sun* (1993), *The Hudsucker Proxy* (1994), *Pulp Fiction* (1994), *Desperado* (1995)

# Gary Busey

**Born:** June 29, 1944; Goose Creek, TX

**Years Active in the Industry:** by decade

| 10s | 20s | 30s | 40s | 50s | 60s | 70s | 80s | 90s |
|-----|-----|-----|-----|-----|-----|-----|-----|-----|
|     |     |     |     |     |     |     |     |     |

Although American leading man Gary Busey has made distinguished appearances in many films, he has yet to attain the consistent popularity that would make him a major star. Born in Texas, Busey first few years were spent on an Oklahoma ranch where he learned to be a bull rider. He attended three different colleges before finally graduating in 1963, the year he became a professional drummer with the rock group The Rubber Band. Later, he billed himself as Teddy Jack Eddy and played percussion for Leon Russell, Kris Kristofferson, and Willie Nelson. In 1970, Busey made his acting debut in an episode of the TV western *High Chaparel.* This led to his feature film debut as a biker in *Angels Hard as They Come* (1971) the following year. After that Busey went on to play supporting roles (typically cast as renegades, daredevils, or good ol' boys with dubious morals) until 1978 when he made a major splash playing the lanky lead in *The Buddy Holly Story,* for which he did all the guitar and vocal work. His impersonation of Holly was remarkable and won him considerable acclaim and an Oscar nomination for Best Actor. Busey then went on to play leads in many films of varying quality during the early to mid-1980s. In the late '80s he returned to supporting roles and co-leads. In 1988, Busey almost died in a motorcycle accident and his near death resulted in enactment of tougher helmet laws in California. **Selected Works:** *Firm* (1993), *Lethal Weapon* (1987), *Point Break* (1991), *Rookie of the Year* (1993), *Under Siege* (1992)

# David Butler

**Born:** December 17, 1894; San Francisco, CA
**Died:** June 14, 1979; Santa Rosa, CA

**Years Active in the Industry:** by decade

| 10s | 20s | 30s | 40s | 50s | 60s | 70s | 80s | 90s |
|-----|-----|-----|-----|-----|-----|-----|-----|-----|
|     |     |     |     |     |     |     |     |     |

David Butler's filmmaking career spans forty years. He is best remembered as a prolific director of musicals and romantic comedies. Prior to becoming a director, the San Francisco born Butler began his career as a three year old child actor. In 1918, he debuted on film in D.W. Griffith's *The Greatest Thing in Life.* He then went on to star in a series of films until 1929; concurrently Butler also appeared on the stage. In 1923, he became the stage manager of the Morosco Theater in Los Angeles, and four years later, became a director for Fox. He has also directed for Paramount, and Warner Bros. where he was popular for his dependability, and his consistent, quality work. In addition to directing, Butler also occasionally produced, and co-scripted his films.

# Charles Butterworth

**Born:** July 26, 1896; South Bend, IN
**Died:** June 14, 1946; Los Angeles, CA

**Years Active in the Industry:** by decade

| 10s | 20s | 30s | 40s | 50s | 60s | 70s | 80s | 90s |
|-----|-----|-----|-----|-----|-----|-----|-----|-----|
|     |     |     |     |     |     |     |     |     |

A master at playing diffident, absentminded middle-aged bachelors, American actor and Notre Dame alumnus Charles Butterworth was an established Broadway musical comedy star when he made his first film, *Life of the Party* (1930). Butterworth's heyday was in the 1930s, when he appeared as either the hero's silly best friend or a besotted society twit in one film after another. An off-screen drinking buddy of such literary wits as Robert Benchley and Corey Ford, Butterworth became so famous for his dry quips and cynical asides that Hollywood screenwriters began writing only fragmentary scripts for him, hoping that the actor would "fill in the blanks" with his own bon mots. Butterworth hated this cavalier treatment, complaining "I need material as much as anyone else!" By the early 1940s, material of all sorts began running thin, and Butterworth was accepting assignments at such lesser studios as Monogram and PRC, with the occasional worthwhile role in A-films like *This Is the Army* (1943). Two years after completing his last picture, *Dixie Jamboree* (1946), the still relatively youthful Butterworth was killed in an automobile accident. His memory was kept alive in the early 1960s by actor Daws Butler, who used a Butterworth-type voice for the cartoon commercial spokesman Cap'n Crunch.

# Red Buttons (Aaron Chwatt)

**Born:** February 5, 1919; Bronx, NY

**Years Active in the Industry:** by decade

| 10s | 20s | 30s | 40s | 50s | 60s | 70s | 80s | 90s |
|-----|-----|-----|-----|-----|-----|-----|-----|-----|
|     |     |     |     |     |     |     |     |     |

American actor Red Buttons, born and raised on New York's Lower East Side, won an amateur night contest at age 12. By age 16 he was working in a Bronx tavern as a bellboy-singer; here he took the name "Red Buttons," in reference to his uniform. He went on to work the Catskills Mountains "Borscht Belt" and to perform as a burlesque comedian. He debuted on Broadway as a supporting player in *Vickie* in 1942. He served in the Army during World War II, appearing in the play *Winged Victory*; he played the same role in the film version (1944), marking his big-screen debut. After briefly starring in his own TV show in 1953 he had a weak career until he landed the role of Sargeant Joe Kelly in the film *Sayonara* (1957), his second movie role; for his work in that film he won a Best Supporting Actor Oscar, going on from there to appear frequently in films, usually as a comedy actor. **Selected Works:** *Ambulance* (1990), *Longest Day* (1962), *One, Two, Three* (1961), *Poseidon Adventure* (1972), *They Shoot Horses, Don't They?* (1969)

# Spring Byington

**Born:** October 17, 1893; Colorado Springs, CO
**Died:** 1971

**Years Active in the Industry:** by decade

| 10s | 20s | 30s | 40s | 50s | 60s | 70s | 80s | 90s |
|-----|-----|-----|-----|-----|-----|-----|-----|-----|
|     |     |     |     |     |     |     |     |     |

American actress Spring Byington, orphaned as a child, debuted onstage with a Denver stock company at age 14. She went on work in the theater with several touring companies, eventually debuting on Broadway in 1924. She made her feature film debut as Marmee in *Little Women* (1933) with Katherine Hepburn. Byington then went on to appear in more than 100 films, usually cast as forever-young, happy, warm, high-spirited, somewhat dizzy women. For her work in *You Can't Take It With You* (1938) she received a Best Supporting Actress Oscar nomination. She was a regular in the "Jones family" series of films (1936-40). She later starred in the TV series *December Bride* and was a regular in the TV series *Laramie*. Her last film was *Please Don't Eat the Daisies* (1960). **Selected**

**Works:** *Devil and Miss Jones* (1941), *Enchanted Cottage* (1945), *Heaven Can Wait* (1943), *Meet John Doe* (1941), *Louisa* (1950)

# Gabriel Byrne

**Born:** 1950; Dublin, Ireland

**Years Active in the Industry:** by decade

| 10s | 20s | 30s | 40s | 50s | 60s | 70s | 80s | 90s |
|-----|-----|-----|-----|-----|-----|-----|-----|-----|
|     |     |     |     |     |     |     |     |     |

British actor Gabriel Byrne came to acting later in life. After earning his college degree, he worked for three years as an archeologist, then spent four years as a Spanish and Gaelic teacher at a  convent school; there he started a drama class, and after taking part in a school production, one of the student's parents, a member of Dublin's Abbey Theater, suggested he become a professional actor. At the end of the school year, he left his job, going to work in community theater; shortly thereafter he was accepted at the Abbey, where he remained for two years. He joined London's Royal Court Theater in 1979, and by the early '80s he was much in demand for TV miniseries. He debuted onscreen in John Boorman's *Excalibur* (1981). He went on to a fairly busy screen career but was unable to land roles in any hit films. He is separated from actress Ellen Barkin, with whom he appeared in *Siesta* (1987). **Selected Works:** *Miller's Crossing* (1990), *Point of No Return* (1993), *Trial by Jury* (1994), *Little Women* (1994), *Usual Suspects* (1995)

James Caan
Sean Connery
Cher
Richard Crenna
Peter Cushing

# C

## James Caan

**Born:** March 26, 1939; Bronx, NY

**Years Active in the Industry:** by decade

| 10ˢ | 20ˢ | 30ˢ | 40ˢ | 50ˢ | 60ˢ | 70ˢ | 80ˢ | 90ˢ |
|---|---|---|---|---|---|---|---|---|

After college, American actor James Caan joined New York's Neighborhood Playhouse in 1960, going on to debut on-stage in an off-Broadway production of *La Ronde*. He did some TV

work, then debuted on-screen in an unbilled bit part in *Irma La Douce* (1963); his first sub-stantial role was as a young thug in *Lady in a Cage* (1964). For much of the next decade he continued to have an unmemorable film ca-reer, but became well-known in 1972 as the result of two perfor-mances: in the TV movie *Brian's Song* he played the dying foot-ball player Brian Piccolo, and in Francis Ford Coppola's block-buster *The Godfather* he portrayed tough-guy Sonny Corleone. Following this he became one of the hottest properties in Holly-wood, but he never went on to achieve the level of star status that might have been expected. In 1979 he made his directorial debut with the film *Hide in Plain Sight*. He also engaged in professional rodeo, an enthusiasm that earned him the nickname "The Jewish Cowboy"; he also owns a stable of racehorses. In the '80s his ca-reer stagnated after a series of poor films, but he seemed to be on his way up again after co-starring in Rob Reiner's hit *Misery* (1990). **Selected Works:** *Dick Tracy* (1990), *The Godfather* (1972), *The Godfather, Part 2* (1974), *Honeymoon in Vegas* (1992), *Thief* (1981)

## Bruce Cabot (Jacques Etienne de Bujac)

**Born:** April 20, 1904; Carlsbad, NM
**Died:** 1972

**Years Active in the Industry:** by decade

| 10ˢ | 20ˢ | 30ˢ | 40ˢ | 50ˢ | 60ˢ | 70ˢ | 80ˢ | 90ˢ |
|---|---|---|---|---|---|---|---|---|

Actor Bruce Cabot was a handsome, macho-man hero of many '30s action-adventure movies. After holding jobs ranging from cowboy to boxer, he met filmmaker David O. Selznick at a party and talked him into allowing him to do a screen test. Cabot made his feature film debut in *Roadhouse Murder* (1932) and then began his string of he-man roles, most memorably that of the hero who saved Fay Wray from the giant ape in *King Kong* (1933). After serving as an intelligence and operations officer in World War II, he returned to Hollywood, then spent much of the 50s in Europe. Coming back again to Hollywood in the '60s he continued his forty-year career with character roles and was frequently cast as villains in Westerns occasionally playing alongside John Wayne (as in *The Comancheros*, 1961). His three wives included ac-tresses Adrienne Ames and Francesca de Scaffa. **Selected Works:** *Cat Ballou* (1965), *Fury* (1936)

## Sid Caesar

**Born:** September 8, 1922; Yonkers, NY

**Years Active in the Industry:** by decade

| 10ˢ | 20ˢ | 30ˢ | 40ˢ | 50ˢ | 60ˢ | 70ˢ | 80ˢ | 90ˢ |
|---|---|---|---|---|---|---|---|---|

Influential American comedian Sid Caesar appeared infrequently in films; he is best-known for his work on the '50s TV sketch-comedy series *Your Show of Shows*. Before becoming a comedian, Caesar studied the saxophone and clarinet at Manhattan's Juilliard School of Music then played with various bands. During his time with the Coast Guard in WW II, he became a featured comedian in the service show *Tars and Spars*, and then again in its film version (1946). He then appeared in nightclubs and in the Broadway hit *Make Mine Manhattan*. Caesar began performing on TV in the late 40s; *Your Show of Shows* started shortly thereafter, a live comedy show with few equals in the history of TV. He began to take pills and drink to excess, however, and after his TV show was canceled he found little work in subsequent years, occasionally turning up in films, usually in cameo or novelty roles. A feature-length compilation of his TV sketches, *Ten from Your Show of Shows*, was released theatrically in 1973. He authored an autobiography, *Where Have I Been?* (1979).

# Nicolas Cage (Nicholas Coppola)

**Born:** January 7, 1964; Long Beach, CA

### Years Active in the Industry: by decade

| 10s | 20s | 30s | 40s | 50s | 60s | 70s | 80s | 90s |
|-----|-----|-----|-----|-----|-----|-----|-----|-----|
|     |     |     |     |     |     |     |     |     |

American actor Nicolas Cage is the nephew of filmmaker Francis Ford Coppola. He enrolled in San Francisco's American Conservatory Theater when he was 15, getting his first experience onstage in lead roles. Later he studied acting with the renowned drama teacher Peggy Feury. He debuted onscreen in Coppola's *Rumble Fish* (1983), the last film in which he was billed as "Nicholas Coppola"; he went on to appear in two other Coppola films, *The Cotton Club* (1984) and *Peggy Sue Got Married* (1986). His breakthrough film was *Valley Girl* (1983), while his most memorable performance was in *Birdy* (1984); for the latter film he had two teeth extracted to simulate shrapnel damage, an example of the lengths he will go to in achieving realism onscreen. **Selected Works:** *Honeymoon in Vegas* (1992), *Moonstruck* (1987), *Wild at Heart* (1990), *Red Rock West* (1993), *Guarding Tess* (1994), *Leaving Las Vegas* (1995)

# James Cagney (James Francis Cagney, Jr.)

**Born:** July 17, 1904; New York, NY
**Died:** March 30, 1986; Stanfordville, NY

### Years Active in the Industry: by decade

| 10s | 20s | 30s | 40s | 50s | 60s | 70s | 80s | 90s |
|-----|-----|-----|-----|-----|-----|-----|-----|-----|
|     |     |     |     |     |     |     |     |     |

With his raspy voice, and staccato vocal inflections James Cagney is one of the brightest stars in American cinema history. Cagney was the son of an Irish father and a Norwegian mother who

lived and worked in New York's Lower Eastside. To help support his family, Cagney did a variety of odd jobs including working as a waiter, and a poolroom racker; he even joined a Yorkville revue as a female impersonator. This humble beginning led to his joining the chorus in the Broadway show *Pitter-Patter* followed by a vaudeville tour with his wife Francis. By 1925, Cagney had begun to play Broadway leads; he was particularly successful in the musical *Penny Arcade*, which lead him to be cast in the Hollywood version, renamed *Sinner's Holiday*. Within a year, Cagney had been signed to Warner Bros. where he, in his fifth movie role, played the ruthless gangster in *Public Enemy* (1931), the film that made him a star. Cagney was a small, rather plain looking man; he had few of the external qualities that made up the traditional Hollywood leading man during the 1930's, yet inside he was a dynamo able to project a contentiousness, and arrogant confidence that made him the ideal Hollywood tough-guy, the role in which he is best remembered. Of Cagney's energetic acting style Will Rogers once exclaimed: "Every time I see him work, it looks to me like a bunch of firecrackers going off all at once." But Cagney was not content to simply play one type of role and soon proved his range and versatility appearing in musicals (*Yankee Doodle Dandy*, 1945—for which he won an Oscar for his portrayal of George M. Cohen.); Shakespearean drama (as Bottom in *A Midsummernight's Dream*, 1935); and satire (as a gung-ho American businessman in *One Two Three*,1961). Cagney even tried directing with *Short Cut to Hell* a remake of *This Gun for Hire*, but it was not a commercial success. After *One Two Three* Cagney announced his retirement. Even then, he continued to receive respect and adulation from his peers and his public. Fifteen years after retiring, Cagney was the first actor to receive the Life Achievement Award of the American Film Institute. In 1980 he earned a similar award from Kennedy center, and finally, in 1984, he received the US government's highest civilian honor, the Medal of Freedom. In 1975, he published his autobiography *Cagney by Cagney*. While retired, Cagney's health, he suffered from diabetes, circulatory problems, and recurring strokes, began rapidly deteriorating. Though he had been refusing movie offers for years, his doctors finally convinced him that a little work would do him good. He made his critically acclaimed comeback playing a small, but crucial role in Milos Forman's *Ragtime* (1981). This encouraged Cagney to appear as a grumpy ex-prizefighter in a television movie *Terrible Joe Moran* in 1984. It was his final film; two years later he died of a heart attack on his isolated farm in upstate New York. At his funeral, longtime friend and colleague President Ronald Reagan delivered the eulogy and said "America lost one of her finest artists." **Selected**

**Works:** *Angels with Dirty Faces* (1938), *Love Me or Leave Me* (1955), *Man of a Thousand Faces* (1957), *White Heat* (1949), *Mister Roberts* (1955)

# Michael Caine (Maurice Joseph Micklewhite)

**Born:** March 14, 1933; London, England

**Years Active in the Industry:** by decade

| 10ˢ | 20ˢ | 30ˢ | 40ˢ | 50ˢ | 60ˢ | 70ˢ | 80ˢ | 90ˢ |
|---|---|---|---|---|---|---|---|---|
|  |  |  |  |  |  |  |  |  |

The son of a fish-porter father and a charwoman mother, British actor Michael Caine got his first taste of life outside his dank South London neighborhood when he was evacuated to the countryside during World War II. A misfit in school, in service during the Korea conflict, and in the job pool, Caine found himself truly "at home" only after he answered a want ad for an assistant stage manager at the Horsham Repertory Company. Already showbiz-struck by incessantly haunting the movie houses, Caine took to acting like a fish to water, even though the life of a British regional actor was one step away from abject poverty. Changing his last name from "Micklewhite" to "Caine" in tribute to one of his favorite movies, *The Caine Mutiny*, the actor toiled in obscure unbilled film bits and TV walk-ons from 1956 through 1962, occasionally obtaining leads on a TV series based on the Edgar Wallace mysteries. The Big Break finally occurred with the role Lt. Bromhead in the expensive, star-studded historical adventure film *Zulu* (1963). Caine was next cast as Harry Palmer, the bespectacled, iconoclastic secret agent protagonist of *The Ipcress File* (1965) (he would play Palmer in two subsequent films, *Funeral in Berlin* and *Billion Dollar Brain*). Hailed as an "overnight star" - after twelve years in the business - Caine gained international fame in his next film, *Alfie* (1966), in which he played a cheeky cockney womanizer who shared his innermost thoughts directly with the audience. A real scrapper in his youth, Caine curbed his violent streak as his star ascended, though he still liked to take a nip or two of alcoholic spirits in the company of his fellow "angry young men" British actors. One of the most popular action stars in the films of the late 1960s - early 1970s, Caine could also hold his own dramatically with such established acting champs as Laurence Olivier (*Sleuth* [1972]), Sean Connery (*The Man Who Would Be King* [1976]) and a literal honor role of major British and American talent (*A Bridge too Far* [1975]). Though he must surely turn down *some* roles, Caine has in recent years gained the reputa-

tion as one of the most prolific actors of his stature; in 1986 alone, he appeared in five films - managing to win an Academy Award for one of them, Woody Allen's *Hannah and Her Sisters*. **Selected Works:** *California Suite* (1978), *Death Becomes Her* (1992), *Educating Rita* (1983), *Mona Lisa* (1986), *Noises Off* (1992)

# James Cameron

**Born:** August 16, 1954; Kapuskasing, Ontario, Canada

**Years Active in the Industry:** by decade

| 10ˢ | 20ˢ | 30ˢ | 40ˢ | 50ˢ | 60ˢ | 70ˢ | 80ˢ | 90ˢ |
|---|---|---|---|---|---|---|---|---|
|  |  |  |  |  |  |  |  |  |

The top action director of his generation, Canadian-born James Cameron is the son of an electrical engineer. He started out in movies as an art director for Roger Corman on *Battle Beyond The Stars* (1980), and was the production designer on the low budget science fiction chiller *Galaxy of Terror* (1981). His first film as a director, *Piranha II—The Spawning* (1982), was a minor hit. The following year, in 1984, he made *The Terminator*, which established Cameron as a major money director and a ferociously talented filmmaker. He has since gone on to become the maker of such enormous hits as *Aliens* (1986), *The Abyss* (1989), and *Terminator 2* (1991). **Selected Works:** *Point Break* (1991), *True Lies* (1994)

# Jane Campion

**Born:** 1955; Waikanae, New Zealand

**Years Active in the Industry:** by decade

| 10ˢ | 20ˢ | 30ˢ | 40ˢ | 50ˢ | 60ˢ | 70ˢ | 80ˢ | 90ˢ |
|---|---|---|---|---|---|---|---|---|
|  |  |  |  |  |  |  |  |  |

Possibly the most recognizable name in the New Zealand film industry, director/writer Jane Campion is the product of a performing family: her mother was actor/writer Edith Campion, and her father was theatre and opera director Richard Campion. After graduation from the Sydney College of the Arts and the Australian Film, Television and Radio School, Ms. Campion worked in London as an assistant documentary filmmaker. Campion had begun directing short subjects while still in college; her 1982 short *Peel* won a Cannes festival prize. In the mid-1980s, she directed several

films for Australian and New Zealand television, a few of which have since been released theatrically. Expanding on her favorite TV-movie theme, strained family relationships (especially between siblings), Campion turned out her first theatrical film, *Sweetie*, in 1989. Her next project was *Angel at My Table* (1990), a three-hour made-for-TV biography of tormented New Zealand author Janet Frame which, unlike the controversial *Sweetie*, met with almost universal approval. Campion made a spectacular entree into the worldwide popularity pool with her sexy, Bronte-esque period drama *The Piano* (1992), which won the Palme d'Or at Cannes for Best Film and the Academy Award for Best Foreign Screenplay.

ers and fans - even when this lovability was stretched to the breaking point in substandard films. He scored in supporting roles (*Splash* [1984], *Brewster's Millions* [1985]), but such thinnish starring features as *Summer Rental* (1985) and *Who's Harry Crumb* (1989) seemed to suggest that Candy couldn't carry a film by himself. Then he starred in *Uncle Buck* (1989), a disarming comedy about a ne'er-do-well with hidden nobility. Receiving relatively little promotion, *Uncle Buck* was a surprise hit, and stands today as perhaps Candy's best-ever vehicle. Unfortunately most of his follow-up films were on a par with the disastrous *Nothing But Trouble* (1990) and *Delirious* (1992). At the same time, Candy's leading role in *Only the Lonely* (1991) and his supporting performance in *JFK* (1992) proved that a major talent was being squandered by the film industry. Candy was as frustrated as his fans, manifesting this frustration in excessive eating, drinking and smoking. The actor's superlative seriocomic turn as a disgraced Olympic star in *Cool Runnings* (1993), which Candy also co-produced, seemed to point towards a career upswing. But while filming *Wagons East* in Mexico, 43-year-old John Candy suffered a heart attack and died in his sleep. *Wagons East* was released in the summer of 1994, utilizing Candy's existing footage as well as possible; it proved, sadly, an inadequate epitaph for one of film comedy's funniest and most ingratiating stars. **Selected Works:** *Home Alone* (1990), *Little Shop of Horrors* (1986), *Rescuers Down Under* (1990)

# John Candy (John Franklin Candy)

**Born:** October 31, 1950; Toronto, Ontario, Canada
**Died:** March 4, 1994; Durango, Mexico

### Years Active in the Industry: by decade

| 10s | 20s | 30s | 40s | 50s | 60s | 70s | 80s | 90s |
|-----|-----|-----|-----|-----|-----|-----|-----|-----|
|     |     |     |     |     |     |     |     |     |

Canadian comic actor John Candy was geared toward a performing career even while studying for a journalism degree in college. Candy's bulky frame and built-in liability enabled him to secure small roles in Canadian film and TV productions. In the early 1970s, Candy joined Canada's Second City Troupe, sharing the spotlight with such potent talent (and subsequent close friends) as Joe Flaherty, Eugene Levy, Dave Thomas, Andrea Martin and Catherine O'Hara. *Second City TV*, popularly known as *SCTV*, entered the Canadian TV airwaves in 1975 and was syndicated to the United States two years later. Candy scored an instant hit with such characters as porcine *poseur* Johnny LaRue, overly unctuous talkshow sidekick William B., and ever-grinning "Lutonian" musician Yosh Shmenge. So popular did Candy become that suddenly many of his obscurer pre-starring Canadian films (*It Seemed Like a Good Idea at the Time*, *The Clown Murders*) became hot properties on the video rental circuit. Candy stayed with the various *SCTV* syndicated and network programs until 1983, earning two Emmies in the process. One of the few genuine nice guys in the realm of comedy, Candy was beloved by both cowork-

# Dyan Cannon (Samille Diane Friesen)

**Born:** Janurary 4, 1939; Tacoma, WA

### Years Active in the Industry: by decade

| 10s | 20s | 30s | 40s | 50s | 60s | 70s | 80s | 90s |
|-----|-----|-----|-----|-----|-----|-----|-----|-----|
|     |     |     |     |     |     |     |     |     |

Actress Dyan Cannon studied anthropology in college before she moved to Los Angeles to work as a model. She was spotted by writer-producer Jerry Wald, who came up with her pseudonym and helped her get hired by MGM as an actress. In the late '50s she debuted before the camera on TV's *Playhouse 90*, appearing with Art Carney in *The Ding-A-Ling Girl*. Billed as "Diane Cannon," she debuted onscreen as a member of a teenage gang in *This Rebel Breed* (1960). She made another film and appeared on Broadway with Jane Fonda in *The Fun Couple*, and also did some work on TV, but her career advancement was slow. In the mid-'60s she met actor Cary Grant and moved in with him; they were married in 1965 and had a child, at which point she put her career on hold. They were divorced acrimoniously in 1968, when she accused Grant of overindulging in LSD and beating her in front of the servants. She returned to the screen as an insecure housewife contemplating a swinger's life in *Bob & Carol & Ted & Alice* (1969), for which she won the New York Film Critics Best Supporting Actress award and received an Oscar nomination. She went on to appear in five films released in 1971, then continued a fairly steady screen career until the early '80s, when she took six years off before returning to movies in 1988; since then she has worked only infrequently. In 1976 she wrote, produced, directed, and co-edited *Number One*, a 42-minute film made under the sponsorship of the American Film Institute; it received an Oscar nomination. She went on to direct *For the First Time* (1979) and to write, direct, and star in *The End of Innocence* (1990). For her portrayal of a cuckolding wife in *Heaven Can Wait* (1981) she received a second Best Supporting Actress Oscar nomination. **Selected Works:** *Christmas in Connecticut* (1992), *The Pickle* (1993)

# Eddie Cantor (Edward Israel Itskowitz)

**Born:** January 31, 1892; New York, NY
**Died:** 1964

**Years Active in the Industry:** by decade

| 10ˢ | 20ˢ | 30ˢ | 40ˢ | 50ˢ | 60ˢ | 70ˢ | 80ˢ | 90ˢ |
|-----|-----|-----|-----|-----|-----|-----|-----|-----|

Orphaned in early childhood, American actor Eddie Cantor began performing professionally at age 14. Over the following decade he worked his way up to great popularity in vaudeville and burlesque. He was launched into stardom after he appeared in *The Midnight Frolics* (1916). He later starred in the Ziegfeld Follies and on Broadway. He debuted onscreen in 1926; as soon as the sound era arrived he became a very popular screen personality. During the '30s he starred in a popular radio show. A heart attack in 1952 ended his career. In 1956 he received a special Oscar "for distinguished service to the film industry." He was portrayed by Keefe Brasselle in the poor biopic *The Eddie Cantor Story* (1953). He authored four volumes of memoirs.

# Yakima Canutt (Enos Edward Canutt)

**Born:** November 29, 1895; Colfax, WA
**Died:** May 24, 1986; North Hollywood, CA

**Years Active in the Industry:** by decade

| 10ˢ | 20ˢ | 30ˢ | 40ˢ | 50ˢ | 60ˢ | 70ˢ | 80ˢ | 90ˢ |
|-----|-----|-----|-----|-----|-----|-----|-----|-----|

Legendary Hollywood stuntman Yakima Canutt was also an actor and assistant director. He began working on ranches as a boy, and joined a Wild West show at 17, going on to win many prizes for his riding and roping. Eventually he was named Rodeo World Champion, a title leading to work as a stuntman and in bit parts in Westerns of the early '20s. Canutt began acting in lead cowboy roles in 1924, making fast-paced action-packed adventure films in which he did all his own stunts; unfortunately, most of his films were produced by small companies that got only limited distribution, so he never became a front-rank cowboy hero. When the sound era began, his voice was deemed inadequate, so he ceased starring in films and went back to stunt work; at the same time, he found work as a screen villain in Westerns headlined by others.

While going on to be a stunt double for (among others) Roy Rogers, Gene Autry, and John Wayne (who styled the way he walked after Canutt's manner), in the same films he often played supporting characters, heavies, and Indians. In the late '30s, his work setting up stunt sequences grew into full-fledged directing as a second-unit director; in this role he directed the breathtaking action sequences in some of the screen's most spectacular films (for example, he staged the chariot race in 1959's *Ben-Hur*). Finally, in the '40s he directed a number of Westerns and co-directed serials. In 1966 he was awarded a special Oscar "for creating the profession of stuntman as it exists today and for the development of many safety devices used by stuntmen everywhere."

# Frank Capra

**Born:** May 18, 1897; Palermo, Sicily
**Died:** September 3, 1991; La Quinta, CA

**Years Active in the Industry:** by decade

| 10ˢ | 20ˢ | 30ˢ | 40ˢ | 50ˢ | 60ˢ | 70ˢ | 80ˢ | 90ˢ |
|-----|-----|-----|-----|-----|-----|-----|-----|-----|

The most honored and well-liked director of his generation, Sicilian-born Frank Capra graduated from the California Institute of Technology as a chemical engineering major. Down on his luck after service during World War I, he bluffed his way into the movie business and learned films from the bottom up, from the film lab to the prop department to the editing department. He settled in as a gagman during the 1920s, and soon became a director specializing in comedy, and after a stint with Mack Sennett, moved to Columbia Pictures, where he came into his own as a filmmaker. Displaying a good feel for drama as well as comedy, and a common touch to which the ordinary viewer could resonate, Capra quickly became the star among the tiny studio's stable of directors. His pictures, starting with *American Madness* in 1932, displayed themes that audiences regarded as important and uplifting during the worst days of the Great Depression, and Capra, despite the relatively modest budgets that he had to work with, became one of the most popular serious filmmakers of the 1930s. After *It Happened One Night* (1934), a comedy starring Claudette Colbert and Clark Gable that earned an armload of Oscars and nominations, his career was made. Some critics regarded the messages of movies such as *Mr. Deeds Goes To Town* (1936) and *Mr. Smith Goes To Washington* (1939)—often dealing with the rights and dignity of the common man—as corn (the phrase "Capra-corn" was an often used derision), but the public loved them. Capra finished the 1930s as one of Hollywood's most honored filmmakers, with three Best Director Oscars to his credit. He turned more serious at the end of the decade, with the rise of fascism, and attempted to address this in *Lost Horizon* (1937) and his first independent production, *Meet John Doe*. He returned to pure comedy just prior to entering the army, with *Arsenic and Old Lace*, and during his wartime service directed the U.S. Army's *Why We Fight* series. After the war, he made the most ambitious and personal of his movies, *It's A Wonderful Life* (1946), which originally didn't find its audience—only during the 1970s and early 1980s, when it temporarily passed out of copyright protection (a situation since remedied by its owner) did the wide showings of this poignant comedy/fantasy turn the movie into a piece of definitive film-Americana. Capra's subsequent films, including *State of the Union* (1948) and *A Hole In The Head* (1959), although they were successful, lacked the urgency and immediacy of his pre-war work, and he fell increasingly out of touch with the changing tastes and attitudes of both audiences and movie studios during the 1950s and early 1960s. He made several industrial films during this period, but his career in feature films had effectively ended after the 1961 release of *Pocketful of Miracles*, a very sentimental (and big-budget, widescreen) remake of his 1933 hit *Lady For a Day*. **Selected Works:** *You Can't Take It with You* (1938)

# Kate Capshaw (Kathy Sue Nail)

**Born:** 1953; Fort Worth, TX

**Years Active in the Industry:** by decade

| 10s | 20s | 30s | 40s | 50s | 60s | 70s | 80s | 90s |
|-----|-----|-----|-----|-----|-----|-----|-----|-----|
|     |     |     |     |     |     |     |     |     |

After receiving a degree in learning disabilities, Kate Capshaw worked for a while as a teacher, then joined New York's Ford Agency to become a model. This led to work in a TV soap opera, *The Edge of Night*. Her screen debut was in *A Little Sex* (1982), but the role that made her well-known was as Harrison Ford's sidekick in Steven Spielberg's *Indiana Jones and the Temple of Doom* (1984). She went on to marry Spielberg, meanwhile continuing to appear regularly in films; however, she has never landed another role as prominent (in terms of box-office receipts) as that in *Indiana Jones*. **Selected Works:** *Black Rain* (1990), *My Heroes Have Always Been Cowboys* (1991), *Love Affair* (1994)

# Jack Cardiff

**Born:** September 18, 1914; Yarmouth, Norfolk, England

**Years Active in the Industry:** by decade

| 10s | 20s | 30s | 40s | 50s | 60s | 70s | 80s | 90s |
|-----|-----|-----|-----|-----|-----|-----|-----|-----|
|     |     |     |     |     |     |     |     |     |

By the age of four, Cardiff was acting in British films; at 13, he was working as a camera assistant. A camera operator by the mid 1930s, Cardiff worked on many notable productions, including *As You Like It* (1936), *The Four Feathers* (1939), and England's first Technicolor film, *Wings Of The Morning* (1937). As a director of photography, he worked with such major filmmakers as Michael Powell and Emeric Pressburger (*Stairway To Heaven* [1946], *The Red Shoes* [1948]), Alfred Hitchcock (*Under Capricorn* [1949]), and John Huston (*The African Queen* [1951]). He began directing in the late 1950s, scoring his biggest success with the D.H. Lawrence adaptation *Sons And Lovers*. **Selected Works:** *Black Narcissus* (1947), *Fanny* (1961)

# Harry Carey, Sr.

**Born:** January 16, 1878; Bronx, NY
**Died:** May 21, 1947; Brentwood, CA

**Years Active in the Industry:** by decade

| 10s | 20s | 30s | 40s | 50s | 60s | 70s | 80s | 90s |
|-----|-----|-----|-----|-----|-----|-----|-----|-----|
|     |     |     |     |     |     |     |     |     |

Western film star Harry Carey was the Eastern-born son of a Bronx judge. Carey's love and understanding of horses and horsemanship was gleaned from watching the activities of New York's mounted policemen of the 1880s. He worked briefly as an actor in stock, then studied law until a bout of pneumonia forced him to quit the job that was paying for his education. He reactivated his theatrical career in 1904 by touring the provinces in *Montana*, a play he wrote himself. In 1911, Carey signed with the Bronx-based Biograph film company, playing villain roles for pioneer director D. W. Griffith. Though only in his mid-30s, Carey's face had already taken on its familiar creased, weatherbeaten look; it was an ideal face for westerns, as Carey discovered when he signed with Hollywood's Fox Studios. Under the guidance of fledgling director John Ford, Carey made 26 features and two-reelers in the role of hard-riding frontiersman Cheyenne Harry. Throughout the 1920s, Carey remained an audience favorite, supplementing his acting income with occasional scripting, producing and co-directing assignments. At the dawn of the talkie era, Carey had been around so long that he was considered an old-timer, and had resigned himself to playing supporting parts. His starring career was revitalized by the 1931 jungle epic *Trader Horn*, in which he appeared with his wife Olive Golden. While he still accepted secondary roles in "A" features (he earned an Oscar nomination for his performance as the Vice President in Capra's *Mr. Smith Goes to Washington* [1939]), Carey remained in demand during the 1930s as a leading player, notably in the autumnal 1936 western *The Last Outlaw* and the rugged 1932 serial *Last of the Mohicans*. In 1940, Carey made his belated Broadway debut in *Heavenly Express*, following this engagement with appearances in *Ah, Wilderness* (1944) and *But Not Goodbye* (1944). By the early 1940s, Carey's craggy face had taken on Mount Rushmore dimensions; his was the archetypal "American" countenance, a fact that director Alfred Hitchcock hoped to exploit. Hitchcock wanted to cast Carey against type as a Nazi ring-leader in 1942's *Saboteur*, only to have these plans vetoed by Mrs. Carey, who insisted that her husband's fans would never accept such a radical deviation from his image. Though Carey and director John Ford never worked together in the 1930s and 1940s, Ford acknowledged his indebtedness to the veteran actor by frequently casting Harry Carey Jr. (born 1921), a personable performer in his own right, in important screen roles. When Carey Sr. died in 1948, Ford dedicated his film *Three Godfathers* to Harry's memory. A more personal tribute to Harry Carey Sr. was offered by his long-time friend John Wayne; in the very last shot of 1955's *The Searchers*, Wayne imitated a distinctive hand gesture that Harry Carey had virtually patented in his own screen work.

# Marcel Carné

**Born:** August 18, 1909; Paris, France

**Years Active in the Industry:** by decade

| 10s | 20s | 30s | 40s | 50s | 60s | 70s | 80s | 90s |
|-----|-----|-----|-----|-----|-----|-----|-----|-----|

Carné began working in films as an assistant cameraman on Jacques Feyder's *Les Nouveaux Messieurs* in 1928. The next year he was assistant director to René Clair on *Sous Les Toits De Paris*, and went on to assist Feyder on *Le Grand Jeu*, *Pension Mimosa*, and *La Kermesse Héroéque*. He graduated to directing features in 1936, and with scriptwriter Jacques Prévert made a series of landmark films in the late '30s: *Dréle De Drame/Bizarre, Bizarre*, *Quai Des Brumes/Port Of Shadows*, and *Le Jour Se Léve/Daybreak*. During the Nazi occupation, the two made the classic period love story *Les Enfants Du Paradis/Children Of Paradise*. Their partnership ended after the liberation, but Carné went on to co-script and direct many handsome French dramas in the 1950s and '60s, most notably *Thérése Raquin/The Adulteress* and *Trois Chambres A Manhattan*. **Selected Works:** *Jour Se Leve (Daybreak)* (1939)

# Art Carney (Arthur William Matthew Carney)

**Born:** November 4, 1918; Mount Vernon, NY

**Years Active in the Industry:** by decade

| 10s | 20s | 30s | 40s | 50s | 60s | 70s | 80s | 90s |
|-----|-----|-----|-----|-----|-----|-----|-----|-----|

Distinguished actor Art Carney began as a comedian, moving into a sidekick role for other comedians such as Fred Allen, Edgar Bergen, and Bert Lahr. While serving in World War II, Carney was hit by shrapnel (leaving him with a slight limp) at Omaha Beach during the Normandy landing. After the war he found much work on Broadway, both as a dramatic and comic actor. He is best known, however, for his role as Ed Norton, Jackie Gleason's pal in the classic '50s TV sitcom *The Honeymooners*. Later, mental instability and alcoholism caused him to leave the Broadway run of Neil Simon's *The Odd Couple* in order to stay

(briefly) in a mental hospital. Soon returned to work as an actor, going on the win the Best Actor Oscar for his performance as a 72-year-old in Paul Mazursky's *Harry and Tonto* (1974); he has also won several Emmys for his work on TV. His film appearances were few and far between before the mid-'70s, when he began to make movies fairly regularly. **Selected Works:** *Going in Style* (1979), *Late Show* (1977)

# John Carpenter

**Born:** January 16, 1948; Bowling Green, KY

**Years Active in the Industry:** by decade

| 10s | 20s | 30s | 40s | 50s | 60s | 70s | 80s | 90s |
|-----|-----|-----|-----|-----|-----|-----|-----|-----|

American filmmaker John Carpenter is known as one of the masters of contemporary horror movies. Born and raised in Bowling Green, Kentucky, the son of a music professor, Carpenter be-gan making homemade fantasy movies when he was only eight. In 1968, he abruptly dropped out of Western Kentucky University to enroll in the film school at the University of Southern California. There he made over 12 short films; he also collaborated on *The Resurrection of Broncho Billy* (1970), which won an Academy Award for best action-short. Soon after, Carpenter and fellow classmate Dan O'Bannon (who aspired to become special-effects wizard but went on to become a director and screenwriter) received a $1,000 grant from USC, and began production on *Dark Star*, a sci-fi film shot on less than $60,000 that would go on to become a cult classic following its 1974 release. Though his subsequent film *Assault on Precinct 13* (1976) had a bigger budget and was well-received, Carpenter did not hit the big-time until he made the slasher classic *Halloween* (1978), a movie he made on a shoestring budget that ended up raking in over $60 million internationally, and becoming the top-grossing independent film of its time. In addition to directing the film, Carpenter also co-wrote the screenplay and contributed to its musical score, a trend he has frequently repeated on subsequent films. In his horror and sci-fi films, Carpenter is especially noted for his ability to create genuine suspense while exploring the darkest underpinnings of American culture. He is also notable for using special effects, which at times are so spectacular that they detract from his stories. **Selected Works:** *Memoirs of an Invisible Man* (1992), *In the Mouth of Madness* (1994)

# Russell Carpenter

**Born:** Not Available

**Years Active in the Industry:** by decade

| 10ˢ | 20ˢ | 30ˢ | 40ˢ | 50ˢ | 60ˢ | 70ˢ | 80ˢ | 90ˢ |
|-----|-----|-----|-----|-----|-----|-----|-----|-----|
|     |     |     |     |     |     |     | ■ | ■ |

Russell Carpenter has been an active Hollywood cinematographer since 1988. His earliest credits include the horror films *Critters 2: The Main Course* (1988), *Lady in White* (1988) and *Cameron's Closet* (1989). Remaining with the scare genre into the 1990s, Carpenter occasionally ventured into the action/adventure field with projects like *Perfect Weapon* (1991). Some of Carpenter's most effective (and most stomach-churning) camerawork has been for the Stephen King-inspired *Lawnmower Man* (1992) and *Pet Sematary II* (1993). **Selected Works:** *Death Warrant* (1990), *Hard Target* (1993), *Solar Crisis* (1992), *True Lies* (1994)

# David Carradine (John Arthur Carradine)

**Born:** December 8, 1936; Hollywood, CA

**Years Active in the Industry:** by decade

| 10ˢ | 20ˢ | 30ˢ | 40ˢ | 50ˢ | 60ˢ | 70ˢ | 80ˢ | 90ˢ |
|-----|-----|-----|-----|-----|-----|-----|-----|-----|
|     |     |     |     |     | ■ | ■ | ■ | ■ |

Known for his unorthodox behavior and spontaneity, the lanky, sad-eyed American actor David Carradine is the son of actor John Carradine and half-brother of actors Keith and Robert Carradine. After a bit part in, *Taggart* (1964), he worked on Broadway in *The Royal Hunt of the Sun* in 1965, then appeared briefly in the title role of the unsuccessful TV series *Shane* (1966); there followed a string of supporting and character roles in Hollywood films, in most of which he was cast as ruthless or villainous types. In 1972 he gained international recognition as the star of the TV series *Kung Fu*, which led to starring roles in films, most notably the role of folksinger Woody Guthrie in the acclaimed *Bound for Glory* (1976); as Guthrie, he did his own work as a singer and guitarist, and elsewhere he has performed in folk concerts as a singer-songwriter. Other notable roles include that of the male lead opposite Liv Ullman in Ingmar Bergman's *The Serpent's Egg* (1977). **Selected Works:** *Animal Instincts* (1992), *Bird on a Wire* (1990), *Deadly Surveillance* (1991), *Roadside Prophets* (1992), *Think Big* (1990)

# John Carradine (Richmond Reed Carradine)

**Born:** February 5, 1906; Greenwich Village, NY
**Died:** November 27, 1988; Milan, Italy

**Years Active in the Industry:** by decade

| 10ˢ | 20ˢ | 30ˢ | 40ˢ | 50ˢ | 60ˢ | 70ˢ | 80ˢ | 90ˢ |
|-----|-----|-----|-----|-----|-----|-----|-----|-----|
|     | ■ | ■ | ■ | ■ | ■ | ■ | ■ |     |

With his long face, straight hair, and distinctively funereal voice, John Carradine, is considered one of Hollywood's greatest, and most prolific character actors. The father of actors David, Keith, and Robert Carradine, he first worked as a painter and sculptor, sketching portraits in Southern office-building lobbies. He then decided to become an actor and in 1925 made his stage debut in a New Orleans production of *Camille*, later joining a Shakespeare stock company. He hitchhiked to Hollywood in 1927, but found only stage work until 1930, when he made his screen debut in *Tol'able David*. His earliest roles, mostly small ones, were done under the name "John Peter Richmond," which he changed to "John Carradine" upon being signed by Fox in 1935. His reputation became firmly established following his performance in director John Ford's *The Prisoner of Shark Island* (1936); he went on to appear in nine more of Ford's films. In the '30s and '40s he landed many fine character roles, but as his career progressed he tended increasingly to take parts (often playing mad doctors) in cheap horror flicks, eventually appearing in more films of that genre than virtually any other actor; he also toured in one-man Shakespeare productions. He has played every imaginable sort of role, from Presidents to Nazis to eccentrics; he portrayed Dracula three times. In-between films he continued to do stage work (often Shakespeare) and, later, made many appearances on TV. He had a reputation in Hollywood as an eccentric and a ham, and became known as the "Bard of the Boulevard" because he often recited Shakespeare in booming tones while strolling the Hollywood streets. **Selected Works:** *Bride of Frankenstein* (1935), *Captains Courageous* (1937), *Grapes of Wrath* (1940), *Man Who Shot Liberty Valance* (1962), *Stagecoach* (1939)

# Keith Carradine (Keith Ian Carradine)

**Born:** August 8, 1951; San Mateo, CA

**Years Active in the Industry:** by decade

| 10ˢ | 20ˢ | 30ˢ | 40ˢ | 50ˢ | 60ˢ | 70ˢ | 80ˢ | 90ˢ |
|-----|-----|-----|-----|-----|-----|-----|-----|-----|
|     |     |     |     |     |     | ■ | ■ | ■ |

Keith Carradine, the son of actor John Carradine, brother of actor Robert and half-brother of actor David Carradine, began acting in high school. He dropped out of college after one semester as a drama student to seek acting jobs; got a role in the Los Angeles production of the rock-musical *Hair* in 1969, leading to a small role in Robert Altman's film *McCabe and Mrs. Miller* (1971). Later he played leads in films by Altman and others, most notably Altman's *Nashville* (1975), in which he played an amoral rock singer; the song he composed for and sang in that film, "I'm Easy," won the Best Song Academy Award. **Selected Works:** *Bachelor* (1993), *Ballad of the Sad Cafe* (1991), *Crisscross* (1992), *Eye on the Sparrow* (1991), *Thieves Like Us* (1974)

# Tia Carrere

**Born:** 1966; Honolulu, HI

**Years Active in the Industry:** by decade

| 10s | 20s | 30s | 40s | 50s | 60s | 70s | 80s | 90s |
|-----|-----|-----|-----|-----|-----|-----|-----|-----|
|     |     |     |     |     |     |     | ■   | ■   |

An alumnus of the ABC daytime drama *General Hospital* (she played Jade Soong), Hawaii-born actress Tia Carrere has been appearing in films since 1988. Most of her earlier efforts were

along the forgettable lines of *Alpha Summer* (1988) and *Fatal Mission* (1990), with a few career high points like the well-received TV miniseries *James Clavell's Noble House*. In 1991, the poor girl was cast as the goonish Mike Myers' somewhat unlikely lady love in *Wayne's World*; one suspects that she received more gratification from having a snake wrapped around her in one scene than from Myers' fadeout embrace. Carrere gamely entered the breach once more in 1993's *Wayne's World 2*. **Selected Works:** *Rising Sun* (1993), *True Lies* (1994)

# Jim Carrey

**Born:** January 17, 1962

**Years Active in the Industry:** by decade

| 10s | 20s | 30s | 40s | 50s | 60s | 70s | 80s | 90s |
|-----|-----|-----|-----|-----|-----|-----|-----|-----|
|     |     |     |     |     |     |     | ■   | ■   |

Arguably the Numero Uno screen comedian of the 1990s, Canadian-born entertainer Jim Carrey has taken equal parts of his idol Jerry Lewis, his spiritual ancestor Harry Ritz, and loose-limbed eccentric dancer Ray Bolger, and combined them with a gloriously uninhibited screen image uniquely his own. Carrey's life has not always been a barrel of laughs; he was born into a peri-

patetic household that regularly ran the gamut from middle-class comfort to abject poverty. Not surprisingly, Carrey became a classic over-achiever, excelling in academics even while keeping his classmates in stitches with his wild improvisations and elastic facial expressions. His comedy-club debut at age 16 was a dismal failure, but Carrey had already resolved not to be beaten down by life's disappointments (as his father, a frustrated musician, had been). By age 22, Carrey was making a good living as a standup comic, and was starring on the short-lived sitcom *The Duck Factory*—a series which curiously did little to take advantage of its star's uncanny physical dexterity. Throughout the 1980s, Carrey appeared in supporting roles in such films as *Peggy Sue Got Married* (1986) and *Earth Girls are Easy* (1990). Full stardom came Carrey's way in 1990 as the resident "white guy" on Keenan Ivory Wayans' Fox TV Network comedy weekly *In Living Color*. The most popular of Carrey's many characterizations on this program was the grotesquely disfigured Fire Marshal Bob, whose dubious safety tips brought down the wrath of real-life fire prevention groups—and also earned Carrey the ultimate accolade of being imitated by *other* comics. 1994 was the Year of Carrey, with three top-grossing comedy films to his credit: *Ace Ventura, Pet Detective, The Mask* and *Dumb and Dumber;* by the end of the year, Carrey was commanding seven to ten million dollars per picture. Unlike many of the me-oriented comics of previous decades, Carrey has attributed much of his success to God, and to the love and support of his parents. In 1995, Jim Carrey took over for Robin Williams as The Riddler in the 1995 blockbuster *Batman Forever*. **Selected Works:** *Ace Ventura: When Nature Calls* (1995

# Madeleine Carroll (Marie-Madeleine Bernadette O'Carroll)

**Born:** February 26, 1906; West Bromwich, Staffordshire, England
**Died:** October 2, 1987; Marbella, Spain

**Years Active in the Industry:** by decade

| 10s | 20s | 30s | 40s | 50s | 60s | 70s | 80s | 90s |
|-----|-----|-----|-----|-----|-----|-----|-----|-----|
|     | ■   |     |     |     |     |     |     |     |

With her ladylike aura of British gentility, blonde actress Madeleine Carroll was among the first English leading ladies to find a career in Hollywood. Prior to becoming an actress, she worked as a French teacher and hat model, then in 1927 made her London stage debut; began appearing in British films (at first silents) in 1928, going on to become England's biggest female star. She made 22 films in England, including the two Hitchcock films *The 39 Steps*, (1935), and *Secret Agent* (1936) that brought her to Hollywood's attention. She moved there in 1936 to sign a contract with 20th Century-Fox. She became an American citizen in 1943. Following her sister's death during the London blitz of WW II, Carroll largely abandoned films to work in England for war relief. She participated in USO and war-bond drives, and served as a Red Cross volunteer in Italy and France; such work led her to receive France's Legion of Honor and the U.S. Medal of Freedom. Carroll appeared in three more films before retiring, lastly *The Fan* (1949). She then went on to work for UNESCO while also occasionally appearing on stage, radio, and TV. Her four husbands included actor Sterling Hayden and French film producer Henri Lavorel. **Selected Works:** *General Died at Dawn* (1936), *Prisoner of Zenda* (1937)

# Jack Carson (John Elmer Carson)

**Born:** October 27, 1910; Carmen, Manitoba, Canada
**Died:** January 2, 1963; Los Angeles, CA

**Years Active in the Industry:** by decade

| 10s | 20s | 30s | 40s | 50s | 60s | 70s | 80s | 90s |
|-----|-----|-----|-----|-----|-----|-----|-----|-----|
|     |     |     |     |     |     |     |     |     |

Actor Jack Carson was born in Canada but raised in Milwaukee, which he always regarded as his hometown. After attending Carleton College, Carson hit the vaudeville trail in an act with his old friend Dave Willock (later a prominent Hollywood character actor in his own right). Carson's first movie contract was at RKO, where he spent an uncomfortable few years essaying bits in A picutres and thankless supporting parts in Bs. His fortunes improved when he moved to Warner Bros. in 1941, where after three years' apprenticeship in sizeable secondary roles achieved his first starring vehicle, *Make Your Own Bed* (1944); he was cast in this film opposite Jane Wyman, as part of an effort by Warners to create a Carson-Wyman team. While the studio hoped that Carson would become a comedy lead in the manner of Bob Hope, he proved himself an able dramatic actor in films like *The Hard Way* (1943) and *Mildred Pierce* (1945). Still, he was built up as Warners' answer to Hope, especially when teamed in several films with the studio's "Bing Crosby", Dennis Morgan. Continuing to alternate comic and dramatic (sometimes villainous) roles throughout the 1950s, Carson starred in his own Jack Benny-style radio series, appeared successfully as a standup comedian in Las Vegas, and was one of four rotating hosts on the 1950 TV variety series *All-Star Revue*. Belying his roly-poly frame and on-camera bumptuousness, Carson was reportedly quite the ladies' man; he was married four times (once to Lola Albright) and allegedly had affairs with several of his leading ladies, notably Doris Day. Shortly after completing his role in the Disney TV comedy *Sammy the Way Out Seal* (1962), Carson died of stomach cancer on January 2, 1963 (the same day that actor/producer Dick Powell succumbed to cancer). **Selected Works:** *Cat on a Hot Tin Roof* (1958), *Mr. Smith Goes to Washington* (1939), *Stage Door* (1937), *Star Is Born* (1954)

# Dana Carvey

**Born:** April 2, 1955; Missoula, MT

**Years Active in the Industry:** by decade

| 10s | 20s | 30s | 40s | 50s | 60s | 70s | 80s | 90s |
|-----|-----|-----|-----|-----|-----|-----|-----|-----|
|     |     |     |     |     |     |     |     |     |

Comic actor Dana Carvey led a near-monastic existence while growing up in Montana, not out of choice but because the truly popular kids were bigger and better-looking. "I was a fetus in  shoes" commented Carvey on his high school years. While attending San Francisco State University, Carvey launched his career as a standup comic. The going was rugged for a while, but by 1981 Carvey had built up enough of a reputation to earn second billing on the Mickey Rooney TV sitcom *One of the Boys*. Though the show was history by mid-1982, Carvey was now on a roll. In 1984, he showed up as a regular on the TV police adventure series *Blue Thunder*, and was spotlighted in the parody rockumentary film *This is Spinal Tap* (1984); two years later he was signed as a regular on NBC's *Saturday Night Live*. Carvey's gallery of comic characterizations is too vast to fully recount here, but his greatest popularity rested on two recurring characters. As "The Church Lady" (an amalgam of all the well-meaning pious neighbors Carvey had known while growing up), Carvey entered the Catchphrase Lexicon with his oft-repeated "Isn't that special?" and "Could it be....SATAN?" And as mop-topped teenage couch potato Garth (again drawn from life—this time based on Dana's brother Brad), Carvey was teamed with Mike "Wayne" Myers in a flawless ongoing parody of cheap cable-access television. After a misfire movie vehicle, *Opportunity Knocks* (1990), Carvey became a major box-office commodity by costarring with Mike Myers in the megahit *Wayne's World* (1992). While the 1993 sequel *Wayne's World 2* didn't quite match the take of the original, Carvey was artistically satisfied that same year with an Emmy award for his performance as H. Ross Perot (among others) on TV's *Saturday Night Live Presidential Bash*.

# John Cassavetes

**Born:** December 9, 1929; New York, NY
**Died:** February 3, 1989; Los Angeles, CA

**Years Active in the Industry:** by decade

| 10s | 20s | 30s | 40s | 50s | 60s | 70s | 80s | 90s |
|-----|-----|-----|-----|-----|-----|-----|-----|-----|
|     |     |     |     |     |     |     |     |     |

John Cassavetes was an intense, lean-faced, wiry, compact actor who went on to produce and direct independent films. After graduating from college as an English major, he enrolled at the American Academy of Dramatic Arts. Debuting onstage with a Providence, Rhode Island, stock company, he soon found work in films and live TV. A starring role in the TV detective series *Johnny Staccato* provided the funds to finance his first film as a filmmaker, a semi-improvised work, *Shadows* (1961), made on a $40,000 budget; after the film won the Critics Award at the Venice Film Festival he was hired to direct two studio films, *Too Late Blues* (1962) and *A Child is Waiting* (1963), both of which were unsuccessful critically and financially. He broke away from the studios after that and began to make a string of experimental independent films which relied heavily on improvisation. Some criticize his films as being self-indulgent, sloppy, and erratic, while others hail him as an "auteur." His best-known work is probably *A Woman Under the Influence* (1974), which departed from his usual work in that it was fully scripted; the crew consisted mostly of friends working on reduced salaries (much of the money for the film was put up by one of its co-stars, Peter Falk), and Cassavetes traveled from coast to coast promoting the film and finding bookings for it—making it a truly "independent" feature. As an actor he is probably best remembered as Mia Farrow's husband in *Rosemary's Baby* (1968), but most of his roles have been as gangsters and other undesirables in violent films. He was nominated for Oscars for Best Supporting Actor (in *The Dirty Dozen*, 1967), Best Script (*Faces*, 1968), and Best Director (for *A Woman Under the Influence*). He was married to actress Gena Rowlands, who was featured in most of his films; his son is actor Nick Cassavetes. He died of cirrhosis of the liver. **Selected Works:** *Opening Night* (1977), *Edge of the City* (1957)

# William Castle (William Schloss)

**Born:** April 24, 1914; New York, NY
**Died:** May 31, 1977; Beverly Hills, CA

**Years Active in the Industry:** by decade

| 10s | 20s | 30s | 40s | 50s | 60s | 70s | 80s | 90s |
|-----|-----|-----|-----|-----|-----|-----|-----|-----|
|     |     |     |     |     |     |     |     |     |

New York-born William Castle was known to some industry wags as one of the movies' great schlockmeisters, but his films are also among the most beloved B-pictures of the late 1950s and early 1960s, and he did produce one unabashed classic, *Rosemary's*

*Baby* (1968). Starting out as an actor on stage, he got to Hollywood in the late 1930s and became a director in 1943. He made numerous low budget pictures, most notably as part of the *Whistler and Crime Doctor* series, but it was as an independent producer during the late 1950s that Castle made his mark. Recognizing the growing enthusiasm for shock thrillers and horror films, he devised various exploitation campaigns to go with his films—thus, a good haunted house chiller like *The House On Haunted Hill* (1958) was marketed around a new process called "Emergo," which consisted of a luminous skeleton swung out over the audience during scenes involving a disembodied skeleton's appearance on screen. Other pictures, such as *The Tingler*, gave selected members of the audience mild electric shocks through their seats during appropriately tense sequences. Even without these "effects," however, these films were good, solid competent pictures that hold up well on television. Castle soon began infusing his own personality into the marketing of his movies, appearing in opening wrap-around scenes and trailers, a kind of poor man's Alfred Hitchcock. *Homicidal*, Castle's near-parody of Hitchcock's *Psycho*, was one of his strangest films, and bears watching on that basis alone. Later on, as his string of exploitation titles ran out, Castle left the director's chair and produced his best, and best-known movie, *Rosemary's Baby*, directed by Roman Polanski. He died in 1977, soon after publishing his autobiography, *Step Right Up! I'm Gonna Scare the Pants Right Off America*. In 1993, Universal released *Matinee*, a Joe Dante-directed comedy built around a producer/director (played by John Goodman) loosely based on William Castle.

# Phoebe Cates

**Born:** 1964; New York, NY

**Years Active in the Industry:** by decade

| 10s | 20s | 30s | 40s | 50s | 60s | 70s | 80s | 90s |
|-----|-----|-----|-----|-----|-----|-----|-----|-----|
|     |     |     |     |     |     |     | ■   | ■   |

Leading lady and former juvenile actress Phoebe Cates is the daughter of producer-director Joseph Cates. She began dancing as a child and was something of a prodigy; in her teens, she became a model. She debuted onscreen at age 18 in the forgettable *Paradise* (1982), becoming well-known after her appearances in the hits *Fast Times at Ridgemont High* (1982) and *Gremlins* (1984); she greatly increased her visibility with a lead role in the TV mini-series *Lace* (1984). She is married to actor Kevin Kline, and took a four-year break from films between 1984-88 to concentrate on her new family. **Selected Works:** *Bodies, Rest & Motion* (1993), *Gremlins 2: The New Batch* (1990), *Princess Caraboo* (1994)

# Claude Chabrol

**Born:** June 24, 1930; Paris, France

**Years Active in the Industry:** by decade

| 10s | 20s | 30s | 40s | 50s | 60s | 70s | 80s | 90s |
|-----|-----|-----|-----|-----|-----|-----|-----|-----|
|     |     |     |     |     | ■   | ■   | ■   | ■   |

A film critic for "Cahiers Du Cinema," Chabrol co-authored a study of Alfred Hitchcock with Eric Rohmer in 1957. He directed his first film, *Le Beau Serge*, the next year, using his own financing. Other writers at "Cahiers" soon followed Chabrol's lead, and his production company AJYM helped launch the careers of Rohmer, Phillipe de Broca, and Jacques Rivette. As a writer/director, Chabrol is best known for his provocative looks at the French bourgeoisie, such as *Les Cousins* and *Les Biches*, and his Hitchcock-inspired thrillers, most notably *La Femme Infidéle/Unfaithful Wife*, *Que La Béte Meure\This Man Must Die* and *Le Boucher*. **Selected Works:** *Madame Bovary* (1991), *Wedding in Blood* (1974), *Femme Infidele* (1969), *Cry of the Owl* (1992), *L'enfer* (1994)

# Lon Chaney, Sr. (Alonso Chaney)

**Born:** April 1, 1883; Colorado Springs, CO
**Died:** August 26, 1930; Hollywood, CA

**Years Active in the Industry:** by decade

| 10ˢ | 20ˢ | 30ˢ | 40ˢ | 50ˢ | 60ˢ | 70ˢ | 80ˢ | 90ˢ |
|-----|-----|-----|-----|-----|-----|-----|-----|-----|
|     |     |     |     |     |     |     |     |     |

Even after 65 years, the designation "Man of a Thousand Faces" brings to mind only one name: Lon Chaney Sr. The son of deaf-mute parents, Chaney learned at an early age to rely on pan-

tomime as a communications skill. The stagestruck Chaney worked in a variety of backstage positions at the opera house in his home town of Colorado Springs; eventually he was allowed to appear onstage, and before his 17th birthday he was on tour with a play he'd cowritten with his brother. Sensitive about his extreme youth and plain features, Chaney hid behind a variety of elaborate makeup when appearing onstage. Forced into single parenthood after divorcing his unstable first wife Clever Creighton (the mother of his son Creighton), Chaney had to find a more steady source of income than the theater world. He began picking up extra work at Universal studios in 1912, making himself valuable—and ultimately indispensable—through his expertise with character makeup. He rose from featured player to star at Universal in the years between 1913 and 1920, sometimes doubling as director and scriptwriter. Chantey's breakthrough film was 1919's *The Miracle Man,* in which he played a phony cripple. It was the first of many films in which he underwent severe physical discomfort to achieve a convincing screen effect; in *The Penalty* (1920), for example, he not only bound up his legs to play a dou-

ble amputee, but also contrived to jump from great heights and land on his knees. Much has been written "explaining" the psychological reasons that Chaney continued utilizing makeup and disguises even after attaining stardom. Psychology aside, it's likely that Chaney realized he needed a gimmick to survive in an increasingly competitive Hollywood—and what better gimmick than to have an entirely different face in each film? *The Hunchback of Notre Dame* (1923), in which, as Quasimodo, Chaney wore a rubber hump weighing anywhere from 30 to 70 pounds, was the film that put him into the Big Box-office category. After Universal's *Phantom of the Opera* (1925) (in which his skull-like makeup was so sturdy that it withstood frequent drenchings in a studio river), Chaney moved to MGM, where he starred in several Grand Guignol horror films directed by Tod Browning. Wildly successful upon their original release, these films all seem cut from the same cloth when seen today, even allowing for Chaney's elaborate makeup. Some of his best work during this period was *without* makeup, in such bread-and-butter vehicles as *Tell it to the Marines* (1927) and *The Big City* (1928). Offscreen, Chaney was a loner, preferring to live far from Hollywood with his son and second wife. Assessments of his true personality vary; coworkers found him affable and cooperative, if somewhat distant (one actor referred to the fortyish Chaney as a "grand old guy"), while his son Creighton, who later acted under the name Lon Chaney Jr., considered his father repressive and arbitrarily cruel (a contrast to the idyllic father-son setup in the 1957 biopic *Man of a Thousand Faces*). When talking pictures took hold in 1929, Chaney at first refused to participate, concerned that he'd have to come up with a different voice for each performance; he finally acquiesced with 1930's *The Unholy Three* (a remake of his 1925 silent success), in which he not only utilized four different vocal characterizations but also proved to be a superior performer in his natural voice. It was planned for Chaney to star in Universal's *Dracula*, but a growth in his throat (aggravated by fake snowflakes that had lodged in his esophagus during the filming of an earlier film) developed into bronchial cancer. Lon Chaney died in August of 1930 at the age of 47; in his last days, his cancer rendered him speechless, forcing him to rely on the pantomimic gestures of his youth to communicate with his friends and loved ones.

# Lon Chaney, Jr. (Creighton Chaney)

**Born:** February 10, 1906; Oklahoma City, OK
**Died:** July 12, 1973; San Clemente, CA

**Years Active in the Industry:** by decade

| 10ˢ | 20ˢ | 30ˢ | 40ˢ | 50ˢ | 60ˢ | 70ˢ | 80ˢ | 90ˢ |
|-----|-----|-----|-----|-----|-----|-----|-----|-----|
|     |     |     |     |     |     |     |     |     |

The son of actors Lon Chaney and Cleva Creighton, Creighton Tull Chaney was raised in an atmosphere of Spartan strictness by his father. The elder Chaney refused to allow Creighton to enter show business, wanting his son to prepare for a more "practical" profession; thus, young Chaney trained to be a plumber. After Chaney Sr. died in 1930, Creighton entered movies with an RKO contract, but nothing much happened until Creighton was (by his own recollection) "starved" into changing his name to Lon Chaney Jr. Chaney would spend the rest of his life competing with his father's reputation as "The Man With a Thousand Faces", hoping against hope to someday "top" Lon Sr. professionally. He would have little opportunity to do this in the poverty-row quickies that were his lot in the 1930s, nor was his tenure (1937-40) as a 20th Century-Fox contract player artistically satisfying. Hoping to convince producers that he was a fine actor in his own right, Chaney appeared as the retarded giant Lennie in a Los Angeles stage production of Steinbeck's *Of Mice and Men*. This led to his being cast as Lennie in the 1939 film version of the Steinbeck play—which turned out to be a mixed blessing; his reviews were excellent, but the character "typed" him in the eyes of many, forcing him to play variations of Lennie for the next thirty years (most amusingly in the 1947 Bob Hope comedy *My Favorite Brunette*). In 1939, Chaney was signed by Universal Pictures, where once his father had appeared in *Hunchback of Notre Dame* (1923) and *Phantom of the Opera* (1925). Universal was launching a new cycle of horror films, and hoped to cash in on the Chaney name. Billing Lon Jr. as "the screen's master character actor", Universal cast him as Dynamo Dan the Electric Man in *Man Made Monster* (1939), a role originally intended for Boris Karloff. In 1941, Lon was starred as the unfortunate lycanthrope Lawrence Talbot in *The Wolf Man* (1941), the highlight of which was a "transformation" sequence deliberately evoking memories of Chaney Sr.'s makeup expertise (unfortunately, union rules were such than Lon Jr. was not permitted to apply his own Wolfman makeup). Universal would recast Chaney as the Wolf Man in four subsequent films, and also starred him as the Frankenstein Monster in *Ghost of Frankenstein* (1942) and the title role in *Son of Dracula* (1943). Chaney also headlined two "B" horror series, one based on radio's *Inner Sanctum* anthology, the other spun off from the 1932 film *The Mummy* (there is still some speculation as to whether it was Chaney or his stand-in under all those mummy bandages). Though well paid, Chaney was irritated that he had still not matched the fame and reputation of his father; this frustration was intensified when Universal refused to cast Chaney in the 1942 remake of one of his father's biggest silent successes, *The Phantom of the Opera*. Chaney began drinking more heavily than usual, and word got out to directors around the studio to finish the actor's scenes early in the day before he "gets thirsty." The soul of kindness and cooperation when sober, Chaney was a real-life monster when drunk, and this coupled with an executive decision to eliminate the B-picture unit ended Chaney's association with Universal. Chaney would occasionally be cast in a worthwhile role in the 1950s, notably in the films of producer/director Stanley Kramer (*High Noon*, *Not as a Stranger* and especially *The Defiant Ones*); he also costarred in the popular TV series *Hawkeye and the Last of the Mohicans*. But for the most part, Chaney's last two decades as a performer were "distinguished" by a steady stream of cheap, threadbare horror films, reaching a nadir with such fare as *Hillbillies in a Haunted House* (1967) and *Dracula vs. Frankenstein* (1971). In the late 1960s, Chaney fell victim to the same throat cancer that had killed his father, though publicly he tried to pass this affliction as an acute case of laryngitis. In his last months on Earth,

Lon Chaney Jr. was unable to speak at all, though he grimly insisted upon seeking out film assignments, vainly holding out hope that somewhere, sometime, he'd get the one role that would finally "top" his legendary dad.

# Stockard Channing (Susan Stockard)

**Born:** February 13, 1944; New York City

**Years Active in the Industry:** by decade

| 10s | 20s | 30s | 40s | 50s | 60s | 70s | 80s | 90s |
|-----|-----|-----|-----|-----|-----|-----|-----|-----|
|     |     |     |     |     |     | ███ | ███ | ███ |

American actress Stockard Channing became interested in theater while in college, and after graduating she joined Boston's Theater Company, an experimental group, where her theater career began in the '60s. After working in repertory and trying unsuccessfully to get Broadway roles, she landed a lead role in a Los Angeles production of *Two Gentlemen of Verona*; eventually she became a regular on Broadway, ultimately appearing in more than 25 Broadway productions and receiving three Tony nominations, winning the award for her work in *A Day in the Death of Joe Egg*. In the early '70s she landed bit parts in several films and did some TV work, but her big break came when director Mike Nichols cast her opposite Warren Beatty and Jack Nicholson in *The Fortune* (1975). Aside from a memorable performance in the musical film *Grease* (1978), in which she played a teenager while in her early '30s, most of her later career success was on the stage, and many of the films she appeared in were sub-par; meanwhile she starred in a number of TV movies. She received a Best Supporting Actress Oscar nomination for her work in *Six Degrees of Separation* (1993) and can most recently be seen on-screen in *Smoke* (1995). **Selected Works:** *Hospital* (1971), *Meet the Applegates* (1992), *Six Degrees of Separation* (1994)

# Sir Charles Chaplin

**Born:** April 16, 1889; London, England
**Died:** December 25, 1977

**Years Active in the Industry:** by decade

| 10s | 20s | 30s | 40s | 50s | 60s | 70s | 80s | 90s |
|-----|-----|-----|-----|-----|-----|-----|-----|-----|
| ███ | ███ | ███ | ███ | ███ | ███ | ███ |     |     |

The first great screen comedian, Charles Chaplin was also one of the most gifted directors in history, and a formidable talent as a writer and composer as well. The son of music hall performers from England, he began working on the stage at age five. He was a popular child dancer and got work on the London stage, eventually moving up to acting roles. It was while touring America in 1912 that Chaplin was spotted by Mack Sennett, the head of Keystone studios, and he was signed to the studio a year later. After a disappointing, relatively non-descript debut, Chaplin began evolving the

screen persona that would emerge as his most famous screen portrayal, *The Little Tramp*, and it was after his first 11 movies that Chaplin manifested the desire to direct films. By his 13th movie, he had shifted into the director's chair, and also emerged as a writer. Chaplin's 35 films at Keystone Studios established him as a major screen comedian, and afforded him the chance to adapt his stage routines to the screen. He next moved on to Essanay Studios, where he had virtually complete creative freedom, and *The Little Tramp* became an established big-screen star. In 1916, Chaplin went to Mutual, earning an astronomical $10,000 per week under a contract that gave him absolute control of his films—the Mutual title, most notably *The Immigrant* and *Easy Street*, are still counted among the greatest comedies ever made. These modestly proportioned two-reelers were followed by Chaplin's move to First National Studios, where he made lengthier, more ambitious, but fewer films including the comedy *The Kid*, which was the second highest grossing silent film after D.W. Griffith's *The Birth of a Nation*, and made an overnight sensation of his co-star, Jackie Coogan. By this time, Chaplin was an international celebrity of a status that modern audiences can only wonder at because he achieved his status through comedy. With three other screen giants, Mary Pickford, Douglas Fairbanks Sr., and D.W. Griffith, he founded United Artists, the first modern production and distribution company, and achieved further renown as a director with *A Woman of Paris* two years later. In 1925, he made what is generally considered his magnum opus, *The Gold Rush*. Chaplin's success continued into the sound era, although he resisted using sound until *Modern Times* in 1936. He had his first failure with the anti-Hitler political satire *The Great Dictator*, in 1940, at around the same time that Chaplin's personal life—he had been involved in several awkward problems with various women, including a paternity suit filed against him by aspiring actress Joan Barry began to catch up with him. Chaplin's career during the immediate post-World War II period was marred by continuing problems, as his pacifism and alleged anti-American views led to investigations. He also made the black comedy *Monsieur Verdoux*, which failed at the box office. It was followed, however, by the best of his sound comedies, *Limelight*, which—because of his legal difficulties—didn't open in Los Angeles until two decades later—at which time its score, written by Chaplin, received an Oscar. *A King in New York*, in 1957, and *The Countess from Hong Kong*, made nine years later, closed out his career on a lackluster note. After D.W. Griffith, Chaplin was the most important filmmaker of the silent film era. Through his clear understanding of film and its capabilities, and his constant experimentation—he frequently ran though hundreds of takes to get just the right shot and effect he wanted—he set most of the rules for screen comedy that are still being followed 80 years later, and his on-screen image remains one of the most familiar. **Selected Works:** *City Lights* (1931), *Circus* (1928)

# Geraldine Chaplin

**Born:** July 31, 1944; Santa Monica, CA

**Years Active in the Industry:** by decade

| 10s | 20s | 30s | 40s | 50s | 60s | 70s | 80s | 90s |
|-----|-----|-----|-----|-----|-----|-----|-----|-----|

Willowy Geraldine Chaplin, the daughter of actor-filmmaker Charlie Chaplin and playwright Eugene O'Neill, made her feature film debut at the age of eight with a brief appearance in her father's film *Limelight* (1952); later she had a bit part in his *The Countess from Hong Kong* (1967). Educated in Switzerland, she studied dance and began her professional career with England's Royal Ballet. She debuted onscreen (as an adult) as Omar Sharif's wife in David Lean's *Doctor Zhivago* (1965), which had a long shoot on location in Spain; there she became romantically involved with Spanish filmmaker Carlos Saura, going on to star in six of his films beginning with *Peppermint Frappe* (1967). Besides working in Hollywood and British productions, she has appeared in many films made in continental Europe; she was very busy as a screen actress throughout the '70s, after which she still worked steadily but in fewer productions. She has worked frequently with directors Robert Altman and Alan Rudolph. Her stage work includes a co-starring role in the Broadway revival of *The Little Foxes*. **Selected Works:** *Duel of Hearts* (1992), *Nashville* (1975), *Three Musketeers* (1974), *Age of Innocence* (1993)

# Michael Chapman

**Born:** November 21, 1935; New York, NY

**Years Active in the Industry:** by decade

| 10s | 20s | 30s | 40s | 50s | 60s | 70s | 80s | 90s |
|-----|-----|-----|-----|-----|-----|-----|-----|-----|

After an apprenticeship as a documentary cameraman, Manhattan-born cinematographer Michael Chapman became another of the many talented lensmen given a professional leg-up by legendary photographer Gordon Willis. Chapman was a camera operator on such well-regarded 1970s films as *The Godfather* (1972) and *Jaws* (1974); in 1973 he finally attained director of photography status on *The Last Detail* (1973). Some of his best work in the 1980s was in old-fashioned but highly stylish black-and-white: *Raging Bull* (1980) and *Dead Men Don't Wear Plaid* (1982). In 1983, Chapman gave directing a try with the laudable *All the Right Moves* (1983); his next and (thus far) last directorial gig was the beautifully lensed but dramatically threadbare *Clan of the Cave Bear* (1986). **Selected Works:** *Fugitive* (1993), *Kindergarten Cop* (1990), *Quick Change* (1990), *Rising Sun* (1993)

# Cyd Charisse (Tula Ellice Finklea)

**Born:** March 8, 1922; Amarillo, TX

**Years Active in the Industry:** by decade

| 10s | 20s | 30s | 40s | 50s | 60s | 70s | 80s | 90s |
|-----|-----|-----|-----|-----|-----|-----|-----|-----|
|     |     |     |     |     |     |     |     |     |

Cyd Charisse is considered one of the finest dancers in American cinema. She spent her childhood studying ballet; at 13 she joined the Ballet Russe; five years later, during a tour of Europe, she married her ballet instructor, Nico Charisse. In 1943 she began appearing in bit parts in films, billed as "Lily Norwood." After changing her name, she began rising to stardom in 1946 and eventually appeared in screen musicals as the dance partner of Fred Astaire and Gene Kelly. In the late '50s, with the decline of Hollywood musicals, she was obliged to focus on straight acting, and soon was relegated to lower status as a screen personality. She made few films after 1963. In the '60s she performed in a nightclub revue with her second husband, singer Tony Martin. She starred in an Australian stage production of *No No Nanette* in 1972. She and Martin authored a dual memoir, *The Two of Us* (1976). **Selected Works:** *Band Wagon* (1953), *It's Always Fair Weather* (1955), *Singin' in the Rain* (1952), *Ziegfeld Follies* (1946)

# Charlie Chase (Charles Parrott)

**Born:** October 20, 1893; Baltimore, MD
**Died:** 1940

**Years Active in the Industry:** by decade

| 10s | 20s | 30s | 40s | 50s | 60s | 70s | 80s | 90s |
|-----|-----|-----|-----|-----|-----|-----|-----|-----|
|     |     |     |     |     |     |     |     |     |

Toothbrush-mustached comedic actor, director, screenwriter Charley Chase began in vaudeville and musical comedy, then found work as a second-string comedian with Mack Sennett's Keystone in 1914. After appearing in several Chaplin vehicles, he moved to Triangle and Fox. In 1915, Chase began to direct his own comedies as well as some for comedians Fatty Arbuckle and Ford Sterling. Greater success came when he joined the Hal Roach studios as a writer-director in 1921, working under his real name; he directed some of Roach's brightest comedies of the early '20s. In 1924, he returned to acting under the name "Charley Chase," and became very popular in two-reel comedies where he tended to play a dapper but bashful man-about-town who runs into trouble, or else a meek, hen-pecked husband. The sound era did not ruin his career; his speaking and singing voices were both good, and he went on to find work as a supporting player, as well as continuing to direct comedic shorts. However, he began drinking heavily and died of a heart attack at age 46.

# Chevy Chase (Cornelius Crane Chase)

**Born:** October 8, 1943; New York, NY

**Years Active in the Industry:** by decade

| 10s | 20s | 30s | 40s | 50s | 60s | 70s | 80s | 90s |
|-----|-----|-----|-----|-----|-----|-----|-----|-----|
|     |     |     |     |     |     |     |     |     |

The son of a plumbing-company heiress, Cornelius Crane Chase was nicknamed "Chevy" (after the wealthy Maryland community of the same name) by his grandmother. After graduating from Bard college with a BA in English, Chevy held down several jobs (tennis pro, truck driver, bartender) before seeking work as a comedy writer; throughout his twenties Chase wrote for the Smothers Brothers, *National Lampoon*, and (just once) *Mad* magazine. His performing career began with "Channel One", a New York-based comedy video workshop, which evolved into the 1974 feature film *Groove Tube*. Chase's quick wit and smart-alecky stage presence led to his being hired by producer Lorne Michaels for the first season of NBC's *Saturday Night Live* in 1975. Ostensibly an ensemble show, *S.N.L.* quickly became a star vehicle for Chase on the strength of his satirical "Weekend Update" news reports ("I'm Chevy Chase - and you're not") and also because of Chevy's spectacular slapstick falls and his devastating lampoons of President Gerald Ford. Chase left *S.N.L.* in 1976 to embark upon a movie career of variable success: for every huge hit like *National Lampoon's Vacation* (1983) there have been major misses like *Nothing But Trouble* (1991). His highly publicized return to TV as host of a late-night talk show for Fox resulted in one of 1993's biggest bombs, canceled less than two months after its debut. Taking an uncharacteristic "mea culpa" attitude for the disaster, Chase resumed his spotty but occasionally rewarding movie career. **Selected Works:** *Hero* (1992), *Memoirs of an Invisible Man* (1992), *Man of the House* (1995)

# Ruth Chatterton

**Born:** December 24, 1893; New York, NY
**Died:** 1961

**Years Active in the Industry:** by decade

| 10s | 20s | 30s | 40s | 50s | 60s | 70s | 80s | 90s |
|-----|-----|-----|-----|-----|-----|-----|-----|-----|
|     |     |     |     |     |     |     |     |     |

Ruth Chatterton was a dignified, sophisticated, brittle, blonde leading lady. At age 12, she debuted onstage in a stock production; reached Broadway by age 18, then triumphed at 20 as the star of *Daddy Long Legs*. She didn't break into films until her mid-30s, starting with *Sins of the Fathers* (1928) opposite Emil

Jannings. She was subsequently nominated for Best Actress Oscars for her work in *Madame X* (1929) and *Sarah and Son* (1930), but is perhaps best remembered as Walter Huston's spoiled, selfish wife in *Dodsworth* (1936), after the making of which she left Hollywood. She went on to appear in two British productions, then retired from the screen. She continued a successful and variety-filled career on the stage, once directing a play but more usually starring in Broadway productions. She authored a Broadway play, *Monsieur Brotonneau* (1930), as well as several novels in the 50s. Chatterton was also a licensed pilot who flew her own plane cross-country. She was married three times, each time to an actor: Ralph Forbes (1924-32), George Brent (1932-34), and Barry Thomson (1942-his death in 1960).

# Paddy Chayefsky

**Born:** January 29, 1923; Bronx, NY
**Died:** August 1, 1981; New York, NY

**Years Active in the Industry:** by decade

| 10s | 20s | 30s | 40s | 50s | 60s | 70s | 80s | 90s |
|-----|-----|-----|-----|-----|-----|-----|-----|-----|

Playwright/scenarist Paddy Chayefsky originally harbored dreams of becoming a comedian, but turned to writing while convalescing from a war wound. His entry into movies was by way of a bit part in the New York-based *A Double Life* (1947). He began securing writing work in the world of live television in the early 1950s, contributing to virtually every major Golden Age anthology. Though he was pigeonholed early on as a specialist in "kitchen sink" drama, Chayefsky preferred to think of himself as a satirist: even his best-known TV drama, *Marty*, was intended as a parody of the dreary lives and pointless small talk of Bronx tenement dwellers. *Marty* did so well as a 1953 TV drama that it was expanded by Chayefsky into a 1955 film, which won that year's Best Picture Oscar. The author continued in a relatively realistic vein until his 1959 play *Gideon*, an irreverent Biblical retelling wherein the title character spends most of his time kvetching with the Angel of the Lord. Chayefsky made the transition to satire pure and simple with his dark 1971 film farce *The Hospital*, which won him another Oscar. Five years later, he skewered the world of TV journalism with his screenplay for *Network* (1976), introducing the now-legendary mantra "I'm mad as hell, and I'm not going to take it any more." Chayefsky's last screenplay was the 1980 adaptation of his own novel *Altered States*. So unhappy was he with the cavalier treatment given his dialogue in the finished film that he had his name removed from the screen credits. Chayefsky died shortly afterward; at the 1982 Oscar ceremony, a loving tribute was offered to the prolific playwright by his long-ago *Marty* star, Rod Steiger.

# Maury Chaykin

**Born:** Not Available

**Years Active in the Industry:** by decade

| 10s | 20s | 30s | 40s | 50s | 60s | 70s | 80s | 90s |
|-----|-----|-----|-----|-----|-----|-----|-----|-----|

It is somehow reassuring to see movies going back to the tradition of casting familiar faces in small, offbeat roles—roles guaranteed to invoke the audience response "I've seen that actor before, but who *is* that?" Potato-faced Maury Chaykin is one of those familiar-but-anonymous actors. Whether playing a supporting role in *Sommersby* (1993) or the lead as a insanely misguided family provider in the Canadian *Cold Comfort* (1988), Chaykin is certain to make an indelible impression on the audience. Perhaps Chaykin's most-talked-about performance was as the glazed-eyed cavalry officer at the beginning of Kevin Costner's *Dances with Wolves* (1991) wherein he introduces himself by gleefully announcing that he's just wet his pants—and later bids the film adieu by blowing his brains out. **Selected Works:** *Adjuster* (1991), *Hero* (1992), *Leaving Normal* (1992), *My Cousin Vinny* (1992)

# Joan Chen (Chen Chong)

**Born:** 1961; Shanghai, China

**Years Active in the Industry:** by decade

| 10s | 20s | 30s | 40s | 50s | 60s | 70s | 80s | 90s |
|-----|-----|-----|-----|-----|-----|-----|-----|-----|

Chinese actress Joan Chen became a star in China through her portrayals of frail "flowers" possessed of metallic inner strength. She first appeared on screen in 1980, achieving international acclaim with 1986's *Tai Pan*. Even better received was her assignment as John Lone's love interest in the Oscar-winning *The Last Emperor* (1987). David Lynch fanatics will recall Chen as sawmill proprietress Jocelyn "Josie" Packard in Lynch's cult TV series *Twin Peaks*. **Selected Works:** *Deadlock* (1991), *Strangers* (1991), *Heaven and Earth* (1993)

# Cher (Cherilyn Sarkesian)

**Born:** May 20, 1946; El Centro, CA

**Years Active in the Industry:** by decade

| 10s | 20s | 30s | 40s | 50s | 60s | 70s | 80s | 90s |
|-----|-----|-----|-----|-----|-----|-----|-----|-----|

Born into a disintegrating lower-income California family, actress/singer Cher attempted to escape her poverty by entering show business at age 16 as a "go go" dancer. She met and married singer/promoter Sonny Bono, who with what some have described as a Svengalilike hold over his wife lifted her from obscurity as half of the immensely popular singing duo Sonny and Cher. Gaining fame at a period in which the odder a performer looked the more bookings he or she received, the diminutive, ebullient Sonny and the tall, deadpan Cher became a top recording team (their big hit was "I Got You, Babe") and a regular guest act on the many variety shows of the period: The pair also starred in an interesting but fragmentary feature film, *Good Times* (1967). Beloved by some and ridiculed by others, Sonny and Cher continued their upward climb until musical tastes changed in the early 1970s, whereupon they began concentrating on comedy sketches and kidding-on-the-square insults directed at one another in a 1971 TV variety weekly, *The Sonny and Cher Comedy Hour*, which enjoyed a successful three year network run. It was on this program that Cher, regarded previously as a soulless mannequin and "prop" for Sonny, began sharpening her acting versatility in such sketch roles as brash housewife Laverne, sardonic waitress Rosa, and a whole slew of historical "vamps". But Cher began to chafe at control-freak Sonny's hold on her career and her private life, and in 1974 the couple divorced. In the fall of that year, both Sonny and Cher were starring on separate TV series: Cher's program was the more successful of the two (but only slightly), perhaps due as much to her censor-baiting outfits - favoring plunging necklines and bare midriffs - as to her talent. Faced with diminishing ratings, Sonny and Cher decided to team up again professionally for a new *Sonny and Cher Show*, even though Cher was now Mrs. Greg Allman. The chemistry was no longer there, and the new program was axed in 1977. Sonny eased out of show business for a successful political career, while Cher began seeking out film work. At first treated condescendingly by critics, Cher matured into a first-rate actress in such films as *Come Back to the Five and Dime, Jimmy Dean Jimmy Dean* (1982) (repeating her Broadway role), *Silkwood* (1983), *Mask* (1985), *Suspect* (1987) and *Moonstruck* (1987) - this last film earning her an Academy Award. Something of an enigma in the show business world, Cher has managed to remain her stature as a highly respected film actress, even while continuing her rambunctious private life, selling her celebrity to promote exercise videos and a line of cosmetics, and appearing in music videos. No longer Trilby to Sonny Bono's Svengali, Cher is indubitably Her Own Woman. **Selected Works:** *Mermaids* (1990)

# Maurice Chevalier

**Born:** September 12, 1888; Paris, France
**Died:** 1972

**Years Active in the Industry:** by decade

| 10s | 20s | 30s | 40s | 50s | 60s | 70s | 80s | 90s |
|-----|-----|-----|-----|-----|-----|-----|-----|-----|
|     |     |     |     |     |     |     |     |     |

In the eyes of many film-buffs, actor Maurice Chevalier with his sophisticated charm, zest for life, and wit is the consummate movie Frenchman. Chevalier, born in Paris, was the youngest of nine children. His father was an alcoholic housepainter and did not work steadily. To help out, the 11-year-old Chevalier quit school to work as an apprentice engraver and a factory worker. After some performing briefly as an acrobat, he was injured and changed to singing in Paris cafes and halls. It is odd that he should turn to music as Chevalier had a no-

toriously weak, and average singing voice; to compensate, he added a touch of comedy to his act and soon became the toast of the town. Though only 21, he got his biggest break when he became the revue partner of the infamous musical star Mistinguett in the Folies-Bergere. Soon she became his lover as well. While serving in World War I, Chevalier was captured and spent two years in a POW camp; later he was awarded a *Croix de Guerre*. After the war he rose to world fame as a star of music halls. His trademarks were his boulevardier outfit of a straw hat and bow tie, his suggestive swagger, his aura of Epicurean enjoyment. Having appeared in a number of silent films, he moved to Hollywood in 1929 and was popular with American audiences as the light-hearted, sophisticated star of romantic films. He left Hollywood in 1935, angered over having gotten second billing in a film, but continued making movies elsewhere. In 1938 he was decorated a Chevalier of the Legion of Honor. In 1951 he was refused re-entry to the United States because he had signed an anti-nuclear-weapons document, the "Stockholm Appeal." In 1958 he was allowed to return to Hollywood and receive a special Oscar "for his contributions to the world of entertainment for more than half a century." **Selected Works:** *Fanny* (1961), *Gigi* (1958), *Love in the Afternoon* (1957), *Love Parade* (1929), *One Hour with You* (1932)

# Rae Dawn Chong

**Born:** 1961; Vancouver, BC, Canada

**Years Active in the Industry:** by decade

| 10s | 20s | 30s | 40s | 50s | 60s | 70s | 80s | 90s |
|-----|-----|-----|-----|-----|-----|-----|-----|-----|
|     |     |     |     |     |     |     | ■   | ■   |

Slim, attractive, intelligent actress Rae Dawn Chong is the daughter of comedian-actor Tommy Chong (of Cheech and Chong). At age 12, she debuted in front of the camera in the TV show *The Whiz Kid of Riverton*. Her big-screen debut came seven years later, when she played a prehistoric cave-dweller in *Quest for Fire* (1981). She went three years before her next screen role, in her father's directorial debut *The Corsican Brothers* (1984); within a year she appeared in three more releases, then was in four more films the following year. Since then she has maintained a fairly steady career; though her films have not been very successful. She appeared again with her father in *Far Out Man* (1990). **Selected Works:** *Common Bonds* (1991), *Curiosity Kills* (1990), *Time Runner* (1992), *When the Party's Over* (1993), *Boulevard* (1994)

# Tommy Chong

**Born:** May 24, 1938; Edmonton, Alberta, Canada

**Years Active in the Industry:** by decade

| 10s | 20s | 30s | 40s | 50s | 60s | 70s | 80s | 90s |
|-----|-----|-----|-----|-----|-----|-----|-----|-----|
|     |     |     |     |     |     |     | ■   | ■   |

Canadian born Thomas Chong could boast a curious mixed lineage: Chinese, French, Scotch and Irish. A musician by inclination, Chong dropped out of high school as a sophomore, frequently working as a band member to support himself. At one point, Chong was playing with The Vancouvers, for whom he helped write a hit song, "Does Your Mama Know About Me?" Chong was exposed to quite a few improvisational comedy groups during his musical career; he developed a knack for getting laughs on his own, forming an improv group called City Works, which performed at a Vancouver nitery run by Tommy's brother. It is here that Chong met erstwhile humorist Richard "Cheech" Marin, who'd left his native Los Angeles for Canada in order to avoid the draft. Breaking away from City Works two years later, Cheech and Chong (as the act was now known) developed several routines built around the characters of two dimwitted dopers who aspired to nothing more than "good grass". By 1972, the team had won a Grammy award for their scatalogically hilarious comedy albums, which seemed to strike a nerve with the then-thriving Head Generation. Cheech and Chong's record producer Lou Adler decided that the boys were movie material; boy, was he right. The team's first film *Up in Smoke* (1978) turned out to be one of Warner Bros.' highest grossing films (in every sense of the word). Subsequent Cheech and Chong films didn't do quite so well; perhaps their time had past, or perhaps their material was just too thin for a stream of comedy hits. In recent years, Cheech and Chong have worked separately and together with variable success, and both have contributed their vocal talents to Disney cartoon features. A firm believer in nepotism, Thomas Chong frequently hired his friends and family to work on the Cheech and Chong movies he directed; his daughter is the highly regarded action-film stalwart Rae Dawn Chong. **Selected Works:** *After Hours* (1985)

# Julie Christie (Julie Frances Christie)

**Born:** April 14, 1940; Chukua, Assam, India

**Years Active in the Industry:** by decade

| 10s | 20s | 30s | 40s | 50s | 60s | 70s | 80s | 90s |
|-----|-----|-----|-----|-----|-----|-----|-----|-----|
|     |     |     |     |     | ■   |     |     |     |

The daughter of an India-based British tea planter, actress Julie Christie was educated in England and the Continent, planning to become an artist or linguist. Julie altered her life's goals by enrolling in the Central School of Speech Training in London. In 1957, she first stepped onstage as a paid professional with the Frinton Repertory of Essex. Celebrated less for her stage work than for her continuing role in a popular British TV serial, *A For Andromeda*, Julie made her film debut in a micro role in *Crooks Anonymous* (1962). After a rather charming ingenue stint in *The Fast Lady* (1963) (the lady was a car, not the ingenue), Julie received her first prestige part in *Billy Liar* (1963), gaining critical appraisal for this and her subsequent supporting part in *Young Cassidy* (1964). Thus, Julie was not the "newcomer" that some perceived her to be when she shook film audiences to their foundation in *Darling* (1965), a poignant time capsule about a "mod" sexual butterfly. Julie won numerous awards for *Darling*, not the least of which were the British Film Academy award and the American Oscar. Her star ascended into box-office heaven when she was cast as Lara in the big-budget *Doctor Zhivago* (1965), where she was radiant despite having some of the most clumsy dialogue lines in the history of movie epics. She followed this with a dual role in *Fahrenheit 451* (1967), where unfortunately her performance was as detached as Francois Truffaut's direction. Roles of wildly varying quality followed, until in 1971 Christie began a professional and romantic liaison with Warren Beatty. The romance was over within a few years, but the films that resulted from the alliance - *McCabe and Mrs. Miller* (1971), *Shampoo* (1975), *Heaven Can Wait* (1978) - were at best brilliant, at worst worth a look. Few of Christie's films of the 1970s and 1980s seemed worthy of her talents, though in fact she was less interested in pursuing a career than she was grandstanding for various social and political causes. Christie's most recent performance, in the British TV movie *The Railway Station Man* (1992), was a choice example of her devotion to Issues with a capital "I" - in this case, the ongoing ideological (and shooting) war in Ireland. **Selected Works:** *Go-Between* (1971), *Petulia* (1968)

# Michael Cimino

**Born:** 1943; New York, NY

**Years Active in the Industry:** by decade

| 10s | 20s | 30s | 40s | 50s | 60s | 70s | 80s | 90s |
|-----|-----|-----|-----|-----|-----|-----|-----|-----|
|     |     |     |     |     | ■   |     |     |     |

Cimino directed documentaries, industrial films, and television commercials in the 1960s. He began writing for films in the early 1970s, co-scripting the science-fiction film *Silent Running* (1971) and the Clint Eastwood actioner *Magnum Force* (1973). The latter film led to Cimino's writing and directing the popular Eastwood caper film *Thunderbolt And Lightfoot* (1974). Cimino's next effort as a writer/director was the hit film *The Deer Hunter* (1978), a look at the lives of a group of friends before, during, and after their tour of duty in Vietnam. Cimino damaged his success with the failure of his costly epic western *Heaven's Gate* (1981), and has gone on to specialize in violent crimes films: *Year Of The Dragon* (1985), *The Sicilian* (1987), *Desperate Hours* (1990).

# René Clair (René-Lucien Chomette)

**Born:** November 11, 1898; Paris, France
**Died:** March 15, 1981; Paris, France

**Years Active in the Industry:** by decade

| 10ˢ | 20ˢ | 30ˢ | 40ˢ | 50ˢ | 60ˢ | 70ˢ | 80ˢ | 90ˢ |
|---|---|---|---|---|---|---|---|---|
| | ▓ | ▓ | ▓ | ▓ | ▓ | | | |

In 1920 René-Lucien Chomette began acting in films under the name René Clair. He performed in Louis Feuillade's 1921 serials *L'Orpheline* and *Parisette*, but in 1924 he began writing and directing his own films with the comic fantasy *Paris Qui Dort* (*The Crazy Ray*). Over the '20s Clair would make some of the most original and admired works of early French cinema, including the avant-garde short *Entr'acte*, the landmark early musicals *Sous Les Toits De Paris* and *Le Million*, and the classic satire *A Nous La Liberté*. Working in England and the United States during the 1930s and '40s, his films were dominated (sometimes overly so) by fantasy and whimsy, but he managed to inject some healthy venom into the Agatha Christie mystery *And Then There Were None*. He returned to Europe for his films of the 1950s and '60s, most notably *La Beauté Du Diable* (*Beauty And The Devil*) and *Les Belles De Nuit* (*Beauties Of The Night*). **Selected Works:** *Nous La Liberté* (1931), *Break the News* (1939)

# Bob Clampett

**Born:** May 8, 1913; San Diego, CA
**Died:** May 2, 1984; Detroit, MI

**Years Active in the Industry:** by decade

| 10ˢ | 20ˢ | 30ˢ | 40ˢ | 50ˢ | 60ˢ | 70ˢ | 80ˢ | 90ˢ |
|---|---|---|---|---|---|---|---|---|
| | | ▓ | ▓ | ▓ | | | | |

Clampett joined the Harman-Ising Studio in 1931, and in the early '30s began animating for the Warner Brothers' "Loony Tunes" cartoons. He graduated to directing in the late 1930s, and until 1946 made some of the most hilarious and outrageous of the Warner cartoons: *Porky In Wackyland*, highlighted by some of Clampett's most surreal humor; *A Tale Of Two Kitties*, which introduced Tweety Bird; *A Corny Concerto*, his Fantasia send-up; the race parody *Coal Black And De Sebben Dwarfs*; *Russian Rhapsody*, in which gremlins from the Kremlin sock it to Hitler; *Draftee Daffy*, with the little black duck trying to dodge the man from the draft board; *Kitty Kornered*, with Porky Pig bested by his pet cats; and *The Big Snooze*, a slapstick psychodrama with Bugs Bunny and Elmer Fudd, which marked Clampett's final cartoon for Warners. After a brief stint at Screen Gems, Clampett turned to television and created the popular puppet show *Time For Beany*. In the late '50s he animated his characters for the television cartoon series "Beany And Cecil."

# Jill Clayburgh

**Born:** April 30, 1944; New York, NY

**Years Active in the Industry:** by decade

| 10ˢ | 20ˢ | 30ˢ | 40ˢ | 50ˢ | 60ˢ | 70ˢ | 80ˢ | 90ˢ |
|---|---|---|---|---|---|---|---|---|
| | | | | | | ▓ | ▓ | ▓ |

American actress Jill Clayburgh was fortunate enough to find work in her field of endeavor directly after graduation from Sarah Lawrence University. She acted with the Williamstown Theatre Festival, the Charles Playhouse in Boston, and, with such future film luminaries as Al Pacino (her sometimes boyfriend) she appeared in several off-Broadway productions A tentative stab at film acting in *The Wedding Party*, filmed at Sarah Lawrence in 1963 but released in 1969, might have been forgotten save for its roster of celebrities-to-be: Jill Clayburgh, Robert DeNiro and director Brian De Palma. Otherwise, Clayburgh's "official" stepping stones into stardom would include her continuing role on the TV daytime drama *Search for Tomorrow* and her Broadway appearances in such successes as *The Rothschilds* and *Pippin*. The actress' earliest mainstream films - *Portnoy's Complaint* (1972) *The Thief Who Came to Dinner* (1974) - were not exactly vehicles for her talent. It would take her vivid performance as a battered prostitute on the 1974 TV-movie *Hustling* to make audiences aware of her extraordinary talents. Unfortunately, her turn as Carole Lombard in the 1976 stinker *Gable and Lombard* set her back a few steps, the bad press surrounding the film helped not at all by her tempestuous on-set behavior. It helped to be in the box-office winner *Silver Streak* (1977), though the actress wasn't served well playing second fiddle to Gene Wilder and Richard Pryor; she was given a better chance to shine opposite Burt Reynolds and Kris

Kristofferson in *Semi-Tough* (1977). In 1978 came the turn-around: *An Unmarried Woman*, in which Clayburgh's richly textured performance as a thirtyish divorcee trying to make sense of her disoriented life should have won her an Academy Award. It didn't, but Clayburgh was now firmly an A-List actress. Bucking the usual trend, she decided not to complacently go the "moneymaking vehicle" route but risked her success to stretch her talent in such films as director Bernardo Bertolucci's *Luna* (1979) and Costa-Gavras' *Hannah K* (1983). As expected, these non-blockbuster appearances put her career in the doldrums, compelling her to toil for her paycheck in such indifferent films as the 1986 thriller *Where are the Children?*. But Clayburgh is one of those rare American film stars to whom the work itself is more important than the fame. **Selected Works:** *Rich in Love* (1993), *Starting Over* (1979), *Whispers in the Dark* (1992), *Unspeakable Acts* (1990), *Naked in New York* (1994)

# John Cleese (John Marwood Cleese)

**Born:** October 27, 1939; Weston-Super-Mare, England

**Years Active in the Industry:** by decade

| 10s | 20s | 30s | 40s | 50s | 60s | 70s | 80s | 90s |
|-----|-----|-----|-----|-----|-----|-----|-----|-----|
|     |     |     |     |     |     |     |     |     |

Born into comfortable upper-class British surroundings, comic actor John Cleese developed a knack for making people laugh while in childhood. Attending Cambridge University with the intent of practicing law, Cleese tried to get into Cambridge's fabled Footlights revue, but was rejected because he could neither sing nor dance. His entree into the Footlights came from his collaboration with a friend on several comic sketches, setting a professional precedent for nearly always working as a "team" player. Cleese was a staffer on the radio series *I'm Sorry I'll Read That Again*, wrote for TV comedian David Frost in *The Frost Report*, worked in concert with Marty Feldman, Graham Chapman and Tim-Brooke Taylor on the revue-like *At Last the 1948 Show*, and together with Chapman helped form the groundbreaking *Monty Python's Flying Circus* in 1969. Specializing in playing the sort of upper-class twits he'd grown up around, Cleese shone in the company of fellow Pythons Chapman, Eric Idle, Terry Jones, Michael Palin and Terry Gilliam. With his very close friend and *Monty Python* supporting actress Connie Booth, Cleese moved on to his self-created situation comedy, *Fawlty Tow-*

*ers* (1975), based on a character Cleese had played on the long-running British comedy series *Doctor in the House*. Popular in America thanks to Public Television, Cleese and the *Python* crew made their first completely original film, *Monty Python and the Holy Grail*, in 1975, wherein among many other parts Cleese played the Black Knight, who refused to end his sword duel with King Arthur even though his own arms and legs had been chopped off! Several Python films (and an excellent Petruchio in Jonathan Miller's TV version of Shakespeare's *Taming of the Shrew*) later, Cleese landed the starring role of an obtuse military commander in *Privates on Parade* (1981). He'd been in films in supporting roles since 1968's *Interlude*, but *Privates* was Cleese's first real solo showcase. Following an odd but welcome appearance as a western bad guy in the American film *Silverado* (1985), Cleese starred again in *Clockwise* (1985), a parody of the British obsession with correctness, and *A Fish Called Wanda* (1986), wherein Cleese's clandestine relation with criminal Jamie Lee Curtis resulted in his having french fries stuffed up his nose by the "villain" of the piece, Kevin Kline. His fame enhanced by numerous commercial endorsements, Cleese has continued contributing comic cameos to films, and has costarred with his old *Python* cohort Eric Idle in *Splitting Heirs* (1993). In the fall of 1994, Cleese could be seen in the company of some very formidable British talent in Kenneth Branagh's filmization of *Frankenstein*. Despite his extroverted comic style, Cleese has the offscreen reputation of a shy loner, and has endured spells of depression that have resulted in psychotherapy: this in turn led to yet another collaboration, this time on a non-comic book titled *Families and How to Survive Them*, cowritten with psychiatrist Robin Skynner. **Selected Works:** *Mary Shelley's Frankenstein* (1994), *Swan Princess* (1994)

# Montgomery Clift (Edward Montgomery Clift)

**Born:** October 17, 1920; Omaha, NE
**Died:** July 23, 1966; New York, NY

**Years Active in the Industry:** by decade

| 10s | 20s | 30s | 40s | 50s | 60s | 70s | 80s | 90s |
|-----|-----|-----|-----|-----|-----|-----|-----|-----|
|     |     |     |     |     |     |     |     |     |

At age 14 American actor Montgomery Clift began appearing in summer stock and soon moved onto Broadway, where he landed several important roles. He had rejected a number of Hollywood offers before making his screen debut in *The Search* (1948), for which he received a Best Actor Oscar nomination. He soon became known as one of Hollywood's most promising young stars, and went on to make a number of movies in which he portrayed introspective, sensitive, sometimes doomed young men, always with strong and deep psychological undertones; he received three additional Oscar nominations, for *A Place in the Sun* (1951), *From Here to Eternity* (1953), and *Judgment at Nuremberg* (1961). An unhappy man offscreen, he had a reputation as a loner and nonconformist. An automobile accident in 1957 permanently scarred his face, following

which he was rumored to be involved in drugs and heavy drinking. With his good looks ruined by the accident, he went on to play roles with greater strength and pathos. He died of a heart attack at age 45. **Selected Works:** *Heiress* (1949), *Red River* (1948), *Judgement at Nuremburg* (1961), *Wild River* (1960)

# Glenn Close

**Born:** March 19, 1947; Greenwich, CT

**Years Active in the Industry:** by decade

| 10s | 20s | 30s | 40s | 50s | 60s | 70s | 80s | 90s |
|-----|-----|-----|-----|-----|-----|-----|-----|-----|
|     |     |     |     |     |     |     | ■   | ■   |

Before she was famous, distinguished star of stage and screen Glenn Close studied anthropology and acting in college, then acted with a repertory theater group called Fingernails; later

she toured America with a folk-singing group. She debuted as a professional actress at New York's Phoenix Theater, working in a season of plays, then moved on to Broadway; there she appeared in several productions, earning her first Tony nomination for *Barnum* and winning the Tony in 1984 for Tom Stoppard's *The Real Thing*. She debuted onscreen in *The World According to Garp* (1982), for which she received a Best Supporting Actress nomination. Over the next decade she established herself as one of the most talented and versatile film actresses of her generation; her status as a star was confirmed with her portrayal of a psychotic in the hit *Fatal Attraction* (1987). Altogether, as of 1994 she has received five Oscar nominations, three for Best Supporting Actress and two for Best Actress. In 1989 she was tenth on the list of a Top Ten Box Office Stars poll taken by the film industry.She most recently won another Tony for her role as Norma Desmond in the Broadway smash *Sunset Boulevard*. **Selected Works:** *Dangerous Liaisons* (1988), *Hamlet* (1990), *Reversal of Fortune* (1990), *Sarah, Plain & Tall* (1991), *Big Chill* (1983)

# Henri-Georges Clouzot

**Born:** November 20, 1907; Niort, France
**Died:** January 12, 1977; Paris, France

**Years Active in the Industry:** by decade

| 10s | 20s | 30s | 40s | 50s | 60s | 70s | 80s | 90s |
|-----|-----|-----|-----|-----|-----|-----|-----|-----|
|     |     | ■   | ■   | ■   | ■   |     |     |     |

Clouzot began collaborating on the scripts of numerous French films in 1931, and co-scripted and directed the short *La Terreur Des Batignolles*. An assistant director to Anatole Litvak and E.A. Dupont, he had to leave cinema due to ill health in 1933, but resumed scriptwriting in 1938. Four years later he directed his first feature, the thriller *L'Assassin Habite Au 21* (*The Murderer Lives At Number 21*). Clouzot's next suspense film, *Le Corbeau* (The Raven) was produced by a Nazi-owned company; its harsh portrait of smalltown France was also considered unpatriotic, and after the liberation Clouzot was briefly banned from the film industry. In the '50s he wrote and directed two of the screen's finest thrillers, Le Salaire De La Peur (*The Wages Of Fear*) and *Les Diaboliques*, both featuring his wife, actress Vera Clouzot. The fascinating documentary Le Mystére Picasso (aka The Mystery Of Picasso) followed, but ill health eventually took its toll and Clouzot's output became increasingly sporadic. He made his last film in 1969, the controversial study of obsession *La Prisonnére*.

# Lee J. Cobb (Leo Jacob)

**Born:** December 9, 1911; New York, NY
**Died:** 1976

**Years Active in the Industry:** by decade

| 10s | 20s | 30s | 40s | 50s | 60s | 70s | 80s | 90s |
|-----|-----|-----|-----|-----|-----|-----|-----|-----|
|     |     | ■   | ■   | ■   | ■   | ■   |     |     |

Heavy-faced, round-eyed, jowly American character actor of stage, screen, and TV Lee J. Cobb was usually seen scowling and smoking a cigar. As a child, Cobb showed artistic promise as a virtuoso violinist, but any hope for a musical career was ended by a broken wrist. He ran away from home at age 17, going to Hollywood. Unable to find film work there, he returned to New York and acted in radio dramas while going to night school at CCNY to learn accounting. He returned to California in 1931 where he made his stage debut with the Pasadena Playhouse. Back in New York in 1935, he joined the celebrated Group Theater and appeared in several plays with them, including *Waiting for Lefty* and *Golden Boy*. He began his film career in 1937, going on to star and play supporting roles in dozens of films straight through to the end of his life. Cobb was most frequently cast as menacing villains, but sometimes appeared as a brooding business executive or community leader. His greatest triumph on stage came in the 1949 production of Arthur Miller's *Death of a Salesman* in which he played the lead role, Willy Loman (he repeated his performance in a 1966 TV version). Between 1962-66, he also appeared on TV in the role of Judge Garth in the long-running series *The Virginian*. He was twice nominated for Best Supporting Actor Oscars for his work in *On the Waterfront* (1954) and *The Brothers Karamazov* (1958). **Selected Works:** *Exodus* (1960), *Song of Bernadette* (1943), *Three Faces of Eve* (1957), *Twelve Angry Men* (1957), *Luck of the Irish* (1948)

# Charles Coburn

**Born:** June 19, 1877; Macon, GA
**Died:** August 30, 1961; Lenox Hill, NY

### Years Active in the Industry: by decade

| 10s | 20s | 30s | 40s | 50s | 60s | 70s | 80s | 90s |
| --- | --- | --- | --- | --- | --- | --- | --- | --- |

The quintessential "foxy grandpa," American actor Charles Coburn had already put in nearly forty years as a stage actor, producer, and director (specializing in Shakespeare) before making his screen debut at age 61 in *Of Human Hearts* (1938). At home in any kind of film, Coburn was most popular in comedies, and in 1943 won an Academy Award for his role in *The More the Merrier* as the bombastic but likable business executive forced by the wartime housing shortage to share a Washington DC apartment with Jean Arthur and Joel McCrea. Coburn continued playing variations on his elderly scalawag character (he was the living image of the Monopoly-board millionaire) throughout the late 1940s and 1950s, most notably as Marilyn Monroe's erstwhile "sugar daddy" in *Gentlemen Prefer Blondes* (1953). The actor also kept busy on stage, touring with the Theatre Guild as Falstaff in *Merry Wives of Windsor* and supervising the annual Mohawk Drama Festival at Schenectady's Union College, which he'd founded in 1934. Moving into television work with the enthusiasm of a novice, the octogenarian Coburn continued acting right up to his death. Coburn's last appearance, one week before his passing, was as Grandpa Vanderhoff in an Indianapolis summer-stock production of *You Can't Take It With You*. **Selected Works:** *Devil and Miss Jones* (1941), *Heaven Can Wait* (1943), *Lady Eve* (1941), *Wilson* (1944), *Kings Row* (1942)

# James Coburn

**Born:** August 31, 1928; Laurel, NE

### Years Active in the Industry: by decade

| 10s | 20s | 30s | 40s | 50s | 60s | 70s | 80s | 90s |
| --- | --- | --- | --- | --- | --- | --- | --- | --- |

American actor James Coburn studied his craft extensively before garnering critical praise for his La Jolla Playhouse stage debut in *Billy Budd*. He came to Hollywood during the same period that onetime movie villain Lee Marvin was being promoted to stardom; producers took advantage of Coburn's slight resemblance to

Marvin, casting the young actor in the sort of secondary "heavy" roles that Marvin had previously been essaying. In 1960, Coburn landed the starring role of adventurer Jeff Durain on the TV series *Klondike*. The series lasted a mere 13 weeks before the producers decided to retain the services of Coburn and costar Ralph Taeger for another adventure series, *Acapulco*—which likewise expired after 13 weeks and sent Coburn back to movie supporting roles. With the 1966 spy spoof *Our Man Flint*, Coburn finally achieved movie stardom. Organizing his own production company, Coburn himself produced the 1967 satire *The President's Analyst*, which made very little of a box-office dent but has since earned cult status (the film's megalomaniac "villain" turns out to be the Telephone Company!). A favorite of macho director Sam Peckinpah, Coburn was given an opportunity to direct the second unit of Peckinpah's *Convoy* (1978); he also co-wrote the screenplay for another Peckinpah project, *Circle of Iron* (1979). In recent years, Coburn has frequently shown up in colorful, John Hustonesque character roles, as in the 1994 Mel Gibson vehicle *Maverick*.

# Jean Cocteau (Jean Maurice Eugéne Clément Cocteau)

**Born:** July 5, 1889; Maisons-Lafitte, France
**Died:** October 11, 1963

### Years Active in the Industry: by decade

| 10s | 20s | 30s | 40s | 50s | 60s | 70s | 80s | 90s |
| --- | --- | --- | --- | --- | --- | --- | --- | --- |

Jean Cocteau was a true Renaissance man whose work in cinema included directing, writing, and acting in films. A child prodigy, he began writing at age 10; by age 16 he was a published poet, magazine editor, and the young darling of intellectuals the world over. Between the World Wars, while only a teen, he became a leading figure in French cultural life, active in many art movements and involved in nearly every variety of art. In the mid-'20s he became severely depressed and turned to opium. Fortunately, he was eventually cured of his subsequent addiction. Cocteau's first film, *The Blood of a Poet* (1930), was made with financial assistance from the Vicomte de Noailles; such backing provided him with complete freedom from the conventions of film, about which he knew little. Expanding on the themes of his first film (the poet's inner life, his fears and obsessions, his connection to the outer world, and his preoccupation with death), he also made *Orpheus* (1950) and *The Testament of Orpheus* (1960), and all three films have been criticized as being pretentious and self-centered; other critics, however, claim that the films are among the most inventive and aesthetically impressive in the history of cinema. His other important films are *Beauty and the Beast* (1945) and *Les Parents terribles* (1948), the latter being an adaptation of his own stage play. Besides making his own films, he also contributed screenplays or dialogue to other directors. He was honorary President of the Cannes Film Festival and the author of a film manifesto, *Entretiens autour de Cinematographe* (1952).

# Ethan Coen

**Born:** September 21, 1957; Minneapolis, MN

**Years Active in the Industry:** by decade

| 10s | 20s | 30s | 40s | 50s | 60s | 70s | 80s | 90s |
|-----|-----|-----|-----|-----|-----|-----|-----|-----|
|     |     |     |     |     |     |     |     |     |

Ethan Coen and his brother Joel are considered amongst the most talented of modern American filmmakers. While his brother primarily directs, Ethan produces; they often write their films together. They are most known for their distinctive style and ability to evoke the qualities that made older films classic on the modern screen. Much of this ability stems from the many films they watched and loved as boys. Ethan attended Princeton where he studied philosophy. Soon after college, the two brothers began writing their first screenplays. Brother Joel also edited several low-budget horror movies, including the popular 1983 film *The Evil Dead*. Their first film was a critically acclaimed tribute to film noir, *Blood Simple* (1984). Their next film, *Raising Arizona* (1987), a black comedy about a desperate childless couple who kidnap a baby, was even more acclaimed and was quite popular. Since then, the Coens have produced a remarkably consistent yet varied body of work—many of them paying homage to Hollywood's most popular film genres. **Selected Works:** *Barton Fink* (1991), *Miller's Crossing* (1990)

# Joel Coen

**Born:** November 29, 1954; St. Louis Park, MN

**Years Active in the Industry:** by decade

| 10s | 20s | 30s | 40s | 50s | 60s | 70s | 80s | 90s |
|-----|-----|-----|-----|-----|-----|-----|-----|-----|
|     |     |     |     |     |     |     |     |     |

American writer/director Joel Coen trained at New York University, then moved into films in the 1980s. Working in tandem with his producer/writer brother Ethan, Coen burst into the big time with a modestly budgeted "film noir" melodrama, *Blood Simple* (1984). The picture had one of those setpiece scenes that everybody talked about, thus increasing its box-office appeal; it was the scene wherein a murderer discovered that it's not so easy to clean a blood-soaked wooden floor, especially when company is coming in a few minutes. Joel and Ethan's next hit was *Raising Arizona* (1987), a determinedly nonconformist kidnap caper in which no one in the audience was sure who exactly to root for or whether or not to laugh. *Arizona* also established what has become a cliché in Hollywood films of the 1990s: the floor-level chase sequence. The Coens pursued the unorthodox so diligently that by 1990 they were in the "love them or hate them" classification. *Miller's Crossing* (1990) was a labyrinthine gangster film that alternated between spoofery and deadly seriousness, while *Barton Fink* (1991), a hallucinatory tale about Hollywood in the 1940s, had so many plot twists that the major critics came to a gentleman's agreement not to mention anything about the film except the cast and the photogra-phy. Joel Coen's 1994 directorial project *The Hudsucker Proxy* was a bit more conservative (and a lot more expensive) than his earlier films, though its skewering of American big-business intrigues had more in common with Fellini than Madison Avenue.

# Larry Cohen

**Born:** April 20, 1938; New York, NY

**Years Active in the Industry:** by decade

| 10s | 20s | 30s | 40s | 50s | 60s | 70s | 80s | 90s |
|-----|-----|-----|-----|-----|-----|-----|-----|-----|
|     |     |     |     |     |     |     |     |     |

Holding degrees from City College and New York University, American writer/director Larry Cohen kicked off his professional career as an NBC page. This position has historically been an excellent launching pad for creative people, and within a year Cohen had made enough contacts to gain a scriptwriter post at NBC. Cohen then moved into Hollywood production, writing scripts for such films as *Return of the Seven* (1966) and *Daddy's Gone A-Hunting* (1969). The writer gradually eased into direction with the low-budget blaxploitation flicks *Black Caesar* and *Hell Up in Harlem* (both 1973). Cohen then turned out the film that moved him into cult-worship circles: *It's Alive* (1974), a gruesome but undeniably effective yarn about a killer baby (with music by old suspense stand-by Bernard Herrmann!). Despite oddball directorial items like *The Private Files of J. Edgar Hoover* (1976) (again with an incongruously lush Hollywood music score, this time by Miklos Rosza) and traditionalist writing assignments like *I the Jury* (1982), Cohen found himself typed as a horror director - not that it bothered him in the least. Never slick or expensive, Cohen's film always maintained interest by dwelling in the unexpected. *Q* (1982) includes a scuzzy dirtbag of a character (Michael Moriarty) who, much to everyone's surprise, winds up the hero of the piece. *The Stuff* (1985) brightened up its standard humongous-blob terror plot with cameos by several TV commercial spokespeople, including Clara "Where's the Beef?" Peller. And *Wicked Stepmother* (1989), though nothing resembling a classic, did allow Bette Davis her valedictory screen appearance. Apparently happiest when the budget is tightest, Cohen has continued to ply his trade into the 1990s with such direct-to-video epics as *The Man Who Loved Hitchcock* (1991) and *The Apparatus* (1992). **Selected Works:** *Ambulance* (1990), *Guilty As Sin* (1993), *Maniac Cop, Part 2* (1990), *Body Snatchers* (1994)

# Claudette Colbert (Claudette Lily Chauchoin)

**Born:** September 13, 1907; Paris, France

**Years Active in the Industry:** by decade

| 10s | 20s | 30s | 40s | 50s | 60s | 70s | 80s | 90s |
|-----|-----|-----|-----|-----|-----|-----|-----|-----|
|     |     |     |     |     |     |     |     |     |

Paris-born actress Claudette Colbert was brought to New York at age 7 by her father, a banker. She planned an art career after high school graduation, studying at the Art Student's League. Attending a party with actress Anne Morrison, the 18-year-old was offered a three-line bit in Morrison's new play, *The Wild Westcotts*. That ended her art aspirations, and Colbert embarked on a stage career in 1925, scoring her first big critical success in the 1926 Broadway play *The Barker*, in which she played a duplicitous snake charmer. One year later the actress made her first film at Long Island's Astoria studio, *For the Love of Mike* (1927), but the film was a turkey and she enjoyed neither the experience nor her young director, Frank Capra. Back she went to Broadway, returning to films during the talkie revolution in *The Hole in the Wall* (1929), which was also the talkie debut of Edward G. Robinson. Once again, Colbert disliked film acting, but movie audiences responded to her beauty and cultured voice, so she forsook the stage for Hollywood. Colbert's popularity (and salary) skyrocketed after she was cast as "the wickedest woman in history," Nero's unscrupulous wife Poppaea, in the Biblical epic *Sign of the Cross* (1932). Though she wasn't fond of disrobing for the camera, audiences got to see plenty of the Colbert epidermis, notably in the famous scene in which she bathed in ass's milk. Colbert expanded her range as a street-smart smuggler's daughter in *I Cover the Waterfront* and in the pioneering "screwball comedy" *Three Cornered Moon* (both 1933), but it was for a role she nearly refused to have anything to do with that the actress secured her box office stature. Virtually every other actress in Hollywood had turned down the role of spoiled heiress Ellie Andrews in Columbia's *It Happened One Night* (1934), and when director Frank Capra approached an unenthusiastic Colbert, she wearily agreed to play it only on the condition that Columbia pay twice her normal salary and that the film be completed before she was scheduled to go on vacation in four weeks. The actress considered the experience one of the worst in her life - until the 1935 Academy Awards ceremony, in which *It Happened One Night* won in virtually all major categories, including a Best Actress Oscar for Colbert. She spent the next decade alternating between comedy and drama, frequently in the company of her most popular costar, Fred MacMurray. She gained a reputation of giving 110% percent of her energies while acting, which compensated for her occasional imperviousness and her insistence that only one side of her face be photographed (which frequently necessitated redesigning movie sets just to accommodate her phobia about her "bad side"). Colbert remained a top moneymaking star until her last big hit, *The Egg and I* (1947), after which she lost some footing, partly because of producers' unwillingness to meet her demands that she could only film a short time each day at her doctor's orders (her doctor was her husband). A potential career jump-start in the role of Margo Channing in *All About Eve* was squelched when she injured her back and had to relinquish the role to Bette Davis. Colbert went the usual "fading star" route of making films in Europe and a budget western in the U.S., but she survived in the business by returning triumphantly to Broadway, first in 1956's *Janus*, then in the long-running 1958 comedy *Marriage Go Round*. The actress also appeared on television, though reportedly she had trouble adjusting to "live" productions in which she couldn't stop the cameras if she messed up her lines. In 1961, she returned to films as Troy Donahue's mother in *Parrish*, where she looked lovely but had little worthwhile to do. It would be her last film appearance until the 1987 TV movie, *The Two Mrs. Grenvilles* - where again she far outclassed her material. Still a prominent figure in the Hollywood hierarchy, Colbert retired to her lavish home in California, where she frequently entertained her old friends President and Mrs. Ronald Reagan. **Selected Works:** *Drums Along the Mohawk* (1939), *Since You Went Away* (1944), *So Proudly We Hail* (1943)

# Dabney Coleman

**Born:** Janurary 3, 1932; Austin, TX

**Years Active in the Industry:** by decade

| 10ˢ | 20ˢ | 30ˢ | 40ˢ | 50ˢ | 60ˢ | 70ˢ | 80ˢ | 90ˢ |
|-----|-----|-----|-----|-----|-----|-----|-----|-----|
|     |     |     |     |     | ■   | ■   | ■   | ■   |

Those who've reveled in the cinematic "corporate villainy" of actor Dabney Coleman should not be surprised that the sharkish, snake-eyed actor once aspired to be an attorney (not *all* attorneys are corporate villains, but...) While attending the University of Texas, Coleman became attracted to acting, and headed to New York, where he studied at the Neighborhood Playhouse. After stage experience and TV work, Coleman made his movie debut in 1965's *The Slender Thread*. Minus his trademarked mustache for the most part in the mid-1960s, Coleman specialized in secondary character roles that were not outright villains, but were somehow lacking in leading-man integrity. The first inkling that Coleman could handle comedy occurred during his supporting stint as obstetrician Leon Bessemer on the Marlo Thomas sitcom *That Girl*. In 1976, Coleman was cast as self-serving Mayor Jeeter (a role the actor still regards as a favorite) on Norman Lear's soap opera spoof *Mary Hartman, Mary Hartman*. Four years later, Coleman burst forth in full hissable glory as the nasty, chauvinistic boss in *9 to 5* (1980); he is so thoroughly trounced by Jane Fonda and Lily Tomlin in this film that one wonders how he was able to subsequently costar with both Fonda and Tomlin (in *On Golden Pond* [1981] and *The Bev-*

erly *Hillbillies* [1993] respectively) without flinching. After *9 to 5*, Coleman's film roles became increasingly stereotyped; he was better served on television, where he starred in the groundbreaking sitcom *Buffalo Bill* (1983), playing TV's first thoroughly, unremittingly despicable "hero." The series didn't last (audiences laughed at but did not love Buffalo Bill), but made enough of an impression for Coleman to ever afterward find himself playing cantankerous, mean-spirited sitcom leads; as recently as 1994, Coleman sneered his way through the starring role of a reactionary newspaper columnist in NBC's short-lived *Madman of the People*. Reportedly, Coleman is just as contentious and caustic offscreen as on, giving his portrayals the extra bite lacking in the performances of certain movie and TV villains who go out of their way to be pussycats in private life. **Selected Works:** *Melvin and Howard* (1980), *North Dallas Forty* (1979), *Short Time* (1990), *Tootsie* (1982), *Meet the Applegates* (1992)

# Joan Collins

**Born:** May 23, 1933; London, England

**Years Active in the Industry:** by decade

| 10ˢ | 20ˢ | 30ˢ | 40ˢ | 50ˢ | 60ˢ | 70ˢ | 80ˢ | 90ˢ |
|---|---|---|---|---|---|---|---|---|

British actress Joan Collins, daughter of a London theatrical booking agent, made her showbiz bow in a production of *The Doll's House* - in a male role. She was 9 years old, and it would be the last time there would be any doubt as to her gender. With the sort of glamorous countenance that prompted people to ask "why aren't you in movies?," Collins first appeared before the cameras in a small role as a beauty contestant in *Lady Godiva Rides Again* (1953). Thanks to a brief but torrid romance with Charlie Chaplin's son Sydney, she was able to make all the right connections and make an auspicious American debut as an Egyptian temptress in *Land of the Pharoahs* (1955). Much attention was centered on her revealing costume, notably the jewel in her navel, which was fine since it distracted viewers from her minimal acting ability. This assignment led to a contract with 20th Century-Fox, where despite a few good dramatic parts (*Girl on the Red Velvet Swing* [1955] in particular) and an adroit comic characterization in *Rally Round the Flag, Boys* (1958), she was written off by critics as decorative but nothing more. She was perilously close to "perennial starlet" status in the 1960s, and by the 1970s was the uncrowned queen of B pictures. Offscreen she cut quite a swath through the tabloid headlines; if her autobiography, *Past Imperfect*, is to be believed, she dallied with virtually every male actor in Hollywood except Wile E. Coyote. Her maturation from mere personality to superstar came about when she was cast in 1981 as glamorous bitch supreme Alexis Carrington on *Dynasty*. It was a part she played beautifully, if with a touch of high camp, and one which she exploited for publicity to the utmost with stories about the lofty cost of her wardrobe and jewelry and her actual or alleged tilting with the cast members. While professionally at the summit, she has had her share of woes

in her private life. In 1980, her daughter was seriously injured in an auto accident, and Collins stayed diligently by her side until she fully recovered; and a few years later, her latest husband sued for divorce and demanded the equivalent of a third-world treasury for alimony. Despite these setbacks, Collins has managed to survive in an industry that swallows up lesser starlets on an average of ten per hour. Nor is Joan the only Collins with talent and charisma; her sister Jackie Collins is a highly successful romance novelist, whose books *The Bitch* and *The Stud* were turned into films, both starring sibling Joan.

# Phil Collins

**Born:** Janurary 31, 1951; London, England

**Years Active in the Industry:** by decade

| 10ˢ | 20ˢ | 30ˢ | 40ˢ | 50ˢ | 60ˢ | 70ˢ | 80ˢ | 90ˢ |
|---|---|---|---|---|---|---|---|---|

Many film and TV viewers who have been impressed by singer Phil Collins' occasional acting performances are probably unaware that he started out in the acting end of the business. A busy child performer, Collins played the Artful Dodger in the London production of *Oliver* and was also fleetingly seen in the Beatles film *A Hard Days' Night* (1964). Upon joining the rock band Genesis in 1970, Collins abandoned acting in favor of a fruitful music-only career. In the mid-1980s, Collins began easing back before the cameras with recurring villainous appearances on the hit American TV series *Miami Vice*. With 1988's *Buster*, Collins made his film starring debut, playing a notorious bank robber. Since that time, Collins has sporadically returned to films; if you watch closely in the opening scenes of Steven Spielberg's *Hook* (1991), you'll spot Collins in the atypically businesslike role of a Scotland Yard detective. **Selected Works:** *And the Band Played On* (1993)

# Ray Collins

**Born:** December 10, 1889; Sacramento, CA
**Died:** July 11, 1965; Santa Monica, CA

**Years Active in the Industry:** by decade

| 10ˢ | 20ˢ | 30ˢ | 40ˢ | 50ˢ | 60ˢ | 70ˢ | 80ˢ | 90ˢ |
|---|---|---|---|---|---|---|---|---|

A descendant of one of California's pioneer families, American actor Ray Collins' interest in the theater came naturally: His father was drama critic of the *Sacramento Bee*. Taking to the stage at age 14, Collins moved to British Columbia, where he briefly headed his own stock company, then went on to Broadway. An established theater and radio performer by the mid-1930s, Collins began a rewarding association with Orson Welles' Mercury Theatre. He played the "world's last living radio announcer" in Welles' legendary *War of the Worlds* broadcast of 1938, then moved to Hollywood with the Mercury troupe in 1939.

Collins made his film debut as Boss Jim Gettys in Welles's film classic *Citizen Kane* (1940). After the Mercury disbanded in the early 1940s, Collins kept busy as a film and stage character actor, usually playing gruff business executives. Collins is most fondly remembered by TV fans of the mid-1950s for his continuing role as the intrepid Lt. Tragg on the weekly series *Perry Mason*. **Selected Works:** *Double Life* (1947), *Heiress* (1949), *Magnificent Ambersons* (1942), *Seventh Cross* (1944), *Leave Her to Heaven* (1946)

# Ronald Colman

**Born:** February 9, 1891; Richmond, Surrey, England
**Died:** May 19, 1958; Santa Barbara, CA

**Years Active in the Industry:** by decade

| 10s | 20s | 30s | 40s | 50s | 60s | 70s | 80s | 90s |
|-----|-----|-----|-----|-----|-----|-----|-----|-----|
|     |     |     |     |     |     |     |     |     |

Born to middle-class British parents (his father was an import merchant), actor Ronald Colman was raised to be as much a gentleman as any "high born" Englishman, and strove to maintain

that standard both on and off screen all his life. Acting was merely a hobby to Colman while he attended the Hadley School at Littlehampton, Sussex, but after a few years' drudgery as a bookkeeper with the British Steamship Company, the theater seemed a more alluring (if not more lucrative) life's goal. As he could not pass the military physical Colman did not join the fight during World War I in 1915. Instead he went into acting full-time, making his debut in a tiny role in the play *The Maharanee of Arakan* (1916). A subsequent better role in a production of *Damaged Goods* led to Colman's being hired to star in a two-reel film drama, *The Live Wire*. The film was never released, which is why Colman's "official" debut is often listed as his first feature film *The Toilers* (1919). The money wasn't good in the British film industry of the period - in fact it was a step away from starvation wages - so Colman arrived in New York City with about $37 to his name, making his American movie debut in *Handcuffs or Kisses?* (1920). His next film was also his "Big Break": *The White Sister* (1923), directed in Italy by Henry King, in which Colman was co-starred opposite prestigious actress Lillian Gish. The association with King and Gish was Colman's entry into Hollywood, and by 1925 he'd begun his nine-year association with producer Sam Goldwyn. Most of Colman's silent films were lush romantic cos-

tume dramas, in which he usually costarred with the lovely Vilma Banky. This sort of glorious nonsense was rendered anachronistic by the advent of talking pictures, but Goldwyn wisely cast Colman in a sophisticated up-to-date adventure, *Bulldog Drummond* (1929), for the actor's talkie debut. Colman scored an instant hit with his beautifully modulated voice and his roguishly elegant manner, and was one of the biggest and most popular screen personalities of the 1930s. A falling out with Goldwyn in 1934 prompted Colman to avoid long-term contracts for the rest of his career. As good as his pre-1935 films were, Colman was even more effective as a freelancer in such films as *Tale of Two Cities* (1935), *Lost Horizon* (1937), *The Prisoner of Zenda* (1937), *The Light That Failed* (1939), and *Talk of the Town* (1942). The actor also began a fruitful radio career during this period, first as host of an intellectual celebrity round-robin discussion weekly called *The Circle* in 1939; ten years later, he and his actress wife Benita Hume starred in a witty and well-written sitcom about a college professor and his spouse, *The Halls of Ivy*, which became a TV series in 1954. Perhaps the most famous of Colman's radio appearances were those he made on *The Jack Benny Program* as Jack's long-suffering next door neighbor. Colman won an Academy Award for his atypical performance in *A Double Life* (1947) as an emotionally disturbed actor who becomes so wrapped up in his roles that he commits murder. Curtailing his film activities in the 1950s, Colman planned to write his autobiography, but was prevented from doing so by ill health - and in part by his reluctance to speak badly of anyone. Colman died shortly after completing his final film role as the Spirit of Man in *The Story of Mankind* (1957), a laughably wretched extravaganza from which Colman managed to emerge with his dignity and reputation intact.

# Robbie Coltrane

**Born:** 1950; Rutherglen, Scotland

**Years Active in the Industry:** by decade

| 10s | 20s | 30s | 40s | 50s | 60s | 70s | 80s | 90s |
|-----|-----|-----|-----|-----|-----|-----|-----|-----|
|     |     |     |     |     |     |     |     |     |

Stocky Scottish comic actor Robbie Coltrane was trained for his craft in Glasgow and Edinburgh. During the 1970s, he rose to prominence as an improvisational nightclub comedian, usually working in ensemble (one of his partners was actress Emma Thompson). In films since 1979, Coltrane gained an American following with his antic performances in *Nuns on the Run* (1990) and *The Pope Must Die* (1991); when the latter film's title courted censorship, it was Coltrane himself who suggested that it be altered to *The Pope Must Diet*. In 1993, Coltrane launched the British TV detective series *Cracker*, in which he essayed the dramatic role of a volcanic, neurosis-ridden detective. When *Cracker* was broadcast in America over the A&E cable service, the series earned Coltrane a Cable Ace Award. **Selected Works:** *Adventures of Huck Finn* (1993), *Mona Lisa* (1986), *Perfectly Normal* (1991), *Henry V* (1989)

# Chris Columbus (Christopher Columbus)

**Born:** September 10, 1958; Spangler, PA

**Years Active in the Industry:** by decade

| 10ˢ | 20ˢ | 30ˢ | 40ˢ | 50ˢ | 60ˢ | 70ˢ | 80ˢ | 90ˢ |
|-----|-----|-----|-----|-----|-----|-----|-----|-----|
|     |     |     |     |     |     |     | ■   | ■   |

Screenwriter Chris Columbus, sold his first movie script, *Jocks*, while he was a film student at New York University; though heavily rewritten by others for the screen, this piece got Columbus' foot in the big-time door. Columbus' breakthrough script for producer Steven Spielberg, *Gremlins*, was allegedly inspired by Chris' dreams of mice at his fingers. *Gremlins*, which blended warmth and whimsy with violent slapstick and some truly mean-spirited moments, was even *more* vicious than what we saw on screen before it was cleaned up by Spielberg himself. The success of *Gremlins* secured Columbus future writing assignments on such Spielberg projects as *Young Sherlock Holmes* (1985) and *Goonies* (1986). He also came up with the concept for a 1986 TV cartoon series, *Galaxy High School*, about an extraterrestrial school populated by weird-looking space aliens. Columbus was given a chance to direct the medium-budget teen comedy *Adventures in Babysitting* in 1988. He followed this with *Home Alone* (1990), directed from a script by John Hughes, which made obscene amounts of money and which planted Columbus firmly on the Hollywood "A" list. Continuing to alternate between writing and directing into the 1990s, Columbus has admittedly had a few down days (you can't get much down-er than the script for 1993's *Dennis the Menace*), but these have been offset by such box-office bonanzas as *Home Alone 2: Lost in New York* (1992), and *Mrs. Doubtfire* (1993). **Selected Works:** *Only the Lonely* (1991)

# Betty Comden (Elizabeth Cohen)

**Born:** May 3, 1916; Brooklyn, NY

**Years Active in the Industry:** by decade

| 10ˢ | 20ˢ | 30ˢ | 40ˢ | 50ˢ | 60ˢ | 70ˢ | 80ˢ | 90ˢ |
|-----|-----|-----|-----|-----|-----|-----|-----|-----|
|     |     |     | ■   | ■   | ■   | ■   | ■   |     |

Though they were never married or even related, writer/lyricists Betty Comden and Adolph Green were joined at the hip so far as the public was concerned. Early studio publicity even suggested that Comden and Green were born within a few months of each other, though this is open for debate. Whatever the case, Betty Comden was doing just fine as an NYU grad and just adequately as a theater actress when she met fellow performers Green, Judy Holliday, and Alvin Hammer. Forming a comedy/revue act called The Revellers, the four young performers were a hit on the New York nightclub circuit when they were brought to Hollywood to appear in the 1944 musical *Greenwich Village*. Only Judy Holliday was able to go on to success as a solo performer, but Comden and Green flourished as a writing/acting collaboration in such Broadway musicals as *On the Town* and *Billion Dol-*

*lar Baby*, then as non-performing writers and lyricists for such major MGM musicals as *Good News* (1947), *Take Me Out to the Ball Game* (1949), *The Barkleys of Broadway* (1949), *Singin' in the Rain* (1952), and *The Band Wagon* (1953) (this last film included an ersatz Comden-Green team in the form of Nanette Fabray and Oscar Levant). After their MGM years, Betty and Adolph collaborated on Broadway hits like *Bells are Ringing* (1956) and films like *What a Way to Go* (1964), deftly blending coherent continuity with stinging satire. They were also responsible for the 1967 ABC musical special *I'm Getting Married*, and have packed the houses with their own two-person stage show. More recently, the team has won Tony awards for the Broadway hits *On the Twentieth Century* and *The Will Rogers Follies*. Like Adolph Green, Betty Comden has made recent acting appearances, notably as Greta Garbo in the closing scenes of *Garbo Talks* (1984). **Selected Works:** *It's Always Fair Weather* (1955)

# Joyce Compton (Eleanor Hunt)

**Born:** Janurary 27, 1907; Lexington, KY

**Years Active in the Industry:** by decade

| 10ˢ | 20ˢ | 30ˢ | 40ˢ | 50ˢ | 60ˢ | 70ˢ | 80ˢ | 90ˢ |
|-----|-----|-----|-----|-----|-----|-----|-----|-----|
|     | ■   | ■   | ■   | ■   | ■   |     |     |     |

American actress Joyce Compton was born into a traveling family; she received her schooling bit by bit in classrooms from Texas to Toronto. In the company of her parents, Compton made the Hollywood casting-office rounds in the mid-1920s, finally landing a role in *What Fools Men* (1925). In 1926 she was designated a Wampas Baby Star (a publicity ploy created by the Western Association of Motion Picture Advertisers), in the company of such future luminaries as Mary Astor, Joan Crawford, Dolores Del Rio, Janet Gaynor, and Fay Wray. Compton's career never quite reached the heights of these contemporaries; small and delicate, she was advised by her parents not to go out for large roles for fear of endangering her health. When talkies came in, she cornered the market in squeaky-voiced dumb blondes, often applying her natural Southern accent for full comic effect. She worked frequently in two-reel comedies with such funsters as Clark and McCullough, Walter Catlett, and Charley Chase. Compton's feature appearances were confined to supporting roles as waitresses, good-time girls, and ditzy Southern belles. Occasionally a big part would come her way, and she'd make the most of it; her best role of the 1930s was nightclub singer Dixie Belle Lee in *The Awful Truth*, whose striptease number "Gone with the Wind" is later hilariously imitated by the film's star, Irene Dunne. Among Compton's favorite films was *Sky Murder* (1939), an MGM "Nick Carter" mystery in which she played a deceptively dimwitted female private eye. She married once, very briefly, in 1956; she lived in her well-appointed California home with her parents until their deaths. Retiring from the screen in 1961, Compton worked from time to time as a private nurse, preferring to spend her spare hours painting and designing clothes.

# Jennifer Connelly

**Born:** 1970; New York, NY

**Years Active in the Industry:** by decade

| 10ˢ | 20ˢ | 30ˢ | 40ˢ | 50ˢ | 60ˢ | 70ˢ | 80ˢ | 90ˢ |
|-----|-----|-----|-----|-----|-----|-----|-----|-----|
|     |     |     |     |     |     |     |     |     |

Loose-limbed American actress Jennifer Connelly was 18 when she first attracted notice as the very odd lady friend of Patrick Dempsey in the European film *Some Girls* (1988). She has remained busy, if not always ideally cast, in films ever since. She raised temperatures in several movie houses with her brief nude scene in *Hot Spot* (1990), and won the hearts of comic-book aficionados with her athletic portrayal of the plucky heroine in *The Rocketeer* (1992). Jennifer Connelly's more recent film work has included director John Singleton's *Higher Learning*, and (potentially) an oft-shelved, as-yet-untitled medieval swashbuckler with Arnold Schwarzenegger.

# Sean Connery (Thomas Sean Connery)

**Born:** August 25, 1930; Edinburgh, Scotland

**Years Active in the Industry:** by decade

| 10ˢ | 20ˢ | 30ˢ | 40ˢ | 50ˢ | 60ˢ | 70ˢ | 80ˢ | 90ˢ |
|-----|-----|-----|-----|-----|-----|-----|-----|-----|
|     |     |     |     |     |     |     |     |     |

One of the few movie "superstars" truly worthy of the designation, actor Sean Connery was born to a middle-class Scots family in the first year of the worldwide Depression. Dissatisfied with his

austere surroundings, Connery quit school at 15 to join the Navy (he still bears his requisite tattoos, one reading "Scotland Forever" and the other "Mum and Dad"). Holding down several minor jobs, not the least of which was as a coffin polisher, Connery became interested in body building, which led to several advertising modeling jobs and a bid at Scotland's "Mr. Universe" title. Mildly intrigued by acting, Connery joined the singing-sailor chorus of the London Production of *South Pacific* in 1951; he later claimed that his only qualification for the job was that he was "straight." *South Pacific* whetted his appetite for stage work; Connery worked for a while in repertory, then moved to television, where he scored a success in the BBC's re-staging of the American teledrama *Requiem for a Heavyweight.* The actor moved on to films, playing bits (he was an extra in the 1954 Anna Neagle musical

*Lilacs in the Spring*) and working up to supporting parts. Connery's first important movie role was as Lana Turner's vis-a-vis in *Another Time, Another Place* (1958); though he was killed off fifteen minutes into the picture, Connery allegedly carried his amorous activities with Ms. Turner into his off-camera life, which nearly got him killed by Lana's then-boyfriend Johnny Stompanato. After several more years in increasingly larger film and TV roles, Connery was cast as James Bond in 1962's *Dr. No*; he was far from the first choice, but the producers were impressed by Connery's refusal to kowtow to them when he came in to read for the part. The actor played Bond again in *From Russia With Love* (1963), but it wasn't until the third Bond picture, *Goldfinger* (1964), that both Connery and his secret-agent alter ego became major box-office attractions. While the money steadily improved, Connery was already weary of Bond at the time of the fourth 007 flick *Thunderball* (1965). He tried to prove to audiences and critics that there was more to his talents than James Bond by playing a villain in *Woman of Straw* (1964), an enigmatic Hitchcock hero in *Marnie* (1964), a cockney POW in *The Hill* (1965), and a wacked-out Greenwich Village poet in *A Fine Madness* (1966). Despite the excellence of his characterizations, audiences preferred the Bond films, while critics always qualified their comments with references to Bond. With *You Only Live Twice* (1967), Connery swore he was through with James Bond; with *Diamonds are Forever* (1970), he really meant what he said. Rather than coast on his celebrity, the actor sought out the most challenging movie assignments possible; this time audiences were more responsive, though Connery was still most successful with action films like *The Wind and the Lion* (1974), *The Man Who Would Be King* (1975), and *The Great Train Robbery* (1981). With his patented glamorous worldliness, Connery was also ideal in films about international political intrigue like *The Next Man* (1976), *Cuba* (1979), *Hunt for Red October* (1990), and *The Russia House* (1990). One of Connery's personal favorite performances was also one of his least typical: In *The Offence* (1973), he played a troubled police detective whose emotions—and hidden demons—are agitated by his pursuit of a child molester. In 1981, Connery briefly returned to the James Bond fold with *Never Say Never Again* (1981), but his difficulties with the production staff turned what should have been a fond throwback to his salad days into a nightmarish experience for the actor. At this point, he hardly needed Bond to sustain his career; Connery had not only the affection of his fans but the respect of his industry peers, who honored him with the British Film Academy award for *Name of the Rose* (1986) and the American Oscar for *The Untouchables* (1987) (this last film also helped make a star of Kevin Costner, who repaid the favor by casting Connery as Richard the Lionhearted in *Robin Hood: Prince of Thieves* [1991]—the most highly publicized "surprise" cameo of the year). Although his mercurial temperament and occasional overbearing nature is well known, Connery is nonetheless widely sought out by actors and directors who crave the thrill of working with him. Among those so anointed in recent years were Harrison Ford, Steven Spielberg, and George Lucas, who collaborated with Connery on *Indiana Jones and the Last Crusade*, wherein the actor played Indy's father. Still a megastar in the 1990s, Sean Connery commands one of moviedom's highest salaries—not so much for his own ego-massaging as for the good of his native Scotland, to whom Connery donates a sizable chunk of his earnings. **Selected Works:** *Longest Day* (1962), *Murder on the Orient Express* (1974), *Rising Sun* (1993), *First Knight* (1995)

# Walter Connolly

**Born:** April 8, 1887; Cincinnati, OH
**Died:** May 28, 1940; Beverly Hills, CA

**Years Active in the Industry:** by decade

| 10s | 20s | 30s | 40s | 50s | 60s | 70s | 80s | 90s |
|-----|-----|-----|-----|-----|-----|-----|-----|-----|
|     |     |     |     |     |     |     |     |     |

Rotund American character actor Walter Connolly cornered the market on film portrayals of exasperated businessmen and newspaper men in the 1930s. A successful stage actor, Connolly refused all entreaties by Hollywood producers to enter films. His resistance was broken down a little by an appearance in the 1930 short *Many Happy Returns*, then he gave in altogether to Columbia Pictures president Harry Cohn. Connolly made his feature film debut in *Washington Merry-Go-Round* (1932), then appeared in *The Bitter Tea of General Yen* (1933), wherein he worked for Columbia's premier director, Frank Capra. In later years, Capra would recall affectionately the devious means by which Connolly, who hated any kind of physical exertion, was coerced into moving his body as dexterously as he moved his mouth. Connolly was featured in Capra's next two films, *Broadway Bill* (1934) and the Award-winning *It Happened One Night* (1934), then spent the rest of the 1930s bouncing between Columbia and the other major studios in meaty supporting roles - most enjoyably as the volcanic newspaper editor in David O. Selznick's *Nothing Sacred* (1937). Generally billed just below the title, Connolly was awarded star status when he essayed the title role in his final film, *The Great Victor Herbert* (1939). **Selected Works:** *Good Earth* (1937), *Lady for a Day* (1933), *Libeled Lady* (1936), *Twentieth Century* (1934), *King Steps Out* (1936)

# William Conrad

**Born:** September 27, 1920; Louisville, KY
**Died:** February 11, 1994; Los Angeles, CA

**Years Active in the Industry:** by decade

| 10s | 20s | 30s | 40s | 50s | 60s | 70s | 80s | 90s |
|-----|-----|-----|-----|-----|-----|-----|-----|-----|
|     |     |     |     |     |     |     |     |     |

Actor/director/producer William Conrad started his professional career as a musician. After World War II service, he began building his reputation in films and on Hollywood-based radio programs. Due to his bulk and shifty-eyed appearance, he was cast in films as nasty heavies, notably in *The Killers* (1946) (his first film), *Sorry Wrong Number* (1948), and *The Long Wait* (1954). On radio, the versatile Conrad was a fixture on such moody anthologies as

*Escape* and *Suspense*; he also worked frequently with Jack "Dragnet" Webb during this period, and as late as 1959 was ingesting the scenery in the Webb-directed film *30*. Conrad's most celebrated radio role was as Marshal Matt Dillon on *Gunsmoke*, which he played from 1952 through 1961 (the TV *Gunsmoke*, of course, went to James Arness, who physically matched the character that the portly Conrad had shaped vocally). In the late 1950s, Conrad went into the production end of the business at Warner Bros., keeping his hand in as a performer by providing the hilariously strident narration of the cartoon series *Rocky and His Friends* and its sequel *The Bullwinkle Show*. During the early 1960s, Conrad also directed such films as *Two on a Guillotine* (1964) and *Brainstorm* (1965). Easing back into acting in the early 1970s, Conrad enjoyed a lengthy run as the title character in the detective series *Cannon* (1971-76), then all too briefly starred as a more famous corpulent crime solver on the weekly *Nero Wolfe*. Conrad's final TV series was as one-half of *Jake and the Fatman* (Joe Penny was Jake), a crime show which ran from 1987 through 1991. **Selected Works:** *Body and Soul* (1947), *Desert Song* (1953)

# Hans Conried

**Born:** April 15, 1917; Baltimore, MD
**Died:** January 5, 1982; Burbank, CA

**Years Active in the Industry:** by decade

| 10s | 20s | 30s | 40s | 50s | 60s | 70s | 80s | 90s |
|-----|-----|-----|-----|-----|-----|-----|-----|-----|
|     |     |     |     |     |     |     |     |     |

You read it correctly; actor Hans Conried, whose public image was that of the rotund Shakespearean ham, was born not in England but in Baltimore. Scrounging for work during the Depression era, Conried offered himself to a radio station as a performer, and at 18 became a professional. One of his earliest jobs was appearing in uncut radio adaptations of Shakespeare's plays, and before he was twenty he was able to recite many of the Bard's lengthier passages from memory. After several years in summer stock and radio, Conried made his screen debut in *Dramatic School* (1938). Conried's saturnine features and reedy voice made him indispensable for small character roles, and until he entered the service in World War II the actor fluctuated between movies and radio. Given a choice, Conried would have preferred to stay in radio, where the money was better and the parts larger, but despite the obscurity of much of his film work he managed to sandwich in memorable small (often unbilled) appearances in such "A" pictures as *Once Upon a Honeymoon* (1942), *The Big Street* (1942), and *Passage to Marseilles* (1944). While in the army, Conried was put in charge of Radio Tokyo in postwar Japan, where he began his lifelong hobby of collecting rare Japanese artifacts; the actor also had a near-encyclopedic knowledge of American Indian lore. As big-time radio began to fade during the late 1940s and early 1950s, Conried concentrated more on film work. He was awarded the starring role in the bizarre musical *5000 Fingers of Dr. T.* (1952), written by his friend Dr. Seuss; unfortunately, the studio, not knowing how to handle this unorthodox project, cut it to ribbons, and the film was a failure. Somewhat ruefully, Conried thereafter referred to *Dr. T* as the film that ruined his chances to become a major star, but in retrospect, he didn't do badly at all in the 1950s. He was engaged for a choice costarring role in Cole Porter's Broadway musical *Can Can*; in addition, he became a favorite guest on Jack Paar's late-night TV program, popped up frequently and hilariously as a game show contestant, and in 1957 made the first of many special-guest visits as the imperishable Uncle Tonoose on *The Danny Thomas Show*. Cartoon producers also relied heavily on Conried, notably Walt Disney, who cast the actor as Captain Hook in the animated feature *Peter Pan*, and Jay Ward, for whom Conried played Snidely Whiplash on *The Bullwinkle Show* and Uncle Waldo on *Hoppity Hooper*. In 1963, Jay Ward hired Conried as the supercilious host of the syndicated comedy series *Fractured Flickers*. Conried cut down on his TV show appearances in the 1970s and 1980s, preferring to devote his time to stage work; for well over a year, the actor costarred with Phil Leeds in an Atlanta production of Neil Simon's *The Sunshine Boys*. Just before his death, Conried was cast in a recurring role on the "realistic" drama series *American Dream*, where he was permitted to drop the high-tone Shakespearean veneer in the gruff, down-to-earth part of Jewish oldster Abe Berlowitz. **Selected Works:** *Bus Stop* (1956)

# Tom Conti

**Born:** November 22, 1941; Glasgow, Scotland

**Years Active in the Industry:** by decade

| 10s | 20s | 30s | 40s | 50s | 60s | 70s | 80s | 90s |
|-----|-----|-----|-----|-----|-----|-----|-----|-----|
|     |     |     |     |     |     |     |     |     |

Scotsman Tom Conti was trained to be a classical pianist at Glasgow's Royal Scottish Academy of Music. It was while in Glasgow that Conti switched artistic gears to become an actor. One year after his London stage bow in 1973, Conti made his first film, *Flame* (1974). In both his stage and screen work, Conti has specialized in quixotic characters with tormented psyches; he won a 1979 Tony award for his Broadway debut in the role of a paralyzed, suicidal sculptor in *Whose Life Is it Anyway?* In 1983, Conti was Oscar-nominated for his performance as a Brendan Behanesque drunken poet in *Reuben, Reuben*. More recently, Conti starred in a gritty law-enforcement TV weekly which briefly supplanted *Murder She Wrote*

on CBS's Sunday evening schedule in the spring of 1995. **Selected Works:** *That Summer of White Roses* (1990), *Voices Within: The Lives of Truddi Chase* (1990)

# Tim Conway

**Born:** December 15, 1933; Willoughby, OH

**Years Active in the Industry:** by decade

| 10s | 20s | 30s | 40s | 50s | 60s | 70s | 80s | 90s |
|-----|-----|-----|-----|-----|-----|-----|-----|-----|
|     |     |     |     |     |     |     |     |     |

American actor Tim Conway was born in Willoughby, Ohio (not far from Cleveland), but grew up in the curiously named community Chagrin Falls, a fact that he'd later incorporate for a quick laugh in many of his comedy routines, TV films, and movies. After majoring in speech and radio at Bowling Green State University, Conway went into the Eighth Army Assignment Team, where, much in the manner of his later bumbling screen characters, he managed to "misplace" a boatload of 7500 replacement troops. Once the Army was through with him (and vice versa), Conway secured a job answering mail for a Cleveland radio deejay; his letters were so amusing that he was given a job as a writer in the promotional department, then went on to direct a TV program called *Ernie's Place*. Whenever Ernie was short a guest, Conway showed up as "Doug Hereford," a so-called authority on several subjects who'd reveal himself to be a blithering simpleton. Comedienne Rose Marie happened to be in Cleveland in 1961, and upon catching Conway's routine recommended the young erstwhile comic to Steve Allen; Conway redid the Hereford bit for Allen's ABC variety series in the fall of '61, fracturing the audiences (and Allen) in three memorable appearances. Now that he was a full fledged comic, he knew he couldn't continue performing under his real name, Tom Conway, since that was also the name of a well-known British actor; Allen advised Tom to "dot the O", and thereafter he was known as Tim Conway. In 1962, Conway was engaged to play the Doug Hereford-like role of Ensign Doug Parker on the wartime sitcom *McHale's Navy*, which lasted six seasons and made Conway a star. The actor has made several attempts over the last three decades to succeed as a solo TV star, but none of his post-*McHale's Navy* series have been anything resembling hits. Still, Conway was always welcome as a supporting comic, as with his hysterically funny appearances opposite Harvey Korman on *The Carol Burnett Show* in the 1970s; Conway also enjoyed a measure of success as star or costar of a number of Disney films and low-budget "regional" comedy pictures like *The Prize Fighter* (1978) and *The Private Eyes* (1980). More recently, Conway has starred in a popular series of satirical "how-to" home videos, playing a diminutive, dim-bulbed Scandinavian named Dorf.

# Jackie Coogan (Jack Leslie Coogan)

**Born:** October 26, 1914; Los Angeles, CA
**Died:** March 1, 1984; Santa Monica, CA

**Years Active in the Industry:** by decade

| 10ˢ | 20ˢ | 30ˢ | 40ˢ | 50ˢ | 60ˢ | 70ˢ | 80ˢ | 90ˢ |
|-----|-----|-----|-----|-----|-----|-----|-----|-----|

American actor Jackie Coogan belonged to a family of vaudevillians. At age four Coogan was already a stage attraction performing with his father when he caught the eye of Charles Chaplin, who immediately hired him (and his father as well). After giving him a bit part in the short *A Day's Pleasure* (1919), he made Coogan his co-star in the masterpiece *The Kid* (1921). This launched Coogan's film career and he went on to become one of the highest paid film actors of the day. Movie audiences world-wide doted on him, but his career as a child star petered out when he was 13 and too old to be "cute." In 1935 when his mother and stepfather refused to let him have the $4 million that he had amassed during his child acting days, he filed suit against them. When the settlement finally came, he received a mere $126,000, but the legal fight brought attention to such abuses, and resulted in the "California Child Actor's Bill" also known as the "Coogan Act" which protected the earnings of child actors. He was married to Betty Grable for 3 years, and to three other showgirls in succession afterwards. He occasionally appeared in films playing character roles during his adulthood and worked frequently in television, most notably as Uncle Fester in *The Adams Family TV* series.

# Elisha Cook, Jr.

**Born:** December 26, 1906; San Francisco, CA

**Years Active in the Industry:** by decade

| 10ˢ | 20ˢ | 30ˢ | 40ˢ | 50ˢ | 60ˢ | 70ˢ | 80ˢ | 90ˢ |
|-----|-----|-----|-----|-----|-----|-----|-----|-----|

American actor Elisha Cook Jr. was the son of an influential theatrical actor/writer/producer who died early in the 20th Century. The younger Cook was in vaudeville and stock by the time he was fourteen years old. In 1928, Cook enjoyed critical praise for his performance in the play *Her Unborn Child*, a performance he would repeat for his film debut in the 1930 film version of the play. The first ten years of Cook's Hollywood career found the slight, baby-faced actor playing innumerable college intellectuals and hapless freshmen (he's given plenty of screen time in 1936's *Pigskin Parade*). In 1940, Cook was cast as a man wrongly convicted of murder in *Stranger on the Third Floor* (1940),

and so was launched the second phase of Cook's career as Helpless Victim. The actor's ability to play beyond this stereotype was first tapped by director John Huston, who cast Cook as Wilmer, the hair-trigger homicidal "gunsel" of Sidney Greenstreet in *The Maltese Falcon* (1941). So far down on the Hollywood totem pole that he wasn't billed in the *Falcon* opening credits (you'll find him buried in the closing credits, however), Cook suddenly found his services much in demand. Sometimes he'd be shot full of holes (as in the closing gag of 1941's *Hellzapoppin'*) sometimes he'd fall victim to some other grisly demise (poison in *The Big Sleep* [1946]), and sometimes he'd be the squirrely little guy who turned out to be the last-reel murderer (*I Wake Up Screaming* [1941]; *The Falcon's Alibi* [1946]). At no time, however, was Cook ever again required to play the antiseptic "nerd" characters that had been his lot in the 1930s. Seemingly born to play "film noir" characters, Cook had one of his best extended moments in *Phantom Lady* (1944), wherein he plays a set of drums with ever-increasing orgiastic fervor. Another career high point was his death scene (again!) in *Shane* (1953); Cook is shot down by hired gun Jack Palance and plummets to the ground like a dead rabbit. A near-hermit in real life who lived in a remote mountain home and had to receive his studio calls by courier, Cook nonetheless never wanted for work, even late in life. Fans of the 1980s series *Magnum PI* will remember Cook in a recurring role as a the snarling elderly mobster Ice Pick. Having appeared in so many "cult" films, Elisha Cook Jr. has always been one of the most eagerly sought out interview subjects by film historians; his comments are invariably matter-of-fact, iconoclastic, and usually obscene. **Selected Works:** *Killing* (1956), *Rosemary's Baby* (1968)

# Martha Coolidge

**Born:** August 17, 1946; New Haven, CT

**Years Active in the Industry:** by decade

| 10ˢ | 20ˢ | 30ˢ | 40ˢ | 50ˢ | 60ˢ | 70ˢ | 80ˢ | 90ˢ |
|-----|-----|-----|-----|-----|-----|-----|-----|-----|

American director Martha Coolidge did not emerge full-grown out of nowhere in 1983 to direct the amiable sleeper *Valley Girl*; by the time of this "debut," she had nearly two decades' experience to her credit. A film crew worker in her teens, Coolidge polished her skills at the NYU film school, and for a while produced a Canadian children's program. After a professional apprenticeship as a documentary filmmaker, Coolidge helmed her first feature, a rape-awareness drama titled *Not a Pretty Picture* (1976) (yes, we know; *we* can't find it anywhere either). Desultory professional associations with Francis Ford Coppola and Peter Bogdanovich slowed down her career momentum, but in 1983 Coolidge entered the Hollywood mainstream with *Valley Girl*. Coolidge has since remained bankable, even without any blockbusters to her credit; arguably her best post-*Valley Girl* effort was the 1991 nostalgia piece *Rambling Rose*. **Selected Works:** *Crazy in Love* (1992), *Lost in Yonkers* (1993), *Angie* (1994)

# Gary Cooper (Frank James Cooper)

**Born:** May 7, 1901; Helena, MT
**Died:** May 13, 1961; Beverly Hills, CA

**Years Active in the Industry:** by decade

| 10s | 20s | 30s | 40s | 50s | 60s | 70s | 80s | 90s |
|-----|-----|-----|-----|-----|-----|-----|-----|-----|
|     |     |     |     |     |     |     |     |     |

American actor Gary Cooper was born on the Montana ranch of his wealthy father, and educated in a prestigious school in England. This dichotomy goes a long way in explaining how the adult

Cooper was able to combine the ruggedness of the frontiersman with the poise of a cultured gentleman. Injured in an auto accident while attending Wesleyan College, he convalesced on his dad's ranch, perfecting the riding skills that would see him through many a future Western film. Unable to make a living at his chosen avocation of political cartoonist,
Cooper was encouraged by two of his friends to seek employment as a cowboy extra in movies. Actor's agent Nan Collins felt she could get more prestigious work for the handsome, gangling Cooper, and in 1926 she was instrumental in obtaining the actor an important role in The Winning of Barbara Worth. Movie star Clara Bow also took an interest (some say carnal) in Cooper, seeing to it that he was cast in a couple of her films. Cooper really couldn't act at this point, but he applied himself to his work in a brief series of silent Westerns for his home studio, Paramount Pictures, and by 1929 both his acting expertise and his popularity had soared. Cooper's first talking-picture success was The Virginian (1929), in which he developed his taciturn, laconic speech patterns that became fodder for every impressionist on radio, nightclubs, and TV (Coop actually did say more in films than "Yup" and "Nope", but you'd never know it from those imitators). Cooper alternated between tie-and-tails parts in Design for Living (1933) and he-man adventurer roles in Lives of the Bengal Lancers (1935) for most of the 1930s, and in 1941 was honored with an Academy Award for Sergeant York (1941), a part for which he was World War I hero Alvin York's personal choice. One year later, Cooper scored in another film biography, Pride of the Yankees; as baseball great Lou Gehrig, the actor was utterly convincing (despite the fact that he'd never played baseball and wasn't a southpaw like Gehrig), and left few dry eyes in the audiences with his fadeout "luckiest man on the face of the Earth" soliloquy. Too old for World War II service, Cooper gave tirelessly of his time in hazardous South Pacific personal appearance tours. Cooper had married Veronica "Rocky"

Balfe in 1933, though it is no secret that he conducted affairs with several other women even into the 1950s, notably his frequent costar Patricia Neal. Ignoring this extamarital activity and the actor's indirect participation in the Communist witch-hunt of the 1940s, Hollywood held Cooper in the highest regard as an actor and a man. Even those coworkers who thought that Cooper wasn't exerting himself at all when filming were amazed to see how, in the final product, Cooper was actually outacting everyone else in a subtle, unobtrusive manner. Consigned mostly to Westerns by the 1950s (including the classic High Noon [1952]), Cooper retained his box-office stature; privately he was plagued with painful recurring illnesses, one of these developing into cancer. Discovering the extent of his illness, Cooper kept the news a secret, though hints of his condition were accidentally blurted out by his close friend Jimmy Stewart during the 1961 Academy Awards ceremony, wherein Cooper was being given an honorary Oscar. Less than two months after his final public appearance as narrator of a TV documentary on the "Real West," Cooper died; to fans still reeling from the death of Clark Gable six months earlier, it seemed that Hollywood's Golden Era had suddenly died as well. **Selected Works:** Meet John Doe (1941), Morocco (1930), Mr. Deeds Goes to Town (1936), For Whom the Bell Tolls (1943)

# Dame Gladys Cooper

**Born:** December 18, 1888; Lewisham, England
**Died:** November 17, 1971; Henley-on-Thames, England

**Years Active in the Industry:** by decade

| 10s | 20s | 30s | 40s | 50s | 60s | 70s | 80s | 90s |
|-----|-----|-----|-----|-----|-----|-----|-----|-----|
|     |     |     |     |     |     |     |     |     |

Widely acclaimed as one of the great beauties of the stage, British actress Gladys Cooper had the added advantage of great talent. Daughter of a London magazine editor, she made her stage bow at age 17 in a Colchester production of Bluebell in Fairyland; at 19, she was a member of the "Gaiety Girls," a famous and famously attractive chorus-girl line. Graduating to leading roles, Cooper was particularly popular with young stage door johnnies; during World War I, she was the British troops' most popular "pin-up" (albeit not in cheesecake poses). Switching from light comedy to deep drama in the 1920s, Cooper retained her following, even when leaving England for extended American appearances after her 1934 Broadway debut in The Shining Hour. She made subsequent New York appearances in Shakespearean roles, thereafter achieving nationwide fame with her many Hollywood film appearances (she'd first acted before the cameras way back in 1911 in a British one-reeler, Eleventh Commandment). Now past fifty but still strikingly attractive, Cooper was often cast as aristocratic ladies whose sharp-tongued cattiness was couched in feigned politeness; her film parts ranged from Bette Davis' overbearing mother in Now Voyager (1941) to the hidden murderess in a Universal "B" horror, The Black Cat (1941). Returning to the London stage in 1947, Cooper remained there for several years before returning to Broadway in *The Chalk Garden* (1955). New York was again regaled by her in 1962 when she played Mrs. Moore in *A Passage to India* (the role which won Peggy Ashcroft an Oscar when *Passage* was filmed over 20 years later). The years 1960-1964 were particularly busy for Cooper on TV and in films; she won her third Oscar nomination for her role as Henry Higgins' mother in *My Fair Lady* (1964), starred as the matriarch of a family of genteel swindlers on the TV series *The Rogues* (1964), and even found time to costar with a very young Robert Redford on a 1962 episode of *The Twilight Zone*. Made a Dame Commander of the O.B.E. in 1967, Cooper had no plans for slowing down in her eighties, even though she was appalled by the "let it all hang out" theater offerings of the era. Cooper was planning to tour in a Canadian revival of *Chalk Garden* in 1971 when prevented by a bout with pneumonia, which was terminated fatally in November of that year. **Selected Works:** *Bishop's Wife* (1947), *Kitty Foyle* (1940), *Mrs. Parkington* (1944), *Rebecca* (1940), *Song of Bernadette* (1943)

# Jackie Cooper

**Born:** September 15, 1922; Los Angeles, CA

**Years Active in the Industry:** by decade

| 10s | 20s | 30s | 40s | 50s | 60s | 70s | 80s | 90s |
|-----|-----|-----|-----|-----|-----|-----|-----|-----|

American actor Jackie Cooper was in movies at the age of three; his father had abandoned the family when Jackie was two, forcing his mother to rely upon the boy's acting income to keep food on the table. Shortly after earning his first featured part in *Fox Movietone Follies of 1929,* Cooper was hired for producer Hal Roach's "Our Gang" two-reeler series, appearing in 15 shorts over the next two years. The "leading man" in many of these comedies, he was most effective in those scenes wherein he displayed a crush on his new teacher, the beauteous Miss Crabtree. On the strength of "Our Gang," Paramount Pictures signed Cooper for the title role in the feature film *Skippy* (1931), which earned the boy an Oscar nomination. A contract with MGM followed, and for the next five years Cooper was frequently costarred with blustery character player Wallace Beery (while Jackie and Wally were "pals" on screen, they were anything but in real life, due to Beery's dislike of anyone who might upstage him). Cooper outgrew his preteen cuteness by the late 1930s, and was forced to accept whatever work came along, enjoying the occasional plum role in such films as *The Return of Frank James* (1940) and *What a Life!* (1941). His priorities rearranged by his wartime Naval service, Cooper returned to the states determined to stop being a mere "personality" and to truly learn to be an actor. This he did on Broadway and television, notably as the star of two popular TV sitcoms of the 1950s, *The People's Choice* and *Hennessy*. Cooper developed a taste for directing during this period (he would earn an Emmy for his directorial work on *M*A*S*H* in 1973), and also devoted much of his time in the 1960s to the production end of the business; in 1965 he was appointed vice-president in charge of production at Screen Gems,

the TV subsidiary of Columbia Pictures. From the early 1970s onward, Cooper has juggled acting, producing, and directing with equal aplomb. Modern audiences know Cooper best as the apoplectic Perry White in the Christopher Reeve *Superman* films. In 1981, Cooper surprised (and sometimes shocked) his fans with a warts-and-all autobiography, *Please Don't Shoot My Dog*. **Selected Works:** *Passport to Pimlico* (1949), *Champ* (1931)

# Merian C. Cooper

**Born:** October 24, 1893; Jacksonville, FL
**Died:** 1973

**Years Active in the Industry:** by decade

| 10s | 20s | 30s | 40s | 50s | 60s | 70s | 80s | 90s |
|-----|-----|-----|-----|-----|-----|-----|-----|-----|

American producer and director Merian C. Cooper met his partner Ernest B. Schoedsack in Poland just after serving as a lieutenant colonel with the Kosciusko Flying Squadron during World War I. Together the two went on to co-direct two documentaries. Their success lead Cooper and Schoedsack to begin working in fictional features notable for their exotic backgrounds. Their most famous film is the classic *King Kong* (1933), in which Cooper also acted. In 1933, he gave up directing in favor of full time producing when he succeeded long-time friend David O. Selznick as vice president in charge of production at RKO. Selznick then appointed Cooper his vice-president of Selznick International Pictures in 1936. Cooper entered the US Army Air Corps during World War II where he became a colonel and chief of staff to General Claire Chennault in China. When he finally retired from the military, he was a brigadier general in the US Air Force. In 1947, he and director John Ford formed Argosy Pictures where Cooper co-produced many of Ford's movies. In addition to working in films and the military, Cooper is also the author of several books including *The Sea Gypsy, Under the White Eagle,* and *King Kong*. He co-produced the first Cinerama presentation in 1952; that year, he also won an honorary Oscar for his many contributions to American cinema.

# Francis Ford Coppola

**Born:** April 7, 1939; Detroit, MI

**Years Active in the Industry:** by decade

| 10s | 20s | 30s | 40s | 50s | 60s | 70s | 80s | 90s |
|-----|-----|-----|-----|-----|-----|-----|-----|-----|

The son of a musician, Francis Ford Coppola was born in Detroit, and raised in New York. He became an amateur filmmaker at a very early age and, while studying drama at Hofstra University, became involved in writing for the stage. He studied in the film department at UCLA, and began making low budget features in the early 1960s. He worked as a screenwriter, contributing to *This Property Is Condemned*, and *Is Paris Burning?* After a period work-

ing for Roger Corman, for whom he directed *Dementia 13*, Coppola was four years away from the director's chair, until 1967 when Coppola made *Finian's Rainbow*, starring Fred Astaire, at Warner Bros. In 1972, Coppola established himself as a leading director of his generation with his drama *The Godfather*, which yielded two sequels of varying quality, as well as multiple variant editions. His subsequent work failed to live up to the commercial success of this blockbuster, but much of it, including *The Conversation*, achieved critical acclaim around the world. *Apocalypse Now* was a massive hit, although some critics chided its maker for his bombast and pretentions, and *The Black Stallion*, which Coppola produced, became one of the most popular children's films of the 1970s. Coppola's attempt at founding an independent studio failed, but not before it yielded a major hit from the silent era in the form of the reconstruction of Abel Gance's *Napoleon*, whose restoration Coppola helped finance. Coppola's own films have failed financially not through any faults on their part, but because of the often unusual subject matter that he has chosen to film. However, the success of Bram Stoker's *Dracula* in 1993 proved that he still has a popular and defiantly individualistic stylistic touch. **Selected Works:** *Bram Stoker's Dracula* (1992), *Godfather, Part 2* (1974), *Godfather, Part 3* (1990), *Patton* (1970)

# Roger Corman

**Born:** April 5, 1926; Los Angeles, CA

**Years Active in the Industry:** by decade

| 10s | 20s | 30s | 40s | 50s | 60s | 70s | 80s | 90s |
|-----|-----|-----|-----|-----|-----|-----|-----|-----|
|     |     |     |     |     |     |     |     |     |

A former engineering student, Roger Corman entered the picture business as a messenger and ended up a producer/director, after a stint as a story analyst and a brief detour to Oxford University. After returning to Hollywood, he saw an opportunity to make money and gain experience by making low budget films to feed the drive-in and neighborhood theater circuits, which had been abandoned in large part by the major studios—working from budgets of as little as $50,000, he quickly learned the act of making bargain basement entertainment and making money at it, producing and directing pictures for American International Pictures and Allied Artists: *Five Guns West, Apache Woman, The Day The World Ended, It Conquered The World, Not of This Earth, The Undead, Attack of the Crab Monsters, Teenage Doll, Machine Gun*

*Kelly, The Wasp Woman,* and *Sorority Girl* were only a few of the titles, and these are indicative of their subjects. These films were short (some as little as 62 minutes in length) and threadbare in production values (distributor Samuel Z. Arkoff used to look at the rushes and telephone Corman, telling him, "Roger, for chrissake, hire a couple more extras and put a little more furniture on the set!") but were also extremely entertaining, and endeared Corman to at least two generations of young filmgoers. During the early 1960s, Corman became more ambitious—he made the serious school desegregation drama *The Intruder*, adapted to the screen by his brother Gene from Charles Beaumont's novel, the only one of his movies to lose money (although it is one of the finest B-movies ever made) because no theaters would book it, and he also began working in color, most notably on a series of Edgar Allan Poe adaptations starring Vincent Price that won the respect of younger critics and aspiring filmmakers alike. Corman also employed many young film students and writers during this period, including Francis Ford Coppola, Curtis Harrington, and author Robert Towne. His output decreased as his budgets went up, and Corman moved away from directing and into producing. In the 1970s, Corman was still producing exploitation films (*Humanoids From the Deep*), but his New World films also distributed several important foreign movies, including Bergman's *Cries and Whispers* and the groundbreaking Jamaican crime-drama *The Harder They Come*. **Selected Works:** *Frankenstein Unbound* (1990), *Godfather, Part 2* (1974), *Little Miss Millions* (1993), *Silence of the Lambs* (1991), *Philadelphia* (1993)

# Bud Cort (Walter Edward Cox)

**Born:** March 29, 1950; New Rochelle, NY

**Years Active in the Industry:** by decade

| 10s | 20s | 30s | 40s | 50s | 60s | 70s | 80s | 90s |
|-----|-----|-----|-----|-----|-----|-----|-----|-----|
|     |     |     |     |     |     |     |     |     |

Inasmuch as there was already a Wally Cox, American actor Walter Edward Cox chose the stage name Bud Cort when applying for his Equity card. Straight off the stage, Cort was cast in the small role of an intern browbeaten into tears by Robert Duvall in *M\*A\*S\*H* (1970). This brief appearance was enough to encourage *M\*A\*S\*H* director Robert Altman to entrust Cort with the lead in his next film, *Brewster McCloud* (1971), a Vonnegut-like pastiche about a flying boy. Cort was not "standard leading man" material, thus many of his roles were in this offbeat vein of *Brewster McCloud*, even in more down-to-earth material like *The Strawberry Statement* (1971). Thus Cort was in many ways perfect for the suicidal teen protagonist of Hal Ashby's *Harold and Maude* (1972), whose life would be turned inside out (and back on track) by septuagenarian "free spirit" Ruth Gordon. It wasn't that Cort quit acting after *Harold and Maude*; it's simply that many of his subsequent films tried too hard to emulate *H and M*'s cult status, and fell so short of this goal as to be forgettable. The later Cort films in this "midnight movie wanna-be" vein included *Electric Dreams* (1984),

*Invaders From Mars* (1989), *Love at Stake* (1991), and *Ted & Venus* (1992), a charmingly outdated "crazy for love" opus which Cort also directed. **Selected Works:** *And the Band Played On* (1993), *Going Under* (1991)

## Stanley Cortez (Stanley Krantz)

**Born:** November 4, 1908; New York, NY

**Years Active in the Industry:** by decade

| 10$^s$ | 20$^s$ | 30$^s$ | 40$^s$ | 50$^s$ | 60$^s$ | 70$^s$ | 80$^s$ | 90$^s$ |
|---|---|---|---|---|---|---|---|---|

American cinematographer Stanley Cortez's given name was Krantz; he had it changed professionally following the lead of his older brother, film star Ricardo Cortez. While attending New York University, Cortez became an assistant cameraman for the various movie studios operating in Manhattan. He briefly pursued the occupation of portrait photographer before returning full-time to movie work at the end of the silent era. He remained an assistant and associate photographer during the early 1930s, with time out to direct the 1932 short subject *Scherzo*. By 1937, Cortez was a director of photography at Universal Pictures, confined to the studio's "B" product. Beyond such mood pieces as the 1941 comedy/horror film *The Black Cat*, there was little opportunity for Cortez to develop a style of his own, though word got around that he could attain evocative results with a minimum of fuss. Orson Welles signed Cortez to shoot his *Citizen Kane* follow-up *The Magnificent Ambersons* in late 1941. Throwing out all the economy and efficiency he'd learned on his Universal "B"s, Cortez proceeded to eat up valuable production time in achieving his admittedly marvelous photographic effects. RKO held Cortez partially responsible for the cost overrun (and ultimate failure) of *Ambersons*, and as a result his next two important assignments— Universal's *Flesh and Fantasy* (1943) and *Since You Went Away* (1944)—were filmed in collaboration with other, less time-consuming cinematographers. Nonetheless, it is *Magnificent Ambersons* for which Cortez will always be remembered, and for which he won an award from the Film Critics of America. Cortez's first Technicolor assignment, *The Man on the Eiffel Tower* (1949), made quite an impression on Charles Laughton, the film's star; when Laughton directed the deliberately stylized *Night of the Hunter* (1955) six years later, Cortez was behind the camera. While there would be the occasional "A" picture to his credit, most of Cortez's subsequent photography was confined to such low-budget films as *The Naked Kiss* (1964), *Dillinger* (1965), and *Ghost in the Invisible Bikini* (1966)— all magnificently shot if nothing else. Perhaps Cortez's oddest assignment in the latter stages of his career was the mid-1950s melodrama *Madmen of Mendora*, which was never released in its original form; in 1964, Cortez's superb camerawork for this project was spliced together with artlessly shot new footage, and the result was the notorious *They Saved Hitler's Brain* (1964). Several of Cortez's assignments in the 1970s were in the "special photography" or title-sequence category, e.g. *Tell Me That You Love Me Junie Moon* (1970), *Damien—The Omen II* (1978), and *When Time Ran Out*

(1980). Cortez also dabbled in television work from time to time, notably on the all-star TV-movie suspensor *Do Not Fold, Spindle or Mutilate* (1971).

## Bill Cosby (William H. Cosby, Jr.)

**Born:** July 12, 1937; Philadelphia, PA

**Years Active in the Industry:** by decade

| 10$^s$ | 20$^s$ | 30$^s$ | 40$^s$ | 50$^s$ | 60$^s$ | 70$^s$ | 80$^s$ | 90$^s$ |
|---|---|---|---|---|---|---|---|---|

African-American entertainer Bill Cosby, in his own words, "started out as a child," the son of an $8-a-day maid and an alcoholic absentee father. A product of grinding poverty, Cosby escaped his rundown Philadelphia neighborhood by dropping out of high school and joining the navy. He earned his diploma via correspondence course, then earned a football scholarship to Temple University. Working nights as a bartender, Cosby discovered he had the ability to make people laugh, so he temporarily shelved his plans to become an athletics teacher and set out to become a nightclub comedian. Most black comics of the era used the race issue in their act; this didn't quite work for Cosby, but relating humorous reminiscences about himself and his childhood buddies worked beautifully. After numerous TV guest shots and several top-selling record albums, Cosby was signed by producer Sheldon Leonard to costar with Robert Culp in a weekly TV espionage series, *I Spy*. This was an era of acute racial tension; many NBC executives were wary about a black leading man, and quite a few Southern affiliates threatened not to run the show, but Leonard, a street scrapper from way back, refused to back down. *I Spy* was a hit, earning Cosby an Emmy. As the series progressed, the camaraderie between Cosby and Culp deepened, and by the end of the series, Culp was talking and ad-libbing in the same low-key, offbeat cadence that Cosby had adopted for his club appearances! After *I Spy*, Cosby signed a sweetheart deal with NBC, which guaranteed him a two-year run on his next program, whether the ratings were good or not. *The Bill Cosby Show* cast the star as high school coach Chet Kincaid, and was unusual for the time in that it was a sitcom minus a laughtrack. At times it was a sitcom minus laughs as well, but NBC had made its promise, and Cosby did his best. Viewers who think of Cosby in terms of one success after another have forgotten such failed 1970s TV projects as *The New Bill Cosby Show* and *Cos*, both variety programs that suffered from saggy writing and an ever-increasing "take it or leave it" attitude from the star. On the opposite end of the spectrum, there was *The Cosby Show*, the eight-season wonder that singlehandedly rescued the sitcom format from oblivion in 1984 and enabled the woebegone NBC network to crack the Number One slot in the ratings week after week. And there was *Fat Albert and the Cosby Kids* (1969-84), a superlative Saturday morning cartoon show supervised by Cosby that managed to be what is now called "prosocial" without losing any of the fun. As one of the wealthiest entertainers in the history of mankind, one would think that Cosby would also be one of the most serene. But stories persist of his unpredictable temper, his alternately currying favor with fans and then turning his back on them, and his genius at bearing long grudges. Too, it must gall Cosby to know that he hasn't been able to build any kind of movie career, certainly not with such stinkers as *Leonard Part Six* (1986) and *Ghost Dad* (1990). And there are those observers (notably Eddie Murphy) who've noticed that Cosby's nightclub act can veer dangerously from pure charm to raw arrogance. But to the majority of TV fans, Cosby is Show Business Royalty, and nothing—not even recent fiascoes like his *I Spy* reunion film—can alter that status. **Selected Works:** *California Suite* (1978)

# Constantin Costa-Gavras

**Born:** February 12, 1933; Peloponnesus, Greece

**Years Active in the Industry:** by decade

| 10ˢ | 20ˢ | 30ˢ | 40ˢ | 50ˢ | 60ˢ | 70ˢ | 80ˢ | 90ˢ |
|-----|-----|-----|-----|-----|-----|-----|-----|-----|

Constantin Costa-Gavras gleaned his political activism literally from his father's knee. The senior Gavras was a Greek government functionary who performed heroically in the resistance movement against the occupying Nazi forces in World War II. At war's end, the outspoken Gavras found himself labeled a Communist by the new regime. As a result, young Costa-Gavras was denied entrance to the U.S., where he hoped to study filmmaking. He moved instead to Paris, studying literature at the Sorbonne and working as an assistant to several of France's top directors. Costa-Gavras displayed both the techniques he'd learned from such masters as Renoir and Demy (and the tricks he'd picked up through incessant viewings of American films) in his first directorial effort, *The Sleeping Car Murders* (1966). It would be the last pure-entertainment effort in Costa-Gavras' career; once the Greek government was toppled in a military junta, the director concentrated all his energies in turning out fast-moving, entertaining cinematic tracts. *Z*, a 1969 indictment of the repressiveness of the Greek "Colonels," was an international smash (even yielding a hit soundtrack); it won multiple awards, including the "Best Foreign Language Film" Oscar. Most often in collaboration with his favorite actor Yves Montand, Costa-Gavras continued pouring out his hatred of political oppression in such subsequent films as *The Confession*, *State of Siege,* and *Special Section*. His style was several degrees removed from subtlety, and his films drove home their messages with the force of a jackhammer. In his first American film, *Missing* (1982), Costa-Gavras casts Jack Lemmon in the role that Yves Montand might have played in other circumstances; the film (which won a "best screenplay adaptation" Oscar for the director) was based on the true story of an American kidnapped in Chile, a tragic consequence of the American-backed dictatorial regime. Making films for his own edification and not for those of the "politically correct" elite, Costa-Gavras lost many of his adherents (and gained many others) with his pro-Palestinian *Hannah K* (1983). In 1982, Costa-Gavras was appointed president of the Cinematheque Francaise. Constantin Costa-Gavras' last film to date was 1989's *The Music Box*, an un-

characteristically restrained fact-based story of a respected naturalized American citizen (Armin Mueller-Stahl) accused of being a Nazi war criminal; the film was not a financial success, but did win the Golden Bear Award at the Berlin Film Festival.

# Kevin Costner

**Born:** January 18, 1955; Lynwood, CA

**Years Active in the Industry:** by decade

| 10ˢ | 20ˢ | 30ˢ | 40ˢ | 50ˢ | 60ˢ | 70ˢ | 80ˢ | 90ˢ |
|-----|-----|-----|-----|-----|-----|-----|-----|-----|

While a marketing student at California State University in Fullerton, American actor Kevin Costner became involved with community theater. Upon graduation in 1978, Costner took a marketing job that lasted all of 30 days before he decided to take a crack at acting. At least that's the official story; though Costner would probably like to cremate the memory, the fact is that he made his film debut in 1974 in the ultra-cheapie *Sizzle Beach USA*. No matter. When Costner *seriously* decided to take up acting, he went the usual theater-workshop, multiple-audition route. Casting directors saw potential, but weren't quite sure how to use Costner; besides, the novice actor had a bad habit of speaking up if something bothered him on the set. That may be why his Big-Studio debut in *Night Shift* (1982) consisted of little more than background decoration and the subsequent *Frances* (1982) featured Costner as an offstage voice. Director Lawrence Kasdan liked Costner enough to cast him in the important role of the suicide victim who motivated the plot of *The Big Chill* (1983), but when the film was released, all we saw of Costner were his dress suit and necktie as the undertaker prepared him for burial during the opening credits. Two years later, a guilt-ridden Lawrence Kasdan chose Costner for a major part as a hell-raising gunfighter in the "retro" Western *Silverado* (1985)—and this time he was on camera for virtually the entire film. Costner's big breakthrough came with a brace of baseball films, released within months of one another: in *Bull Durham* (1988), the actor was taciturn minor-league ballplayer Crash Davis, and in *Field of Dreams* he was Ray Kinsella, a farmer who constructed a baseball diamond in his Iowa cornfield when The Voice said "If you build it, he will come." His Hollywood clout amplified by the combined box-office success of these films enabled Costner to make his directing debut. With a minuscule budget of $18 million, Costner went off to the Black Hills of South Dakota to film the first Western epic that Hollywood had seen in years, a revisionist look at Indian-white relationships titled *Dances With Wolves* (1990). Detractors had a field day with this supposedly foredoomed project, labeling the film "Costner's Folly" and "Kevin's Gate." But he who laughs last. . . *Dances with Wolves* was not only one of 1990's biggest moneymakers but also that year's Academy Award-winning film; additionally, Costner copped an Oscar as Best Director. A curious costume epic *Robin Hood: Prince of Thieves* (1991) followed, with Costner as the world's first Oklahoma-accented Robin Hood; this, too, made money, though it seriously strained Costner's longtime friendship with the film's director, the notoriously erratic Kevin Reynolds. *The Bodyguard* (1992), an improbable concoction which teamed Costner with Whitney Houston, did so well at the box-office that it seemed the actor could do no wrong. But *A Perfect World* (1993), directed by Clint Eastwood and casting Costner against type as a half-psycho, half-benign prison escapee, was a major disappointment, even though Costner came through with one of his best performances. Unfortunately, Costner followed *Perfect World* with another cast-against-type failure, the 1994 sagebrush dud *Wyatt Earp*, which proved that even director Lawrence Kasdan can have his off days. Costner's most recent film *Waterworld* received an enormous amount of negative publicity prior to opening because it was way over budget and schedule, however, it opened to good critical reviews and so far has been enjoying box-office success. **Selected Works:** *JFK* (1991), *Untouchables* (1987), *The War* (1994)

# Joseph Cotten (Joseph Cheshire Cotten)

**Born:** May 15, 1905; Petersburg, VA
**Died:** February 6, 1994; Los Angeles, CA

**Years Active in the Industry:** by decade

| 10s | 20s | 30s | 40s | 50s | 60s | 70s | 80s | 90s |
|-----|-----|-----|-----|-----|-----|-----|-----|-----|
|     |     |     |     |     |     |     |     |     |

American actor Joseph Cotten trained at the Hickman School of Expression in Washington, D.C. Cotten was a member of Orson Welles' Mercury Theatre and went with him to Hollywood to co-star in *Citizen Kane* (1941). He then starred in Welles' ill-fated *The Magnificent Ambersons* and their joint collaboration *Journey Into Fear* (both 1942). Cotten continued on as a "thinking man's leading man" throughout the 1940s and early 50s. He was cast against type but to great effect as a bluebeard in Hitchcock's *Shadow of a*

*Doubt* (1943) and as Ingrid Bergman's savior in Cukor's *Gaslight* (1944). He appeared with Jennifer Jones four times, most notably in *Portrait of Jennie* (1948), which garnered him the best actor award at the Venice Film Festival. He again teamed with Welles for possibly his most memorable role in *The Third Man* (1949) and found steady work as a supporting player up and through the 1980s. He died of pneumonia on February 6, 1994. **Selected Works:** *Duel in the Sun* (1946), *Farmer's Daughter* (1947), *Petulia* (1968), *Since You Went Away* (1944), *Love Letters* (1945)

# Tom Courtenay

**Born:** February 25, 1937; Hull, Yorkshire, England

**Years Active in the Industry:** by decade

| 10s | 20s | 30s | 40s | 50s | 60s | 70s | 80s | 90s |
|-----|-----|-----|-----|-----|-----|-----|-----|-----|
|     |     |     |     |     |     |     |     |     |

Actor Tom Courtenay studied acting at the Royal Academy of Dramatic Arts before making his theatrical debut in the Old Vic production of *The Seagull* in 1960; in 1961 he took over Albert Finney's role in *Billy Liar*, a part he would later play in the film version. In his first British film, *The Loneliness of the Long Distance Runner* (1962), he made a big impression on audiences and critics alike. Courtenay went on to play numerous lead roles in American and British films, often as a misunderstood, underprivileged, nonconformist youth. He was nominated for a Best Supporting Actor Oscar for his work in *Doctor Zhivago* (1965) and for a Best Actor Oscar for *The Dresser* (1983). His screen career mysteriously came to a near-halt after 1971, but he continued to succeed as a stage actor, making his belated Broadway debut in 1977's *Otherwise Engaged*. He is married to stage actress Cheryl Kennedy. **Selected Works:** *Let Him Have It* (1991), *King and Country* (1964), *Last Butterfly* (1993)

# Jerome Cowan

**Born:** October 6, 1897; New York, NY
**Died:** January 24, 1972; Encino, CA

**Years Active in the Industry:** by decade

| 10s | 20s | 30s | 40s | 50s | 60s | 70s | 80s | 90s |
|-----|-----|-----|-----|-----|-----|-----|-----|-----|
|     |     |     |     |     |     |     |     |     |

From vaudeville and stock companies, actor Jerome Cowan graduated to Broadway in the now-forgotten farce *We've Gotta Have Money*. While starring in the 1935 Broadway hit *Boy Meets Girl*, Cowan was spotted by movie producer Sam Goldwyn, who cast (or miscast) Cowan as a sensitive Irish rebel in 1936's *Beloved Enemy*. Most of Cowan's subsequent films found him playing glib lawyers, shifty business executives, and jilted suitors. A longtime resident at Warner Bros., the pencil-moustached Cowan appeared in several substantial character parts from 1940 through 1949, notably the doomed private eye Miles Archer in *The Maltese Falcon*. Warners gave Cowan the opportunity to be a romantic leading man in two B films, *Crime By Night* (1942) and *Find the Blackmailer* (1943). As the years rolled on, Cowan's air of slightly unscrupulous urbanity gave way to respectability, and in this vein he was ideally suited for the role of Dagwood Bumstead's new boss Mr. Radcliffe in several installments of Columbia's *Blondie* series; he also scored in such flustered roles as the hapless district attorney in *Miracle on 34th Street*. Cowan briefly left Hollywood in 1950 to pursue more worthwhile roles on stage and TV; he starred in the Broadway play *My Three Angels* and was top-billed on the 1951 TV series *Not for Publication*. In his fifties and sixties, Cowan continued essaying roles calling for easily deflated dignity (e.g. The Three Stooges' *Have Rocket Will Travel* [1959] and Jerry Lewis' *Visit to a Small Planet* [1960]) and made regular supporting appearances on several TV series, among them *Valiant Lady*, *The Tab Hunter Show*, *Many Happy Returns,* and *Tycoon*. **Selected Works:** *Great Lie* (1941), *Hurricane* (1937), *Mr. Skeffington* (1944)

# Alex Cox

**Born:** December 15, 1954; Cheshire, England

**Years Active in the Industry:** by decade

| 10s | 20s | 30s | 40s | 50s | 60s | 70s | 80s | 90s |
|-----|-----|-----|-----|-----|-----|-----|-----|-----|
|     |     |     |     |     |     |     | ■   | ■   |

English director Alex Cox studied law at Oxford—at least until being deflected into theater through his participation in the University's drama department. Cox switched to a film studies program at University of Bristol, received a Fulbright scholarship, then traveled across the Big Pond to attend the UCLA film school. His plans to become the next Welles or Scorcese were muddied by several years' inactivity, during which time he took a job repossessing automobiles. Drawing from the experience, Cox made his feature-film directorial bow with the wildly inconsistent but very entertaining *Repo Man* (1984), which served as one of Emilio Estevez's first starring assignments. *Repo Man*'s musical score was drenched in punk-rock, a symbolic form of violent rebellion explored further in Cox's *Sid and Nancy* (1987), a fascinating if depressing chronicle of the life and death of "punk" musician Sid Vicious and groupie Nancy Spungen. Eventually Cox fell deeply in love with his own technique, turning out such wearisome exercises in self-indulgence as *Walker* (1987) and the barely released *Highway Patrolman* (1991).

# Courteney Cox

**Born:** June 15, 1964; Birmingham, AL

**Years Active in the Industry:** by decade

| 10s | 20s | 30s | 40s | 50s | 60s | 70s | 80s | 90s |
|-----|-----|-----|-----|-----|-----|-----|-----|-----|
|     |     |     |     |     |     |     | ■   | ■   |

At age 21, Alabama-born actress Courteney Cox made her series TV debut as a teenaged juvenile delinquent with a genius IQ

in the sci-fi series *Misfits of Science*. Both the series and Cox's role were soon forgotten, but she enjoyed a longer run starting in 1986 as Lauren Miller, Alex Keaton's (Michael J. Fox) girlfriend, on the popular sitcom *Family Ties*. Cox replaced Tracy Pollan, who left the series but married Fox in real life; in Cox's *own* real life she became the longtime companion of another Keaton, this one an actor whose first name is Michael. After appearing in several films, notably the Jim Carrey vehicle *Ace Ventura Pet Detective* (1994), Cox was cast as New York career woman/neatness freak Monica Geller on the instant-hit 1994 TV comedy *Friends*. **Selected Works:** *Blue Desert* (1991), *Curiosity Kills* (1990), *Mr. Destiny* (1990)

# Ronald Cox

**Born:** August 23, 1938; Cloudcroft, NM

**Years Active in the Industry:** by decade

| 10s | 20s | 30s | 40s | 50s | 60s | 70s | 80s | 90s |
|-----|-----|-----|-----|-----|-----|-----|-----|-----|
|     |     |     |     |     |     | ■   | ■   | ■   |

An alumnus of Eastern New Mexico University, American actor Ronny Cox received one of the best early film showcases an actor could ask for. In 1972, he was cast as one of the four unfortunate rafters in *Deliverance*; it was Cox who engaged in the celebrated "dueling banjos" sequence with enigmatic albino boy Hoyt J. Pollard. Two years later, Cox found himself in *Apple's Way*, a homey TV dramatic weekly described (often derogatorily) as a "modern *Waltons*." Most of his subsequent roles were in this benign, All-American vein—and then Cox shocked his followers by portraying Jerry Rubin in the 1975 PBS TV drama *The Trial of the Chicago Seven*. During this telecast, Cox became one of the first (if not *the* first) actors to mouth a now-familiar expletive of disgust on American television. As his physique thickened and his hairline thinned in the 1980s, Cox was much in demand in films as a corporate villain, notably in Paul Verhoeven's *Robocop* (1984) and *Total Recall* (1990). The flip side of this hard-nosed screen image was his portrayal of the apoplectic but scrupulously honest police chief in Eddie Murphy's *Beverly Hills Cop* films. **Selected Works:** *Bound for Glory* (1976), *When Hell Was in Session* (1982)

# Peter Coyote (Peter Cohon)

**Born:** 1942; Englewood, NJ

**Years Active in the Industry:** by decade

| 10s | 20s | 30s | 40s | 50s | 60s | 70s | 80s | 90s |
|-----|-----|-----|-----|-----|-----|-----|-----|-----|
|     |     |     |     |     |     |     | ■   | ■   |

There are several theories as to why Peter Cohon chose the stage name of Peter Coyote; for his part, the actor is reluctant to discuss an event that apparently was the end result of an evening's experimentation with controlled substances. In the late 1960s, Coyote quit his job as a dockworker to "turn on, tune in and drop out." With hair so long that he could sit on it (by his own admis-

sion), Coyote was a "fringie" with such varied organizations as the Grateful Dead and the Hell's Angels, and also worked for a while with a guerilla mime group. After years of deprivation, Coyote dropped back into society in 1975, accepting a job as a drama teacher at a public school. Rapidly approaching middle age, Coyote entered films with 1980's *Die Laughing*. Throughout the 1980s, he alternated between good guys, villains, and a vaguely defined stereotype known as "loser boy friends." As the vengeful public prosecutor in *The Jagged Edge* (1985), Coyote turns out *not* to be the film's principal heavy; even so, we leave the picture disliking his character more than anyone else's. Leading roles came his way in such films as *Exposure* (1991), but even here he could not completely escape an aura of slime (his ostensibly heroic character burrows through the seamy underside of Rio in search of a prostitute's murderer). One of Coyote's few unconditionally "nice" roles was as the enigmatic scientist Keys in the champion moneymaker *E.T.* (1982). **Selected Works:** *E.T.: The Extra-Terrestrial* (1982), *The Jagged Edge* (1985), *Keeper of the City* (1992), *Bitter Moon* (1994), *Kika* (1994)

# Larry "Buster" Crabbe (Clarence Lindon Crabbe)

**Born:** February 7, 1908; Oakland, CA
**Died:** 1983

**Years Active in the Industry:** by decade

| 10s | 20s | 30s | 40s | 50s | 60s | 70s | 80s | 90s |
|-----|-----|-----|-----|-----|-----|-----|-----|-----|
|     |     |     |     |     |     |     |     |     |

Athletic actor Buster Crabbe grew up in Hawaii, where he developed into a first-rate swimmer and athlete, going on to win the gold medal in 400-meter swimming at the 1932 Olympics (he broke the record held by another actor-athlete, Johnny Weissmuller). After the Olympics he found work in Hollywood playing Tarzan, branching out from this character to eventually play Flash Gordon, Billy the Kid, and Buck Rogers, among other action heroes. He became enormously popular with young audiences for his appearances in many serials and action flicks of the '30s and '40s, and ultimately starred in over 100 films. He also made Westerns (in the '40s he was teamed with sidekick Al "Fuzzy" St. John), and was on the list for Top Ten Western stars at the box office in 1936. Crabbe went on to star in the '50s TV series *Captain Gallant*, which also featured his son Cullen "Cuffy" Crabbe. He considerably slowed down his acting output in the '50s and '60s, becoming the

athletic director for a resort hotel in the Catskills and investing in the swimming pool business. He also authored *Energetics*, a book on physical fitness for people over 50. Crabbe returned to the screen once, for a large role in *The Alien Dead* (1980).

# Jeanne Crain

**Born:** May 25, 1925; Barstow, CA

**Years Active in the Industry:** by decade

| 10s | 20s | 30s | 40s | 50s | 60s | 70s | 80s | 90s |
|-----|-----|-----|-----|-----|-----|-----|-----|-----|
|     |     |     |     |     |     |     |     |     |

At age 16, Jeanne Crain won a beauty contest as "Miss Long Beach" and became a model; the next year she was named "Camera Girl of 1942," leading to contacts in Hollywood. She debuted onscreen in 1943 in *The Gang's All Here*, beginning a starring career that lasted through the 50s. She rose to prominence through her performance in Henry Hathaway's *Home in Indiana* (1944). Crain was frequently cast as the "girl next door," and was generally employed to be a "pretty face" in the midst of light films, but occasionally she got more serious roles, as in *Pinky* (1949) in which she played a black girl passing for white; for that performance she was nominated for a Best Actress Oscar, repeating a nomination she got for her role in *Margie* (1946). Her career waned in the '60s, but she continued to appear in films through the '70s. **Selected Works:** *Letter to Three Wives* (1949), *Leave Her to Heaven* (1946), *Model and the Marriage Broker* (1951)

# Frank Craven

**Born:** August 24, 1875; Boston, MA
**Died:** September 1, 1945; Beverly Hills, CA

**Years Active in the Industry:** by decade

| 10s | 20s | 30s | 40s | 50s | 60s | 70s | 80s | 90s |
|-----|-----|-----|-----|-----|-----|-----|-----|-----|
|     |     |     |     |     |     |     |     |     |

American actor/playwright Frank Craven enjoyed a long stage career as both performer and writer. As an actor, he specialized in wry middle-aged small town types; as a writer, he favored domestic comedies, usually centered around the tribulations of "normal" family life. Craven was so firmly locked into his particular style that he felt lost doing anything else. For several years during the silent film era, Craven had begged Harold Lloyd to allow him to sit in on the "gag sessions" for Lloyd's films, in order to contribute comedy ideas; after a particularly harrowing session with Lloyd's writers, who tossed gag ideas about at the tops of their voices, Craven admitted that slapstick wasn't his brand of humor and returned to the stage. Craven made his film bow in the 1928 "ethnic melting pot" drama *We Americans*, but when he was finally brought to Hollywood under contract to Fox in 1932, it was as a writer. One of Craven's best-known screenplays was for the Laurel and Hardy vehicle *Sons of the Desert* (1933), one of the comedy team's few feature films with a solid plot structure. Concentrating mainly on performing for most of his film career, Craven returned to Broadway in 1939 to play the Stage Manager in Thornton Wilder's Pulitzer Prize-winning *Our Town*. The actor was called upon to repeat the role in the 1940 film version, and thereafter most of his film roles were variations of the Stage Manager, complete with his ubiquitous pipe. Craven died in 1945 at age 70, shortly after completing his role in *Colonel Effingham's Raid* (1945). **Selected Works:** *State Fair* (1933)

# Wes Craven (Wesley Earl Craven)

**Born:** August 2, 1939; Cleveland, OH

**Years Active in the Industry:** by decade

| 10s | 20s | 30s | 40s | 50s | 60s | 70s | 80s | 90s |
|-----|-----|-----|-----|-----|-----|-----|-----|-----|
|     |     |     |     |     |     |     |     |     |

After earning an MA in Philosophy from Johns Hopkins University, American director Wes Craven taught for a while, then plunged into filmmaking as production assistant and editor for several "B" companies. His first directorial job was *Last House on the Left* (1972), a gruesome little effort that affected different people differently. Some viewers found this repellently staged "revenge for rape" story profound, citing the fact that Craven based the movie on Ingmar Bergman's *Virgin Spring*; others, including such mainstream commentators as Siskel, Ebert, and Maltin, have condemned *Last House on the Left* as utter excrement. No matter how one felt about Craven, one could not deny his power to manipulate his audience. *The Hills Have Eyes* (1972) again met with radically divided opinions—and made a fortune. With *Swamp Thing* (1982), Craven graduated to big budgets, and also revealed a wicked gift for comedy that we hadn't seen before. *Nightmare on Elm Street* (1984) was an equally effective blend of gore and grim humor which spawned several sequels and served to introduce the world to Freddy Krueger, vengeful spectre *par excellance*. Still a potent force in Hollywood horror into the 1990s, Craven has recently made yet another *Nightmare on Elm Street* sequel, *Wes Craven's New Nightmare* (1994), a Pirandellian affair in which Craven and *Nightmare* cast regulars Robert Englund, Heather Langenkamp, and John Saxon played "themselves"—as did Freddy Krueger! (Huh?) Craven has occasionally curbed his stomach-churning tendencies (though not his willingness to run viewers through an emotional wringer) with his

TV work, including selected episodes of the *Twilight Zone* revival of the mid-1980s. In 1989, Craven flummoxed his followers by producing a situation comedy (!), 1989's *The People Next Door*, all about a cartoonist who had the ability to imagine his drawings into existence (should this have been retitled *The Wes Craven Story*, or what?) **Selected Works:** *Freddy's Nightmares: Dreams That Kill* (1990), *Freddy's Nightmares: Freddy's Tricks and Treats* (1990), *Freddy's Nightmares: Lucky Stiff* (1990), *Freddy's Nightmares: No More Mr. Nice Guy* (1990), *People Under the Stairs* (1991)

# Broderick Crawford (William Broderick Crawford)

**Born:** December 9, 1911; Philadelphia, PA
**Died:** April 26, 1986; Rancho Mirage, CA

**Years Active in the Industry:** by decade

| 10s | 20s | 30s | 40s | 50s | 60s | 70s | 80s | 90s |
|-----|-----|-----|-----|-----|-----|-----|-----|-----|
|     |     |     |     |     |     |     |     |     |

Big, burly, broken-nosed leading man Broderick Crawford, the son of vaudevillian Lester Crawford and famed comedienne Helen Broderick, began as a vaudeville and radio performer before debuting on the London stage in 1932; following a stint on Broadway in 1935, he was signed by Goldwyn to a film contract and began appearing onscreen in minor roles. He had a great success portraying Lennie in John Steinbeck's *Of Mice and Men* on Broadway in 1937; despite this, in the movies he made over the next 12 years he was given unsubstantial roles requiring little acting skill. That string broke with his portrayal of ruthless politico Willie Stark in *All the King's Men* (1949), for which he won the Best Actor Oscar; the following year he played opposite Judy Holliday in *Born Yesterday* (1950), further demonstrating his skills as an actor. Nevertheless, throughout the rest of his career he tended to land tough-guy parts in conformance with his looks. One notable exception was his role as a swindler in Fellini's *Il Bidone* (1955), the last great film performance of his career. In the '60s he tended to make low-budget Westerns and adventure epics in Italy and Spain, but in the '70s he got some more substantial parts in American films, such as the title role in *The Private Files of J. Edgar Hoover* (1978). He was featured in three TV series, *Highway Patrol* (in which he achieved perhaps his greatest fame), *King of Diamonds*, and *The Interns*. **Selected Works:** *Beau Geste* (1939), *Not As a Stranger* (1955)

# Joan Crawford (Lucille Le Sueur)

**Born:** March 23, 1908; San Antonio, TX
**Died:** May 10, 1977; New York, NY

**Years Active in the Industry:** by decade

| 10s | 20s | 30s | 40s | 50s | 60s | 70s | 80s | 90s |
|-----|-----|-----|-----|-----|-----|-----|-----|-----|
|     |     |     |     |     |     |     |     |     |

Joan Crawford is the quintessential movie star, complete with humble beginnings and tumultuous personal life. With her broad shoulders and serious face, she was never considered a great beauty, nor a truly great actress, but the versatile and hardworking Crawford, whose career spans over 50 years during which she played the lead in more than 80 films, did possess a rare, genuine glamour that allowed her star to shine long after others had dimmed. Born Lucille Fay Le Sueur, the Texas-born Crawford worked as a laundress, a waitress, and a shop clerk before entering and subsequently winning a Charleston contest, appearing under the name Billie Cassin. Her win lead her to a modest dancing career in Detroit and Chicago nightclubs. While in a Broadway chorus line she was spotted by MGM executive Harry Rapf, who invited her to Hollywood and offered her a contract. To choose a screen name for her and to publicize their newest "star," the studio sponsored a nationwide contest. The newly named Crawford began in silent films; before long she had come to be an icon for "flapper"-era youth, rivaling Clara Bow. In her first talkies she tended to play working girls struggling through the Depression era in search of better lives. In the late '30s through the early '40s she became the epitome of Tinseltown glamour. But then she appeared in a series of flops and became considered "box office poison" and was released from her MGM contract in 1943. She came back strong with Warner Bros., re-establishing her superstar status by playing heroines of melodramas; in 1945 she won a Best Actress Oscar for her work in *Mildred Pierce*. By the '50s she was playing mature, sensual women often involved with younger men (usually creeps and scoundrels). In the early '60s her career took another turn when she appeared with Bette Davis, her former rival, in the surprise hit *Whatever Happened to Baby Jane* (1962), the first of a series of horror films she appeared in. Three of her four husbands were actors: Douglas Fairbanks, Jr., Franchot Tone, and Philip Terry. After the death of her fourth husband, a Pepsi-Cola executive, she became active as a board member and publicity executive for Pepsi. She authored two volumes of memoirs, *A Portrait of Joan* (1962) and *My Way of Life* (1971). After her death, her daughter Christina depicted her as a cruel, manipulative witch of a mother in the best-selling biography *Mommie Dearest* (1978). **Selected Works:** *Grand Hotel* (1932), *Humoresque* (1946), *Possessed* (1947), *What Ever Happened to Baby Jane?* (1962), *Sudden Fear* (1952)

# Richard Crenna

**Born:** November 30, 1926; Los Angeles, CA

**Years Active in the Industry:** by decade

| 10s | 20s | 30s | 40s | 50s | 60s | 70s | 80s | 90s |
|-----|-----|-----|-----|-----|-----|-----|-----|-----|
|     |     |     |     |     |     |     |     |     |

American actor Richard Crenna started out as a radio performer at age 11, demonstrating an astonishing range for one so young. The momentum of his career was unaffected by an army hitch and time spent earning an English degree at the University of Southern California. But even though he was by then in his twenties, Crenna found himself still playing adolescents, notably squeaky-voiced high schooler Walter Denton on the radio comedy *Our Miss Brooks*. That he was able to play characters of virtually any age was overlooked by movie and TV casting directors, who could see Crenna only in callow-juvenile roles. After making an excellent impression as ballplayer Daffy Dean in the 1953 film *Pride of St. Louis*, for example, Crenna wasn't cast in another film until the 1955 movie version of *Our Miss Brooks*—in which, at 29, he was Walter Denton once more. The following year, Crenna decided "to sorta let Walter Denton die," and took a decidedly mature role in the sleazy exploitation film *Over-Exposed* (1956). It was a fully grown Dick Crenna who took on the role of Luke McCoy on the Walter Brennan TV series *The Real McCoys*, which ran from 1957 through 1963 and which gave Crenna his first opportunities as a director. After *McCoys*, Crenna found himself facing potential career standstill again, since it seemed that now he was typed as the rubeish Luke McCoy. This time, however, the actor had impressed enough producers with his dogged work ethic and the range displayed in guest-star appearances. In 1964, Crenna was cast in a prestigious TV drama *For the People* as assistant DA David Koster, and though the program lasted only one season, Crenna was firmly established as a compelling dramatic actor. Still, and despite solid film performances in *The Sand Pebbles* (1966), *Body Heat* (1981), and *The Flamingo Kid* (1985), the actor has never completely escaped the spectre of Walter Denton. Crenna was able to conjure up the old adenoidal Denton voice on talk shows of the 1980s and 1990s, and in the action-film spoof *Hot Shots: Part Deux*, the actor, with an absolute straight face, portrayed Colonel Denton Walters! **Selected Works:** *Hot Shots! Part Deux* (1993), *Intruders* (1992), *Last Flight Out* (1990), *And the Sea Will Tell, Part 1* (1991), *Murder in Black and White* (1990)

# Michael Crichton (John Michael Crichton)

**Born:** October 24, 1942; Chicago, IL

**Years Active in the Industry:** by decade

| 10s | 20s | 30s | 40s | 50s | 60s | 70s | 80s | 90s |
|-----|-----|-----|-----|-----|-----|-----|-----|-----|
|     |     |     |     |     |     |     |     |     |

The son of an *Advertising Age* executive editor, Chicago-born Michael Crichton has become one of the most distinguished medical scholars in academic history. Recognized for his brilliance while a Harvard undergrad, Crichton moved on to Cambridge, where he taught anthropology. But Crichton's "guilty pleasure" was writing thriller novels, an activity he pursued under the nom de plume of John Lange (one of several pen names adopted by the fantastically prolific Crichton over the years). Under his own name, Crichton utilized his scientific and medical know-how to add credibility to his nail-biting best-sellers *The Andromeda Strain*, *The Terminal Man*, and *Jurassic Park*; each of these works resulted in high-grossing film adaptations—most notably *Jurassic Park*, which under the guidance of Steven Spielberg, became one of the biggest moneymakers of all time. In 1972, Crichton made his directing debut with a TV-movie adaptation of his own novel *Binary*. Subsequent Crichton-directed efforts have included *Westworld* (1973), *Coma* (1976), *The Great Train Robbery* (1978), and *Runaway* (1983). While most of his works have been universally popular, Crichton brewed up a storm of controversy with his 1991 novel *Rising Sun*, which was perceived in some circles to be a "Japanese basher" (the subsequent 1993 film version was considerably toned down). In 1994, Crichton returned to television as the creative force and executive producer of the top-rated NBC medical series *ER*. **Selected Works:** *Disclosure* (1994)

# Donald Crisp

**Born:** July 27, 1880; Aberfeldy, Perthshire, Scotland
**Died:** May 26, 1974; Los Angeles, CA

**Years Active in the Industry:** by decade

| 10s | 20s | 30s | 40s | 50s | 60s | 70s | 80s | 90s |
|-----|-----|-----|-----|-----|-----|-----|-----|-----|

"Was he ever young?" asked film historian Ted Sennett of venerable British actor Donald Crisp. The answer is, yes; while a mere lad of 26, Crisp, already a veteran of the Boer War, came to the U.S., where he toured in opera companies and did a bit of stage directing for producer-star George M. Cohan. Despite his imperious attitude toward "the flickers," Crisp was compelled by an empty wallet to go to work for D. W. Griffith at Biograph studios in 1910, functioning as both character actor and assistant director. Crisp played General Grant in Griffith's 1915 epic *Birth of a Nation*, and in later years the actor would claim that he directed some of the battle scenes as well, though the quality of the films Crisp actually did direct in the 1920s would seem to confirm that Griffith was the one and only "auteur" on *Birth*. As his acting career prospered in the 1920s, 1930s and 1940s—most frequently in patriarch or priest roles—Crisp supplemented his considerable income with wise real-estate investments. At one point, he was a board member of the Bank of America, where his notorious frugality did not endear him with independent movie producers looking for financing. Crisp's lengthy movie career as a "professional oldster" concluded in 1963 with a sizable role in *Spencer's Mountain*. **Selected Works:** *Charge of the Light Brigade* (1936), *How Green Was My Valley* (1941), *Lassie Come Home* (1943), *Private Lives of Elizabeth and Essex* (1939), *Sea Hawk* (1940)

# John Cromwell (Elwood Dager Cromwell)

**Born:** December 23, 1888; Toledo, OH
**Died:** September 26, 1979; Santa Barbara, CA

**Years Active in the Industry:** by decade

| 10s | 20s | 30s | 40s | 50s | 60s | 70s | 80s | 90s |
|-----|-----|-----|-----|-----|-----|-----|-----|-----|

American director John Cromwell spent the first phase of his career as a romantic stage leading man. As a theatrical director, he was spirited to Hollywood to "show" silent filmmakers how to do things right, but his cinematic flair in such early pictures as *The Racket* (1928), *Close Harmony* (1929), and *Tom Sawyer* (1931) indicate that Cromwell learned a lot from the Hollywood veterans. Film critic Andrew Sarris has summed up Cromwell's career as "cherchez la femme," meaning that he seemed to have a knack for drawing first-rate performances out of actresses. Directorial assignments like *Ann Vickers* (1933) starring Irene Dunne, *Of Human Bondage* (1934) starring Bette Davis, and *I Dream Too Much* (1935) starring Opera diva Lily Pons would appear to bear out Sarris's typecasting of Cromwell. Like most such auteurist theories, however, Sarris's assessment was limited: Cromwell was also capable of turning out male-dominated historical dramas like *Prisoner of Zenda* (1937) and *Abe Lincoln in Illinois* (1940). Cromwell was additionally one of the prime contributors to the film noir genre, as witnessed by *Dead Reckoning* (1947), *Night Song* (1947), and *Caged* (1950); he was among *Dead Reckoning* star Humphrey Bogart's favorite directors. Long out of films, Cromwell made a return as an actor in his eighties, becoming one of director Robert Altman's inner circle in the films *Three Women* (1977) and *A Wedding* (1978). Despite his many cinematic accomplishments, Cromwell wasn't very fond of any of his films, and was given to responding to the queries of movie buffs over this or that movie by turning his thumbs down or holding his nose! **Selected Works:** *Algiers* (1938)

# David Cronenberg

**Born:** May 15, 1943; Toronto, Ontario, Canada

**Years Active in the Industry:** by decade

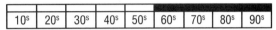

| 10s | 20s | 30s | 40s | 50s | 60s | 70s | 80s | 90s |
|-----|-----|-----|-----|-----|-----|-----|-----|-----|

A prime candidate for the title of Duke of Disgusting, Canadian director/writer David Cronenberg studied for a literature degree at the University of Toronto, winning a writing prize his first year at college. After a few student film productions, Cronenberg made his first feature, *Stereo*, in 1969. Most of his subsequent films were grotesque low-budget horrors which played the drive-in circuit. The director entered the realm of Cult with *The Brood* (1978), which had among its highlights a scene in which new mother Samantha Eggar eats her own afterbirth. Repulsive, true, but Cronenberg was undeniably talented and his films were com-

pelling, even when difficult to watch. *Scanners* (1981) gained fame for its close-up scene in which a human head explodes, while *Videodrome* (1982), a bloody study of how excessively violent TV videos could brainwash unwary viewers, was so potent that it was heavily edited in the United Kingdom after an outbreak of bloody real-life incidents in that country which were allegedly tied in with the viewing of gory horror videos. *Dead Zone* (1983), based on a Stephen King story, was Cronenberg's most disciplined film to date; this story of a man able to read the future by touching people had bloody and apocalyptic special effects aplenty, but all were crucial to the plotline. Cronenberg's 1985 remake of the 1959 chiller *The Fly* was one of the few instances wherein the gratuitous horror vignettes common to the 1980s actually improved upon a more restrained original. *Dead Ringers* (1988) was a haunting tale of malevolent twin brothers, featuring seamless split screen work involving star (or perhaps "stars") Jeremy Irons. With *Naked Lunch* (1992), based upon William Burroughs' semi-autobiographical novel about a drug-and-booze-obsessed writer, Cronenberg gained more critical attention than his previous works, though even his staunchest defenders were appalled by the scenes of typewriters turning into copulating cockroaches. That Cronenberg could turn out a work of sedate subtlety was proven with 1993's *M. Butterfly*, the "believe it or not" true story about a male Chinese opera singer who disguised himself as a woman so successfully that even his male lover was hoodwinked!

# Hume Cronyn

**Born:** July 18, 1911; London, Ontario, Canada

**Years Active in the Industry:** by decade

| 10s | 20s | 30s | 40s | 50s | 60s | 70s | 80s | 90s |
|-----|-----|-----|-----|-----|-----|-----|-----|-----|
|     |     |     |     |     |     |     |     |     |

Canadian-born actor Hume Cronyn was the son of a well-known Ontario politician. At his father's insistence, young Cronyn studied law at McGill University, but had already been hooked by the aroma of greasepaint; he made his stage bow with the Montreal Repertory Company at 19, while still a student. After taking classes at the American Academy of Dramatic Arts and working with regional companies in Washington D.C. and Virginia, Cronyn made it to Broadway in 1934. His first important role was as the imbibing, jingle-writing hero of *Three Men on a Horse*, directed and cowritten by George Abbott. He remained with Abbott to work in

*Room Service* and *Boy Meets Girl*—not only establishing himself as a versatile stage actor but also gleaning a lifelong appreciation of strict artistic discipline from the authoritarian Mr. Abbott. Cronyn went from one taskmaster to another when he made his film debut in Alfred Hitchcock's *Shadow of a Doubt*. The 32-year-old Cronyn quietly stole several scenes in the film as a fiftyish mystery-novel fanatic. Cronyn would remain beholden to Hitchcock for the rest of his career: He acted in Hitch's *Lifeboat* (1944) and worked several times thereafter on the director's TV series; he adapted the stage play *Rope* and the novel *Under Capricorn* for Hitchcock's film adaptations; and he sprang to the late director's defense when a scabrous biography of Hitchcock was published in the mid-1980s. Though well versed in Shakespeare and Moliere on stage, Cronyn was often limited to unpleasant, weasely, and sometimes sadistic characters in films; one of his nastiest portrayals was as the Hitleresque prison guard Munsey in *Brute Force* (1947). A somewhat less hissable Cronyn appeared in *The Green Years* (1946), wherein he portrayed the father of his real-life wife Jessica Tandy, who was in fact two years older than he. Cronyn had married Tandy in 1942, a union that was to last until the actress' death in 1994. They worked together often on stage (*The Fourposter*, *The Gin Game*) and in films (*Batteries Not Included*), and delighted in giving joint interviews where they'd confound and misdirect the interviewer; their daughter, Tandy Cronyn, matured into a fine actress in her own right. Seemingly indefatigable despite health problems and the loss of one eye, Cronyn remained gloriously active in films, television and stage into the 1990s, encapsulating many of his experiences in his breezy autobiography *A Terrible Liar*. **Selected Works:** *Age Old Friends* (1989), *Cocoon* (1985), *Seventh Cross* (1944), *World According to Garp* (1982), *Pelican Brief* (1993)

# Bing Crosby (Harry Lillis Crosby)

**Born:** May 2, 1901; Tacoma, WA
**Died:** October 14, 1977; outside Madrid, Spain

**Years Active in the Industry:** by decade

| 10s | 20s | 30s | 40s | 50s | 60s | 70s | 80s | 90s |
|-----|-----|-----|-----|-----|-----|-----|-----|-----|
|     |     |     |     |     |     |     |     |     |

American actor/singer Bing Crosby acquired his nickname as a child in Washington State. As the legend goes, little Harry Lillis Crosby's favorite comic strip was "The Bingville Bungle," in which the leading character was called Bingo. After that the boy was "Bingo Crosby" until the "O" dropped out as he got older. An eternally restless youth, Crosby tried studying law at Gonzaga University, but spent more time as a drummer and singer in a Spokane band. Crosby and his pal Al Rinker worked up a musical act, and were later joined by Harris Barris. As the Rhythm Boys, the three young entertainers were hired by bandleader Paul Whiteman, who featured them in his nightclub appearances and in his film debut, *The King of Jazz* (1930). Crosby was undeniably talented but also undeniably undisciplined; warned several times by Whiteman to

cut down his heavy drinking, Bing managed to alienate his boss by being arrested on a drunk driving charge. The massive booze intake also affected Crosby's voice, lowering it from a tenor to his more familiar "boo-boo-boo-boo" baritone. Crosby's intemperate behavior got him and the Rhythm Boys blacklisted from several important professional gigs. Bing managed to score on radio in 1931, and a series of two-reel comedies made for Mack Sennett helped him launch a screen career. During this period he married singer Dixie Lee, the mother of his sons Gary, Dennis, Philip, and Lindsay. Crosby's starring feature debut was *The Big Broadcast of 1932*, where he played himself—or at least the smooth, casual "self" that the public knew. As one of Paramount's most popular stars of the 1930s, Crosby began cultivating the public image of an easygoing, golf-happy regular guy, generous contributor to charities, devoted husband, father, and friend. That this image was at odds with the truth has been thoroughly documented elsewhere in the years after Crosby's death, with "shocking" exposés of Bing's womanizing, his drinking (which admittedly decreased in the late 1930s, even as his wife descended into alcoholism), his calculated cruelties to his sons, his aloofness towards friends, and his rude demeanor when approached by fans. Oddly, many of these stories were in circulation while Crosby was alive; it's simply that the public had made Bing an icon, and didn't want to hear anything bad about him. In 1940, Crosby made the first of several appearances with his golfing buddy Bob Hope, resulting in seven "Road" pictures which seem as fresh today as they did 50 years ago thanks to the stars' improvisational style and inveterate ad-libbing. Another milestone occurred in 1944 when director Leo McCarey asked Crosby to play a priest in an upcoming film. Crosby, who despite his character blemishes was a devout Catholic, refused at first on the grounds that his playing a man of the cloth would be bad taste. But McCarey persisted, and Crosby ended up collecting an Academy Award for his performance in *Going My Way* (1944). Bing ushered in a new technological era a few years later when he signed a contract to appear on a weekly ABC variety show, on the proviso that it not be live but tape-recorded—a first in network radio—so that Crosby could spend more time on the golf course. In 1952, Bing's wife Dixie died; despite his philandering he was devastated, and dropped out of moviemaking for a full year. His life took an upswing when he married young actress Kathryn Grant in 1957, then raised a whole new family with his new wife—and as rough as he'd been on his older sons, he was loving and generous to his younger children. His film roles were few in the 1960s, but Bing was a television fixture in these years, and could be counted on each Yuletide to appear on just about everyone's program

singing his signature tune, "White Christmas." Burdened by life-threatening illnesses in the mid-1970s, Crosby nonetheless embarked on singing tours throughout the world, surviving even a dangerous fall into an orchestra pit. When death finally came to Crosby in the form of a heart attack in 1977, it was on a golf course in Spain, just as Bing had finished 18 holes. As banal as this comment is, one can't help but feel that this is the precise manner in which Crosby would have wanted to go. **Selected Works:** *Bells of St. Mary's* (1945), *Country Girl* (1954), *Holiday Inn* (1942), *Star Spangled Rhythm* (1942)

# Tom Cruise (Thomas Cruise Mapother IV)

**Born:** July 3, 1962; Syracuse, NY

**Years Active in the Industry:** by decade

| 10s | 20s | 30s | 40s | 50s | 60s | 70s | 80s | 90s |
|-----|-----|-----|-----|-----|-----|-----|-----|-----|
|     |     |     |     |     |     |     | ■  |     |

American actor Tom Cruise led a peripatetic existence in childhood, moving from town to town with his rootless family. A high school wrestler, Cruise went into acting after being sidelined

by a knee injury. This new activity served a dual purpose: Performing satiated Cruise's need for attention, while the memorization aspect of acting helped him come to grips with his dyslexia. Moving to New York in 1980, Cruise held down odd jobs until getting his first movie break in *Endless Love* (1981). Cruise's first big hit was *Risky Business* (1982) in which he entered movie-trivia heaven with the scene wherein he celebrates his parent's absence by dancing around the living room in his underwear. The Hollywood press corps began touting Cruise as one of the "Brat Pack," a group of twenty-something young actors that seemed on the verge of taking over the movie industry in the early 1980s. But Cruise chose not to play the sort of teen-angst roles that the other Bratpackers specialized in—a wise decision, in that he has sustained his stardom while many of his contemporaries have fallen by the wayside or retreated into direct-to-video cheapies. *Top Gun* (1985) established Cruise as an "action" star, but again he refused to be pigeonholed, and followed up *Top Gun* with a solid characterization as a fledgling pool shark in *The Color of Money* (1986), the film that earned costar Paul Newman an Academy Award. In 1988, Cruise took on his most challenging assignment to date as the brother of autistic savant Dustin Hoffman in *Rain Man*. "Old" Hollywood chose to give all the credit for that film's success to Hoffman, but a closer look at *Rain Man* proves that Cruise is the true central character in the film, the one who "grows" in humanity and maturity while Hoffman's character, though brilliantly portrayed, remains the same. Finally, Cruise was given an opportunity to carry a major dramatic film without an older established star in tow. As physically challenged Vietnam vet Ron Kovic in *Born on the Fourth of July* (1989), Cruise delivered a performance that seemed to make the Oscar a foregone conclusion—except that Daniel Day-Lewis copped the honor for *his* portrayal of a disabled man in *My Left Foot* (1989). Cruise's bankability faltered a bit with the expensive disappointment *Far and Away* (1990) (though it did give him a chance to costar with his wife Nicole Kidman), but with *A Few Good Men* (1992) Cruise was back in form; again, however the critical plaudits went to his veteran costar, in this instance Jack Nicholson, whose performance was as excessive as Cruise's was expertly restrained. Most recently Cruise appeared as the vampire Lestat in the long-delayed filmization of the Anne Rice novel *Interview with the Vampire*. We take pleasure in reporting that, although she was violently opposed to Cruise's casting, Anne Rice has reversed her decision upon seeing the actor's performance. It's a safe bet that Cruise will continue to be a name to contend with into the next century—and if the fates are kind, he'll get that Oscar. **Selected Works:** *Days of Thunder* (1990), *The Firm* (1993), *Interview with the Vampire* (1994)

# Jon Cryer

**Born:** April 16, 1965; New York, NY

**Years Active in the Industry:** by decade

| 10s | 20s | 30s | 40s | 50s | 60s | 70s | 80s | 90s |
|-----|-----|-----|-----|-----|-----|-----|-----|-----|
|     |     |     |     |     |     |     |     |     |

The son of American actors David and Gretchen Cryer, Jon Cryer received his own theatrical training at London's Royal Academy of Dramatic Arts. Cryer made his film debut when he was not yet twenty in *No Small Affair* (1984). As Molly Ringwald's misfit admirer in *Pretty in Pink* (1986), Cryer stole the show, no mean feat in a film that contains a bravura performance from veteran Harry Dean Stanton. And in *Hot Shots* (1991), Cryer distinguished himself in an ensemble of formidable comic talents with his performance as Jim "Washout" Pfaffenbach, a fearless air ace suffering from "walleye vision." Cryer also starred on TV as an inexperienced talent agent in the 1990 sitcom *The Fabulous Teddy Z.* **Selected Works:** *Noon Wine* (1984), *Penn & Teller Get Killed* (1990), *Heads* (1994)

# Billy Crystal

**Born:** March 14, 1947; Long Island, NY

**Years Active in the Industry:** by decade

| 10s | 20s | 30s | 40s | 50s | 60s | 70s | 80s | 90s |
|-----|-----|-----|-----|-----|-----|-----|-----|-----|
|     |     |     |     |     |     |     |     |     |

The son of a jazz concert producer, American actor/director Billy Crystal grew up in the company of such music legends as Billie Holliday, Pee Wee Russell, and Eddy Condon. His mind made up by age 5, Crystal knew he wanted to become a performer—not in music but in baseball or comedy. As he later explained to *TV GUIDE*, Crystal chose comedy "because God made me short"—though from all reports he is one of the best ballplayers in show business. Learning how to make people laugh by studying the works of past masters Laurel and Hardy, Ernie Kovacs, and Jonathan Winters, Crystal began making the club rounds at 16. He was sidetracked briefly by New York University's film school, where he studied to be a director under Martin Scorsese, but upon graduation it was back to comedy when Crystal formed his own troupe, 3's Company. On his own, Crystal developed into an "observational" comic, his humor based on his own experiences and the collective experiences of his audience. He came to media attention via his impression of Howard Cosell interviewing Muhammad Ali. After doing time as an opening act for such musicians as Barry Manilow, Crystal struck out for Hollywood, in hopes of finding regular work on a TV series. In 1977, Crystal was hired to play the gay character Jodie Dallas on *Soap*. Though many people expected the performer to be typecast in this sort of part, Crystal transcended the "sissy" stereotype, making the character so three-dimensional that audiences and potential employers were fully aware that there was more to Crystal's talent than what they saw in Jodie. Thanks to *Soap*, Crystal became and remained a headliner, and in 1978 had his first crack at movie stardom as a pregnant man in *Rabbit Test*. The movie wound up as much of a stiff as that rabbit, but Crystal's star had not been eclipsed by the experience; he was even entrusted with a dramatic role in the 1980 TV movie *Enola Gay*. His career accelerating with comedy records, choice club dates, regular appearances on *Saturday Night Live,* and TV guest shots, Crystal had a more successful stab at the movies in such films as *This is Spinal Tap* (1984), *The Princess Bride* (1987), *Throw Momma From the Train* (1987), and *When Harry Met Sally* (1989). Riding high after a memorable emceeing stint at the Oscar ceremony, Crystal executive produced and starred in his most successful film project to date, an uproarious middle-age-angst comedy called *City Slickers* (1991). In 1992, the actor mounted his most ambitious film endeavor, *Mr. Saturday Night,* the bittersweet chronicle of a self-destructive comedian. The film had great potential (as indicated by the outtakes contained in its videocassette version), but the end result was an exercise in repetitive self-indulgence, and it died at the box office. The following year, Crystal hosted the Oscar awards for the last time, a strained performance that seemed drenched in flop-sweat. But Crystal has given every indication of learning from his career missteps, and as of this writing his fans are anxiously waiting for the movie or TV project that will prove to be Crystal's healthy recovery.

# George Cukor (George Dewey Cukor)

**Born:** July 7, 1899; New York, NY
**Died:** Janurary 24, 1983; Hollywood, CA

**Years Active in the Industry:** by decade

| 10s | 20s | 30s | 40s | 50s | 60s | 70s | 80s | 90s |
|-----|-----|-----|-----|-----|-----|-----|-----|-----|

A successful stage director in New York by the late 1920s, Cukor began working in films as a dialogue director, his credits including *All Quiet On The Western Front*. In 1930 he co-directed his first features: *Grumpy* with Cyril Gardner, *The Virtuous Sin* with Louis Gasnier, and *The Royal Family Of Broadway* with Gardner. Cukor had his solo debut the following year, directing Tallulah Bankhead in *Tarnished Lady*. For the next fifty years he'd show a flair for bringing out the best in actors, particularly women. That specialty could work against him, as when he was removed from *Gone With The Wind* at the insistence of Clark Gable. But it defined his best work, starting in 1932 with Katharine Hepburn's first film, *A Bill Of Divorcement*; Cukor also directed her idiosyncratic 1930s performances in *Little Women*, *Sylvia Scarlett*, and *Holiday*. In that decade he also made the all-star comedies *Dinner At Eight* and *The Women*; the prestigious adaptations *David Copperfield* and *Romeo And Juliet*; and Greta Garbo's iconic *Camille*. In the 1940s he made the award-winning dramas *Gaslight* and *A Double Life*, as well as the classic comedies *The Philadelphia Story* and *Adam's Rib*. Comedy remained his forte in the '50s, with *Born Yesterday* and *Pat And Mike*. One of Cukor's finest films was the 1954 musical *A Star Is Born* with Judy Garland and James Mason (despite its having been cut to ribbons by the studio). A musical was also his biggest hit of the '60s: *My Fair Lady*. In the 1970s he reunited with Katharine Hepburn for the television films *Love Among The Ruins* and *The Corn Is Green*.

# Macaulay Culkin

**Born:** August 26, 1980; New York, NY

**Years Active in the Industry:** by decade

| 10s | 20s | 30s | 40s | 50s | 60s | 70s | 80s | 90s |
|-----|-----|-----|-----|-----|-----|-----|-----|-----|

The most successful child performer since Shirley Temple (Mickey Rooney wasn't a star until his teen years), Macaulay Culkin first stepped on a New York stage at the age of four. Extensively trained for his craft, including a stint with Balanchine's School of the American Ballet, young "Mack" became a familiar TV-commercial face and was spotlighted in several film supporting roles, the best of which was as John Candy's inquisitive nephew in *Uncle Buck* (1989). After appearing in a Michael Jackson video, Mack became a regular guest at Jackson's lavish Wonderland estate (back when there were no dark implications attached to such a friendship). After an unbilled cameo in *Jacob's Ladder* (1990), he was cast as the preteen protagonist of *Home Alone* (1990), a Three Stooge-ish combo of violent slapstick and sappy sentiment that brought in enough at the box office to feed a Third World nation. With *Home Alone*, Culkin became the highest-paid child actor of all time, and one of the few under-13 performers that could be counted on to "open" a picture. His career was at this time under the tight control of his father Kit, an erstwhile actor who also managed the careers of Mack's younger, equally photogenic siblings. Story upon story began to emerge from Tinseltown concerning Kit Culkin's dictatorial on-set behavior, which ranged from vetoing directors in mid-production to demanding that Kevin Kline's narration be removed from Mack's 1993 film version of *The Nutcracker* (it wasn't). Meanwhile, Mack's box office appeal began waning, partly because of the indifferent response to pedestrian vehicles like *The Good Son* (1992), *Getting Even With Dad* (1993) and *Richie Rich* (1994), but chiefly because Mack was outgrowing his cuteness and spontaneity. In June of 1995, Macaulay Culkin's mother went to court to remove the boy from Kit's custody, insisting that Culkin Senior's contentiousness was ruining the boy's chances of revitalizing his career. **Selected Works:** *Home Alone 2: Lost in New York* (1992), *My Girl* (1991), *Only the Lonely* (1991)

# Bob Cummings

**Born:** July 9, 1908; Joplin, MO
**Died:** December 2, 1990; Woodland Hills, CA

**Years Active in the Industry:** by decade

| 10s | 20s | 30s | 40s | 50s | 60s | 70s | 80s | 90s |
|-----|-----|-----|-----|-----|-----|-----|-----|-----|

American actor Bob Cummings' mother was a minister and his father a doctor. Cummings studied for an engineer's degree at several colleges before concentrating his energies at the American School of Dramatic Arts. After returning from a trip to England, he became possessed with the notion that he could best conquer Hollywood if he passed himself off as a British actor, so for a brief uncomfortable period he called himself Blade Stanhope Conway. The best he could get was an extra part in Laurel and Hardy's *Sons of the Desert* (1933) (there's someone who looks like Cummings in the scene at the Honolulu Steamship Company); after that, he renamed himself Brice Hutchens, under which name he played on Broadway with a magic act in *Ziegfeld Follies of 1934*. As plain old Robert Cummings, the actor made his film debut in Paramount's *So Red the Rose* (1935), in which he was killed off in the Civil War before the first reel was over. He finally got a meaty hysteria scene as a condemned prisoner in *The Accusing Finger* (1936)—but thereafter played almost nothing but comedy at Paramount. Stronger dramatic roles came Cummings' way in *Kings Row* (1941) and Hitchcock's *Saboteur* (1942), though these performances don't stand up very well today (in fact, Cummings was not the first choice for either of these, his best known 1940s films). By the early 1950s, the formerly callow Cummings had matured enough to be convincing as the "other man" in the Hitchcock thriller *Dial M for Murder* (1954), and in the difficult role of the compassionate Juror Number 8 in the original 1955 TV production of *Twelve Angry Men*. He also gained valuable off-camera prestige as an officer in the Air Force Reserves (he'd been a licensed pilot since age 17). Still, Cummings' main reputation in this decade rested on two lighthearted TV situation comedies: *My Hero*, which lasted 39 episodes in 1952, and the more famous *Bob Cummings Show*, a.k.a. *Love That Bob*, which ran from 1955 through 1958. Playing glamour photographer Bob Collins in the latter series, Cummings perpetuated public TV reputation as an eternally youthful ladies' man (though the biggest laughs went to supporting actress Ann B. Davis as "Schultzy"). Newspaper and magazine articles of the period made much of Cummings' seeming agelessness, which the actor chalked up to careful dieting, plenty of vitamins and exercise. That anyone would find it unusual that a 50-year-old man could retain his looks and sex appeal is astonishing in these days of such over-50 movie idols as Harrison Ford and Sean Connery, but such was the state of press agentry in the *Love That Bob* days. Two later TV series didn't do so well for Cummings, nor did his performances in such negligible 1960s films as *The Carpetbaggers* (1963); still, critics would marvel at how well the now sixtyish actor was "holding up." Unfortunately, Cummings fell victim to Parkinson's disease in the 1980s, and the once virile actor deteriorated rapidly both in mind and body before his death at age 82. In his prime, however, Cummings was one of those rare film actors who managed to retain his fame and popularity even though he made relatively few films of importance.

# Dean Cundey

**Born:** California

**Years Active in the Industry:** by decade

| 10s | 20s | 30s | 40s | 50s | 60s | 70s | 80s | 90s |
|-----|-----|-----|-----|-----|-----|-----|-----|-----|
|     |     |     |     |     |     | ■   | ■   | ■   |

Cinematographer Dean Cundy may well be a household name someday; for the moment, he is among those unsung master photographers whose names appear parenthetically next to the names of their more celebrated directors. Cundy's first feature credit was *Where the Red Fern Grows* (1974). Thereafter, he worked on such John Carpenter films as *Halloween* (1978), *The Fog* (1980) and *The Thing* (1981). Few films have so successfully captured the wet, overgrown ambience of central America as have the Cundy-lensed *Romancing the Stone* (1984), directed by Robert Zemeckis. One year later, Cundy successfully coordinated flashy special effects with two vastly different time-frames (the 1950s and the 1980s) in Zemeckis' *Back to the Future*. Cundy's prowess at seamlessly melding live action with laboratory effects prompted Zemeckis to re-engage Cundy for the landmark live/cartoon combo *Who Framed Roger Rabbit?*, which earned Cundy an Academy Award nomination. As late as 1993, Cundy was still convincingly juggling reality with computer-generated artifice in *Jurassic Park*. **Selected Works:** *Back to the Future, Part 1* (1985), *Back to the Future, Part 3* (1990), *Death Becomes Her* (1992), *Hook* (1991)

# Tim Curry

**Born:** April 19, 1946; Cheshire, England

**Years Active in the Industry:** by decade

| 10s | 20s | 30s | 40s | 50s | 60s | 70s | 80s | 90s |
|-----|-----|-----|-----|-----|-----|-----|-----|-----|
|     |     |     |     |     |     | ■   | ■   | ■   |

For several years, the name of British actor Tim Curry was known only to the privileged few who'd seen his performance as transvestite mad scientist Dr. Frank N. Furter in the stage and screen versions of *The Rocky Horror Picture Show*. By one of those wondrous quirks of fate, the 1975 *Rocky Horror* film was resuscitated from its disappointing initial run and became the archetypal "midnight movie"; for nearly two decades the Faithful have lined up each weekend evening in front of theatres playing *Rocky Horror* in bizarre costumes and makeup, toting toilet paper and toast (suitable for throwing at the screen). Unlike these fans, Curry was not content to relive his past triumphs, but moved ahead to such prestige assignments as the role of Mozart in the Broadway production of *Amadeus* and the part of William Shakespeare in a TV movie biography. A polished farceur, Curry was seen at his best in comedy film roles, notably the repressed music teacher in *Oscar* (1991) and the supercilious concierge in *Home Alone 2: Lost in New York* (1992). But audiences must have their villains, and Curry has aimed to please in such insidious roles as Cardinal Richelieu in the 1993 *Three Musketeers* (possibly the most lascivious Richelieu ever—so much so that Milady DeWinter pulls out a knife and threatens to "change his religion".) Curry's heart remained in the theatre, and for an unfortunately short period in the early 1990s he excelled in the Peter O'Toole role in a musical stage version of the 1982 film *My Favorite Year*. He has also contributed his vocal talents to such animated cartoon series as *Peter Pan and the Pirates*, winning an Emmy for his con brio portrayal of Captain Hook. Curry's reputation preceded him when he was hired to give voice to a nasty character on Hanna-Barbera's *Paddington Bear* cartoon series in 1988; the character's name was Mr. Curry! **Selected Works:** *Hunt for Red October* (1990), *Passed Away* (1992), *Shadow* (1994)

# Jamie Lee Curtis

**Born:** November 22, 1958; Los Angeles, CA

**Years Active in the Industry:** by decade

| 10s | 20s | 30s | 40s | 50s | 60s | 70s | 80s | 90s |
|-----|-----|-----|-----|-----|-----|-----|-----|-----|
|     |     |     |     |     |     |     |     |     |

The daughter of film stars Tony Curtis and Janet Leigh, American actress Jamie Lee Curtis launched her film career as a "scream queen." After a nondescript supporting role on the TV  series *Operation Petticoat*, Curtis played the straightlaced teenage babysitter imperiled by an unknown slasher in *Halloween* (1978). Upon appearing in the sequel of this film and in such spookers as *The Fog* (1980) and *Prom Night* (1980), she seemed in danger of being limited to bloodspattered horror films. But she wasn't about to be typed this early in the game. With a meaty secondary role as a prostitute—with several well-publicized nude scenes—in the big-budget comedy *Trading Places* (1983), Curtis made the transition from imperiled teen type to knowing adult with nary a hitch. The actress didn't exactly have a string of box-office smashes after that (did anyone see *Perfect* [1985]?), but she was always worth watching even when the films weren't. And when the good parts did come along, notably her roles in *A Fish Called Wanda* (1987) and *My Girl* (1991), she proved she was an actress of range and stature, and not just another "movie star's kid". Taking a potentially humiliating role as the unknowing wife of a secret agent in the megabucks Schwartzenegger adventure *True Lies* (1994), Curtis delivered a sparkling performance, emerging as the only truly likable character in a very loud and extremely misogynistic melodrama. In private life, Curtis is married to actor/writer Christopher Guest. **Selected Works:** *Blue Steel* (1990), *Forever Young* (1992), *Queens Logic* (1991), *Mother's Boys* (1994)

# Tony Curtis (Bernard Schwartz)

**Born:** June 3, 1925; Bronx, NY

**Years Active in the Industry:** by decade

| 10s | 20s | 30s | 40s | 50s | 60s | 70s | 80s | 90s |
|-----|-----|-----|-----|-----|-----|-----|-----|-----|
|     |     |     |     |     |     |     |     |     |

Good-looking, curly-haired leading man with a Bronx accent, Tony Curtis, born to an immigrant tailor, grew up in poverty and by age 11 was a member of a notorious street gang. He served with the Navy in World War II, getting injured in Guam. After the war he attended CCNY and studied drama at the Dramatic Workshop in New York. Curtis began acting professionally on the Catskills Mountains "Borscht Circuit," touring with a stock company, and did some work off-Broadway. After he was signed to a contract with Universal in 1949, his career quickly took off with the help of both the studio's publicity machine (Universal felt he had star quality) and also thousands of pieces of fan mail from adoring female viewers, most of them "bobby soxers". At first Curtis was considered just a teen idol with a hint of delinquency, and typecast as swashbuckling heroes, in 1957 he stunned critics with his excellent performance in *The Sweet Smell of Success*, in which he played the nervous, energetic, unprincipled press agent Sidney Falco. From there he continued making more serious films and soon was considered a top-notch actor as well as a star. In 1958 he received a Best Actor Oscar nomination for his work in *The Defiant Ones*. His comedic performance as a cross-dressed musician in *Some Like it Hot* (1959) led him to get lighter roles in the '60s, along with his usual dramatic ones. After 1975, he tended to appear in poor, unmemorable films. Two of his three marriages were to actresses: Janet Leigh (who gave birth to his daughter, actress Jamie Lee Curtis) and Christine Kauffmann. He starred in the early '70s TV series *The Persuaders*. He is the author of several novels, beginning with *Kid Andrew Cody & Julie Sparrow* (1977). **Selected Works:** *Captain Newman, M.D.* (1963), *Christmas in Connecticut* (1992), *Spartacus* (1960), *Naked in New York* (1994)

# Michael Curtiz (Mihézly Kertéz)

**Born:** December 24, 1888; Budapest, Hungary
**Died:** April 11, 1962; Hollywood, CA

**Years Active in the Industry:** by decade

| 10s | 20s | 30s | 40s | 50s | 60s | 70s | 80s | 90s |
|-----|-----|-----|-----|-----|-----|-----|-----|-----|
|     |     |     |     |     |     |     |     |     |

A stage actor while still a teenager, Curtiz began acting in and directing Hungarian films in 1912. He directed films in Germany and Austria after World War I, and came to America in 1926 at the behest of Harry Warner. A prolific director, he made dozens of films at Warner Bros. during the 1930s and '40s, proving himself a master at whatever genre he attempted, including action (*Captain Blood*, *The Charge Of The Light Brigade*), horror (*The Mystery Of The Wax Museum*, *The Walking Dead*), crime (*Angels*

*With Dirty Faces*), detective (*The Kennel Murder Case*), drama (*The Sea Wolf, Casablanca, Mildred Pierce*), musical (*Yankee Doodle Dandy*) and western (*Dodge City, Santa Fe Trail*). His films of the 1950s showed a slackening off, but included the popular musicals *White Christmas* and *King Creole*. **Selected Works:** *Four Daughters* (1938)

# Joan Cusack

**Born:** October 11, 1962; Evanston, IL

**Years Active in the Industry:** by decade

| 10ˢ | 20ˢ | 30ˢ | 40ˢ | 50ˢ | 60ˢ | 70ˢ | 80ˢ | 90ˢ |
|---|---|---|---|---|---|---|---|---|
| | | | | | | | | |

Dark-haired, versatile, offbeat actress Joan Cusack typically plays comedic character roles. She started performing as a member of Ark, a Madison, Wisconsin-based improvisational group, then did a series of plays with the River Theater Workshop. She had four fleeting appearances in films before being cast in a co-lead in *The Allnighter* (1987); meanwhile, she was a regular cast member in the weekly sketch-comedy TV series *Saturday Night Live* in 1985-86. Cusack went on to appear in a number of films, mostly light fair in which she played kooky types. She received a Best Supporting Actress Oscar nomination for her performance in *Working Girl* (1988). She is the sister of actor John Cusack, with whom she appeared in *Sixteen Candles* (1984) and in an unbilled role in *Say Anything* (1989). **Selected Works:** *Broadcast News* (1987), *Hero* (1992), *Married to the Mob* (1988), *My Blue Heaven* (1990), *Addams Family Values* (1993)

# John Cusack

**Born:** June 26, 1966; Evanston, IL

**Years Active in the Industry:** by decade

| 10ˢ | 20ˢ | 30ˢ | 40ˢ | 50ˢ | 60ˢ | 70ˢ | 80ˢ | 90ˢ |
|---|---|---|---|---|---|---|---|---|
| | | | | | | | | |

Actor John Cusack, the son of documentary film-maker Richard Cusack, began acting at age nine as a member of the River Theater Workshop. As a high school student, he worked in industrial films, made commercials, and did voice-overs; he also wrote and staged two musical comedies, both of which were shown on cable TV. He debuted onscreen in *Class* (1983), going on to supporting roles in two other teen-oriented films before landing the lead in Rob Reiner's *The Sure Thing* (1985). He has since alternated comedic films with serious dramas. Meanwhile, he remains a resident of his native Chicago, where he has continued to work in theater and has both produced and directed plays. His sister is actress Joan Cusack, with whom he appeared in *Sixteen Candles* (1984) and *Say Anything* (1989). **Selected Works:** *The Grifters* (1990), *Map of the Human Heart* (1993), *The Player* (1992), *Roadside Prophets* (1992), *Bullets over Broadway* (1994)

# Peter Cushing

**Born:** May 26, 1913; Kenley, Surrey, England
**Died:** August 11, 1994; Canterbury, England

**Years Active in the Industry:** by decade

| 10ˢ | 20ˢ | 30ˢ | 40ˢ | 50ˢ | 60ˢ | 70ˢ | 80ˢ | 90ˢ |
|---|---|---|---|---|---|---|---|---|
| | | | | | | | | |

The distinguished actor Peter Cushing is best remembered for his supporting roles in the Hammer horror films where he usually played wan, cold blooded mad scientists who created and dealt

with all manner of monsters. Prior to beginning his film career, Cushing worked as a surveyor's clerk until he began training at London's Guildhall School of Music and Drama. In 1935, he debuted on stage; he subsequently came to the U.S. where he appeared on Broadway and then played supporting roles in several Hollywood films such as *The Man in the Iron Mask* (1939). By 1948, he had returned to England where he made his film debut in *Hamlet*. After his discovery by Hammer Films, Cushing began to work in horror movies where he often worked with Christopher Lee. He has also played in science-fiction films, most notably 1977's *Star Wars*. **Selected Works:** *Moulin Rouge* (1952)

Beverly D'Angelo

Danny DeVito

Bo Derek

Vincent Philip D'Onofrio

George Dzundza

# Beverly D'Angelo

**Born:** 1954; Columbus, OH

**Years Active in the Industry:** by decade

| 10ˢ | 20ˢ | 30ˢ | 40ˢ | 50ˢ | 60ˢ | 70ˢ | 80ˢ | 90ˢ |
|---|---|---|---|---|---|---|---|---|
| | | | | | | | | |

After attending school in Europe and living in Italy, actress Beverly D'Angelo worked as a cartoonist for Hanna-Barbera Productions. She also sang in Canadian coffee-houses and with a rock group, Elephant; besides being an excellent singer she also plays piano and guitar. She gained her first stage experience with the Charlotte Town Festival Company. Her Broadway debut came in the rock musical *Rockabye Hamlet*, in which she played Ophelia. She debuted onscreen in a supporting role in the horror film *The Sentinel* (1977), going on to gain much exposure in Clint Eastwood's comedy *Every Which Way But Loose* (1979); she also had the female lead in the film version of the rock musical *Hair* (1979) and played country singer Patsy Cline in *Coal Miner's Daughter* (1980). However, other than three *National Lampoon* "vacation" movies, the films she has subsequently appeared in have generally failed to be very successful. Although she has remained a busy stage, screen, and TV actress, she has never lived up to her early star potential. **Selected Works:** *Daddy's Dyin'... Who's Got the Will?* (1990), *Lonely Hearts* (1991), *Miracle* (1991), *Pacific Heights* (1990)

# Vincent Philip D'Onofrio

**Born:** 1960; Brooklyn, NY

**Years Active in the Industry:** by decade

| 10ˢ | 20ˢ | 30ˢ | 40ˢ | 50ˢ | 60ˢ | 70ˢ | 80ˢ | 90ˢ |
|---|---|---|---|---|---|---|---|---|
| | | | | | | | | |

Vincent D'Onofrio first gained prominence in a series of off-Broadway productions, notably *Open Admission*. For several years, the actor was most closely associated with the American Stanislavsky Theatre. On TV, D'Onofrio received excellent notices for his performance as a retarded man accused of murder on the adventure series *The Equalizer*. Because of his chameleonlike ability to "become" the character he's playing, D'Onofrio has been compared by some observers to the young Robert DeNiro. In 1987, D'Onofrio delivered a dynamic performance as Pvt. "Gomer Pyle" Dawson in Stanley Kubrick's *Full Metal Jacket*, convincingly transforming in the course of the film from backwoods innocent to self-hating killing machine. From this career peak, D'Onofrio once more switched gears with a comedy role in *Adventures in Babysitting* (1988). Since that time, Vincent D'Onofrio has scored with distinctive supporting roles in *Dying Young* (1991) *JFK* (1991), *The Player* (1992) and *Mr. Wonderful* (1993). **Selected Works:** *Malcolm X* (1992), *Household Saints* (1993), *Ed Wood* (1994), *Imaginary Crimes* (1994)

# Willem Dafoe

**Born:** July 22, 1955; Appleton, WI

**Years Active in the Industry:** by decade

| 10ˢ | 20ˢ | 30ˢ | 40ˢ | 50ˢ | 60ˢ | 70ˢ | 80ˢ | 90ˢ |
|---|---|---|---|---|---|---|---|---|
| | | | | | | | | |

American actor Willem Dafoe began as a set-builder and eventually an actor for a Milwaukee-based avant garde group, Theater X. In 1977, he moved to New York, where he joined the Wooster group, which specializes in "performance pieces." Besides a small part in *Heaven's Gate* (cut from the theatrical version), his debut onscreen came in Kathryn Bigelow's *The Loveless* (1982), in which he played a Brandoesque biker. His first films cast

him as strange-looking villains, but he achieved a great breakthrough in his performance as the good sergeant in Oliver Stone's *Platoon* (1986). He later went on to play Jesus in Martin Scorsese's controversial *The Last Temptation of Christ* (1988). **Selected Works:** *Light Sleeper* (1992), *Mississippi Burning* (1988), *Wild at Heart* (1990), *Tom and Viv* (1994), *Clear and Present Danger* (1994)

# Timothy Dalton

**Born:** March 21, 1944; Colwyn Bay, Clywd, Wales

**Years Active in the Industry:** by decade

| 10s | 20s | 30s | 40s | 50s | 60s | 70s | 80s | 90s |
|-----|-----|-----|-----|-----|-----|-----|-----|-----|
|     |     |     |     |     |     |     |     |     |

Welsh actor Timothy Dalton has the looks and bearing of a young Peter O'Toole and the on-stage brooding temperament of a Richard Burton. As such, Dalton has excelled in roles calling for

both panache and psychological complexity. His stage training has included stints at the National Youth Theatre, the Royal Academy of Dramatic Art, and the starmaking Birmingham Rep. Dalton's extensive work in the classics with the Royal Shakespeare Company led to his being cast as King Philip of France in the quasi-classical film *The Lion in Winter* (1968).

In 1971, Dalton appeared in *Mary Queen of Scots*, simultaneously launching a lengthy romantic involvement with that film's star, Vanessa Redgrave. When Roger Moore quit the James Bond film series in 1986, it looked for a while as though his successor would be TV star Pierce Brosnan; instead, the *Bond* producers made the eleventh-hour decision to cast Timothy Dalton as Secret Agent 007 in *The Living Daylights*. Though dashing in a tuxedo and more than willing to perform his own stunts, Dalton seemed ill at ease in his two Bond appearances, as though he'd be more comfortable playing the villain. Timothy Dalton's weight as a performer was

more effectively felt in the role of the dastardly movie swashbuckler-cum-Nazi spy (patterned after the much-maligned Errol Flynn) in the breezy sci-fier *The Rocketeer* (1991). **Selected Works:** *Jane Eyre* (1983), *King's Whore* (1990), *Naked in New York* (1994)

# Dorothy Dandridge

**Born:** November 9, 1923; Cleveland, OH
**Died:** 1965

**Years Active in the Industry:** by decade

| 10s | 20s | 30s | 40s | 50s | 60s | 70s | 80s | 90s |
|-----|-----|-----|-----|-----|-----|-----|-----|-----|
|     |     |     |     |     |     |     |     |     |

Actress, singer, dancer Dorothy Dandridge, the daughter of stage and screen actress Ruby Dandridge, began performing professionally in the song-and-dance duo "The Wonder Children"

with her sister Vivian at age four; they toured parts of the South, performing at churches, schools, and social gatherings. In the 1930s her family relocated to Los Angeles, and she and her sister appeared briefly in the Marx brothers comedy *A Day at the Races* (1937). In their teens she and her sister enlisted a third singer and formed a new group, the Dandridge Sisters; they worked with Jimmie Lunceford's Orchestra and Cab Calloway, appeared at the Cotton Club, and turned up with Louis Armstrong and Maxine Sullivan in the film *Going Places* (1939). She started performing solo in the early '40s, appearing in a string of musical shorts made in 1941 and 1942; she also performed in several features in the same years, including *Sun Valley Serenade* (1942), during the production of which she met her first husband, the dancer Harold Nicholas. After her marriage she put her career on hold for a while, but the birth of a severely brain-damaged daughter strained her marriage and it soon ended in divorce, following which she put most of her energy into her career. She joined the cast of the radio series *Beulah*, and went on to perform in its TV incarnation. She became popular and famous as a sultry nightclub entertainer, then began to make her mark in movies with her notable appearance in *Tarzan's Peril* (1951), in which she played a sexy African princess. For her work in Otto Preminger's *Carmen Jones* (1954) she received a Best Actress Oscar nomination, becoming the first black women to do so. Three years went by before her next role, in *Islands in the Sun* (1957), in which she again made history by being the first black actress cast romantically with a white actor in a film. For her work in Preminger's

*Porgy and Bess* (1959) she won the Golden Globe Award as Best Actress in a Musical. After a few more years she found it difficult to get lead roles in films, and went back to nightclubs, which she hated. Shortly afterwards a disastrous marriage and bad investments forced her to file bankruptcy. In 1965 she signed a new film contract, but her rebounding luck was short-lived—she was found dead from an overdose of anti-depressants.

# Rodney Dangerfield

**Born:** November 22, 1921; Babylon, NY

**Years Active in the Industry:** by decade

| 10ˢ | 20ˢ | 30ˢ | 40ˢ | 50ˢ | 60ˢ | 70ˢ | 80ˢ | 90ˢ |
|-----|-----|-----|-----|-----|-----|-----|-----|-----|
|     |     |     |     |     |     |     |     |     |

If ever there was a "late bloomer," it was American comedian Rodney Dangerfield. His father was a vaudeville pantomimist who was known professionally as Phil Roy, thus when Dangerfield struck out on his own standup comedy career at age 19 (he'd been writing jokes for other comics since 15), he called himself Jack Roy. For nine years he labored in some of the worst dives on the East Coast, giving it all up at age 28 in order to support his new wife. The marriage was an unhappy one, soon ending in divorce. Dangerfield's professional life was none too smooth either, since one doesn't become a millionaire selling paint door-to-door. In 1963 the comic returned to performing, using the name "Rodney Dangerfield" to distance himself from his miserable "Jack Roy" days. Four more years passed before Dangerfield finally got his big break on *The Ed Sullivan Show*, for which he'd auditioned by sneaking in during a dress rehearsal. By this time, Dangerfield had fully developed his belligerently neurotic stage persona, tugging at his tie and mopping his brow while he delineated the variety of ways in which he "don't get no respect." On top at last, Dangerfield opened his own nightclub in 1969, where many major comics of the 1970s and 1980s got their first opportunities; fiercely competitive onstage, Dangerfield is known to be more than generous to new talent offstage (Not *all* new talent, however. One well-known TV talk show host, who once opened for Dangerfield as a singer, has sworn publicly that she'll never forgive him for his unspecified behavior towards her). In films since his turn as a nasty theatre manager in the 1970 low-budgetter *The Projectionist*, Dangerfield has exuded a movie image somewhat different than his paranoid nightclub character; he often plays a crude-and-rude "nouveau riche" type who delights in puncturing the pomposity of his "old money" opponents. Rodney Dangerfield's best screen role was, significantly, his nicest—in *Back to School* (1985), he played a blunt but decent self-made millionaire who decides to join his son in getting an expensive college education. **Selected Works:** *Rover Dangerfield* (1991), *Natural Born Killers* (1994)

# Henry Daniell

**Born:** March 5, 1894; London, England
**Died:** October 31, 1963; Santa Monica, CA

**Years Active in the Industry:** by decade

| 10ˢ | 20ˢ | 30ˢ | 40ˢ | 50ˢ | 60ˢ | 70ˢ | 80ˢ | 90ˢ |
|-----|-----|-----|-----|-----|-----|-----|-----|-----|
|     |     |     |     |     |     |     |     |     |

With his haughty demeanor and near-satanic features, British actor Henry Daniell was the perfect screen "gentleman villain" in such major films of the 1930s and 1940s as *Camille* (1936) and *The Great Dictator* (1940). An actor since the age of 18, Daniell worked in London until coming to America in an Ethel Barrymore play. He costarred with Ruth Gordon in the 1929 Broadway production *Serena Blandish*, in which he won critical plaudits in the role of Lord Iver Cream. Making his movie debut in *Jealousy* (1929)—which costarred another stage legend, Jeanne Eagels—Daniell stayed in Hollywood for the remainder of his career, most often playing cold-blooded aristocrats in period costume. He was less at home in action roles; he flat-out refused to participate in the climactic dueling scene in *The Sea Hawk* (1940), compelling star Errol Flynn to cross swords with a none too convincing stunt double. Daniell became something of a regular in the Basil Rathbone-Nigel Bruce Sherlock Holmes films made at Universal in the 1940s—he was in three entries, playing Professor Moriarity in *The Woman in Green* (1945). Though seldom in pure horror films, Daniell nonetheless excelled in the leading role of *The Body Snatcher* (1945)—though, as usual, top billing was denied him (he was listed under the bigger box-office names Boris Karloff and Bela Lugosi, the latter in a very minor role). Coworkers in this film recalled in later years that Daniell was a thorough, no-nonsense professional, and rather cold and forbidding. When the sort of larger-than-life film fare in which Daniell specialized began disappearing in the 1950s, the actor nonetheless continued to prosper in both films (*Man in the Grey Flannel Suit* [1956], *Witness for the Prosecution* [1957]) and television (*Thriller*, *The Hour of St. Francis*, and many other programs). While portraying Prince Gregor of Transylvania in *My Fair Lady* (1964), under the direction of his old friend George Cukor, Daniell died suddenly; his few completed scenes remained in the film, though his name was removed from the cast credits. **Selected Works:** *Holiday* (1938), *Lust for Life* (1956), *Philadelphia Story* (1940), *Private Lives of Elizabeth and Essex* (1939), *Watch on the Rhine* (1943)

# Bebe Daniels (Phyllis Daniels)

**Born:** January 14, 1901; Dallas, TX
**Died:** March 15, 1971; London England

**Years Active in the Industry:** by decade

| 10ˢ | 20ˢ | 30ˢ | 40ˢ | 50ˢ | 60ˢ | 70ˢ | 80ˢ | 90ˢ |
|-----|-----|-----|-----|-----|-----|-----|-----|-----|
|     |     |     |     |     |     |     |     |     |

American actress Bebe Daniels and the motion picture industry virtually grew up together. After touring with her stage-actor parents, Daniels made her film debut at age seven in the silent one-reeler *A Common Enemy* (1908). After unsuccessfully applying for a job as a Mack Sennett bathing beauty (she was well under the age of consent), Daniels secured a job at Hal Roach's comedy studio in

1915, co-featured with Roach's biggest (and only) star Harold Lloyd in a series of zany slapstick comedies. In 1919, Daniels was signed by producer-director Cecil B. DeMille to star in a group of slick, sophisticated feature films in the company of DeMille regulars Gloria Swanson and Thomas Meighan. Though successful in these glamorous ventures, Daniels found herself more at home in fast-moving comedy roles, in which she specialized while contracted with Paramount Pictures in the mid-1920s; the actress played everything from a female Zorro type in *Senorita* (1927) to a "lady Valentino" in *She's a Shiek* (1927). When talking pictures came around, Paramount dropped Daniels' contract, worried that she wouldn't be able to make the transition to sound. But Daniels surprised everyone by scoring a hit in RKO's expensive musical feature *Rio Rita* (1929), managing to keep her career in high gear until her last American film, *Music in Magic* (1935). Upon her retirement from Hollywood, Daniels moved to England with her actor husband Ben Lyon in 1935. Enormously popular with London audiences, Daniels and Ben Lyon starred in stage plays and films, and in the 1940s, headlined the successful radio series *Life with the Lyons*, which graduated to an even more successful TV program in the 1950s. **Selected Works:** *42nd Street* (1933)

# Jeff Daniels

**Born:** February 19, 1955; Georgia

**Years Active in the Industry:** by decade

| 10s | 20s | 30s | 40s | 50s | 60s | 70s | 80s | 90s |
|-----|-----|-----|-----|-----|-----|-----|-----|-----|

American actor Jeff Daniels distinguished himself early in his stage career by winning an Obie award for his performance in the off-Broadway production *Johnny Got His Gun*. Making his

screen bow in *Ragtime* (1981), Daniels quickly gained film fame via his portrayal of Debra Winger's vacillating husband in the Oscar-winning *Terms of Endearment* (1983). He also shone in the dual role of a callous 1930s movie star and his nicer on-screen alter ego in Woody Allen's *Purple Rose of Cairo* (1984). Taking occasional time out from movies to manage his own theatrical company, Daniels has chalked up several prestigious credits, and not a few financially satisfying ones; among his most profitable endeavors was playing the spider-hating hero of the cheap but effective horror flick *Arachnophobia* (1990). Since then he has continued to work steadily and has re-

cently appeared on television as well as in feature films. **Selected Works:** *Gettysburg* (1992), *Radio Days* (1987), *Rain Without Thunder* (1993), *Dumb and Dumber* (1994), *Speed* (1994)

# William H. Daniels

**Born:** 1895; Cleveland, OH
**Died:** June 1970; Los Angeles, CA

**Years Active in the Industry:** by decade

| 10s | 20s | 30s | 40s | 50s | 60s | 70s | 80s | 90s |
|-----|-----|-----|-----|-----|-----|-----|-----|-----|

Following his graduation from USC, 22-year-old Ohioan William H. Daniels secured an assistant cameraman job at Triangle Studios. In 1918, less than a year later, he was chief photographer at Universal. His association with Erich Von Stroheim's *Greed* brought Daniels to MGM in 1924, where he would remain for most of his career. While at MGM, Daniels became Greta Garbo's favorite cameraman; he responded to this honor by drawing up an annotated list of the various photographic techniques that showed off the actress to best advantage. At times, Daniels and his crew were the only people permitted on the set when Garbo went into a particularly delicate scene. In his heyday of the 1930s and early 1940s, Daniels was publicly praised by his contemporaries for his ability to convey his own personal "signature" on each film, without ever repeating himself or taking any glory away from the director. In the mid-1940s, a contract dispute and an illness briefly kept him out of films; his "comeback" was the 1947 Universal crime drama *The Naked City*, which won Daniels an Academy Award. During the 1950s, Daniels adapted his formerly lush, diffused MGM style to the gritty, hard-edged demands of such Universals as *Brute Force* (1918) and *Winchester 73* (1950). Still active in the 1960s, Daniels turned producer for two Frank Sinatra films, and also served two years as president of the ASC. Daniels died shortly after shooting his last film, the Elliot Gould vehicle *Move* (1970). **Selected Works:** *Cat on a Hot Tin Roof* (1958), *How the West Was Won* (1963)

# Blythe Danner

**Born:** February 3, 1944; Philadelphia, PA

**Years Active in the Industry:** by decade

| 10s | 20s | 30s | 40s | 50s | 60s | 70s | 80s | 90s |
|-----|-----|-----|-----|-----|-----|-----|-----|-----|

American actress Blythe Danner might have come into the world with the first name Pauline, but her aunt decided that the girl would either be an actress or a writer (the rest of her family was packed with musical and artistic talent), hence the name "Blythe." The daughter of a bank executive, Danner enjoyed an expensive education at prep school and at Bard College. Her earliest theatrical work was with the Theater Company of Boston and the Trinity

Square Playhouse of Boston; by the time she was 25 she'd won the Theatre World Award for her performance in the Lincoln Center Rep's production of *The Miser*. In 1969, she played the free-spirit ingenue in *Butterflies are Free*, which was based on the life story of a blind attorney and which won the actress a Tony Award. Given the tenor of 1970s newspaper publicity, Danner was featured in several magazine and newspaper photo spreads because she spent much of *Butterflies'* first act clad in nothing but her underwear. The actress was frequently cast opposite fellow up-and-comer Ken Howard, notably in the short-lived 1973 TV sitcom *Adam's Rib*. She worked so well with Howard that many fans assumed the two were married; in fact, Blythe's longtime husband was Broadway and TV producer Bruce Paltrow. A "critic's darling" thanks to her husky voice and pleasantly mannered acting style, Danner has worked with distinction in TV and on stage, though her film roles are few and far between; she was memorable as Robert Duvall's long-suffering wife in *The Great Santini* (1979) and as Nick Nolte's suicidal sister in *The Prince of Tides* (1991), while in 1986's *Brighton Beach Memoirs*, the decidedly WASPish Danner surprised fans by portraying a middle-aged Jewish lady. Frequently seen in TV guest roles (she managed to make her Mrs. Albert Speer in 1982's *Inside the Third Reich* sympathetic—no mean feat), Danner was last seen on television on a regular basis in the brief 1988 series *Tattinger's*, produced by husband Bruce Paltrow. **Selected Works:** *Alice* (1990), *Hearts of the West* (1975), *Husbands and Wives* (1992), *Mr. & Mrs. Bridge* (1991), *Oldest Living Confederate Widow Tells All* (1994)

# Ted Danson

**Born:** December 29, 1947; San Diego, CA

**Years Active in the Industry:** by decade

| 10s | 20s | 30s | 40s | 50s | 60s | 70s | 80s | 90s |
|-----|-----|-----|-----|-----|-----|-----|-----|-----|
|     |     |     |     |     |     |     |     |     |

The son of a prominent archeologist/museum director, American actor Ted Danson grew up near a Navajo reservation in Arizona. He played basketball while at Kent School Connecticut, and played the field with the ladies (by his own admission) when he moved on to Stanford University. It was in the process of getting acquainted with an aspiring actress at Stanford that Danson found himself attending his first audition—and by years' end had transferred to the drama department at Carnegie Tech. Marking time in non-speaking roles, Danson left the stage for the more lucrative world of TV commercials, some of which have been well circulated on videotape since Danson has become famous. Danson's first steady TV work was as a slimy villain on the NBC soap opera *Somerset*. Shortly afterward, the actor attained his first film role, as a murdered cop, in *The Onion Field* (1978). After seeing Danson in the movie *Body Heat* (1981) and in an episode of the TV series *Taxi*, producer Glen Charles cast the actor as Sam Malone, ex-sports star and fulltime barkeeper and womanizer, on the sitcom *Cheers* He won Emmys for the 1989-90 and 1992-93 seasons.

Danson's subsequent celebrity was as much due to his many off-camera squabbles with *Cheers* costar Shelley Long as it was to his considerable comic talent. Frequently making attempts at film stardom during the 11-season run of *Cheers*, Danson finally struck gold in *Three Men and a Baby* (1987) and its sequel *Three Men and a Little Lady* (1990). Admired in private life for caring and nurturing his wife following her debilitating stroke, Danson scuttled much of that goodwill by leaving his wife (by then recovered) for actress Whoopi Goldberg. It was not a match made in Heaven, as witness the lukewarm Danson-Goldberg film vehicle *Made in America* (1993) and Danson's notorious appearance in blackface (purportedly at Goldberg's behest) at a 1993 Friar's Club roast. Since the end of *Cheers* and his breakup with Goldberg, Danson has been casting about for the right film roles and personal choices (he has recently been romantically linked with actress Mary Steenburgen) to get himself back on the fast track. **Selected Works:** *Pontiac Moon* (1994)

# Joe Dante

**Born:** 1948; Morristown, NJ

**Years Active in the Industry:** by decade

| 10s | 20s | 30s | 40s | 50s | 60s | 70s | 80s | 90s |
|-----|-----|-----|-----|-----|-----|-----|-----|-----|
|     |     |     |     |     |     |     |     |     |

Born and raised in New Jersey, Joe Dante was one of those garrulous, semi-obsessed "movie nuts" you remember from high school. As a teenager, Dante wrote articles and criticism for *Castle of Frankenstein*, a popular "fanzine" for horror-film aficionados. While attending the Philadelphia College of Art, Dante and his friend Jon Davidson put together *Movie Orgy* (1968), a 7-hour compilation of kitschy film clips that was screened on the college-campus circuit under the sponsorship of Schlitz beer. Dante went on to write for *The Film Bulletin*, then joined Roger Corman's New World Pictures, starting out editing trailers. When Dante made noises about becoming a director, Corman challenged him to whip up a picture for $50,000; the result was *Hollywood Boulevard*, an elongated (and frequently sidesplitting) inside joke about low-budget moviemaking. With *Piranha* (1978) and *The Howling* (1980), Dante began attracting critical attention as a director to keep an eye on. For producer Steven Spielberg, Dante directed his most profitable film, *Gremlins* (1984), a funny/frightening compendium of filmic "quotes" from past movie classics, chock full of cameo appearances by such pop-culture icons as Chuck Jones, Dick Miller, and Robby the Robot. For television, Dante has directed episodes of *Police Squad*, *Amazing Stories*, *Twilight Zone* (he was responsible for the "It's a Good Life" segment in 1982's *Twilight Zone: The Movie*) and *Tales from the Crypt*. While Dante is best known for his stylish "scare" pictures, one of the director's finest and most personal projects was *Matinee* (1993), a nostalgic (and very movie-savvy) glance back at what it was like to grow up as a film buff in the white-bread early 1960s. **Selected Works:** *Gremlins 2: The New Batch* (1990)

# Tony Danza (Anthony Ladanza)

**Born:** April 21, 1950; Brooklyn, NY

**Years Active in the Industry:** by decade

| 10s | 20s | 30s | 40s | 50s | 60s | 70s | 80s | 90s |
|-----|-----|-----|-----|-----|-----|-----|-----|-----|

A graduate of the University of Dubuque, Tony Danza was busy with a profitable if not spectacular career as a boxer when he began tentatively moving into acting. His first important TV role was, appropriately, as erstwhile boxer Tony Banta on the popular sitcom *Taxi*. During his *Taxi* years, Danza built up the screen image of the pugnacious, not overly bright lug with a golden heart; off-screen, Danza was capable of shedding his lovability in an instant, as his occasional public brawls demonstrated. In 1984, Danza was cast as Tony Micelli, the widowed housekeeper of divorced career woman Angela Bower (Judith Light), on the weekly domestic comedy *Who's the Boss?* Reports vary as to Danza's deportment during the eight-season run of the series. Danza's first starring film role in *She's Out of Control* (1988), as the overprotective father of teenager Ami Dolenz, was more or less an extension of his TV work; the actor demonstrated a wider range in the supporting role of a dying baseball player in the 1994 remake of *Angels in the Outfield*.

# Linda Darnell (Monetta Eloyse Darnell)

**Born:** October 16, 1923; Dallas, TX
**Died:** April 10, 1965; Chicago, IL

**Years Active in the Industry:** by decade

| 10s | 20s | 30s | 40s | 50s | 60s | 70s | 80s | 90s |
|-----|-----|-----|-----|-----|-----|-----|-----|-----|

Daughter of a Texas postal clerk, actress Linda Darnell trained to be a dancer, and came to Hollywood's attention as a photographer's model. Though only 15, Darnell looked quite mature and sexy in her first motion picture, *Hotel For Women* (1937), and before she was twenty she found herself the leading lady of such 20th Century-Fox male heartthrobs as Tyrone Power and Henry Fonda. Weary of thankless good-girl roles, Darnell scored a personal triumph when loaned out to United Artists for *September Storm* (1944), in which she played a "Scarlett O'Hara" type Russian vixen. 20th Century-Fox thereafter assigned the actress meatier, more substantial parts, culminating in the much-sought-after leading role in 1947's *Forever Amber*. Director Joseph L. Mankiewicz followed up this triumph by giving Darnell two of her best parts—Paul Douglas' "wrong side of the tracks" wife in *A Letter To Three Wives* (1949) and Richard Widmark's racist girlfriend in *No Way Out* (1950) (though befitting her star status, Darnell "reformed" at the end of both films). When her Fox contract ended in 1952, Darnell found herself cast adrift in Hollywood, the good roles fewer and farther between; by the mid-1960s, she was appearing as a nightclub singer, touring in summer theatre, and accepting supporting roles on television. The victim of a turbulent private life and an on-

and-off drinking problem, Darnell died in 1965 of severe burns suffered in a house fire. Ironically, Darnell had had a lifelong fear of dying in flames, speaking publicly of her phobia after appearing in a "burned at the stake" sequence in the 1946 film *Anna and the King of Siam*. **Selected Works:** *Letter to Three Wives* (1949), *Mark of Zorro* (1940), *It Happened Tomorrow* (1944)

# Jane Darwell (Patti Woodward)

**Born:** October 15, 1879; Palmyra, MO
**Died:** August 14, 1967

**Years Active in the Industry:** by decade

| 10s | 20s | 30s | 40s | 50s | 60s | 70s | 80s | 90s |
|-----|-----|-----|-----|-----|-----|-----|-----|-----|

American actress Jane Darwell was the daughter of a Missouri railroad executive. Despite her father's disapproval, she spent most of her youth acting in circuses, opera troupes and stock companies, making her film debut in 1912. Even in her early thirties, Darwell specialized in formidable "grande dame" roles, usually society matrons or strict maiden aunts. Making an easy transition to talking pictures, Darwell worked primarily in small character parts (notably as governesses and housekeepers in the films of Shirley Temple) until 1939, when her role as the James Brothers' mother in *Jesse James* began a new career direction—now she would most often be cast as indomitable frontierswomen, unbending in the face of hardship and adversity. It was this quality that led Darwell to be cast in her favorite role as Ma Joad in *The Grapes of Wrath* (1940), for which she won an Oscar. Darwell continued to work until she became ill in the late 1950s. Even so, Darwell managed to essay a handful of memorable parts on TV and in movies into the 1960s; her last film role was as the "Bird Woman" in Disney's *Mary Poppins* (1964). **Selected Works:** *Devil and Daniel Webster* (1941), *Gone with the Wind* (1939), *Last Hurrah* (1958), *Ox-Bow Incident* (1943), *Caged* (1950)

# Jules Dassin

**Born:** December 18, 1911; Middletown, CT

**Years Active in the Industry:** by decade

| 10s | 20s | 30s | 40s | 50s | 60s | 70s | 80s | 90s |
|-----|-----|-----|-----|-----|-----|-----|-----|-----|

One of the most defiantly visible survivors of the Hollywood Blacklist was American director Jules Dassin. Following high school in the Bronx and drama school in Europe (paying his own way), Dassin made his stage debut at age 25 with the Yiddish Theatre in New York. In Hollywood, Dassin worked his way up to a directorial spot at MGM's short subjects unit, where he handled a brilliant 20-minute adaptation of Poe's *The Tell-Tale Heart* (1941). This led to a promotion to features like *Nazi Agent* (1942), *Reunion in France* (1942) and *The Canterville Ghost* (1944). From MGM, Dassin went to work for producer Mark Hellinger at Universal Studios, where he turned out two full-blooded crime classics: *Brute Force* (1947) and *The Naked City* (1948). Unfortunately, the late 1940s were difficult times for anyone with even the slightest leftist political leanings. After being identified as a Communist by director Ed Dmytrk during a House UnAmerican Activities Committee hearing, Dassin found himself completely shut out by Hollywood. The last 1950s film which Dassin directed for a major studio was 20th Century-Fox's *Night and the City*, which was shot in London. Then he moved to France, where he helmed one of the most influential "crime caper" movies ever made, *Riffifi* (1954). So successful was this melodrama that it spawned numerous ripoffs (*Riffifi in Tokyo* was one of the most blatant) and parodies, including Dassin's own *Topkapi* (1964). Operating in Greece by 1959, Dassin directed his second wife Melina Mercouri in *Never On Sunday* (1960), a robust comedy about a joyous prosititute; Mercouri's performance was superb enough for viewers to forgive Dassin's own lackluster performance as a stuffy American moralist. Permitted back in the U.S. studio system in the mid-1960s, Dassin directed *Uptight* (1968), a black-oriented remake of *The Informer* which proved beyond doubt that Dassin's alleged "Communistic" tendencies were a just a bit old hat. Not many of Jules Dassin's later, more personal films (notably an indictment of the Greek junta leaders, *The Rehearsal* [1974]) were seen in America, but the director's reputation, so idiotically maligned in the early 1950s, had been completely restored so far as Hollywood was concerned— even though the man himself chose to shun the U.S. for self-imposed Swiss exile. **Selected Works:** *Rififi* (1954)

# Robert Davi

**Born:** 1953; Astoria, NY

**Years Active in the Industry:** by decade

| 10s | 20s | 30s | 40s | 50s | 60s | 70s | 80s | 90s |
|-----|-----|-----|-----|-----|-----|-----|-----|-----|
|     |     |     |     |     |     |     | ■   |     |

After attending Hofstra University, New York-born Robert Davi studied at the Actors Studio, then commenced a career of portraying stone-faced antagonists. Davi worked on the New York stage and in regional rep before making his feature film bow in 1984's *City Heat*. Among the earliest of Davi's attention-getting film roles was as villainess Anne Ramsey's brutish son in *Goonies* (1985). Davi's showiest movie assignment was as the ecologically incorrect villain in the 1989 James Bond flick *License to Kill* (1989). **Selected Works:** *Deceptions* (1990), *Die Hard* (1988), *Illicit Behavior* (1991), *Legal Tender* (1990), *White Hot: The Mysterious Murder of Thelma Todd* (1991)

# Lolita Davidovich

**Born:** July 1961; Ontario, Canada

**Years Active in the Industry:** by decade

| 10s | 20s | 30s | 40s | 50s | 60s | 70s | 80s | 90s |
|-----|-----|-----|-----|-----|-----|-----|-----|-----|
|     |     |     |     |     |     |     | ■   |     |

Actress Lolita Davidovich made her flamboyant film debut by playing the notorious Louisiana stripper Blaze Starr who became the mistress of Governor Earl Long in *Blaze* (1988). With her

voluptuous body (much of which was faked for the film—something Davidovich is not embarrassed to admit), bright red hair, and lively acting style, she accurately captured the qualities that made the real Blaze a living legend. Born of Yugoslavian parents, Davidovich was raised speaking Serbo-Croatian. When she was 10, her parents divorced and she stayed with her mother. Davidovich was determined to become an actress, and as a young woman moved to Chicago to take classes. There she found some stage work under the name Lolita David. She gradually began getting bit parts in feature films like *Adventures In Babysitting* (1987). It took six months of fiercely competitive auditioning to land the part of Blaze. A wide variety of subsequent roles have allowed her to demonstrate her considerable abilities. **Selected Works:** *Inner Circle* (1991), *JFK* (1991), *Keep the Change* (1992), *Object of Beauty* (1991), *Prison Stories: Women on the Inside* (1991)

# Marion Davies (Marion Cecilia Douras)

**Born:** January 3, 1897; Brooklyn, NY
**Died:** September 22, 1961; Los Angeles, CA

**Years Active in the Industry:** by decade

| 10s | 20s | 30s | 40s | 50s | 60s | 70s | 80s | 90s |
|-----|-----|-----|-----|-----|-----|-----|-----|-----|
|     | ■   |     |     |     |     |     |     |     |

American actress Marion Davies became a Broadway chorus dancer through the auspices of her brother-in-law, the powerful theatrical producer George W. Lederer. There are many stories of how Davies came to the attention of newspaper tycoon William Randolph Hearst, the most popular of which relates how, when watching her perform as a solo singer-dancer in the 1916 edition of *Ziegfeld Follies*, Hearst became so enchanted that for eight weeks thereafter he never missed a performance, reserving two seats per show (one seat for his hat). Hearst, who in addition to his publishing empire also dabbled in moviemaking, cast Marion in the 1917 silent film *Runaway Romany*. For the rest of her career, Davies appeared only in Hearst-produced movies, a professional association which spilled over into her private life; she became Hearst's mistress, and might very well have married him had Mrs. Hearst not refused him a divorce. The Hearst press promoted Davies' film career to the point of the ridiculous, over-praising each movie as though it were the Second Coming; in retaliation, rival newspapers mercilessly panned Davies, suggesting that she'd still be a chorus girl without Hearst's sponsorship. The truth lay somewhere in between—when viewing such Davies films as *Show People* (1928), *Blondie of the Follies* (1932) and *Cain and Mabel* (1936), one is struck by her deft comic skills and superior musical talent; at the same time, she is nowhere near the Greatest Actress in the Universe promoted by the Hearst publicity machine. Davies retired from the screen after *Ever Since Eve* (1937), settling down as the popular hostess of San Simeon, Hearst's gigantic estate on the California coast. After Hearst died in 1951, Davies married Capt. Horace G. Brown of the California State Guard and divided her time between managing her considerable financial holdings and maintaining the Marion Davies Childrens' Clinic, a charitable organization. Davies was much loved by her friends and by Hollywood in general; alas, most people today "know" Davies only through the vulgar, abrasive character of "Susan Alexander" in filmmaker Orson Welles' thinly disguised chronicle of William Randolph Hearst's life, *Citizen Kane* (1941).

# Bette Davis (Ruth Elizabeth Davis)

**Born:** April 5, 1908; Lowell, MA
**Died:** October 6, 1989; Neuilly-sur-Seine, France

**Years Active in the Industry:** by decade

| 10s | 20s | 30s | 40s | 50s | 60s | 70s | 80s | 90s |
|-----|-----|-----|-----|-----|-----|-----|-----|-----|

The daughter of a Massachusetts lawyer, American actress Bette Davis was demanding attention almost from the moment of her birth. Her early show-off tendencies matured into a desire to be-

come an actress upon her graduation from Cushing Academy, but she was turned away from Eva LeGallienne's Manhattan Civic Repertory in New York—LeGallienne regarded Davis as frivolous and insincere. Undaunted, Davis enrolled in John Murray Anderson's Dramatic School, where everyone (including classmate Lucille Ball) regarded her the star pupil. After a 1928 summer season with director George Cukor's stock company in Rochester, NY (where she worked with future costar—and rival—Miriam Hopkins), Davis went on to Broadway, starring in *Broken Dishes* and *Solid South* before Hollywood called. Dazzling on stage, Davis was somewhat plain and mousy in civilian clothes; when signed for a contract by Universal in 1930, one of the higher-ups complained that she had "as much sex appeal as Slim Summerville." An unimpressive debut in *Bad Sister* (1930) did little to change the studio's mind about Davis, and by 1931 she was out of work, only to be picked up by Warner Bros. a year later. Here Davis applied herself with white-hot intensity to become a star, and after a major role in the 1932 George Arliss vehicle *The Man Who Played God*, a star she became. Still, the films at Warners were uneven, and it wasn't until the studio loaned Davis out to play the bravura role of Mildred in RKO's *Of Human Bondage* (1934) that the critics began to take notice. An Academy Award nomination seemed inevitable for *Bondage*, but Davis was let down by Warners, which didn't like the fact that her best appearance had been in a rival series and failed to get behind her Oscar campaign (however, there was a significant write-in vote for the actress). But in 1935, Davis excelled as a self-destructive actress in the otherwise turgid Warners film *Dangerous*; the Oscar was finally hers. When Warners failed to give Davis the top roles she felt her award had merited, the actress went on strike and headed for England. She lost a legal battle with Warners and came back, but the studio acknowledged her grit and talent by increasing her salary and giving her much better roles. In 1939 alone, Davis starred in *Dark Victory*, *Juarez*, *The Private Lives of Elizabeth and Essex* and *The Old Maid*—but she didn't get the plum role of the season, Scarlet O'Hara in *Gone With the Wind*, because Warners wouldn't loan her to David Selznick unless Errol Flynn was engaged to play Rhett Butler (a piece of casting both Selznick *and* Davis opposed violently). But Davis had already had her turn at playing a Southern belle in *Jezebel* (1938), winning her second Oscar in the process. As her star status increased in the 1940s, Davis found that stardom would have to be at the expense of her private life—she would be married and divorced four times, admitting towards the end of her life that her career came first, last and always. A fling at being her own producer in 1946 was disappointing, and her Warners' contract petered out in 1949 with a string of turkeys, the worst of which was *Beyond the Forest* (that's the one where Davis said "What a dump!"). Davis made a spectacular comeback in 1950 when she replaced an ailing Claudette Colbert in the role of Margot Channing in the Oscar-winning *All About Eve* (1950). The actress seemed to be summing up both her career and her on-screen persona with her immortal *Eve* line "Fasten your seat belts, folks. It's going to be a bumpy ride." Though suffering from a bone disease that required part of her jaw to be removed, Davis continued to work in films throughout the 1950s, but in 1961 things came to a standstill, forcing the actress to take out a famous "job wanted" ad in the trade papers. In 1962, Davis began the next phase of her career when she accepted the role of a whacked-out former child star in *Whatever Happened to Baby Jane?*. This led to a string of gothic horror films that did little to advance Davis' reputation, but kept her in the public eye. Working in movies, TV, on stage and in one-woman lecture tours into the 1970s, Davis may have been older but no less feisty and combative; her outspokenness may have un-nerved some of her costars, but made her an ideal interview subject for young film historians and fans. In 1977, Davis received a Life-time Achievement Award from the American Film Institute, an honor usually bestowed on performers who were retired or inactive. Not Davis. She kept at her craft into the 1980s, even after a stroke imposed serious limitations on her speech and movement. Amidst many TV movies and talk-show appearances, Davis gave one last memorable film appearance in *The Whales of August* (1987), in which she worked with another venerable screen legend, Lillian Gish (*Whales* wasn't Davis' final film, but given the unremitting silliness of 1989's *Wicked Stepmother*, it should have been). Though plagued with illness and such personal reverses as her daughter's scabrous "Mommie Dearest"-type autobiography, Davis was formidable to the last—so much so that, when she died at age 82 in France, a lot of her fans refused to believe it. **Selected Works:** *Death on the Nile* (1978), *Letter* (1940), *Little Foxes* (1941), *Mr. Skeffington* (1944), *Now, Voyager* (1942)

## Brad Davis (Robert Davis)

**Born:** November 6, 1949; Tallahassee, FL
**Died:** September 8, 1991; Los Angeles, CA

**Years Active in the Industry:** by decade

| 10ˢ | 20ˢ | 30ˢ | 40ˢ | 50ˢ | 60ˢ | 70ˢ | 80ˢ | 90ˢ |
|-----|-----|-----|-----|-----|-----|-----|-----|-----|
|     |     |     |     |     |     |     |     |     |

American actor Brad Davis set out for a show business life after winning a music talent contest in his teens. After studying at the American Academy of Dramatic Arts, Davis worked in a number of New York stage productions. On TV, he was one of many cast members of the 1977 miniseries *Roots*, he played an American soldier in Vietnam in the 1981 TV movie *A Rumor of War*, essayed the title role in 1985's *Robert Kennedy and His Times*, and played the classic paranoid Lt. Cmdr. Queeg in Robert Altman's 1988 production of *The Caine Mutiny Court Martial*. In films, Davis' stardom was secured by his intense portrayal of Billy, a young American imprisoned in Turkey for drug charges, in *Midnight Express* (1978); he also shone in *Chariots of Fire* (1981), and in the lead of *Querelle* (1983), Rainer Werner Fassbinder's adaptation of a once-censorable Jean Genet novel. Davis died of AIDS at the age of 42. **Selected Works:** *The Player* (1992), *Habitation of Dragons* (1992), *Unspeakable Acts* (1990)

## Geena Davis (Virginia Davis)

**Born:** January 21, 1957; Wareham, MA

**Years Active in the Industry:** by decade

| 10ˢ | 20ˢ | 30ˢ | 40ˢ | 50ˢ | 60ˢ | 70ˢ | 80ˢ | 90ˢ |
|-----|-----|-----|-----|-----|-----|-----|-----|-----|
|     |     |     |     |     |     |     |     |     |

While attending Boston University in 1979, tall, vivacious American actress Geena Davis enrolled in a professional Actor's Training Program. Later she joined the Mount Washington Repertory Company in New England. In the early '80s she appeared in and wrote an episode of the TV series *Buffalo Bill*, marking her debut before the camera, then went on to get roles in TV movies; her big-screen debut came in a supporting role in the hit comedy *Tootsie* (1982) with Dustin Hoffman. Although she didn't appear in another film until 1985, her screen career after that was busy and successful, helped along by co-starring roles in two highly successful films, the horror movie *The Fly* (1986) and Tim Burton's dark comedy *Beetlejuice* (1987). For her work in *The Accidental Tourist* (1988) she won a Best Supporting Actress Oscar, and she was nominated for a Best Actress Oscar for *Thelma and Louise* (1991). She has tended to play quirky, unconventional, off-beat, eccentric characters. Divorced from actor Jeff Goldblum, she married director Renny Harlin in 1993. **Selected Works:** *Hero* (1992), *A League of Their Own* (1992), *Thelma & Louise* (1991), *Angie* (1994)

## Judy Davis

**Born:** 1956; Perth, Australia

**Years Active in the Industry:** by decade

| 10ˢ | 20ˢ | 30ˢ | 40ˢ | 50ˢ | 60ˢ | 70ˢ | 80ˢ | 90ˢ |
|-----|-----|-----|-----|-----|-----|-----|-----|-----|
|     |     |     |     |     |     |     |     |     |

Australian born actress Judy Davis has thusfar had a highly distinguished career. Before becoming an actress, she was a rock singer—she left convent-school to make that career move. She

later attended the Western Australia Institute of Technology and the National Institute of Dramatic Art. She made her big screen debut in feminist director Gillian Armstrong's 1979 blockbuster *My Brilliant Career*, which won Davis a British Film Academy Best Actress award. Throughout the '80s, she has been noted for her portrayals of strong, vital women unafraid to thumb their noses at traditional notions of womanhood in films such as *High Tide* (1987) and *A Passage to India* (1984). In recent years, she has begun to break out of those roles into edgier, more highly-strung women in a variety of roles ranging from the whimsical (*Alice* [1990]) to the horrific (*Naked Lunch* [1991]) to the sympathetic (*The Ref* [1994]). **Selected Works:** *Barton Fink* (1991), *Husbands and Wives* (1992), *Impromptu* (1990), *One Against the Wind* (1991), *Where Angels Fear to Tread* (1991)

# Ossie Davis

**Born:** December 18, 1917; Cogdell, GA

**Years Active in the Industry:** by decade

| 10s | 20s | 30s | 40s | 50s | 60s | 70s | 80s | 90s |
|-----|-----|-----|-----|-----|-----|-----|-----|-----|
|     |     |     |     |     |     |     |     |     |

Actor, director, producer, playwright, screenwriter Ossie Davis attended Howard and Columbia, then moved to New York with the hope of becoming a writer. However, he also studied acting with the Rose McClendon Players in Harlem. During 32 months in the army in World War II, he wrote and performed in several shows for the troops. After the war, he landed a role in the Broadway show *Jeb Turner* in 1946; the play closed after nine performances, but the cast included actress Ruby Dee, whom Davis married two years later. In the late '40s and '50s he continued finding stage roles, and appeared in one film, *No Way Out* (1950), which also featured Ruby Dee; he also appeared in two TV dramas. However, for the most part, this period of his career was a struggle. He began to do better in the '60s, when television opened up to African-American actors; he appeared in episodes of numerous TV shows. His greatest triumph came in 1961, when he wrote and appeared in the Broadway play *Purlie Victorious*; two years later he repeated his success with the film version, *Gone Are the Days!* (1963). He began directing films in the early 70s, beginning with *Cotton Comes to Harlem* (1970). In the early '70s he also founded and headed Third World Cinema, a film production company meant to encourage the work of black and Puerto Rican filmmakers. **Selected Works:** *Do the Right Thing* (1989), *Jungle Fever* (1991), *Malcolm X* (1992), *Grumpy Old Men* (1993), *The Client* (1994)

# Sammy Davis, Jr.

**Born:** December 28, 1925; New York, NY
**Died:** May 16, 1990

**Years Active in the Industry:** by decade

| 10s | 20s | 30s | 40s | 50s | 60s | 70s | 80s | 90s |
|-----|-----|-----|-----|-----|-----|-----|-----|-----|
|     |     |     |     |     |     |     |     |     |

Actor, singer, dancer Sammy Davis, Jr., the son of vaudeville entertainer Sammy Davis, began performing professionally at the age of three, appearing in his uncle Will Mastin's family act of seven men and seven women; during the early Depression the act was reduced in size to Davis, Jr., his father, and his uncle, and was called the Will Mastin trio. Soon he developed into a very versatile entertainer, skilled at singing, dancing, telling jokes, doing mimicry, and playing several instruments. He debuted onscreen at age seven in the short *Rufus Jones for President* (1933), in which he acted and danced. He toured the country with the Trio until the '40s, when he spent two years in the army; when he returned, the act was renamed "The Will Mastin Trio, Starring Sammy Davis, Jr.," and began playing big variety theaters and top nightclubs. In the '50s he performed solo, soon becoming a popular TV entertainer as well; some critics considered him the world's greatest living entertainer. A car accident in 1954 cost him his left eye and caused other injuries that jeopardized his career. However, he quickly bounced back, and in the mid-'50s he began getting work in films, debuting onscreen in *The Benny Goodman Story* (1956) and playing his first dramatic lead role in *Anna Lucasta* (1958). Also, in 1956 he debuted on Broadway as the star of *Mr. Wonderful*; later he starred in the Broadway show *Golden Boy*. As a screen actor he became best known for his work with the "Rat Pack," comprised of Frank Sinatra, Dean Martin, Peter Lawford, and Joey Bishop, who socialized and worked together; although the inclusion of a black man in the group was at the time considered egalitarian, his roles tended to be tokenistic and occasionally involved benign racist jokes at his expense. He somewhat alienated himself from black audiences, who occasionally booed him as a sell-out; and in a controversial move he converted to Judaism. He was also a popular recording star with several hits including "Mr. Bojangles" and "The Candy Man." He was frequently a guest star on TV specials and episodes of TV series, and twice hosted his own variety-talk shows, *The Sammy Davis Jr. Show* (NBC, 1966) and *Sammy and Company* (syndicated, 1975-77). He authored the autobiography *Yes I Can* (1965). He married and divorced Swedish actress Mai Britt. **Selected Works:** *Ocean's 11* (1960), *Robin and the Seven Hoods* (1964), *Cannonball Run* (1981), *Tap* (1989), *Kid Who Loved Christmas* (1990)

# Bruce Davison

**Born:** June 28, 1946; Philadelphia, PA

**Years Active in the Industry:** by decade

| 10s | 20s | 30s | 40s | 50s | 60s | 70s | 80s | 90s |
|-----|-----|-----|-----|-----|-----|-----|-----|-----|
|     |     |     |     |     |     |     |     |     |

Bruce Davison studied acting at New York University's prestigious School of the Arts, then at age 21 made his stage debut on Broadway in *Tiger At the Gate*. He went on to a prosperous stage career, performing in works ranging from Shakespeare to American standards to provocative modern dramas. He won the Drama-logue Award three times, first for his portrayal of the deformed John Merrick in the title role of Broadway's *The Elephant Man*; he won it the third time for his work in *Streamers*, for which he also won a Los Angeles Critics Award. He debuted onscreen in *Last Summer* (1969), portraying the "bad boy" among four teenagers coming of age in a sinister way. Although he has remained fairly busy as a screen actor, he has generally appeared in forgettable films and has yet to establish himself as a well-known screen presence; the highlight of his film career came when he received a Best Supporting Actor Oscar nomination for his work in *Longtime Companion* (1990), the first major feature film to deal with the subject of AIDS. Since 1978 he has also worked frequently on TV, appearing in TV movies as well as co-starring in the sitcom *Harry and the Hendersons*. For his portrayal of an escaped POW in the TV movie *Summer of My German Soldier* (1978), he received an Emmy nomination. He is most skilled at portraying caring, sharing, sensitive types and victims of circumstance. **Selected Works:** *Steel and Lace* (1990), *Short Cuts* (1993), *Six Degrees of Separation* (1993)

# Doris Day (Doris von Kappelhoff)

**Born:** April 3, 1922; Cincinnati, OH

**Years Active in the Industry:** by decade

| 10s | 20s | 30s | 40s | 50s | 60s | 70s | 80s | 90s |
|-----|-----|-----|-----|-----|-----|-----|-----|-----|

On screen, Doris Day was the epitome of perkiness and sunshine, but off-screen her life was not always so cheerful. Born Doris von Kappelhoff, her teenage aspirations of becoming a dancer were crushed when she was injured in a serious auto accident at age 15. Instead of giving up entirely, the plucky Day became a singer, performing in clubs and on the radio. By the early '40s she achieved popularity singing with the Bob Crosby and Les Brown bands; by the mid-'40s she was a very successful recording star. In 1948, she made her feature film debut in *Romance on the High Seas*, which lead her to be cast as the eternally wholesome "girl next door" in a series of light musicals and occasional dramas. During the early 50s, Day had become the most popular female star in the U.S. She is best remembered for playing innocent virgin to big handsome "wolves" such as Rock Hudson and Cary Grant in a series of frothy bedroom farces in the '50s; for one of these films, *Pillow Talk* (1959), she received a Best Actress Oscar nomination. In 1975, Day authored an autobiography, *Doris Day: Her Own Story* (1975), revealing that her life was not all sunshine and daisies; in it she discussed her unhappy childhood that included a year's hospitalization when she

was 13, life on the road at 16, and her brief marriage to a psychopath at 17. In 1968, she suffered a mental breakdown and retired from films after discovering that her recently deceased third husband, manager, and producer Marty Melcher had either mishandled or embezzled her $20 million fortune, leaving her nearly destitute. But Day, still as plucky as she was when she was 15, quickly recovered; she then went on to star in the popular TV series *The Doris Day Show*. In 1974, Day sued her former lawyer, who had shared responsibility with Melcher for her fortune, and was awarded $22 million as a settlement. In the '80s she briefly hosted a cable TV show, *Doris Day and Friends*. **Selected Works:** *Love Me or Leave Me* (1955), *Lover Come Back* (1961)

# Laraine Day (Laraine Johnson)

**Born:** October 13, 1917; Roosevelt, UT

**Years Active in the Industry:** by decade

| 10s | 20s | 30s | 40s | 50s | 60s | 70s | 80s | 90s |
|-----|-----|-----|-----|-----|-----|-----|-----|-----|

American actress Laraine Day, a descendant of a prominent Mormon pioneer leader, moved with her family from Utah to California, where she began her acting career with the Long Beach Players. In 1937 she debuted onscreen in a bit part in *Stella Dallas*; shortly afterwards she won lead roles in several George O'Brien Westerns at RKO, in which she was billed as "Laraine Hays" and then "Laraine Johnson." In 1939 she signed with MGM, going on to become popular and well-known (billed as "Laraine Day") as Nurse Mary Lamont, the title character's fiancee in a string of seven "Dr. Kildare" movies beginning with *Calling Dr. Kildare* (1939); Lew Ayres played Dr. Kildare. During the '40s and '50s she played a variety of leads in medium-budget films made by several studios. She rarely appeared in films after 1960, but later occasionally appeared on TV, portraying matronly types. She was married to famous baseball player Leo Durocher from 1947-60, when she was sometimes referred to as "the first lady of baseball." Her first husband was singer Ray Hendricks, and her third, TV producer Michael Grilkhas. She is the author of a book of memoirs, *Day With Giants* (1952), and an inspirational book, *The America We Love*; in the '70s she was the official spokeswoman for the Make America Better program of the National Association of Real Estate Boards, traveling across the country speaking on environmental issues. **Selected Works:** *Foreign Correspondent* (1940), *The High and the Mighty* (1954)

# Daniel Day-Lewis

**Born:** April 29, 1957; London, England

**Years Active in the Industry:** by decade

| 10s | 20s | 30s | 40s | 50s | 60s | 70s | 80s | 90s |
|-----|-----|-----|-----|-----|-----|-----|-----|-----|

To some, it might have seemed as though British actor Daniel Day-Lewis burst out of nowhere to star in 1989's *My Left Foot*, but in fact he'd been in films since 1971. The grandson of British film executive Michael Balcon, Day-Lewis had neither the time nor the inclination for boarding schools and social training, and by age 13 he'd dropped out of his privileged life style. Thanks to his granddad's influence, Day-Lewis managed to secure a bit part as a teenage hoodlum in John Schlesinger's *Sunday, Bloody, Sunday* (1971), but he didn't take acting seriously until he was 15. He trained at the Bristol Old Vic and made his legitimate stage debut in 1982, and shortly afterward appeared in small roles in such films as *Gandhi* (1983) and *The Bounty* (1985). Day-Lewis first caught the eyes of critics with his performance as an insufferable young aristocrat in Merchant-Ivory's *A Room with a View* (1985); other early performances of note could be seen in *My Beautiful Launderette* (1984) and *The Unbearable Lightness of Being* (1988)—films that, though designed for limited audience, managed to break into big-time distribution. Day-Lewis won an Academy Award for the role of true-life paralyzed artist/writer Christy Brown in *My Left Foot* (1989), then assured the film extra publicity attention with his near-monastic protection of his own privacy. *My Left Foot* opened the doors for subsequent superlative Daniel Day-Lewis appearances: he was a virile Hawkeye in *Last of the Mohicans* (1992); offered an astonishingly restrained performance in *The Age of Innocence* (1993) as a man trapped by the sexual mores of the 19th century; and in *In the Name of the Father* (1993), Day-Lewis played another real-life character—a Belfast man falsely imprisoned for a terrorist bombing.

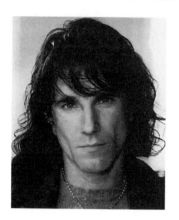

more's theater group and got bit parts in several movies, as well as work in TV commercials. In 1951, Dean moved to New York, where he worked as a busboy to support himself until he landed a part in the Broadway play *See the Jaguar*. He then remained in the Big Apple to observe classes at the Actors' Studio and played small roles on television until he again returned to Broadway to appear in *The Immoralist* in 1954; this lead him to test for Warner Bros. Within a year, Dean had starred in three films, all which had a tremendous effect on mid-'50s youth who came to see Dean (especially in his signature film *Rebel Without a Cause* [1955]) as the embodiment of their own restlessness. The films were also critically acclaimed; for his roles in *East of Eden* (1955), and *Giant* (1956)—his final film—Dean was nominated for Oscars for Best Actor. His career came to a sudden stop on September 30, 1955, when he was involved in a high speed car crash en route to a road race in Salinas. Following his death, his popularity exploded and he became almost a mystical figure to his most rabid fans. As with Valentino in the late '20s and Elvis in the '70s, some of Dean's fans even refused to believe that he was really dead and fostered multiple theories on his actual fate. Following his demise, many authors have cashed in on Dean's cultish following by publishing biographies; among them was one published by his former roommate James Bast that was made into the 1976 television movie *James Dean*. Filmmakers Robert Altman and James Bridges have also made movie tributes to Dean, a screen legend who will remain forever young, tormented, and fascinating.

# James Dean (James Byron Dean)

**Born:** February 8, 1931; Marion, IN
**Died:** September 30, 1955

**Years Active in the Industry:** by decade

| 10ˢ | 20ˢ | 30ˢ | 40ˢ | 50ˢ | 60ˢ | 70ˢ | 80ˢ | 90ˢ |
|-----|-----|-----|-----|-----|-----|-----|-----|-----|
|     |     |     |     |     |     |     |     |     |

During his all-to-brief career, actor James Dean rose to become a true pop-icon in American culture. When he was five, the Indiana born Dean moved with his family to L.A. Four years later, following his mother's death, he was sent back to Indiana to be raised by relatives. After high school he moved to California and attended college; there he also began acting with James Whit-

# Jan DeBont

**Born:** October 22, 1943; Holland

**Years Active in the Industry:** by decade

| 10ˢ | 20ˢ | 30ˢ | 40ˢ | 50ˢ | 60ˢ | 70ˢ | 80ˢ | 90ˢ |
|-----|-----|-----|-----|-----|-----|-----|-----|-----|
|     |     |     |     |     |     |     |     |     |

Cinematographer Jan DeBont rose to fame with a fellow Hollander, director Paul Verhoeven. A graduate of the Amsterdam Film Academy, DeBont lensed Verhoeven's *Turkish Delight* (1973), *Keetje Tippel* (1975) and *Soldier of Orange* (1979). DeBont's first American film, *Private Lessons* (1981), was, in keeping with its visual style, directed in a quasi-European fashion by Alan Myerson. During his Hollywood years, DeBont has emerged as one of the foremost lensers of slam-bang action fare, as witnessed in *Jewel of the Nile* (1985), *Die Hard* (1988) and *Hunt for Red October* (1990);

he chose to stick to the genre for his first directorial effort, the thrilling blockbuster *Speed* (1994). **Selected Works:** *Basic Instinct* (1992), *Flatliners* (1990), *Lethal Weapon, Part 3* (1992), *Shining Through* (1992)

# Rosemary DeCamp

**Born:** November 14, 1914; Prescott, AZ

**Years Active in the Industry:** by decade

| 10s | 20s | 30s | 40s | 50s | 60s | 70s | 80s | 90s |
|-----|-----|-----|-----|-----|-----|-----|-----|-----|

From her earliest stage work onward, American actress Rosemary DeCamp played character roles that belied her youth and fresh-scrubbed attractiveness. On radio, DeCamp developed the vocal timbre that enabled her to portray a rich variety (and age-range) of characters. A peripheral performer on *One Man's Family* at 21, DeCamp showed up on several radio soap operas and anthologies before settling into the role of secretary Judy Price on the *Dr. Christian* series in 1937. DeCamp made her film bow in *Cheers for Miss Bishop* (1941), in which she and most of the cast were required to "age" several decades. With *The Jungle Book* (1941), the actress played the first of her many mother roles. The most famous examples of DeCamp's specialized film work are *Yankee Doodle Dandy* (1942), in which she was the Irish-American mother of George M. Cohan (James Cagney, who was 14 years her senior), and *Rhapsody in Blue* (1945), in which she played George Gershwin's Jewish mother (Gershwin was impersonated by Robert Alda, one year younger than DeCamp). Even when playing a character close to her own age, such as the Red Cross worker in *Pride of the Marines* (1945), DeCamp's interest in the leading man (in this case the same-aged John Garfield) was strictly maternal. On television, DeCamp was Peg Riley to Jackie Gleason's Chester A. Riley on the original 1949 run of *The Life of Riley*. She also played rakish Bob Cummings' levelheaded sister Margaret in *Love That Bob* (1955-59), and later was seen as Marlo Thomas' mother on *That Girl* (1966-70). In 1965, Rosemary subbed for her old friend Ronald Reagan as host on *Death Valley Days*; FCC rules of the time compelled the removal of Reagan's scenes when the show was telecast in California, where he was running for governor. Upon Reagan's election, Robert Taylor took over as host, but DeCamp was installed as permanent commercial spokesperson for 20 Mule Team Borax. Semi-retired for several years, DeCamp reemerged in 1981 for a "de-campy" cameo part in the horror spoof *Saturday the 14th*. **Selected Works:** *Hold Back the Dawn* (1941)

# Sandra Dee (Alexandra Zuck)

**Born:** April 23, 1942; Bayonne, NJ

**Years Active in the Industry:** by decade

| 10s | 20s | 30s | 40s | 50s | 60s | 70s | 80s | 90s |
|-----|-----|-----|-----|-----|-----|-----|-----|-----|

American actress Sandra Dee began her career as a model at age 12, moving on to TV commercials. Dee's film break came when producer Ross Hunter, balking at Natalie Wood's lofty salary demands, decided to use a newcomer to play Lana Turner's daughter in *Imitation of Life* (1959). The result for Dee was a long-term contract at Universal, though one of her biggest moneymakers was the 1959 Warner Bros. "date picture" *A Summer Place*. In 1961 Dee married singer/actor Bobby Darin, with whom she appeared in three lightweight but high-grossing film comedies. After her divorce from Darin, Dee's career began a downhill slide (she could no longer convey her patented perky-teen charm); her decline was occasionally slowed a bit by such curious highlights as the pseudo-hip sex comedy *Doctor, You've Got to Be Kidding* (1967) and the nail-biting psychological scare film *The Dunwich Horror* (1970). Out of movies completely by 1971, Dee retreated to private life, occasionally popping up on TV and granting interviews with nostalgia-happy young film buffs. Much of the actress' latter-day fame has rested upon the satiric 1950s-style rock ballad in the Broadway smash *Grease* titled "Look at Me, I'm Sandra Dee".

# Olivia de Havilland (Olivia Mary de Havilland)

**Born:** July 1, 1916; Tokyo, Japan

**Years Active in the Industry:** by decade

| 10s | 20s | 30s | 40s | 50s | 60s | 70s | 80s | 90s |
|-----|-----|-----|-----|-----|-----|-----|-----|-----|

Born in Japan to a British patent attorney and his actress wife, Olivia de Havilland was the older sister of actress Joan Fontaine (that there was never any love lost between the two sisters

is something that won't be dwelled upon here). Succumbing to the lure of Thespis while attending high school in Los Angeles, de Havilland played Hermia in an amateur production of *A Midsummer Night's Dream*. She was spotted by famed director Max Reinhardt, who cast De-Havilland in his legendary Hollywood Bowl production of *Midsummer*. This led to her being cast in Warner Bros.' film version of *Midsummer* in 1935, and to being signed to a long-term contract. Considering herself a classical actress, de Havilland tried to refuse the traditional ingenue roles offered her by Warners, but the studio countered by telling her she'd be ruined in Hollywood if she didn't cooperate. Her haughty behavior on the set of Joe E. Brown's *Alibi Ike* (1935) made her the target of the crew's pranks and practical jokes, but de Havilland finally let down her guard and became "one of the guys" by pulling a few pranks of her own. On loan-out to David O. Selznick, de Havilland portrayed Melanie Hamilton in *Gone with the Wind* (1939), earning an Oscar nomination in the process. When she lost to Hattie McDaniel, de Havilland was heartbroken, but was lectured by Selznick's wife Irene, who told the girl that it was sociologically important for an African American to win the Oscar and that her time would come. Indeed it did—in fact, de Havilland would win two Oscars, the first for 1946's *To Each His Own*, the second for 1949's *The Heiress* (she also deserved a nomination for her portrayal of a mentally ill woman in 1949's *The Snake Pit*). De Havilland also made news of a legal rather than artistic nature when she sued Warner Bros. for extending her seven-year contract by tacking on the months she'd been on suspension for refusing to take a part. De Havilland spent three long years off the screen, but in the end she won her case, and the "de Havilland Law", as it would become known, effectively destroyed the studios' ability to virtually enslave their contractees by unfairly extending their contract time. After completing *The Heiress* (1949), de Havilland spent several years on Broadway, cutting down her subsequent film appearances to approximately one per year. In 1955 she moved to France with her second husband, *Paris Match* editor Pierre Galante; she later recalled her Paris years with the semiautobiographical *Every Frenchman Has One*. In the 1960s, de Havilland showed up in a brace of those profitable "fading star" horror films, *Lady in a Cage* (1964) and *Hush Hush Sweet Charlotte* (1965), in which she replaced Joan Crawford. During the next decade, she appeared in a number of TV productions and in such all-star film efforts as *Airport '77* (1977) and *The Swarm* (1978). After years of retirement, De Havilland once more found herself in the limelight in 1989, on the occasion of the 50th anniversary of *Gone with the Wind*; as the only surviving star from this film, she was much sought after for interviews and reminiscences, but graciously refused virtually every request. **Selected Works:** *Adventures of Robin Hood* (1938), *Captain Blood* (1935), *Private Lives of Elizabeth and Essex* (1939), *Hold Back the Dawn* (1941), *My Cousin Rachel* (1952)

# Dana Delaney

**Born:** 1956; New York, NY

**Years Active in the Industry:** by decade

| 10s | 20s | 30s | 40s | 50s | 60s | 70s | 80s | 90s |
|-----|-----|-----|-----|-----|-----|-----|-----|-----|
|     |     |     |     |     |     |     | ■   | ■   |

American actress Dana Delaney can thank the restrooms of America for her family's financial security; Dana's grandfather invented the Delaney flush valve. A graduate of Phillips Academy and Wesleyan University, Delaney began making television appearances in the mid-1980s on such programs as *Moonlighting* and the movie *A Winner Never Quits* (1986). In 1988, she was cast as Army nurse Lt. Colleen McMurphy in the Vietnam-era TV drama *China Beach*, which ran until 1990. In her film appearances (*Moon Over Parador* [1988], *Patty Hearst* [1988], *Light Sleeper* [1992]), Delaney has leaned toward characters governed by their neuroses

and eccentricities. In 1994, Delaney began showing up in publicity photos wearing a skimpy leather dominatrix outfit and brandishing a whip. No, she hadn't switched careers: it was all for a much-touted "bondage" comedy/mystery *Exit to Eden*. When the film deservedly laid an egg, Delaney immediately recovered with a strong portrayal as birth control pioneer Margaret Sanger (whom she closely resembled) in a made-for-cable TV biopic. **Selected Works:** *Housesitter* (1992), *Tombstone* (1993)

# Georges Delerue

**Born:** March 12, 1925; Roubaix, France
**Died:** March 20, 1992; Los Angeles, CA

**Years Active in the Industry:** by decade

| 10s | 20s | 30s | 40s | 50s | 60s | 70s | 80s | 90s |
|-----|-----|-----|-----|-----|-----|-----|-----|-----|
|     |     |     |     |     | ■   | ■   | ■   |     |

French film composer Georges Delerue studied his craft under prestigious movie musician Darius Milhaud. More interested in establishing mood than churning out hit theme songs, Delerue contributed the scores to over 150 motion pictures. In his native France, Delerue wrote music for such highly regarded New Wave films as *Hiroshima Mon Amour* (1959), *Shoot the Piano Player* (1960) and *Jules et Jim* (1961). Equally busy in England and the U.S., Delerue worked on *A Man for All Seasons* (1966), *Anne of a Thousand Days* (1969), *Day of the Dolphin* (1973), *A Little Romance* (1979), *Platoon* (1986) and *Steel Magnolias* (1989). He also penned music for stage and TV productions during his long career. Delerue's final score was for the bizarre American romantic comedy *Joe Versus the Volcano* (1990).

# Alain Delon

**Born:** November 8, 1935; Sceaux, France

**Years Active in the Industry:** by decade

| 10s | 20s | 30s | 40s | 50s | 60s | 70s | 80s | 90s |
|-----|-----|-----|-----|-----|-----|-----|-----|-----|
|     |     |     |     |     | ■   | ■   | ■   | ■   |

Aggressive, dynamic, handsome, romantic-looking, sexy French lead actor Alain Delon, after being expelled from several Catholic schools, enlisted in the French marines at age 17; he served as a parachutist and participated in the disastrous Dienbienphu

siege. His good looks helped him break into films shortly after he returned to civilian life. He debuted onscreen in *Quand la Femme s'en mele* (1957), and within a few years he was much in demand for lead roles in both French and international films; however, although he worked with such illustrious directors as Clement, Visconti, and Antonioni, it was difficult for him to be seen as anything but a pretty face. Partly to compensate, in 1964 he set up his own film production company, Adel, and within a decade he was as much a producer as an actor. In 1968, the body of his bodyguard was found in a garbage dump, leading to a major scandal involving murder, drugs, and sex; he and his wife, actress Natalie Delon, became the central figures in the scandal, which also involved many politicians and show business people. Delon was cleared of any wrong-doing, but he admitted to having had close connections with underworld figures since his youth; the result of the scandal (which was quickly hushed up) was to help rather than hurt his career, giving him an aura of toughness offscreen as well as on. **Selected Works:** *Nouvelle Vague* (1990)

# Julie Delpy

**Born:** 1969; Paris, France

**Years Active in the Industry:** by decade

| 10ˢ | 20ˢ | 30ˢ | 40ˢ | 50ˢ | 60ˢ | 70ˢ | 80ˢ | 90ˢ |
|-----|-----|-----|-----|-----|-----|-----|-----|-----|
|     |     |     |     |     |     |     |     |     |

Discovered at age 14 by director Jean-Luc Goddard, blonde French actress Julie Delpy gained worldwide prominence with her performance as a fervent anti-Nazi in *Europa Europa* (1991). Efforts

to make Delpy a mainstream Hollywood actress in such films as *The Three Musketeers* (1994) have been resisted by Delpy herself, who prefers appearing in the small, thought-provoking films best appreciated at cinema festivals. *Killing Zoe* (1993), *White* (1994) and *Before Sunrise* (1995) are among the more esoteric entries in her resume.

While much in demand as an actress, Delpy has evinced an interest in becoming a director, enrolling in the summer directing course at New York University. **Selected Works:** *Voyager* (1991), *Three Colors: Blue* (1993), *Three Colors: Red* (1994), *Three Colors: White* (1994)

# Dolores Del Rio (Lolita Dolores Martinez Asunsolo Lopez Negrette)

**Born:** August 3, 1905; Durango, Mexico
**Died:** April 11, 1983; Newport Beach, CA

**Years Active in the Industry:** by decade

| 10ˢ | 20ˢ | 30ˢ | 40ˢ | 50ˢ | 60ˢ | 70ˢ | 80ˢ | 90ˢ |
|-----|-----|-----|-----|-----|-----|-----|-----|-----|
|     |     |     |     |     |     |     |     |     |

Born into an aristocratic Mexican family, actress Dolores Del Rio was the daughter of a prominent banker. After a convent education, she was married at age 16 to writer Jaime Del Rio, whose name she retained long after the marriage had dissolved. The second cousin of silent film star Ramon Novarro, Del Rio was a regular guest at Hollywood parties; at one of these, director Edwin Carewe, struck by her dazzling beauty (and who wasn't?), felt she'd be perfect for a role in his upcoming film *Joanna* (1925). Stardom followed rapidly, with Del Rio achieving top billing in several major silent productions, including *What Price Glory?* (1927), as the French coquette Charmaine, and *The Loves of Carmen* (1927), in the title role. Since Del Rio spoke fluent English, the switch-over to sound posed no problem for her, though her marked Hispanic accent limited her range of roles. Most often, she was cast on the basis of beauty first, talent second; she is at her most alluring in 1932's *Bird of Paradise*, in which she appears all but nude in some sequences. Del Rio looked equally fetching when fully clothed, as in the title role of *Madame DuBarry* (1934). Upon the breakup of her second marriage to art director Cedric Gibbons, the graceful, intelligent Del Rio became the most eligible "bachelor girl" in Hollywood; one of her most ardent suitors was Orson Welles, ten years her junior, who cast her in his 1942 RKO production *Journey Into Fear*. In 1943, Del Rio returned to Mexico to star in films, negotiating a "percentage of profits" deal which increased her already vast fortune. Enormously popular in her native country, Del Rio returned only occasionally to Hollywood, usually at the request of such long-standing industry friends as director John Ford. Her seemingly ageless beauty and milk-smooth complexion was the source of envy and speculation; from all accounts, she used no cosmetic surgery, maintaining her looks principally through a diligent (and self-invented) diet and exercise program. Even as late as 1960, she looked far too young to play Elvis Presley's mother in *Flaming Star*. Del Rio retired from filmmaking in 1978, choosing to devote her time to managing her financial and real estate holdings, and to her lifelong hobbies of writing and painting. **Selected Works:** *The Fugitive* (1948)

# Dom DeLuise

**Born:** August 1, 1933; Brooklyn, NY

**Years Active in the Industry:** by decade

| 10s | 20s | 30s | 40s | 50s | 60s | 70s | 80s | 90s |
|-----|-----|-----|-----|-----|-----|-----|-----|-----|
|     |     |     |     |     | ■ | ■ | ■ | ■ |

Rotund comedic character actor Dom DeLuise has had success on stage, TV, and in films. After working in Cleveland repertory, he became popular as Dominick the Great, an inept magician, on the TV series *The Garry Moore Show*. He next went on to star in his own TV variety program and appeared on Broadway, most notably in *The Last of the Red Hot Lovers*. He debuted onscreen in 1964, going on to work frequently with Mel Brooks, Gene Wilder, and Burt Reynolds; in the mid- '80s he began to be in demand to do voice-overs for feature cartoons. He directed himself in *Hot Stuff* (1980). He is married to actress Carol Arthur and is the father of actors Peter DeLuise and Michael DeLuise. **Selected Works:** *Almost Pregnant* (1991), *Blazing Saddles* (1974), *Driving Me Crazy* (1991), *Happily Ever After* (1991), *Robin Hood: Men in Tights* (1993)

# William Demarest

**Born:** February 27, 1892; St. Paul, MN
**Died:** December 28, 1983; Palm Springs, CA

**Years Active in the Industry:** by decade

| 10s | 20s | 30s | 40s | 50s | 60s | 70s | 80s | 90s |
|-----|-----|-----|-----|-----|-----|-----|-----|-----|
|     | ■ | ■ | ■ | ■ | ■ | ■ |     |     |

Famed for his ratchety voice and cold-fish stare, William Demarest was an "old pro" even when he was a young pro. He began his stage career at age 13, holding down a variety of colorful jobs (including professional boxer) during the off-season. After years in carnivals and as a vaudeville headliner, Demarest starred in such Broadway long-runners as *Earl Carroll's Sketch Book*. He was signed with Warner Bros. pictures in 1926, where he was briefly paired with Clyde Cook as a "Mutt and Jeff"-style comedy team. Demarest's late-silent and early-talkie roles varied in size, becoming more consistently substantial in the late 1930s. His specialty during this period was a bone-crushing pratfall, a physical feat he was able to perform into his 60s. While at Paramount in the 1940s, Demarest was a special favorite of writer/director Preston Sturges, who cast Demarest in virtually all his films: *The Great McGinty* (1940); *Christmas in July* (1940); *The Lady Eve* (1941); *Sullivan's Travels* (1942); *The Palm Beach Story* (1942); *Hail the Conquering Hero* (1944); *Miracle of Morgan's Creek* (1944), wherein Demarest was at his bombastic best as Officer Kockenlocker; and *The Great Moment* (1944). For his role as Al Jolson's fictional mentor Steve Martin in *The Jolson Story* (1946), Demarest was Oscar-nominated (the actor had, incidentally, appeared with Jolie in 1927's *The Jazz Singer*). Demarest continued appearing in films until 1975, whenever his increasingly heavy TV schedule would allow. Many Demarest fans assumed that his role as Uncle Charlie in *My Three Sons* (66-72) was his first regular TV work: in truth, Demarest had previously starred in the shortlived 1960 sitcom *Love and Marriage*. **Selected Works:** *Devil and Miss Jones* (1941)

# Cecil Blount DeMille

**Born:** August 12, 1881; Ashfield, MA
**Died:** January 21, 1959; Hollywood, CA

**Years Active in the Industry:** by decade

| 10s | 20s | 30s | 40s | 50s | 60s | 70s | 80s | 90s |
|-----|-----|-----|-----|-----|-----|-----|-----|-----|
| ■ | ■ | ■ | ■ | ■ |     |     |     |     |

An actor and general manager with his mother's theatrical troupe since the mid-1900s, Cecil B. DeMille formed a filmmaking partnership in 1913 with vaudeville artist Jesse L. Lasky and businessman Samuel Goldfish (soon to be known as Samuel Goldwyn); their first venture was *The Squaw Man* (1913), which DeMille co-directed and co-produced with Victor Apfel. This successful and elaborate six-reeler launched DeMille on a lifelong career in films. His first solo effort was the western *The Virginian* (1914), which he also co-scripted. He edited and wrote (or co-scripted) almost all his successful films, with the notable exception of the popular melodrama *The Cheat* (1915). Writer Jeanie Macpherson began working for DeMille in 1914 with *The Captive* (1915), and scripted most of his later silent films: hits that included witty romantic farces (*Don't Change Your Husband*); epic morality tales that combine modern dramas with visions of history (*Joan The Woman* [1916]) or the Bible (*The Ten Commandments* [1923]); and perhaps DeMille's greatest artistic success, the handsome and moving life of Christ, *The King of Kings* (1927). Macpherson also wrote DeMille's first three talkies, ending their collaboration in 1930 with the bizarre comedy *Madam Satan* (1930). In the '30s DeMille continued to score hits with epics (*Sign of the Cross* [1932], *Cleopatra* [1934]) and westerns (*The Plainsman* [1937], *Union Pacific* [1939]). His output became more sporadic over the 1940s, but he still pleased the public with his rugged actioners *Northwest Mounted Police* (1940) and *Reap the Wild Wind* (1942). DeMille's last three films—*Samson and Delilah* (1950), *The Greatest Show on Earth* (1952), and *The Ten Commandments* (1956)—were the most successful releases of their year; *The Ten Commandments* was also the 1950s' box office champ.

# Jonathan Demme

**Born:** February 22, 1944; Baldwin, NY

**Years Active in the Industry:** by decade

| 10s | 20s | 30s | 40s | 50s | 60s | 70s | 80s | 90s |
|-----|-----|-----|-----|-----|-----|-----|-----|-----|
|     |     |     |     |     |     | ■ | ■ | ■ |

A publicist for Joseph E. Levine in the late 1960s and Roger Corman in the early '70s, Jonathan Demme began making low-budget exploitation films in 1971, producing and co-scripting the biker tale *Angels Hard as They Come* (1971) and the woman's-prison actioner *The Hot Box* (1972). The latter genre became something of a specialty, with Demme co-writing *Black Mama, White Mama* and making his directing debut with *Caged Heat* (1974) starring Barbara Steele. He began attracting critical atten-

tion with his 1978 comedy *Citizens Band* (aka *Handle With Care*) and showed himself to be an eclectic director in the '80s, his range including the comedies *Melvin and Howard* (1980) and *Married to the Mob* (1988), the Talking Heads concert film *Stop Making Sense* (1984), and the dark farce *Something Wild* (1986). Demme had his biggest hits in the '90s with the thriller *The Silence of the Lambs* (1991), which won five Oscars (including Best Picture and Best Director) as well as numerous other critical awards, and the AIDS-themed drama *Philadelphia* (1993), which was also nominated for the Best Picture Oscar. **Selected Works:** *Cousin Bobby* (1992), *Miami Blues* (1990), *Household Saints* (1993)

# Rebecca De Mornay

**Born:** August 29, 1961; Santa Rosa, CA

**Years Active in the Industry:** by decade

| 10ˢ | 20ˢ | 30ˢ | 40ˢ | 50ˢ | 60ˢ | 70ˢ | 80ˢ | 90ˢ |
|-----|-----|-----|-----|-----|-----|-----|-----|-----|
|     |     |     |     |     |     |     |     |     |

Though there is (thankfully) no discernable family resemblance, actress Rebecca De Mornay is the daughter of "gonzo" TV talk host Wally George. Raised in Europe and educated in Austria, she studied acting at America's Lee Strasberg Institute. While apprencting at Francis Ford Coppola's Zoetrope Studios, she made her screen debut in a one-lit bit ("I ordered waffles!") in Coppola's *One From the Heart* (1982). Her big movie break was as the likeable hooker who "invades" the suburban home of honors student Tom Cruise in *Risky Business.* Too many indifferent roles in too many terrible films like *The Slugger's Wife* (1985) threatened to sabotage her career before it truly got under way. Fortunately, De Mornay rebounded with smiler-with-a-knife villainous assignments in *The Hand That Rocks the Cradle* (1992) and *The Three Musketeers* (1993). **Selected Works:** *Backdraft* (1991), *Guilty As Sin* (1993), *Inconvenient Woman* (1991), *Runaway Train* (1985), *Trip to Bountiful* (1985), *Getting Out* (1994)

# Patrick Dempsey

**Born:** 1966; Lewiston, ME

**Years Active in the Industry:** by decade

| 10ˢ | 20ˢ | 30ˢ | 40ˢ | 50ˢ | 60ˢ | 70ˢ | 80ˢ | 90ˢ |
|-----|-----|-----|-----|-----|-----|-----|-----|-----|
|     |     |     |     |     |     |     |     |     |

Contemporary American actor Patrick Dempsey is a rising star in Hollywood already noted for playing quirky and charmingly shy young men. In high school, Dempsey was a state downhill skiing champion. At this time, he also began performing non-professionally as a juggler, magician and puppeteer for local groups. In 1981, the multi-talented youth won second place at the 1981 International Jugglers Competition. This led to a stage career in which he worked with different troupes around the U.S. He made his feature film debut playing a bit part in *Heaven Help Us* (1985). This led to his being cast as a regular on the TV series, *Fast Times at Ridgemont High*; he was eventually nominated for an Emmy for that role. Dempsey has since returned to feature films where he has worked steadily. Though Dempsey is primarily a comic actor, in the 1991 film *Mobsters* he showed considerable talent for drama. He most recently appeared in *Outbreak* (1995). **Selected Works:** *Coupe De Ville* (1990), *Mobsters* (1991)

# Catherine Deneuve (Catherine Dorléac)

**Born:** October 22, 1943; Paris, France

**Years Active in the Industry:** by decade

| 10ˢ | 20ˢ | 30ˢ | 40ˢ | 50ˢ | 60ˢ | 70ˢ | 80ˢ | 90ˢ |
|-----|-----|-----|-----|-----|-----|-----|-----|-----|
|     |     |     |     |     |     |     |     |     |

The screen persona of strikingly beautiful blond French actress Catherine Deneuve combines the aloofness of an ice queen with the smoldering sexuality of the femme fatale. Born Catherine

Dorleac, she is the daughter of stage and screen actor Maurice Dorleac and the sister of the late actress Francoise Dorleac. Taking her mother's maiden name, at age 13 she debuted onscreen in *Les Collegiennes* (1956). Director and star-maker Roger Vadim became her mentor, but she did not have much success until her appearance in Demy's *The Umbrellas of Cherbourg* (1963); her international reputation was established after her performance in Luis Bunuel's *Belle du Jour* (1967). Soon Deneuve became one of the brightest stars of French cinema, leading her to international stardom. She had a son by Vadim in 1963 and a daughter by actor Marcello Mastroianni in 1972; however, her first and only marriage (which ended in divorce) was to British photographer David Bailey. A virtual institution in her native country, Deneuve continues to appear in an average of one film per year, mostly French productions; she was nominated for the Best Actress Oscar for her role in *Indochine* (1992), and appeared with her daughter Chiara Deneuve in *Ma Saison Preferee* (1993). **Selected Works:** *Last Metro* (1980), *Repulsion* (1965), *Tristana* (1970), *Belle De Jour* (1968)

# Robert De Niro

**Born:** August 17, 1943; New York, NY

**Years Active in the Industry:** by decade

| 10s | 20s | 30s | 40s | 50s | 60s | 70s | 80s | 90s |
|-----|-----|-----|-----|-----|-----|-----|-----|-----|

Distinguished actor, producer and director Robert De Niro, a student of Stella Adler and Lee Strasberg, is today considered to be the quintessential "actor's actor." De Niro's immersions into roles seem effortless when compared to similar work by Dustin Hoffman or Al Pacino, a quality which suggests that he is able to accomplish the purist form of method acting by practically replacing his inner-self with that of any given character. De Niro entered films in the late 1960s, but wasn't noticed until he portrayed slow-wits in *Bang the Drum Slowly* and *Mean Streets*, both in 1973. He won an Oscar the following year for playing the young Vito Corleone in *The Godfather Part II* (1974) and has continued to consistently amaze audiences and critics alike with one truly remarkably nuanced performance after another. Several of note include the demented Travis Bickle in *Taxi Driver* (1976); the strong, idealistic steelworker/soldier in *The Deer Hunter* (1978); an Oscar-winning performance as boxer Jake La Motta in *Raging Bull* (1980); the hapless, would-be comic Rupert Pupkin in *The King of Comedy* (1981); a love-struck, married man in *Falling in Love* (1983); a merciless slaver/turned fervent missionary in *The Mission* (1986); Al Capone in *The Untouchables* (1987); tough, wise-cracking bounty hunter Jack Walsh in *Midnight Run* (1988); the catatonic Leonard Lowe in *Awakenings* (1990); the cool wiseguy in *Goodfellas* (1990); a crazed criminal in *Cape Fear* (1991); a psychotic stepfather in *This Boy's Life* (1993); and as a caring but shortsighted father/busdriver in *A Bronx Tale* (1993), which also marked his directorial debut. In 1994, De Niro played a role completely different from his others when he was cast as the philosophical but horrific Creature in Kenneth Branagh's horror film *Mary Shelley's Frankenstein.* De Niro is the owner/founder of the Tribeca Film Center in New York City, a venture he started as a home for and to encourage New York film production. **Selected Works:** *Cape Fear* (1991), *Godfather 1902-1959: The Complete Epic* (1981), *Godfather, Part 2* (1974), *Goodfellas* (1990), *Night and the City* (1992), *Casino* (1995)

# Brian Dennehy

**Born:** July 9, 1939; Bridgeport, CT

**Years Active in the Industry:** by decade

| 10s | 20s | 30s | 40s | 50s | 60s | 70s | 80s | 90s |
|-----|-----|-----|-----|-----|-----|-----|-----|-----|

An ex-Marine with a large frame and authoritative demeanor, American actor Brian Dennehy is well suited to playing leads and supporting roles in feature films, stage and television. Dennehy began acting while attending Columbia University; after graduating, he was drafted and served in 1965-66 in Vietnam with the Marine Corps, during which he was the Dear America voice in radio broadcasts to the home front. He returned to America and completed his studies at Yale, supporting himself with a variety of odd jobs. He then began working off-Broadway, before getting his big break in David Rabe's play *Streamers* on Broadway. Currently, Dennehy frequently works on television, and appearing frequently in movies and starring in the short-lived series *Birdland.* He debuted in films with *Semi-Tough* (1977), gradually moving his way up the cast lists in many later films, including *First Blood* (1982), *Cocoon* (1985), *Silverado* (1985), and *Presumed Innocent* (1990). For his performance in the made-for-cable movie *Foreign Affairs* (1993), co-starring Joanne Woodward, Dennehy won a Cable ACE award for Best Actor. **Selected Works:** *Killing in a Small Town* (1990), *Teamster Boss: The Jackie Presser Story* (1992), *To Catch a Killer* (1992)

# Sandy Dennis (Sandra Dale Dennis)

**Born:** April 27, 1937; Hastings, NE
**Died:** March 2, 1992; Westport, CT

**Years Active in the Industry:** by decade

| 10s | 20s | 30s | 40s | 50s | 60s | 70s | 80s | 90s |
|-----|-----|-----|-----|-----|-----|-----|-----|-----|

Sandy Dennis was a distinctive actress with a flighty demeanor and mumbling style of delivering lines. The Nebraska born Dennis began her career in local stock companies, then studied at New York's Actors' Studio, where she embraced method acting. She debuted onscreen in *Splendor in the Grass* (1961) with Natalie Wood and Warren Beatty. On Broadway, she won two Tony Awards in successive years, for *A Thousand Clowns* (1963) and *Any Wednesday* (1964). For her second screen performance, as George Segal's academic wife in the Richard Burton and Elizabeth Taylor film *Who's Afraid of Virginia Woolf?* (1966), Dennis won the Best Supporting Actress Oscar. She went on to get leads and co-starring roles in a number of films, but remained primarily a stage actress; after 1971 her film work was sporadic. She died of cancer in 1992. **Selected Works:** *Indian Runner* (1991)

# Reginald Denny (Reginald Leigh Daymore)

**Born:** November 20, 1891; Richmond, Surrey, England
**Died:** 1967

**Years Active in the Industry:** by decade

| 10s | 20s | 30s | 40s | 50s | 60s | 70s | 80s | 90s |
|-----|-----|-----|-----|-----|-----|-----|-----|-----|
|     | ■   | ■   | ■   | ■   | ■   |     |     |     |

Leading man Reginald Denny, usually played an energetic man of action in the Douglas Fairbanks mold. From the age of eight he appeared on the London stage, and then moved to Hollywood in his late teens. He debuted onscreen in 1919 and went on to star in numerous comedy-adventure films. Denny continued starring in films in the early sound era, but as he aged he began using his British accent in character roles as amiable but dim-witted Englishmen; he had a continuing role as Algy in the "Bulldog Drummond" film series. Offscreen, he developed the first pilotless radio-controlled aircraft successfully flown in the U.S. After 1948 Denny's screen appearances were infrequent, though he went on to work on TV and the stage. **Selected Works:** *Anna Karenina* (1935), *Lost Patrol* (1934), *Rebecca* (1940), *Romeo and Juliet* (1936), *Love Letters* (1945)

# Brian De Palma (Brian Russell De Palma)

**Born:** September 11, 1940; Newark, NJ

**Years Active in the Industry:** by decade

| 10s | 20s | 30s | 40s | 50s | 60s | 70s | 80s | 90s |
|-----|-----|-----|-----|-----|-----|-----|-----|-----|
|     |     |     |     |     | ■   | ■   | ■   | ■   |

American director Brian De Palma has always insisted that he gained his fascination with all things gory by watching his father, an orthopedic surgeon, at work. It's more likely that the principal influence on De Palma's career was Alfred Hitchcock, a fascination he has claimed to have outgrown professionally. Sure. Whatever the case, De Palma's first film work was in amateur short subjects while at Columbia University. Thanks to one of these films, he won a writing fellowship to Sarah Lawrence College,

where he made his first feature, *The Wedding Party*, between 1962 and 1964. In the cast of *The Wedding Party*, which wouldn't be released until 1969, were Sarah Lawrence student Jill Clayburgh and a Brooklyn kid who called himself "Bobby De Nero." De Palma's first film to gain a release was 1967's *Murder a la Mode* (try to find it), and the first to accrue critical approval was a trendy antiwar tome called *Greetings* (1968), again with that Brooklyn boy who *now* spelled his name "Robert De Niro." *Hi, Mom* (1970) was a similarly irreverent comedy, but De Palma was prescient enough to realize that the vogue for anti-establishment films would soon pass. Thus he began emulating Alfred Hitchcock with *Sisters* (1973), utilizing the split-screen technique popularized by such late 1960s pictures as *Grand Prix* and *The Boston Strangler*. De Palma not only admitted borrowing from Hitchcock in *Sisters*, but also underlined the tribute by having the film scored by Hitch's frequent musical director Bernard Herrmann. *Obsession* (1976), again scored by Herrmann, was one of several De Palma imitations of Hitchcock's *Vertigo* (see also *Blow-Out* and *Body Double*), and also established the director's fascination with 360-degree camera pans. *Carrie* (1976), De Palma's most successful film to that time (and still one of the most successful Stephen King adaptations), returned to the *Sisters* split screen and wrapped the story up with *another* of De Palma's trademarks, the "false shock" ending which turns out to be a nightmare. There was a similar finale (again staged as a dream) in *Dressed to Kill* (1980), which audaciously included a shower scene a la *Psycho* (but the director fooled us and staged the murder in an elevator). By the time *Body Double* came around in 1984, De Palma was all but parodying himself with gratuitous gore, slow motions, lyrical panning shots, Hermannesque musical scores, characters who weren't who they seemed to be, and twistaround endings. With *Scarface* (1983), the director inaugurated his "crime is not nice" period, ladling out grimly violent sequences in such films as *Wise Guys* (1986) and *The Untouchables* (1987) to show us that the bad guys weren't the lovable lugs Damon Runyon had made them out to be. *Raising Cain* (1992) was a full-blooded return to terror, with one of De Palma's favorite actors, John Lithgow, given free reign to express his wildest, darkest passions. *Carlito's Way* (1993) was another crime flick, this time with Al Pacino (who'd worked with De Palma in *Scarface*), proving by example that crime is bad. With only *Bonfire of the Vanities* (1989) a full-out failure, De Palma is one of a handful of truly bankable Hollywood directors, and one of the few that can open a picture on the basis of his own name rather than the names of the stars. Subtlety may be a stranger to his work, but one never has any trouble remembering who the director is when watching a Brian De Palma film.

# Gérard Depardieu

**Born:** December 27, 1948; Chateauroux, France

**Years Active in the Industry:** by decade

| 10s | 20s | 30s | 40s | 50s | 60s | 70s | 80s | 90s |
|-----|-----|-----|-----|-----|-----|-----|-----|-----|
|     |     |     |     |     |     | ■   | ■   | ■   |

Even Gerard Depardieu himself has noted that, in terms of looks, he is not a probable candidate for leading-man stardom. It is hopefully not an insult to note that the uniquely visaged Depardieu was an ideal choice for the 1990 remake of *Cyrano de Bergerac*. And yet, physical attractiveness (or lack of same) has had no bearing on the French-born Depardieu's success: On screen he is the personification of the words "sexy" and "dynamic", with full and brilliant control over his chosen craft. A onetime juvenile delinquent (he has frequently and convincingly portrayed two-bit street criminals on screen), Depardieu spent much of his childhood indulging in petty thievery and rape (or so he has claimed). He was straightened out by a social worker, who steered him into acting. In films and on stage since the age of 16, the versatile Depardieu developed a strong following during the 1970s, extending his popularly to the rest of the world with his multilayered performances in such films as *1900* (1975), *Get Out Your Handkerchiefs* (1978) and *Danton* (1982). He won France's Cesar Award for *The Last Metro* (1980) and *Cyrano de Bergerac* (1990), for which he also earned an Oscar nomination. In 1984, he made his film directorial bow with *Le Tartuffe*. Sporadic efforts to make Depardieu a mainstream Hollywood film star with such films as *Green Card* (1990), *1492* (1992) and *My Father the Hero* (1994) have fallen victim to spotty scriptwork and half-hearted promotion. **Selected Works:** *Camille Claudel* (1989), *Jean De Florette* (1987), *Tous Les Matins Du Monde* (1993), *Germinal* (1993), *Colonel Chabert* (1994)

# Johnny Depp

**Born:** June 9, 1963; Owensboro, KY

**Years Active in the Industry:** by decade

| 10ˢ | 20ˢ | 30ˢ | 40ˢ | 50ˢ | 60ˢ | 70ˢ | 80ˢ | 90ˢ |
|-----|-----|-----|-----|-----|-----|-----|-----|-----|
|     |     |     |     |     |     |     |     |     |

Popular American actor Johnny Depp is noted for his versatility and his tendency to play off-beat, quirky characters. Depp came to L.A. at age 20 as an aspiring rock musician with his band, The Kids. It was actor Nicolas Cage who suggested that Depp try acting in the mid-'80s. After meeting with Cage's agent, Depp was given a role in *Nightmare on Elm Street* (1984). He next played a small part in *Platoon* (1986). Depp began to attract real notice after appearing as a regular on the 1980's TV show *21 Jump Street* and being named by *Rolling Stone* magazine as one of the "Hot Faces of 1988." Simultaneously, *US* magazine

voted him as one of the "Ten Sexiest Bachelors in the Entertainment Industry." Although *Jump Street* helped his career and made him a teen-idol, Depp did not become a major star until appearing as the tragi-comic lead in Tim Burton's *Edward Scissorhands* (1990). Since then Depp continues to gain critical acclaim and increasing popularity for his performances, most notably in *What's Eating Gilbert Grape?* (1993), Burton's *Ed Wood* (1994), and *Don Juan DeMarco* (1995), in which he starred with Marlon Brando. Depp has garnered nearly as much attention for his off-screen life, including his romances with Wynona Ryder and model Kate Moss, his proprietorship of the L.A. nightspot The Viper Room (on the front sidewalk of which River Phoenix died), his rock band P, and his moody, hotel room-trashing temperament. **Selected Works:** *Benny and Joon* (1993), *Nick of Time* (1995)

# Bo Derek

**Born:** November 20, 1956; Long Beach, CA

**Years Active in the Industry:** by decade

| 10ˢ | 20ˢ | 30ˢ | 40ˢ | 50ˢ | 60ˢ | 70ˢ | 80ˢ | 90ˢ |
|-----|-----|-----|-----|-----|-----|-----|-----|-----|
|     |     |     |     |     |     |     |     |     |

Voluptuous, blond, blue-eyed actress Bo Derek, born Mary Cathleen Collins, is most noted for playing scantily-clad, irresistable women. She owes her career to her husband, actor/director John Derek, who began managing her while she was still a teen. They rejected numerous scripts for her before accepting a role in *10* (1979), her first major film (she did have a small part in *Orca: The Killer Whale* [1977]). Playing Dudley Moore's ideal woman (the title refers to a "perfect score" for her looks), she quickly became an international sex symbol. Never considered much of an actress, she has gone on to several more films which have emphasized her physical appearance and little else; besides starring in them, she also produced both *Tarzan, the Ape Man* (1981) and *Bolero* (1984), both of which were directed by her husband. She has made few film appearances following *Bolero*. **Selected Works:** *Hot Chocolate* (1992), *Woman of Desire* (1993)

# Bruce Dern

**Born:** June 4, 1936; Chicago, IL

**Years Active in the Industry:** by decade

| 10ˢ | 20ˢ | 30ˢ | 40ˢ | 50ˢ | 60ˢ | 70ˢ | 80ˢ | 90ˢ |
|-----|-----|-----|-----|-----|-----|-----|-----|-----|
|     |     |     |     |     |     |     |     |     |

Versatile, off-beat actor Bruce Dern is the grandson of a former governor of Utah, and the nephew of both poet-playwright Archibald MacLeish and Roosevelt's Secretary of War. He dropped out of college to become an actor, and studied with Lee Strasberg and Elia Kazan at the Actors' Studio. Soon Dern began landing roles on TV and on and off Broadway, then debuted onscreen in a bit part in Kazan's *Wild River* (1960). In the mid-'60s he played a psychotic hillbilly in an episode of the TV series *Alfred Hitchock Presents*; his work was so convincing that for years he became typecast as crazed loners, drugged-out wackos, and wild-eyed freaks. However, he also found other types of roles that displayed his versatility as an actor; for his portrayal of a crippled, suicidal Vietnam War vet in *Coming Home* (1978) he received a Best Supporting Actor Oscar nomination. He married and divorced actress Diane Ladd (with whom he appeared in *The Wild Angels* [1966]); their daughter is actress Laura Dern. **Selected Works:** *After Dark, My Sweet* (1990), *Carolina Skeletons* (1992), *Court Martial of Jackie Robinson* (1990), *Diggstown* (1992), *Into the Badlands* (1992)

# Laura Dern

**Born:** February 10, 1966; Santa Monica, CA

**Years Active in the Industry:** by decade

| 10ˢ | 20ˢ | 30ˢ | 40ˢ | 50ˢ | 60ˢ | 70ˢ | 80ˢ | 90ˢ |
|-----|-----|-----|-----|-----|-----|-----|-----|-----|
|     |     |     |     |     |     |     |     |     |

American actress Laura Dern, the daughter of actors Bruce Dern and Diane Ladd, debuted onscreen at age seven in Martin Scorsese's *Alice Doesn't Live Here Anymore* (1975). At the age of

11 she lied and said she was in her mid-teens for her audition for the film *Foxes* (1980); she got the role, her first featured screen performance. During her teens she studied acting at the Lee Strasberg Institute, a move that wasn't approved by her actor parents. She started landing regular film roles in the mid-'80s, originally typecast in innocent, virginal teenager roles; for her performance in *Smooth Talk* (1986) she won the prestigious Los Angeles Film Critics New Generation Award. An advocate of method acting, she wore a blindfold for two weeks before playing the role of a blind girl in *Mask* (1985); because her character in *Teachers* (1984) gets an abortion, Dern pretended to be pregnant and checked into a private clinic to observe how teenage girls actually deal with abortion. Her appearance in David Lynch's controversial *Blue Velvet* (1986) gained her much recognition, and resulted in the lead female role in Lynch's award-winning *Wild at Heart*, the first film in which she was able to manifest mature sexuality. For her work in *Rambling Rose* (1991) she received a Best Actress Oscar nomination; uniquely, her mother received a Best Supporting Actress Oscar nomination for her work in the same film. Later Dern co-

starred in the massive blockbuster *Jurassic Park* (1993) with longtime love Jeff Goldblum. **Selected Works:** *Afterburn* (1992), *Perfect World* (1993)

# Caleb Deschanel

**Born:** September 21, 1941; Philadelphia, PA

**Years Active in the Industry:** by decade

| 10ˢ | 20ˢ | 30ˢ | 40ˢ | 50ˢ | 60ˢ | 70ˢ | 80ˢ | 90ˢ |
|-----|-----|-----|-----|-----|-----|-----|-----|-----|
|     |     |     |     |     |     |     |     |     |

After attending Johns Hopkins University and the University of Southern California film school, American cinematographer Caleb Deschanel was trained at the American Film Institute. He launched his professional career as assistant to veteran photographer Gordon Willis, then handled the second unit photography for Francis Ford Coppola's *Apocalypse Now* (1978). One of his first major cinematography credits was for the Coppola-produced *The Black Stallion* (1979), one of the most beautifully lensed films of the 1970s. Deschanel was Oscar-nominated for his work on *The Right Stuff* (1983) and *The Natural* (1984); he was instrumental in developing the Steadicam system that assured rock-steady camera movement under any circumstances, which he would later refine into his own "skycam" system for aerial photography. In addition to his camera credits, Deschanel has directed two films, one of which was the quirky "success d'estime" *The Escape Artist* (1982). **Selected Works:** *It Could Happen to You* (1994), *Cop Gives Waitress $2 Million Tip* (1994)

# Vittorio De Sica

**Born:** July 7, 1902; Sora, Italy
**Died:** 1974

**Years Active in the Industry:** by decade

| 10ˢ | 20ˢ | 30ˢ | 40ˢ | 50ˢ | 60ˢ | 70ˢ | 80ˢ | 90ˢ |
|-----|-----|-----|-----|-----|-----|-----|-----|-----|
|     |     |     |     |     |     |     |     |     |

Vittorio De Sica became interested in acting while still a teenager in Naples, and even appeared in one film when he was 16 (*The Clemenceau Affair*, 1918). The real beginning of his acting career, however, came in 1923, when he joined Tatiana Pavlova's stage company. By the late '20s he had become a matinee idol, soon founding his own company to produce stage plays; he starred in many of these alongside his first wife, Giuditta Rissone. Around the same time he began to establish himself in Italian films, primarily light comedies; a suave, strikingly handsome leading man, he was especially popular with women. Eventually De Sica acted in more than 150 films, a few of which were British or Hollywood productions. He is, however, best remembered as a director, a vocation he took up in the early '40s; one of his films, *The Bicycle Thief* (1948), is frequently found at or near the top of "All-Time Greatest Movies" lists. The films he directed are known

for their neo-realist style, in which many or all of the actors are non-professionals. Throughout his years as a director he continued acting in films in order to finance his directorial efforts; for his performance in the Hollywood film *A Farewell to Arms* (1957) he received a Best Supporting Actor Oscar nomination. Four of the 25 films he directed won the Best Foreign Film Oscar. **Selected Works:** *Garden of the Finzi-Continis* (1971), *Miracle in Milan* (1951), *Two Women* (1961), *Umberto D.* (1955), *Yesterday, Today, and Tomorrow* (1964)

## Andy Devine (Jeremiah Schwartz)

**Born:** October 7, 1905; Flagstaff, AZ
**Died:** 1977

**Years Active in the Industry:** by decade

| 10s | 20s | 30s | 40s | 50s | 60s | 70s | 80s | 90s |
|-----|-----|-----|-----|-----|-----|-----|-----|-----|
|     |     |     |     |     |     |     |     |     |

With his high-pitched, raspy voice, movie cowboy sidekick Andy Devine was readily recognizable. Born Jeremiah Schwartz, he moved to Hollywood at 20 and appeared in bit parts onscreen, then moved into light supporting roles. His trademark voice was due to a childhood accident; at first his voice was deemed unsuitable for the newly established talkies, but it wound up an asset, leading him to be typecast as a funny-sounding country bumpkin. Later Devine did much work as a comic sidekick for such screen cowboys as Roy Rogers. He played Jingles, Guy Madison's sidekick, in the early '50s TV series *Wild Bill Hickok*, and later starred in his own series, *Andy's Gang*; meanwhile, he continued appearing fairly frequently in films through 1970. For several years he was the honorary mayor of Van Nuys, California. **Selected Works:** *Red Badge of Courage* (1951), *Romeo and Juliet* (1936), *Stagecoach* (1939), *Star Is Born* (1937), *In Old Chicago* (1938)

## Danny DeVito

**Born:** November 17, 1944; Asbury Park, NJ

**Years Active in the Industry:** by decade

| 10s | 20s | 30s | 40s | 50s | 60s | 70s | 80s | 90s |
|-----|-----|-----|-----|-----|-----|-----|-----|-----|
|     |     |     |     |     |     |     |     |     |

A dyed-in-the-wool New Jerseyite, actor/director Danny DeVito was born in Neptune, New Jersey, and raised in Asbury Park. After graduation from a Catholic boarding school, DeVito worked as a cosmetician in his sister's beauty parlor, assuming the outlandish moniker "Mr. Danny." He entered New York's American Academy of Dramatic Arts, not to study acting but to pick up some additional expertise in makeup. Nevertheless, the acting bug bit, and DeVito pursued a stage career, where his short height and volatile demeanor assured him a lifetime of character parts. Losing a starring role in the 1967 movie *In Cold Blood* to Robert Blake, DeVito decided to concentrate on stage work in the 1970s, during which time he met his longtime companion and future bride, actress Rhea Perlman; Danny's screen debut finally occurred in *Lady Liberty* (1972). A stage stint in the role of Martini in *One Flew Over the Cuckoo's Nest* led to DeVito's recreation of the part in the Oscar-winning 1975 film version, produced by DeVito's old friend Michael Douglas. DeVito's star ascended when he was cast as despicable dispatcher Louie on the long-running sitcom *Taxi* in 1978; it is said that he walked into the audition with script in hand, exclaimed "Who wrote this s—t?", and earned the role on the spot. In addition to his film acting roles, DeVito has also made his mark as a first-rate director with such films as *Throw Mama from the Train* (1987), *The War of the Roses* (1989), and *Hoffa* (1992); he also served as producer of the acclaimed hit *Pulp Fiction* (1994) and *Reality Bites* (1994). **Selected Works:** *Batman Returns* (1992), *Other People's Money* (1991), *Romancing the Stone* (1984), *Terms of Endearment* (1983)

## I.A.L. Diamond (Itek Dommnici)

**Born:** June 27, 1920; Ungeny, Romania
**Died:** April 21, 1988; Beverly Hills, CA

**Years Active in the Industry:** by decade

| 10s | 20s | 30s | 40s | 50s | 60s | 70s | 80s | 90s |
|-----|-----|-----|-----|-----|-----|-----|-----|-----|
|     |     |     |     |     |     |     |     |     |

The I. A. L. in I. A. L. Diamond stands for Interscholastic Algebra League (at least that's *one* of his stories). Diamond was of course not born with this moniker, but chose it for himself while working on the campus newspaper at Columbia University. Born in Romania, Diamond was raised in Brooklyn, where he gained attention early on for his stellar academic achievements. Upon finishing his college education, Diamond headed for Hollywood, where he worked in collaboration on several B-picture screenplays before his "A" break with the Errol Flynn vehicle *Never Say Goodbye* (1946). During his 20th Century-Fox years, Diamond specialized in comedy, working on the mirth-provoking scripts of such films as *Love Nest* (1951), *Monkey Business* (1952) and *Something for the Birds* (1952). In 1957, Diamond teamed with director Billy Wilder to pen the screenplay for *Love in the Afternoon*. Though the men had their share of rows, Wilder sensed in Diamond the sort of kindred spirit that would result in the perfect team. Thereafter, Diamond would work almost exclusively with Wilder, sharing an Oscar for *The Apartment* (1960) and collaborating on such additional productions as *Some Like It Hot* (1959), *One-Two-Three* (1961), *Irma La Douce* (1963), *Kiss Me Stupid* (1964), *The Fortune Cookie* (1966), *The Pri-*

*vate Life of Sherlock Holmes* (1969), *Avanti!* (1972), *The Front Page* (1974) and *Fedora* (1978). Though nearly two decades younger, Diamond decided to retire before Wilder did; his presence was sorely missed on Wilder's final film, the chaotic *Buddy Buddy* (1981).

# Leonardo DiCaprio

**Born:** 1975

**Years Active in the Industry:** by decade

| 10s | 20s | 30s | 40s | 50s | 60s | 70s | 80s | 90s |
|-----|-----|-----|-----|-----|-----|-----|-----|-----|
|     |     |     |     |     |     |     |     | ▮   |

As a child actor, Leonardo DiCaprio was rejected by a casting agent for having an "inappropriate" haircut. DiCaprio was 15 when he made his first film appearance in director Ron Howard's *Parenthood* (1990). After some TV work, DiCaprio was selected at the age of 17 for the demanding role of the stepson of bullying Robert De Niro in *This Boy's Life* (1993); despite their on-screen hostility, the actors got along splendidly off-camera, and DiCaprio has since credited De Niro for providing him with encouragement and invaluable acting tips. The young actor followed this critical triumph with his Oscar-nominated performance as a retarded teenager in *What's Eating Gilbert Grape?* (1993). So convincing was his portrayal that many moviegoers believed the *Gilbert Grape* producers had hired a genuine developmentally-delayed youngster for the role. Though not yet twenty, DiCaprio found himself a celebrity, able to turn down a lucrative offer to co-star in *Hocus Pocus* (1994) in favor of a less financially remunerative but more artistically satisfying assignment in the film version of Jim Carroll's novel *The Basketball Diaries* (1995). "My parents love it", Leonardo DiCaprio recently commented on the subject of his stardom. "My dad and I have creative talks, and my mom loves to see me in magazines."

# Angie Dickinson (Angeline Brown)

**Born:** September 30, 1931; Kulm, ND

**Years Active in the Industry:** by decade

| 10s | 20s | 30s | 40s | 50s | 60s | 70s | 80s | 90s |
|-----|-----|-----|-----|-----|-----|-----|-----|-----|
|     |     |     |     | ▮   |     |     |     | ▮   |

Sexy Angie Dickinson became an actress after winning a beauty contest. She debuted onscreen in a Doris Day musical,

*Lucky Me* (1954), then went on to play bits and small roles for several years, finally landing a lead role in Howard Hawks's *Rio Bravo* (1959). For a while she averaged one or two films a year, playing desirable leading ladies in mostly sub-standard films, (her role in Brian De Palma's *Dressed to Kill* in 1980 is a notable exception); she has rarely appeared onscreen since 1981. In the '70s she starred in the TV series *Police Woman*, and has done a fair amount of other TV work, including a co-starring role in the mini-series *Wild Palms* (1993). **Selected Works:** *Captain Newman, M.D.* (1963), *Texas Guns* (1990), *Treacherous Crossing* (1992)

# William S. Dieterle (Wilhelm Dieterle)

**Born:** July 15, 1893; Ludwigshafen, Germany
**Died:** December 9, 1972; Ottobrun, Germany

**Years Active in the Industry:** by decade

| 10s | 20s | 30s | 40s | 50s | 60s | 70s | 80s | 90s |
|-----|-----|-----|-----|-----|-----|-----|-----|-----|
|     | ▮   |     |     | ▮   |     |     |     |     |

A stage actor in Germany and Switzerland while a teenager, William Dieterle began acting in movies by 1913, and appeared in such memorable '20s films as Paul Leni's *Waxworks* (1924) and F. W. Murnau's *Faust* (1926). In 1923 Dieterle also began directing himself in a series of films, including *Geschlecht In Fesseln* (*Sex in Chains* [1928]). He began his Hollywood career in 1930, directing German-language versions of *Those Who Dance* (1930), *The Way of All Men* (1930), and *Kismet* (1944). At Warner Bros., Dieterle scored with *The Last Flight* (1931), the W. C. Fields comedy *Her Majesty* (1931), and the elaborate *A Midsummer Night's Dream* (1935), which he co-directed with Max Reinhardt. In the late '30s he helmed Warners' prestigious biopics for actor Paul Muni: *The Story of Louis Pasteur* (1936), *The Life of Emile Zola* (1937), and *Juarez* (1939). Moving to RKO in 1939, Dieterle delivered two classics with *The Hunchback of Notre Dame* (1939), starring Charles Laughton as Quasimodo; and *The Devil and Daniel Webster* (aka *All That Money Can Buy* [1941]), with Walter Huston as the Devil. His subsequent Hollywood work of the '40s and '50s was well crafted but impersonal, notable chiefly for his romantic dramas *Love Letters* (1945) and *Portrait of Jennie* (1948), and the crime films *Rope of Sand* (1949) and *Dark City* (1950). In the late '50s he returned to Europe and directed films in Italy and Germany.

# Marlene Dietrich (Maria Magdalene Dietrich)

**Born:** December 27, 1904; Berlin, Germany
**Died:** May 6, 1992; Paris, France

**Years Active in the Industry:** by decade

| 10s | 20s | 30s | 40s | 50s | 60s | 70s | 80s | 90s |
|-----|-----|-----|-----|-----|-----|-----|-----|-----|
|     | ▮   |     |     |     | ▮   |     |     |     |

Legendary actress Marlene Dietrich took up acting in her late teens; after failing an audition with Max Reinhardt in 1921, she joined the chorus line of a touring music revue. In 1922 she re-auditioned with Reinhardt  and this time was accepted in his drama school. Shortly thereafter she began playing small roles on the stage and in German films, never getting anything more substantial than a supporting role; however, by the late '20s she had risen to playing leads with moderate success. Her big break came when she was spotted onstage by American director Josef von Sternberg, who cast her to play a sexy, seductive vamp in *The Blue Angel* (1930), filmed in Germany. Von Sternberg became a dominant force in her life, molding her into a glamorous, sensuous star; she got a Hollywood contract and left her husband and daughter behind, going on to star in six films for Von Sternberg (out of the first seven she made). Their collaboration made her a star equal in magnitude to Garbo. She became an American citizen in 1939; meanwhile, her films were banned in Germany because she had refused a lucrative offer from the Nazis to return and star in German films. During World War II she entertained U.S. troops, participated in war bond drives, and made anti-Nazi broadcasts in German; she was awarded the Medal of Freedom for "meeting a grueling schedule of performances under battle conditions ... despite risk to her life." She was also named Chevalier of the French Legion of Honor. In the '50s, as her film career slowed, Dietrich began a second career as a recording star and cabaret performer, singing to packed houses in major cities all over the world. Late in her life she was rarely seen in public, but she agreed to provide the voice-over for Maximillian Schell's screen biography of her, *Marlene* (1984). She wrote three volumes of memoirs: *Marlene Dietrich's ABC* (1961), *My Life Story* (1979), and *Marlene* (1987). **Selected Works:** *Around the World in 80 Days* (1956), *Morocco* (1930), *Shanghai Express* (1932), *Witness for the Prosecution* (1957), *Judgement at Nuremburg* (1961)

# Kevin Dillon

**Born:** August 19, 1965; Mamaroneck, NY

**Years Active in the Industry:** by decade

| 10s | 20s | 30s | 40s | 50s | 60s | 70s | 80s | 90s |
|-----|-----|-----|-----|-----|-----|-----|-----|-----|
|     |     |     |     |     |     |     |     |     |

The younger brother of actor Matt Dillon, Kevin Dillon may have unknowingly predetermined his movie career by being born in Mamaroneck, New York—once the home of the D. W. Griffith studios. This might be stretching things, of course, but the fact remains that Dillon was a movie leading man by age 20. Originally planning to study art, Dillon became an actor when was spotted by an agent at the premiere of older brother Matt's *Tex* (1985). Often cast in lightweight roles (*Heaven Help Us* [1985], *The Blob* [1988]), Dillon has distinguished himself in the films of director Oliver Stone with a brace of powerful characterizations: the baby-faced but homicidal teenage soldier Bunny in *Platoon* (1986), and real-life rock musician John Densmore in *The Doors* (1991). **Selected Works:** *Midnight Clear* (1992), *When He's Not a Stranger* (1989)

# Matt Dillon

**Born:** February 18, 1964; New Rochelle, NY

**Years Active in the Industry:** by decade

| 10s | 20s | 30s | 40s | 50s | 60s | 70s | 80s | 90s |
|-----|-----|-----|-----|-----|-----|-----|-----|-----|
|     |     |     |     |     |     |     |     |     |

Actor Matt Dillon was born into a pop-culture milieu: he was named for the protagonist of TV's *Gunsmoke*, and was the nephew of comic-strip artist Alex Raymond, of *Flash Gordon*, *Jungle Jim*  and *Rip Kirby* fame. Discovered by a casting director at 14, Dillon was cast as one of the dead-end teens in 1979's *Over the Edge*. After making an excellent impression as a high school bully in *My Bodyguard* (1980), Dillon settled into tough-but-decent leading roles, where he has flourished ever since. Recently, Dillon has made successful efforts to divest himself of his teen-idol image with his unsympathetic portrayals of a strung-out slacker in *Drugstore Cowboy* (1989) and a consciousless killer in *A Kiss Before Dying* (1991). Matt Dillon is the older brother of film star Kevin Dillon. **Selected Works:** *Little Darlings* (1980), *Malcolm X* (1992), *Singles* (1992), *Women and Men 2* (1991), *To Die For* (1995)

# Melinda Dillon

**Born:** October 13, 1939; Hope, AR

**Years Active in the Industry:** by decade

| 10s | 20s | 30s | 40s | 50s | 60s | 70s | 80s | 90s |
|-----|-----|-----|-----|-----|-----|-----|-----|-----|
|     |     |     |     |     |     |     |     |     |

Supporting actress Melinda Dillon is perhaps best known for her distinguished Broadway career, beginning with her appearance as Honey in the original production of *Who's Afraid of Virginia Woolf?* Aside from a bit part in *The April Fools* (1969), she debuted onscreen in Hal Ashby's biopic *Bound for Glory* (1976), in which she played the first Mrs. Woody Guthrie. As a film actress she is probably best-known for her third prominent role, as a mother whose child is taken by aliens in Steven Spielberg's *Close Encounters of the Third Kind* (1977), for which she received a Best Supporting Actress Oscar nomination. She was nominated for the same award for her work in Sydney Pollack's *Absence of Malice* (1981). Her film work has been sporadic, but she has shown good taste and discrimination in choosing her roles, including a recent appearance in *The Prince of Tides* (1991). **Selected Works:** *Christmas Story* (1983), *Prince of Tides* (1991)

# Carlo DiPalma

**Born:** April 17, 1925; Rome, Italy

**Years Active in the Industry:** by decade

| 10ˢ | 20ˢ | 30ˢ | 40ˢ | 50ˢ | 60ˢ | 70ˢ | 80ˢ | 90ˢ |
|-----|-----|-----|-----|-----|-----|-----|-----|-----|

A director of photography in his native Italy since 1954, Carlo DiPalma was virtually unknown until his lavish color work on director Michelangelo Antonioni's *Red Desert* (1966). Then came *Blow-Up* (1968), Antonioni's biggest commercial success and one of the finest (and most often imitated) photographic achievements of the last 40 years, bar none. DiPalma continued contributing superior camerawork for other directors before making his own megging debut with 1973's *Teresa la Landra*. From 1985 onward, DiPalma has been principal photographer of the films of director Woody Allen. He has reluctantly found himself the subject of controversy thanks to Allen fans who aren't partial to the jerky, *cinema verite* hand-held photography in such Allen films as *Manhattan Murder Mystery* (1993). **Selected Works:** *Alice* (1990), *Hannah and Her Sisters* (1986), *Husbands and Wives* (1992), *Bullets over Broadway* (1994), *Monster* (1994)

# Walt Disney

**Born:** December 5, 1901; Chicago, IL
**Died:** 1966

**Years Active in the Industry:** by decade

| 10ˢ | 20ˢ | 30ˢ | 40ˢ | 50ˢ | 60ˢ | 70ˢ | 80ˢ | 90ˢ |
|-----|-----|-----|-----|-----|-----|-----|-----|-----|

The smallest of five children, Walt Disney endured a Dickensian childhood of profound cruelty and deprivation. Forced to work on the family farm from sun-up to sundown, Disney sought escape from the drudgery by swapping tall tales with his protective older brother Roy—and by drawing pictures. At age fourteen, he was an

accomplished enough caricturist to be accepted into the Kansas City Art Institute. Two years later, he lied about his age so that he could serve in the Red Cross Ambulance Corps of World War I. Back in Kansas City in 1919, Disney secured work at a commercial art studio, where he befriended fellow artist Ub Iwerks. Walt and Ub set up their own company in 1920, though they had to give it up within the year to accept paying jobs at the Kansas City Film Ad Company, which produced short animated commercials for local movie theatres. After several of their filmed collaborations scored a hit with KC's Newman Theatre, Disney and Iwerks went into business together again, forming a cartoon firm called Laugh-O-Grams. Disney's first independent animated efforts, including *Puss and Boots* (1922) and *The Bremen Town Musicians* (1923), were minimally animated, but demonstrated an artistic and creative skill far exceeding the standard potboiler theatrical cartoons of the era. The cost of these cartoons could not be recouped in the small Kansas City market, so Disney moved to Los Angeles in hopes of setting up a bigger operation—and of finding a larger audience. His first regular cartoon series was *Alice in Cartoonland*, which combined animation with live action; it was picked up for theatrical release in 1924 by cartoon executive M.J. Winkler. When *Alice* showed signs of flagging at the box-office in 1927, Winkler encouraged Disney to produce a series based on a new character, Oswald the Lucky Rabbit. These cartoons did well enough theatrically to embolden Disney to ask for a raise from Winkler; instead, he was told that he'd have to take a cut in salary, or else Winkler would hire away Disney's staff and continue producing the *Oswald* cartoons without him. Disney refused, whereupon Winkler made good his threat; only Iwerks remained loyal to Disney during this darkest period in his career. Vowing to create a cartoon character that couldn't be taken away from him, Disney dreamed up an insouciant little mouse named Mickey (who, as has been noted by many cartoon historians, was at base a redesigned Oswald). Disney's first two silent Mickey Mouse cartoons didn't sell; for the third, *Steamboat Willie* (1928), Disney decided to jump on the talking-picture bandwagon, utilizing a bootlegged sound system owned by distributor Pat Powers. Bowling audiences over with its innovative synchronized music score and sound effects, *Steamboat Willie* was an enormous success, and Disney's future was secured. In 1929, he officially launched his "Silly Symphonies" series with the harmlessly macabre *The Skeleton Dance*. Switching distributors throughout the 1930s (from Powers to Columbia to United Artists to RKO), Disney became the foremost cartoon producer in the business, the one whom everyone else in the animation industry wanted to emulate. There was no one "secret" to Disney's success, though much of it was due to his emphasis on appealing characters and strong storylines in his seven-minute epics. While Mickey Mouse remained the mainstay of his organization, Disney found himself trapped by Mickey's popularity, unable to indulge in the hilariously vulgar humor that the Mouse had been permitted in his pre-star days. As a result, Disney started developing several other characters—including Goofy and Donald Duck—who could perform the slapstick gags now considered "beneath" the mighty Mickey. In 1932, Disney struck an exclusive deal with the Technicolor company, producing his first fully-hued cartoon, the Oscar-winning *Flowers and Trees*. One year later, Disney was gratified to see his studio's *Three Little Pigs* (complete with signature tune "Who's Afraid of the Big Bad Wolf?") open at New York's prestigious Radio City Music Hall. Disney's fame was solidified when he was embraced by the intellectuals, who insisted upon reading all sorts of subliminal messages in his humble efforts. But this was only the beginning. Having put his career and his bank account on the line several times in the past, Disney embarked on a project that elicited loud forewarnings of doom from his rivals: the first full-length animated feature film, *Snow White and the Seven Dwarfs* (1937). Once again, Disney emerged triumphant with a box-office smash. From this point onward, Disney concentrated on feature-film work, using his short subjects as a training program for his fledgling animators. His second cartoon feature, *Pinocchio* (1939), was another success, but his third, the ambitious "concert feature" *Fantasia* (1940), was a financial disappointment. To add to this headache, Disney's animators went on strike in 1941, citing low wages, poor working conditions and lack of on-screen credit. Shortly after the strike was settled, Disney's studio was commandeered by the government for the purpose of producing wartime propaganda films, the best of which were the "strategic bombing" paean *Victory Through Air Power* (1942) and the "Good Neighbor Policy" musical *Saludos Amigos* (1943). After the war, Disney lost a lot of his intellectual following by producing bread-and-butter musical-revue cartoons like *Make Mine Music* (1948) and *Melody Time* (1949). During this period, he began moving into live-action production with such films as *So Dear to My Heart* (1948) and *Song of the South* (1948). He also produced several films in England to take advantage of "frozen funds" accrued during the war: *Treasure Island* (1950) *The Story of Robin Hood* (1952), etc. He returned to old-style cartoon features with 1950's *Cinderella*, though the innovation and freshness of his 1930s efforts had eroded, and his cartoons began taking on an assembly-line look. His most successful venture in the early 1950s was a series of live-action nature films released under the blanket title *True-Life Adventures*. In 1953, he ended his long distribution relationship with RKO Radio, setting up his own releasing company, Buena Vista; for the first time in his career, he was a truly independent moviemaker. At this point in time, most of Disney's energies were concentrated on building a huge amusement park. The ABC television network agreed to pour funds into this venture, so long as Disney agreed to produce a weekly TV show for ABC in exchange. In 1954, the *Disneyland* anthology series went on the air; one year later, the Disneyland amusement park opened its doors to the public in Burbank, California (This studio/network correlation resurfaced in 1995, when in one of the largest business mergers ever conceived, the Disney Company pur-

chased ABC outright). Thanks in great part to its "Davy Crockett" episodes, *Disneyland* became the first ABC series ever to crack the "Top 25" list of TV shows. Subsequent Disney TV projects for ABC included *The Mickey Mouse Club* and *Zorro*. Meanwhile, Disney was becoming aware that small-scale family films like *The Shaggy Dog* were bringing in more box-office revenue than loftier cartoon efforts like *Sleeping Beauty* (1959); thus it was that Disney stepped up his live-action activities, with his animated productions fewer and farther between. In 1961, Disney moved his weekly TV series to NBC to take advantage of that network's color facilities; *Walt Disney's Wonderful World of Color* (later *Wonderful World of Disney*) would remain a Sunday-night NBC fixture for the next two decades. With many critics writing off Disney's theatrical features as "more of the same" in the 1960s, the producer responded with what many consider his *magnum opus*, the lavish 1964 musical fantasy *Mary Poppins*. At time of his death of acute circulatory collapse in 1966, the indefatigable Disney was laying the groundwork for what would later become Florida's Epcot Center. Many bizarre stories concerning Walt Disney have circulated since his death—none sillier than the claim that he'd had his body cryogenically "frozen." Disney's detractors never seem to lack for reasons to dislike the man, ranging from his very real anti-union sentiments to his alleged anti-semitism (one recent biography went so far as to intimate that Disney attended Nazi bund rallies in the 1930s, and also exhibited an unnatural affection for his adopted daughter!). None of this really matters in the final analysis: whatever one thinks of the man, it cannot be denied that he brought more pleasure to more people than anyone else in the film industry. If this fact is too intangible for your tastes, remember that Disney was the recipient of 29 Academy Awards, and dozens of additional industry honors. The shadow of Walt Disney continues to loom large into the 1990s; it is not uncommon for people to still refer to the Walt Disney Company as "he" rather than "it."

# Divine (Harris Glenn Milstead)

**Born:** October 19, 1945; Baltimore, MD
**Died:** March 7, 1988; Hollywood, CA

**Years Active in the Industry:** by decade

| 10s | 20s | 30s | 40s | 50s | 60s | 70s | 80s | 90s |
|-----|-----|-----|-----|-----|-----|-----|-----|-----|
|     |     |     |     |     | ■   | ■   | ■   |     |

How shall we classify Divine? An American...actor? actress? Biologically, Divine was a certified male. Professionally, Divine was a woman—a woman of balloonlike proportions whose dress code and cosmetic skills were only slightly less tasteless and outrageous than "her" acting style. Discovered by cult director John Waters while standing on a Baltimore street corner for several days running, with a different hair color each day, Divine was cast in Waters' underground farrago *Mondo Trasho* (1969). Several other subculture films followed, but none more conspicuous than Waters' gutter masterpiece, *Pink Flamingos* (1972). As Babs Johnson, prime candidate for "the most disgusting person on earth," Divine capped all of Bab's screen excesses—including murder—by eating a heaping handful of doggie doo on camera. Waters took his bizarre "repertory company" with him—including Divine, Paul Bartel and Mary Woronov—as he moved into (comparatively) mainstream films. No one who has seen Divine as the heroine of director Paul Bartel's *Lust in the Dust* (1985) will forget the performer's torrid clinches with Tab Hunter (TAB HUNTER!), nor the closeups of the treasure map tattooed on Divine's Cinemascopesized backside. Those who could get past the unremitting weirdness of Divine's performance discovered that the actor/actress had genuine talent, including a natural sense of comic timing and an uncanny gift for slapstick. Occasionally, Divine would shed feminine garb and play male roles, such as the villain of *Trouble in Mind* (1985), but fans wanted the truly divine Divine. In his/her last appearance for Waters, *Hairspray*, Divine played a dual role, one male, one female, and was quite effective in both parts. Divine died suddenly of an enlarged heart at the age of 42, while preparing a guest appearance on Fox TV's *Married...With Children*. Even the more "conservative" showbiz columnists mourned the passing of Divine, who if nothing else was a one-of-a-kind entertainer.

## Richard Dix (Ernest Carlton Brimmer)

**Born:** July 18, 1894; St. Paul, MN
**Died:** 1949

**Years Active in the Industry:** by decade

| 10s | 20s | 30s | 40s | 50s | 60s | 70s | 80s | 90s |
|-----|-----|-----|-----|-----|-----|-----|-----|-----|

American actor Richard Dix, was a square-jawed, stalwart, leading man. He began acting in school plays while studying medicine in college, eventually deciding on a theater career. He worked in stock and served in World War I before debuting on Broadway in *The Hawk* (1919). In 1921 he debuted onscreen and soon became a silent star, usually playing the strong, silent type, a hero able to deal calmly with any situation. He started the sound era strongly, receiving an Oscar nomination for his work in *Cimarron* (1931); however, he failed to sustain his star status and began working in B-movies, usually action-oriented. No longer a star, he continued to make plenty of films, and portrayed "The Whistler" in a series of adventure flicks in the mid-'40s. He died of a heart attack at 55. He was the father of actor Robert Dix.

## Edward Dmytryk

**Born:** September 4, 1908; Grand Forks, BC, Canada

**Years Active in the Industry:** by decade

| 10s | 20s | 30s | 40s | 50s | 60s | 70s | 80s | 90s |
|-----|-----|-----|-----|-----|-----|-----|-----|-----|

A messenger boy at Paramount in the mid 1920s, Edward Dmytryk became an editor in the 1930s and began directing in

1935. By the mid '40s he had such impressive credits as *The Devil Commands* (1941) with Boris Karloff; the anti-fascist *Hitler's Children* (1943); the noirs *Murder, My Sweet* (1944) and *Cornered* (1945), starring Dick Powell; and *Crossfire* (1947), one of the first Hollywood films to confront anti-Semitism. In 1948 Dmytryk became one of the "Hollywood Ten" and was sentenced to a year in prison for contempt of Congress. Afterwards he directed three films in England, but returned to the States in 1951 and was a friendly witness before the House Un-American Activities Committee. He then resumed his American career and directed four films for producer Stanley Kramer, most notably *The Sniper* (1952) and *The Caine Mutiny* (1954). Dmytryk went on to make several notable films in the 1950s, including the westerns *Broken Lance* (1954) with Spencer Tracy and *Warlock* (1959) with Henry Fonda, and the World War II drama *The Young Lions* (1958), starring Marlon Brando and Montgomery Clift. His subsequent work was well made but unremarkable. **Selected Works:** *Give Us This Day* (1949)

## Shannen Doherty

**Born:** April 12, 1971; Memphis, TN

**Years Active in the Industry:** by decade

| 10s | 20s | 30s | 40s | 50s | 60s | 70s | 80s | 90s |
|-----|-----|-----|-----|-----|-----|-----|-----|-----|

From all accounts, Memphis-born Shannen Doherty was once an obedient, toe-the-line child actress. During this early period, she supplied several cartoon voices (notably in the animated feature *Secret of NIMH* [1982]) and was featured as Jenny Wilder during the 1982-83 season of TV's *Little House on the Prairie*. While appearing as Kris on the family "dramedy" *Our House* (1986-88), Doherty was praised both privately and publicly for her cooperation and professionalism. So what happened during her four-year stint on Fox's *Beverly Hills 90210*? As her TV character of Brenda Walsh metamorphosed from goody two-shoes to Rich Bitch, Doherty's real life began mirroring her "reel" life. The actress' well-publicized after-hours shenanigans have included alcohol and drug abuse, nightclub brawls, and a down-in-flames marriage to Ashley Hamilton. The blurred line between Brenda the character and Doherty the star resulted in a curious phenomenon: a "non-fan" club, whose members published a well-circulated "I Hate Brenda" newsletter. In 1994, Doherty was invited to leave *Beverly Hills 90210*; she went on to pursue a film career that has yet to catch fire. **Selected Works:** *Freeze Frame* (1992), *Mallrats* (1995)

## Roger Donaldson

**Born:** November 15, 1945; Ballarat, Australia

**Years Active in the Industry:** by decade

| 10s | 20s | 30s | 40s | 50s | 60s | 70s | 80s | 90s |
|-----|-----|-----|-----|-----|-----|-----|-----|-----|

Director Roger Donaldson is an important figure in the development of modern New Zealand cinema. When he emigrated to New Zealand from Australia in 1965 to set up a still photography business, the Kiwi film industry was all but non-existent. He was interested in filmmaking, but had to make do with creating television commercials and documentaries; he then went on to do seven short dramas titled *Winners and Losers*. By 1977, he was finally able to scrape up enough cash to make his film debut with the futuristic political drama *Sleeping Dogs*; the first feature made in New Zealand in 15 years, it was also the first to be shown in American theaters. Donaldson then went on to co-found the country's Film Commission. He did not direct again until 1982. In 1984 his version of the famous mutiny *Bounty* was released to critical acclaim; unfortunately, the powerful all-star drama sank at the box office. He continued trying to make quality films, but unfortunately, most of them suffered the same fate until he made the Kevin Costner vehicle *No Way Out* (1987), which became a hit. He then scored again Tom Cruise in the vacuous comedy *Cocktail* (1988), which became a box office smash. Since then Donaldson has had moderate box office success, with so-so fare such as *Cadillac Man* (1990) and *The Getaway* (1994). **Selected Works:** *White Sands* (1992)

# Robert Donat

**Born:** March 18, 1905; Withington, Manchester, England
**Died:** 1958

**Years Active in the Industry:** by decade

| 10s | 20s | 30s | 40s | 50s | 60s | 70s | 80s | 90s |
|-----|-----|-----|-----|-----|-----|-----|-----|-----|
|     |     |     |     |     |     |     |     |     |

At age 11, Robert Donat began taking elocution lessons to overcome a stutter, going on to develop an exceptional and versatile voice. At 16 he debuted onstage and later played a number of Shakespearean and classical roles in repertory and with touring companies; it was almost ten years, however, before he made his London debut. In the early '30s he attracted the attention of filmmakers, and signed a contract with Alexander Korda; almost immediately he was internationally famous for his romantic lead in *The Private Life of Henry VIII* (1933), his third film. He made one film in Hollywood but he didn't like the town or the prospect of becoming a conventional movie star. For his work in *Goodbye Mr. Chips* (1939), in which he aged from 25 to 83 onscreen, he won the Best Actor Oscar. Although very successful, his career was hampered by chronic asthma and an insecure, self-doubting personality; he turned down many more films than he accepted, and for an actor of his time, his filmography is unusually thin. He appeared in only three films in the '50s, and was seriously ill during the production of his last, requiring oxygen tanks to complete his work. Donat died at 53. He was married to actress Renee Asherson. **Selected Works:** *Citadel* (1938), *Ghost Goes West* (1936), *Inn of the Sixth Happiness* (1958), *Winslow Boy* (1949)

# Stanley Donen

**Born:** April 13, 1924; Columbia, SC

**Years Active in the Industry:** by decade

| 10s | 20s | 30s | 40s | 50s | 60s | 70s | 80s | 90s |
|-----|-----|-----|-----|-----|-----|-----|-----|-----|
|     |     |     |     |     |     |     |     |     |

A dancer since he was child, Stanley Donen made his Broadway debut at age 16 in *Pal Joey*, which starred Gene Kelly. In 1941 he and Kelly choreographed *Best Foot Forward*, and when the

show was filmed by MGM in 1943, Donen was hired as a dancer and assistant choreographer. He went on to choreograph such musicals as Kelly's *Cover Girl* (1944) and *Take Me Out to the Ball Game* (1949), and debuted as a director in 1949, co-helming *On the Town* (1949) with Kelly. The two went on to make the beloved musicals *Singin' in the Rain* (1952) and *It's Always Fair Weather* (1955). With George Abbot, Donen also co-directed *Damn Yankees* (1958) and *The Pajama Game* (1957). His solo musicals include *Seven Brides for Seven Brothers* (1954) and *Funny Face* (1957) with Fred Astaire and Audrey Hepburn. He went on to direct Hepburn in the comic thriller *Charade* (1963) and the romantic comedy/drama *Two for the Road* (1967). Donen's later films as a producer/director include such offbeat projects as the Faust parody *Bedazzled* (1968), the Lerner and Loewe musical *The Little Prince* (1974), and the double-feature spoof *Movie Movie* (1978).

# Brian Donlevy

**Born:** February 9, 1889; Portadown, Ireland
**Died:** 1972

**Years Active in the Industry:** by decade

| 10s | 20s | 30s | 40s | 50s | 60s | 70s | 80s | 90s |
|-----|-----|-----|-----|-----|-----|-----|-----|-----|
|     |     |     |     |     |     |     |     |     |

American actor Brian Donlevy joined the Army in his teens, going on to become a pilot in World War I. In 1924 he began his career in bit parts on Broadway and in New York films. Gradually he began landing bigger roles, but his screen career didn't begin in earnest until the mid-'30s when he began playing tough, sadistic villain roles. For his work in *Beau Geste* (1939), Donlevy received a Best Supporting Actor Oscar nomination. Besides playing heavies, he also played numerous tough-guy heroes, and occasionally had comedic roles. He remained fairly busy onscreen through the late

'60s. He was married to actress Marjorie Lane **Selected Works:** *Great McGinty* (1940), *Kiss of Death* (1947), *Miracle of Morgan's Creek* (1944), *Wake Island* (1942), *Hangmen Also Die* (1943)

# Richard D. Donner

**Born:** 1939; New York, NY

**Years Active in the Industry:** by decade

| 10s | 20s | 30s | 40s | 50s | 60s | 70s | 80s | 90s |
|-----|-----|-----|-----|-----|-----|-----|-----|-----|
|     |     |     |     |     | ■   | ■   | ■   | ■   |

Working briefly as an actor in the late 1950s, American director Richard Donner first wielded the megaphone for a group of TV commercials, then graduated to the weekly western *Wanted: Dead or Alive*. Some of Donner's best early work was concentrated on the fantasy anthology *Twilight Zone*, including the imperishable 1963 episode "Nightmare at 20,000 Feet" (unofficially known as "William Shatner and the Gremlin on the Wing.") Donner also worked for Hanna-Barbera, directing several episodes of "Danger Island," a component of the 1968 kid's series *The Banana Splits*; there was, however, very little that was "kiddie" about "Mystery Island," an hallucinatory symphony of hand-held camerawork which Donner described as appearing to be "totally improvised on Acapulco Gold." A film director since 1961 (the film was *X-15*, which if nothing else represented the only screen teaming of Wayne Rogers and Mary Tyler Moore), Donner turned to movie work full time with 1968's *Salt and Pepper*. *The Omen* (1976), a demonic-possession opus, was Donner's first major moneymaker, leading to his directing assignment on the first *Superman* film in 1978. Perhaps the most schizophrenic adventure movie of all time (it started out deadly serious, then switched to campy comedy 40 minutes in), *Superman* was popular enough to inspire three sequels, the first of which contained so much uncredited Donner-directed footage that the director was compelled to sue. Donner has struck gold at the box office several times since 1978, notably with the three action-packed *Lethal Weapon* films starring Mel Gibson and Danny Glover, and with another Gibson vehicle, *Maverick* (1994). **Selected Works:** *Lethal Weapon, Part 3* (1992)

# Amanda Donohoe

**Born:** 1962; London, England

**Years Active in the Industry:** by decade

| 10s | 20s | 30s | 40s | 50s | 60s | 70s | 80s | 90s |
|-----|-----|-----|-----|-----|-----|-----|-----|-----|
|     |     |     |     |     |     |     | ■   | ■   |

An alumnus of London's Central School of Speech and Drama, English actress Amanda Donohoe's first film role was a supporting one in the door-slamming sex farce *Foreign Body* (1986). She then starred in a handful of British TV movies, usually cast as the slinky femme fatale. Briefly a member of director Ken Russell's informal stock company, Donohoe was stunning as the wicked snake woman in Russell's *Lair of the White Worm* (1988); in the same director's *The Rainbow* (1989), she played the worldly seductress to whom sexual *naif* Judy Davis turns to for advice. Donohoe was also starred as the alluring desert-island companion of Oliver Reed in director Nicholas Roeg's *Castaway* (1987), and was seen in a rare sympathetic role in 1990's *Paper Mask*. It was back to "black widows" again in 1993's made-for-cable *The Substitute*—one of several recent TV appearances for Donohoe, the most well-publicized of which was her weekly assignment as lesbian attorney C. J. Lamb on the popular TV series *LA Law*. **Selected Works:** *Dark Obsession* (1990), *Double Cross* (1992), *Shame* (1992), *Madness of King George* (1994)

# Kirk Douglas (Issur Danielovitch)

**Born:** December 9, 1916; Amsterdam, NY

**Years Active in the Industry:** by decade

| 10s | 20s | 30s | 40s | 50s | 60s | 70s | 80s | 90s |
|-----|-----|-----|-----|-----|-----|-----|-----|-----|
|     |     |     |     | ■   | ■   | ■   | ■   | ■   |

American he-man actor Kirk Douglas, born to Russian immigrants, waited tables to put himself through St. Lawrence University, where he was a top-notch wrestler. While there he also did a little work in theater. Later he became a professional wrestler and held various odd jobs, including a stint as a bell-hop, to put himself through the American Academy of Dramatic Arts. In 1941 he debuted on Broadway, but had only two small roles before he enlisted in the Navy and served in World War II. After his discharge, Douglas returned to Broadway in 1945, where he began getting meatier roles; he also did some work on radio. After being spotted and invited to Hollywood by producer Hal Willis, he debuted onscreen in *The Strange Love of Martha Ivers* (1946), but did not emerge as a full-fledged star until his role as an unscrupulously ambitious boxer in *Champion* (1949); with this role he defined one of his main character-types as an actor, that of a cocky, selfish, intense, powerful man. In 1955 he formed his own company, Bryna Productions, through which he produced both his own films and those of others, including two by Stanley Kubrick, *Paths of Glory* (1957) and *Spartacus* (1960); later he also formed Joel Productions. In 1963 he appeared on Broadway in Ken Kesey's *One Flew Over the Cuckoo's Nest,* but was never able to interest Hollywood in a film version of the work; he passed it along to his son Michael Douglas (a powerful, popular contemporary actor/filmmaker), who eventually brought it to the screen to great success. During the 1960s, he continued to play leading men. Douglas began directing some of his films in the early '70s. Though he continues to appear in films, by the 1980s he began volunteering much of his time to civic duties. Since 1963, Douglas has worked as a Goodwill Ambassador for the State Department and the USIA. In 1981, his many contributions earned him the highest civilian award given in the U.S., the Presidential Medal of Freedom. For his public service he was given the Jefferson Award in 1983. Two years later the French government dubbed him Chevalier of the Legion of Honor for his artisitic contributions. Other awards received include the American Cinema Award (1987), the German Golden Kamera Award (1988), and the National Board of Review's Career Achievement Award (1989). Douglas has also published two novels: *Dance with the Devil* (1990) and *The Secret* (1992). He published his autobiography, *The Ragman's Son*, in 1988. **Selected Works:** *Bad & the Beautiful* (1952), *Detective Story* (1951), *Lust for Life* (1956), *Posse* (1975), *Seven Days in May* (1964), *Greedy* (1994)

## Melvyn Douglas (Melvyn Edouard Hesselberg)

**Born:** April 5, 1901; Macon, GA
**Died:** August 4, 1981; New York, NY

**Years Active in the Industry:** by decade

| 10s | 20s | 30s | 40s | 50s | 60s | 70s | 80s | 90s |
|-----|-----|-----|-----|-----|-----|-----|-----|-----|
|     |     |     |     |     |     |     |     |     |

American actor Melvyn Douglas began his stage career shortly after being mustered out of World War I Army service. Douglas secured a position with the Owens Repertory Company, making his debut in a production of *Merchant of Venice*. He spent the first part of the 1920s touring with Owens Rep and with the Jessie Bonstelle Company, reaching Broadway in the 1928 drama *A Free Soul*. Brought to Hollywood in the early talkie "gold rush" for stage-trained actors, Douglas made his film bow in 1931's *Tonight or Never*. With *The Old Dark House* (1932), the actor established his standard screen character: a charming, blase young socialite who could exhibit great courage and loyalty when those attributes were called upon. After a brief return to Broadway in 1933, Douglas returned to films in 1935, signing a joint contract with Columbia and MGM. Most often appearing in sophisticated comedies, Douglas was one of the busiest stars in Hollywood, playing in as many as eight films per year. One of the actor's better roles was a supporting one: as Cary Grant's beleaguered lawyer and business adviser in *Mr. Blandings Builds His Dream House* (1947), who spends most of the film trying to keep Grant from spending himself into bankruptcy. Douglas found movie roles scarce in the early 1950s thanks to the "Red Scare". The actor was married to Congresswoman Helen Gahagan, the woman labeled by Richard Nixon as the "pink lady" friendly to Communism. The more rabid anti-Communists in Washington went after Douglas himself, suggesting that because he was Jewish and had changed his name for professional reasons, he was automatically politically suspect. Douglas began recovering his

career with an early-1950s detective program, *Hollywood Off-Beat* - ironically playing a disbarred lawyer trying to regain his reputation. He headed back to Broadway, gaining high critical praise for his "emergence" as a topnotch character actor (as though he *hadn't* been acting in all those movies!) Some of Douglas' stage triumphs included *Inherit the Wind* (replacing Paul Muni in the Clarence Darrow part) and *The Best Man* (which had a character based on Richard Nixon). Douglas' long-overdue Academy Award was bestowed upon the actor for his role as Paul Newman's dying father in *Hud* (1963); other highlights of Douglas' final Hollywood days included *I Never Sang for My Father* (1971) and *Being There* (1979), the latter film winning the actor his second Oscar. Melvyn Douglas died at age 80, just before the release of his final film, *Ghost Story* (1981). **Selected Works:** *Billy Budd* (1962), *Candidate* (1972), *Captains Courageous* (1937), *Ninotchka* (1939), *Theodora Goes Wild* (1936)

# Michael Douglas

**Born:** September 25, 1944; New Brunswick, NJ

**Years Active in the Industry:** by decade

| 10s | 20s | 30s | 40s | 50s | 60s | 70s | 80s | 90s |
|-----|-----|-----|-----|-----|-----|-----|-----|-----|
|     |     |     |     |     |     |     |     |     |

Michael Douglas is one of the most powerful actors and filmmakers in Hollywood. The son of screen star Kirk Douglas and British actress Diana Dill, began his career in his late teens and  early 20s when he worked as an assistant director on *Lonely Are the Brave* (1962). He studied drama in California and New York and appeared off Broadway; shortly thereafter he debuted onscreen in *Hail, Hero!* (1969). After a few more film appearances he landed a co-starring role in the TV police series *The Streets of San Francisco*, remaining with that show till 1975 and directing two episodes. His career took a surprising turn in the mid-'70s when his father handed over to him the film rights to the play *One Flew Over the Cuckoo's Nest*, which the elder Douglas had acquired after appearing in the play the previous decade; he co-produced the screen version (1975), which was one of the biggest box-office successes in film history and swept the Oscars for Best Picture, Director, Actor, Actress, and Screenplay. He returned to acting in films with *Coma* (1978), then surprisingly became one of the highest-paid actors in Hollywood after his successes in a series of films beginning with *Romancing* the *Stone* (1984). For his performance in Oliver Stone's *Wall Street* (1987) he won the Best Actor Oscar. He has also continued to produce films, including *The China Syndrome* (1979) and *The Jewel of the Nile* (1985). In *The Star Chamber* (1983) he appeared with his mother as a supporting actress. By 1991, he commanded a $15 million salary to appear in *Basic Instinct*, and is one of the most in demand leading men on the scene; he beat out several younger actors to star opposite Demi Moore in *Disclosure* (1994) . **Selected Works:** *Black Rain* (1990), *Falling Down* (1993), *Fatal Attraction* (1987), *The American President* (1995)

# Brad Dourif

**Born:** March 18, 1950; Huntington, WV

**Years Active in the Industry:** by decade

| 10ˢ | 20ˢ | 30ˢ | 40ˢ | 50ˢ | 60ˢ | 70ˢ | 80ˢ | 90ˢ |
|-----|-----|-----|-----|-----|-----|-----|-----|-----|

Brad Dourif is a slightly-built co-starring actor with large blue eyes, whose performances have an unpredictable edginess. After attending college he had a three-year apprenticeship with New York's Circle Repertory. He studied with the celebrated drama coach Sanford Meisner. Dourif debuted onscreen as Billy, a vulnerable, stuttering patient of a mental hospital, in *One Flew Over the Cuckoo's Nest* (1975), for which he received a Best Supporting Actor nomination. His first lead role came in his fourth movie, John Huston's *Wise Blood* (1979), in which he portrayed the obsessed preacher of the Church Without Christ. After appearing in several more films which, like *Wise Blood*, failed to succeed at the box office, he took three years off from the screen and taught directing at Columbia University. After 1984 he began working in films fairly often, but most of them have been forgettable B-movies; one exception has been Alan Parker's *Mississippi Burning* (1988), in which he played a bigoted, wife-beating deputy sheriff of a small town in the '60s. **Selected Works:** *Common Bonds* (1991), *Hidden Agenda* (1990), *Jungle Fever* (1991), *Ragtime* (1981), *Trauma* (1993)

# Lesley-Anne Down

**Born:** March 17, 1954; London, England

**Years Active in the Industry:** by decade

| 10ˢ | 20ˢ | 30ˢ | 40ˢ | 50ˢ | 60ˢ | 70ˢ | 80ˢ | 90ˢ |
|-----|-----|-----|-----|-----|-----|-----|-----|-----|

British actress Lesley-Anne Down was a celebrity before reaching the age of consent, thanks to her winning several teen beauty contests. In films since the age of 15, Lesley achieved international prominence for her recurring appearances as Lady Georgina on the British TV serial *Upstairs, Downstairs*, which ran from 1976 through 1977. At that same time, she became an alluring movie sex symbol by virtue of her co-starring turn in *The Pink Panther Strikes Again* (1976). The bulk of her subsequent movie work has often been of negligible quality, though she herself is always worth watching. Down's television work has been more rewarding, including a starring role as bewitching southern belle Madeline Main in the 1985 miniseries *North and South* and its 1986 sequel. As colorful a personality off-camera as on, Down has been linked romantically with several high-profile males, and was briefly and tempestuously wed to director William Friedkin. **Selected Works:** *Hunchback of Notre Dame* (1982)

# Robert Downey, Jr.

**Born:** April 4, 1965; New York, NY

**Years Active in the Industry:** by decade

| 10ˢ | 20ˢ | 30ˢ | 40ˢ | 50ˢ | 60ˢ | 70ˢ | 80ˢ | 90ˢ |
|-----|-----|-----|-----|-----|-----|-----|-----|-----|

American actor Robert Downey, Jr., the son of a filmmaker, first appeared onscreen at the age of five in his father's film *Pound* (1970); he went on to make cameo appearances in five more of his  father's films between 1972-90. His first significant role, in *Baby, It's You* (1983), largely ended up on the cutting-room floor. He went on to supporting parts in a series of teen-oriented films, finally landing the male lead opposite Molly Ringwald in *The Pick-Up Artist* (1987). Meanwhile, he gained much recognition during a year spent in the regular cast of the weekly sketch-comedy TV series *Saturday Night Live*. He has maintained a steady film career but has yet to appear in a major hit. His most compelling performance was in the title role of Richard Attenborough's biopic *Chaplin* (1992), for which he earned an Oscar nomination for Best Actor. He continues to garner both leading (*Heart and Souls* [1993], *Only You* [1994]) and supporting (*Natural Born Killers [1994]* roles). **Selected Works:** *Soapdish (1991),* Natural Born Killers *(1994),* Only You *(1994),* Restoration *(1995)*

# Marie Dressler (Leila Marie Koerber)

**Born:** November 9, 1869; Cobourg, Ontario, Canada
**Died:** 1934

**Years Active in the Industry:** by decade

| 10ˢ | 20ˢ | 30ˢ | 40ˢ | 50ˢ | 60ˢ | 70ˢ | 80ˢ | 90ˢ |
|-----|-----|-----|-----|-----|-----|-----|-----|-----|

A homely, mugging, rowdy actress of enormous girth, Marie Dressler was a leading American comedienne during the silent era. At age 14 she joined a stock company, going on to become a seasoned veteran in light opera and on the legitimate stage. In 1892 she debuted on Broadway; by the turn of the century she was a vaudeville headliner. Dressler debuted onscreen opposite Charlie Chaplin in the silent feature *Tillie's Punctured Romance* (1914), based on one of her stage vehicles; she appeared in two more "Tillie" films plus a couple of other comedies, then after 1918 went almost a decade without appearing onscreen; she remained mainly a vaudeville and musical comedy star. She re-entered films in 1927 with the help of MGM screenwriter Frances Marion; her stage career had undergone a severe setback in the mid-'20s, largely due to her involvement in a labor dispute. Soon Dressler was a popular star, her appeal increased by comedies in which she co-starred with Polly Moran. She became even more popular in the sound era; her range of roles increased after her unexpected casting in a serious character part, as the waterfront hag/barfly Marthy in *Anna Christie* (1930). For her tragicomic performance opposite Wallace Beery in *Min and Bill* (1930) she won the Best Actress Oscar, then was nominated again for the same award for her work in *Emma* (1932). An unlikely-looking star, for four years in the early '30s Dressler was the nation's top box office attraction. She authored an autobiography, *The Life Story of an Ugly Duckling*.

# Carl Theodor Dreyer

**Born:** February 3, 1889; Copenhagen, Denmark
**Died:** March 20, 1968

**Years Active in the Industry:** by decade

| 10ˢ | 20ˢ | 30ˢ | 40ˢ | 50ˢ | 60ˢ | 70ˢ | 80ˢ | 90ˢ |
|-----|-----|-----|-----|-----|-----|-----|-----|-----|

Considered the finest Danish film director of all time, Carl Theodor Dreyer was born out of wedlock and raised by an inordinately strict Lutheran family. This, plus his discovery at age 18 that his mother had died as a result of a botched abortion, helped formulate the two most prevalent themes in Dreyer's films: the use and misuse of religion, and the ill-treatment of the less fortunate (particularly women) at the hands of the intolerant. He began his writing career as a newspaper journalist in 1909, then moved into movie scriptwriting in 1913. Six years later, he directed his first film, *Praesidenten*. From the outset, Dreyer was less interest in the nuances of film technique and production polish than he was in recording the innermost feelings and long-hidden emotions of his characters; as a result, Dreyer's films have some of the longest, tightest close-ups in movie history. In his first major film, 1921's *Leaves From Satan's Book*, Dreyer concentrated on past female martyrs of religious and political persecution, a theme that would come to full and brilliant fruitition with his finest silent work, *The Passion of Joan of Arc* (1928). A journeyman filmmaker in the best sense, Dreyer worked in several countries during the silent

era, with stopovers at Berlin's UFA and Paris' Societie Generale de Films. After the financial failure of *Joan of Arc*, Dreyer went back to journalism, making his talking debut with the multilingual *Vampyr*. This nightmarish, hallucinatory horror film was another box-office disappointment, compelling Dreyer to leave the movie industry for nearly ten years. His one major film of the 1940s, an extremely downbeat witch-burning saga titled *Day of Wrath* (1943), combined many of the horrific elements of *Vampyr* with the religious and feminist overtones of his silent films. The psychological impact of *Day of Wrath* is such that at times the audience is forced to turn away rather than endure the terrors that threaten to avail themselves at every turn; not surprisingly, the film was another money-loser. For the rest of the 1940s, Dreyer attempted to assemble a film on the life of Christ, vestiges of which could be found in his one feature film of the 1950s, *Ordet* (1955), the story of a man with a pronounced Messianic complex who suffers the ridicule of his allegedly pious neighbors. Derided by Dreyer's detractors as being just another "dull" tract, the questions of religious tradition vs. spiritual emotionalism raised in *Ordet* struck a nerve with the more receptive audiences of the era; the film did quite well internationally, winning the Golden Lion award at the Venice Film Festival. Dreyer's last film was 1964's *Gertrud*, the slowly unfolding tale of an unhappy woman to whom "love is all;" almost universally panned upon its first release, *Gertrud*, like many previously underappreciated Dreyer efforts, is now an acknowledged classic. Definitely not a director for all tastes, Dreyer has nonetheless exerted a far-reaching influence on the cinema of personal expression, an influence especially obvious in the works of Ingmar Bergman and Michelangelo Antonioni.

# Richard Dreyfuss

**Born:** October 29, 1947; Brooklyn, NY

**Years Active in the Industry:** by decade

| 10ˢ | 20ˢ | 30ˢ | 40ˢ | 50ˢ | 60ˢ | 70ˢ | 80ˢ | 90ˢ |
|-----|-----|-----|-----|-----|-----|-----|-----|-----|

After spending his childhood in New York, actor Richard Dreyfuss, at age nine, moved with his family to Los Angeles; there, a few years later, he began acting at the Beverly Hills Jewish Center. By the late '60s and early '70s he was working on both coasts, performing on and off Broadway, working in repertory and improvisational comedy, and making TV appearances. After bit parts in *The Valley of the Dolls* and *The Graduate* (both 1967), he had his first big-screen supporting role in *The Young Runaways* (1968). After an impressive performance as Baby Face Nelson in *Dillinger* (1973), he achieved stardom with an appearance in George Lucas's highly successful *American Graffiti* (1973). Dreyfuss went on to appear in two more all-time box office champs, the Steven Spielberg films *Jaws* (1975) and *Close Encounters of the Third Kind* (1977). For his work in Neil Simon's *The Goodbye Girl* (1977) he won a Best Actor Oscar, becoming at age 29 the youngest actor to have won that award. So much success so quickly led him to a hedonistic, self-destructive lifestyle, in which he consumed two grams of cocaine, twenty Percodan pills, and two quarts of alcohol a day; after being involved in a car crash he was arrested on drug charges. He cleaned up his life with the help of his friends, taking time off from films until the mid-'80s, when he made a successful cinema comeback with films such as *Stake Out* (1987), *Once Around* (1991), and *What About Bob?* (1991). **Selected Works:** *Apprenticeship of Duddy Kravitz* (1974), *Lost in Yonkers* (1993), *Once Around* (1991), *Silent Fall* (1994)

# David Duchovny

**Born:** August 7, 1960; New York, NY

**Years Active in the Industry:** by decade

| 10ˢ | 20ˢ | 30ˢ | 40ˢ | 50ˢ | 60ˢ | 70ˢ | 80ˢ | 90ˢ |
|-----|-----|-----|-----|-----|-----|-----|-----|-----|
|     |     |     |     |     |     |     |     | ■ |

Manhattan-born David Duchovny did his undergraduate work at Princeton, then moved on to earn a Master's at Yale, where he was a teaching assistant. He was working on his PhD dissertation in literature when he made his acting debut in a beer commercial. In 1991, Duchovny made his first film appearance in *Julia Has Two Lovers*. Other films followed in rapid progression: *Don't Tell Mom the Babysitter's Dead* (1991), *The Rapture* (1991), *Chaplin* (1992) and *Kalifornia* (1993). In his own words, Duchovny "imagined hopping from one glorious movie to another," but TV work was more steady and the money came faster. His television bow was as Denise, the transvestite detective, in *Twin Peaks* (1990). Since 1993, Duchovny has starred as FBI agent Fox Mulder in the Fox Network's Emmy-nominated sci-fi series *The X Files*; at the risk of disillusioning his fans, we must note that, unlike Mulder, Duchovny still harbors doubts concerning the existence of space aliens. **Selected Works:** *Beethoven* (1992), *Red Shoe Diaries* (1992), *Red Shoe Diaries 2: Double Dare* (1992), *Ruby* (1992)

# John Duigan

**Born:** 1949; Hartney-Witney, Hampshire, England

**Years Active in the Industry:** by decade

| 10ˢ | 20ˢ | 30ˢ | 40ˢ | 50ˢ | 60ˢ | 70ˢ | 80ˢ | 90ˢ |
|-----|-----|-----|-----|-----|-----|-----|-----|-----|
|     |     |     |     |     |     | ■ |     |     |

Director John Duigan first attracted attention with such low-budget films as *The Trespassers* (1976) and *Mouth to Mouth* (1978), which he also wrote and directed. These films were centered in Duigan's adopted homeland of Australia, but their theme of youthful alienation and confusion struck a universal chord. Duigan's *The Year My Voice Broke* (1988) is perhaps the best of his many explorations of the painful coming-of-age process. Duigan has since varied his subject matter with *Romero* (1989), a heartfelt but objective biography of controversial Salvadorian clergyman Oscar Romero, and *Sirens* (1994), a likeably erotic story of artistic expression in the Outback of the 1920s. **Selected Works:** *Flirting* (1992)

# Olympia Dukakis

**Born:** June 20, 1931; Lowell, MA

**Years Active in the Industry:** by decade

| 10ˢ | 20ˢ | 30ˢ | 40ˢ | 50ˢ | 60ˢ | 70ˢ | 80ˢ | 90ˢ |
|-----|-----|-----|-----|-----|-----|-----|-----|-----|
|     |     |     |     |     | ■ | ■ | ■ | ■ |

American actress Olympia Dukakis, the daughter of Greek immigrants, co-founded the famous Charles Playhouse in Boston after college and some stage work. Dukakis worked there from 1957-60. Later she taught acting at New York University and Yale. She and her husband, actor Louis Zorich, have made great contributions to the Whole Theater in Montclair, New Jersey; she has adapted plays and directed dinner theater for the company, as well as directing plays at summer festivals in other parts of the U.S. Dukakis has appeared in more than 100 plays on and off-Broadway and in various regional theaters across the country. She debuted onscreen in *Lilith* (1964), but her central vocation remained the theater and she appeared in only five more films over the next 15 years. However, after she won the Best Supporting Actress Oscar for her work in *Moonstruck* (1987)—in which she played Cher's mother—she began working more frequently in high-profile films, including *Steel Magnolias* (1989), *Look Who's Talking* (1989), and *I Love Trouble* (1994). She is the cousin of Michael Dukakis, the 1988 Democratic candidate for President. **Selected Works:** *Cemetery Club* (1993), *Sinatra* (1992), *Steel Magnolias* (1989), *Wanderers* (1979), *Working Girl* (1988)

# Douglas Dumbrille

**Born:** October 13, 1890; Hamilton, Ontario, Canada
**Died:** April 2, 1974; Woodland Hills, CA

**Years Active in the Industry:** by decade

| 10ˢ | 20ˢ | 30ˢ | 40ˢ | 50ˢ | 60ˢ | 70ˢ | 80ˢ | 90ˢ |
|-----|-----|-----|-----|-----|-----|-----|-----|-----|
|     | ■ | ■ | ■ | ■ | ■ |     |     |     |

Silver-tongued actor Douglas Dumbrille played just about every type in his long screen career, but it was as a dignified villain that he is best remembered. Born in Canada, Dumbrille did most of his stage work in the United States, breaking into films with *His Woman* in 1931. He bounced between supporting parts and unbilled bits in the early 1930s, usually at Warner Bros., where his sleek brand of skullduggery fit right in with the gangsters, shysters and political phonies popping up in most of the studio's 1930s product. Superb in modern dress roles, Dumbrille also excelled at costume villainy: it is claimed that, in *Lives of the Bengal Lancers* (1935), he was the first bad guy to growl, "We have ways of making you talk." The actor's pompous demeanor made him an ideal foil for such comedians as the Marx Brothers, with whom he appeared twice, and Abbott and Costello, who matched wits with Dumbrille in four different films. Sometimes, Dumbrille's reputation as a no-good was used to lead the audience astray; he was frequently cast as red-herring suspects in such murder mysteries as *Castle in the Desert* (1942), while in the Johnny Mack Brown western *Flame of the West* (1945), Dumbrille piqued the viewer's interest by playing a thoroughly honest, decent sheriff (surely he'd turn bad by the end, thought the audience—but he didn't). In real life a gentle man whose diabolical features were softened by a pair of spectacles, Dumbrille mellowed his image as he grew older, often playing bemused officials and judges who couldn't make head nor tails of Gracie Allen's thought patterns on TV's *The Burns and Allen Show*. Late in life, a widowed Douglas Dumbrille married Patricia Mobray, daughter of his close friend—and fellow screen villain—Alan Mobray. **Selected Works:** *Broadway Bill* (1934), *Day at the Races* (1937), *Lives of a Bengal Lancer* (1935), *Mr. Deeds Goes to Town* (1936), *Kentucky* (1938)

## Margaret Dumont (Margaret Baker)

**Born:** October 20, 1889; Brooklyn, NY
**Died:** March 6, 1965; Los Angeles, CA

**Years Active in the Industry:** by decade

| 10s | 20s | 30s | 40s | 50s | 60s | 70s | 80s | 90s |
|-----|-----|-----|-----|-----|-----|-----|-----|-----|

Originally an opera singer, American actress Margaret Dumont was engaged in 1925 to act in *The Cocoanuts*, a Broadway musical comedy starring the Marx Brothers. As wealthy widow Mrs. Potter, Dumont became the formidable stage target for the rapid-fire insults and bizarre lovemaking approach of Groucho Marx. So impressive was her "teaming" with Groucho that she was hired for their next Broadway production, *Animal Crackers* (1928), in which she portrayed society dowager Mrs. Rittenhouse. Though Groucho would later insist that Dumont never understood his jokes, she more than held her own against the unpredictable Marxes, facing their wild ad-libs, practical jokes and roughhouse physical humor with the straightfaced aplomb of a school principal assigned a classroom of unruly children. Dumont continued appearing opposite the Marx Brothers when they began making motion pictures, co-starring in seven of the team's films, most notably as hypochondriac Emily Upjohn in *A Day at the Races* (1937). It was for this picture that Dumont won a Screen Actor's Guild award; upon this occasion, film critic Cecilia Ager suggested that a monu-

ment be erected in honor of Dumont's courage and steadfastness in the face of the Marx invasion. Although she appeared in many other films (sometimes in the company of other famous comedy teams such as Laurel and Hardy, Wheeler and Woolsey, and Abbott and Costello), it is for her Marx appearances that Dumont—often dubbed "the Fifth Marx Brother"—is best remembered. Dumont made her last professional appearance a week before her death, on the TV variety series *Hollywood Palace*; appropriately, it was in support of Groucho Marx in a recreation of the "Hooray for Captain Spaulding" production number from *Animal Crackers*.

## Faye Dunaway

**Born:** January 14, 1941; Bascom, FL

**Years Active in the Industry:** by decade

| 10s | 20s | 30s | 40s | 50s | 60s | 70s | 80s | 90s |
|-----|-----|-----|-----|-----|-----|-----|-----|-----|

A tall, green-eyed blonde with high cheekbones, American actress Faye Dunaway was an "Army brat" and grew up in a number of towns. After college she went to New York to find an acting  career. In 1962 she joined the Lincoln Center Repertory Company, going on to appear in a number of plays between 1962-67, including *A Man for All Seasons* and Elia Kazan's production of Arthur Miller's *After the Fall* (in which she played the character based on Marilyn Monroe). Dunaway's big break came with a role off-Broadway in *Hogan's Goat*, which led to her debut onscreen in *The Happening* (1967); that same year she became an international star with her portrayal of gangster Bonnie Parker in Arthur Penn's influential *Bonnie and Clyde* (1967), thus rising from "unknown" to star in a matter of months. In the following decades she kept up a steady stream of film work, gaining a reputation as a very difficult worker ("insane," in the words of director Roman Polanski). She was nominated for Best Actress Oscars for both *Bonnie and Clyde* and *Chinatown* (1974), then won the award for her work in Paddy Chayefsky's *Network* (1976). She gave a brilliant performance as Joan Crawford in *Mommie Dearest* (1981), and has continued to deliver frequent film appearances, most notably in the star-powered *Don Juan DeMarco* with Marlon Brando and Johnny Depp. In 1993 she starred in the short-lived TV sitcom *It Had to Be You*. **Selected Works:** *Handmaid's Tale* (1990), *Little Big Man* (1970), *Three Days of the Condor* (1975), *Three Musketeers* (1974)

# James Dunn

**Born:** November 2, 1901; New York, NY
**Died:** September 3, 1967; Santa Monica, CA

**Years Active in the Industry:** by decade

| 10s | 20s | 30s | 40s | 50s | 60s | 70s | 80s | 90s |
|-----|-----|-----|-----|-----|-----|-----|-----|-----|
|     |     |     |     |     |     |     |     |     |

American actor James Dunn's early career embraced bit parts in silent pictures, vaudeville, and Broadway before he made his talking picture bow in *Bad Girl* (1931). For the next several years, Dunn appeared in sentimental "lovable scamp" leading roles; he also helped introduce Shirley Temple to feature films by costarring with the diminutive dynamo in *Stand Up and Cheer*, *Baby Take a Bow*, and *Bright Eyes*, all released in 1934. When Fox merged with 20th Century Pictures in 1935, the type of domestic comedy-dramas and freewheeling musicals in which Dunn specialized came to an end; by the end of the 1930s Dunn's appearance were confined to B pictures and poverty-row quickies. Heavy drinking began to blunt Dunn's leprechaunish features, and the added weight made him unconvincing in the lighthearted roles he'd once specialized in. Thanks to the kindness of his show business friends, Dunn was given a comeback chance as Peggy Ann Garner's irresponsible alcoholic father in the 1945 drama *A Tree Grows in Brooklyn*. The actor won an Academy Award for his performance, and it seemed as though his future was secure, but in 1951 the notoriously improvident Dunn filed for bankruptcy during a Connecticut summer stock appearance as Willy Loman in *Death of a Salesman*. Eight years passed before Dunn would be seen in films again, though he found occasional solace in TV work, getting a year's worth of paychecks as the star of a 1955 sitcom, *It's a Great Life*. Dunn's final movie role, filmed two years before his death, was a minor part as an agent in the all-star "trash classic" *The Oscar* (1966).

# Griffin Dunne

**Born:** June 8, 1955; New York, NY

**Years Active in the Industry:** by decade

| 10s | 20s | 30s | 40s | 50s | 60s | 70s | 80s | 90s |
|-----|-----|-----|-----|-----|-----|-----|-----|-----|
|     |     |     |     |     |     |     |     |     |

The son of producer-author Dominick Dunne and the nephew of author-screenwriter John Gregory Dunne, American actor Griffin Dunne trained with Uta Hagen at the Neighborhood Playhouse. He went on to work on stage and TV and in films, and also set up his own film production company, Double Play Productions, with partner Amy Robinson. Dunne debuted onscreen in *The Other Side of the Mountain* (1975), then went five years before his next screen role. He first made an impression in his fourth film, *An American Werewolf in London* (1981), in which he played a decomposing corpse; after that he again went several years without appearing in films, meanwhile producing John Sayles's *Baby, It's You* (1983). In 1985 he starred in and co-produced Martin Scors-

ese's *After Hours*, in which he played a hyperactive computer programmer involved in a weird, surreal, action-packed night; the role increased his visibility, as did his work in *Who's That Girl* (1987) with Madonna, but he has found it hard to sustain a career as a screen actor. He has gone on to work in several more films and on TV, while continuing to produce or co-produce on occasion. His sister was actress Dominique Dunne, who was murdered shortly after her first film appearance. **Selected Works:** *My Girl* (1991), *Once Around* (1991), *I Like It Like That* (1994), *Quiz Show* (1994)

# Irene Dunne (Irene Marie Dunn)

**Born:** December 20, 1904; Louisville, KY
**Died:** September 4, 1990; Hollywood, CA

**Years Active in the Industry:** by decade

| 10s | 20s | 30s | 40s | 50s | 60s | 70s | 80s | 90s |
|-----|-----|-----|-----|-----|-----|-----|-----|-----|
|     |     |     |     |     |     |     |     |     |

The daughter of a boat manufacturer and a concert pianist, American actress Irene Dunne began voice training lessons before the age of thirteen. Dunne's diligence won her a scholarship to the Chicago Musical College, but her dreams of a career with New York City's Metropolitan opera faded when she failed the audition. Still, there was an outlet for her talents in musical comedy, which she began in a touring company of the popular stage production *Irene*. After her Broadway debut in 1923, Dunne was able to secure leading roles in several musicals and marry Francis J. Griffin, a New York dentist, with whom she remained married until his death in 1965—despite of, or perhaps *because* of, his disinterest in the theatrical world. In 1929, Dunne was cast as Magnolia in the Chicago company of *Show Boat*; her superlative performance led to a movie contract with RKO, where after a few inconsequential programmers like *Leathernecking* (1930), she became one of the top dramatic stars at that studio. Her strong early film appearances are all the more remarkable in that many of the characters held to ethical and moral beliefs that went against the grain of Dunne's strongly held Catholic religious values. In *Ann Vickers* (1933), for example, her character, a lady doctor, undergoes an illegal abortion. Another RKO performance might be of interest to contemporary filmgoers; in *The Age of Innocence* (1934), Dunne played the same role reprised by Michelle Pfeiffer in the 1994 remake of that film. Dunne was finally permitted to show off her singing talents in *Sweet Adeline* (1935), and in 1936 Universal Pictures cast her in her stage role as Magnolia in the studio's definitive film version of *Show Boat* (1936). After this film, Dunne entered the second phase of her movie career as a comedienne, contributing hilarious performances to such screwball farces as *Theodora Goes Wild* (1936), *The Awful Truth* (1937), and *My Favorite Wife* (1940). It was back to dramatic roles in the early 1940s, and as age crept up on Dunne, she made a seamless transition to starring character roles in such films as *Anna and the King of Siam* (1946) and *Life with Father* (1947). Approaching fifty, Dunne retained the classically beautiful features and svelte figure; in fact, Hollywood makeup artists were compelled to draw lines on her face and fit her with heavy body suits for her "aged" roles in *I Remember Mama* (1948)—for which she won her only Academy Award—and *The Mudlark* (1950). Upon completion of *It Grows on Trees* (1952), Dunne retired from films, though she remained active on television, notably in such Catholic-oriented programs as *The Christophers*. In recognition of her charitable work and interest in conservative political causes, Dunne was appointed by President Eisenhower as one of five alternative delegates to the United Nations in 1957. Contentedly retired in the 1980s—and as beloved by her former coworkers as her fans—Dunne could truthfully boast that she was one of the few motion picture actors who had none of the neuroses or hangups that plague performers; even when recalling her less prestigious films or rare unpleasant on-set experiences for interviewers, Dunne insisted that she had enjoyed every minute of her career. **Selected Works:** *Love Affair* (1939)

# Mildred Dunnock

**Born:** January 25, 1900; Baltimore, MD
**Died:** July 25, 1991; Oak Bluffs, MA

**Years Active in the Industry:** by decade

| 10$^s$ | 20$^s$ | 30$^s$ | 40$^s$ | 50$^s$ | 60$^s$ | 70$^s$ | 80$^s$ | 90$^s$ |
|---|---|---|---|---|---|---|---|---|
| | | | ■ | ■ | ■ | | | |

Educated at Goucher College and at Johns Hopkins and Columbia University, American actress Mildred Dunnock was introduced to films in her stage role as Miss Ronsberry in *The Corn Is Green* (1945). Her next major assignment was as Willy Loman's long-suffering wife Linda in Arthur Miller's 1948 Pulitzer Prize-winning play *Death of a Salesman*, a part that she also essayed in the 1952 film version. Dunnock preferred stage work and college lecture tours to the movies, but returned before the cameras occasionally in such films as 1952's *Viva Zapata* (directed by the director of *Salesman*, Elia Kazan), Hitchcock's *The Trouble with Harry* (1955), and *Sweet Bird of Youth* (1962). One of Dunnock's most spectacular film appearances was her unbilled role in the gangster melodrama *Kiss of Death* (1948); she was the wheelchair-bound old lady pushed down a flight of stairs by giggling psychopath Richard Widmark! **Selected Works:** *Baby Doll* (1956), *Nun's Story* (1959), *Peyton Place* (1957), *Viva Zapata!* (1952)

# Kirsten Dunst

**Born:** Los Angeles, CA

**Years Active in the Industry:** by decade

| 10$^s$ | 20$^s$ | 30$^s$ | 40$^s$ | 50$^s$ | 60$^s$ | 70$^s$ | 80$^s$ | 90$^s$ |
|---|---|---|---|---|---|---|---|---|
| | | | | | | | | ■ |

11-year-old Kirsten Dunst was shopping with her mother in Beverly Hills when she was approached by two very efficient-looking gentlemen. They asked the golden-haired Kirsten if she was an actress; when she answered that she had previously appeared in several films, notably *Greedy* and *Oedipus Wrecks*, the men replied that they wanted the girl to audition for the difficult role of the child vampire in the upcoming *Interview With the Vampire* (1994). Director Neil Jordan selected Kirsten over 5000 applicants. Some viewers were disturbed by the sensual overtones of Dunst's performance in *Interview With the Vampire*; for her part, the girl hated kissing Brad Pitt, but enjoyed the scenes where she bared her prosthetic fangs and chowed down on human and animal blood. **Selected Works:** *Little Women* (1994)

# Jimmy Durante (James Francis Durante)

**Born:** February 10, 1893; New York, NY
**Died:** January 29, 1980; San Diego, CA

**Years Active in the Industry:** by decade

| 10$^s$ | 20$^s$ | 30$^s$ | 40$^s$ | 50$^s$ | 60$^s$ | 70$^s$ | 80$^s$ | 90$^s$ |
|---|---|---|---|---|---|---|---|---|
| | | | | | | | | |

Known to friends, family and fans as "The Schnozzola" because of his Cyrano-sized nose, American entertainer Jimmy Durante was the youngest child of an immigrant Italian barber. Fed up with his schooling by the second grade, Durante dedicated himself to becoming a piano player, performing in the usual dives, beer halls and public events. He organized a ragtime band, playing for such spots as the Coney Island College Inn and Harlem's Alamo Club. He secured two long-lasting relationships in 1921 when he married Maud Jeanne Olson and formed a professional partnership with dancer Eddie Jackson; two years later Durante and Jackson combined with another dancer, Lou Jackson, to form one of the best-known roughhouse teams of the 1920s. Clayton, Jackson and Durante opened their own speakeasy, the Club Durant (they couldn't afford the "E" on the sign), which quickly became the "in" spot for show business celebrities and the bane of Prohibition agents. Durante was clearly the star of the proceedings, adopting his lifelong stage character of an aggressive, pugnacious singer, yelling "Stop the music" at the slightest provocation and behaving as though he had to finish his song before the authorities hauled him away for having the nerve to perform. Durante's trio went uptown in the Ziegfeld musical *Show Girl* in 1929, the same year that Durante made his screen debut in *Roadhouse Nights*. Though popular in personal appearances, Durante's overbearing personality was too much of

a good thing in movies, especially when MGM had the misguided notion to team the megawatt Durante with stone-faced comedian Buster Keaton. Though Durante and Keaton liked each other, their comedy styles were as compatible as a mongoose and a rattlesnake. Durante wore out his welcome in films by 1934, and was thereafter used only as a specialty or in supporting roles. On stage, however, Durante was still a proven audience favorite: he stopped the show with the moment in the 1935 Billy Rose stage musical *Jumbo*, wherein, while leading a live elephant away from his creditors, he was stopped by a cop. "What are you doing with that elephant?" demanded the cop. Durante looked askance and bellowed, "*What* elephant?" In hit after hit on Broadway, Durante was a metropolitan success, expanding his popularity nationwide with a radio program costarring young comedian Garry Moore, which began in 1943, the year of his first wife's death (she may or may not have been the "Mrs. Calabash" to whom he said goodnight at the end of each broadcast). Virtually out of films by the 1950s, Durante continued to thrive on TV and in nightclubs, finding solace in his private life with his 1960 marriage to Margie Little. By the mid-1960s, Durante was capable of fracturing a TV audience simply by mangling the words written for him on cue cards; a perennial of ABC's weekly *Hollywood Palace*, he took on a weekly series in his 76th year in a variety program co-starring the Lennon Sisters. Suffering several strokes in the 1970s, Durante decided to retire completely, though he occasionally showed up (in a wheelchair) for such celebrations as MGM's 50th anniversary. Few stars were as beloved as Durante, and even fewer were spoken of so highly and without any trace of jealousy or rancor after his death in 1980; perhaps this adulation was due in part to Durante's ending each performance by finding a telephone, dialing G-O-D, and saying "Thanks!" **Selected Works:** *Man Who Came to Dinner* (1941)

carefully crafted musicals, beginning in 1936 with *Three Smart Girls*. This and subsequent films—notably *One Hundred Men and a Girl* (1937)—craftily exploited Durbin's remarkable operatic voice, but at the same time cast her as a "regular kid" who was refreshingly free of diva-like behavior. The strategy worked, and Durbin almost single-handedly saved Universal from oblivion; she was awarded a 1938 special Oscar "for bringing to the screen the spirit and personification of youth," and when she received her first screen kiss (from Robert Stack) in *First Love* (1939), the event knocked the European crisis off the front pages. She remained popular throughout the first years of the 1940s despite a fluctuating weight problem and an offstage predilection for marrying and divorcing older men. When the box office receipts began to flag, Universal attempted to alter Durbin's screen image with such heavy dramas as *The Amazing Mrs. Holliday* (1942) and *Christmas Holiday* (1944), but these films failed to make the turnstiles click. In 1945, Durbin had her best "grown up" role in the murder mystery *Lady on a Train* (1945), which allowed her to dress a bit more glamorously than in previous appearances. By this time, however, Durbin was tired of filmmaking, and began exhibiting a conspicuous lack of interest in performing and an utter inability to hold down her weight while shooting. After *For the Love of Mary* (1948), Durbin retired, escaping to France with her third husband, *Lady on a Train* director Charles David. She so thoroughly disappeared from public view that rumors persisted she had died. Actually, as one writer has pointed out, the "Deanna Durbin" that fans had known and loved *had* died, to be replaced by a fabulously wealthy matron who had absolutely no interest in the past. Though having lived in comfortable anonymity for the past five decades, Durbin has retained her fervent fan following (particularly strong among otherwise reserved film historians!) and has recently gained a whole new following thanks to exposure of the vintage Durbin films on cable TV and through video.

# Deanna Durbin (Edna Mae Durbin)

**Born:** December 4, 1921; Winnipeg, Manitoba, Canada

**Years Active in the Industry:** by decade

| 10s | 20s | 30s | 40s | 50s | 60s | 70s | 80s | 90s |
|-----|-----|-----|-----|-----|-----|-----|-----|-----|
|     |     |     |     |     |     |     |     |     |

Canadian actress/singer Deanna Durbin learned at a very early age that she was blessed with a strong and surprisingly mature set of vocal chords. After studying with coach Andres de Segurola, Durbin set her sights on an operatic career, but was sidetracked into films with a 1936 MGM short subject, *Every Sunday*. This one-reeler was designed as an audition for both Durbin and her equally youthful costar Judy Garland; MGM decided to go with Durbin and drop Garland, but by a front-office fluke the opposite happened and it was Durbin who found herself on the outside looking in. But MGM's loss was Universal's gain. That studio, threatened with receivership due to severe losses, decided to gamble on her potential. Under the guiding influence of Universal executive Joseph Pasternak, Durbin was cast in a series of expensive,

# Charles Durning

**Born:** February 28, 1923; Highland Falls, NY

**Years Active in the Industry:** by decade

| 10s | 20s | 30s | 40s | 50s | 60s | 70s | 80s | 90s |
|-----|-----|-----|-----|-----|-----|-----|-----|-----|
|     |     |     |     |     |     |     |     |     |

Irish-American actor Charles Durning, one of the busiest and most recognizable character actors in American films, debuted in a touring stage production of *The Andersonville Trial* in 1960; he went on to more stage work and appeared in the TV soap opera *Another World* in 1964. His film debut was in *Harvey Middleman, Fireman* (1965), but it wasn't until he appeared in *Sisters* (1973) and *The Sting* (1973) that he began to become well-known; in the latter film he played an Irish-American cop, a role which (thanks to his hefty frame and working-man looks) became a standard one for him in the years to come. Durning went on to play supporting roles in many films, including such hits as *Dog Day Afternoon* (1975),

*Tootsie* (1982), and *Dick Tracy* (1990). He has also worked in TV movies and miniseries, and starred on the Burt Reynolds sitcom *Evening Shade*. **Selected Works:** *Dick Tracy* (1990), *North Dallas Forty* (1979), *True Confessions* (1981), *Water Engine* (1992), *The Hudsucker Proxy* (1994)

# Robert Duvall

**Born:** September 30, 1929; San Diego, CA

**Years Active in the Industry:** by decade

| 10ˢ | 20ˢ | 30ˢ | 40ˢ | 50ˢ | 60ˢ | 70ˢ | 80ˢ | 90ˢ |
|-----|-----|-----|-----|-----|-----|-----|-----|-----|

Distinguished American leading and supporting actor Robert Duvall is one of Hollywood's most popular and versatile actors, noted for his rare talent for totally immersing himself in his

roles. The son of an admiral, Duvall fought in Korea for two years after graduating from Principia College. Upon his Army discharge, he moved to New York to study acting with the Neighborhood Playhouse, where he won much acclaim for his portrayal of a longshoreman in *A View from the Bridge*. Later he acted in stock and off Broadway. He debuted onscreen as Gregory Peck's simple-minded neighbor Boo Radley in *To Kill a Mockingbird* (1963). During his early film career, Duvall, with his intense expressions and chiseled features, was frequently cast as troubled, lonely characters in films such as *The Chase* (1966). Whatever the role, be it a lead or character part, when Duvall plays a role, he brings to it an almost palpable intensity tempered by an ability to make his characters seem real (this is in contrast to certain contemporary actors who never let the viewer forget that they are watching a *star* playing a role). Though well-respected and popular, Duvall largely eschews the traditionally glitzy life of a Hollywood star. During his career, he has worked with some of contemporary Hollywood's greatest directors, including a

long association with Francis Ford Coppola for whom he worked in two *Godfather* movies (1972 and 1974) and *Apocalypse Now* (1979), and has received several Oscar nominations before finally winning the Best Actor Oscar for his work in *Tender Mercies* (1983). He also directed and co-produced *Angelo, My Love* (1984), and made an acclaimed appearance in *Rambling Rose* (1991). Throughout his film career, Duvall continued to also work on stage; in addition, he occasionally appears in TV miniseries such as *Lonesome Dove* (1989) and *Stalin* (1992). **Selected Works:** *The Great Santini* (1980), *Network* (1976), *True Confessions* (1981), *The Paper* (1994), *Something to Talk About* (1995)

# Shelley Duvall

**Born:** July 7, 1949; Houston, TX

**Years Active in the Industry:** by decade

| 10ˢ | 20ˢ | 30ˢ | 40ˢ | 50ˢ | 60ˢ | 70ˢ | 80ˢ | 90ˢ |
|-----|-----|-----|-----|-----|-----|-----|-----|-----|

Distinctive-looking American actress and television producer Shelley Duvall was discovered by director Robert Altman at a party in Houston. A lawyer's daughter, the 20 year-old Duvall had zero acting experience when Altman cast her in *Brewster McCloud* (1970). She has spent most of her feature film acting career in Altman films, including *Nashville* (1975), *Three Women* (1977), and *Popeye* (1980). For *Three Women* she received the Best Actress award at the Cannes Film Festival. She became known for her offbeat, eccentric performances in such films as Stanley Kubrick's *The Shining* (1979). Since 1981 she has appeared in few films. In the late '80s and early '90s Duvall hosted a star-studded cable TV show devoted to retelling classic fairy tales and myths. **Selected Works:** *Annie Hall* (1977), *McCabe and Mrs. Miller* (1971), *Thieves Like Us* (1974)

# Ann Dvorak (Ann McKim)

**Born:** August 2, 1912; New York, NY
**Died:** December 10, 1979; Honolulu, HI

**Years Active in the Industry:** by decade

| 10ˢ | 20ˢ | 30ˢ | 40ˢ | 50ˢ | 60ˢ | 70ˢ | 80ˢ | 90ˢ |
|-----|-----|-----|-----|-----|-----|-----|-----|-----|

American actress Ann Dvorak was the daughter of silent film director Sam McKim and stage actress Anne Lehr ("Dvorak" was her mother's maiden name). Educated at Page School for Girls in Los Angeles, Dvorak secured work as a chorus dancer in early talking films: she is quite visible amongst the female hoofers in *Hollywood Revue of 1929* (1929). Reportedly it was her friend Joan Crawford, a headliner in *Hollywood Revue*, who introduced Dvorak to multimillionaire Howard Hughes, then busy putting together his film *Scarface* (1931). Dvorak was put under contract and cast in *Scarface* as gangster Paul Muni's sister, and despite the strictures of film censorship at the time, the actress' piercing eyes and subtle body language made certain that the "incest" subtext in the script came through loud and clear. Hughes sold Dvorak's contract to Warner Bros., who intended to pay her the relative pittance she'd gotten for *Scarface* until she decided to retreat to Europe. Warners caved in with a better salary, but it might have been at the expense of Dvorak's starring career. Though she played roles in such films as *Three on a Match* (1932) and *G-Men* (1935) with relish, the characters were the sort of "life's losers" who usually managed to expire just before the fadeout, leaving the hero to embrace the prettier, less complex ingenue. Dvorak cornered the market in portraying fore-doomed gangster's molls with prolonged death scenes, but they were almost always secondary roles. One of her rare forays into comedy occurred in producer Hal Roach's *Merrily We Live* (1938), an amusing *My Man Godfrey* ripoff. In 1940, Dvorak followed her first husband to England, starring there in such wartime films as *Squadron Leader X* (1941) and *This Was Paris* (1942). Upon her return to Hollywood in 1945, Dvorak found very little work beyond westerns and melodramas; she did have a bravura role as a cabaret singer held prisoner by the Japanese in *I Was an American Spy* (1951), but it was produced at second-string Republic Pictures and didn't get top bookings. After *Secret of Convict Lake* (1951), Dvorak quit film work; she had never found it to be as satisfactory as her stage career, which included a year's run in the 1948 Broadway play *The Respectful Prostitute*. During her retirement she divided her time between her homes in Malibu and Hawaii with her third husband, and her passion for collecting rare books.

## Allan Dwan (Joseph Aloysius Dwan)

**Born:** April 3, 1885; Toronto, Ontario, Canada
**Died:** December 21, 1981; Woodland Hills, CA

**Years Active in the Industry:** by decade

| 10s | 20s | 30s | 40s | 50s | 60s | 70s | 80s | 90s |
|-----|-----|-----|-----|-----|-----|-----|-----|-----|
|     |     |     |     |     |     |     |     |     |

Allan Dwan worked for a lighting company, and in 1909 was in Chicago dealing with one of their customers, the Essanay studios. He soon got a job there as a writer, and by 1911 was direct-ing films in California. After making hundreds of one-reel westerns, comedies, and documentaries, he graduated to features, and in the late teens guided such stellar talents as Mary Pickford, the Gish sisters, and Douglas Fairbanks. In the '20s, Dwan's memorable films included the Fairbanks swashbucklers *Robin Hood* (1922) and *The Iron Mask* (1929); he also produced and directed several Gloria Swanson films, including *Zaza* (1923), *Manhandled* (1924), and *Her Love Story* (1924). In the 1930s Dwan was relegated mostly to low-budget fare, but managed to score with the Shirley Temple films *Heidi* (1937) and *Rebecca of Sunnybrook Farm* (1938), and the period drama *Suez* (1938). His '40s work includes a quartet of clever farces for producer Edward Small (*Up in Mabel's Room* [1944], *Abroad with Two Yanks* [1944], *Brewster's Millions* [1945], and *Getting Gertie's Garter* [1945]) and the John Wayne war film *Sands of Iwo Jima* (1949). In the '50s, Dwan capped his career with a series of westerns, including *Silver Lode* (1954) and *Tennessee's Partner* (1955).

## George Dzundza

**Born:** July 19, 1945; Rosenheim, Germany

**Years Active in the Industry:** by decade

| 10s | 20s | 30s | 40s | 50s | 60s | 70s | 80s | 90s |
|-----|-----|-----|-----|-----|-----|-----|-----|-----|
|     |     |     |     |     |     |     |     |     |

Heavyset German-born actor George Dzundza is best known to the general public for his starring role as Detective Sgt. Max Greevey on the first few seasons of the TV series *Law and Order*. It was a high point of a long career that included several seasons on the New York stage and a score of movie roles. At first principally cast as a buckshot-eyed, steel-hearted corporate villain, Dzundza's screen image softened to the point that his characters were not so much wicked as ill-tempered. Compared to the perfidy of Sharon Stone in *Basic Instinct* (1993), Dzundza, in the role of Michael Douglas' partner (remember his facial expressions in the interrogation scene?) was practically benign. In late 1992, the familiar clipped tones of Dzundza could be heard in the role of "The Ventriloquist" on the TV cartoon series *Batman*. **Selected Works:** *Deer Hunter* (1978), *White Hunter, Black Heart* (1990)

# E

## Clint Eastwood (Clinton Eastwood, Jr.)

**Born:** May 31, 1930; San Francisco, CA

**Years Active in the Industry:** by decade

| 10ˢ | 20ˢ | 30ˢ | 40ˢ | 50ˢ | 60ˢ | 70ˢ | 80ˢ | 90ˢ |
|-----|-----|-----|-----|-----|-----|-----|-----|-----|

Clint Eastwood is one of the few actors whose name on a movie marquee can still guarantee a hit. Less well known, until he won the Academy Award as Best Director for *Unforgiven*, is the fact that Eastwood is also a producer/director, with a notable record of successes. Born in San Francisco, he worked as a logger and gas pumper, among other jobs, before coming to Hollywood in the mid-1950's, where he played small roles in several Universal features (he's the pilot of the plane that napalms the giant spider at the end of *Tarantula* [1955]) before achieving some limited star status on the television series *Rawhide*. It was as the star of the three Italian-made Sergio Leone westerns *A Fistful of Dollars* (1964), *For a Few Dollars More* (1965), and *The Good, The Bad and the Ugly* (1966) that Eastwood became an international star. Upon his return to the U.S., he set up his own production company, Malpaso, which had a hit right out of the box with the revenge western *Hang 'em High* (1967). He extended his relatively limited acting range in a succession of roles—most notably in the hit *Dirty Harry* (1971)—during the late 1960's and early 1970's, and directed several of his most popular movies, including 1971's *Play Misty for Me* (a forerunner to *Fatal Attraction*), *High Plains Drifter* (1973), and *The Outlaw Josey Wales* (1976). Although Eastwood became known for his violent roles, he also showed a gentler side to his persona that came through in pictures such as *Bronco Billy* (1980), a romantic comedy that he directed and starred in. As a filmmaker, Eastwood learned from the best of the men who had previously directed him, Don Siegel and Sergio Leone, knowing just when to add some stylistic or visual flourish to a scene that otherwise should play straightforward, and just how effective a small nuance can be on the big screen. Their approaches perfectly suited Eastwood's restrained acting style, and he integrated their approach to his filmmaking technique with startling results, culminating in 1993 with his Best Director Oscar for *Unforgiven*. In 1995, Eastwood scored a hit with the film adaptation of the best-selling book *The Bridges of Madison County*, a chronicle of the romance between two older adults in which he stars opposite Meryl Streep; he served as star, director, and producer. **Selected Works:** *In the Line of Fire* (1993), *Outlaw Josey Wales* (1976), *White Hunter* (1990), *Black Heart* (1990), *Perfect World* (1993)

## Buddy Ebsen (Christian Rudolph Ebsen)

**Born:** April 2, 1908; Belleville, IL

**Years Active in the Industry:** by decade

| 10ˢ | 20ˢ | 30ˢ | 40ˢ | 50ˢ | 60ˢ | 70ˢ | 80ˢ | 90ˢ |
|-----|-----|-----|-----|-----|-----|-----|-----|-----|

Unlike other actors who gained fame for the roles they played, American actor/dancer Buddy Ebsen was best known in the first half of his career for two parts he *didn't* get. A dancer from childhood, Ebsen headlined in vaudeville in an act with his sister Velma. In 1935, Ebsen was signed by MGM as a specialty performer in *The Broadway Melody of 1936*, wherein he was shown to good advantage in several solos. He worked in a number of subsequent musicals, including Shirley Temple's *Captain January* (1936), teaming with Shirley for the delightful number "At the Codfish Ball." MGM assigned Ebsen to the role of the Scarecrow in 1939's *The Wizard of Oz*, but Ray Bolger, who'd been cast as the Tin Man, talked Ebsen into switching roles. The move proved to be Ebsen's undoing; he found that he was allergic to the silver makeup required for the Tin Man, fell ill, and was forced to bow out of the film, to be replaced by Jack Haley (however, Ebsen's voice can still be heard in the reprises of "We're Off to See the Wizard"). Any other performer might have considered this setback to be disastrous, but in fact Ebsen wasn't all that happy in Hollywood. When MGM head Louis B. Mayer offered the actor a long-term contract, Ebsen turned him down cold—enraging Mayer, who warned Buddy that he'd never work in Hollywood again. Ebsen returned to the stage, taking time out to provide the dancing model for a electronically operated wooden marionette which later was used at Disneyland. In 1950 Ebsen returned to films as comical sidekick to Rex Allen, gradually working his way into good character parts in A pictures like *Night People* (1955). Walt Disney, who'd remembered Ebsen from that dancing marionette, offered the actor the lead in his 1954 three-part TV production of *Davy Crockett*, but at the last moment engaged Fess Parker as Davy and recast Buddy as Crockett's pal George Russel. If Ebsen was upset by this turn of events, he didn't show it, at least not in public. He continued to pop up in films like 1961's *Breakfast at Tiffany's* (as Audrey Hepburn's abandoned hometown husband), and in TV westerns, where he often cast his image to the winds by playing cold-blooded murderers. Comfortably wealthy in 1962 thanks to his film work and wise business investments, Ebsen added to his riches by signing on to play Jed Clampett in the TV sitcom *The Beverly Hillbillies*, which ran for nine years to excellent ratings. A millionaire several times over, Ebsen planned to ease off after *Hillbillies*, but in 1972 he was back in the title role of *Barnaby Jones*. Few observers gave this easygoing detective series much of a chance, but they weren't counting on Ebsen's built-in popularity. *Barnaby Jones* lasted until 1980, earning Ebsen *another* fortune. The actor now confined himself to special events appearances and occasional guest star roles, though he did play the recurring part of Lee Horsley's uncle in the final season of the TV mystery show *Matt Houston* (1983-85). By this time Ebsen was so much of an icon that even the negative publicity attending the breakup of his long marriage didn't dent his fan following. Buddy Ebsen's most recent appearance was in the 1993 theatrical film version of *The Beverly Hillbillies*—not as Jed Clampett but in a cameo as Barnaby Jones!

# Nelson Eddy

**Born:** June 29, 1901; Providence, RI
**Died:** 1967

**Years Active in the Industry:** by decade

| 10s | 20s | 30s | 40s | 50s | 60s | 70s | 80s | 90s |
|-----|-----|-----|-----|-----|-----|-----|-----|-----|

Nelson Eddy was an actor and singer noted for his rich baritone voice and wooden acting. He sang soprano in church choirs as a boy. He moved to Philadelphia as a teenager, and after a number of odd jobs he won a competition in 1922 to join the Philadelphia Civic Opera; he went on to perform frequently with the group, and played Tonio in *Pagliacci* at the New York Metropolitan Opera in 1924. In the early '30s Eddy began appearing on radio and had a successful concert tour; this led to a movie contract with MGM, and he debuted onscreen in 1933. In 1935 he and Jeanette MacDonald were teamed together, going on to appear in a series of sentimental operettas beginning with *Naughty Marietta* (1935); billed as "America's Sweethearts" or the "Singing Sweethearts," the team became extraordinarily popular, and for a time they were

the screen's most popular duo, appearing in one box office smash after another. After their last film, *I Married An Angel* (1942), Eddy's career quickly went into decline, and he made no films after 1947. He continued to appear in concerts and nightclubs and made some recordings; during an Australian tour in 1967, he collapsed onstage and died of a stroke.

# Barbara Eden

**Born:** August 22, 1934; Tuscon AZ

**Years Active in the Industry:** by decade

| 10s | 20s | 30s | 40s | 50s | 60s | 70s | 80s | 90s |
|-----|-----|-----|-----|-----|-----|-----|-----|-----|

An Arizona native, actress Barbara Eden was three years old when her family moved to San Francisco, where as a teenager she plunged into acting and singing classes at San Francisco State College's Conservatory of Music. After a traumatic debut as a band singer (she opened her mouth and nothing came out), Eden took up residence at Hollywood's Studio Club, an inexpensive rooming house for aspiring actresses. Other Studio Club residents would note in later years that Eden would look at the club's bulletin board and apply for every show business job available, even those that she was advised would "ruin" her career. Persistence paid off, and in 1956 Eden made her film debut in *Back from Eternity*. She worked steadily in television, finally attaining leading-lady status on the 1958 sitcom *How to Marry a Millionaire*, in which she played a myopic "Marilyn Monroe" type golddigger. Good film and TV roles followed for the lovely blonde actress, and full stardom arrived with the NBC comedy series *I Dream of Jeannie*. Eden played the curvaceous bottle imp (who thanks to network censors was evidently born without a navel) from 1965-70, reviving the character in a brace of TV movies, the last one produced in 1991 (she still looked terrific in her harem togs). Eden's post-Jeannie career has included several films, TV guest star appearances, theatrical and nightclub engagements, and still another sitcom, 1981's *Harper Valley P.T.A.*

# Anthony Edwards

**Born:** July 19, 1962; Santa Barbara, CA

**Years Active in the Industry:** by decade

| 10s | 20s | 30s | 40s | 50s | 60s | 70s | 80s | 90s |
|-----|-----|-----|-----|-----|-----|-----|-----|-----|

Currently, the lanky blond and balding actor Anthony Edwards' career is flying high with his role as the easy-going Dr. Green on the hit NBC television series *ER*. But while his rise to fame seems sudden, the 33-year old actor has been in the business since he was 12 years old. At that young age, Edwards began acting on stage. For the next five years he would act in over 30 plays before going to study at the prestigious Royal Academy of

Arts in London in 1980 for formal training. He also studied drama at USC, Los Angeles. While there he made his feature film debut in *Fast Times At Ridgemont High* (1982). Unlike many actors who are typecast into certain roles in particular genres, such as comedy, or action roles, Edwards has remained firmly between genres, having played in everything from teen exploitation flicks (*Revenge of the Nerds* [1984]), and serious drama (*Mr. North* [1988]), to actioners (*Top Gun* [1986]) and thrillers (*Downtown* [1990]). In 1992, Edwards had a recurring, but memorable role as the environmentally-hypersensitive Bubbleman on the popular CBS TV show *Northern Exposure*. **Selected Works:** *Delta Heat* (1992), *El Diablo* (1990), *Client* (1994)

# Blake Edwards (William Blake McEdwards)

**Born:** July 26, 1922; Tulsa, OK

**Years Active in the Industry:** by decade

| 10s | 20s | 30s | 40s | 50s | 60s | 70s | 80s | 90s |
|-----|-----|-----|-----|-----|-----|-----|-----|-----|

American filmmaker Blake Edwards was the grandson of J. Gordon Edwards, director of such silent film epics as *The Queen of Sheba* (1922). Edwards started his own film career as an actor

in 1943; he played bits in A pictures and leads in B's, paying his dues in such trivialities as *Gangs of the Waterfront* (1945) and *Strangler of the Swamp* (1946). He turned to writing radio scripts, distinguishing himself on the above-average Dick Powell detective series *Richard Diamond*. As a screenwriter and staff producer at Columbia, Edwards was frequently teamed with director Richard Quine for such lightweight entertainment as *Sound Off* (1952), *Rainbow 'Round My Shoulder* (1953) and *Cruisin' Down the River* (1953). He also served as associate producer on the popular syndicated Rod Cameron TV vehicle *City Detective* in 1953. Given his first chance at movie directing in 1955, Edwards turned out a Richard Quine-like musical, *Bring Your Smile Around*; ironically, as Edwards' prestige grew, his style would be imitated by Quine! A felicitous contract at Universal led Edwards to his first big box office successes, including the Tony Curtis film *Mister Cory* (1957) and Cary Grant's *Operation Petticoat* (1959). In 1958, Edwards produced, directed and occasionally wrote a "hip" TV detective series, *Peter Gunn*, which was distinguished by its film noir camerawork and its driving jazz score by Henry Mancini. A second TV series, *Mr. Lucky* (1959),

contained many of the elements that made *Peter Gunn* popular, but suffered from a bad time slot and network interference (Lucky was a gambler, a profession frowned upon by the more sanctimonious CBS execs); the series did, however, introduce Edwards to actor Ross Martin, who later showed up to excellent advantage as an asthmatic criminal in the Edwards-directed *Experiment in Terror* (1962). Continuing to turn out box-office bonanzas like *Breakfast at Tiffany's* (1961) and *The Days of Wine and Roses* (1962), Edwards briefly jumped on the "comedy spectacular" bandwagon of the mid-1960s with the slapstick epic *The Great Race* (1965), which the director dedicated to his idols, "Mr. Laurel and Mr. Hardy" (Edwards' next homage to the duo was the far less successful 1986 comedy *A Fine Mess*). In 1964, Edwards introduced Inspector Clouseau to an unsuspecting world in *The Pink Panther*, leading to a string of moneyspinning Clouseau films starring Peter Sellers; actually, *The Pink Panther* was Edwards' *second* Clouseau film, since *A Shot in the Dark*, though released after *Panther*, was filmed first. Despite the carefree spirit of his comedies, Edwards was known to carry on long and bitter feuds, notably with studio executives. Things came to a head with *Darling Lili* (1969), a World War I musical starring Edwards' wife Julie Andrews. The film was a questionable piece to begin with (audiences were asked to sympathize with a German spy who cheerfully sent young British pilots to their deaths), but was made incomprehensible by Paramount's ruthless editing. *Darling Lili* all but ruined Edwards in Hollywood, though he came back with the 1979 comedy hit *10*, and then exercised his revenge on Tinseltown with his scabrous satirical film *S.O.B.* (1981). Edwards' track record in the 1980s has been uneven, with plenty of projects that looked great on paper but fell apart before the cameras (*Blind Date* [1987], *Sunset* [1988], *Switch* [1991]); the director has also faltered in his attempts to revive the "Pink Panther" comedies minus the services of the late Peter Sellers as Clouseau. Still, Edwards has always seemed able to find someone to bankroll his projects; in addition, he has left something of a legacy to Hollywood through his actress daughter Jennifer Edwards and his screenwriter son Geoffrey Edwards.

# Sergei Mikhailovich Eisenstein

**Born:** February 4, 1898; Riga, Latvia
**Died:** February 11, 1948; Moscow, Russia

**Years Active in the Industry:** by decade

| 10s | 20s | 30s | 40s | 50s | 60s | 70s | 80s | 90s |
|-----|-----|-----|-----|-----|-----|-----|-----|-----|

In the early 1920s, Sergei Mikhailovich Eisenstein was a set designer and co-director with Moscow's Proletkult Theater. Heading his own troupe in 1922, he made his first film the following year: the five-minute newsreel parody *Glumov's Diary* for his play

*The Wise Man.* After a short time in Lev Kuleshov's film workshop, Eisenstein completed his first feature, *Strike*, in 1925. Recreating an actual factory strike in Tsarist Russia, *Strike* introduced the violent editing and imagery which dominated Eisenstein's silent films. That same year saw his classic *The Battleship Potemkin* (aka *Potemkin*), dramatizing the 1905 uprising by oppressed sailors and the Odessa people. *Potemkin* had a profound impact on filmmaking, above all its celebrated "Odessa Steps" montage sequence of Cossacks slaughtering civilians. Eisenstein was then assigned *October* (aka *Ten Days That Shook The World* [1927]) for the tenth anniversary of the Russian Revolution. This recreation of the Bolshevik rise to power in 1917 used metaphoric, non-realistic images; although less successful than his earlier work, *October* is one of his most original efforts. His last silent, *Old And New* (aka *The General Line* [1929]), looked at the collectivization of agriculture. After failing to find financing for an American film in 1930, Eisenstein got the backing of writer Upton Sinclair to make a film about Mexico. He ultimately lost control of the footage, which was released in various bowdlerizations (his assistant, Grigori Alexandrov, prepared an authoritative edition of *Que Viva Mexico!* in 1979.) Upon returning to the USSR, Eisenstein began *Bezhin Meadow* in 1935, but the state production head halted the politically scathing film. Like other Soviet artists in the Stalin years, Eisenstein had to publicly admit his error before he he could make *Alexander Nevsky* (1938), a rousing account of the 13th-century Russian prince who fought off Teutonic invaders. *Nevsky* was a propaganda coup against Nazi Germany, but after Stalin signed a non-aggression pact with Hitler in 1939, it was withdrawn from circulation. In 1943 Eisenstein began *Ivan the Terrible*, an epic account of the notorious 16th-century Tsar. Two years later Part I premiered to great praise at home; critics abroad were divided, some considering the film a masterpiece, others finding it even more operatic and artificial than *Nevsky* had been, and a further abandonment of Eisenstein's original artistic principles of montage. He completed Part II in 1946, but Stalin hated it and the film wasn't released until 1958. Nevertheless, he got Stalin's permission to film Part III. Ill health forced Eisenstein to abandon the project, and his death of a heart attack ended the career of one of cinema's most influential artists.

# Jack Elam

**Born:** November 13, 1916; Miami, FL

**Years Active in the Industry:** by decade

| 10ˢ | 20ˢ | 30ˢ | 40ˢ | 50ˢ | 60ˢ | 70ˢ | 80ˢ | 90ˢ |
|---|---|---|---|---|---|---|---|---|

A graduate of Santa Monica Junior College, Jack Elam spent the immediate post-World War II years as an accountant, numbering several important Hollywood stars among his clients. Already blind in one eye from a childhood fight, Elam was in danger of losing the sight of his other eye as a result of his demanding profession. Several of his show business friends suggested that Elam give acting a try; after all, with that wavering eye and those

pitbull facial features, Elam would be a natural as a villain. A natural he was, and throughout the 1950s Elam cemented his reputation as one of the meanest-looking and most reliable "heavies" in the movies. Few of his screen roles gave him the opportunity to display his natural wit and sense of comic timing, but inklings of these skills were evident in his first regular TV series assignments: *The Dakotas* and *Temple Houston*, both 1963. In 1967, Elam was given his first all-out comedy role in *Support Your Local Sheriff*, after which he found his villainous assignments dwindling and his comic jobs increasing. Elam starred as the patriarch of an itinerant Southwestern family in the 1974 TV series *The Texas Wheelers* (his sons were played by Gary Busey and Mark Hamill), and in 1979 played a benign Frankenstein-monster type in the weekly horror spoof *Struck By Lightning*. Later TV series in the Elam manifest included *Detective in the House* (1985) and *Easy Street* (1987). Though well established as a comic actor, Elam would never completely abandon the western genre that had sustained him in the 1950s and 1960s; in 1993, a proud Elam was inducted into the Cowboy Hall of Fame.

# Danny Elfman

**Born:** 1954; Los Angeles, CA

**Years Active in the Industry:** by decade

| 10ˢ | 20ˢ | 30ˢ | 40ˢ | 50ˢ | 60ˢ | 70ˢ | 80ˢ | 90ˢ |
|---|---|---|---|---|---|---|---|---|

American composer Danny Elfman can be described as the Prokofiev of fantasy movies. Launching his career as a member of the group Oingo Boingo, Elfman wrote his first complete film score for *Pee-Wee's Big Adventure* (1985), directed by his friend and fellow movie "virgin" Tim Burton. The Elfman/Burton team held firm through *Beetlejuice* (1988), *Batman* (1989), *Edward Scissorhands* (1990), *Batman Returns* (1992) and *The Nightmare Before Christmas* (1993), in which Elfman also provided the singing voice for leading character, Jack Skellington. Elfman is at his best with "motion" music, ranging from the bicycle leitmotif in *Pee-wee's Big Adventure* to the skateboard-driven opening theme for TV's *The Simpsons.* **Selected Works:** *Army of Darkness* (1992), *Darkman* (1990), *Dick Tracy* (1990), *Sommersby* (1993)

# Hector Elizondo

**Born:** December 22, 1936; New York, NY

**Years Active in the Industry:** by decade

| 10ˢ | 20ˢ | 30ˢ | 40ˢ | 50ˢ | 60ˢ | 70ˢ | 80ˢ | 90ˢ |
|---|---|---|---|---|---|---|---|---|

An actor of seemingly boundless range, New York-born Hector Elizondo began his career as a dancer. His initial training was at the Ballet Arts school of Carnegie Hall, from which he

moved on to the Actors Studio. After several years' stage work, Elizondo made an inauspicious movie debut as "The Inspector" in the low-budget sex film *The Vixens* (1969). He was shown to better advantage in his next film, Hal Ashby's *The Landlord* (1970), which he followed up with strong character parts in such Manhattan-based productions as *The Taking of Pelham One Two Three* (1974) and *Thieves* (1977). With *Young Doctors in Love* (1982), Elizondo began his long association with director Garry Marshall, who has since cast the actor in all of his films, in roles both sizable (Matt Dillon's dad in *The Flamingo Kid* [1984], the cafe owner in *Frankie and Johnny* [1991]), and microscopic (*Overboard* [1987]). Elizondo's screen roles have run the gamut from scrungy garbage scow captains to elegant concierges. In addition, he has been a regular on several mediocre television series: *Popi, Freebie and the Bean, Casablanca* (in the old Claude Rains role of Inspector Renault), *a.k.a. Pablo, Foley Square*, and *Down and Out in Beverly Hills*, In 1994, Elizondo took on a co-starring role as a demanding chief of surgery on the popular TV medical drama *Chicago Hope*. **Selected Works:** *Final Approach* (1991), *Necessary Roughness* (1991), *Pretty Woman* (1990), *There Goes the Neighborhood* (1992), *Being Human* (1994)

# Denholm Elliott

**Born:** May 31, 1922; London, England
**Died:** October 6, 1992; Ibiza, Spain

**Years Active in the Industry:** by decade

| 10s | 20s | 30s | 40s | 50s | 60s | 70s | 80s | 90s |
|-----|-----|-----|-----|-----|-----|-----|-----|-----|

Educated at Malvern College, British actor Denholm Elliot went on stage just after World War II, and made his first film, *Dear Mr. Prohack*, in 1949. A sort of British Ralph Bellamy, Elliot specialized in playing pleasant but ineffectual types during the 1950s, switching to dignified and slightly stuffy characters as he grew grayer. In 1964, he made a major impression on international audiences by playing the tattered gentleman who teaches Alan Bates the tricks of social and financial climbing in *Nothing but the Best*—only to be strangled by Bates with his old school tie. With tight lips and taciturn glances, Elliot was the official who closed down Elliot Gould's burlesque house in *The Night They Raided Minsky's* (1968). A gentler but no less authoritative role came in 1981 as Harrison Ford's immediate superior Brody in *Raiders of*

the *Lost Ark* (reprising the part in 1989's *Indiana Jones and the Last Crusade*), while in 1984 Elliot was unforgettably waspish as the dying social lion who dictates his own death notice in *The Razor's Edge* (the role played by Clifton Webb in the 1946 version). In between these engagements, Elliot was Dan Aykroyd's—and then Eddie Murphy's—sneering butler in *Trading Places* (1983). Shortly after completing 1992's *Noises Off*, Elliot died of AIDS. **Selected Works:** *Boys from Brazil* (1978), *Codename: Kyril* (1991), *One Against the Wind* (1991), *Room with a View* (1986), *Love She Sought* (1990)

# Sam Elliott

**Born:** August 9, 1944; Sacramento, CA

**Years Active in the Industry:** by decade

| 10s | 20s | 30s | 40s | 50s | 60s | 70s | 80s | 90s |
|-----|-----|-----|-----|-----|-----|-----|-----|-----|

Through a cruel twist of fate, American actor Sam Elliott came to films at just the point that the sort of fare in which he should have thrived was dying at the box office. A born cowboy star if ever there was one, the stage-trained Elliot made his debut in a tiny role in the 1969 western *Butch Cassidy and the Sundance Kid*. Within a few years, the western market had disappeared, and Elliot had to settle for standard good-guy roles in such contemporary films as *Lifeguard* (1976). Never tied down to any one type, Elliot's range has embraced sexy "other men" (*Sibling Rivalry* [1989]) and vicious rapist/murderers (the TV movie *A Death in California* [1986]). Still, one yearned to see Elliot playing frontiersmen: fortunately, the western genre had not completely disappeared on television, and Elliot was well served with such hard-riding projects as *The Sacketts* (1977), *I Will Fight No More Forever* (1981), *The Shadow Riders* (1982), *Houston: The Legend of Texas* (1986) and *Conagher* (1991), in which he appeared with his wife, actress Katherine Ross. When westerns began showing up on the big screen again in the 1990s, Elliot was there, prominently cast as Virgil Earp in *Tombstone* (1993) and the made-for-cable sagebrusher *The Desperate Trail* (1995). **Selected Works:** *Gettysburg* (1992), *Mask* (1985)

# Cary Elwes

**Born:** October 26, 1962; London, England

**Years Active in the Industry:** by decade

| 10s | 20s | 30s | 40s | 50s | 60s | 70s | 80s | 90s |
|-----|-----|-----|-----|-----|-----|-----|-----|-----|
|     |     |     |     |     |     |     |     |     |

The son of well-known painter Dominic Elwes, British actor Cary Elwes has chalked up a number of excellent stage and screen appearances in his relatively short career. Elwes started out as aristocratic "old school" brats in such films as *Another Country* (1984) and *Oxford Blues* (1984), then was swept along with Sting, Jennifer Beals and Quentin Crisp in the publicity maelstrom attending the silly horror spoof *The Bride* (1985). The actor was shown to better advantage as the feckless hero of *The Princess Bride* (1986), director Rob Reiner's deliciously anachronistic fairy tale. Elwes' British cadence melted nicely into a Southern drawl for the Civil War epic *Glory* (1989), and the actor did his best as a murderous gang punk in the negligible *Leather Jackets* (1990). Elwes was permitted a full-out comedy lead in Mel Brooks' *Robin Hood: Men in Tights* (1993), in which he had one of the film's best moments, delivering a honeyed insult in the direction of Kevin Costner: "Unlike other Robin Hoods, *I* have an English accent." In addition to his comedic turns, Elwes has appeared in dramas such as *Bram Stoker's Dracula* (1992), *The Crush* (1993), and *The Chase* (1994). **Selected Works:** *Bram Stoker's Dracula* (1992), *Days of Thunder* (1990), *Hot Shots* (1991)

# Robert Englund

**Born:** June 6, 1949; Glendale, CA

**Years Active in the Industry:** by decade

| 10s | 20s | 30s | 40s | 50s | 60s | 70s | 80s | 90s |
|-----|-----|-----|-----|-----|-----|-----|-----|-----|
|     |     |     |     |     |     |     |     |     |

American actor is probably best known as his scary screen alter-ego Freddy Krueger. But Englund has ben around much longer than has the *Nightmare on Elmstreet* series. At age 12 he

joined a children's theater program. After attending two colleges he studied acting at the MIchigan Academy of Dramatic Arts. He then went on to a busy theater career, starting with an appearance in a Cleveland production of *Godspell*. Englund eventually found success as a supporting player in more than 30 feature and made-for-TV films. While playing a sympathetic alien in the TV miniseries *V*, he was spotted by director Wes Craven, who enlisted him to play the diabolical dream-

haunting monster Freddy in *A Nightmare on Elm Street* (1984) and its numerous sequels (including a turn as himself in *Wes Craven's New Nightmare* [1994]), plus the TV show *Freddy's Nightmares*; he has since reaped the benefits of a huge "Freddy" marketing campaign, complete with t-shirts, books, and models. He directed the film *976-Evil* (1988) and appeared in the title role of *The Phantom of the Opera* (1990). However, thanks to his identification in the public mind with Freddy, Englund has found it difficult to find other roles. **Selected Works:** *Freddy's Dead: The Final Nightmare* (1991), *Danse Macabre* (1991)

# Nora Ephron

**Born:** May 19, 1941; New York, NY

**Years Active in the Industry:** by decade

| 10s | 20s | 30s | 40s | 50s | 60s | 70s | 80s | 90s |
|-----|-----|-----|-----|-----|-----|-----|-----|-----|
|     |     |     |     |     |     |     |     |     |

The daughter of author/screenwriters Phoebe and Henry Ephron, Nora Ephron was educated at Wellesley. She first made her mark as humorist, satirist and dead-on parodist in book form (*Crazy Salad*) and in magazine articles. Ephron's first movie assignment was the Oscar-nominated screenplay for *Silkwood* (1983). Her stormy marriage with Washington Post reporter Carl Bernstein provided grist for her *roman a clef Heartburn*, which she adapted into a film in 1985. After years of courting cynicism and waspishness in her work, Nora turned romantic with her script for the extremely popular *When Harry Met Sally...* (1989), and has remained in this vein ever since. After a few so-so writing and producing assignments, Ephron made her directing bow with *This Is My Life* (1991), allegedly based on Roseanne, which she cowrote with sister Delia Ephron. She then scored as director and writer of *Sleepless in Seattle* a big-time hit of 1993. Alas, 1994's *Mixed Nuts*, a comedy set at a suicide prevention clinic, was a tasteless misfire. **Selected Works:** *Husbands and Wives* (1992), *My Blue Heaven* (1990)

# Julius J. & Philip G. Epstein

**Born:** August 22, 1909; New York, NY

**Years Active in the Industry:** by decade

| 10s | 20s | 30s | 40s | 50s | 60s | 70s | 80s | 90s |
|-----|-----|-----|-----|-----|-----|-----|-----|-----|
|     |     |     |     |     |     |     |     |     |

Identical-twin screenwriters Julius J. and Philip G. Epstein were the sons of a prosperous New York livery stable owner. Both Epsteins attended Penn State, then went off to seek their separate fortunes as journalists. Julius was employed as a press agent when, in 1933, he headed to Hollywood to help out a couple of old college friends who'd sold a story to Warner Bros. but were having trouble finishing the script. He continued to contribute anonymously to other screenwriter's efforts, finally receiving a credit for

1935's *Broadway Gondolier*. Around that same time, Julius' brother Philip arrived in Hollywood to work at RKO; in 1938, the brothers formed a writing team that would flourish until Philip's sudden death in 1952. Before long, it became common Hollywood practice for producers, directors and writers to cry out "Get me the Epsteins!" whenever a script became mired down. Among the films that the Epsteins worked on (credited and uncredited) were *The Strawberry Blonde* (1941), *Yankee Doodle Dandy* (1942), *The Male Animal* (1942), *My Foolish Heart* (1948) and *Forever Female* (1952). Their prolific output is all the more remarkable in that they never typed a script, choosing instead to write in longhand. To hear the brothers tell it, they were of equal talent, though an argument can be made that Julius was the better raconteur and Philip was more skilled at bypassing censorship (it was Philip who saved the ending of *Arsenic and Old Lace* (1942) by purifying the line "I'm a bastard!" into "I'm the son of a sea cook!") The Epsteins' best-known credit was the award-winning *Casablanca*; Julius was fond of referring to this classic as "slick s—t," though he found himself late in life defending his contribution to the film after his collaborator Howard Koch insisted upon grabbing most of the glory for himself. Outside of his work with Philip, Julius wrote or cowrote four plays (including the popular *Chicken Every Sunday*), and wrote the scripts for *The Tender Trap* (1956), *Kiss Them For Me* (1957), *Return From the Ashes* (1965), *Any Wednesday* (1967) and *Pete 'N' Tillie* (1973), also functioning as producer on several of these films. Philip G. Epstein's credits without his brother include *The Bride Walks Out* (1936) and *The Mad Miss Manton* (1938). In 1983, the 74-year-old Julius J. Epstein won the fourth of his Oscar nominations for *Reuben, Reuben*.

# Leon Errol

**Born:** July 3, 1881; Sydney, Australia
**Died:** 1951

**Years Active in the Industry:** by decade

| 10ˢ | 20ˢ | 30ˢ | 40ˢ | 50ˢ | 60ˢ | 70ˢ | 80ˢ | 90ˢ |
|-----|-----|-----|-----|-----|-----|-----|-----|-----|

Small, bald, rubber-legged Australian comedic actor Leon Errol moved to the U.S. in his youth. He starred in vaudeville, burlesque, and on the legitimate stage; from 1911-15 he was a star of the *Ziegfeld Follies*. He debuted onscreen in *Yolanda* (1924), then made a few silents before successfully making the transition to sound. He played leads and supporting roles, but was most successful as a comic actor in over 100 comedy shorts made between 1933-51; in these he usually played a nervous, henpecked husband getting in trouble for drinking and having affairs. A scene-stealer skilled in slapstick, he portrayed Uncle Matt in the "Mexican Spitfire" series of comedies, in which he also often played bumbling, bowlegged, dim-witted Lord Epping. He was at the height of his popularity in the '40s, and shortly before his death, he was negotiating a TV series deal.

# Stuart Erwin

**Born:** February 14, 1902; Squaw Valley, CA
**Died:** December 21, 1967; Beverly Hills, CA

**Years Active in the Industry:** by decade

| 10ˢ | 20ˢ | 30ˢ | 40ˢ | 50ˢ | 60ˢ | 70ˢ | 80ˢ | 90ˢ |
|-----|-----|-----|-----|-----|-----|-----|-----|-----|

Though the characters he played often seemed utterly bereft of brains, American actor Stuart Erwin attended the University of California at Berkeley. After stage experience in Los Angeles, Erwin made his earliest screen appearances in silent films, notably a classic two-reel comedy for Hal Roach, *A Pair of Tights* (1928), in which Stu and Edgar Kennedy played roles evidently written for Laurel and Hardy (a generous portion of this film appears in the 1960 compilation *When Comedy Was King*). After his first talking picture, *Happy Days* (1929), Erwin found himself typed as the vague, ingenuous young man who always seemed to have the cards stacked against him. Contrary to popular belief, Erwin's screen character *did* get the girl on occasion; in *The Big Broadcast* (1932), for example, Erwin not only won Leila Hyams away from Bing Crosby, but he was also billed *above* Crosby in the opening credits. The actor was nominated for an Academy Award for his performance as a rustic football hero in *Pigskin Parade* (1936), which also served as the screen debut for Judy Garland (as Erwin's kid sister). In 1942, Erwin made his Broadway bow in the title role of *Mr. Sycamore*, an odd little failure wherein he played a man who turned into a tree! When TV came in, Erwin made the most of it, costarring with his wife June Collyer on a sitcom titled *The Stu Erwin Show* (aka *The Trouble With Father*). From 1950-55, Erwin played one "Stuart Erwin," a small town high school principal; among the supporting cast, in the role of his youngest daughter, was Sheila James, later the memorable Zelda Gilroy on TV's *Dobie Gillis*. Still very active in the 1960s—though he was certainly wealthy enough to retire had he wanted to—Erwin appeared in a few Disney pictures and as a circus advance man on the 1963 TV series *The Greatest Show on Earth*. **Selected Works:** *Our Town* (1940), *Viva Villa!* (1934)

# Emilio Estevez

**Born:** May 12, 1962; New York, NY

**Years Active in the Industry:** by decade

| 10ˢ | 20ˢ | 30ˢ | 40ˢ | 50ˢ | 60ˢ | 70ˢ | 80ˢ | 90ˢ |
|-----|-----|-----|-----|-----|-----|-----|-----|-----|

The son of actor Martin Sheen and brother of actor Charlie Sheen, Emilio Estevez ("Estevez" is his father's *real* last name) began acting in amateur productions while still a child. In high school he wrote and starred in a play which was directed by his friend, Sean Penn. He debuted onscreen in *Tex* (1982), then appeared alongside a number of other up-and-coming young stars (later called "The Brat Pack") in Francis Ford Coppola's *The Out-*

*siders* (1983). His career became firmly founded after lead roles in two consecutive hits, *Repo Man* (1984) and *The Breakfast Club* (1985). He wrote and starred in *That Was Then, This Is Now* (1985), and wrote, directed, and starred in *Wisdom* (1986) and *Men At Work* (1990). He scored an unlikely hit as a reluctant hockey coach in the comedy *The Mighty Ducks* (1992), although its sequel was less than successful, and took a stab at actioners with *Freejack* (1992) and *Judgment Night* (1993). Estevez also served as producer of *The Jerky Boys* (1995). After a broken engagement to actress Demi Moore (who co-starred in *Wisdom*) he married and divorced pop singer Paula Abdul. **Selected Works:** *Another Stakeout* (1993), *Young Guns, Part 2* (1990)

# Joe Eszterhas

**Born:** 1944; Gaskanydoroszlo, Hungary

**Years Active in the Industry:** by decade

| 10s | 20s | 30s | 40s | 50s | 60s | 70s | 80s | 90s |
|-----|-----|-----|-----|-----|-----|-----|-----|-----|
|     |     |     |     |     |     |     |     |     |

Hungarian-born Joe Eszterhas began his journalistic career as a reporter for *Rolling Stone*. In 1974, Eszterhas authored the popular, award-winning novel *Charlie Simpson's Apocalypse*. The book was optioned by Hollywood, and though it has not as yet been filmed, it served as the key for Eszterhas' entree into scriptwriting. He is best known for his vicious, sexy, highly literate crime and mystery scripts: *The Jagged Edge* (1985), *Betrayed* (1988), and the Sharon Stone starmaker *Basic Instinct* (1989). At one point Eszterhas was the highest-paid writer in Hollywood, receiving $3 million up-front money for *Basic Instinct* alone. Never one to shirk from a fracas, Eszterhas has fought publicly with producers, directors, powerful agents and even crime bosses (especially after accepting the responsibility of penning the John Gotti biopic). Given his reputation for censor-baiting, it is surprising to learn that one of Eszterhas' biggest battles was aimed at convincing director Paul Verhoeven to *tone down* the sex-and-violence excesses that Verhoeven had added to *Basic Instinct*. Nonetheless, it was Eszterhas who in 1995 issued a sarcastic response to Senator Bob Dole's call for Hollywood to clean up its act; kidding on the square, Eszterhas argued that some of the political misdeeds of the Nixon, Reagan and Bush administrations were far more "obscene" than anything found in an R-rated movie.

# Dame Edith Evans

**Born:** February 8, 1888; London, England
**Died:** October 14, 1976; Cranbrook, Kent, England

**Years Active in the Industry:** by decade

| 10s | 20s | 30s | 40s | 50s | 60s | 70s | 80s | 90s |
|-----|-----|-----|-----|-----|-----|-----|-----|-----|
|     |     |     |     |     |     |     |     |     |

Formidable English character actress Edith Evans was celebrated for her unique voice and speech pattern. As a young woman, she held down a job while studying acting at night. In 1912 she made her professional stage debut, going on to become famous for her glorious performances of the classics both on the London stage and later on Broadway. Evans appeared in two silent films, *A Welsh Singer* (1915) and *East Is East* (1917), then went three decades before her next screen appearance, in *The Queen of Spades* (1948); in the meantime she devoted herself to the stage. After three films she again went seven years without a screen role, then after 1959 she began appearing in films more frequently. For her work in both *Tom Jones* (1963) and *The Chalk Garden* (1964) she received Best Supporting Actress Oscar nominations; for *The Whisperers* (1967) she won the New York Critics Award for Best Actress, and was nominated for a Best Actress Oscar. Evans was an inspiration to generations of younger British stars, many of whom considered her to be their greatest influence in their professional lives. In 1946 she was made a Dame Commander of the Order of the British Empire. Her authorized biography is *Dame Edith Evans: Ned's Girl* (1978) by writer-director Bryan Forbes. **Selected Works:** *Importance of Being Earnest* (1952), *Nun's Story* (1959)

# Rupert Everett

**Born:** May 29, 1959; Norfolk, England

**Years Active in the Industry:** by decade

| 10s | 20s | 30s | 40s | 50s | 60s | 70s | 80s | 90s |
|-----|-----|-----|-----|-----|-----|-----|-----|-----|
|     |     |     |     |     |     |     |     |     |

Not yet as widely known as he should be, British actor Rupert Everett has been in show business since age 15. A restless spirit, Everett could not adapt to formalized theatrical training, but he had no problem holding down his first professional job as an apprentice with the Citizen's Theatre of Glasgow. He made his film debut in 1984's *Another Country* as a younger version of notorious spy Guy Burgess (here named Guy Bennett). Two years earlier, he had created this role in the well-received BBC TV version of *Another Country*. Everett's American work has included the nominal male lead in the TV miniseries *Princess Daisy* (1983) and the title role (a teen idol-turned-screenwriter) in *Inside Monkey Zetterland* (1993). **Selected Works:** *Comfort of Strangers* (1991), *Madness of King George* (1994)

# Tom Ewell

**Born:** April 29, 1909; Owensboro, KY

**Years Active in the Industry:** by decade

| 10ˢ | 20ˢ | 30ˢ | 40ˢ | 50ˢ | 60ˢ | 70ˢ | 80ˢ | 90ˢ |
|-----|-----|-----|-----|-----|-----|-----|-----|-----|
|     |     |     |     |     |     |     |     |     |

Born Samuel Yewell Tompkins, actor Tom Ewell began his career acting in college plays. In 1928 the teenaged Ewell made his professional stage debut. He moved to New York and worked at

Macy's before debuting on Broadway in 1934; over the next fifteen years he established himself as a Broadway character comedian. He had small roles in two films before landing an important supporting role in *Adam's Rib* (1949) opposite Judy Holliday. He went on to a sporadic screen career, usually in roles in which he caricatured the foibles of the ordinary man; his most memorable appearance was in *The Seven Year Itch* (1955) opposite Marilyn Monroe, in which he reprised his triumphant 1952 Broadway role. He briefly starred on the TV series *The Tom Ewell Show* in 1960, then in the '70s co-starred with Robert Blake in the series *Baretta*.

# Jeff Fahey

**Born:** 1954; Olean, New York

**Years Active in the Industry:** by decade

| 10ˢ | 20ˢ | 30ˢ | 40ˢ | 50ˢ | 60ˢ | 70ˢ | 80ˢ | 90ˢ |
|-----|-----|-----|-----|-----|-----|-----|-----|-----|
|     |     |     |     |     |     |     |     |     |

One of 13 children in an Irish-American family, Jeff Fahey worked in odd jobs, including crewman on a fishing boat and ambulance driver before becoming an actor. He spent three years with the Joffrey Ballet, and appeared in musical revivals before doing a two-and-a-half year stint on the TV soap opera *One Life to Live*. He made his feature film debut in *Silverado* (1985), then went on to appear in a number of other unmemorable films while continuing to work in off-Broadway productions, notably, the London production of *Orphans*, in which he appeared opposite Albert Finney. His career was sustained by a critically-acclaimed performance in *White Hunter, Black Heart* (1990) and his starring role in the surprise horror hit *The Lawnmower Man* (1992). In 1995 he assumed the title role of the ABC drama *The Marshal*. **Selected Works:** *Hit List* (1993), *Sketch Artist* (1992), *Blindsided* (1992), *Wyatt Earp* (1994)

# Douglas Fairbanks, Jr. (Douglas Elton Ullman Fairbanks, Jr.)

**Born:** December 9, 1909; New York, NY

**Years Active in the Industry:** by decade

| 10ˢ | 20ˢ | 30ˢ | 40ˢ | 50ˢ | 60ˢ | 70ˢ | 80ˢ | 90ˢ |
|-----|-----|-----|-----|-----|-----|-----|-----|-----|
|     |     |     |     |     |     |     |     |     |

American actor Douglas Fairbanks Jr. was—now prepare yourself—the son of film star Douglas Fairbanks Sr. The elder Fairbanks wasn't too keen on his son entering "the business", but there were too many Hollywood people putting pressure on Doug Jr. to give acting a try. So he did, in 1923's *Stephen Steps Out*,

which was remarkable only in how quickly it went out of circulation. Young Fairbanks was more impressive as Lois Moran's fiancé in 1926's *Stella Dallas*, though it did give Doug Sr. pause to see his teenaged son sporting a Fairbanksian mustache. Even as a youth, Fairbanks' restlessness would not be satisfied by mere film work; before he was 20 he'd written an amusing article about the Hollywood scene for *Vanity Fair* magazine. In 1927, Fairbanks appeared in a stage play, *Young Woodley*, which convinced detractors that he truly had talent and was not merely an appendage to his father's fame. When talking pictures came in, he demonstrated a well-modulated speaking voice and as a result worked steadily in the early 1930s. Married at that time to actress Joan Crawford, Fairbanks was a fixture of the Tinseltown social whirl, and many acquaintances of the time wondered how a man so seemingly shallow and carefree would survive in the business. But he had a lot more going for him than suspected, and in 1935 offered the earliest evidence of his sharp business savvy by setting up his own production company, Criterion Films—the first of six such companies created under the Fairbanks imprimatur. The actor had his best role in 1937's *The Prisoner of Zenda*, in which he was alternately charming and cold-blooded as the villainous Rupert of Hentzau. Upon his father's death in 1939, Fairbanks began to extend his activities into politics and service to his country. He helped to organize the Hollywood branch of the William Allen White Committee, designed to aid the allied cause in the European war. From 1939 through 1944, Fairbanks, ever an Anglophile, headed London's Douglas Voluntary Hospitals, which took special care of war refugees. Fairbanks was appointed by President Roosevelt to act as envoy for the Special Mission to South America in 1940, and one year later was commissioned as a lieutenant j.g. in the Navy. In 1942 he was chief officer of Special Operations, and in 1943 participated in the allied invasion of Sicily and Elba. Fairbanks worked his way up from Navy lieutenant to commander and finally, in 1954 to captain. After the war's end, the actor spent five years as chairman of CARE, sending food and aid to war-torn countries. How he had time to resume his acting career is anybody's guess, but Fairbanks was back before the cameras in 1947 with *Sinbad the Sailor*, taking up scriptwriting with 1948's *The Exile*; both films were swashbucklers, a genre he'd stayed away from while his father was alive (Fairbanks Sr. had *invented* the swashbuckler; it wouldn't have been right for his son to bank on that achievement during the elder Fairbanks' lifetime). Out of films as an actor by 1951 (except for a welcome return in 1981's *Ghost Story*), Fairbanks concentrated on the production end for the next decade; he also produced and starred in a high-quality TV anthology, *Douglas Fairbanks Jr. Presents* (1952-55), which belied its tiny budget with excellent scripts and superior actors. Evidently the only setback suffered by Fairbanks in the last forty years was his poorly received appearance as Henry Higgins in a 1968 revival of *My Fair Lady*; otherwise, the actor has retained his status as a respected and concerned citizen of the world, sitting in with the U.S. delegation at SEATO in 1971 and accruing many military and humanitarian awards. He has published two autobiographies, *The Salad Days* in 1988 and *A Hell of a War* in 1993. **Selected Works:** *Gunga Din* (1939), *Little Caesar* (1930), *Young in Heart* (1938), *Great Manhunt* (1949)

# Douglas Fairbanks, Sr.

**Born:** May 23, 1883; Denver, CO
**Died:** December 12, 1939; Santa Monica, CA

**Years Active in the Industry:** by decade

| 10s | 20s | 30s | 40s | 50s | 60s | 70s | 80s | 90s |
|-----|-----|-----|-----|-----|-----|-----|-----|-----|

American actor Douglas Fairbanks Sr., instilled with a love of dramatics by his Shakespearean-scholar father, was never fully satisfied with theatrical work. A born athlete and extrovert, Fairbanks felt the borders of the stage were much too confining, even when his theatrical work allowed him to tour the world. The wide open spaces of the motion picture industry were more his style, and in 1915 Fairbanks jumped at the chance to act in the film version of the old stage perennial *The Lamb*. Fairbanks became the top moneymaker for the Triangle Film Company, starring in an average of 10 pictures a year for a weekly salary of $2000. He specialized in comedies—not the slapstick variety, but freewheeling farces in which he usually played a wealthy young man thirsting for adventure. Fairbanks was a savvy businessman, and in 1919 he reasoned that he could have more control—and a larger slice of the profits—if he produced as well as starred in his pictures. Working in concert with his actress-wife Mary Pickford (a star in

her own right, billed as "America's Sweetheart"), his best friend Charlie Chaplin, and pioneer director D. W. Griffith, Fairbanks formed a new film company, United Artists. The notion of actors making their own movies led one film executive to wail, "The lunatics have taken over the asylum!", but Fairbanks' studio was a sound investment, and soon other actors were dabbling in the production end of the business. Still most successful in contemporary comedies in 1920, Fairbanks decided to try a momentary change of pace, starring in the swashbuckling *The Mark of Zorro* (1920). The public was enthralled, and for the balance of his silent career Fairbanks specialized in lavish costume epics with plenty of fast-moving stunt work and derring-do. While several of these films still hold their fascination today, notably *The Thief of Baghdad* (1924) and *The Black Pirate* (1926), some historians argue that Fairbanks' formerly breezy approach to moviemaking became ponderous, weighed down in too much spectacle for the Fairbanks personality to fully shine. When talkies came, Fairbanks wasn't intimidated, since he was stage-trained and had a robust speaking voice; unfortunately, his first talking picture, 1929's *Taming of the Shrew* (in which he costarred with Mary Pickford), was an expensive fiasco. Fairbanks' talking pictures failed to click at the box office; even the best of them, such as *Mr. Robinson Crusoe* (1932), seemed outdated rehashes of his earlier silent successes. Fairbanks' last film, the British-made *Private Life of Don Juan* (1934), unflatteringly revealed his advanced years and his flagging energy. Marital difficulties, unwise investments and health problems curtailed his previously flamboyant lifestyle considerably, though he managed to stave off several takeover bids for United Artists and retained the respect of his contemporaries. Fairbanks died in his sleep, not long after he'd announced plans to come out of retirement. He was survived by his actor son Douglas Fairbanks Jr., who'd inherited much of his dad's professional panache and who after his father's death began a successful career in film swashbucklers on his own.

# Peter Falk

**Born:** September 16, 1927; New York, NY

**Years Active in the Industry:** by decade

| 10s | 20s | 30s | 40s | 50s | 60s | 70s | 80s | 90s |
|-----|-----|-----|-----|-----|-----|-----|-----|-----|

With his squinty gaze (the result of the loss of an eye at the age of 3) and rumpled demeanor, character and lead actor Peter Falk is probably best known as the cigar chewing, raincoat wearing TV detective Columbo. Until his mid-20s he pursued an ordinary career in public administration, working as an efficiency expert for the Connecticut Budget Bureau. Bored with his work, he became involved in amateur dramatics. In 1955 with the encouragement of Eva La Gallienne, he turned professional. His performance in the off-Broadway production of *The Iceman Cometh* brought him much attention, leading to work on Broadway, in TV, and films; Falk debuted onscreen in *Wild Across the Everglades* (1958). At first he was cast as hoodlums, often with a hint of humor, and blue-

collar types. As an actor, he showed his skill most effectively in two independent films made by his friend John Cassavetes, *Husbands* (1970) and *A Woman Under the Influence* (1974), both of which he helped finance. He won an Emmy for his portrayal of a truck driver in the TV play *Price of Tomatoes*; later, Falk won another Emmy for playing the title role in the popular TV detective series *Columbo*. He received Oscar nominations for his work in the movies *Murder Inc.* (1960) and *Pocketful of Miracles* (1961). Also, he won a Tony for his 1972 performance on Broadway in Neil Simon's comedy *The Prisoner of Second Avenue*. **Selected Works:** *Player* (1992), *Princess Bride* (1987), *Tune in Tomorrow* (1990), *Wings of Desire* (1988), *Roommates* (1995)

## Frances Farmer

**Born:** September 19, 1913; Seattle, WA
**Died:** 1970

**Years Active in the Industry:** by decade

| 10s | 20s | 30s | 40s | 50s | 60s | 70s | 80s | 90s |
|-----|-----|-----|-----|-----|-----|-----|-----|-----|

Frances Farmer is one of Hollywood's most tragic figures. In 1936, she made her feature film debut. One year later, she defied the studios and simultaneously began appearing on stage with

New York's Group Theater, where she played the female lead in *Golden Boy* and other Broadway plays of the late '30s. After gaining great critical praise for her dual role in the film *Come and Get It* (1936), Farmer became a sensation, and it was expected that she would become Paramount's greatest star. However, she suffered from alcoholism and mental illness and had some run-ins with the law, forcing her retirement in 1942. Declared insane, Farmer went on to spend seven years in various mental-health hospitals before attempting a comeback in the '50s, when she worked in stock, appeared in one film, and

made some TV appearances, including the hosting of a local TV program in Indianapolis. She died of cancer at 57. She was married from 1934-42 to actor Leif Erickson. Her autobiography, *Will There Really Be a Morning?* was published posthumously, and she became the subject of two books. Her life was also the subject of two off-Broadway plays, a TV movie starring Susan Blakely (*Committed*), and the film *Frances* (1982), for which Jessica Lange (in the title role) received a Best Actress Oscar nomination.

## Glenda Farrell

**Born:** June 30, 1904; Enid, OK
**Died:** May 1, 1971; New York, NY

**Years Active in the Industry:** by decade

| 10s | 20s | 30s | 40s | 50s | 60s | 70s | 80s | 90s |
|-----|-----|-----|-----|-----|-----|-----|-----|-----|

American actress Glenda Farrell, like so many other performers born around the turn of the century, made her stage debut in a production of *Uncle Tom's Cabin*. Her first adult professional job was with Virginia Brissac's stock company in San Diego, after which she worked up and down the California coast until leaving for Broadway in the late 1920s. Farrell's performance in the stage play *Skidding* established her reputation, and in 1929 she was wooed to Hollywood along with many other stage actors in the wake of the "talkie" revolution. Uncharacteristically cast as the ingenue in *Little Caesar* (1930), Farrell would thereafter be cast in the fast-talking, "hardboiled dame" roles that suited her best. Though her characters had a tough veneer, Farrell was sensitive enough to insist upon script changes if the lines and bits of business became *too* rough and unsympathetic; still, she seemed to revel in the occasional villainess, notably her acid performance as Paul Muni's mercenary paramour in *I Am a Fugitive From a Chain Gang* (1932). In 1937, Farrell was assigned by Warner Bros. to portray dauntless news reporter Torchy Blaine in a series of brisk B pictures. She was gratified by the positive fan mail she received for Torchy, and justifiably proud of her ability to spout out 390 words per minute in the role, but Farrell decided to leave Warners and freelance after five "Torchy Blaines." The actress's character roles in the 1940s and 1950s may have been smaller than before, but she always gave 100 percent to her craft. Farrell moved into television with ease, appearing on virtually every major dramatic weekly series and ultimately winning an Emmy for her work on the two-part *Ben Casey* episode of 1963, "A Cardinal Act of Mercy." Perhaps Farrell might have preferred a worthier exit from movies than the 1964 Jerry Lewis farce *The Disorderly Orderly*; even so, she plunged into this assignment with all the enthusiasm and sheer professionalism that she'd brought to the rest of her screen career. **Selected Works:** *Lady for a Day* (1933), *Talk of the Town* (1942)

## Mia Farrow (Maria de Lourdes Villiers Farrow)

**Born:** February 9, 1945; Santa Monica, CA

**Years Active in the Industry:** by decade

| 10s | 20s | 30s | 40s | 50s | 60s | 70s | 80s | 90s |
|-----|-----|-----|-----|-----|-----|-----|-----|-----|
|     |     |     |     |     |     |     |     |     |

American actress Mia Farrow was the third of seven children born to film star Maureen O'Sullivan and director John Farrow. She enjoyed the usual pampered Hollywood kid lifestyle until she fell victim to polio at age 9; her upward struggle from this illness was the first of many instances in which the seemingly frail Farrow exhibited a will of iron. Educated in an English convent school, Farrow returned to California with plans to take up acting (she'd had a minor taste of this in a bit part in her father's 1959 film *John Paul Jones*). With precious little prior experience, she debuted on Broadway in a 1963 revival of *The Importance of Being Earnest*. In 1964 the actress was cast as Alison McKenzie in the nighttime TV soap opera *Peyton Place,* which made her an idol of the American teen set. That people over the age of 18 were interested in Farrow was proven in the summer of 1965, when she became the third wife of singer Frank Sinatra, thirty years her senior. The marriage provided fodder for both the tabloids and leering nightclub comics for a while, and while the union didn't last long, it put Farrow into the international film-going consciousness. The actress' first important movie appearance was in *Rosemary's Baby* (1968) as the unwitting mother of Satan's offspring—a part that plunked her name in the headlines once more due to a nude scene that required an unconvincingly svelte body double for the pencil-thin Farrow. She toiled away in damsel-in-distress parts capitalizing on *Rosemary's Baby* and in "trendy" pop-culture roles for several years thereafter, in the meantime marrying musician Andre Previn and starting a family almost as large as her mother's and father's. Her skills as an actress increased, even if her films didn't bring in large crowds; Farrow's performance as Daisy Buchanan in *The Great Gatsby* (1974) is one of the few high points of that disappointing film. By the early 1980s, newly divorced Farrow had taken up with comedian-director Woody Allen, for whom she did some of her best work in such films as *Zelig* (1983), *Purple Rose of Cairo* (1984), *Hannah and Her Sisters* (1986), *Radio Days* (1987) and *Broadway Danny Rose* (1984), wherein she was barely recognizable in a brilliant turn as a bosomy blonde bimbo. Farrow and Allen were soulmates in private as well as cinematic life; she had a child by him named Sacha, who was Allen's first son—though certainly not hers. Farrow once more commanded newspaper headlines in 1992 when she discovered that Allen had been having an affair with her adopted daughter Soon-Yi Previn, and those fans who knew Farrow only through her film roles were astounded at the length and breadth of rancor and recrimination of which she was capable. While her film career is in abeyance, it is certain that Farrow will remain a conspicuous (and unavoidable) public figure for years to come. **Selected Works:** *Alice* (1990), *Crimes and Misdemeanors* (1989), *Death on the Nile* (1978), *Husbands and Wives* (1992)

# Rainer Werner Fassbinder

**Born:** May 31, 1945; Bad Worishofen, Bavaria, Germany
**Died:** June 10, 1982; Munich, Germany

**Years Active in the Industry:** by decade

| 10s | 20s | 30s | 40s | 50s | 60s | 70s | 80s | 90s |
|-----|-----|-----|-----|-----|-----|-----|-----|-----|
|     |     |     |     |     |     |     |     |     |

A lifelong movie buff, German filmmaker Rainer Werner Fassbinger studied acting at Munich's Fridl-Leonhard school. Though he was not accepted into the West Berlin Film and Television academy, Fassbinder decided to pick up practical experience on his own beginning in 1965, acting, writing and directing (under the pseudonym Franz Walsch) short amateur films. He joined Munich's *action-theater* as an actor/playwright 1967; here he met actress Hanna Schygulla, who would later star in many of his best films (explosive and divisive personal differences notwithstanding). Fassbinder founded the Brechtian *anti-theater* troupe in 1968, utilizing his stage actors for his films, which he financed with government grants, small festival prizes, and occasional hocking of his own possessions. Throughout his film career, Fassbinder remained active with such theatrical organizations as Theatre am Turm and Albatross Productions, and also contributed scripts to radio. The first film that Fassbinder directed under his own name rather than his "Franz Walsch" alias was *Pioneers in Ingolstadt*, made for German television in 1971. The director gained national attention for such "alternative" films as *Fear Eats the Soul* (1973) and *Mother Kuster's Trip To Heaven* (1975); his style of preference during this period was to move along at a slow pace with humdrum characters and dialogue, then jolt the audiences out of their seats with unexpected bursts of violence or onslaughts of bitter cynicism (in his *Why Does Herr R Run Amok?*, the bland leading character expresses displeasure at being ignored by his dull little family by suddenly killing them with a blunt instrument!) Fassbinder's first international success was *The Marriage of Maria Braun* (1975), a story of a tragic case of wartime *coitus interruptus*, constructed in the manner of an old Joan Crawford picture. Like his idol Bertolt Brecht, Fassbinder loved American "B" romances and crime melodramas, and would utilize some of the best (and many of the worst) aspects of these genres in his own films. The Fassbinder style would mature into a heady combination of Hollywood tawdriness and avant-garde theatricality. Off-camera, Fassbinder seemed determined to behave like one of his own self-destructive movie characters, deliberately straining his closest relationships with carefully calculated cruelties. In the eyes of many critics, Fassbinder's masterpiece was his 14-part TV series *Berlin Alexanderplatz*, the epic story of a harmless nebbish whose unsuccessful efforts to fit into society transform him into a criminal lunatic; the project, which like many of Fassbinder's works was a remake of an earlier German film, was later released as a feature film—lasting 931 minutes! Fassbinder's last films, which he photographed as well as directed, were *Veronika Voss* and *Querelle*; both were released in 1982, the year that Fassbinder died of a presumed drug overdose. **Selected Works:** *Effi Briest* (1974)

# Farrah Fawcett

**Born:** February 2, 1947; Corpus Christi, TX

**Years Active in the Industry:** by decade

| 10s | 20s | 30s | 40s | 50s | 60s | 70s | 80s | 90s |
|-----|-----|-----|-----|-----|-----|-----|-----|-----|
|     |     |     |     |     |     |     |     |     |

American actress Farrah Fawcett was an art student at the University of Texas before she deduced that she could make more money posing for pictures than painting them. A supermodel before that phrase had fallen into common usage, Fawcett moved from Wella Balsam ads into acting, though one suspects that she doesn't include her first film, the appalling *Myra Breckenridge* (1970), in her resume. She worked in TV bits and full supporting parts, obtaining steady employment in 1974 with a small recurring role on the cop series *Harry O*, but true stardom was still some two years down the road. In 1976, producer Aaron Spelling cast Fawcett, Kate Jackson and Jaclyn Smith in a pilot for an adventure series titled *Charlie's Angels*. The pilot graduated to a series, and the rest was TV history; not precisely the most talented of the three leading actresses, Fawcett was the most visible, adorning magazine covers and pin-up posters, which set sales records. There were even Farrah Fawcett dolls before the first season of *Charlie's Angels* was over, though posterity does not record how many were bought by little boys and their bigger daddies. Now in the hands of high-profile agents and advisers, Fawcett (billed Farrah Fawcett-Majors after her marriage to Lee Majors) decided she'd outgrown *Angels* and left the series, even though she had another year on her contract. While the studio drew up legal papers to block her move, she was replaced by Cheryl Ladd; Fawcett settled her dispute by agreeing to a set number of guest appearances on the program. Some industry cynics suggested that Fawcett would have problems sustaining her popularity. Certainly such lukewarm film projects as *Sunburn* (1979), *Somebody Killed Her Husband* (1978) and *Saturn 3* (1980) would seem to bear this theory out. But Fawcett (who dropped the "Majors" and her husband at the same time) took matters into her own hands and decided to make her own opportunities—and like many other performers who strive to be taken seriously, she chose the most extreme, demanding method of proving her acting mettle. Playing a vengeful rape victim in both the play and 1986 film version of *Extremities* (an apt title) and making a meal of her role as a battered wife who murders her husband out of self-defense in the TV movie *The Burning Bed* (1984), Fawcett confounded her detractors and demonstrated she was more than a head of hair and a pair of long legs. Other TV movie appearances of varying quality cast her as everything from a child killer to a Nazi hunter to famed LIFE photographer Margaret Bourke-White. Never as big a name as she was in 1976, Fawcett has nonetheless affirmed her reputation as an actress of importance. Her fans were even willing to forgive her misbegotten fling at situation comedy in the 1991 series *Good Sports*, in which she costarred with her longtime "significant other" Ryan O'Neal. **Selected Works:** *Criminal Behavior* (1992), *Man of the House* (1995), *Substitute Wife* (1994)

# Alice Faye (Alice Jeanne Leppert)

**Born:** May 4, 1912; New York, NY

**Years Active in the Industry:** by decade

| 10s | 20s | 30s | 40s | 50s | 60s | 70s | 80s | 90s |
|-----|-----|-----|-----|-----|-----|-----|-----|-----|
|     |     |     |     |     |     |     |     |     |

American actress Alice Faye began singing and dancing professionally at age 14. In 1931, while in her late teens, she was working as a chorus girl in Broadway's *George White's Scandals* when actor-singer Rudy Vallee spotted her and signed her to tour with his band as a singer. During the filming of the screen version of *George White's Scandals* in 1934, its star walked off the set, and despite the objections of George White, Faye was given the lead at the insistence of Vallee. Later that year Vallee was involved in an acrimonious divorce, and his wife named Faye as a source of their break-up. She then signed a screen contract with Fox, where she was at first cast as a bleached-blond Harlow-type. Soon, however, her good singing voice helped land her in a string of musical films, and within a few years she was a leading star of that genre. Faye remained very active in films until the early '40s, when she began having frequent disputes with studio boss Darryl F. Zanuck, who retaliated by banning her radio appearances and signing Betty Grable to a Fox contract as a threat to Faye. Soon Grable replaced Faye as Fox's major musical star, surpassing her in popularity. Faye had only a bit part in one film in 1944, and in 1945 she had a disastrous appearance in the drama *Fallen Angel* and ended up walking out on her contract to retire from the screen. She did not appear in another film until *State Fair* (1962), then made two more films in the '70s; her other acting credits included performing on Broadway and on tour in a revival of the musical *Good News*, in which she appeared with former screen partners John Payne (on Broadway) and Don Ameche (on tour). She was married to singer Tony Martin from 1936-40, and after 1941 to bandleader-actor Phil Harris. **Selected Works:** *Alexander's Ragtime Band* (1938), *In Old Chicago* (1938)

# Frank Faylen

**Born:** 1909; St. Louis, MO
**Died:** August 2, 1985

**Years Active in the Industry:** by decade

| 10s | 20s | 30s | 40s | 50s | 60s | 70s | 80s | 90s |
|-----|-----|-----|-----|-----|-----|-----|-----|-----|
|     |     |     |     |     |     |     |     |     |

American actor Frank Faylen was born into a vaudeville act; as an infant, he was carried on stage by his parents, the song-and-dance team Ruf and Clark. Traveling with his parents from one engagement to another, Faylen somehow managed to complete his education at St. Joseph's Prep School in Kirkwood, Missouri. Turning pro at age eighteen, Faylen worked on stage until getting a Hollywood screen test in 1936. For the next nine years, Faylen played a succession of bit and minor roles, mostly for Warner Bros.; of these minuscule parts he would later say, "If you sneezed, you missed me." Better parts came his way during a brief stay at Hal Roach Studios in 1942 and 1943, but Faylen's breakthrough came at Paramount in 1945, where he was cast as Bim, the chillingly cynical male nurse at Bellevue's alcoholic ward in the Oscar-winning *The Lost Weekend*. Though the part lasted all of four minutes' screen time, Faylen was so effective in this unpleasant role that he became entrenched as a sadistic bully or cool villain in his subsequent films. TV fans remember Faylen best for his more benign but still snarly role as grocery store proprietor Herbert T. Gillis on the 1959 sitcom *Dobie Gillis*. For the next four years, Faylen gained nationwide fame for such catch-phrases as "I was in World War II—the big one—*with* the good conduct medal!", and, in reference to his screen son Dobie Gillis, "I gotta kill that boy someday. I just gotta." Faylen worked sporadically in TV and films after *Dobie Gillis* was canceled in 1963, receiving critical plaudits for his small role as an Irish stage manager in the 1968 Barbra Streisand starrer *Funny Girl*. The actor also made an encore appearance as Herbert T. Gillis in a *Dobie Gillis* TV special of the 1970s, where his "good conduct medal" line received an ovation from the studio audience. Faylen was married to Carol Hughes, an actress best recalled for her role as Dale Arden in the 1939 serial *Flash Gordon Conquers the Universe*, and was the father of another actress, also named Carol. **Selected Works:** *Detective Story* (1951), *It's a Wonderful Life* (1946), *Gunfight at the O.K. Corral* (1957)

# Corey Feldman

**Born:** July 16, 1971; Reseda, CA

**Years Active in the Industry:** by decade

| 10s | 20s | 30s | 40s | 50s | 60s | 70s | 80s | 90s |
|-----|-----|-----|-----|-----|-----|-----|-----|-----|
|     |     |     |     |     |     |     |     |     |

Corey Feldman began his career at the age of three, appearing in more than 60 TV commercials over the next four years. After a recurring role on the TV sitcom *Mork and Mindy,* he debuted onscreen in *Born Again* (1978), going on to a number of small "cute kid" parts in films. Feldman's first substantial film role was in Rob Reiner's *Stand by Me* (1986). Now a teen idol, he soon found work in a fairly steady string of films (often co-starring fellow teen dream Corey Haim), including *The Lost Boys* (1987), *License to Drive* (1988), and *Dream a Little Dream* (1989), which he choreographed as well; he also supplied the voice of Donatello in *Teenage Mutant Ninja Turtles* (1990) and its sequels. Drug problems and arrests clouded his career and image in the late '80s and early '90s, and Feldman's subsequent film appearances (sometimes with Haim) have mostly been straight-to-video fare. **Selected Works:** *Round Trip to Heaven* (1992), *Maverick* (1994)

# Marty Feldman

**Born:** July 8, 1934; London, England
**Died:** December 2, 1982; Mexico City, Mexico

**Years Active in the Industry:** by decade

| 10s | 20s | 30s | 40s | 50s | 60s | 70s | 80s | 90s |
|-----|-----|-----|-----|-----|-----|-----|-----|-----|
|     |     |     |     |     |     |     |     |     |

Wild-haired, pop-eyed British comedian Marty Feldman dropped out of school at 15 in hopes of becoming a jazz trumpeter. Instead he found steady work as a radio comedy writer, first for the popular BBC weekly *Educating Archie* (which in the tradition of Edgar Bergen starred a ventriloquist and his dummy), and most famously for Kenneth Horne's *Round the Horne,* which ran from 1965 to 1969. *Round the Horne* would become something of a cult favorite when it was rebroadcast on American public radio in the 1970s to capitalize on Feldman's latter-day fame. Toiling away on many of Britain's best satirical TV and radio series of the 1960s, Feldman avoided the cameras, feeling that he was a bit too grotesque looking for public consumption. Once he did start acting as well as writing, the public loved him and begged for more. His biggest British TV break was *The Marty Feldman Comedy Machine*, in which he appeared in lightning-paced sketches (often artificially sped up, "Benny Hill" style) with some of the best English comedy talent available, most notably the great Spike Milligan. Feldman was introduced to American TV audiences when he co-starred on *Dean Martin Presents the Golddiggers in London*, the 1970 summer replacement for *The Dean Martin Show* (an Americanized *Marty Feldman Comedy Machine* would be broadcast briefly two years later). Having made his film debut in *The Bed Sitting Room* (1969), Feldman became a U.S. movie favorite with his role as Igor, Gene Wilder's bemused hunchbacked assistant (whose hump switched shoulders from scene to scene), in director Mel Brooks' *Young Frankenstein* (1973). Feldman later co-starred with Brooks and Dom DeLuise as a Ritz Brothers-like team of movie producers in *Silent Movie* (1975); his manic tango with Anne Bancroft, wherein the actress deftly imitated Feldman's cross-eyed squint, was the highlight of the film. In 1977, Feldman followed the footsteps of fellow Mel Brooks alumnus Gene Wilder by directing as well as starring in *The Last Remake of Beau Geste* (1977), an uneven but hilarious spoof in which Feldman cast himself as the twin brother of Michael Caine! A second directorial effort, the organized-religion takeoff *In God We Trust* (1979), was such a disaster that Feldman was obliged to confine himself to acting assignments for the rest of his career. While filming the all-star "comedy salad" *Yellowbeard* in Mexico City, Feldman died suddenly of heart failure. He is buried at Hollywood's Forest Lawn Cemetary in close proximity to the grave of his lifelong idol, Buster Keaton.

# Federico Fellini

**Born:** January 20, 1920; Rimini, Italy
**Died:** October 31, 1993; Rome, Italy

**Years Active in the Industry:** by decade

| 10s | 20s | 30s | 40s | 50s | 60s | 70s | 80s | 90s |
|-----|-----|-----|-----|-----|-----|-----|-----|-----|
|     |     |     |     |     |     |     |     |     |

While Italian director Federico Fellini so disliked being interviewed that he deliberately dispensed misleading information about his early life, the bare bones of his pre-movie career would

seem to be as follows: the son of middle-class parents who hoped he'd become an attorney, Fellini was an aimless, troublesome child, whose only discernible skill in school was drawing pictures. At various junctures he was a street vagrant, a circus worker, a newspaper comic strip artist and a journalist—experiences he would later romanticize in his films. Fellini attended college in Florence, principally to avoid the draft. He then joined the traveling theatrical troupe of actor Aldo Fabrizi, after which he wrote radio scripts. Barely squeezing out of military service in 1943, Fellini married actress Guiletta Masina; to support himself and his wife after the Liberation, he opened a small novelty shop in Rome, sketching caricatures of the occupying GIs and making comic recordings. When director Roberto Rosselini dropped into the shop, he was impressed by the range of Fellini's artistic skills, and hired Fellini to script his neorealist classic *Open City* (1945). After several subsequent scriptwriting gigs, Fellini decided to try directing himself, drawing upon his experiences with Aldo Fabrizi for his first feature, *Variety Lights* (1951), which he co-directed with Alberto Lattuda. Even in this early project, Fellini was pursuing his lifelong goal of seeking out beauty and optimism in the most tawdry of surroundings. Fellini's first solo directorial effort was *The White Sheik* (1952), a lampoon of the comic books that the director used to sell in his own shop. Neither of his first films were successful, but the restless Fellini had at last found a direction in life, and vowed to pursue moviemaking. *I Vitelloni* (*The Young and the Passionate* [1953]) once more dipped into Fellini's past life for material, relating the tale of five provincial young layabouts whose grandiose dreams are compromised by the realities of adult life. For the first time, Fellini used an autobiographical character (played by Franco Interlenghi) as the principle protagonist. In 1954 Fellini directed his first international hit, *La Strada*, an allegorical circus story starring Masina; the film won several industry awards, including Hollywood's Oscar. *La Strada, Il Bidone* (1955) and the Oscar-winning *Nights of Cabiria* (1957) represented Fellini's "melancholy" period in which he abandoned his search for beauty in favor of bleak pessimism; even in this doleful trio, however, he could not quench the upbeat spirits of Masina, whose characters kept bouncing back from the worst catastrophes with a crinkly smile and a warm heart. In *La Dolce Vita* (1960), Fellini brought back the Alter Ego character he'd created for *I Vitelloni*: the protagonist (Marcello Mastrioanni) is a journalist who disdains the decaying, immoral society all around him—but who is incapable of escaping life's seductions, possibly because he secretly enjoys the decadent passing parade. *La Dolce Vita* was so enormous a success that Fellini wondered how he'd ever top him-

self. Unable to come up with a workable storyline, the director decided to make a film about his creative crisis; the result was *8 1/2*, a fascinatingly self-indulgent film about a world-famous director (Mastrioanni again) who is given carte blanche on his latest movie—but finds that the freedom to do everything results in his inability to do anything. The film also takes time to jab away at the "money men" of the movie industry, who consider artistic genius just another gimmick. In addition, *8 1/2* is a detailed resumé of Fellini's early experiences, including his tenure in the circus and his first sexual encounter (represented by a fat, undulating whore). When people use the word "Felliniesque" in describing a dreamlike film chock-full of social satire, colorfully costumed peripheral characters, theatrical setpieces, and symbolism both subtle and blatant, the Fellini film they have in mind is *8 1/2*. The director's next project, a valentine to his wife titled *Juliette of the Spirits* (1963), completely dispenses with coherency, offering one garish visual highlight after another. After *Juliet*, Fellini's honeymoon with the critics was over. Upon the release of such cinematic excesses as *Fellini Satyricon* (1969) and *Fellini's Roma* (1972), the director was accused of merely trotting out all his old tricks, jumbling them about in kaleidoscopic fashion, and serving them up with style but no substance. His best-received project of this period was *The Clowns* (1970), a straightforward TV film celebrating the circus folk whom Fellini adored. The director regained his critical following with *Amarcord* (1973), which, though not bereft of his patented surrealism (in one scene, a parade float in the shape of Mussolini's head comes to life), was a subtle and heartfelt nostalgic piece about growing up in the provincial town of Rimini during the 1930s. *Amarcord* won Fellini his third and final Best Foreign Picture Oscar. In his last decade, Fellini experimented with a variety of cinematic forms, sometimes brilliantly (as in the gently satirical *Ginger and Fred* [1985]), sometimes backtracking into self-absorption (*Intervista* [1987], an ersatz documentary, is essentially *The Fellini Story*, right down to a recreation of the *La Dolce Vita* beach scene with Marcello Mastrioanni and Anita Ekberg). Fellini's last film was 1990's *La Voce de La Luna*; two years later he was honored with a Lifetime Achievement Award at the Academy Awards ceremony, where his ingratiating smile and naughty-schoolboy demeanor stole the show.

# Sherilyn Fenn

**Born:** February 1, 1965; Detroit, MI

**Years Active in the Industry:** by decade

| 10s | 20s | 30s | 40s | 50s | 60s | 70s | 80s | 90s |
|-----|-----|-----|-----|-----|-----|-----|-----|-----|
|     |     |     |     |     |     |     |     |     |

Actress Sherlyn Fenn had her first taste of show business while touring the country with her mother, a rock musician. Fresh out of high school, Fenn decided to put her stunning physical attributes to good use as a Playboy bunny—but alas, she failed to survive the first year of "bunny school". After posing for perfume and designer jean ads, Fenn made her film debut in *The Wild Life*

(1984). In early 1990, she skyrocketed to fame in the role of Audrey Horne in David Lynch's cult TV series *Twin Peaks;* her singular series highlight was the scene in which she tied a knot in a cherry stem with her tongue. In 1993, Fenn replaced a recalcitrant Kim Basinger in the role of a haughty beauty whose arms and legs are amputated by a love-obsessed surgeon in *Boxing Helena,* directed by David Lynch's daughter, Jennifer Lynch. The apex of Fenn's career may well turn out to be her take-no-prisoners 1995 TV performance as screen goddess Elizabeth Taylor. **Selected Works:** *Diary of a Hitman* (1991), *Of Mice and Men* (1992), *Ruby* (1992), *Three of Hearts* (1993), *Wild at Heart* (1990)

# Abel Ferrara

**Born:** 1952; Bronx, NY

**Years Active in the Industry:** by decade

| 10s | 20s | 30s | 40s | 50s | 60s | 70s | 80s | 90s |
|-----|-----|-----|-----|-----|-----|-----|-----|-----|
|     |     |     |     |     |     | ███ | ███ | ███ |

Independent New York filmmaker Abel Ferrara is best known for his low-budget, shockingly violent films that explore the rottenest parts of the Big Apple. These films (such as *China Girl* [1987], his unique version of *Romeo and Juliet*) have generated a devoted following of fans. Ferrara was born in the Bronx, but he spent most of his childhood in Peekskill, where he met the two young men who would eventually become his screenwriter and sound engineer, Nicholas St. John and John McIntyre. As boys they would play around with 8mm cameras. Later, in the mid-70s, the three reunited and founded Navaron Films, where they produced *Nine Lives* (1975). In 1979 they released their most notorious film, *Driller Killer,* in which Ferrara starred, edited, and wrote the songs under the pseudonym Jimmie Laine. In this film, a young man goes berserk and begins killing vagrants with a portable power drill. He continued making low budget shockers until the late '80s. when he began making more mainstream (although hardly subtle) films, including *The King of New York* (1990), *The Bad Lieutenant* (1992), and *Body Snatchers* (1994). During the '80s, he also worked on television shows such as *Miami Vice* and *Crime Story.* **Selected Works:** *Dangerous Game* (1993), *Addiction* (1995)

# José Luis Ferrer (José Vincente Ferrer De Otero y Cintron)

**Born:** January 8, 1912; Santurce, Puerto Rico
**Died:** January 26, 1992; Coral Gables, FL

**Years Active in the Industry:** by decade

| 10s | 20s | 30s | 40s | 50s | 60s | 70s | 80s | 90s |
|-----|-----|-----|-----|-----|-----|-----|-----|-----|
|     |     | ███ | ███ | ███ | ███ | ███ | ███ |     |

José Ferrer decided to become an actor while in college. Early in his career he appeared with James Stewart and Joshua Lo-

gan at the Triangle Theater. In 1935 he debuted on Broadway with a walk-on part; he soon began to land bigger roles and quickly established his reputation as a highly versatile actor, performing in roles ranging from the comic title role in *Charlie's Aunt* to the evil Iago in *Othello,* and he began directing Broadway productions in 1942. Ferrer debuted onscreen as the Dauphin opposite Ingrid Bergman in *Joan of Arc* (1948), for which he received a Best Supporting Actor Oscar nomination. He later became internationally famous, and won a Best Actor Oscar for reprising his theatrical lead in the film version of *Cyrano de Bergerac* (1950). Ferrer earned another Oscar nomination for his portrayal of painter Toulouse-Lautrec in *Moulin Rouge* (1952). While both roles definitely enhanced his career, he later complained that they lead him to become typecast, and sometimes went years between film offers. In the mid-'50s he began directing films (usually ones in which he appeared), starting with *The Shrike* (1955). Also in the mid-'50s he made several successful recordings with his third wife, singer Rosemary Clooney. After 1962 he gave up directing and concentrated on stage and screen character acting, usually being typecast in his films as a swarthy foreigner. He continued to appear frequently in films into the '90s, meanwhile doing much TV work. His first wife was actress Uta Hagen. **Selected Works:** *Caine Mutiny* (1954), *Lawrence of Arabia* (1962), *Old Explorers* (1990), *Ship of Fools* (1965), *Perfect Tribute* (1991)

# Mel Ferrer (Melchior Gaston Ferrer)

**Born:** August 25, 1917; Elberon, NJ

**Years Active in the Industry:** by decade

| 10s | 20s | 30s | 40s | 50s | 60s | 70s | 80s | 90s |
|-----|-----|-----|-----|-----|-----|-----|-----|-----|
|     |     | ███ | ███ | ███ | ███ | ███ | ███ |     |

Mel Ferrer dropped out of Princeton University in his sophomore year to become an actor in summer stock; meanwhile he worked as an editor for a small Vermont newspaper and wrote a children's book. He debuted on Broadway in 1938 as a chorus dancer; two years later, he made his debut as an actor. A bout with polio interrupted his career, leading to work in radio, first as a small-station disc jockey and later as a writer, producer, and director of radio shows for NBC. Having not acted in any films, Ferrer directed his first movie, *The Girl of the Limberlost,* in 1945, the year in which he also returned to Broadway. After assisting John Ford on the film *The Fugitive* (1947), he debuted onscreen in *Lost Boundaries* (1949). Ferrer went on to appear in numerous movies where he was usually cast as a sensitive, quiet, somewhat stiff leading man; his best-known role was as the lame puppeteer in *Lili* (1953). He continued to direct films, most of which were unexceptional, then began producing in the late '60s. Since 1960 he has worked primarily in Europe, appearing infrequently in American film and TV productions. His third wife was actress Audrey Hepburn, whom he directed in *Green Mansions* (1959) . He later produced her film *Wait Until Dark* (1967). **Selected Works:** *Longest Day* (1962)

# Stepin Fetchit (Lincoln Theodore Monroe Andrew Perry)

**Born:** May 30, 1902; Key West, FL
**Died:** 1985

**Years Active in the Industry:** by decade

| 10ˢ | 20ˢ | 30ˢ | 40ˢ | 50ˢ | 60ˢ | 70ˢ | 80ˢ | 90ˢ |
|-----|-----|-----|-----|-----|-----|-----|-----|-----|
|     |     |     |     |     |     |     |     |     |

African American comedic character actor Stepin Fetchit left his home in 1914 to pursue a show business career. He first joined the Royal American Shows plantation revues adopting the stage name "Stepin Fetchit." He went on to spend several years on the vaudeville circuit. In the late '20s, he arrived in Hollywood where he made an immediate impact; by the time he appeared in *Hearts in Dixie* (1929) he was being hailed by some as one of the greatest screen comedians. In these politically correct days, Fetchit's screen persona of the lazy, inarticulate, and easily frightened Negro is considered extremely racist and offensive, but back in the unenlightened '30s, audience found him hysterically funny, and he was the most celebrated black comic actor in Hollywood. He is said to have made $2 million in the '30s, but he squandered it (at one time he owned 16 cars) and had to declare bankruptcy in 1947. He made few films after 1940, drifting into obscurity before resurfacing in the late '60s as a member of boxer Muhammed Ali's entourage (he had converted to the Black Muslim faith); he was also the litigant in a suit against CBS, whom he felt had negatively represented him in a 1968 TV documentary. He made two more films in the '70s, *Amazing Grace* (1974) and *Won Ton Ton, the Dog Who Saved Hollywood* (1976).

# Betty Field

**Born:** February 8, 1918; Boston, MA
**Died:** 1973

**Years Active in the Industry:** by decade

| 10ˢ | 20ˢ | 30ˢ | 40ˢ | 50ˢ | 60ˢ | 70ˢ | 80ˢ | 90ˢ |
|-----|-----|-----|-----|-----|-----|-----|-----|-----|
|     |     |     |     |     |     |     |     |     |

Betty Field was a versatile character and lead actress said to have never repeated a characterization. She attended the American Academy of Dramatic Arts before appearing professionally in summer stock in 1933. The following year, Field made her Broadway debut and soon became a popular ingenue in George Abbott's comedies of the late '30s. She made her premiere feature film appearance in *What a Life* (1939), reprising her role in a Broadway play of the same name. With her provocative performance in *Of Mice and Men* (1940), she established herself as a significant actress. Throughout the '40s, Field alternated between Broadway plays and Hollywood films. On screen she tended to play neurotic, hard-bitten women. After making one film around 1950, Field returned to steady film work until after 1956, when she became a character actress frequently cast as unkempt but well-meaning mothers. One of

her three marriages was to playwright Elmer Rice, who wrote several plays as vehicles for her. She died of a cerebral hemorrhage in 1973. **Selected Works:** *Birdman of Alcatraz* (1962), *Bus Stop* (1956), *Peyton Place* (1957), *Picnic* (1955)

# Sally Field

**Born:** November 6, 1946; Pasadena, CA

**Years Active in the Industry:** by decade

| 10ˢ | 20ˢ | 30ˢ | 40ˢ | 50ˢ | 60ˢ | 70ˢ | 80ˢ | 90ˢ |
|-----|-----|-----|-----|-----|-----|-----|-----|-----|
|     |     |     |     |     |     |     |     |     |

American actress Sally Field was the daughter of another actress, Margaret Field, who is perhaps best known to film buffs as the leading lady of the sci-fier *The Man From Planet X* (1951). Field's stepfather was actor/stuntman Jock Mahoney, who despite a certain degree of alienation between himself and his stepdaughter was the principal influence in her pursuance of an acting career. Active in high school dramatics, Field bypassed college to enroll in a summer acting workshop at Columbia studios. Her energy and determination enabled her to win the coveted starring role on the 1965 TV series *Gidget* over hundreds of other aspiring actresses. *Gidget* lasted only one season, but Field had become popular with teen fans, and in 1967 was given a second crack at a sitcom, *The Flying Nun*; this one lasted three seasons and is still flying around in reruns. Somewhere along the way Field made her film debut in *The Way West* (1967), but was more or less ignored by moviegoers over the age of 21. Juggling sporadic work on stage and TV with a well-publicized first marriage (she was pregnant during *Flying Nun's* last season), Field set about shedding her "perky" image in order to get more substantial parts. Good as she was as a reformed junkie in the 1970 TV movie *Maybe I'll Come Home in the Spring,* Field was mired again in the sitcom treadmill by 1972 with the short-lived weekly *The Girl With Something Extra*. Freshly divorced and with a new agent, she tried to radically alter her persona with a nude scene in the 1975 film *Stay Hungry*, resulting in little more than embarrassment for all concerned. Finally in 1976, Field proved her mettle as an actress in the TV movie *Sybil*, winning an Emmy for her virtuoso performance as a woman suffering from multiple personalities stemming childhood abuse. Following this triumph, Field entered into a long romance with Burt Reynolds, working with the actor in numerous films that were short on prestige but big at the box office. By 1979, Field found herself in another career crisis; now she had to jettison the "Burt Reynolds' girlfriend" image. She did so with her powerful portrayal of a small town union organizer in *Norma Rae* (1979), for which she earned her first Academy Award. At last taken completely seriously by fans and industryites, Field spent the next four years in films of fluctuating merit (she also ended her relationship with Burt Reynolds and married again), rounding out 1984 with her second Oscar for *Places in the Heart.* It was at the 1985 Academy Awards ceremony that Field earned a permanent place in the lexicon of comedy writers, talk show hosts and impressionists everywhere by reacting to her Oscar with a tearful "You LIKE me! You REALLY LIKE me!" Few liked her in such subsequent missteps as *Surrender* (1987) and *Soapdish* (1991), but as in past years, Field has always managed to cap her cinematic dry spells with one or two first-rate performances, such as her triumph as the doggedly determined mother of Tom Hanks in the 1994 box office bonanza *Forrest Gump.* **Selected Works:** *Absence of Malice* (1981), *Murphy's Romance* (1985), *Not Without My Daughter* (1990), *Steel Magnolias* (1989)

# W.C. Fields

**Born:** January 29, 1880; Philadelphia, PA
**Died:** December 25, 1946; Pasadena, CA

**Years Active in the Industry:** by decade

| 10s | 20s | 30s | 40s | 50s | 60s | 70s | 80s | 90s |
|-----|-----|-----|-----|-----|-----|-----|-----|-----|
|     |     |     |     |     |     |     |     |     |

A Charles Dickens character come to life, American comedian W. C. Fields ran away from a very abusive home at age 11. Continuous exposure to cold weather gave his voice its distinctive hoarse timbre, while constant fights with bigger kids gave Fields his trademarked red, battered nose. Perfecting his skills as a juggler until his fingers bled, Fields became a vaudeville headliner before the age of 21, traveling the world with his pantomimed comedy juggling act. After making his Broadway debut in the musical comedy *The Ham Tree* (1906), "W.C. Fields—Tramp Juggler", as he then billed himself, achieved the pinnacle of stage stardom by signing on with impresario Flo Ziegfeld. Somewhere along the line the comedian decided to speak on stage, to the everlasting gratitude of Fields fans everywhere. Though his flowery, pompous comic dialogue would seem

to have been indispensable, Fields did rather well in silent films (the first was the 1915 one-reeler *Pool Sharks*) thanks to his keen juggler's dexterity. In 1923, Fields took Broadway by storm with a part specially written for him in the musical *Poppy.* As larcenous snake-oil peddler Eustace McGargle, the comedian cemented his familiar stage and screen persona as Confidence Man Supreme. *Poppy* was filmed as *Sally of the Sawdust* by director D.W. Griffith in 1925; incredible as it may seem, Fields was not the first choice for the film, but once ensconced in celluloid (to use a Fields-like turn of phrase), he became a favorite of small-town and rural movie fans—even though it was those very fans who were often the targets of Field's brand of social satire. From 1930 through 1934, Fields appeared in talking feature films and short subjects, truly hitting his stride in *It's a Gift* (1934), which contained his famous "sleeping on the back porch" stage sketch. By this time, audiences responded to his characterization of the bemused, beleaguered everyman, attacked from all sides by nagging wives, bratty children, noisy neighbors and pesky strangers. His film characters also embraced his offstage adoration of alcoholic beverages; it is no news to anyone familiar with Fields that he was one of the more conspicuous and prolific drinkers of his time. In private life, Fields was perhaps Hollywood's most enigmatic personality. He was simultaneously an inveterate ad-libber and improviser who meticulously prepared his ad-libs and improvisations on paper ahead of time; a nasty, obstinate man surrounded by loyal and lasting friends; a racial bigot whose closest chums included Jewish entertainer Eddy Cantor and African American comic Bert Williams; a man disliked by directors and producers, beloved by most of his fellow actors; and a man who showed up late and hung over on the film set, but who never missed a performance and finished all his films on schedule and under budget. Though most fans prefer Fields' freewheeling starring comedies, which he wrote under such colorful pseudonyms as "Otis Cribblecrossis" and "Mathatma Kane Jeeves," he also shone in at least one prestige picture, MGM's *David Copperfield* (directed by George Cukor, who contrary to expectation got along splendidly with Fields), wherein Fields portrayed Mr. Micawber. A serious illness curtailed Fields' film work in 1936, but he made a comeback trading insults with ventriloquist's dummy Charlie McCarthy on radio in 1938. Fields' final films for Universal are a mixed bag; teaming with Mae West in *My Little Chickadee* (1940), was more surreal than funny, and *Never Give a Sucker an Even Break* (1941) makes very little sense, but *The Bank Dick* (1940), starring Fields as Egbert Souse is an unadulterated classic. Too ill to contribute anything but guest appearances in his final films, W. C. Fields died at age 67 on the one holiday he claimed he despised: Christmas Day.

# Ralph Fiennes

**Born:** December 22, 1962

**Years Active in the Industry:** by decade

| 10s | 20s | 30s | 40s | 50s | 60s | 70s | 80s | 90s |
|-----|-----|-----|-----|-----|-----|-----|-----|-----|
|     |     |     |     |     |     |     |     |     |

British actor Ralph Fiennes, known for his piercing stare and skeletal grin, received his training at the Royal Academy of Dramatic Arts. While performing with the Royal Shakespeare Com-

pany, Fiennes starred in the British TV movie *A Dangerous Man: Lawrence After Arabia*. This multi-faceted performance was observed with awe by director Steven Spielberg, who selected Fiennes to play the role of odious Nazi workcamp commandant Amon Goeth in *Schindler's List* (1993). To match existing photographs of this human vermin, the normally pencil-thin Fiennes gained a great deal of weight, resulting in an obscene but appropriate pot belly. Fiennes was so despicable in *Schindler* that one might suppose he would never be able to evoke pity from an audience—but he did just that in the role of the tragically flawed Charles Van Doren in director Robert Redford's *Quiz Show* (1994). In 1995, Fiennes was back on stage, starring in a Broadway production of *Hamlet*, and back on screen, starring in the futuristic thriller *Strange Days*.

# Harvey Fierstein

**Born:** June 6, 1954; New York, NY

**Years Active in the Industry:** by decade

| 10s | 20s | 30s | 40s | 50s | 60s | 70s | 80s | 90s |
|-----|-----|-----|-----|-----|-----|-----|-----|-----|
|     |     |     |     |     |     |     | ■   | ■   |

A graduate of the Pratt Institute, actor/playwright Harvey Fierstein made his off-Broadway debut in something called *Pork*. Outspokenly homosexual, Fierstein has successfully smashed

previous "gay" stereotypes with his deep, ratchety voice and his engaging "You got a problem with that?" belligerence. In 1982, Fierstein wrote and starred in the stage play *Torch Song Trilogy*, a bittersweet three-part comedy concerning the homosexual experience in the AIDS era; the play won two Tony Awards and became

one of longest-running Broadway productions in history, toting up 1,222 performances. Fierstein repeated his stage characterization of Arnold Beckoff for the heavily rewritten and severely shortened 1988 movie version of *Torch Song Trilogy*. The actor's crossover performances in mainstream roles have often been quite successful, notably his appearance as the likable cosmetician brother of Robin Williams in *Mrs. Doubtfire* (1993). In 1994, Fierstein co-starred in the short-lived TV series *Daddies' Girls*, unfortunately lapsing into some of the cliched gay mannerisms which he had so successfully avoided in his previous work. **Selected Works:** *Bullets over Broadway* (1994)

# Mike Figgis

**Born:** February 28, 1948; Kenya

**Years Active in the Industry:** by decade

| 10s | 20s | 30s | 40s | 50s | 60s | 70s | 80s | 90s |
|-----|-----|-----|-----|-----|-----|-----|-----|-----|
|     |     |     |     |     |     | ■   | ■   | ■   |

Born in Kenya, director Mike Figgis studied music in London, where he helped form a rhythm and blues group called the Gas Band (later, he would write the scores for many of his films). He went on to work with a experimental British comedy/variety group known as The People Show. When turned down by the National Film School, Figgis bankrolled his own 60-minute TV movie *The House* (1976), gaining entree into mainstream filmmaking. In 1988, he directed and wrote his first theatrical feature, *Stormy Monday*. Figgis is probably best known for his successful direction of the variable Richard Gere in *Internal Affairs* (1991) and the near-surrealistic *Mr. Jones* (1993). More recently, Figgis directed the 1994 remake of *The Browning Version* (1994). **Selected Works:** *Liebestraum* (1991), *Women and Men: Stories of Seduction, Part 2* (1991), *Women and Men: In Love There Are No Rules* (1991)

# Peter Finch (William Mitchell)

**Born:** September 28, 1916; London, England
**Died:** 1977

**Years Active in the Industry:** by decade

| 10s | 20s | 30s | 40s | 50s | 60s | 70s | 80s | 90s |
|-----|-----|-----|-----|-----|-----|-----|-----|-----|
|     |     | ■   | ■   | ■   | ■   | ■   |     |     |

Ruddy-faced British star Peter Finch was raised by relatives in France, India, and Australia after his parents divorced when he was two. He had several odd jobs during the Depression before working as a comedian's stooge in vaudeville. He began working in the legitimate theater in 1935, then in 1936 debuted onscreen in the Australian film *Dave and Dad Come to Town*. While sporadically appearing in Australian films over the next decade-plus, Finch continued working on stage and formed his own company; eventually he also became Australia's top radio actor. His work impressed Laurence Olivier, who brought him to London in 1949,

where he performed impressively on the stage and landed supporting roles in numerous films. In the mid-'50s he began getting better film roles, becoming one of Britain's leading male stars. Between 1956-71 he won the British Film Academy best actor award four times. For his portrayal of a gay doctor in *Sunday Bloody Sunday* (1971) he received a Best Actor Oscar nomination. His last film was *Network* (1976); during a promotional campaign for the film, he died of a massive coronary. That year he was posthumously awarded the Oscar for Best Actor—making him the first actor in Academy Award history to do so. **Selected Works:** *Flight of the Phoenix* (1965), *Nun's Story* (1959), *Pumpkin Eater* (1964)

# Albert Finney

**Born:** May 9, 1936; Salford, Lancashire, England

**Years Active in the Industry:** by decade

| 10$^s$ | 20$^s$ | 30$^s$ | 40$^s$ | 50$^s$ | 60$^s$ | 70$^s$ | 80$^s$ | 90$^s$ |
|------|------|------|------|------|------|------|------|------|

A 1955 graduate of the Royal Academy of Dramatic Arts, British actor Albert Finney arrived just at the time that the English theater was beginning to be peopled by young working-class actors seething with rage at the social structure and the broken promises of the prewar years. Finney could certainly have spent his career in a string of roles comparable to his hostile, hard-drinking working stiff in the 1959 film *Saturday Night and Sunday Morning*, but his classical and repertory training led him into the direction of versatility. As in the case of Paul Muni, no two Finney performances are exactly alike. He was the lusty, low-born protagonist of the internationally popular *Tom Jones* (1963), the cold-blooded murderer of *Night Must Fall* (1964), the well-to-do wayfaring husband of Audrey Hepburn in *Two For the Road* (1967), the superannuated title character in *Scrooge* (1970) and the immaculately groomed, insufferably self-important Belgian detective Hercule Poirot in *Murder on the Orient Express* (1974). Directing as well as starring in *Charlie Bubbles* (1968), Finney used this tale of a philandering author to convey the creature-comfort emptiness of privileged youth in a flashy, fragmentary style anticipating MTV by nearly two decades (he also allowed Liza Minelli her screen debut). In the 1980s Finney leaned precariously toward caricature in his role as a Donald Wolfit-style "grand old actor" in *The Dresser* (1981), and his John Huston-like interpretation of Daddy Warbucks in *Annie* (1982) (directed by Huston!); still, he was too good

an actor ever to make these outrageous performances anything less than believable. As active as ever in films, stage and TV work, Finney has been Oscar-nominated for *Shoot the Moon* (1982) and *Under the Volcano* (1984), and recently lent his master's touch to the roles of a shiftless American southerner in *Rich in Love* (1993) and a mild, theater-loving Irishman in *A Man of No Importance* (1994). **Selected Works:** *Green Man* (1991), *Miller's Crossing* (1990), *Playboys* (1992), *Browning Version* (1994)

# Linda Fiorentino (Clorinda Fiorentino)

**Born:** March 9, 1960; Philadelphia, PA

**Years Active in the Industry:** by decade

| 10$^s$ | 20$^s$ | 30$^s$ | 40$^s$ | 50$^s$ | 60$^s$ | 70$^s$ | 80$^s$ | 90$^s$ |
|------|------|------|------|------|------|------|------|------|

Before deciding upon an acting career, Philadelphia-born Linda Fiorentino briefly flirted with the notion of becoming a political science major. Fiorentino's fans consider her first year of filmmaking her most rewarding, and her inaugural movie role as an erstwhile, lovestruck artist in *Vision Quest* (1985) among her finest performances. After a conventional heroine stint in *Gotcha* (1985), Fiorentino raised eyebrows (and temperatures) as a mellow sculptress with a predilection for sex games in the bizarre *After Hours* (1985). After 1985, Fiorentino was seldom well served in pictures, hampered by too many nondescript performances in ensemble films. Then came her startling performance as the utterly conscienceless "black widow" Bridget in the low-budget sleeper *The Last Seduction* (1994). In a less rule-bound world, Fiorentino would have been nominated for an Academy Award, but unfortunately *The Last Seduction* was shown on cable TV before its theatrical release, thus rendered ineligible for the Oscar race. **Selected Works:** *Queens Logic* (1991), *Strangers* (1991), *Jade* (1995)

# Laurence Fishburne

**Born:** July 30, 1961; Augusta, GA

**Years Active in the Industry:** by decade

| 10$^s$ | 20$^s$ | 30$^s$ | 40$^s$ | 50$^s$ | 60$^s$ | 70$^s$ | 80$^s$ | 90$^s$ |
|------|------|------|------|------|------|------|------|------|

Laurence Fishburne is a dramatic actor whose star is on the rise. He was first drawn to acting at age ten, when he made his New York stage debut. When he was 12, Fishburne scored a major role in *Cornbread, Earl and Me* (1975). Since then, he has gone on to play lead or supporting roles under some of the most distinguished contemporary directors, including Coppola, Spielberg, and Spike Lee. In the late '70s and '80s, he acted in several of Coppola's films, most notably *Apocalypse Now* (1979). In the '90s he has become a most prolific actor, delivering strong supporting performances in such films as *Boyz N the Hood* (1991), *Searching* for *Bobby Fischer* (1993), and *Higher Learning* (1995). He received much acclaim and an Oscar nomination for his realistic portrayal of the abusive, meglomaniacal Ike Turner in *What's Love Got to Do with It?* (1993), a bio-pic about the struggles of singer Tina Turner. Although primarily a dramatic actor, Fishburne is not without a sense of fun, which was seen in his recurring role as Cowboy Curtis on *Pee-Wee's Playhouse*, an enormously popular children's television show that ran during the late 1980s. In addition to his work in cinema, Fishburne has also established a distinguished stage career, winning a Tony in 1992 for his role in August Wilson's *Two Trains Running*. **Selected Works:** *Class Action* (1991), *Deep Cover* (1992), *King of New York* (1990)

# Carrie Fisher

**Born:** October 21, 1956; Los Angeles, CA

**Years Active in the Industry:** by decade

| 10s | 20s | 30s | 40s | 50s | 60s | 70s | 80s | 90s |
|-----|-----|-----|-----|-----|-----|-----|-----|-----|

American actress Carrie Fisher, the daughter of singer Eddie Fisher and actress Debbie Reynolds, began her professional career performing in her mother's Las Vegas nightclub act when she was twelve. At 15 she dropped out of high school to pursue an acting career, and a year later appeared in the chorus of her mother's Broadway show *Irene*. After studying at London's Central School of Speech and Drama, she landed a small role in *Shampoo* (1975), in which her character seduces Warren Beatty. She became internationally famous as the result of playing Princess Leia, the female lead, in the enormous blockbuster *Star Wars* (1977) and its two sequels, *The Empire Strikes Back* (1980) and *Return of the Jedi* (1983). Her early success led to personal problems including drug addiction, a subject she later discussed in her semi-autobiographical novel *Postcards from the Edge*; she wrote the screenplay for the 1990 film version, which was directed by Mike Nichols. Fisher has gone on to write two additional novels. While maintaining an occasional screen career (including a nifty turn as Meg Ryan's best friend in *When Harry Met Sally* [1989]), she also works as an uncredited script "doctor" for Hollywood films. She was briefly married to singer-songwriter Paul Simon. **Selected Works:** *Hannah and Her Sisters* (1986), *Soapdish* (1991), *Sweet Revenge* (1990), *This Is My Life* (1992)

# Geraldine Fitzgerald

**Born:** November 24, 1914; Dublin, Ireland

**Years Active in the Industry:** by decade

| 10s | 20s | 30s | 40s | 50s | 60s | 70s | 80s | 90s |
|-----|-----|-----|-----|-----|-----|-----|-----|-----|

Geraldine Fitzgerald began acting professionally while in her late teens. There she met another newcomer, Orson Welles.

She began appearing in low-budget British films in 1934 and soon was a busy screen actress. In 1938 she moved to New York, where Welles gave her a role in the Mercury Theater production of *Wuthering Heights;* it was her first American role. Fitzgerald moved to Hollywood in 1939 and went on to play intense, sometimes stern leads in melodramas of the early '40s. For her work in the film *Wuthering Heights* (1939), she received a Best Supporting Actress Oscar nomination. Dissatisfied with the sorts of roles she was getting, she continuously fought with the studio bosses. Unfortunately, her efforts were unsuccessful, and by the early '50s her once-promising screen career had ground to a halt. Fitzgerald appeared in only a few films over the next two decades, but made a triumphant comeback in 1971, winning rave reviews for her performance in the Broadway revival of O'Neill's *Long Day's Journey Into Night*; after that she began appearing occasionally as a character actress in films. Her son is British director Michael Lindsay-Hogg. **Selected Works:** *Dark Victory* (1939), *Harry and Tonto* (1974), *Pawnbroker* (1965), *Watch on the Rhine* (1943), *Wilson* (1944)

# Paul Fix

**Born:** March 13, 1901; Dobbs Ferry, NY
**Died:** October 14, 1983; California

**Years Active in the Industry:** by decade

| 10s | 20s | 30s | 40s | 50s | 60s | 70s | 80s | 90s |
|-----|-----|-----|-----|-----|-----|-----|-----|-----|

The son of a brewery owner, steely-eyed American character actor Paul Fix went the vaudeville and stock-company route before settling in Hollywood in 1926. During the 1930s and 1940s he appeared prolifically in varied fleeting roles: a transvestite jewel thief in the Our Gang two-reeler *Free Eats* (1932), a lascivious zookeeper (appropriately named Heinie) in *Zoo in Budapest* (1933), a humorless gangster who puts Bob Hope "on the spot" in *The Ghost Breakers* (1940), and a bespectacled ex-convict who muscles his way into Berlin in *Hitler: Dead or Alive* (1943), among others. During this period, Fix was most closely associated with westerns, essaying many a villainous (or at least untrustworthy) role at various B-picture mills. In the mid-1930s, Fix befriended young John Wayne, and helped coach the star-to-be in the whys and wherefores of effective screen acting. Fix ended up appearing in 27 films with "The Duke," among them *Pittsburgh* (1942), *The Fighting Seabees* (1943), *Tall in the Saddle* (1944), *Back to Bataan* (1945), *Red River* (1948) and *The High and the Mighty* (1954). Busy in TV during the 1950s, Fix often found himself softening his bad-guy image to portray crusty old gents with golden hearts—characters not far removed from the real Fix, who by all reports was a 100% nice guy. His most familiar role was as the honest but often ineffectual sheriff Micah Torrance on the TV series *The Rifleman*. In the 1960s, Fix was frequently cast as sagacious backwoods judges and attorneys, as in *To Kill a Mockingbird* (1962). **Selected Works:** *Hondo* (1953)

# Robert Flaherty (Robert Joseph Flaherty)

**Born:** February 16, 1884; Iron Mountain, MI
**Died:** July 23, 1951; Vermont

**Years Active in the Industry:** by decade

| 10s | 20s | 30s | 40s | 50s | 60s | 70s | 80s | 90s |
|-----|-----|-----|-----|-----|-----|-----|-----|-----|

Michigan-born filmmaker Robert J. Flaherty was the son of a miner/prospector who dragged his son along on his many wealth-seeking expeditions to northernmost America. Thus the young Flaherty was exposed to many different cultures. As an adult, Flaherty offered his services as an explorer, guide and "native" specialist (though he reportedly despised that condescending word and avoided using it). From 1910 through 1916, he handled numerous expeditions into the Canadian wastes and wilderness on behalf of Sir William McKenzie, the builder of the Canadian Northern Railway. Allegedly it was McKenzie who suggested that Flaherty record his explorations on film. While fiddling with his camera out of boredom, Flaherty discovered that the Hudson Bay Eskimos, for whom he acted as interpreter, were natural and willing movie subjects. After several false starts, he produced his first feature-length record of Eskimo life, *Nanook of the North* in 1922. His backers were the Revillon brothers, who hoped to use the film to promote their fur business. While he claimed to disdain "showmanship," Flaherty was not above a little fakery in getting the best effect; Nanook's igloo is patently fake, while the famous harpooning sequence was comprised of several different harpooning expeditions filmed over a series of days. Nonetheless, *Nanook* was an impressive achievement, and though it was not (as has often been claimed) the first feature-length "true life" film ever made, it was the first big box office success of its genre. Four years after *Nanook*, Paramount Pictures commissioned Flaherty to make a similar record of Samoan life. Though unfamiliar with this South Seas culture (his specialty was the Great White North), Flaherty put together 1926's *Moana*; this was the film for which the word "documentary" was coined by British critic John Grierson. *Moana* was not a success, suggesting to Hollywood that *Nanook* had been a fluke. When engaged by MGM to make *White Shadows on the South Seas* in Tahiti in 1928, Flaherty found himself butting up against the highly organized studio system—and if there was anything Flaherty was *not*, it was highly organized. Flaherty handled only the documentary sequences, while W. S. Van Dyke was assigned the dramatic scenes; when Flaherty proved too slow for MGM's taste, Van Dyke took over the production completely. Flaherty's next project, the South Seas-based *Tabu*, was likewise a collaboration, this time with director F. W. Murnau. Again, Flaherty withdrew (the problems this time were monetary rather than artistic), but when released in 1931, *Tabu* was heralded as a Flaherty-Murnau production. Working solo on his next project, the Irish-filmed *Man of Aran* (1934), Flaherty went back to his catch-as-catch-can, "take your time" production technique. He went on to direct exteriors for Alexander Korda's *Elephant Boy* (1937), and produced and directed two subsequent "sponsored"

documentaries: *The Land* (1942) for the Department of Agriculture, and *Louisiana Story* (1948) for Standard Oil. After Flaherty's death in 1951, his wife Frances (daughter of Michigan geologist Dr. Lucien Hubbard) was the flamekeeper for her husband's memory, organizing reissues of his work for college seminars and lecture tours. One of the first presentations of the National Educational Television service (the forerunner of PBS) was a 13-week retrospective, *Flaherty and Film*.

# Dave Fleischer

**Born:** July 14, 1894; Austria
**Died:** June 25, 1979; Woodland Hills, CA

**Years Active in the Industry:** by decade

| 10s | 20s | 30s | 40s | 50s | 60s | 70s | 80s | 90s |
|-----|-----|-----|-----|-----|-----|-----|-----|-----|

A cutter at Pathé Films in the early teens, Dave Fleischer and his brother Max made the first of their imaginative "Out of the Inkwell" cartoons starring Koko the Clown for Paramount in 1916. They took this popular series into the 1920s, when they also devised the audience sing-along "Song Car-Tunes" series. In the '30s, the Fleischers had even greater success with their beloved characters Betty Boop (*Boop-Ooop-A-Doop, Is My Palm Red?*) and Popeye the Sailor (*Beware of Barnacle Bill, Popeye the Sailor Meets Sinbad the Sailor*). By the end of the decade, they branched out into animated features with an adaptation of Jonathan Swift's *Gulliver's Travels* (1939); they followed it with their insect-filled feature *Mr. Bug Goes To Town* (aka *Hoppity Goes To Town* [1941]), but found greater success with their handsome series of short Superman cartoons in the early '40s. After leaving Paramount, Dave Fleischer became head of animation at Columbia until 1944; afterwards, he served as a gag writer for live-action comedies at Universal into the late 1950s.

# Victor Fleming

**Born:** February 23, 1883; Pasadena, CA
**Died:** January 6, 1949; Cottonwood, AZ

**Years Active in the Industry:** by decade

| 10s | 20s | 30s | 40s | 50s | 60s | 70s | 80s | 90s |
|-----|-----|-----|-----|-----|-----|-----|-----|-----|

An assistant cameraman for director Alan Dwan in the early teens, Victor Fleming was a director of photography by 1915, and worked under D. W. Griffith's supervision as well as for Dwan on several films with Douglas Fairbanks. Fairbanks also starred in Fleming's first two films as a director: 1919's *When the Clouds Roll By,* co-directed by Theodore Reed, and his solo effort of the following year, *The Mollycoddle.* Fleming helmed several rugged actioners in the 1920s, and became a reliable craftsman of impersonal but handsome films at MGM in the 1930s. Skilled at films for young audiences—*Treasure Island, Captains Courageous, The Wizard of Oz*—Fleming was also a favorite director of actor Clark Gable, and having guided him in *Red Dust* (1932) and *Test Pilot* (1938), was brought in to take over the direction of *Gone with the Wind* (1939). His most notable films of the '40s were the Spencer Tracy films *Dr. Jekyll & Mr. Hyde* (1941), *Tortilla Flat* (1942), and *A Guy Named Joe* (1944), and his final film, *Joan of Arc* (1948), starring Ingrid Bergman.

# Robert Florey

**Born:** September 14, 1900; Paris, France
**Died:** May 16, 1979; Santa Monica, CA

**Years Active in the Industry:** by decade

| 10s | 20s | 30s | 40s | 50s | 60s | 70s | 80s | 90s |
|-----|-----|-----|-----|-----|-----|-----|-----|-----|

Frenchman Robert Florey began to assistant direct, write, and act in Swiss one-reelers in 1919; that same year, he directed *Isidore A La Deveine*. Back in France he assisted famed director Louis Feuillade. After acting in his serial *L'Orpheline* in 1921, he came to America and was technical advisor on *Monte Christo*. Florey then began writing shorts for comic Al St. John and resumed acting. In 1923 he directed a comic two-reeler, *Fifty-Fifty*, and began to assist several directors, including Joseph von Sternberg, King Vidor, and Louis Gasnier. Florey finished the direction of his script for *That Model from Paris* after Gasnier took ill, and in 1927 directed his first feature. While keeping busy helming low-budget films, Florey also made a quartet of fascinating avant-garde shorts: *The Life and Death of 9413—A Hollywood Extra* (1928), *The Loves of Zero* (1928), *Johann the Coffin Maker* (1928) and *Skyscraper Symphony* (1928). In 1929, he and Joseph Stanley co-directed the first Marx Brothers feature, *The Cocoanuts* (1929). Florey helmed a stream of programmers in the '30s and '40s, highlighted by his special affinity for horror: *Murders in the Rue Morgue* (1932) with Bela Lugosi, and *The Face Behind the Mask* (1941) and *The Beast with Five Fingers* (1946), both starring Peter Lorre. In the 1950s and '60s he turned his attention to television.

# Errol Flynn

**Born:** June 20, 1909; Hobart, Tasmania
**Died:** October 14, 1959; Vancouver, British Columbia

**Years Active in the Industry:** by decade

| 10s | 20s | 30s | 40s | 50s | 60s | 70s | 80s | 90s |
|-----|-----|-----|-----|-----|-----|-----|-----|-----|

It could be said that actor Errol Flynn was the original Tasmanian Devil. He was indeed born on the isle of Tasmania, the son of distinguished Australian marine biologist/zoologist Prof. Theodore Thomson Flynn. It was clear from childhood onward that Flynn would never follow in the scholarly footsteps of his dad. He

was expelled from a number of exclusive schools, though in all of them he displayed a keen propensity for athletics. Flynn couldn't make a go at government service work either, nor was he an efficient plantation overseer; he did however have an abiding love of the sea and sailing, an activity to which he'd habitually return after his many business ventures failed. Involved in several rather shady endeavors (he once reportedly had a hand in slave trading!), Flynn seemed destined to a life of dodging law enforcement officers when an Australian film producer happened to see photographs of the young man, which led to his being cast as Fletcher Christian in the low-budget film *In the Wake of the Bounty* (1933). Acting seemed a safer and more glamorous venture than his previous shenanigans, so Flynn headed to London for film work, stopping over for a year of stage repertory so that he could at least learn to act. Attaining a contract at Warner Bros. in 1935, Flynn languished in tiny parts until star Robert Donat suddenly dropped out of the big-budget swashbuckler *Captain Blood* (1935). Warners took a chance on Flynn, and the result was virtual overnight stardom. Though he'd make stabs at modern dress dramas and light comedies, Flynn was most effective in period costume, leading his men "into the Valley of Death" in *Charge of the Light Brigade* (1936), trading swordplay and sarcasm with Basil Rathbone in *The Adventures of Robin Hood* (1938), and even making the west safe for women and kids in *Dodge City* (1939). One of Warners' most popular and highest-priced stars by the early 1940s, Flynn was also one of the most troublesome; offscreen he was constantly entangled with fascinating young women and booze. The actor's chickens came home to roost in 1942 when Flynn was brought up on a statutory rape charge involving two teenage girls aboard his yacht. The whole affair reeked of a frame, and Flynn's lawyer was able to beat the rap by impugning the reputation of the teenage plaintiff. Instead of finding his career in ruins, Flynn was suddenly more popular than ever—particularly with female fans. But while Flynn's pictures continued to score at the box office, the actor himself was declining; already demoralized by his inability to fight in World War II due to a bad heart, Flynn's drinking and carousing increased, and though he remained a loyal and good friend to his cronies, the actor's overall behavior became erratic and downright abusive. By the time he starred in *The Adventures of Don Juan* (1949)—a role he could have done blindfolded ten years earlier—Flynn could barely remember a line or take a step without faltering. The 1950s found Flynn in a series of indifferent or misbegotten films, though he rallied late in the decade with excellent performances in *The Sun Also Rises* (1957), *The Roots of Heaven* (1958) and *Too Much too Soon* (1958). In the last film, Flynn played another self-destructive matinee idol, John Barrymore; it was virtually impossible to tell where the film ended and reality began. Strapped for cash during this period, Flynn, an erstwhile writer, penned his memoirs, *My Wicked Wicked Ways*, which if nothing else insured him a spot on the TV guest-star rounds; his final film was the pathetic Grade-Z *Cuban Rebel Girls* (1958), in which he appeared with his current girlfriend, 17-year-old Beverly Aadland. Flynn died four months after his fiftieth birthday; to quote Flynn biographer Tony Thomas, "To anyone who knew Flynn at all well it came as a shock but no surprise that he died at the age of fifty. The surprise was that he lasted that long." **Selected Works:** *Objective, Burma!* (1945), *Private Lives of Elizabeth and Essex* (1939), *Sea Hawk* (1940)

# Bridget Fonda

**Born:** January 27, 1964; Los Angeles, CA

**Years Active in the Industry:** by decade

| 10s | 20s | 30s | 40s | 50s | 60s | 70s | 80s | 90s |
|-----|-----|-----|-----|-----|-----|-----|-----|-----|

Bridget Fonda is the daughter of Peter Fonda, the granddaughter of Henry Fonda and the niece of Jane Fonda. So you expected her to go into the aluminum siding business? When Fonda

was seven, her parents divorced and she went to live with her mother, actress Susan Brewer; still, she has always maintained a strong relationship with her father, which (according to at least one network newsmagazine) borders on the telepathic at times. After studying drama at New York University, Fonda did some stage work, then made her movie bow in *Aria* (1988). Deceptively fragile and vulnerable looking, Fonda *can* play a victim if need be (as in *Single White Female* [1992]), but is more effectively cast as manipulators, neurotics and iconoclasts. She came to prominence as British goodtime-girl Mandy Rice Davies in *Scandal* (1989), and later convincingly essayed the almost unplayable part of an evening-gowned political assassin in *Point of No Return* (1993). Fonda has also displayed the Fonda family predilection for razor-sharp comic timing in such films as *Singles* (1992), *It Could Happen to You* (1994) and *The Road to Wellville* (1994). She has sus-

tained a long term romance with actor Eric Stolz, with whom she appeared in *Bodies, Rest & Motion* (1993). **Selected Works:** *Godfather, Part 3* (1990), *Strapless* (1990), *Little Buddha* (1994), *Camilla* (1994)

# Henry Fonda

**Born:** May 16, 1905; Grand Island, NE
**Died:** 1982

**Years Active in the Industry:** by decade

| 10s | 20s | 30s | 40s | 50s | 60s | 70s | 80s | 90s |
|-----|-----|-----|-----|-----|-----|-----|-----|-----|

With his honest, chiseled face and flat, unaccented voice, Nebraska born actor Henry Fonda exuded an air of quiet decency and amiable wisdom and served as the personification of Midwest-

ern American values. After two years of college (majoring in journalism) and work as an office boy, he starred in an amateur production at the Omaha Community Playhouse, then quit his job to remain with the theater company; he stayed for three years, receiving a small salary for acting and working as the manager's assistant. While acting in New England summer stock in 1928, Fonda met the University Players, a young group of actors who included Joshua Logan and Myron McCormick; he joined the group, as did James Stewart, Margaret Sullivan, and Mildred Natwick. With the group, Fonda developed his style as a leading man; he was often cast opposite Margaret Sullivan, whom he married in 1931 and divorced in 1933. Having had a couple of bit roles on Broadway, in 1934 he landed his first important Broadway part in the first edition of *New Faces;* later that year he got excellent reviews for his work in the title role of *The Farmer Takes a Wife*, and in 1935 went to Hollywood to reprise the role in his screen debut. His career took off with astonishing speed, and within a year he was a star, sustaining a very busy screen career in westerns, comedies, and melodramas before landing the most important role of his career, that of Tom Joad in *The Grapes of Wrath* (1940), for which he received a Best Actor Oscar nomination; by then he had gained international fame and admiration. Fonda served in the Navy from 1942-45, and was commissioned in the Pacific as an assistant operations and air combat intelligence officer; he became a lieutenant and was awarded a Bronze Star and a Presidential Citation. After World War II, he returned to the screen in more mature roles. Fonda had his greatest stage triumph in 1948 in the title role in Broadway's *Mister*

*Roberts;* he stayed with the play for three years, then (after a six-year absence from the screen) appeared in its film version (1955). Meanwhile, he suffered a tragedy when his wife, Frances Brokaw, whom he had married in 1936, committed suicide in a rest home after having a nervous breakdown; Brokaw was the mother of his children Jane and Peter Fonda, both of whom later became actors. Later, Fonda married three more times and divorced twice. He went on to work on stage, in films, and on TV, where he starred in the series *The Deputy* and *The Smith Family* and in specials and TV films. In 1978, the American Film Institute gave him its Life Achievement Award. He appeared with his daughter Jane in the film *On Golden Pond* (1982), for which he won his first Best Actor Oscar. In 1981 he was awarded a special Oscar for a half-century of "brilliant accomplishments and his enduring contribution to the art of motion pictures." **Selected Works:** *Lady Eve* (1941), *Mr. Roberts* (1955), *Ox-Bow Incident* (1943), *Twelve Angry Men* (1957), *Young Mr. Lincoln* (1939)

# Jane Fonda (Jane Seymour Fonda)

**Born:** December 21, 1937; New York, NY

**Years Active in the Industry:** by decade

| 10s | 20s | 30s | 40s | 50s | 60s | 70s | 80s | 90s |
|-----|-----|-----|-----|-----|-----|-----|-----|-----|
|     |     |     |     |     | ■   | ■   | ■   | ■   |

Hollywood legend has it that Bette Davis was forced to talk to a blank wall rather than her costar Henry Fonda during filming of her close-ups in *Jezebel;* the reason was that Fonda had returned to New York to attend the birth of his daughter Jane. A child of privilege, the young Jane Fonda exhibited the imperious, headstrong attitude and ruthlessness—as she demonstrated by bullying her younger brother Peter—that would distinguish both her film work and her private life. The teenage Jane wasn't keen on acting until she worked with her father in a 1954 Omaha Community Theatre production of *The Country Girl.* Slightly interested in pursuing a stage career at this point, Fonda nonetheless studied art both at Vassar and in Europe, returning to the states to work as a fashion model. Studying acting in earnest at Lee Strasberg's Actors' Studio, Fonda ultimately starred on Broadway in *Tall Story,* then made her film debut by recreating this stage appearance in 1960. A talented but not really distinctive player at this time, Fonda astonished everyone (none as much as her father) by becoming one of the first major American actresses to appear nude in a foreign film. This was *La Ronde* (1964), directed by her lover (and later her first husband) Roger Vadim. The event was heralded by a giant promotional poster in New York's theatre district, with Fonda's naked backside in full view for all Manhattan to see. Vadim decided to mold Fonda into a "sex goddess" in a series of lush but forgettable films; the best Fonda/Vadim collaboration was *Barbarella* (1968), which scored as much on the actress' sharp comic timing (already evidenced in such American pictures as *Cat Ballou* [1968]) as it did on her kinky costuming. In the late 1960s, Fonda underwent another career metamorphosis when she

took up the cudgel of the anti-Vietnam War movement. Her notorious visit to North Vietnam at the height of the conflict earned her the sobriquet "Hanoi Jane" as well as the enmity of virtually every ex-GI who fought in Southeast Asia (her belated 1988 apology for her behavior during this time was fully accepted only by those who'd spent the Vietnam era yelling "baby killer" and spitting on returning servicemen). Even so, Fonda's film stardom ascended in the early 1970s; in 1971, she won the first of two Oscars for her portrayal of a high-priced prostitute in *Klute* (her other Oscar was for *Coming Home* [1978]) and Fonda's career flourished despite a sub-rosa Hollywood campaign to discredit the actress and spread idiotic rumors about her subversive behavior (one widely circulated fabrication had Fonda destroying the only existing negative of *Stagecoach* because she despised John Wayne). In the 1980s, the actress realized several personal and career milestones: she worked with her father on film for the only time in *On Golden Pond* (1981); she married former peace activist Tom Hayden, assisting him in his successful bid for the California State Assembly; and she launched the first of several best-selling exercise videos. She also won an Emmy for her performance in the TV movie *The Dollmaker* (1984). After her marriage to Hayden ended, Fonda married media mogul Ted Turner in 1984, and began curtailing her film appearances; her most recent film appearance is 1989's *Stanley and Iris.* Though she's been sometimes seen performing the "tomahawk chop" at Atlanta Braves games, Fonda is no less the social activist in the 1990s than she was twenty years earlier. Her most recent project was the production of several "revisionist" dramatic specials and documentaries about the history of Native Americans, duly telecast on Turner's various worldwide cable services. **Selected Works:** *Barefoot in the Park* (1967), *China Syndrome* (1979), *Julia* (1977), *They Shoot Horses, Don't They?* (1969)

# Peter Fonda

**Born:** February 23, 1939; New York, NY

**Years Active in the Industry:** by decade

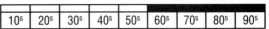

| 10s | 20s | 30s | 40s | 50s | 60s | 70s | 80s | 90s |
|-----|-----|-----|-----|-----|-----|-----|-----|-----|
|     |     |     |     |     | ■   | ■   | ■   | ■   |

Actor, producer, and director Peter Fonda, the son of actor Henry Fonda and brother of actress Jane Fonda, acted in college productions before debuting on Broadway in *Blood, Sweat and Stanley Poole* in 1961. He began appearing in films in 1963, at first playing strait-laced types. Beginning with *The Wild Angels* (1966), he soon cultivated a motorcycle-riding hippie-rebel image, culminating in the enormous hit *Easy Rider* (1969), which he also produced and co-wrote. His directorial debut was the lyrical western *The Hired Hand* (1971), in which he also starred; he has since directed several other films. His subsequent acting career has been dominated by low-budget films, and he has not gone on to achieve much of a reputation as a film actor. He is the father of actress Bridget Fonda. **Selected Works:** *Montana* (1990)

# Joan Fontaine (Joan de Beavoir de Havilland)

**Born:** October 22, 1917; Tokyo, Japan

**Years Active in the Industry:** by decade

| 10s | 20s | 30s | 40s | 50s | 60s | 70s | 80s | 90s |
|-----|-----|-----|-----|-----|-----|-----|-----|-----|
|     |     |     |     |     |     |     |     |     |

Born Joan de Beauvoir de Havilland, Joan Fontaine began her acting career in her late teens with various west coast stage companies under the name Joan Burfield. She also used that name when she made her fea-

ture film debut in *No More Ladies* (1935), in which she had a minor role. After two more years of stage work, she returned to the screen as Joan Fontaine, going on to appear primarily in B movies; two exceptions were *A Damsel in Distress* (1937) opposite Fred Astaire, and *Gunga Din* (1939) opposite Douglas Fairbanks, Jr. In the early '40s her career took off, largely due to leads in two Hitchcock films. She received Best Actress Oscar nominations for her work in Hitchcock's *Rebecca* (1940) and *The Constant Nymph* (1943), and won the Best Actress Oscar for her work in Hitchcock's *Suspicion* (1941). She went on from there to star in many films, at first playing innocent, well-bred types and later maturing into roles as sophisticated, worldly, often hot-headed or maliciously calculating women. Her sister was actress Olivia de Havilland, with whom she supposedly had many feuds (some of which were probably press inventions) in the '40s and '50s. She appeared in few films after 1958. Besides acting, Fontaine was also a licensed pilot, champion balloonist, prize-winning tuna fisherman, expert golfer, licensed interior decorator, and Cordon Bleu cook. The first three of her four husbands were actor Brian Aherne, producer William Dozier, and producer-screenwriter Collier Young. She authored an autobiography, *No Bed of Roses* (1978). **Selected Works:** *This Above All* (1942)

# Glenn Ford (Gwyllyn Samuel Newton)

**Born:** May 1, 1916; Quebec, Canada

**Years Active in the Industry:** by decade

| 10s | 20s | 30s | 40s | 50s | 60s | 70s | 80s | 90s |
|-----|-----|-----|-----|-----|-----|-----|-----|-----|
|     |     |     |     |     |     |     |     |     |

Though actor Glenn Ford was born in Canada, he was raised from age eight in California. He began his career working in high school plays, then landed roles as juveniles and eventually leads in various west coast productions. In 1939, he was tested and signed by Columbia, debuting onscreen that same year and going on to make many films over the next several years. His budding career was interrupted by service with the Marines in World War II, but he became very popular after the war as the result of his lead roles opposite Rita Hayworth in *Gilda* (1946) and Bette Davis in *A Stolen Life* (1946). From there his career was assured and he landed many lead roles, playing everything from comedy to drama to action-adventure. Ford tended to be cast as amiable and easygoing heroes who were nevertheless tough and introspective. He starred in the TV series *Cade's County* in 1971-72 and *The Family Holvak* in 1975. He was married to actress Eleanor Powell from 1943-59. **Selected Works:** *3:10 to Yuma* (1957), *Big Heat* (1953), *Blackboard Jungle* (1955), *Teahouse of the August Moon* (1956), *Sheepman* (1958)

# Harrison Ford

**Born:** July 13, 1942; Chicago, IL

**Years Active in the Industry:** by decade

| 10s | 20s | 30s | 40s | 50s | 60s | 70s | 80s | 90s |
|-----|-----|-----|-----|-----|-----|-----|-----|-----|
|     |     |     |     |     |     |     |     |     |

Harrison Ford began acting while in college, then worked briefly in summer stock. In the mid-60s he moved to Hollywood, where he signed as a contract player with Columbia and then Uni-

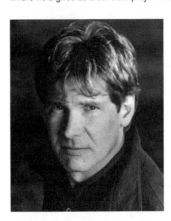

versal. After debuting onscreen in a bit as a bellboy in *Dead Heat on a Merry-Go-Round* (1966) he played secondary roles, typically as a cowboy, in several films of the late 60s and in such TV series as *Gunsmoke*, *The Virginian*, and *Ironside*. Depressed at the course of his career, he quit acting for a while and worked as a carpenter. His luck turned around when a casting director friend helped him get a part in George Lucas's *American Graffiti* (1973), a film which became a blockbuster and greatly increased his familiarity. Still, his career remained stagnant until Lucas cast him as space pilot Han Solo in the megahit *Star Wars* (1977), after which he became a minor star. He advanced to major stardom with his portrayal of action-adventure hero Indiana Jones in *Raiders of the Lost Ark* (1981), yet another enormous hit. Having appeared in several of the biggest money-makers of all time, he was able to pick and choose his roles in the 80s and 90s. In 1992 he signed an unprecedented $50 million contract to play CIA agent Jack Ryan in a series of five films based on the novels of Tom Clancy. His wife is screenwriter Melissa Mathison, whose credits include *E.T. The Extra-Terrestrial* (1982).

# John A. Ford (Sean Aloysius O'Fearna)

**Born:** February 1, 1895; Cape Elizabeth, Maine
**Died:** August 31, 1973; Palm Desert, CA

**Years Active in the Industry:** by decade

| 10ˢ | 20ˢ | 30ˢ | 40ˢ | 50ˢ | 60ˢ | 70ˢ | 80ˢ | 90ˢ |
|---|---|---|---|---|---|---|---|---|

Maine-born John Ford originally went to Hollywood in the shadow of his older brother Francis, an actor-writer-director who had worked on Broadway. Originally a laborer, a propman's assistant, and sometime stuntman for his brother, he rose to assistant director and became a supporting actor before turning to directing in 1917. He became best known for his westerns, of which he did dozens through the 1920s, but he didn't achieve status as a major director until the mid-1930's when his films for RKO (*The Lost Patrol* [1934], *The Informer* [1935]), 20th Century-Fox (*Young Mr. Lincoln* [1939], *The Grapes of Wrath* [1940]), and Walter Wanger (*Stagecoach* [1939]), won over the public, the critics, and earned various Oscars and Oscar nominations. His 1940's films included one military-produced documentary co-directed by Ford and cinematographer Greg Toland, *December 7th* [1943] which creaks badly today (especially compared with Frank Capra's *Why We Fight* series), a major war film (*They Were Expendable* [1945]), the historically-based drama *My Darling Clementine* (1946), and the "cavalry trilogy" of *Fort Apache* (1948) *She Wore a Yellow Ribbon* (1949), and *Rio Grande* (1950), all starring John Wayne. *My Darling Clementine* and the cavalry trilogy contain some of the most powerful images of the American West ever shot, and are considered definitive examples of the western. Ford also had a weakness for Irish and Gaelic subject matter, in which a great degree of sentimentality was evident, most notably *How Green Was My Valley* (1941) and *The Quiet Man* (1952), which was his most personal film, and one of his most popular as well; it also earned more Academy Awards and nominations than any other movie ever produced at Republic Pictures. Poor health dogged Ford's career during the 1950s, but he still managed to create *The Sun Shines Bright* (1953)—one of his favorite films, dealing with politics and race relations in the nineteenth century South—*Mogambo* (1953), and *The Searchers* (1956), which is considered one of the most powerful western dramas ever made. *The Horse Soldiers* (1959) showed some of Ford's flair, but was marred by production problems, and Ford later directed the John Wayne/Harry Morgan section of *How The West Was Won* (1963). His concern with social justice, which manifested itself in *The Sun Shines Bright* also became more evident during the early 1960s, in films such as *Sergeant Rutledge* (1960), *Donovan's Reef* (1963), and *Cheyenne Autumn* (1964), all of which sought to address problems of racial prejudice. Ford was the recipient of the first Life Achievement Award bestowed by the American Film Institute, and was the subject of Peter Bogdanovich's documentary, *Directed by John Ford*

(1971). **Selected Works:** *Fugitive* (1948), *Last Hurrah* (1958), *Mister Roberts* (1955)

# Wallace Ford (Samuel Jones Grundy)

**Born:** February 12, 1898; Batton, England
**Died:** 1966

**Years Active in the Industry:** by decade

| 10ˢ | 20ˢ | 30ˢ | 40ˢ | 50ˢ | 60ˢ | 70ˢ | 80ˢ | 90ˢ |
|---|---|---|---|---|---|---|---|---|

Wallace Ford's long, fruitful career as a lead and supporting actor of stage and screen spanned close to five decades, nearly four of which were spent in film. Ford had a childhood straight out of a Dickens novel. Raised in a London orphanage, much of his childhood was spent in assorted foster homes until he ran away at 11 to join a vaudeville troupe. In time, Ford made it to the legitimate theater. Once in the United States, Ford began appearing in many Broadway shows where he often played the lead. In 1930, he began his film career where he played character leads and supporting roles until the mid-'60s. **Selected Works:** *Informer* (1935), *Set-Up* (1949), *Shadow of a Doubt* (1943), *Spellbound* (1945), *Secret Command* (1944)

# Milos Forman

**Born:** February 18, 1932; Caslav, Czechoslovakia

**Years Active in the Industry:** by decade

| 10ˢ | 20ˢ | 30ˢ | 40ˢ | 50ˢ | 60ˢ | 70ˢ | 80ˢ | 90ˢ |
|---|---|---|---|---|---|---|---|---|

Czechoslovakian director Milos (pronounced Mee-losh) Forman lost his Jewish father and Protestant mother to Hitler's concentration camps. Raised by family members, Forman studied

at the Academy of Music and Dramatic Art in Prague, serving his professional apprenticeship as a writer of the pioneering Laterna Magika mixed-media presentations of the 1950s. Already an award-winning filmmaker thanks to a brace of short subjects, Forman directed his first feature, *Black Peter*, in 1963. *Loves of a Blonde* (1964) and *Firemen's Ball* (1968), two sweet-tempered films with a distinctively Czech sense of humor, brought Forman to the attention of the American critical intelligentsia. With the increasing artistic freedom prevalent in his country, Forman intended to spend the rest of his career in Prague, but when Russian troops marched into Czechoslovakia in 1968, the director shifted his base of operations to France. From here he went to Hollywood for his first English-language film, *Taking Off* (1971), a modest comedy about changing family values of the '70s (featured in the cast were such stars-to-be as Georgia Engel and Carly Simon). Forman directed the decathlon sequences of the multi-national Olympic documentary *Visions of Eight* (1972), then moved on to what many consider his masterpiece, *One Flew Over the Cuckoo's Nest* (1975). A celebration of the individual spirit staged in the depressing confines of a mental institution, *Cuckoo's Nest* became the first American film since *It Happened One Night* (1934) to win Oscars in all the major categories—including Best Director. *Hair* (1979), the overdue filmization of the 1967 Broadway rock musical, could have been anachronistic in lesser hands, but under Forman's guidance became a delectable time-capsule of what the '60s seemed to represent to those who lived through it. *Ragtime* (1981) had potential for greatness; unfortunately, post-production cutting whittled down what could have been a fascinating mosaic of the early 20th century into the wearisome story of a black man's quest for justice. With *Amadeus* (1984), Forman returned to Prague for the first time since his 1968 exile, filming location shots for a liberal retelling of the life of Mozart (as seen through the eyes of Mozart's mortal enemy Salieri). *Amadeus* won another Oscar for Forman, not to mention the Academy statuette for Best Picture. Since this film, Forman has continued his activities as director of Columbia University's film division; he has also acted in other director's films and has himself directed *Valmont* (1989), the least famous variation of the thrice-filmed *Les Liasons Dangereuse*.

# Frederic Forrest

**Born:** December 23, 1938; Waxahachie, TX

**Years Active in the Industry:** by decade

| 10s | 20s | 30s | 40s | 50s | 60s | 70s | 80s | 90s |
|-----|-----|-----|-----|-----|-----|-----|-----|-----|
|     |     |     |     |     |     | ■ | ■ | ■ |

Frederic Forrest studied acting with Sanford Meisner and Lee Strasberg. He then began working off-Broadway and also in experimental theater. Among the troupes he became involved with was Tom O'Horgan's La Mama troupe, with whom he appeared in the screen version of their stage show *Futz* (1972). He was spotted by a casting director while appearing in a show in Los Angeles, and was subsequently given the role of a young Indian in *When the Legends Die* (1972), for which he received a Golden Globe Best Newcomer nomination. Forrest then went on to work with impressive directors in disappointing films. He broke through with his roles as the "cook" in Francis Ford Coppola's *Apocalypse Now* (1979) and as Bette Midler's lover in *The Rose* (1979), for which he received an Oscar nomination. He was the first actor signed by Coppola as a contract player at Zoetrope Studios, but financial confusion there made the contract unimportant after only two films (*One From the* 

*Heart*, [1982], and *Hammett* [1983]). For the rest of the '80s he tended to play burned-out, introspective types, though he had some impressive TV work such as *Lonesome Dove*. During the '90s, Forrest has been working as a character actor in such films as *The Two Jakes* (1990), *Citizen Cohn* (1992), and *Falling Down* (1993). **Selected Works:** *Habitation of Dragons* (1992), *Rain Without Thunder* (1993)

# Robert Forster

**Born:** July 13, 1941; Rochester, NY

**Years Active in the Industry:** by decade

| 10s | 20s | 30s | 40s | 50s | 60s | 70s | 80s | 90s |
|-----|-----|-----|-----|-----|-----|-----|-----|-----|
|     |     |     |     |     | ■ | ■ | ■ | ■ |

After attending several universities, American actor Robert Forster took to the stage; his real name was Foster, but he added the extra "r" in order to stand out. Stand out he did in a 1967 revival of *A Streetcar Named Desire*, which led to his being cast in John Huston's film *Reflections in A Golden Eye* (1969), as the handsome object of lust for bisexual Army officer Marlon Brando. *Reflections* (1967) required a nude scene for Forster, as did his subsequent picture *Medium Cool* (1969), in which he played a socially conscious cameraman patterned after Haxwell Wexler (who directed the film). Frequently described as the "new John Garfield," Forster found himself cast in the Garfield mold as a 1930s private eye in the 1971 TV movie *Banyon*, which led to a brief series in 1972. Amidst numerous stage and film roles, Forster has made periodic returns to series TV; in 1974 he starred in the adventure series *Nakia*, and in 1987 he co-starred as Gumshoe, a comic-book character come to life, on the fantasy TV series *Once a Hero* (which lasted all of three weeks), and has since made several direct-to-video films. In 1985, Forster made his first foray into film directing with *Harry's Machine* (aka *Hollywood Harry*). **Selected Works:** *29th Street* (1991), *Committed* (1991), *Diplomatic Immunity* (1991)

# Bob Fosse (Robert Louis Fosse)

**Born:** June 23, 1927; Chicago, IL
**Died:** September 23, 1987

**Years Active in the Industry:** by decade

| 10s | 20s | 30s | 40s | 50s | 60s | 70s | 80s | 90s |
|-----|-----|-----|-----|-----|-----|-----|-----|-----|
|     |     |     |     | ■ | ■ | ■ | ■ |     |

The son of a vaudeville performer, director, choreographer, dancer, and actor Bob Fosse began his own distinguished career as a child; by the time he was 13 he was a seasoned veteran of burlesque shows. After serving in World War II, he and his first wife, Mary-Ann Niles, began working as a dance team in nightclubs and stage musicals. Soon he began appearing as a dancer and actor in Hollywood films, including *Kiss Me Kate* (1953) and *My Sister*

*Eileen* (1955). He separated from his wife and married Joan Mc-Cracken, his dance partner. In 1954 he choreographed the Broadway show *Pajama Game,* for which he won a Tony; this began a successful period as a Broadway choreographer, during which he also occasionally choreoraphed the screen versions of Broadway shows. In 1959 he directed the Broadway musical *Redhead* (which starred his third wife, dancer Gwen Verdon), going on to direct many other shows. In 1969 he directed his first film, *Sweet Charity;* he won the Best Director Oscar for his second effort, *Cabaret* (1972). In the mid-'70s he suffered a coronary as the result of overwork and substance abuse; after recovering he continued directing for the stage and screen. Included is the cynically semi-autobiographical film *All That Jazz* (1979), a chronicle of the events leading up to his heart attack, and *Star 80* (1983), the story of murdered *Playboy* Playmate Dorothy Stratten. **Selected Works:** *Daughter of the Puma* (1994), *Lenny* (1974)

# Jodie Foster (Alicia Christian Foster)

**Born:** November 19, 1962; Los Angeles, CA

**Years Active in the Industry:** by decade

| 10ˢ | 20ˢ | 30ˢ | 40ˢ | 50ˢ | 60ˢ | 70ˢ | 80ˢ | 90ˢ |
|---|---|---|---|---|---|---|---|---|
| | | | | | | | | |

The youngest of four children born to Evelyn "Brandy" Foster, Jodie Foster was christened Alicia, but earned her "proper" name when her siblings insisted upon Jodie. A stage mother supreme, Brandy Foster dragged her kids from one audition to another, securing work for son Buddy in the role of Ken Berry's son on the popular sitcom *Mayberry RFD.* It was on *Mayberry* that Jodie, already a professional thanks to her stint as the Coppertone girl (the little kid whose swimsuit was being pulled down by a dog on the ads for the suntan lotion), made her TV debut in a succession of minor roles. Buddy would become disenchanted with acting, but Jodie stayed at it, taking a mature, businesslike approach to the disciplines of line memorization and following directions that belied her years. Janet Waldo, a voice actress who worked on the 1970s cartoon series *The Addams Family,* would recall in later years that Foster, cast due to her raspy voice in the male role of Puggsley Addams, took her job more seriously and with more dedication than many adult actors. After her film debut in Disney's *Napoleon and Samantha* (1972), Foster was much in demand, though usually in "oddball" child roles by virtue of her unstarlike facial features. She was cast in the Tatum O'Neil part in the 1974 TV series based on the film *Paper Moon*—perhaps the last time she would ever be required to pattern her performance after someone else's. In 1975, Foster was cast in her most controversial role to date, as the preteen prostitute Iris in Martin Scorcese's *Taxi Driver.* Both the director and the on-set supervisors made certain that she would not be psychologically damaged by the sleaziness of her character's surroundings and lifestyle; alas, the film apparently did irreparable damage to the psyche of at least one of its viewers. In 1981, John Hinckley Jr. attempted to assassinate President Rea-

gan, and when captured, Hinckley insisted he'd done it to impress Foster—a recreation of a similar incident in *Taxi Driver.* The resultant negative publicity made Foster (who'd been previously stalked by Hinckley) extremely sensitive to the excesses of the media; through absolutely no fault of her own, she'd become the quarry of every tabloid and "investigative journalist" in the world. Thereafter, she'd stop an interview cold whenever the subject of Hinckley was mentioned, and even ceased answering fan mail or giving out autographs. This (justifiable) shunning of "the public" had little if any effect on Foster's professional life; after graduating cum laude from Yale University, the actress appeared in a handful of "small" films of little commercial value just to recharge her acting batteries, then came back stronger than ever with her Oscar-winning performance in *The Accused* (1988), in which she played a rape victim seeking justice. Foster followed up this triumph with another Oscar for her work as FBI investigator Clarisse Starling (a role turned down by several prominent actresses) in the 1991 chiller *The Silence of the Lambs.* Not completely satisfied professionally, Foster went into directing with a worthwhile drama about (perhaps significantly) the tribulations of a child genius, *Little Man Tate* (1991)—a logical extension, according to some movie insiders, of Foster's tendency to wield a great deal of authority on the set. Foster has in recent years managed to balance the artistic integrity of her award-winning work with the more commercial considerations of such films as *Maverick* (1994). She made her debut as producer in 1994 with the acclaimed *Nell,* in which she also gave a stunning Oscar-nominated performance as a backwoods wild child brought into the modern world. Still smarting from the public scrutiny thrust upon her by the Hinckley incident, Foster keeps out of the glare of publicity as much as possible, by dressing simply and by frequenting malls and fast-food restaurants instead of all the "hip" Hollywood hot-spots. **Selected Works:** *Alice Doesn't Live Here Anymore* (1974), *Sommersby* (1993)

# Meg Foster

**Born:** May 10, 1948; Reading, PA

**Years Active in the Industry:** by decade

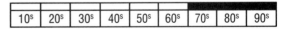

| 10ˢ | 20ˢ | 30ˢ | 40ˢ | 50ˢ | 60ˢ | 70ˢ | 80ˢ | 90ˢ |
|---|---|---|---|---|---|---|---|---|
| | | | | | | | | |

American actress Meg Foster was trained at New York's Neighborhood Playhouse, a rigorous and exacting establishment that lets practically everyone in for one year and practically no one in for their second year. Foster survived the entire program with the steely-eyed grit that characterized her best film and stage roles. With such notable exceptions as *The Osterman Weekend* (1983) and *The Emerald Forest* (1986), many of Foster's films have been cheapjack exploitation efforts unworthy of her skills. She has racked up her most impressive credits on TV, including the lead role of Hester Prynne in the 1979 PBS multi-part adaptation of *The Scarlet Letter.* In 1982, she was cast as Chris Cagney opposite Tyne Daly's Mary Beth Lacey on the TV series *Cagney and Lacey.*

When the series went into its second season, Foster was replaced by Sharon Gless; the official reason was that she played her character "too tough, too hard," but unofficial sources noted that audiences perceived Foster's performance as too "butch." This setback slowed down her TV career though she was always welcome (if not always well served) on the big screen. **Selected Works:** *Blind Fury* (1990), *Diplomatic Immunity* (1991), *Jezebel's Kiss* (1990), *Relentless 2: Dead on* (1991), *Shrunken Heads* (1994)

# Douglas V. Fowley

**Born:** May 30, 1911; New York, NY

**Years Active in the Industry:** by decade

| 10s | 20s | 30s | 40s | 50s | 60s | 70s | 80s | 90s |
|-----|-----|-----|-----|-----|-----|-----|-----|-----|

     Born and raised in the Greenwich Village section of New York, Douglas Fowley did his first acting while attending St. Francis Xavier Military Academy. A stage actor and nightclub singer/dancer during the regular theatrical seasons, Fowley took such jobs as athletic coach and shipping clerk during summer layoff. He made his first film, *The Mad Game*, in 1933. Thanks to his somewhat foreboding facial features, Fowley was usually cast as a gangster, especially in the Charlie Chan, Mr. Moto and Laurel and Hardy B films churned out by 20th Century-Fox in the late 1930s and early 1940s. One of his few romantic leading roles could be found in the 1942 Hal Roach "streamliner" *The Devil with Hitler*. While at MGM in the late 1940s and early 1950s, Fowley essayed many roles both large and small, the best of which was the terminally neurotic movie director in *Singin' in the Rain* (1952). Fowley actually did sit in the director's chair for one best-forgotten programmer, 1960's *Macumba Love*, which he also produced. On television, Fowley made sporadic appearances as Doc Holliday in the weekly series *Wyatt Earp* (1955-61). In the mid-1960s, Fowley grew his whiskers long and switched to portraying Gabby Hayes-style old codgers in TV shows like *Pistols and Petticoats* and *Detective School: One Flight Up*, and movies like *Homebodies* (1974) and *North Avenue Irregulars* (1979); during this period, the actor changed his on-screen billing to Douglas V. Fowley. **Selected Works:** *High and the Mighty* (1954)

# Edward Fox

**Born:** April 13, 1937; London, England

**Years Active in the Industry:** by decade

| 10s | 20s | 30s | 40s | 50s | 60s | 70s | 80s | 90s |
|-----|-----|-----|-----|-----|-----|-----|-----|-----|

     The brother of film star James Fox, British actor Edward Fox spent the first few years of his career in the shadow of his longer-established younger sibling. All this changed when Edward was cast as the charismatic but cold-blooded international assassin The Jackal in 1973's *Day of the Jackal;* so determined was Fox's

character to go through with his assignment to kill Charles De Gaulle that at times the audience believed he was actually going to get away with it! Never a major box-office attraction, Fox has aged into a dynamic character player, busy throughout the 1980s in such films as *Never Say Never Again* (1983), *The Shooting Party* (1984) and *Wild Geese II*. In 1991, Fox could be seen by TV fans as King Richard in *Robin Hood,* the "rival" production to Kevin Costner's *Robin Hood: Prince of Thieves*. **Selected Works:** *Crucifer of Blood* (1991), *Dresser* (1983), *Gandhi* (1982), *Go-Between* (1971), *Soldier of Orange* (1978)

# James Fox (William Fox)

**Born:** May 19, 1939; London, England

**Years Active in the Industry:** by decade

| 10s | 20s | 30s | 40s | 50s | 60s | 70s | 80s | 90s |
|-----|-----|-----|-----|-----|-----|-----|-----|-----|

     Born into a theatrical family, British actor James Fox made his film bow as a child actor in 1950, using his own name, William Fox. Fox's first movie was *The Miniver Story* (1950), a Hollywood-financed sequel to 1942's *Mrs. Miniver*. The best of the actor's earliest appearance was in *The Magnet* (1950), in which 11-year-old Fox played a fun-loving young boy at play with his mates. Fox changed his first name to James when he began assuming adult roles in the early 1960s, a period in which he played upper-class types. It was in one of these roles that Fox appeared with Dirk Bogarde in the brooding, Freudian Harold Pinter drama *The Servant* (1963); that same year, Fox appeared in the "angry young man" exercise *The Loneliness of the Long Distance Runner*, which starred Richard Harris. With his *Servant* vis-a-vis Sarah Miles, Fox headlined an international cast in the comedy extravaganza *Those Magnificent Men in Their Flying Machines* (1965). Fox continued in films into the 1980s, generally in class-A items like *A Passage to India* (1984) and *The Russia House* (1989). Fox continues to play old-blood aristocrats in films, most recently as the foolishly fascistic lord of the manor in *Remains of the Day* (1993); he also appeared in *Mrs. Parker and the Vicious Circle* (1994) and *Heart of Darkness* (1994). **Selected Works:** *Afraid of the Dark* (1992), *Crucifer of Blood* (1991), *Hostage* (1992), *Patriot Games* (1992)

# Michael J. Fox

**Born:** June 9, 1961; Edmonton, Alberta, Canada

**Years Active in the Industry:** by decade

| 10s | 20s | 30s | 40s | 50s | 60s | 70s | 80s | 90s |
|-----|-----|-----|-----|-----|-----|-----|-----|-----|

     Canadian born actor Michael J. Fox is one of the few actors who began in a television sitcom to make it big in the movies. He began his acting career at the age of 15 when he landed a role in the hit Canadian TV show *Leo and Me*. Later he moved to Hollywood, where appeared in two now-obscure films, Disney's first PG-rated movie

*Midnight Madness* (1980)—his screen debut—and *Class of 1984* (1982). Fox became a star when he got the part of Alex P. Keaton, the conservative yuppie son of former flower-child parents, in the hit TV sitcom *Family Ties* (1982-89). After some forgettable teen fare, he got his big break in feature films when he was chosen to replace Eric Stolz in the title role of time-traveling teen Marty McFly in Steven Spielberg's mega-hit *Back to the Future* (1985); he went on to star in the film's two sequels (1989 and 1990), amassing a $40 million fortune for his share of the three films. A turn toward dramatic roles (*Light of Day* [1987], *Bright Lights, Big City* [1988], *Casualties of War* [1989]) wasn't nearly so successful commercially, despite his earnest performances, and his recent comedy efforts have been unimpressive (*Life with Mikey* [1993], *For Love or Money* [1993], *Greedy* [1994]). Fox is married to his former TV-girlfriend from *Ties* Tracey Pollan. **Selected Works:** *Doc Hollywood* (1991), *Life with Mikey* (1993), *Where the Rivers Flow North* (1994)

# John Frankenheimer

**Born:** February 19, 1930; Malba, NY

**Years Active in the Industry:** by decade

| 10ˢ | 20ˢ | 30ˢ | 40ˢ | 50ˢ | 60ˢ | 70ˢ | 80ˢ | 90ˢ |
|---|---|---|---|---|---|---|---|---|
| | | | | ■ | ■ | ■ | ■ | ■ |

Having worked on documentary shorts in the early 1950s while in the Air Force, John Frankenheimer began directing for television, including the prestigious *Playhouse 90* series. He made his first feature in 1957, but returned to television for another four years before finally entering films for good with the social drama *The Young Savages* (1961) starring Burt Lancaster. Over the '60s, Frankenheimer made several popular, well crafted, and intelligent films with Lancaster, most notably the prison drama *Birdman of Alcatraz* (1962) and the thriller *Seven Days in May* (1964). He also directed two of the decade's strongest films: the satiric political thriller *The Manchurian Candidate* (1962) and the psychological horror tale *Seconds* (1966). Frankenheimer faced several career setbacks in the '70s, but also made such accomplished—and neglected—films as *The Iceman Cometh* (1973), *99 and 44/100% Dead* (1974), and *French Connection II* (1975). He scored a hit with his thriller *Black Sunday* in 1977 but has made mostly unremarkable actioners since. **Selected Works:** *Train* (1965), *Fixer* (1968)

# Freddie Francis (Frederick Francis)

**Born:** 1917; Islington, London, England

**Years Active in the Industry:** by decade

| 10ˢ | 20ˢ | 30ˢ | 40ˢ | 50ˢ | 60ˢ | 70ˢ | 80ˢ | 90ˢ |
|---|---|---|---|---|---|---|---|---|
| | | | ■ | ■ | ■ | ■ | ■ | ■ |

A clapper boy in British films while a teenager, Freddie Francis became a camera assistant and in the mid-1950s was an operator for Oswald Morris, the director of photography on John Huston's *Moulin Rouge* (1953) and *Beat the Devil* (1954); he also directed second-unit footage for Huston's *Moby Dick* (1956). As a director of photography himself, Francis worked for directors Karel Reisz (*Saturday Night and Sunday Morning* [1961], *Night Must Fall* [1964]), Jack Cardiff (*Sons and Lovers* [1960]), and fellow Huston-alumnus Jack Clayton (*Room at the Top* [1959], *The Innocents* [1961]). In the early 1960s he began directing but has occasionally shot films for such directors as Reisz (*The French Lieutenant's Woman* [1981]) and David Lynch (*The Elephant Man* [1980], *Dune* [1984]). As a director, Francis has specialized in horror films, notably at Hammer (*Paranoiac* [1963], *Dracula Has Risen from the Grave* [1968]) and for producers Max J. Rosenberg and Milton Subotsky (*The Skull* [1965], *The Psychopath* [1966], and the anthology films *Dr. Terror's House of Horrors* [1965], *Torture Garden* [1967], and *Tales from the Crypt* [1972]). **Selected Works:** *Cape Fear* (1991), *Glory* (1989), *School Ties* (1992), *Man in the Moon* (1991), *Princess Caraboo* (1994)

# Brendan Fraser

**Born:** 1967; Indianapolis, IN

**Years Active in the Industry:** by decade

| 10ˢ | 20ˢ | 30ˢ | 40ˢ | 50ˢ | 60ˢ | 70ˢ | 80ˢ | 90ˢ |
|---|---|---|---|---|---|---|---|---|
| | | | | | | | | ■ |

Born in Indianapolis, darkly handsome actor Brendan Fraser is the son of a Canadian tourism official. After an early appearance in *Dogfight* (1991), Fraser got his break in 1992's *Encino Man* as a Stone Age man unfrozen in modern-day California and gained audience prominence with in diverse roles such as a Jewish football player in an all-WASP environment in *School Ties* (1992), a grunged-out musician in *Airheads* (1994), a Harvard student who loses his thesis in *With*

*Honors* (1994), and a quirky baseball phenom in *The Scout* (1994). Fraser has proven equally capable in both comedic and dramatic roles; according to one magazine article, he seeks out roles combining "silliness and sexiness."

# William Frawley

**Born:** February 26, 1887; Burlington, IA
**Died:** March 3, 1966

**Years Active in the Industry:** by decade

| 10s | 20s | 30s | 40s | 50s | 60s | 70s | 80s | 90s |
|-----|-----|-----|-----|-----|-----|-----|-----|-----|
|     |     |     |     |     |     |     |     |     |

American actor William Frawley had hopes of becoming a newspaperman, but was sidetracked by a series of meat-and-potatoes jobs. At 21, he found himself in the chorus of a musical comedy in Chicago; his mother forced him to quit, but Frawley had already gotten greasepaint in his veins. Forming a vaudeville act with his brother Paul, Frawley hit the show business trail; several partners later (including his wife Louise), Frawley was a headliner, and in later years laid claim to having introduced the beer-hall chestnut "Melancholy Baby." Whether he introduced the song or not, chances are Frawley sang it incessantly, for when he wasn't on stage he could usually be found propped up against a bar rail. Entering films in the early 1930s (he'd made a few desultory silent-movie appearances), Frawley became typecast as irascible, pugnacious Irishmen, not much of a stretch from his off-camera personality. Though he worked steadily into the late 1940s, Frawley's drinking got the better of him, and by 1951 most producers found him virtually unemployable. Not so Desi Arnaz, who cast Frawley as neighbor Fred Mertz on the *I Love Lucy* TV series when Gale Gordon proved unavailable. Frawley promised to stay away from the booze during filming, and in turn Arnaz promised to give Frawley time off whenever the New York Yankees were in the World Series (a rabid baseball fan, Frawley not only appeared in a half dozen baseball films, but also was one of the investors of the minor league Hollywood Stars ball team). Frawley played Fred Mertz until the last *I Love Lucy* episode was filmed in 1960, then moved on to a five-year assignment as Bub, chief cook and bottle-washer to son-in-law Fred MacMurray's all male household on *My Three Sons.* Though Bub was a more benign character than Fred Mertz, Frawley remained as cantankerous as ever in private life; he had few friends beyond his coworkers (some weren't overly fond of him, notably his *Lucy* co-star Vivian Vance), and took delight in being as profane and opinionated as possible. Still, despite his many "warts," Frawley had become a highly regarded and beloved TV star at the time of his death. When a close associate recalled that Frawley "hated everybody and everything," he did so with a curious tone of affection. **Selected Works:** *General Died at Dawn* (1936), *Monsieur Verdoux* (1947), *Miracle on 34th Street* (1947)

# Stephen Frears

**Born:** June 20, 1941; Leicester, England

**Years Active in the Industry:** by decade

| 10s | 20s | 30s | 40s | 50s | 60s | 70s | 80s | 90s |
|-----|-----|-----|-----|-----|-----|-----|-----|-----|
|     |     |     |     |     |     |     |     |     |

Internationally recognized British filmmaker Stephen Frears is known for his keen imagery and his provocative stories. Before getting involved with film, Frears studied law at Cambridge; while there he got involved with London's Royal Court Theater. In 1966 the unemployed Frears was offered a job as assistant director by Karel Reisz, with whom he worked (along with Lindsey Anderson and Albert Finney) until 1972, when he made his directorial debut with the satirical *Gumshoe.* Frears then went on to create a large body of television work. Some of his most famous theatrical films were in fact originally designed for television—most notably, *My Beautiful Laundrette* (1985), a satirical comedy of manners that earned him international recognition. All of Frear's early and subsequent work contains certain elements that distinguish his films: sly references to classic genres; economically told stories; sympathetic, often stylized portraits of people on society's fringe (both socially and sexually); and intense but seldom over-the-top performances. In 1988, Frears released his first Hollywood film *Dangerous Liasons,* a critical and box office success that won Oscars for its screenplay, art direction, and costumes. He then made *The Grifters* (1990), a gritty homage to film noir that won lead actresses Anjelica Huston and Annette Bening Oscar nominations; Frears himself was also nominated as Best Director. Although his first few films gained little recognition outside of Britain, his more recent films (including *The Snapper* [1993]) prove that he is truly an international talent. **Selected Works:** *Hero* (1992) *Mary Reilly* (1995)

# Arthur Freed (Arthur Grossman)

**Born:** September 9, 1894; Charleston, SC
**Died:** April 12, 1973; Hollywood, CA

**Years Active in the Industry:** by decade

| 10s | 20s | 30s | 40s | 50s | 60s | 70s | 80s | 90s |
|-----|-----|-----|-----|-----|-----|-----|-----|-----|
|     |     |     |     |     |     |     |     |     |

American filmmaker Arthur Freed began his lifelong love affair with popular music while working as a song plugger and vaudeville performer. His first big hit as a songwriter was the plaintive ballad "I Cried For You." After playing the nightclub circuit, Freed was hired by MGM in 1928 to write songs for the studio's new musical department. Usually teamed with Nacio Herb Brown, Freed was responsible for most of the top tunes heard in MGM's early-talkie manifest, including "Broadway Melody," "My Lucky Star," "Wedding of the Painted Doll," and the Oscar-winning "Singin' in the Rain." Even after the first cycle of musical films had passed, Freed was still churning out such classics as "Temptation." Appointed associate producer of MGM's 1939 *The Wizard of Oz,* Freed became fascinated with the concept of the "integrated" musical, wherein the songs are important to the storyline (and vice versa) rather than being mere disposable "highlights." After *Wizard*, Freed was given his own production unit at MGM, where he immediately went to work changing the face of filmed musicals. When one uses the phrase "MGM musicals," one is generally speaking of such Freed-produced films as *Meet Me in St. Louis* (1944) and *The Harvey Girls* (1948) rather than the conventional operetta-style endeavors filmed by the rival Joe Pasternak unit. Freed developed and nurtured such talents as Judy Garland, Gene Kelly, Debbie Reynolds, Stanley Donen, Vincente Minelli, Andre Previn and Michael Kidd. He also gave Fred Astaire's flagging career a shot in the arm with such productions as *Easter Parade* (1948) and *The Band Wagon* (1953). While it was *An American in Paris* (1951) and *Gigi* (1958) that attracted all the Oscars, Freed's masterpiece was *Singin' in the Rain* (1952), a brilliant musical spoof of the early-talkie era (Millard Mitchell's portrayal in *Rain* of studio head R. K. Simpson is said to be based on Freed himself). Though widely respected in Hollywood, Freed was known to make mincemeat of tender egos by insisting that his was the only way; there were also stories circulating that he was a firm proponent of the Casting Couch (Shirley Temple has claimed that, as a mere 13-year-old, she was nearly pounced upon by a trouserless Freed). Most observers, however, prefer to ignore Freed's personal quirks and let his films stand as his testament. Freed left MGM in 1961, at a time when his brand of pure-cinema musical was on the outs and big-budget adaptations of Broadway hits (*West Side Story, The Music Man*) were the current rage. From 1963 through 1966, Freed served as president of the Academy of Motion Picture Arts and Sciences, applying his showmanship savvy to the annual Oscar telecast.

# Morgan Freeman

**Born:** June 1, 1937; Memphis, TN

**Years Active in the Industry:** by decade

| 10s | 20s | 30s | 40s | 50s | 60s | 70s | 80s | 90s |
|---|---|---|---|---|---|---|---|---|
| | | | | | | | | |

After college and a five-year stint in the Air Force, Morgan Freeman began to study acting; soon he had a role in the off-Broadway play *The Niggerlovers*, which led to his Broadway debut

in the all-black version of *Hello Dolly!* (opposite Pearl Bailey). Freeman continues on to have a distinguished stage career; he has won three Obies, a Drama Desk Award, and a Clarence Derwent Award. From 1971-76 he played the "Easy Reader" on the Public Television educational show *The Electric Company*. Aside from a film

or two made earlier, his movie career did not take off until the early '80s, particularly after he received the Best Supporting Actor Awards from the New York and Los Angeles Critics and the National Board of Review for his role as a pimp in *Street Smart* (1987). He received a Best Actor Oscar nomination for his portrayal of the chauffeur in *Driving Miss Daisy* (1989), a role he had previously won an Obie for in its stage version. Other impressive performances from Freeman include *Lean on Me* (1989), *Unforgiven* (1992) and *The Shawshank Redemption* (1994). In 1993 he directed the anti-Apartheid film *Bopha!*. **Selected Works:** *Glory* (1989), *Power of One* (1992), *Seven* (1995)

# Fritz Freleng

**Born:** August 21, 1906; Kansas City, MO

**Years Active in the Industry:** by decade

| 10s | 20s | 30s | 40s | 50s | 60s | 70s | 80s | 90s |
|---|---|---|---|---|---|---|---|---|
| | | | | | | | | |

Isadore "Fritz" Freleng began animating cartoons with Hugh Harman and Ub Iwerks at United Film Ad Service in the mid-1920s, then moved with his associates to the Disney studios. Freleng left Disney in 1929 and after directing his first cartoon for Walter Lantz at Universal (*Wicked West*), joined the Warner Brothers animation department. There his black-and-white cartoons of the mid-'30s showed a special flair for integrating music and action, especially in his "Bosko" series. Freleng began directing Warners' color series of Merrie Melodies cartoons in 1934, and over the next three decades made many of Warners' funniest cartoons, creating such memorable characters as Yosemite Sam (said to be a self-caricature) and Speedy Gonzalez, as well as developing the identities of such iconic figures as Porky Pig (*Porky's Hired Hand*), Bugs Bunny (*Racketeer Rabbit, Rhapsody Rabbit*), Daffy Duck (*Ain't That Ducky*), and Sylvester and Tweety (*Tweetie Pie, Birds Anonymous*). After Warners' cartoon unit folded, Freleng formed DePatie-Freleng Enterprises with David H. DePatie in 1963; there he reprised several of his Warners' characters, but achieved his greatest success with their Pink Panther cartoons, starting with *The Pink Phink*, co-directed with Hawley Pratt. In the early '80s Freleng created linking animation scenes for feature-length reissue anthologies of Warners cartoons: *Fritz Freleng's Looney Looney Looney Bugs Bunny Movie, Bugs Bunny's 3rd Movie: 1001 Rabbit Tales*, and *Daffy Duck's Movie: Fantastic Island*.

# William Friedkin

**Born:** August 29, 1939; Chicago, IL

**Years Active in the Industry:** by decade

| 10s | 20s | 30s | 40s | 50s | 60s | 70s | 80s | 90s |
|---|---|---|---|---|---|---|---|---|
| | | | | | | | | |

A television director by the late 1950s, William Friedkin directed his first theatrical feature in 1967, *Good Times*, starring

Sonny and Cher. An eclectic series of films followed—the Pinter adaptation *The Birthday Party* (1968), the farce *The Night They Raided Minsky's* (1968), the gay-themed *The Boys in the Band* (1970)—until Friedkin scored with two blockbusters in the mid '70s: the exciting police actioner *The French Connection* (1971) and the lurid horror tale *The Exorcist* (1973). Friedkin's subsequent career was derailed by the expensive flops *Sorcerer* (1977), the second American remake of Clouzot's *The Wages of Fear*, *The Brink's Job* (1978); and *Cruising* (1980). He has regained some attention with his later crime films, *To Live And Die in L.A.* (1985) and *Rampage* (1987), and the basketball drama *Blue Chips* (1994). **Selected Works:** *Jade* (1995)

# Samuel Fuller (Samuel Michael Fuller)

**Born:** August 12, 1911; Worcester, MA

**Years Active in the Industry:** by decade

| 10ˢ | 20ˢ | 30ˢ | 40ˢ | 50ˢ | 60ˢ | 70ˢ | 80ˢ | 90ˢ |
|-----|-----|-----|-----|-----|-----|-----|-----|-----|

Samuel Fuller is a true Hollywood maverick known for his controversial B movies that pummel audiences with graphic violence, unlovable characters, and contradictory political views vacillating between rabid right-wing patriotism to an almost liberal sympathy for the world's underdogs. He directs, writes his own screenplays and produces most of his films, which are often based on his early experiences as a crime reporter, a drifter, and a soldier. At 17, he became a crime reporter for the San Diego Sun. When the Great Depression hit, Fuller hit the road, hopping trains, and doing what he could to get by. In 1935, he published the first of several pulp fiction novels, *Burn Baby Burn*. By the following year, he was writing screenplays. He did this until World War II broke out; he then joined the First Infantry Division, where he was awarded the Bronze Star, the Silver Star, and a Purple Heart. By 1949, he had returned to Hollywood to direct his first film *I Shot Jesse James*. He continued making westerns until 1951, when he made his first war film *The Steel Helmet*. Fuller's best film is *Pickup on South Street* (1953), an artful blend of brutality, sentimentality. and anti-Communist propaganda. Fuller, dubbed "an authentic American primitive" by critic Andrew Sarris, has been a driving force in American cinema. He is also admired in Europe, particularly in France, where a devoted cult of followers considers him one of the most influential directors of postwar times. **Selected Works:** *Pierrot Le Fou* (1965), *Big Red One* (1980), *Vie De Boheme* (1993)

# Edward Furlong

**Born:** August 2, 1977; Glendale, CA

**Years Active in the Industry:** by decade

| 10ˢ | 20ˢ | 30ˢ | 40ˢ | 50ˢ | 60ˢ | 70ˢ | 80ˢ | 90ˢ |
|-----|-----|-----|-----|-----|-----|-----|-----|-----|

Child actor Edward Furlong catapulted into prominence with his role as Linda Hamilton's son in *Terminator 2: Judgement Day* (1991). He followed this with an affecting performance as Jeff Bridges' son in the little-seen *American Heart* (1991). In a way, this appearance constituted a character part, since the 13-year-old Edward was playing a 15-year-old. Whenever film work is scarce, young Furlong concentrates on his first love, music; Furlong has evolved into a enormously popular singer in Japan, thanks to his best-selling first album *Hold on Tight*. **Selected Works:** *Home of Our Own* (1993), *Brainscan* (1994)

Jean Gabin

Whoopi Goldberg
Teri Garr
Edmund "Hoot" Gibson

Edmund Gwenn

# G

## Jean Gabin (Jean-Alexis Moncorgé)

**Born:** May 17, 1904; Mériel, France
**Died:** 1976

**Years Active in the Industry:** by decade

| 10ˢ | 20ˢ | 30ˢ | 40ˢ | 50ˢ | 60ˢ | 70ˢ | 80ˢ | 90ˢ |
|-----|-----|-----|-----|-----|-----|-----|-----|-----|

French star Jean Gabin, with his craggy, impassive face and sardonic demeanor, is famed for his portrayals of earthy, courageous, lower-class loners and outsiders who have given up on love and happiness. Known as "Gabin the Magnificent," he was the most durably popular personality in French films for over four decades, becoming a national institution. The son of cafe entertainers, he was urged by his father to enter show business, and at age 19, became a dancer with the Folies-Bergere; later he played supporting parts in music halls and operettas, then returned to the Folies as Mistinguette's leading man. He debuted onscreen in 1930, quickly achieving prominence. He secured his stature as a star after his appearance in Duvivier's *Maria Chapdelaine* (1934), and had earned an international reputation by the late '30s. He starred in many of the greatest milestones of French cinema, and worked with such directors as Renoir and Carne; he was also very popular in a series of films about novelist Simenon's detective, Maigret. Besides his classic "anti-hero" performances, he has played a wide range of roles, from hobo to tycoon. He moved to Hollywood during the

Nazi occupation of France, appearing in two mediocre films, *Moontide* (1942) with Ida Lupino, and *The Imposter* (1944). During that time he was involved in a romance with actress Marlene Dietrich. Having regained his stature in French films by 1950, he went on to play successful, confident, authoritative middle-aged men. In partnership with French actor Fernandel, he founded Gafer Films, a production company, in 1963. Having been an unusually busy screen actor in the '50s, after 1962 he tended to appear in only one film a year, continuing to work until the year before his death. **Selected Works:** *Grand Illusion* (1937), *Pepe Le Moko* (1937), *Jour Se Leve (Daybreak)* (1939)

## Clark Gable (William Clark Gable)

**Born:** February 1, 1901; Meadville, PA
**Died:** November 16, 1960; Hollywood, CA

**Years Active in the Industry:** by decade

| 10ˢ | 20ˢ | 30ˢ | 40ˢ | 50ˢ | 60ˢ | 70ˢ | 80ˢ | 90ˢ |
|-----|-----|-----|-----|-----|-----|-----|-----|-----|

The son of an Ohio oil driller and farmer, American actor Clark Gable had a relatively sedate youth until, at 16, he was talked into traveling to Akron with a friend to work at a tire factory. It was in Akron that Gable saw his first stage play, and from that point on he was hooked; even though he was forced to work with his father on the oil fields for a time, Gable used a $300 inheritance he'd gotten on his 21st birthday to launch a theatrical career. Several years of working for bankrupt stock companies and crooked theatre managers and doing odd jobs followed until Gable was taken under the wing of veteran actress Josephine Dillon. The older Dillon coached Gable in speech and movement, paid to fix his teeth, and became the first of his five wives in 1924. As the marriage deteriorated, Gable's career built up momentum as he appeared in regional theatre, road shows and movie extra roles. He tackled Broadway at a time when producers were looking for rough-hewn, down-to-earth types as a contrast to the standard cardboard stage leading men.

Gable fit this bill, though he'd been imbued in certain necessary social graces by his second wife, the wealthy (and again older) Ria Langham. A 1930 Los Angeles stage production of *The Last Mile* starring Gable as Killer Mears brought the actor to the attention of the film studios, though many producers felt that Gable's ears were too large for him to pass as a leading man. Making his talkie debut in *The Painted Desert* (1931), the actor's first roles were as villains and gangsters, but as it turned out, the rougher he treated his leading ladies on-screen, the more he was adored by female film fans. By 1932, Gable was a star at MGM, where except for loan-outs he'd remain for the next 22 years. On one of those loan-outs, Gable was punished for insubordination by being sent to Columbia Studios, then a low-budget factory. The actor was cast by Columbia's ace director Frank Capra in *It Happened One Night* (1934), an amiable comedy which swept the Academy Awards in 1935—one of those Oscars going to Gable. After that, except for the spectacular failure of Gable's 1937 film *Parnell*, it seemed as though the actor could do no wrong. In 1939, Gable—despite his initial reluctance—was cast as Rhett Butler in *Gone With the Wind* (1939), leading him to be dubbed "The King" of Hollywood. A happy marriage to wife number three, Carole Lombard, and a robust off-camera life as a sportsman and athlete (a he-man image created by the MGM publicity department which Gable happened to enjoy and decide to perpetuate on his own) seemed to bode well for Gable's future contentment. But when Lombard was killed in a 1942 plane crash, a disconsolate Gable seemed to lose all interest in life. Though well over draft age, he entered the Army Air Corps and served courageously in World War II as a fighter pilot; what started out as a death wish renewed his vitality and increased his popularity (ironically, he was the favorite film star of Adolf Hitler, who offered a reward to his troops for the capture of Gable—alive). Gable's postwar films for MGM were for the most part disappointing, as was his 1949 marriage to Lady Sylvia Ashley. Dropped by both his wife and his studio, Gable ventured out as a free-lance actor in 1955, quickly regaining lost ground and becoming the highest paid non-studio actor in Hollywood. He again found happiness with his fifth wife, Kay Spreckels, and Gable continued his career as a box-office champ, even though many the films were toothless confections like *Teacher's Pet* (1959). In 1960, Gable was signed for the introspective "modern western" *The Misfits*, which had a prestigious production lineup: costars Marilyn Monroe, Montgomery Clift and Eli Wallach, scripter Arthur Miller and director John Huston. The troubled and tragic history of this film has been well documented, but despite the on-set tension, Gable took on the task uncomplainingly, going so far as to perform several grueling stunt scenes involving wild horses. The strain of filming, however, coupled with his ever-robust life style, proved too much for the actor. Clark Gable suffered a heart attack two days after the completion of *The Misfits* and died at age 59, a scant few months before the birth of his first son. Most of the nation's newspapers announced the death of Clark Gable with a four-word headline: "The King is Dead." **Selected Works:** *Mutiny on the Bounty* (1935), *San Francisco* (1936), *Test Pilot* (1938)

# Peter Gallagher

**Born:** August 19, 1955; Yonkers, NY

**Years Active in the Industry:** by decade

| 10s | 20s | 30s | 40s | 50s | 60s | 70s | 80s | 90s |
|-----|-----|-----|-----|-----|-----|-----|-----|-----|
|     |     |     |     |     |     |     |     |     |

Lead actor with saturnine good looks and intense, brooding dark eyes, Peter Gallagher studied at Tufts University outside Boston, working every summer with local theater groups. After  graduating in 1977, he landed a singing and dancing role in the Broadway revival of the rock musical *Hair;* this led to the lead role of Danny Zuko in the Broadway revival of another rock musical, *Grease.* Having played a '50s "type" in *Grease,* he got a similar role in his debut film, *The Idolmaker* (1980), leading to top billing in his second movie, *Summer Lovers* (1982), an empty-headed film that prompted him to go back to the stage for a few more years. In 1986 he played Jack Lemmon's alcoholic son in Jonathan Miller's Broadway production of Eugene O'Neill's *Long Day's Journey Into Night,* for which he received a Tony nomination. He also performed (again opposite Lemmon) in the TV movie *The Murder of Mary Phagan,* cast as an accused murderer; this led to a central role in Robert Altman's TV movie version of *The Caine Mutiny Court-Martial* (1988). In movies, his big break came in the acclaimed comedy of manners *sex, lies and videotape* (1989), which led to much better roles in films, including that of Tim Robbins's rival studio power-player in Robert Altman's *The Player* (1992). **Selected Works:** *Late for Dinner* (1991), *Watch It* (1993), *Hudsucker Proxy* (1994), *The Underneath* (1995)

# Abel Gance

**Born:** October 25, 1889; Paris, France
**Died:** November 10, 1981; Paris, France

**Years Active in the Industry:** by decade

| 10s | 20s | 30s | 40s | 50s | 60s | 70s | 80s | 90s |
|-----|-----|-----|-----|-----|-----|-----|-----|-----|
|     |     |     |     |     |     |     |     |     |

A stage actor at 19, Frenchman Abel Gance appeared in his first film, *Moliere*, in 1909. Two years later, with *La Digue,* he was writing and directing as well. He quickly earned distinction both as an innovator, with the distorted-mirror sequence of his 1915 mad-scientist comedy *La Folie Du Docteur Tube,* and for his romantic dramas of the late teens, *Mater Dolorosa* and *La Dixiéme Symphonie.* Briefly conscripted late in World War I, Gance re-enlisted so he could return with cameras and film the soldiers under fire. That footage was woven into his anti-war drama *J'Accuse,* which overwhelmed postwar audiences with its realism and its stylized, high-velocity editing. In *La Roue,* a romantic-triangle drama played out against images of railroad trains, Gance threw himself further into violent cutting and vivid locations. The lengthy film made him internationally famous, and Gance found funding for *Napoleon* (also known as *Napoleon Vu Par Abel Gance*), an epic biography which traces Bonaparte from his boyhood to the start of the Italian campaign. Gance's camerawork achieved a new fluidity and daring in *Napoleon,* the camera flying through the air on wires or strapped to a horse. His editing also became more intense, both his crosscutting in the "Double Tempest" scene, and even within a single frame, when a schoolboy pillow fight erupts into multiple split screens. To capture the geographic vista and legions of extras for Napoleon's entry in Italy, Gance created Polyvision, a Cinerama prototype employing three synchronized cameras. But the Polyvision finale of *Napoleon* doesn't restrict itself to a single new frame; Polyvision can also be a central panel with symmetrical wings of action, or even three separate frames, each crackling with its own hallucinatory editing and superimposition. *Napoleon* caused a sensation when it was premiered in 1927, but the complexities of its exhibition proved its undoing, especially with the changeover in technology from silent films to sound. Gance's masterpiece eventually became a lost work, and his career never recovered; his sound output was mostly assigned projects over which he had no creative control. The exceptions are two visionary films from the mid 1930s: *Un Grand Amour De Beethoven* (also known as *Beethoven*), where his treatment of sound is as daring as his editing, and his remake *J'Accuse,* with disfigured combat veterans portraying the resurrected war dead. Periodic efforts to revive *Napoleon* proved futile until the 1980 premiere of film historian Kevin Brownlow's reconstruction. Shown in Polyvision with a live

orchestral score, Napoleon became an international triumph—which Gance lived long enough to enjoy.

# Lowell Ganz

**Born:** August 31, 1948; New York, NY

**Years Active in the Industry:** by decade

| 10s | 20s | 30s | 40s | 50s | 60s | 70s | 80s | 90s |
|-----|-----|-----|-----|-----|-----|-----|-----|-----|
|     |     |     |     |     |     |     |     |     |

Screenwriter Lowell Ganz was 23 years old when he was taken under the wing of TV producer Gary Marshall as a member of the writing staff of the popular sitcom *The Odd Couple*. Marshall liked Ganz's offbeat sense of humor and his willingness to work long hours for the sake of a laugh; by 1974, Ganz was a coproducer of *Happy Days*. During his tenure on *Laverne and Shirley*, which he helped develop, Ganz and writer Mark "Babaloo" Mandel formed a screenwriting team, distinguished by a fondness for unorthodox comic situations. A prime example of this style was Ganz and Mandel's first movie screenplay, *Night Shift* (1982), the story of a morgue attendant who runs a prostitution service in his off-hours. *Night Shift* reunited Ganz and Mandel with *Happy Days* confreres Henry Winkler (the star) and Ron Howard (the director); it was Howard who insisted that the writing team pen his next project, *Splash* (1984), a man-and-mermaid romance. With this hit under their belts, Ganz and Mandel became one of the hottest duos in Hollywood, turning out such subsequent hits as *Parenthood* (1989) and *City Slickers* (1991). When Ganz and Mandel's *A League of Their Own* (1992) (which costarred their mentor Gary Marshall) was spun off into a TV series, the team came full circle, once more burning the midnight oil as sitcom scriveners. **Selected Works:** *Who Framed Roger Rabbit?* (1988), *Mr. Saturday Night* (1992)

# Greta Garbo

**Born:** September 18, 1905; Stockholm, Sweden
**Died:** April 15, 1990; New York, NY

**Years Active in the Industry:** by decade

| 10s | 20s | 30s | 40s | 50s | 60s | 70s | 80s | 90s |
|-----|-----|-----|-----|-----|-----|-----|-----|-----|
|     |     |     |     |     |     |     |     |     |

Few who knew Swedish actress Greta Garbo in her formative years would have predicted the illustrious career that awaited her. Greta grew up in a rundown Stockholm district, the daughter of an itinerant laborer. In school, Greta had few friends and did little to distinguish herself academically; nor was her first job, as a barber shop lather girl, indicative of future greatness. But even as a youth she photographed beautifully, a fact that enabled her to get a few modeling jobs for the Stockholm department store where she worked. Her body had a peasant's chunkiness, so her modeling was confined to head shots; even in her first film, a 1921 publicity

short financed by her employers titled *How Not to Dress,* she was seldom seen full figure. Greta followed this first movie appearance with *Our Daily Bread,* a one reel commercial for a local bakery. Then she played a bathing beauty (with a notably unflattering swimsuit) in a 1922 two-reel comedy, *Luffar Peter* (*Peter the Tramp*). Billed under her own last name (Gustaffson), Greta gained a couple of good trade reviews, and also enough confidence to seek out and win a scholarship to the Royal Dramatic Theatre. While studying acting, she was spotted by director Mauritz Stiller, who in the early '20s was Sweden's foremost filmmaker. Stiller cast Greta in *The Atonement of Gosta Berling* (1923) an overlong but internationally successful film which made her a minor star. The director became Greta's mentor and (according to most reports) lover, glamorizing her image and changing her professional name to Garbo. On the strength of *Gosta Berling,* Garbo was cast in the important German film drama *The Joyless Street* (1925), which was directed by G. W. Pabst. Hollywood's MGM studios, seeking to "raid" the European film industry and spirit away its top talents, signed Maurice Stiller to a contract. MGM head Louis Mayer was unimpressed by Garbo's two starring roles, but Stiller insisted on bringing her to America, thus Mayer had to contract her as well. The actress spent most of 1925 posing for nonsensical publicity photos which endeavored to create a "mystery woman" image for her (a campaign that had worked for previous foreign film actresses like Pola Negri), but it was only after shooting commenced on Garbo's first American film, *The Torrent* (1926), that MGM realized it had a potential gold mine on its hands. As Maurice Stiller withered on the vine due to continual clashes with the MGM brass, Garbo's star ascended. But MGM refused to pay her commensurate to her worth, so Garbo threatened to walk out; the studio counter-threatened to have the actress deported, but in the end they buckled under and increased her salary. In *Flesh and the Devil* (1927), Garbo costarred with John Gilbert, and it became obvious that theirs was not a mere movie romance. The Garbo/Gilbert team went on to make an adaptation of Tolstoy's *Anna Karenina* titled *Love* (its original title was *Heat,* but this was scrapped to avoid an embarrassing ad campaign which would have started with "John Gilbert and Greta Garbo in..."). The couple planned to marry, but Garbo, in one of her frequent attacks of self-imposed solitude, did not show up for the wedding; over the years the actress would have several other discreet affairs with such luminaries as orchestra conductor Leopold Stokowsky and director Rouben Mamoulien, but she never would marry. In 1930, MGM's concerns that Garbo's thick Swedish accent (tinged with "stage British") would not register well in talkies were abated by the success *Anna Christie,* which

was heralded with the famous ad tag "GARBO TALKS". Some noted that the slogan could also have been "GARBO ACTS," for the advent of talkies obliged the actress to drop the "mysterious temptress" characterization she'd used in silents in favor of more richly textured performances as worldly, somewhat melancholy women to whom the normal pleasures of love and contentment would always be just out of reach. In this vein, Garbo starred in *Grand Hotel* (1932), *Queen Christina* (1933), *Anna Karenina* (1935) and *Camille* (1936), which served to increase her worshipful fan following, even if the films weren't the box office smashes her silent pictures had been. The actress's legendary aloofness and desire to "be alone" (a phrase she used often in her films, once to comic effect in *Ninotchka*) added to her appeal, though less starry-eyed observers like radio comedians and animated-cartoon directors found Garbo a convenient target for satire and lampoon. Always more popular overseas than in the US, Garbo became less and less a moneymaker as the war clouds gathered in Europe; this was briefly stemmed by *Ninotchka* (1939), a bubbly comedy which was advertised *Anna Christie* style with "GARBO LAUGHS". But by 1940, it was clear that the valuable European market would soon be lost, as would Garbo's biggest following. The actress's last film, *Two Faced Woman* (1941), was a pedestrian domestic comedy that some observers believe was deliberately badly made by MGM in order to kill her career. Actually it wasn't any worse than several other comedies of its period, but for Garbo it was a distinct step downward. She retired from movies directly after *Two Faced Woman* , and though she came close to returning to films with Hitchcock's *The Paradine Case* (1947), she opted instead for total and permanent retirement. A millionaire many times over, Garbo had no need to act, nor any desire to conduct an active social life. She traveled frequently, but always incognito—which didn't stop photographers from ferreting her out. A solitary woman but not really a recluse, Garbo could frequently be spotted strolling the streets near her New York apartment; in fact, "Garbo sightings" became as much a topic of conversation in some icon-worshipping circles as "Elvis sightings" would be in the 1970s, the major difference being of course that Garbo was alive to be sighted. Even after her death in 1990, the legend of Greta Garbo was undiminished. Few of her fans talk of her in human terms; to her devotees, Greta Garbo was not so much Film Legend as Film Goddess.

# Andy Garcia

**Born:** April 12, 1956; Havana, Cuba

**Years Active in the Industry:** by decade

| 10s | 20s | 30s | 40s | 50s | 60s | 70s | 80s | 90s |
|-----|-----|-----|-----|-----|-----|-----|-----|-----|
|     |     |     |     |     |     |     | ■   | ■   |

Actor Andy Garcia is a Cuban-American immigrant whose family fled Havana for Miami when he was a child. Before making his feature film debut in *Blue Skies Again* (1983), Garcia worked in regional theater, did some improvisational work, and appeared at the Comedy Store. His breakthrough came with his electrifying performance in *Eight Million Ways to Die* (1986); this caught the

attention of director Brian De Palma, who cast him as a rookie cop in *The Untouchables* (1987). Previously a supporting player, this performance led Garcia to an uncontested lead role in Francis Ford Coppola's *The Godfather Part III* (1990), launching him into a new league as a screen actor, including leads or co-leads in *Jennifer 8* (1992) and *When a Man Loves a Woman* (1994). Garcia also directed a documentary on Cuban musician Israel Lopez, *Cachao*, in 1993. **Selected Works:** *Dead Again* (1991), *Hero* (1992), *Steal Little, Steal Big* (1995)

# Vincent Gardenia (Vincente Scognamiglio)

**Born:** January 7, 1922; Naples, Italy
**Died:** December 9, 1992; Philadelphia, PA

**Years Active in the Industry:** by decade

| 10s | 20s | 30s | 40s | 50s | 60s | 70s | 80s | 90s |
|-----|-----|-----|-----|-----|-----|-----|-----|-----|
|     |     |     |     |     |     |     |     |     |

Paternal, sad-faced, character actor Vincent Gardenia, specialized in Italian-American roles. At age two he moved with his family to New York where his father established an Italian-language theater company. Gardenia performed in the company, and at age 14 he left school to devote more time to it. He continued to appear with the company until 1960. He spent two years as a U.S. Army private during World War II. Because he was very active in New York's Italian theatrical community, he did not begin his film career until he was in his mid-'30s; he debuted onscreen in *Cop Hater* (1958) and within a few years he gained a reputation as a top-notch character actor. He went on to a busy screen career in the early '60s, but then tapered off, appearing only once until 1970 when he resumed his career. He has also had a busy and successful Broadway career, winning several Obies; he won a Tony Award for his work in *The Prisoner of Second Avenue*. He has twice received Best Supporting Actor Oscar nominations for *Bang the Drum Slowly* (1973) and *Moonstruck* (1987). **Selected Works:** *Hustler* (1961), *Heaven Can Wait* (1978), *Little Shop of Horrors* (1986), *Age Old Friends* (1989), *Tragedy of Flight 103: The Inside Story* (1991)

# Reginald Gardiner

**Born:** February 27, 1903; Wimbledon, Surrey, England
**Died:** July 7, 1980; Westwood, CA

**Years Active in the Industry:** by decade

| 10s | 20s | 30s | 40s | 50s | 60s | 70s | 80s | 90s |
|-----|-----|-----|-----|-----|-----|-----|-----|-----|
|     |     |     |     |     |     |     |     |     |

The son of an insurance man who'd aspired to appear onstage but never had the chance, British-born actor Reginald Gardiner more than made up for his dad's unrealized dreams with a career lasting fifty years. Graduating from the Royal Academy of Dramatic Art, Gardiner started as a straight actor but drifted into musical revues, frequently working in the company of such favorite British entertainers as Bea Lillie. His Broadway bow occurred in the 1935 play *At Home Abroad,* and though he'd made his film debut nearly ten years earlier in Hitchcock's silent *The Lodger* (1926), he suddenly became a "new" Hollywood find. Handsome enough to play romantic leads had he so chosen (he gets away with it in the 1939 Laurel and Hardy comedy *Flying Deuces*), Gardiner preferred the sort of kidding-on-the-square comedy he'd done in his revue days. His turn as a traffic cop who imagines himself a symphony conductor in his first American film *Born to Dance* (1936) was so well received that he virtually repeated the bit—this time as a butler who harbors operatic aspirations—in *Damsel in Distress* (1937). For most of his film career, Gardiner played suave but slightly untrustworthy British gentlemen; a break from this pattern occurred in Charlie Chaplin's *The Great Dictator* (1940), in which Gardiner played a fascist military man who turns his back on dictator "Adenoid Hinkel" to cast his lot with a community of Jews. Devoting his private life to the enjoyment of classical music, rare books, painting, and monitoring the ghost that supposedly haunted his Beverly Hills home, Reginald Gardiner flourished as a stage, film and television actor into the 1960s; one of his latter-day assignments was his weekly dual role in the 1966 Phyllis Diller sitcom, *Pruitts of Southampton.* **Selected Works:** *Man Who Came to Dinner* (1941)

# Ava Gardner (Ava Lavinia Gardner)

**Born:** December 24, 1922; Smithfield, NC
**Died:** January 25, 1990; London, England

**Years Active in the Industry:** by decade

| 10s | 20s | 30s | 40s | 50s | 60s | 70s | 80s | 90s |
|-----|-----|-----|-----|-----|-----|-----|-----|-----|
|     |     |     |     |     |     |     |     |     |

From dirt-poor childhood surroundings, Ava Gardner fought her way up to social respectability first as a model, then as a contract player at MGM. Her gawky "hillbilly" demeanor was totally made over by the studio into an image of inaccessible glamour. Gardner toiled in tiny bit roles (her starring appearance in Monogram's *Ghosts on the Loose* [1943] was so unremarkable that Ava couldn't even remember the plot correctly in her autobiography), finally getting a worthwhile role on loan-out to Universal in *The Killers* (1946). MGM was never too comfortable with the bad-girl persona she displayed so well in this film, thus most of her starring appearances at her home studio were relatively sympathetic roles in

*The Hucksters* (1949) and *Show Boat* (1952). Her cinema reputation as "The World's Most Beautiful Animal" (in the words of a '50s publicity campaign) was once again manifested in loan-outs like *Pandora and the Flying Dutchman* (1951) and *Snows of Kilimanjaro* (1952). MGM eventually came to terms with the elements that made Ava Gardner popular, notably in the gutsy *Mogambo* (1953), in which Ava made an excellent partner to the equally earthy Clark Gable. Director George Cukor was much taken by Ava, and cast her in her best and most complex MGM role in *Bhowani Junction* (1956) wherein she was torn not only by love but by clashing East-Indian cultural values. Ms. Gardner was equally well served in *The Barefoot Contessa* (1954), which in many ways was a replay of her own rags-to-riches personal story. Off camera, Ava was the personification of Temperamental Movie Queen, clashing with costars, directors and film executives alike, and driving MGM's "damage doctors" crazy with her turbulent romances and marriages (her three husbands were Mickey Rooney, Frank Sinatra and Artie Shaw). Otherwise easygoing performers like Charlton Heston were left dumbfounded by Ava's deplorable behavior, and would reluctantly say so in print years later. In the 1960s, Ava was cast in some of her best parts, notably in *Seven Days in May* (1964) and *Night of the Iguana* (1966), but the pace of her jet-setting lifestyle and an increasing reliance upon booze were beginning to tell on her. With roles and public appearances decreasing while her own self-destruction gathered momentum, Ava Gardner did not so much pass away as burn out in the early days of 1990. **Selected Works:** *On the Beach* (1959), *55 Days at Peking* (1962)

# John David Garfield (Julius Garfinkle)

**Born:** March 4, 1913; Los Angeles, CA
**Died:** May 21, 1952

### Years Active in the Industry: by decade

| 10s | 20s | 30s | 40s | 50s | 60s | 70s | 80s | 90s |
|-----|-----|-----|-----|-----|-----|-----|-----|-----|
|     |     |     |     |     |     |     |     |     |

American actor John Garfield, grew up poor on the tough Lower East Side of New York where he verged on juvenile delinquency, and ended up attending a school for problem children. As the result of winning a state debating contest sponsored by *The New York Times,* he received an open-ended scholarship, and chose to attend the Ouspenskaya Drama School. Later he worked with Eva Le Gallienne's Civic Repertory Theater. Afterwards he

went traveling cross-country on freight trains and working as a farm-hand; he also appeared in a bit part in the film *Footlight Parade* (1933). Soon he returned to New York and joined the Group Theater, and by 1936 he was playing leads on Broadway. He was signed by Warner Brothers in 1938, landing his first major screen role as a supporting player in *Four Daughters* (1938), for which he received a Best Supporting Actor Oscar nomination. The following year he appeared in six films, and his film career was firmly established. Immediately, he developed a screen persona similar to his real personality, that of an angry and cynical lower-class rebel whose tough-guy exterior concealed a gentle soul. He began his own production company in the mid-'40s and remained popular for several more years. For his work in *Body and Soul* (1947) he received a Best Actor Oscar nomination. His career came to a complete stop when he was called before the House Un-American Activities Committee in the early '50s, and was blacklisted for refusing to name names. In 1952 he died of a heart attack, which his friends attributed to the pressures of being blacklisted. He was the father of actors John Garfield, Jr., and Julie Garfield. **Selected Works:** *Sea Wolf* (1941), *Tortilla Flat* (1942), *Pride of the Marines* (1945), *Humoresque* (1946), *Gentleman's Agreement* (1947)

# William Gargan

**Born:** July 17, 1905; Brooklyn, NY
**Died:** 1979

### Years Active in the Industry: by decade

| 10s | 20s | 30s | 40s | 50s | 60s | 70s | 80s | 90s |
|-----|-----|-----|-----|-----|-----|-----|-----|-----|
|     |     |     |     |     |     |     |     |     |

Actor William Gargan began his career 1924, shortly after leaving high school, and made it to Broadway within a year. In 1932 he won great acclaim for his work in the play *The Animal Kingdom,* leading to an invitation from Hollywood where he made his film debut in 1932. During the '30s he played high-energy, gregarious leads in many B-movies and second leads in major films; later he moved into character roles. For his work in *They Knew What They Wanted* (1940), he received a Best Supporting Actor Oscar nomination. He made few films after 1948, but from 1949 to 1951 he starred in the title role of the TV series *Martin Kane, Private Eye,* then reprised the role in 1957 in *The New Adventures of Martin Kane.* He was stricken by cancer of the larynx, and in 1960 his voice box was removed in surgery, ending his career. He learned esophageal speech, then taught this method for the American Cancer Society; the same group enlisted him as an anti-smoking campaigner. Two years after losing his speech, he gave his final performance, portraying a mute clown on TV in *King of Diamonds.* He authored an autobiography, *Why Me?* (1969), recounting his struggle with cancer. His brother was actor Edward Gargan. **Selected Works:** *Bells of St. Mary's* (1945)

# Judy Garland (Frances Gumm)

**Born:** June 10, 1922; Grand Rapids, MI
**Died:** June 22, 1969; London, England

**Years Active in the Industry:** by decade

| 10ˢ | 20ˢ | 30ˢ | 40ˢ | 50ˢ | 60ˢ | 70ˢ | 80ˢ | 90ˢ |
|-----|-----|-----|-----|-----|-----|-----|-----|-----|

Entertainer Judy Garland was both one of the greatest and one of the most tragic figures in American show business. The daughter of the Stage Mother from Hell, Judy and her sisters were

forced into a vaudeville act called the Gumm Sisters (her real name), appearing in movie shorts and at the 1933 Chicago World's Fair. It was clear from the outset that Judy was the star of the act, and as such was engaged by MGM as a solo performer in 1936. The studio adored Judy's adult-sounding singing but were concerned about her puffy facial features and her curvature of the spine. MGM decided to test both Judy and another teenage contractee, Deanna Durbin, in a musical "swing vs. the classics" short subject, *Every Sunday* (1936). The studio had planned to keep Durbin and drop Garland, but through a corporate error, the opposite took place. Whatever the case, MGM decided to allow Judy her feature-film debut in another studio's production, just in case the positive audience response to *Every Sunday* was a fluke. Loaned to 20th Century-Fox, Judy was ninth billed in *Pigskin Parade* (1936), but stole the show with her robust renditions of "Balboa" and "Texas Tornado." Judy returned to MGM in triumph and was given better opportunities to show her stuff: the "Dear Mr. Gable" number in *Broadway Melody of 1938,* "Zing Went the Strings of My Heart" in *Listen Darling* (1938), and so on. Judy almost didn't get her most celebrated role: MGM had planned to star 20th Century Fox's

Shirley Temple in *The Wizard of Oz,* but the deal fell through and Garland was cast as Dorothy. Even after this, the actress nearly lost out on her definitive screen moment when the studio decided to cut the song "Over the Rainbow," finally keeping the number after it tested well in previews. *The Wizard of Oz* made Garland a star, but MGM couldn't see beyond the little-girl image and insisted upon casting her in "Hey, kids, let's put on a show" roles opposite Mickey Rooney (a life-long friend of Judy's, whose own life was no bed of roses). Judy proved to the world that she was a grown-up by marrying composer David Rose in 1941, after which MGM began giving her adult roles in such films as *For Me and My Gal* (1942)—though still her most successful film of the early '40s was in another blushing-teen part in *Meet Me in St. Louis* (1944). Once very popular on the set due to her infectious high spirits, Judy became moody and irritable in the mid-'40s, as well as undependable insofar as showing up on time and being prepared. The problem was an increasing dependency upon barbiturates, an addiction allegedly inaugurated in the 1930s when the studio had Judy "pepped up" with prescription pills so that she could work longer hours. Judy also began drinking heavily and her marriage was deteriorating; in 1945 she married director Vincent Minelli, with whom she had a daughter, Liza, in 1946. By 1948 Judy's moodswings and suicidal tendencies were getting the better of her, and in 1950 she had to quit the musical *Annie Get Your Gun.* That same year, she barely got through *Summer Stock,* her health problems painfully evident upon viewing this film. Before 1950 was half over, Judy attempted suicide, and upon recovery, she was fired by MGM. Judy and Vincent Minelli divorced in 1951, whereupon she married Sid Luft, who took over management of his wife's career and choreographed Garland's triumphant comeback at the London Palladium, a success surpassed by her 1951 appearance at New York's Palace Theatre. Luft strong-armed Warner Bros. to bankroll *A Star is Born* (1954), providing Judy with her first film role in four years. *A Star is Born* was Judy's best film to date, allowing her a wealth of songs and a full range of emotions. Riding high once more, Judy was reduced to the depths of depression when she lost the Academy Award to Grace Kelly. Her subsequent live appearances were wildly inconsistent, and her film performances ranged from excellent (*Judgment at Nuremberg* [1961]) to appallingly undisciplined (*A Child is Waiting* [1963]). Her third marriage on the rocks, Judy nonetheless pulled herself together for an unforgettable 1961 appearance at Carnegie Hall, which led indirectly to her 1963 weekly CBS series, *The Judy Garland Show.* As with most of the significant moments in Garland's life, much contradictory information has emerged regarding her CBS series and her behavior therein; the end result, however, was cancellation after one year, due less to the wavering quality of the program (it started poorly, but finished big with several "concert" episodes) as to the competition of NBC's *Bonanza.* Garland's marriage to Sid Luft, which produced her daughter Lorna, ended in divorce in 1965, and from here on in Judy's life and career hit a rapid downslide. She made a comeback attempt in London in 1968, but audiences ranged from enthusiastic to indifferent—as did her performances. A 1969 marriage to discotheque manager Mickey Deems did neither party any good, nor did a three-week engagement in a London nightclub, during which Garland was booed offstage. On June 22, 1969, Judy Garland was found dead in her London apartment, the victim of an ostensibly accidental overdose of barbiturates. Despite of (or perhaps *because* of) the deprivations of her private life, Judy Garland has remained a Show Business Legend. As to her untimely demise, Ray Bolger summed it up best in his oft-quoted epitaph: "Judy didn't die. She just wore out." **Selected Works:** *Ziegfeld Follies* (1946), *Easter Parade* (1948), *Pirate* (1948), *Judgement at Nuremburg* (1961)

# James Garner (James Scott Baumgarner)

**Born:** April 7, 1928; Norman, OK

**Years Active in the Industry:** by decade

| 10s | 20s | 30s | 40s | 50s | 60s | 70s | 80s | 90s |
|-----|-----|-----|-----|-----|-----|-----|-----|-----|
|     |     |     |     | ■   | ■   | ■   | ■   | ■   |

The son of an Oklahoma carpet layer, American actor James Garner did stints in the Army and merchant marines before working as a male model. His professional acting career commenced with a non-speaking part in the Broadway play *The Caine Mutiny Court Martial* (1954), in which he was also assigned to run lines with stars Lloyd Nolan, Henry Fonda and John Hodiak. Given that talent roster and the fact that the director was Charles Laughton, Garner managed to earn his salary and receive a crash course in acting all at once. After a few TV commercials, Garner was signed as a contract player by Warner Bros. studios in 1956. He barely had a part in his first film, *The Girl He Left Behind* (1956), though he was given special attention by director David Butler, who felt Garner had far more potential than the film's nominal star, Tab Hunter. Due in part to Butler's enthusiasm, Garner was cast in the Warner Bros. TV western *Maverick*. The series was originally supposed to have alternate stars: Gambler Bart Maverick (Jack Kelly) would carry the ball one week, while his brother Brett (James Garner) would handle things the next week. After a few months, it was clear to Warners that the public regarded Garner as the only true star of the series (something that Kelly would fully and respectfully acknowledge in later years). The scriptwriters latched on to Garner's gift for understated humor, and before long *Maverick* had as many laughs as shoot-outs. Garner was promoted to starring film roles during his *Maverick* run, but by the third season he chafed at his low salary and insisted on better treatment. Warners refused, so Garner walked. Lawsuits and recriminations were exchanged, but the end result was that Garner

was a free agent as of 1960. He did quite well as a freelance actor for several years, turning in commendable work in such films as *Boy's Night Out* (1962) and *The Great Escape* (1963), but soon was perceived by filmmakers as something of a less expensive Rock Hudson - never more so than when he played Hudsonish parts opposite Doris Day in *Move Over, Darling* (1963) and *The Thrill of It All* (1963). He fared rather better in variations of his "Maverick" persona in such westerns as *Support Your Local Sheriff* (1969) and *Skin Game* (1971), but he tired of eating warmed-over stew - besides, being a cowboy star had made him a walking mass of injuries and broken bones. Garner tried to play a more peaceable westerner in the TV series *Nichols* (1971), but when audiences failed to respond his character was killed off and replaced by his more athletic twin brother (also Garner). The actor finally shed the *Maverick* cloak with his long running TV series *The Rockford Files* (1973-78) wherein he played a John McDonaldesque private eye who never seemed to meet anyone capable of telling the truth. *Rockford* resulted in even more injuries for the increasingly bethumped Garner, and soon he was showing up on TV talk shows telling the world the many physical activities he *couldn't* do anymore. *Rockford* ended in a spirit of recrimination when Garner, expecting a percentage of profits, learned that "creative bookkeeping" had resulted in the series posting no profits! (Another lawsuit transpired. When Garner wasn't in the hospital, he was in court). To the public, Garner was the rough-hewn but basically affable fellow they'd seen in his fictional roles and as Mariette Hartley's partner (not husband) in a series of Polaroid commercials. Offscreen, Garner was a complicated, moody man, willing to give the shirt off his back to people he liked, but eager to crack the skulls of those who'd wronged him. Perhaps in reflection of this, Garner's later film and TV-movie roles had a dark edge to them, notably his likable but mercurial pharmacist in *Murphy's Romance* (1985), for which he was nominated for an Oscar, and his multifaceted co-starring stints with James Woods in the TV movies *The Promise* (1988) and *My Name is Bill* (1989). In 1994, James Garner came full circle in the profitable feature film *Maverick* (1994), wherein the title role was played by Mel Gibson. **Selected Works:** *Sayonara* (1957), *Children's Hour* (1961), *Decoration Day* (1990), *Distinguished Gentleman* (1992)

# Teri Garr

**Born:** December 11, 1944; Lakewood, OH

**Years Active in the Industry:** by decade

| 10s | 20s | 30s | 40s | 50s | 60s | 70s | 80s | 90s |
|-----|-----|-----|-----|-----|-----|-----|-----|-----|
|     |     |     |     |     | ■   | ■   | ■   | ■   |

The daughter of actor-comedian Edward Garr, American actress Teri Garr first appeared onscreen in a bit role in one of Elvis Presley's mid-'60s films, but her first real screen role was in *Head* (1968), which starred the pop group the Monkees. Most of her early experience came on TV, where she got guest shots on TV shows such as *Star Trek* and regularly appeared on *The Sonny and Cher Show* as Cher's friend Olivia. Her first notable screen roles were in Mel Brooks's *Young Frankenstein* and Francis Ford Coppola's *The Conversation* (both 1974). She went on to appear as Richard Dreyfuss's wife in Steven Spielberg's blockbuster *Close Encounters of the Third Kind* (1977) and Dustin Hoffman's girlfriend in the hit comedy *Tootsie* (1982). Generally she has played supporting roles, with which she has maintained a busy screen career into the '90s. **Selected Works:** *After Hours* (1985), *Waiting for the Light* (1990), *Player* (1992), *Dumb and Dumber* (1994)

# Greer Garson

**Born:** September 29, 1908; Dublin, Ireland

**Years Active in the Industry:** by decade

| 10ˢ | 20ˢ | 30ˢ | 40ˢ | 50ˢ | 60ˢ | 70ˢ | 80ˢ | 90ˢ |
|-----|-----|-----|-----|-----|-----|-----|-----|-----|

Irish-born actress Greer Garson graduated with honors from the University of London and finished her post-grad work at the University of Grenoble in France. For many years, she worked efficiently as supervisor of an advertising firm, spending her spare time working in community theatre. By age 24, Garson decided to take a risk and try a full-time acting career. She was accepted by the Birmingham Repertory, making her first stage appearance as an American Jewish tenement girl in *Street Scene*. Her London debut came in 1934 in *The Tempest,* after which she headlined several stage plays and musicals. While vacationing in London, MGM mogul Louis B. Mayer happened to see Greer in *Old Music;* entranced by her elegant manner and flaming red hair, Mayer signed the actress to an MGM contract, showcasing her in the Anglo-American film production *Goodbye, Mr. Chips* (1939). Garson became MGM's resident aristocrat, appearing most often as costar of fellow contractee Walter Pidgeon. It was with Pidgeon that she appeared in *Mrs. Miniver* (1942), a profitable wartime morale-booster which won Oscars for Greer, for supporting actress Teresa Wright, and for the picture itself. Legend has it that Garson's acceptance speech at the Academy Awards ceremony rambled on for 45 minutes; in fact, it wasn't any more than 5 or 6 minutes, but the speech compelled the Academy to limit the time any actor could spend in accepting the award. Though not overly fond of being so insufferably ladylike in her films, Garson stayed at MGM until her contract expired in 1954; it was surprising but at the same time refreshing to see her let her hair down in the 1956 western *Strange Lady in Town*. In 1960, Gar-

son received her second Oscar nomination for her astonishingly accurate portrayal of Eleanor Roosevelt in *Sunrise at Campobello*. After that, Garson was given precious few opportunities to shine in films, though she was permitted to exhibit her still-vibrant singing voice in her last picture, 1967's *The Happiest Millionaire*. **Selected Works:** *Random Harvest* (1942), *Madame Curie* (1943), *Mrs. Parkington* (1944), *Valley of Decision* (1945), *Julius Caesar* (1953)

# Vittorio Gassman

**Born:** September 1, 1922; Genoa, Italy

**Years Active in the Industry:** by decade

| 10ˢ | 20ˢ | 30ˢ | 40ˢ | 50ˢ | 60ˢ | 70ˢ | 80ˢ | 90ˢ |
|-----|-----|-----|-----|-----|-----|-----|-----|-----|

Prolific, versatile Italian actor Vittorio Gassman gave up law studies to enroll at the Accademia Nazionale Arte Dramatica in Rome. After appearing in more than 40 plays, he debuted onscreen in 1946; because of his arrogant good looks, he was typecast as a self-centered hero or insensitive creep in adventure films and romantic melodramas. Within a few years he was one of Italy's top leading men; meanwhile, his work onstage gradually won him much prestige as a theatrical star. He married actress Shelley Winters in 1952, and within a year he moved to Hollywood where he quickly appeared in a string of films. Both the marriage and the American screen career fizzled rapidly, however, and he returned to Italy. He founded his own stage company, Teatro Popolare Italiano, and went back to making Italian films. He directed himself in the film *Kean* (1957), and was heavily criticized for his overacting. In the late '50s he switched gears and began taking roles as a comedic actor, renewing his popularity. For the next two-plus decades he sustained a busy and consistent screen career, mostly in Italian productions but occasionally in Hollywood and international films as well. For his portrayal of a blind thief in the first (Italian) version of *Scent of a Woman* (1975), he won the Cannes Film Festival Best Actor award. **Selected Works:** *Big Deal on Madonna Street* (1958)

# Janet Gaynor (Laura Gainor)

**Born:** October 6, 1906; Philadelphia, PA
**Died:** September 14, 1984; Palm Springs, CA

**Years Active in the Industry:** by decade

| 10ˢ | 20ˢ | 30ˢ | 40ˢ | 50ˢ | 60ˢ | 70ˢ | 80ˢ | 90ˢ |
|-----|-----|-----|-----|-----|-----|-----|-----|-----|

American actress Janet Gaynor was a star of the late silent era and early talkies who was able to project vulnerability and naiveté in any role. She attended high school in San Francisco; hoping to find work in films, she moved to L.A. shortly after graduation, supporting herself through odd jobs while appearing as an extra. This led her to some bit roles in Hal Roach comedy shorts and a lead in a two-reel Western. Signed to a contract by Fox, she had her first significant role in *The Johnstown Flood* (1926). She soon went on to appear in two successful films, Murnau's masterpiece *Sunrise* and Borzage's hit *Seventh Heaven* (both 1927); as a result, within a year she was Fox's biggest star. At the very first Academy Awards ceremony she won the Best Actress Oscar for her work in several films in 1927-28 (the early Oscars were often given for cumulative work). Her charming, gentle voice was ideally suited to talkies, and she made the transition to the sound era with great success. She often co-starred with romantic idol Charles Farrell. Their popularity as a team was at its peak in the early '30s, when they were known as "America's favorite lovebirds." She was Hollywood's top box-office attraction in 1934. She retired from the screen in 1939, around the time of her second marriage, to Hollywood's most renowned costume designer, Gilbert Adrian; much of her later years were spent on a Brazilian ranch. In the '50s she came back occasionally to work on radio and TV, and had a role in one more film, *Bernadine* (1957). Widowed in 1959, she married producer Paul Gregory in 1964. She also took up painting, and in 1976 her still-lifes were exhibited in a New York gallery. In the early '80s she appeared in the Broadway show *Harold and Maude*. **Selected Works:** *State Fair* (1933), *Star Is Born* (1937), *Young in Heart* (1938)

## Mitzi Gaynor (Franceska Mitzi von Gerber)

**Born:** September 4, 1930; Chicago, IL

**Years Active in the Industry:** by decade

| 10ˢ | 20ˢ | 30ˢ | 40ˢ | 50ˢ | 60ˢ | 70ˢ | 80ˢ | 90ˢ |
|-----|-----|-----|-----|-----|-----|-----|-----|-----|
|     |     |     |     |     |     |     |     |     |

Vivacious American actress Mitzi Gaynor, the daughter of a ballerina, began studying dance at age four. By the time she was 12, she was in the corps de ballet of the Los Angeles Civic Light Opera. She debuted onscreen in 1954, going on to perform with vivacity and charm in a string of musicals; however, her films did poorly at the box office and her contract was dropped in 1954. That same year she married talent agent Jack Bean, and within two years he helped her renew her career. She made several successful films, and then was selected by Joshua Logan to star in the screen version of *South Pacific* (1958); the film bombed and her screen career never recovered. She made a few more films, then retired from the screen after 1963, going on to appear successfully in stock and nightclubs and on TV; for some time she hosted an annual TV special.

## Leo Genn

**Born:** August 9, 1905; London, England
**Died:** January 26, 1978

**Years Active in the Industry:** by decade

| 10ˢ | 20ˢ | 30ˢ | 40ˢ | 50ˢ | 60ˢ | 70ˢ | 80ˢ | 90ˢ |
|-----|-----|-----|-----|-----|-----|-----|-----|-----|
|     |     |     |     |     |     |     |     |     |

Smooth, refined British star Leo Genn is known for his relaxed charm and "black velvet voice." Before becoming an actor, he received a law degree at Cambridge and worked as a barrister in the early '20s. In 1930 he debuted onstage; for several years he continued earning money with legal services, meanwhile gaining experience in both plays and films. In 1939 he finally gave up the law to make his Broadway debut. He served with the Royal Artillery during World War II; in 1943 he was promoted to lieutenant colonel, and in 1945 he was awarded the *Croix de Guerre*. On several occasions during the war he was granted leave to appear in films. At war's end he became one of Britain's investigators of war crimes at the Belsen concentration camp, and went on to be an assistant prosecutor for the Belsen trial. After his small but noteworthy role as the Constable of France in Laurence Olivier's film *Henry V* (1944), he was invited to the U.S., where he had a great theatrical triumph in the 1946 Broadway production of Lillian Hellman's *Another Part of the Forest*. His stage and screen career flourished afterwards in both the U.S. and England. Onscreen he was usually cast in smart, likable, subtle character leads and supporting roles. For his portrayal of Gaius Petronius, Nero's counselor, in *Quo Vadis* (1951), he received a Best Supporting Actor Oscar nomination. **Selected Works:** *Mourning Becomes Electra* (1947), *Snake Pit* (1948)

## Richard Gere

**Born:** August 31, 1948; Syracuse, NY

**Years Active in the Industry:** by decade

| 10ˢ | 20ˢ | 30ˢ | 40ˢ | 50ˢ | 60ˢ | 70ˢ | 80ˢ | 90ˢ |
|-----|-----|-----|-----|-----|-----|-----|-----|-----|
|     |     |     |     |     |     |     |     |     |

Sexy leading man Richard Gere began as a musician, playing a number of instruments in high school and writing music for high school productions. He dropped out of college to pursue act-

ing, eventually landing a lead role in the London production of the rock musical *Grease* in 1973. His work earned him a season with the Young Vic Company (an unusual opportunity for an American actor), during which he appeared in such plays as *Taming of the Shrew* (1974). He debuted onscreen in a small role as a pimp in *Report to the*

*Commissioner* (1974), after which he made one or more films a year while continuing to do stage work. His breakthrough screen performance was in the title role of *American Gigolo* (1979), which established him as a major sex symbol. After that success he took a big career risk in accepting the role of a gay concentration-camp prisoner in the Broadway play *Bent,* for which he received excellent reviews. His next film, *An Officer and a Gentleman* (1982), confirmed his star status, but it was followed by a long dry spell of poor or unsuccessful movies; that period was ended with his starring role in the smash hit *Pretty Woman* (1990) playing opposite Julia Roberts. Off-screen, he is a devout Buddhist and remains active in ecological and political causes. His marriage to supermodel Cindy Crawford ended in 1995. **Selected Works:** *Days of Heaven* (1978), *Final Analysis* (1992), *And the Band Played On* (1993), *Sommersby* (1993), *First Knight* (1995)

# Edmund "Hoot" Gibson

**Born:** August 6, 1892; Takamah, NE
**Died:** August 23, 1962

**Years Active in the Industry:** by decade

| 10s | 20s | 30s | 40s | 50s | 60s | 70s | 80s | 90s |
|-----|-----|-----|-----|-----|-----|-----|-----|-----|

Actor Edmund "Hoot" Gibson is said to have been given his unusual nickname because of his boyhood habit of hunting owls. He joined a circus at age 13; later he got stranded in Colorado and began to work as a cowpuncher. By age 16 he was a skilled performer in Wild West rodeo shows, going on to win the title of "World's All-Around Champion Cowboy" in 1912. In 1911 or 1912 he began working in films as an extra and stuntman, frequently acting as a double for Harry Carey and other Western stars; during the teens he appeared in many Western two-reelers, but his career progressed slowly. In 1917 he started getting supporting roles in John Ford-Harry Carey Westerns at Universal, but this work was interrupted by service in the Army Tank Corps during World War I. He was discharged in 1919 and went back to supporting roles in Ford Westerns; soon he got his own two-reel series in which he was billed as "The Smiling Whirlwind." He shot to fame in 1921 after starring in his first feature films, John Ford's five-reelers *Action* and *Sure Fire.* He went on to become the cowboy idol of millions of American kids in the '20s and well into the '30s. However, he was an atypical Western hero as he rarely carried a gun and was more of a comedian than action hero. He was Universal's #1 cowboy star throughout the '20s, earning $14,000 a week as star and producer. His only significant rival was Fox's Tom Mix. His popularity continued until 1936, the last year in which he was on the Top Ten Money-Making Western Stars list; Gene Autry's cowboy style took over after that, and Gibson retired from the screen after making a serial in 1937. He occasionally did a little more film work, though, including the low-budget 1944 *Trail Blazers* series as well as guest appearances in a few movies. He married and divorced silent screen actress Helen Wegner Gibson and actress Sally Eilers.

# Mel Gibson

**Born:** January 3, 1956; Peekskill, NY

**Years Active in the Industry:** by decade

| 10s | 20s | 30s | 40s | 50s | 60s | 70s | 80s | 90s |
|-----|-----|-----|-----|-----|-----|-----|-----|-----|

With his rugged, rakish smile and 10,000 watt blue eyes, actor and filmmaker Mel Gibson is one of the few performers who can truly be labeled a superstar. Though generally considered an Australian because he has

adopted the country's native accent, Gibson was actually born and raised in Peekskill, New York. At age 12 he moved with his family to Sydney, Australia because his father wanted to protect the family's boys from being drafted to serve in Vietnam. As a young man he attended Sydney's National Institute of Dramatic Art; there he was so nervous in his first play that he was unable to stand and had to play the role sitting down. He debuted onscreen in *Summer City* (1977), after which he joined the South Australia Theater Company, going on to appear in Shakespearean productions and such plays as *Waiting for Godot* and *Death of a Salesman.* Shortly before he auditioned for the film *Mad Max* (1979), he was in a street fight that left his face badly bruised; fortunately, this gave him the edge over other auditioners and director George Miller selected him for the lead. Although the film was only moderately popular outside Australia (where it was the nation's biggest commercial success ever), its sequel, *The Road Warrior* (1981), was an international smash hit and made him a star. His star status was further confirmed by his next film, the internationally successful *Gallipoli* (1981). While going on to take serious roles, including the title role in a film production of *Hamlet* (1990), he has sustained his career with action films, such as three *Lethal Weapon* films (1987, 1989, and 1992) and the third *Mad Max* movie (1985). He made his directorial debut in *The Man Without A Face* (1993), in which he also starred, and served as director, producer, and star of the acclaimed epic *Braveheart* (1995). He has won a number of Australian acting awards, including the best actor and "sammy" awards for his work in *Tim* (1979), and the best actor award for *Gallipoli* (1981). **Selected Works:** *Year of Living Dangerously* (1982), *Lethal Weapon, Part 2* (1989), *Forever Young* (1992), *Lethal Weapon, Part 3* (1992)

# Sir John Gielgud (Arthur John Gielgud)

**Born:** April 14, 1904; London, England

**Years Active in the Industry:** by decade

| 10$^s$ | 20$^s$ | 30$^s$ | 40$^s$ | 50$^s$ | 60$^s$ | 70$^s$ | 80$^s$ | 90$^s$ |
|---|---|---|---|---|---|---|---|---|
| | | | | | | | | |

"Progressive" dramatic coaches have tended to deride British actor Sir John Gielgud for "merely" acting with his voice alone. That's probably their way of saying, "God, what I'd give for a voice like that!" A grandnephew of fabled actress Ellen Terry, Gielgud attended the Royal Academy of Dramatic Art and made his professional bow at age 17. Shakespeare was Gielgud's forte, and his famous interpretation of Hamlet is the stuff of which legends are made (Lillian Gish, who played Ophelia opposite Gielgud's Hamlet on Broadway in the 1930s, noted that despite his expertise, Gielgud took direction like an obedient child—a trait he has retained into his eighties). Fortunately, we have a record of his Hamlet on film, albeit in truncated form, courtesy of a 1939 documentary. The rest of Gielgud's film appearances have run hot and cold, possibly due to his willingness to accept roles purely for the money, in order to finance his stage work and such independent projects as his mid-'60s series of Chekhov TV specials. An uncomfortable romantic lead in Hitchcock's *The Secret Agent* (1936), Gielgud has been better served in roles calling for larger-than-life theatricality: as Disraeli in *The Prime Minister* (1941), Cassius in *Julius Caesar* (1953), Clarence in *Richard III* (1955), and King Louis VII in *Becket* (1968). These are far more representative of Gielgud's technique than his bread-and-butter performances in the likes of *The Loved One* (1965), *Assignment to Kill* (1968), *Lost Horizon* (1973) and *Murder By Decree* (1978). Curiously, it was for one of his "take the money and run" assignments that John Gielgud won his only Academy Award: the role of Dudley Moore's fatherly butler in *Arthur* (1981). **Selected Works:** *Murder on the Orient Express* (1974), *Chariots of Fire* (1981), *Prospero's Books* (1991), *Power of One* (1992)

# Billy Gilbert

**Born:** September 12, 1894; Louisville, KY
**Died:** September 23, 1971

**Years Active in the Industry:** by decade

| 10$^s$ | 20$^s$ | 30$^s$ | 40$^s$ | 50$^s$ | 60$^s$ | 70$^s$ | 80$^s$ | 90$^s$ |
|---|---|---|---|---|---|---|---|---|
| | | | | | | | | |

Tall, rotund, popular comedic supporting actor Billy Gilbert is best remembered for his ability to sneeze on cue. The son of opera singers, he was 12 when he started performing. Later, in vaudeville and burlesque, he perfected a suspenseful sneezing routine; this became his trademark as a screen actor (he provided the voice of "Sneezy," one of the Seven Dwarfs, in Disney's feature cartoon *Snow White and the Seven Dwarfs*, [1938]). He appeared in some silent films, then began a busier screen career during the sound era, eventually appearing in some 200 feature films and shorts where he was usually cast in light character roles as comic relief to straight performers and as support for major comedians, notably Laurel and Hardy. He also frequently had accented roles, including Field Marshall Herring in Chaplin's *The Great Dictator* (1940). In the late '40s, he directed two Broadway shows; he also wrote a play, *Buttrio Square,* which was produced in New York in 1952. **Selected Works:** *One Hundred Men and a Girl* (1937), *Block-Heads* (1938)

# John Gilbert (John Pringle)

**Born:** July 10, 1895; Logan, UT
**Died:** January 9, 1936

**Years Active in the Industry:** by decade

| 10$^s$ | 20$^s$ | 30$^s$ | 40$^s$ | 50$^s$ | 60$^s$ | 70$^s$ | 80$^s$ | 90$^s$ |
|---|---|---|---|---|---|---|---|---|
| | | | | | | | | |

American leading man and supporting actor John Gilbert was the son of the Pringle Stock company's leading comic. It was his father who helped Gilbert break into showbusiness as an extra

and bit player in 1916. Within a year he was playing featured roles and occasional leads, usually as an unlikable character or the "other man"; until mid-1921 he was billed as "Jack Gilbert." He also collaborated on some scripts. In 1919 he began landing excellent lead roles opposite such actresses as Mary Pickford, and by the early '20s he was very popular and developing into a dashing leading man. In the mid- to late-'20s he appeared in one box-office hit after another, becoming one of the great screen idols of the decade; he was second only to Valentino as a romantic lead, and after Valentino's death in 1926 he had no competition. His popularity peaked in the late '20s, when he appeared in three films with Greta Garbo; the studio publicized his mad infatuation with Garbo, though she later claimed that there had been no romance between them. He went on to appear in ten talkies, but by the time of the sound era took hold, his type of melodramatic romance was no longer popular. Unfortunately he was not skilled enough as an actor to carry other types of films. He retired from the screen after 1934, then began drinking heavily. He died of a heart attack a few years later. He had been married to actresses Leatrice Joy, Ina Claire, and Virginia Bruce; each marriage ended in divorce. **Selected Works:** *Queen Christina* (1933)

# Terry Gilliam

**Born:** November 22, 1940; Minneapolis, MN

**Years Active in the Industry:** by decade

| 10s | 20s | 30s | 40s | 50s | 60s | 70s | 80s | 90s |
|-----|-----|-----|-----|-----|-----|-----|-----|-----|

Innovative animator, actor, writer, and director Terry Gilliam was born in America, where he briefly worked as a writer-illustrator for *Mad* magazine before emigrating to England in 1967. There he began developing his unique animated cartoons involving cut-outs (stolen from magazines, photos, and actual copies of famous works of art) while working on the children's TV show *Do Not Adjust Your Set.* Gilliam's surreal animations were done as short stream-of-consciousness segments often containing jet-black humor that fortunately sailed right over the heads of the children. In 1969 his work found a more appropriate audience when he teamed up with the comedy troupe Monty Python and begin providing animated segues for their British TV show, *Monty Python's Flying Circus.* Not only did he animate segments, he also contributed as a writer. Interestingly, he was never given plotlines or ideas for his part of the show; instead, the others would ring him up in his cramped attic studio and simply tell him how much time he would need to fill. Later he co-directed Python's first original film, *Monty Python and the Holy Grail* (1975), and the following year had his first outing as a solo director with *Jabberwocky* (1976). He went on to appear in and help create two more Python films, as well as to become a well-respected director of such films as *Time Bandits* (1979), *Brazil* (1985) and *The Fisher King* (1991), usually writing the films he directs. As with his art, his films offer a surreal, often darkly humorous view of the world.

# Annabeth Gish (Anne Elizabeth Gish)

**Born:** March 1971; Albuquerque, NM

**Years Active in the Industry:** by decade

| 10s | 20s | 30s | 40s | 50s | 60s | 70s | 80s | 90s |
|-----|-----|-----|-----|-----|-----|-----|-----|-----|

Annabeth Gish, a natural ingenue, began acting in children's theater when she was only eight. By the time she was 11 she had appeared in a number of amateur, children's, and college stage productions. She also began modeling in ads when she was 11. When she was in her early teens, an impressive audition at a cast-

ing call led to her screen debut in *Desert Bloom* (1986), in which she had the central role opposite Jon Voight. Gish gained popularity with her role in the suprising *Mystic Pizza* (1988), and followed up with another coming-of-ager, *Shag* (1989). She has gone on to co-star in several more films and TV movies. **Selected Works:** *When He's Not a Stranger* (1989), *Coupe De Ville* (1990), *Wyatt Earp* (1994)

# Lillian Gish (Lillian de Guiche)

**Born:** October 14, 1896; Springfield, OH
**Died:** February 27, 1993; New York, NY

**Years Active in the Industry:** by decade

| 10s | 20s | 30s | 40s | 50s | 60s | 70s | 80s | 90s |
|-----|-----|-----|-----|-----|-----|-----|-----|-----|

American silent screen actress Lillian Gish was the daughter of actress Mary Gish (aka Mae Barnard) and sister of actress Dorothy Gish. At age five she made her theatrical debut in the

melodrama *In Convict Stripes.* Shortly before, during one of her restless father's frequent absences, her mother had taken up acting to earn money, and was soon persuaded by friends to supplement the family income by getting her daughters in on the act. As a child, Lillian (billed "Baby Lillian") traveled with touring companies, usually with her mother and sister but occasionally by herself; at one point she had a dancing part in a Sarah Bernhardt production in New York. She and her sister also posed for artists and photographers. Their big break came in 1912, when they went to seek work at Manhattan's American Biograph Company. There they ran into an old friend, a former child actress they had known as "Gladys Smith." Smith was Mary Pickford, soon to be a major star, and she introduced them to director D.W. Griffith, who cast all three of them in *An Uneasy Enemy,* filmed that same day. Lillian became a favorite of Griffith's, who found that beneath her outer fragility was a spiritual depth and physical strength that made her the ideal choice for his melodramas. Under his guidance, she became the most skilled actress in silent films, known as "The First Lady of the Silent Screen." Griffith directed all of her films until the early '20s, when Gish began choosing her own scripts and directors. In 1920, Lillian tried her hand at directing with *Remodeling Her Husband* starring her sister. After a few more smash successes in the mid-'20s, her bright star began to slowly fade in the public's fickle eye. All the while, her studio, MGM, began grooming her replacement, Greta Garbo. In

1928, MGM released Gish, and she left Hollywood to appear in several Broadway plays during the '30s. During the early '40s, she occasionally appeared in character roles in films, but most of her professional energy went to the stage and, later, to TV and lecture tours. For her work in *Duel in the Sun* (1947), she received a Best Supporting Actress Oscar nomination. In 1970 she received a special Academy Award "for superlative artistry and distinguished contributions to the progress of motion pictures." She authored two autobiographies, *Life and Lillian Gish* (1932) and *The Movies, Mr. Griffith, and Me* (1969). She never married. **Selected Works:** *Portrait of Jennie* (1948), *Whales of August* (1987)

# Robin Givens

**Born:** November 27, 1964; New York, NY

**Years Active in the Industry:** by decade

| 10ˢ | 20ˢ | 30ˢ | 40ˢ | 50ˢ | 60ˢ | 70ˢ | 80ˢ | 90ˢ |
|-----|-----|-----|-----|-----|-----|-----|-----|-----|

African American model/actress Robin Givens first gained national prominence as a regular on the TV series *Head of the Class*. From 1986 through 1991, she played Darlene Merriman, a prep-school type attending a high school honors program. Though she was but one of an ensemble, Givens's participation in the series was hyped by the network on the occasion of her marriage to boxing champ Mike Tyson (reportedly, her ego grew in direct proportion to her tabloid-press notoriety). The marriage ended in divorce after only a few years, amidst accusations of brutality and infidelity. Givens has proven she is not merely an adjunct to Mike Tyson's fame with excellent performances in such TV and movie projects as *The Women of Brewster Place* (1989) and *A Rage in Harlem* (1991), and the TV series *Courthouse*. **Selected Works:** *Boomerang* (1992), *Penthouse* (1992), *Foreign Student* (1994)

# Jackie C. Gleason (Herbert John Gleason)

**Born:** February 26, 1916; Brooklyn, NY
**Died:** June 24, 1987; Fort Lauderdale, FL

**Years Active in the Industry:** by decade

| 10ˢ | 20ˢ | 30ˢ | 40ˢ | 50ˢ | 60ˢ | 70ˢ | 80ˢ | 90ˢ |
|-----|-----|-----|-----|-----|-----|-----|-----|-----|

Rotund comedian-actor Jackie Gleason broke into show business at age 15 by winning an amateur-night contest, going on to perform in vaudeville, carnivals, nightclubs, and roadhouses. In 1940 he was signed to a film contract by Warner Bros., and he debuted onscreen in *Navy Blues* (1941). His career was interrupted by World War II, but at the war's end, Gleason returned to films, this time playing character roles in a number of films. His film work, however, lent little strength to his career, and he performed

in several Broadway shows before achieving major success as the star of such TV comedy series as *The Life of Riley, The Honeymooners,* and *The Jackie Gleason Show*. It was during his reign on television that Gleason created such enduring characters as Ralph Kramden (the loud-mouth busdriver from *The Honeymooners*), Reggie Van Gleason, and Joe the Bartender. As a result of the comedic talents he displayed on TV, he became known as "The Great One." He returned to films in the early '60s in lead roles, both comic and dramatic (he earned an Academy Award nomination for his performance in *The Hustler* [1961]), but he never had as much success in movies as he did on TV. He did have some success in the late '70s and early '80s playing a good-ole'-boy Southern sheriff in the *Smokey and the Bandit* series of action-comedies. His long career also included a period when he composed, arranged, and conducted recordings of mood music. Gleason died in 1987 of cancer. His grandson is actor Jason Patric.

# James Gleason

**Born:** May 23, 1886; New York, NY
**Died:** 1959

**Years Active in the Industry:** by decade

| 10ˢ | 20ˢ | 30ˢ | 40ˢ | 50ˢ | 60ˢ | 70ˢ | 80ˢ | 90ˢ |
|-----|-----|-----|-----|-----|-----|-----|-----|-----|

Character actor James Gleason usually played tough-talking, world-weary, guys with a secret heart-of-gold. He is easily recognized for his tendency to talk out of the side of his mouth. His parents were actors, and after serving in the Spanish-American War, Gleason joined their stock company in Oakland, California. His career was interrupted by service in World War I, following which he began to appear on Broadway. He debuted onscreen in 1922, but didn't begin to appear regularly in films until 1928. Meanwhile, during the '20s he also wrote a number of plays and musicals, several of which were later made into films. In the early sound era, he collaborated on numerous scripts as a screenwriter or dialogue specialist; he also directed one film, *Hot Tip* (1935). As an actor, he appeared in character roles in over 150 films, playing a wide range of hard-boiled (and often semi-comic) urban characters, including detectives, reporters, marine sergeants, gamblers, fight managers, and the heroes' pals. In a series of films in the '30s, he had a recurring lead role as slow-witted police inspector Oscar Piper. He was married to actress Lucille Webster Gleason; their son was actor Russell Gleason. **Selected Works:** *Here Comes Mr. Jordan* (1941), *Meet John Doe* (1941), *Crash Dive* (1943), *Tree Grows in Brooklyn* (1945), *Bishop's Wife* (1947)

# Scott Glenn

**Born:** January 26, 1942; Pittsburgh, PA

**Years Active in the Industry:** by decade

| 10s | 20s | 30s | 40s | 50s | 60s | 70s | 80s | 90s |
|-----|-----|-----|-----|-----|-----|-----|-----|-----|
|     |     |     |     |     |     | ■ | ■ | ■ |

Rugged character actor Scott Glenn attended college, served in the Marines, and worked as a journalist in Wisconsin before breaking into show business. In 1967 he moved to New York to study acting at Lee Strasberg's Actors' Studio (where he remains an associate); by 1968 he had found some success off-Broadway in heavyweight productions such as *Long Day's Journey Into Night*. He made his screen debut with a supporting role in *The Baby Makers* (1970), but did little film work until 1975 when he appeared in Robert Altman's *Nashville*. This lead him to play roles in films such as *Apocalypse Now* (1979); *Urban Cowboy* (1980); and *The Right Stuff* (1983), in which he portrayed astronaut Alan Shepard; and *Silverado* (1985); indeed, Glenn tends to continue to play gruff, macho characters. **Selected Works:** *Hunt for Red October* (1990), *Backdraft* (1991), *My Heroes Have Always Been Cowboys* (1991), *Silence of the Lambs* (1991), *Extreme Justice* (1993)

# Crispin Glover

**Born:** 1964; New York, NY

**Years Active in the Industry:** by decade

| 10s | 20s | 30s | 40s | 50s | 60s | 70s | 80s | 90s |
|-----|-----|-----|-----|-----|-----|-----|-----|-----|
|     |     |     |     |     |     |     | ■ | ■ |

American actor Crispin Glover, the son of actor and drama coach Bruce Glover, debuted onstage at the Dorothy Chandler Pavilion in Los Angeles at age 14 in *The Sound of Music*. He made his feature film debut at age 18 in *My Tutor* (1982). Glover is known for his peculiar acting style that includes nearly whispered speech punctuated by small karate-like gesticulations. His breakthrough came in the role of the wimpy, nerdy father, George McFly, in Steven Spielberg's *Back to the Future* (1985), after which he landed increasingly important roles. He has a reputation as an eccentric, in part borne out of his personal editing and republishing of books titled *Rat Catching* ( a modernized version of a 100-year-old text to which he added new pictures of mutilated rats) and the equally strange *Concrete Inspection*. During a bizarre appearance on David Letterman's talk-show *Late Night* , the seemingly paranoid, almost psychotic Glover, apparently in the midst of a breakdown, nearly kicked Letterman's head with his grossly oversized shoes. In addition to that, Glover also recorded an album of songs by murderer Charles Manson with a cover graced by Adolf Hitler. Despite his disturbing eccentricities, Crispin Glover is considered by some to be one of the more original and intense actors of his generation. **Selected Works:** *River's Edge* (1987), *Wild at Heart* (1990), *Little Noises* (1991), *Rubin & Ed* (1992), *What's Eating Gilbert Grape* (1993)

# Danny Glover

**Born:** July 22, 1947; San Francisco, CA

**Years Active in the Industry:** by decade

| 10s | 20s | 30s | 40s | 50s | 60s | 70s | 80s | 90s |
|-----|-----|-----|-----|-----|-----|-----|-----|-----|
|     |     |     |     |     |     | ■ | ■ | ■ |

Versatile leading man Danny Glover studied acting at the Black Actors' Workshop, then launched into an acclaimed career on the stage. He won a New York Theater Award for his performance in *Master Harold and the Boys*. After three bit parts, he landed his first important screen role as Moze the farmworker in Robert Benton's Oscar-winning *Places in the Heart* (1984). His handsome, muscular build coupled with his amiable on-screen charisma has lead him to more substantial roles in a number of films. He truly became a star when he was teamed up with Mel Gibson in the *Lethal Weapon* series of buddy-cop action films, beginning with *Lethal Weapon* (1987). Glover served as executive producer of *To Sleep with Anger* (1990), in which he starred as well, and was praised for his performance in the anti-Apartheid film *Bopha!* (1993), which was directed by Morgan Freeman. **Selected Works:** *Lonesome Dove* (1989), *The Color Purple* (1985), *Grand Canyon* (1991), *Angels in the Outfield* (1994)

# John Glover

**Born:** August 7, 1944; Salisbury, MD

**Years Active in the Industry:** by decade

| 10s | 20s | 30s | 40s | 50s | 60s | 70s | 80s | 90s |
|-----|-----|-----|-----|-----|-----|-----|-----|-----|
|     |     |     |     |     |     | ■ | ■ | ■ |

First appearing off-Broadway in 1969, actor (and Towson State Teacher's College graduate) John Glover began the slow transition from stage to screen in the mid-1970s. He had small parts in such films as *Annie Hall* (1977) and *Julia* (1977), but moviemakers didn't start using Glover to full advantage until he became established as a hissable villain in films like *The Evil That Men Do* (1985) and *52 Pick-Up* (1986). Even when he showed up as a goodnatured, childlike Trump/Turner billionaire in *Gremlins 2: The New Batch* (1990), audiences were primed for a final-scene unmasking of Glover as the heavy of the piece (which didn't happen, by the way). On television, Glover has acquitted himself nicely with roles of depth in such TV movies as *An Early Frost* (1985) and *The Two Mrs. Greenvilles* (1986). **Selected Works:** *El Diablo* (1990), *Dead on the Money* (1991), *Season of Giants* (1991), *What Ever Happened to Baby Jane?* (1991), *Drug Wars: The Cocaine Cartel, Part 1* (1992)

# Jean-Luc Godard

**Born:** December 3, 1930; Paris, France

**Years Active in the Industry:** by decade

| 10s | 20s | 30s | 40s | 50s | 60s | 70s | 80s | 90s |
|-----|-----|-----|-----|-----|-----|-----|-----|-----|

Having grown up with all the luxuries and privileges of his wealthy Parisian family, French film director Jean-Luc Godard attended the Sorbonne, purportedly to be educated in ethnology. Instead he devoted his waking hours to studying film, befriending several influential French new-wave filmmakers and turning his hobby into a vocation by writing for *Cahiers du Cinema.* Cut off from all funding by his disapproving father, Godard drifted about for several years—a clouded period from which legends of various petty thefts, jail terms and exotic adventures have sprung. Supporting himself as a laborer (the writing barely paid the rent), Godard was able to finance his first directorial project, a short subject about the construction of a dam. Four other shorts followed before Godard made his first feature from a script by Francois Truffault: *A Bout de Souffle* (1959) (released in English-speaking countries as *Breathless*), the free-form, improvisational tale of a small time crook (and Humphrey Bogart fan). The film made a star of Jean-Paul Belmondo, revitalized the career of American actress Jean Seberg, and put Godard in the forefront of a hand-held cinema genre popularly known as *Nouvelle Vague.* Godard let the world know of his Marxist leanings with his next film, *Le Petit Soldat* (1961), a damnation of France's involvement in Algeria that served as a model for the many later anti-Vietnam films. It was so contemptuous of the French government that it was banned from Godard's homeland until 1963. The director's subsequent films were similarly controversial, some of them provoking fist-fights between pro- and anti-Godard factions. Hollywood's Joseph E. Levine and Italy's Carlo Ponti, impressed by the publicity and by the director's excellent reputation with the New York Film Festival, waved a million-dollar budget in front of Godard and invited him to film a Technicolor "A" picture starring Brigette Bardot. Godard responded by delivering a hate-filled indictment of the whole Hollywood system, significantly titled *Contempt* (1963). In addition to laying bare the perceived vulgarities of Levine and Ponti, Godard mocked their financing by deliberately making a picture that looked as cheap (if not cheaper) than *Breathless;* one scene in a rundown deserted house went on for half an hour! Even though he despised Hollywood, Godard did not despise the films

made there. His lifelong idols included John Ford and Orson Welles, while *Breathless* was dedicated to the old B-picture factory, Monogram Studios. Seemingly reveling in baiting international censors and refusing to descend to conventionalism, Godard continued making films with no obvious commercial notions in mind; as long as they pleased him and his followers, that was fine. Even when handling a purely formula science fiction picture like *Alphaville* (1965), Godard followed his own drumbeat, resulting in one of the most intensely personal "futuristic" films ever made. *Weekend* (1968), Godard's last big critical success, explored humanity's obsession with violence by concentrating upon an apocalyptic traffic jam. In the early 1970s, Godard began renouncing his own early work and moved toward becoming a full-time revolutionary, preaching to the converted with filmed tracts rather than narrative movies; he also briefly ceased to work by himself, choosing to collaborate with those whom (he thought) shared his political views. Returning to solo directing in the 1980s, Jean-Luc Goddard mellowed a bit, becoming less outrageous and more introspective in his filmmaking. Still, Godard refused to turn out anything for bourgeois audiences, and his "quiet" films (including *Hail Mary* [1985] and *Woe Is Me* [1993]) are just as idiosyncratic as his rebellious projects of the 1950s and 1960s. **Selected Works:** *Woman Is a Woman* (1960), *My Life to Live* (1962), *Pierrot Le Fou* (1965), *Masculine Feminine* (1966), *Tout Va Bien* (1973)

# Paulette Goddard (Pauline Marion Levee)

**Born:** June 3, 1911; Long Island, NY
**Died:** April 23, 1990; Ronco, Switzerland

**Years Active in the Industry:** by decade

| 10s | 20s | 30s | 40s | 50s | 60s | 70s | 80s | 90s |
|-----|-----|-----|-----|-----|-----|-----|-----|-----|

American actress Paulette Goddard spent her teen years as a Broadway chorus girl, gaining attention when she was featured reclining on a prop crescent moon in the 1928 Ziegfeld musical *Rio Rita.* In Hollywood as early as 1929, Paulette reportedly appeared as an extra in several Hal Roach two-reel comedies, making confirmed bit appearances in a handful of these short subjects wearing a blonde wig over her naturally raven-black hair. Continuing as a blonde, she appeared as a "Goldwyn Girl" in the 1932 Eddie Cantor film *Kid From Spain,* where she was awarded several closeups. Paulette's career went into full gear when she met Charlie Chaplin, who was looking for an unknown actress to play "The Gamin" in his 1936 film *Modern Times.* Struck by the actress's breathtaking beauty and natural comic sense, Chaplin not only cast her in the film, but fell in love with her. It is still a matter of contention in some circles as to whether or not Charlie and Paulette were ever legally married (Chaplin claimed they were; it was his third marriage and her second), but whatever the case the two lived together throughout the 1930s. Goddard's expert performances in such films as *The Young in Heart* (1938) and *The Cat and the Canary* (1939) enabled her to ascend to stardom without Chaplin's sponsorship, but the role she truly craved was that of Scarlett

O'Hara in the 1939 epic *Gone With the Wind.* Existing test footage indicates that she would have made an excellent Scarlett, but the tide of public opinion was against her; since no one knew the state of her marital status with Chaplin, she was deemed a "moral risk," one whose casting as Scarlett would not sit well in America's Bible-belt states. After working together in *The Great Dictator* (1940), Paulette and Chaplin's relationship crumbled; by the mid-1940s she was married to another extremely gifted performer, Burgess Meredith. The actress remained a box-office draw for her home studio Paramount until 1949, when (presumably as a result of a recent flop titled *Bride of Vengeance*) she received a phone call at home telling her bluntly that her contract was dissolved. Goddard's film appearances in the 1950s were in such demeaning B pictures as *Vice Squad* (1953) and *Babes in Baghdad* (1953). Still quite beautiful, and possessed of a keener intellect than most movie actors, she retreated to Europe with her fourth (or third?) husband, German novelist Erich Maria Remarque (*All Quiet on the Western Front*). This union was successful, lasting until Remarque's death. Coaxed out of retirement for one made-for-TV movie in 1972 (*The Snoop Sisters*), Goddard preferred to remain in her lavish Switzerland home for the last two decades of her life. **Selected Works:** *Hold Back the Dawn* (1941), *Star Spangled Rhythm* (1942), *So Proudly We Hail* (1943), *Kitty* (1945)

# Whoopi Goldberg (Caryn Johnson)

**Born:** November 13, 1949; New York, NY

**Years Active in the Industry:** by decade

| 10s | 20s | 30s | 40s | 50s | 60s | 70s | 80s | 90s |
|-----|-----|-----|-----|-----|-----|-----|-----|-----|
|     |     |     |     |     |     |     |     |     |

Distinguished comedienne and actress, Whoopi Goldberg began performing at New York's Helena Rubenstein Children's Theater at age eight. She was also enrolled in the Hudson Guild children's arts program. Later she attended the famed New York High School for the Performing Arts, and after graduation she moved to California, becoming a founding member of the San Diego Repertory Theater. There she appeared in such serious dramas as Brecht's *Mother Courage.* She went on to join Spontaneous Combustion, an improvisational group, then appeared in fringe drama at Berkeley's Blake Street Hawkeyes Theater. In the early '80s she began appearing in a solo satirical act called *The Spook Show,* first in San Francisco and then on the road in the U.S. and Europe. This led in 1983 to a one-woman show on Broadway, directed by Mike Nichols; for her work she won both Drama Desk and Theater World Awards. She debuted onscreen in Steven Spielberg's *The Color Purple* (1985), for which she won a Best Actress Golden Globe Award and an Oscar nomination; also in 1985 she won a Grammy Award for the album of her Broadway show, which was named Best Comedy Recording. After her initial film success, she appeared in a string of poor or unsuccessful films; this period was ended with her Oscar winning portrayal of a fake medium in

the mega-hit *Ghost* (1990), a role which many felt saved her film career. She again found public acclaim for her stint as a tawdry night-club singer who invades a convent in the films *Sister Act* (1991), and *Sister Act 2: Back in the Habit* (1993). She has also been active in the Comic Relief charity projects, has done other solo shows, and has worked on TV, where she received an Emmy nomination for her work in an episode of *Moonlighting,* co-starred briefly in the TV series *Bagdad Cafe,* and was a semi-regular on the syndicated hit *Star Trek The Next Generation* playing the ever-wise, alien bartender Guinan. **Selected Works:** *The Player* (1992), *Sarafina!* (1992), *Star Trek Generations* (1994), *Boys on the Side* (1995), *Moonlight and Valentino* (1995)

# Jeff Goldblum

**Born:** October 22, 1952; Pittsburgh, PA

**Years Active in the Industry:** by decade

| 10s | 20s | 30s | 40s | 50s | 60s | 70s | 80s | 90s |
|-----|-----|-----|-----|-----|-----|-----|-----|-----|
|     |     |     |     |     |     |     |     |     |

American actor Jeff Goldblum began studying acting shortly after graduating from high school, working at New York City's Neighborhood Playhouse; since the early '70s he has

worked both on and off-Broadway, appearing in everything from Shakespeare to musicals. His first notable role was as a guard in Joe Papp's New York production of *Two Gentlemen of Verona.* He debuted onscreen with a small role in the Charles Bronson vehicle *Death Wish* (1974). While performing in the comic review *El Grande de Coca Cola,* he was spotted by director Robert Altman, who cast him in small roles in *California Split* (1974) and in the ensemble movie *Nashville* (1975). From there he tended to appear in small or cameo roles, or in films that attracted little attention. In the early '80s he co-starred in the TV series *Tenspeed and Brown Shoe.* He became well-known after appearing in *The Right Stuff* and *The Big Chill* (both 1983), resulting in a string of leading roles in major productions through the '90s. He has also worked in a number of TV movies, notably as Nobel Prize-winner James Watson in the BBC production *Life Story* (1987). He married and divorced actress Geena Davis and has maintained a long-time romance with actress Laura Dern, with whom he co-starred in *Jurassic Park* (1993). **Selected Works:** *Fly* (1986), *Deep Cover* (1992), *The Player* (1992)

# William Goldman

**Born:** August 12, 1931; Chicago, IL

**Years Active in the Industry:** by decade

| 10s | 20s | 30s | 40s | 50s | 60s | 70s | 80s | 90s |
|-----|-----|-----|-----|-----|-----|-----|-----|-----|

The younger brother of writer James Goldman, William Goldman has successfully tackled every sort of professional writing, from children's books to novels to essays to plays to screenplays. He is even more prolific than some people might assume: several of Goldman's works were published under the *nom de plume* Harry Longbaugh. Goldman is at his best with iconoclastic historical pieces, notably his Oscar-winning screenplays for *Butch Cassidy and the Sundance Kid* (1969) and *All the President's Men* (1976). He has also expertly adapted many of his own novels to the screen: *Marathon Man* (1976) (another Oscar winner), *Magic* (1978), *Heat* (1979) and *The Princess Bride* (1987). Goldman has earned a reputation as an ace "script doctor", offering his uncredited services to projects that might otherwise be unfilmable. A perceptive inside observer of the movie business, Goldman has written two revelatory nonfiction books, *Adventures in the Screen Trade* (1983) and *Hype and Glory* (1990). He recently returned to the "revisionist" western format he'd popularized in *Butch Cassidy* with his screenplay for Mel Gibson's *Maverick* (1994). **Selected Works:** *Right Stuff* (1983), *Misery* (1990)

# Jerry Goldsmith (Jerrald Goldsmith)

**Born:** February 10, 1929; Los Angeles, CA

**Years Active in the Industry:** by decade

| 10s | 20s | 30s | 40s | 50s | 60s | 70s | 80s | 90s |
|-----|-----|-----|-----|-----|-----|-----|-----|-----|

American film composer Jerry Goldsmith was classically trained in piano and composition before studying the "science" of film scores at the University of Southern California, under the tutelage of Hollywood veteran Miklos Rozsa. Much of Rozsa's stylistic influence stayed with Goldsmith in his subsequent TV and radio work, notably the use of bass drums and deliberately discordant "stings" during action or suspense sequences. Goldsmith's first film score was for the inexpensive western *Black Patch* in 1957; since that time he has received numerous Oscar nominations, and in 1976 won the coveted statuette for *The Omen*. Among Goldsmith's best scores have been those for *Gremlins* (1984), *Rambo: First Blood II* (1985), *Total Recall* (1990) and *Basic Instinct* (1991). One project with which Jerry Goldsmith has been closely associated was Rod Serling's classic TV series *The Twilight Zone;* many of Goldsmith's scores for the series (notably the one heard on the 1960 episode "Back There") have since been absorbed into television's standard stock-music catalog. **Selected Works:** *Planet of the Apes* (1968), *Patton* (1970), *Chinatown* (1974), *Poltergeist* (1982), *Hoosiers* (1986)

# Samuel Goldwyn (Samuel Goldfish)

**Born:** August 27, 1882; Warsaw, Poland
**Died:** 1974

**Years Active in the Industry:** by decade

| 10s | 20s | 30s | 40s | 50s | 60s | 70s | 80s | 90s |
|-----|-----|-----|-----|-----|-----|-----|-----|-----|

One of the most distinguished of the old Hollywood film moguls, Goldwyn arrived in America in 1893 without a penny to his name. He became a glovemaker's apprentice and studied in his 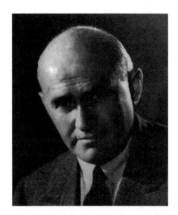 spare time. In 1913, he and his brother-in-law, the vaudeville producer Jesse L. Lasky, formed a film company at Goldfish's suggestion. The company's debut release, *The Squaw Man,* was an enormous hit, and it had a good three years before merging with Adolph Zukor's Famous Players studio. Soon after, Goldfish went into partnership with Edgar Selwyn in a company whose name took the first syllable of Goldfish's name and the last one of Selwyn's—the Goldwyn name, which Goldfish soon adopted, was born. The original Goldwyn studio merged with Metro Studios and L. B. Mayer's production company in the early 1920s to form Metro-Goldwyn-Mayer, but Samuel Goldwyn wasn't long in that partnership. In 1923 he formed Samuel Goldwyn Productions, the company that he was to run for the next four decades. Goldwyn's philosophy, in contrast to the major studios, was to make one picture at a time, but make it very well, sparing no expense in bringing the best actors, directors, designers, composers, and writers together to create only the finest in feature films— Goldwyn never made "B" pictures, and every Samuel Goldwyn Production was an important film, getting the full devotion of its producer's resources and attention. The company came into its own with the arrival of sound; included in Goldwyn's illustrious talent pool were Ronald Colman, Gary Cooper, Laurence Olivier, Merle Oberon, Eddie Cantor, Danny Kaye, David Niven, Will Rogers, Walter Huston, Susan Hayward, and Joel McCrea; director William Wyler; the composers George and Ira Gershwin and Aaron Copland; choreographer Busby Berkeley; and the authors Lillian Hellman, Sinclair Lewis, and Robert Sherwood. Goldwyn's films, whether serious dramas like *These Three* (1936) (a partly censored version of Hellman's play *The Children's Hour*), *Dodsworth* (1936), or *The Best Years of Our Lives* (1946), or comedies like *Ball Of Fire* (1941), were all quality entertainment—indeed, his family films such as *Hans Christian Andersen* (1952) rivaled the best live-action movies that Disney created, while his musicals, including numerous Eddie Cantor vehicles (*Whoopee!* [1930], *Palmy Days* [1931], and *Roman Scandals* [1933], up through *Guys and Dolls* [1955]) were more than a match for any contemproary releases by Warner Bros. or MGM. Like many of the other moguls, Goldwyn's judgement and business fortunes faltered in the years after World War II as audiences and American popular culture began changing rapidly. His *Guys and Dolls* (1955) was a hit, but Goldwyn's attempt to produce Gershwin's *Porgy and Bess* (1959) was a colossal failure, partly because of major production problems, including a fire that destroyed its expensive sets. As a man who arrived in America during the 1890's and whose entertainment sense was formed in vaudeville, he seemed unable to cope with a fast-paced post-war world fueled by television and rock 'n roll as major cultural forces. He ceased production in 1959, and, because his company still owns virtually every picture it ever produced, his films continue to enjoy prestige on home video, in television and in theatrical presentation.

# Tony Goldwyn (Anthony Goldwyn)

**Born:** 1960; Los Angeles, CA

**Years Active in the Industry:** by decade

| 10s | 20s | 30s | 40s | 50s | 60s | 70s | 80s | 90s |
|-----|-----|-----|-----|-----|-----|-----|-----|-----|
|     |     |     |     |     |     |     | ■   | ■   |

The grandson of movie mogul Samuel Goldwyn, actor Tony Goldwyn favored his grandmother's side of the family (she was onetime film actress Frances Howard) by pursuing an acting rather than an executive career. Tony's first major film was 1987's *Gaby: A True Story*, in which he was eighth-billed. His breakthrough feature was 1990's *Ghost*, in which Goldwyn played Carl, the "lying snake" who sets up the murder of Patrick Swayze and then callously moves in on Swayze's grieving girlfriend (Demi Moore). A master at playing charming but shallow yuppies, Goldwyn appeared in *The Pelican Brief* (1994). **Selected Works:** *Iran: Days of Crisis* (1991)

# Valeria Golino

**Born:** October 22, 1966; Naples, Italy

**Years Active in the Industry:** by decade

| 10s | 20s | 30s | 40s | 50s | 60s | 70s | 80s | 90s |
|-----|-----|-----|-----|-----|-----|-----|-----|-----|
|     |     |     |     |     |     |     | ■   | ■   |

Wholesomely sexy Italian actress Valeria Golino was a teen model when she appeared in her first film, Lina Wertmuller's *Joke of Destiny* (1984). Conversant (if not proficient) in several languages, Golino thrived in international films bearing such provocative titles as *Little Fires* (1985), *Last Summer in Tangiers* (1987) and *Love Story* (1987). One of her first important American roles was as Tom Cruise's voice-of-conscience girlfriend in the Oscar-winning *Rain Man* (1988), after which she portrayed the

trapeze artist who falls in love with Pee-Wee Herman in *Big Top Pee-Wee* (1988). Blessed with a subtle, sparkle-eyed sense of humor, Golino has been seen to good advantage in the adventure-film spoofs *Hot Shots!* (1991) and *Hot Shots Part Deux* (1992); her deadly serious delivery of the most ridiculous of lines ("What do you do with an elephant with three balls?") has been attributed by some to expert comic timing, and by others to Golino's alleged habit of learning her English dialogue by rote. **Selected Works:** *Indian Runner* (1991), *Immortal Beloved* (1994), *Four Rooms* (1995)

# John Goodman

**Born:** June 20, 1952; St. Louis, MO

**Years Active in the Industry:** by decade

| 10s | 20s | 30s | 40s | 50s | 60s | 70s | 80s | 90s |
|-----|-----|-----|-----|-----|-----|-----|-----|-----|
|     |     |     |     |     |     |     | ■   | ■   |

Six-foot three-inch, portly character and lead actor John Goodman attended college on a football scholarship but was sidelined by an injury, after which he concentrated on drama studies. He moved to New York in 1975, working his way from off-off-Broadway to Broadway, where he appeared in *Loose Ends* and the musical *Big River;* he also made TV commercials. He debuted on-screen in a small role in *Eddie Macon's Run* (1983). His first major role was as a policeman in *The Big Easy* (1985). Goodman has worked steadily in a wide variety of genres through out the 1980s, but he did not have a lead role until *King Ralph* (1991). In 1994, he appeared as a larger-than-life version of Fred Flintstone in *The Flintstones*. Most recently he received critical acclaim for his powerful portrayal of the controversial Louisana senator in *Huey Long* (1995). Despite his respectable and growing body of filmwork, Goodman is still best known as Roseanne's TV husband, Dan, on her long-running TV sitcom. **Selected Works:** *Sea of Love* (1989), *Arachnophobia* (1990), *Barton Fink* (1991), *Babe* (1992), *Matinee* (1992)

# Frances Goodrich

**Born:** 1891; Belleville, NJ
**Died:** January 29, 1984; Manhattan, NY

**Years Active in the Industry:** by decade

| 10s | 20s | 30s | 40s | 50s | 60s | 70s | 80s | 90s |
|-----|-----|-----|-----|-----|-----|-----|-----|-----|
|     | ■   | ■   | ■   | ■   | ■   |     |     |     |

Completing her education at Vassar, American screenwriter Frances Goodrich began her career as an actress, first appearing on Broadway in 1916. Her stage career was slightly more successful than her marital experiences; by 1929 she had been divorced twice, first from actor Robert Ames, then from historian Henrik Willem Van Loon (the author of *The Story of Mankind*). Thus she was not predisposed to romantic entanglements when, in the late

1920s, she met fellow actor Albert Hackett; moreover, he was to her a "fresh kid" (he was nine years her junior). As it happened, both Goodrich and Hackett shared a mutual goal: to leave acting behind in favor of playwrighting. The two were married while collaborating on their first Broadway hit, *Up Pops the Devil* (1929). This success eventually led to the pair being signed as a writing team by MGM, where they launched the popular *Thin Man* series, allegedly basing the characterizations of Nick and Nora Charles on their good friends Dashiel Hammett (who wrote the novel upon which *Thin Man* was based) and Lillian Hellman. While there would be another Broadway production on the Goodrich/Hackett docket in the 1940s, *The Great Big Doorstep*, for the most part the couple devoted their time to screenwriting. They were particularly skilled at adapting the works of others to meet the restrictions and requirements of the movies; among their most famous film credits were adaptations of Owen Wister's *The Virginian* (1946), S. N. Behman's *The Pirate* (1948), Edward Streeter's *Father of the Bride* (1950), and the musical version of Stephen Vincent Benet's *Sobbin' Women*, released as *Seven Brides for Seven Brothers* (1954). Goodrich and Hackett were also among the many writers who toiled on Frank Capra's *It's A Wonderful Life* (1946); when apprised that Capra was passing off their scriptwork as his own "inspirations", Goodrich characterized the director as "that dreadful man!", a position which she held even after *Wonderful Life* was acknowledged a screen classic. One of the Goodrich/Hackett projects at MGM was to have been an film version of *The Diary of Anne Frank;* when the studio nixed the project as too downbeat, the couple labored for two years on their own adaptation, which ultimately opened on Broadway in 1954 and won a Pulitzer Prize. Goodrich and Hackett retired to their lavish New York apartment after completing work on their last film, an adaptation of Peter Shaffer's play *Five Finger Exercise* (1962).

# Ruth Gordon (Ruth Gordon Jones)

**Born:** October 30, 1896; Quincy, MA
**Died:** August 28, 1985; Edgartown, MA

**Years Active in the Industry:** by decade

| 10ˢ | 20ˢ | 30ˢ | 40ˢ | 50ˢ | 60ˢ | 70ˢ | 80ˢ | 90ˢ |
|-----|-----|-----|-----|-----|-----|-----|-----|-----|
|     |     |     |     |     |     |     |     |     |

The daughter of a former ship's captain, American actress Ruth Gordon knew what she wanted to do with her life after witnessing a performance by stage actress Hazel Dawn. Over the initial objections of her father, Gordon decided upon a stage career, studying at the American Academy of Dramatic Arts. After the usual deprivations and barnstorming (and a few extra roles in such films as *Camille* [1915]), she got her first positive newspaper notice for her appearance in a 1915 production of *Peter Pan*. "Ruth Gordon was ever so gay as Nibs," wrote influential critic Alexander Wolcott, who became a valued and powerful friend to Gordon and did what he could to encourage her and promote her career. With such stage hits as *Seventeen, Serena Blandish,* and *Ethan Frome,* Gor-

don was one of Broadway's biggest stars of the 1920s and 1930s; privately her life was blotted by the premature death of her first husband, actor Gregory Kelly. Not anxious to marry again, Gordon conducted long affairs with two of Broadway's biggest producers, causing shock waves in a more Puritanical age by acknowledging her "out of wedlock" son, the result of her liason with producer Jed Harris. Finally she married again , to the brilliant playwright Garson Kanin, some 16 years her junior—a marriage that would last over four decades. Combining stage work with appearances in such films as *Abe Lincoln in Illinois* (1940) and *Action in the North Atlantic* (1943), Gordon began to collaborate with Kanin on writing projects, with such delightful results as the Tracy-Hepburn film comedies *Adam's Rib* (1949) and *Pat and Mike* (1952), and the Judy Holliday feature *The Marrying Kind* (1952). Long absent from movies, Gordon returned to the cameras for *Inside Daisy Clover* (1966), then took on the kinky role of an elderly witch in *Rosemary's Baby* (1968). Upon receiving her Academy Award for this role, the 72-year-old Ruth brought down the house at the Oscar ceremonies by saying "You have no idea how encouragin' a thing like this can be." Though few of her subsequent film assignments were this prestigious, Gordon managed to enter cult-film Valhalla with unforgettable roles in two films: *Where's Poppa?* (1970), in which she played the obscenely senile mother of George Segal; and *Harold and Maude* (1972), as the freewheeling soulmate of suicidal teen Bud Cort. **Selected Works:** *Dr. Ehrlich's Magic Bullet* (1940), *Double Life* (1947), *My Bodyguard* (1980)

# Lou Gossett, Jr.

**Born:** May 27, 1936; Brooklyn, NY

**Years Active in the Industry:** by decade

| 10ˢ | 20ˢ | 30ˢ | 40ˢ | 50ˢ | 60ˢ | 70ˢ | 80ˢ | 90ˢ |
|-----|-----|-----|-----|-----|-----|-----|-----|-----|
|     |     |     |     |     |     |     |     |     |

Versatile lead and supporting actor Louis Gossett, Jr. began dabbling in acting after injuring his leg in high school while playing basketball. He continued playing basketball, however, going on after college to play briefly with the New York Knicks. After studying acting with Lloyd Richards and Frank Silvera, he went on to appear on Broadway in the lead role of *Take a Giant Step;* for his performance he won the Donaldson Award as Best Newcomer of the Year. His stage work led him to TV, and eventually to his feature film debut in *A Raisin in the Sun* (1961), reprising the role he'd played on Broadway. Gossett did not make another film until the '70s, but he did continue on with his stage and TV work (he also sang occasionally in nightclubs). He appeared in several films in the '70s, did guest spots on TV shows, and briefly starred in his own show ,*The Lazarus Syndrome.* For his work in the smash hit TV miniseries *Roots,* Gossett won an Emmy, but he did not become really well-known until he won the Oscar for Best Supporting Actor for his portrayal of a tough drill instructor in *An Officer and a Gentleman* (1982), for which he also won a Golden Globe and the NAACP Image Award. This "tough guy" role led to much work in action-adventure movies in the '80s and '90s, including the three *Iron Eagle* movies (1986, 1987, 1992). **Selected Works:** *Sudie and Simpson* (1990), *Murder on the Bayou* (1991), *Carolina Skeletons* (1992), *Diggstown* (1992), *Monolith* (1993)

# Elliott Gould (Elliott Goldstein)

**Born:** August 29, 1938; Brooklyn, NY

**Years Active in the Industry:** by decade

| 10ˢ | 20ˢ | 30ˢ | 40ˢ | 50ˢ | 60ˢ | 70ˢ | 80ˢ | 90ˢ |
|-----|-----|-----|-----|-----|-----|-----|-----|-----|

Tall, distinctive-looking actor with a quirky comedic style, Elliott Gould the son of an ambitious "stage mother," began taking lessons in drama, diction, singing, and dancing at the age of eight. His earliest performances were in temples and hospitals, where he did song-and-dance routines; he also modeled and occasionally worked on TV. He attended Manhattan's Professional Children's School and spent his summers performing in the Catskill "borscht belt." A student of ballet, at age 18 he debuted on Broadway in a chorus line. For several years held odd jobs while struggling to find theatrical work. His first break came with a chorus job in David Merrick's *Irma La Douce,* which got him in line for an audition for the Broadway play *I Can Get It for You Wholesale;* he landed the lead role and got excellent reviews, but the show was only a minor success. However, the show was a turning point for his co-star Barbara Streisand, who was rapidly becoming a major star. Following the play, he and Streisand had a love affair which led to their marriage in 1963. He debuted onscreen in *Quick, Let's Get Married* (1964), but the film went unreleased; it was followed by a role in another failure, *The Confession* (1964). For several years his career went nowhere while hers soared, and he occupied himself by managing her TV enterprises; he began to be called "Mr. Streisand," driving him to despair and psychiatric therapy. In 1968 he got a supporting role in the film *The Night They Raided Minsky's,* after which his rise was swift; he next landed a co-starring role in *Bob & Carol & Ted & Alice* (1969), for which he received a Best Supporting Actor Oscar nomination. He became a full-fledged star after his third film, Robert Altman's smash hit Korean War comedy *M\*A\*S\*H* (1970); now one of the hottest actors in Hollywood, he began getting one big role after another. Around the same time, he separated from Streisand. In 1971 he became the first non-Swede to star in an Ingmar Bergman film, *The Touch.* Unfortunately, his career soon began to spiral downward after he chose to do several sub-par and unsuccessful movies; by the end

of the '70s he was no longer in demand, and he went on to work onscreen steadily but unmemorably. His most recent appearances have been in character or supporting roles, including a graceful cameo in *Bugsy* (1991).

# Edmund Goulding

**Born:** March 20, 1891; London, England
**Died:** December 24, 1959; Hollywood, CA

**Years Active in the Industry:** by decade

| 10ˢ | 20ˢ | 30ˢ | 40ˢ | 50ˢ | 60ˢ | 70ˢ | 80ˢ | 90ˢ |
|-----|-----|-----|-----|-----|-----|-----|-----|-----|

A child actor in British theater, Goulding came to the States after World War I and began writing for films in 1921, most notably for producer/director Henry King with *Tol'able David, The Seventh Day,* and *Fury* (from Goulding's own novel). Goulding debuted as a writer/director with MGM in 1925, and helmed two memorable Greta Garbo films, the silent *Love* and the talkie *Grand Hotel.* At Warner Bros. in the late '30s, he directed Bette Davis in *Dark Victory* (1939), *The Old Maid* (1939), and *The Great Lie* (1941). His strongest work of the 1940s were his films with Tyrone Power, *The Razor's Edge* and *Nightmare Alley.*

# Betty Grable (Elizabeth Ruth Grable)

**Born:** December 18, 1916; South St. Louis, MO
**Died:** July 2, 1973; Los Angeles, CA

**Years Active in the Industry:** by decade

| 10ˢ | 20ˢ | 30ˢ | 40ˢ | 50ˢ | 60ˢ | 70ˢ | 80ˢ | 90ˢ |
|-----|-----|-----|-----|-----|-----|-----|-----|-----|

The celebrated "pin-up girl" of World War II, American actress Betty Grable was the daughter of a stockbroker and an aggressive "stage mother." When her older sister Marjorie balked at

a show business career, Grable was taken in hand by her mother and trained to sing, dance, tell jokes and play the ukulele and saxophone. Despite her father's objections, Grable begged her mother to take her to Los Angeles for a movie career, preparing herself with a two-girl musical act while attending Hollywood Professional School. Lying about her age, 13-year-old Grable was hired as a chorus girl for short subjects, getting her first important exposure as the energetic blonde "cowgirl" who sings the first chorus of the first song in the Eddie Cantor film musical *Whoopee!* (1930). She played supporting parts in two-reelers and bits in features for the next couple of years, attaining her first major role in *Hold 'Em Jail* (1932), a comedy starring the comedy team of Wheeler and Woolsey. Bert Wheeler had promised Grable's mother several years earlier that he'd get the girl a break in pictures if she came to Hollywood, and with this film, Wheeler kept his word. More bits and indifferent supporting roles followed until Grable was signed by Paramount, who loaned her to 20th Century-Fox for *Pigskin Parade* (1936), which established her with the public. Grable finally landed top billing in Paramount's *Million Dollar Legs* (1939)—the title referred not to the star but to a college athletic team—which costarred her first husband, Jackie Coogan. Grable's career stalled at Paramount, but a Broadway appearance in the Cole Porter musical *DuBarry Was a Lady* led to a contract with 20th Century-Fox, where she remained a number one box office attraction from 1940 through 1955. Fox wisely allowed Grable to shed her "college co-ed" image for a more salable screen persona as a wholesomely sexy musical comedy star, emphasizing her greatest attributes: her shapely figure and shapelier legs. After a misfire attempt at heavy dramatics in *I Wake Up Screaming* (1941), Grable insisted that she be required only to sing and dance, not act, and Fox complied with a string of nonsensical but lavish Technicolor musicals. Grable was enormously popular with American GIs during the war, most of this popularity resting on her famous "pin-up" picture in which, dressed in a one-piece bathing suit and with her back to the camera, Grable glanced saucily over one shoulder. This rear-view image was borne not out of a desire to titilate but from necessity: she was several months pregnant when the picture was taken! Grable furthered her acceptance with the overseas troops when she married trumpeter-bandleader Harry James in 1943. Her popularity undimmed by war's end, Grable continued making Technicolor frolics, though her frequent tiffs with the Fox executives led the studio to try out any number of potential replacements, including Vivian Blaine, June Haver, and even Marilyn Monroe. A few miscalculated breakaways from her accepted screen image—*Mother Wore Tights* (1947), *The Beautiful Blonde From Bashful Bend* (1949) and *The Shocking Miss Pilgrim* (1949)—hurt Grable's box-office status, even though these films hold up better than some of her wartime hits. Freelancing after her last film, the lackluster *How to Be Very, Very Popular* (1955), Grable inadvertently offended producer Sam Goldwyn, thereby losing out on the chance of playing the plum role of Adelaide in Goldwyn's *Guys and Dolls* (1955); this and a few disappointing TV appearances prompted the actress into semi-retirement, save for a few nightclub appearances. After divorcing Harry James in 1965, Grable made a triumphal return to Broadway as Carol Channing's replacement in *Hello, Dolly;* later foray into musical comedy, *Belle Starr,* was less satisfying, closing its London run after two weeks. Shortly before her death, Grable appeared in advertisements for a number of low-calorie food products, her alluring figure and beautiful "gams" belying her age. **Selected Works:** *Gay Divorcee* (1934)

# Gloria Grahame (Gloria Grahame Hallward)

**Born:** November 28, 1924; Los Angeles, CA
**Died:** 1981

**Years Active in the Industry:** by decade

| 10s | 20s | 30s | 40s | 50s | 60s | 70s | 80s | 90s |
|-----|-----|-----|-----|-----|-----|-----|-----|-----|
| | | | ■ | ■ | ■ | ■ | | |

American actress Grahame began performing onstage with the Pasadena Community Playhouse at age nine. She later acted in Hollywood High School plays and in stock. In 1943 she debuted on Broadway (billed "Gloria Hallward"); the following year, MGM signed her to a film contract. However, not until the early '50s did she come into her own as a sexy leading lady, often playing fallen women or cheating wives. For her portrayal of a somewhat classy tart in *The Bad and the Beautiful* (1952), she won a Best Supporting Actress Oscar. Until the mid-'50s she landed a number of excellent roles, but after that her career gradually diminished and she retired from the screen in the late '50s. Years later she returned to play character roles, mostly in low-budget films. She married and divorced actor Stanley Clements, director Nicholas Ray, and writer Cy Howard; later she raised eyebrows by marrying Nicholas Ray's son (her former step-son), actor-producer Tony Ray. She spent her last days working on the stage in England while battling cancer. **Selected Works:** *Crossfire* (1947), *Sudden Fear* (1952), *Big Heat* (1953), *Not As a Stranger* (1955)

# Stewart Granger (James Stewart)

**Born:** May 6, 1913; London, England
**Died:** August 16, 1993; Los Angeles, CA

**Years Active in the Industry:** by decade

| 10s | 20s | 30s | 40s | 50s | 60s | 70s | 80s | 90s |
|-----|-----|-----|-----|-----|-----|-----|-----|-----|
| | | ■ | ■ | ■ | ■ | ■ | | |

British actor Stewart Granger studied acting at the Webber-Douglas School of Dramatic Art and began getting work as an extra in British films in 1933. In the late '30s he adopted his professional name to avoid confusion with recent star James Stewart. He worked with various stage companies before getting his first lead role onscreen in *So This Is London* (1939). In the '40s he was one of British films' two top romantic leading men (along with James Mason) and a steady box-office draw, attracting the interest of Hollywood. He signed with MGM in 1950, and for the next seven years played a variety of virile "he-man" types such as romantic swashbucklers and white hunters. He became a U.S. citizen in 1956. In the late '50s he began free-lancing, appearing again in British films as well as in international productions in the following decade. He began accepting starring roles on TV in the early '70s. From 1950-60 he was married to actress Jean Simmons, the second of his three wives. **Selected Works:** *King Solomon's Mines* (1950)

# Cary Grant (Archibald Alexander Leach)

**Born:** January 18, 1904; Bristol, England
**Died:** November 29, 1986; Davenport, IA

**Years Active in the Industry:** by decade

| 10s | 20s | 30s | 40s | 50s | 60s | 70s | 80s | 90s |
|-----|-----|-----|-----|-----|-----|-----|-----|-----|
|     |     |     |     |     |     |     |     |     |

British-born actor Cary Grant escaped his humble Bristol environs and unstable home life (his father was a philanderer, his mother had suffered a nervous breakdown) by joining an acrobatic troupe, where he became a stilt-walker. Numerous odd jobs kept him going until he tried acting, and after moving to the United States he managed to lose his cockney accent, developing a clipped mid-Atlantic speaking style uniquely his own. After acting in Broadway musicals, Grant was signed in 1932 by Paramount Pictures to be built into leading-man material. His real name, Archie Leach, would never do for marquees, so the studio took the first initials of their top star Gary Cooper, reversed them, then filled in the C and the G to come up with Cary Grant. After a year of nondescript roles, Cary was selected by Mae West to be her leading man in *She Done Him Wrong* (1933) and *I'm No Angel* (1934). A bit stiff-necked but undeniably sexy, Grant was vaulted to stardom, though Paramount continued wasting his potential in second rate films. Free at last from his Paramount obligations in 1935, Grant vowed never to be strictly bound to any one studio ever again, so he signed a dual contract with Columbia and RKO which allowed him to choose any "outside" roles he pleased. *Sylvia Scarlett* (1936) was the first film to fully demonstrate Grant's inspired comic flair, which would be utilized to the utmost in such knee-slappers as *The Awful Truth* (1937), *Bringing Up Baby* (1938), *His Girl Friday* (1939) and *The Bachelor and the Bobby Soxer* (1947) (only in *Arsenic and Old Lace* [1941] did he overplay his hand and lapse into mugging). The actor was also accomplished at straight drama, as evidenced in *Only Angels Have Wings* (1939), *Destination Tokyo* (1942), *Crisis* (1950), and in his favorite role as an irresponsible cockney in *None But the Lonely Heart* (1942), for which Grant was nominated for an Oscar (he didn't win, although was awarded a special Oscar for career achievement in 1970). As smooth and effortless as his performances seemed to be, offstage Grant was a workaholic, a worrier, an occasional grouch, an evidently poor husband (five marriages), and one of Hollywood's most notorious tightwads. Nonetheless, most of his co-workers had nothing but praise for his craftsmanship and willingness to work *with* co-stars rather than *at* them. Among Grant's yea-sayers was director Alfred Hitchcock, who cast the actor in three of his best films, most notably the quintessential Hitchcock thriller *North by Northwest* (1959). Seemingly growing handsomer and more charming as he got older, Grant retained his stardom into the 1960s, enriching himself with lucrative percentage-of-profits deals on such box-office hits as *Operation Petticoat* (1959) and *Charade* (1964). Upon completing *Walk, Don't Run* in 1966, Grant decided he was through with filmmaking—and he meant it. Devoting his remaining years to an executive position at a major cosmetics firm, Grant never appeared on a TV talk show and seldom granted newspaper interviews. In the 1980s, however, he became restless, and decided to embark on a nationwide lecture tour, confining himself exclusively to small towns in which the residents might otherwise never have the chance to see a Hollywood superstar in person. It was while preparing to lecture in Davenport, Iowa, that the 82-year-old Cary Grant suffered a sudden and fatal stroke. **Selected Works:** *Topper* (1937), *My Favorite Wife* (1940), *Philadelphia Story* (1940), *Suspicion* (1941), *Bishop's Wife* (1947)

# Hugh Grant

**Born:** 1962; London, England

**Years Active in the Industry:** by decade

| 10s | 20s | 30s | 40s | 50s | 60s | 70s | 80s | 90s |
|-----|-----|-----|-----|-----|-----|-----|-----|-----|
|     |     |     |     |     |     |     |     |     |

British actor Hugh Grant would seem to be better suited to Cambridge University, the spawning ground of Monty Python's Flying Circus, than his actual alma mater of Oxford. Though handsome enough for serious romantic leads, Grant is blessed with an iconoclastic sense of humor, which he has displayed (sometimes to excess) in his many TV award-show appearances. Grant made his screen bow in *Privileged* (1982), a minor Oxford-financed film, then worked in repertory before forming his own comedy troupe, the Jockeys of Norfolk. Grant's first professional film appearance in *Maurice* (1987) earned him a Best Actor award at the Venice Film Festival. While his more prestigious film assignments include his performances as Lord Byron in *Rowing With the Wind* (1989) and Chopin in *Impromptu* (1990), Hugh Grant has continued to register most strongly in eccentric, Ealing Studios-type comedy roles, notably the sanctimonious clergyman in *Sirens* (1994) and the befuddled title character in *The Englishman Who Went Up a Hill and Came Down a Mountain* (1995). Grant's biggest American hit was *Four Weddings and Funeral* (1994), although *Nine Months* (1995) gained an enormous box-office take with its release hot on the heels of Grant's highly publicized arrest for soliciting the services of an L.A. prostitute—and his sheepish, truant-schoolboy public apology to his longtime girlfriend, model Elizabeth Hurley. **Selected Works:** *Restoration* (1995), *Sense and Sensibility* (1995)

# Lee Grant (Lyova Haskell Rosenthal)

**Born:** October 31, 1927; New York, NY

**Years Active in the Industry:** by decade

| 10s | 20s | 30s | 40s | 50s | 60s | 70s | 80s | 90s |
|---|---|---|---|---|---|---|---|---|
| | | | | ■ | ■ | ■ | ■ | ■ |

American actress Lee Grant daughter of an actress-model, debuted onstage in a Metropolitan Opera production when she was only four years old. She became a member of the American Ballet at age 11. After graduating high school, she won a scholarship to the Neighborhood Playhouse; in a showcase production there, she was spotted by filmmaker Sidney Kingsley, who cast her as a shoplifter in the Broadway show *Detective Story* in 1949. For her performance she won a Critics Circle Award, and she went on to reprise her role in the play's film version (1951); for this, her screen debut, she received a Best Supporting Actress Oscar nomination and won the Cannes Film Festival Best Actress award. Her career was halted when her husband, playwright Arnold Manoff, was blacklisted during the peak of the McCarthy Era; she refused to testify against him and was blacklisted herself, going 12 years with almost no film or TV work. She continued working on the stage, then in the '60s came back to films in a number of memorable leads and character parts; she excelled as tough older women who aggressively pursue their interests. For her work in *Shampoo* (1975) she won the Best Supporting Actress Oscar; altogether, she has been Oscar-nominated four times. She also did much work on TV, winning two Emmys—one for the series *Peyton Place* in 1966, the other for the drama *Neon Ceiling* in 1971. Having reclaimed her acting career with great success, she turned to directing in the '80s, becoming the only Hollywood actress of her generation to succeed behind the camera; her directorial debut was *Tell Me a Riddle* (1980), and she went on to direct *Wilmar Eight* (1980) and *Staying Together* (1989). She is married to producer Joe Feury. **Selected Works:** *In the Heat of the Night* (1967), *Landlord* (1970), *Plaza Suite* (1971), *Defending Your Life* (1991), *Citizen Cohn* (1992)

# Richard E. Grant

**Born:** May 5, 1957; Mbabane, Swaziland, South Africa

**Years Active in the Industry:** by decade

| 10s | 20s | 30s | 40s | 50s | 60s | 70s | 80s | 90s |
|---|---|---|---|---|---|---|---|---|
| | | | | | | | ■ | ■ |

American actor Richard E. Grant tends to appear in large roles in small-budget films and small roles in large-budget ones. Before coming to the big-screen, Grant attended the acting school of Cape Town University, co-founding the Troupe Theater Company in 1977. He moved to London in 1982 with no contacts and no agents. There he met playwright Jonathan Miller and got a job sweeping the stage at the Donmar Warehouse. After working on-stage for two years in fringe theater and repertory, *Plays and Play-*

*ers* magazine nominated him as the most promising newcomer of 1984, leading to some TV work which included *Honest, Decent, and True*, a celebrated improvised satire on advertising. Grant debuted onscreen in *Withnail and I* (1987), leading to numerous supporting roles in important films. **Selected Works:** *Mountains of the Moon* (1990), *L.A. Story* (1991), *Bram Stoker's Dracula* (1992), *Age of Innocence* (1993)

# Rupert Graves

**Born:** June 30, 1963; Weston-Super-Mare, England

**Years Active in the Industry:** by decade

| 10s | 20s | 30s | 40s | 50s | 60s | 70s | 80s | 90s |
|---|---|---|---|---|---|---|---|---|
| | | | | | | | ■ | ■ |

British actor Rupert Graves has been appearing on screen since the mid-1980s. His first film role of significance was Freddy Honeychurch, wastrel brother of heroine Helena Bonham-Carter, in *A Room with a View* (1986). Graves' forte thus far seems to be convincingly conveying the snottiest examples of the Upper Class, as in 1988's *A Handful of Dust*. Graves was more recently cast as the son of British MP Jeremy Irons in *Damage* (1992), wherein he loses his fiancee (Juliette Binoche) to his own philandering father. **Selected Works:** *Madness of King George* (1994)

# Spalding Gray

**Born:** June 5, 1941; Barrington, RI

**Years Active in the Industry:** by decade

| 10s | 20s | 30s | 40s | 50s | 60s | 70s | 80s | 90s |
|---|---|---|---|---|---|---|---|---|
| | | | | | | | ■ | ■ |

It takes guts to stand on stage for four hours and talk about making a movie—and Spalding Gray is possessed of such intestinal fortitude. A cofounder of the experimental Wooster Theatre Group (whose most famous alumnus is actor Willem Dafoe), Gray made ends meet with traditional stage and movie roles, then began monologizing with an engaging piece titled "Sex and Death at the Age of 14," a rambling discourse on Gray's angst-ridden youth in Rhode Island. He toured the U.S., Australia and Europe with his one-man shows, aggravating some, delighting many others. After appearing in a small role in 1985's *The Killing Fields*, Gray parlayed this experience into his best-known monologue, *Swimming to Cambodia*, which was filmed by Jonathan Demme (wisely telescoped from its original 240 minutes to 87) in 1987. One year later, Gray made his "mainstream" Broadway debut as the Stage Manager in a revival of *Our Town*—and this not altogether pleasant experience inspired a *second* monologue film, 1992's *Monster in a Box*. **Selected Works:** *King of the Hill* (1993)

# Peter Greenaway

**Born:** April 5, 1942; London, England

**Years Active in the Industry:** by decade

| 10$^s$ | 20$^s$ | 30$^s$ | 40$^s$ | 50$^s$ | 60$^s$ | 70$^s$ | 80$^s$ | 90$^s$ |
|---|---|---|---|---|---|---|---|---|
| | | | | | | | | |

A painter in the early 1960s, Peter Greenaway was a film editor for the Central Office of Information from 1965-67. During this time he began making experimental short films, including *Train, Tree,* and *Five Postcards from Capital Cities.* He began making features in 1980 with *The Falls,* and attracted critical attention with his stylish 17th-century drama *The Draughtsman's Contract* (1982). After helming documentaries about American composers Robert Ashley, John Cage, Philip Glass, and Meredith Monk, Greenaway made a series of provocative, thiny plotted, and self-consciously cerebral features which offered his meditations on decay (*A Zed and Two Noughts* [1985]), art (*The Belly of an Architect* [1987]), and mortality (*Drowning by Numbers* [1988]). His recent works include *The Cook, The Thief, His Wife And Her Lover* (1990), a gross-out theatrical allegory of contemporary England, and *Prospero's Books* (1991), a reinvention of Shakespeare's *The Tempest* with Sir John Gielgud and a lot of naked people. **Selected Works:** *Comment Faire L'Amour Avec Un Negre Sans Se Fatiguer* (1990), *The Baby of Macon* (1995)

# Sydney Greenstreet

**Born:** December 27, 1879; Sandwich, England
**Died:** 1954

**Years Active in the Industry:** by decade

| 10$^s$ | 20$^s$ | 30$^s$ | 40$^s$ | 50$^s$ | 60$^s$ | 70$^s$ | 80$^s$ | 90$^s$ |
|---|---|---|---|---|---|---|---|---|
| | | | | | | | | |

British character actor Sydney Greenstreet moved to Sri Lanka at age 18, hoping to make his fortune as a tea planter, but a drought bankrupted him and he returned to England. He took sev-

eral odd jobs, and as a pastime he attended an acting school. In 1902 he debuted onstage in London, playing a murderer in *Sherlock Holmes.* He went on tour in the U.S. in 1904, later debuting on Broadway in *Everyman;* he went on to play a wide range of roles in many productions in New York and on the road, performing in everything from Shakespeare to musical comedy. In the '30s he worked with the Lunts at the Theatre Guild. He debuted onscreen in 1941, playing the mysterious, ruthless Kaspar Gutman in John Huston's classic thriller *The Maltese Falcon.* He appeared in two dozen films over the next decade; his urbane, enigmatic style made him a popular favorite, and he ranks as one of the screen's all-time great villains. He retired from the screen in 1951. Greenstreet died at 75, having long suffered from diabetes and Bright's disease. **Selected Works:** *Casablanca* (1942)

# Jennifer Grey

**Born:** March 26, 1960; New York, NY

**Years Active in the Industry:** by decade

| 10$^s$ | 20$^s$ | 30$^s$ | 40$^s$ | 50$^s$ | 60$^s$ | 70$^s$ | 80$^s$ | 90$^s$ |
|---|---|---|---|---|---|---|---|---|
| | | | | | | | | |

American actress Jennifer Grey, the daughter of Broadway and screen actor Joel Grey, began studying dance as a child; her first professional work was as a dancer in TV commercials. She graduated from the Neighborhood Playhouse School of Theater in New York, then worked off-Broadway in *Album* and performed at both the acclaimed American Conservatory Theater and the Williamstown Theater in Massachusetts. She went on to appear in several TV movies, and her screen debut was in the youth-oriented *Reckless* (1984). A few small parts followed, including a humorous turn as the revenge-minded sister in *Ferris Bueller's Day Off* (1986) with then-boyfriend Matthew Broderick. Her breakthrough role was in the suprise coming-of-ager hit *Dirty Dancing* (1987), in which she convincingly played a idealistic girl who learns about life, love, and dancing from hunky Patrick Swayze, but her subsequent films have failed to attract much attention. **Selected Works:** *Criminal Justice* (1990), *Murder in Mississippi* (1990), *Eyes of a Witness* (1991), *Wind* (1992)

# Joel Grey (Joel Katz)

**Born:** April 11, 1932; Cleveland, OH

**Years Active in the Industry:** by decade

| 10$^s$ | 20$^s$ | 30$^s$ | 40$^s$ | 50$^s$ | 60$^s$ | 70$^s$ | 80$^s$ | 90$^s$ |
|---|---|---|---|---|---|---|---|---|
| | | | | | | | | |

American entertainer Joel Grey was the son of Mickey Katz, the famous "gurgler" of the Spike Jones Orchestra and a legend in his own right as a performer/producer of nightclub, resort and Broadway satirical revues. Growing up around some of the best comics, musical performers and second bananas in the business, Joel was all but predestined to enter show business himself. An accomplished singer and dancer, Grey was rather wasted in such early film roles as *About Face* (1953) and *Come September* (1961), though he achieved minor fame on TV variety shows and in the lead of a televised musical version of *Jack and the Beanstalk;* ironically, one of his best TV parts was as a second-rate comic unable to live up to the accomplishments of a famous relative on an episode of *77 Sunset Strip*. Grey's career was boosted in 1966 when he was cast in the Broadway musical *Cabaret* as the Master of Ceremonies, a white-faced, smirking, sexually ambivalent observer of changing mores and philosophies in pre-Hitler Berlin. Grey won a Tony Award for his brilliant portrayal (which has since been imitated by countless "wannabes" in college and summer theater productions of the musical), and copped an Academy Award for repeating the role in the 1972 film version of *Cabaret*. Grey enjoyed a second Broadway triumph as George M. Cohan in the 1969 musical *George M.,* a virtuoso performance he recreated on TV in the early 1970s. Thanks to his highly stylized Broadway roles, Joel Grey has not been easy to cast in "normal" movie parts; among his better roles were that of an Austrian petty criminal in *The Seven Per Cent Solution* (1976) and an ancient and irredeemably sarcastic oriental martial arts master in *Remo Williams* (1985). On the final episode of the TV serial *Dallas* in 1991, Grey was a red-eyed satanic chap who showed a suicidal J.R. (Larry Hagman) how much better the world would have been without him (*It's a Terrible Life?*) Joel Grey is the father of actress Jennifer Grey, whose breakthrough role was in *Dirty Dancing*, which coincidentally was set in a Catskills resort not unlike those in which her dad Joel learned his craft. **Selected Works:** *Marilyn and Me* (1991)

# Pam Grier (Pamela Grier)

**Born:** 1949; Winston-Salem, NC

**Years Active in the Industry:** by decade

| 10ˢ | 20ˢ | 30ˢ | 40ˢ | 50ˢ | 60ˢ | 70ˢ | 80ˢ | 90ˢ |
|-----|-----|-----|-----|-----|-----|-----|-----|-----|
|     |     |     |     |     |     |     |     |     |

African American actress Pam Grier is best known for her starring roles in '70s "exploitation" films aimed at black audiences. An "army brat" who grew up on European bases and in Denver, Grier left home for Hollywood at a young age. She found work as a switchboard operator for American International Pictures, where she gradually landed supporting roles in low-budget action and exploitation films. In the early '70s she began starring in films, most of which were rowdy, low-budget crowd-pleasers; soon she was a sex symbol and, briefly, the "Queen of B-movies," usually cast as a sexy, foul-mouthed woman of action who carried a gun and resorted to a variety of violent acts to get herself out of dangerous situations. She often disrobed in her films, and furthered her sexy image by posing nude in the magazine *Players*. For some time she had a large following, and her picture appeared on the covers of such magazines as *Ms.* and *New York*. When Grier tried to make more serious films later in the '70s, however, her popularity quickly waned. Nevertheless, she managed to sustain her career through movie and TV work, including an appearance in *Posse* (1993). She is a niece of actor and former football star Rosie Grier. **Selected Works:** *Class of 1999* (1990), *Bill & Ted's Bogus Journey* (1991)

# D.W. Griffith (David Wark Griffith)

**Born:** January 22, 1875; La Grange, KY
**Died:** July 23, 1948; Hollywood, CA

**Years Active in the Industry:** by decade

| 10ˢ | 20ˢ | 30ˢ | 40ˢ | 50ˢ | 60ˢ | 70ˢ | 80ˢ | 90ˢ |
|-----|-----|-----|-----|-----|-----|-----|-----|-----|
|     |     |     |     |     |     |     |     |     |

One of the pioneers of contemporary filmmaking (and often cited as the single most important figure in the history of American filmmaking), D. W. Griffith was also one of the most controversial figures in the history of Hollywood. The son of a physician and Confederate hero during the Civil War, Griffith grew up in poverty in Louisville, Kentucky, and gravitated to acting at an early age.

During the turn-of-the-century, he worked as a performer in various touring companies with mixed success and in virtual poverty. After years of frustration on the stage, he turned to movies, and became an actor and a writer, establishing himself at New York's Biograph Studio. He eventually became a producer and, later, a director in 1908. He directed every Biograph release through the end of 1909, and later as chief of production, supervised the making of every film released by the company for the next three years, personally directing all of the major films. Most of these 450 films were comedies, although a significant minority were dramas, but it was in 1913 that Griffith's ambitions became clear with *Judith of Bethulia*; violating the restrictions of the studio heads, Griffith made the Old Testament drama into a four-reel film, almost double the length that had been approved, and an epic by the existing standards of the film medium.

After leaving Biograph, Griffith embarked on an ambitious production based on Thomas Dixon's novel *The Clansmen*, which ultimately became known as *Birth of a Nation* (1915). The first great epic film of American cinema, this movie, more than any other, defined what film was capable of. Assisted by his cameraman Billy Bitzer, Griffith had already seized upon such techniques of film construction and design as the close-up, rhythmic editing, parallel action, and dramatic lighting, which had been used before Griffith, but not with his coherence or purpose—*Birth of a Nation* was the culmination of his efforts, drawing these techniques together in an epic length story that carried viewers through the Civil War and into Reconstruction, with in-depth, detailed drama involving dozens of characters.

Griffith single-handedly elevated American film—which had previously stood in the shadow of its European cousins (Italian filmmakers, in particular, had been more ambitious much earlier) to world-class stature, and forced Americans who had thought of movies as light entertainment to perceive movies as serious creations, worthy of respect equal to the greatest stage dramas and capable of creating drama that the stage couldn't hope to match. The movie's Civil War setting, however, was to prove a blemish on Griffith's reputation—a Southerner by birth and family history with a deep resentment of the toll that Reconstruction played on his homeland, Griffith was outspoken on his views regarding the races, and black audience members all over the country rose up in protest over the depiction of slaves and ex-slaves in the movie.

Demonstrations began almost from the instant the film was released, and Griffith—despite including a plea for reconciliation of all mankind's differences in his subsequent film *Intolerance* (1916)—never fully recovered from the controversy (a film answering Griffith's, *Birth of a Race*, was even produced, presenting a completely different view of black Americans and their ancestors; the film's ripple effect also moved in other directions—the news that Griffith was doing an eight-reel drama also led his former mentor, Mack Sennett, to make the hour-long *Tillie's Punctured Romance*, the first comedy to run longer than two reels).

Griffith never had another success as great as *Birth of a Nation*, and, indeed, faced ongoing financial problems for much of the rest of his career. Additionally, while his filmmaking technique was beyond reproach, his dramatic sensibilities were rooted in the touring theater of the first decade of the century. While he expanded the structural boundaries and storytelling capability of film with *Intolerance*, whose parallel action took place across several time periods, and ventured into topical filmmaking with a vengeance in the World War I story *Hearts of the World* (1918), his characters and the surrounding dramas seemed dated and one-dimensional. His smaller scale productions, such as *True Heart Susie* (1925) and *Broken Blossoms* (1919), worked better and have endured, but increasingly Griffith fell behind the rest of the country and the filmmaking community in the kinds of stories he told. He co-founded United Artists with Mary Pickford, Douglas Fairbanks Sr., and Charles Chaplin, but his involvement with the new studio failed to give him the financial independence that he needed to sustain his productions.

By the end of the 1920s, Griffith was looking desperately for a financial and critical comeback. He thought he'd found it in *Abraham Lincoln,* his first talking picture, but the film failed despite a huge publicity push by United Artists, and Griffith's career as a major filmmaker was over. He made one more movie, *The Struggle* (1931), a drama about alcoholism made in New York City, and worked uncredited on parts of Hal Roach's 1940 prehistoric drama *One Million B.C.* but otherwise became a sad, unfulfilled relic of film history.

# Melanie Griffith

**Born:** August 9, 1957; New York, NY

**Years Active in the Industry:** by decade

| 10s | 20s | 30s | 40s | 50s | 60s | 70s | 80s | 90s |
|-----|-----|-----|-----|-----|-----|-----|-----|-----|

The daughter of actress Tippi Hedren (with whom she appeared in 1981's *Roar!* and 1990's *Pacific Heights*), Melanie Griffith debuted onscreen while still a teenager in *Night Moves* (1975). Often cast as dimwitted, breathy blondes, she appeared in a number of films between 1975-81 then took three years off. In 1984, she made her breakthrough in Brian De Palma's *Body Double* (1984), which resulted in a string of leads in major productions. For her performance in the hit *Working Girl* (1988), she won a Golden Globe Award and was nominated for a Best Actress Oscar.

Griffith survived a wild youth: at 14 she ran away with actor Don Johnson, whom she later married and divorced, and she battled drug and alcohol addictions as well. After a brief marriage to actor Steven Bauer, Griffith and Johnson were remarried in 1989. They appeared together in *Paradise* (1991) and *Born Yesterday* (1993). Griffith split from Johnson in 1995 and entered into a torrid romance with actor Antonio Banderas. **Selected Works:** *Shining Through* (1992), *Stranger among Us* (1992), *Milk Money* (1994), *Nobody's Fool* (1994)

# Raymond Griffith

**Born:** January 23, 1890; Boston, MA
**Died:** November 23, 1957; Hollywood, CA

**Years Active in the Industry:** by decade

| 10s | 20s | 30s | 40s | 50s | 60s | 70s | 80s | 90s |
|-----|-----|-----|-----|-----|-----|-----|-----|-----|

Born into a theatrical family, American actor Raymond Griffith was trained from an early age in the exacting art of pantomime. His ability to convey thoughts and emotions physically came in handy when Griffith went to work in silent pictures in 1914. After an apprenticeship at Vitagraph, Griffith became a staff writer and lead comic at Keystone Studios; his early buffoon roles bear little resemblance to his sleek, sophisticated characterizations of the 1920s. Signed as a supporting actor by Paramount, Griffith gained critical attention by stealing scenes in a series of wry social comedies. While everyone around him concerned themselves with the plotline, the mustachioed, tuxedoed Griffith would sit in a corner, react coolly and agreeably to the events, and then drink another cocktail. Promoted to leading roles, Griffith further developed his implacable, nonchalant characterization in such comedies as *Paths to Paradise* (1926). *Hands Up* (1927) is considered Griffith's masterpiece; as a dapper Civil War spy, he responds to the most horrendous of dangers as if calmly ordering breakfast. Offscreen, Griffith developed a swelled head, insisting upon running every aspect of his productions and refusing to heed anyone's advice. While this may not have been an laudable method of handling the responsibilities of stardom, Griffith's take-charge attitude served him well when he became a producer at Warner Bros. and 20th Century-Fox in the 1930s. Griffith was forced to switch from acting to producing in the sound era because he literally had no voice: as a result of straining his vocal chords in childhood, Griffith could barely manage a hoarse whisper. But before retiring from acting, Raymond Griffith was assigned his most famous (albeit uncredited) screen role, as the bayonetted French soldier in *All Quiet on the Western Front,* whose facial features freeze into a hauntingly quizzical death mask.

# Charles Grodin

**Born:** April 21, 1935; Pittsburgh, PA

**Years Active in the Industry:** by decade

| 10ˢ | 20ˢ | 30ˢ | 40ˢ | 50ˢ | 60ˢ | 70ˢ | 80ˢ | 90ˢ |
|-----|-----|-----|-----|-----|-----|-----|-----|-----|
|     |     |     |     |     |     |     |     |     |

Lead and supporting actor Charles Grodin is often cast in comedic roles as "the perfect jerk." He became interested in acting while still a teenager; after college he studied drama with Uta Hagen and Lee Strasberg,

then began performing at the Pacific Playhouse. His Broadway debut was in *Tchin-Tchin* (1962) with Anthony Quinn, while he debuted onscreen in *Sex and the College Girl* (1964); he appeared in only one more movie, however, during the '60s. His first lead was in *The Heartbreak Kid* (1972), directed by his friend and mentor Elaine May. He has had a fairly busy screen career since then, meanwhile acting and directing for the stage. He passed over the chance to play the role Richard Dreyfuss accepted in the mega-hit *Jaws* (1974) because he was directing the Broadway play *Thieves;* later he appeared in the film version of that play (1977). He has tended to play supporting roles, a notable exception being in the smash hit comedy *Beethoven* (1992) and its sequel (1993). He is the author of an autobiography, *It Would Be So Nice If You Weren't Here,* and began hosting his own self-titled talk show in 1995. **Selected Works:** *Heaven Can Wait* (1978), *Midnight Run* (1988), *Dave* (1993), *Heart and Souls* (1993)

# Sir Alec Guinness (Alec Guinness de Cuffe)

**Born:** April 2, 1914; Marylebone, West London, England

**Years Active in the Industry:** by decade

| 10ˢ | 20ˢ | 30ˢ | 40ˢ | 50ˢ | 60ˢ | 70ˢ | 80ˢ | 90ˢ |
|-----|-----|-----|-----|-----|-----|-----|-----|-----|
|     |     |     |     |     |     |     |     |     |

British actor Alec Guinness was known in prep school as Alec Stiven; he had been registered under the name of his stepfather because the boy's biological father had never married his mother ("Guinness" was the name of Alec's real dad's best friend, a complicated situation best understood by students of British protocol). With little money and no social standing, young Alec took on one of the few professions open to a boy of his background: he became an actor. Despite discouragement from the higher-ups and a few traumatic on-stage experiences, Guinness won a scholarship with the Fay Compton School of Acting in 1933, secured his first film work (as an extra) that same year, and by 1935 was working in John Gielgud's acting company. Guinness' reputation increased as he worked with the Old Vic and the Queen's Theatre, and during wartime service in the Royal Navy, the actor's ship's was assigned to New Jersey, allowing Guinness to make his American stage debut in *Flare Path.* Established on both sides of the Atlantic by 1946, Guinness made his "official" film debut as Pocket in the highly popular British picture *Great Expectations*—his first collaboration with director Carol Reed. As in his stage work, Guinness' strong suit in films was his astonishing versatility: before he was forty the actor played Fagin (with controversial exaggerated "Jewish" makeup) in *Oliver Twist* (1948), Disraeli in *The Mudlark* (1951), a mild-mannered criminal mastermind in *The Lavender Hill Mob* (1951), a bemused inventor in *Man in the White Suit* (1952), a bigamous skipper in *The Captain's Paradise* (1953), the portly, middle-aged title character in *Father Brown, Detective* (1954), and no fewer than eight different roles (one of them a woman!) in *Kind Hearts and Coronets* (1949). One of the most popular of British film stars, Guinness was knighted in 1955, and two years later won both the Academy Award and the British Film Award for his performance as stubborn POW Col. Nicholson in *Bridge on the River Kwai* (1957). Guinness' willingness to tackle any sort of role has resulted in a misstep or two over the last few decades, notably his bold but ineffectual portrayal of a Japanese gentleman in *A Majority of One* (1961) and his curiously British take on the title role in *Hitler: The Last Ten Days* (1973). But even a Guinness failure holds a lot more interest than the successes of most other actors. Ironically, the biggest box-office success with which Alec Guinness was involved was one that he initially rejected and one that he would act in for minimal salary: *Star Wars* (1977), wherein Sir Alec was Obi-Wan Kenobi, guardian of The Force. **Selected Works:** *Horse's Mouth* (1958), *Tunes of Glory* (1960), *Lawrence of Arabia* (1962), *Empire Strikes Back* (1980), *Kafka* (1992)

# Steve Guttenberg

**Born:** August 24, 1958; Brooklyn, NY

**Years Active in the Industry:** by decade

| 10s | 20s | 30s | 40s | 50s | 60s | 70s | 80s | 90s |
|-----|-----|-----|-----|-----|-----|-----|-----|-----|
|     |     |     |     |     |     |     |     |     |

American actor Steve Guttenberg attended the celebrated School of the Performing Arts, studied drama with John Houseman at the prestigious Juilliard School, and later worked with acting teachers Uta Hagen and Lee Strasberg. His professional stage debut came in the off-Broadway production of *The Lion in Winter*. He moved to California and first appeared before the camera in the TV movie *Something for Joey* (1977). He made his big-screen debut in *The Chicken Chronicles* (1977), but his first notable screen role was as a young Nazi hunter in *The Boys from Brazil* (1978). He has become well-known as the result of his appearance in the comedy *Police Academy* (1984) and three of its sequels (1985, 1986, 1987). He has proved most capable in comedic parts. **Selected Works:** *Diner* (1982), *Cocoon* (1985), *Three Men and a Baby* (1987), *The Big Green* (1995)

# Edmund Gwenn

**Born:** September 26, 1875; Glamorgan, Wales, England
**Died:** September 7, 1959; Woodland Hills, CA

**Years Active in the Industry:** by decade

| 10s | 20s | 30s | 40s | 50s | 60s | 70s | 80s | 90s |
|-----|-----|-----|-----|-----|-----|-----|-----|-----|
|     |     |     |     |     |     |     |     |     |

The son of a traveling British civil servant, Edmund Gwenn was ordered to leave his home at age 17 when he announced his intention to become an actor. Working throughout the British empire in a variety of theatrical troupes, Gwenn finally settled in London in 1902 when he was personally selected by playwright George Bernard Shaw for a role in Shaw's *Man and Superman*. Thanks to Shaw's sponsorship, Gwenn rapidly established himself as one of London's foremost character stars, his career interrupted only by military service as a captain during World War I. Gwenn's film career, officially launched in 1916, took a back seat to his theatrical work for most of his life; still, he was a favorite of both American and British audiences for his portrayals of blustery old men, both comic and villainous. At age 71, Gwenn was cast as Kris Kringle, a lovable old eccentric who imagined that he was Santa Claus, in the comedy classic *Miracle on 34th Street* (1947); his brilliant portrayal was honored with an Academy Award, and transformed the veteran actor into an "overnight" movie star. Edmund Gwenn died shortly after making his final film, an oddball Mexican comedy titled *The Rocket From Calabuch* (1958); one of his surviving family members was his cousin Cecil Kellaway, a respected character actor in his own right. **Selected Works:** *Foreign Correspondent* (1940), *Devil and Miss Jones* (1941), *Lassie Come Home* (1943), *Life with Father* (1947), *Mister 880* (1950)

# H

## Lukas Haas

**Born:** April 16, 1976; West Hollywood, CA

**Years Active in the Industry:** by decade

| 10ˢ | 20ˢ | 30ˢ | 40ˢ | 50ˢ | 60ˢ | 70ˢ | 80ˢ | 90ˢ |
|-----|-----|-----|-----|-----|-----|-----|-----|-----|
|     |     |     |     |     |     |     |     |     |

California-born actor Lukas Haas was discovered at age four. Haas's kindergarten principal spotted potential in the young performer, and encouraged his parents to set their sights on a movie career for the boy. His first film was *Testament* (1983), in which he played the youngest of the doomed children of post-apocalyptic housewife Jane Alexander. Haas's best movie assignment was in the title role of *Witness* (1985), playing an Amish boy who witnesses a murder and must accept the protection of cop Harrison Ford. His older roles have not always been of this high a calibre, though he was very effective as a sexually inquisitive 1960s adolescent in *Rambling Rose* (1991). **Selected Works:** *Music Box* (1989), *Convicts* (1991), *Perfect Tribute* (1991)

## Albert Hackett

**Born:** February 16, 1900; New York, NY

**Years Active in the Industry:** by decade

| 10ˢ | 20ˢ | 30ˢ | 40ˢ | 50ˢ | 60ˢ | 70ˢ | 80ˢ | 90ˢ |
|-----|-----|-----|-----|-----|-----|-----|-----|-----|
|     |     |     |     |     |     |     |     |     |

Manhattan-born Albert Hackett's mother was stage star Florence Hackett, and his brother was matinee idol Raymond Hackett. Albert made his own stage bow at age six, studying his trade at New York's Professional Children's School. Though a moderately successful actor, Hackett longed to break into playwrighting, but would not realize this dream until meeting and marrying another performer with writing ambitions, Frances Goodrich. Hackett and his wife collaborated on the 1929 play *Up Pops the Devil*. The show was a success, and Hackett was invited to Hollywood to work as dialogue director of the film version. But Hackett refused to leave his wife behind in New York; nor did he want Goodrich to be regarded as merely a "writer's wife". When Hackett finally did come to Hollywood, it was as his wife's writing partner, a collaboration that lasted professionally until the team's 1962 retirement—and personally until Goodrich's death in 1984 (a cross-section of the Goodrich/Hackett projects will be found in the essay on Frances Goodrich). Once he'd dedicated himself to writing, Hackett halted his acting career; he returned to the stage just once in the 1940 Broadway play *Mr. and Mrs. North*—and then only as a favor to an old friend, playwright Owen Davis Jr. **Selected Works:** *Thin Man* (1934), *Father of the Bride* (1950), *Seven Brides for Seven Brothers* (1954), *Diary of Anne Frank* (1959)

## Taylor Hackford

**Born:** December 3, 1944; Santa Barbara, CA

**Years Active in the Industry:** by decade

| 10ˢ | 20ˢ | 30ˢ | 40ˢ | 50ˢ | 60ˢ | 70ˢ | 80ˢ | 90ˢ |
|-----|-----|-----|-----|-----|-----|-----|-----|-----|
|     |     |     |     |     |     |     |     |     |

American producer/director Taylor Hackford was hired by a Los Angeles TV station after his two-year hitch in the Peace Corps. On his own, he created New Visions Productions, which he would eventually merge into the New Century Company before giving up producing to concentrate on directing. In 1978, he won an Academy Award for *Teenage Father*, a short-subject elaboration of a TV news story he'd previously worked on. Hackford's first feature was *The Idolmaker* (1980), a jaundiced recreation of the "Philadelphia school" of 1950s rock 'n roll; he would later return to the rarefied world of vintage rock 'n roll in his 1988 Richie Valens biopic *La Bamba* and his revelatory 1987 documentary *Chuck Berry: Hail! Hail! Rock 'N' Roll*. Though Hackford has toted up some impressive credits, few of his films have matched the audience appeal or box office bankability of his biggest hit, *An Officer and A Gentleman* (1982). **Selected Works:** *Queens Logic* (1991)

# Gene Hackman (Eugene Alden Hackman)

**Born:** January 30, 1931; San Bernardino, CA

**Years Active in the Industry:** by decade

| 10s | 20s | 30s | 40s | 50s | 60s | 70s | 80s | 90s |
|-----|-----|-----|-----|-----|-----|-----|-----|-----|
|     |     |     |     |     |  ■  |  ■  |  ■  |  ■  |

Distinguished American character and lead actor Gene Hackman is one the most versatile actors in contemporary American cinema, noted for his ability to convincingly portray "regular joes." Before becoming an actor, Hackman dropped out of school at 16 to do a three year stint in the Marines. He then moved to New York, going from job to job for two years before studying commercial drawing, journalism, and TV production on the GI Bill. Following that, he drifted across the country from one town to another, working any available odd jobs, all the while secretly dreaming of becoming an actor. When he was in his early 30s, Hackman enrolled in California's Pacific Playhouse school (one of his classmates was Dustin Hoffman, and legend has it that while there, he and Hoffman were voted "Least Likely to Succeed"). He returned to New York and began getting small roles in summer stock, off-Broadway, and TV. He got his big break in 1964 when he received the lead role in the Broadway comedy *Ash Wednesday* opposite Sandy Duncan; this led to a brief but impressive scene in the film *Lilith* (1964), starring Warren Beatty. Three years later Beatty cast Hackman as Clyde Barrow's brother Buck in the huge hit *Bonnie and Clyde* (1967), a role for which he received a Best Supporting Actor Oscar nomination. From there he landed a string of prime roles. He received another Best Supporting Actor Oscar nomination for *I Never Sang for My Father* (1970), then went on to win the Best Actor Oscar for *The French Connection* (1971), in which he played tough narcotics cop Popeye Doyle, the part with which he is most identified. He was also nominated for a Best Actor Oscar for his work in *Mississippi Burning* (1988). From 1985-90, the hardworking Hackman was dubbed as Hollywood's busiest movie star by TV's *Entertainment Tonight*. He is also among the highest paid. Although Hackman suffered a heart attack in 1990, he continues to be a prolific and impressive performer; his turn as the crooked sheriff in *Unforgiven* (1992) earned him several honors, including the Oscar for Best Supporting Actor.

**Selected Works:** *Conversation* (1974), *Hoosiers* (1986), *The Quick and the Dead* (1995), *Get Shorty* (1995)

# Corey Haim

**Born:** December 23, 1972; Toronto, Ontario, Canada

**Years Active in the Industry:** by decade

| 10s | 20s | 30s | 40s | 50s | 60s | 70s | 80s | 90s |
|-----|-----|-----|-----|-----|-----|-----|-----|-----|
|     |     |     |     |     |     |     |  ■  |     |

An actor since the age of ten, Canadian Corey Haim is one of the few juvenile performers to thrive in wacky comedy roles. He started out with relatively straight parts in films like *Lucas* (1986), in which he effectively played one of filmdom's rare three-dimensional "nerds". But in laughgetters like *License to Drive* (1988) and *Dream Machine* (1991), Haim has demonstrated comic skills above and beyond those of the films' comparatively unimaginative screenwriters. He was also a regular on the TV sitcom *Roomies* (1987), where once again he was markedly better than his material. His recent appearances in theatrical bombs and direct-to-video potboilers have somewhat diminished Haim's industry clout, but give him time. Haim is frequently costarred (and frequently confused) with his contemporary namesake Corey Feldman. **Selected Works:** *Murphy's Romance* (1985), *Prayer of the Rollerboys* (1991), *Double O Kid* (1992)

# Alan Hale, Sr. (Rufus Alan McKahan)

**Born:** February 10, 1892; Washington, DC
**Died:** January 22, 1950; Hollywood, CA

**Years Active in the Industry:** by decade

| 10s | 20s | 30s | 40s | 50s | 60s | 70s | 80s | 90s |
|-----|-----|-----|-----|-----|-----|-----|-----|-----|
|  ■  |  ■  |  ■  |  ■  |     |     |     |     |     |

The son of a patent medicine manufacturer, American actor Alan Hale chose a theatrical career at a time when, according to his son Alan Hale Jr., boarding houses would post signs reading "No Dogs or Actors Allowed." Undaunted, Hale spent several years on stage after graduating from Philadelphia University, entering films as a slapstick comedian for Philly's Lubin Co. in 1911. Bolstering his acting income with odd jobs as a newspaperman and itinerant inventor (at one point he considered becoming an osteopath!), Hale finally enjoyed a measure of security as a much-in-demand character actor in the 1920s, usually as hardhearted villains. One of his more benign roles was as Little John in Douglas Fairbanks' *Robin Hood* (1922), a role he would repeat opposite Errol Flynn in 1938 and John Derek in 1950. Talkies made Hale more popular than ever, especially in his many roles as Irishmen, blusterers and "best pals" for Warner Bros. Throughout his career, Hale never lost his love for inventing things, and reportedly patented or financed items as commonplace as auto brakes and as esoteric as greaseless potato chips. Alan Hale contacted pneumonia and died while working on the Warner Bros. western *Montana* (1950), which starred Hale's perennial screen cohort Errol Flynn. **Selected Works:** *Lost Patrol* (1934), *Stella Dallas* (1937), *Adventures of Robin Hood* (1938), *Sea Hawk* (1940)

# Anthony Michael Hall

**Born:** April 14, 1968; Boston, MA

**Years Active in the Industry:** by decade

| 10s | 20s | 30s | 40s | 50s | 60s | 70s | 80s | 90s |
|-----|-----|-----|-----|-----|-----|-----|-----|-----|
|     |     |     |     |     |     |     | ■ | ■ |

Actor Anthony Michael Hall began his film career at the age of 14 in Kenny Rogers' family comedy *Six Pack* (1982) as one of six precocious orphans foisted upon a gruff stock-car driver. He then appeared in the 1983 comedy *National Lampoon's Vacation.* Hall is perhaps best remembered for his role as skinny nerds in *Sixteen Candles* (1984) and *The Breakfast Club* (1985). After that he continued to play in teen comedies, but none of them did well at the box office. He served for a season as part of the ensemble cast of TV's *Saturday Night Live* and played a more mature and serious role as the dangerously jealous (and not at all nerd-like) boyfriend in *Edward Scissorhands* (1990). **Selected Works:** *Into the Sun* (1992), *Six Degrees of Separation* (1993)

# Conrad L. Hall

**Born:** 1926; Papeete, Tahiti

**Years Active in the Industry:** by decade

| 10s | 20s | 30s | 40s | 50s | 60s | 70s | 80s | 90s |
|-----|-----|-----|-----|-----|-----|-----|-----|-----|
|     |     |     |     |     | ■ | ■ | ■ | ■ |

The son of American writer James Norman Hall, co-author of *Mutiny on the Bounty,* cinematographer Conrad Hall was born on the family estate in Tahiti. After flunking out of journalism school at the University of Southern California, Hall changed his major to cinema. Inspired by department chairman Slavko Vorkapich (best known as Hollywood's foremost "montage" expert), he branched out into independent filmmaking with the experimental picture *Sea Theme.* With several fellow students he created Canyon Films, though few of their projects received widespread theatrical play. Virtually frozen out of the cinematographer's union, Hall first tried creating a union of his own, then worked on the independent non-"shop" films of such producers as Benedict Bogeaus; he also wielded the 16-millimeter color camera on many of Disney's "True Life Adventure" features of the early 1950s. Hall's first solo director of photography credits were on the 1960s TV series *Stoney Burke* and *The Outer Limits,* both produced by Leslie Stevens. Hall went on to lens Stevens' offbeat Esperanto-language feature film *Incubus* (1965). In the major studio mainstream by the mid-1960s, Hall preferred to work in black and white; one of his best achievements in this field was 1967's *In Cold Blood,* directed by Hall's frequent employer Richard Brooks. When compelled by the studios to work in color, Hall strove to avoid the artificial "Hollywood" look, opting for naturalistic and sometimes impressionistic tints. Hall's best color work includes *Harper* (1966), *Cool Hand Luke* (1967), and *Butch Cassidy and the Sundance Kid* (1969), for which he won an Oscar. After 1976's *Marathon Man,* Conrad Hall left films for over a decade, returning to an Oscar nomination for 1988's *Tequila Sunrise.* During his 1970s heyday, Conrad Hall was a public proponent of photographic experimentation in the field of videotape; some of his published notions were expanded upon by the earliest and most adventuresome music video directors of the 1980s. **Selected Works:** *Professionals* (1966), *Day of the Locust* (1975), *Class Action* (1991), *Searching for Bobby Fischer* (1993)

# Mark Hamill

**Born:** September 25, 1952; Oakland, CA

**Years Active in the Industry:** by decade

| 10s | 20s | 30s | 40s | 50s | 60s | 70s | 80s | 90s |
|-----|-----|-----|-----|-----|-----|-----|-----|-----|
|     |     |     |     |     |     | ■ | ■ | ■ |

American actor Mark Hamill will be forever remembered on film as the naive but courageous sci-fi hero Luke Skywalker from George Lucas' *Star Wars* films. An "army brat," Hamill grew up in different cities in America and in Japan. He majored in drama at the Los Angeles City College. While still a student there in 1970, he made his professional acting debut in an episode of the old *Bill Cosby Show.* He went on to appear in TV shows and movies, had a stint in the cast of the soap opera *General Hospital,* and co-starred in the short-lived TV series *The Texas Wheelers.* But it was not until he earned the role of Luke that Hamill became a bona-fide star. Unfortunately, his identification in the public mind with the role of Skywalker severely restricted his later career, and he went eight years after the last *Star Wars* movie before making another big-screen appearance (in the sci-fi film *Slipstream* [1989]). However, he did continue to have a good theatrical career, debuting on Broadway in the title role of *The Elephant Man* and doing a number of other plays off-Broadway. In the late '70s, Hamill was involved in a serious car accident that caused him to have extensive reconstructive facial surgery. **Selected Works:** *Big Red One* (1980), *Empire Strikes Back* (1980), *Return of the Jedi* (1983)

# Linda Hamilton (Linda Carroll Hamilton)

**Born:** September 26, 1957; Salisbury, MD

**Years Active in the Industry:** by decade

| 10s | 20s | 30s | 40s | 50s | 60s | 70s | 80s | 90s |
|-----|-----|-----|-----|-----|-----|-----|-----|-----|
|     |     |     |     |     |     |     | ■ | ■ |

The stepdaughter of the fire chief of Salisbury, Maryland, Linda Hamilton began her acting career with local children's theatre groups. After college training and dramatic lessons conducted by former director Nicholas Ray, Hamilton was cast in a handful of inexpensive film programs. She was briefly costarred in the prime time TV soap opera *Secrets of Midland Heights* (1980) which led to an equally short stint on the weekly series *King's Crossing* (1982). Hamilton's stock in the film industry rose substantially when she was cast as Sarah Connor, the target for the homicidal intentions of futuristic android Arnold Schwarzenegger in *The Terminator* (1984). No shivering ingenue, the agile and athletic Linda proved a formidable foe for the forces of evil in both *The Terminator* and its sequel, *Terminator 2: Judgment Day,* where at times she came off tougher than the "kinder, gentler" Arnold. From 1987-89, Hamilton starred as Catherine Chandler on the cult TV fantasy series *Beauty and the Beast.* She has a son with director James Cameron. **Selected Works:** *Mr. Destiny* (1990), *Silent Fall* (1994), *A Mother's Prayer* (1995)

# Harry Hamlin (Harry Robinson Hamlin)

**Born:** October 30, 1951; Pasadena, CA

**Years Active in the Industry:** by decade

| 10s | 20s | 30s | 40s | 50s | 60s | 70s | 80s | 90s |
|-----|-----|-----|-----|-----|-----|-----|-----|-----|
|     |     |     |     |     |     |     |     |     |

Handsome American actor Harry Hamlin studied his craft at San Francisco's American Conservatory Theatre. Hamlin made his film debut as a John Garfieldesque prizefighter in the 1930s spoof *Movie Movie* (1978). Three years later, he played Perseus in the Ray Harryhausen sexfest *Clash of the Titans* (1981). Also appearing in this film was international sex symbol Ursula Andress, who became Hamlin's "constant companion" over the next few years, a liaison that resulted in a son. Even as his film career dwindled down to such forgettable fare as *Blue Skies Again* (1983), in which he played an immature Ted Turner type, Hamlin's career flourished on television. He starred in a 1979 TV miniseries adaptation of James T. Farrell's *Studs Lonigan,* played a courageous astronaut on the 1985 multiepisode production *Space,* and essayed the role of a straying politician in the 1988 two-parter *Favorite Son.* Hamlin's best-known TV assignment, which he launched in 1986, was the role of amorous litigation attorney Michael Kuzak on the popular NBC series *L.A. Law.* He is divorced from actress Nicollette Sheridan. **Selected Works:** *Deceptions* (1990), *Deadly Intentions... Again?* (1991)

# Tom Hanks

**Born:** July 9, 1956; Concord, CA

**Years Active in the Industry:** by decade

| 10s | 20s | 30s | 40s | 50s | 60s | 70s | 80s | 90s |
|-----|-----|-----|-----|-----|-----|-----|-----|-----|
|     |     |     |     |     |     |  ■  |  ■  |  ■  |

American leading actor Tom Hanks has become one of the most popular stars in contemporary American cinema. Hanks spent much of his childhood moving about with his divorced father, an itinerant cook, and continually attempting to cope with constantly changing schools, religions, and stepmothers. After settling in Oakland, California, he began performing in high school plays. He continued acting while attending Cal State, Sacramento, but left to pursue his vocation full-time. In 1978, Hanks went to find work in New York; while there he married actress-producer Samantha Lewes, whom he later divorced. He debuted onscreen in the low-budget slasher movie *He Knows You're Alone* (1979). Shortly afterwards he moved to Los Angeles and landed a co-starring role in the TV sitcom *Bosom Buddies;* he also worked occasionally in other TV series such as *Taxi* and *Family Ties,* as well as in the TV movie *Mazes and Monsters.* Hanks finally became a star when he starred opposite Darryl Hannah in the Disney comedy *Splash!,* which became the sleeper hit of 1984. Audiences were drawn to the lanky, curly headed actor's amiable, laid back style and keen sense of comic-timing. He went on to appear in a string of mostly unsuccessful comedies before starring *Big* (1988), in which gave a delightful performance as a child in a grown man's body. His 1990 film *Bonfire of the Vanities* was one of the biggest bombs of the year, but audiences seemed to forgive his lapse. In 1992, Hank's star again rose when he played the outwardly disgusting, inwardly warmhearted coach in Penny Marshall's *A League of Their Own.* This led to a starring role in the smash hit romantic comedy *Sleepless in Seattle* (1993). Although a fine comedic actor, Hanks earned critical respect and an even wider audience when he played the tormented AIDS afflicted homosexual lawyer in the drama *Philadelphia* (1993) and won that year's Oscar for Best Actor. In 1994 he won again for his convincing portrait of the slow-witted but phenomenally lucky *Forrest Gump,* and his success continued with the smash space epic *Apollo 13* (1995). Hanks is married to actress Rita Wilson, with whom he appeared in *Volunteers* (1985). **Selected Works:** *Joe Versus the Volcano* (1990)

# William Hanna

**Born:** July 14, 1910; Melrose, NM

**Years Active in the Industry:** by decade

| 10ˢ | 20ˢ | 30ˢ | 40ˢ | 50ˢ | 60ˢ | 70ˢ | 80ˢ | 90ˢ |
|-----|-----|-----|-----|-----|-----|-----|-----|-----|
|     |     |     |     |     |     |     |     |     |

A writer, lyricist, and composer for the Harman-Ising studios in the early '30s, William Hanna joined MGM's animation department in 1937. There he teamed with Joseph Barbera, with whom he made a series of "Tom & Jerry" cartoons between 1940 and 1958, most notably *Mouse Trouble, The Cat Concerto, Kitty Foiled, The Two Mouseketeers,* and *Johann Mouse.* They also made animated sequences for the MGM musicals *Anchors Aweigh, Holiday in Mexico, Dangerous When Wet,* and *Invitation To The Dance.* Hanna and Barbera turned to television in the 1960s and created several beloved animated series, including *The Flintstones, Huckleberry Hound, Yogi Bear, Top Cat, The Jetsons,* and *Johnny Quest.* Their shows led to the '60s theatrical animated features *Hey There, It's Yogi Bear* and *A Man Called Flintstone,* as well as the recent *Jetsons: The Movie.*

# Daryl Hannah

**Born:** 1960; Chicago, IL

**Years Active in the Industry:** by decade

| 10ˢ | 20ˢ | 30ˢ | 40ˢ | 50ˢ | 60ˢ | 70ˢ | 80ˢ | 90ˢ |
|-----|-----|-----|-----|-----|-----|-----|-----|-----|
|     |     |     |     |     |     |     |     |     |

Statuesque leading lady Daryl Hannah began studying drama in Chicago after working as a classical dancer in her teens. She then went on to study with Stella Adler. While still a high school student she was chosen for a small role in the horror film *The Fury* (1978), and after several more films she got her breakthrough role as an android in *Bladerunner* (1982) as well as a part in the abysmal *Summer Lovers* (1982). Her first major film role was in the hit comedy *Splash!* (1984), in which she played a mermaid who charms Tom Hanks, and her turn as the title character in the 1987 comedy *Roxanne* was particularly delightful. She has since gone on to work steadily, playing assorted leads and supporting roles, but Hannah garnered just as much attention with the details of her long-term romances with singer Jackson Browne and John F. Kennedy Jr. She is the sister of actress Page Hannah. **Selected Works:** *At Play in the Fields of the Lord* (1991), *Memoirs of an Invisible Man* (1992), *Attack of the 50 ft. Woman* (1993), *Grumpy Old Men* (1993)

# Ann Harding (Dorothy Walton Gatley)

**Born:** August 7, 1901; Fort Sam Houston, TX
**Died:** 1981

**Years Active in the Industry:** by decade

| 10ˢ | 20ˢ | 30ˢ | 40ˢ | 50ˢ | 60ˢ | 70ˢ | 80ˢ | 90ˢ |
|-----|-----|-----|-----|-----|-----|-----|-----|-----|
|     |     |     |     |     |     |     |     |     |

American actress Ann Harding spent her childhood as an "army brat" constantly moving around the U.S. and Cuba. In her late teens, she worked as a freelance script reader for the Famous Players-Lasky company. In 1921 she made her stage acting debut with the Provincetown Players of Greenwich Village; later that year she appeared on Broadway. Soon she was a well-respected leading lady on Broadway and in stock, and as a result, was signed to a movie contract with Pathe in 1929. She was a Hollywood star within a year. Especially popular with women, she was usually cast as a gentle, refined heroine. For her work in *Holiday* (1930) she received a Best Actress Oscar nomination. For several years she remained a top star, but her career was hurt by typecasting; again and again she appeared in sentimental tearjerkers in which she played the noble woman who makes a grand sacrifice. After marrying symphony conductor Warner Janssen, she quit making films in 1937. Five years later she returned to the screen as a character actress, going on to make a number of films over the next decade, followed by another break of several years and then one last spurt of film acting in 1956. Later she went on to star on Broadway and appear in guest-star roles on TV. Her first husband was actor Harry Bannister. **Selected Works:** *Magnificent Yankee* (1950)

# Sir Cedric Hardwicke

**Born:** February 19, 1883; Lye, Stourbridge, Worcester, England
**Died:** 1964; Los Angeles, CA

**Years Active in the Industry:** by decade

| 10ˢ | 20ˢ | 30ˢ | 40ˢ | 50ˢ | 60ˢ | 70ˢ | 80ˢ | 90ˢ |
|-----|-----|-----|-----|-----|-----|-----|-----|-----|
|     |     |     |     |     |     |     |     |     |

British actor Sir Cedric Hardwicke's physician father was resistant to his son's chosen profession; nonetheless, the elder Hardwicke paid Cedric's way through the Royal Academy of Dramatic Arts. The actor was fortunate enough to form a lasting friendship with playwright George Bernard Shaw, who felt that Hardwicke was the finest actor in the world (Shaw's other favorites were the Four Marx Brothers). Working in Shavian plays like *Heartbreak House, Major Barbara* and *The Apple Cart* throughout most of the 1920s and 1930s in England, Hardwicke proved that he was no one-writer actor with such roles as Captain Andy in the London production of the American musical *Show Boat.* After making his first film *The Dreyfus Case* in 1931, Hardwicke worked with distinction in both British and American films, though his earliest attempts at becoming a Broadway favorite were disappointments. Knighted for his acting in 1934, Hardwicke's Hollywood career ran the gamut from prestige items like *Wilson* (1944), in which he played Henry Cabot Lodge, to low-budget gangster epics like *Baby Face Nelson* (1957), where he brought a certain degree of tattered dignity to the role of a drunken gangland doctor. As proficient at directing as he was at acting, Hardwicke unfortunately was less successful as a businessman. Always a step away from his creditors, he found himself taking more and more journeyman assignments as he got older. Better things came his way with a successful run in the 1960 Broadway play *A Majority of One* and several tours with Charles Laughton, Agnes Moorehead and Charles Boyer in the "reader's theatre" staging of Shaw's *Don Juan in Hell*. A talented writer, Hardwicke wrote two autobiographies, the last of these published in 1961 as *A Victorian in Orbit*. It was here that he wittily but ruefully observed that "God felt sorry for actors, so he gave them a place in the sun and a swimming pool. The price they had to pay was to surrender their talent." **Selected Works:** *Hunchback of Notre Dame* (1939), *Invisible Man Returns* (1940), *Suspicion* (1941), *Winslow Boy* (1949), *Richard III* (1955)

# Oliver Hardy

**Born:** January 18, 1892; Harlem, GA
**Died:** August 7, 1957; North Hollywood, CA

**Years Active in the Industry:** by decade

| 10ˢ | 20ˢ | 30ˢ | 40ˢ | 50ˢ | 60ˢ | 70ˢ | 80ˢ | 90ˢ |
|-----|-----|-----|-----|-----|-----|-----|-----|-----|
|     |     |     |     |     |     |     |     |     |

Unlike his future screen partner Stan Laurel, American comedian Oliver Hardy did not come from a show business family. His father was a lawyer who died when Hardy was ten; his mother was a hotel owner in both his native Georgia and in Florida. The young Hardy became fascinated with show business through the stories spun by the performers who stayed at his mother's hotel, and at age eight he ran away to join a minstrel troupe. Possessing a beautiful singing voice, Hardy studied music for a while, but quickly became bored with the regimen; the same boredom applied to his years at Georgia Military College (late in life, Hardy claimed to have briefly studied law at the University of Georgia, but chances are that he never got any farther than filling out an application). Heavy-set and athletic, Hardy seemed more interested in sports than in anything else; while still a teenager, he umpired local baseball games, putting on such an intuitively comic display of histrionics that he invariably reduced the fans to laughter. In 1910, he opened the first movie theater in Milledgeville, Georgia, and as a result became intrigued with the possibilities of film acting. Traveling to Jacksonville, Florida in 1913, he secured work at the Lubin Film Company, where thanks to his 250-pound frame he was often cast as a comic villain. From 1915-25, Hardy appeared in support of such comedians as Billy West (the famous Chaplin imitator), Jimmy Aubrey, Larry Semon (Hardy played the Tin Woodman in Semon's 1925 version of *The Wizard of Oz*), and Bobby Ray. An established "heavy" by 1926, Hardy signed with the Hal Roach studios, providing support to such headliners as Our Gang and Charley Chase. With the rest of the Roach stock company, Hardy appeared in the Comedy All-Stars series, where he was frequently directed by fellow Roach contractee Stan Laurel (with whom Hardy had briefly appeared on-screen in the independently produced 1918 two-reeler *Lucky Dog*). At this point, Laurel was more inter-

ested in writing and directing than performing, but was lured back before the cameras by a hefty salary increase. Almost inadvertently, Laurel began sharing screen time with Hardy in such All-Stars shorts as *Slipping Wives* (1927), *Duck Soup* (1927) and *With Love and Hisses* (1927). Roach's supervising director Leo McCarey, noticing how well the pair worked together, began teaming them deliberately, which led to the inauguration of the "Laurel and Hardy" series in late 1927. At first, the comedians indulged in the cliched fat-and-skinny routines, with Laurel the fall guy for the bullying Hardy. Gradually the comedians developed the multidimensional screen characters with which we're so familiar today. The corpulent Hardy was the pompous know-it-all, whose arrogance and stubbornness always got him in trouble; the frail Stan was the blank-faced man-child, whose carelessness and inability to grasp an intelligent thought prompted impatience from his partner. Underlining all this was the genuine affection the characters held for each other, emphasized by Hardy's courtly insistence upon introducing Stan as "my friend, Mr. Laurel." Gradually Hardy adopted the gestures and traits that rounded out the "Ollie" character: The tie-twiddle, the graceful panache with which he performed such simple tasks as ringing doorbells and signing hotel registers, and the "camera look," in which he stared directly at the camera in frustration or amazement over Laurel's stupidity. Fortunately Laurel and Hardy's voices matched their characters perfectly, so they were able to make a successful transition to sound, going on to greater popularity than before. Sound added even more ingredients to Hardy's comic repertoire, not the least of which were such catchphrases as "Why don't you do something to *help* me?" and "Here's *another* nice mess you've gotten me into." Laurel and Hardy graduated from two-reelers to feature films with 1931's *Pardon Us*, though they continued to make features and shorts simultaneously until 1935. While Laurel preferred to burn the midnight oil as a writer and film editor, Hardy stopped performing each day at quitting time. He occupied his leisure time with his many hobbies, including cardplaying, cooking, gardening, and especially golf. The team nearly broke up in 1939, not because of any animosity between them but because of Stan's contract dispute with Hal Roach. While this was being settled, Hardy starred solo in *Zenobia* (1939), a pleasant but undistinguished comedy about a southern doctor who tends to a sick elephant. Laurel and Hardy reteamed in late 1939 for two more Roach features and for the Boris Morros/RKO production *The Flying Deuces* (1939). Leaving Roach in 1940, the team performed with the USO and the Hollywood Victory Caravan, then signed to make features at 20th Century-Fox and MGM. The resultant eight films, produced between 1941 and 1945, suffered from too much studio interference and too little creative input from Laurel and Hardy, and as such are but pale shadows of their best work at Roach. In 1947, the team was booked for the first of several music hall tours of Europe and the British Isles, which were resounding successes and drew gigantic crowds wherever Stan and Ollie went. Upon returning to the States, Hardy soloed again in a benefit stage production of *What Price Glory* directed by John Ford. In 1949, he played a substantial supporting role in *The Fighting Kentuckian,* which starred his friend John Wayne; as a favor to another friend, Bing Crosby, Hardy showed up in a comic cameo in

1950's *Riding High*. Back with Laurel, Hardy appeared in the French-made comedy *Atoll K* (1951), an unmitigated disaster that unfortunately brought the screen career of Laurel and Hardy to a close. After more music hall touring abroad, the team enjoyed a resurgence of popularity in the U.S. thanks to constant showings of their old movies on television. Laurel and Hardy were on the verge of starring in a series of TV comedy specials when Stan Laurel suffered a stroke. While he was convalescing, Hardy endured a heart attack, and was ordered by his doctor to lose a great deal of weight. In 1956, Hardy was felled a massive stroke that rendered him completely inactive; he held on, tended day and night by his wife Lucille, until he died in August of 1957. Ironically, Oliver Hardy's passing occurred at the same time that he and Stan Laurel were being reassessed by fans and critics as the greatest comedy team of all time. **Selected Works:** *Way out West* (1937), *Block-Heads* (1938)

# Renny Harlin

**Born:** 1958; Helsinki, Finland

**Years Active in the Industry:** by decade

| 10s | 20s | 30s | 40s | 50s | 60s | 70s | 80s | 90s |
|-----|-----|-----|-----|-----|-----|-----|-----|-----|
|     |     |     |     |     |     |     |     |     |

Finnish director Renny Harlin did not come from an artistically-inclined family (his parents were in the medical profession), but Renny himself had determined his future before he was 12, via

extensive use of a home movie camera. Harlin was a twentyish film school graduate when he set up his own production company; while he was fairly successful marketing documentaries and commercial shorts, young Harlin could not get anyone in Finland to bankroll him for a feature. He moved to the presumably greener pastures of Hollywood, where he finally realized his goal with the 1986 feature *Born American*. His direction of 1990's *Die Hard 2* seemed to bode well for steady work in action films; unfortunately Harlin's next effort (released the same month as *Die Hard 2*) was the ill-fated Andrew Dice Clay vehicle *The Adventures of Ford Fairlane* (1990). The collapse of this enterprise resulted in reams of magazine copy about the "once-promising" and "washed-up" Har-

lin. But in 1993, he responded with the successful *Cliffhanger*, which managed the remarkable feat of being an actor's picture (the star was Sylvester Stallone) *and* a director's picture all in one. Renny Harlin is married to actress Geena Davis, whom he directed in the 1995 swashbuckler *Cutthroat Island*. **Selected Works:** *Die Hard 2: Die Harder* (1990)

# Jean Harlow (Harlean Carpenter)

**Born:** March 3, 1911; Kansas City, MO
**Died:** 1937

**Years Active in the Industry:** by decade

| 10s | 20s | 30s | 40s | 50s | 60s | 70s | 80s | 90s |
|-----|-----|-----|-----|-----|-----|-----|-----|-----|
|     |     |     |     |     |     |     |     |     |

Jean Harlow, with her soft come-hither body, platinum blonde hair, and keen sense of humor, is recognized as one of the most gifted and blatantly sensual stars of the 1930s. Harlow endured much pain during her 26 years. Born Harlean Carpenter in Kansas City, she was the daughter of Jean Harlow Carpenter (whose name the actress appropriated for the marquee), the complex, often oppressive force behind her daughter's sudden rise to fame. When she was only 16, the young Harlow eloped with a businessman and moved to

Los Angeles, where she began appearing as an extra in silent films. She was particularly noticed for her appearance in a 1929 Laurel and Hardy short *Double Whoopee*. That year she also played a small role opposite reigning sex symbol Clara Bow in *The Saturday Night Kid*. In 1930, Harlow got her first real break from Howard Hughes, who cast her in his World War I drama *Hell's Angels* after he found the film's original star Greta Nissen's Swedish accent incomprehensibly thick. It was in this film that she uttered the immortal words "Would you be shocked if I changed into something more comfortable?" Harlow's wise-cracking presence in the film soon attracted much attention, and Hughes sent her out on a publicity tour and loaned her to other studios. In 1931 she appeared in six films; while her performances were often panned by critics and audiences were initially shocked by her almost lurid onscreen sexuality, she gradually began to develop a following. She achieved real fame in 1932 when MGM bought her contract and decided to give her more substantial parts. In films such as *Red-Headed Woman* and *Red Dust* (both 1932) Harlow demonstrated that she was not only extremely sexy and funny, she was also a first-rate actress; by the year's end she was a bonafide star playing opposite some of the industry's most popular men, including Clark Gable and Spencer Tracy. Unfortunately, as her professional career flourished, her personal life began to deteriorate, beginning with the alleged suicide of her second husband Paul Bern. Though there was a subsequent scandal surrounding his demise, it did not impact Harlow's popularity. Later she ended up briefly married to cinematographer Harold Rosson, and then had a long engagement with MGM star William Powell. While filming *Saratoga* in 1937, Harlow suddenly fell ill; ten days later, on June 7, she died at age 26. During her reign, Harlow had starred in less than twenty films. At the time of her death, no details as to why she died were released, but several years later it was revealed that Harlow had suffered from kidney disease most of her life, and that she died of acute uremic poisoning. Her life has been chronicled in several biographies and two subsequent movies, both named *Harlow*. **Selected Works:** *Public Enemy* (1931), *Libeled Lady* (1936)

# Mark Harmon

**Born:** September 2, 1951; Burbank, CA

**Years Active in the Industry:** by decade

| 10s | 20s | 30s | 40s | 50s | 60s | 70s | 80s | 90s |
|-----|-----|-----|-----|-----|-----|-----|-----|-----|
|     |     |     |     |     |     |     |     |     |

Let us dispense with the family tree of actor Mark Harmon as expeditiously as possible. Mark is the son of football great Tom Harmon and 1940s film star Elyse Knox; he is the brother of Kris Harmon—ex-wife of Ricky Nelson—and uncle of Kris and Ricky's actress daughter Tracy Nelson (Harmon was briefly put in custody of Kris' other children when she proved unable to care for them); and finally, Harmon is the husband of *Mork and Mindy* star Pam Dawber. Harmon emulated his dad by playing football at UCLA, then followed in mom's footsteps by turning to acting; his first movie was 1978's *Comes a Horseman*. Most of Harmon's starring film appearances are easy to take but unmemorable, such as his lackadaisical high school teacher in *Summer School* (1988). A baseball fan, Harmon was once part-owner of the minor-league San Bernardino Spirit, a team which figured prominently in his 1988 film vehicle *Stealing Home*. Harmon is best known for his work on 1980s series TV: he has costarred in *Flamingo Road* and *Moonlighting*, and played the lead role of AIDs-stricken Dr. Bob Calswell on *St. Elsewhere*. In mid-1995, promotional ads on the NBC television network proudly trumpetted that "Mark Harmon is *back!*" for a tire-screeching private eye series "Charlie Grace." **Selected Works:** *Deliberate Stranger* (1986), *Dillinger* (1991), *Shadow of a Doubt* (1991), *Wyatt Earp* (1994), *Magic in the Water* (1995)

# Jessica Harper

**Born:** October 10, 1949; Chicago, IL

**Years Active in the Industry:** by decade

| 10s | 20s | 30s | 40s | 50s | 60s | 70s | 80s | 90s |
|-----|-----|-----|-----|-----|-----|-----|-----|-----|
|     |     |     |     |     |     |     |     |     |

Birdlike, wide-eyed, brunette American actress Jessica Harper headed for New York after graduation from Sarah Lawrence College; her first professional gig was an understudy in the "tribal love rock musical" *Hair*. It would be one of the few major financial successes that Harper would ever be associated with. The actress is considered the uncrowned queen of "cult" films, among them such esoterica as *Phantom of the Paradise* (1974), *Inserts* (1977), and *The Blue Iguana* (1988), in which she played a female Castro! Even when selecting a "mainstream" role, Harper's choices have been somewhat offbeat: as Steve Martin's put-upon wife in *Pennies from Heaven* (1981), she has a musical number in which he imagines hacking her husband to death with a knife! Harper was at her most normal, and most appealing, in the nostalgic comedy *My Favorite Year* (1982), in which she played the girlfriend of Mel Brooksish comedy writer Mark-Linn Baker. In *Stardust Memories* (1980), she was one of many stellar contributors to Woody Allen's impressionistic vision of fame. Offscreen, Jessica Harper is the wife of motion picture executive Thomas E. Rothman.

# Tess Harper

**Born:** 1952; Mammoth Springs, AR

**Years Active in the Industry:** by decade

| 10s | 20s | 30s | 40s | 50s | 60s | 70s | 80s | 90s |
|-----|-----|-----|-----|-----|-----|-----|-----|-----|
|     |     |     |     |     |     |     |     |     |

Straight out of Southwest Missouri State College, actress Tess Harper entered the professional acting pool via children's and dinner theatre. She showed up in such TV productions as *Starflight One* (1982) before making her impressive screen debut as Robert Duvall's pious lady love in the critically acclaimed *Tender Mercies* (1983). It would be nice to report that all of her films were of this calibre, but such cannot be said of such efforts as *Amityville 3-D* (1983) and *My Heroes Have Always Been Cowboys* (1993). In 1986, Harper was Oscar-nominated for her violets-and-vitriol portrayal of the spiteful cousin of Diane Keaton, Jessica Lange and Sissy Spacek in *Crimes of the Heart*. **Selected Works:** *Silkwood* (1983), *Dark River: A Father's Revenge* (1990), *Man in the Moon* (1991), *My New Gun* (1992)

# Woody Harrelson

**Born:** July 23, 1961; Midland, TX

**Years Active in the Industry:** by decade

| 10s | 20s | 30s | 40s | 50s | 60s | 70s | 80s | 90s |
|-----|-----|-----|-----|-----|-----|-----|-----|-----|
|     |     |     |     |     |     |     |     |     |

The son of convicted killer Charles Voyde Harrelson, Woody Harrelson was a rootless, trouble-prone youngster who spent much of his early life in a school for kids with learning disabilities. He learned to channel his restlessness while appearing in high school plays in Lebanon, Ohio. He went professional around this time, making his film debut in *Harper Valley PTA* (1978). While studying acting in earnest, Harrelson attended Indiana's Hanover College, where he was member of Sigma Chi. His first on-film line was "I like her tits!" in 1986's *Wildcats,* On stage, Harrelson understudied in the Neal Simon Broadway comedy *Biloxi Blues* (he was briefly married to Simon's daughter Nancy), and at one point wrote a play titled *Furthest from the Sun.* Though many of his film roles were extensions of his own quarrelsome, opinionated nature, Harrelson gained national fame in the role of sweet-natured, ingenuous bartender Woody Boyd on the TV sitcom *Cheers,* which he played from 1985 until the series' conclusion in 1993, and for which he won an Emmy in 1988. Still a restless, iconoclastic spirit, Harrelson is very particular in his selection of film roles (he was sued by MGM for dropping out of *Benny and Joon*). In 1994, he electrified audiences with his complex performance as a publicity-hound serial murderer in Oliver Stone's controversial *Natural Born Killers.* **Selected Works:** *Doc Hollywood* (1991), *White Men Can't Jump* (1992), *Indecent Proposal* (1993), *Money Train* (1995)

# Ed Harris

**Born:** November 28, 1950; Tenafly, NJ

**Years Active in the Industry:** by decade

| 10s | 20s | 30s | 40s | 50s | 60s | 70s | 80s | 90s |
|-----|-----|-----|-----|-----|-----|-----|-----|-----|
|     |     |     |     |     |     |     | ■   |     |

American actor Ed Harris played football for two years at Columbia, then transferred to Oklahoma State and began taking acting classes and appearing in summer stock. He went on to the California Institute of the Arts, working extensively after graduation in West Coast stage productions. It is said that Sam Shepard's play *Fool for Love* was written for him. He got some television roles, including a substantial part in *The Amazing Howard Hughes* (1977). He debuted onscreen as a killer in the Charles Bronson action flick *Borderline* (1980). His career took off in 1983, when he gave contrasting performances in two films, *Under Fire* and *The Right Stuff,* in which he played astronaut John Glenn. He continues to deliver meaty performances in both supporting and lead roles, including an impressive

turn as a NASA engineer who guides the lost crew back to Earth in *Apollo 13* (1995). He is married to actress Amy Madigan, with whom he co-starred in *Places in the Heart* (1984) and *Alamo Bay* (1985). **Selected Works:** *State of Grace* (1990), *Glengarry Glen Ross* (1992), *Running Mates* (1992), *Milk Money* (1994), *Apollo 13* (1995)

# Richard Harris

**Born:** October 1, 1932; Limerick, Ireland

**Years Active in the Industry:** by decade

| 10s | 20s | 30s | 40s | 50s | 60s | 70s | 80s | 90s |
|-----|-----|-----|-----|-----|-----|-----|-----|-----|
|     |     |     |     | ■   | ■   | ■   | ■   | ■   |

After studying acting at the London Academy of Music and Dramatic Art, British actor Richard Harris debuted onstage in 1956; two years later he made his screen debut in *Alive and Kicking* (1958). He worked in films steadily for the next few years, finally becoming an international star with his robust performance in *This Sporting Life* (1963), for which he won the Cannes Film Festival Best Actor Award and received a Best Actor Oscar nomination. He is perhaps best remembered for portraying King Arthur in the stage and screen versions of the musical *Camelot* (1967). Both on and offscreen his persona is that of the "man's man," a rugged, charismatic, earthy, pugnacious, unconventional rebel with earthy desires. In addition to acting, Harris has also been a singer (with his unforgettably campy classic "MacArthur Park," which he also wrote) and poet. In 1982 he published a thriller novel, *Honor Bound.* Harris renewed his film career in the late 1980's and has continued to work steadily ever since. **Selected Works:** *Field* (1990), *Patriot Games* (1992), *Unforgiven* (1992), *Wrestling Ernest Hemingway* (1993), *Silent Tongue* (1994)

# Rex Harrison (Reginald Carey Harrison)

**Born:** March 5, 1908; Huyton, England
**Died:** June 2, 1990

**Years Active in the Industry:** by decade

| 10s | 20s | 30s | 40s | 50s | 60s | 70s | 80s | 90s |
|-----|-----|-----|-----|-----|-----|-----|-----|-----|
|     |     | ■   | ■   | ■   | ■   | ■   | ■   |     |

Debonair and distinguished British star of stage and screen for over fifty years, Sir Rex Harrison is best remembered for playing charming, slyly mischievous characters. Born Reginald Carey, he made his theatrical debut at age 16 with the Liverpool Repertory Theater, remaining with that group for three years. He first appeared on the British stage and in films in 1930. Harrison made the first of many appearances on Broadway in *Sweet Aloes* in 1936. That year, he became a bonafide British star when he played in the theatrical production *French Without Tears,* in which he showed himself to be very skilled in black-tie comedy. He served as a flight lieutenant in the RAF during World War II; this interruption in his career was quickly followed by several British films. Harrison moved to Hollywood in 1945, where he continued to prosper in films. Among his many roles was that of the King in the 1946 production of *Anna and the King of Siam.* Three of his six marriages were to actresses, namely Lilli Palmer, Kay Kendall, and Rachel Roberts. When Hollywood actress Carole Landis committed suicide in 1948, Harrison's name was linked to her, and led to his being dubbed "Sexy Rexy" in the gossip columns. Harrison is perhaps best known for his performance as Professor Henry Higgins in the musical *My Fair Lady,* in which he appeared on Broadway from 1956-58 (winning a Tony) and again in its revival in 1981, as well as for a year in London in the late '50s. In 1964, he won an Oscar for his onscreen version of the role. Previously, he had received a Best Actor Oscar nomination for his portrayal of Julius Caesar in *Cleopatra* (1963). In 1975 his autobiography, *Rex,* was published; four years later, he edited and published an anthology of poetry *If Love Be Love.* He was knighted in 1989. Harrison continued to act (his final appearance was in the Broadway revival of Sommerset Maugham's *The Circle,* in which he starred with Stewart Granger and Glynis Johns) until one month before he died of pancreatic cancer. **Selected Works:** *Citadel* (1938), *Major Barbara* (1941), *Blithe Spirit* (1945), *Ghost and Mrs. Muir* (1947)

# Ray Harryhausen

**Born:** 1921; Los Angeles, CA

**Years Active in the Industry:** by decade

| 10ˢ | 20ˢ | 30ˢ | 40ˢ | 50ˢ | 60ˢ | 70ˢ | 80ˢ | 90ˢ |
|-----|-----|-----|-----|-----|-----|-----|-----|-----|

Although he is neither producer, director, nor actor, Ray Harryhausen has carved out a special niche in motion picture history, and a unique worldwide fandom, as the creator and designer of several of the most beloved fantasy films of all time. An early fan of the stop-motion animation work of Willis O'Brien (*King Kong*), Harryhausen began devising his own stop-motion creations at home while still a boy, and eventually received guidance from O'Brien, with whom he later worked. After a few attempts at mounting projects of his own and a stint in the Army, where his stop-motion work served him well in creating instructional and training films, Harryhausen worked as an animator for George Pal in the middle and late 1940's. At the end of the decade, he went to work for O'Brien on *Mighty Joe Young,* the last of O'Brien's major projects—although, as Harryhausen pointed out, O'Brien was so involved in producing the film, that 80 percent of the animation in the picture was his. In the early 1950s, Harryhausen devised a relatively low-cost stop-motion procedure allowing the production of less expensive effects and relatively low budget films. The first of these films, *The Beast from 20,000 Fathoms* (1953), began as an independent production but was bought by Warner Bros. and became one of the studio's top-grossing movies of that year. Harryhausen began his association with producer Charles H. Schneer during the mid-1950s with *It Came From Beneath The Sea* (1955) and *Earth vs. The Flying Saucers* (1956), the success of which led to the creation of Morningside Productions. Harryhausen and Schneer produced a string of popular fantasy films: *20 Million Miles To Earth* (1957), *The Seventh Voyage of Sinbad* (1958), *The Three Worlds of Gulliver* (1959), *Mysterious Island* (1961), *Jason and the Argonauts* (1963), *The First Men In The Moon* (1964), *The Valley of Gwangi* (1969), *The Golden Voyage of Sinbad* (1973), *Sinbad and the Eye of the Tiger* (1977), and *Clash of the Titans* (1981), all featuring beautifully detailed, lifelike stop-motion animation of such mythical creatures as Cyclopes, giant birds and dragons, and towering Olympian gods. In addition to devising the special effects of these films, Harryhausen also helped create storylines and work out the precise details of their production and direction, which left relatively little for their directors to do apart from work with the actors in exactly predetermined fashion. He directed much second-unit footage, and occasionally appeared in his films as well. In 1992, Harryhausen received an Academy Award for his work as a creator and designer of special effects.

# William S. Hart

**Born:** December 6, 1865; Newburgh, NY
**Died:** 1946

**Years Active in the Industry:** by decade

| 10ˢ | 20ˢ | 30ˢ | 40ˢ | 50ˢ | 60ˢ | 70ˢ | 80ˢ | 90ˢ |
|-----|-----|-----|-----|-----|-----|-----|-----|-----|

Actor William S. Hart developed a strong attachment to the American West in his youth, which was spent traveling around the country with his father, an itinerant laborer. At 19 he began acting onstage in New York, going on to make his name as a Shakespearean actor on Broadway; by his 30s he was a highly popular stage performer, particularly in western plays. He began working in films in 1914 at age 44, when he was employed by his friend Thomas H. Ince. He played villains in a couple of two-reelers before moving into starring roles. Soon he began directing and occasionally writing the films he appeared in, becoming one of the three top male stars of 1910-12. Basing his westerns on his own memories of the West, he insisted on stark realism, using bare, unglamorous storylines that emphasized plot and character over action. For some time his films were popular and critical favorites, but in the early '20s other western stars emerged who emphasized spectacular action and larger-than-life heroics, and Hart's popularity faded. In 1925 he made his final film, *Tumbleweeds,* which was successful but no smash hit; Hart sued United Artists for negligent distribution, eventually winning $278,000 in damages. The litigation ended his career, and he went into retirement. He wrote several western novels and an autobiography, *My Life—East and West* (1929). During his film career he had a habit of proposing to his leading ladies, and was briefly married to one of them, Winifred Westover.

# Hal Hartley

**Born:** 1960; Lindenhurst, NY

**Years Active in the Industry:** by decade

| 10ˢ | 20ˢ | 30ˢ | 40ˢ | 50ˢ | 60ˢ | 70ˢ | 80ˢ | 90ˢ |
|-----|-----|-----|-----|-----|-----|-----|-----|-----|
|     |     |     |     |     |     |     | ■ | ■ |

All but unknown at the outset of the 1990s, American director Hal Hartley was prominent enough at mid-decade for at least one actress to be labelled in the press as a "typical Hal Hartley player." Hartley's graduate project at State University of New York was the short subject *Kid* (1986), in which he displayed the Keatonesque "dark" humor that would characterize his later work. In his first feature *The Unbelievable Truth* (1988), which he completed in a brisk eleven days, Hartley further developed his black-comedy sense by relating the tale of an ex-prisoner whose return to his home town sets off a chain of unexpected reactions from his former neighbors. *Simple Men,* the 1992 film that had critics falling all over themselves "discovering" Hartley, is a study of an odd-couple pairing (a favorite theme of the director), in this instance two brothers who hope to be reunited with their political fugitive father. **Selected Works:** *Surviving Desire* (1991), *Trust* (1991), *Amateur* (1994)

# Laurence Harvey (Lauruska Mischa Skikne)

**Born:** October 1, 1928; Yomishkis, Lithuania
**Died:** 1973

**Years Active in the Industry:** by decade

| 10ˢ | 20ˢ | 30ˢ | 40ˢ | 50ˢ | 60ˢ | 70ˢ | 80ˢ | 90ˢ |
|-----|-----|-----|-----|-----|-----|-----|-----|-----|
|     |     |     | ■ | ■ | ■ | ■ |     |     |

Actor Laurence Harvey was a popular leading man during the 1950s. As a child he emigrated to South Africa with his parents to escape persecution for their Jewish faith. At age 14 he lied about his age and enlisted in the South African Navy; he was soon discovered and sent home. At 15 he debuted onstage with the Johannesburg Repertory Theater; later that year (1943) he joined the army and served until the end of World War II. He went to England in 1946 and enrolled at the Royal Academy of Dramatic Art, staying there three months before joining a Manchester repertory company where he soon began to play leads. He debuted onscreen in 1948 and soon became a busy performer in British films. Meanwhile he gained in stature on both the London and New York stage. A highlight of his theatrical career was his work in the title role of *Henry V* in the 1958-59 Old Vic tour of the U.S. Harvey's breakthrough screen role was as a ruthless social climber in *Room At the Top* (1958), which established him as a star and for which he received a Best Actor Oscar nomination. He went on to star in numerous top-budget Hollywood films and important British films. He married and divorced actress Margaret Leighton. Harvey died of cancer at 45. **Selected Works:** *Manchurian Candidate* (1962), *Darling* (1965)

# Henry Hathaway (Henri Leopold de Fiennes)

**Born:** March 13, 1898; Sacramento, CA
**Died:** February 11, 1985; Los Angeles, CA

**Years Active in the Industry:** by decade

| 10ˢ | 20ˢ | 30ˢ | 40ˢ | 50ˢ | 60ˢ | 70ˢ | 80ˢ | 90ˢ |
|-----|-----|-----|-----|-----|-----|-----|-----|-----|
|     | ■ | ■ | ■ | ■ | ■ | ■ |     |     |

Henry Hathaway was a child actor in western one-reelers (often for director Allan Dwan) of the early 1900s, and appeared in numerous films through the teens. An assistant director in the '20s, he became a director with a string of Randolph Scott westerns in the early '30s, and soon made his mark with the Gary Cooper films *Now and Forever* (1934), *The Lives Of A Bengal Lancer* (1935), and *Peter Ibbetson* (1935). He also directed the Mae West comedy *Go West, Young Man* (1936). In the '40s he made several memorable crime films, including *Johnny Apollo* (1940), *Kiss Of Death* (1947), and *Call Northside 777* (1948), as well as two documentary-style espionage thrillers for producer Louis de Rochemont, *The House on 92nd Street* (1945) and *13 Rue Madeleine* (1946). He continued to make solid and exciting films in a range of genres through the mid '70s, but is most fondly remembered for his westerns *From Hell To Texas* (1958) and *True Grit* (1969). **Selected Works:** *Trail of the Lonesome Pine* (1936)

# Rutger Hauer

**Born:** January 23, 1944; Breukelen, Holland

**Years Active in the Industry:** by decade

| 10s | 20s | 30s | 40s | 50s | 60s | 70s | 80s | 90s |
|-----|-----|-----|-----|-----|-----|-----|-----|-----|
|     |     |     |     |     |     |     |     |     |

Tall, strikingly handsome Dutch actor Rutger Hauer, the son of drama teachers, ran away from his Amsterdam home at age 15 and spent a year aboard a freighter. After coming home, he took a variety of odd jobs while attending night classes to study acting. Afterwards he joined an experimental theater troupe, remaining with them for five years. He then landed a role in a Dutch TV series in which he played a swashbuckler. He debuted onscreen as the lead in Paul Verhoeven's erotically graphic film *Turkish Delight* (1973); his English-speaking debut came two years later in Ralph Nelson's *The Wilby Conspiracy* (1975), but it failed to establish him in Hollywood and he returned to making European films. He finally broke through in America as the sociopathic cold-blooded terrorist in the Sylvester Stallone vehicle *Nighthawks* (1981), after which he was frequently cast as steel-cold heavies in American films. However, his range extends beyond bad guys, as shown (for example) in his role opposite Michelle Pfeiffer in the medieval romance *Ladyhawke* (1985). Most of his films since 1981 have been made in America. **Selected Works:** *Soldier of Orange* (1978), *Blade Runner* (1982), *Legend of the Holy Drinker* (1988), *Buffy the Vampire Slayer* (1992), *Beans of Egypt, Maine* (1994)

# Wings Hauser

**Born:** December 12, 1947

**Years Active in the Industry:** by decade

| 10s | 20s | 30s | 40s | 50s | 60s | 70s | 80s | 90s |
|-----|-----|-----|-----|-----|-----|-----|-----|-----|
|     |     |     |     |     |     |     |     |     |

The years of struggle and near-starvation for actor Wings Hauser began paying off when, in 1977, he was cast as Greg Foster on the daytime drama *The Young and the Restless*. Fans of the series may remember that, at the time, the actor billed himself as J.D. Hauser. In the 1982 movie melodrama *Vice Squad*, Hauser forever sealed his cinematic future by playing the most scurrilous, hate-inducing bad guy this side of Richard Widmark. While he'd occasionally show up in a sympathetic role, Hauser spent most of his time "down and dirty" in B actioners and direct-to-video flicks. A much pleasanter chap in his TV appearances, Hauser has been seen on

two TV sitcoms, 1986's *The Last Precinct* (as Lt. Hobbs) and the still-running *Roseanne* (as the Conners' off-and-on next door neighbor). **Selected Works:** *Art of Dying* (1990), *Exiled in America* (1990), *Frame Up* (1991), *Pale Blood* (1991), *Watchers 3* (1994)

# June Havoc (Ellen Evangeline Hovick)

**Born:** November 8, 1916; Seattle, WA

**Years Active in the Industry:** by decade

| 10s | 20s | 30s | 40s | 50s | 60s | 70s | 80s | 90s |
|-----|-----|-----|-----|-----|-----|-----|-----|-----|
|     |     |     |     |     |     |     |     |     |

The sister of the notorious stripper Gypsy Rose Lee, with whom she was driven into performance by an ambitious stage mother, June Havoc began playing bits in silent film shorts at age two, appearing in 24 Hal Roach comedies. She was earning $1500 a week as a vaudeville headliner by the time she was five. At age 13 she married the first of three husbands, and in her late teens, during the Depression and the demise of vaudeville, she modeled and participated in dance marathons (she still holds a record for marathon dancing in 1933), then went on to perform in Catskill Mountain resorts and in stock. In 1936 she made her Broadway debut. Four years later, she scored a big success in the 1940 production of *Pal Joey*, after which she was invited to Hollywood. She debuted onscreen as an adult in 1941, and over the next decade played leads and second leads in many films. However, Havoc never became a top star and found herself cast in routine films; she rarely appeared onscreen after 1952. Her stage work was more successful, and in 1944 she won a Donaldson Award for *Mexican Hayride*; she also did much work on TV. She wrote and directed the autobiographical Broadway play *Marathon 33* (1963), and authored an autobiography, *Early Havoc* (1959). She was portrayed as a juvenile stage performer in the Broadway show *Gypsy* and its screen version. She married actor-director William Spier. **Selected Works:** *My Sister Eileen* (1942), *Gentleman's Agreement* (1947)

# Ethan Hawke

**Born:** November 6, 1970; Austin, TX

**Years Active in the Industry:** by decade

| 10s | 20s | 30s | 40s | 50s | 60s | 70s | 80s | 90s |
|-----|-----|-----|-----|-----|-----|-----|-----|-----|
|     |     |     |     |     |     |     |     |     |

Texas-born Ethan Hawke made his inaugural film, *Explorers* (1984), at the age of 14. No flash-in-the-pan kid actor, Hawke studied acting with Princeton's McCarter Theatre, the British Theatre Association, and Carnegie-Mellon. While still in school, Hawke gave an excellent account of himself in the role of Tod Anderson in the 1989 film *Dead Poets Society*. By the time he was 22, Hawke was more than prepared for his Broadway bow in Chekhov's

*The Seagull.* Nothing Hawke ever did on stage or screen, however, received more press coverage than his 1994 "night on the town" with the then-married Julia Roberts. **Selected Works:** *Midnight Clear* (1992), *Rich in Love* (1993), *Reality Bites* (1994), *Before Sunrise* (1994)

# Jack Hawkins (John Edward Hawkins)

**Born:** September 1, 1910; London, England
**Died:** 1973

**Years Active in the Industry:** by decade

| 10s | 20s | 30s | 40s | 50s | 60s | 70s | 80s | 90s |
|-----|-----|-----|-----|-----|-----|-----|-----|-----|
|     |     |     |     |     |     |     |     |     |

Handsome, popular British star with a husky voice, Jack Hawkins began acting onstage at age 13, and made his screen debut in 1930. Playing both leads and character roles, he became one of British cinema's strongest personalities, often cast as resilient, resolute, active men, both in and out of uniform. He maintained a busy screen career for over three decades, and was still very much in demand in the mid-'60s, until he was stricken by cancer of the larynx and lost his voice after an operation in 1966. He continued appearing in films, with his speaking parts dubbed by others. He married and divorced actress Jessica Tandy, and authored an autobiography, *Anything for a Quiet Life* (published posthumously). **Selected Works:** *Prisoner* (1955), *Bridge on the River Kwai* (1957), *Ben-Hur* (1959), *Lawrence of Arabia* (1962)

# Howard Hawks (Howard Winchester Hawks)

**Born:** May 30, 1896; Goshen, IN
**Died:** December 26, 1977; Palm Springs, CA

**Years Active in the Industry:** by decade

| 10s | 20s | 30s | 40s | 50s | 60s | 70s | 80s | 90s |
|-----|-----|-----|-----|-----|-----|-----|-----|-----|
|     |     |     |     |     |     |     |     |     |

One of the most distinctive and popular stylists of Hollywood's Golden Age, Howard Hawks's reputation has only grown in the decades since his death. A graduate of Philips-Exeter Academy, Hawks first started working in movies in the prop department of Famous Players-Lasky Studios. He served as a flyer during World War I, and returned to the picture business as a cutter, grad-ually moving up to assistant director and story editor. He began directing during 1922, and by the middle of the decade was also a successful screenwriter. From 1925 onward, Hawks was established as a director, and for the next 45 years, he moved easily between comedy and drama, musical and action film, western and detective thriller, and even science fiction, racking up successes in each area. The most distinctive element in his films is the frequent use of "overlapping dialogue," in which characters frequently start sentences before other characters have finished theirs—this technique, if used properly (as Hawks always did), lent greater speed, tension, and snap to the scene, and made watching Hawks's films a riveting experience. He also had a tendency to include very subtle comic relief in otherwise tense scenes, and his female characters were among the most formidable in screen history, with his leading ladies (most notably Barbara Stanwyck, Rosalind Russell, Margaret Sheridan, and Lauren Bacall) seemingly chosen partly on the basis of their ability to project strength and hold their own against the men around them. Among Hawks's many classics, *Red River* (1948), *The Thing* (1951), *The Big Sleep* (1946), *To Have and Have Not* (1944), *Ball of Fire* (1941), *His Girl Friday* (1940), and *Rio Bravo* (1959) have aged the best, although numerous others have followings that are just as dedicated and wide. **Selected Works:** *Twentieth Century* (1934), *Sergeant York* (1941)

# Goldie Hawn (Goldie Studlendgehawn)

**Born:** November 21, 1945; Washington, DC

**Years Active in the Industry:** by decade

| 10s | 20s | 30s | 40s | 50s | 60s | 70s | 80s | 90s |
|-----|-----|-----|-----|-----|-----|-----|-----|-----|
|     |     |     |     |     |     |     |     |     |

American actress Goldie Hawn made her professional acting debut at age 16 playing Juliet in a Virginia Stage Company Shakespeare production. She studied drama in college while op-

erating a dance studio (she had been taking ballet and tap lessons since she was three) to cover tuition. After dropping out at age 18, she moved to New York to find work as a dancer, ending up as a chorus line can-can dancer at the 1964 World's Fair. She went on to work as a go-go dancer and occasionally in stock. After appearing as a dancer on an episode of the TV series *The Andy Griffith Show,* she was spotted by an agent, who landed her a role in the short-lived comedy TV series *Good Morning World*; this in turn led to membership in the original cast of the sketch-comedy TV series *Laugh-In*, on which she affected a dizzy, giggling, saucer-eyed "dumb blonde" persona. Now nationally known, she was chosen for her kooky image to appear in the comedy *Cactus Flower* (1969) with Walter Matthau; for this, only her second film (she debuted onscreen in a bit part in Disney's *The One and Only Genuine Original Family Band*, in 1968), she won the Best Supporting Actress Oscar. She went on to sustain a busy and generally successful film career, usually cast in the "dizzy blonde" mode established early in her work. She produced several of her later films, and received a Best Actress Oscar nomination for her work in *Private Benjamin* (1980). Twice divorced, she has a long-term live-in relationship with actor Kurt Russell, with whom she is raising her four children; she and Russell appeared together in *Swing Shift* (1984) and *Overboard* (1987). **Selected Works:** *Bird on a Wire* (1990), *Deceived* (1991), *Death Becomes Her* (1992), *Housesitter* (1992)

# Nigel Hawthorne

**Born:** April 5, 1929; Coventry, England

**Years Active in the Industry:** by decade

| 10$^s$ | 20$^s$ | 30$^s$ | 40$^s$ | 50$^s$ | 60$^s$ | 70$^s$ | 80$^s$ | 90$^s$ |
|--------|--------|--------|--------|--------|--------|--------|--------|--------|

Nigel Hawthorne had been acting in his native England for nearly a quarter of a century before making his American debut in a 1974 production of *As You Like It*. Sixteen years later, Hawthorne prompted critical acclaim for his performance in the stage version of *Shadowlands*. In 1994, he wowed movie audiences with his brilliant, outrageous performance as British regent George III in *The Madness of King George*. Nominated for an Academy Award, Nigel Hawthorne might very well have claimed the trophy had 1994 not been The Year of *Forrest Gump*.

# Sessue Hayakawa (Kitaro Hayakawa)

**Born:** June 10, 1889; Honshu, Japan
**Died:** 1973

**Years Active in the Industry:** by decade

| 10$^s$ | 20$^s$ | 30$^s$ | 40$^s$ | 50$^s$ | 60$^s$ | 70$^s$ | 80$^s$ | 90$^s$ |
|--------|--------|--------|--------|--------|--------|--------|--------|--------|

Japanese actor Sessue Hayakawa joined a Japanese stage troupe directed by his uncle after a partial loss of hearing denied him access into the navy, which he had dreamed of joining. He

moved to the U.S. at age 19 and enrolled at the University of Chicago. After returning to Japan he founded the Japanese Imperial Company, with which he toured the American West in 1913. Silent filmmaker Thomas Ince saw him perform and signed him to a film contract, and in 1914 he appeared in several silents. Within two years he was as popular as any big Hollywood star, particularly after his appearance in *The Typhoon* (1914), in which he co-starred was his wife, Tsuru Aoki. He went on to frequently appear with Aoki. His acting style has been described as a combination of "the Method" and Zen; his restrained performances contrasted sharply with the exaggerations of other silent actors. He played both exotic heroes and charming villains in many Hollywood films until 1923, when he moved to Europe; there he continued his busy screen career, mostly in France. He also occasionally worked in Japan and the U.S. He lived in France in the '30s and '40s, and during the Nazi occupation he painted to earn a living. He returned to Hollywood in the late '40s and over the next decade-plus appeared in numerous character roles. For his portrayal of a Japanese camp commander in *The Bridge on the River Kwai* (1957) he received a Best Supporting Actor Oscar nomination. He retired from the screen in the '60s, returning to Japan; there he became an ordained Zen priest and taught acting. During his lifetime he also wrote a novel, a play, and the screenplay for *The Swamp* (1921).

# Sterling Hayden (Sterling Relyea Walter)

**Born:** March 26, 1916; Montclair, NJ
**Died:** May 23, 1986; Sausalito, CA

**Years Active in the Industry:** by decade

| 10$^s$ | 20$^s$ | 30$^s$ | 40$^s$ | 50$^s$ | 60$^s$ | 70$^s$ | 80$^s$ | 90$^s$ |
|--------|--------|--------|--------|--------|--------|--------|--------|--------|

American actor Sterling Hayden was a Hollywood leading man of the '40s and '50s who went on to become a character actor in later years. At age 16 he dropped out of school to become a mate on a schooner, beginning a life-long love affair with the sea; by age 22 he was a ship's captain. Extremely good looking, he modeled professionally to earn enough money to buy his own vessel; this led to a movie contract with Paramount in 1940. Within a year he was famous, having starred in two technicolor movies, *Virginia* (1941) and *Bahama Passage* (1942); both featured the somewhat older actress Madeleine Carroll, to whom he was married from 1942-46. With these films, Paramount began trumpeting him as "The Most Beautiful Man in the Movies" and "The Beautiful Blond Viking God." Shortly after making these two films he joined the Marines to serve in World War II. After the war he landed inconsequential roles until a part as a hoodlum in *The Asphalt Jungle* (1950) demonstrated his skill as an actor. After this his career was spotty, marked for the most part by inferior films (with some notable exceptions, such as *Dr. Strangelove* [1964]) and frequent abandonment of the screen in favor of the sea. It was said that Hayden was never particularly interested in his work as an actor, vastly preferring the life of a sailor. His obsession with the sea and his various voyages are described in his 1963 autobiography, *Wanderer*, in which he also expresses regret for having cooperated with the House Un-American Activities Commission during the early '50s McCarthy-Era "witch trials." He published a novel in 1976, *Voyage: A Novel of 1896*; it was named as a selection of the Book of the Month Club. **Selected Works:** *Killing* (1956)

# George "Gabby" Hayes

**Born:** May 7, 1885; Wellsville, NY
**Died:** February 9, 1969; NV

**Years Active in the Industry:** by decade

| 10s | 20s | 30s | 40s | 50s | 60s | 70s | 80s | 90s |
|-----|-----|-----|-----|-----|-----|-----|-----|-----|
|     |     |     |     |     |     |     |     |     |

Virtually the prototype of all grizzled old-codger western sidekicks, George "Gabby" Hayes professed in real life to hate westerns, complaining that they all looked and sounded alike. For his first few decades in show business, he appeared in everything *but* westerns, including travelling stock companies, vaudeville, and musical comedy. He began appearing in films in 1928, just in time to benefit from the talkie explosion. In contrast to his later unshaven, toothless screen persona, George Hayes (not yet Gabby) frequently showed up in clean-faced, well groomed articulate characterizations, sometimes as the villain. In 1933 he appeared in several of the Lone Star westerns featuring young John Wayne, alternating between heavies and comedy roles. Wayne is among the many cowboy stars who has credited Hayes with giving them valuable acting tips in their formative days. In 1935, Hayes replaced an ailing Al St. John in a supporting role in the first *Hopalong Cassidy* film, costarring with William Boyd; Hayes' character died halfway through this film, but audience response was so strong that he was later brought back into the *Hoppy* series as a regular. It was while sidekicking for Roy Rogers at Republic that Hayes, who by now never appeared in pictures with his store-bought teeth, earned the soubriquet "Gabby", peppering the

soundtrack with such slurred epithets as "Why, you goldurned whipersnapper" and "Consarn it!" He would occasionally enjoy an A-picture assignment in films like *Dark Command* (1940) and *Tall in the Saddle* (1944), but from the moment he became "Gabby", Hayes was more or less consigned exclusively to "B"s. After making his last film appearance in 1952, Hayes turned his attentions to television, where he starred in the popular Saturday-morning *Gabby Hayes Show* ("Hullo out thar in televisium land!") and for a while was the corporate spokesman for Popsicles. Retiring after a round of personal appearance tours, Hayes settled down on his Nevada ranch, overseeing his many business holdings until his death at age 83.

# Helen Hayes (Helen Hayes Brown)

**Born:** October 10, 1900; Washington, DC
**Died:** March 17, 1993; Nyack, NY

**Years Active in the Industry:** by decade

| 10s | 20s | 30s | 40s | 50s | 60s | 70s | 80s | 90s |
|-----|-----|-----|-----|-----|-----|-----|-----|-----|
|     |     |     |     |     |     |     |     |     |

Helen Hayes, the First Lady of the American Theater, made most of her infrequent film appearances after an allergy to theater dust forced her to retire from the stage. Her stage career began when she was five; at age nine, she made her first Broadway appearance. By 1918, she was a star. When she married playwright Charles MacArthur in 1928, the couple came to Hollywood briefly, where she won her first Oscar for *The Sin of Madelon Claudet* (1931). Other memorable roles during that time included her role as a nurse in *A Farewell to Arms* (1932) with a very young Gary Cooper, and *What Every Woman Knows* (1934). Unhappy in Hollywood, she returned to the stage, where she reigned as one of the outstanding American stage actresses. One of her most famous roles was Queen Victoria in *Victoria Regina*. She won a Tony Award the first year they were presented, in 1947, for *Happy Birthday,* and another in 1958 for *Time Remembered*. Throughout the '40s, '50s, '60s and into the '70s, Hayes made numerous television appearances, winning an Emmy as Best Actress in 1952 and starring in the short-lived comic mystery series *The Snoop Sisters* with Mildred Natwick in 1971. She returned to films in the 1950s, making an impressive showing as the Dowager Empress in *Anastasia* (1956) and winning another Oscar for her role in *Airport* (1970). In her later years, she often played kind but mischievous old ladies. Her son is actor James MacArthur. Hayes wrote several memoirs, prompted to write originally by the death of her daughter.

# Louis Hayward (Seafield Grant)

**Born:** March 19, 1909; Johannesburg, South Africa
**Died:** February, 1985

**Years Active in the Industry:** by decade

| 10s | 20s | 30s | 40s | 50s | 60s | 70s | 80s | 90s |
|-----|-----|-----|-----|-----|-----|-----|-----|-----|
|     |     |     |     |     |     |     |     |     |

Upon his father's death, Louis Hayward, moved with his family to London where he was raised. After acting on the British stage, he debuted onscreen in 1932. Following his 1935 Broadway debut, Hayward was invited to Hollywood. For the next two decades he primarily played swashbuckling heroes in historical adventures. His career was broken up by a long stint in the Marines, and Hayward earned a Bronze star for heroism during World War II. Later he became one of the first stars to negotiate for a percentage of his films' revenues; he also had a financial interest in his 1954 TV series *The Lone Wolf.* In the '60s he starred in the TV series *The Pursuers* and *The Survivors.* He was rarely onscreen after 1956. From 1939-45 he was married to actress Ida Lupino.

# Susan Hayward (Edythe Marrener)

**Born:** June 30, 1918; Brooklyn, NY
**Died:** 1975

**Years Active in the Industry:** by decade

| 10s | 20s | 30s | 40s | 50s | 60s | 70s | 80s | 90s |
|-----|-----|-----|-----|-----|-----|-----|-----|-----|
|     |     |     |     |     |     |     |     |     |

Energetic red-haired leading lady Susan Hayward specialized in portraying gutsy women who rebound from adversity. While in high school, she began working as a photographer's model. When open auditions were held in 1937 for the role of Scarlett O'Hara in the upcoming *Gone With the Wind,* she arrived in Hollywood with scores of other actresses. Unlike most of the others, she managed to become a contract player. At first her roles were discouragingly small, but gradually she was able to work her way up to stardom. For her role in *Smash-Up: The Story of a Woman* (1947), the first in which she played a strong-willed, courageous woman, Hayward received the first of five Oscar nominations; her other nominations were for performances in *My Foolish Heart* (1950), *With a Song in My Heart* (1952), *I'll Cry Tomorrow* (1956), and *I Want to Live* (1958), though she won only for the last of these. Although she maintained her star status through the late '50s, in the early '60s she appeared in several unmemorable tearjerkers, prompting her to retire from films in 1964; she later returned to the screen for a few more roles. She was married from 1944-54 to actor Jess Barker. Following their bitter child-custody dispute in 1955, she attempted suicide. After a two-year struggle with a brain tumor, she died at age 56. **Selected Works:** *Beau Geste* (1939), *I Married a Witch* (1942), *Star Spangled Rhythm* (1942)

# Rita Hayworth

**Born:** October 17, 1918; Brooklyn, NY
**Died:** May 14, 1987

**Years Active in the Industry:** by decade

| 10s | 20s | 30s | 40s | 50s | 60s | 70s | 80s | 90s |
|-----|-----|-----|-----|-----|-----|-----|-----|-----|
|     |     |     |     |     |     |     |     |     |

The definitive femme fatale of the 1940s, Rita Hayworth was the Brooklyn-born daughter of Spanish dancer Eduardo Cansino and Ziegfeld Follies showgirl, Volga Haworth. She joined the family dancing act in her early teens and made a few '30s films under her real name, Margarita Cansino, and with her real hair color (black); *Charlie Chan in Egypt* (1935) and *Meet Nero Wolfe* (1936) are among them. Over the next few years, she (at the urging of Columbia Studios and her first husband) reshaped her hairline with electrolysis, dyed her hair auburn, and adopted the name Rita Hayworth. Following her performance in *Only Angels Have Wings* (1939), Hayworth became a major leading lady to most of the big stars, including Tyrone Power, Fred Astaire, Charles Boyer, Gene Kelly and her second and soon to be ex-husband Orson Welles in *Lady From Shanghai* (1948). She then became involved in a tempestuous romance with the already married Aly Khan, son of the Moslem leader, and they married in 1949. Following their divorce in 1951, she was married to singer Dick Haymes from 1953 to 1955, and then for three years to James Hill, producer of her film *Separate Tables* (1958). Her career had slowed down in the 1950s and virtually came to a standstill in the 1960s, when rumors of erratic and supposedly drunken behavior began to circulate. In reality she was suffering from the first symptoms of Alzheimer's Disease. For years, she would be cared for by her daughter Princess Yasmin Khan, and her death from the disease years later gave it public attention that led to increased funding for medical research to find a cure. **Selected Works:** *You Were Never Lovelier* (1942), *Gilda* (1946), *Pal Joey* (1957)

# Glenne Headly

**Born:** March 13, 1955; New London, CT

**Years Active in the Industry:** by decade

| 10s | 20s | 30s | 40s | 50s | 60s | 70s | 80s | 90s |
|-----|-----|-----|-----|-----|-----|-----|-----|-----|
|     |     |     |     |     |     |     |     |     |

With her gentle, innocent demeanor, American actress Glenne Headly seems to be a throwback to the ingenues of the 1930s. A graduate of New York's High School of the Performing Arts, she attended the Herman Berghof Studios and the American College of Switzerland, then joined Chicago's New Works Ensemble. Later she moved on to Chicago's acclaimed Steppenwolf Theater Company, where she won four Jefferson Awards for her performances; there, she also met and married actor John Malkovich, whom she later divorced. She directed a play and appeared off-Broadway in *Arms and the Man* and on Broadway in *Extremities*. During the early '80s she played small supporting parts in films, but didn't make an impact until her co-starring role in *Dirty Rotten Scoundrels* (1988). She appeared with Malkovich in *Eleni* (1985) and *Making Mr. Right* (1987). She also appeared in the TV western mini-series *Lonesome Dove* (1989), and played Tess Trueheart, Warren Beatty's fiancee, in *Dick Tracy* (1990). **Selected Works:** *Purple Rose of Cairo* (1985), *Mortal Thoughts* (1991), *Grand Isle* (1992), *And the Band Played On* (1993)

helped produce. She has since gone on to direct a number of moderately successful mainstream comedies. With her 1989 feature *Look Who's Talking*, she scored her first real hit. In 1995 she wrote and directed *Clueless*, another teen comedy which she loosely based on Jane Austen's *Emma*. She is married to writer Neal Israel.

# John Heard

**Born:** March 7, 1946; Washington, DC

**Years Active in the Industry:** by decade

| 10s | 20s | 30s | 40s | 50s | 60s | 70s | 80s | 90s |
|-----|-----|-----|-----|-----|-----|-----|-----|-----|
|     |     |     |     |     |     | ■   | ■   | ■   |

John Heard began his career with the Organic Theater, with whom he received critical acclaim in the Chicago and New York productions of *Warp*. He went on to win a Theater World Award for his work in *Streamers* in 1977, and to win an Obie in 1979 for two off-Broadway roles in *Othello* and *Split*. In the meantime, he debuted onscreen in Joan Micklin Silver's *Between the Lines* (1977), in which he played the star reporter of an underground radical paper. Heard went on to appear in numerous films (six released in 1988 alone), including playing the forgetful father in the successful *Home Alone* (1990) and *Home Alone 2: Lost in New York* (1992). He has also done TV work, most notably in an adaptation of *The Scarlet Letter* for PBS. **Selected Works:** *Mindwalk* (1991), *Dead Ahead: The Exxon Valdez Disaster* (1992), *Waterland* (1992), *Pelican Brief* (1993)

# Dan Hedaya

**Born:** July 24, 1940; Brooklyn, NY

**Years Active in the Industry:** by decade

| 10s | 20s | 30s | 40s | 50s | 60s | 70s | 80s | 90s |
|-----|-----|-----|-----|-----|-----|-----|-----|-----|
|     |     |     |     |     |     |     | ■   | ■   |

Dan Hedaya is one of the most prolific and versatile of contemporary character actors on the stage, screen, and television. He is perhaps most recognizable for his recurring role as Nick Tortelli, the sleazeball ex-husband of Carla the barmaid on the television comedy *Cheers*. He began acting professionally after studying literature at Tufts University. He then went on to act in the New York Shakespeare Festival for many years. Since 1980, Hedaya has appeared in over 20 feature films where he frequently plays cops, criminals, or rough-edged regular joes. In *Blood Simple* (1984), he got the opportunity to play a leading role as Marty, the jealous husband who hires a creepy detective to kill his faithless wife. **Selected Works:** *Pacific Heights* (1990), *Benny and Joon* (1993), *Rookie of the Year* (1993), *Searching for Bobby Fischer* (1993), *Clueless* (1995)

# Amy Heckerling

**Born:** May 7, 1954; New York, NY

**Years Active in the Industry:** by decade

| 10s | 20s | 30s | 40s | 50s | 60s | 70s | 80s | 90s |
|-----|-----|-----|-----|-----|-----|-----|-----|-----|
|     |     |     |     |     |     |     | ■   | ■   |

Contemporary filmmaker Amy Heckerling graduated from New York's Art and Design High School. Later she studied film and television at New York University. Prior to coming to Hollywood, Heckerling made three short 16mm films with money from the American Film Institute: *Modern Times*, *High Finance* and *Getting It Over With*. This lead her to direct *Fast Times at Ridgemont High* (1982), a popular comedy about high school life. The success of this lively little film spawned a *Fast Times* television series that she

# Mariel Hemingway

**Born:** November 22, 1961; Ketchum, ID

**Years Active in the Industry:** by decade

| 10s | 20s | 30s | 40s | 50s | 60s | 70s | 80s | 90s |
|-----|-----|-----|-----|-----|-----|-----|-----|-----|
|     |     |     |     |     |     | ■   | ■   | ■   |

A scant three months after her grandfather, author Ernest Hemingway, took his own life with a shotgun, Mariel Hemingway came into the world. By the time Hemingway was ready to launch her career, it appeared as though she would remain in the shadow of two famous relatives: her grandfather Ernest, and her older sister, model Margaux Hemingway, who was just about to star in her first feature film, *Lipstick* (1976). As the publicity hounds sought out Margaux for interviews and photo ops, Mariel quietly took a supporting role in her sister's first starring vehicle. Within a few years, Margaux was out of the movie-star race, but Mariel had only just begun, costarring as Woody Allen's teenaged lover in *Manhattan* (1979). Oscar-nominated for her natural, relaxed performance in the Allen picture, Hemingway followed this triumph with the chancy role of a lesbian athlete in *Personal Best*. Thereafter, Hemingway couldn't seem to stay out of the headlines: she underwent a well-publicized session of cosmetic surgery and breast enhancement to portray the unfortunate *Playboy* centerfold Dorothy Stratten in *Star 80*, then caused bluenosed media monitors to have palpatations by appearing in the nude (actually *appearing* to be appearing in the nude) in an episode of the TV lawyer series *Civil Wars*. Possessed of a keen business sense, Mariel Hemingway has acted as executive producer of one of her pictures, *The Suicide Club*, and has also been the owner of a popular New York eating establishment, Sam's Place. **Selected Works:** *Falling from Grace* (1992), *Into the Badlands* (1992)

# Lance Henriksen

**Born:** May 5, 1940; New York, NY

**Years Active in the Industry:** by decade

| 10s | 20s | 30s | 40s | 50s | 60s | 70s | 80s | 90s |
|-----|-----|-----|-----|-----|-----|-----|-----|-----|
|     |     |     |     |     |     |     |     |     |

Upon graduation from the Actor's Studio, Manhattan-born Lance Henriksen spent nearly two decades playing villains. An agreeable-looking fellow offscreen, Henriksen portrayed the foulest of murderers, rapists, perverts, extraterrestrials and other antisocial types on stage (*Richard III*) and screen. He made his first film, *It Ain't Easy,* in 1972 (his studio bios list his screen debut as *Dog Day Afternoon* [1975]), then concentrated his skills on the melodramatic requirements of *The Jagged Edge* (1986), *Johnny Handsome* (1990), *Jennifer Eight* (1992) and many others. In interviews, Henriksen claims to "live" his parts while portraying them, which he admits is a self-defeating practice. A close friend of director James Cameron, Lance posed for Cameron's preliminary character sketches for the robotic antagonist of the 1984 thriller *The Terminator*. The producers went for the sketches but not for Henriksen; the role instead went to Arnold Schwarzenegger. In compensation, James Cameron saw to it that Lance Henriksen was cast as a *heroic* android in his 1986 film *Aliens*. **Selected Works:** *Pit & the Pendulum* (1991), *Alien 3* (1992), *Hard Target* (1993)

# Buck Henry (Buck Henry Zuckerman)

**Born:** December 9, 1930; New York, NY

**Years Active in the Industry:** by decade

| 10s | 20s | 30s | 40s | 50s | 60s | 70s | 80s | 90s |
|-----|-----|-----|-----|-----|-----|-----|-----|-----|
|     |     |     |     |     |     |     |     |     |

Comedic actor, writer and filmmaker Buck Henry, born Buck Henry Zuckerman, the son of actress Ruth Taylor, began his long career at age 16 as a minor member of the cast of Broadway's *Life with Father*. During the Korean War, he spent his years of service touring Germany with the Seventh Army Repertory Company in a musical comedy that he wrote, directed, and starred in. He found little work as an actor and writer in the '50s, but he gained some fame for an elaborate hoax: he and a friend formed SINA, the Society for Indecency to Naked Animals, and he appeared on talk shows to propagate the idea that the nudity of animals was detrimental to human morality. In 1960 he joined The Premise, an off-Broadway improvisational group. Next he moved to Hollywood, where he wrote comedy for the TV shows of Steve Allen and Garry Moore and for the TV satirical show *That Was the Week That Was*. In 1964 he and Mel Brooks began collaborating on the TV sitcom *Get Smart!;* that same year he co-wrote and acted in the comedy film *The Troublemaker*. His next screenplay collaboration was for the smash hit *The Graduate* (1967), following which he became one of the hottest scriptwriters in Hollywood. He went on to write and/or act in a number of films, and co-directed (with Warren Beatty) *Heaven Can Wait* (1978), for which they received an Oscar nomination. In the mid-'70s he frequently hosted the TV sketch-comedy series *Saturday Night Live*. **Selected Works:** *Defending Your Life* (1991), *Keep the Change* (1992), *Player* (1992), *Grumpy Old Men* (1993), *Short Cuts* (1993)

# Jim Henson (James Muary Henson)

**Born:** September 24, 1936; Greenville, MS
**Died:** May 16, 1990; New York, NY

**Years Active in the Industry:** by decade

| 10s | 20s | 30s | 40s | 50s | 60s | 70s | 80s | 90s |
|-----|-----|-----|-----|-----|-----|-----|-----|-----|
|     |     |     |     |     |     |     |     |     |

For as long as he could remember, Massachusetts native Jim Henson was a devoted fan of puppeteers and ventriloquists; his idols included Edgar Bergen, Burr Tillstrom and Bil and Cora Baird. While attending high school in Maryland (where his meteorologist father had been relocated), Henson was hired for the staff of the Washington D.C. kiddy show *Sam and His Friends*. By the time he was a freshman at the University of Maryland, the lanky, goateed Henson was in charge of the TV show's puppets, with his future wife Jane

Nebel as his assistant. It was during the Washington years that Henson hit upon the concept of the Muppet: part marionette, part puppet. His most popular character was Kermit the Frog, whom Henson fashioned out of his mom's overcoat in 1959. TV commercial appearances by the Muppets led to guest stints on *The Jack Paar Show, The Today Show, The Tonight Show* and *The Jimmy Dean Show.* While Henson and his partner Frank Oz handled the voices for most of the characters, the ever-expanding Muppet cast required a retinue of willing (and quick-witted) assistants. Henson's first taste of moviemaking was the Oscar-nominated 1965 short *Time Piece,* but at the time he preferred television to films. In 1969, the Muppets became a regular feature on the spectacularly popular PBS daily *Sesame Street,* which turned out to be both a blessing and a curse for Henson: his characters were now highly marketable, but he was being perceived as exclusively a "children's entertainer." As such, he lost a lot of adult-oriented assignments. This "kiddy" onus prevented ABC from picking up Henson's half-hour *The Muppet Show* in 1975, whereupon Henson offered the program to syndication. As a result, *The Muppet Show* became one of the biggest non-network hits in TV history, as well as a great international success. Capitalizing on the popularity of "star" muppets Kermit and Miss Piggy, Henson and his staff concocted the 1979 all-star feature film *The Muppet Movie.* With 1981's *The Great Muppet Caper,* Henson made his feature-film directorial debut; he would later direct *Labyrinth* (1985), and with Frank Oz co-directed *The Dark Crystal* (1982). After many years of avoiding Saturday morning network TV, Henson collaborated with Marvel Studios on the weekly cartoon series *Muppet Babies* (1984), which added more Emmy awards to his already top-heavy trophy shelf; less successful was the 1986 animated version of Henson's HBO series *Fraggle Rock.* During the late 1980s, Henson expanded his activities to designing "creatures" for other producer's projects, notably the 1990 movie blockbuster *Teenage Mutant Ninja Turtles.* In May of 1990, Henson was poised to sell his Muppet empire to Disney Studios. Suddenly stricken with streptococcus pneumonia, Jim Henson checked himself into New York Hospital, where he died a few days later at the age of 53. The Muppet operation was taken over by Jim Henson's son Brian.

Although she was born into wealth and influence in Belgium (her father was a banker, her mother a baroness), the young Hepburn was soon struggling in Nazi-occupied Holland, where she attempted to study dancing. After working as a model and dancer and taking acting classes from British character actor Felix Aylmer, Hepburn came to the U.S. and instantly became a star with her first American film, *Roman Holiday* (1953), for which she won an Academy Award. Her charm, intelligence and grace brightened all of her subsequent (although rare) appearances and she would receive four more Oscar nominations, for *Sabrina* (1954), *The Nun's Story* (1959), *Breakfast at Tiffany's* (1961) and *Wait Until Dark* (1967). Though most of her time during the '70s was spent raising her two sons, she would occasionally make a film appearance, as in *Robin and Marian* (1976) opposite Sean Connery as Robin. Her stage appearances were rare, but she did win a Tony for *Ondine* (1954). In the late 1980s, Hepburn became Danny Kaye's successor as a representative of UNICEF. Her unceasing efforts on behalf of the world's children earned her international admiration and her public statements about abhorrent conditions in Somalia are considered in great part responsible for the international community's involvement in attempting to bring peace to and feed the Somali population. She was awarded the Jean Hersholt Humanitarian Award posthumously in 1993. **Selected Works:** *Funny Face* (1957), *Love in the Afternoon* (1957), *Charade* (1963), *My Fair Lady* (1964), *Two for the Road* (1967)

# Katharine Hepburn (Katharine Houghton Hepburn)

**Born:** 1907; Hartford, CT

**Years Active in the Industry:** by decade

| 10s | 20s | 30s | 40s | 50s | 60s | 70s | 80s | 90s |
| --- | --- | --- | --- | --- | --- | --- | --- | --- |

"I'm a personality as well as an actress," Katharine Hepburn once declared. "Show me an actress who isn't a personality, and you'll show me a woman who isn't a star." Hepburn's bold, distinctive personality was apparent almost from birth. She inherited from her lawyer father and suffragette mother her three most pronounced traits: an open and ever-expanding mind, a healthy body (maintained through constant rigorous exercise), and an inability to tell anything less than the truth. She was more a personality than an actress when she took the professional plunge after graduating

# Audrey Hepburn (Edda van Heemstra Hepburn-Ruston)

**Born:** May 4, 1929; Ixtelles, Belgium
**Died:** January 20, 1993; Tolochenaz, Switzerland

**Years Active in the Industry:** by decade

| 10s | 20s | 30s | 40s | 50s | 60s | 70s | 80s | 90s |
| --- | --- | --- | --- | --- | --- | --- | --- | --- |

When Audrey Hepburn died of colon cancer in 1993, she was hailed not only as a magical screen personality, but as a tireless and significant crusader for children's rights around the world.

from Bryn Mawr in 1928; her first stage parts were bits, but she always attracted attention with her distinct New England accent and her bony, sturdy frame. Hepburn's outspokenness lost her more jobs than she received, but in 1932 she finally scored on Broadway with the starring role in *The Warrior's Husband.* She didn't want to sign the film contract offered her by RKO, so she made several "impossible" demands concerning salary and choice of scripts. The studios agreed to her terms, and in 1932 she made her film debut opposite John Barrymore in *A Bill of Divorcement* (despite legends to the contrary, the stars got along quite well). Critical reaction to Hepburn's first film set the tone for the next decade: some thought that she was the freshest and most original actress in Hollywood, while others were irritated by her mannerisms and "artificial" speech patterns. For her third film, *Morning Glory* (1933), Hepburn won the first of her four Academy Awards (a still unbeaten record). Despite initial good response to her films, Hepburn lost a lot of popularity during her RKO stay because of her refusal to play the Hollywood Game. She dressed in unfashionable slacks and paraded about without makeup; refused to pose for pin-up pictures, give autographs or grant interviews; and avoided mingling with her co-workers. As stories of her arrogance and self-absorption leaked out, moviegoers responded by staying away from her films. The fact that Hepburn was a thoroughly dedicated professional—letter-perfect in lines, completely prepared and researched in her roles, the first to arrive to the set each day and the last to leave each evening—didn't matter in those days, when style superseded substance. Briefly returning to Broadway in 1933's *The Lake,* Hepburn received devastating reviews from the same critics who found her personality so bracing in *Warrior's Husband.* The grosses on her RKO films diminished with each release—understandably so, since many of them (*Break of Hearts* [1935], *Mary of Scotland* [1936]) were dogs. She reclaimed the support of the RKO executives after appearing in the moneymaking *Alice Adams* (1935)—only to lose it again by insisting upon starring in *Sylvia Scarlett* (1936), a curious exercise in sexual ambiguity that lost a fortune. Efforts to "humanize" the haughty Hepburn personality in *Stage Door* (1937) and the delightful *Bringing Up Baby* (1938) came too late; in 1938, she was adjudged "box office poison" by an influential exhibitor's publication. Hepburn's career might have ended then and there, but she hadn't been raised to be a quitter. She went back to Broadway in 1938 with a part written especially for her in Phillip Barry's *The Philadelphia Story.* Certain of a hit, she bought the film rights to the play; thus, when *The Philadelphia Story* ended up a success, she was able to negotiate her way back into Hollywood on her own terms, including choice of director and

co-stars. Produced by MGM in 1940, the film version of *The Philadelphia Story* was a box-office triumph, and Hepburn had beaten the "poison" onus. In her next MGM film, *Woman of the Year* (1942), Hepburn costarred with Spencer Tracy, a copacetic teaming that endured both professionally and personally until Tracy's death in 1967. After several years of off-and-on films, Hepburn scored another success with 1951's *The African Queen,* marking her switch from youngish sophisticates to middle-aged character leads. After 1962's *Long Day's Journey into Night,* Hepburn withdrew from performing for nearly five years, devoting her attention to her ailing friend and lover Tracy. She made the last of her eight screen appearances with Tracy in *Guess Who's Coming to Dinner* (1967), which also featured her niece Katharine Houghton. Hepburn won her second Oscar for this film, and her third the following year for *A Lion in Winter;* the fourth Academy Award was bestowed upon her thirteen years later for *On Golden Pond* (1981). When she came back to Broadway for the 1969 musical *Coco,* Hepburn proved that the years had not mellowed her; she readily agreed to preface her first speech with a then-shocking profanity, and during one performance she abruptly dropped character to chew out an audience member for taking flash pictures. Hepburn made the first of her several TV movies in 1975, co-starring with Sir Laurence Olivier in *Love Among the Ruins*—and winning an Emmy as well. Her last Broadway appearance was in 1976's *A Matter of Gravity.* Throughout the 1970s and 1980s, Hepburn continued to star on TV and in films, announcing on each occasion that it would be her last performance. She also began writing magazine articles and books, each of them an extension of her personality: self-centered, well organized, succinct, and brutally frank (especially regarding herself). While she remained a staunch advocate of physical fitness, Hepburn was plagued by a progressive neurological disease which caused her head to shake uncontrollably—an affliction she blithely incorporated into her screen characters. In 1994, Warren Beatty coaxed Hepburn out of her latest retirement to appear as his aristocratic grand-aunt in *Love Affair.* Though appearing frailer than usual, Katharine Hepburn was in complete control of herself and her craft, totally dominating her brief scenes. On the threshold of her tenth decade, Katharine Hepburn remains the consummate personality, actress and star. **Selected Works:** *Holiday* (1938), *Adam's Rib* (1950), *Summertime* (1955), *Man Upstairs* (1993), *Love Affair* (1994)

# Pee-Wee Herman (Paul Rubenfeld)

**Born:** 1952; Peekskill, NY

**Years Active in the Industry:** by decade

| 10s | 20s | 30s | 40s | 50s | 60s | 70s | 80s | 90s |
|-----|-----|-----|-----|-----|-----|-----|-----|-----|
|     |     |     |     |     |     |     | ■ | ■ |

American comic actor Pee-Wee Herman was born Paul Rubenfeld, which he later shortened professionally to Paul Reubens. While growing up in Sarasota, Florida, Reubens began acting in junior high school, carrying this extra-curricular interest through several colleges before graduating from the California Institute of the Arts. A natural-born clown, Reubens joined an improv group called The Groundlings, which during its existence would boast such formidable talent as Phil Hartman and Jon Lovitz. In 1978, Reubens developed the comic persona of Pee-Wee Herman, a childlike, squeaky-voiced kiddie show host reminiscent of Pinky Lee (with a little Soupy Sales thrown in). Soon "The Pee-Wee Herman Show" became a nightclub act unto itself; this multilayered skewing of the whole children's entertainment ethic included a huge supporting cast, deliberately repulsive puppets, bizarre props and of course Pee-Wee himself, who cavorted about the set like a baby speed freak. Reubens, who for all intents and purposes *was* Pee-Wee Herman at this point, was given frequent TV exposure thanks to *Late Night With David Letterman* and the home-video version of *The Pee-Wee Herman Show*. With former Groundling Phil Hartman, Pee-Wee/Reubens co-scripted the 1985 film *Pee-Wee's Big Adventure*. Though it was the inaugural project of director Tim Burton, it was *not* Pee-Wee's first film (he'd already shown up in *The Blues Brothers* [1980] and *Cheech and Chong's Nice Dreams* [1981]). A surrealistic reworking of the classic Italian film *The Bicycle Thief*, *Pee-Wee's Big Adventure* was a tad *too* bizarre for its distributor Warner Bros. The studio chose to release the film slowly on a regional basis—but when the box-offices began to bulge, Warners gave the film a major big-city push. Audiences immediately understood that *Pee-Wee's Big Adventure* was meant to be a nine-year-old's notion of the Perfect World; critics, to whom nothing is ever simple, insisted upon reading all sorts of motivation and subtext into the film, and suddenly Pee-Wee Herman was the darling of the wine-and-cheese crowd. In 1986, Pee-Wee launched a Saturday morning kid's show, *Pee-Wee's Playhouse*, which immediately scored a hit, attracting as many adults as children (some of those adults began renting the original *Pee-Wee Herman Show* for their children, assuming that it would be as "safe" as the Saturday morning program—only to be amazed at how raunchy the earlier Pee-wee could be!) The performer's popularity peaked in 1988, at which time his second film, *Big Top Pee-Wee,* was released. This film was not as cohesive nor as funny as the first, and was a disappointment for both Reubens and his fans. The actor began announcing plans to "kill" his alter-ego and become Paul Reubens again in public, at which time stories began to surface about Reubens' tendency to be a control freak and credit-grabber. But Pee-Wee would have been dead after 1991 anyway, after Reubens was arrested for exposing himself at a screening of a porno movie. Backlash from the incident effectively forced the performer to largely abandon the Pee-Wee character. Since his fateful night at the movies, Reubens has appeared as the Penguin's father in *Batman Returns* (1992), a hand-me-down Dracula in *Buffy the Vampire Slayer* (1992), and a voice in Tim Burton's animated feature *The Nightmare Before Christmas* (1993).

# Bernard Herrmann

**Born:** June 29, 1911; New York, NY
**Died:** December 24, 1975; New York, NY

**Years Active in the Industry:** by decade

| 10ˢ | 20ˢ | 30ˢ | 40ˢ | 50ˢ | 60ˢ | 70ˢ | 80ˢ | 90ˢ |
|-----|-----|-----|-----|-----|-----|-----|-----|-----|
|     |     |     | ■   | ■   | ■   | ■   |     |     |

A composition prize winner at age 13, Manhattan-born composer Bernard Herrmann studied at New York University and Julliard before accepting his first conductor's post at age 20. While he wrote for virtually every branch of the musical theater—ballet, concert hall, opera—Herrmann's latter-day fame rests squarely on his prolific film work. As one of several composer/conductors retained by the CBS radio network in the mid-1930s (he was briefly married to radio writer Lucille Fletcher, of *Sorry Wrong Number* fame), Herrmann worked on Orson Welles' *Mercury Theatre of the Air*. When Welles headed to Hollywood to direct *Citizen Kane* (1941), he invited Herrmann to write the film's score, promising the young composer full artistic freedom. Welles so respected Herrmann's talent that many scenes in *Kane* were tailored to fit the music, rather than the other way around. Herrmann capped his first year in Hollywood with an Academy Award—not for *Kane,* but for another RKO production, *All That Money Can Buy* (1941). He was engaged to score Welles' second picture, *The Magnificent Ambersons* (1942), but angrily demanded that his name be removed from the credits after his music was extensively rearranged by RKO contractee Roy Webb. It was not the first example of Herrmann's volatile temperament, and it would not be the last. Autocratic, imperious and stubborn, Herrmann invoked fear in musicians and film directors alike; despite his troublesome nature, the range of his talent was so enormous that he remained in demand until his death in 1975. With *Jane Eyre* (1944), Herrmann began a lengthy association with 20th Century-Fox, best exemplified by the scores for such films as *The Ghost and Mrs. Muir* (1947), *Five Fingers* (1952), *The Snows of Kilimanjaro* (1953) and *The Man in the Grey Flannel Suit* (1954). At his best, Herrmann was tirelessly creative, ever finding new ways to match his scores to the mood and locale of his films. As one of many examples, Herrmann wrote an orchestration incorporating authentic native African musical instruments for the 1954 jungle actioner *White Witch Doctor*. Many of his innovations have since become cinematic clichés, notably his vibraphonic score for the 1951 sci-fi classic *The Day the Earth Stood Still* and the screeching violins for 1960's *Psycho*. In the 1950s, Herrmann inaugurated two long associations with a brace of notable filmmakers: special-effects maven Ray Harryhausen (*Seventh Voyage of Sinbad* [1957], *Mysterious Island* [1961], *Three Worlds of Gulliver* [1962], *Jason and the Argonauts* [1963]) and suspense specialist Alfred Hitchcock (*The Trouble With Harry* [1955], *The Wrong Man* [1956], *Vertigo* [1958], *North by Northwest* [1959], *Psycho* [1960], *Marnie* [1964] and *The Birds* [1963], for which Herrmann orchestrated genuine bird sounds). After acrimoniously severing his ties with Hitchcock over a dispute arising from the score of 1966's *Torn Curtain*, Herrmann accepted assignments from a number of Hitchcock emulators, including Francois Truffault (*The Bride Wore Black* [1967]), Larry Cohen (*It's Alive!* [1974]) and Brian De Palma (*Obsession* [1976]). Herrmann also kept busy on TV, principally on Rod Serling's *Twilight Zone* series; for the 1962 *Zone* episode "Little Girl Lost," the composer was billed *above* the director. Herrmann's final score was for Martin Scorcese's *Taxi Driver* (1975), which was posthumously dedicated to Herrmann. **Selected Works:** *Devil and Daniel Webster* (1941), *Cape Fear* (1991), *Hundred and One Nights* (1995)

# Barbara Hershey

**Born:** February 5, 1948; Hollywood, CA

**Years Active in the Industry:** by decade

| 10s | 20s | 30s | 40s | 50s | 60s | 70s | 80s | 90s |
|-----|-----|-----|-----|-----|-----|-----|-----|-----|
|     |     |     |     |     |     |     |     |     |

American actress Barbara Hershey, born Barbara Herzstein, debuted professionally while still a teen as a regular on the "country family saga" TV series *The Monroes.* This led to her big-screen debut in *With Six You Get Eggroll* (1968). For the next few years she tended to be typecast as a "swinging chick" or hippie, doing much film work in primarily unmemorable productions; she lived up to her film persona offscreen during a "free-spirit" period when she had a live-in relationship with actor David Carradine, changed her name to Barbara Seagull, and gave birth to a son she named Free. Later she changed her name back to Hershey. Although busy, her film career remained unimpressive until the mid-'80s, when she began getting parts in much better films, beginning with her work in *The Right Stuff* (1983). She won the Cannes Film Festival Best Actress Award two years in a row, for her work in *Shy People* (1987) and *A World Apart* (1988), and she won an Emmy for her work in the TV movie *A Killing in a Small Town.* Also among her memorable films are *The Natural* (1984), *Hannah and Her Sisters* (1986), and *Beaches* (1988). **Selected Works:** *Last Temptation of Christ* (1988), *Tune in Tomorrow* (1990), *Falling Down* (1993), *Last of the Dog Men* (1995)

# Werner Herzog (Werner Stipetic)

**Born:** September 5, 1942; Munich, Germany

**Years Active in the Industry:** by decade

| 10s | 20s | 30s | 40s | 50s | 60s | 70s | 80s | 90s |
|-----|-----|-----|-----|-----|-----|-----|-----|-----|
|     |     |     |     |     |     |     |     |     |

Filmmaker Werner Herzog began attracting attention with his short films of the mid-'60s, and his first feature, *Signs of Life,* in 1968. As a writer/director, he made a series of provocative, highly personal works, including *Even Dwarfs Started Small* (1968), the cryptic desert journey *Fata Morgana,* and the stunning *Heart Of Glass* (1974), perhaps his finest film, in which he hypnotized his actors to get properly somnambulistic performances. He cast Bruno S., a lifelong inmate of mental institutions and prisons, to play a real-life man who was raised in a dark basement in *Every Man for Himself and God Against All* (aka *The Mystery Of Kasper Hauser* [1975]) and as an uncomprehending visitor to the United States in *Stroszek* (1977). With actor Klaus Kinski, Herzog made his most famous '70s films: his conquistador drama *Aguirre, the*

*Wrath Of God* (1974), his Murnau remake *Nosferatu the Vampyre* (1979), and *Wozzeck* (1978), his adaptation of Georg Buchner's classic play. Notorious for dragging his cast and crew to remote and arduous locations, Herzog has made fewer feature films since the '80s; his notable recent work includes *Fitzcarraldo* (1982) and *Cobra Verde* (1988), both with Kinski. Herzog is also widely admired as a superb documentary filmmaker for such works as *Land of Silence and Darkness,* about the deaf and blind. **Selected Works:** *Cry of Stone* (1991)

# Charlton Heston (John Charlton Carter)

**Born:** October 4, 1924; Evanston, IL

**Years Active in the Industry:** by decade

| 10s | 20s | 30s | 40s | 50s | 60s | 70s | 80s | 90s |
|-----|-----|-----|-----|-----|-----|-----|-----|-----|
|     |     |     |     |     |     |     |     |     |

American leading actor Charlton Heston, studied speech and drama at Northwestern University, where he played the title role in an amateur student film production of *Peer Gynt* (1942) and performed on Chicago radio. During World War II, Heston served three

years in the Air Force. He debuted onstage in stock in 1947; that same year he made his first Broadway appearance as a cast-member in Katherine Cornell's production of *Anthony and Cleopatra.* After playing prominent roles in a series of TV specials, including such characters as Antony in *Julius Caesar* and Heathcliff in *Wuthering Heights* (he also played Antony in an amateur film version of *Julius Caesar* [1949]), he began to gain national recognition. He made his feature film debut in *Dark City* (1950). At first cast in tough but down-to-earth roles, he went on to make his name as Hollywood's main epic hero, playing larger-than-life characters in a string of screen spectaculars; among others, he has played Moses, John the Baptist, Michelangelo, Ben-Hur, El Cid, Andrew Jackson, and General "Chinese" Gordon. His breakthrough role was as Moses in Cecil B. De Mille's huge box office hit *The Ten Commandments* (1956). For his work in the title role of *Ben-Hur* (1959) he won a Best Actor Oscar. He served six terms as president of the Screen Actors Guild and was chairman of the American Film Institute. In the 1977 Oscar ceremony he received the Jean Hersholt Humanitarian Award. He is the author of *The Actor's Life: Journals 1956-76.* **Selected Works:** *Crucifer of Blood* (1991), *Solar Crisis* (1992), *In the Mouth of Madness* (1994), *True Lies* (1994), *The Avenging Angel* (1995)

# George Roy Hill

**Born:** December 20, 1922; Minneapolis, MN

**Years Active in the Industry:** by decade

| 10ˢ | 20ˢ | 30ˢ | 40ˢ | 50ˢ | 60ˢ | 70ˢ | 80ˢ | 90ˢ |
|---|---|---|---|---|---|---|---|---|
| | | | | | ■ | ■ | ■ | ■ |

Not to be confused with early-1930s MGM director George Hill (many historians do mix up the names, even though the earlier Hill died in 1934), American director George Roy Hill started out as a musician. He studied both at Yale and Trinity College in Dublin; it was there that Hill began an acting career with Cyril Cusack's company. After World War II, Hill shifted his interest to stage directing, and after further military service in Korea, he moved into TV as both director and writer. Hill directed for various live anthologies of the 1950s, including *Kraft Television Theater, The Kaiser Aluminum Hour* and *Studio One.* He came to films relatively late, directing his first feature, *Period of Adjustment,* in 1962. Hill rapidly built up a reputation for being commercially reliable after such hits as *The World of Henry Orient* (1964) and *Hawaii* (1967); even relative misfires like *Thoroughly Modern Millie* (1966) were at least attractively assembled. All the same, Hill was no Hollywood bootlicker; he was fired during post-production of both *Millie* and *Hawaii* due to heated arguments over the editing. Thus, no one was certain what the mood on the set would be when Hill was contracted to direct Paul Newman in *Butch Cassidy and the Sundance Kid* (1969). Hill's first move turned out to be the film's lifesaver: he vetoed several co-starring choices, including Steve McQueen and Warren Beatty, in favor of Robert Redford, and the resultant chemistry between Newman and Redford was sheer box office nirvana. Hill won an Oscar for his direction, which doubtless compensated for the back injury that forced him to do much of his directing in a supine position. *Butch Cassidy* had built-in audience appeal—more than can be said for Hill's next project, a filmization of Kurt Vonnegut's almost unfilmable novel *Slaughterhouse Five* (1971). It was a noble failure, but Hill was feted by the Cannes Film Festival for the effort. The director reunited Newman and Reford for *The Sting* (1973), which did even better than *Butch Cassidy* and copped a Best Picture Academy Award. *The Sting* stars demonstrated their thanks to Hill by entrusting him with many later projects: the director guided Reford through *The Great Waldo Pepper* (1973) and Newman through *Slap Shot* (1977). Not all of George Roy Hill's subsequent projects were as successful, though there are excellent moments in the first twenty minutes of *The Little Drummer Girl* (1981) once we get past Diane Keaton's miscasting as a Vanessa Redgrave-type activist; and Hill's *Funny Farm* (1988) makes up for its misfire slapstick set-pieces involving nature-lover Chevy Chase with a rousing comedy climax.

# Walter Hill

**Born:** January 10, 1942; Long Beach, CA

**Years Active in the Industry:** by decade

| 10ˢ | 20ˢ | 30ˢ | 40ˢ | 50ˢ | 60ˢ | 70ˢ | 80ˢ | 90ˢ |
|---|---|---|---|---|---|---|---|---|
| | | | | | | ■ | ■ | ■ |

The son of a ship's riveter, director/writer Walter Hill studied art in Mexico City, hoping to become a cartoonist; he later transferred to the journalism department at the University of Michigan. Following several years in various jobs, Hill wrote a few documentary films and gained work as an assistant director on such major productions as *The Thomas Crown Affair* (1968) and *Bullitt* (1968). Establishing himself in Hollywood as a screenwriter (*The Getaway* [1972], *The Drowning Pool* [1975] and others), Hill received his first directing opportunity with *Hard Times* (1975), a virile tale about bare-knuckles boxing starring Charles Bronson and James Coburn. Hill's reputation was both enhanced and tarnished by *The Warriors* (1979), a nightmarish, deliberately exaggerated story of gang violence that was banned from several theaters for allegedly inciting real-life gang wars. The director's biggest moneymaker of the early 1980s was *48 Hours* (1982), which deftly shifted from grim violence to laugh-out-loud comedy and which made a star of Eddie Murphy. *Streets of Fire* (1984), which like *The Warriors* placed a ruggedly realistic story in a near-fantasy setting, didn't do as well as expected, and Hill found himself settling for lesser directing projects for the next few years. Recently, his *Geronimo: An American Legend* (1993) was somewhat lost amidst a sea of competing "revisionist" westerns. Though his R-rated style is not altogether suited for TV, Hill has nonetheless had his name on the credits of two series since 1989: since he owns the rights to several horror stories from the days of the classic E.C. comic books, Hill is listed as one of the producers of *Tales from the Crypt* (for which he directed several segments) and its cartoon spinoff *Tales from the Cryptkeeper.* **Selected Works:** *Aliens* (1986), *Aliens 3* (1992), *Trespass* (1992), *Fugitive* (1993), *Wild Bill* (1995)

# Arthur Hiller

**Born:** November 22, 1923; Edmonton, Alberta, Canada

**Years Active in the Industry:** by decade

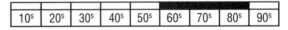

| 10ˢ | 20ˢ | 30ˢ | 40ˢ | 50ˢ | 60ˢ | 70ˢ | 80ˢ | 90ˢ |
|---|---|---|---|---|---|---|---|---|
| | | | | ■ | ■ | ■ | ■ | ■ |

After wartime service with the Royal Canadian Air Force, Edmontonian Arthur Hiller began his show business career in Canadian radio and television. In the mid-1950s, Hiller left the CBC for American television, directing such live anthologies as *Playhouse 90* and such filmed weeklies as *Alcoa/Goodyear Theatre, Alfred Hitchcock Presents* and *The Naked City.* He directed his first theatrical film in 1957, moving on to such 1960s big-budgeters as *The Americanization of Emily* (1964), where he proved himself a superb technician with only a trace of personal style. In 1970, Hiller was fortunate enough to be in the director's chair for that year's biggest hit, *Love Story,* which earned him an Oscar nomination. Extremely successful for the past four decades, Arthur Hiller has continued to turn out such slick, efficient products as *Silver Streak* (1974), *The In-Laws* (1976), *The Lonely Guy* (1984) and *The Babe* (1992), works that were always as good as (but seldom better than) their scripts. One of Hiller's most admirable professional accomplishments was establishing a strong rapport with notoriously argumentative actor George C. Scott, whom Hiller directed in *The Hospital* (1971) and *Plaza Suite* (1971), and about whom Hiller wrote an article for the 1977 compendium *Closeups: The Movie Star Book*. In 1993, Hiller was appointed president of the Academy of Motion Picture Arts and Sciences.

# Dame Wendy Hiller

**Born:** August 15, 1912; Bramshall, Cheshire, England

**Years Active in the Industry:** by decade

| 10<sup>s</sup> | 20<sup>s</sup> | 30<sup>s</sup> | 40<sup>s</sup> | 50<sup>s</sup> | 60<sup>s</sup> | 70<sup>s</sup> | 80<sup>s</sup> | 90<sup>s</sup> |
|---|---|---|---|---|---|---|---|---|

Educated at Winceby House, a girl's school in Sussex, British actress Wendy Hiller made her stage debut at age 18 with the Manchester Repertory troupe. Her stardom came as a result of her performance in the popular London "everyday folks" drama *Love on the Dole* in 1935 (written by her future husband Ronald Gow), later repeating this triumph on Broadway. Hiller's stage performance in George Bernard Shaw's *St. Joan* prompted Shaw to recommend her for the role of Eliza Doolittle in the film version of *Pygmalion* (1938). The actress was nominated for an Oscar (well deserved, since the film was actually made twice, one version "sanitized" for American audiences), but for many years thereafter her performance was unseen due to legal tangles arising from the musical remake of *Pygmalion, My Fair Lady*. Wendy later starred in another filmization of a Shaw play, *Major Barbara* (1941). Though she preferred the stage, Hiller would return to films sporadically if the part offered was worthwhile; she finally won an Oscar for her supporting role in *Separate Tables* (1958), and would rack up a future nomination for *A Man For All Seasons* (1966). She received the Order of the British Empire in 1966 and was made a Dame of the Empire in 1975, all the while plying her acting trade in a brilliantly workmanlike fashion. Most of her 1970s roles weren't up to her earlier appearances, but she gave her all to such parts as the foredoomed Lawyer Crosbie (a role originally written for a man!) in the 1978 remake of *Cat and the Canary*. Hiller also did a great deal of television both in England and America; she was starred in a 1964 episode of *Profiles in Courage*, played a pivotal role in the 1982 TV movie *Witness for the Prosecution*, and headlined "All Passion Spent," a three-part 1989 offering of PBS' *Masterpiece Theatre*. **Selected Works:** *Sons and Lovers* (1960), *Murder on the Orient Express* (1974), *Elephant Man* (1980), *Anne of Avonlea* (1987)

# Samuel S. Hinds

**Born:** April 4, 1875; Brooklyn, NY
**Died:** 1948

**Years Active in the Industry:** by decade

| 10<sup>s</sup> | 20<sup>s</sup> | 30<sup>s</sup> | 40<sup>s</sup> | 50<sup>s</sup> | 60<sup>s</sup> | 70<sup>s</sup> | 80<sup>s</sup> | 90<sup>s</sup> |
|---|---|---|---|---|---|---|---|---|

Before he became a character actor, Samuel Hinds spent most of his adult life as a practicing lawyer. A Harvard graduate, he participated in amateur theater for 35 years before turning pro in the early 1930s when he was nearly 60 years old. He made his feature film debut in 1933 and subsequently appeared in over 150 films, including many in the enduring *Dr. Kildare* series. With his kindly face and sagacious manner, Hinds was frequently cast as a father or amiable gentleman, though occasionally he got to play disreputable lawyers and other good-men-gone-bad. Hinds was also a co-founder of the Pasadena Community Playhouse. **Selected Works:** *Berkeley Square* (1933), *Test Pilot* (1938), *You Can't Take It with You* (1938), *It's a Wonderful Life* (1946)

# Gregory Hines

**Born:** February 14, 1946; New York, NY

**Years Active in the Industry:** by decade

| 10<sup>s</sup> | 20<sup>s</sup> | 30<sup>s</sup> | 40<sup>s</sup> | 50<sup>s</sup> | 60<sup>s</sup> | 70<sup>s</sup> | 80<sup>s</sup> | 90<sup>s</sup> |
|---|---|---|---|---|---|---|---|---|

Talented, amiable American actor and dancer Gregory Hines began tap dancing at age four with his brother Maurice in an act called the Hines Kids; the two later studied with tap whiz Henry LeTang, renamed themselves the Hines Brothers in 1962, and in 1964, teamed up with their father in an act called Hines, Hines, and Dad. The trio appeared on *The Tonight Show* and opened for big-name performers at a number of top-flight clubs. Hines left the trio in 1973, then spent five years in Venice, California, living what he called a "hippie" lifestyle and working with a jazz-rock band. In 1978 he returned to New York and, helped by his brother, auditioned for new shows, ultimately landing excellent parts in three musicals (*Eubie!*, *Comin' Uptown*, and *Sophisticated Ladies*); he received Tony nominations for each of the three shows. He finally received a Tony for his performance as Jelly Roll Morton in the Broadway show *Jelly's Last Jam*. All of this led to invitations from Hollywood, and he debuted onscreen in 1981's horror film *Wolfen*. He went on to make a few more films before landing a breakthrough role in Robert Evans's and Francis Ford Coppola's *The Cotton Club* (1984), one of the year's biggest movies; he also served as choreographer for that film. In 1988 he released an album titled *Gregory Hines*. **Selected Works:** *Rage in Harlem* (1991), *T Bone N Weasel* (1992), *White Man's Burden* (1994)

# Alfred Hitchcock (Alfred Joseph Hitchcock)

**Born:** August 13, 1899; London, England
**Died:** April 28, 1980

**Years Active in the Industry:** by decade

| 10<sup>s</sup> | 20<sup>s</sup> | 30<sup>s</sup> | 40<sup>s</sup> | 50<sup>s</sup> | 60<sup>s</sup> | 70<sup>s</sup> | 80<sup>s</sup> | 90<sup>s</sup> |
|---|---|---|---|---|---|---|---|---|

Alfred Hitchcock was the most well-known director to the general public, by virtue of both his many thrillers and his appearances on television in his own series from the mid-1950s through the early 1960s. Proba-

bly more than any other filmmaker this side of Steven Spielberg, his name evokes instant expectations on the part of audiences—they know to expect at least two or three great chills (and a few more good ones), some striking black comedy, and an eccentric characterization or two in every one of the director's movies. Originally trained at a technical school, Hitchcock gravitated to movies through art courses and advertising, and by the mid-1920s he was making his first films. He had his first major success in 1926 with *The Lodger,* a thriller loosely based on the career of Jack the Ripper. While he worked in a multitude of genres over the next six years, he found his greatest acceptance working with thrillers. His early work in this genre, including *Blackmail* (1929) and *Murder* (1930), seem primitive by modern standards but have many of the essential elements of Hitchcock's subsequent successes, even if they are presented in technically rudimentary terms. Hitchcock came to international attention in the middle and late 1930s with *The Man Who Knew Too Much* (1934), *The 39 Steps* (1935), and most notably, *The Lady Vanishes* (1938). By the end of the 1930s, having gone as far as the British film industry could take him, he signed a contract with David O. Selznick and came to America. From the outset, with the multi-Oscar winning psychological chiller *Rebecca* (1940) and the topical anti-Nazi thrillers *Foreign Correspondent* (1940) and *Saboteur* (1942), Hitchcock was one of Hollywood's "money" directors whose mere presence on a marquee attracted audiences. Although his relationship with Selznick was stormy, he created several fine and notable features while working for the producer, either directly for Selznick or on loan to RKO and Universal, including *Spellbound* (1945), probably the most romantic of Hitchcock's movies; *Notorious* (1946); and *Shadow of a Doubt* (1943), considered by many to be his most unsettling film. In 1948, after leaving Selznick, Hitchcock went through a fallow period, in which he experimented with new techniques and made his first independent production, *Rope,* but he found little success. In the early and middle 1950s, he returned to form with the thrillers *Strangers on a Train* (1951), which was remade in 1987 by Danny DeVito as *Throw Momma from the Train; Dial M for Murder* (1954), which was among the few successful 3-D movies; and *Rear Window* (1954). By the mid-1950s, Hitchcock's persona became the basis for a television anthology series called *Alfred Hitchcock Presents,* which ran for eight seasons (although he only directed, or even participated as producer, in a mere handful of the shows). His films of the late 1950s became

more personal and daring, particularly *The Trouble With Harry* (1955) and *Vertigo* (1958), in which the dark side of romantic obsession was explored in startling detail. *Psycho* (1960) was Hitchcock's great shock masterpiece, mostly for its haunting performances by Janet Leigh and Anthony Perkins and its shower scene, and *The Birds* (1963) became the unintended forerunner to an onslaught of films about nature-gone-mad, and all were phenomenally popular—*The Birds,* in particular, managed to set a new record for its first network television showing in the mid-1960s. By then, however, Hitchcock's films had slipped seriously at the box office, and understandably so—both *Marnie* (1964) and *Torn Curtain* (1966) suffered from major casting problems, and the script of *Torn Curtain* was terribly unfocused. He was also hurt by the sudden departure of composer Bernard Herrmann (who had scored all of Hitchcock's movies from 1957 onward) during the making of *Torn Curtain,* as Herrmann's music had become a key element of the success of Hitchcock's films. Of his final three movies, only *Frenzy* (1972), which marked his return to British thrillers after 30 years, was successful, although his last film, *Family Plot* (1976) has achieved some respect from cult audiences. In the early 1980s, several years after his death, Hitchcock's box office appeal was once again displayed with the re-release of *Rope, The Trouble With Harry,* the 1956 remake of *The Man Who Knew Too Much,* and *Vertigo,* all of which had been withheld from distribution for several years, and which earned millions of dollars in new theatrical revenues. **Selected Works:** *Suspicion* (1941), *Lifeboat* (1944), *Wrong Man* (1956), *North by Northwest* (1959)

# Dustin Hoffman

**Born:** August 8, 1937; Los Angeles, CA

**Years Active in the Industry:** by decade

| 10s | 20s | 30s | 40s | 50s | 60s | 70s | 80s | 90s |
|-----|-----|-----|-----|-----|-----|-----|-----|-----|
|     |     |     |     |     |     |     |     |     |

Versatile superstar of stage and screen Dustin Hoffman differs from other "traditional" leading men by playing antiheroes, making him a trendsetter for other stars during the '70s, '80s, and

'90s. He dropped out of college to attend the Pacific Playhouse and began acting at 19. In search of a stage career, he moved to New York in the late '50s, but struggled professionally for several years, studying with Lee Strasberg at the Actors' Studio. He managed to get small roles on TV and in summer stock, and finally made it to an off-

Broadway production in 1965. In 1966 he won the Best Actor Obie for his work in *The Journey of the Fifth Horse,* and in 1967 received much acclaim for his performance in the British farce *Eh?*; this led to his big break when director Mike Nichols attended *Eh?* and insisted that Hoffman play the lead in *The Graduate* (1967), which was enormously successful and made Hoffman a star (he had played small roles in two previous movies, *The Tiger Makes Out* and *Madigan's Millions,* both 1967.) He went on to a spectacularly successful film and stage career. A dedicated "Method actor," he does great preparation for his roles; for example, when playing a victim of torture in *Marathon Man* (1976) he went without sleep for two days and did strenuous, sweat-inducing exercises before filming the torture scenes. He was nominated for Academy Awards three times before finally winning the Best Actor Oscar twice, for *Kramer vs. Kramer* (1979) and *Rain Man* (1988). He has done much stage work, including portraying Willy Loman in *Death of a Salesman* and Shylock in *The Merchant of Venice.* **Selected Works:** *Midnight Cowboy* (1969), *Lenny* (1974), *Tootsie* (1982), *Billy Bathgate* (1991), *Hero* (1992), *Outbreak* (1995)

# Paul Hogan

**Born:** 1939; Parramutta, Australia

**Years Active in the Industry:** by decade

| 10s | 20s | 30s | 40s | 50s | 60s | 70s | 80s | 90s |
|-----|-----|-----|-----|-----|-----|-----|-----|-----|
|     |     |     |     |     |     |     |     |     |

Australian actor Paul Hogan was mellow-voiced and rugged enough to succeed as an action hero, but he loved making people laugh, something he'd been doing on a professional basis since his debut as a blindfolded, tap dancing knife thrower on the Aussie TV amateur contest *New Faces.* With his late-1970s weekly half hour TV show *The Paul Hogan Show,* he became the most popular comedian in Australia. His material was limited to a handful of subjects—breasts, bums, beer and soccer—but the series' selling card was Hogan's ability to play a wide variety of distinct characterizations, sometimes making the transition from one character to another so quickly that he literally seemed to be two different people. Hogan was able to expand his popularity to England with a series of commercials for Australian Lager Beer; but though *The Paul Hogan Show* had been shown on a smattering of American independent and PBS stations, he was largely unknown in the U.S. While visiting New York in 1985, Hogan was struck by the wide cultural gaps between the Big Apple and the Outback. With his manager John Cornell as director, Hogan took a big chunk of his TV earnings and produced an amiable culture-clash comedy *Crocodile Dundee* (Hogan and Cornell owned 65 percent of the picture, the rest going to the circle of friends who'd invested in the project). To make sure that American audiences would be primed for this film, Hogan agreed to film a series of "visit Australia" ads for no salary. The strategy worked: *Crocodile Dundee* opened big in the U.S. in the fall of 1986, ultimately posting a worldwide gross of $375 million. While filming *Dundee,* the long-married Hogan fell in love with leading lady Linda Kozlowski; after divesting himself of wife number one (he claimed that the marriage was on the rocks anyway), Hogan made Kozlowski his bride—and his most frequent costar in subsequent productions. Those later Paul Hogan vehicles failed to match the popularity of *Crocodile Dundee;* even the very carefully contrived sequel *Crocodile Dundee 2* was a box-office dud. Hogan's most recent project, 1994's *Lightning Jack,* was a retrogressive western comedy that didn't even make back the publicity costs.

# Hal Holbrook (Harold Rowe Holbrook, Jr.)

**Born:** February 17, 1925; Cleveland Heights, OH

**Years Active in the Industry:** by decade

| 10s | 20s | 30s | 40s | 50s | 60s | 70s | 80s | 90s |
|-----|-----|-----|-----|-----|-----|-----|-----|-----|
|     |     |     |     |     |     |     |     |     |

American actor Hal Holbrook broke into performing as a monologist at various esoteric nightspots in San Francisco and Greenwich Village. Holbrook worked on stage in the early 1950s and appeared on the CBS TV soap opera *The Brighter Day.* He might have spent the rest of his career as a talented but unremarkable performer had Holbrook not decided to bank upon his lifelong fascination with humorist Mark Twain. Donning elaborate Twain makeup and constume and memorizing several hours' worth of the writer's material, Holbrook put together a one man show, *Mark Twain Tonight.* After touring in small towns, Holbrook brought Mark Twain to an off-Broadway theater, scoring an immediate hit which led to some 2000 subsequent appearances as Twain (one of these in a 1967 CBS one-hour special) and a top-selling record album. The fame attending *Mark Twain Tonight* enabled Holbrook to flourish as a starring actor in numerous non-Twain projects. Among Holbrook's films are *The Group* (1966), *Wild in the Streets* (1968), *Magnum Force* (1973), *The Star Chamber* (1987), *Wall Street* (1987) and *The Firm* (1993); in 1976 the actor was Oscar-nominated for his portrayal of the shadowy amalgam character "Deep Throat" in *All the President's Men.* Holbrook has also stayed busy in TV, starring on the weekly series *The Senator* (1970) and appearing several times as Abraham Lincoln in various network specials. A multi-Emmy winner, Hal Holbrook was most recently seen as a regular on the CBS sitcoms *Designing Women,* costarring with his third wife Dixie Carter, and *Evening Shade* in the role of Burt Reynolds' father. **Selected Works:** *Great White Hope* (1970), *Julia* (1977), *When Hell Was in Session* (1982)

# William Holden (William Franklin Beedle, Jr.)

**Born:** April 17, 1918; O'Fallon, IL
**Died:** November 16, 1981; Santa Monica, CA

**Years Active in the Industry:** by decade

| 10s | 20s | 30s | 40s | 50s | 60s | 70s | 80s | 90s |
|-----|-----|-----|-----|-----|-----|-----|-----|-----|
|     |     |     |     |     |     |     |     |     |

American actor William Holden, the son of a chemical analyst, plunged into high school and junior college sport activities as a means of "proving himself" to his demanding father. Nonetheless, Holden's forte would be in what he'd always consider a "sissy" profession—acting. Spotted by a talent scout during a stage production at Pasadena Junior College, Holden was signed by both Paramount and Columbia, who would share his contract for the next two decades. After one bit role, Holden was thrust into the demanding leading part of boxer Joe Bonaparte in *Golden Boy* (1939). He was so green and nervous that Columbia considered replacing him, but costar Barbara Stanwyck took it upon herself to coach the young actor and build up his confidence—a selfless act for which Holden would be grateful until the day he died. After serving as a lieutenant in the Army's special services unit, Holden returned to films, mostly in light, inconsequential roles. Director Billy Wilder changed all that by casting Holden as Joe Gillis, embittered failed screenwriter and "kept man" of Gloria Swanson in the Hollywood-bashing classic *Sunset Boulevard* (1950). Wilder also directed Holden in the role of the cynical, conniving but ultimately heroic American POW Sefton in *Stalag 17* (1953), for which the actor won an Academy Award. The private Holden began to develop a reputation during this period as a loyal friend, cooperative actor and tireless activist in the Screen Actor's Guild when sober—but a nasty, vindictive monster when drunk. Holden was known to put up his dukes at the slightest provocation; and despite his long marriage to Ardis Ankerson, an actress known professionally as Brenda Marshall, Holden conducted several serious affairs with such leading ladies as Audrey Hepburn, Grace Kelly and Capucine. Holden became a man of the world, as it were, when he moved to Switzerland to avoid heavy taxation on his earnings; while traversing the globe, Holden developed an interest in African wildlife preservation, spending much of his off-camera time campaigning for humane treatment of animals and raising funds for that purpose. Free to be selective in his film roles in the 1960s and 1970s, Holden evinced an erratic sensibility: for every *Counterfeit Traitor* (1962) and *Network* (1976) there would be a walk-through part in *The Towering Inferno* (1974) or *Ashanti* (1978). His final film role was in *S.O.B.* (1981), which like *Sunset Boulevard* was a searing and satirical indictment of Hollywood; but times had changed, and one of the comic highlights of *S.O.B.* was a drunken film executive urinating on the floor of an undertaking parlor. Holden's incessant imbibing had alienated him from most of his friends and all but destroyed his relationship with actress Stefanie Powers, and sadly, his alcohol dependency resulted in his death. When Holden died in 1981,

it was not as a result of a movie stunt or a mishap during an African safari, but from tripping on a rug, gashing his head on a table, and bleeding to death. Holden was too drunk to comprehend the extent of his injury or to help himself. **Selected Works:** *Born Yesterday* (1950), *Executive Suite* (1954), *Picnic* (1955), *Bridge on the River Kwai* (1957), *Wild Bunch* (1969)

# Agnieszka Holland

**Born:** November 28, 1948; Warsaw, Poland

**Years Active in the Industry:** by decade

| 10s | 20s | 30s | 40s | 50s | 60s | 70s | 80s | 90s |
|-----|-----|-----|-----|-----|-----|-----|-----|-----|
|     |     |     |     |     |     |     | ██  |     |

Best recognized for her highly politicized contributions to Polish New Wave cinema, Agnieszka Holland is considered one of Poland's most prominent filmmakers. She graduated from Prague Film School in 1971 and went on to become assistant director to Kryzstof Zanussi on his 1973 film *Illuminacja*. After that she became involved in directing stage plays and TV movies. Holland drew upon her theatrical experience to create her 1978 feature *Aktorzy prowincjonalni*, a chronicle of the often tense backstage relations of a small town theater company that was actually a metaphor for the political situation in Poland. This film won the FIPRESCI prize at the 1980 Cannes Film Festival. Just before Polish martial law was declared in December, 1981, Holland moved her operations to Paris. Her 1985 feature film *Bittere Ernte* (*Angry Harvest*), an examination of the relationship between a gentile farmer and the Jewess he conceals during World War II, was nominated for an Academy Award for Best Foreign Language Film. In addition to making her own films, Holland has also collaborated with legendary filmmaker Andrzej Wajda on several films including 1982's *Danton*. **Selected Works:** *Fever* (1981), *Europa, Europa* (1991), *Olivier, Olivier* (1992)

# Judy Holliday (Judith Tuvim)

**Born:** June 21, 1923; New York, NY
**Died:** June 7, 1965; New York, NY

**Years Active in the Industry:** by decade

| 10s | 20s | 30s | 40s | 50s | 60s | 70s | 80s | 90s |
|-----|-----|-----|-----|-----|-----|-----|-----|-----|
|     |     |     | ██  |     |     |     |     |     |

Although her film career rested on portraying dumb blondes, American actress Judy Holliday scored 172 on her early IQ tests. A voracious reader and theater devotee, Holliday was determined to become a classical actress even though she was rejected for admission to Yale Drama School. She worked as a switchboard operator and a stage manager for Orson Welles' Mercury Theater, then took a job in a comedy revue at a Greenwich Village nightclub in 1938. In the company of her friends Adolph Green, Betty Comden, Alvin Hammer and John Frank, Holliday was a member of the Revuers, an

aggregation specializing in wildly satirical songs and sketches. Working their way up the club date grapevine, the Revuers caught the attention of a 20th Century-Fox talent scout, who wanted to hire only Holliday. She loyally refused to enter movies without her co-workers—to little avail, since the group's premiere performance in *Greenwich Village* (1944) was trimmed down to near-nonexistence. Holliday stayed at Fox for a bit in *Something for the Boys* (1944) and a good supporting role in *Winged Victory* (1944), but was dropped by the studio as having limited potential. The seriocomic role of a prostitute in the 1945 stage play *Kiss Them for Me* revitalized her career somewhat, but her biggest break came when Jean Arthur dropped out of the Garson Kanin play *Born Yesterday.* With less than three days' rehearsal, Judy stepped into the role of Billie Dawn, the dimwitted "kept girl" of crooked junk dealer Paul Douglas, and overnight became the hottest new "find" on Broadway. Columbia Pictures bought the film rights for *Born Yesterday,* but Columbia president Harry Cohn didn't care for Holliday, so her chances at being hired for the movie were slim. She took an excellent part as a would-be husband killer in *Adam's Rib* (1949), and it was this performance that convinced Columbia to allow Holliday to recreate Billie Dawn for the screen version of *Born Yesterday* (1950). The result was an Academy Award for Holliday and a lucrative Columbia contract. Some of her Columbia pictures tended to recast Holliday as Billie Dawn (under different names) over and over again. Though this dum dum characterization was irritating to the star, it came in handy when she was called to testify for the House Un-American Activities Committee. By playing "stupid," Holliday managed to survive accusations of Communist activity that would have killed her career. Tired of Hollywood by 1956, she signed to star in a musical comedy written by her old Revuers companions Comden and Green. *Bells Are Ringing,* which cast Holliday as a "Miss Fixit" telephone operator, ran several seasons, and was ultimately adapted as a film in 1960; this time there was no question that she would repeat her stage role for the movie. Unhappily, *Bells Are Ringing* was Holliday's last film. Domestic problems and the debilitating failures of her 1960 play based on the life of Laurette Taylor and the bedeviled Broadway musical *Hot Spot* were only part of the problem; an earlier bout with cancer had recurred, and this time proved fatal. Holliday died at the age of 42—a brilliant, singular talent allowed to perform at only half steam in most of her Hollywood films.

# Lauren Holly

**Born:** October 28, 1966; Bristol, PA

**Years Active in the Industry:** by decade

| 10s | 20s | 30s | 40s | 50s | 60s | 70s | 80s | 90s |
|-----|-----|-----|-----|-----|-----|-----|-----|-----|
|     |     |     |     |     |     |     | ■   | ■   |

American actress Lauren Holly has herself admitted that turning down the female lead in the Jim Carrey vehicle *Ace Ventura, Pet Detective* (1994) may not have been the wisest career move. Holly was acting

on instinct, having co-starred with another highly individual comedian, Andrew Dice Clay, in 1990's forgettable *The Adventures of Ford Fairlane.* But when profits from *Ace Ventura* soared, Holly was more than willing to sign on for the subsequent Carrey vehicle, *Dumb and Dumber* (1995), during the filming of which she and Carrey became an item. The blonde/then redhead/then blonde again actress has kept busy ever since her first important TV role as Betty in *Archie: To Riverdale and Back Again* (1990) and a stint on the ABC soap opera *All My Children.* Prior to her recent film success, Holly was perhaps best known for her role as Deputy Maxine Stewart on the CBS drama *Picket Fences.* **Selected Works:** *Dragon: The Bruce Lee Story* (1993), *Sabrina* (1995)

# Celeste Holm

**Born:** April 29, 1919; New York, NY

**Years Active in the Industry:** by decade

| 10s | 20s | 30s | 40s | 50s | 60s | 70s | 80s | 90s |
|-----|-----|-----|-----|-----|-----|-----|-----|-----|
|     |     |     | ■   | ■   | ■   | ■   | ■   | ■   |

American actress Celeste Holm made her first stage appearance in 1936 with a Pennsylvania stock company. Sophisticated and poised beyond her years, Holm was cast shortly afterward in a touring company of the ultra-chic Clare Boothe Luce comedy *The Women,* then played New York in such high-profile productions as *The Time of Your Life.* Rodgers and Hammerstein cast her as soubrette Ado Annie in *Oklahoma* in 1943; both the production itself and Annie's show-stopping song "I Cain't Say No" affirmed Holm's future stardom. Following her film debut in *Three Little Girls in Blue* (1946), she was cast by her studio, 20th Century-Fox, in the role of the love-starved fashion editor in the prestige feature *Gentlemen's Agreement* (1947), for which she won an Academy Award. The important role of Bette Davis' understanding friend in another Oscar-winner, *All About Eve* (1950), has immortalized Holm amongst the film cultists. Stage, nightclub and television assignments followed (she starred in the short-lived 1950s sitcom *Honestly, Celeste*), and from the late 1950s onward, Holm was more at home on stage than in films. Her performance in the touring company of *Mame* won Holm the Sara Siddons Award—coincidentally the same award presented to the title character at the beginning of *All About Eve*. Always choosy about her roles, Holm has remained active in the 1980s and 1990s whenever a good part struck her fancy; one of her most frequently rebroadcast assignments was as a custody court judge in an early-1980s episode of *Archie Bunker's Place*. When giving on-camera interviews on the occasion of the 50th anniversary of *Oklahoma!*, Holm appeared much too youthful to have participated in the landmark musical. **Selected Works:** *Gentleman's Agreement* (1947), *Snake Pit* (1948), *Three Men and a Baby* (1987)

## Tim Holt (Charles John Holt, Jr.)

**Born:** February 5, 1918; Beverly Hills, CA
**Died:** 1973

**Years Active in the Industry:** by decade

| 10s | 20s | 30s | 40s | 50s | 60s | 70s | 80s | 90s |
|-----|-----|-----|-----|-----|-----|-----|-----|-----|
|  |  |  |  |  |  |  |  |  |

The son of actor Jack Holt and brother of actors David and Jennifer Holt, Tim Holt debuted onscreen at age ten (playing his father's character as a child) in *The Vanishing Pioneer* (1928). He went on to play earnest teenagers in the mid-to-late '30s, moving into roles as boyish Western heroes in many B-movies; from 1941-43 and 1948-52 he was a top ten box office star, and at one point was very popular among teenage girls. He occasionally got higher quality roles, and will probably be best remembered as the arrogant aristocrat George Amberson in Orson Welles' *The Magnificent Ambersons* (1942) and as Curtin, Humphrey Bogart's conscientious partner, in John Huston's *The Treasure of the Sierra Madre* (1948). During World War II, he was an oft-decorated B-29 bomber in the Pacific arena. He was rarely onscreen after 1952, and he retired from acting in the mid-'50s to go into business; later he did occasional radio and TV work. He died of cancer in 1973. **Selected Works:** *Stella Dallas* (1937), *Stagecoach* (1939), *Swiss Family Robinson* (1940)

## Oscar Homolka

**Born:** August 12, 1898; Vienna, Austria
**Died:** 1978

**Years Active in the Industry:** by decade

| 10s | 20s | 30s | 40s | 50s | 60s | 70s | 80s | 90s |
|-----|-----|-----|-----|-----|-----|-----|-----|-----|
|  |  |  |  |  |  |  |  |  |

Beetle-browed, heavily-accented Viennese character actor Oscar Homolka graduated from the Royal Dramatic Academy in Vienna before going on to work on the Austrian and German stage,

which led him to appear in many German silent and sound films. After Hitler came to power, he moved first to England, then to the U.S. in 1936. In Hollywood films and on Broadway he played imposing character roles, usually scheming or villainous but sometimes humorous or sympathetic. For his portrayal of gruff Uncle Chris in *I Remember Mama* (1948) he received a Best Supporting Actor Oscar nomination. Because of his coarse, Slavic features, he was frequently cast as heavies in films about foreign intrigue. He returned to England in the mid-'60s, intending to retire; instead, he continued appearing in films, and in 1975 came back to Hollywood to make two made-for-TV movies, *One of Our Own* and *The Legendary Curse of the Hope Diamond*, co-starring his wife, actress Joan Tetzel. **Selected Works:** *Ball of Fire* (1941), *Seven Year Itch* (1955), *A Farewell to Arms* (1957)

## Tobe Hooper

**Born:** 1943; Austin, TX

**Years Active in the Industry:** by decade

| 10s | 20s | 30s | 40s | 50s | 60s | 70s | 80s | 90s |
|-----|-----|-----|-----|-----|-----|-----|-----|-----|
|  |  |  |  |  |  |  |  |  |

American film director Tobe Hooper started out like most people in his field, working on industrial films and TV advertisements. Using student help, Hooper began making fictional films while an instructor at the University of Texas. Hooper exploded onto the public scene in 1974 with *The Texas Chainsaw Massacre,* a creepy variation on the unhappy career of cannibalistic killer Ed Gein. Despite its lurid title, the film scored more on the *threat* of violence than its actual violent action, which was minimal. While critics either condemned the picture or flat-out refused to review it, *Texas Chain Saw Massacre* became a cult favorite; within five years of its release it was being written up and analyzed by intellectual film periodicals. Hooper remained on the outside looking in so far as Hollywood was concerned, though his cheaply produced *Eaten Alive* (1976) and *The Funhouse* (1981) had a loyal following. Television was more responsive to Hooper, and in 1979 he was entrusted with a TV movie version of Stephen King's *Salem's Lot*. In 1982, Hooper was given his first mainstream assignment, the Steven Spielberg-produced *Poltergeist* (1982). It was a bit too reliant upon special effects for Hooper's taste, but it proved his ability to set and sustain an eerie mood and highlighted his cheerful disregard for logic and consistency. Hooper's most recent output has included a 1985 remake of that kiddy-matinee perennial *Invaders From Mars* (1985), a mishmash 1986 sequel to *Texas Chainsaw Massacre,* and the ponderously paced thriller *Spontaneous Combustion* (1990). Hooper continues to be a "promising" talent—it's just that lately he's promised more than he's delivered. **Selected Works:** *I'm Dangerous Tonight* (1990)

## Bob Hope (Leslie Townes Hope)

**Born:** May 29, 1903; Standiforth Court, Eltham, England

## Years Active in the Industry: by decade

| 10ˢ | 20ˢ | 30ˢ | 40ˢ | 50ˢ | 60ˢ | 70ˢ | 80ˢ | 90ˢ |
|-----|-----|-----|-----|-----|-----|-----|-----|-----|

Entertainer Bob Hope is unquestionably an American institution, and never mind that he was born in England. Hope's father was a stonemason and his mother a one-time concert singer; when Hope was two, his parents moved him and his brothers to Cleveland, where relatives awaited them. Since everyone in the Hope clan was expected to contribute to the family bank account, he took on several part-time jobs early in life. One of these was as a concessionaire at Cleveland's Luna Park, where Hope had his first taste of show business by winning a Charlie Chaplin imitation contest (he later claimed he'd gotten his brothers to strong-arm all the neighborhood kids to vote for him). At 16, Hope entered the work force full-time as a shoe salesman for a department store, then as a stock boy for an auto company. At night, Hope and a friend picked up spare change singing at local restaurants and saloons, and for a brief time he was an amateur boxer calling himself "Packy East." Picking up dancing tips from older vaudevillians, Hope decided to devote himself to a show business career, first in partnership with his girlfriend Mildred Rosequist, then with a pal named Lloyd Durbin. Comedian Fatty Arbuckle, headlining a touring revue, caught Hope and Durbin's comedy/dancing act and helped the boys get better bookings. Following the accidental death of Durbin, Hope took on another partner, George Byrne, with whom he developed a blackface act. After several career reversals, Hope and Byrne were about to pack it in when they were hired to emcee Marshall Walker's Whiz Bang review in New Castle, Pennsylvania. As the more loquacious member of the team, Hope went out on stage as a single and got excellent response for his seemingly ad-libbed wisecracks. It was in this and subsequent vaudeville appearances that Hope learned how to handle tough audiences by having the guts to wait on stage until everyone in the crowd had gotten his jokes; he was still using this technique seven decades later. Dropping his blackface makeup and cannibalizing every "college humor" magazine he could get his hands on, Hope took on yet another partner (Louise Troxell) in 1928 and started getting choice vaudeville bookings on the Keith Circuit. A year later, he was given a movie screen test, but was told his ski nose didn't photograph well. With material from legendary gagster Al Boasberg, Hope appeared as a single in *The Antics of 1931*, which led to a better theatrical gig with *The Ballyhoo of 1932*, in which Hope was encouraged to ad-lib to his heart's content. He then went back to vaudeville and squeezed in his first radio appearance in 1933 before being hired as the comedy second lead in an important Jerome Kern Broadway musical, *Roberta*. During the long run of this hit, Hope met and married nightclub singer Dolores Reade, who became still *another* of his onstage partners when the play closed and Hope returned to vaudeville. He scored a major success in *The Ziegfeld Follies of 1936,* which spotlighted Hope's talent for sketch comedy, then co-starred with Ethel Merman and Jimmy Durante in *Red, Hot and Blue*. In 1937 he was brought to Hollywood for Paramount's *The Big Broadcast of 1938*, wherein he dueted with Shirley Ross in the Oscar-winning song "Thanks for the Memory," which has been his signature theme ever since. Hope's first few years at Paramount found him appearing in relatively sedate comedy leads, but with *The Cat and the Canary* (1939) he solidified his screen persona as the would-be great lover and "brave coward" who hides his insecurities by constantly wisecracking. In 1940, Hope was teamed with Bing Crosby and Dorothy Lamour for *Road to Singapore* (1940), the first of the still-uproarious "Road" series that featured everything from in-jokes about Bob and Bing's private lives to talking camels. While continuing to build up his movie box office, Hope was also starring in his long running NBC radio program, which was distinguished by its sharp topical humor and censor-baiting risqué material. It was not so much his show business earnings as his profitable real estate deals and holdings that formed the basis of Hope's immense personal fortune (perhaps his rather parsimonious dealings with his writing staff also had something to do with his fat bank account). In the midst of all his media clowning in World War II, Hope worked tirelessly as a USO entertainer for troops in the U.S. and abroad— so much so that he was unable to make any films at all in 1944. In 1950, Hope inaugurated a long-term television contract with NBC, which resulted in 40-plus years' worth of periodic specials that have never failed to sweep the ratings, and also in a 1960's anthology series, *The Bob Hope Chrysler Theatre*. With his film box office receipts flagging in the early 1950s (audiences didn't quite buy a 50-year-old man playing a thirtyish girl chaser), Hope took the advice of writer/directors Norman Panana and Melvin Frank and attempted a straight dramatic film role as Eddie Foy Sr. in *The Seven Little Foys* (1955). He succeeded in both pulling off the character and in packing a relatively maudlin script with humanity and humor. Hope's last "straight" film part was as New York City Mayor Jimmy Walker in *Beau James* (1957), in which he again acquitted himself quite nicely. Having long taken a percentage of profits on his Paramount releases, Hope became his own producer in 1957, which at first resulted in such fine pictures as *Alias Jesse James* (1959) and *The Facts of Life* (1960) (with frequent costar Lucille Ball). But in the 1960s, the quality of Hope's films took a depressing downward spiral; even hard-core Hope fans were hard-pressed to suffer though such dogs as *Boy, Did I Get a Wrong Number* (1966) and *The Private Navy of Sgt. O'Farrell* (1968). It has been theorized that Hope was too wealthy and much too busy with a multitude of other projects to care about the sorry state of his films. Besides, even the worst of the Hope pictures posted a profit, which to him evidently meant more than whether or not the films were any good. It's hardly necessary to enumerate the accomplishments, patriotic services, charitable donations, awards, medals and honorariums pertaining to Hope—nor does it serve any purpose to delve into his "secret" private life of alleged philandering, penny-pinching and backing of questionable American foreign policy decisions. A bit slower of tongue but no less energetic in his ninetieth decade, Bob Hope is a man for whom the word "legend" seems somehow inadequate. **Selected Works:** *Star Spangled Rhythm* (1942)

# Sir Anthony Hopkins

**Born:** December 31, 1937; Port Talbot, South Wales, England

**Years Active in the Industry:** by decade

| 10ˢ | 20ˢ | 30ˢ | 40ˢ | 50ˢ | 60ˢ | 70ˢ | 80ˢ | 90ˢ |
|-----|-----|-----|-----|-----|-----|-----|-----|-----|
|     |     |     |     |     |     |     |     |     |

The only son of a baker, British actor Anthony Hopkins was drawn to the theatre while attending the YMCA at age 17, and later learned the basics of his craft at the Royal Academy of Dramatic Art. In 1960, Hopkins made his stage bow in *The Quare Fellow,* then spent four years in regional repertory before his first London success in *Julius Caesar.* Combining the best elements of the British theater's classic heritage and its burgeoning "angry young man" school, Hopkins worked well in both ancient and modern pieces. His film debut was not, as has often been cited, his appearance as Richard the Lionhearted in *The Lion in Winter* (1968), but in an odd, "pop art trendy" film, *The White Bus* (1967). Though already familiar to some sharp-eyed American viewers after his film performance as Lloyd George in *Young Winston* (1971), Hopkins burst full-flower onto the American scene in 1974 as an ex-Nazi doctor in *QB VII,* the first television miniseries. Also in 1974, Hopkins made his Broadway debut in *Equus,* eventually directing the 1977 Los Angeles production. The actor became typed in intense, neurotic roles for the next several years: in films he portrayed the obsessed father of a girl whose soul has been transferred into the body of another child in *Audrey Rose* (1976), an off-the-wall ventriloquist in *Magic* (1978), and the much-maligned Captain Bligh (opposite Mel Gibson's Fletcher Christian) in *Bounty* (1982). On TV, Hopkins played roles as varied (yet somehow intertwined) as Adolph Hitler, accused Lindbergh-baby kidnapper Bruno Richard Hauptmann, and the Hunchback of Notre Dame. Offscreen, Hopkins' life was almost as troubled as the characters he played, with periodic bouts of all-consuming anger and substance abuse. Hopkins rechanneled his personal life in the

1980s, allowing whatever demons that plagued him to manifest themselves in his acting. This psychological turnaround resulted in more private peace of mind and a series of unforgettable film parts. In 1991, Hopkins won an Academy Award for his bloodcurdling portrayal of murderer Hannibal "The Cannibal" Lecter in *The Silence of the Lambs* (1991). With the aplomb of a thorough professional, Anthony Hopkins was able to follow up his chilling Lecter with characters of great kindness, courtesy and humanity: the conscience-stricken butler of a British fascist in *The Remains of the Day* (1992) and compassionate author C. S. Lewis in *Shadowlands* (1993). **Selected Works:** *Elephant Man* (1980), *Bram Stoker's Dracula* (1992), *Efficiency Expert* (1992), *Howard's End* (1992), *Nixon* (1995)

# Miriam Hopkins

**Born:** October 18, 1902; Bainbridge, GA
**Died:** October 9, 1972; New York, NY

**Years Active in the Industry:** by decade

| 10ˢ | 20ˢ | 30ˢ | 40ˢ | 50ˢ | 60ˢ | 70ˢ | 80ˢ | 90ˢ |
|-----|-----|-----|-----|-----|-----|-----|-----|-----|
|     |     |     |     |     |     |     |     |     |

American actress Miriam Hopkins studied to be a dancer, but her first major opportunity with a touring ballet troupe was cut short when she broke her ankle. Opting for an acting career, Hopkins drew upon her Georgia background to specialize in playing Southern belles, most notably in the 1933 Broadway play *Jezebel.* Entering films with 1930's *Fast and Loose,* Hopkins became a popular film star, though many critics and film historians deemed her histrionic, uninhibited style as "an acquired taste." During the early stages of her film career, Hopkins contributed at least two memorable performances: Champagne Ivy, the doomed cockney songstress in the Fredric March version of *Dr. Jeckell and Mr. Hyde* (1931), and the title role in *Becky Sharp* (1935), the first feature film to be shot in the three-strip Technicolor process. Relatively charming offscreen, Hopkins could be a terror on the set, driving co-stars to distraction with her lateness, lack of concentration and self-centered attitude towards camera angles; she owned the distinction of being one of the few actors ever reprimanded in full view of the production crew by the otherwise gentlemanly Edward G. Robinson. Still, she had her following, and was able to continue her stage career (she was particularly good in the 1958 Pulitzer Prize winner *Look Homeward Angel*) after her movie popularity waned. One of Hopkins' best later roles was her character part in 1961's *The Children's Hour;* 25 years earlier, Miriam had starred in the first film version of that Lillian Hellman play, *These Three* (1936). **Selected Works:** *Dr. Jekyll & Mr. Hyde* (1931), *Heiress* (1949)

# Dennis Hopper

**Born:** May 17, 1936; Dodge City, KS

**Years Active in the Industry:** by decade

| 10s | 20s | 30s | 40s | 50s | 60s | 70s | 80s | 90s |
|-----|-----|-----|-----|-----|-----|-----|-----|-----|
|     |     |     |     |     |     |     |     |     |

Acting since his teens, quirky but talented actor Dennis Hopper got his professional start in juvenile roles in the TV series *Medic*. A friend of James Dean, whom he emulated, he landed roles in two of Dean's films, *Rebel Without a Cause* (1955) and *Giant* (1956). He went on to play small roles in a number of big films, but soon gained a reputation among directors and producers as being very difficult to work with; he was said to be argumentative, rebellious, and violent, with a bad temper and an inability to take direction, insisting on playing each role as he (not the director) saw fit. This led to a long dry spell when no one would hire him. He then reversed his previous tendencies and started playing big roles in minor films. He began to get recognition from the '60s generation through his performance in the LSD-influenced *The Trip* (1967), written by Jack Nicholson and starring Peter Fonda. The same trio then made the hippie-era motorcycle film *Easy Rider* (1969), which Hopper directed and co-wrote. *Easy Rider,* made on a $400,000 budget, became a counter-culture hit and grossed $16 million. This success persuaded the studios to allow him to make a semiautobiographical documentary, *American Dreamer* (1971), and then to go to Peru to film *The Last Movie* (1971), which he wrote, directed, edited and starred in; although it won the Best Picture award at the Venice film festival, the film was panned as being too self-indulgent, and was a failure at the box office. He then spent 15 years on the outskirts of the film industry, making films that went nowhere, often for European companies. He directed another film, the well-received *Out of the Blue* (1980), then bounced back in the mid-'80s, making six films in one year; these included his portrayal of a psychotic rapist in *Blue Velvet* (1986), a breakthrough for him among a new generation of viewers, and his role as an alcoholic in *Hoosiers* (1986), for which he received a Best Supporting Actor nomination. Following that highly successful year his career continued to prosper, and included three more directorial efforts; one of these was *Colors* (1988), whose theme of gang warfare led to a debate over the question of whether the movie merely reflected violence or actually encouraged it. For some time he had the reputation of being "the most freaked-out man in films," but by his mid-50s he had shaken that image. **Selected Works:** *Indian Runner* (1991), *True Romance* (1993), *Speed* (1994), *Waterworld* (1995)

# James Horner

**Born:** August 14, 1953; Los Angeles, CA

**Years Active in the Industry:** by decade

| 10s | 20s | 30s | 40s | 50s | 60s | 70s | 80s | 90s |
|-----|-----|-----|-----|-----|-----|-----|-----|-----|
|     |     |     |     |     |     |     | ■   | ■   |

American composer James Horner attended the Royal College of Music, UCLA and USC. Before moving into big-budget movie projects, Horner composed for Roger Corman's New World Pictures (including *The Lady in Red* [1979] and *Humanoids of the Deep* [1980] ) and for special projects put together by the American Film Institute. Unlike many modern film composers who tend to emulate the swashbuckling swagger of a Max Steiner or an Erich Wolfgang Korngold, Horner prefers to write in lush, tone-poem fashion, in the manner of Aaron Copeland. Among the many films scored by Horner are *Aliens* (1986), *Field of Dreams* (1988) and *Glory* (1989), for which he won a Grammy. In typical fashion, Horner's music for 1995's *Apollo 13* brilliantly emphasizes the heroism of the story without relying upon *Star Wars*-style pageantry. **Selected Works:** *Swing Kids* (1993), *Pelican Brief* (1993), *Bopha* (1993), *Searching for Bobby Fischer* (1993), *Clear and Present Danger* (1994)

# Edward Everett Horton

**Born:** March 18, 1886; Brooklyn, NY
**Died:** September 29, 1970; San Fernando Valley, CA

**Years Active in the Industry:** by decade

| 10s | 20s | 30s | 40s | 50s | 60s | 70s | 80s | 90s |
|-----|-----|-----|-----|-----|-----|-----|-----|-----|
| ■   |     |     |     |     |     |     |     |     |

Often mistaken for an Englishman, actor Edward Everett Horton was actually born in Brooklyn, the son of newspaper print-machine operator. Horton left Oberlin College in his junior year to pursue his dreams of becoming a stage actor, receiving his training at Brooklyn's Polytechnic Institute and then at Columbia University, where he made his first stage appearance in a varsity variety show. Knocking about professionally as a chorus boy and stage manager, Horton was given his first leading role as a Japanese prince (hardly typecasting for the gangly, puck-faced actor) in the venerable stage melodrama *The Typhoon*. Thereafter, despite a few forays into heavy drama, Horton specialized in comedy, occasionally giving movies a try as a light leading man; his film debut was 1921's *Too Much Business*. By the end of the 1920s, Horton was managing the Majestic Theatre in Los Angeles, casting his fellow character actors in the meaty, demanding roles often denied them by the movies. He also helped train several silent film leading men and ingenues to use their voices properly in stage work, to prepare them for talking pictures. Horton was pretty much locked into second lead and supporting roles in the 1930s and 1940s, most notably in the delightful Fred Astaire-Ginger Rogers musicals at RKO; during this period he also established himself as a reliable radio actor, frequently enlivening second-rate scripts with his own amusing elaboration. After a decade-long concentration on theater, usually touring as star of the reliable stage vehicle *Springtime for Henry,* Horton resumed his film career in 1957, which he maintained until his death. In the 1950s and 1960s, Horton suddenly found himself a favorite of the younger set thanks to his narration of the "Fractured Fairy Tales" segment on the legendary TV cartoon series *Rocky and His Friends,* and his semi-regular appearances as medicine man Roaring Chicken on the western situation comedy *F Troop*. **Selected Works:** *Gay Divorcee* (1934), *Here Comes Mr. Jordan* (1941), *Holiday* (1938), *Lost Horizon* (1937), *Top Hat* (1935)

# Bob Hoskins

**Born:** October 26, 1942; Greenville, SC

**Years Active in the Industry:** by decade

| 10ˢ | 20ˢ | 30ˢ | 40ˢ | 50ˢ | 60ˢ | 70ˢ | 80ˢ | 90ˢ |
|-----|-----|-----|-----|-----|-----|-----|-----|-----|
|     |     |     |     |     |     |     |     |     |

A burly actor with a Cockney working-man persona, Bob Hoskins had a fateful beginning to his career. It began when he, then in his mid-20s was sitting around in a pub where a play was to be staged by a small troupe. They needed an extra hand, he was there, and the rest is history. Hoskins went on to become a distinguished character actor in a variety of productions from classical to avant-garde, and performed with three of Britain's most prestigious companies, the Royal Court, the Royal Shakespeare Company, and the National Theater. He debuted onscreen in *The National Health* (1973) and appeared in a few more films in the '70s, but his movie career didn't really take off until his appearance in John Mackenzie's *The Long Good Friday* (1980); able to affect an American accent, he made his U.S. film debut in *The Honorary Consul* (1983), also made by Mackenzie. After that, he appeared in many films, including the highly successful *Who Framed Roger Rabbit?* (1988) in which he played opposite a cartoon character. He directed and co-wrote *The Raggedy Rawney* (1988). He received a Best Actor Oscar nomination for his work in Neil Jordan's *Mona Lisa* (1986). **Selected Works:** *Heart Condition* (1990), *Hook* (1991), *Inner Circle* (1991), *Mermaids* (1990), *Shattered* (1991)

# John Houseman (Jacques Haussmann)

**Born:** September 22, 1902; Bucharest, Romania
**Died:** October 31, 1988; Malibu, CA

**Years Active in the Industry:** by decade

| 10ˢ | 20ˢ | 30ˢ | 40ˢ | 50ˢ | 60ˢ | 70ˢ | 80ˢ | 90ˢ |
|-----|-----|-----|-----|-----|-----|-----|-----|-----|
|     |     |     |     |     |     |     |     |     |

Before entering the entertainment industry, actor, producer, scriptwriter, playwright and stage director John Houseman first worked for his father's grain business after graduating from college, then began writing magazine pieces and translating plays from German and French. Living in New York, he was writing, directing, and producing plays by his early 30s; soon he had a stel-

lar reputation on Broadway. In 1937, he and Orson Welles founded the Mercury Theater, at which he produced and directed radio specials and stage presentations; at the same time he was a teacher at Vassar. He produced Welles' never-completed first film, *Too Much Johnson* (1938). Houseman then went on to play a crucial role in the packaging of Welles's first completed film, the masterpiece *Citizen Kane* (1941): he developed the original story with Herman Mankiewicz, motivated Mankiewicz to complete the script, and worked as a script editor and general advisor for the film. Shortly afterwards, he and Welles had a falling out and Houseman became a vice president of David O. Selznick Productions, a post he quit in late 1941 (after Pearl Harbor) to become chief of the overseas radio division of the OWI. After returning to Hollywood he produced many fine films and commuted to New York to produce and direct Broadway plays and TV specials; in all, the films he produced were nominated for 20 Oscars and won seven. Later he became the artistic director of the touring repertory group the Acting Company, with which he toured successfully in the early '70s. He debuted onscreen at the age of 62 in *Seven Days in May* (1964), and then in the '70s and '80s played character roles in a number of films. As an actor he was best known as Kingsfield, the stern Harvard law professor, in the film *The Paper Chase* (1973), his second screen appearance, for which he won a Best Supporting Actor Oscar; he reprised the role in the TV series of the same name. He authored two autobiographies, *Run-Through* (1972) and *Front and Center* (1979). **Selected Works:** *My Bodyguard* (1980), *Three Days of the Condor* (1975)

# Whitney Houston

**Born:** August 9, 1963

**Years Active in the Industry:** by decade

| 10ˢ | 20ˢ | 30ˢ | 40ˢ | 50ˢ | 60ˢ | 70ˢ | 80ˢ | 90ˢ |
|-----|-----|-----|-----|-----|-----|-----|-----|-----|
|     |     |     |     |     |     |     |     |     |

The daughter of Cissy Houston and a cousin of Dionne Warwick, singer Whitney Houston burst on the music scene with her inaugural album in 1985, becoming the first woman performer to debut at the number one slot in the *Billboard* charts. Houston could have remained merely a fabulously successful songstress, but in 1992 she decided to make her film debut in *The Bodyguard*. Playing an ill-tempered rock star, Houston was paired with Kevin Costner, who portrayed an ex-cop hired to protect her from a stalking fan. Written

years earlier by Lawrence Kasdan as a vehicle for Steve McQueen, *The Bodyguard* was overbaked and utterly illogical. It also made a pile at the box office, providing Whitney Houston with yet another vocal hit: a new version of the Dolly Parton standard "I Will Always Love You", which became the biggest-selling single in the history of pop music. Houston is married to oft-arrested funk singer Bobby Brown, with whom she has a daughter, Bobbi. **Selected Works:** *Waiting to Exhale* (1995)

# John C. Howard (John R. Cox, Jr.)

**Born:** April 14, 1913; Cleveland, OH

**Years Active in the Industry:** by decade

| 10ˢ | 20ˢ | 30ˢ | 40ˢ | 50ˢ | 60ˢ | 70ˢ | 80ˢ | 90ˢ |
|-----|-----|-----|-----|-----|-----|-----|-----|-----|
|     |     |     |     |     |     |     |     |     |

An honor student in high school, American actor John Howard was also an accomplished pianist, and in this capacity won a position in the musical department at the Cleveland radio station WHK. While appearing in a stage production at Western Reserve University, Howard was spotted by a Paramount talent scout and signed for films. Looking much older than his 26 years, the actor assumed the role of suave adventurer Bulldog Drummond in a series of seven Paramount B pictures, beginning in 1937. The first actor to play Drummond in talking pictures was Ronald Colman, and it was with Colman whom Howard co-starred in his most famous film, *Lost Horizon* (1937). Howard played Colman's younger brother, whose recklessness led to the classic scene in which Margo, playing a woman spirited away from Shangri-La by Howard, aged 50 years before audiences' eyes. Modern day audiences viewing *Lost Horizon* aren't too kind to Howard; laughing uproariously at his fevered histrionics; but Howard was the first to admit in latter-day interviews that he was overacting—in fact, he was rougher on himself than any audience had been. Otherwise, Howard's film roles were played competently if not colorfully, though he certainly deserves some credit for convincingly reacting to and making love with the Invisible Woman in the 1941 film comedy of the same name. Howard became a pioneer of sorts when in 1947 he starred in *Public Prosecutor,* the first filmed television series. Eight years later, the actor enjoyed a two-season run on the syndicated hospital drama *Dr. Hudson's Secret Journal,* in which all traces of the *Lost Horizon* ham were completely obliterated by Howard's calm, persuasive performance. A third TV series starring Howard, *Adventures of the Sea Hawk,* was filmed in 1958, but didn't hit the tube until 1961, and it was subsequently a flop. Howard was philosophical about his screen career, noting that he was always somewhat indifferent about stardom (though he did dearly covet the role of Ashley Wilkes in *Gone With the Wind* [1939], which went to Leslie Howard); the actor was, however, justifiably proud of his Broadway appearances in *The Philadelphia Story* and *Hazel Flagg.* Completely out of the film business in the early 1970s, Howard taught drama and English at a private high school in Brentwood, California. **Selected Works:** *Butch Cassidy and the Sundance Kid* (1969), *High and the Mighty* (1954)

# Leslie Howard (Leslie Stainer)

**Born:** April 3, 1893; London, England
**Died:** June 2, 1943; Bay of Biscay

**Years Active in the Industry:** by decade

| 10ˢ | 20ˢ | 30ˢ | 40ˢ | 50ˢ | 60ˢ | 70ˢ | 80ˢ | 90ˢ |
|-----|-----|-----|-----|-----|-----|-----|-----|-----|
|     |     |     |     |     |     |     |     |     |

Son of a London stockbroker, British actor Leslie Howard worked as a bank clerk after graduating from London's Dulwich School. Serving briefly in World War I, Howard was mustered out for medical reasons in 1918, deciding at that time to act for a living. Working in both England and the U.S. throughout the 1920s, Howard specialized in playing disillusioned intellectuals in such plays as *Outward Bound,* the film version of which served as his 1930 film debut. Other films followed on both sides of the Atlantic, the best of these being Howard's masterful star turn in *The Scarlet Pimpernel* (1934). In 1935, Howard portrayed yet another disenchanted soul in *The Petrified Forest,* which co-starred Humphrey Bogart as a gangster patterned after John Dillinger. Howard was tapped for the film version, but refused to make the movie unless Bogart was also hired (Warner Bros. had planned to use their resident gangster type, Edward G. Robinson). Hardly a candidate for "Mr. Nice Guy"—he was known to count the lines of his fellow actors and demand cuts if they exceeded his dialogue—Howard was nonetheless loyal to those he cared about. Bogart became a star after *The Petrified Forest,* and in gratitude named his first daughter Leslie Bogart. Somehow able to hide encroaching middle-age when on screen, Howard played romantic leads well into his late 40s, none more so than the role of—yes—disillusioned intellectual Southern aristocrat Ashley Wilkes in the 1939 classic *Gone with the Wind.* In the late 1930s, Howard began dabbling in directing, notably in his starring films *Pygmalion* (1938) and *Pimpernel Smith* (1941). Fiercely patriotic, Howard traveled extensively on behalf of war relief; on one of these trips, he boarded a British Overseas Airways plane in 1943 with several other British notables, flying en route from England to Lisbon. The plane was shot down over the Bay of Biscay and all on board were killed. Only after the war ended was it revealed that Howard had selflessly taken that plane ride knowing it would probably never arrive in Lisbon; it was ostensibly carrying Prime Minister Winston Churchill, and was sent out as a decoy so that Churchill's actual plane would be undisturbed by enemy fire. **Selected Works:** *Intermezzo: A Love Story* (1939), *Romeo and Juliet* (1936), *49th Parallel* (1941), *Smilin' Through* (1932), *Berkeley Square* (1933)

# Ron Howard

**Born:** March 1, 1954; Duncan, OK

**Years Active in the Industry:** by decade

| 10ˢ | 20ˢ | 30ˢ | 40ˢ | 50ˢ | 60ˢ | 70ˢ | 80ˢ | 90ˢ |
|-----|-----|-----|-----|-----|-----|-----|-----|-----|
|     |     |     |     |     |     |     |     |     |

At age two, filmmaker and former juvenile actor Ron Howard, the son of actors Rance and Jean Howard, appeared on-stage with his parents in a Baltimore stage production of *The Seven Year Itch*. At age five he debuted on-screen in *The Journey* (1959), going on to play child roles in a number of other Hollywood films, including that of the lisping lad in 1962's *The Music Man*. In his late teens and early 20s he appeared in several other films, notably George Lucas's block-buster *American Graffiti* (1973). As an actor, Howard is best known for his roles in two TV series: as a boy he played Opie Taylor, Sheriff Andy Taylor's son, in *The Andy Griffith Show;* and as a young adult he played Richie Cunningham in *Happy Days*. He appeared in only two films after 1980. In the late '70s he directed his first film, a fast paced B movie, *Grand Theft Auto*. He then went on to direct such hits as *Night Shift* (1982), *Splash* (1984), and *Cocoon* (1985). As a director, Howard is known for his well crafted films, and his ability to choose stories (often scripted by Lowell Ganz and Babaloo Mandel) with mass appeal and guaranteed entertainment value, as evidenced by the critical acclaim and huge success of *Apollo 13* (1995). He is co-founder of one of the industry's most successful production studios, Imagine Films Entertainment. His brother is actor Clint Howard, with whom he appeared in *Eat My Dust!* (1976). **Selected Works:** *Backdraft* (1991), *Far and Away* (1992), *Parenthood* (1989), *The Paper* (1994), *Apollo 13* (1995)

# Trevor Howard

**Born:** September 29, 1916; Cliftonville, England
**Died:** January 7, 1988; Bushey, England

### Years Active in the Industry: by decade

| 10ˢ | 20ˢ | 30ˢ | 40ˢ | 50ˢ | 60ˢ | 70ˢ | 80ˢ | 90ˢ |
|-----|-----|-----|-----|-----|-----|-----|-----|-----|
|     |     |     |     |     |     |     |     |     |

British actor Trevor Howard trained at the Royal Academy of Dramatic Art, and while there he made his London stage debut in 1934; however, his subsequent work onstage gained little attention until the mid-'40s. While fighting World War II with the Royal Artillery, he was injured and discharged. Howard made his feature film debut in 1944; soon he attained star status as the result of playing the romantic lead in David Lean's *Brief Encounter* (1945). Thus began a long and consistently successful film career. At first, Howard was cast in romantic leads, but then began playing more heroic leads before eventually moving into character roles. Regard-

less of his role, he was known as a consistent, polished actor with an understated, true-to-life style. At first appearing exclusively in British films, he began appearing occasionally in Hollywood productions in the mid-'50s. For his performance as the father in *Sons and Lovers* (1960) he received a Best Actor Oscar nomination. He was married to actress Helen Cherry, with whom he appeared in *A Soldier for Christmas* (1944). **Selected Works:** *Gandhi* (1982), *Third Man* (1949), *Von Ryan's Express* (1965), *Mary, Queen of Scots* (1971)

# James Wong Howe (Wong Tung Jim)

**Born:** August 28, 1899; Kwantung (Canton), China
**Died:** July 12, 1976; Los Angeles, CA

### Years Active in the Industry: by decade

| 10ˢ | 20ˢ | 30ˢ | 40ˢ | 50ˢ | 60ˢ | 70ˢ | 80ˢ | 90ˢ |
|-----|-----|-----|-----|-----|-----|-----|-----|-----|
|     |     |     |     |     |     |     |     |     |

Canton-born James Wong Howe was one of the few Hollywood cinematographers whom the average movie fan knew by name. Arriving in America with his family at age five, Howe set-

tled in Washington state. At 11, he was given a cheap brownie camera as payment for doing odd jobs for a local druggist. After World War I service and a desultory career as a prizefighter, he went to work as a handyman for the Famous Players-Lasky studio in Hollywood, shooting still pictures of various costume tests just for the experience. While taking a photo of film star Mary Miles Minter, Howe hit upon a method of making her blue eyes photograph darker; Minter began talking up Howe to everyone she met, and thus his cinematography career was underway. Overcoming the racial prejudice of certain Hollywood cameramen, Howe turned out some of the best, most evocatively lit and composed work in the business; he also developed a close working association with prestigious director William K. Howard. Howe took a vacation to China during the industry's switch to talkies, and upon returning to the states discovered he was considered "old fashioned" and unemployable. His old friend

Howard came to his rescue again, engaging Howe to photograph *Transatlantic* (1931), in which he pioneered the use of low-hanging ceilings (ten years before Orson Welles was lauded for this "innovation" in *Citizen Kane!*) Howe also shot Howard's *The Power and the Glory* (1933), another critical success. In the late 1930s, he interrupted his thriving Hollywood career for a brief stopover in England, again collaborating with Howard on the Laurence Olivier vehicle *Fire over England* (1937). Howe was a particular favorite of female stars because of his inherent ability to emphasize their best features and obscure their facial flaws—especially in close-up. Arguably, Howe's most creative years were the late 1940s onward. He shot the boxing sequence in *Body and Soul* (1947) holding the camera in his hands and gliding about on roller skates; he economically conveyed the diverging emotions of the climax in *Picnic* (1956) with an overhead shot of a train leaving in one direction, a bus in the other; and illuminated a crucial scene in *The Molly Maguires* (1970) using only candlelight. His work on *The Rose Tattoo* (1958) and *Hud* (1963) won Academy Awards, while his riveting exploitation of a fisheye lens in the closing scene of *Seconds* (1966) set the standard for most "paranoia" camera shots in subsequent films. Twice during his career, Howe left camerawork for directing. He helmed the 1954 Harlem Globetrotters drama *Go Man Go;* and, on location in New Orleans, Howe co-directed two pilot episodes for a TV version of *The Shadow*, which were spliced together and released theatrically as *Invisible Avenger* (1959). **Selected Works:** *Abe Lincoln in Illinois* (1940), *Algiers* (1938), *King's Row* (1942), *Old Man and the Sea* (1958)

# C. Thomas Howell

**Born:** December 7, 1966; Los Angeles, CA

**Years Active in the Industry:** by decade

| 10<sup>s</sup> | 20<sup>s</sup> | 30<sup>s</sup> | 40<sup>s</sup> | 50<sup>s</sup> | 60<sup>s</sup> | 70<sup>s</sup> | 80<sup>s</sup> | 90<sup>s</sup> |
|---|---|---|---|---|---|---|---|---|
| | | | | | | | | |

American actor C. Thomas Howell (the "C" is for Christopher) began his acting career at the age of four, when he was a regular on the TV series *Little People*; he went on to appear on two other series: *Two Marriages* and *Into the Homeland*. This led to a big break when he was cast at the age of 16 in a secondary role in Steven Spielberg's *E.T.: The Extra-Terrestrial* (1982), one of the most successful films of all time. Following that, Francis Ford Coppola gave him the lead (in part due to Howell's "pretty-boy" good looks) in *The Outsiders* (1983), which has led to a consistent film career. However, most of his movies (with the exception of *The Hitcher*, 1986, in which he is stalked by a killer) have fared badly at the box office. Besides being an actor, Howell is also a former junior rodeo circuit champion. He is married to actress Rae Dawn Chong, with whom he co-starred in *Soul Man* (1986). **Selected Works:** *Curiosity Kills* (1990), *Gettysburg* (1992), *Kid* (1990), *Nickel and Dime* (1992), *To Protect and Serve* (1992)

# Rock Hudson (Roy Harold Scherer, Jr.)

**Born:** November 17, 1925; Winnetka, IL
**Died:** October 2, 1985; Beverly Hills, CA

**Years Active in the Industry:** by decade

| 10<sup>s</sup> | 20<sup>s</sup> | 30<sup>s</sup> | 40<sup>s</sup> | 50<sup>s</sup> | 60<sup>s</sup> | 70<sup>s</sup> | 80<sup>s</sup> | 90<sup>s</sup> |
|---|---|---|---|---|---|---|---|---|
| | | | | | | | | |

American actor Rock Hudson was born Roy Scherer, adopting the last name Fitzgerald when his mother remarried in the mid-1930s. A popular but academically unspectacular student at New Trier High School in Winnetka, Illinois, he decided somewhere in his high school years to become an actor, but a wartime stint in the navy put these plans on hold. Uninspiring postwar jobs as a moving man, postman, telephone company worker and truck driver in his new home, California, only fueled his desire to break into movies, which was accomplished after he had professional photos of himself taken and sent out to the various studios. A few dead-end interviews later, he took dramatic lessons; his teacher advised him to find a shorter name if he hoped to become a star, and after rejecting Lance and Derek, he chose Rock (the Hudson part was inspired by the automobile of that name). Signed by Universal-International, Hudson was immediately loaned to Warner Bros. for his first film, *Fighter Squadron* (1948); despite director Raoul Walsh's predictions of stardom for the young actor, Hudson did the usual contract player bits, supporting roles and villain parts when he returned to Universal. A good part in *Winchester 73* (1950) led to better assignments; the studio chose to concentrate its publicity on Hudson's physical attributes rather than his acting ability, which may explain why the actor spent an inordinate amount of screen time with his shirt off. A favorite of teen-oriented fan magazines, Hudson ascended to stardom, his films gradually reaching the "A" category with such important releases as *Magnificent Obsession* (1954) and *Battle Hymn* (1957). Director George Stevens cast Hudson in one of his best-ever roles, Bick Benedict, in the epic film *Giant* (1956); critics finally decided that, since Hudson not only worked well with such dramatic league leaders as Elizabeth Taylor and James Dean but frequently outacted them in *Giant*, he was due better, less condescending reviews. Hudson's career took a giant leap forward in 1959 when he was cast in *Pillow Talk*, the first of several profitable co-starring gigs with Doris Day. Again taken for granted by the mid-1960s, Hudson turned in another first rate performance as a middle-aged man given a newer, younger body in the mordant fantasy film *Seconds* (1966). A longtime TV hold-out, Hudson finally entered the weekly video race in 1971 with the popular detective series *McMillan and Wife,* which co-starred Susan St. James, and appeared on the prime time soap opera *Dynasty* in the early 1980s. Regarded by his coworkers as a good sport, hard worker and all-around nice guy, Hudson endured a troubled private life; though the studio flacks liked to emphasize his womanizing, Hudson was in reality a homosexual. This had been hinted at for years by the Hollywood underground, but it was only in the early 1980s that Hudson confirmed the rumors by announcing that he'd contacted the deadly AIDS virus. Staunchly defended by friends, fans and coworkers, Rock Hudson lived out the remainder of his life with dignity, withstanding the ravages of his illness, the intrusions of the tabloid press and the poor-taste snickerings of the judgmental and misinformed. It is a testament to his courage—and a tragedy in light of his better film work—that Hudson will be remembered principally as the first star of his magnitude to go public with details of his battle with AIDS. **Selected Works:** *Lover Come Back* (1961), *Written on the Wind* (1956), *A Farewell to Arms* (1957)

# John Hughes

**Born:** February 18, 1950; Lansing, MI

**Years Active in the Industry:** by decade

| 10ˢ | 20ˢ | 30ˢ | 40ˢ | 50ˢ | 60ˢ | 70ˢ | 80ˢ | 90ˢ |
|-----|-----|-----|-----|-----|-----|-----|-----|-----|
|     |     |     |     |     |     |     | ■   | ■   |

Like many baby-boomers who grew up in Chicago, director/writer John Hughes was an unregenerate fan of the Three Stooges, whose old comedies were telecast without interruption in the Windy City from 1958 onward. Hughes hoped one day to perpetuate the Stooges' brand of violent slapstick in Hollywood feature films, but his dream was detoured after he dropped out of college and became an advertising copywriter. He returned to the comedy field as a joke writer for standup comics in the Chicago area. Joining the irreverent *National Lampoon* as an editor in 1979, Hughes found an ideal outlet for his gleefully sadistic sense of humor. He worked on the screenplays of such *National Lampoon* film projects as *Class Reunion* (1982) and *Christmas Vacation* (1989). In 1984, he directed his first film, *Sixteen Candles,* which led to the subsequent teen-angst flicks *The Breakfast Club* (1985) and *Pretty in Pink* (1986). By probing the various triumphs and failures in the lives of 1980s

teenagers, Hughes developed a sense of warmth and understanding not evident in his *Lampoon* work—though he always found time to insert a gratuitous slapstick gag here and there. The success of Hughes' teen-oriented films enabled him to set up his own production company, which entered into a multipicture deal with Universal in 1988. *Uncle Buck* (1988) starring John Candy as a terminal misfit, is probably the best example of Hughes' curious blend of humanity, pathos, and mean-spirited broad comedy. It was a blend he carried over into 1990's *Home Alone,* an incredibly successful film that Hughes has essentially been remaking ever since. After several years of hit-and-miss projects which he produced, directed and/or wrote, Hughes came out with an unexpectedly subdued, gently funny 1994 remake of the 1947 classic *Miracle on 34th Street.* This change-of-pace endeavor ended up as one Hughes' few flat-out failures. **Selected Works:** *Beethoven* (1992), *Dennis the Menace* (1993), *Home Alone 2: Lost in New York* (1992), *Baby's Day Out* (1994)

# Tom Hulce

**Born:** December 6, 1953; White Water, WI

**Years Active in the Industry:** by decade

| 10ˢ | 20ˢ | 30ˢ | 40ˢ | 50ˢ | 60ˢ | 70ˢ | 80ˢ | 90ˢ |
|-----|-----|-----|-----|-----|-----|-----|-----|-----|
|     |     |     |     |     |     | ■   | ■   | ■   |

American stage actor Tom Hulce made his film debut in *September 30, 1955* (1977) (the title referred to the day James Dean died), and attained his first starring role as Larry Kroger in *National Lampoon's Animal House* (1978). The sincerity of Hulce's portrayal was somewhat lost in the enthusiasm over co-star John Belushi, but Hulce was impressive enough to be cast in *Those Lips, Those Eyes* (1980), a heartfelt tribute to summer theater actors. Over several possible candidates, Hulce was selected to play Mozart in *Amadeus* (1984), earning an Oscar nomination for his virtuoso portrayal of that outrageously immature musical genius. Again, however, the honors went to a co-star, in this case F. Murray Abraham, who won the Oscar for his performance as Mozart's vindictive nemesis Salieri. Few of Hulce's subsequent roles have taken as full advantage of his gifts as did *Amadeus,* though the actor had some good moments as a family "black sheep" in *Paternity* (1989). Hulce has also occasionally shown up on television, notably in the 1990 TV movie about three martyred civil rights workers, *Murder in Mississippi.* **Selected Works:** *Black Rainbow* (1991), *Inner Circle* (1991), *Parenthood* (1989), *Fearless* (1993), *Mary Shelley's Frankenstein* (1994)

# Helen Hunt

**Born:** June 15, 1963; Los Angeles, CA

**Years Active in the Industry:** by decade

| 10ˢ | 20ˢ | 30ˢ | 40ˢ | 50ˢ | 60ˢ | 70ˢ | 80ˢ | 90ˢ |
|-----|-----|-----|-----|-----|-----|-----|-----|-----|
|     |     |     |     |     |     |     | ■   | ■   |

A precociously talented youngster, New Jerseyite Helen Hunt was trained for the arts at Michigan's Interlochen School and at Chicago's Goodman Theater. From age ten, Hunt was drawing paychecks as a TV actress; before she was 17, she had appeared as a regular on two series, *Swiss Family Robinson* (1975) and *The Fitzpatricks* (1977). Hunt proved she was more than just a workaday kid actress with her starring performance in the fact-based 1979 TV movie *The Miracle of Kathy Miller,* in which she played a high school athlete who overcame severe mental and physical damage brought on by a highway accident. While she had been appearing in films as early as 1977's *Rollercoaster,* Hunt was never groomed as a star player; it is possible that her close resemblance to another child actress, Jodie Foster, held her back from more important roles. After taking on her first adult role in the 1982 sitcom *It Takes Two,* Hunt's film assignments improved, with sizable roles in *Peggy Sue Got Married* (1986), *Project X* (1987) and *Next of Kin* (1991); she gained a small measure of cult status by appearing in a brace of sci-fi films, *Trancers 2* (1991) and *Trancers 3* (1992). In 1992, Hunt landed her longest-lasting acting assignment to date, as co-star of the Paul Reiser-created comedy series *Mad About You,* with which she has earned Emmy and Golden Globe Awards. **Selected Works:** *Into the Badlands* (1992), *Mr. Saturday Night* (1992), *Murder in New Hampshire: The Pamela Smart Story* (1991), *The Waterdance* (1991), *Kiss of Death* (1995)

# Linda Hunt

**Born:** April 2, 1945; Morristown, NJ

**Years Active in the Industry:** by decade

| 10s | 20s | 30s | 40s | 50s | 60s | 70s | 80s | 90s |
|-----|-----|-----|-----|-----|-----|-----|-----|-----|
|     |     |     |     |     |     |     |     |     |

While still a child, Linda Hunt decided to become an actress, and began taking drama lessons at age 13. As she was quite small (4'9") and not a great beauty, she also studied directing, in case she never landed any acting roles. Hunt majored in directing at the prestigious Goodman Theater School in Chicago, and went on to spend several years in New York, working as a stage manager, director, and occasionally as an actress; during some of that time she worked in alternative theater with companies such as La Mama and the Open Theater. Following years of getting bit parts and directing for a children's theater, Hunt finally started landing good roles and ultimately won two Obie Awards and a Tony nomination. She debuted onscreen in Robert Altman's *Popeye* (1980), but it was her second film, *The Year of Living Dangerously* (1983), that made her internationally known; for her portrayal of a male Indonesian dwarf, she won a Best Supporting Actress Oscar. She went on to have a fairly busy and successful film career as a character and supporting actress, often winning raves for her performances. **Selected Works:** *If Looks Could Kill* (1991), *Kindergarten Cop* (1990), *Maverick* (1994), *Rain Without Thunder* (1993)

# Marsha Hunt

**Born:** October 17, 1917; Chicago, IL

**Years Active in the Industry:** by decade

| 10s | 20s | 30s | 40s | 50s | 60s | 70s | 80s | 90s |
|-----|-----|-----|-----|-----|-----|-----|-----|-----|
|     |     |     |     |     |     |     |     |     |

American actress Marsha Hunt, born Marcia Hunt, attended the Theodore Irving School of Dramatics while still a teenager. Simultaneously, she worked as a Powers model until she debuted onscreen in *The Virginia Judge* (1935) at age 18. Hunt went on to become a very busy screen actress through the early '50s. In the '30s she appeared in supporting roles such as bridesmaids and coeds, while in the '40s she played leads in second features and second leads and supporting roles in major productions. In the early '50s, during the heyday of the McCarthy Era "witch hunts," she was blacklisted by the studios for her liberal political beliefs, and after 1952 she appeared in only a handful of films, as well as the TV series *Peck's Bad Girl.* Through the '80s, however, she still turned up occasionally in character roles on TV. From 1938-43 she was married to editor (now director) Jerry Hopper. After 1946 she was married to movie/TV scriptwriter Robert Presnell Jr., who died in 1986. She remains active in social issues, lending her help to organizations involved with such issues as peace, poverty, population, and pollution; she is a frequent speaker on the issues that concern her, and she serves on nearly a dozen Boards of Directors. She was last onscreen in *Johnny Got His Gun* (1971). **Selected Works:** *Double Cross* (1992), *Human Comedy* (1943), *Valley of Decision* (1945)

# Holly Hunter

**Born:** March 20, 1958; Conyers, GA

**Years Active in the Industry:** by decade

| 10s | 20s | 30s | 40s | 50s | 60s | 70s | 80s | 90s |
|-----|-----|-----|-----|-----|-----|-----|-----|-----|
|     |     |     |     |     |     |     |     |     |

Diminutive Southern actress of stage and screen Holly Hunter was raised on a large cattle and hay farm in Georgia. As a young woman, she moved to New York in search of an acting career; there she studied drama at the Carnegie Mellon Institute and landed roles off-Broadway, notably in the Beth Henley plays *Crimes of the Heart* and *The Miss Firecracker Contest.* Hunter debuted onscreen in a small role in the horror film *The Burning* (1981), going on to small roles in three more movies before landing her first substantial part as a woman who steals a baby in the Coen Brothers' comedy *Raising Arizona* (1987). For her portrayal of a TV executive in *Broadcast News* (1987) she won Best Actress Awards from the New York and Los Angeles Film Critics and the National Board of Review, as well as an Oscar nomination. Hunter also earned an Emmy for her work in the TV movie *Roe vs. Wade* (1989). Her most widely acclaimed performance, however, is that of a Scottish mute who expresses her emotions through music in *The Piano* (1993), for which she won the Oscar for Best Actress as well as numerous other critical awards. **Selected Works:** *The Firm* (1993), *Once Around* (1991), *The Positively True Adventures of the Alleged Texas Cheerleader-Murdering Mom* (1993)

# Kim Hunter (Janet Cole)

**Born:** November 12, 1922; Detroit, MI

**Years Active in the Industry:** by decade

| 10s | 20s | 30s | 40s | 50s | 60s | 70s | 80s | 90s |
|-----|-----|-----|-----|-----|-----|-----|-----|-----|

American actress Kim Hunter trained at the Actors Studio. At age 17 she debuted onscreen in *The Seventh Victim* (1943), then went on to several subpar films. Her popularity was renewed with her appearance in the British fantasy *A Matter of Life and Death* (1946). In 1947 she created the role of Stella Kowalski on Broadway in Tennessee Williams's *A Streetcar Named Desire,* then reprised the role in the film version (1951); for her performance she won the Best Supporting Actress Oscar. Shortly afterwards her career was dealt a terrible blow when her name appeared without cause in *Red Channels,* a Red-scare pamphlet, and she was blacklisted. Several years later she was called as the star witness in a court case instigated by another *Red Channels* victim, and her testimony discredited the pamphlet and made it possible for dozens of other performers to reclaim their careers. After this she returned to films sporadically, and also did much work on stage and TV; among other roles, she appeared as a female ape in three *Planet of the Apes* films. She is the author of *Loose in the Kitchen,* a combination autobiography-cookbook. She is married to writer Robert Emmett. **Selected Works:** *Stairway to Heaven* (1946)

# Ross Hunter (Martin Fuss)

**Born:** May 6, 1916; Cleveland, OH

**Years Active in the Industry:** by decade

| 10s | 20s | 30s | 40s | 50s | 60s | 70s | 80s | 90s |
|-----|-----|-----|-----|-----|-----|-----|-----|-----|

Upon his graduation from Western Reserve University, American producer Ross Hunter was content to settle into a school teaching career. But his Glenn Ford-like good looks weren't easily ignored; he was offered a contract with Columbia pictures in 1944. Hunter appeared prominently but not memorably in such B musicals as *Louisiana Hayride* (1944), *Ever Since Venus* (1945) and

*The Sweetheart of Sigma Chi* (1946). When the contract ended, Hunter's career stalled, and he went back to teaching temporarily. He re-entered movies on the production end, attaining a staff producer post at Universal in 1953 on the strength of his previous credits as a theatrical producer and director. With 1954's *Magnificent Obsession,* Hunter hit upon the winning formula that would sustain him for the next two years: beautiful stars (male and female), beautiful costumes, beautiful sets, beautiful music, and an abundance of reliable story elements ranging from old-fashioned tear-wringing to tickle 'n' tease sexual humor. Under Hunter's auspices, Rock Hudson became a major name; Lana Turner's flagging career received a coiffed and permed boost; and Doris Day was reinvented as America's most popular middle-aged virgin. While many of Hunter's productions were screen originals (*Pillow Talk* [1959], *Portrait in Black* [1960], and *That Touch of Mink* [1962]), the producer also displayed an absolute genius for attractively updating old warhorses like *Imitation of Life* (1959), *Back Street* (1961), and *Madame X* (1965). He also knew how to make the cash registers ring with screen adaptations of stage hits like *Flower Drum Song* (1961) and *The Chalk Garden* (1964), even if these overproduced properties lost a lot of their charm along the way. After closing out his Universal career with the blockbuster *Airport* (1970), Hunter moved to Columbia, where his 1973 musical remake of *Lost Horizon* all but ruined the studio, earning the unflattering nickname "Lost Investments." While his foolproof formula had finally been proven foolish, Hunter moved on to TV, where he continued for several years to turn out high-gloss, big-star TV movies and pilot films.

# Isabelle Huppert

**Born:** March 16, 1955; Paris, France

**Years Active in the Industry:** by decade

| 10s | 20s | 30s | 40s | 50s | 60s | 70s | 80s | 90s |
|-----|-----|-----|-----|-----|-----|-----|-----|-----|

Even while approaching her fourth decade, French actress Isabelle Huppert has retained her fresh, gamine-like beauty. A graduate of the Conservatoire National d'Art Dramatique, Huppert made her first film, *Growing Up,* at age 16. Exhibiting a range that permits her to convincingly play everything from innocents to trollops and murderers, Huppert has gained fame (and several international awards) in such films as *The Lacemaker* (1977), *Entre Nous* (1983), *Story of Women* (1988), *A Woman's Revenge* (1990) and *Madame Bovary* (1991). Such was Huppert's talent and fan following that she was able to emerge from the career-busting fiasco *Heaven's Gate* (1980) with her reputation and prestige intact. **Selected Works:** *Loulou* (1980), *Amateur* (1994)

# John Hurt

**Born:** January 22, 1940; Shirebrook, Derbyshire, England

**Years Active in the Industry:** by decade

| 10s | 20s | 30s | 40s | 50s | 60s | 70s | 80s | 90s |
|-----|-----|-----|-----|-----|-----|-----|-----|-----|
|     |     |     |     |     | ■   | ■   | ■   | ■   |

Originally, versatile British actor of stage and screen John Hurt aspired to be a painter and trained at the Grimsby Art School and St. Martin's School of Art, but he switched directions and enrolled in the Royal Academy of Dramatic Arts. In 1962 he made his professional stage debut and also appeared in his first film, *The Wild and the Willing*. He first made an impression onscreen as the ambitious Rich in *A Man for All Seasons* (1966), his third film. From there he alternated stage and screen work, and also played the insane Emperor Caligula in the BBC TV production *I, Claudius*, which won him his great public acclaim. For his portrayal of a drug addict in *Midnight Express* (1978), he received a Best Supporting Actor Oscar nomination. He earned tremendous praise (and a Best Actor Oscar nomination) for his work as the deformed title character in *The Elephant Man* (1980), a role which required him to hide his face entirely beneath a great deal of prosthetic make-up. His film work in the '80s was inconsistent, and his career moved in the direction of character parts and away from leads. He has also done voice-over acting for such animated features as *Watership Down* (1978), *The Plague Dogs* (1982), and *The Black Cauldron* (1985). **Selected Works:** *Alien* (1979), *Field* (1990), *King Ralph* (1991), *Monolith* (1993), *Second Best* (1994)

# Mary Beth Hurt (Mary Beth Supinger)

**Born:** September 26, 1948; Marshalltown, IA

**Years Active in the Industry:** by decade

| 10s | 20s | 30s | 40s | 50s | 60s | 70s | 80s | 90s |
|-----|-----|-----|-----|-----|-----|-----|-----|-----|
|     |     |     |     |     |     | ■   | ■   | ■   |

American actress Mary Beth Hurt trained for the theater at New York University's School of the Arts. She then spent a year in London, where she performed with the Questers, a well-known amateur theater troupe. In 1972 she made her professional debut with the New York Shakespeare Festival, then went on to a very successful stage career on Broadway and elsewhere; she won two Obie awards (one for her work in the play *Crimes of the Heart*) and was nominated for a Tony for *Trelawney of the Wells*. Her theater work impressed filmmaker Woody Allen, who cast her in a supporting role in her screen debut, *Interiors* (1978), Allen's first non-comedy. This won her the co-lead in Joan Micklin Silver's *Head Over Heels* (1979). Hurt has remained primarily a stage actress, appearing in films every two years or so. From 1972-82 she was married to actor William Hurt. She is now married to writer-director Paul Schrader, and co-starred in his film *Light Sleeper* (1992). **Selected Works:** *Defenseless* (1991), *World According to Garp* (1982), *Age of Innocence* (1993), *Six Degrees of Separation* (1993)

# William Hurt

**Born:** March 20, 1950; Washington, DC

**Years Active in the Industry:** by decade

| 10s | 20s | 30s | 40s | 50s | 60s | 70s | 80s | 90s |
|-----|-----|-----|-----|-----|-----|-----|-----|-----|
|     |     |     |     |     |     |     | ■   | ■   |

Distinguished American actor William Hurt, one of the top leading men in 1980's, is notable for his intensity and ability to effectively portray complex characters. Although born in Washington

DC, Hurt had already seen much of the world by the time he was grown, as his father worked for the State Department. His early years were spent in the South Pacific near Guam. When he was six years old, Hurt's parents divorced, and he moved to Manhattan with his mother, summering with his father in a variety of international locales, including Sudan. When he was ten, Hurt's life dramatically changed when he became a stepson to Henry Luce III, the heir to the Time-Life empire. Soon after the wedding he was sent to a boarding school in Massachusetts. There he found comfort in acting. Later his stepfather convinced him to study theology, which Hurt did for three years before marrying aspiring actress Mary Beth Hurt and heading for London to study drama during his senior year. Upon their return to the U.S., Hurt studied drama at Julliard. By this time his marriage was failing so he divorced his wife, got a motorcycle and headed cross-country for the Shakespeare festival in Ashland, Oregon, where he made his professional debut. Later he joined the New York's Circle Repertory Company, and went on to receive critical acclaim, including an Obie Award in 1977 for his work in the play *My Life*. He made his feature film debut in Ken Russell's *Altered States* (1980), but it was not until he appeared opposite Kathleen Turner in *Body Heat* (1981) that he became a star and sex symbol. For his sensitive portrayal of a gay prisoner in *Kiss of the Spider Woman* (1985), Hurt won an Oscar for Best Actor and a similar honor at Cannes. Hurt was again nominated for Best Actor Oscars for his two subsequent films *Children of a Lesser God* (1986) and *Broadcast News* (1987). As bright as his star shone on stage and screen, by the end of the '80s, a darker side of Hurt was exposed when he was sued by his former live-in love and mother of his daughter Alex, ballet dancer Sandra Jennings, who claimed to be his common-law wife. In court, allegations of his heavy drinking, depressive incidents and violent temper were aired to the public. He was also involved for several years with *Lesser God* co-star Marlee Matlin. Despite his personal problems, Hurt remains a fine and busy actor. He later married Heidi Henderson, daughter of bandleader Skitch Henderson. **Selected Works:** *Doctor* (1991), *I Love You to Death* (1990), *Until the End of the World* (1991), *Trial by Jury* (1994), *Second Best* (1994)

# Angelica Huston

**Born:** July 9, 1951; Los Angeles, CA

**Years Active in the Industry:** by decade

| 10s | 20s | 30s | 40s | 50s | 60s | 70s | 80s | 90s |
|-----|-----|-----|-----|-----|-----|-----|-----|-----|
|     |     |     |     |     |     |     |     |     |

Distinctive, versatile American actress Anjelica Huston, the daughter of celebrated filmmaker John Huston, was brought up in Ireland and moved to London at age 11 after her parents' divorce. She debuted onscreen at age 16 in her father's *A Walk with Love and Death* (1969), then appeared in only two more movies during the '70s. For some time she was a successful model for *Vogue*, and at age 30 Huston began working with the famed acting coach Peggy Fleury. After a few small parts she co-starred with Jack Nicholson (with whom she was romantically involved for 17 years) in her father's Mafia semi-comedy, *Prizzi's Honor* (1985), for which she won the Best Supporting Actress Oscar; from there she went on to a number of widely varied lead roles in commendable films. For her portrayal of a con artist in *The Grifters* (1990) she received a Best Actress Oscar nomination. Huston has also made acclaimed TV appearances in two miniseries, *Lonesome Dove* (1989) and *Buffalo Girls* (1995). **Selected Works:** *Manhattan Murder Mystery* (1993), *Addams Family Values* (1993)

# John Huston

**Born:** August 5, 1906; Nevada, MO
**Died:** August 28, 1987; Middletown, RI

**Years Active in the Industry:** by decade

| 10s | 20s | 30s | 40s | 50s | 60s | 70s | 80s | 90s |
|-----|-----|-----|-----|-----|-----|-----|-----|-----|
|     |     |     |     |     |     |     |     |     |

The son of actor Walter Huston, John Huston lived a freewheeling childhood, moving between the vaudeville stage and legitimate theater with his father, becoming a champion amateur boxer in high school, and serving a stint in the cavalry. Huston then went on to become a writer. It was as a screenwriter that he first went to Hollywood, where his father helped him secure work. He then drifted to London to work in the British film industry and studied painting for a time before returning to America to have a try at acting on the stage. He returned to Hollywood in 1937 and once again established himself as a screenwriter. It was at Warner Bros. that he broke into directing, in his own adaptation of the novel *The Maltese Falcon* (1941), which made Huston into one of the company's top filmmakers and Humphrey Bogart into a major leading man. Over the next four and a half decades, Huston made his reputation as one of Hollywood's most distinctive directors, with a liter-

ate, idiosyncratic style that gave his actors a chance to project a full range of characteristics—some of them very offbeat and often disturbing—that other directors suppressed. Though this technique was not always suited to the material that he was dealing with, his work was always interesting and frequently entertaining to watch, even in failed films such as *The Kremlin Letter* (1970). He seemed equally adept in all genres, except musicals—his only one, *Annie* (1982) is something of a dud. Among his most notable pictures were *The Treasure of the Sierra Madre* (1948), *The Asphalt Jungle* (1950), *Moulin Rouge* (1952), *The African Queen* (1951), *Beat The Devil* (1953), *Moby Dick* (1956), *The Unforgiven* (1960), *The Misfits* (1961), *The Life and Times of Judge Roy Bean* (1972), *The Man Who Would Be King* (1975), *Wise Blood* (1979), and *Prizzi's Honor* (1985). Huston also made many notable appearances as an actor, in his own and in many other people's films, of which the best was probably his work in Roman Polanski's *Chinatown* (1974). **Selected Works:** *Dead* (1987), *Sergeant York* (1941), *Under the Volcano* (1984), *Dr. Ehrlich's Magic Bullet* (1940), *Heaven Knows, Mr. Allison* (1957)

# Walter Huston (Walter Houghston)

**Born:** April 6, 1884; Toronto, Ontario, Canada
**Died:** April 7, 1950; Beverly Hills, CA

**Years Active in the Industry:** by decade

| 10s | 20s | 30s | 40s | 50s | 60s | 70s | 80s | 90s |
|-----|-----|-----|-----|-----|-----|-----|-----|-----|
|     |     |     |     |     |     |     |     |     |

Canadian-born actor Walter Huston enjoyed an early theatrical life of roller-coaster proportions which he doggedly pursued, despite a lifelong suffering of "stage fright." Taking nickel and dime performing jobs, quitting to pursue "real" work—an engineering job came to an end when his inept attempts to fix a town's reservoir nearly resulted in a flood—then returning to bit roles were all part of Huston's early days. Before 1910, Huston had toured in vaudeville, worked in stock companies, tried to maintain a normal married life (though temptations to stray sexually were at times irresistable), and fathered a son whose life was twice as tempestuous as Walter's: future director John Huston. The barnstorming days ended when Huston got his first major Broadway role in *Mr. Pitt* (1924), which led to several successful New York seasons for the actor in a variety of plays. His stage and vaudeville training made him an excellent candidate for talkies; Huston launched his movie career with *Gen-*

*tlemen of the Press* (1929), and spent the 1930s playing everything from a Mexican bandit to President Lincoln. Returning to Broadway in 1938 for the musical comedy *Knickerbocker Holiday*, Huston, in the role of 17th century New Amsterdam governor Peter Minuit, achieved theatrical immortality with his poignant rendition of the show's top tune, "September Song," the recording of which curiously became a fixture of the Hit Parade *after* Huston's death in 1950. Throughout the 1940s, Huston offered a gallery of memorable screen portrayals, from the diabolical Mr. Scratch in *All That Money Can Buy* (1941) to George M. Cohan's father in *Yankee Doodle Dandy* (1942). Still, it was only after removing his expensive false teeth and trading his fancy duds for a dusty bindlestiff's outfit that the actor would win an Academy Award, for his portrayal of the cackling old prospector Howard in *The Treasure of the Sierra Madre* (1948), directed by his son. At the time of his death, Huston was preparing to take on the part of the "world's oldest counterfeiter" in *Mr. 880*, a role ultimately played by fellow Oscar winner Edmund Gwenn. **Selected Works:** *Devil and Daniel Webster* (1941), *Dodsworth* (1936), *Duel in the Sun* (1946), *Prizefighter and the Lady* (1933), *Of Human Hearts* (1938)

# Betty Hutton (Betty June Thornburg)

**Born:** February 26, 1921; Battle Creek, MI

**Years Active in the Industry:** by decade

| 10s | 20s | 30s | 40s | 50s | 60s | 70s | 80s | 90s |
|-----|-----|-----|-----|-----|-----|-----|-----|-----|
|     |     |     |     |     |     |     |     |     |

As a child, American actress Betty Hutton sang on street corners to help support her family after her father died. She was singing with bands by the time she was 13, eventually becoming the vocalist for the Vincent Lopez orchestra. Because of her exuberance and energy she became known as "The Blonde Bombshell." She debuted on Broadway in *Two for the Show* in 1940, then in 1941 signed a film contract with Paramount. Hutton debuted onscreen in *The Fleet's In* (1942), and for the next decade appeared in tailor-made comedic roles and occasional dramatic roles. She sabotaged her own career in 1952, however, when she demanded that her husband (choreographer Charles O'Curran) direct her films; the studio refused and she walked out on her contract, after which she appeared in only one more film. Over the next fifteen years she worked occasionally on stage and in nightclubs, and co-starred on Broadway in *Fade In Fade Out* in 1965. Her career going nowhere, she attempted suicide in 1972; a friendly priest helped her find work in a Catholic rectory, and eventually she enrolled in college and earned a master's degree. She went on to teach acting at two New England colleges. Her sister is actress Marion Thornburg. **Selected Works:** *Greatest Show on Earth* (1952), *Miracle of Morgan's Creek* (1944)

# Jim Hutton

**Born:** May 31, 1933; Binghamton, NY
**Died:** June 2, 1979; Los Angeles, CA

**Years Active in the Industry:** by decade

| 10s | 20s | 30s | 40s | 50s | 60s | 70s | 80s | 90s |
|-----|-----|-----|-----|-----|-----|-----|-----|-----|
|     |     |     |     |     |     |     |     |     |

American actor Jim Hutton was performing in a military show in Germany when he was discovered by director Douglas Sirk. Sirk promptly cast Hutton in *A Time to Love and a Time to Die* (1958), which though released by Universal, led to an MGM contract for the young actor. Evidently MGM had plans to turn Hutton into the new Jimmy Stewart, for the studio insisted upon casting their young star in roles calling for ingenuous clumsiness. Perhaps the quintessential Hutton role was as *The Horizontal Lieutenant* (1962), in which his constant bumbling eventually transforms him into a war hero. MGM frequently paired Hutton with another player of acute comic skill, Paula Prentiss; they worked so well together that many fans assumed Hutton and Prentiss were married—which must have been amusing to Paula's longtime husband Richard Benjamin. Hutton was allowed a few non-comedy "outdoors" roles in *Major Dundee* (1965) and *The Green Berets* (1969), but for the most part was locked into playing gangling young goofs. Oddly, Hutton's screen persona worked quite well for his TV-series role as Ellery Queen in the mid-1970s. The actor was charming and convincing as the self-effacing, deceptively preoccupied criminologist, especially when he turned to the camera 45 minutes into each *Ellery Queen* episode and invited the folks at home to help him solve the mystery. Hutton died of cancer at age 46—too soon to fully realize the success of his son, actor Timothy Hutton.

# Lauren Hutton

**Born:** November 17, 1943; Charleston, SC

**Years Active in the Industry:** by decade

| 10s | 20s | 30s | 40s | 50s | 60s | 70s | 80s | 90s |
|-----|-----|-----|-----|-----|-----|-----|-----|-----|
|     |     |     |     |     |     |     |     |     |

Born in South Carolina and raised in rural Florida, Lauren Hutton embarked on a modelling career in roundabout fashion by becoming a Playboy bunny at age 20. It wasn't long thereafter that the statuesque Hutton became a top fashion model, cover girl and commercial spokesperson. Though advised early on to correct the slight gap in her teeth, Hutton wisely retained this "imperfection," which gave her on-camera persona a down-home sensibility that other, more ethereal models lacked. She began appearing in films in 1968, hitting her stride with such movies as *Gator* (1976), *American Gigolo* (1978), and *Zorro, the Gay Blade* (1981). Unlike other actresses-turned-models, Hutton achieved critical acceptance fairly rapidly, earning respectable reviews for such projects as the 1977 TV miniseries *The Rheinman Exchange* and the 1984 adventure film *Lassiter* (in which she played a literally bloodthirsty villainess). Following the lead of Farrah Fawcett, Hutton made her stage debut in the harrowing revenge-for-a-rape stage play *Extremities* in 1983. In recent years, Hutton has cut down on her acting appearances to return successfully to modeling; she has also become a staunch and powerful activist for several political causes. **Selected Works:** *Fear* (1990), *My Father The Hero* (1994)

# Timothy Hutton

**Born:** August 16, 1960; Malibu, CA

**Years Active in the Industry:** by decade

| 10s | 20s | 30s | 40s | 50s | 60s | 70s | 80s | 90s |
|-----|-----|-----|-----|-----|-----|-----|-----|-----|

While still in high school, American actor Timothy Hutton, son of actor Jim Hutton, toured with his father in a stage production of *Harvey*. After high school he moved to southern California and managed to land roles in several TV films, notably *Friendly Fire* and *Young Love, First Love* (both 1979). He debuted onscreen as a troubled teenager in Robert Redford's first directorial effort, *Ordinary People* (1980). For his work in that film he won an Oscar for Best Supporting Actor, at the time the youngest actor to earn such an honor. Hutton soon became typecast as sensitive, somewhat wimpy youths in a string of major films, a mold he didn't break out of until the late '80s. Despite his auspicious beginning, most of Hutton's films have been financially unsuccessful. In 1984 he made his New York stage debut in *Orpheus Descending,* and in 1990 starred on Broadway in the hit romance *Prelude to a Kiss*. He has also done some directing, including an episode of the TV show *Amazing Stories* and a rock video made by the band The Cars. He married and divorced actress Debra Winger. **Selected Works:** *Dark Half* (1991), *Oldest Living Graduate* (1982), *Q & A* (1990), *Strangers* (1991), *French Kiss* (1995)

# Peter Hyams

**Born:** July 26, 1943; New York, NY

**Years Active in the Industry:** by decade

| 10s | 20s | 30s | 40s | 50s | 60s | 70s | 80s | 90s |
|-----|-----|-----|-----|-----|-----|-----|-----|-----|

An alumnus of Syracuse University and Hunter College, director/writer Peter Hyams entered show business as a CBS TV newscaster. His first feature film assignment was *T.R. Baskin* (1971), which he wrote and produced. His maiden directorial efforts were the well-received TV movies *The Rolling Man* and *Good-night My Love*, both broadcast in 1972. The films Hyams has directed for theatrical release have included such slick, satisfying fare as *Busting* (1974) (which stirred up negative publicity with its alleged anti-gay stance), *Peeper* (1976) and *Telefon* (1976). Perhaps his best film work was concentrated in the Alan Pakula/Oliver Stone school of sociopolitical paranoia: *Capricorn One* (1978) and *The Star Chamber* (1983). Much castigated for "daring" to follow Stanley Kubrick's *2001* with the only fitfully successful sequel *2010* (1983), Hyams exhibited a considerable amount of directorial skill in glossing over the plot holes that he himself, as screenwriter, concocted (he also handled the photography on *2010*, again doing a better job than many critics would admit). Among Hyams' most recent films are *Stay Tuned* (1992), a satire of cable TV, and *Timecop* (1994), a futuristic actioner. **Selected Works:** *Narrow Margin* (1990)

# Wilfrid Hyde-White

**Born:** May 12, 1903; Bourton-on-the-Water, England
**Died:** May 6, 1991; Woodland Hills, CA

**Years Active in the Industry:** by decade

| 10s | 20s | 30s | 40s | 50s | 60s | 70s | 80s | 90s |
|-----|-----|-----|-----|-----|-----|-----|-----|-----|

British actor Wilfrid Hyde-White entered the Royal Academy of Dramatic Art upon graduation from Marlborough College. After some stage work, he made his first film in 1934 and became a stalwart in British movies like *Rembrandt* (1936) and *The Demi-Paradise* (1943), often billed as merely "Hyde White" and specializing in benign but stuffy upper-class types. Hyde-White received a somewhat larger role than usual in *The Third Man* (1949), principally because his character was an amalgam of *two* characters who were originally written for the erstwhile British comedy team Basil Radford and Naunton Wayne. Working both sides of the continent, Hyde-White appeared in such American productions as *In Search of the Castaways* (1962) and *Gaily Gaily* (1969). His best-loved role was as Colonel Pickering in the 1964 Oscar-winner *My Fair Lady*, wherein he participated in two musical numbers, "The Rain in Spain" and "You Did It." Remaining in films until 1983, Hyde-White was still inducing audience chuckles in such films as *The Cat and the Canary* (1979), in which he appeared "posthumously" in a pre-filmed last will and testament. **Selected Works:** *Browning Version* (1951), *Winslow Boy* (1949), *Mudlark* (1950)

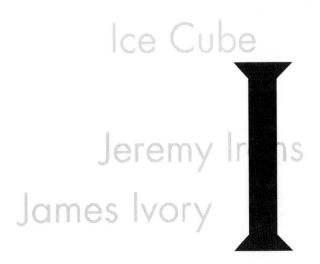

Amy Irving

Ice-T

Ice Cube

Jeremy Irons

James Ivory

# Ice Cube (Oshea Jackson)

**Born:** June 15, 1969

**Years Active in the Industry:** by decade

| 10ˢ | 20ˢ | 30ˢ | 40ˢ | 50ˢ | 60ˢ | 70ˢ | 80ˢ | 90ˢ |
|-----|-----|-----|-----|-----|-----|-----|-----|-----|
|     |     |     |     |     |     |     |     | ■   |

L.A.-born African American singer Ice Cube is one of the few performers in the rap-music world with strong academic credentials; while still using his given name, Oshea Jackson, the performer attended the Phoenix Institute of Technology. Ice Cube rose to prominence as lead singer of two popular groups: N.W.A. (the last two letters stand for "With Attitude") and the Lynch Mob. In 1991, director John Singleton cast Ice Cube in the pivotal and brilliantly essayed role of cynical ex-con Doughboy in Singleton's debut feature, *Boyz N the Hood* (1991) (the title was taken from Ice Cube's bestselling 1986 album); Ice Cube also appeared in Singleton's *Higher Learning* (1995). **Selected Works:** *The Freshman* (1990), *Trespass* (1992)

# Ice-T

**Born:** Not Available

**Years Active in the Industry:** by decade

| 10ˢ | 20ˢ | 30ˢ | 40ˢ | 50ˢ | 60ˢ | 70ˢ | 80ˢ | 90ˢ |
|-----|-----|-----|-----|-----|-----|-----|-----|-----|
|     |     |     |     |     |     |     | ■   |     |

Although he can't be much older than his mid-thirties, African American rap artist Ice-T prefers to keep mum about nearly everything in his past, including his birth date. What's known is that he spent a substantial portion of his youth in L.A. street gangs, that he did time in jail, and that he was in the Army for four years. In 1982, Ice-T became one of the first major West Coast rap performers with the release of his single "The Coldest Rap." Two years later he made his film bow in the popular *Breakin'* (1984), which he followed up with (what else?) *Breakin' II* (1985). His best film showing thus far has been in director Mario Van Peebles' 1991 film *New Jack City*. A 1990 Grammy winner for *Back on the Block*, Ice-T later churned up controversy on both political and showbiz fronts with his 1993 single "Cop Killer." **Selected Works:** *Ricochet* (1991), *Trespass* (1992)

# Rex Ingram (Reginald Ingram Montgomery Hitchcock)

**Born:** January 15, 1893; Dublin, Ireland
**Died:** 1969; North Hollywood, CA

**Years Active in the Industry:** by decade

| 10ˢ | 20ˢ | 30ˢ | 40ˢ | 50ˢ | 60ˢ | 70ˢ | 80ˢ | 90ˢ |
|-----|-----|-----|-----|-----|-----|-----|-----|-----|
| ■   | ■   | ■   | ■   | ■   | ■   |     |     |     |

Not to be confused with the African American actor of the same name, Irish-born actor/director Rex Ingram was a set designer and painter before entering films as a performer in 1914's *Necklace of Rameses*. Handsome enough to thrive as a film star, Ingram was more attracted to directing, making his debut in this capacity with the 1916 feature *The Great Problem*. A consummate artist, Ingram disliked the crass business haggling of Hollywood, and was particularly disenchanted with the level of American writing. He was drawn to the mystical, tragic novels of Spanish author Vicente Blasco Ibanez; many of these were unfilmable, but one Ibanez adaptation, *Four Horsemen of the Apocalypse* (1922), was not only a hit for Ingram but secured the stardom of Rudolph Valentino. Unwilling to submit to rushed production schedules and tight budgets, Ingram was not well loved in Hollywood, though he found a kindred spirit in fellow director Erich Von Stroheim, who like Ingram was meticulous in detail but careless in spending studio money. When Von Stroheim completed the eight-hour film drama *McTeague*, Ingram volunteered out of friendship to cut the film down to a more playable length. When Ingram's cut was whittled down further by MGM and released as *Greed* (1924), Ingram decided that he was sick of the so-called "butchers" of Hollywood and retreated to France, where he set up his own studios in Nice to direct films of his own choosing with his wife Alice Terry as star. Visually exquisite, with richly toned photography and beautifully tinted film stock, Ingram's features were artistic successes but box office disappointments. Seen today, such Ingram films as *Mare Nostrum* (1926) and *The Magician* (1927) are feasts for the eye, but rather stodgy and slow; moreover, though he fancied himself a writer, Ingram's screenplays are often confusing and disorganized. Still, he was a staunch individualist in a world of cookie-cutter studio directors, and Ingram had a loyal following, even if his films lost money for his American distributors. Utterly opposed to the introduction of talking pictures, Ingram made one sound film, *Baroud* (1931), which was filmed in Morocco. Thereafter, Ingram abandoned filmmaking for the tenets of Islam, devoting the last two decades of his life to introspective worship, writing, and sculpting. **Selected Works:** *Elmer Gantry* (1960), *Sahara* (1943), *Talk of the Town* (1942), *Thousand and One Nights* (1945), *Thief of Bagdad* (1940)

# Jeremy Irons

**Born:** 1948; Cowes, Isle of Wight, England

**Years Active in the Industry:** by decade

| 10s | 20s | 30s | 40s | 50s | 60s | 70s | 80s | 90s |
|-----|-----|-----|-----|-----|-----|-----|-----|-----|
|     |     |     |     |     |     |     | ■   | ■   |

Elegant, low-key, and handsome British lead actor Jeremy Irons, born into the upper class, trained at the Bristol Old Vic School for two years, then joined the Bristol Old Vic repertory company where he gained much experience working in everything from Shakespeare to contemporary dramas. He moved to London in 1971 and had a number of odd jobs before landing the role of John the Baptist in the hit musical *Godspell*. He went on to a successful early career in the West End Theatre and on TV, and debuted onscreen in *Nijinsky* (1980). In the early '80s he gained international attention with his starring role in a BBC TV serial adaptation of *Brideshead Revisited*, after which he was much in demand as a romantic leading man and went on to a steady film career. In 1984 he debuted on Broadway opposite Glenn Close in Tom Stoppard's *The Real Thing*, and in the mid-'80s he appeared in three lead roles with the Royal Shakespeare Company. For his work in David Cronenberg's *Dead Ringers* (1988) he won the New York Critics Best Actor Award, and for his work in *Reversal of Fortune* (1990) he won the Best Actor Oscar. He is married to actress Sinead Cusack, with whom he appeared in *Waterland* (1992) and in the Royal Shakespeare Company plays. He appeared with his son Sam and his father-in-law Cyril Cusack in the film *Danny the Champion of the World* (1987). Though he typically plays in dramatic films, Irons recently turned in a marvelous performance as the voice of the villainous lion Scar in Disney's *The Lion King* (1994) and portrayed a cool terrorist in the 1995 actioner *Die Hard with a Vengeance*. **Selected Works:** *Betrayal* (1983), *Damage* (1992), *Moonlighting* (1982)

# Amy Irving

**Born:** September 10, 1953; Palo Alto, CA

**Years Active in the Industry:** by decade

| 10s | 20s | 30s | 40s | 50s | 60s | 70s | 80s | 90s |
|-----|-----|-----|-----|-----|-----|-----|-----|-----|
|     |     |     |     |     |     | ■   | ■   | ■   |

American actress Amy Irving, daughter of actress Priscilla Painter, trained at San Francisco's American Conservatory Theater and in London. She went on to do much work on stage work and on TV, notably in the miniseries *The Far Pavilions*. She debuted onscreen as a sympathetic teenager in Brian De Palma's horror movie *Carrie* (1978), and was enlisted again by De Palma for her second film, *The Fury* (1979). Her film work has been only occasional, but is highlighted by her performance in Barbra Streisand's *Yentl* (1983), for which she received a Best Supporting Actress Oscar nomination. For her performance in the New York production of Athol Fugard's play *The Road to Mecca* she won an Obie award in 1988. She was married to filmmaker Steven Spielberg; upon their divorce she received a huge settlement. **Selected Works:** *Micki and Maude* (1984)

# Judith Ivey

**Born:** September 4, 1951; El Paso, TX

**Years Active in the Industry:** by decade

| 10s | 20s | 30s | 40s | 50s | 60s | 70s | 80s | 90s |
|-----|-----|-----|-----|-----|-----|-----|-----|-----|
|     |     |     |     |     |     |     | ■   | ■   |

Judith Ivey's acting career followed a direct line from Illinois State University to Chicago's Goodman Theatre. She was a notable Broadway success, with award-winning comedy performances in the plays *Steaming* and *Hurlyburly* to her credit. Judith's first film was the 1984 farce *The Lonely Guy*, in which she jilts title character Steve Martin in favor of nightclub star Steve Lawrence, then is reunited with Martin while throwing herself off a bridge (you had to be there). Most of her film roles have continued in this comic vein, though unlike *The Lonely Guy* these films have yet to find an appreciative audience. In 1990, Judith Ivey starred in her own TV sitcom, *Down Home*, and in 1992 she became a regular as on the long-running series *Designing Women*. **Selected Works:** *Decoration Day* (1990), *There Goes the Neighborhood* (1992)

# James Ivory

**Born:** June 7, 1928; Berkeley, CA

**Years Active in the Industry:** by decade

| 10s | 20s | 30s | 40s | 50s | 60s | 70s | 80s | 90s |
|-----|-----|-----|-----|-----|-----|-----|-----|-----|
|     |     |     |     |     | ■   | ■   | ■   | ■   |

Though born in California and raised in Oregon, film director James Ivory is often mistaken for an East Indian by fans and

less knowledgeable critics. This is because Ivory did the bulk of his earliest work in India, having been sent to that country by the Asia Society in 1960 on the strength of his documentary on Indian artifacts, *The Sword and the Flame.* Ivory first gained mass media fame for 1965's *Shakespeare Wallah,* an amusing but poignant study of a rundown British repertory theatre troupe touring India. The American-financed *The Guru* (1969) allowed Ivory to explore the then-current fascination amongst rock stars with transcendental meditation; it was a bit too Hollywood to be considered one of the director's best works, but it did lead to future American projects like *The Wild Party* (1975) (based on the Fatty Arbuckle scandal) and *Roseland* (1977). Meanwhile, Ivory was allowed more personal expression in his lower budgeted Indian-based films, notably *Bombay Talkie* (1969), *Mahatma and the Mad Boy* (1973) and *An Autobiography of a Princess* (1975). Since the early 1960s, Ivory had been in partnership with Indian-producer Ismail Merchant, a relationship which, despite innumerable heated arguments between the two men (many conducted during televised interviews!), has resulted in some of the finest films in the last three decades. The Merchant-Ivory combination came to full flower in the 1980s with such exquisite period pieces as *The Bostonians* (1984), *A Room with a View* (1986), *Howard's End* (1992) and *The Remains of the Day* (1992), each film distinguished by sumptuous decor, diligent attention to detail, and cast lists chock-full of some of Britain's finest acting talent. Ivory's signature as a director has been his ability to imbue a big-budget look to films that in fact were *very* economically produced, an achievement partly due to the willingness of major actors to toil for minimal salaries just for the privilege of working in a Merchant-Ivory production. **Selected Works:** *Mr. & Mrs. Bridge* (1991); *Jefferson in Paris* (1995)

# J

Glenda Jackson
Don Johnson
Al Jolson
Ruth Prawer Jhabvala
Curt Jurgens

## Glenda Jackson

**Born:** May 9, 1936; Birkenhead, Cheshire, England

**Years Active in the Industry:** by decade

| 10ˢ | 20ˢ | 30ˢ | 40ˢ | 50ˢ | 60ˢ | 70ˢ | 80ˢ | 90ˢ |
|-----|-----|-----|-----|-----|-----|-----|-----|-----|
|     |     |     |     |     |     |     |     |     |

Distinguished British leading lady Glenda Jackson is noted for her portrayals of intelligent, iron-willed characters on stage, screen, and television. A bricklayer's daughter, she dropped out of school to join an amateur theater group at age 16; she then spent a decade acting in provincial British repertory while supporting herself with a variety of odd jobs. Jackson went on to study at the Royal Academy of Dramatic Art, and in 1964 she joined the Royal Shakespeare Company. Her break came from playwright-director Peter Brook, who first cast her in his "Theater of Cruelty" revue in 1964, then as the mad Charlotte Corday on both the London and New York stage in *Marat/Sade;* in 1966 she reprised the role in the play's film version (her screen debut). This led to lead roles in two Ken Russell films, *Women in Love* (1969) and *The Music Lovers* (1971), which established her a significant and powerful screen personality. For her work in *Women in Love,* she won the Best Actress Oscar and the New York Film Critics Award for Best Actress. She went on to a number of lead roles in films of uneven quality through the '70s, and after 1980 appeared onscreen much less frequently as she devoted herself to the stage and politics. For her work in *A Touch of Class* (1973) she won another Best Actress Oscar. For her portrayal of Elizabeth I in the six-part BBC TV mini-series *Elizabeth R* she won an Emmy Award. She is known as a woman who holds strong convictions that are forcefully expressed. Long active in politics as a passionate and eloquent member of the British Labour Party, in 1992 she was elected Member of Parliament for Hampstead. **Selected Works:** *Sunday, Bloody Sunday* (1971), *Mary, Queen of Scots* (1971)

## Janet Jackson

**Born:** May 16, 1966

**Years Active in the Industry:** by decade

| 10ˢ | 20ˢ | 30ˢ | 40ˢ | 50ˢ | 60ˢ | 70ˢ | 80ˢ | 90ˢ |
|-----|-----|-----|-----|-----|-----|-----|-----|-----|
|     |     |     |     |     |     |     |     |     |

Of the many siblings of mega-star Michael Jackson, Michael's youngest sister Janet is one of the few with enough genuine talent to succeed without her family ties. Jackson's fame rests largely on her successful, elaborately produced music videos, wherein the talented singer and dancer projects a more accessible, realistic image than her otherworldly brother. She is also a skilled and agreeable actress, as witness her series-TV stints on *Good Times* (1977-78), *Diff'rent Strokes* (1981-82) and *Fame* (1984). In 1993, Janet Jackson made her movie debut as a South Central L.A. beautician in director John Singleton's *Poetic Justice* (1993); the film was no classic, but Jackson dominated every scene she was in, even those shared with notorious rap artist Tupac Shakur.

## Samuel L. Jackson

**Born:** 1949; Atlanta, GA

**Years Active in the Industry:** by decade

| 10ˢ | 20ˢ | 30ˢ | 40ˢ | 50ˢ | 60ˢ | 70ˢ | 80ˢ | 90ˢ |
|-----|-----|-----|-----|-----|-----|-----|-----|-----|
|     |     |     |     |     |     |     |     |     |

While African American actor Samuel L. Jackson prefers to keep the details of his formative years to himself, it is known that he graduated from Morehouse College in Atlanta, and that he was co-founder of Atlanta's black-oriented Just Us Theater (the name of the company was taken from a famous Richard Pryor routine). Jackson arrived in New York in 1977, and has acted continuously on stage, screen and TV ever since. After a plethora of character roles of varying sizes, Jackson was "discovered" by the public in the role of the hero's tempestuous drug-addict brother in 1991's *Jungle Fever,* directed by another Morehouse College alumnus, Spike Lee. *Jungle Fever* won Jackson a special acting prize at the Cannes Film Festival, and thereafter his career soared. Confronted

with sudden celebrity, Jackson stayed grounded by continuing to live in the Harlem brownstone where he'd resided since his stage days. 1994 was a particularly felicitous year for Jackson; while his appearances in *Jurrasic Park* (1993) and *Menace II Society* (1993) were still being seen in second-run houses, he co-starred with John Travolta as a mercurial hit man in Quentin Tarantino's *Pulp Fiction,* a performance that earned him an Oscar nomination; his performance in the quieter *Fresh* was acclaimed as well. The following year, one-time journeyman character actor was third-billed in the blockbuster action flick *Die Hard with a Vengeance.* **Selected Works:** *Juice* (1992), *Jurassic Park* (1993), *Patriot Games* (1992), *True Romance* (1993), *Losing Isaiah* (1995)

## Iréne Jacob

**Born:** 1966; Paris, France

**Years Active in the Industry:** by decade

| 10ˢ | 20ˢ | 30ˢ | 40ˢ | 50ˢ | 60ˢ | 70ˢ | 80ˢ | 90ˢ |
|---|---|---|---|---|---|---|---|---|
| | | | | | | | | |

French actress Irene Jacob entered the cult-icon realm with her first starring film. In director Krzystof Kieslowksi's *The Double Life of Veronique* (1991), Jacob plays two roles, a Polish girl named Veronika and her French counterpart Veronique. As their lives unfold in parallel fashion, Veronika is punished for her blind ambition, while Veronique is rewarded for thinking of others—and it is obvious that both characters represent the "flip sides" of one single personality. For her astonishing dual portrayal, she won a Cannes film festival prize. More recently, Jacob won acclaim from the critics with her starring role in Kieslowski's *Three Colors: Red.*

## Richard Jaeckel

**Born:** October 10, 1926; Long Beach, NY

**Years Active in the Industry:** by decade

| 10ˢ | 20ˢ | 30ˢ | 40ˢ | 50ˢ | 60ˢ | 70ˢ | 80ˢ | 90ˢ |
|---|---|---|---|---|---|---|---|---|
| | | | | | | | | |

Born R. Hanley Jaeckel (the "R" stood for nothing), young Richard Jaeckel arrived in Hollywood with his family in the early

1940s. Columnist Louella Parsons, a friend of Jaeckel's mother, got the boy a job as a mailman at the 20th Century-Fox studios. When the producers of Fox's *Guadalcanal Diary* found themselves in need of a baby-faced youth to play a callow marine private, Jaeckel was given a screen test. Despite his initial reluctance to play-act, Jaeckel accepted the *Guadalcanal Diary* assignment and remained in films for the next five decades, playing everything from wavy-haired romantic leads to crag-faced villains. In 1971, Jaeckel was nominated for a best supporting actor Oscar on the strength of his performance in *Sometimes a Great Notion.* Jaeckel has also been a regular in several TV series, usually appearing in dependable, authoritative roles: he was cowboy scout Tony Gentry in *Frontier Circus* (1962), Lt. Pete McNeil in *Banyon* (1972), firefighter Hank Myers in *Firehouse* (1974), federal agent Hank Klinger in *Salvage 1* (1979), Major Hawkins in *At Ease* (1983) (a rare—and expertly played—comedy role), and Master Chief Sam Rivers in *Supercarrier* (1988). **Selected Works:** *3:10 to Yuma* (1957), *Battleground* (1949), *Dirty Dozen* (1967), *Gunfighter* (1950), *Sands of Iwo Jima* (1949)

## Dean Jagger

**Born:** November 7, 1903; Lima, OH
**Died:** February 1991

**Years Active in the Industry:** by decade

| 10ˢ | 20ˢ | 30ˢ | 40ˢ | 50ˢ | 60ˢ | 70ˢ | 80ˢ | 90ˢ |
|---|---|---|---|---|---|---|---|---|
| | | | | | | | | |

Amiable lead and character actor Dean Jagger worked as a vaudeville and stage actor before debuting onscreen in 1929. During his long career (spanning over five decades), he played a wide variety of roles. The first few years of his screen career were spent in minor films, prompting him to quit making films in the mid-'30s and focus on Broadway; having made his name on stage, Jagger came back to films in 1940 to play lead roles. For his work in *Twelve O'Clock High* (1950), he won the Best Supporting Actor Oscar. He did much TV work, and in the '60s was popular as high school principal Albert Vance in the TV series *Mr. Novak.* **Selected Works:** *Bad Day at Black Rock* (1954), *Elmer Gantry* (1960), *Executive Suite* (1954), *Nun's Story* (1959), *Men in Her Life* (1941)

## Mick Jagger (Michael Philip Jagger)

**Born:** July 26, 1946; Dartford, Kent, England

**Years Active in the Industry:** by decade

| 10ˢ | 20ˢ | 30ˢ | 40ˢ | 50ˢ | 60ˢ | 70ˢ | 80ˢ | 90ˢ |
|---|---|---|---|---|---|---|---|---|
| | | | | | | | | |

Swaggering, thick-lipped Brit Mick Jagger has been the lead singer and (along with guitarist Keith Richards) main songwriter for the consistently popular and influential rock band the

Rolling Stones since 1962. His first feature film appearance, in 1969's *Sympathy for the Devil*, was in the company of the Stones. One year later, Jagger made his solo acting bow in *Ned Kelly*, in which he was ideally cast as "Australia's Jesse James." Since that time, Jagger's movie assignments have been confined to concert films, with the exception of his spirited turn as a bounty hunter in the otherwise wearisome *Freejack* (1992).

# Henry Jaglom

**Born:** January 26, 1943; London, England

**Years Active in the Industry:** by decade

| 10s | 20s | 30s | 40s | 50s | 60s | 70s | 80s | 90s |
|-----|-----|-----|-----|-----|-----|-----|-----|-----|

American actor/director/writer Henry Jaglom studied acting at the University of Pennsylvania, then completed his training at the Actors Studio in New York. Jaglom acted on stage and in TV, marking time in small roles until 1967, when Jaglom found a project that could provide his big break: a marathon documentary of the Israeli six-day war, which he filmed, wrote and edited, but which was never generally released. Back in the U.S. as an actor in 1968, Jaglom was able to attain backing for his first film directorial job, *A Safe Place* (1971). While capable of turning out a "safe" commercial film like *Always* (1985), Jaglom has preferred to work in a European-style cinema verite fashion, encouraging his actors to improvise within a "party" framework. The director's *Someone to Love* (1987), set during a birthday celebration, allowed Orson Welles in his last screen appearance to expose his philosophies to his heart's content. Jaglom's *Eating* (1990), which took place during *another* birthday bash, contained an incredibly self-revealing scene featuring Frances Bergen, Candice's mother. Jaglom's work is not always to everyone's taste, especially those films in which he self-indulgently cast himself in the leading role, but those willing to go along for the ride are in for a treat, albeit a long-winded one. **Selected Works:** *Babyfever* (1994), *House in the Hamptons* (1994)

# Emil Jannings (Theodor Friedrich Emil Janenz)

**Born:** July 23, 1884; Rorschach, Switzerland
**Died:** 1950

**Years Active in the Industry:** by decade

| 10s | 20s | 30s | 40s | 50s | 60s | 70s | 80s | 90s |
|-----|-----|-----|-----|-----|-----|-----|-----|-----|

Born into a middle-class home, German actor Emil Jannings ran away from home at age 16 to become a sailor, and ended up working as an assistant cook on a ocean liner. He returned home disillusioned, but soon took up the theater; at 18 he made his professional stage debut, going on to tour with several companies in numerous provincial towns. In 1906 he was invited to join Max Reinhardt's theater in Berlin, then considered to be the finest stage

troupe in the world. Over the following decade, he established himself as a significant stage actor. Jannings debuted onscreen in 1914, but the first five years of his film career were routine. In 1919 he began appearing in a string of Germanic-slanted historical dramas, portraying imposing historical figures such as Louis XV, Henry VIII, and Peter the Great; next he starred in a series of literary adaptations. By the mid-'20s he had an international reputation, and many considered him the world's greatest screen actor. In 1927 Paramount signed him and he moved to Hollywood, appearing in a number of films designed to showcase his gift for tragedy. Jannings won the very first Best Actor Academy Award for his first two American films, *The Last Command* (1928) and *The Way of All Flesh* (1927). Because of his thick German accent, the advent of sound ended his American career. He returned to Germany in 1929. When the Nazis came to power in 1933, he was enlisted to participate in the state's propaganda machine; an enthusiastic supporter of the Nazis, he spent the next decade-plus making films that supported Nazi ideology. Propaganda Minister Goebbels awarded him in 1938 with a medal and an appointment to head Tobis, the company that produced his films, and he was honored as "Artist of the State" in 1941. At war's end Jannings was blacklisted by the Allied authorities, and he never made another film. He died five years later, lonely and bitter.

# Derek Jarman

**Born:** January 31, 1942; Northwood, Middlesex, England
**Died:** February 19, 1994; London, England

**Years Active in the Industry:** by decade

| 10s | 20s | 30s | 40s | 50s | 60s | 70s | 80s | 90s |
|-----|-----|-----|-----|-----|-----|-----|-----|-----|

An accomplished painter, Derek Jarman entered films in the early '70s, designing sets for Ken Russell's *The Devils* (1971) and *Savage Messiah* (1972). After making numerous experimental

shorts, mostly in Super-8, he began helming features in 1979 with *Sebastiane*, a controversial gay-themed account of Saint Sebastian, in which all the dialogue was spoken in Latin. Over the next twenty years Jarman frequently interwove historical evocation and unexpected anachronisms, particularly in his biopics *Caravaggio* (1986) and *Wittgenstein* (1993). His landmark non-narrative features of the '80s, *The Angelic Conversation* (1985) and *The Last of England* (1987), offer a painter's sense of texture, with Jarman transferring Super-8 footage onto video for his editing, and then transferring the video onto 35-mm film. Radical gay politics, a constant theme in his films, emerged most forcefully in the '90s with *The Garden* (1990), which re-enacts incidents from the life of Christ with two gay lovers in place of Jesus; *Edward II* (1992), his fiery adaptation of Christopher Marlowe's 16th-century tragedy; and his last film *Blue* (1993), in which the sole visual element is an unchanging field of blue, while the soundtrack describes Jarman's thoughts and emotions in the face of his imminent death from AIDS.

# Jim Jarmusch

**Born:** January 22, 1954; Akron, OH

**Years Active in the Industry:** by decade

| 10s | 20s | 30s | 40s | 50s | 60s | 70s | 80s | 90s |
|-----|-----|-----|-----|-----|-----|-----|-----|-----|
|     |     |     |     |     |     |     | ■   | ■   |

Before becoming an off-beat filmmaker, Jim Jarmusch went to Paris in the early '70s to be a Beat poet. Exposure to the archives of the Cinematheque Francaise changed his direction to filmmaking. After getting a B.A., he worked as a teaching assistant for director Nicholas Ray at New York University Film School. In 1982 he shot his first film, *Permanent Vacation,* in 16mm at a cost of $12,000; this film featured many of his future trademarks, such as bizarre humor, minimalist camerawork, and a semi-improvised script comprised of a series of episodes. His second film was *Stranger Than Paradise* (1984); made for $150,000, it gained excellent distribution and became a cult hit, establishing his reputation as a filmmaker. His subsequent films have established him as one of today's most original American directors. **Selected Works:** *In the Soup* (1992), *Night on Earth* (1991)

# Maurice Jarre (Maurice Alexis Jarre)

**Born:** September 13, 1924; Lyons, France

**Years Active in the Industry:** by decade

| 10s | 20s | 30s | 40s | 50s | 60s | 70s | 80s | 90s |
|-----|-----|-----|-----|-----|-----|-----|-----|-----|
|     |     |     |     |     | ■   | ■   | ■   | ■   |

A student of the Paris Conservatoire, French composer Maurice Jarre was the musical director at Paris' Theatre National Populaire, when, in the early 1950s, he became intrigued with film work. His first movie assignment was the Georges Franju-directed short subject, *Hotel des Invalides* (1952). Here as in future projects, Jarre preferred to avoid the obvious in his scores, opting for muted and romantic effects where other film musicians might rely upon bombast. Jarres' three Oscar have all been for his work on the films of David Lean: *Lawrence of Arabia* (1962), *Doctor Zhivago* (1965) and *A Passage to India* (1984). The composer's *Zhivago* leitmotif "Lara's Theme" became a best-selling single—though it caused a brief rift with director Lean, who disapproved of hit songs that detracted from the films themselves. Jarre has also scored the films of directors as diverse as Alfred Hitchcock (*Topaz* [1969]), John Huston (*The Man Who Would Be King* [1975]), Peter Weir (*The Year of Living Dangerously* [1982]) and even satirist Jerry Zucker (*Top Secret!* [1984]). When Zucker decided to forego parody for romantic fantasy in 1990's *Ghost*, he engaged Jarre for the score—and the composer had yet another hit (with the help of Alex North's "Unchained Melody"). Jarre is the father of Jean-Michael Jarre, a popular composer in his own right. **Selected Works:** *Enemies, a Love Story* (1989), *Gorillas in the Mist* (1988), *Witness* (1985), *Fearless* (1993), *Hundred and One Nights* (1995)

# Allen Jenkins (Alfred McGonegal)

**Born:** April 9, 1900; New York, NY
**Died:** June 20, 1974; Los Angeles, CA

**Years Active in the Industry:** by decade

| 10s | 20s | 30s | 40s | 50s | 60s | 70s | 80s | 90s |
|-----|-----|-----|-----|-----|-----|-----|-----|-----|
|     | ■   | ■   | ■   | ■   | ■   | ■   |     |     |

The screen's premier "comic gangster," Allen Jenkins studied at the American Academy of Dramatic Arts and worked several years in regional stock companies and on Broadway before talking pictures created a demand for his talents in Hollywood. One of his first films was *Blessed Event* (1932), in which Jenkins played the role he'd originated in the stage version. This and most subsequent Allen Jenkins films were made at Warner Bros., where the actor made so many pictures that he was sometimes referred to as "the fifth Warner Brother." As outspoken and pugnacious off screen as on, Jenkins was a member in good standing of Hollywood's "Irish Mafia", a rotating band of Hibernian actors (including James Cagney, Pat O'Brien, Matt McHugh and Jimmy Gleason) who palled around incessantly. It is rumored that drinks were sometimes consumed, and that foremost of the non-abstainers was Jenkins, though his old friend and onetime roommate Jimmy Cagney insisted that Allen had gone "absolutely A.A." just before his death. Popular but undisciplined and profligate with his money, Jenkins was reduced to B films by the 1940s and 1950s, including occasional appearances in RKO's *Falcon* films and the *Bowery Boys* epics at Monogram; still, he was as game as ever, and capable of taking any sort of physical punishment meted out to his characters. TV offered several opportunities for Jenkins in the 1950s and 1960s, notably his supporting role on 1956's *Hey Jeannie,* a sitcom starring Scottish songstress Jeannie Carson, and 30 weeks' worth of voice-over work as Officer Dibble on the 1961 animated series *Top Cat.* Going the dinner theater and summer stock route in the 1960s, Jenkins was as wiry as ever onstage, but his eyesight had deteriorated to the point that he had to memorize where the furniture was set. Making ends meet between acting jobs, Jenkins took on work as varied as tool-and-die making for Douglas Aircraft and selling cars for a Santa Monica dealer. Asked in 1965 how he felt about "moonlighting", Jenkins (who in his heyday had commanded $4000 per week) growled, "I go where the work is and *do* what the work is! Moonlighting's a fact. The rest is for the birds." Towards the end of his life, Jenkins was hired for cameo roles by directors who fondly remembered the frail but still feisty actor from his glory days; one of Jenkins' last appearances was as a telegrapher in the final scene of Billy Wilder's *The Front Page* (1974). **Selected Works:** *Ball of Fire* (1941), *Dead End* (1937), *I Am a Fugitive from A Chain Gang* (1932), *Pillow Talk* (1959), *Tortilla Flat* (1942)

# Norman Jewison

**Born:** July 21, 1921; Toronto, Ontario, Canada

**Years Active in the Industry:** by decade

| 10ˢ | 20ˢ | 30ˢ | 40ˢ | 50ˢ | 60ˢ | 70ˢ | 80ˢ | 90ˢ |
|-----|-----|-----|-----|-----|-----|-----|-----|-----|

A writer and actor for the BBC, Norman Jewison returned to Canada to direct television. He started directing American television in the early 1960s, and helmed his first film in 1963. Jewison displayed a special flair for comedy with his films of the mid '60s, most notably *Send Me No Flowers* (1964) and *The Russians Are Coming, The Russians Are Coming* (1966); at the same time, he also showed a sure hand for guiding actors through provocative dramas with *The Cincinnati Kid* (1965), *In The Heat Of The Night* (1967), and *Jesus Christ Superstar* (1973). Drama has been Jewison's main interest in recent years, most notably with *A Soldier's Story* (1984), *Agnes Of God* (1985), although his romantic comedy *Moonstruck* (1987) achieved great success. **Selected Works:** *Fiddler on the Roof* (1971), *Other People's Money* (1991), *Just in Time* (1994), *Only You* (1994)

# Ruth Prawer Jhabvala

**Born:** May 7, 1927; Cologne, Germany

**Years Active in the Industry:** by decade

| 10ˢ | 20ˢ | 30ˢ | 40ˢ | 50ˢ | 60ˢ | 70ˢ | 80ˢ | 90ˢ |
|-----|-----|-----|-----|-----|-----|-----|-----|-----|

Ruth Prawer Jhabvala, born Ruth Prawer in Cologne, Germany and the daughter of Polish-Jewish parents, came to England as a young refugee with her family in 1939. She attended London University where she was an English major. She married Indian architect C.S.H. Jhabvala in 1951 and moved to New Delhi. There she began writing; during the mid '50s, many of her novels and short stories were published in England—many of her stories centered on the culture clash between the Indians and the British colonialists. By the mid '60s she was writing screenplays and began a long, productive association with the filmmaking team of James Ivory and Ismail Merchant who wanted to film her novel *The Householder*. She worked with them until the mid '80s and, together, the three created many distinguished films that focused on post-colonialist life. In 1984, after their usual type of film began to lose popularity, the three changed tactics and Jhabvala began adapting period novels, particularly those of Henry James and E.M. Forster. This change, with films such as *The Bostonians* (1984) and *A Room with a View* (1985), brought Merchant, Ivory, and Jhabvala acclaim from both critics and the public. The latter film also won Jhabvala an Oscar; she won again in 1992 with her adaptation of Forster's *Howards End.* Though she primarily works with Merchant-Ivory, she also occasionally writes for others as with her screenplay for John Schlesinger's *Madame Sousatzka* (1988). In 1993, she earned another Oscar nomination for her adaptation of Ishiguro's novel *The Remains of the Day.* **Selected Works:** *Mr. & Mrs. Bridge* (1991)

# Roland Joffe

**Born:** November 17, 1945; London, England

**Years Active in the Industry:** by decade

| 10ˢ | 20ˢ | 30ˢ | 40ˢ | 50ˢ | 60ˢ | 70ˢ | 80ˢ | 90ˢ |
|-----|-----|-----|-----|-----|-----|-----|-----|-----|

Briton Roland Joffe (*accent ague* over the E) was educated at Manchester University before pursuing a theatrical career. Joffe was one of the organizers and leading lights of the Young Vic, a troupe dedicated to experimenting with fresh and more chancy material. Eventually, Joffe would move to the *Old* Vic and the equally traditional National Theatre as a director. During his TV years, Joffe became established as a documentary director; he carried over the best of his "reality" techniques to his first feature film, *The Killing Fields* (1984), a harrowing account of Cambodia's Pol Pot regime. Many of Joffe's images, notably his shots of helicopters weaving eerily in and out of shimmering smoke, have since entered the standard lexicon of Vietnam-era films. For this debut film, Joffe was nominated for an Oscar for Best Director. Likewise impressive was his next Oscar-nominated effort, *The Mission* (1986), a tragic story of 18th century Brazil which was as hauntingly effective in recreating disastrous historical events as *Killing Fields* had been. Joffe's most recent period picture was *City of Joy* (1992), a Calcutta-based tale that served as a compendium all of Joffe's favorite film elements: altruism, disillusionment, clash of cultures, unbearable scenes of suffering and isolated images of breathtaking beauty.

# Don Johnson

**Born:** December 15, 1949; Flat Creek, MO

**Years Active in the Industry:** by decade

| 10ˢ | 20ˢ | 30ˢ | 40ˢ | 50ˢ | 60ˢ | 70ˢ | 80ˢ | 90ˢ |
|-----|-----|-----|-----|-----|-----|-----|-----|-----|

American actor Don Johnson debuted onscreen at age 16 as a well-off '60s "California boy" in *Good Morning ... And Goodbye* (1967), then went on to a string of roles as sexy or drugged-out youths in college-oriented films of the early '70s. His first notable lead role came in the cult classic *A Boy and His Dog* (1975). Johnson's film career entirely ceased from 1976-81, when he worked frequently in TV movies and had some theater roles. He became famous in the early '80s for his portrayal of flashy, well-dressed police detective Sonny Crockett in the hit TV series *Miami Vice*, which somewhat resuscitated his film career, although none of his movies has been a hit. He married actress Melanie Griffith while she was still in her teens; shortly thereafter they divorced, only to be remarried in 1989 and divorced again in 1995. They appeared together in *Paradise* (1991) and *Born Yesterday* (1992). **Selected Works:** *Guilty As Sin* (1993), *Hot Spot* (1990), *Tales of the Unexpected* (1991)

# Nunnally Johnson

**Born:** December 5, 1897; Columbus, GA
**Died:** March 24, 1977; Hollywood, CA

**Years Active in the Industry:** by decade

| 10s | 20s | 30s | 40s | 50s | 60s | 70s | 80s | 90s |
|-----|-----|-----|-----|-----|-----|-----|-----|-----|
| | | | | | | | | |

Starting out as a reporter in his native Georgia, Nunnally Johnson worked his way up the journalistic ladder to the New York *Herald Tribune*. A prolific writer, Johnson contributed fiction to such periodicals as *The New Yorker* and *The Saturday Evening Post*; one of his *Post* stories was adapted for the screen as the 1927 Clara Bow vehicle *Rough House Rosie*. Unlike other Manhattan-based writers, Johnson was attracted to film work. When his proposal to write movie criticism for *The New Yorker* was turned down by editor Harold Ross in 1933, Johnson decided to move to Hollywood, where he immediately found work for a screenwriter. Well known for his laconic, biting wit, Johnson became a close friend of several other well-known Tinseltown quipsters, notably Groucho Marx. His movie career was briefly jeopardized in the late 1930s when, under a pseudonym, he wrote a less than flattering *Saturday Evening Post* profile of powerful gossip columnist Louella Parsons. The crisis passed, and Johnson remained incredibly busy, particularly at 20th Century-Fox, where from 1935 onward he toiled as both screenwriter and associate producer. Among the many films benefitting from Johnson's expertise was 1940's *The Grapes of Wrath*, which costarred Dorris Bowden, a budding leading lady who gave up her career to become Johnson's wife. In partnership with one time Fox executive William Goetz, Johnson formed International Pictures in 1943, turning out such projects as *Woman in the Window* (1944) and *The Stranger* (1946) until International merged with Universal in 1946. Johnson returned to Fox as a producer, handling many of the best early CinemaScope efforts, notably 1953's *How to Marry a Millionaire*. He turned to directing in 1954 with the literate murder mystery *Black Widow*; though not terribly proficient visually, he had a sharp ear for intelligent, scintillating dialogue, as proven by such films as *The Man in the Grey Flannel Suit* (1956). Johnson's best directorial efforts include the pioneering multiple-personality drama *Three*

*Faces of Eve* (1957) and the sprightly all-star comedy *Oh, Men, Oh Women* (1957). While sweating through a difficult location shoot during the making of *The Angel Wore Red* (1960), Johnson suddenly decided he was too old and too wealthy to continue knocking himself out as a director, and he returned exclusively to screenwriting. Two years after his last film, *The Dirty Dozen* (1968), Johnson announced his formal retirement ("I simply put on my top hat and tails—and retired"); a collection of his letters to and from famous friends was published posthumously in 1981.

# Van Johnson (Charles Van Johnson)

**Born:** August 20, 1916; Newport, RI

**Years Active in the Industry:** by decade

| 10s | 20s | 30s | 40s | 50s | 60s | 70s | 80s | 90s |
|-----|-----|-----|-----|-----|-----|-----|-----|-----|
| | | | | | | | | |

Actor Van Johnson was a popular teen idol of the '40s and early '50s. With his Nordic blue eyes, strawberry hair and freckles, Johnson typified the mythical boy-next-door of WASPy World War II America. He was so popular amongst the bobby-soxers that he was dubbed "The Voiceless Sinatra." He was born in Newport, Rhode Island. As a youth, he worked as a Broadway chorus boy before coming to motion pictures. From the late '50s on, Johnson tried to become a more serious actor, but his boyish image continued to dog him. Since the '70s, Johnson has appeared in TV movies and has worked the dinner theater circuit. In 1985, he made a cameo appearance in Woody Allen's *The Purple Rose of Cairo*. **Selected Works:** *Battleground* (1949), *Caine Mutiny* (1954), *Human Comedy* (1943), *Madame Curie* (1943), *Thirty Seconds over Tokyo* (1944)

# Al Jolson (Asa Yoelson)

**Born:** June 7, 1886; Srednik, Lithuania
**Died:** October 23, 1950; San Francisco, CA

**Years Active in the Industry:** by decade

| 10s | 20s | 30s | 40s | 50s | 60s | 70s | 80s | 90s |
|-----|-----|-----|-----|-----|-----|-----|-----|-----|
| | | | | | | | | |

Legendary entertainer Al Jolson and his family left Russia when he was a child. The son of a cantor, he first sang in a synagogue. His first show business job was with a circus, which he ran away from home to join; in 1906 he became a black-faced cafe and vaudeville entertainer. After he began working on the New York stage in 1909, he rose to stardom, and was considered by many to be the greatest entertaining talent of his time. In 1923 he was signed by D. W. Griffith to appear in *Mammy's Boy*, but the film was never made. Three years later he sang three songs in an experimental sound short, *April Showers* (1926). The following year Jolson became immortal when he starred in *The Jazz Singer*, the world's first talkie (though most of the sound was background mu-

sic), in which he spoke several sentences including the famous line "You ain't heard nothin' yet." He next appeared in the part-talkie *The Singing Fool* (1928), which grossed more money than any film until *Gone with the Wind* (1939). Through the mid-'30s he starred in a number of formula musicals, but changing public tastes led to a gradual decline in his popularity. After Jolson received some attention for singing for troops in World War II, his life was the subject of the film *The Jolson Story* (1946), in which he dubbed the songs for star Larry Parks. The film was a great box office success, resulting in a sequel, *Jolson Sings Again* (1949); once more Jolson dubbed the songs, and this time appeared in a cameo face-to-face with Parks. From 1928-39 he was married to actress Ruby Keeler, with whom he appeared in *Go Into Your Dance* (1935). He went on to entertain troops in Korea, shortly after which he died of a heart attack.

# Buck Jones (Charles Frederick Gebhard)

**Born:** December 4, 1889; Vincennes, IN
**Died:** 1942

**Years Active in the Industry:** by decade

| 10s | 20s | 30s | 40s | 50s | 60s | 70s | 80s | 90s |
|-----|-----|-----|-----|-----|-----|-----|-----|-----|

Buck Jones was a very popular cowboy star with good looks, a great physique, outstanding riding skills, and a horse named Silver. An expert rider since childhood, he joined the U.S. cavalry at 17 and fought in Mexico and the Philippines. After 7 years he was discharged, going on to appear in circuses (he was a trick rider for Ringling Brothers) and wild west shows. In 1917 he began appearing as an extra and stuntman in films; within a year after his first lead role in *The Last Straw* (1920), he was an established star. Over the next seven years he starred in 57 films, surpassing Tom Mix and William S. Hart as the top cowboy star. Some of his films were boxing or car-chase flicks, in which he was billed as "Charles Jones." He then went on to make over 100 Buck Jones westerns exclusively through the early '40s. In 1936 he was the top western money maker, and ranked in the top ten from 1937-39; he also directed a number of films in the mid-'30s. In 1941-42 he was demoted to co-starring status in the *Rough Rider* series. While on a campaign to sell U.S. war bonds in December 1942, he died heroically trying to save others in a Boston nightclub fire.

# Chuck Jones

**Born:** September 21, 1912; Spokane, WA

**Years Active in the Industry:** by decade

| 10s | 20s | 30s | 40s | 50s | 60s | 70s | 80s | 90s |
|-----|-----|-----|-----|-----|-----|-----|-----|-----|

A cel washer for Ub Iwerks at Celebrity Pictures, Chuck Jones joined the Warner Bros. animation unit in 1933, and after writing and animating numerous cartoons, became a director of the Merrie Melodies series in 1938 with *The Night Watchman*. Over the next two decades he established himself as perhaps America's greatest maker of cartoons—a master at creating slapstick comedy who also had a special fondness for sudden moments of sophisticated repartee or subtle character expression. Working regularly with writer Michael Maltese, Jones brought new heights to Warners' greatest characters, particularly Daffy Duck (*The Scarlet Pumpernickel, Duck Dodgers In The 24-1/2 Century, Duck Amuck*) and Bugs Bunny (*Hair-Raising Hare, Rabbit Fire, What's Opera, Doc?*); he also created such beloved figures as the Road Runner and the Coyote (*Fast and Furry-ous*), Pepe Le Pew (*For Scent-Imental Reasons*), and the Three Bears (*A Bear for Punishment*). Jones further distinguished himself with numerous outstanding one-shot cartoons, including *The Dover Boys, Feed the Kitty*, and his classic, the singing-frog morality tale *One Froggy Morning*. In the mid-1960s he made several Tom & Jerry cartoons at MGM. More impressive was his work in the animated feature *The Phantom Tollbooth* (1969), co-directed by Abe Levitow; and his television adaptations of Rudyard Kipling (*Rikki-Tikki-Tavi* [1975]) and Dr. Seuss (*How The Grinch Stole Christmas* [1965]). In 1979 Jones created linking animation scenes for a feature-length reissue anthology of his Warners cartoons, *The Bugs Bunny/Road Runner Movie* (aka *The Great American Chase*). Most recently he has provided animated sequences for *Gremlins 2: The New Batch* (1990) and *Stay Tuned* (1992).

# James Earl Jones

**Born:** January 17, 1931; Arkabutla, MS

**Years Active in the Industry:** by decade

| 10s | 20s | 30s | 40s | 50s | 60s | 70s | 80s | 90s |
|-----|-----|-----|-----|-----|-----|-----|-----|-----|

James Earl Jones is a distinguished African American actor instantly recognizable for his deep, resonant Shakespearean voice and wide smile. The son of prizefighter and actor Robert Earl Jones, he was raised on a farm. In college, he briefly studied medicine but switched to drama. After serving with the Army he enrolled at the American Theater Wing in New York. He made his Broadway debut in 1957, then went on to appear in many plays before spending several seasons with Joseph Pap's New York Shakespeare Festival. Jones' biggest success onstage was as the star of *The Great White Hope* on Broadway (1966-68); for his work (por-

traying heavyweight champion Jack Jefferson) he received a Tony award. He had a small part in Stanley Kubric's *Dr. Strangelove* (1964), but did not begin to appear onscreen much until the '70s. In addition to stage and occasional film work, he also appeared as an African chieftain in the TV series *Tarzan* and was one of the first black actors to be cast as a regular on the soap opera *The Guiding Light* in 1967. Reprising his stage role, he received a Best Actor Oscar nomination and won a Golden Globe award for his work in the screen version of *The Great White Hope* (1970) and went on from there to have a busy screen career. He starred in the TV series *Paris* in 1979-80. Beginning in 1977, he provided the melodiously wicked voice of the villainous Darth Vader in the three *Star Wars* films. Since then he has continued to appear on stage, screen, and television. He also continues to provide voiceovers (he can frequently be heard on the CNN television network). His portrayal of the grouchy, reclusive writer opposite Kevin Costner in *Field of Dreams* (1989) is among his most notable turns. In 1987 he won another Tony Award, this time for his portrayal of a frustrated baseball player in August Wilson's *Fences*. Most recently, Jones provided the voice for Mufasa, the regal patriarch in Disney's animated film *The Lion King* (1994). **Selected Works:** *Hunt for Red October* (1990), *Patriot Games* (1992), *Sneakers* (1992), *Sommersby* (1993), *Clear and Present Danger* (1994)

## Jeffrey Jones

**Born:** September 28, 1947; Buffalo, NY

**Years Active in the Industry:** by decade

| 10s | 20s | 30s | 40s | 50s | 60s | 70s | 80s | 90s |
|-----|-----|-----|-----|-----|-----|-----|-----|-----|
|     |     |     |     |     |     |     |     |     |

Spindly blond American actor Jeffrey Jones studied premed at Lawrence University in Wisconsin before focusing his energies towards an acting career. After several seasons with Minneapolis' Guthrie Theater, Jones worked in South America, London and Canada, making his off-Broadway debut in 1973's *Lotta*. His first film was Robert Altman's *A Wedding* (1978), but to most moviegoers Jones' true "unveiling" was as Austria's Emperor Joseph II in the 1984 Oscar-winner *Amadeus*. Most of Jones' subsequent screen roles were of the corporate-villain variety, though he was capable of eliciting a great deal of audience empathy as the henpecked, ghost-plagued father of Wynona Rider in *Beetlejuice* (1989). This, as it turned out, was *not* the strangest

assignment in Jones' career: in 1989, he starred in the brief fantasy sitcom *The People Next Door,* as a comic-strip artist whose creations came to life at the most inopportune moments. **Selected Works:** *Hunt for Red October* (1990), *Ed Wood* (1994), *Houseguest* (1995)

## Shirley Jones

**Born:** March 31, 1934; Smithton, PA

**Years Active in the Industry:** by decade

| 10s | 20s | 30s | 40s | 50s | 60s | 70s | 80s | 90s |
|-----|-----|-----|-----|-----|-----|-----|-----|-----|
|     |     |     |     |     |     |     |     |     |

A singer almost from the time she learned to talk, American actress Shirley Jones was entered by her vocal coach in the Miss Pittsburgh contest at age 18. The attendant publicity led Jones to an audition with Rodgers and Hammerstein for potential stage work. Much taken by Jones' beautifully trained voice, the producers cast her as the leading lady in the expensive, prestigious film production of their theatrical smash *Oklahoma!* (1955). In 1956 Jones starred in another Rodgers and Hammerstein film adaptation, *Carousel;* this and her first film tended to limit her to sweet, peaches 'n' cream roles for the next several years. Thankfully, and with the full support of director Richard Brooks, Jones was able to break away from her screen stereotype with her role as a vengeful prostitute in *Elmer Gantry* (1960)—a powerfully flamboyant performance which won her an Academy Award. Alas, filmgoers preferred the "nice" Shirley, and it was back to goody-goody roles in such films as *The Music Man* (1962) and *A Ticklish Affair* (1963)—though critics heartily praises Jones' performances in these harmless confections. It was again for Brooks that Shirley had her next major dramatic film role, in 1969's *The Happy Ending,* which represented one of her last movie appearances before her four-year TV stint as the glamorous matriarch of *The Partridge Family.* This popular series did less for Jones than it did for her stepson, teen idol David Cassidy, but *The Partridge Family* is still raking in ratings (and residuals) on the rerun circuit. Her unhappy marriage to the late actor Jack Cassidy long in the past, Jones found domestic stability as the wife of actor/agent Marty Ingels, with whom she recently wrote a refreshingly candid dual biography.

## Tommy Lee Jones

**Born:** September 15, 1946; San Saba, TX

**Years Active in the Industry:** by decade

| 10s | 20s | 30s | 40s | 50s | 60s | 70s | 80s | 90s |
|-----|-----|-----|-----|-----|-----|-----|-----|-----|
|     |     |     |     |     |     |     |     |     |

An 18th generation Texan, actor Tommy Lee Jones attended Harvard University, where he roomed with future U.S. vice presi-

dent Al Gore. Though several of his less knowledgable fans have tended to dismiss Jones as a roughhewn redneck, the actor is equally at home on the polo fields (he's a champion player) as he was on the oil fields, where he made his living for many years. Jones made his stage bow in 1969 in *A Patriot for Me*; in 1970 he appeared in his first film, *Love Story* (listed way, way down the cast as one of Ryan O'Neal's frat buddies). Jones' first film leading role was in the obscure Canadian film *Eliza's Horoscope* (1970). After a stint on the daytime soap opera *One Life to Live*, Jones gained national attention in 1976, when he was cast in the title role in the TV miniseries *The Amazing Howard Hughes* (the resemblance, both vocally and visually, was positively uncanny). In 1982, he won an Emmy for his startling performance as murderer Gary Gilmore in *The Executioner's Song*. Eleven years later, Jones was honored with both an Oscar and a Golden Globe for his work in the movie blockbuster *The Fugitive* (1993). In recent years, the prolific Jones has adopted two distinct acting styles: subtle and sensitive for roles that call for such qualities, and over-the-top, Armour Star hamminess for such assignments as *Under Siege* (1993) and *Natural Born Killers* (1994). There was absolutely no controlling Jones in his broad portrayal of Two-Face in *Batman Forever* (1995), the film that put him in the same action-figure category as the "cast" of *Jurassic Park*. Reputed to be as irascible and unpredictable offscreen as on, Jones prefers to shun the Hollywood scene by living in San Antonio, Texas. **Selected Works:** *Coal Miner's Daughter* (1980), *JFK* (1991), *Lonesome Dove* (1989), *Client* (1994), *Blue Sky* (1994), *Cobb* (1994)

# Neil Jordan

**Born:** February 25, 1950; County Sligo, Ireland

**Years Active in the Industry:** by decade

| 10ˢ | 20ˢ | 30ˢ | 40ˢ | 50ˢ | 60ˢ | 70ˢ | 80ˢ | 90ˢ |
|-----|-----|-----|-----|-----|-----|-----|-----|-----|
|     |     |     |     |     |     |     | ■   | ■   |

An acclaimed author of fiction, Neil Jordan entered films in 1981 as script consultant on John Boorman's King Arthur tale *Excalibur*. He made a documentary on the making of Boorman's film, and after scripting *Traveler*, wrote and directed his first film, the stylish drama *Angel* (aka *Danny Boy*) in 1982. Jordan attracted international attention with his horror tale *The Company Of Wolves* (1985) and his crime drama *Mona Lisa* (1986). He then came to

the U.S., where he helmed two unimpressive comedies, *High Spirits* (1988) and *We're No Angels* (1989). Back in Ireland, Jordan strengthened his reputation with *The Miracle* (1991), a touching drama about Irish teens, and then scored a major hit with his striking drama of the IRA, *The Crying Game* (1992). Most recently he has returned to horror and Hollywood with his big-budget Anne Rice adaptation *Interview with the Vampire* (1994).

# Victor Jory

**Born:** November 23, 1902; Dawson City, AK
**Died:** 1982

**Years Active in the Industry:** by decade

| 10ˢ | 20ˢ | 30ˢ | 40ˢ | 50ˢ | 60ˢ | 70ˢ | 80ˢ | 90ˢ |
|-----|-----|-----|-----|-----|-----|-----|-----|-----|
|     |     | ■   | ■   | ■   | ■   | ■   |     |     |

With his burly physique, dark, saturnine face and lugubrious voice, Victor Jory was among the most commanding character actors ever to appear in American film. Before becoming an actor, Jory was the Coast Guard's boxing and wrestling champion. He made his feature film debut in 1932, going on to appear in more than 120 films over the next five decades. Early in his screen career Jory played occasional leads, then moved into character roles in a wide range of Hollywood films, most of them B-movies in which he was typecast as an evil-eyed heavy or villain. From 1929 he maintained an active stage career, going on to play leads in several Broadway productions; he also wrote two plays that were produced in New York, *Bodies by Fisher* and *Five Who Were Mad*. His wife was actress Jean Innes. **Selected Works:** *Adventures of Tom Sawyer* (1938), *Gone with the Wind* (1939), *King Steps Out* (1936), *State Fair* (1933)

# Raul Julia

**Born:** March 9, 1940; San Juan, Puerto Rico
**Died:** October 24, 1994

**Years Active in the Industry:** by decade

| 10ˢ | 20ˢ | 30ˢ | 40ˢ | 50ˢ | 60ˢ | 70ˢ | 80ˢ | 90ˢ |
|-----|-----|-----|-----|-----|-----|-----|-----|-----|
|     |     |     |     |     |     | ■   | ■   | ■   |

Born to a prosperous Puerto Rican family, suave and handsome leading man Raul Julia acted in school plays and in college before coming to the U.S. in 1964. After studying drama with Wynn

Handman, he made his New York stage debut in 1964 in a Spanish play. In 1966 he began a long association with Joseph Papp and the New York Shakespeare Festival. After debuting onscreen in *The Organization* (1971) with Sidney Poitier, he did another film the same year, then went until 1976 before getting another screen role; meanwhile he built his reputation on stage and TV, and frequently appeared on the children's educational show *Sesame Street.* For his portrayal of Macheath in *The Threepenny Opera,* Julia won a Tony award. His screen career did not take off until the early '80s, when Francis Ford Coppola enlisted him for the short-lived Zoetrope Studios stock company; he went on to appear in Coppola's *One from the Heart* (1982). The role for which Julia received the most acclaim was as a political prisoner in *Kiss of the Spider Woman* (1985). Although never making it into the realm of stardom, he sustained a busy screen career; he appeared in five films released in 1988 and four in 1990. He gained recognition from a younger generation for his portrayal of Gomez Addams in the popular comedy *The Addams Family* (1991) and its sequel. Julia died suddenly shortly after the filming of *Street Fighter* in 1994. **Selected Works:** *Havana* (1990), *Presumed Innocent* (1990), *Addams Family Values* (1993)

# Curt Jurgens

**Born:** December 13, 1915; Munich, Germany
**Died:** 1982

**Years Active in the Industry:** by decade

| 10ˢ | 20ˢ | 30ˢ | 40ˢ | 50ˢ | 60ˢ | 70ˢ | 80ˢ | 90ˢ |
|-----|-----|-----|-----|-----|-----|-----|-----|-----|
|     |     |     |     |     |     |     |     |     |

German actor Curt Jurgens worked as a journalist until his first wife, actress Louise Basler, persuaded him to take up acting. In 1935 he began appearing on the German stage and screen, and gradually increased his career status until 1944, when he was sent to a concentration camp at the order of Dr. Goebbels. After his release he continued to appear in German films, gaining international recognition with his work in *The Devil's General* (1955). Jurgens went on to be a leading star of the European stage and international films; onscreen he often played urbane villains, and sometimes was cast as a Nazi. Although he appeared in over 100 films, he considered himself primarily a stage actor. He directed a few films with limited success, and also wrote screenplays. Jurgens was married five times; one of his wives was actress Eva Bartok. He authored an autobiography, *Sixty and Not Yet Wise.* **Selected Works:** *Inn of the Sixth Happiness* (1958), *Longest Day* (1962)

Madeline Kahn

Guy Kibbee

Carol Kane

B... Kirby

...ane Kurys

## Madeline Kahn

**Born:** September 29, 1942; Chelsea, MA

**Years Active in the Industry:** by decade

| 10ˢ | 20ˢ | 30ˢ | 40ˢ | 50ˢ | 60ˢ | 70ˢ | 80ˢ | 90ˢ |
|-----|-----|-----|-----|-----|-----|-----|-----|-----|
|     |     |     |     |     |     |     |     |     |

Comedic actress of the American stage, screen, and TV, Madeline Kahn originally trained to be an opera singer, then sang and acted on and off Broadway, making her Broadway debut in *Faces of 1968*. She debuted onscreen in Peter Bogdanovich's *What's Up Doc?* (1972), and for her work in both *Paper Moon* (1973) and *Blazing Saddles* (1974) she received Best Supporting Actress Oscar nominations. Her screen career dwindled in the '80s, but she starred in the TV series *Oh Madeline* and *Mr. President;* she also appeared in several TV specials and movies, one of which, *Wanted: The Perfect Guy* (1986), earned her an Emmy Award. She also performed in operas with the Washington Opera Society and the New York Philharmonic. She has been nominated three times for Tony Awards, most recently for her work in the Broadway revival of *Born Yesterday* (1989). **Selected Works:** *Betsy's Wedding* (1990), *For Richer, for Poorer* (1992), *Young Frankenstein* (1974)

## Chen Kaige

**Born:** 1952

**Years Active in the Industry:** by decade

| 10ˢ | 20ˢ | 30ˢ | 40ˢ | 50ˢ | 60ˢ | 70ˢ | 80ˢ | 90ˢ |
|-----|-----|-----|-----|-----|-----|-----|-----|-----|
|     |     |     |     |     |     |     |     |     |

Chen Kaige is the premiere director amongst China's daring Fifth Generation of filmmakers. Kaige and his peers graduated from the Beijing Film Institute. Created after the Cultural Revolution to help Chinese cinema earn international respect, the films of the Fifth Generation are characterized by a focus on imagery and sound rather than traditional narrative structures; they also contain strong political messages that have met with opposition from censors thus making the films accessible only to students and intellectuals within China. Though his films such as *Yellow Earth* (1983) and *Red Sorghum* (1987) have had limited release in his own country, Kaige's films are critically acclaimed worldwide, and he has been awarded the highest honors in Tokyo, Cannes, and Berlin. One of Kaige's most recent films, *Farewell, My Concubine* (1993), the epic saga of the homoerotic relationship between two Beijing opera stars, provides a good example of Fifth Generation cinema. In the film, the trials and triumphs of the two singers are framed by a rich background of China at peace, at war, occupied by the Japanese, and in the throes of the Cultural Revolution. The film caused quite a stir amongst censors and authorities who considered the film potentially embarrassing to the government; the film was banned until it was reedited to suit state officials. In the west, *Concubine* was well received, sharing the Palme d'Or with *The Piano* at Cannes 1993.

## Carol Kane

**Born:** June 18, 1952; Cleveland, OH

**Years Active in the Industry:** by decade

| 10ˢ | 20ˢ | 30ˢ | 40ˢ | 50ˢ | 60ˢ | 70ˢ | 80ˢ | 90ˢ |
|-----|-----|-----|-----|-----|-----|-----|-----|-----|
|     |     |     |     |     |     |     |     |     |

A professional actress since age 14, Ohio-born Carol Kane is best known for essaying a staggering variety of characterizations in her three-decade career. Most of her early film roles were fleeting but memorable, such as that of the hippie girlfriend of Art Garfunkel in *Carnal Knowledge* (1971), the "sailor's plaything" in *The Last Detail* (1973) and the terrified bank teller in *Dog Day Afternoon* (1973). Kane's first starring appearance was in *Hester Street* (1975), wherein she was Oscar-nominated for her portrayal of a Jewish newlywed in turn-of-the-century New York. From 1981 through 1983, Kane played Simka, the wife of immigrant mechanic Latka Gavras (Andy Kaufman) on the TV sitcom *Taxi*. Simka's country of origin was fictitious, but Kane and Kaufman managed between them to "create" a Slavic language peppered with ridiculous, non-sequitur terms of endearment. The actress won an Emmy for her work on *Taxi*, and might have continued in the role were it not for Kaufman's untimely death at the age of 34. Other regular TV sitcom assignments for Kane have included 1986's *All Is Forgiven* and 1990's *American Dreamer*. In her more recent films, Kane has excelled in bizarre character roles, notably the kvetching old peasant wife in *Willow* (1986), the abusive "Ghost of Christmas Present" in *Scrooged* (1988), and the toothless, witchlike Grandmama in the two *Addams Family* theatrical features. **Selected Works:** *Baby on Board* (1992), *In the Soup* (1992), *My Blue Heaven* (1990), *Addams Family Values* (1993)

# Garson Kanin

**Born:** November 24, 1912; Rochester, NY

**Years Active in the Industry:** by decade

| 10ˢ | 20ˢ | 30ˢ | 40ˢ | 50ˢ | 60ˢ | 70ˢ | 80ˢ | 90ˢ |
|-----|-----|-----|-----|-----|-----|-----|-----|-----|
|     |     | ■ | ■ | ■ | ■ |     |     |     |

Younger brother of scriptwriter Michael Kanin, Garson Kanin acted in and directed theatrical productions in the 1930s, and in 1938 began directing films. His notable early films include the comedies *The Great Man Votes* (1938), *Bachelor Mother* (1939), and *Tom, Dick And Harry* (1941). During World War II he produced and directed several documentaries for the Office of Emergency Management; he also collaborated on documentaries with Carol Reed (*The True Glory* [1945]) and Jean Renoir (*Salute to France* [1945]). After the war he collaborated with his wife Ruth Gordon on a series of memorable screenplays for director George Cukor: *A Double Life* (1947), *Adam's Rib* (1950), *The Marrying Kind* (1952), *Pat and Mike* (1952) and *The Actress*. Kanin also helmed two minor comedies in 1969, *Where It's At* (1969) and *Some Kind of a Nut* (1969). **Selected Works:** *My Favorite Wife* (1940)

# Jonathan Kaplan

**Born:** November 5, 1947; Paris, France

**Years Active in the Industry:** by decade

| 10ˢ | 20ˢ | 30ˢ | 40ˢ | 50ˢ | 60ˢ | 70ˢ | 80ˢ | 90ˢ |
|-----|-----|-----|-----|-----|-----|-----|-----|-----|
|     |     |     |     |     |     | ■ | ■ | ■ |

Parisian-born American film director Jonathan Kaplan may have held degrees from the University of Chicago and New York University, but he gained his hands-on education at the Roger Corman School of Makin' 'Em Cheap. Kaplan apprenticed at Corman's New World Pictures, making his directorial bow with the energetic if parsimonious *Student Nurses* (1971). After a few more low-budgeters, Kaplan was allowed to spend a little more time and money on *White Line Fever* (1975), then enjoyed his most lavish budget to date on *Mr. Billion* (1976), a lighthearted and empty-headed caper film starring Terence Hill, Valerie Perrine and Jackie Gleason. Kaplan made Hollywood's A-list with *The Accused* (1988), a fact-based account of a rape victim's quest for justice which featured Jodie Foster in her first Academy Award-winning role. **Selected Works:** *Fallen Angels, Vol. 1* (1993), *Love Field* (1991), *Unlawful Entry* (1992)

# Boris Karloff (William Henry Pratt)

**Born:** November 23, 1887; London, England
**Died:** 1969

**Years Active in the Industry:** by decade

| 10ˢ | 20ˢ | 30ˢ | 40ˢ | 50ˢ | 60ˢ | 70ˢ | 80ˢ | 90ˢ |
|-----|-----|-----|-----|-----|-----|-----|-----|-----|
| ■ | ■ | ■ | ■ | ■ | ■ |     |     |     |

British actor Boris Karloff, the star of many horror films of the early sound era, will forever be most associated with the Monster in the 1931 classic *Frankenstein*. Headed for a diplomatic ca-

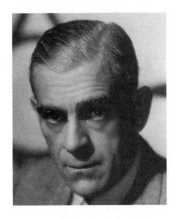

reer, at age 21 he emigrated to Canada and became a farm-hand. Karloff joined touring companies and acted for a decade, playing supporting parts all over Canada and the U.S. During a brief stay in Los Angeles in 1916, he made his screen debut as an extra in *The Dumb Girl of Portici*. Three years later, while out of work, he returned to Hollywood and began appearing regularly as extras and bit players in films. Karloff, supporting himself as a truck driver, began receiving better roles in the mid-'20s. He appeared in 40 silent films altogether, typically playing a villain, but gained little recognition. He fared better in the sound era, when he could employ his theatrically-trained voice. Karloff's first important role was in *The Criminal Code* (1931), in which he repeated a previous stage performance. His great breakthrough came later that same year, when James Whale cast him in *Frankenstein*. The film's tremendous success guaranteed him a place in many subsequent horror films. Along with frequent co-star Bela Lugosi, he became one of the central actors in the Universal horror cycle of the '30s and in many similar films afterwards; however, he also played straight roles, notably that of a religious fanatic in John Ford's *The Lost Patrol* (1934). Meanwhile, he intermittently continued his stage career, appearing to great acclaim as Jonathan Brewster (a madman driven to homicidal rage whenever anyone said he looked like Boris Karloff!) in the Broadway production of *Arsenic and Old Lace* (1941) and as Captain Hook in *Peter Pan* (1950). He continued appearing in films through the late 1960s, and in 1968 Karloff gave one of his finest performances playing a man very similar to himself in Bogdanovich's directorial debut, *Targets*. **Selected Works:** *Bride of Frankenstein* (1935), *Scarface* (1931), *House of Rothschild* (1934)

# Lawrence Kasdan

**Born:** January 14, 1949; Miami, FL

**Years Active in the Industry:** by decade

| 10s | 20s | 30s | 40s | 50s | 60s | 70s | 80s | 90s |
|-----|-----|-----|-----|-----|-----|-----|-----|-----|

The archetypal Hollywood Baby-Boomer, American director Lawrence Kasdan planned to be an English teacher upon graduation from the University of Michigan. Instead, Kasdan moved into writing for Chicago-based TV commercials, winning several awards in the process. He tried his hand at screenwriting, and after numerous disappointments he attained a credit on *The Empire Strikes Back* (1980), which led to Kasdan's scripting of George Lucas' story for *Raiders of the Lost Ark* (1981). Kasdan's first directing job was *Body Heat* (1981), "film noir" for the 1980s which inevitably echoed the 1940s classics in this genre, but which nonetheless made a great deal of money, and also secured the stardom of newcomer Kathleen Turner. *Continental Divide* (1981), based in part on the roisterous career of Chicago columnist Mike Royko, didn't do as well as *Body Heat*, but Kasdan made up for this lapse with *The Big Chill* (1983), a tale of thirtysomething angst which struck a chord with many disillusioned children of the 1960s (the film was remarkably similar to John Sayles' earlier and cheaper *Return of the Secaucus Seven*, but not enough to invoke lawsuits). Kasdan had planned to use *The Big Chill* to showcase his actor friend Kevin Costner, but circumstances forced him to cut Costner from the release print. The director made it up to Costner by casting him in a plum role in *Silverado* (1985), a rousing return to the western genre that Kasdan and most others his age had grown up with. *The Accidental Tourist* (1988), like *The Big Chill*, had a plot motivated by the sudden death of a loved one; the film was a dextrous blend of high comedy and deep tragedy, and won an Oscar for supporting actress Geena Davis. After an all-stops-out zany comedy, *I Love You to Death* (1990), Kasdan returned to many of the search-for-meaning

themes found in *The Big Chill* with *Grand Canyon* (1991), which furthered the director's contention that one must find peace of mind beyond the boundaries of materialism and social status. Kasdan put his sensibilities (and many of his senses) on hold with *The Bodyguard* (1992), a melodrama which he'd written for Steve McQueen nearly two decades earlier but which he filmed with old pal Kevin Costner in the lead. *The Bodyguard* journeyed into the Twilight Zone of silliness and incredibility, but made a fortune. Kasdan's most recent project, again in tandem with Costner, was 1994's *Wyatt Earp*, a lavish but extremely disappointing western epic which ended up one of the most conspicuous money-losers of the 1990s.

# Philip Kaufman

**Born:** October 23, 1936; Chicago, IL

**Years Active in the Industry:** by decade

| 10s | 20s | 30s | 40s | 50s | 60s | 70s | 80s | 90s |
|-----|-----|-----|-----|-----|-----|-----|-----|-----|

An independent filmmaker in the mid-1960s, Phillip Kaufman collaborated with Benjamin Manaster to write, produce, and direct his first film, the Martin Buber adaptation *Goldstein* (1964). In the '70s Kaufman was working within the industry, making such notable films as the revisionist Jesse James western *The Great Northfield, Minnesota Raid* (1972); the Arctic adventure tale *The White Dawn* (1975); *Invasion Of The Body Snatchers* (1978), a remake of the classic Don Siegel science-fictioner; and *The Wanderers* (1979), a stylish reminiscence of high-school life in early-1960s New York. In the '80s Kaufman established himself as a major writer/director with *The Right Stuff* (1983), a chronicle of the American space program adapted from Tom Wolfe's book; *The Unbearable Lightness Of Being* (1988), based on Milan Kundera's novel; and the bisexual romance *Henry and June* (1990), taken from Anais Nin's memoirs of her relationship with Henry Miller and his wife June. **Selected Works:** *Raiders of the Lost Ark* (1981)

# Julie Kavner

**Born:** September 7, 1951; Los Angeles, CA

**Years Active in the Industry:** by decade

| 10s | 20s | 30s | 40s | 50s | 60s | 70s | 80s | 90s |
|-----|-----|-----|-----|-----|-----|-----|-----|-----|

When the decision was made in 1974 to transform Rhoda Morgenstern (Valerie Harper) from frumpy kvetcher to desirable bachelorette on the TV series *Rhoda*, somebody had to inherit all those self-deprecating jokes told by Rhoda on *The Mary Tyler Moore Show*. The decision was made to create a new character: Rhoda's pudgy, insecure younger sister, Brenda. The actress chosen for the role sounded as though she'd been a New Yorker since the womb, but in fact Julie Kavner was born and raised in California.

A theatre student at USC-San Francisco, Kavner came to *Rhoda* with no professional experience, but before the series ran its course, she had won an Emmy for her portrayal. With her performance in the 1986 film *Hannah and Her Sisters*, Kavner became one of the most prominent members of director Woody Allen's stock company, essaying very un-Brendalike roles in *Radio Days* (1987), the "Oedipus Wrecks" segment of *New York Stories* (1989), *Alice* (1990) and *Shadows and Fog* (1992). Kavner's regular stint as an ensemble player on the Fox TV network's *Tracy Ullman Show* led to her long-running assignment as the gravelly voice of Marge Simpson on the weekly animated series *The Simpsons*. **Selected Works:** *Awakenings* (1990), *This Is My Life* (1992)

# Danny Kaye (David Daniel Kominski)

**Born:** January 18, 1913; Brooklyn, NY
**Died:** March 3, 1987

**Years Active in the Industry:** by decade

| 10s | 20s | 30s | 40s | 50s | 60s | 70s | 80s | 90s |
|-----|-----|-----|-----|-----|-----|-----|-----|-----|

Inimitable, multi-talented entertainer Danny Kaye first gained fame on Broadway by upstaging the great Gertrude Lawrence in *Lady in the Dark* in 1941 with an unforgettable rendition of the "Tchaikovsky," in which he rapidly fired off the names of 54 Russian composers in 38 seconds. Born David Daniel Kaminski, a garment worker's son in Brooklyn, New York, Kaye left school at age 13 to work as a mischievous busboy in the popular "borscht belt" resorts of the Catskill Mountains. While endeavoring to break into vaudeville and nightclub acts as a singer and dancer, Kaye also occasionally worked as a soda jerk and an insurance salesman. In 1939, he made his Broadway debut in *Straw Hat Revue* with Imogene Coco. Following the run of *Lady in the Dark,* he began making a series of educational films during the '30s. In 1943, he signed a movie contract with producer Sam Goldwyn, and became a star when he appeared in *Up in Arms* (1944). A talented mimic, physical comedian, singer and dancer, he was unlike any performer who had come before him. Kaye specialized in playing multiple roles or personalities in such films as *Wonder Man* (1945), *The Kid From Brooklyn* (1946), *The Secret Life of Walter Mitty* (1947), *The Inspector General* (1949), and *On the Riviera* (1951). Probably his best films are *The Court Jester* (1956), which contains the unforgettable "pellet with the poison's

in the vestle with the pestle" routine, based on similar but less effective bits in earlier films, and *White Christmas* (1954). His wife, composer-lyricist Sylvia Fine, wrote most of his best gags and patter numbers throughout his career. Though tremendously popular during the mid-'40s through the '50s—most particularly in Great Britain, where he played to record-breaking crowds in the Palladium in 1948 and 1949 (he even made personal visits to Buckingham Palace)—his bright star began to wane in the late 1950s when he began spending most of his time working for UNICEF, and traveling the world-over to entertain impoverished children. In the early to mid-'60s, he starred in *The Danny Kaye Show,* a comedy-variety television series for which he won an Emmy in 1964. He also found time to conduct symphony orchestras and appear in *Two by Two* on Broadway. In 1955, Kaye was awarded an honorary Oscar; the Motion Picture Academy also awarded him the Jean Hersholt Award in 1982 for his selfless work with UNICEF.

# Elia Kazan (Elia Kazanjoglou)

**Born:** September 7, 1909; Kadi-Kev, Constantinople, Turkey

**Years Active in the Industry:** by decade

| 10s | 20s | 30s | 40s | 50s | 60s | 70s | 80s | 90s |
|-----|-----|-----|-----|-----|-----|-----|-----|-----|

At age four, Elia Kazanjoglou came to America with his Greek parents and settled in New York City. A stage actor in the early '30s, he directed his first play in 1935, and guided several celebrated plays in the '40s, including *A Streetcar Named Desire* and *Death of a Salesman.* After acting in the 1934 short film *Pie in the Sky,* Kazan helmed two documentaries: the 1937 short *The People of The Cumberlands* and the 1941 feature *It's Up to You.* In the early '40s he also played supporting roles in director Anatole Litvak's *City for Conquest* (1940) and *Blues in the Night* (1941). In 1945 Kazan scored directing his first narrative feature, *A Tree Grows in Brooklyn,* and soon established his reputation with several provocative social dramas: *Boomerang* (1947), *Gentlemen's Agreement* (1947), *Pinky* (1949), and *Panic in the Streets* (1950). In the '50s Kazan's gift for guiding actors was showcased in a series of films starring Marlon Brando: *A Streetcar Named Desire* (1951), *Viva Zapata!* (1952), and *On the Waterfront* (1954). He also introduced audiences to actor James Dean with *East Of Eden* (1954). In the late '50s and early '60s, Kazan continued to impress filmgoers with his controversial tales of adolescent sexuality, *Baby Doll* (1956) and *Splendor in the Grass* (1961), and his handsome, thoughtful social dramas, *A Face in the Crowd* (1957) and *Wild River* (1960). He adapted two of his own novels for *America America* (1963) and *The Arrangement* (1969); neither were commercial successes, and he made only two more films: *The Visitors* (1972), an independent, low-budget thriller; and *The Last Tycoon* (1976), a prestigious adaptation of F. Scott Fitzgerald's last novel.

## Stacy Keach (Walter Stacy Keach, Jr.)

**Born:** June 2, 1941; Savannah, GA

**Years Active in the Industry:** by decade

| 10s | 20s | 30s | 40s | 50s | 60s | 70s | 80s | 90s |
|-----|-----|-----|-----|-----|-----|-----|-----|-----|
|     |     |     |     |     |     |     |     |     |

The son of a drama teacher and dialogue director, American actor Stacy Keach began performing in college productions, then studied at the Yale Drama School. He spent a year at the London Academy of Music and Dramatic Art on a Fulbright scholarship, then acted in Shakespeare in the Park productions, where he first established his reputation; he soon worked both off and on Broadway, winning a Tony for his work in *Indians.* Keach debuted onscreen as a drunken drifter in *The Heart Is a Lonely Hunter* (1968), then went on to play leads and supporting roles in a number of films; his screen appearances after 1982, however, have been infrequent. He wrote and directed the short film *The Repeater* (1972); he also directed a TV version of Pirandello's classic *Six Characters in Search of an Author.* In 1975 he starred in the short-lived TV series *Caribe,* and after starring in several TV movies, Keach assumed the title role of the TV series *Mike Hammer* in 1983. His career came to an abrupt halt in the mid-'80s when he was arrested and imprisoned in England for cocaine possession; after serving nine months and participating in drug rehabilitation, he returned to *Mike Hammer.* He is the brother of actor James Keach, with whom he co-starred in *The Long Riders* (1980), a film he also co-wrote and co-produced. He is married to Polish actress Malgosia Tomassi. **Selected Works:** *False Identity* (1990), *Fat City* (1972), *Mission of the Shark* (1991), *Rio Diablo* (1993)

## Buster Keaton (Joseph Francis Keaton, Jr.)

**Born:** October 4, 1895; Piqua, KS
**Died:** February 1, 1966; Woodland Hills, CA

**Years Active in the Industry:** by decade

| 10s | 20s | 30s | 40s | 50s | 60s | 70s | 80s | 90s |
|-----|-----|-----|-----|-----|-----|-----|-----|-----|
|     |     |     |     |     |     |     |     |     |

Joseph Francis Keaton Jr. was a child star in his family's roughhouse slapstick vaudeville act The Three Keatons, where the young Buster developed the acrobatic skill and comic timing which

would distinguish his great silent films. In 1917 he began acting in support of Fatty Arbuckle in numerous short comedies, including *The Butcher Boy, Fatty At Coney Island,* and *The Garage,* which gained Keaton enough attention to be chosen to star in the 1920 feature-length farce *The Saphead.* His uniquely personal brand of comedy, with an unsmiling Buster persevering in a confounding world of willful machines, not-very-bright girlfriends, menacing heavies, and even-more menacing police, was launched with a series of brilliant shorts in the early '20s. He co-wrote and co-directed most of those films with Eddie Cline, among them the classics *The Playhouse, The Boat,* and *Cops;* Cline also shared the honors on Keaton's first official feature, the Intolerance-parody *The Three Ages* (1923). A series of hilarious, uniquely cinematic comedy features followed, highlighted by Keaton's extraordinary stunts and the unexpected dark twists which occasionally surfaced in his humor. Unsurpassed at constructing elaborate and original sight gags, Keaton brought a new vision to silent comedy with his masterpieces *Our Hospitality* (1923), *Sherlock Jr.* (1924), *The Navigator* (1924), *Seven Chances* (1925), *The General* (1927), *College* (1927), and *Steamboat Bill Jr.* (1928)—films which made him second only to Chaplin as an internationally beloved comedy star. Signing with MGM in 1928, Keaton scored with his last silents, *The Cameraman* (1928) and *Spite Marriage* (1929), both nominally directed by Edward Sedgwick. The studio demanded more control over Keaton's talking films, and his career quickly collapsed as he delivered ordinary jokes in a series of low-budget comedies, frequently teamed with Jimmy Durante. An uncredited gagman for Red Skelton in the 1940s, Keaton's reputation began to rise again in the '50s, thanks in part to his live stage shows and his appearance in Charlie Chaplin's *Limelight* (1952). Although Keaton would never again create the kind of films that made him one of the giants of world cinema, his final years nevertheless included memorable performances in *Film,* Alan Schneider's production of Samuel Beckett's original screenplay, and director Richard Lester's comic musical *A Funny Thing Happened on the Way to the Forum* (1966). **Selected Works:** *Around the World in 80 Days* (1956), *Sunset Boulevard* (1950)

## Diane Keaton (Diane Hall)

**Born:** January 5, 1946; Los Angeles, CA

**Years Active in the Industry:** by decade

| 10s | 20s | 30s | 40s | 50s | 60s | 70s | 80s | 90s |
|-----|-----|-----|-----|-----|-----|-----|-----|-----|
|     |     |     |     |     |     |     |     |     |

Distinctive looking American actress Diane Keaton dropped out of college after three semesters to study theater at the Neighborhood Playhouse in New York. She appeared for several months in summer stock in Woodstock, New York, then landed a supporting part in the Broadway rock musical *Hair;* she was also the understudy for the lead, and in 1968 she took over the starring role. In 1969 she co-starred with Woody Allen in Allen's Broadway play *Play It Again, Sam;* she also appeared in the play's film version (1972). She and Allen began a romance (which later became a friendship), and she went on to appear in a number of his films. For her work in Allen's *Annie Hall* (1977), she won the Best Actress Oscar (the "Hall" in the title was adopted from Keaton's real name). Having made her screen debut in *Lovers and Other Strangers* (1970), she went on to a steady career onscreen, and also appeared in TV dramas. Her first important screen role was as Al Pacino's wife in Francis Ford Coppola's *The Godfather* (1972), and she went on to appear in both of that movie's sequels (1974 and 1990). For her portrayal of real-life journalist Louise Bryant in Warren Beatty's *Reds* (1981), Keaton received another Best Actress Oscar nomination. She directed the documentary *Heaven* (1987) and 1995's *Unstrung Heroes* as well as some rock videos and an episode of the David Lynch TV series *Twin Peaks;* she also produced and co-starred in the film *The Lemon Sisters* (1989), a flop that never made it to major distribution. She has published two books of photographs. **Selected Works:** *Manhattan* (1979), *Manhattan Murder Mystery* (1993), *Radio Days* (1987), *Running Mates* (1992)

## Michael Keaton (Michael Douglas)

**Born:** September 5, 1952; Coraopolis, PA

**Years Active in the Industry:** by decade

| 10ˢ | 20ˢ | 30ˢ | 40ˢ | 50ˢ | 60ˢ | 70ˢ | 80ˢ | 90ˢ |
|-----|-----|-----|-----|-----|-----|-----|-----|-----|
|     |     |     |     |     |     |     |     |     |

Before becoming a popular leading man, Michael Keaton dropped out of college after two years, then took a variety of odd jobs while attempting to establish himself as a stand-up comic. Af-

ter three years of work as a TV technician, he moved to Hollywood and managed to get small roles on TV shows such as *The Tony Randall Show* and *Maude.* In 1982 he got a major break when Ron Howard cast him in a supporting role in the comedy *Night Shift;* this led to a lead role in another successful comedy, *Mr. Mom* (1983).

For the next five years he made poor choices in his cinematic work, but landed the part of the manic title character in Tim Burton's box-office winner *Beetlejuice* (1988). The next year he broke out of the comedic film mode in the title role of the hugely successful *Batman* (1989). He reprised the role in *Batman Returns* (1992), but balked at playing the Caped Crusader in the series' third installment over a money dispute, and Val Kilmer took over the role. He has assumed other dramatic roles in less popular but otherwise respectable works such as *Pacific Heights* (1990), *My Life* (1993), and *The Paper* (1994), and lent a delightful spark as Dogberry in *Much Ado About Nothing* (1993). **Selected Works:** *Batman Returns* (1992), *Clean & Sober* (1988), *My Life* (1993)

## Harvey Keitel

**Born:** May 13, 1947; New York, NY

**Years Active in the Industry:** by decade

| 10ˢ | 20ˢ | 30ˢ | 40ˢ | 50ˢ | 60ˢ | 70ˢ | 80ˢ | 90ˢ |
|-----|-----|-----|-----|-----|-----|-----|-----|-----|
|     |     |     |     |     |     |     |     |     |

Lead and supporting actor Harvey Keitel brings a rare intensity and believability to the roles he portrays. Straight out of high school he joined the Marine Corps; he later studied acting with

Frank Corsaro, Stella Adler, and Lee Strasberg. After joining the Actors Studio he performed off-off-Broadway in coffee houses, and in 1965 debuted off-Broadway. Also in 1965, he made his Broadway debut opposite George C. Scott in a revival of *Death of a Salesman.* Keitel began working with director Martin Scorsese in 1968 when he was cast in Scorsese's thesis project, *Who's That Knocking at My Door?*, this led to several other appearances in Scorsese films, launching his career onscreen. Though Keitel has played a variety of roles, many of his most memorable roles are as hard-bitten, streetwise characters in films such as *Mean Streets* (1973), *Taxi Driver* (1976), *Bad Lieutenant* (1992), and *Reservoir Dogs* (1992); a favorite of director Quentin Tarantino, Keitel also had a bit role in *Pulp Fiction* (1994). In 1993, he changed directions and gave a strong, sensual performance in the erotic love story *The Piano.* Keitel also received a Best Supporting Actor Oscar nomination for his work in Warren Beatty's *Bugsy* (1991). **Selected Works:** *Rising Sun* (1993), *Thelma & Louise* (1991), *Imaginary Crimes* (1994), *Clockers* (1995)

# Brian Keith (Robert Keith Richey, Jr.)

**Born:** November 14, 1921; Bayonne, NJ

**Years Active in the Industry:** by decade

| 10s | 20s | 30s | 40s | 50s | 60s | 70s | 80s | 90s |
|-----|-----|-----|-----|-----|-----|-----|-----|-----|
|     |     |     |     | ■ | ■ | ■ | ■ |     |

The son of actor Robert Keith, burly blond lead and supporting actor Brian Keith appeared in the silent film *Pied Piper Malone* (1924) at age three. After acting in stock and on radio, and serving during World War II as a machine gunner in the Marines, he made his adult screen debut in 1953. Keith then went on to a steady film career for the next two-plus decades, appearing on-screen much less frequently after the early '70s. In the '50s he often appeared in westerns, and later appeared in several Disney films, including *The Parent Trap* (1961). At first he tended to be cast in heavy character parts, then gradually moved into sympathetic, more important roles, often of a "good-hearted curmudgeon" nature. He starred in the TV series *The Westerner*, *Family Affair*, and *Hardcastle and McCormick*.

# David Keith

**Born:** May 8, 1954; Knoxville, TN

**Years Active in the Industry:** by decade

| 10s | 20s | 30s | 40s | 50s | 60s | 70s | 80s | 90s |
|-----|-----|-----|-----|-----|-----|-----|-----|-----|
|     |     |     |     |     |     |     | ■ | ■ |

A graduate of the University of Tennessee, David Keith made his first significant theatrical appearance in Chicago. Keith has the distinction of starring in the 1979 sitcom *Co-Ed Fever*, which was pulled from the CBS lineup after one episode. Luckily, his more enduring movie career also began in 1979. Keith quickly became a specialist in portraying all-American boy roles who were cursed with a fatal character flaw or two, as witnessed in his performance in *An Officer and a Gentleman* (1982). Retaining his military buzz-cut from *Officer*, Keith had his first above-the-title starring role in 1983's *The Lords of Discipline*. And with an uncharacteristic full head of hair, Keith played Elvis in the 1990 fantasy *Heartbreak Hotel*. An able director, Keith has thus far helmed two films: *The Curse* (1985) and *Further Adventures of Tennessee Buck* (1987). One of Keith's more unorthodox recent screen appearances was as a foot-tall toy figure who comes to life in 1995's *The Indian in the Cupboard*. **Selected Works:** *Liar's Edge* (1992), *Two Jakes* (1990), *Desperate Motive* (1992)

# Cecil Kellaway

**Born:** August 22, 1893; Cape Town, South Africa
**Died:** 1973

**Years Active in the Industry:** by decade

| 10s | 20s | 30s | 40s | 50s | 60s | 70s | 80s | 90s |
|-----|-----|-----|-----|-----|-----|-----|-----|-----|
|     |     | ■ | ■ | ■ | ■ |     |     |     |

Cecil Kellaway, a portly character actor with a devilish sparkle in his eye, was typecast into playing aged rogues. He was a prolific actor, appearing in over 100 films in Australia and the U.S. in a career spanning close to 40 years. Though Kellaway looked Irish, he was actually born in South Africa. As a young man, he moved to Australia where he began a successful stage and screen career. He emigrated to the U.S. in 1939, where he worked in Hollywood films such as *Wuthering Heights* (1939) and *Intermezzo* (1939). Though generally a supporting actor, Kellaway played the lead in *The Good Fellows* (1943). He was nominated for an Oscar twice: first for his role as a leprechaun in *The Luck of the Irish* (1948), and again in 1967 for his performance in *Guess Who's Coming to Dinner?* **Selected Works:** *I Married a Witch* (1942), *Intermezzo: A Love Story* (1939), *Invisible Man Returns* (1940), *Portrait of Jennie* (1948), *Kitty* (1945)

# Sally Kellerman

**Born:** June 2, 1937; Long Beach, CA

**Years Active in the Industry:** by decade

| 10s | 20s | 30s | 40s | 50s | 60s | 70s | 80s | 90s |
|-----|-----|-----|-----|-----|-----|-----|-----|-----|
|     |     |     |     | ■ | ■ | ■ | ■ | ■ |

Tall, blonde, somewhat quirky supporting and occasional lead actress with a throaty voice, Sally Kellerman attended Hollywood High School, where she became interested in acting after appearing in a play. After graduating, she first studied drama at the Actors' Studio West, then with Jeff Corey, and finally, at the Actors' Studio. After debuting onscreen in *Reform School Girl* (1957), she struggled for a decade, getting only small stage and screen roles. Kellerman's lucky break came when she was cast as Major Margaret "Hot Lips" Houlihan in Robert Altman's highly successful Korean War comedy *M*A*S*H* (1970), which made her a star and earned her a Best Supporting Actress Oscar nomination. She has never been able to capitalize on this success, though, and went on to make mostly mediocre, forgettable films and do voiceover work. She is married to TV director Rick Edelstein. **Selected Works:** *Happily Ever After* (1991), *Victim of Beauty* (1991), *Boris and Natasha* (1992), *Drop Dead Gorgeous* (1991), *Mirror, Mirror 2: Raven Dance* (1994)

# Gene Kelly (Eugene Curran Kelly)

**Born:** August 23, 1912; Pittsburgh, PA

**Years Active in the Industry:** by decade

| 10s | 20s | 30s | 40s | 50s | 60s | 70s | 80s | 90s |
|-----|-----|-----|-----|-----|-----|-----|-----|-----|
|     |     |     | ■ | ■ | ■ | ■ | ■ | ■ |

Dancer, actor, choreographer, and director Gene Kelly began dancing as a child. He later supported himself in a variety of odd jobs, including a turn as a dance instructor. In 1938 he debuted on Broadway in the chorus of *Leave It to Me*. In 1940 he choreographed *Billy Rose's Diamond Horseshoe*, then landed the lead in *Pal Joey;* the following year he choreographed another hit Broadway musical, *Best Foot Forward.* Kelly's first onscreen appearance came in 1942 opposite Judy Garland in *For Me and My Gal;* from there he became increasingly popular as a star of '40s MGM musicals and occasional dramas. From the time he made *Cover Girl* (1944), his dance routines revolutionized the Hollywood musical, giving it a new, free-flowing, imaginative vitality. For his work in *Anchors Aweigh* (1945) he received a Best Actor Oscar nomination; in that film he danced a duet with Jerry, the animated mouse from Tom & Jerry cartoons. He co-directed (with Stanley Donen) three musicals, beginning with the highly successful *On the Town* (1949); the others were *An American in Paris* (1951) and *Singin' In the Rain* (1952). From then on he assumed the mantle of Hollywood's premier master of dance, succeeding the aging Fred Astaire in that position. Kelly's work as a straight dramatic actor, however, has been less successful. He received a special Academy Award in 1951 "in appreciation of his versatility as actor, singer, director, and dancer, and specifically for his brilliant achievements in the art of choreography on film." He won the Grand Prize at the West Berlin Film Festival for his first film as a solo director, *Invitation to the Dance* (1956), a musical with no dialogue. Kelly continued directing and starring in films for the next two-plus decades; his other directorial efforts include *A Guide for the Married Man* (1967) and *Hello Dolly!* (1969). Kelly made a few movie and TV appearances in the '70s and '80s, but nothing that compares to his earlier greatness. From 1940-57 he was married to actress Betsy Blair. **Selected Works:** *Inherit the Wind* (1960), *It's Always Fair Weather* (1955), *Pirate* (1948), *Ziegfeld Follies* (1946)

# Grace Kelly

**Born:** November 12, 1929; Philadelphia, PA
**Died:** 1982

**Years Active in the Industry:** by decade

| 10s | 20s | 30s | 40s | 50s | 60s | 70s | 80s | 90s |
|-----|-----|-----|-----|-----|-----|-----|-----|-----|
|     |     |     |     |     |     |     |     |     |

Serenely beautiful and coolly elegant, American actress Grace Kelly lived a fairy-tale life. Her mother was a former cover girl, her father a wealthy industrialist and former world champion oarsman; her uncle was the Pulitzer Prize-winning playwright George Kelly. At age ten she made her stage debut in a Philadelphia production, and in her late teens she moved to New York, working as a model while studying acting at the American Academy of Dramatic Arts. Numerous auditions for plays led only to parts in TV cigarette commercials; finally, in 1949 she debuted on Broadway in a revival of Strindberg's *The Father* starring Raymond Massey. From there she got a bit part in the film *Fourteen Hours* (1951), then soon landed her first screen starring role in *High Noon* (1952) opposite Gary Cooper. From then on Kelly appeared only in lead roles. For her portrayal of an adulteress in *Mogambo* (1953), she received a Best Supporting Actress Oscar nomination.

For her performance as the embittered but staunchly loyal wife of an alcoholic entertainer (Bing Crosby) in *The Country Girl* (1954), she won the Best Actress Oscar and the New York Film Critics Best Actress award. In 1955, while working on location in the French Riviera for Hitchcock's *To Catch a Thief,* she met Prince Rainier III, the ruler of Monaco; the following year they were married, and she permanently retired from acting to become Princess Grace of Monaco. She died at 54 as the result of an automobile crash. **Selected Works:** *Bridges at Toko-Ri* (1955), *Rear Window* (1954)

# Arthur Kennedy (John Arthur Kennedy)

**Born:** December 17, 1914; Worcester, MA
**Died:** January 5, 1990; Branford CT

**Years Active in the Industry:** by decade

| 10s | 20s | 30s | 40s | 50s | 60s | 70s | 80s | 90s |
|-----|-----|-----|-----|-----|-----|-----|-----|-----|
|     |     |     |     |     |     |     |     |     |

American actor Arthur Kennedy was usually cast in western or contemporary roles in his films; on stage, it was another matter. A graduate of the Carnegie-Mellon drama department, Kennedy's first professional work was with the Globe Theatre Company touring the midwest in abbreviated versions of Shakespearian plays. From here he moved into the American company of British stage star Maurice Evans, who cast Kennedy in his Broadway production of *Richard III.* Kennedy continued doing Shakespeare for Evans and agit-prop social dramas for the Federal Theatre, but when time came for his first film, *City for Conquest* (1940), he found himself in the very ordinary role of James Cagney's boxer brother. Throughout his first Warner Bros. contract, Kennedy showed promise as a young character lead, but films like *Bad Men of Missouri* (1941), *They Died with Their Boots On* (1942) and *Air Force* (1943) did little to tap the actor's classical training. After World War II service, Kennedy returned to Broadway, creating the role of Chris Keller in Arthur Miller's *All My Sons* (1947). This led to an even more prestigious Miller play, the Pulitzer Prize winning *Death of a Salesman* (1948), in which Kennedy played Biff. Sadly, Kennedy was not permitted to repeat these plum roles in the film versions of these plays, but the close association with Miller continued on stage; Kennedy would play John Proctor in *The Crucible* (1957) and the doctor brother in *The Price* (1965). While his film work during this era resulted in several Academy Award nominations, Kennedy never won; he was honored, however, with the New York Film Critics award for his on-target portrayal of a newly blinded war veteran battling not only his handicap but also his in-bred racism in *Bright Victory* (1951). The biggest box office success with which Kennedy was associated was *Lawrence of Arabia* (1962), wherein he replaced the ailing Edmund O'Brien in the role of the Lowell Thomas character. Working continually in film and TV projects of wildly varying quality, Kennedy quit the business cold in the mid-1980s, retiring to live with family members in a small eastern town. Kennedy was so far out of the Hollywood mainstream in the years before his death that, when plans were made to restore the fading *Laurence of Arabia* prints and Kennedy was needed to re-record his dialogue, the restorers were unable to locate the actor through Screen Actor's Guild channels—and finally had to trace him through his hometown telephone directory. **Selected Works:** *Champion* (1949), *Elmer Gantry* (1960), *Peyton Place* (1957), *Some Came Running* (1958), *Trial* (1955)

# Edgar Kennedy

**Born:** April 26, 1890; Monterey, CA
**Died:** November 9, 1948; Woodland Hills, CA

**Years Active in the Industry:** by decade

| 10ˢ | 20ˢ | 30ˢ | 40ˢ | 50ˢ | 60ˢ | 70ˢ | 80ˢ | 90ˢ |
|---|---|---|---|---|---|---|---|---|

American comic actor Edgar Kennedy left home in his teens, smitten with the urge to see the world. He worked a number of manual labor jobs and sang in touring musical shows before returning to his native California in 1912 to break into the infant movie industry. Hired by Mack Sennett in 1914, Kennedy played innumerable roles in the Keystone comedies. He would later claim to be one of the original Keystone Kops, but his specialty during this period was portraying mustache-twirling villains. By the early 1920s, Kennedy's screen image had mellowed; now he most often played detectives or middle-aged husbands. He joined Hal Roach Studios in 1928, where he did some of his best early work: co-starring with Laurel and Hardy, Charlie Chase and Our Gang; directing two-reelers under the stage name E. Livingston Kennedy; and receiving top billing in one of Roach's most enduring comedies, *A Pair of Tights* (1928). Kennedy was dropped from the Roach payroll in a 1930 economy drive, but he'd already made a satisfactory talkie debut—even though he'd had to lower his voice to his more familiar gravelly growl after it was discovered that his *natural* voice sounded high-pitched and effeminate. During his Roach stay, Kennedy developed his stock-in-trade "slow burn," wherein he'd confront a bad situation or personal humiliation by glowering at the camera, pausing, then slowly rubbing his hand over his face. In 1931, Kennedy was hired by RKO studios to star in a series of two-reelers, unofficially titled "Mr. Average Man." These films, precursors to the many TV sitcoms of the 1950s, cast Kennedy as head of a maddening household consisting of his dizzy wife (usually Florence Lake, sister of Arthur "Dagwood" Lake), nagging mother-in-

law and lazy brother-in-law. Kennedy made six of these shorts per year for the next 17 years, taking time out to contribute memorable supporting roles in such film classics as *Duck Soup* (1933), *San Francisco* (1936), *A Star Is Born* (1937) and *Anchors Aweigh* (1944). Some of Kennedy's most rewarding movie assignments came late in his career: the "hidden killer" in one of the *Falcon* B mysteries, the poetic bartender in Harold Lloyd's *Sin of Harold Diddlebock* (1946), and the classical music-loving private detective in *Unfaithfully Yours* (1948), which like *Diddlebock* was directed by Preston Sturges. On November 9, 1948, shortly after completing his 103rd "Average Man" two-reeler and 36 hours before a Hollywood testimonial dinner was to be held in his honor, Kennedy died of throat cancer; his last film appearance as Doris Day's long-suffering father in *Romance on the High Seas* (1948) was released posthumously. **Selected Works:** *Twentieth Century* (1934), *It Happened Tomorrow* (1944)

# George Kennedy

**Born:** February 18, 1925; New York, NY

**Years Active in the Industry:** by decade

| 10ˢ | 20ˢ | 30ˢ | 40ˢ | 50ˢ | 60ˢ | 70ˢ | 80ˢ | 90ˢ |
|---|---|---|---|---|---|---|---|---|

American actor George Kennedy, the son of an orchestra leader and a ballet dancer began appearing onstage at age two, and spent many years in his youth as a radio performer; he was seven when he first worked as a disc jockey. After enlisting in the Army during World War II, he went on to serve for 16 years, later as an armed forces radio and TV officer. Kennedy then worked as a technical adviser on the TV series *Sergeant Bilko,* and with that "foot in the door" he began acting on TV and then, from the early '60s, in films. At first he tended to play tough guys, but he gradually evolved into more important, subtle, and often sympathetic roles. For his work in *Cool Hand Luke* (1967) he won a Best Supporting Actor Oscar. He also appeared in the TV series *The Blue Knight.* Kennedy has gained recognition with current audiences with his appearances in the zany *The Naked Gun: From the Files of Police Squad* (1988) and its sequels. **Selected Works:** *Airport* (1970), *Dirty Dozen* (1967), *Flight of the Phoenix* (1965), *Naked Gun 2 1/2: The Smell of Fear* (1991), *Naked Gun 33 1/3: The Final Insult* (1994)

# Jerome Kern

**Born:** January 27, 1885; New York, NY
**Died:** 1945; New York, NY

**Years Active in the Industry:** by decade

| 10ˢ | 20ˢ | 30ˢ | 40ˢ | 50ˢ | 60ˢ | 70ˢ | 80ˢ | 90ˢ |
|---|---|---|---|---|---|---|---|---|

American composer Jerome Kern was trained at home by his mother, then went in for formal study at the New York College of Music and Heidelberg University. Gravitating to the lucrative fields of operetta and popular music, Kern wrote his first hit song in 1905, and seven years later composed his first Broadway score for the now-forgotten *The Red Petticoat*. Public recognition of Kern's skills accelerated after he contributed several new songs to the pre-packaged British musical *The Girl From Utah* (1914). With his close friends Guy Bolton and P.G. Wodehouse, Kern became a leading light of New York's Princess Theatre, which eschewed the pomp and spectacle of the European operettas in favor of small casts, "intimate" stories, and well-integrated songs. Kern's biggest Broadway success of the 1920's was *Show Boat*, though when it was first filmed in 1929 the producers threw out most of Kern's songs because they were already "too familiar" to the audience (subsequent filmizations of *Show Boat* in 1936 and 1951 not only restored the Jerome Kern-Oscar Hammerstein score, but also—in the case of the 1936 version—added two new tunes to the manifest). In addition to the film adaptations of Kern's stage shows, including *Sunny* (1941) and *Roberta* (1935), the composer has written several scores expressly for the screen, beginning with his orchestra accompaniment for the silent 1916 serial *Gloria's Romance*. He wrote the songs for the 1936 Astaire-Rogers musical *Swing Time*, including the Oscar-winning "The Way You Look Tonight," and also labored on the solo Astaire vehicle *You Were Never Lovelier*. Kern's movie assignments ranged from the celebrated (*Cover Girl*, *Centennial Summer* ) to the disappointing (*High Wide and Handsome*, *One Night in the Tropics*). In 1941, he won his second Oscar for *The Last Time I Saw Paris,* which was the highlight of the otherwise negligible *Lady Be Good* (1941). Though well known for being helpful and solicitous to up-and-coming composers like George Gershwin, Kern had his darker side—especially when insisting that radio orchestras play his songs exactly as written or face legal action. Kern had just inherited *Annie Get Your Gun* from the too-busy Rodgers and Hammerstein, and was busy fashioning songs to suit the style of star Ethel Merman, when he died suddenly at the age of 60 (he was succeeded on *Annie* by Irving Berlin). Jerome Kern was portrayed on screen by a grey-templed Robert Walker in the 1946 biopic *Till the Clouds Roll By.*

years, often playing cool, reserved, well-bred young ladies; she also appeared in London stage productions. Her portrayal of a nun in *Black Narcissus* (1947) earned a New York Film Critics Best Actress Award and led to an invitation from Hollywood to co-star opposite Clark Gable in *The Hucksters* (1947), after which she remained in Hollywood. She continued to play long-suffering, prim, proper, ladylike types until 1953, when she broke her typecast mold by portraying a passionate adulteress in *From Here to Eternity,* a role she had fought for; after that her range of roles broadened, and she also began to appear in British films again. In 1953 Kerr debuted on Broadway to great acclaim in *Tea and Sympathy,* later reprising her role in the play's screen version (1956). She retired from the screen in 1969, having received six Best Actress Oscar nominations but never winning. In 1986 she appeared in the film *The Assam Garden*. She is married to novelist-screenwriter Peter Viertel. **Selected Works:** *King and I* (1956), *Separate Tables* (1958), *Sundowners* (1960), *Edward, My Son* (1949), *Heaven Knows, Mr. Allison* (1957), *Night of the Iguana* (1964)

# Guy Kibbee

**Born:** March 6, 1882; El Paso, TX
**Died:** May 24, 1956; Los Angeles, CA

**Years Active in the Industry:** by decade

| 10s | 20s | 30s | 40s | 50s | 60s | 70s | 80s | 90s |
|-----|-----|-----|-----|-----|-----|-----|-----|-----|

It is possible that when actor Guy Kibbee portrayed newspaper editor Webb in the 1940 film version of *Our Town*, he harked back to his own father's experiences as a news journalist. The cherubic, pop-eyed Kibbee first performed on Mississippi riverboats as a teenager, then matriculated to the legitimate stage. The 1930 Broadway play *Torch Song* was the production that brought Kibbee the Hollywood offers. From 1931 onward, Kibbee was one of the mainstays of the Warner Bros. stock companies, specializing in dumb politicos (*The Dark Horse* [1932]), sugar daddies (*42nd Street* [1933]) and the occasional straight, near-heroic role (*Captain Blood* [1935]). In 1934, Kibbee enjoyed one of his rare leading roles, essaying the title character in *Babbitt* (1934), a role he seemed born to play. During the 1940s, Kibbee headlined the *Scattergood Baines* B-picture series at RKO. He retired in 1949, after completing his scenes in John Ford's *Three Godfathers*. Kibbee was the brother of small-part play Milton Kibbee, and the father of

# Deborah Kerr (Deborah Jane Kerr-Trimmer)

**Born:** September 30, 1921; Helensburgh, Scotland

**Years Active in the Industry:** by decade

| 10s | 20s | 30s | 40s | 50s | 60s | 70s | 80s | 90s |
|-----|-----|-----|-----|-----|-----|-----|-----|-----|

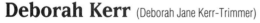

Cultured actress Deborah Kerr, born Deborah Kerr-Trimmer in Scotland, was first trained as a dancer at her aunt's drama school in Bristol, England. After winning a scholarship to the Sadler's Wells ballet school, she made her London debut at age 17 in the *corps de ballet* of *Prometheus;* meanwhile, she developed an interest in acting, and began getting bit parts and walk-ons in Shakespearean productions. Kerr debuted onscreen in 1940 and went on to appear in a number of British films over the next seven

Charles Kibbee, City University of New York chancellor. **Selected Works:** *Gold Diggers of 1933* (1933), *Lady for a Day* (1933), *Mr. Smith Goes to Washington* (1939), *Three Comrades* (1938), *Of Human Hearts* (1938)

# Margot Kidder (Margaret Ruth Kidder)

**Born:** October 17, 1948; Yellowknife, NW Territories, Canada

**Years Active in the Industry:** by decade

| 10s | 20s | 30s | 40s | 50s | 60s | 70s | 80s | 90s |
|-----|-----|-----|-----|-----|-----|-----|-----|-----|
|     |     |     |     |     |     |     |     |     |

The daughter of a mining engineer, Canadian actress Margot Kidder spent her first two-and-a-half years living in a caboose. While attending the University of British Columbia, Kidder was talked into appearing in a college stage production of *Take Me Along;* she was hooked, though she later learned there was more to acting than crying on cue and partying. In her first professional years with the Canadian Broadcasting Corporation headquarters in Vancouver, Kidder played everything from simpering ingenues to an unhinged murderess. She made her first film in 1969, an American production titled *Gaily Gaily,* then worked with Gene Wilder in the British-made *Quackser Fortune Has a Cousin in the Bronx* (1970). Kidder disliked the seamier side of the movie business and retreated to Canada in hopes of learning how to become a film editor, but was brought back to the U.S. in 1971 for a continuing role in the James Garner TV series *Nichols.* She liked Garner but not the hassles of making a weekly series, and for the next decade concentrated on film work, plunging headfirst into a kinky Brian DePalma chiller titled *Sisters* (1972). Kidder's best-known work in the '70s and '80s was as Lois Lane in the *Superman* films starring Christopher Reeve. Other movie roles and a stint on 1987 TV series *Shell Game* followed; although her acting has been limited by injuries she suffered in an on-set accident in the late 1980s, she has nonetheless sustained her career with such voice-only assignments as the character of Gaia on the TV cartoon series *Captain Planet and the Planeteers.* Kidder married and divorced writer Tom McGuane and actor John Heard (their union lasted six days!) and remains a vocal activist for political and ecological causes. **Selected Works:** *To Catch a Killer* (1992), *Maverick* (1994)

# Nicole Kidman

**Born:** 1966; Hawaii

**Years Active in the Industry:** by decade

| 10s | 20s | 30s | 40s | 50s | 60s | 70s | 80s | 90s |
|-----|-----|-----|-----|-----|-----|-----|-----|-----|
|     |     |     |     |     |     |     |     |     |

Born in Hawaii to Australian parents, Nicole Kidman began studying ballet while still a child; at age ten she enrolled in drama school, and later studied acting at the St. Martin's Youth Theater in Melbourne and in Sydney at both the Australian Theater for Young

People and (under the direction of Peter Williams) the Philip Street Theater. At age 14, her portrayal of a 50-year-old American in a small production gained the attention of a casting director, who gave her a role in her debut film, *Bush Children* (1982); this led to a lead role in the children's movie *BMX Bandits* (1983). Kidman went on to make an average of one film a year, but gained her greatest recognition on Australian TV, winning the Australian Film Institute's Best Actress Award two years in a row for her work in the TV movies *Vietnam* (1988) and *Bangkok Hilton* (1989); she was also voted 1988's Actress of the Year by the Australian public. She also won awards for her work on the stage; for her portrayal of a doomed Southern belle in *Steel Magnolias* she was named the best newcomer of the year by the Sydney Theater Critics. Kidman's first major international film was *Dead Calm* (1989), prompting Tom Cruise and his co-producers to cast her as Cruise's love interest in *Days of Thunder* (1990). In late 1990 she and Cruise were married, and went on to appear together in *Far and Away* (1992) and adopt two children. Her popularity with American audiences has grown steadily, although her dramatic turns in *My Life* (1993) and *Malice* (1993) received only a lukewarm response. Most recently she starred as the love interest of the Caped Crusader in the blockbuster *Batman Forever* (1995) and gained great reviews for her performance in *To Die For* (1995). **Selected Works:** *Billy Bathgate* (1991), *Malice* (1993), *My Life* (1993), *Flirting* (1992)

# Krzysztof Kieslowski

**Born:** 1941; Warsaw, Poland

**Years Active in the Industry:** by decade

| 10s | 20s | 30s | 40s | 50s | 60s | 70s | 80s | 90s |
|-----|-----|-----|-----|-----|-----|-----|-----|-----|
|     |     |     |     |     |     |     |     |     |

Polish filmmaker Krzysztof Kieslowski was in his mid-20s when he attended the Lodz School of Cinema and Theatre. Kieslowksi directed his first film, a documentary entitled *Picture*, in 1969, but it would be ten years before he would gain attention outside of Poland for his 1979 effort *Camera Buff*. Like many directors of Eastern Europe's "new cinema" movement, Kieslowski found his films forever at the mercy of government censors. The director has financed many of his projects by teaching in the radio and television department of the University of Silesia. In addition, he served as vice-president of the Union of Polish Cinematographers from 1978 through 1981. He has won prizes at the Mannheim Festival, the Moscow Festival, the Polish Ministry of Foreign Affairs, and the Cannes Festival. Kieslowski's most ambitious project was the ten-part *Dekalog*, a political-allegory series based on the Ten Commandments, which he directed for Polish television in 1988; one *Dekalog* chapter, *A Short Film About Killing*, received a "best foreign film" Oscar nomination. Kieslowski's *Three Colors* trilogy was inspired by the French tricolor and won him international recognition. *Blue* (liberty), *White* (equality), and *Red* (brotherhood) marked Kieslowski's retirement from filmmaking in 1994. **Selected Works:** *Double Life of Veronique* (1991), *Three Colors: Blue* (1993), *Three Colors: White* (1994), *Three Colors: Red* (1994)

# Val Kilmer

**Born:** December 31, 1959; Los Angeles, CA

### Years Active in the Industry: by decade

| 10s | 20s | 30s | 40s | 50s | 60s | 70s | 80s | 90s |
|-----|-----|-----|-----|-----|-----|-----|-----|-----|
|     |     |     |     |     |     |     |     |     |

Tall, handsome and versatile leading man Val Kilmer is probably best known for his powerful portrayal of and eerie resemblance to self-destructive rock singer Jim Morrison in Oliver Stone's epic *The Doors* (1991), but during his brief career, he has appeared in films of almost every major genre. As a youngster, the L.A.-born actor studied at the Hollywood Professional School. He then went on to Julliard before breaking into film with his debut in the 1984 comedy *Top Secret*. While making films, Kilmer has also maintained a successful career on the New York stage. Currently he has replaced Michael Keaton as the tortured Caped Crusader in *Batman Forever* (1995). He separated in 1995 from his wife, actress Joanne Whalley-Kilmer, with whom he has two children. **Selected Works:** *Thunderheart* (1992), *True Romance* (1993), *Tombstone* (1993)

# Henry King

**Born:** June 24, 1888; Christiansburg, VA
**Died:** June 29, 1982; Toluca Lake, CA

### Years Active in the Industry: by decade

| 10s | 20s | 30s | 40s | 50s | 60s | 70s | 80s | 90s |
|-----|-----|-----|-----|-----|-----|-----|-----|-----|
|     |     |     |     |     |     |     |     |     |

After a start as a stage actor, Henry King began appearing in films in 1912, and by 1915 was directing. King made numerous dramas, westerns, and actioners over the teens, achieving special distinction with his 1919 comedy *23-1/2 Hours Leave*. Two years later he co-wrote, produced, and directed the landmark rural drama *Tol'able David;* his other important works of the '20s include *The White Sister* (1923), *Romola* (1925), and *The Winning of Barbara Worth* (1926). A prolific and reliable craftsman, King made numerous handsome films into the early 1960s, most notably two outstanding films with Gregory Peck: a psychological drama of World War II, *Twelve O'Clock High* (1942), and the moody, intelligent western *The Gunfighter* (1950). King's career is also notable for his feeling for Americana, as found in 1930s projects as different as *State Fair* (1933), *Jesse James* (1939), and *In Old Chicago* (1938), as well as in such later films as *Remember the Day* (1941) and *Wait 'Til the Sun Shines, Nellie* (1952). He was also skilled at helming historical dramas (*Lloyds of London* [1936], *The Song of Bernadette* [1943]) and adventure tales (*The Black Swan* [1942], *Prince of Foxes* [1949]). **Selected Works:** *Wilson* (1944), *Alexander's Ragtime Band* (1938)

# Ben Kingsley

**Born:** December 31, 1943; Snaiton, Yorkshire, England

### Years Active in the Industry: by decade

| 10s | 20s | 30s | 40s | 50s | 60s | 70s | 80s | 90s |
|-----|-----|-----|-----|-----|-----|-----|-----|-----|
|     |     |     |     |     |     |     |     |     |

Chameleon-like British actor Ben Kingsley has proven he can play just about everything, though for many viewers he will always be inextricably linked with one single film role—in which his "costume" consisted of a white sheet. Of English, Indian and South African extraction, Kingsley started out in amateur theatricals in Manchester, before making his professional debut at age 23. In 1967 he made his first London appearance at the Aldwych theatre, then joined the Royal Shakespearean Company, devoting himself almost exclusively to stage work for the next fifteen years (with the exception of two obscure films, *Fear Is the Key* [1972] and *Hard Labour* [1973]). When asked his favorite stage roles, he listed Hamlet, Ariel (from *The Tempest*) and Mosca (from *Volpone*). American audiences first saw Kingsley in 1971, when he made his Broadway debut with the Royal Shakespearian. In 1982, director/actor Richard Attenborough selected Kingsley for the demanding title role in his lifelong-ambition epic *Gandhi*. The film swept the international awards that year, earning the 39-year-old "overnight success." Kingsley was awarded an Oscar as well as several other honors. Adamantly refusing to chew his cabbage twice, Kingsley has since appeared as an Arab potentate in *Harem* (1985), a "born loser" in *Turtle Diary* (1985), Dmitri Shostakovich in *Testimony* (1988), Sherlock Holmes' Doctor Watson in *Without a Clue* (1988), the title character in *Murderers Among Us: The Simon Weisenthal Story* (1989), an incorruptible American vice president in *Dave* (1992), New York gangster Meyer Lansky in *Bugsy* (1992), the voice-of-conscience Jewish bookkeeper in *Schindler's List* (1993), and a suspected Nazi war criminal in *Death and the Maiden* (1994). So many of his characters have been either taciturn or downright villainous that, upon being cast in a good-guy role in the escapist sci-fier *Species* (1995), Kingsley publicly expressed his relief in several widely circulated magazine articles. Kingsley has also taken Broadway by storm with his one-man show *Edward Kean* (later taped for cable), which was directed by his wife Alison Sutcliffe. **Selected Works:** *Betrayal* (1983), *Sneakers* (1992), *Searching for Bobby Fischer* (1993)

# Klaus Kinski (Nikolaus Gunther Nakszynski)

**Born:** October 8, 1926; Sopot (now Gdansk), Poland
**Died:** November 23, 1991; Lagunitas, CA

**Years Active in the Industry:** by decade

| 10s | 20s | 30s | 40s | 50s | 60s | 70s | 80s | 90s |
|-----|-----|-----|-----|-----|-----|-----|-----|-----|

Though he invariably looked sickly and tubercular, Polish/German actor Klaus Kinski rose to fame in roles calling for near-manic aggressiveness. His war career consisted primarily of a year and a half in a British POW camp. After this experience, Kinski took to the theatre, where he rapidly built a reputation for on-stage brilliance and offstage emotional instability. He made his first German film, *Morituri*, in 1948; three years later he made his English-language movie debut with a fleeting bit in *Decision before Dawn* (1951). Villainy was Kinski's film stock in trade during the 1950s and 1960s, with several appearances in Germany's Edgar Wallace second-feature series and in such Italian spaghetti westerns as *For a Few Dollars More* (1966). International stardom came Kinski's way via his off-the-beam appearances in the films of director Werner Herzog, notably *Aguirre, the Wrath of God* (1973), *Nosferatu the Vampyre* (1979) and *Fitzcarraldo* (1982). With 1989's *Paganini*, Kinski proved to be as colorful and chaotic a director as he was an actor. Kinski was the father of actress Nastassja Kinski, though it is matter of record that the two seldom saw each other and were never close. **Selected Works:** *Doctor Zhivago* (1965)

# Nastassja Kinski

**Born:** January 24, 1959; Berlin, Germany

**Years Active in the Industry:** by decade

| 10s | 20s | 30s | 40s | 50s | 60s | 70s | 80s | 90s |
|-----|-----|-----|-----|-----|-----|-----|-----|-----|

The long-estranged daughter of the late film star Klaus Kinski, German actress Nastassja Kinski began her career in her teens.

According to most sources, her first film was director Wim Wenders' *The Wrong Move* (1975), though there is evidence that a German TV movie directed by Wolfgang Petersen, *For Your Love Only* (1976), was produced first. Still not yet twenty, Kinski fell in love with the much-older filmaker Roman Polanski, who subsidized her training as an actress. After taking drama classes in New York and London, Kinski was deemed ready by Polanski to star in *Tess* (1980), a lavishly produced filmization of Thomas Hardy's *Tess of the D'Urbervilles*. Shortly thereafter Kinski became the dream of male college undergrads everywhere by posing for a Richard Avedon poster wearing nothing save the large live python which spiralled around her body. Kinski's next few films tended to capitalize on her physical attributes rather than her very real talent; in *Cat People* (1982), directed by her then-lover Paul Schrader, the actress' character transformed into a panther after having sex; and in *Exposed* (1982), she participated in one of the goofiest moments of screen erotica in history when costar Rudolph Nureyev "played" her body with a cello bow. Compared to scenes like these, Kinski's appearance as Dudley Moore's wife in *Unfaithfully Yours* (1983) was downright puritanical—but it was back to the bizarre with her role as a woman dressed in a bear suit in *Hotel New Hampshire* (1985). At this point, Kinski's film output was getting a bit too beyond the fringe for most filmgoers, and she spent much of the next decade in "artistic" movies of little box office appeal (*Torrents of Spring* [1989], *Faraway, So Close* [1991]). For a brief time she remained in the public eye thanks to several well-publicized romances and because she gave birth to a baby without (at first) revealing the name of the father, allowing the world press to go into a torrent of speculation (the father turned out to be Egyptian producer Ibrahim Moussa, who briefly became her husband). In the early 1990s, Kinski dropped from view altogether, devoting herself to her marriage to pop-music maestro Quincy Jones. In 1994, Kinski made a surprising reappearance in the "normal" role of a KGB agent in the popular movie thriller *Terminal Velocity* (1994)—managing to remain clothed in her big scene, wherein she was locked in the trunk of a car and thrown from a plane in flight. **Selected Works:** *Paris, Texas* (1983), *Night Sun* (1990)

# Bruno Kirby (Bruno Quidaciolu, Jr.)

**Born:** 1949; New York, NY

**Years Active in the Industry:** by decade

| 10s | 20s | 30s | 40s | 50s | 60s | 70s | 80s | 90s |
|-----|-----|-----|-----|-----|-----|-----|-----|-----|

Early in his career, Bruno Kirby, Jr. was sometimes billed as "B. Kirby Jr." The son of actor Bruce Kirby, he studied acting with Stella Adler and Peggy Feury. He began his career with a regular role on the TV series *Room 222,* and he has since appeared in numerous TV movies. He debuted onscreen in *Cinderella Liberty* (1973), then landed a noteworthy small role with Robert DeNiro in *The Godfather Part II* (1974); after that promising beginning he spent a decade in bit parts and bombs. His screen career became more fruitful after a prominent supporting role as an uptight, idiotic army lieutenant in *Good Morning, Vietnam* (1987). He has gone on to a string of important supporting roles in mostly successful films. **Selected Works:** *City Slickers* (1991), *The Freshman* (1990), *Good Morning, Vietnam* (1987), *When Harry Met Sally* (1989)

# Sally Kirkland

**Born:** October 31, 1944; New York, NY

**Years Active in the Industry:** by decade

| 10s | 20s | 30s | 40s | 50s | 60s | 70s | 80s | 90s |
|-----|-----|-----|-----|-----|-----|-----|-----|-----|

The daughter of the fashion editor of *Life* magazine, Sally Kirkland often appeared in *Vogue* and other magazines as a model. After high school, she studied with Uta Hagen and Lee Strasberg at the Actors' Studio, then appeared in off- and off-off-Broadway productions; her appearance in *Sweet Eros* won her a great deal of notoriety (her part required her to sit onstage for 45 minutes, tied up and nude). She debuted on Broadway in *Step on a Crack* (1962). In 1964 Kirkland attempted suicide; she then went on to be a member of Andy Warhol's Factory, where she had some drug problems. She appeared in a number of underground and avant-garde films, leading to supporting roles in Hollywood films. In 1983 she founded the Sally Kirkland Acting Workshop, a traveling seminar; her workshop emphasized the positive effects of meditation and yoga. For her work in Yurek Bogayevicz's *Anna* (1987) she received both an Oscar nomination and a Golden Globe Award nomination, plus a Los Angeles Critics Best Actress Award. Her subsequent movies have been mostly forgettable actioners and dramas. **Selected Works:** *Cheatin' Hearts* (1993), *Double Jeopardy* (1992), *Primary Motive* (1992), *Two Evil Eyes* (1990), *Haunted* (1991)

# Robert Klein

**Born:** February 8, 1942; New York, NY

**Years Active in the Industry:** by decade

| 10s | 20s | 30s | 40s | 50s | 60s | 70s | 80s | 90s |
|-----|-----|-----|-----|-----|-----|-----|-----|-----|

A graduate of Alfred University, American actor Robert Klein spent the 1960s and 1970s amassing a respectable list of stage and film credits (he played George Segal's befuddled roomie in *The Owl and the Pussycat* [1970]), but his bread and butter turned out to be his career as a stand-up comic. First gaining national attention as host of the 1970 TV variety series *Comedy Tonight,* Klein went on to transcribe his comedy routines in a series of popular record albums. A "reporter" of humor, the raspy-voiced, heavily eyebrowed Klein is at his best commenting offhandedly on the absurdities of everyday life. Some of his best routines involve the dissection of such pop-culture icons as The Little Rascals, *My Lit-*

*tle Margie,* and Babe Ruth; other monologues recall such childhood experiences as civil defense drills and the first dance (complete with imitations of the Johnny Mathis records heard on the PA). Klein continued taking acting jobs into the 1970s and 1980s: one of his longer engagements during this period was in the Neil Simon Broadway musical *They're Playing Our Song.* In 1991, Robert Klein found himself the unofficial spokesperson for the Comedy Central cable service, hosting the weekly series *Dead Comics Society* and *Stand Up Stand Up.* He also appeared occasionally on the NBC drama *Sisters.*

# Kevin Kline

**Born:** October 24, 1947; St. Louis, MO

**Years Active in the Industry:** by decade

| 10s | 20s | 30s | 40s | 50s | 60s | 70s | 80s | 90s |
|-----|-----|-----|-----|-----|-----|-----|-----|-----|

Kevin Kline is an acclaimed Juilliard-trained actor who has demonstrated panache in his widely varied film and stage roles. Kline has played everything from a swashbuckling Douglas Fairbanks in Richard Attenborough's *Chaplin* to intensely dramatic parts in *Sophie's Choice* (1982), *The Big Chill* (1983) and *Cry Freedom* (1987), and wild comedic parts in *A Fish Called Wanda* (1988), for which he won an Oscar, and *Dave* (1993). He is also a gifted musical performer, winning two Tony Awards, for *On the Twentieth Century* and *The Pirates of Penzance,* which he repeated on film in 1983. In the '90s, Kline became associate producer of the New York Shakespeare Festival, with which he had long been affiliated. Kline is married to actress Phoebe Cates. **Selected Works:** *Grand Canyon* (1991), *I Love You to Death* (1990), *Soapdish* (1991), *French Kiss* (1995)

# Jack Klugman

**Born:** April 27, 1922; Philadelphia, PA

**Years Active in the Industry:** by decade

| 10s | 20s | 30s | 40s | 50s | 60s | 70s | 80s | 90s |
|-----|-----|-----|-----|-----|-----|-----|-----|-----|

Most famous for playing Oscar Madison to Tony Randall's Felix Unger on TV's *The Odd Couple* (1970-75), Jack Klugman has been in films and on stage since the 1950s. On stage, he performed in *Gypsy* with Ethel Merman, and on film made strong dramatic appearances in *Twelve Angry Men* (1957) and *Days of Wine and Roses* (1962). He won his first Emmy Award for his role in a 1964 episode of *The Defenders* about the entertainment industry's blacklist, followed by two more for *The Odd Couple* in 1971 and 1973. As a medical examiner in TV's *Quincy, M.D.* (1976-83), Klugman displayed humor and dramatic intensity. His other TV series include *Harris Against the World* (1964-65) and *You Again?* (1986-87). Over the years, following surgery for throat cancer in the 1990s, Klugman has reprised the role of Oscar Madison on stage around the country with Randall. **Selected Works:** *Days of Wine & Roses* (1962)

# Shirley Knight

**Born:** July 5, 1937; Goessel, KS

**Years Active in the Industry:** by decade

| 10ˢ | 20ˢ | 30ˢ | 40ˢ | 50ˢ | 60ˢ | 70ˢ | 80ˢ | 90ˢ |
|-----|-----|-----|-----|-----|-----|-----|-----|-----|
|     |     |     |     |     |     |     |     |     |

Shirley Knight trained at the Pasadena Playhouse, then debuted onscreen in 1959. The following year she received a Best Supporting Actress Oscar nomination for her work in Delbert Mann's *The Dark at the Top of the Stairs* (1960); two years later she was again nominated, this time for portraying Paul Newman's childhood sweetheart in *Sweet Bird of Youth* (1962). Candid about her dissatisfaction with Hollywood, Knight concentrated on the stage in the mid '60s and had several successes on Broadway. She moved to London in 1966 with her husband, stage producer Gene Person, to appear in his film *Dutchman* (1967). She remained in England for several years, appearing in films and TV productions; there she divorced Person and married British playwright John Hopkins, after which she was sometimes billed as "Shirley Knight Hopkins." In the mid '70s she returned to Broadway. Her screen appearances since 1971 have been sporadic, although she did have a role in the 1994 thriller *Color of Night.* **Selected Works:** *Petulia* (1968), *Playing for Time* (1980), *Bump in the Night* (1991), *Shadow of a Doubt* (1991)

# Alexander Knox

**Born:** January 16, 1907; Strathroy, Ontario, Canada

**Years Active in the Industry:** by decade

| 10ˢ | 20ˢ | 30ˢ | 40ˢ | 50ˢ | 60ˢ | 70ˢ | 80ˢ | 90ˢ |
|-----|-----|-----|-----|-----|-----|-----|-----|-----|
|     |     |     |     |     |     |     |     |     |

Canadian actor Alexander Knox launched his stage career in Britain in 1929; two years later he made his film film, *The Ringer.* After a successful British stage career, Knox came to America in 1941, where he found steady film work playing learned types. In *The Sea Wolf* (1941), Knox was the pedantic Weyland, the opponent/doppelganger of brutish sea captain Wolf Larsen (Edward G. Robinson); while in *This Above All* (1942), Knox lent credibility to his role as clergyman who does but really doesn't condone a clandestine love affair. Knox's most daunting American film assignment was the title role in *Wilson* (1944), producer Darryl F. Zanuck's budget-busting valentine to the 28th president of the United States. Too healthy and fit to be totally convincing as Woodrow Wilson, Knox nonetheless sustained audience interest in an otherwise ponderous film marathon, and received an Oscar nomination—which he might have won had not *Wilson* been one

of the most conspicuous failures in Hollywood history. Nonetheless, the film allowed Knox to command star billing for his next few American pictures, including the enjoyable 1949 outing *The Judge Steps Out,* a light comedy loosely based on the Judge Crater disappearance. In the early 1950s, Knox found himself playing a few villains, at least until Hollywood's doors closed on him during the Blacklist era (that a man who once played a U.S. president should even be suspected of subversive leanings is quite ironic). The actor returned to Britain for choice character roles in such films as *The Sleeping Tiger* (1954), *The Night My Number Came Up* (1955) and *Oscar Wilde* (1957). In 1967, Knox was signed up for a term as a fictional U.S. president in the James Bond extravaganza *You Only Live Twice* (1967). Active in films until the mid 1980s, Knox also kept busy as a screenwriter and mystery novelist.

# Sir Alexander Korda

**Born:** September 16, 1893; Turkeve, Hungary
**Died:** 1956

**Years Active in the Industry:** by decade

| 10ˢ | 20ˢ | 30ˢ | 40ˢ | 50ˢ | 60ˢ | 70ˢ | 80ˢ | 90ˢ |
|-----|-----|-----|-----|-----|-----|-----|-----|-----|
|     |     |     |     |     |     |     |     |     |

The first motion picture producer ever to receive a knighthood, Alexander Korda was the founder and guiding force behind the British film industry throughout the 1930s, and continued as a major producer until his death in 1956. Although synonymous to the world with British films, Korda was Hungarian born, and worked in movies in Austria, Germany, and America before coming to England in 1930. A crafty businessman as well as a flamboyant personality (Michael Powell and Emeric Pressburger modeled Boris Lermontov, the egotistical ballet impressario of *The Red Shoes,* partly on Alexander Korda), by 1933 he had a major (though always financially shaky) studio in London Films, and managed to pull off a seemingly impossible feat by directing and producing *The Private Life of Henry VIII* (1933). This film became a hit in America, turned its star Charles Laughton (who won the Best Actor Oscar) into an international star, and earned a nomination as Best Picture. London Films, built on Korda's production genius and the work of his brothers Zoltan (one of England's greatest directors) and Vincent (an art director) with a small colony of expatriate Hungarians, seemed bent on "selling" the British Empire all over the world. Many of these films failed financially, but were also glorious in their failures: *Rembrandt* (1936), starring Laughton, is still considered by many to be the best drama ever made on the life of a painter (not a surprise, since Korda himself was a devoted art enthusiast); *Clouds over Europe* (1939), starring Laurence Olivier and Ralph Richardson, was an espionage comedy that anticipated the 1960s series "The Avengers" (as well as one James Bond movie) in spirit and content; *The Four Feathers* (1939) was the finest action adventure film of the 1930s, and one of the greatest films ever shot in Technicolor; and *The Thief of Baghdad* (1940), starring Sabu, remains a prime example of great fantasy filmmaking. The outbreak of the World War II in Europe forced Korda to move his operations to America, where he made several less distinguished movies, including *The Jungle Book* (1942) with Sabu, before returning in 1945. Korda's postwar activities were spent somewhat in the shadow of J. Arthur Rank, but the departure from Rank's company of such talented filmmakers as Michael Powell, Emeric Pressburger, Laurence Olivier, David Lean and Carol Reed gave London Films new opportunities—the company didn't make many movies, but the quality of the films was staggering. Among its successes were *The Third Man* (1949), *The Tales of Hoffmann* (1951), *The Sound Barrier, Summertime* (1955), and *Richard III* (1955). Korda's death early 1956 resulted in the closing of London Films, but thanks to Korda's having sold his library to television in the mid 1950s, long before any American studios had made their films available for broadcast, the company and its Big Ben logo remain among the most familiar in motion pictures. Among Korda's productions, *The Thief of Baghdad* has proved the most enduring for its opulence and grandeur, and received a whole new national theatrical release to great acclaim during the late 1970s. Known for moviemaking on a grand scale, Korda was probably the most articulate producer-showman in the history of motion pictures.

# Yaphet Kotto

**Born:** November 15, 1937; New York, NY

**Years Active in the Industry:** by decade

| 10s | 20s | 30s | 40s | 50s | 60s | 70s | 80s | 90s |
|-----|-----|-----|-----|-----|-----|-----|-----|-----|
|     |     |     |     |     |     |     |     |     |

African American actor Yaphet Kotto was one of the most prominent beneficiaries of the upsurge in black-oriented theatrical pieces of the late 1950s; he appeared in many prestigious Broadway and off-Broadway productions, taking regional theatre work rather than accept stereotypical "mainstream" roles in movies and TV. Kotto's first film was *Nothing But a Man* (1964), an independently produced study of black pride in the face of white indifference. In 1972, Kotto produced, directed and wrote the feature film *Speed Limit 65* (aka *The Limit* and *Time Limit*), a one-of-a-kind "black biker" film which was seen by about three people. The biggest production with which Kotto was associated with in the early 1970s was the James Bond film *Live and Let Die*, in which, as the villainous Mr. Big, he was blown up in the final scene (a similarly grisly fate awaited Kotto in *Alien*). On television, Yaphet Kotto was a regular on the TV series *For Love and Honor* and *Homicide: Life on the Streets*, and was seen as Ugandan president Idi Amin in the 1977 TV movie *Raid on Entebbe*. **Selected Works:** *After the Shock* (1990), *Chrome Soldiers* (1992), *Extreme Justice* (1993), *Freddy's Dead: The Final Nightmare* (1991), *Robert A. Heinlein's The Puppet Masters* (1994)

# Ernie Kovacs

**Born:** January 23, 1919
**Died:** 1962

**Years Active in the Industry:** by decade

| 10s | 20s | 30s | 40s | 50s | 60s | 70s | 80s | 90s |
|-----|-----|-----|-----|-----|-----|-----|-----|-----|
|     |     |     |     |     |     |     |     |     |

Actor, television writer, director and producer Ernie Kovacs started in radio and was already established as a truly unique comic personality when he broke into television. His immediate fascination with the whole television concept led to his acquiring an unprecedented command of the medium not seen since. Throughout the '50s and early '60s, Kovacs dazzled and bewildered audiences with his repertoire of zany characters, his "back-of-the-head" humor and his newly discovered innovations such as "blue screen/chroma key;" he was truly television's comic genius. Kovacs embarked on a film career, and to his frustration found himself often cast as authoratative military figures. A highlight was his comic portrayal of a bewitched, drunken author in *Bell, Book and Candle* (1958). Kovac's death in a car accident on January 13, 1962 remains particularly tragic when one considers the possibilities of what he had in store for the future.

# Laszlo (Leslie) Kovacs

**Born:** May 14, 1933; Hungary

**Years Active in the Industry:** by decade

| 10s | 20s | 30s | 40s | 50s | 60s | 70s | 80s | 90s |
|-----|-----|-----|-----|-----|-----|-----|-----|-----|
|     |     |     |     |     |     |     |     |     |

Educated at Budapest's Academy of Drama and Film Art, Hungarian cinematographer Laszlo Kovacs fled to the U.S. during his country's 1956 revolution. Unable to crack the tight Hollywood cameraman's union, Kovacs took whatever jobs he could, principally on the independently produced quickies of such entrepreneurs as Arch Hall Sr. and Ray Dennis Steckler (he was billed as Leslie Kovacs during this period). He then moved on to American International, where his camerawork on a string of cheap motorcycle epics was frequently singled out for critical praise. Even in his least prepossessing projects, Kovacs displayed a keen sense of color schematics, a quality that attracted him to shoestring impresario Roger Corman. Fellow Corman protege Peter Bogdanovich engaged Kovacs to lens Bogdanovich's maiden directorial effort, *Targets* (1969), which has a brilliant photographic range far in excess of the usual low-budget film. Kovacs was then hired by yet another Corman alumnus, Peter Fonda, to shoot *Easy Rider* (1969); at first Kovacs balked, insisting that he didn't want to be typed as a cycle-flick cameraman, but he was persuaded that *Easy Rider* was to be of more value and meaning than the average "Hell's Angels" effort. While Kovacs failed to earn the Oscar nomination he so richly deserved for *Rider,* the film's reputation enabled him to move upward to increasingly important assignments. While in the employ of still another Corman trainee, Bob Rafaelson, Kovacs provided the brilliantly atmospheric camerwork for *Five Easy Pieces* (1970). Bogdanovich came calling again, and the result was Kovacs' brilliant photography for *What's Up Doc?* (1971); *Paper Moon* (1973) a rare opportunity to work in black and white; *At Long Last Love* (1975); and *Nickelodeon* (1976). While Kovacs would have been recognized as a master of his trade even without a box office hit to his name, he has fortunately been associated with several huge money-makers, including *Close Encounters of the Third Kind* (1978) and *Ghostbusters* (1984). **Selected Works:** *Mask* (1985), *Shattered* (1991), *The Next Karate Kid* (1994), *The Scout* (1994)

# Jeroen Krabbé

**Born:** December 5, 1944; Amsterdam, Holland

**Years Active in the Industry:** by decade

| 10s | 20s | 30s | 40s | 50s | 60s | 70s | 80s | 90s |
|-----|-----|-----|-----|-----|-----|-----|-----|-----|
|     |     |     |     |     |     |     |     |     |

Heavy-set, dour Dutch supporting actor of international films, Jeroen Krabbe tends to be typecast as a villain. He began to study acting at age 17, when he was the youngest student ever accepted at the Amsterdam Academy of Performing Arts. As a young man he founded a touring theater company, designed costumes, translated plays into Dutch, and directed. He is also an accomplished painter. He hosted a television talk show and a radio music program in Holland, and is the author of *The Economy Cookbook*. Aside from a role in a children's movie, *The Little Ark* (1972), Krabbe's debut onscreen came in Paul Verhoeven's *Soldier of Orange* (1979); he went on to play the lead in Verhoeven's *The Fourth Man* (1983), an international hit that led him to begin making movies outside Holland. His first British film was *Turtle Diary* (1985), and his Hollywood debut was *Jumpin' Jack Flash* (1986). He has continued a steady film career in English-speaking parts. **Selected Works:** *Fugitive* (1993), *King of the Hill* (1993), *Stalin* (1992), *Immortal Beloved* (1994)

# Stanley Kramer

**Born:** September 29, 1913; New York, NY

**Years Active in the Industry:** by decade

| 10s | 20s | 30s | 40s | 50s | 60s | 70s | 80s | 90s |
|-----|-----|-----|-----|-----|-----|-----|-----|-----|
|     |     |     |     |     |     |     |     |     |

Stanley Kramer was an editor and writer by the mid-'30s, and in the late '40s formed an independent production company, Screen Plays Inc. (which he'd bring into the fold of Columbia in 1951). Into the mid-'50s he produced a series of powerful and provocative films, most notably with directors Mark Robson (*Champion* [1949], *Home of the Brave* [1949]) and Fred Zinnemann (*The Men* [1950], *High Noon* [1942]). Many of his pictures dealt with long-ignored social issues, a commitment Kramer held to when he began directing (after helming two minor films he'd hoped would make some needed profits: the sudsy hospital drama *Not as a Stranger* [1955] and the period war tale *The Pride and the Passion* [1957]). In the late '50s, Kramer began making the films for which he's best known, starting with *The Defiant Ones* (1958), a

look at American racism, and *On the Beach* (1959), a prediction of life after a nuclear war. In the '60s he began an association with actor Spencer Tracy, making two landmark courtroom films, *Inherit the Wind* (1960) and *Judgment at Nuremberg* (1961), and two comedies, the slapstick epic *It's A Mad, Mad, Mad, Mad World* (1963) and Tracy's last film, *Guess Who's Coming to Dinner?* (1967), a charming romantic comedy of interracial love. Although critics typed Kramer as a message-monger, the public made these comedies his biggest box office hits. He went on to do some of his best work in the '70s with *Bless the Beasts and Children* (1971), *Oklahoma Crude* (1973), and *The Runner Stumbles* (1979), but the public stayed away. **Selected Works:** *Ship of Fools* (1965)

# Kris Kristofferson

**Born:** June 22, 1936; Brownsville, TX

**Years Active in the Industry:** by decade

| 10s | 20s | 30s | 40s | 50s | 60s | 70s | 80s | 90s |
|-----|-----|-----|-----|-----|-----|-----|-----|-----|
|     |     |     |     |     |     |     |     |     |

Attractive, usually bearded, blue-eyed singer-actor Kris Kristofferson has a devilish grin and definite sex appeal. A creative writing major in college, then an Oxford Rhodes Scholar, he served with the Army in Germany for five years and taught at West Point. Later began to become well known as a singer-songwriter, and eventually was a major country music recording star, perhaps best known for "Me and Bobby McGee." His first onscreen appearance was a bit part in Dennis Hopper's peculiar *The Last Movie* (1971), for which he also did the music; he then landed the title role in *Cisco Pike* (1972). Since then he has appeared in many films, often cast in rugged, quasi-cowboy roles. Kristofferson made three films with Sam Peckinpah, *Pat Garret and Billy the Kid* (in which he played Billy, 1973), *Bring Me the Head of Alfredo Garcia* (1974), and *Convoy* (1978). His career suffered after he appeared in the lead role of the disastrous *Heaven's Gate* (1981), and in the '80s he worked onscreen less and focused more on his recording career, especially as a member of The Highwaymen with music legends Willie Nelson, Johnny Cash, and Waylon Jennings. He married and divorced singer-actress Rita Coolidge, with whom he appeared in *Pat Garrett and Billy the Kid*. **Selected Works:** *Alice Doesn't Live Here Anymore* (1974), *A Star is Born* (1976), *Another Pair of Aces: Three of a Kind* (1991), *Cheatin' Hearts* (1993), *Christmas in Connecticut* (1992), *Miracle in the Wilderness* (1991)

# Stanley Kubrick

**Born:** July 26, 1928; Bronx, NY

**Years Active in the Industry:** by decade

| 10ˢ | 20ˢ | 30ˢ | 40ˢ | 50ˢ | 60ˢ | 70ˢ | 80ˢ | 90ˢ |
|-----|-----|-----|-----|-----|-----|-----|-----|-----|
|     |     |     |     | ■   |     |     |     |     |

A former staff photographer for *Look* magazine, Stanley Kubrick was a movie buff from an early age who made good in his childhood hobby. Beginning as a maker of documentary shorts—which he sold to RKO—he borrowed money to make his first feature, *Fear and Desire*, in 1953, and followed it up with the low-budget feature *Killer's Kiss* (1955). In partnership with James B. Harris, Kubrick formed his own production company in the mid-1950s and made his first major feature, *The Killing*, for United Artists in 1956. Kubrick's next film, *Paths of Glory* (1957), was a critical success that died at the box office, and he was without film assignments for the two years following its release. He replaced Anthony Mann as the director of *Spartacus* after the latter was fired, and transformed it into a superbly crafted cosutme epic which, as a major hit, validated Kubrick's capabilities as a money director. Kubrick's next two movies, *Lolita* (1962) and *Dr. Strangelove* (1964) establsihed him as a filmmaker with a penchant for black humor who often stretched the envelope of what was considered acceptable entertainment—*Strangelove,* in particular, with its jokes about the end of the world through nuclear accident peopled with half-lunatic military and political officials, was a breath of fresh air in an American popular culture that had been stifled by its own seriousness. *2001: A Space Odyssey* (1968) managed to be both pretentious and witty, while setting new technical and production standards for science fiction cinema, and *A Clockwork Orange* (1971) violated an armload of a taboos about sex, violence, and language while becoming a major hit, despite its original X-rating. *Barry Lyndon* (1975) and *The Shining* (1980) both suffered from excessive tedium in the course of presenting their stories, although *The Shining* became a hit because of its association with Stephen King, on whose novel it was based, and a manic but charismatic lead performance by Jack Nicholson. Kubrick's production output, never great—he is a meticulous craftsman, and even in his early days only made a film a year, and took three years between pictures in the 1960s—has decreased since the early 1980's, with 1987's *Full Metal Jacket* his most recent picture.

# Akira Kurosawa

**Born:** March 23, 1910; Omori, Tokyo, Japan

**Years Active in the Industry:** by decade

| 10ˢ | 20ˢ | 30ˢ | 40ˢ | 50ˢ | 60ˢ | 70ˢ | 80ˢ | 90ˢ |
|-----|-----|-----|-----|-----|-----|-----|-----|-----|
|     |     |     | ■   |     |     |     |     |     |

The most well-known of all Japanese directors, the great irony about Akira Kurosawa's career is that he is far more popular outside of Japan than he is in Japan. The son of an army officer, Kurosawa studied art before gravitating to film as a means of sup-porting himself. He served seven years as an assistant to director Kajiro Yamamoto before he began his own directorial career with *Sanshiro Sugata* (1943), a film about the 19th-century struggle for supremacy between adherents of judo and ju-jitsu that so impressed the military government, he was prevailed upon to make a sequel (*Sanshiro Sugata Part II*). Following the end of World War II, Kurosawa's career gathered speed with a series of films that cut across all genres, from crime thrillers to period dramas—among the latter, his *Rashomon* (1951) became the first postwar Japanese film to find wide favor with Western audiences, and simultaneously introduced leading man Toshiro Mifune to Western viewers. It was Kurosawa's *The Seven Samurai* (1954), however, that made the largest impact of any of his movies outside of Japan. Although heavily cut on its original release, this three-hour-plus medieval action drama, shot with painstaking attention to both dramatic and period detail, became one of the most popular of Japanese films of all time in the West, and every subsequent Kurosawa film has been released in the U.S. in some form, even if many—most notably *The Hidden Fortress* (1958)—were cut down in length. At the same time, American and European filmmakers began taking a serious look at Kurosawa's movies as a source of plot material for their own work—*Rashomon* was remade as *The Outrage*, in a western setting, while *Yojimbo* was remade by Sergio Leone as *A Fistful of Dollars* (1964). *The Seven Samurai* (1954) fared best of all, serving as the basis for John Sturges's *The Magnificent Seven* (which had been the original title of Kurosawa's movie), in 1960; the remake actually did better business in Japan than the original film did. In the early 1980s, an unfilmed screenplay of Kurosawa's also served as the basis for *Runaway Train* (1985), a popular action thriller. Kurosawa's movies subsequent to his period thriller *Sanjuro* (1962) abandoned the action format in favor of more esoteric and serious drama, including his epic length medical melodrama *Red Beard* (1965). In recent years, despite ill-health and the problems getting financing for his more ambitious films, Kurosawa has remained the most prominent of Japanese filmmakers. With his Westernized style, Kurosawa has always found a wider audience and more financing opportunities in Europe and America than he has in his own country. A sensitive romantic at heart, with a sentimental streak that occasionally rises forcefully to the surface of his movies, his work probably resembles that of John Ford more closely than it does any of his fellow Japanese filmmakers. **Selected Works:** *Kagemusha: The Shadow Warrior* (1980), *Ran* (1985), *Throne of Blood* (1957), *Dreams* (1990)

# Swoosie Kurtz

**Born:** September 6, 1944; Omaha, NE

**Years Active in the Industry:** by decade

| 10ˢ | 20ˢ | 30ˢ | 40ˢ | 50ˢ | 60ˢ | 70ˢ | 80ˢ | 90ˢ |
|-----|-----|-----|-----|-----|-----|-----|-----|-----|
|     |     |     |     |     |     | ■   |     |     |

Stage, screen, and TV actress Swoosie Kurtz's father was a colonel in the U.S. Air Force, and she was named after a plane he flew in World War II. After college she attended a drama school in London, and debuted onstage in a series of regional theater plays in the late '60s. In 1970 she appeared in an off-Broadway production of *The Effects of Gamma Rays on Man-in-the-Moon Marigolds,* for which she won an Obie Award; she went on to a successful stage career, winning two Tony Awards, a Drama Desk Award, and an Outer Critics' Circle Award. Eventually Hollywood took an interest, and she became a regular on the TV sitcom *Love, Sydney* winning an Emmy for her work. She debuted onscreen in a small role in Slap Shot (1977), then appeared in two successive flops; it was four years before her next screen role. Since 1982 she has had an intermittently busy film career, mostly in well-respected but not particularly successful productions. In the '90s she has co-starred in the TV series *Sisters.* **Selected Works:** *And the Band Played On* (1993), *Shock to the System* (1990), *Stanley and Iris* (1990), *Positively True Adventures of the Alleged Texas Cheerleader-Murdering Mom* (1993), *Reality Bites* (1994)

# Diane Kurys

**Born:** December 3, 1948; Lyons, France

**Years Active in the Industry:** by decade

| 10s | 20s | 30s | 40s | 50s | 60s | 70s | 80s | 90s |
|-----|-----|-----|-----|-----|-----|-----|-----|-----|
|     |     |     |     |     |     |     |     |     |

French filmmaker Diane Kurys began as an actress with Jean-Louis Barrault's company. She went on to nominal film stardom, but didn't like roles she was getting and wasn't fond of taking orders from others. With a government grant, Kurys wrote a screenplay which developed into her first directorial effort: *Peppermint Soda* (*Diabolo Menthe*, 1979), the first of several films which delved into Kurys' own life as a child of divorce, as well as her relationships with her parents and siblings. The divorce issue manifested itself into Kurys most popular film, 1983's *Entre Nous* (originally *Coup de Foudre*), which afforded actress Isabelle Huppert the opportunity for an excellent characterization as the heroine's mother. Kurys' autobiographical cinematic odyssey continued with 1990's *C'est la Vie*, in which her alter-ego leading character returned to the adolescent years previously explored in *Peppermint Soda.* **Selected Works:** *Love After Love* (1994), *Six Days, Six Nights* (1994)

# Alan Ladd

**Born:** September 3, 1913; Hot Springs, AR
**Died:** 1964

**Years Active in the Industry:** by decade

| 10ˢ | 20ˢ | 30ˢ | 40ˢ | 50ˢ | 60ˢ | 70ˢ | 80ˢ | 90ˢ |
|-----|-----|-----|-----|-----|-----|-----|-----|-----|
|     |     |     |     |     |     |     |     |     |

Alan Ladd was a short (5' 5"), unexpressive lead actor with icy good looks and a resonant voice. He worked in a variety of odd jobs before entering films in his late teens as a bit player and grip; he also worked on radio and in local theater. In the mid-'30s he began appearing regularly in minor screen roles. Hollywood agent Sue Carol discovered him and began trumpeting him as star material; she helped him land a major role in *This Gun for Hire* (1942) oppposite Veronica Lake. He quickly became a major star, and was teamed with Lake in other films, all hits. He and Carol married in 1942, and she remained his agent the rest of his life. Ladd was on the Top Ten Box Office Attractions list in 1947, 1953, and 1954. He continued to star in films through the '50s, but—with the exception of *Shane* (1953)—few of his films were noteworthy; most were entertaining adventure films featuring Ladd bare-chested and in fistfights, but by the late '50s their appeal was waning. A sensitive and insecure man suffering from alcoholism, he was nearly killed in the early 1960s by an "accidental" self-inflicted gunshot wound that some thought resulted from a suicide attempt. In 1964 he died from an overdose of sedatives mixed with alcohol, and again it was thought to have been intentional. He was the father of actors Alan Ladd Jr. and David Ladd, and former child actress Alana Ladd. **Selected Works:** *Joan of Paris* (1942), *Star Spangled Rhythm* (1942)

# Diane Ladd (Rose Diane Ladner)

**Born:** November 29, 1939; Meridian, MO

**Years Active in the Industry:** by decade

| 10ˢ | 20ˢ | 30ˢ | 40ˢ | 50ˢ | 60ˢ | 70ˢ | 80ˢ | 90ˢ |
|-----|-----|-----|-----|-----|-----|-----|-----|-----|
|     |     |     |     |     |     |     |     |     |

Diane Ladd moved to New York City as a teenager, finding work as a model and as a dancer at the Copacabana nightclub. Ladd went on to make her New York stage debut in Tennessee Williams's *Orpheus Descending*. She debuted onscreen in *Something Wild* (1961), but during the '60s made few films and concentrated on the stage. In 1966 she appeared in the film *Wild Angels* with Bruce Dern, whom she later married and divorced; they are the parents of actress Laura Dern. For her performance as the tough waitress Flo in Martin Scorsese's *Alice Doesn't Live Here Anymore* (1975), she received nominations for an Oscar, a Golden Globe Award, and a BAFTA award. In 1990 she appeared with her daughter in David Lynch's *Wild At Heart,* playing Dern's mother; she received a Best Supporting Actress Oscar nomination while her daughter got a Best Actress Oscar nomination, a unique event in the history of the movies. She also appeared with Dern in *Rambling Rose* (1991). **Selected Works:** *Cemetery Club* (1993), *Chinatown* (1974), *Lookalike* (1990), *Hold Me, Thrill Me, Kiss Me* (1993), *Rock Hudson* (1990)

# Christine Lahti

**Born:** April 4, 1950; Birmingham, MS

**Years Active in the Industry:** by decade

| 10s | 20s | 30s | 40s | 50s | 60s | 70s | 80s | 90s |
|-----|-----|-----|-----|-----|-----|-----|-----|-----|
|     |     |     |     |     |     |     | ■   |     |

Unpredictable American actress Christine Lahti majored in drama at the University of Michigan, then toured Europe with a group of pantomimists. She studied with Uta Hagen in New York, taking whatever stage work that came along (including her Obie award-winning performance in an off-Broadway revival of *Little Murders*) before being steadily employed on TV. In 1978, Lahti was costarred in *The Harvey Korman Show* as Korman's daughter. The following year, she made her first film, *...And Justice for All.* A scene stealer par excellence, Lahti often found her film roles reduced in the cutting room, usually at the behest of nervous stars. Her performance as Hazel Zenutti in *Swing Shift* (1984) was severly pared down after previews, allegedly on star Goldie Hawn's orders, but that didn't prevent Lahti from being nominated for an Oscar. The endearingly off-balance nature of many of Christine Lahti's screen characters is best summed up by her scene in *Housekeeping* (1987), in which she calmly carries on a conversation while her living room fills up with water. **Selected Works:** *Crazy from the Heart* (1991), *Doctor* (1991), *Fear Inside* (1992), *Good Fight* (1992), *Running on Empty* (1988)

# Arthur Lake (Arthur Silverlake)

**Born:** April 17, 1905; Corbin, KY
**Died:** September 25, 1987; Indian Wells, CA

**Years Active in the Industry:** by decade

| 10s | 20s | 30s | 40s | 50s | 60s | 70s | 80s | 90s |
|-----|-----|-----|-----|-----|-----|-----|-----|-----|
|     | ■   | ■   |     |     |     |     |     |     |

Truly a single-note man, American actor Arthur Lake spent most of his adult life portraying only one screen role: Dagwood Bumstead. The son of circus acrobats and the brother of character actress Florence Lake (famed for her ongoing portrayal of Mrs. Edgar Kennedy in nearly 100 two-reel comedies), Lake began his professional career as one of the "Fox Kiddies" in a series of silent-film takeoffs of famous fairy tales, featuring casts comprised completely of children. Lake graduated to a succession of collegiate and office boy roles in feature films, gaining a degree of stardom in the late 1920s and early 1930s after appearing in the title role of *Harold Teen* (1928). The actor's high-pitched voice and mama's boy features were amusing for a while, but audiences became bored with Lake by 1934, and the actor found himself shunted to supporting parts and bits. An amusing role as a flustered bellboy in *Topper* (1937) rejuvenated his career, but Lake's comeback wouldn't be complete until Columbia Pictures cast him as woebegone suburbanite Dagwood Bumstead in *Blondie* (1938), based on Chic Young's internationally popular comic strip. The strip's characterizations were altered to fit the personalities of Lake and his costar Penny Singleton; in the films, Dagwood was the dope and Blondie the brains of the family, precisely the opposite of the

comic-strip situation. A few scattered "straight" performances aside, Lake was nothing other than Dagwood in films from 1938 through 1950; he not only starred in 28 "Blondie" pictures, but repeated the role on radio and starred in an unsuccessful 1954 TV series based on the property. Not at all the blithering idiot that he played on screen, Lake was a sagacious businessman in real life, his wise investments increasing the fortune he'd already accumulated by playing Dagwood—and also bolstering the moneys inherited by his socialite wife, Patricia Van Cleve. Though he often remarked that it would be wonderful to play Dagwood forever, Lake parted company with the role in the mid-1950s; when another *Blondie* TV series appeared briefly in 1968, it starred Will Hutchins. Appearing publicly only rarely in the 1960s and 1970s (usually in summer theatres and revivals of 1920s musicals like *No, No Nanette*), Lake retired before his 70th birthday, a far more prosperous and secure man than his alter ego Dagwood Bumstead—who's *still* being fired regularly by boss Mr. Dithers in the funny papers—ever would be.

# Veronica Lake (Constance Frances Marie Ockelman)

**Born:** November 14, 1919; Brooklyn, NY
**Died:** July 7, 1973

**Years Active in the Industry:** by decade

| 10s | 20s | 30s | 40s | 50s | 60s | 70s | 80s | 90s |
|-----|-----|-----|-----|-----|-----|-----|-----|-----|
|     |     |     | ■   |     |     |     |     |     |

When Brooklyn-born Constance Ockleman was prodded into a performing career by her ambitious mother, she chose her stepfather's name, Keane, for her *nom de stage*. After a year of thankless bit parts, she was dropped by RKO Radio Pictures. When she re-emerged at MGM in a small role in the Eddie Cantor vehicle *40 Little Mothers* (1940), she was known as Veronica Lake. While posing for publicity pictures, Lake inadvertently allowed her blonde hair to obscure one eye, thereby creating her movie persona as "the girl with the peek-a-boo bang." Signed by Paramount in 1941, Lake quickly ascended to leading roles—and with equal swiftness earned a reputation for being temperamental and unprofessional. Certain directors like Preston Sturges and Rene Clair had the patience to draw genuine performances from Lake, but for the most part she was cast on the basis of her beauty and popularity, with acting hardly a

matter of consideration. In *This Gun for Hire* (1942), Lake was teamed with up-and-coming Alan Ladd, thereby launching one of Paramount's most successful screen duos. Even at the peak of her popularity, however, the studio was paying Lake only a pittance, so it's somewhat understandable that she was testy on the set and spent most of her off-hours in the company of rich and influential men. Eventually renegotiating her contact and finding brief domestic happiness with her second husband, director Andre De Toth, Lake flourished professionally and financially until 1948, when she was hit with the double whammy of being dropped by Paramount and being sued for support payments by her mother. DeToth wangled a good role for Lake in the 20th Century-Fox film *Slattery's Hurricane* (1949), but it failed to rekindle her stardom or save her tottering marriage. She left Hollywood in the early 1950s, making a living with stage appearances. An unhappy third marriage, an increasing dependence on alcoholism, and a stage injury effectively ended her career, and by 1959 she was working as a Manhattan barmaid. Lake staged a comeback as a Baltimore TV host in the early 1960s; viewers who remembered her glory days were willing to ignore the fact that she'd lost her looks and her trim figure. Lake financed two cheap film vehicles for herself in 1966 (*Footsteps in the Snow*) and 1970 (*Flesh Feast*), and also penned a tell-all autobiography in 1969 in which she placed blame on everyone but herself for her current condition. After seeking stage work in England, Lake returned to the U.S. in 1971; two years later, after several more alcoholic episodes and failed comeback attempts, she died of hepatitis while visiting friends in Burlington, Vermont. **Selected Works:** *I Married a Witch* (1942), *Sullivan's Travels* (1941), *So Proudly We Hail* (1943), *Star Spangled Rhythm* (1942)

# Hedy Lamarr

**Born:** November 9, 1914; Vienna, Austria

**Years Active in the Industry:** by decade

| 10ˢ | 20ˢ | 30ˢ | 40ˢ | 50ˢ | 60ˢ | 70ˢ | 80ˢ | 90ˢ |
|-----|-----|-----|-----|-----|-----|-----|-----|-----|

The daughter of a Vienesse banker, Hedy Lamarr began her acting career at 16 under the tutelage of German impresario Max Reinhardt. She began appearing in German films in 1930, but garnered little attention until her star turn in Czech director Gustav Machaty's *Extase* (*Ecstacy*) in 1933. It wasn't just because Lamarr appeared briefly in the nude; *Extase* was filled to overflowing with orgasmic imagery, including tight closeups of Lamarr in the throes of delighted passion. Though her first husband, Austrian businessman Fritz Mandl, tried to buy up and destroy all prints of *Extase*, the film enjoyed worldwide distribution, the result being that Lamarr was famous in America before ever setting foot in Hollywood. She was signed by producer Walter Wanger to co-star with Charles Boyer in the American remake of the French *Pepe Le Moko*, titled *Algiers* (1938). That Lamarr wasn't much of an actress was compensated for with several scenes in which was required to merely stand around silently and look beautiful (she would later downgrade these performances, equating sex appeal with "looking

stupid"). The prudish Louis B. Mayer was willing to forgive Lamarr the "indiscretion" of *Extase* by signing her to a long MGM contract in 1939. Most of her subsequent roles were merely decorative (never more so than as Tondelayo in *White Cargo* [1940]), though she was first rate in the complex role of the career woman who "liberates" stuffy Bostonian Robert Young in *H.M. Pulham Esq.* (1942). In 1949, Lamarr, tastefully underdressed, appeared opposite the equally attractive Victor Mature in Cecil B. DeMille's *Samson and Delilah* (1949), a coupling that moved Groucho Marx to comment, "First picture I ever saw where the male lead's tits were bigger than the female's." Lamarr's limited thespic skills became more pronounced in her 1950s films, especially when she gamely tried to play Joan of Arc in the all-star disaster *The Story of Mankind* (1957). She disappeared from films in 1958; seven years later she was arrested for shoplifting, resulting in an outpouring of public sympathy for her current reduced financial state. An autobiography, *Ectasy and Me,* enabled her to pay many of her debts, though she'd later sue her collaborators for distorting the facts. In another legal action, Lamarr took on director Mel Brooks for using the character name "Hedley Lamarr" in his 1974 western spoof *Blazing Saddles.* In 1990, Lamarr made an unexpected return before the cameras in the obscure low-budget Hollywood satire *Instant Karma,* in which she was typecast in the role of "Movie Goddess." **Selected Works:** *Tortilla Flat* (1942)

# Christopher Lambert

**Born:** March 29, 1957; New York, NY

**Years Active in the Industry:** by decade

| 10ˢ | 20ˢ | 30ˢ | 40ˢ | 50ˢ | 60ˢ | 70ˢ | 80ˢ | 90ˢ |
|-----|-----|-----|-----|-----|-----|-----|-----|-----|

Born in New York City and brought up by his French parents in Geneva, Christopher Lambert briefly worked at the London Stock Exchange, then studied acting at the National Conservatory in Paris, where he was expelled after three years. He soon landed a role in the French film *Le Bar Du Telephone* (1980) and within two years had appeared in three French films. His English language debut was in *Greystoke: The Legend of Tarzan* (1984); an attractive, well-built man, he soon attracted a large following among women as a movie sex symbol, and in France he is something of a "pin-up." Lambert went on to work steadily in both American and French films, often in actioners. He is married to actress Diane Lane, with whom he appeared in *Knight Moves* (1992). **Selected Works:** *Fortress* (1993), *Highlander: The Final Dimension* (1995)

# Dorothy Lamour (Maryleta Dorothy Kaumeyer)

**Born:** December 10, 1914; New Orleans, LA

**Years Active in the Industry:** by decade

| 10ˢ | 20ˢ | 30ˢ | 40ˢ | 50ˢ | 60ˢ | 70ˢ | 80ˢ | 90ˢ |
|-----|-----|-----|-----|-----|-----|-----|-----|-----|

American actress/singer Dorothy Lamour graduated from Spencer Business College, after spending a few teen years as an elevator operator in her home town of New Orleans. By 1930, she'd

turned her back on the business world and was performing in the Fanchon and Marco vaudeville troupe. In 1931, she became vocalist for the Herbie Kay Band, and soon afterward married Kay (it didn't last). In the years just prior to her film debut, Lamour built up a solid reputation as a radio singer, notably on the 1934 series *Dreamer of Songs.* Paramount Pictures signed Lamour to a contract in 1936, creating an exotic southseas image for the young actress: she wore her fabled sarong for the first time in *Jungle Princess* (1936), the first of three non-sensical but high-grossing "jungle" films in which the ingenuous island girl asked her leading man what a kiss was. A more prestigious "sarong" role came about in Goldwyn's *The Hurricane* (1937), wherein Lamour, ever the trouper, withstood tons of water being thrust upon her in the climactic tempest of the film's title. A major star by 1939, Lamour had developed enough onscreen self awareness to amusingly kid her image in *St. Louis Blues* (1939), in which she played a jaded movie star who balked at playing any more southseas parts. Lamour's latter-day fame was secured in 1940, when she co-starred in *Road to Singapore* (1940), the first of six "Road" pictures teaming Lamour with Bob Hope and Bing Crosby. It represented both a career summit and a downslide: as the "Road" series progressed, Lamour found herself with fewer and fewer comic lines, and by 1952's *Road to Bali* she was little more than a decorative "straight woman" for Bob and Bing. Very popular with the troops during World War II, Lamour gave selflessly of her time and talent in camp tours, USO shows and bond drives throughout the early 1940s. A tough cookie who brooked no non-sense on the set, Lamour was nonetheless much loved by Paramount casts and crews, many of which remained friends even after the studio dropped her contract in the early 1950s. Occasionally retiring from films during her heyday to devote time to her family, Lamour was out of Hollywood altogether between 1952 and 1962, during which time she developed a popular nightclub act. She returned to films for Hope and Crosby's *Road to Hong Kong* (1962), not as leading lady (that assignment was given to Joan Collins) but as a special guest star—this time she was allowed as many joke lines as her co-stars in her one scene. More on stage than on film in the 1960s and 1970s, Lamour was one of several veteran actresses to star in *Hello Dolly,* and spent much of her time in regional productions of such straight plays as *Barefoot in the Park.* Lamour's latest film acting job to date was in the 1976 TV movie *Death at Love House,* though she has been a most loquacious par-

ticipant in the many Bob Hope TV birthday specials and was recently the sprightly subject of an interview conducted by Prof. Richard Brown on cable's American Movie Classics channel. **Selected Works:** *Greatest Show on Earth* (1952), *Star Spangled Rhythm* (1942)

# Burt Lancaster (Burton Stephen Lancaster)

**Born:** November 2, 1913; New York, NY
**Died:** October 20, 1994

**Years Active in the Industry:** by decade

| 10s | 20s | 30s | 40s | 50s | 60s | 70s | 80s | 90s |
|-----|-----|-----|-----|-----|-----|-----|-----|-----|
|     |     |     |     |     |     |     |     |     |

A handsome, strapping leading man with a boyish grin and athlete's physique, Burt Lancaster grew up in the tough East Harlem section of Manhattan's Upper East Side, excelling in bas-

ketball and other high school sports. An athletic scholarship got him into NYU; but he soon quit college and formed an acrobatic team called Lang and Cravat with a diminutive childhood friend, Nick Cravat (who went on to appear in several films, including Lancaster's). They toured with circuses and appeared in vaudeville and night-clubs over the next several years. In 1941 he was obliged to take day jobs, then joined the Army and served in World War II with Special Services in North Africa and Italy. According to his studio biographers, he was "discovered" after the war in an elevator by a stage director who mistook him for a well-known actor and invited him to read for a Broadway part; he went on to appear in *The Sound of Hunting* (1945) for its three-week run on Broadway, during which he was spotted by Hollywood scouts. Lancaster's screen debut came in *The Killers* (1946), which immediately established him as a star; he was careful to avoid typecasting in "beefcake" adventure roles, and seached for parts that could demonstrate his versatility and sensitivity as an actor. While pursuing a busy screen career, in 1948 he became an independent producer and formed the Hecht-Lancaster company with his agent, James Hecht. He directed one film, *The Kentuckian* (1955), in which he also starred. His company produced a number of significant films in the '50s, including *Marty* (1951). For his performance as the charlatan title character of *Elmer Gantry* (1960) he received a Best Actor Oscar; in 1962 he won the Venice Film Festival Award for his work in *Birdman of Alcatraz.* He continued to find good roles straight up to *Field of Dreams* (1989), his final film appearance. **Selected Works:** *At-*

*lantic City* (1981), *From Here to Eternity* (1953), *Local Hero* (1983), *Seven Days in May* (1964), *Voyage of Terror: The Achille Lauro Affair* (1990), *The Sweet Smell of Success* (1957)

## Elsa Lanchester (Elizabeth Sullivan)

**Born:** October 28, 1902; London, England
**Died:** December 26, 1986

**Years Active in the Industry:** by decade

| 10ˢ | 20ˢ | 30ˢ | 40ˢ | 50ˢ | 60ˢ | 70ˢ | 80ˢ | 90ˢ |
|-----|-----|-----|-----|-----|-----|-----|-----|-----|
|     |     | ██  | ██  | ██  | ██  | ██  |     |     |

Eccentric, high-voiced British comedienne/actress Elsa Lanchester started her career as a modern dancer, appearing with Isadora Duncan. Lanchester can be seen bringing unique and usually humorous interpretations to roles in *The Private Life of Henry VIII* (1933), opposite husband Charles Laughton; *The Bride of Frankenstein* (1934), where she appears both as a subdued Mary Shelley and a hissing bride; *David Copperfield* and *Naughty Marietta* (both 1935); *Tales of Manhattan* (1942) and *Forever and a Day* (1943), both with Laughton; *Lassie Come Home* (1943), in which she is unusually subdued as the mother; *The Bishop's Wife* (1947); *The Inspector General* and *The Secret Garden* (1949); and *Come to the Stable* (1949), for which she was nominated for an Oscar. She and Laughton are riotous together in *Witness for the Prosecution* (1957), for which she was also Oscar-nominated, and she also appeared in *Bell, Book and Candle* (1958) and the Disney films *Mary Poppins* (1964), as the departing nanny Katie Nanna, and in *That Darn Cat* (1965). One of her best late performances was in *Murder by Death* (1976). Lanchester was also an actress at London's Old Vic, an outlandish singer, and a nightclub performer; she co-starred on *The John Forsythe Show* (1965-66), and was a regular on *Nanny and the Professor* in 1971. **Selected Works:** *Ghost Goes West* (1936), *Razor's Edge* (1946), *Rembrandt* (1936), *Spiral Staircase* (1946)

## Martin Landau

**Born:** June 20, 1931; Brooklyn, NY

**Years Active in the Industry:** by decade

| 10ˢ | 20ˢ | 30ˢ | 40ˢ | 50ˢ | 60ˢ | 70ˢ | 80ˢ | 90ˢ |
|-----|-----|-----|-----|-----|-----|-----|-----|-----|
|     |     |     |     | ██  | ██  | ██  | ██  | ██  |

Saturnine character actor Martin Landau was a staff cartoonist for the *New York Daily News* before switching to acting. Extremely busy in the days of live, Manhattan-based television, Landau made his cinematic mark with his second film appearance, playing James Mason's implicitly homosexual henchman in Hitchcock's *North by Northwest* (1959). In 1966, Landau and his actress wife Barbara Bain were both cast on the TV adventure/espionage series *Mission: Impossible*. For three years, Landau portrayed Rollin Hand, a master of disguise with the acute ability to impersonate virtually every villain who came down the pike (banana-re-

public despots were a specialty). Unhappy with changes in production personnel and budget cuts, the Landaus left the series in 1969. Six years later, they costarred in *Space: 1999,* a popular syndicated sci-fier; the performances of Landau, Bain, and third lead Barry Morse helped to gloss over the glaring gaps in continuity and logic which characterized the series' two-year run. The couple would subsequently act together several times (*The Harlem Globetrotters on Gilligan's Island* [1981] was one of the less distinguished occasions) before their marriage dissolved. Working steadily in variable projects throughout the 1980s, Landau enjoyed a career renaissance with two consecutive Oscar nominations, the first for Francis Ford Coppola's *Tucker: A Man and His Dream* (1988), and the second for Woody Allen's *Crimes and Misdemeanors* (1989). Landau finally won an Academy Award for his portrayal of Bela Lugosi in 1994's *Ed Wood;* Landau's justifiably heated refusal to cut his acceptance speech short when ordered to do so was one of the high points of the 1995 Oscar ceremony. **Selected Works:** *Legacy of Lies* (1992), *Max & Helen* (1990), *Mistress* (1991)

## John Landis

**Born:** August 30, 1950; Chicago, IL

**Years Active in the Industry:** by decade

| 10ˢ | 20ˢ | 30ˢ | 40ˢ | 50ˢ | 60ˢ | 70ˢ | 80ˢ | 90ˢ |
|-----|-----|-----|-----|-----|-----|-----|-----|-----|
|     |     |     |     |     |     | ██  | ██  | ██  |

Chicago-born John Landis began his film career on the crew of *Kelly's Heroes* (1970), and his first film was *Schlock* (1973), a parody of the Joan Crawford Neanderthal man thriller *Trog* among other films. His subsequent *Kentucky Fried Movie* (1977) became a

cult favorite, but it was *National Lampoon's Animal House* (1978) that put Landis on the map, earning over $40 million and making film stars of several of its cast members, most of whom had previously worked only in television. Landis' subsequent career has been somewhat uneven, veering between successful satire such as *The Blues Brothers* (1980) and *Amazon Women on the Moon* (1987) and big-budget failures like *The Twilight Zone: The Movie* (1983), whose production—with the accidental death of three cast members—created a major scandal at the time, although the director was later absolved of responsibility for the accident. **Selected Works:** *Innocent Blood* (1992), *Oscar* (1991), *Sindbad The Dream Quest* (1992)

# Diane Lane

**Born:** January 22, 1965; New York, NY

**Years Active in the Industry:** by decade

| 10ˢ | 20ˢ | 30ˢ | 40ˢ | 50ˢ | 60ˢ | 70ˢ | 80ˢ | 90ˢ |
|-----|-----|-----|-----|-----|-----|-----|-----|-----|
|     |     |     |     |     |     |     |     |     |

Actress Diane Lane, notable for playing sultry women in films such as *The Cotton Club* (1984), began her career as a distinguished child actress. The daughter of drama coach Burt Lane, she made her acting debut at age six when she joined Cafe La Mama, a renowned experimental group from New York. With them she toured Europe in *Medea, Electra* and *The Trojan Women*. She then worked for Joseph Papp, appearing in his productions of *The Cherry Orchard* and *Agamemnon* at Lincoln Center. Her portrayal of the lead in the off-Broadway hit *Runaways* won her critical acclaim in 1978. She made her film debut playing opposite Laurence Olivier in *A Little Romance* (1979) when she was only fourteen. She went on to play in several more features and TV movies until she met director Francis Ford Coppola, who became a mentor. She appeared in his films *The Outsiders* (1983), *Rumble Fish* (1983), and *The Cotton Club*. She is married to actor Christopher Lambert. **Selected Works:** *Lonesome Dove* (1989), *My New Gun* (1992), *Knight Moves* (1993), *Oldest Living Confederate Widow Tells All* (1994)

# Fritz Lang (Friedrich Christian Anton Lang)

**Born:** December 5, 1890; Vienna, Austria
**Died:** August 2, 1976

**Years Active in the Industry:** by decade

| 10ˢ | 20ˢ | 30ˢ | 40ˢ | 50ˢ | 60ˢ | 70ˢ | 80ˢ | 90ˢ |
|-----|-----|-----|-----|-----|-----|-----|-----|-----|
|     |     |     |     |     |     |     |     |     |

Trained as an artist and architect, Fritz Lang served in the Austrian army during World War I and was discharged after being wounded four times. While recovering, he began writing screenplays, and joined the German film industry as a writer and story editor. He made his first film in 1919, and a year later was established as a promising and commercially successful filmmaker. By the mid-1920s, he was one of Germany's top directors, with a ferociously individualistic Expressionist style which manifested itself in his series of films built around the charismatic criminal figure of Dr. Mabuse. A visit to New York helped give Lang the inspiration for the first of his two

best known German movies, *Metropolis* (1926), a dazzling futuristic work that carried the angular sets and perspectives of German Expressionism to its extreme. In 1931, Lang directed *M* (1931), a tale of the manhunt for a serial murderer of children that made a star of Peter Lorre and held audiences around the world spellbound with its vivid depiction of an underworld made up of grifters, thugs, and general lowlifes who were never so well represented on the screen. Lang left Germany after Hitler came to power and, following a stay in Paris (where he directed *Liliom* [1935]) he came to America. His first U.S. film, *Fury* (1936) was one of the most controversial and important films made at MGM during the 1930s, but its serious anti-lynching theme didn't set well with the studio. Lang found difficulty at first working with an American crew, and he didn't remain at the studio. After a brief stay with independent producer Walter Wanger, he moved to 20th Century-Fox, where he made a string of successes with *The Return of Frank James* (1940) and *Man Hunt* (1941). Lang worked independently for the remainder of the 1940s and created hits in the thrillers *The Woman in the Window*, *Scarlet Street*, and *Ministry of Fear*, all in 1945. His doom-laden psychological western *Rancho Notorious* (1952) has remained well regarded, and his 1956 urban manhunt drama *While the City Sleeps* (based on the novel *The Bloody Spur*) is still thought of as one of the best of its kind. Lang returned to Europe in the late 1950s and found mixed, limited success with various projects, including a revival of his Dr. Mabuse character from the 1920's. He subsequently turned to acting, very briefly, before retiring in America. **Selected Works:** *Hangmen Also Die* (1943)

# Harry Langdon

**Born:** June 15, 1884; Council Bluffs, IA
**Died:** 1944

**Years Active in the Industry:** by decade

| 10ˢ | 20ˢ | 30ˢ | 40ˢ | 50ˢ | 60ˢ | 70ˢ | 80ˢ | 90ˢ |
|-----|-----|-----|-----|-----|-----|-----|-----|-----|
|     |     |     |     |     |     |     |     |     |

After working several odd jobs, Harry Langdon joined an Omaha medicine show and went on to spend 20 years traveling with minstrel shows, circuses, burlesque, and vaudeville; he had some success with a comedy act called "Jimmy's New Car." Langdon was in his late 30s when he joined Mack Sennett's film company in 1923. He quickly appeared in numerous two-reel comedies, in the course of which he developed his own screen persona: his childlike face covered by traditional pantomime white make-up, he wore a tightly buttoned jacket as though he were a boy who had outgrown it. Juvenile in appearance, he played the bewildered, clumsy, wide-eyed simpleton out of step with the behavior of normal adults, eerily baffled by erotic situations and naively trusting in the world's goodness. The character caught on, and by 1926 he was one of the Big Four of American screen comedy (along with Chaplin, Lloyd, and Keaton). His best work was done in collaboration with director Harry Edwards and writer Frank Capra. Langdon's enormous success fuelled his ego, and after a year or two he dispensed with Edwards and Capra and took sole responsibility for his films. However, his talent was limited, and his efforts were disastrous; furthermore, he stubbornly refused to adapt his style to changing tastes. He was also a poor businessman, and he once spent the entire $150,000 budget of a film before a word of it had been written. Much of his own substantial salary went to alimony payments. Langdon was soon fired by his film company, after which he returned to vaudeville for almost two years. When he returned to Hollywood, the sound era was underway and he was out of touch with prevailing fashions. By 1931 he had to file for bankruptcy. He went on to appear in numerous films as a character player, and also starred in dozen of talkie shorts, never reclaiming his earlier popularity.

# Jessica Lange

**Born:** April 20, 1949; Cloquet, MN

**Years Active in the Industry:** by decade

| 10s | 20s | 30s | 40s | 50s | 60s | 70s | 80s | 90s |
|-----|-----|-----|-----|-----|-----|-----|-----|-----|
|     |     |     |     |     |     |     |     |     |

After two years of college, native Minnesotan Jessica Lange studied mime in Paris and danced for several months in the Opera Comique's chorus. After returning to the U.S., she became a model in New York. One of many unknowns screen-tested by producer Dino De Laurentiis for the lead in his remake of *King Kong* (1976), Lange got the part and signed a seven-year contract with De Laurentiis that later proved to be restrictive to her career; three years passed before she appeared in her second film, *All That Jazz* (1979), in which she gave a much better performance than she had in *King Kong*. Her breakthrough role came in Bob Rafelson's *The Postman Always Rings Twice* (1981), a sexually-charged film in which she played opposite Jack Nicholson. The attention Lange gained led to her next role, as a starlet in the Dustin Hoffman vehicle *Tootsie* (1982), for which she won the Best Supporting Actress Oscar; the same year she earned another Oscar nomination (for Best Actress) for her work in *Frances* (1982), a film she initiated and in which she played tragic real-life actress Francis Farmer. She had a child with ballet star Mikhail Baryshnikov, before entering into a long-term relationship with playwright-actor Sam Shepard; she costarred with him in *Country* (1984), which she also co-produced and for which she received another Best Actress Oscar nomination (she

also received the same nomination for her work in *Sweet Dreams*, [1985] and *Music Box* [1989]). In 1991 she played Blanche Dubois in a Broadway revival of *A Streetcar Named Desire*. Lange finally captured the Best Actress Oscar with her fifth nomination for her portrayal as the eccentric military wife in *Blue Sky*, released in 1994 after being shelved for three years by financially troubled Orion. **Selected Works:** *Cape Fear* (1991), *Night and the City* (1992), *Losing Isaiah* (1995)

# Frank Langella

**Born:** January 1, 1940; Bayonne, NJ

**Years Active in the Industry:** by decade

| 10s | 20s | 30s | 40s | 50s | 60s | 70s | 80s | 90s |
|-----|-----|-----|-----|-----|-----|-----|-----|-----|
|     |     |     |     |     |     |     |     |     |

American actor Frank Langella has been on the verge of screen stardom at several junctures in his career, but has always preferred to return to his first love, the theatre. After his first flurry of professional experience in stock and at the Lincoln Center Repertory, 23-year-old Langella made his Broadway bow in *The Immoralist*, a play that had served as a vehicle for James Dean ten years earlier. Most of his subsequent stage work was off-Broadway, earning him three Obie Awards. In 1970, Langella made his film debut as Carrie Snodgress' handsome but shallow extramarital assignation in *Diary of a Mad Housewife;* that same year, he starred in Mel Brooks' zany *The Twelve Chairs,* which has since built up a cult following but which died at the box office upon its first release. A handful of films followed, after which Langella went back to Broadway, winning a Tony for his 1977 performance in *Seascape.* The following season, he played to SRO crowds in a revival of the Balderstone-Deane play *Dracula,* carrying over his charismatic portrayal of the Count into an elaborate 1979 screen version (a later regional stage appearance as another literary icon, Sherlock Holmes, was videotaped and telecast on cable TV in the mid-1980s). In 1980, Langella garnered some of his best-ever movie reviews for his portrayal of a charming but ageing stock company leading man in *Those Lips, Those Eyes;* since that time, his movie roles have become fewer and farther between, while his always welcome and well-received stage appearances have increased. **Selected Works:** *Dave* (1993), *True Identity* (1991), *Junior* (1994)

# Angela Lansbury

**Born:** October 16, 1925; London, England

**Years Active in the Industry:** by decade

| 10s | 20s | 30s | 40s | 50s | 60s | 70s | 80s | 90s |
|-----|-----|-----|-----|-----|-----|-----|-----|-----|
|     |     |     |     |     |     |     |     |     |

Angela Lansbury garnered an Academy Award nomination for her first film, *Gaslight,* in 1944, and has been winning acting awards and audience favor ever since. Born in London of a family that included both politicians and performers, Lansbury came to the U.S. during World War II. She made notable early film appearances as the snooty sister in *National Velvet* (1944), the pathetic singer in *The Picture of Dorian Gray* (1945), which garnered her another Oscar nomination, and the evil-with-a-heart-of-gold saloon singer in *The Harvey Girls* (1946). She turned evil as the manipulative publisher in *State of the Union* (1948), but was just as convincing as the good queen in *The Three Musketeers* (1948) and the petulant daughter in *The Court Jester* (1956). She received another Oscar nomination for her chilling performance as the mother in *The Manchurian Candidate* (1962) and appeared as the addled witch in *Bedknobs and Broomsticks* (1971), among other later films. On Broadway, she won Tony Awards for the musicals *Mame* (1966), *Dear World* (1969), the revival of *Gypsy* (1975) and *Sweeney Todd* (1979). Despite a season in the '50s on the game show *Pantomime Quiz*, she came to series television late, starring since 1984 as Jessica Fletcher on *Murder, She Wrote*. She took over producing chores for the show in the 1990s. She returned to the Disney studios to record the voice of Mrs. Potts in *Beauty and the Beast* (1991) and to sing the title song. Lansbury is the sister of TV producer Bruce Lansbury. **Selected Works:** *Death on the Nile* (1978), *Samson and Delilah* (1950), *World of Henry Orient* (1964), *Dark at the Top of the Stairs* (1960), *Love She Sought* (1990)

## Mario Lanza (Alfred Arnold Coccozza)

**Born:** January 31, 1921; Philadelphia, PA
**Died:** 1959

**Years Active in the Industry:** by decade

| 10ˢ | 20ˢ | 30ˢ | 40ˢ | 50ˢ | 60ˢ | 70ˢ | 80ˢ | 90ˢ |
|-----|-----|-----|-----|-----|-----|-----|-----|-----|
|     |     |     |     |     |     |     |     |     |

Powerful tenor Mario Lanza studied singing from childhood, and in 1942 gained an audition with conductor Serge Koussevitzky; as a result, he won a scholarship and appeared at the Berkshire Summer Festival in Tanglewood. He was soon signed to a concert tour contract by Columbia, but the tour was interrupted by his World War II service. After his discharge, MGM signed him to a film contract and he starred in a number of tailor-made musical vehicles, beginning with *That Midnight Kiss* (1949). For several years he was greatly popular; his muscular appearance and powerful voice won many fans, and his rise was rapid. However, he had a problem with alcohol and barbituates and constantly had to fight against obesity; this plus his volatile personality led to a dramatic, quick decline in his career. By the late-'50s he was appearing only in minor films. He died at 38 from a heart attack, partly attributable to the effects of a crash diet.

## Anthony LaPaglia

**Born:** 1958; Adelaide, Australia

**Years Active in the Industry:** by decade

| 10ˢ | 20ˢ | 30ˢ | 40ˢ | 50ˢ | 60ˢ | 70ˢ | 80ˢ | 90ˢ |
|-----|-----|-----|-----|-----|-----|-----|-----|-----|
|     |     |     |     |     |     |     |     |     |

Australian actor Anthony LaPaglia has the face of a kindly city cop, which describes his typical role. When he arrived in the U.S. at age 25, LaPaglia had plans to become a teacher. Those plans receded farther into the background the more his agent called him on the phone, so by 1988 LaPaglia was a full time actor. Usually safely enscored in the supporting cast list, LaPaglia has been seen in such films as *Betsy's Wedding* (1990), *So I Married an Axe Murderer* (1993), and three 1991 films: *He Said She Said, 29th Street,* and *One Good Cop.* On TV, LaPaglia strayed to the wrong side of the law as Capone-era gangster Frank Nitti in *Nitti: The Enforcer* (1988). **Selected Works:** *Innocent Blood* (1992), *Keeper of the City* (1992), *Whispers in the Dark* (1992), *The Client* (1994)

## John Larroquette

**Born:** November 25, 1947; New Orleans, LA

**Years Active in the Industry:** by decade

| 10ˢ | 20ˢ | 30ˢ | 40ˢ | 50ˢ | 60ˢ | 70ˢ | 80ˢ | 90ˢ |
|-----|-----|-----|-----|-----|-----|-----|-----|-----|
|     |     |     |     |     |     |     |     |     |

American actor John Larroquette began gaining public attention as a disc jockey. For several years, he paid the bills with TV and movie voiceovers, notably as the (uncredited) narrator of Tobe Hooper's *The Texas Chainsaw Massacre* (1974). Larroquette started getting on-camera assignments in the mid-1970s, making his network TV bow in the role of Dr. Paul Herman in the prime time weekly *Doctors' Hospital* (1975-76); this was followed by a two-year stint as Robert Anderson on the Robert Conrad TV vehicle *Black Sheep Squadron* (1976-78). From 1984 through 1992, Larroquette portrayed assistant DA and self-styled ladies man Dan Fielding on the popular sitcom *Night Court*, a role which won him four Emmy awards. In 1994, the actor starred in his own series, *The John Larroquette Show*, playing an erudite recovering alcoholic who manages a St. Louis bus depot. The character was to some extent drawn from Larroquette's own life; for several years, his chronic drinking compromised his ability to work at peak performance level. Unlike his character in *The John Larroquette Show*, however, Larroquette overcame his problem on his own, without the aid of Alcoholics Anonymous. He has also appeared in several forgettable movie roles, mostly in madcap comedies. **Selected Works:** *Richie Rich* (1995)

# Jack LaRue

**Born:** May 3, 1900; New York, NY
**Died:** January 11, 1984; Santa Monica, CA

**Years Active in the Industry:** by decade

| 10s | 20s | 30s | 40s | 50s | 60s | 70s | 80s | 90s |
|-----|-----|-----|-----|-----|-----|-----|-----|-----|
|     |     |     |     |     |     |     |     |     |

American actor Jack LaRue is frequently mistaken for Humphrey Bogart by casual fans. In both his facial features and his choice of roles, LaRue did indeed resemble Bogart, in every respect but one; Bogart became a star, while LaRue remained in the supporting ranks. After stage work in his native New York, LaRue came to Hollywood for his first film, *The Mouthpiece*, in 1932. For the next few years he played secondary hoodlums (for example, the hot-head hit man in the closing sequences of *Night World* [1932]) and unsavory lead villains—never more unsavory than as the sex-obsessed kidnapper in *The Story of Temple Drake* (1933). LaRue decided to shift gears and try romantic leading roles, but this "new" LaRue disappeared after the Mayfair Studios cheapie, *The Fighting Rookie* (1934). He was at his most benign as "himself", trading gentle quips with Alice Faye at an outdoor carnival in the MGM all-star short *Cinema Circus* (1935). Otherwise, it was back to gangsters and thugs, with a few exceptions like his sympathetic role in *A Gentleman from Dixie* (1941). By the 1940s, LaRue had spent most of his movie savings and was compelled to seek out any work available. Awaiting his cue to appear in a small role on one movie set, LaRue was pointed out to up-and-coming Anne Shirley on a movie set as an example of what happens when a Hollywood luminary doesn't provide for possible future career reverses. Things improved a bit when LaRue moved to England in the late 1940s to play American villains in British pictures. His most memorable appearance during this period was as Slim Grissom in the notorious *No Orchids for Miss Blandish* (1948)—a virtual reprisal of his part in *The Story of Temple Drake*. LaRue worked often in television during the last two decades of his career; in the early 1950s, he was the eerily-lit host of the spooky TV anthology *Lights Out*. **Selected Works:** *A Farewell to Arms* (1932)

success in *The Private Life of Henry VIII* for Alexander Korda on film in 1933, he won a Best Actor Oscar. Known both for his fascination with the darker side of human behavior and for his comic touch, Laughton should be watched as a frightening Nero in *Sign of the Cross* (1932), the triumphant employee in *If I Had a Million* (1932), the evil doctor in *Island of Lost Souls* (1932), the incestuous father in *The Barretts of Wimpole Street* (1934), the irrepressible Ruggles in *Ruggles of Red Gap* (1935), the overbearing Captain Bligh in *Mutiny on the Bounty* (1935), which garnered him another Oscar nomination, and the haunted hunchback in *The Hunchback of Notre Dame* (1939), with a very young Maureen O'Hara. During the war years, he played some light roles in *Tales of Manhattan* (1942), *Forever and a Day* (1943) and *The Canterville Ghost* (1944), among others. By the late '40s, Laughton sought greater challenges and returned to the stage in *The Life of Galileo*, which he translated from Bertolt Brecht's original and co-directed. As stage director and/or performer, he made *Don Juan in Hell* in 1951, *John Brown's Body* in 1953, *The Caine Mutiny Court Martial* in 1954, and *Shaw's Major Barbara* in 1956, all in New York. When he returned to England in 1959, he appeared in Stratford-upon-Avon productions of *A Midsummer Night's Dream*, and *King Lear*. Later film appearances include *O. Henry's Full House* (1952), *Hobson's Choice* (1954), *Witness for the Prosecution* (1957) (which gave him another Oscar nomination), *Spartacus* (1960) and *Advise and Consent* (1962). Although he was homosexual, Laughton was married from 1929 to his death to actress Elsa Lanchester, with whom he occasionally appeared. His direction of the film *The Night Is a Hunter* (1955) is critically acclaimed. **Selected Works:** *Miserables* (1935), *Rembrandt* (1936), *They Knew What They Wanted* (1940)

# Charles Laughton

**Born:** July 1, 1899; Scarborough, England
**Died:** 1962

**Years Active in the Industry:** by decade

| 10s | 20s | 30s | 40s | 50s | 60s | 70s | 80s | 90s |
|-----|-----|-----|-----|-----|-----|-----|-----|-----|
|     |     |     |     |     |     |     |     |     |

Tortured but brilliant British actor Charles Laughton's unique performances made him a compelling performer both on stage and in film. After starting his career as an hotel manager, Laughton switched to acting. His performances in London's West End plays brought him early acclaim, which eventually led to the Old Vic, Broadway and Hollywood. When he repeated his stage

# Stan Laurel (Arthur Stanley Jefferson)

**Born:** June 16, 1890; Ulverston, England
**Died:** February 23, 1965

**Years Active in the Industry:** by decade

| 10s | 20s | 30s | 40s | 50s | 60s | 70s | 80s | 90s |
|-----|-----|-----|-----|-----|-----|-----|-----|-----|
|     |     |     |     |     |     |     |     |     |

Actor, screenwriter and producer Stan Laurel was born to British stage performers. He started acting on stage in his midteens in music halls and theatres before touring the U.S. in 1910 and 1912 as Charlie Chaplin's understudy. He remained in the States to perform in vaudeville and in 1917 supplemented his stage work by appearing as clownish misfit types in comedy shorts often spoofing dramatic films of the period. One of these was a two-reeler called *Lucky Dog* (1917), in which he appeared totally by accident with Oliver Hardy. They were not to appear together again until 1926, when they both found themselves working for comedy producer Hal Roach. Laurel, who had been hired by Roach as a gagman/director, was persuaded to appear in front of the camera and thus auspiciously again with Hardy. It soon became obvious that the two men had a certain comic chemistry on screen, and they starred together as an incredibly popular comedy team in over fifty films through the '30s and early '40s. Their three-reeler *The Music Box* (1932) won an Oscar for best short subject. Laurel, the creative member of the team, had numerous run-ins with producer Hal Roach. Laurel wanted the team's films to aspire to the higher quality productions of their contemporaries, while Roach was firmly content with maintaining a low-budget norm. Laurel had a few short lived victories, acting as producer on the team's *Our Relations* (1936) and *Way Out West* (1937). The team left Roach in 1940 to seek more artistic control over their work, but were given even less at Fox and MGM. In the late '40s and early '50s they enjoyed touring the English Music Halls. After Hardy's death in 1957, Laurel stopped performing but kept active. **Selected Works:** *Block-Heads* (1938)

# Peter Lawford (Peter Sidney Ernest Aylen Lawford)

**Born:** September 7, 1923; London, England
**Died:** December 23, 1984; Los Angeles, CA

**Years Active in the Industry:** by decade

| 10s | 20s | 30s | 40s | 50s | 60s | 70s | 80s | 90s |
|-----|-----|-----|-----|-----|-----|-----|-----|-----|
|     |     |     |     |     |     |     |     |     |

Peter Lawford was a bushy-browed, slender, aristocratic, good-looking British leading man in Hollywood films. At age eight he appeared in the film *Poor Old Bill* (1931); seven years later he visited Hollywood and appeared in a supporting role as a Cockney boy in *Lord Jeff* (1938). In 1942 he began regularly appearing on-screen, first in minor supporting roles; by the late 1940s he was a breezy romantic star, and his studio promised him (incorrectly) that he would be the "new Ronald Colman." His clipped British accent, poise, looks, and charm made him popular with teenage girls and young women, but he outgrew his typecast parts by the mid '50s and spent several years working on TV, starring in the series *Dear Phoebe* and *The Thin Man*. Off screen he was known as a jet-setter playboy; a member of Frank Sinatra's "Rat Pack," he married Patricia Kennedy and became President John F. Kennedy's brother-in-law. From the 1960s he appeared mainly in character roles; his production company, Chrislaw, made several feature films, and he was credited as executive producer of three films, two in co-producer partnership with Sammy Davis Jr. In 1971-72 he was a regular on the TV sitcom *The Doris Day Show*. He divorced Kennedy in 1966 and later married the daughter of comedian Dan Rowan. He rarely acted onscreen after the mid-'70s. **Selected**

**Works:** *Easter Parade* (1948), *The Longest Day* (1962), *Mrs. Miniver* (1942), *Mrs. Parkington* (1944), *Picture of Dorian Gray* (1945)

# Marc Lawrence

**Born:** February 17, 1910; Bronx, NY

**Years Active in the Industry:** by decade

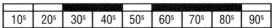

| 10s | 20s | 30s | 40s | 50s | 60s | 70s | 80s | 90s |
|-----|-----|-----|-----|-----|-----|-----|-----|-----|
|     |     |     |     |     |     |     |     |     |

After attending City College of New York, Marc Lawrence studied acting with Eva Le Gallienne. Among the many stage productions in which Lawrence appeared were *Sour Mountain* and *Waiting for Lefty*. First signed for films by Columbia in 1932, Lawrence's scarred face and growly voice made him indispensable for gangster parts, though he generally displayed an intelligence far higher than the average goon or gunman. Though usually limited to villainy, Lawrence was not always confined to urban roles, as witness his successful portrayals of a mountaineer in *Shepherd of the Hills* (1942) and a western saddle tramp in *The Ox-Bow Incident* (1943). The actor's own favorite role was Corio in 1947's *Captain from Castille*. During the House Un-American Activities Committee investigations of the 1950s, Lawrence reluctantly offered testimony implicating several of his coworkers as alleged Communist sympathizers; the experience virtually destroyed his American career and left him embittered and defensive (he would always refuse to be interviewed by historians of the "Blacklist" era, referring to them as "ghouls"). Lawrence was forced to seek out work in Europe, where he'd emerge in the early 1960s as a director of crime films and U.S. spaghetti westerns. Back in the U.S. in the 1980s, Lawrence made several TV appearances and showed up in such films as *The Big Easy* (1987) and *Newsies* (1992), typecast once more as gangsters. In 1993, Lawrence privately published his memoirs, in which for the first time in print he addressed his dark days as an HUAC "friendly witness." **Selected Works:** *Asphalt Jungle* (1950), *Key Largo* (1948), *Life with Mikey* (1993), *Ruby* (1992)

# Cloris Leachman

**Born:** April 30, 1926; Des Moines, IA

**Years Active in the Industry:** by decade

| 10s | 20s | 30s | 40s | 50s | 60s | 70s | 80s | 90s |
|-----|-----|-----|-----|-----|-----|-----|-----|-----|
|     |     |     |     |     |     |     |     |     |

Cloris Leachman seems capable of playing any kind of role, and has consistently demonstrated her versatility in films and on TV since the 1950s. On film, she can be seen in *Kiss Me Deadly* (1955); *Butch Cassidy and the Sundance Kid* (1969); *The Last Picture Show* (1971), for which she won an Oscar; and *Young Frankenstein* (1974). On TV, she played the mother on *Lassie* from 1957-58, and Phyllis Lindstrom on *The Mary Tyler Moore Show* from 1970-77 and on her own series, *Phyllis* (1975-77). She was a staple on many of the dramatic shows of the 1950s, and a regular on *Charlie Wild, Private Detective* (1950-52) and *The Facts of Life*. She has won three Emmy Awards and continues to make TV, stage, and film appearances, including a turn as Granny in the film version of *The Beverly Hillbillies* (1993). **Selected Works:** *Oldest Living Graduate* (1982), *Texasville* (1990), *In Broad Daylight* (1991), *A Troll in Central Park* (1994)

# Sir David Lean

**Born:** March 25, 1908; Croydon, England
**Died:** April 16, 1991; London, England

**Years Active in the Industry:** by decade

| 10s | 20s | 30s | 40s | 50s | 60s | 70s | 80s | 90s |
|-----|-----|-----|-----|-----|-----|-----|-----|-----|

Director, writer, and producer David Lean came out of a strict religious background in which movies were forbidden to become one of the world's most celebrated filmmakers. Beginning as a tea-

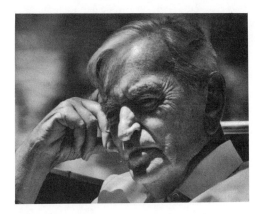

boy in the mid-1920s, he was lucky enough to move into editing just as sound films—with their special requirements—were coming in, and by the mid-1930s was regarded as one of the top men in his field. Lean turned down several chances to become a director in low budget films, and got his first chance to direct (unofficially) on *Major Barbara* (1941), one of the most celebrated movies of the early 1940s. Noel Coward hired Lean as his directorial collaborator on his wartime classic *In Which We Serve* (1943), and from there Lean's career was made—for the next 15 years, he became known throughout the world for his close, intimate, serious film dramas. Some (*This Happy Breed* [1944], *Blithe Spirit* [1945], and *Brief Encounter* [1945]) were based on Coward's plays, which the author had given Lean virtual cart blanche to film. Others ranged from Charles Dickens adaptations (*Oliver Twist* [1948], *Great Expectations* [1946]) to stories about aviation (*The Sound Barrier* [1952]). In 1957, in association with producer Sam Spiegel, Lean moved out of England and into international production with his epic adapta-

tion of Pierre Boulle's Japanese prisoner-of-war story *The Bridge on The River Kwai,* a superb drama starring Alec Guinness, Jack Hawkins, and William Holden that expanded the dimensions of serious filmmaking. Lean's next film, *Lawrence of Arabia* (1962), based on the life and military career of World War I British hero T. E. Lawrence, became the definitive dramatic film epic of its generation. *Doctor Zhivago* (1965), a complex romantic tale about life in Russia before and during the revolution, opened to mixed reviews but went on to become one of the top-grossing movies of the 1960s, despite a three-hour running time. With an armload of Oscars behind him from his three most recent pictures, and box office earnings of as much as $300 million between them, Lean was established as one of the top "money" directors of the 1960s. But his next movie, the multi-million dollar, 200-minute *Ryan's Daughter* (1970) fared far less well, especially before the critics, who nearly universally condemned the slowness and seeming self-indulgence of its drama and scale. Disheartened by its reception, Lean took over 10 years to release his next movie, the critical and box office success *A Passage to India* (1984). He was working on his next movie, *Nostromo,* based on Joseph Conrad's book, at the time of his death. **Selected Works:** *Summertime* (1955)

# Denis Leary

**Born:** 1957; Boston, MA

**Years Active in the Industry:** by decade

| 10s | 20s | 30s | 40s | 50s | 60s | 70s | 80s | 90s |
|-----|-----|-----|-----|-----|-----|-----|-----|-----|

Boston-born Denis Leary is the snearing, tousle-haired comedian who popularized the cautionary phrase "two words." Leary's routine goes something like this: "Regarding Bill Clinton's foreign policy, *two words*: Jimmy...Carter." Best known for his many MTV appearances, Leary excells in playing characters who wavered between quiet sarcasm and howling insanity. His one-man show *No Cure for Cancer* premiered in New York in 1991, scoring a hit with its "intellectual guerilla" comedy. Leary's several film stints have included *National Lampoon's Loaded Weapon* (1993), *Judgment Night* (1993), and *Operation Dumbo Drop* (1995). Thus far, Leary's best screen showing has been as the beleagered burglar and reluctant kidnapper in *The Ref* (1994). **Selected Works:** *The Sandlot* (1993)

# Bruce Lee (Lee Yenn Kam)

**Born:** November 27, 1940; San Francisco, CA
**Died:** 1973

**Years Active in the Industry:** by decade

| 10s | 20s | 30s | 40s | 50s | 60s | 70s | 80s | 90s |
|-----|-----|-----|-----|-----|-----|-----|-----|-----|

Cult hero Bruce Lee studied philosophy in college, but then turned to acting; he also established Kung Fu training schools on

the West Coast. In the mid '60s he appeared on TV in several episodes of *Batman* as Kato; Lee continued playing this role in the series *The Green Hornet*. He went on to get supporting roles in a couple of Hollywood films, then in the early '70s established himself as the hugely popular star of a number of Hong Kong-made martial arts films, the first of which was *Fists of Fury* (1973). Lee soon became a cult figure among fans of the martial-arts genre; he had fan clubs around the world. Lee died mysteriously at the age of 32, but left behind the outline for a story that was turned into the film *Circle of Iron* (1979), starring David Carradine in the role Lee had created for himself. He was the father of actor Brandon Lee, who himself died suddenly while filming the movie *The Crow* (1993).

# Christopher Lee (Christopher Frank
Carandini Lee)

**Born:** May 27, 1922; London, England
**Died:** March 31, 1993

**Years Active in the Industry:** by decade

| 10ˢ | 20ˢ | 30ˢ | 40ˢ | 50ˢ | 60ˢ | 70ˢ | 80ˢ | 90ˢ |
|-----|-----|-----|-----|-----|-----|-----|-----|-----|
|     |     |     |     |     |     |     |     |     |

Contrary to popular belief, Christopher Lee and Peter Cushing did not first appear together in *The Curse of Frankenstein*. In Laurence Olivier's *Hamlet* (1948), in which Cushing plays the minor role of Osric, he played the cadaverous candle-bearer in the "frighted with false fires" scene—one of his first film roles. After several years in secondary film roles, Lee achieved horror-flick stardom as the Monster in 1957's *The Curse of Frankenstein*, the first of his 21 Hammer Studios films. In 1958, Lee made his inaugural appearance as "the Count" in *Curse of Dracula*, with Peter Cushing as Van Helsing. It would remain the favorite of Lee's *Dracula* films; the actor later noted that he was grateful to be allowed to convey "the sadness of the character. The terrible sentence, the doom of immortality..." One year after *Curse*, Lee added another legendary figure to his gallery of characters: Sherlock Holmes, the protagonist of *The Hound of the Baskervilles*. With the release ten years later of *The Private Life of Sherlock Holmes*, Lee became the first actor ever to portray both Sherlock Holmes *and* Holmes' brother Mycroft on screen. Other Christopher Lee roles of note include the title characters in 1959's *The Mummy* and the *Fu Manchu* series of the 1960s, and the villainous Scaramanga in the 1973 James Bond effort *Man with the Golden Gun*. In one brilliant casting coup, Christopher Lee was costarred with fellow movie bogeymen Peter Cushing, Vincent

Price and John Carradine in the otherwise unmemorable *House of Long Shadows* (1982). **Selected Works:** *Double Vision* (1992), *Gremlins 2: The New Batch* (1990), *Sherlock Holmes and the Leading Lady* (1991), *Incident at Victoria Falls* (1991)

# Jason Scott Lee

**Born:** 1966; Los Angeles, CA

**Years Active in the Industry:** by decade

| 10ˢ | 20ˢ | 30ˢ | 40ˢ | 50ˢ | 60ˢ | 70ˢ | 80ˢ | 90ˢ |
|-----|-----|-----|-----|-----|-----|-----|-----|-----|
|     |     |     |     |     |     |     |     |     |

The similarity in name and physique has led some people to mistakenly assume that actor Jason Scott Lee is in some way related to the late and legendary Bruce Lee; indeed, he is not. Confusion was compounded when Lee starred in the moderately acclaimed 1993 biopic *Dragon: The Bruce Lee Story* (1993). It is possible that the younger Lee's "association" with Bruce has prevented him from getting parts of wider range. Lee also starred in the notorious Kevin Reynolds-directed Easter Island fiasco *Rapa Nui* (1994), and garnered positive reviews for his work in *Rudyard Kipling's The Jungle Book* (1994). **Selected Works:** *Map of the Human Heart* (1993)

# Spike Lee (Shelton Jackson Lee)

**Born:** March 20, 1956; Atlanta, GA

**Years Active in the Industry:** by decade

| 10ˢ | 20ˢ | 30ˢ | 40ˢ | 50ˢ | 60ˢ | 70ˢ | 80ˢ | 90ˢ |
|-----|-----|-----|-----|-----|-----|-----|-----|-----|
|     |     |     |     |     |     |     |     |     |

Actor and filmmaker Spike Lee is often a figure of controversy for his outspoken views and arrogant manner. Raised in Brooklyn, New York, he attended college and did a summer internship at Columbia Pictures. After returning to

New York he gained recognition while still at NYU film school; there he made a student film, *Joe's Bed-Stuy Barbershop: We Cut Heads* (1982), which became the first student work ever shown in Lincoln Center's "New Directors, New Films" showcase, and also won a student award from the American Academy of Motion Picture Arts and Sciences. This led to offers from high-power agents, but no studio funding. He raised $175,000 to produce his first professional feature, *She's Gotta Have It* (1986), which he directed, wrote, and performed in (as he has for each of his subsequent films); the film won the Prix Jeunesse at the Cannes Film Festival and made $10 million. At the same time, Lee wrote *Inside Guerrilla Filmmaking,* a textbook for others who might follow in his footsteps. After his first success, he made a string of Hollywood-produced films, including the controversial *Do the Right Thing* (1989), for which he received a Best Screenplay Oscar nomination, and the epic-scaled *Malcolm X* (1992), for which solicited large financial gifts from a number of wealthy black entertainers to ensure financing. He continues to feature complex urban themes in his latest work, including *Crooklyn* (1994), for which Lee collaborated with his sisters, Joie Lee and Cinque Lee; and *Clockers* (1995). **Selected Works:** *Jungle Fever* (1991)

# John Leguizamo

**Born:** July 22, 1965; Bogota, Colombia

**Years Active in the Industry:** by decade

| 10s | 20s | 30s | 40s | 50s | 60s | 70s | 80s | 90s |
|-----|-----|-----|-----|-----|-----|-----|-----|-----|
|     |     |     |     |     |     |     |     | ■ |

Colombian-American comic actor John Leguizamo has had a substantial film career, including *Casualties of War* (1988), *Hangin' with the Homeboys* (1991) *The Super Mario Brothers* (1993) as brother Luigi, *Carlito's Way* (1993) with his idol Al Pacino, and *To Wong Foo,Thanks for Everything, Julie Newmar* (1995). Often a victim of ethnic stereotyping in his film roles, Leguizamo decided to begin affording himself better opportunities by creating a one-man show titled *Mambo Mouth*, which scored a success off-Broadway and as an 1992 HBO special. Leguizamo followed this triumph with a second one-man effort, *Spic O Rama*, a wildly scatalogical piece about a dysfunctional Latino family. In 1994, Leguizamo codeveloped and starred in the Fox TV network series *House of Buggin'*, described in the trades as an Hispanic *In Living Color.* **Selected Works:** *Whispers in the Dark* (1992), *Die Hard 2* (1990)

# Janet Leigh (Jeanette Helen Morrison)

**Born:** July 6, 1926; Merced, CA

**Years Active in the Industry:** by decade

| 10s | 20s | 30s | 40s | 50s | 60s | 70s | 80s | 90s |
|-----|-----|-----|-----|-----|-----|-----|-----|-----|
|     |     | ■ | ■ | ■ | ■ | ■ |     |     |

The only child of a very young married couple, American actress Janet Leigh spent her childhood moving from town to town due to her father's changing jobs. A bright child who skipped several grades in school, Leigh took music and dancing lessons, making her public debut at age 10 as a baton twirler for a marching band. Her favorite times were the afternoons spent at the local movie house, which she referred to as her "babysitter." In 1946,

Leigh's mother was working at a ski lodge where actress Norma Shearer was vacationing; impressed by a photograph of Leigh, Norma arranged for the girl (whose prior acting experience consisted of a college play) to be signed with the MCA talent agency. One year later Leigh was at MGM, playing the ingenue in the 1947 film *Romance of Rosy Ridge.* The actress became one of the busiest contractees at the studio, building her following with solid performances in such films as *Little Women* (1949), *The Doctor and the Girl* (1950) and *Scaramouche* (1951)—and catching the eye of RKO Radio's owner Howard Hughes, who hoped that the actress' several RKO appearances (on loanout from MGM) would lead to something substantial in private life. Instead, Leigh married Tony Curtis (her second husband), and the pair became the darlings of fan magazines and columnists, as well as occasional costars (*Houdini* [1954], *The Vikings* [1958], *Who Was That Lady?* [1960]). Even as this "perfect" Hollywood marriage deteriorated, Leigh's career prospered. Among her significant roles in the 1960s were that of Frank Sinatra's enigmatic lady friend in *The Manchurian Candidate* (1962), Paul Newman's ex-wife in *Harper* (1966), and, of course, the unfortunate embezzler in Hitchcock's *Psycho* (1960), who met her demise in the nude (actually covered by a moleskin) and covered with blood (actually chocolate sauce, which photographed better) in the legendary "shower scene." Curtailing her film and TV appearances in the 1980s, Leigh is best known to today's younger film fans not only as the star/victim of *Psycho* but as the mother of another fine actress, Jamie Lee Curtis. **Selected Works:** *Naked Spur* (1953), *Touch of Evil* (1958), *American Dream* (1966)

# Jennifer Jason Leigh

**Born:** February 5, 1962; Los Angeles, CA

**Years Active in the Industry:** by decade

| 10s | 20s | 30s | 40s | 50s | 60s | 70s | 80s | 90s |
|-----|-----|-----|-----|-----|-----|-----|-----|-----|
|     |     |     |     |     |     |     | ■ | ■ |

American actress Jennifer Jason Leigh is the daughter of the late actor Vic Morrow and screenwriter Barbara Turner. As a child, she made her film debut in the extremely obscure *Death of a Stranger,* a few years

later, with the token approval of her parents, Leigh dropped out of high school to study acting at the Lee Strasberg Institute. Her first important TV role was as the anorexic heroine of *The Best Little Girl in the World,* for which she voluntarily lost weight before the cameras turned. This "method" approach was typical of

Leigh, who, even after obtaining stardom, indulged in the sort of subtextual preparation that many actors abandon after leaving college—such as writing a diary in the style of the character she is playing. She won a 1994 Golden Globe for her performance in Robert Altman's ensemble film *Short Cuts*. More recently, Leigh has exhibited a fondness for flamboyant, curiously accented characterizations, notably her maniacal "roomate from hell" in *Single White Female* (1991), her Katharine Hepburn-style comic turn in *The Hudsucker Proxy* (1994) and her deliberately artifice-laden portrayal of writer Dorothy Parker in *Mrs. Parker and the Vicious Circle* (1994). **Selected Works:** *Backdraft* (1991), *Last Exit to Brooklyn* (1990), *Miami Blues* (1990), *Rush* (1991)

# Mike Leigh

**Born:** 1943; Salford, England

**Years Active in the Industry:** by decade

| 10ˢ | 20ˢ | 30ˢ | 40ˢ | 50ˢ | 60ˢ | 70ˢ | 80ˢ | 90ˢ |
|-----|-----|-----|-----|-----|-----|-----|-----|-----|

British-born writer/director Mike Leigh is a qualified success: extremely well known and highly respected in England, he has yet to completely match that success with American critics and audiences. This is principally because Leigh deals with distinctly British social and political themes, most of which hold little significance for American filmgoers. Originally an acting trainee at the Royal Academy of Dramatic Art, Leigh decided he preferred directing and writing, and eventually transferred to the London Film School. His most important stage works, *The Box Play* and *Bleak Moments*, grew from collaborative experimentation during rehearsals. It's not always easy to transfer this improvisational technique to film, but Leigh managed the trick in his 1972 movie version of *Bleak Moments*. The film won several awards, but public response was sparse and Leigh returned to the stage, with occasional TV stopovers. Two of his British made-for-TV films, *Meantime* (1983) and *Four Days in July* (1984), were given limited theatrical release, while *Nuts in May* (1976) and *Who's Who* (1978) have been issued on videocassette. Leigh's 1988 film *High Hopes*, the slyly funny story of a family comprised exclusively of extreme political and social "types," was a success at the New York Film Festival, but a major distributor was not forthcoming. This was also the fate for *Life Is Sweet*, a 1990 production with a similar storyline and cast of characters. Leigh's 1993 effort *Naked* was, once more, populated with a representative cross-section of modern British humanity; this one did fairly well in the U.S., though its 126-minute running time diluted its effectiveness. **Selected Works:** *My Beautiful Launderette* (1986)

# Vivien Leigh

**Born:** November 5, 1913; Darjeeling, India
**Died:** 1967; London, England

**Years Active in the Industry:** by decade

| 10ˢ | 20ˢ | 30ˢ | 40ˢ | 50ˢ | 60ˢ | 70ˢ | 80ˢ | 90ˢ |
|-----|-----|-----|-----|-----|-----|-----|-----|-----|

Born in India to a British stockbroker and his Irish wife, Vivien Leigh first appeared on stage in convent-school amateur theatricals. Completing her education in England, France, Italy and Germany, Leigh continued pursuing acting at the Royal Academy of Dramatic Art; she was not a particularly impressive pupil, so she was obliged to continue her training with private tutors. In 1932, Leigh briefly interrupted her pursuit of a theatrical career to marry London barrister Herbert Leigh Holman. Three years later, she made her professional stage bow in

*The Sash*, which never made it to London's West End; still, Leigh's bewitching performance caught the eye of producer Sydney Carroll, who cast her in her first London play, *The Mask of Virtue*. She alternated between stage and film work, usually in flighty, kittenish roles, until being introduced to Shakespeare (and vice versa) at the Old Vic. It was there that she met Laurence Olivier, appearing with him on stage as Ophelia in *Hamlet* and Titania in *A Midsummer Night's Dream*, and on screen in 1937's *Fire Over England*. It was the latter picture which brought Leigh to the attention of American producer David O. Selznick, who brought his well-publicized search for the "perfect" Scarlett O'Hara to a sudden conclusion when he cast Leigh as the resourceful Southern belle in 1939's *Gone With the Wind*. The role won Leigh her first Academy Award, after which she kept her screen appearances to a minimum, preferring to devote her time to Olivier, who would become her second husband in 1940. Refusing to submit to the Hollywood publicity machine, Leigh and her new husband all but disappeared from view for months at a time. Often there were gaps of two to three years between Leigh's films; the stage would forever remain foremost in her heart. One of her rare movie appearances in the 1950s was as Blanche DuBois in *A Streetcar Named Desire* (1951), a performance that won her a second Oscar. In private life, Leigh began developing the severe emotional and health problems that would eventually destroy her marriage to Olivier and seriously impede her ability to perform on stage or before the camera. Despite her ongoing manic-depressive state, she managed to turn in first-rate performances in such films as *The Roman Spring of Mrs. Stone* (1961) and *Ship of Fools* (1965), and maintained a busy theatrical schedule, including a 1963 musical version of *Tovarich* and a 1966 Broadway appearance opposite John Gielgud in *Ivanov*. Leigh was preparing to star in the London production of Edward Albee's *A Delicate Balance* when she was found dead, presumably of tuberculosis, in her London apartment; in tribute to the actress, the lights in London's theatre district were blacked out for an hour.

# Mitchell Leisen

**Born:** October 6, 1898; Menominee, MI
**Died:** October 28, 1972; Woodland Hills, CA

**Years Active in the Industry:** by decade

| 10s | 20s | 30s | 40s | 50s | 60s | 70s | 80s | 90s |
|-----|-----|-----|-----|-----|-----|-----|-----|-----|
|     |     |     |     |     |     |     |     |     |

After being trained as an architect and working as an interior designer, Mitchell Leisen began work in Hollywood as a costume designer. Leisen worked on such notable films as Cecil B. De Mille's *Male and Female* (1919), Ernst Lubitsch's *Rosita,* and the Douglas Fairbanks actioners *Robin Hood* (1922) and *The Thief Of Bagdad* (1924). As a set designer for De Mille in the late '20s and early '30s, Leisen's credits included *The King of Kings* (1927), *Madam Satan* (1930), and *The Sign of the Cross* (1932). Leisen began directing in the mid-'30s, scoring with the allegory *Death Takes a Holiday* (1934) and the bizarre mystery musical *Murder at the Vanities* (1934). He showed a special flair for comedy in the late '30s and early '40s, especially when his scripts were written by Preston Sturges (*Easy Living* [1937], *Remember the Night* [1940]) or Charles Brackett and Billy Wilder (*Midnight* [1939], *Arise My Love* [1940], *Hold Back the Dawn* [1941]). His notable later films include *Lady in the Dark* (1944), *To Each His Own* (1946), and *Golden Earrings* (1947). After his film work waned, he turned to TV directing and became the proprietor of a nightclub.

# Claude Lelouch (Claude Barruck Lelouch)

**Born:** October 30, 1937; Paris, France

**Years Active in the Industry:** by decade

| 10s | 20s | 30s | 40s | 50s | 60s | 70s | 80s | 90s |
|-----|-----|-----|-----|-----|-----|-----|-----|-----|
|     |     |     |     |     |     |     |     |     |

An amateur filmmaker as a boy, French director, writer, and producer Claude Lelouch made the award-winning short *Le Mal Du Siacle* at age 13. He helmed shorts and television comercials in the mid-'50s, and short films for the French army while in the service from 1957-60. He began directing features in 1960, and scored an international hit with the romantic drama *Un Homme Et Une Femme* (*A Man and a Woman,* 1966) in 1966. Lelouch has made numerous films over the years, including *Vivre Pour Vivre* (*Live for Life,* 1967); *Le Chat Et La Souris* (*Cat and Mouse,* 1978); *Un Autre Homme, Une Autre Chance* (*Another Man, Another Chance,* 1977); *Robert Et Robert* (1979), and *Partir Revenir* (*Leave to Come Back,* 1986). **Selected Works:** *And Now My Love* (1974)

# Jack Lemmon (John Uhler Lemmon, III)

**Born:** February 8, 1925; Boston, MA

**Years Active in the Industry:** by decade

| 10s | 20s | 30s | 40s | 50s | 60s | 70s | 80s | 90s |
|-----|-----|-----|-----|-----|-----|-----|-----|-----|
|     |     |     |     |     |     |     |     |     |

Born prematurely in an elevator, American actor Jack Lemmon matured from a slight, sickly child to a star athlete and scholar thanks to the loving diligence of his father, a doughnut company executive. After World War II Navy service, Lemmon attended Harvard, where among other accomplishments he excelled at amateur theatricals. To support himself after hitting New York City, he played piano at the Knickerbocker Music Hall, accompanying silent film comedies (he later insisted that he learned more about comic technique watching these ancient two-reelers than he ever would have in acting school). Taking any acting job available, including a part in an Army sex hygiene film, Lemmon worked in summer stock and early live television. With his first wife Cynthia Stone, the actor starred in two pioneer TV sitcoms, *That Wonderful Guy* and *Heavens for Betsy.* A stint in a less-than-successful revival of the old stage farce *Room Service* brought Lemmon to the attention of a Columbia Pictures talent scout, and in 1954 the actor signed a long contract with Columbia, which paid comparatively little but which gave him invaluable public exposure. Scoring a popular success with his first film, the Judy Holliday vehicle *It Should Happen to You* (1954), Lemmon toiled in potboiler comedies and musicals until Columbia loaned him out to play Ensign Pulver in Warner Bros. *Mister Roberts* (1955). The actor's inspired comic performance, not to mention his ability to hold his own in the company of heavyweight veterans Henry Fonda, James Cagney and William Powell, won Lemmon an Academy Award for Best Supporting Actor. In 1959, Lemmon made the first of several rewarding appearances for director Billy Wilder: *Some Like It Hot* (1959), *The Apartment* (1960), *Irma La Douce* (1963), *The Fortune Cookie* (1966), *Avanti* (1972) and *Buddy Buddy* (1981) contain some of Jack Lemmon's best screen moments. Lemmon won a second Oscar for his decidedly non-comic performace as an end-of-his-rope businessman in *Save the Tiger* (1973), acting the film for virtually no fee when the budget ran out; other significant dramatic Lemmon appearances include *The Days of Wine and Roses* (1962), *The China Syndrome* (1979), and *Glengarry Glen Ross* (1992). Widely regarded as one of the nicest and most generous men in show business, Lemmon has eased into his 60s with the same grace and charm that characterized his film work; one of his most recent appearances, 1994's *Grumpy Old Men,* reunited the actor with Walter Matthau, who next to the late Ernie Kovacs is Lemmon's favorite and most copacetic co-star. **Selected Works:** *Days*

*of Wine & Roses* (1962), *Glengarry Glen Ross* (1992), *Missing* (1982), *Mr. Roberts* (1955), *The Odd Couple* (1968)

# Robert Sean Leonard

**Born:** February 28, 1969; Westwood, NJ

**Years Active in the Industry:** by decade

| 10s | 20s | 30s | 40s | 50s | 60s | 70s | 80s | 90s |
|-----|-----|-----|-----|-----|-----|-----|-----|-----|
|     |     |     |     |     |     |     |     |     |

After several seasons of Broadway work in such plays as *Brighton Beach Memoirs*, American actor Robert Sean Leonard made his film bow at age 17 in *The Manhattan Project* (1986). He attracted positive critical notice for his portrayal of Neil Perry, the sensitive prep-school student whose acting aspirations are crushed by his wealthy father in *Dead Poets Society* (1989). His character's subsequent suicide provided the dramatic core for this quixotic little film. Leonard's most recent film assignments have generally been in such period pieces as *Swing Kids* (1992), *Much Ado About Nothing* (1993), and *The Age of Innocence* (1994). **Selected Works:** *Mr. & Mrs. Bridge* (1991), *Safe Passage* (1994)

# Sergio Leone

**Born:** January 23, 1921; Rome, Italy
**Died:** April 30, 1989; Rome, Italy

**Years Active in the Industry:** by decade

| 10s | 20s | 30s | 40s | 50s | 60s | 70s | 80s | 90s |
|-----|-----|-----|-----|-----|-----|-----|-----|-----|
|     |     |     |     |     |     |     |     |     |

Italian filmmaker Sergio Leone came from show-business stock; his father was a pioneer producer in the Italian film industry and his mother was a popular opera singer. In the movie industry as

a director's assistant and bit player from age 18, Leone made valuable Hollywood contacts by working as a second-unit assistant for American productions filmed in Rome (including *Quo Vadis* [1951] and *Ben-Hur* [1959]). He began receiving screenplay credit on several of the "gladiator" films shot in Italy in the late 1950s, finally earning a full-fledged directing assignment with 1961's *Colossus of Rhodes*. Reasoning that gladiator

directors were a dime a dozen, Leone created his own genre: the "spaghetti western." Expertly staging scenes of bloodsplattered violence and sustaining tension through the use of huge closeups, fast cutaways, and long, pregnant silences, Leone made major stars out of such "washed up" Hollywood personalities as Clint Eastwood and Lee Van Cleef. Leone's "Man with No Name" trilogy—*A Fistful of Dollars* (1964), *For a Few Dollars More* (1965) and *The Good, the Bad and the Ugly* (1966)—owed a lot stylistically to American westerns and to the Japanese samurai films of Akira Kurosawa, but were original enough in execution to spawn an overabundance of ultraviolent European imitators. Hollywood's Paramount pictures, cognisant of Leone's worldwide bankability, gave the director carte blanche for his 1968 film *Once Upon a Time in the West*, which among its many accomplishments cast veteran "good guy" Henry Fonda as the most despicable of all western villains (a fact that attracted Fonda to the project in the first place). While regarded today as his masterpiece, *Once Upon a Time in the West* was a failure on its first release; audiences attuned to formula westerns weren't quite ready for this 165-minute assault on the senses, which spent nearly half an hour setting up its violent premise and nearly as long getting all the opening credits on the screen. Paramount cut the film down by 25 minutes, which rendered the complex storyline incomprehensible. It would be fifteen years before Leone would make another Hollywood-financed film. The result was virtually the same: *Once Upon a Time in America* (1984), an elegiac gangster epic starring Robert DeNiro. The film seemed so unwieldy at its original four-hour length that its U.S. distributors not only cut the film literally in half, but also rearranged the order of scenes. Leone's reputation was salvaged by the videocassette release of *America,* which restored its original running time, but the film was still too much of a good thing to succeed. After Leone's sudden death in 1989, Clint Eastwood dedicated his Oscar-winning *Unforgiven* (1992) to the two men who shaped Eastwood's own directorial vision: Don Siegel and Sergio Leone.

# Mervyn Le Roy

**Born:** October 15, 1900; San Francisco, CA
**Died:** September 13, 1987; Beverly Hills, CA

**Years Active in the Industry:** by decade

| 10s | 20s | 30s | 40s | 50s | 60s | 70s | 80s | 90s |
|-----|-----|-----|-----|-----|-----|-----|-----|-----|
|     |     |     |     |     |     |     |     |     |

A stage actor at age 12, Le Roy won cash prizes in singing competitions and Charlie Chaplin lookalike contests. He broke into film work on the recommendation of his cousin, Paramount executive Jesse Lasky. At first a player of juvenile roles, Le Roy entered the production end as a film cutter. By age 27, he was a "boy wonder" director at Warners Bros., turning out campus comedies and (after the advent of sound) frothy musicals. With *Little Caesar* (1931), Le Roy established himself as a top-rank dramatic director; he also exhibited for the first time his "starmaking" expertise, transforming Edward G. Robinson from a standard character man to a major box-office draw.

When he moved to MGM in 1938, Le Roy forsook the gritty "torn from today's headlines" approach of Warners in favor of glossy glamour. He functioned as both director and producer at MGM, responsible for such films as *Thirty Seconds over Tokyo* (1944) and *Quo Vadis* (1951) as a director, and such films as *The Wizard of Oz* (1939) and the Marx Brothers' *At the Circus* (1939) as producer. Le Roy's habit of putting certain stars under personal contract, thereby earning himself a "through the courtesy of..." credit for those stars' non-MGM appearances, served as joke material for such radio comedians as Le Roy's good friend Jack Benny. Back at Warner Bros. in the mid-1950s, Le Roy produced and directed a string of stage play adaptations (*The Bad Seed, No Time for Sergeants, Gypsy,* and others) for which he abandoned his fluid cinematic sense in favor of a stiff, hidebound theatrical style. While he never received an Academy Award for direction, Le Roy was honored with special Oscars in 1945 and 1975 for his services to the industry. Also in 1975, Le Roy wrote his engagingly inaccurate autobiography, *Take One.* **Selected Works:** *Random Harvest* (1942), *Mister Roberts* (1955)

# Richard Lester

**Born:** January 19, 1932; Philadelphia, PA

**Years Active in the Industry:** by decade

| 10s | 20s | 30s | 40s | 50s | 60s | 70s | 80s | 90s |
|-----|-----|-----|-----|-----|-----|-----|-----|-----|
|     |     |     |     |     |     |     |     |     |

An American TV director in the early 1950s, Lester began directing British TV a few years later, and in 1960 made the short comedy *The Running, Jumping, and Standing Still Film,* with Peter Sellers and members of the TV series *The Goon Show.* Feature-length comedies followed, leading to Lester's helming the two smash Beatles musicals, *A Hard Day's Night* (1964) and *Help!* (1965). Several outstanding films followed in the late '60s: the Stephen Sondheim musical *A Funny Thing Happened on the Way to the Forum* (1966), the military satire *How I Won the War* (1967) starring John Lennon, the offbeat romantic comedy/drama *Petulia* (1968), and a fantasy of post-apocalyptic England, *The Bed Sitting Room* (1969). A prolific and stylish director, Lester enlivened the swashbuckler in the '70s with *The Three Musketeers* (1973) and *The Four Musketeers* (1975); he transcended the genre with his touching look at Robin Hood's last years, *Robin and Marian* (1976). Lester's output has become sporadic since his early-1980s hits *Superman II* (1980) and *Superman III* (1983); his recent work includes *The Return of The Musketeers* (1989) and the Paul McCartney concert-documentary *Get Back* (1992). **Selected Works:** *The Knack ... And How to Get It* (1965)

# Barry Levinson

**Born:** June 2, 1942; Baltimore, MD

**Years Active in the Industry:** by decade

| 10s | 20s | 30s | 40s | 50s | 60s | 70s | 80s | 90s |
|-----|-----|-----|-----|-----|-----|-----|-----|-----|
|     |     |     |     |     |     |     |     |     |

The son of a Baltimore warehouse manager, director Barry Levinson had his eyes on a media career. He studied broadcast journalism in college but never stuck around in school long enough to earn a degree. Levinson switched his interests to acting and stand-up comedy, and after serving a stint as a staff writer on *The Carol Burnett Show,* he was hired by comedy producer Mel Brooks. The first film to carry a screenwriters credit for Levinson (in the company of serveral other writers) was *Silent Movie* (1976); this was followed by Mel Brooks' *High Anxiety* (1977), in which Levinson also played the role of a vengeful bellboy in the film's celebrated *Psycho* parody scene. Levinson's first directorial job was the low-budget *Diner* (1982), the first of three films to celebrate the director's hometown of Baltimore (the others were *Tin Men* [1987] and *Avalon* [1988]); *Diner* also served to showcase several stars-to-be, among them Mickey Rourke, Ellen Barkin, Daniel Stern, Paul Reiser and Michael Tucker. Securing his bankable status with such purely commercial projects as *The Natural* (1984) and *Young Sherlock Holmes* (1985), Levinson tackled his most ambitious project to date in 1988: *Rain Man,* the remarkable saga of a ruthless yuppie's deepening relationship with his autistic savant brother. *Rain Man* won numerous Oscars, including Best Picture, Best Director and Best Actor (Dustin Hoffman). Levinson has had little difficulty imposing his own personal stamp on such star-oriented films as *Good Morning Vietnam* (1988), starring Robin Williams, and *Bugsy* (1991), starring Warren Beatty. Though he has made few missteps in his career, Levinson suffered an intensely personal defeat with *Toys* (1992), a morality tale acted out in a toy manufacturing company. The film had been a pet project of Levinson's for nearly twenty years—and when finally completed, it looked indeed like a relic from the 1970s. Levinson's most recent film was *Jimmy Hollywood* (1994), one of a cycle of 1990s movies (*Serial Mom, Natural Born Killers*) based on the public's fascination with high-profile sociopaths. **Selected Works:** *And Justice for All* (1979), *Quiz Show* (1994), *Disclosure* (1994)

# Jerry Lewis (Joseph Levitch)

**Born:** March 16, 1926; Newark, NJ

**Years Active in the Industry:** by decade

| 10s | 20s | 30s | 40s | 50s | 60s | 70s | 80s | 90s |
|-----|-----|-----|-----|-----|-----|-----|-----|-----|
|     |     |     |     |     |     |     |     |     |

Born to show business parents, Jerry Lewis spent his early summers with his parents as they performed in resorts of the Catskills Mountain "borscht belt;" occasionally he would join their act by singing a song. After one year of high school, he dropped out and started looking for work as an entertainer, supporting himself with a variety of odd jobs. He was an experienced one-night-stand comic by the time he was 18; his act consisted in part of mimicking famous performers whose recordings would be played off-stage. He married Patty Palmer, a singer with the Jimmy Dorsey band, when he was 18, supporting himself and his wife by entertaining in the Catskills during the summers. He met Dean Martin,

another small-time entertainer, in 1946, and the two formed a comedy team. Their first appearance, at Atlantic City's 500 Club, was a big success; soon they were playing to packed houses all over the country. Martin would sing and be interrupted by Lewis' wacky clowning, and the two would ad-lib and trade insults; by the end of the '40s they were the most popular comedy team in America, performing on stage, TV, and in clubs. They were signed to a Paramount movie contract in 1949 by Hal Wallis, debuting as supporting players in *My Friend Irma* (1949). Before splitting up in 1956, they starred in 16 films together, all with the same structure: Martin would play a calm, suave, romantic singer and Lewis would play a hyperkinetic misfit. The films were all solid performers at the box office. Lewis went his own way in order to have more control over his films, and subsequently he often produced, directed, and/or wrote the movies he appeared in. Generally unappreciated (if not panned) in America, his films were considered works of genius in France, where he became known as "Le Roi du Crazy;" two influential French film magazines agreed that his work brilliantly unveiled truths about America. He went to Paris in 1971, receiving a rousing welcome and playing 16 sold-out performances at the Olympia. The same year he published *The Complete Filmmaker,* in which he outlined his theory of film and its techniques. Since 1970 his film work has been very limited, but includes a noteworthy performance as a Johnny Carson-like talk show host in Martin Scorsese's *The King of Comedy* (1983). Every Labor Day Weekend he hosts a telethon to raise money in the battle against muscular dystrophy. **Selected Works:** *Mr. Saturday Night* (1992), *Funny Bones* (1994)

# Juliette Lewis

**Born:** June 21, 1973; Los Angeles, CA

**Years Active in the Industry:** by decade

| 10ˢ | 20ˢ | 30ˢ | 40ˢ | 50ˢ | 60ˢ | 70ˢ | 80ˢ | 90ˢ |
|-----|-----|-----|-----|-----|-----|-----|-----|-----|
|     |     |     |     |     |     |     |     |     |

The daughter of actress Geoffrey Lewis, Juliette Lewis began acting professionally in her teen years. Her first national exposure came in 1987 as a regular on the TV sitcom *I Married Dora,* playing the daughter of series star Daniel Hugh-Kelly. Also in 1987, Lewis took action in court to exempt herself from the California child-labor laws, which limited her five working hours per school day. At age 18, Lewis was Oscar-nominated for her flawless performance as Nick Nolte's troubled daughter in director Martin Scorsese's *Cape Fear* (1991); many observers felt that her scenes

were the only islands of subtlety and credibility in this out-of-control suspenser. Any doubts that Lewis is a mature artist were dispelled with her marrow-chilling performance as a mass murderer in Oliver Stone's *Natural Born Killers* (1994). **Selected Works:** *Husbands and Wives* (1992), *Kalifornia* (1993), *Too Young to Die?* (1990), *Strange Days* (1995)

# Val Lewton (Vladimir Ivan Leventon)

**Born:** May 7, 1904; Yalta, Russia
**Died:** 1951

**Years Active in the Industry:** by decade

| 10ˢ | 20ˢ | 30ˢ | 40ˢ | 50ˢ | 60ˢ | 70ˢ | 80ˢ | 90ˢ |
|-----|-----|-----|-----|-----|-----|-----|-----|-----|
|     |     |     |     |     |     |     |     |     |

A Columbia University graduate and former writer, Val Lewton first made a name for himself in films as an assistant to David O. Selznick in the 1930s, and co-directed the Bastille scene in *A Tale of Two Cities* (1938). In 1942, Lewton became a producer at RKO,

specializing in low budget but extremely effect chillers, such as *Leopard Man* (1943), *Cat People* (1942), *The Seventh Victim* (1943), and *Curse of the Cat People* (1944), co-writing several of them. Lewton hoped to move into A-pictures, but his slightly higher budgeted *Bedlam* (1945) failed to make as much money as was hoped, and he was told to continue with smaller scale films. He left RKO and continued trying to produce movies elsewhere, but none of his subsequent pictures had the style or appeal of those small-scale, atmospheric chillers which Lewton virtually directed himself, so precisely did his scripts indicate what he wanted from his directors. Lewton died of a heart attack in 1951 while trying to revive his career.

# Viveca Lindfors (Elsa Viveca Torstensdotter Lindfors)

**Born:** December 29, 1920; Uppsala, Sweden

**Years Active in the Industry:** by decade

| 10ˢ | 20ˢ | 30ˢ | 40ˢ | 50ˢ | 60ˢ | 70ˢ | 80ˢ | 90ˢ |
|-----|-----|-----|-----|-----|-----|-----|-----|-----|
|     |     |     |     |     |     |     |     |     |

Viveca Lindfors spent three years training at the Royal Dramatic Theater in Stockholm in her teens. She debuted onscreen in 1940, appearing in many films and plays in Sweden during the war years. In 1946 she moved to Hollywood and signed a contract with

Warner Bros., appearing in her first American film in 1948. She went on to work in both Hollywood and international productions, few of which fully utilized her screen talents. For her work in *Die Vier im Jeep* (*Four in a Jeep*, 1951) she won acting honors at the Berlin Film Festival, repeating this feat a decade later for *Huis clos* (*No Exit*, 1962). Lindfors wrote, directed, and acted in the film *Unfinished Business* (1985). She has worked frequently in TV productions and stage plays; her stage work includes *Anastasia, Miss Julie, Brecht on Brecht,* and the one-woman show *I Am a Woman.* From 1949-53 Lindfors was married to director Don Siegel, then later she married playwright/director George Tabori; she is the mother of actor Kristoffer Tabori. **Selected Works:** *Exiled in America* (1990), *Playing for Time* (1980), *Way We Were* (1973)

# Margaret Lindsay (Margaret Kies)

**Born:** September 19, 1910; Dubuque, Iowa
**Died:** 1981

**Years Active in the Industry:** by decade

| 10ˢ | 20ˢ | 30ˢ | 40ˢ | 50ˢ | 60ˢ | 70ˢ | 80ˢ | 90ˢ |
|-----|-----|-----|-----|-----|-----|-----|-----|-----|

Margaret Lindsay was an all-American-looking lead and supporting actress with a low-pitched voice. She trained at the American Academy of Dramatic Arts in New York; unable to find roles in America, she went to London and gained stage experience there. After returning to America, she debuted onscreen in 1932. The following year she gained attention in *Cavalcade,* a Hollywood film with an all-British cast; supposedly, to land the role she lied to the studio and pretended to have an English background. Shortly thereafter she was signed by Warners and went on to appear in many films through the '30s; although appealing and talented, she had leads mostly in low-quality films, getting only supporting roles in major productions. Her B-movie experience included playing the female lead in seven *Ellery Queen* films. After leaving Warners she continued to appear mostly in B-movies, and later moved into character roles. She retired from the screen in 1963, going on to appear only in *The Chadwicks,* an unsuccessful 1973 TV pilot with Fred MacMurray. She never married. **Selected Works:** *Scarlet Street* (1945)

# Richard Linklater

**Born:** 1961; Austin, TX

**Years Active in the Industry:** by decade

| 10ˢ | 20ˢ | 30ˢ | 40ˢ | 50ˢ | 60ˢ | 70ˢ | 80ˢ | 90ˢ |
|-----|-----|-----|-----|-----|-----|-----|-----|-----|

One of the first of the prominent "Generation X" directors, Richard Linklater worked at a variety of odd jobs after leaving Sam Houston University. In the spirit of "film what you know," Linklater aimed his lenses at his home town of Austin, and the result was

*Slacker* (1992), a stylized study of the modern "drop-out" society. The non-professional cast largely improvised its dialogue, which means that you'll either revel in the characters' insights or scream "Get a life!," depending on your perspective. Linklater's next film, *Dazed and Confused* (1993), takes place on the last day of high school in 1976; it has been described by some observers as the *American Graffiti* of the post-postwar generation. Linklater has not made any effort to aim his films at a mass audience; he's satisfied with screening his wares at international film festivals and at such organizations as his own Austin Film Society. Linklater also directed *Before Sunrise* (1995), a slick but still very personal film about a pair of disenfranchised young people (Ethan Hawke and Julie Delpy) cast adrift in Vienna; once more, the festival crowd raved, while "mainstream" critics carped about formlessness and excessive length.

# Ray Liotta

**Born:** December 18, 1955; Union, NJ

**Years Active in the Industry:** by decade

| 10ˢ | 20ˢ | 30ˢ | 40ˢ | 50ˢ | 60ˢ | 70ˢ | 80ˢ | 90ˢ |
|-----|-----|-----|-----|-----|-----|-----|-----|-----|

Tall, good-looking, blue-eyed leading man and supporting player, with a sallow, pock-marked complexion, Ray Liotta received a degree in theater and fine arts. He then moved to New York; within six months he found work in commercials as well as bit parts on stage and television. He launched his career with a three-year stint on the TV soap opera *Another World.* For his performance in *Something Wild* (1986), Liotta received a Golden Globe nomination; he won the part with the help of the film's lead actress, old friend Melanie Griffith. From then on, he has tended to make one film a year, including a notable lead performance as real-life gangster Henry Hill in Martin Scorsese's *GoodFellas* (1990). **Selected Works:** *Article 99* (1992), *Field of Dreams* (1989), *Unlawful Entry* (1992), *Operation Dumbo Drop* (1995)

# John Lithgow

**Born:** October 19, 1945; Rochester, NY

**Years Active in the Industry:** by decade

| 10ˢ | 20ˢ | 30ˢ | 40ˢ | 50ˢ | 60ˢ | 70ˢ | 80ˢ | 90ˢ |
|-----|-----|-----|-----|-----|-----|-----|-----|-----|

John Lithgow is a bulky, six-foot four-inch character actor considered by many to be among the finest supporting players of his generation. The son of theatre people, he grew up playing child roles in his father's productions. He was actively involved in acting and directing while a student at Harvard; Lithgow won a Fulbright scholarship to London's Academy of Music and Dramatic Art. In the early '70s he debuted on Broadway in *The Changing Room*, for his performace he won a Tony Award. He went on to win acclaim for much stage work, then debuted onscreen in Brian De Palma's thriller *Obsession* (1976). His breakthrough as a screen actor came in the role of a transsexual football player in *The World According to Garp* (1982), for which he received a Best Supporting Actor Oscar nomination. From then on he appeared in numerous films in a wide variety of parts, going on to receive another Best Supporting Actor Oscar nomination for his work in *Terms of Endearment* (1983). Lithgow continues to be a prolific performer, usually landing meaty, dynamic roles. He won an Emmy for his work in an episode of the TV series *Amazing Stories*. **Selected Works:** *Memphis Belle* (1990), *Wrong Man* (1993), *Pelican Brief* (1993), *Boys* (1991), *Silent Fall* (1994)

# Anatole Litvak (Mikhail Anatol Litvak)

**Born:** May 10, 1902; Kiev, Russia
**Died:** December 15, 1974; Neuilly, France

**Years Active in the Industry:** by decade

| 10s | 20s | 30s | 40s | 50s | 60s | 70s | 80s | 90s |
|-----|-----|-----|-----|-----|-----|-----|-----|-----|
|     | ■   | ■   | ■   | ■   | ■   | ■   |     |     |

Born in Kiev, Michael Anatole Litvak was a stage actor and assistant director as a teenager. He entered Soviet cinema in 1923, working in Nordkino studios as a set decorator and assistant director. He directed his first film, the 1925 release *Tatiana* (*Hearts and Dollars*), but left the Soviet Union that year for Germany, where he edited G.W. Pabst's *Die Freudlose Gasse* (*The Joyless Street*, 1925), assistant directed, and helmed the early '30s features *Dolly Macht Karriere* (1931), *Nie Wieder Liebe* (1932), and *Das Lied Einer Nacht* (1933). Fleeing the Nazis, Litvak directed films in England and France, among them the international hit *Mayerling* (1936). He came to Hollywood in 1937, where he helmed many handsome and polished features, specializing in crime films (*The Amazing Dr. Clitterhouse* [1938], *Confessions of a Nazi Spy* [1939], *Castle on the Hudson* [1940], *Out of the Fog*, [1941]) and romantic dramas (*The Sisters* [1938], *All This and Heaven Too* [1953]). He worked on several Army documentaries during World War II, and co-directed *The Nazis Strike* (1942), *Divide and Conquer* (1942), and *The Battle of China* (1943) with Frank Capra. Litvak made even stonger films after the war: *Sorry, Wrong Number* (1948), *The Snake Pit* (1948), *Decision Before Dawn* (1951), and *Anastasia* (1956). In the mid-'50s he began making films in Europe; standouts of his late career are the thrillers *The Night of the Generals* (1967) and *The Lady in the Car with Glasses and a Gun* (1970). **Selected Works:** *Deep Blue Sea* (1955)

# Christopher Lloyd

**Born:** October 22, 1938; Stamford, CT

**Years Active in the Industry:** by decade

| 10s | 20s | 30s | 40s | 50s | 60s | 70s | 80s | 90s |
|-----|-----|-----|-----|-----|-----|-----|-----|-----|
|     |     |     |     |     |     | ■   | ■   | ■   |

A reclusive character actor with an elongated, skull-like face, manic eyes and flexible facial expressions, Christopher Lloyd is best known for portraying neurotic, psychotic, or eccentric characters. He worked in summer stock as a teenager, then moved to New York. After studying with Sanford Meisner at the Neighborhood Playhouse, he debuted on Broadway in *Red, White and Maddox* in 1969. Lloyd went on to much success on and off Broadway; for his work in the play *Kaspar* he won both the Obie Award and the Drama Desk Award. His screen debut came in the hugely successful *One Flew Over the Cuckoo's Nest* (1975), in which he played a mental patient. He went on to appear in a number of films, but first achieved national recognition for playing the eccentric, strung out, slightly crazy cab-driver "Reverend" Jim in the TV series *Taxi* from 1979-83; he won two Emmy Awards for his work. He extended his fame to international proportions by playing the well-meaning, wild-haired, mad scientist Doc Brown in *Back to the Future* (1985) and its two sequels; this very unusual character continued the trend in Lloyd's career of portraying off-the-wall nuts and misfits, a character type he took on in a number of other films in the '80s, including *The Addams Family* (1991), in which he played the crazed uncle Fester. His "straight" roles have been infrequent, but include *Eight Men Out* (1989). **Selected Works:** *Back to the Future, Part 3* (1990), *Dead Ahead: The Exxon Valdez Disaster* (1992), *Dennis the Menace* (1993), *T Bone N Weasel* (1992), *Addams Family Values* (1993)

# Emily Lloyd

**Born:** 1970; North London, England

**Years Active in the Industry:** by decade

| 10s | 20s | 30s | 40s | 50s | 60s | 70s | 80s | 90s |
|-----|-----|-----|-----|-----|-----|-----|-----|-----|
|     |     |     |     |     |     |     | ■   | ■   |

Brtiish actress Emily Lloyd is the daughter of National Theatre actor Roger Lloyd Pack; her mother was at one time secretary to playwright Harold Pinter. As a teenager, Lloyd performed with several drama workshops, sometimes essaying boy's roles. She unsuccessfully auditioned for a leading role in director David Leland's film *Wish You Were Here* (1987), but was cast anyway when Leland could find no other actress who fit the part. Portraying a "Lolita" type whose signature line was "Up your bum!," the 16-year-old Lloyd became an overnight critic's darling. Her American debut was in 1989's *Cookie*, where she convincingly played a hardbitten Brooklynite. Surprisingly, Lloyd has been in very few films since; her career high point remains *Wish You Were Here*. **Selected Works:** *A River Runs Through It* (1992)

# Frank Lloyd

**Born:** February 2, 1888; Glasgow, Scotland
**Died:** August 10, 1960; Santa Monica, CA

**Years Active in the Industry:** by decade

| 10ˢ | 20ˢ | 30ˢ | 40ˢ | 50ˢ | 60ˢ | 70ˢ | 80ˢ | 90ˢ |
|-----|-----|-----|-----|-----|-----|-----|-----|-----|
|     |     |     |     |     |     |     |     |     |

An actor in British theater while still a teenager, Scottish-born Frank Lloyd came to the U.S. in 1913, and after acting in films he turned to writing and directing. By the late teens he was helming a series of notable films starring William Farnum, ranging from historic adaptations (a seven-reel version of *A Tale Of Two Cities* [1917] and a ten-reel *Les Miserables* [1918]) to Zane Grey westerns (*Riders of the Purple Sage* [1918], *The Rainbow Trail* [1918]). Lloyd's notable films of the '20s include *Oliver Twist* (1922) with Lon Chaney as Fagin, the Milton Sills swashbuckler *The Sea Hawk* (1924), and his Academy Award-winning historical drama *The Divine Lady* (1929). A prolific and reliable craftsman, Lloyd's enduring popularity resides on his 1930s films: *Cavalcade* (1933), *Mutiny on the Bounty* (1935), and the Preston Sturges-scripted *If I Were King* (1938). His '40s films—an episode of *Forever and a Day* (1943), the James Cagney actioner *Blood on the Sun* (1945)—are also admired. Lloyd also produced several films in the early '40s, most notably Alfred Hitchcock's *Saboteur* (1942).
**Selected Works:** *Drag* (1929)

# Harold Lloyd (Harold Clayton Lloyd)

**Born:** April 20, 1894; Burchard, NE
**Died:** March 8, 1971; Beverly Hills, CA

**Years Active in the Industry:** by decade

| 10ˢ | 20ˢ | 30ˢ | 40ˢ | 50ˢ | 60ˢ | 70ˢ | 80ˢ | 90ˢ |
|-----|-----|-----|-----|-----|-----|-----|-----|-----|
|     |     |     |     |     |     |     |     |     |

An all-American boy with an all-American childhood, comedian Harold Lloyd became entranced with amateur dramatic productions through odd jobs as a theatre usher, call boy, and

stage hand. After working in a stock company where he specialized in intricate character make-up, Lloyd moved from Nebraska to California, where there was more theatrical work. While assisting at a San Diego dramatic school, Lloyd took extra work in several of the silent film companies operating up the coast in Los Angeles. One of his fellow extras was Hal Roach, who had plans to become a film producer. One small inheritance later, Roach set up his own movie company and hired Lloyd as his comedy star. Lloyd's first film character, Willie Work, *didn't* work, though it enabled him to teach himself the skills of film comedy from the ground up. Leaving Roach briefly for bit work at Mack Sennett's Keystone studios, Lloyd returned to Roach and developed a new characterization, Lonesome Luke—which frankly wasn't new at all but a direct steal of Charlie Chaplin's "tramp." Be that as it may, Roach and Lloyd's "Lonesome Luke" two-reelers, which co-starred Bebe Daniels, were very popular, but Lloyd got sick of the imitation and set about creating a more original character. In later years, both Lloyd and Roach took separate credit for coming up with the "glasses" character—a handsome, normal looking youth who wore horned-rimmed glasses. Whoever thought it up, it was manna from heaven for Lloyd, whose star ascended once he got away from heavy character make-up and silly costumes and concentrated on playing a comic variation on the "average guy". Determining to be funny at all times on screen, Lloyd surrounded himself with a crack team of gagmen, who came up with endless comic bits of business for his new character. With their two-reelers doing terrific business, Lloyd and Roach began working their way towards feature films, which would bring in even more revenue. Lloyd's first feature, *Grandma's Boy* (1922), set the tone for his subsequent films: he played a character who "grew" either in strength or integrity as the film progressed. The film itself had a strong plotline to support his character, and the gags flowed freely and naturally from the action, instead of being inserted for their own sake, as often happened in silent film comedy. Though Lloyd would vary his "glasses" character from film to film—a spoiled rich lad in one picture, a humble clerk in the next—he never strayed far from the likeable boy-next-door that he'd established in his short subjects. Lloyd left Hal Roach to form his own production company in 1924, and the annual feature releases which followed—most especially *The Freshman* (1925)—established Harold as the top moneymaking comedian in the movies. "As rich as Croesus," to quote film critic Andrew Sarris, Lloyd invested his savings in a huge Beverly Hills estate, Greenacres, where he would live the rest of his life with his wife (and former co-star) Mildred Davis and their children. Uniquely attuned to the optimistic 1920s, Harold's go-getting screen character had trouble surviving the Depression-era 1930s; though he made a successful transition to sound with 1929's *Welcome Danger,* each of Lloyd's subsequent talking features grossed less than the previous one at the box office. He took up to two years to produce a film, and was more careful than ever to maintain his high standards, but despite excellent films like *Movie Crazy* (1932) and *The Milky Way* (1936), Lloyd's jazz-age character seemed out of step and anachronistic in more desperate times. He left films as an actor in 1938, dabbling briefly as a producer for RKO in the early 1940s and working on occasion in radio. When time seemed ripe for a screen comeback in 1946, it was with *The Sin of Harold Diddlebock,* which might have been a better film had not Lloyd clashed so vehemently with his director, eccentric genius Preston Sturges. A still fabulously wealthy Beverly Hills resident whose activities in charity and municipal work brought him universal respect, Lloyd devoted the 1950s to his favorite hobbies, painting and stereoscopic photography. Feeling somewhat forgotten in the early 1960s, Lloyd began releasing his old films theatrically with modest success, and just before his death agreed to their long-awaited TV distribution; still the creative dynamo, Lloyd insisted upon personally re-editing his old films so that they would play better on TV. While his private life was bruised by his overwhelming self-involvement, his wife's alcoholism, and his children's seeming inability to function outside the family nest, to the world at large Lloyd was one of the richest, nicest, and most accessible film star in Hollywood. **Selected Works:** *Speedy* (1928)

# Ken Loach (Kenneth Loach)

**Born:** June 17, 1936; Nuneaton, Warwickshire, England

**Years Active in the Industry:** by decade

| 10s | 20s | 30s | 40s | 50s | 60s | 70s | 80s | 90s |
|-----|-----|-----|-----|-----|-----|-----|-----|-----|
|     |     |     |     |     |     |     |     |     |

British director Ken Loach planned to study law at Oxford, but instead gravitated to acting with the university's Experimental Theatre Club. After serving with the peacetime RAF, Loach acted in regional repertory. He became a director for BBC television in 1961, where he started out with the long-running cop series *Z Cars*. He moved on to the more prestigious, politically charged *Wednesday Play* anthology, produced by Tony Garnett. It was Garnett who produced Loach's first feature *Up the Junction*, which was initially made for TV but released theatrically. Loach burst onto the international film scene with the 1967 working-class drama *Poor Cow* (Loach's own origins were, by his own admission, as squalid as the living conditions of the film's main characters). The director's subsequent films have focused on factory towns, mining communities, Northern Ireland, and other areas distinguished by hopelessness and deprivation. Loach has won the Cannes Film Festival special jury prize twice, for 1990's *Hidden Agenda* and 1993's *Raining Stones*. **Selected Works:** *Riff Raff* (1992), *Ladybird, Ladybird* (1994)

# Sondra Locke

**Born:** May 28, 1947; Shelbyville, TN

**Years Active in the Industry:** by decade

| 10s | 20s | 30s | 40s | 50s | 60s | 70s | 80s | 90s |
|-----|-----|-----|-----|-----|-----|-----|-----|-----|
|     |     |     |     |     |     |     |     |     |

After working in community theater, Sondra Locke debuted onscreen in *The Heart Is a Lonely Hunter* (1968), for which she received a Best Supporting Actress Oscar nomination. After such a promising start her career quickly went nowhere, and she appeared in a number of unmemorable films. She met Clint Eastwood while appearing with him in *The Outlaw Josey Wales* (1976), and the two of them became romantically involved (Eastwood left his wife for

Locke). He cast her in co-starring roles in several of his films. They split acrimoniously in the mid-'80s; she brought a widely publicized palimony suit against him. Her acting career came to a standstill in the early '80s, and she took up directing; her first two films as a director were *Ratboy* (1986), in which she also appeared, and *Impulse* (1990). **Selected Works:** *Tales of the Unexpected* (1991)

# Heather Locklear

**Born:** September 25, 1961; Los Angeles, CA

**Years Active in the Industry:** by decade

| 10s | 20s | 30s | 40s | 50s | 60s | 70s | 80s | 90s |
|-----|-----|-----|-----|-----|-----|-----|-----|-----|
|     |     |     |     |     |     |     | ■   | ■   |

Blonde and buoyant actress Heather Locklear had the distinction of costarring simultaneously in two weekly series within a year of her 1981 TV debut. Locklear played Steven Carrington's long-suffering wife Sammy Jo on *Dynasty,* then went down the block to essay the role of ever-imperiled lady cop Stacy Sheridan on *T. J. Hooker.* Since that time, Locklear has made several efforts to establish herself as a comedienne, ranging from a forgettable sitcom to her wiselipped heroine in *Return of the Swamp Thing* (1991). Far better at inducing feminine envy than laughs, Locklear has most recently been seen as elegant villainess Amanda Woodward, on the Fox Network series *Melrose Place*, a show she is credited as saving from cancellation with her sexy, bitchy performance. When not participating in series television, Locklear has functioned as spokesperson for the Health and Tennis Corporation of America. Locklear was for several years married to rock star Tommy Lee; after their breakup she wed yet another rocker, Bon Jovi guitarist Richie Sambora. Lee in turn married another blonde TV icon, *Baywatch* star Pamela Anderson. **Selected Works:** *Body Language* (1992), *Illusions* (1991)

# Robert Loggia

**Born:** January 3, 1930; New York, NY

**Years Active in the Industry:** by decade

| 10s | 20s | 30s | 40s | 50s | 60s | 70s | 80s | 90s |
|-----|-----|-----|-----|-----|-----|-----|-----|-----|
|     |     |     |     | ■   | ■   | ■   | ■   | ■   |

A character actor who often plays street-wise tough guys and slimy, high-powered businessmen and politicians, Robert Loggia studied with Stella Adler at the Actors' Studio in New York. He debuted on Broadway in *The Man with the Golden Arm* (1955), and then made his screen debut in *Somebody Up There Likes Me* (1956). His film career came to a decade-long halt after he played Joseph in *The Greatest Story Ever Told* (1965). From there he worked consistently in TV in a number of hit shows and movies, and occasionally as a director. Loggia returned to movies in the mid '70s, going on to average two films a year. He briefly starred

in the TV series *Mancuso FBI*. For his portrayal of a private eye in *Jagged Edge* (1985), he received a Best Supporting Actor Oscar nomination. **Selected Works:** *Innocent Blood* (1992), *Intrigue* (1990), *Marrying Man* (1991), *Necessary Roughness* (1991), *Opportunity Knocks* (1990)

endrick's *The Ladykillers* (1955), King Vidor's *War and Peace* (1956), Jose Ferrer's *I Accuse!* (1958), John Huston's *The Roots Of Heaven* (1958) and Frank Borzage's *The Big Fisherman* (1959). In the early '60s Lom scored as Captain Nemo in *Mysterious Island* (1961) and in the title role of *The Phantom of the Opera* (1962); he also created the role of the crazed Chief Inspector Dreyfuss to Peter Seller's Inspector Clouseau in Blake Edwards' comedy *A Shot in the Dark* (1964), and returned to play the character in Edwards' many *Pink Panther* sequels over the next three decades. Lom's later films include Jesus Franco's *Count Dracula* (1971), Ronald Neame's *Hopscotch* (1980), and David Cronenberg's *The Dead Zone* (1983). **Selected Works:** *Gambit* (1966), *Spartacus* (1960), *Great Manhunt* (1949)

# Gina Lollobrigida (Luigina Lollabrigida)

**Born:** July 4, 1928; Subiaco, Italy

**Years Active in the Industry:** by decade

| 10ˢ | 20ˢ | 30ˢ | 40ˢ | 50ˢ | 60ˢ | 70ˢ | 80ˢ | 90ˢ |
|-----|-----|-----|-----|-----|-----|-----|-----|-----|

Sensual, voluptuous actress Gina Lollobrigida was a sex symbol in her native Italy before becoming a Hollywood star. Under the name Diana Loris she worked as a model for illustrated novels, then participated successfully in several beauty contests. She debuted onscreen in 1946, and by the early '50s she was among the most popular stars (known as "La Lollo") of Continental Europe. A contract dispute with Howard Hughes prevented her for several years from appearing in Hollywood films. She finally made her Hollywood debut in 1956, soon becoming very popular with American audiences; for years her name was synonymous with beauty and glamour. In the early '70s she retired from the screen, going on to be a successful photojournalist (she had a celebrated interview with Fidel Castro) and an executive with a cosmetics company. **Selected Works:** *Bread, Love and Dreams* (1953), *Fanfan the Tulip* (1952)

# Herbert Lom (Herbert Charles Angelo Kuchacevich ze Schluderpacheru)

**Born:** January 9, 1917; Prague, Czechoslovakia

**Years Active in the Industry:** by decade

| 10ˢ | 20ˢ | 30ˢ | 40ˢ | 50ˢ | 60ˢ | 70ˢ | 80ˢ | 90ˢ |
|-----|-----|-----|-----|-----|-----|-----|-----|-----|

Herbert Lom acted in theater and films in his native Czechoslovakia in the late 1930s, and at the end of the decade relocated to England. He appeared in numerous supporting roles British and American films in the '40s and '50s, most notably Compton Bennett's *The Seventh Veil* (1946), Jules Dassin's *Night and the City* (1950), Sidney Gilliat's *State Secret* (1950), Alexander Mack-

# Carole Lombard

**Born:** October 6, 1908; Fort Wayne, IN
**Died:** January 19, 1942

**Years Active in the Industry:** by decade

| 10ˢ | 20ˢ | 30ˢ | 40ˢ | 50ˢ | 60ˢ | 70ˢ | 80ˢ | 90ˢ |
|-----|-----|-----|-----|-----|-----|-----|-----|-----|

When Carole Lombard died at the age of 34 in a plane crash following a World War II war bond drive, the American film industry lost one of its most talented and intelligent actresses.

Starting out in silent films as a Mack Sennett bathing beauty, she later epitomized screwball comedy in *Twentieth Century* (1934); *My Man Godfrey* (1936), for which she was Oscar nominated as Irene Bullock, with ex-husband William Powell as Godfrey; and *Nothing Sacred* (1937), playing the not-so-doomed Hazel Flagg. But Lombard was also a capable dramatic actress whose talents can be seen in her subdued performance as a nurse in one of her final roles, in *Vigil in White* (1940), as well as in *The Eagle and the Hawk* (1933), *In Name Only* (1939) and *They Knew What They Wanted* (1940). Other fine appearances include teaming with Fred MacMurray in several films, the best of which are *Hands Across the Table* (1935) and *The Princess Comes Across* (1936), in which Lombard does a humorously accurate Garbo takeoff. Her two final films contain two of her best performances: *Mr. and Mrs. Smith* (1940) and the Lubitsch war satire, *To Be or Not To Be* (1942). She was married to William Powell from 1931-33 and to Clark Gable from 1939 until her death.

# John Lone

**Born:** 1952; Hong Kong

**Years Active in the Industry:** by decade

| 10ˢ | 20ˢ | 30ˢ | 40ˢ | 50ˢ | 60ˢ | 70ˢ | 80ˢ | 90ˢ |
|-----|-----|-----|-----|-----|-----|-----|-----|-----|
|     |     |     |     |     |     |     | ■   |     |

Asian leading man John Lone entered serious training for the stage at the Chin Chiu Academy in Hong Kong when only ten years old; he later came to America and studied at the American Academy of Dramatic Arts in Pasadena. His professional stage debut was in the off-Broadway play *F.O.B.* (1980), which he also choreographed. Lone went on to choreograph and act in numerous New York shows. His first significant screen role came in Michael Cimino's *Year of the Dragon* (1985), in which he portrayed a powerful young Chinatown crimelord. In 1987 he played the title role in Bernardo Bertolucci's glorious Oscar-winning epic, *The Last Emperor*. **Selected Works:** *Shadow of China* (1991)

# Shelley Long

**Born:** August 29, 1949; Fort Wayne, IN

**Years Active in the Industry:** by decade

| 10ˢ | 20ˢ | 30ˢ | 40ˢ | 50ˢ | 60ˢ | 70ˢ | 80ˢ | 90ˢ |
|-----|-----|-----|-----|-----|-----|-----|-----|-----|
|     |     |     |     |     |     |     | ■   |     |

Shelley Long worked as a TV model and spokesperson, then wrote, directed, and produced industrial and educational films. Later, she joined Chicago's famed Second City comedic improvisational troupe, where she was discovered by two Hollywood producers who cast her in a TV pilot, *That Thing On ABC*. The show didn't sell, but led to guest roles on other TV series such as *M*A*S*H* and *The Love Boat*. She also co-hosted, co-wrote, and associate-produced *Sorting It Out* in Chicago. After appearing in three films, she landed the role of pseudointellectual barmaid Diane on the long-running TV sitcom *Cheers,* which made her famous and for which she won a Best Actress Emmy. She left the show after seven seasons to further her screen career, but her films have proved largely unsuccessful, save for *The Brady Bunch Movie* (1995), in which she delivered a dead-on parody of mom Carol Brady. **Selected Works:** *Night Shift* (1982), *The Money Pit* (1986), *Outrageous Fortune* (1987)

# Sophia Loren (Sofia Scicolone)

**Born:** September 20, 1934; Rome, Italy

**Years Active in the Industry:** by decade

| 10ˢ | 20ˢ | 30ˢ | 40ˢ | 50ˢ | 60ˢ | 70ˢ | 80ˢ | 90ˢ |
|-----|-----|-----|-----|-----|-----|-----|-----|-----|
|     |     |     |     | ■   |     |     |     |     |

Sophia Loren was raised in poverty and a one-parent household in the slums of war-torn Naples. At 14 she began entering beauty contests, and over several years won mostly consolation prizes. She modeled for illustrated pulp novels in her mid-teens. After her ambitious mother moved her to Rome, she appeared as an extra in a number of films. At age 15 she participated in a beauty contest whose judges included Italian producer Carlo Ponti; he signed her to a film contract and groomed her for stardom, sending her to drama coaches and casting her in small parts onscreen (billed as Sofia Lazzaro). Gradually the roles got bigger, and by 1954 she was a major star in Italy; after appearing in several films that were distributed in America she began to be much in demand in Hollywood, partly due to her striking figure, which reflected a major fixation of Hollywood films in the '50s. In 1958 Loren arrived in Hollywood after being hyped extensively as the new sex goddess. She went on to appear in numerous Hollywood and international films. For her work in *The Black Orchid* (1959), she won the Venice Film Festival Best Actress Award. For her portrayal of a mother in wartime Italy in De Sica's *Two Women* (1960), she won numerous awards, including an Oscar and a Cannes Film Festival citation. For *Marriage Italian Style* (1964), she won the Moscow festival award. She left Hollywood in the early '60s, and all of her American-sponsored films since then have been made abroad; for her body of work she was awarded a special Oscar in 1991. In 1957, she and Ponti were married, but legal complications in Italy forced them to have the marriage annulled in 1962; they became citizens of France and were remarried in 1966. She is the author of an autobiography, *Sophia—Living and Loving: Her Own Story* (1979). **Selected Works:** *Yesterday, Today, and Tomorrow* (1964), *Ready-to-Wear* (1994)

# Peter Lorre (Ladislav Loewenstein)

**Born:** June 6, 1904; Budapest, Hungary
**Died:** March 23, 1964

**Years Active in the Industry:** by decade

| 10ˢ | 20ˢ | 30ˢ | 40ˢ | 50ˢ | 60ˢ | 70ˢ | 80ˢ | 90ˢ |
|-----|-----|-----|-----|-----|-----|-----|-----|-----|
|     |     | ███ | ███ | ███ | ███ | ███ |     |     |

With the possible exception of Edward G. Robinson, no actor has so often been the target of impressionists as Hungarian-born Peter Lorre. Leaving his family home at the age of 17, Lorre sought out work as an actor, toiling as a bank clerk during down periods. He went the starving-artist route in Switzerland and Austria before settling in Germany, where he became a favorite of playwright Bertolt Brecht. For most of his first seven years as a professional actor, Lorre employed his familiar repertoire of wide eyes, toothy grin, and nasal voice to invoke laughs rather than shudders. In fact, he was appearing in a stage comedy at the same time that he was filming his breakthrough picture *M* (1931), in which he was cast as a snivelling child murderer. When Hitler ascended to power in 1933, Lorre fled to Paris and then to London, where he appeared in his first English-language picture, Hitchcock's *The Man Who Knew Too Much* (1934). Though the monolingual Lorre had to learn his lines phonetically for the Hitchcock film, he picked up English fairly rapidly, and by 1935 he was well equipped both vocally and psychologically to take on Hollywood. On the strength of *M*, Lorre was at first cast in roles calling for varying degrees of madness, such as the love-obsessed surgeon in *Mad Love* (1935) and the existentialist killer in *Crime and Punishment* (1935). Signed to a 20th Century-Fox contract in 1936, Lorre asked for and received a chance to play a good guy for a change. He starred in eight installments of the *Mr. Moto* series, playing an ever-polite (albeit well versed in karate) Japanese detective. When the *Mr. Moto* series folded in 1939, Lorre freelanced in villainous roles at several studios. While under contract to Warner Bros., Lorre played effeminate thief Joel Cairo in *The Maltese Falcon* (1941), launching an unofficial series of Warners films in which Lorre was teamed with his *Falcon* costar Sidney Greenstreet. During this period, Lorre's coworkers either adored or reviled him for his wicked sense of humor and bizarre on-set behavior. As far as Warners director Jean Negulesco was concerned, Lorre was the finest actor in Hollywood; Negulesco fought bitterly with the studio brass for permission to cast Lorre as the sympathetic leading man in *The Mask of Dimitrios* (1946), in which the diminuitive actor gave one of his finest and subtlest performances. In 1951, Lorre briefly returned to Germany, where he directed and starred in the intriguing (if not wholly successful) postwar psychological drama *The Lost One*. The 1950s were a particularly busy time for Lorre: he appeared frequently on such live TV anthologies as *Climax*, guested on comedy and variety shows, and continued to appear in character parts in films. Never a completely happy or healthy man, Lorre began turning to drugs to assuage his private demons, and he also gained a great deal of weight. Still, he remained a popular commodity into the 1960s, especially after costarring with the likes of Vincent Price, Boris Karloff, and Basil Rathbone in a series of tongue-in-cheek Edgar Allan Poe adaptations for filmmaker Roger Corman. Lorre's last film, completed just a few months before his fatal heart attack, was Jerry Lewis' *The Patsy* (1964), in which the dourly demonic Lorre played a director of comedy films (!). **Selected**

**Works:** *20,000 Leagues Under the Sea* (1954), *Casablanca* (1942), *Constant Nymph* (1943)

# Joseph Losey

**Born:** January 14, 1909; La Crosse, WI
**Died:** June 22, 1984; London, England

**Years Active in the Industry:** by decade

| 10ˢ | 20ˢ | 30ˢ | 40ˢ | 50ˢ | 60ˢ | 70ˢ | 80ˢ | 90ˢ |
|-----|-----|-----|-----|-----|-----|-----|-----|-----|
|     |     | ███ | ███ | ███ | ███ | ███ | ███ |     |

Wisconsinite Joseph Losey entered the entertainment industry through the patron's entrance, writing book and theatre reviews in the early 1930s. Attaining work as a stage director, Losey prepared many of the early live presentations at the Radio City Music Hall, participated in theatrical tours of Scandinavia and Russia, and made his Broadway debut in 1936 with the first of the agit-prop *Living Newspaper* productions. His earliest movie work was as director of documentaries for the Rockefeller Foundation; he moved on to industrial shorts, a marionette film for the Petroleum Industry's exhibit at the 1939 New York World's Fair, and a staff director post on MGM's *Crime Does Not Pay* short-subject series. After radio work and World War II service, Losey directed the celebrated 1947 Hollywood stage production of Bertold Brecht's *Galileo*, starring Charles Laughton. This led to Losey's first feature-film directing assignment, RKO's *The Boy with Green Hair* (1949), a sentimental drama with pacifistic overtones. Losey's favorite of his Hollywood films was *The Prowler* (1951), which contained the quintessential Joseph Losey "hero": a man who *knows* he is orchestrating his own downfall, but can't stop himself. While in Italy filming *Stranger on the Prowl* (1951), Losey declined a summons to testify before the House Un-American Activities Committee. Blacklisted as a result, Losey relocated in England, where his film career at long last shifted into high gear. With *The Servant* (1963), Losey directed from a Harold Pinter script for the first time, and thereafter his cinematic style changed radically; where once he had concentrated on fast action and clear-cut storytelling, his films became studied, ponderous, and sometimes downright dull. A muddled attempt to capture the "mod" audience, 1967's *Modesty Blaise*, only emphasized how out of sync Losey's work had become in this period. He regained his momentum with 1971's *The Go-Between* (another Pinter project), which, like *The Servant*, won several international awards. Moving from England to France in the mid 1970s, Losey returned briefly to the theatre, staging an elaborate production of *Boris Godunov* in 1980. While most of Losey's last film projects were shot in France, he went back to England for his final project, *Steaming* (1985); he died in London in 1984, with his fourth wife at his side. **Selected Works:** *King and Country* (1964)

# Lyle Lovett

**Born:** November 1, 1957

**Years Active in the Industry:** by decade

| 10s | 20s | 30s | 40s | 50s | 60s | 70s | 80s | 90s |
|-----|-----|-----|-----|-----|-----|-----|-----|-----|
|     |     |     |     |     |     |     |     | ■ |

With his giraffe-like countenance and unusually tall haircut, American musician/actor Lyle Lovett may look like the archetypal rube, but don't be fooled: he is well educated (he earned journalism and foreign language degrees from Texas A&M), extremely articulate, and highly disciplined. Achieving his first big success in the mid-1980s, Lovett successfully straddled two musical forms on the verge of renewed popularity, folk-rock and country. Lovett also proved himself an adept actor with important roles in three Robert Altman films, *The Player* (1992), *Short Cuts* (1993), and *Ready to Wear* (1994), a reputation he has sustained in a handful of TV guest star shots. Lovett found himself the reluctant recipient of gaudy publicity hype in 1993 when he married movie superstar Julia Roberts, a union that disintegrated (thanks in no small part to incessant and intrusive press coverage) less than two years later.

# Jon Lovitz

**Born:** 1957; Tarzana, CA

**Years Active in the Industry:** by decade

| 10s | 20s | 30s | 40s | 50s | 60s | 70s | 80s | 90s |
|-----|-----|-----|-----|-----|-----|-----|-----|-----|
|     |     |     |     |     |     |     | ■ |     |

Jon Lovitz is a versatile comedic actor instantly recognizable for his distinctive voice, acerbic wit, pear-shaped body, and hangdog eyes. He studied at the University of California, Irvine, and participated in the Film Actors Workshop. He then went on to do guest spots on TV and had a recurring role on *Foley Square*. Lovitz also played small roles in *Last Resort* (1986), and *Ratboy* (1986), and also provided a voice for the animated feature *The Brave Little Toaster* (1987). He got his first real break as a regular on TV's *Saturday Night Live*, where his characters such as Tommy Flanagan of pathological Liars Anonymous, the great Shakespearean ham Master Thespian, and the Devil himself became quite popular. His stint on *SNL* put him in demand as a character actor and television guest star. His friendship with director Penny Marshall helped him get roles in some of her earlier films such as *Big* (1988), and his role as the fast talking baseball recruiter Ernie "Cappy" Capadino in Marshall's *A League of Their Own* (1992) earned him widespread acclaim. Lovitz has also appeared as a guest voice on the TV animated show *The Simpsons* and played lead voice in the critically-acclaimed animated show *The Critic* on ABC and the Fox Network. **Selected Works:** *Coneheads* (1993), *Mr. Destiny* (1990), *City Slickers 2: The Legend of Curly's Gold* (1994), *Trapped in Paradise* (1994)

# Rob Lowe

**Born:** March 17, 1964; Charlottesville, VA

**Years Active in the Industry:** by decade

| 10s | 20s | 30s | 40s | 50s | 60s | 70s | 80s | 90s |
|-----|-----|-----|-----|-----|-----|-----|-----|-----|
|     |     |     |     |     |     |     | ■ |     |

American actors Rob and Chad Lowe were products of a broken home. To satisfy their performing urges and to make financial ends meet, both Lowe brothers became actors in childhood (Chad would ultimately win an Emmy for his TV work). Rob was acting from the age of eight in 1972; seven years later, he was a regular on the TV series *A New Kind of Family*, playing the teenaged son of star Eileen Brennan. That series was shot down quickly, but Lowe's film career picked up when newspaper and magazine articles began aligning the handsome, sensitive young actor with the burgeoning Hollywood "brat pack," which included such new talent as Molly Ringwald, Matt Dillon, Charlie Sheen, and Anthony Michael Hall. Along with several fellow "packers" (Demi Moore, Judd Nelson, Ally Sheedy, and Emilio Estevez), Lowe starred in 1985's *St. Elmo's Fire*; this film and the earlier *Hotel New Hampshire* (1984) represent the most memorable projects in Lowe's otherwise negligible film output. In 1989, Lowe's already flagging film stardom received a severe setback when he was accused of videotaping his sexual activities with an underaged girl (the evidence has since become a choice item on the underground videocassette circuit). Arrested for his misdeeds, Lowe performed several hours' worth of community service, then tried to reactivate his career. Since then, Lowe has matured into something of a brat-pack George Hamilton, successfully lampooning his previous screen image in such comedies as *Wayne's World* (1992) and *Tommy Boy* (1995). **Selected Works:** *Bad Influence* (1990), *Stand* (1994)

# Myrna Loy (Myrna Williams)

**Born:** August 2, 1905; Helena, MT
**Died:** December 14, 1993; New York, NY

**Years Active in the Industry:** by decade

| 10s | 20s | 30s | 40s | 50s | 60s | 70s | 80s | 90s |
|-----|-----|-----|-----|-----|-----|-----|-----|-----|
|     | ■ |     |     |     |     |     |     |     |

The year Clark Gable was named the King of Hollywood, Myrna Loy was the Queen. She started her career as a dancer, moved on into silent films and was typecast for a few years playing

exotic women. Her film titles from those early years include *Arrowsmith* (1931), *Love Me Tonight* (1932), *The Mask of Fu Manchu* (1932), and *Manhattan Melodrama* (1934), the film gangster John Dillinger just had to see the night he was killed. Starting in 1934, with *The Thin Man*, opposite William Powell, she became Hollywood's ideal wife: bright, witty, humorous. She and Powell were often teamed throughout the '30s and '40s, and many of the characters she played were strong, independent, adventurous women. In addition to *The Thin Man* series, Loy's best appearances include *The Great Ziegfeld* (1936), *Libeled Lady* (1936), *Wife vs. Secretary* (1936), *Test Pilot* (1938), and *Too Hot to Handle* (1938). She took a break from filmmaking during World War II to work with the Red Cross and in her later years devoted as much time to politics as to acting. She stands out in *The Best Years of Our Lives* (1946), *Mr. Blandings Builds His Dream House* (1948), *Cheaper by the Dozen* (1950), and its sequel *Belles on Their Toes* (1952). She received an honorary Oscar in 1991. **Selected Works:** *Broadway Bill* (1934), *Prizefighter and the Lady* (1933), *Rains Came* (1939)

# Ernst Lubitsch

**Born:** January 28, 1892; Berlin, Germany
**Died:** November 30, 1947; Bel-Air, CA

**Years Active in the Industry:** by decade

| 10ˢ | 20ˢ | 30ˢ | 40ˢ | 50ˢ | 60ˢ | 70ˢ | 80ˢ | 90ˢ |
|---|---|---|---|---|---|---|---|---|

A stage actor with Max Reinhart's celebrated Deutsches Theater, German-born Ernst Lubitsch entered films in 1912 and soon began starring in a series of short comedies; he was also writing and directing them by the mid-teens. He wore three hats with his first feature *Als Ich Tot War* in 1916, but began directing features in which he didn't act and immediately won acclaim for two films starring Pola Negri, *Die Augen Der Mummie Ma* (*The Eyes of the Mummy*) and *Carmen* (*Gypsy Blood*), both in 1918. He had a major hit in 1919 with *Die Austernprinzessin* (*The Oyster Princess*), a delightful send-up of American mores, and soon built his reputation with opulent historical dramas (*Madame Dubarry* [1919], *Anna Boleyn* [1920]), which he alternated with smaller films such as the comedy *Die Bergkatze* (*The Wildcat*, 1921) and the drama *Die Flamme* (*Montmartre*, 1922). Lubitsch came to Hollywood in 1923, and after directing Mary Pickford in *Rosita* (1923) decided to remain in the States. He turned out a virtually uninterrupted series of successful and influential comedies, inevitably European-located farces wound around the two American obsessions, money and sex. Beloved for such silent comedies as *The Marriage Circle* (1924), *Forbidden Paradise* (1924), *Lady Windermere's Fan* (1925), *So This Is Paris* (1926) and *The Student Prince in Old Heidelberg* (1927), Lubitsch found even greater acclaim in talkies, ingeniously integrating sound and music in his musicals *The Love Parade* (1929) and *Monte Carlo* (1930), both starring Jeanette MacDonald, and *The Smiling Lieutenant* (1931). The latter was Lubitsch's first film with writer Samson Raphaelson, who would script many of the director's best work of the '30s and '40s: *Broken Lullaby* (1932); *One Hour with You* (1932), co-directed by an uncredited George Cukor; *Trouble in Paradise* (1932); *The Merry Widow* (1934); *Angel* (1937); *The Shop Around the Corner* (1940); and *Heaven Can Wait* (1943). Charles Brackett and Billy Wilder also wrote for Lubitsch in the late '30s

on *Bluebeard's Eight Wife* (1938) and the classic *Ninotchka* (1939). Lubitsch continued to helm first-rate work in the early '40s, including his brilliant *To Be Or Not To Be* (1942), which shocked some sensibilities by making a comedy out of a Polish acting troupe's flight from the Nazis. Ill health frustrated Lubitsch's final years, and his films *A Royal Scandal* (1945) and *That Lady in Ermine* (1948) had to be completed by Otto Preminger. **Selected Works:** *Patriot* (1928)

# George Lucas (George Walton Lucas, Jr.)

**Born:** May 14, 1944; Modesto, CA

**Years Active in the Industry:** by decade

| 10ˢ | 20ˢ | 30ˢ | 40ˢ | 50ˢ | 60ˢ | 70ˢ | 80ˢ | 90ˢ |
|---|---|---|---|---|---|---|---|---|

Born in Modesto, California, George Lucas started out as a racing car buff who only gave up those aspirations after a serious crash. He attended Modesto Junior College before enrolling in USC's Cinema School, where he made a prize-winning experimental science fiction short film called *THX-1138* in the mid-1960's. He interned at Warner Bros. during the time that Francis Ford Coppola was working on *Finian's Rainbow* (1968), and became a protege of the director and served as a production assistant on *The Rain People* (1969), which led to Lucas's

documentary about the making of the feature. He worked on David and Albert Maysles's documentary *Gimme Shelter* (1970), and in 1971 was given the chance to transform his old short film into the full-length feature *THX-1138*, starring Robert Duvall, which got enthusiastic reviews and became a major cult movie of the early 1970's. Lucas's career was fully launched, however, with *American Graffiti*, a low budget 1973 feature that he also co-authored, which won over millions of audience members with its witty, wry look back on the early 1960s. The film made $145 million, despite costing only $700,000 and shooting in less than one month, and marked the feature film and pop-culture debuts of an entire generation of performers such as Richard Dreyfuss, Harrison Ford, Paul Le Mat, Cindy Williams, Suzanne Somers, and a dozen others, and the re-introduction as an adult performer of former child star Ron Howard, who has since emerged as a major director. Lucas's next movie, *Star Wars* (1977), became an enormous international hit and a pop-culture fixture that endures two decades later, yielding two sequels (thus far, although Lucas is reportedly creating three additional related projects) and transforming the science fiction genre in the process. Since then, Lucas has become something of an industry unto himself, producing, directing, and writing (most notably the second and third *Indiana Jones* movies and a spin-off television series), and has even managed to survive the debacle of his one unmitigated box office disaster, *Howard The Duck,* with his career unfazed. **Selected Works:** *Raiders of the Lost Ark* (1981)

# Bela Lugosi (Béla Blasko)

**Born:** October 29, 1884; Lugoj, Romania
**Died:** 1956

**Years Active in the Industry:** by decade

| 10s | 20s | 30s | 40s | 50s | 60s | 70s | 80s | 90s |
|-----|-----|-----|-----|-----|-----|-----|-----|-----|

Bela Lugosi was born either Bela Blasko, Bela Belasko, or Bela Ferenc Dezso (the sources are contradictory) in Transylvania. Trained for the stage at the Budapest Academy of Theatrical Arts,

he began landing lead roles on the Hungarian stage in 1901; Lugosi acted in Hungarian films from 1915, sometimes using the name Arisztid Olt. He was active in politics and organized an actors' union during the collapse of the Hungarian monarchy in 1918. In 1919 the Leftists were defeated and he fled to Germany, where he found work in numerous films. He emigrated to the U.S. in 1921 and began playing character parts on stage and screen. In 1927 he played the title role in the Broadway production of *Dracula,* continued the part on the road for two years. He repeated the role in Tod Browning's film version (1931), when his inimitable accent as the vampire made him an instant horror hit. Lugosi went on to dozens of other horror films in the next two decades, accepting work indiscriminately and appearing in both high- and low-quality films, often with Boris Karloff. His personal life was often unsettled, and he came to identify strongly with the Dracula character, giving interviews while lying in a coffin and behaving in other eccentric ways; in his later films he tended to play parodies of himself. Meanwhile, he was almost always in the middle of marital or monetary difficulties. He became a drug addict, and in 1955 had himself committed to a hospital to end his addiction; he then returned briefly to Ed Wood films before dying in August of 1956. He was buried wearing his Dracula cape. **Selected Works:** *Ninotchka* (1939), *The Devil Bat* (1941), *Glen or Glenda?* (1953), *Plan 9 From Outer Space* (1956)

# Sidney Lumet

**Born:** June 25, 1924; Philadelphia, PA

**Years Active in the Industry:** by decade

| 10s | 20s | 30s | 40s | 50s | 60s | 70s | 80s | 90s |
|-----|-----|-----|-----|-----|-----|-----|-----|-----|

American director Sidney Lumet originally planned to follow in the footsteps of his father, Yiddish Art Theatre actor Baruch Lumet. On stage from age five, Sidney studied at Professional Children's School in New York and acted in numerous Broadway productions, most notably *Dead End.* With several other New York-based actors, Lumet was featured in the agit-prop film drama *One Third of a Nation* (1939); he played Sylvia Sidney's crippled kid brother, who sparked the film's climax by setting fire to a disease-ridden tenement house and perishing himself in the conflagration. After wartime service, Lumet decided he'd had enough of acting and focused on the production end of the business. Working his way up the summer stock ladder, Lumet began directing for live TV in 1950, working on such distinguished series as *Omnibus* and *Studio One,* and filmed anthologies like *Alcoa/Goodyear Theatre.* Lumet directed his first film, *Twelve Angry Men* (1957), at the request of producer/star Henry Fonda; the director later confessed that it was a grueling learning experience for both himself and novice producer Fonda, though he took pride in getting the film in the can in 19 days and under budget. Lumet directed a few more films, but drew more satisfaction out of stage and TV work. In 1960, Lumet gained notoriety for directing *The Sacco-Vanzetti Story* on NBC, a drama which drew flack from the state of Massachusetts (where Sacco and Vanzetti were tried and executed) because it was percieved to postulate that the condemned murderers were in fact wholly innocent. The brouhaha actually did Lumet more good than harm, sending several prestigious film assignments his way, including his 1962 artistic triumph *Long Day's Journey into Night.* Proponents of the "auteur" theory, who insist that a director should leave his personal signature on each film, have long been confounded by Lumet, who has refused to do anything twice in his movie work. He directed the cold-war suspenser *Fail-Safe* (1964), the tense war-guilt character study *The Pawnbroker* (1965), the bittersweet Jewish-middle-age-angst film *Bye Bye Braverman* (1969), the rollercoaster police thriller *Serpico* (1973), the shaggy-dog bank robbery account *Dog Day Afternoon* (1974), the slickly stylish mystery *Murder on the Orient Express* (1974), the award-winning media satire *Network* (1976), the hilarious sexual-sparring comedy *Just Tell Me What You Want* (1980), and the grim gangster flick *The Family Business* (1989). Lumet handled these diverse projects brilliantly, and all differently. There is no "Lumet touch," but so professionally assembled are these films that it hardly matters—except to a few college film-theory professors. As full of surprises as ever, Lumet has recently delivered a nail-biting whodunit, *Guilty as Sin* (1993). Plagued with numerous plot holes and illogical character behavior, *Guilty as Sin* was not his best, but even a second-rate Lumet is better than the first-rate work of many other directors. **Selected Works:** *Prince of the City* (1981), *Stranger Among Us* (1992), *Verdict* (1982)

# Dolph Lundgren

**Born:** November 3, 1959; Stockholm, Sweden

**Years Active in the Industry:** by decade

| 10ˢ | 20ˢ | 30ˢ | 40ˢ | 50ˢ | 60ˢ | 70ˢ | 80ˢ | 90ˢ |
|-----|-----|-----|-----|-----|-----|-----|-----|-----|

Swedish-born Dolph Lundgren is a muscular, square-jawed lead actor in action-adventure films of the Stallone-Schwarzenegger mold. He received an M.A. at Stockholm's Royal Institute of Technology, going on to attend Washington State University and the prestigious Massachusetts Institute of Technology. In 1979 he competed with the Swedish national karate team in Japan, then won the championship in 1980; he also became a champion kick-boxer. Lundgren made a workout video called *Maximum Potential,* which brought him to the attention of Hollywood scouts; he won a role in the James Bond film *A View to a Kill* (1985), which also featured singer-actress Grace Jones, whom he later dated. From there he landed the role of Rocky's superhuman Russian boxing opponent in Sylvester Stallone's *Rocky IV* (1985), and then went on to get lead roles in action-adventure films. His characters tend to be men of few words, and some of his films have acquired a cult following. He co-starred with fellow action hero Jean-Claude Van Damme in *Universal Soldier* (1992). **Selected Works:** *I Come in Peace* (1990), *Punisher* (1990), *Showdown in Little Tokyo* (1991)

# William Lundigan

**Born:** December 6, 1914; Syracuse, NY
**Died:** December 21, 1975; Duarte, CA

**Years Active in the Industry:** by decade

| 10ˢ | 20ˢ | 30ˢ | 40ˢ | 50ˢ | 60ˢ | 70ˢ | 80ˢ | 90ˢ |
|-----|-----|-----|-----|-----|-----|-----|-----|-----|

American actor William Lundigan launched his show business career working as an adolescent announcer for a Syracuse radio station, which was housed in a building owned by his father. Abandoning a planned law career, Lundigan spent thirteen years as an announcer before being discovered by a Universal film executive in 1937. Appearing as a lightweight leading man in such films as *Armored Car* (1937) and *Three Smart Girls Grow Up* (1938), and in featured roles in the bigger-budgeted *Dodge City* and *The Old Maid* (both 1939), Lundigan worked steadily in the major studios before being drafted into the Marines for World War II service in 1942. Like many other second-echelon Hollywood actors, Lundigan found the going rough after the war, though as a Fox contractee he managed to land occasional good parts in such pictures as *Pinky* (1949) and *I'll Get By* (1950). When prospects dried up for Lundigan in the mid-1950s, he returned to announcing as the host of the popular CBS dramatic anthology *Climax.* Science fiction fans will remember Lundigan for his role in *Riders to the Stars* (1954), and for his portrayal of TV's first true astronaut, Col. MacCauley, in the 1959 weekly adventure series *Men Into Space.*

# Ida Lupino

**Born:** February 4, 1918; Brixton, South London, England
**Died:** August 3, 1995

**Years Active in the Industry:** by decade

| 10ˢ | 20ˢ | 30ˢ | 40ˢ | 50ˢ | 60ˢ | 70ˢ | 80ˢ | 90ˢ |
|-----|-----|-----|-----|-----|-----|-----|-----|-----|

London-born actress/director/screenwriter Ida Lupino came from a family of performers. She played small parts in Hollywood films through the 1930s until she starred opposite  Humphrey Bogart in *High Sierra* (1941), which led to bigger roles in films of the '40s. Early on, she appeared in *Peter Ibbetson* (1935), *Anything Goes* (1936), *Artists and Models* (1937), *The Adventures of Sherlock Holmes* (1939), and *The Light That Failed* (1939), among others. Later, she appeared in *Ladies in Retirement* (1941), *The Sea Wolf* (1941), *Life Begins at Eight-Thirty* (1942), and *Forever and a Day* (1943), and continued performing on into the 1960s, but not in major films. Starting with *Not Wanted* (1949), which she also co-wrote, she became the only female movie director of her time. She specialized in dramatic and suspense films, including *Never Fear* (1949), *The Hitch-Hiker* (1953), *The Bigamist* (1953), and the comedy *The Trouble with Angels* (1966). She also directed episodes of many television series, including *The Untouchables* and *The Fugitive.* **Selected Works:** *Gay Desperado* (1936)

# John Lurie

**Born:** 1952; Boston, MA

**Years Active in the Industry:** by decade

| 10ˢ | 20ˢ | 30ˢ | 40ˢ | 50ˢ | 60ˢ | 70ˢ | 80ˢ | 90ˢ |
|-----|-----|-----|-----|-----|-----|-----|-----|-----|

Actor/composer John Lurie began his career studying the alto saxophone, then moved to New York with his brother, pianist Evan Lurie; they formed the Lounge Lizards, a freeform jazz combo that went on to gain some distinction. Beginning in 1977 he directed and appeared in his own Super-8 films, and also acted in many New York-made Super-8 films by other filmmakers. In 1980 he began scoring numerous films, most importantly Jim Jarmusch's first feature-length film, *Permanent Vacation*

(1982), in which he also appeared. This began a significant association with Jarmusch; Lurie co-starred in Jarmusch's breakthrough film *Stranger Than Paradise* (1984), provided the music, and has acted in and/or scored other of Jarmusch's films as well. His work with Jarmusch brought him to the attention of other directors, and he has appeared in a handful of movies while maintaining his work as a screen composer. **Selected Works:** *Wild at Heart* (1990)

# David Lynch

**Born:** January 20, 1946; Missoula, MT

**Years Active in the Industry:** by decade

| 10ˢ | 20ˢ | 30ˢ | 40ˢ | 50ˢ | 60ˢ | 70ˢ | 80ˢ | 90ˢ |
|-----|-----|-----|-----|-----|-----|-----|-----|-----|
|     |     |     |     |     |     |     |     |     |

For a man whose specialty is uncovering the bizarre and depraved secrets that exist beneath the surface of small-town normality, American director David Lynch had a remarkably benign childhood.  The son of a government agricultural scientist, Lynch spent much of his early years communing with nature all over the country; he later became a Boy Scout, and in this capacity was an usher at John F. Kennedy's 1961 inauguration. Lynch planned for a career as an artist, and to that end studied at the Corcoran School in Washington DC and later in Europe, where he succumbed to the spell of the avant-gardists. While at the Pennsylvania Academy of Fine Arts, Lynch began to dabble in filmmaking as a means to support himself as a painter. He was living in Philadelphia at the time, which he regarded as the vilest city on Earth, an attitude that doubtless influenced his hobby of collecting dead animals and insects. In 1967 Lynch transferred this morbidity into his first film, an animated cartoon titled *Six Men Getting Sick.* This and a subsequent short subject, *The Alphabet,* earned several awards and brought Lynch to the attention of the artistic intelligentsia. He staged his first art exhibition in 1969, and in 1970, just before taking advanced studies courses at the American Film Institute, he filmed another grim short subject, *The Grandmother.* From 1972-77 Lynch worked on his first feature film, *Eraserhead,* which when released prompted extreme and sometimes violent responses from midnight-movie attendees everywhere. Inadequately described as the story of a man and his sort-of human baby, *Eraserhead* instantly entered the cult film repertoire and led to Lynch's first "mainstream" film, *The Elephant Man* (1980). Now

celebrated as a "freak" director, Lynch traded on his fame by inaugurating a weekly magazine cartoon, "The Angriest Dog in the World," and lining up a science-fiction film project, *Dune* (1984), which he directed and scripted. Based on a complex Frank Herbert novel, *Dune* did not translate well to the big screen; it was so muddled, in fact, that an opening "explanation" of the story was included in the release print—and the explanation was even more bollixed than the picture itself. *Blue Velvet* (1986), Lynch's first big-budget dissection of small-town amorality and corruption, drew praise from some critical circles and boos from others. Lynch's films would never be enormous moneymakers domestically, but played to turnaway business in Europe, where influential film critics and essayists bent over backward finding new adjectives to praise this overwhelmingly individualistic director. American TV fans briefly took Lynch to their hearts in 1990 with the premiere of his weekly series *Twin Peaks,* an aggressively weird serial with enough oddball characters, perverse setpieces, and sidelines peculiarities to fill a dozen series. *Twin Peaks* inevitably collapsed under the weight of its own strangeness, but not before Lynch had twisted the storyline of *The Wizard of Oz* into the zoned-out musical/murder flick *Wild at Heart* (1990). Lynch shows no signs of normalizing his distorted-mirror view of the world, nor does he permit himself to be daunted by such conspicuous film failures as *Twin Peaks: Fire Walk With Me* (1992). Lynch's daughter Jennifer Chambers Lynch is also a director, her most notable effort being 1993's *Boxing Helena.*

# Kelly Lynch

**Born:** 1959; La Jolla, CA

**Years Active in the Industry:** by decade

| 10ˢ | 20ˢ | 30ˢ | 40ˢ | 50ˢ | 60ˢ | 70ˢ | 80ˢ | 90ˢ |
|-----|-----|-----|-----|-----|-----|-----|-----|-----|
|     |     |     |     |     |     |     |     |     |

Contemporary American actress Kelly Lynch has been playing leads in Hollywood films since the late 1980s, but has yet to make it big. The daughter of showpeople, she has been acting since age four. Lynch studied dance and then spent two summers training to be a director at the Guthrie Theater. As a young woman she moved to New York to study drama with Sanford Meisner and Marilyn Fried. After briefly encountering the head of the Elite modeling agency in an elevator, Lynch was signed for a $250,000 per year modeling contract. During the three years she modeled, Lynch made occasional TV appearances. She made her feature film debut playing a bit part in *Bright Lights, Big City* (1988), but did not play her first leading role until the following year in *Road House.* Lynch first gained widespread acclaim for her portrayal of a suburban drug addict in Van Sant's *Drug Store Cowboy* (1989); it was a role she could relate to as she had broken both legs in an auto accident when she was 20 and had come dangerously close to being addicted to a painkiller. Though major stardom has as yet eluded Lynch, she has recently proven herself to be a competent and versatile actress capable of playing in everything from light romantic comedies to high drama. **Selected Works:** *Desperate Hours* (1990), *Three of Hearts* (1993), *Imaginary Crimes* (1994), *Beans of Egypt, Maine* (1994)

# Adrian Lyne

**Born:** 1941; Peterborough, England

**Years Active in the Industry:** by decade

| 10ˢ | 20ˢ | 30ˢ | 40ˢ | 50ˢ | 60ˢ | 70ˢ | 80ˢ | 90ˢ |
|-----|-----|-----|-----|-----|-----|-----|-----|-----|
|     |     |     |     |     |     |     |     |     |

Director Adrian Lyne has offered such mainstream films as *Fatal Attraction* (1987) and *Indecent Proposal* (1993). Like many of his peers, Lyne started out as a director of high-priced television advertisements in Great Britain. For commercials he created in 1976 and 1978, Lyne won Palme D'Ors at the Cannes Commercials Festival. Eventually he came to the U.S. to make feature films. To help drum up cash, he continued to make commercials for Levi-Strauss, Pepsi, and others. Lyne is primarily known for his strong focus on visual style. He made his feature film debut with *Flashdance* (1983), a box office hit. Following the even bigger hit *Fatal Attraction*, Lyne established himself as a strong industry influence. **Selected Works:** *Jacob's Ladder* (1990)

Ralph Macchio

Kelly McGillis

Tom Mix

Mary Elizabeth Mastrantonio

Mike Myers

## Ralph Macchio

**Born:** November 4, 1962; Huntington, NY

**Years Active in the Industry:** by decade

| 10ˢ | 20ˢ | 30ˢ | 40ˢ | 50ˢ | 60ˢ | 70ˢ | 80ˢ | 90ˢ |
|-----|-----|-----|-----|-----|-----|-----|-----|-----|
|     |     |     |     |     |     |     | ▮   |     |

With his short slender build, large brown eyes, and abundant hair, actor Ralph Macchio appears to be the perennial adolescent, a fact which seems to have been hindering his career of late. Best known for his work in the phenomenally popular *Karate Kid* (1984), in which the twenty-two year old actor played a troubled 14-year-old boy who is helped by a sage karate instructor, Macchio has been in show business most of his life. Born in Long Island, he began performing in local musical productions as a young teenager. At 16, he began working in TV commercials, and before he had even graduated from high school had appeared in the adolescent comedy *Up the Academy* (1980). He did not appear in another film until working in Francis Ford Coppola's epic of teenage rivalry *The Outsiders* (1983). Between those first two films, Macchio played on the TV comedy/drama *Eight Is Enough.* Following the *Karate Kid,* he began working in a series of minor films, of which *My Cousin Vinny* (1992) has been most successful. Macchio has also continued to work on television and on stage. In 1986, he appeared on Broadway opposite Robert De Niro in *Cuba and His Teddy Bears.* **Selected Works:** *Naked in New York* (1994), *Crossroads* (1986), *Distant Thunder* (1988)

## Jeanette MacDonald

**Born:** June 18, 1901; Philadelphia, PA
**Died:** January 14, 1965; Beverly Hills, CA

**Years Active in the Industry:** by decade

| 10ˢ | 20ˢ | 30ˢ | 40ˢ | 50ˢ | 60ˢ | 70ˢ | 80ˢ | 90ˢ |
|-----|-----|-----|-----|-----|-----|-----|-----|-----|
|     |     | ▮   |     |     |     |     |     |     |

American actress/singer Jeanette MacDonald made her first public appearance at age three, singing at a benefit show. She trained her own voice by listening to recordings, and honed her dancing and acting skills in school productions. MacDonald entertained notions of starring in grand opera, but her soprano voice, though pleasant and vibrant, was not quite up to operatic standards; she settled instead for supporting roles in Broadway musicals of the 1920s. Director Ernst Lubitsch was impressed by MacDonald's movie screen test and cast her in his 1929 film *The Love Parade* opposite Maurice Chevalier. In this first phase of her film career, MacDonald was not yet the "iron butterfly" that her detractors described but a bewitching, sexy young lady who was seen in her lingerie as often as the censors allowed. One of her best early films was *Monte Carlo* (1930), which reached a wondrous peak of Hollywood artifice as MacDonald sang "Beyond the Blue Horizon" from the observation car of a moving train, with the peasants and farmers standing by the tracks picking up the lyrics as if by ESP. Offstage she could be harshly temperamental, clashing with frequent costar Maurice Chevalier to the extent that neither performer would agree to work with the other after *The Merry Widow* (1934). Under contract to MGM in the mid-1930s, MacDonald (with studio press-agent assistance) altered her image from a kittenish provacateur to a mature, above-reproach prima donna; she also managed to drop six years off her age in official studio biographies. In 1935, MGM teamed MacDonald with baritone Nelson Eddy in *Naughty Marietta,* the first of eight highly popular MacDonald-Eddy film musicals. Though mercilessly lampooned by comedians and by cartoonmaker Jay Ward's "Dudley DoRight" cartoons, the pair's films were consummately produced and strove to entertain every member of the film audience, not merely opera lovers; if there were laughable moments in these films, they were usually intentional. After *I Married an Angel* (1942), the singing team split. Eddy wanted to establish himself in comedy roles (which he didn't), and MacDonald trained diligently to become a bonafide opera star, finally making her operatic debut in a 1943 Montreal production of *Romeo and Juliet;* soon afterward, she headlined a Chicago staging of *Faust* as Marguerite. But MacDonald failed to impress critics, who wrote her off as a mere film personality, unsufficiently gifted to carry off a live opera. She continued making films, spoofing her own image in 1942's *Cairo,* and making a lachrymose attempt at heavy dramatics in *Hills of Home* (1949), in which she shared screen time with canine star Lassie. Throughout the 1950s and 1960s, MacDonald toured in concert and stage productions, playing to large and enthusiastic crowds, though seldom attempting to re-establish herself as an opera diva. In 1965, MacDonald died suddenly of a heart attack, with her longtime husband, actor Gene Raymond, at her side. **Selected Works:** *San Francisco* (1936), *One Hour with You* (1932)

# Andie MacDowell (Rose Anderson MacDowell)

**Born:** 1958; Gaffney, SC

**Years Active in the Industry:** by decade

| 10s | 20s | 30s | 40s | 50s | 60s | 70s | 80s | 90s |
|-----|-----|-----|-----|-----|-----|-----|-----|-----|
|     |     |     |     |     |     |     | ■   | ■   |

Beginning her career as a top-ranked photographic model, Andie MacDowell appeared in TV commercials and hundreds of magazines. She debuted onscreen as Jane in *Greystoke: The Legend of Tarzan* (1984),

but after filming was completed the producers decided to give Jane an English accent, and all of MacDowell's lines were re-dubbed by actress Glenn Close. This unfortunate beginning to her career led to only one more role in the next five years, as a supporting player in the teen-oriented *St. Elmo's Fire* (1985). After doing some work on Italian TV she got her big break when she co-starred in the surprise hit *sex, lies and videotape* (1989), which made her well-known and established that she was indeed a good actress. Still under contract as a model to L'Oreal, she was able to pick and choose her parts after this, and has sustained a successful career highlighted by the runaway success of *Four Weddings and a Funeral* (1994). She is married to actor Paul Qualley. **Selected Works:** *Green Card* (1990), *Groundhog Day* (1993), *Object of Beauty* (1991), *Bad Girls* (1994)

# Ali MacGraw (Alice MacGraw)

**Born:** April 1, 1938; Pound Ridge, NY

**Years Active in the Industry:** by decade

| 10s | 20s | 30s | 40s | 50s | 60s | 70s | 80s | 90s |
|-----|-----|-----|-----|-----|-----|-----|-----|-----|
|     |     |     |     |     |     | ■   | ■   | ■   |

Born Elizabeth Alice MacGraw, Ali MacGraw grew graduated from Wellesley College with a major in art history. In 1960 she joined *Harper's Bazaar* as an editorial assistant, later working as an assistant to a fashion photographer; soon she was modeling, and by 1967 she was a top cover girl. She debuted onscreen in a bit role in *A Lovely Way to Die* (1968); she became a star with her second film, *Goodbye Columbus* (1969), in which she played the archetypal "Jewish princess." She next appeared as a dying woman in the blockbuster *Love Story* (1970), for which she received a Best Actress Oscar nomination; although a major star, she then went on to make only a few more screen appearances. In the '80s and '90s she appeared in a few TV movies and released a popular yoga video. She was married to actor Steve McQueen, with whom she appeared in *The Getaway* (1972); her husband prior to McQueen was Paramount production chief Bob Evans.

# Alexander Mackendrick

**Born:** 1912; Boston, MA
**Died:** December 22, 1993; Los Angeles, CA

**Years Active in the Industry:** by decade

| 10s | 20s | 30s | 40s | 50s | 60s | 70s | 80s | 90s |
|-----|-----|-----|-----|-----|-----|-----|-----|-----|
|     |     | ■   | ■   | ■   | ■   |     |     |     |

An animator for industrial films, Alexander Mackendrick began writing scripts for British features and helming shorts in the late 1930s. During World War II he worked on documentary films, and in the late '40s he began directing features. He made an immediate hit with his debut film, the sparkling satire *Whiskey Galore* (aka *Tight Little Island,* 1948). His major films of the '50s include his memorable Alec Guiness comedies *The Man in the White Suit* (1951) and *The Ladykillers* (1955), and his American film *Sweet Smell of Success* (1957), a stylish drama of a manipulative gossip columnist. Notable among his later work are his adventure films for children, *Sammy Going South* (1963) and *A High Wind in Jamaica* (1965), and the American satire *Don't Make Waves* (1967). After some television directing, he retired in the late '60s and became dean of the California Institute of the Arts film department.

# Kyle MacLachlan

**Born:** February 22, 1959; Yakima, WA

**Years Active in the Industry:** by decade

| 10s | 20s | 30s | 40s | 50s | 60s | 70s | 80s | 90s |
|-----|-----|-----|-----|-----|-----|-----|-----|-----|
|     |     |     |     |     |     |     | ■   | ■   |

Kyle MacLachlan began acting in school productions, and after college he played Romeo at the Oregon Shakespeare Festival.

After working in repertory and summer playhouses he participated in a national casting search for the lead in David Lynch's science-fiction film *Dune* (1984) and won the role. The film was not successful, but Lynch enlisted MacLachlan to play the lead in his next film, the popular and controversial *Blue Velvet* (1986). From there he's gone on to a fairly busy screen career. He came to national attention as the star of Lynch's surreal TV series *Twin Peaks,* which for a time enjoyed considerable cult status and major hype. MacLachlan has also received attention for his highly publicized romances with *Twin Peaks* co-star Lara Flynn Boyle and supermodel Linda Evangelista. **Selected Works:** *Doors* (1991), *Rich in Love* (1993), *Where the Day Takes You* (1992), *The Flintstones* (1994), *Showgirls* (1995)

# Shirley MacLaine (Shirley MacLean Beatty)

**Born:** April 24, 1934; Richmond, VA

**Years Active in the Industry:** by decade

| 10s | 20s | 30s | 40s | 50s | 60s | 70s | 80s | 90s |
|-----|-----|-----|-----|-----|-----|-----|-----|-----|
|     |     |     |     |     |     |     |     |     |

Versatile entertainer Shirley MacLaine began learning to dance at age two and made her first public appearance at four. She continued to dance locally, then from age 16 she spent her summers looking for work as a dancer in New York. After graduating from high school, she moved to New York and eventually made her way into the chorus lines of several Broadway shows, meanwhile earning money as a model. MacLaine's big break occurred in a manner straight out of Hollywood mythology: while working in the chorus line of *The Pajama Game* on Broadway, she was the star's understudy; the star (Carol Haney) broke her leg and MacLaine replaced her in the cast, shortly thereafter getting spotted by Hollywood bigwig Hal Wallis, who signed her to a contract. She debuted onscreen in Hitchcock's comedic *The Trouble with Harry* (1955), then went on to steady work in films. She received Academy Award nominations for her early work in *Some Came Running* (1959), *The Apartment* (1960), and *Irma La Douce* (1963). In her private life she has been active in politics, campaigning for Robert Kennedy in 1968 (when she was a Democratic Convention delegate) and George McGovern in 1972. She travels extensively and has eight dwellings in various places around the globe. She starred in the TV series *Shirley's World* in 1971-72. Beginning with *Don't Fall Off the Mountain* (1970) she has published a number of memoirs; subsequent books she has

written have dealt with New Age ideas such as reincarnation, making her a leading figure in the New Age movement of the '80s. As the result of a tour of mainland China in 1973, she wrote, produced, and co-directed *The Other Half of the Sky: A China Memoir* (1975), a feature-length documentary concerning her trip; she also chronicled this adventure in the book *You Can Get There From Here.* MacLaine returned to the stage in 1976 with a one-woman show, *A Gypsy in My Soul,* and has done a good deal of stage work since. She won the Best Actress Oscar for her work in *Terms of Endearment* (1983), and has delivered top-notch character performances in *Madame Sousatzka* (1988), *Steel Magnolias* (1989), and *Postcards from the Edge* (1990). She is the sister of actor-filmmaker Warren Beatty. **Selected Works:** *Waiting for the Light* (1990), *Guarding Tess* (1994), *Sweet Charity* (1966), *The Children's Hour* (1962), *The Bliss of Mrs. Blossom* (1968)

# Barton MacLane

**Born:** December 25, 1902; Columbia, SC
**Died:** 1969

**Years Active in the Industry:** by decade

| 10s | 20s | 30s | 40s | 50s | 60s | 70s | 80s | 90s |
|-----|-----|-----|-----|-----|-----|-----|-----|-----|
|     |     |     |     |     |     |     |     |     |

As a football player at Wesleyan University in 1924, Barton MacLane gained some attention from the movie industry, leading to a bit role in the football-oriented silent *The Quarterback* (1926). With his foot in the door of Hollywood, MacLane studied acting and landed some roles on Broadway. After returning to Hollywood, he began a three-decade career in which he appeared in more than 300 films as a semi-star (throughout the '30s, when he frequently played leads) and character actor; he often played burly, tough-talking heavies. MacLane co-starred as Detective Lieutenant Steve McBride in a series of seven *Torchy Blane* films. He also starred in the TV series *The Outlaws.* **Selected Works:** *Maltese Falcon* (1941), *Treasure of the Sierra Madre* (1948)

# Fred MacMurray (Frederick Martin MacMurray)

**Born:** August 30, 1908; Kankakee, IL
**Died:** November 5, 1991; Santa Monica, CA

**Years Active in the Industry:** by decade

| 10s | 20s | 30s | 40s | 50s | 60s | 70s | 80s | 90s |
|-----|-----|-----|-----|-----|-----|-----|-----|-----|
|     |     |     |     |     |     |     |     |     |

Fred MacMurray paid his way through college by working as a band vocalist and saxophonist. Later he traveled with several bands, and while on the road through California in the '20s, he worked as an extra in a few films. He joined an acting troupe called the California Collegians, and appeared with them in a 1930

Broadway revue; years later he performed with the group in the musical *Roberta* on Broadway. In 1934 Paramount signed MacMurray to a screen contract and he very quickly played leads in numerous films; his early assignments were varied, but gradually he found a niche in both sophisticated and farcical comedy, usually playing decent, genial, likable men. Occasionally he played a memorable bad guy, as in *Double Indemnity* (1944). His screen career remained busy and consistent for almost three decades, and in the '60s he found new popularity from two ventures: he played leads in several popular Disney comedies, and starred in the long-running TV series *My Three Sons*. Ultimately, MacMurray's salaries and investments made him one of Hollywood's richest actors. He was married to actress June Haver. **Selected Works:** *The Absent-Minded Professor* (1961), *Alice Adams* (1935), *The Apartment* (1960), *Caine Mutiny* (1954), *Trail of the Lonesome Pine* (1936)

# Gordon MacRae

**Born:** March 12, 1921; East Orange, NJ
**Died:** January 24, 1986; Lincoln, NE

**Years Active in the Industry:** by decade

| 10ˢ | 20ˢ | 30ˢ | 40ˢ | 50ˢ | 60ˢ | 70ˢ | 80ˢ | 90ˢ |
|-----|-----|-----|-----|-----|-----|-----|-----|-----|

American actor/singer Gordon MacRae went from winning a hometown talent contest to singing at the 1939 New York World's Fair at the age of 18. Following stage and cabaret work, MacRae

was introduced to film audiences via *The Big Punch* (1948). His robust baritone obscuring his acting deficiencies, MacRae became Warner Bros.' resident male songbird in the early 1950s: he was teamed several times with Doris Day and headlined such Technicolor musicfests as *About Face* (1952) and *The Desert Song* (1953). In 1955, MacRae was selected to play Curley in the splashy, Todd-AO film version of Rodgers and

Hammerstein's *Oklahoma* (1955), where he set female hearts aflutter with such standards as "Surrey with the Fringe on Top," "Oh What a Beautiful Mornin'," "People Will Say We're in Love," and the title song. Though he registered well in *Oklahoma,* MacRae was not the first choice for Billy Bigelow in the 1956 filmization of Rodgers and Hammerstein's *Carousel*. Frank Sinatra was to have played the irresponsible carnival barker Billy Bigelow, but a combination of throat problems and pressing prior commitments forced Sinatra to bow out, allowing MacRae to play what would be his best film role, and to sing *Carousel*'s immortal "Soliloquy." MacRae left films in 1956 in favor of concert work and TV assignments, in which the singer appeared regularly on *The Colgate Comedy Hour, Lux Video Theatre,* and (surprise, surprise) *The Gordon MacRae Show*. At the time of his death, MacRae had been divorced for many years from Sheila MacRae, a multitalented performer in her own right; Gordon and Sheila were the parents of actresses Heather and Meredith MacRae.

# Amy Madigan

**Born:** September 11, 1951; Chicago, IL

**Years Active in the Industry:** by decade

| 10ˢ | 20ˢ | 30ˢ | 40ˢ | 50ˢ | 60ˢ | 70ˢ | 80ˢ | 90ˢ |
|-----|-----|-----|-----|-----|-----|-----|-----|-----|

Actress Amy Madigan is the daughter of Chicago political commentor John Madigan, well known in the Windy City for his WBBM radio signoff, "John Madigan...News Radio Sssssseventy-eight." After studying piano at the Chicago Conservatory and philosophy at Milwaukee's Marquette University, Madigan spent the next decade as a touring rock musician. In the late 1970s, she began preparing for an acting career at L.A.'s Lee Strasberg Institute, making her TV bow on an episode of *Hart to Hart*. While she may have looked like a standard blonde ingenue, Madigan's endearingly raspy voice and '60s-style ebullience secured her a series of offbeat leading roles, culminating with her performance as Kevin Costner's ex-activist wife in *Field of Dreams* (1989). In 1985, Amy Madigan was Oscar-nominated for her performance as Gene Hackman's embittered daughter in *Twice in a Lifetime*. She is married to actor Ed Harris, with whom she has co-starred in *Places in the Heart* (1984) and *Alamo Bay* (1985).

# Madonna (Madonna Louise Ciccone)

**Born:** August 16, 1958; Bay City, MI

**Years Active in the Industry:** by decade

| 10ˢ | 20ˢ | 30ˢ | 40ˢ | 50ˢ | 60ˢ | 70ˢ | 80ˢ | 90ˢ |
|-----|-----|-----|-----|-----|-----|-----|-----|-----|

Born Madonna Ciccone, native Michigander Madonna studied ballet from an early age, going on to study modern dance, jazz and ballet in college and with the Alvin Ailey Dance Company. Later she moved to New York and sang in clubs, meanwhile learning to play the drums, the guitar, and keyboards; she also teamed up with an aspiring producer, John "Jellybean" Benitez. She recorded her first album, *Madonna,* which became a smash hit and launched her into a phenomenally successful pop music career. Having appeared in the low-budget independent film *A Certain Sacrifice* (1982), Madonna got a role in her first major production, *Vision Quest* (1985), in which she played a barroom singer. Next came her first co-leading role, in Susan Seidelman's successful *Desperately Seeking Susan* (1985). Madonna continued getting film roles at the rate of one a year, but none of her films were successful until *A League of Their Own* (1992), in which she had a supporting role; she has yet to star in another hit. In 1988 she appeared on Broadway in David Mamet's *Speed the Plow*. She married and divorced actor Sean Penn and has made no secret of her many other romantic entanglements, including a lengthy affair with Warren Beatty. **Selected Works:** *Dick Tracy* (1990), *Truth or Dare* (1991), *Four Rooms* (1995)

# Michael Madsen

**Born:** 1947; Winnetka, IL

**Years Active in the Industry:** by decade

| 10ˢ | 20ˢ | 30ˢ | 40ˢ | 50ˢ | 60ˢ | 70ˢ | 80ˢ | 90ˢ |
|-----|-----|-----|-----|-----|-----|-----|-----|-----|
|     |     |     |     |     |     |     | ■ | ■ |

The son of a fireman, Michael Madsen was a gas-pump "jockey" before plunging into acting with Chicago's Steppenwolf Theatre. Since that time, Madsen has successfully essayed a number of film supporting roles, usually playing nasty or insensitive types. Among his movie credits are *Thelma and Louise* (1990), *Free Willy* (1992), *The Getaway* (1992) and *Wyatt Earp* (1994); he also made an indelible impression in Quentin Tarantino's *Reservoir Dogs* (1992), portraying a psycho hit man who cuts off a policeman's ear while boogeyin' to a 1970s rock tune. So far as the possibility of major stardom is concerned, Madsen himself has confessed that he's less interested in fame than in delivering a good performance. He is the older brother of movie and TV leading lady Virginia Madsen. **Selected Works:** *Doors* (1991), *End of Innocence* (1990), *Straight Talk* (1992), *Thelma & Louise* (1991)

# Virginia Madsen

**Born:** September 11, 1963; Winnetka, IL

**Years Active in the Industry:** by decade

| 10ˢ | 20ˢ | 30ˢ | 40ˢ | 50ˢ | 60ˢ | 70ˢ | 80ˢ | 90ˢ |
|-----|-----|-----|-----|-----|-----|-----|-----|-----|
|     |     |     |     |     |     |     | ■ | ■ |

The younger sister of actor Michael Madsen, American actress Virginia Madsen grew up in and around the Chicago area, re-

ceiving her acting training at Northwestern University. As the daughter of an Emmy-winning documentary maker, it was logical for Madsen to make her first appearances on public television. She worked in the many independent theatres of Chicago before making her cinematic bow in *Electric Dreams* (1983). Possessed of a cool, classic beauty, Madsen has frequently found critical commentary about her work centered not around her considerable skills but on her willingness to appear in the nude. Even in the made-for-TV *Long Gone* (1987), Madsen first appears lying on her stomach in bed, with nary a stitch. In 1992, Madsen came full circle by returning to her Chicago home base for *Candyman,* a superior horror film which to many observers represents the actress' finest screen work. On television, Madsen has confronted and conquered the daunting assignment of portraying actress Marion Davies in the TV movie *The Hearst and Davies Affair* (1985) where she maintained an even performing keel with veteran Robert Mitchum as William Randolph Hearst. She has a child with heart-throb TV actor Antonio Sabato Jr. **Selected Works:** *Hot Spot* (1990), *Ironclads* (1990), *Love Kills* (1991), *Victim of Love* (1991), *Becoming Colette* (1992)

# Anna Magnani

**Born:** March 7, 1908; Alexandria, Egypt
**Died:** 1973

**Years Active in the Industry:** by decade

| 10ˢ | 20ˢ | 30ˢ | 40ˢ | 50ˢ | 60ˢ | 70ˢ | 80ˢ | 90ˢ |
|-----|-----|-----|-----|-----|-----|-----|-----|-----|
|     |     | ■ | ■ | ■ | ■ |     |     |     |

Fiery, unkempt, earthy, sensual, powerful star of Italian and international films, Anna Magnani was born illegitimate and raised by her grandmother in Rome. She spent her childhood impoverished and in slums. In her teens she enrolled at Rome's Academy of Dramatic Art; while there, she made money singing bawdy ballads in low-class nightclubs. Soon Magnani began working in variety shows, and in 1926 she first performed in dramatic plays in stock. She debuted onscreen in a bit part in *Scampolo* (1927), but did not make another film appearance until 1934; in the meantime her reputation as a stage actress and singer steadily improved. In 1935 she married director Alfredo Alessandrini, going on to appear in his *Cavalleria* (1936); the marriage was annulled after 15 years, during most of which the couple were separated. Her film career did not take off until 1941, when she played the second feminine lead in Vitorio De Sica's

*Teresa Venerdi*. In 1942 she gave birth to a son by actor Massimo Serato. After Rome was liberated Magnani became popular among American servicemen as a singer in racy revues. For her work in *Open City* (1945), she was named by the National Board of Review as the best foreign actress of the year, the first time she had gained attention in the U.S. From then on she gradually achieved star status around the world, although the conventional star qualities were absent in her appearance: she was short and plump, her hair was disheveled, and her eyes were encircled by deep, dark shadows. However, she gave off an aura of earthiness and volcanic temperament. Several directors declared her to be Italy's greatest actress, including De Sica and Renoir. The climax of her career came with her performance in the Hollywood film *The Rose Tattoo* (1955), for which she won the Best Actress Oscar and the New York Critics award. From there her screen career declined, and in her final years she appeared primarily on stage and TV. Magnani's funeral attracted an enormous crowd in Rome, and she was buried in the family mausoleum of actor-director Roberto Rossellini, her longtime friend. **Selected Works:** *Amore* (1948)

# Ann Magnuson

**Born:** January 4, 1956; Charleston, WV

**Years Active in the Industry:** by decade

| 10s | 20s | 30s | 40s | 50s | 60s | 70s | 80s | 90s |
|-----|-----|-----|-----|-----|-----|-----|-----|-----|
|     |     |     |     |     |     |     |     |     |

When actress Ann Magnuson gained nationwide TV exposure in 1990 for her portrayal of high-strung magazine editor Catherine Hughes on the sitcom *Anything But Love*, viewers suddenly recalled how often they'd seen Magnuson in earlier roles, but never connected a name with the face. Starting her career as a singer and ensemble comedian, Magnuson built up a loyal following of New York clubgoers. Her first fleeting movie appearance was in the 1983 horror film *The Hunger*. Few of Magnuson's movies have been blockbusters, but she has always brightened up even the dimmest of productions. **Selected Works:** *Cabin Boy* (1994), *Clear and Present Danger* (1994), *Making Mr. Right* (1986)

# John Mahoney

**Born:** June 20, 1940; Manchester, England

**Years Active in the Industry:** by decade

| 10s | 20s | 30s | 40s | 50s | 60s | 70s | 80s | 90s |
|-----|-----|-----|-----|-----|-----|-----|-----|-----|
|     |     |     |     |     |     |     |     |     |

A distinctive-looking, grey-haired British character actor, Mahoney worked onstage in his teens, and moved to the U.S. at 19. In his mid-30s, while employed as an editor in Chicago, he decided to renew his interest in acting, and he enrolled in classes at a local theater co-founded by playwright David Mamet; he landed a role in a Mamet play and left his job for the part. At the urging of actor John Malkovich, he went on to join Chicago's celebrated Steppenwolf Theater; eventually he appeared in more than 30 plays. For his work in the Broadway play *House of Blue Leaves* he won a Tony and a Clarence Derwent Award. For his work in the lead role of *Orphans* (on Broadway and in Chicago) he won a Theater World Award. He still lives in Chicago, and maintains his connection with Steppenwolf. Mahoney debuted onscreen in *Mission Hill* (1982), but his screen breakthrough came in his fifth film, Barry Levinson's popular comedy *Tin Men* (1987); afterwards he went on to better parts in more noteworthy movies, and has avoided typecasting in a busy screen career. Mahoney's TV credits include *Favorite Son* and *House of Blue Leaves*, in which he reprised his stage role; he has since achieved wide popularity as Martin Crane, Frasier Crane's crochety father, on the NBC sitcom *Frasier*. **Selected Works:** *Article 99* (1992), *Barton Fink* (1991), *In the Line of Fire* (1993), *Water Engine* (1992), *Hudsucker Proxy* (1994)

# Marjorie Main (Mary Tomlinson)

**Born:** February 24, 1890; Acton, IN
**Died:** 1975

**Years Active in the Industry:** by decade

| 10s | 20s | 30s | 40s | 50s | 60s | 70s | 80s | 90s |
|-----|-----|-----|-----|-----|-----|-----|-----|-----|
|     |     |     |     |     |     |     |     |     |

Scratchy-voiced American character actress who appeared in dozens of Hollywood vehicles following years on the Chautauqua and Orpheum circuits, Marjorie Main eventually worked with W. C. Fields on Broadway, where she appeared in several productions. Widowed in 1934, she entered films in 1937, repeating her Broadway stage role as the gangster's mother in *Dead End* (1937). Best known among her close to 100 film appearances, most for MGM, are *Stella Dallas* (1937), *Test Pilot* (1938), *Too Hot to Handle* (1938), *The Women* (1939), *Another Thin Man* (1939), *I Take This Woman* (1940), *Susan and God* (1940), *Honky Tonk* (1941), *Heaven Can Wait* (1943), *Meet Me in St. Louis* (1944), *Murder, He Says* (1945), *The Harvey Girls* (1946), *Summer Stock* (1950), *The Long, Long Trailer* (1954), *Rose Marie* (1954), and *Friendly Persuasion* (1956). Starting with their appearances in *The Egg and I* (1947), which starred Fred MacMurray and Claudette Colbert, Main and Percy Kilbride became starring performers as Ma and Pa Kettle in a series of rural comedies.

# Karl Malden (Karl Mladen Sekulovich)

**Born:** March 22, 1912; Gary, IN

**Years Active in the Industry:** by decade

| 10s | 20s | 30s | 40s | 50s | 60s | 70s | 80s | 90s |
|-----|-----|-----|-----|-----|-----|-----|-----|-----|
|     |     |     |     |     |     |     |     |     |

The son of Yugoslav immigrants, Karl Malden labored in the steel mills of Gary, Indiana before enrolling in Arkansas State

Teachers College. While not a prime candidate for stardom with his oversized nose and bullhorn voice, Malden attended Chicago's Goodman Dramatic School, then moved to New York, where he made his Broadway bow in 1937. Three years later he made his film debut in a microscopic role in *They Knew What They Wanted* (1940), which also featured another star-to-be, Tom Ewell. While serving in the Army Air Force during World War II, Malden returned to films in the all-serviceman epic *Winged Victory* (1944), where he was billed as Corporal Karl Malden. This led to a brief contract with 20th Century-Fox—but not to Hollywood, since Malden's subsequent film appearances were lensed on the east coast. In 1947, Malden created the role of Mitch, the erstwhile beau of Blanche Dubois, in Tennessee Williams' Broadway play *A Streetcar Named Desire;* he repeated the role in the 1951 film version, winning an Oscar in the process. For much of his film career, Malden has been assigned roles that called for excesses of ham; even his Oscar-nominated performance in *On the Waterfront* (1954) was decidedly "Armour Star" in concept and execution. In 1957, he directed the Korean War melodrama *Time Limit,* the only instance in which the forceful and opinionated Malden was *officially* credited as director. Malden was best known to TV fans of the 1970s as Lieutenant Mike Stone, the no-nonsense protagonist of the longrunning cop series *The Streets of San Francisco.* Still wearing his familiar *Streets* hat and overcoat, Malden supplemented his income with a series of ads for American Express. His commercial catchphrases "What will you do?" and "Don't leave home without it!" soon entered the lexicon of TV trivia—and provided endless fodder for such comedians as Johnny Carson. From 1989-93, Malden served as president of the Academy of Motion Picture Arts and Sciences. **Selected Works:** *Baby Doll* (1956), *Birdman of Alcatraz* (1962), *Gunfighter* (1950), *How the West Was Won* (1963), *Patton* (1970)

# John Malkovich

**Born:** December 9, 1953; Benton, IL

**Years Active in the Industry:** by decade

| 10s | 20s | 30s | 40s | 50s | 60s | 70s | 80s | 90s |
|-----|-----|-----|-----|-----|-----|-----|-----|-----|
|     |     |     |     |     |     |     | ■ | ■ |

After attending college, John Malkovich helped to found the Steppenwolf Ensemble in Chicago, an intense, avant-garde group of young actors known for their shocking, hard-hitting early work; the ensemble became well-known across the country. Malkovich went on to work extensively in theater, including the Broadway revival of *Death of a Salesman* and Lanford Wilson's *Burn This,* in which he originated the role of Pale on the Los Angeles stage in 1987 and then reprised it on Broadway in 1990. He has also directed plays and worked in set and costume design. He debuted onscreen as a war photographer in *The Killing Fields* (1984); for his second film, *Places in the Heart* (1984), he received a Best Supporting Actor Oscar nomination, having convincingly portrayed a blind man. From there he sustained a busy

screen career, including dynamic performances in *Of Mice and Men* (1992) and *In the Line of Fire* (1993), and also co-produced the movie *The Accidental Tourist* (1988). **Selected Works:** *Jennifer 8* (1992), *Object of Beauty* (1991), *Mary Reilly* (1995)

# Louis Malle

**Born:** October 30, 1932; Thumeries, France

**Years Active in the Industry:** by decade

| 10s | 20s | 30s | 40s | 50s | 60s | 70s | 80s | 90s |
|-----|-----|-----|-----|-----|-----|-----|-----|-----|
|     |     |     |     | ■ | ■ | ■ | ■ | ■ |

Born into great wealth, French film director Louis Malle had the advantages of an expensive college education, which started in the study of political science but ended up with filmmaking classes. A protege of underwater photographer/director Jacques Cousteau, Malle received his first director's credit on Cousteau's *The Silent World* (1956), which served to introduce both men to the international film scene. After working as an assistant to cult-favorite director Robert Bresson, Malle made his first solo film, the award winning *Frantic* (1957), a mystery melodrama in the *Diabolique* mold distinguished by an improvisational music score by Miles Davis. With *The Lovers* (1958), Malle gained notoriety for staging what were then considered graphic sex scenes—making him a favorite of American French-film afficionados who went to movies not as much for artistic fulfillment as to see as much female epidermis as possible. Actually, *The Lovers* was meant to be an attack on French class consciousness, and as such won Malle several festival awards. The director once more raised eyebrows in America with 1962's *A Very Private Affair,* a Brigette Bardot vehicle allegedly based on her own life. The more serious international critics were impressed by Malle's next film, *The Fire Within* (1963), the alternately repellent and fascinating account of the last days in the life of an alchoholic (played by Maurice Ronet). As with *Frantic, The Fire Within* was enhanced by a strong music score, composed in this case by Erik Satie. Malle drew controversy (again) for his 1969 documentary *Phantom India,* which compelled the Indian government to lodge a complaint against Malle's unblinking look at the country's appalling poverty. *Murmur of the Heart* (1971), an Italian-German coproduction, was a gentle comedy, while *Lacombe, Lucien* (1974) was a dissection of France under Nazi occupation; both, however, tended to solidify Malles' reputation as a "sex" director in the eyes of those who couldn't see beyond this element. Sex once again was a theme in *Pretty Baby* (1978), Malle's first American film, in which Brooke Shields (in her first important role) played a 12-year-old New Orleans prostitute. The film stirred up the would-be censors of the world, but the fuss was truly unnecessary; the film was more atmospheric than erotic. *Atlantic City* (1980) was Malle's best American film, with topnotch performances from Burt Lancaster and Susan Sarandon. What might have become a seamy look at American subculture in lesser hands became a life-affirming romance, even though it made a hero out of an erstwhile drug courier. *My Dinner with Andre* (1982) was Malles' *oddest* American film, little more than a filmed dialogue between two people (Andre Gregory and Wallace Shawn); still, it never bored, even when it dragged. Commuting between Europe and the U.S. in the last decade (often in the company of his wife, actress Candice Bergen), Malle has persisted in offering works of great visual beauty and muted social observation; his most recent film was *Damage* (1992), a disgraced-politician affair which compensated for a monotonous performance from leading lady Juliette Binoche with superb character studies from the always reliable Jeremy Irons and Miranda Richardson. **Selected Works:** *Au Revoir Les Enfants* (1987), *May Fools* (1990), *Lacombe, Lucien* (1974), *Vie De Boheme* (1993), *Vanya on 42nd Street* (1994)

# David Mamet

**Born:** November 30, 1947; Chicago, IL

**Years Active in the Industry:** by decade

| 10s | 20s | 30s | 40s | 50s | 60s | 70s | 80s | 90s |
|-----|-----|-----|-----|-----|-----|-----|-----|-----|
|     |     |     |     |     |     |     |     |     |

A Chicagoan to his fingertips, American writer/director David Mamet returned to work in his hometown shortly after graduating from Vermont's Godard College. Mamet founded Chicago's St. Nicholas Theatre Company, then became the artistic director of that city's Goodman Theatre. He wrote his first play in 1971, winning numerous awards for such works as *Sexual Perversity in Chicago* (1973) (later filmed under the white-bread title *About Last Night* in 1986), *American Buffalo, Edmond,* and *Glengarry Glen Ross* (based on his own experiences in the real estate business). Mamet's reputation rested on his ability to accurately capture the everyday jargon of people trapped by the routine of their lives. Moving into screenwriting, Mamet has contributed such powerful filmed works as *The Verdict* (1982), *The Untouchables* (1987) and *Hoffa* (1991); he has also directed such films as *House of Games* (1986), *Things Change* (1988), and *Homicide* (1991). In 1988, Mamet gained additional fame for his Tony-winning play *Speed the Plow,* which starred Madonna. Mamet has also penned an original script for television, the 1992 cable-TV movie *The Water Engine.* Mamet also directed the film version of his controversial play, *Oleanna* (1994). **Selected Works:** *Malcolm X* (1992)

# Rouben Mamoulian

**Born:** October 8, 1898; Tiflis, Georgia, Russia
**Died:** December 4, 1987; Woodland Hills, CA

**Years Active in the Industry:** by decade

| 10s | 20s | 30s | 40s | 50s | 60s | 70s | 80s | 90s |
|-----|-----|-----|-----|-----|-----|-----|-----|-----|
|     |     |     |     |     |     |     |     |     |

An actor in Russian theater in the teens, Rouben Mamoulian relocated to England and began directing plays in London in 1922. He came to the U.S. the following year and was soon directing opera and theater. He helmed his first film in 1929, the landmark early talkie *Applause.* This backstage drama was noteworthy for its inventive camerawork and resourceful use of sound—qualities that also defined Mamoulian's major works of the early 1930s: the crime drama *City Streets* (1931) with Gary Cooper; the horror tale *Dr. Jekyll and Mr. Hyde* (1931) with Fredric March; the Lubitsch-inspired musical *Love Me Tonight* (1932), with Jeanette MacDonald; the historical drama *Queen Christina* (1933) with Greta Garbo; and the first Technicolor feature from Hollywood, the Thackeray adaptation *Becky Sharp* (1935). In the early '40s, Mamoulian's silent-film remakes, *The Mark Of Zorro* (1940) and *Blood and Sand* (1941), both starring Tyrone Power, were widely admired, but he went on to make only three more films: the comedy *Rings on Her Fingers* (1942) and the musicals *Summer Holiday* (1948), based on Eugene O'Neill's "Ah, Wilderness!," and *Silk Stockings* (1957), based on Lubitsch's film *Ninotchka.* Never one to compromise, Mamoulian started but was replaced on the films *Laura* (1944), *Porgy and Bess,* and *Cleopatra* (1963). He remained busy directing theater and opera, and staged the original productions of such celebrated works as *Porgy and Bess, Oklahoma!, Carousel,* and *Lost in the Stars.* **Selected Works:** *Dr. Jekyll & Mr. Hyde* (1931), *Gay Desperado* (1936)

# Henry Mancini 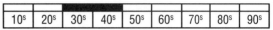 (Enrico Nicola Mancini)

**Born:** April 16, 1924; Cleveland, OH
**Died:** June 14, 1994; Beverly Hills, CA

**Years Active in the Industry:** by decade

| 10s | 20s | 30s | 40s | 50s | 60s | 70s | 80s | 90s |
|-----|-----|-----|-----|-----|-----|-----|-----|-----|
|     |     |     |     |     |     |     |     |     |

American composer Henry Mancini was introduced to music by his Italian immigrant father, who tutored young Henry on piano and flute. After World War II service, Mancini attended Carnegie Tech and Julliard, played piano with the Glenn Miller orchestra, and ultimately became a staff composer at Universal, writing snatches of music for everything from the studio's newsreels to the Abbott and Costello comedies. In 1954 he was given the opportunity to arrange the music for a film that might well have qualified as a labor of love: *The Glenn Miller Story.* The Academy Award nomination he received for this effort elevated Mancini's industry status, as did his long association with producer/director

Blake Edwards. When he wrote the jazzy theme music for Edwards' TV series *Peter Gunn* and *Mr. Lucky*, Mancini was so proud and protective of his work that he had a clause in his contract prohibiting the networks from running spoken "plugs" for upcoming programs over the closing-credit music. Mancini went on to win Oscars for his contributions to the Blake Edwards-directed films *Breakfast at Tiffany's* (1961), for which he wrote "Moon River;" *Days of Wine and Roses* (1962); and *Victor/Victoria* (1982). He also managed to put twenty Grammies on his shelf before his death in 1994. Though arguably the best-known film composer of his time, Henry Mancini was still modest enough in 1989 to title his autobiography *Did They Mention the Music?* **Selected Works:** *Charade* (1963), *Days of Wine & Roses* (1962), *Pink Panther* (1964), *Switch* (1991), *Hundred and One Nights* (1995)

## Babaloo Mandel (Marc Mandel)

**Born:** 1949; New York, NY

**Years Active in the Industry:** by decade

| 10s | 20s | 30s | 40s | 50s | 60s | 70s | 80s | 90s |
|-----|-----|-----|-----|-----|-----|-----|-----|-----|
|     |     |     |     |     |     |     | ■   |     |

Mark "Babaloo" Mandel and his partner Lowell Ganz are responsible for writing some of the most popular comedies in contemporary American cinema. They met in a Hollywood comedy club where Mandel worked as a gag writer. Ganz was also working as a writer on the TV comedy *The Odd Couple*. They found they had a lot in common: both were from New York, and both idolized Billy Wilder. It was Ganz who suggested they team up to write for popular television sitcoms such as *Laverne and Shirley*; it was Laverne, actress Penny Marshall, who later directed one of their most popular hits, *A League of Their Own* (1992). They made their feature film debut with the black comedy *Night Shift* (1982). The stories they tell, such as the Oscar-nominated *Splash* (1984), are easily recognizable for their strong narrative structure and full bodied characterizations. Mandel is also notable as being a master of hardhitting punchlines. **Selected Works:** *City Slickers* (1991), *Mr. Saturday Night* (1992), *Parenthood* (1989), *Who Framed Roger Rabbit?* (1988)

## Herman Mankiewicz

**Born:** November 7, 1897; New York, NY
**Died:** 1953

**Years Active in the Industry:** by decade

| 10s | 20s | 30s | 40s | 50s | 60s | 70s | 80s | 90s |
|-----|-----|-----|-----|-----|-----|-----|-----|-----|
|     | ■   |     | ■   |     |     |     |     |     |

American screenwriter Herman Mankiewicz is the older brother of Joseph L. Mankiewicz. Before joining the film industry, Mankiewicz was educated at Columbia and at the University of Berlin. While in Germany he began working as a Berlin correspondent for the *Chicago Tribune*. He later returned to the U.S. where he gained notoriety among New York's cultural elite as the drama editor of *The New York Times* and *The New Yorker*. In 1926 he moved to Hollywood where he wrote and co-wrote many screenplays and adaptations. His most famous work is the Oscar winning screenplay for *Citizen Kane* (1941); though technically he wrote it in collaboration with Orson Welles, most of the script was penned by Mankiewicz himself. Occasionally he worked as an executive producer on Marx Brothers' comedies such as *Horse Feathers* (1932) and *Duck Soup* (1933).

## Joseph L. Mankiewicz

**Born:** February 11, 1909; Wilkes-Barre, PA
**Died:** February 5, 1993; Bedford, NY

**Years Active in the Industry:** by decade

| 10s | 20s | 30s | 40s | 50s | 60s | 70s | 80s | 90s |
|-----|-----|-----|-----|-----|-----|-----|-----|-----|
|     |     | ■   |     |     |     |     |     |     |

Like his older brother Herman J. Mankiewicz, American producer/ director/ writer Joseph Mankiewicz displayed a streak of brilliance from an early age. Before he was 20, the younger Mankiewicz was the assistant Berlin correspondent for the *Chicago Tribune* and an English translator for the subtitles of German-made films. Brother Herman, ensconced in Hollywood as a high-priced screenwriter, invited Joseph to try his luck in Tinseltown in 1929. His first assignment at Paramount was composing subtitles for the silent versions of the studio's talking pictures. Mankiewicz also concocted special comedy material for the Jack Oakie vehicles, which led to several years' employment on such nonsensical film farces as W. C. Fields' *Million Dollar Legs* (1932) (Fields paid Joseph $50 for the lifetime rights to the phrase "My little chickadee"), and Wheeler and Woolsey's *Diplomaniacs* (1933). He moved to MGM in 1934, where he expressed a desire to direct; MGM head Louis Mayer told him "You have to learn to crawl before you can walk," and made Mankiewicz a producer instead. For the next six years, Mankiewicz produced such enduring MGM films as *Fury* (1936), *The Philadelphia Story* (1940), and *Woman of the Year* (1942). Realizing that Mayer would never give him a directing assignment, Mankiewicz switched to 20th Century-Fox in 1944, where he made his directorial debut with *Dragonwyck* (1944). Mankiewicz's scripts during his Fox period are distinguished by a high level of literacy and wit, most notably *A Letter to Three Wives* (1949) and *All About Eve* (1950), both of which won Mankiewicz Oscars for Best Writer and Best Director. While

Mankiewicz's cameramen have praised his visual sense, his directorial style tended to be flat and perfunctory, with dialogue given precedence over staging and characterization; still, it was superb dialogue, even when there was way too much of it (as in *People Will Talk* [1952]). In 1952, Mankiewicz left Fox to freelance. At MGM, he directed one of the best-ever Shakespeare films, *Julius Caesar,* its appeal heightened by the offbeat (and effective) casting of Marlon Brando as Antony and Edmond O'Brien as Casca. *Barefoot Contessa* (1954) contains all the virtues and vices of the Mankiewicz technique; on the plus side, a complex, involving story and memorably etched individual characters; on the minus side, an excessive running time, interminable dialogue sequences, and too many arbitrarily inserted "Author's Messages" (did we really need a three-minute diatribe about greedy oil companies in the middle of a romantic drama?) Curiously, when Mankiewicz had an opportunity to make a truly volatile political statement in *The Quiet American* (1958), he muffed it by totally altering the message and the denouement of Graham Greene's original novel. Willing to tackle any subject matter, Mankiewicz directed the film version of *Guys and Dolls* (1955) and tried valiantly to bring coherence to the troubled Elizabeth Taylor version of *Cleopatra* (1963). After the *Cleopatra* debacle, Mankiewicz's films became fewer and farther between, and extremely uneven in quality. He was back in the groove with his last film, *Sleuth* (1972), a marvelous cat-and-mouse affair starring Laurence Olivier and Michael Caine. The recipient of dozens of industry awards, Mankiewicz spent his last decade in semi-retirement, regaling TV talk show and college-lecture audiences with his erudite (and admittedly self-aggrandizing) anecdotes of the Hollywood of old. Mankiewicz was the father of screenwriter Tom Mankiewicz, and the uncle of two other writers of note, Don and Frank Mankiewicz. **Selected Works:** *Five Fingers* (1952), *The Ghost and Mrs. Muir* (1947), *Suddenly, Last Summer* (1959)

# Anthony Mann (Emil Anton Bundmann)

**Born:** June 30, 1906; San Diego, CA
**Died:** April 29, 1967; Berlin, Germany

**Years Active in the Industry:** by decade

| 10s | 20s | 30s | 40s | 50s | 60s | 70s | 80s | 90s |
|-----|-----|-----|-----|-----|-----|-----|-----|-----|
|     |     |     |     |     |     |     |     |     |

Born Emil Anton Bundmann, Anthony Mann was a stage actor and director before becoming a casting director for David O. Selznick in the late 1930s. By 1939 he was an assistant director at Paramount, where he worked on Preston Sturges' *Sullivan's Travels* (1941). Mann began directing B-films in the early '40s, most notably *The Great Flamarion* (1945) with Erich von Stroheim, and his crime films of the late '40s, *T-Men* (1947), *Border Incident* (1949), and *Side Street* (1950). In the 1950s Mann distinguished himself as a major director of westerns, starting with *The Devil's Doorway* (1950), which looked at the mistreatment of Native Americans, and the rousing, character-driven *The Furies* (1950), with Walter Huston

and Barbara Stanwyck. Mann is especially regarded for his series of handsomely shot, intelligent westerns starring James Stewart: *Winchester 73* (1950), *Bend of the River* (1952), *The Naked Spur* (1953), *The Far Country* (1955), and *The Man from Laramie* (1955). Mann's other notable '50s oaters are *The Tin Star* ((1957) with Henry Fonda, and *Man of the West* (1958) with Gary Cooper. In the '60s he helmed big-budget epics and actioners, most notably *El Cid* (1961). Mann died while making the espionage drama *A Dandy in Aspic* (1968); the film was completed by its star, Laurence Harvey.

# Michael Mann

**Born:** February 5, 1943; Chicago, IL

**Years Active in the Industry:** by decade

| 10s | 20s | 30s | 40s | 50s | 60s | 70s | 80s | 90s |
|-----|-----|-----|-----|-----|-----|-----|-----|-----|
|     |     |     |     |     |     |     |     |     |

American director Michael Mann studied at both the University of Wisconsin and the London Film School before commencing his career in 1965. At first working on TV commercials, Mann took his rapid-paced, flash-cut approach into documentary filmmaking, producing an award winning short on the 1968 French student riots, *Janpuri*. Mann's fragmented-image technique further manifested itself on such TV detective series of the 1970s as *Starsky and Hutch* and *Vegas,* both of which utilized Mann's scripts (though they were directed by others in the standard conventional style of the period). Mann turned out another prizewinning project, the 1979 TV movie *The Jericho Mile,* before making his big-screen directorial debut with *Thief* (1981). As executive producer of the popular TV cop series *Miami Vice* (1984-90), Mann brought what some considered the "MTV Look" to network television—a look which favored style over substance and technique over storytelling, in the "short attention span" manner of the MTV cable network. In fact, *Miami Vice* was merely a lavish extension of what Mann had been doing since the 1960s, but the MTV label stuck, attracting millions of viewers to Mann's series. When it was announced that Mann would produce and direct the 1992 filmization of *Last of the Mohicans,* purists despaired, complaining that the "youthful" director (age 49!) would unduly modernize, trivialize and homogenize the story. As it turned out, *Last of the Mohicans* (based more on the 1936 film version of the James Fennimore Cooper novel than the book itself) contained more pure storytelling and more raw evocative imagery than any previous Mann project, and remains the director's finest work to date.

# Jayne Mansfield (Vera Jayne Palmer)

**Born:** April 19, 1933; Bryn Mawr, PA
**Died:** 1967

**Years Active in the Industry:** by decade

| 10s | 20s | 30s | 40s | 50s | 60s | 70s | 80s | 90s |
|-----|-----|-----|-----|-----|-----|-----|-----|-----|
|     |     |     |     |     |     |     |     |     |

Born Vera Jane Palmer, Jayne Mansfield was the voluptuous sex symbol of Hollywood films of the '50s and '60s, rivaled only by Marilyn Monroe as a screen sexpot. At 16 she was married; she gave birth within a year. Mansfield attended drama classes at two colleges, and in the early '50s she won several beauty contests, landed several walk-on appearances on TV, and was active in a publicity drive for the Jane Russell film *Underwater* (1955). She debuted onscreen in 1955, but her big break came on Broadway later that year when she appeared in the comedy *Will Success Spoil Rock Hunter?*; cast as a dizzy, breathless blonde bombshell, she went on to play similar roles in most of her films, including the film version of that play (1957). However, by the mid-'60s Mansfield's career was in decline, and she appeared primarily in low-budget European productions (often opposite her second husband, muscleman Mickey Hargitay). She was killed in a car accident in 1967.

# Joe Mantegna

**Born:** November 13, 1947; Chicago, IL

**Years Active in the Industry:** by decade

| 10s | 20s | 30s | 40s | 50s | 60s | 70s | 80s | 90s |
|-----|-----|-----|-----|-----|-----|-----|-----|-----|
|     |     |     |     |     |     |     | ■ | ■ |

The quiet yet dynamic screen presence of actor Joe Mantegna has made him one of the most powerful supporting actors in Hollywood. Born in Chicago, Mantegna made his acting debut in

the 1969 production of *Hair*. He then joined Chicago's Organic Theatre Company. In 1978, he debuted on Broadway in *Working;* he also helped write *Bleacher Bums,* an award-winning play. Still, he did not become well-known until he played a recurring role on the TV show *Soap*. By 1983 he'd returned to Chicago, where he began working with playwright David Mamet. While playing the lead in Mamet's play *Glengarry Glen Ross* (1983), Mantegna won a Tony. When Mamet began making films, Mantegna became his actor of choice in works such as *House of Games* (1987) and *Homicide* (1991). Prior to that, the actor had played small roles in a number of other films. He also continues to play in a variety of movie genres, working with some of Hollywood's top directors. **Selected Works:** *Bugsy* (1991), *Comrades of Summer* (1992), *Water Engine* (1992), *Searching for Bobby Fischer* (1993)

# Jean Marais (Jean Villain-Marais)

**Born:** December 11, 1913; Cherbourg, France

**Years Active in the Industry:** by decade

| 10s | 20s | 30s | 40s | 50s | 60s | 70s | 80s | 90s |
|-----|-----|-----|-----|-----|-----|-----|-----|-----|
|     |     | ■ | ■ | ■ | ■ | ■ | ■ |     |

The extremely good-looking (some have called him beautiful) French actor Jean Marais was hardly a prize-winning performer in his formative years. Turned down by the Paris conservatory, Marais took odd jobs to sustain his nighttime efforts as a stage bit player (one of the productions in which he appeared, *Les Parents Terrible*, would be filmed years later with Marais in the lead). On the basis of his looks and wavy blonde hair, he was able to wangle a few minor film roles from 1933 onward, but the big breaks were not forthcoming until Marais met and befriended director Jean Cocteau. The latter's homosexuality has frequently cast aspersions concerning his real stake in Marais' well-being, but the fact remains that Marais truly blossomed as an actor with starring roles in such Cocteau films as *L'Eternal Retour* (1943), *Beauty and the Beast* (1946), and *Orpheus* (1949). Thanks to Cocteau, Marais became one of the most popular French film personalities of the postwar era, with the country's top directors clamoring for his services. In the early 1960s, the still strikingly handsome Jean Marais became something of a Gallic Roger Moore, appearing in such adventure-film series as *Fantomas* and *The Saint*. After a long retirement, Jean Marais returned to moviemaking in the mid-1980s with choice character roles in such films as *Parking* (1985). **Selected Works:** *The Testament of Orpheus* (1960), *The Donkey Skin* (1970), *White Knights* (1957)

# Fredric March (Ernest Frederick McIntyre Bickel)

**Born:** August 31, 1897; Racine, WI
**Died:** April 14, 1975

**Years Active in the Industry:** by decade

| 10s | 20s | 30s | 40s | 50s | 60s | 70s | 80s | 90s |
|-----|-----|-----|-----|-----|-----|-----|-----|-----|
|     | ■ | ■ | ■ | ■ | ■ | ■ |     |     |

An Academy Award-winning actor (for *Dr. Jekyll and Mr. Hyde* [1932] and *The Best Years of Our Lives* [1946]), Fredric March's movie career spanned more than 40 years, beginning in the late 1920s and ending with *The Iceman Cometh* in 1973. He first gained prominence with his wickedly accurate imitation of John Barrymore on Broadway in George S. Kaufman's hit play *The Royal Family*, a performance that is recorded on the screen in the 1930 film version and for which he was nominated for an Oscar. Among his best-remembered roles are the devil in *Death Takes a Holiday* (1934); Robert Browning in *The Barretts of Wimpole Street* (1934) opposite Norma Shearer; Garbo's Count Vronsky in *Anna Karenina* (1935); Norman Maine in the original *A Star Is Born* (1937) with Janet Gaynor; the reporter in *Nothing Sacred* (1937) with Carole Lombard; Willy Loman in *Death of a Salesman* (1952);

and William Jennings Bryant (renamed Matthew Harrison Brady) in *Inherit the Wind* (1960) opposite Spencer Tracy. March also made an occasional career playing swashbuckling and costume roles in the 30s, including *Les Miserables* (1935) and *Anthony Adverse* (1936). In 1927, March married his second wife, stage actress Florence Eldridge, with whom he occasionally performed, as in *Inherit the Wind.* He won Tony Awards for *Years Ago* (1947) and *Long Day's Journey Into Night* (1957). **Selected Works:** *Bridges at Toko-Ri* (1955), *Dr. Jekyll & Mr. Hyde* (1931), *Executive Suite* (1954), *I Married a Witch* (1942), *Royal Family of Broadway* (1930)

# Richard "Cheech" Marin

**Born:** July 13, 1946; Los Angeles, CA

**Years Active in the Industry:** by decade

| 10s | 20s | 30s | 40s | 50s | 60s | 70s | 80s | 90s |
|-----|-----|-----|-----|-----|-----|-----|-----|-----|

The son of a Los Angeles police officer, American actor/director Richard "Cheech" Marin earned his nickname through his fondness for the Chicano food specialty cheecharone. An excellent student (if something of a class cutup), Marin entered California State University, only to drop out and hightail it to Canada to avoid the draft. While working as an improvisational comedian with Vancouver's City Work troupe, Marin teamed with Tommy Chong; the Hispanic/Asiatic duo created the characters of Cheech and Chong, a pair of zoned-out dopers ever in search of the "perfect joint." On the strength of their bestselling record albums, Cheech and Chong were signed for the inexpensive comedy film *Up in Smoke* (1978), which wound up as one of Warner Bros.' highest-grossing films. As the drug culture lost its momentum, so did the film career of Cheech and Chong, with each of the team's subsequent films making less money than its predecessor. By the time C & C headlined the atrocious *The Corsican Brothers* (1984), the jig was up. Cheech and Chong split up in 1984 (though they remained friends) and went off to their own projects. While it was Chong who directed many of the team's features, Marin sat in the director's chair for the best of his post-team projects, the 1987 film *Born in East L.A.,* inspired by Cheech's own parody music video. Marin's latest starring film is *Shrimp on the Barbie* (1990) which contained no drug jokes and fewer laughs (an indication of its quality is the fact that the director had his name removed from the credits in favor of the pseudonymous "Alan Smithee"). Lately regarded as an elder statesman of the counterculture, Marin has kept busy with cameo roles, cartoon voice-overs (*Oliver and Company, Ferngully, The Lion King*), and a brief stint as a costar of the 1992 TV sitcom "Golden Palace."

# Garry Marshall (Garry Marsciarelli)

**Born:** November 13, 1934; New York, NY

**Years Active in the Industry:** by decade

| 10s | 20s | 30s | 40s | 50s | 60s | 70s | 80s | 90s |
|-----|-----|-----|-----|-----|-----|-----|-----|-----|

Influential screen and TV presence Garry Marshall was born in Brooklyn. His father was an industrial filmmaker; his mother was a dance teacher. He studied journalism, and for a time was a reporter for the *New York Daily News;* he also had a stint in the army and played drums in a jazz band. He later wrote scripts for TV shows, such as *The Joey Bishop Show.* He teamed up with writer Jerry Belson, and the two of them created numerous TV sitcoms, such as *The Lunch Show* and *The Odd Couple;* they also wrote the screenplays to the movies *How Sweet It Is* (1968) and *The Grasshopper* (1970), both of which featured Marshall in small roles. The team split up in the '70s, and Marshall went on to create several enormously successful shows, including *Happy Days, Mork and Mindy,* and *Laverne and Shirley,* which co-starred his sister, Penny Marshall. His big-screen directorial debut was the soap opera spoof *Young Doctors in Love* (1982); he went on to direct and/or write a number of other films, most notably the smash hit *Pretty Woman* (1990). Throughout his career he has also acted, usually in small roles. **Selected Works:** *Frankie and Johnny* (1991), *A League of Their Own* (1992), *Soapdish* (1991)

# George Marshall

**Born:** December 29, 1891; Chicago, IL
**Died:** February 17, 1975; Los Angeles, CA

**Years Active in the Industry:** by decade

| 10s | 20s | 30s | 40s | 50s | 60s | 70s | 80s | 90s |
|-----|-----|-----|-----|-----|-----|-----|-----|-----|

An extra in films of the early teens, George Marshall began writing comedy shorts and by 1916 was directing westerns. He went on to helm serials and short comedies and actioners in the silent era, as well as features. A natural director of comedy, Marshall guided several beloved comedians in the sound era: Laurel and Hardy in their classic shorts *Their First Mistake* and *Towed In A Hole,* and their feature *Pack Up Your Troubles* (1932), which Marshall acted in and co-directed with Raymond McCarey; W. C. Fields in *You Can't Cheat an Honest Man* (1939); Bob Hope in *The Ghost Breakers* (1940), *Monsieur Beaucaire* (1946), *Fancy Pants* (1950), *Boy' Did I Get A Wrong Number* (1966) and *Eight on the Lam* (1967); Martin and Lewis in *My Friend Irma* (1949), *Scared Stiff* (1953) and *Money from Home* (1953); and Jerry Lewis in *The Sad Sack* (1957) and *Hook, Line and Sinker* (1969). Other notable films by this prolific and reliable craftsman include the western spoof *Destry Rides Again* (1939) ,with James Stewart and Marlene Dietrich; the slapstick mystery *Murder, He Says* (1945); the serious mystery *The Blue Dahlia* (1946); and the quirky Glenn Ford comedies *The Sheepman* (1958) and *The Gazebo* (1959).

# Herbert Marshall

**Born:** May 23, 1890; London, England
**Died:** January 22, 1966; Beverly Hills, CA

**Years Active in the Industry:** by decade

| 10s | 20s | 30s | 40s | 50s | 60s | 70s | 80s | 90s |
|-----|-----|-----|-----|-----|-----|-----|-----|-----|

British actor Herbert Marshall was born to a theatrical family, but initially had no intentions of a stage career himself. After graduating from St. Mary's College in Harrow, Marshall became an accounting clerk, turning to acting only when his job failed to interest him. With an equal lack of enthusiasm, Marshall joined a stock company in Brighton, making his stage debut in 1911; he ascended to stardom two years later in the evergreen stage farce, *Brewster's Millions*. Enlisting in the British Expeditionary Forces during World War I, Marshall was severely wounded and his leg was amputated. While this might normally have signalled the end of a theatrical career, Marshall was outfitted with a prosthesis and determined to make something of himself as an actor; he played a vast array of roles, his physical handicap slowing him down not one iota. In tandem with his first wife, actress Edna Best, Marshall worked on stage in a series of domestic comedies and dramas, then entered motion pictures with *Mumsie* (1927). His first talking film was the 1929 version of Somerset Maugham's *The Letter*, which he would eventually film twice, the first time in the role of the heroine's illicit lover, the second time (in 1940) as the cuckolded husband. With Ernst Lubitsch's frothy film *Trouble in Paradise* (1932), Marshall became a popular romantic lead. Easing gracefully into character parts, the actor continued working into the 1960s; he is probably best remembered for his portrayal of author Somerset Maugham in two separate films based on Maugham's works, *The Moon and Sixpence* (1942) and *The Razor's Edge* (1946). Alfred Hitchcock, who'd directed Marshall twice in films, showed the actor to good advantage on the Hitchcock TV series of the 1950s, casting Marshall in one episode as a washed-up matinee idol who wins a stage role on the basis of a totally fabricated life story. Marshall hardly needed to embroider on his real story of his life: he was married five times, and despite his gentlemanly demeanor managed to make occasional headlines thanks to his rambuctious social activities. **Selected Works:** *Duel in the Sun* (1946), *Enchanted Cottage* (1945), *Foreign Correspondent* (1940), *Little Foxes* (1941)

# Penny Marshall

**Born:** October 15, 1943; Bronx, NY

**Years Active in the Industry:** by decade

| 10s | 20s | 30s | 40s | 50s | 60s | 70s | 80s | 90s |
|-----|-----|-----|-----|-----|-----|-----|-----|-----|

Born Carole Penny Marsciarelli in Brooklyn, Penny Marshall's her father was an industrial filmmaker; her mother was a dance coach. At age three she began tapdancing; in her teens she was on TV with a dance troupe composed of her friends, competing on *The Ted Mack Amateur Hour* and appearing on *The Jackie Gleason Show*. After college she moved to Hollywood, where her brother Garry Marshall was already a successful TV writer and sitcom creator. She got a role in the film *How Sweet It Is* (1968), co-written by her brother, and a few other films; she also had guest roles on episodes of numerous TV series, including her brother's creations *The Odd Couple* and *Happy Days*. This led to the costarring role in the sitcom *Laverne and Shirley* (created by her brother), which became a number one hit. Her screen career as an actress never developed, so she took up directing; she did some TV work, then made her big-screen directorial debut with *Jumpin' Jack Flash* (1986). Her second film as a director, *Big* (1988), was an enormous hit, after which she was much in demand behind the camera in Hollywood, scoring other successes with *Awakenings* (1990) and *A League of Their Own* (1992). She married and divorced actor/director Rob Reiner.

# Dean Martin (Dino Paul Crocetti)

**Born:** June 17, 1917; Steubenville, OH

**Years Active in the Industry:** by decade

| 10s | 20s | 30s | 40s | 50s | 60s | 70s | 80s | 90s |
|-----|-----|-----|-----|-----|-----|-----|-----|-----|

The son of a Steubenville, Ohio barber, American singer/actor Dean Martin led a rough-and-tumble childhood; he dropped out of school in the tenth grade and took a string of odd jobs (at one point he was a boxer) before settling into the illicit world of gambling. So good was he at the chips-and-dice table that he could afford to turn down an offer to sing for a local band. Eventually, show business appeared a safer life's venture than gambling, so Martin went to work for the Ernie McKay Orchestra. With wife and children in tow, Martin worked for several bands throughout the early 1940s, scoring more on looks and personality than talent until he developed his own smooth singing style. Failing to achieve a screen test at MGM, Martin seemed destined for the nightclub trail permanently until he met fledgling comic Jerry Lewis at the Glass Hat Club in New York, where both men were performing. Martin and Lewis formed a fast friendship which led to their participating in each other's club acts, and ultimately into forming a music-and-comedy team. Martin and Lewis' official debut occured at Atlantic City's Club 500 on July 25, 1946, and before long club patrons throughout the East Coast were convulsed by the act, which consisted primarily of Lewis interrupting and heckling Martin while the he was trying to sing, then the two of them chasing each other around the stage and having as much fun as possible. A radio series commenced in 1949, the same year that Martin and Lewis were signed by Paramount producer Hal Wallis as comedy relief for the film *My Friend Irma*. Martin and Lewis were the hottest act in nightclubs, films, and TV during the early 1950s, but the pace and the pressure took its toll on the the team.

Fueled by jealousy, hostility, sycophantic hangers-on and strong desires to fly solo, Martin and Lewis broke up in 1956, ten years to the day after their first official teaming. Lewis had no trouble maintaining his film popularity as a single, but Martin, unfairly regarded by much of the public and the motion picture industry as something of a spare tire to Lewis, found the going rough. Martin's first solo starring film, *Ten Thousand Bedrooms* (1957) was a disaster, and when an impoverished Martin was offered a fraction of his former salary to costar in the war drama *The Young Lions* (1957), he was in no position to refuse. *The Young Lions* turned out to be the cornerstone of Martin's spectacular comeback; by the mid-1960s, he was a top movie, recording, and nightclub attraction, even as Lewis' star began to eclipse. In 1965, Martin launched the weekly NBC comedy-variety series *The Dean Martin Show,* which exploited his public image as a lazy, carefree boozer, even though few entertainers worked as hard Martin to make what they were doing look easy. *The Dean Martin Show* behind him in the late 1970s, Martin concentrated on club dates, recordings, and the occasional film, even making an appearance on the Jerry Lewis MDA telethon in 1978 (talk of a complete reconciliation and possible reteaming, however, was dissipated when it was clear that, to paraphrase Jerry, the men may have loved each other but didn't like each other). Martin's even-keel world began to crumble in 1987, when his son Dean Paul was killed in a plane crash. A much-touted tour with old pals Sammy Davis Jr. and Frank Sinatra in 1989 was abruptly cancelled, and the public was led to believe it was due to a falling out between Martin and Sinatra; only intimates knew that Martin was a very sick man, who'd never completely recovered from the loss of his son and who was suffering from an undisclosed illness. Amidst tabloid-press reports that he was at death's door, Martin courageously kept his private life private, emerging briefly and rather jauntily for a public celebration of his 77th birthday with friends, family, and a sympathetic *TV Guide* reporter in tow. Whatever his true state of health, Martin proved in this rare public appearance that he was still the inveterate showman; and perhaps it's worth noting that among the many well-wishers who've communicated with Martin in recent years, few have expressed as much concern as Jerry Lewis. **Selected Works:** *Airport* (1970), *Some Came Running* (1958), *Oceans 11* (1960), *Scared Stiff* (1953), *Bells are Ringing* (1960)

# Steve Martin

**Born:** August 1945; Waco, TX

**Years Active in the Industry:** by decade

| 10s | 20s | 30s | 40s | 50s | 60s | 70s | 80s | 90s |
|-----|-----|-----|-----|-----|-----|-----|-----|-----|
|     |     |     |     |     |     |     |     |     |

Working as a Disneyland concessionaire in his teens, American comedian Steve Martin picked up skills in "a little of this, a little of that:" juggling, tapdancing, sleight of hand, balloon sculpting. Martin then attended UCLA, where he majored in philosophy and theatre, moving on to staff-writer stints for such TV performers as Glen Campbell, The Smothers Brothers, Dick Van Dyke, John Denver, and Sonny and Cher. Occasionally allowed to perform as well as write, Martin didn't go into standup comedy full time until the late 1960s, at which time he moved to Canada, where he appeared as semi-regular on the syndicated TV variety series *Half the George Kirby Comedy Hour.* As the opening act for rock stars in the early 1970s, Martin emulated the fashion of the era with a full beard, shaggy hair, colorful costumes and drug jokes. Comedians of this ilk were common in this market, however, so Martin carefully developed a brand-new persona: the well groomed, immaculately dressed young man who goes against his appearance by behaving like a lunatic. By 1975, Martin was the Comic of the Hour, convulsing audiences with his feigned enthusiasm over the weakest of jokes and the most obvious of comedy props (rabbit ears, head arrows). His entire act a devastating parody of second-rate comedians who rely on preconditioning to get laughs, Martin became internationally famous for such catchphrases as "Excu-u-use me!," "Happy feet!," and "I am...one wild and crazy guy!" It was fun for a while to hear audiences shout out those catchphrases before he'd uttered them, but before long Martin was tired of live standup and anxious to get into films. Ignoring the execrable *Sgt. Pepper's Lonely Hearts Club Band* (1977), Martin's true screen bow was *The Jerk* (1978), in which with the seriousness of Olivier he portrayed a man without a single clue in his brain, a white man who was a self-described "poor black child," an accidental millionaire who truly believed that his status rested upon his ability to order mixed drinks with little umbrellas in the glass. Had he been a lesser performer, Martin could have played variations on *The Jerk* for the remainder of his life, but his was a restless muse ever seeking out new challenges. It took nerve to go against the sensibilities of his fans with an on-edge portrayal of a habitual loser in *Pennies from Heaven* (1981), but Martin was successful, even if the film wasn't. And few other actors could convincingly pull off a project like *Dead Men Don't Wear Plaid* (1983), wherein with utter conviction he acted opposite film clips of dead movie stars. After a first-rate turn in *All of Me* (1984), in which he played a man whose body is inhabited by the soul of a woman (Lily Tomlin), Martin's film work began to fluctuate in quality, only to emerge on top again with *Roxanne* (1987), a potentially silly but ultimately compelling update of *Cyrano de Bergerac.* With as many hits and misses in the late 1980s-early 1990s, Steve Martin was still full of surprises, as witnessed in his unsympathetic portrayal in *Planes, Trains & Automobiles* (1989), his angst-ridden father in *Parenthood* (1989), and his self-justifying porno filmaker in *Grand Canyon* (1991)—though the public still seems to prefer his standard comic performances in *Father of the Bride* (1991) and *L.A. Story* (1991). In real life hardly wild or crazy but a man of tasteful intellectual pursuits (including an extensive art collection), Martin briefly altered his most-eligible-bachelor status with a marriage to his *L.A. Story* costar Victoria Tennant after a long romance with actress Bernadette Peters. More recently, Martin went out on yet another artistic limb with *A Simple Twist of Fate* (1994)—a film updating of that high-school English class perennial *Silas Marner.* **Selected Works:** *Housesitter* (1992), *Leap of Faith* (1992), *Mixed Nuts* (1994), *Father of the Bride II* (1995)

# Lee Marvin

**Born:** February 19, 1924; New York, NY
**Died:** August 29, 1987; Tucson, AZ

**Years Active in the Industry:** by decade

| 10ˢ | 20ˢ | 30ˢ | 40ˢ | 50ˢ | 60ˢ | 70ˢ | 80ˢ | 90ˢ |
|-----|-----|-----|-----|-----|-----|-----|-----|-----|

Lee Marvin had no intention of becoming an actor before, by chance, he was asked to replace an ailing actor in a bit role in summer stock. Afterwards he apprenticed at the American Theater Wing in New York, then appeared in a number of off-Broadway productions. In 1951 he debuted on Broadway in *Billy Budd* and also appeared in his first film, *You're in the Navy Now*. Tall and rugged, his craggy face and throaty voice caused him to be typecast as a brutal villain, primarily in westerns and crime melodramas; some critics considered him the "baddest bad guy" or the screen's "number one sadist." He went on to star in the TV series *M Squad*, and had a couple of more friendly parts in John Wayne movies, and in the '60s he began landing heroic roles. For his work in *Cat Ballou* (1963) he won the Best Actor Oscar, establishing him as a star. He sustained a very busy screen career through the mid '70s, after which he appeared less frequently. He was the subject of a landmark "palimony" case in 1979, when his girlfriend of six years sued him for compensation after their break-up. **Selected Works:** *Big Heat* (1953), *Big Red One* (1980), *Dirty Dozen* (1967), *Man Who Shot Liberty Valance* (1962), *Ship of Fools* (1965)

# Marx Brothers

**Born:** New York, NY

**Years Active in the Industry:** by decade

| 10ˢ | 20ˢ | 30ˢ | 40ˢ | 50ˢ | 60ˢ | 70ˢ | 80ˢ | 90ˢ |
|-----|-----|-----|-----|-----|-----|-----|-----|-----|

When the four Marx Brothers became an overnight sensation on Broadway in *I'll Say She Is* in 1924, they had already spent 20 years in show business. Their uncle, character actor Al Shean (of Gallagher and Shean), helped them get started in the business, spurred on by their mother Minnie. The boys toured the vaudeville circuits, first as singers and eventually as comedians, until they slowly improved enough to make it to Broadway. Ultimately, the Marx Brothers revolutionized American comedy with their anarchistic, faster-than-lightning, anything-goes approach. By the time of their first film, *The Coconuts,* in 1929, which was a filmed version of their second Broadway hit, brother Gummo ( Milton Marx, 1897-1977) had retired from the act and been replaced by the baby, Zeppo (Herbert Marx, 1901-1979). Ultimately, Zeppo retired from performing as well, leaving the three Marxes best known today: Chico (Leonard Marx, 1886-1961), Harpo (Adolph Arthur Marx, 1888-1964), and the one, the only Groucho (Julius Henry Marx, 1890-1977). Each of these three had his own strong screen persona: Chico was the Italian who mangled the English language and played the piano; Harpo never spoke, chased blondes, created general mayhem and played the harp; Groucho, with his greasepaint mustache and tilted walk, was a fast-talker who cracked wise and was often on the dubious side of the law or morality. Off-screen the brothers could be just as wild as they were on-screen, and tended to create chaos wherever they went. Their first five films, all for Paramount, were particularly anti-social and anti-establishment, which made them well suited to the mood of the country in the early years of the Depression. These films, after *The Coconuts,* were *Animal Crackers* (1930), based on their third Broadway hit; *Monkey Business* (1931); *Horse Feathers* (1932); and *Duck Soup* (1933). By 1935, they were working for Irving Thalberg at MGM (thanks to Chico, who played bridge with Thalberg and had worked out the deal). Thalberg insisted on better plot structure and romantic subplots, which made the brothers more popular in their day but in retrospect detract from the inspired anarchy of their earlier comedies. After the first two MGM films, *A Night at the Opera* (1935) and *A Day at the Races* (1937), Thalberg died and the quality of their films began a descent from which they never recovered, culminating in the mostly pathetic *Love Happy* (1950). The Marxes themselves flourished, however. Even Gummo and Zeppo, who had quit performing years earlier, developed financially successful, albeit tangential, careers in show business. Chico formed his own band in 1942, which included a very young Mel Torme. Harpo made numerous comedy/concert tours, including an early trip to Russia. Numerous books have been written about the Marxes' often turbulent personal lives and their zany comedies. Their influence has been widespread, so that many Marx Brothers routines, particularly Groucho's, have slipped into the American vernacular ("I shot an elephant in my pajamas. How he got into my pajamas, I'll never know"). The character of Hawkeye Pierce on *M*A*S*H* was strongly influenced by Groucho's screen persona, and the role of Banjo in George S. Kaufman's *The Man Who Came to Dinner* (1951) was based on Harpo.

# Giulietta Masina (Giulia Anna Masina)

**Born:** February 22, 1921; Giorgio di Piano, Italy
**Died:** March 23, 1994; Rome, Italy

**Years Active in the Industry:** by decade

| 10ˢ | 20ˢ | 30ˢ | 40ˢ | 50ˢ | 60ˢ | 70ˢ | 80ˢ | 90ˢ |
|-----|-----|-----|-----|-----|-----|-----|-----|-----|

Giulietta Masina began acting as a student with a group of university players in Rome. She performed in a radio play written by Frederico Fellini, a fellow student, in 1942; the two were married the following year. She debuted onscreen in a bit role in Rossellini's *Paisa* (1946). For her work in Lattuada's *Without Pity* (1948), her second film, she won the Italian Critics Award for Best Supporting Actress. After returning briefly to the stage, she appeared in Fellini's debut directorial effort, *Variety Lights* (1951), after which she gave up theater permanently and stuck to making films. She went on to appear in two more of Fellini's movies of that decade, the first of which was *La Strada* (1954), which established her as a star; for her portrayal of a prostitute in his *The Nights of Cabria* (1956), she won the Cannes Film Festival Best Actress award. Fellini has said that she was his muse and that many of his films were inspired by her. Her career, however, was hampered after the late '50s by her nearly-exclusive association with Fellini, who went on to include her in *Juliet of the Spirits* (1965) among others. **Selected Works:** *Nights of Cabiria* (1957), *White Sheik* (1952)

# James Mason (James Neville Mason)

**Born:** May 15, 1909; Huddersfield, Yorkshire, England
**Died:** July 27, 1984; Lausanne, Switzerland

**Years Active in the Industry:** by decade

| 10s | 20s | 30s | 40s | 50s | 60s | 70s | 80s | 90s |
|-----|-----|-----|-----|-----|-----|-----|-----|-----|

Darkly handsome, brooding, and cerebral, Mason was an introspective British leading man and character actor. After graduating college he began appearing on stage (among others, he worked with the Old Vic and with Dublin's Gate Company Theater), then debuted onscreen in 1935; for some time he starred in low-budget "quota quickies," British films made to balance out the proportion of Hollywood imports. By the mid-'40s he was England's leading star and box office draw; his breakthrough role was as a romantic villain in *The Man in Grey* (1943), which set his basic screen persona for the next several years: a nasty, evil type who brutalizes sensitive women yet remains attractive to them. In 1948 he moved to Hollywood and began appearing in American films, no longer playing cads so often. A journeyman actor, he sustained a very busy screen career by appearing in productions of wildly variable quality. He married and divorced actress Pamela

(Ostrer) Kellino, with whom he co-starred in *I Met a Murderer* (1939). **Selected Works:** *Georgy Girl* (1966), *Julius Caesar* (1953), *Verdict* (1982), *Star Is Born* (1954), *Child's Play* (1972)

# Marsha Mason

**Born:** April 3, 1942; St. Louis, MO

**Years Active in the Industry:** by decade

| 10s | 20s | 30s | 40s | 50s | 60s | 70s | 80s | 90s |
|-----|-----|-----|-----|-----|-----|-----|-----|-----|

Marsha Mason began her career in New York theater, and also got bit parts in films and TV shows. Later she moved to San Francisco, appearing in a revival of Noel Coward's *Private Lives* directed by Francis Ford Coppola for the American Conservatory Theater. While in California she got her first substantial screen role, a supporting part in *Blume In Love* (1973). Meanwhile, her work in repertory caught the attention of director Mark Rydell, who cast her in the lead of his film *Cinderella Liberty* (1973); she earned an Oscar nomination for her portrayal of a prostitute with a black son. Nevertheless, it was three years berfore her next screen appearance. Mason was again Oscar-nominated for her costarring role in *The Goodbye Girl* (1977), which increased the regularity of her film work for the next five years but still failed to establish her as a star; moreover, she was twice more nominated for Oscars, bringing her total to four nominations with no victories. Her screen appearances since 1983 have been infrequent, though she continued acting on stage and TV. She married and divorced playwright Neil Simon, who wrote several of the films she appeared in; some critics have suggested that her career suffered because she was overly identified with Simon's work.

# Raymond Massey (Raymond Hart Massey)

**Born:** August 30, 1896; Toronto, Ontario, Canada
**Died:** July 29, 1983; Los Angeles, CA

**Years Active in the Industry:** by decade

| 10s | 20s | 30s | 40s | 50s | 60s | 70s | 80s | 90s |
|-----|-----|-----|-----|-----|-----|-----|-----|-----|

Canadian-born Raymond Massey was educated at Oxford and began his London stage career in 1922. He debuted onscreen playing Sherlock Holmes in *The Speckled Band* (1931). Massey became a widely-respected, top-notch character actor; later, he was closely identified with the role of Abraham Lincoln, whom he played in both the theatrical and film versions of *Abe Lincoln in Illinois* (1940), as well as in a small part in *How the West Was Won* (1962). He also tended to play moralists, malicious types, and fanatics. Massey became a U.S. citizen in 1944. Serving with the Canadian army, he was wounded in both World Wars; he became well-known to a new generation of viewers through his portrayal of

Dr. Gillespie in the long-running TV series *Dr. Kildare*. He was married to actress Adrianne Allen, and was the father of actor Daniel Massey and actress Anna Massey. **Selected Works:** *East of Eden* (1954), *Possessed* (1947), *Mourning Becomes Electra* (1947), *Stairway to Heaven* (1946), *Woman in the Window* (1945)

# Mary Stuart Masterson

**Born:** 1966; New York, NY

**Years Active in the Industry:** by decade

| 10ˢ | 20ˢ | 30ˢ | 40ˢ | 50ˢ | 60ˢ | 70ˢ | 80ˢ | 90ˢ |
|-----|-----|-----|-----|-----|-----|-----|-----|-----|
|     |     |     |     |     |     |     |     |     |

In the "People to Watch" section of the 1986 *Motion Picture Guide* annual, Mary Stuart Masterson's performance as Andrew McCarthy's teenaged girl friend in *Heaven Help Us* was praised for its naturalness and maturity. Masterson is the daughter of actress Carlyn Glynn and actor/director Peter Masterson, both of whom have often had the "natural" and "mature" tags affixed to their own work. Masterson made her film debut literally at her father's knee, appearing as Peter Masterson's 7-year-old daughter in *The Step-ford Wives* (1975). She went on to attend NYU and study acting with Estelle Parsons, then did theatrical work until her adult film bow in the aforementioned *Heaven Help Us*. Masterson has since distinguished herself in such film roles as the indomitable restau-ranteur Idgie Threadgood in *Fried Green Tomatoes* (1991) and the mentally challenged girlfriend of Buster Keaton-worshipping Johnny Depp in *Benny & Joon* (1993). **Selected Works:** *Benny and Joon* (1993), *Mad at the Moon* (1992)

# Mary Elizabeth Mastrantonio

**Born:** November 17, 1958; Oak Park, IL

**Years Active in the Industry:** by decade

| 10ˢ | 20ˢ | 30ˢ | 40ˢ | 50ˢ | 60ˢ | 70ˢ | 80ˢ | 90ˢ |
|-----|-----|-----|-----|-----|-----|-----|-----|-----|
|     |     |     |     |     |     |     |     |     |

Dark-haired, dark-eyed, and unconventionally beautiful, this lead and supporting actress trained as an opera singer, then spent a summer singing and dancing at the Opryland Theme Park in Nashville. She was the understudy and vacation replacement for Maria in a revival of *West Side Story*; this role took her to New York, where she soon landed work in a number of Broadway plays including *Amadeus* and *Sunday in the Park with George*. Mastran-tonio's screen debut came in the role of the young sister of mobster Al Capone (played by Al Pacino) in Brian De Palma's *Scarface* (1983). From there she went on to have a steady career in films, re-ceiving an Oscar nomination for her work in Martin Scorsese's *The Color of Money* (1986). **Selected Works:** *Class Action* (1991), *Consenting Adults* (1992), *Robin Hood: Prince of Thieves* (1991), *White Sands* (1992), *Two Bits* (1994)

# Marcello Mastroianni (Marcello Mastrojanni)

**Born:** September 28, 1923; Fontana Liri, Italy

**Years Active in the Industry:** by decade

| 10ˢ | 20ˢ | 30ˢ | 40ˢ | 50ˢ | 60ˢ | 70ˢ | 80ˢ | 90ˢ |
|-----|-----|-----|-----|-----|-----|-----|-----|-----|
|     |     |     |     |     |     |     |     |     |

Italy's most respected and sought-after leading man, Mar-cello Mastroianni projects a darkly handsome, sometimes cynical world-weariness with an air of dignity. During World War II, he was  sent by the Germans to a labor camp; he es-caped and spent the rest of the war hiding in an attic in Venice. He moved to Rome after the war; while working there as a clerk he be-gan acting in the evenings with a group of university players. He debuted onscreen in an Italian version of *Les Miserables* (1947). In 1948, Mastroianni joined Luchino Vis-conti's stage stock company. Over the ensuing years he made a reputation for himself as a talented and good-looking leading man of the Italian stage and screen; this reputation was international by the mid-'50s. After appearing in major films by such filmmakers as Visconti, Fellini, Antonioni, and Germi, he achieved the status of one of the world's leading screen personalities; he came to person-ify the modern-day urban European male. He won British Film Academy Awards for his work in both *Divorce Italian Style* (1962) and *Yesterday, Today, and Tomorrow* (1963). Mastroianni contin-ues to earn film roles in both Italy and the U.S. **Selected Works:** *Everybody's Fine* (1990), *Special Day* (1977), *Used People* (1992), *Pizza Triangle* (1970)

# Richard Masur

**Born:** November 20, 1948; New York, NY

**Years Active in the Industry:** by decade

| 10ˢ | 20ˢ | 30ˢ | 40ˢ | 50ˢ | 60ˢ | 70ˢ | 80ˢ | 90ˢ |
|-----|-----|-----|-----|-----|-----|-----|-----|-----|
|     |     |     |     |     |     |     |     |     |

A graduate of NYU, American actor Richard Masur has been seen in supporting TV and movie roles since the early 1970s. His pliable facial features, boyish demeanor and indeter-minate age have enabled Masur to play a rich variety of roles: a mentally retarded stockboy on *All in the Family*, a hotshot pro-gram manager on *The Mary Tyler Moore Show,* and even a "friendly stranger" child molester in the 1981 TV movie *Fallen Angel*. Masur's film credits include *Semi-Tough* (1977); *Who'll Stop the Rain* (1978); *My Girl* (1991), as Jamie Lee Curtis' prickly ex-husband; and the deservedly maligned *Heaven's Gate* (1980). Masur has also been a regular on several TV series: From 1975 through 1976, for example, he was divorcee Bonnie Franklin's much-younger boyfriend (and almost her second husband) on *One Day at a Time*. In 1987, Masur made his film directorial bow with the Oscar-nominated short subject *Love Struck,* but he continues to work primarily as an actor in both TV and film. **Selected Works:** *Encino Man* (1992), *Man without a Face* (1993), *Six Degrees of Separation* (1993), *Big One: The Great Los Angeles Earthquake, Part 1* (1990), *Story Lady* (1991)

## Tim Matheson

**Born:** December 31, 1947; Burbank, CA

**Years Active in the Industry:** by decade

| 10s | 20s | 30s | 40s | 50s | 60s | 70s | 80s | 90s |
|-----|-----|-----|-----|-----|-----|-----|-----|-----|
|     |     |     |     |     | ■ | ■ | ■ | ■ |

As a child actor, Tim Matheson was billed under his fuller family name of Matthieson. His first weekly TV co-starring assignment was opposite Robert Young in the 1961 "dramedy" *Window on Main Street*. The young actor's voice became familiar to a generation of cartoon fans via his "role" as the title character in Hanna-Barbera's *Jonny Quest*. The handsome Matheson appeared on-screen during his maturation years on such western series as *The Virginian, Bonanza,* and *The Quest*. He remained busy in films during this period, scoring his biggest 1970s success as party animal Otter in *National Lampoon's Animal House* (1978). Matheson also kept his hand in the voiceover business, providing the truculent mutterings of "Blood" the dog in Harlan Ellison's *A Boy and His Dog* (1975) and recording the narration for the 1985 revival of Disney's *Fantasia*. His adult TV appearances have included weekly stints on the TV series *Tucker's Witch* (1982), *Just in Time,* (1988) and *Charlie Hoover* (1991). Turning to directing in 1985, Matheson has been active in episodic television, music videos and direct-to-cassette movies. In 1989, he became CEO of the National Lampoon Company, though he still manages to find time for the occasional acting assignment, appearing in everything from the theatrical feature *Drop Dead Fred* to the live-action prologue for one of the "thrill rides" at Disneyworld. **Selected Works:** *Buried Alive* (1990), *Quicksand: No Escape* (1991), *Solar Crisis* (1992), *Sometimes They Come Back* (1991), *Trial and Error* (1992)

## Samantha Mathis

**Born:** 1970; Los Angeles, CA

**Years Active in the Industry:** by decade

| 10s | 20s | 30s | 40s | 50s | 60s | 70s | 80s | 90s |
|-----|-----|-----|-----|-----|-----|-----|-----|-----|
|     |     |     |     |     |     |     |     | ■ |

Samantha Mathis is the daughter of actress Bibi Besch. Mathis's TV-series bow occured in 1988, when she won the role of Merlin Olson's daughter in the two-month wonder *Aaron's Way*. She could later be found among the supporting cast of another dramatic series, *Knightwatch*, which survived for *three* months. In films since 1990, Mathis made an excellent early impression as the misfit girlfriend of maverick teenage ham-radio operator Christian Slater in *Pump Up the Volume*. Less aesthetically pleasing (but undoubtedly higher salaried) was Mathis' turn as the eminently kidnappable Princess Daisy in *Super Mario Bros*. (1993). **Selected Works:** *Thing Called Love* (1993), *This Is My Life* (1992), *Little Women* (1994)

## Marlee Matlin

**Born:** August 24, 1965; Morton Grove, IL

**Years Active in the Industry:** by decade

| 10s | 20s | 30s | 40s | 50s | 60s | 70s | 80s | 90s |
|-----|-----|-----|-----|-----|-----|-----|-----|-----|
|     |     |     |     |     |     |     | ■ | ■ |

Born deaf, Marlee Matlin attended a high school which had a special education program for deaf students. From the age of eight, she acted as a hobby with the Children's Theater of the Deaf in Des Plaines. While majoring in criminal justice at college, she landed a supporting role in the Chicago stage production of *Children of a Lesser God;* her performance gained the attention of director Randa Haines, who cast her in the lead role in the play's screen version (1986). For this performance, Matlin won the Best Actress Oscar. She has gone on to appear in several other films and in guest spots on TV shows.

## Walter Matthau (Walter Matuschanskayasky)

**Born:** October 1, 1920; New York, NY

**Years Active in the Industry:** by decade

| 10s | 20s | 30s | 40s | 50s | 60s | 70s | 80s | 90s |
|-----|-----|-----|-----|-----|-----|-----|-----|-----|
|     |     |     |     | ■ | ■ | ■ | ■ | ■ |

This dog-faced, jowly, rumpled, tired-looking lead and supporting actor is often cast in grouchy comedic roles. He grew up in poverty as the son of Jewish-Russian immigrants on New York's Lower East Side. As an 11-year-old he began working in a Second Avenue Yiddish theater; soon he got bit roles onstage in the plays there. After high school, where he excelled in theater, he worked a number of odd jobs, then enlisted in the Air Force during World War II. Following the war he took acting classes at the New School's Dramatic Workshop and started acting in summer stock. Soon he was working on Broadway, rising from bit parts to key supporting roles in which he became recognized as a singularly talented and versatile actor. By the mid-'50s he was also working as a character actor in Hollywood films, often playing villains or sleazy types. In 1960 he directed the film *The Gangster*. Also, he

appeared frequently in TV plays and films, eventually starring in the series *Tallahassee 7000*. He seemed to be stuck permanently as a character actor until Neil Simon wrote a part especially for him in the comedy *The Odd Couple;* he appeared in the play on Broadway in 1965 (opposite Jack Lemmon) and rose to sudden stardom. This led to starring roles in a string of film comedies that established him as a Hollywood box-office winner; he got percentages of the profits of several hit films, greatly increasing his wealth. For his work in *The Fortune Cookie* (1966), Matthau won the Best Supporting Actor Oscar; he received Best Actor nominations for both *Kotch* (1971) and *The Sunshine Boys* (1975). He continues to work in both TV and film, and teamed with old pal Jack Lemmon in 1993's *Grumpy Old Men*. **Selected Works:** *California Suite* (1978), *JFK* (1991), *Plaza Suite* (1971), *Against Her Will: An Incident in Baltimore* (1992)

# Victor Mature (Victor John Mature)

**Born:** January 29, 1915; Louisville, KY

**Years Active in the Industry:** by decade

| 10s | 20s | 30s | 40s | 50s | 60s | 70s | 80s | 90s |
|-----|-----|-----|-----|-----|-----|-----|-----|-----|
|     |     |     |     |     |     |     |     |     |

The first male film star to be officially labelled a "hunk,"Victor Mature was the son of Swiss immigrants. When he arrived in California to study acting at the Pasadena Playhouse, Mature was

so broke that he lived in a pup tent in a vacant lot and subsisted on canned sardines and chocolate bars. There was speculation amongst his fellow students that Mature's spartan lifestyle was deliberately engineered to draw publicity to himself; if so, the ploy worked, and by 1938 he'd been signed to a contract by producer Hal Roach. Mature's first starring film role was as Tumack the caveman in Roach's *One Million BC* (1940), which enabled the fledgling actor to display his

physique without being unduly encumbered by dialogue. While still under contract to Roach, Mature made his Broadway debut in the Moss Hart/Kurt Weill musical *Lady in the Dark,* playing a musclebound male model. In 1941, Mature was signed by 20th Century-Fox as the "beefcake" counterpart to the studio's "cheesecake" star Betty Grable; the two attractive stars were frequently cast together in Fox musicals, where a lack of clothes was *de rigeur*. Apparently because of his too-handsome features, the press and fan magazines went out of their way to make Mature look ridiculous and untalented. In truth, he had more *good* film performances to his credit than one might think: he was excellent as the tubercular Doc Holliday in John Ford's *My Darling Clementine* (1948), and also registered well in *Kiss of Death* (1947), *Cry of the City* (1948), *The Egyptian* (1954), *Betrayed* (1954), and *Chief Crazy Horse* (1955). As the slave Demetrius in *The Robe* (1953), Mature is more understated and credible than the film's "distinguished" but hopelessly hammy star Richard Burton. Nonetheless, and thanks to such cinematic folderol as *Samson and Delilah* (1949), Mature was still widely regarded as a lousy actor who survived on the basis of his looks. Rather than fight this ongoing perception, Mature tended to denigrate his own histrionic ability in interviews; later in his career, he hilariously parodied his screen image in such films as *After the Fox* (1966) and *Won Ton Ton, the Dog Who Saved Hollywood* (1976). Semi-retired from acting in the late 1970s, Victor Mature ran a successful television retail shop in Hollywood, although in 1984 he did appear in a TV remake of *Samson and Delilah,* effectively portraying Samson's father.

# Elaine May (Elaine Berlin)

**Born:** April 21, 1932; Philadelphia, PA

**Years Active in the Industry:** by decade

| 10s | 20s | 30s | 40s | 50s | 60s | 70s | 80s | 90s |
|-----|-----|-----|-----|-----|-----|-----|-----|-----|
|     |     |     |     |     |     |     |     |     |

Elaine May is the daughter of Yiddish stage actor Jack Berlin; as a child May toured in several plays with him. She was married and divorced in her teens, and she gave birth to a daughter. She went on to study method acting with veteran actress Maria Ouspenskaya; she also performed with the celebrated improvisational comedy troupe Second City. While a student at the University of Chicago, May met Mike Nichols; the two then teamed up as a satirical comedy duo, eventually becoming very successful and appearing on Broadway in the hit revue *An Evening with Mike Nichols and Elaine May* (1961); they split in 1961. She went on to write and direct for the stage, and in 1967 she appeared in the films *Enter Laughing* and *Luv*. Beginning in the early '70s she wrote and/or directed a number of films, one of which—*The Heartbreak Kid* (1972), which she directed—featured her daughter, Jeannie Berlin; Berlin received a Best Supporting Actress Oscar nomination for her work. May was nominated for a Best Screenplay Oscar for *Heaven Can Wait* (1978), written in collaboration with Warren Beatty. Her career as a director was seriously damaged by her film

*Ishtar* (1987), which was an expensive failure. **Selected Works:** *California Suite* (1978), *Tootsie* (1982), *Wolf* (1994)

# Louis B. Mayer (Eliezer Mayer)

**Born:** July 4, 1885; Minsk, Russia
**Died:** 1957

**Years Active in the Industry:** by decade

| 10s | 20s | 30s | 40s | 50s | 60s | 70s | 80s | 90s |
|-----|-----|-----|-----|-----|-----|-----|-----|-----|
|     |     |     |     |     |     |     |     |     |

Former junkman Louis B. Mayer rose to become one of the most influential and powerful men in Hollywood during the '30s and '40s, when he was the head of Metro-Goldwyn-Mayer, once considered the grandest of Hollywood studios that claimed to have "more stars than there are in the heavens." He was born Eliezer Mayer in Minsk, Russia. The son of a laborer, he emigrated with his family to New York during his childhood. They then moved to St. John, New Brunswick, Canada where young Mayer helped out in his father's successful junk and scrap metal operation. As a young man, Mayer went to Boston and set up his own junk business. He too was successful, and after marrying a kosher butcher's daughter in 1904, he bought a ramshackle motion picture theater in Haverhill, Massachusetts for a song. After renovating it, he vowed only to show the best films. The gambit was successful and he continued buying theaters until he owned New England's largest theater chain. He then began working in film distribution during 1914, and when *The Birth of a Nation* came out, he made a fortune. In 1917, after founding a production company—first called Alco, and then Metro—Mayer moved to L.A. with star Anita Stewart. Metro was purchased by studio helmer Marcus Loew in 1924. Loew also bought up controlling interests in the Goldwyn company and in Louis B. Mayer Pictures; the result was MGM, and Mayer was appointed vice-president. He remained there until he was forcibly ousted in 1951. It was Mayer who set the tone of the studio and he quickly became a grandfather figure to all. He was hot-tempered, perfectionistic and ruthless, and treated his employees as his children. Though not universally beloved, Mayer was respected for his talent for understanding the public's wants. He was adept at picking personnel and stars; very conservative, he sought to impose his high moral standards upon the films MGM produced, thus many of the films were family oriented. To create his high-quality films, he hired only the best. His first production chief was the brilliant Irving Thalberg. At his apex, Mayer was the highest paid person in the United States, making well over a million dollars a year. The conservative Mayer was also politically active and served as the California state chairman of the Republican party for many years. It was Mayer who formed the Academy of Motion Picture Arts and Sciences (the source of the Oscars) in 1927. In 1951, his production chief since 1941, Dore Schary, successfully dethroned King Louis. Mayer then became acting advisor to the Cinerama corporation. The rest of his life was spent unsuccessfully trying to regain some kind of financial control over MGM.

# Ken Maynard

**Born:** July 21, 1895; Vevay, IN
**Died:** 1973

**Years Active in the Industry:** by decade

| 10s | 20s | 30s | 40s | 50s | 60s | 70s | 80s | 90s |
|-----|-----|-----|-----|-----|-----|-----|-----|-----|
|     |     |     |     |     |     |     |     |     |

Ken Maynard performed as a trick rider with the Buffalo Bill and the Ringling Brothers Wild West shows and was once a rodeo champion. In 1923 he entered films, soon becoming a major cowboy star; he was especially popular among children for his riding stunts on his horse Tarzan. Maynard made the transition to sound, and in fact introduced singing to westerns several years before Gene Autry's debut. In the late '20s and early '30s he served as executive producer on a number of his own films. He taught the young John Wayne how to do stunts. In 1936 and 1937, the first two years of the poll, he was one of the top ten western moneymakers at the box office. His popularity decreased in the late '30s, and by 1939 he was off screen and back on the rodeo circuit. From 1943-45 he made some low-budget westerns, then retired from performing altogether; in later years, however, he still occasionally appeared in rodeos, state fairs, and films. Partly due to his alcoholism, Maynard died a poor and forgotten man; after his wife's death, he lived alone in a trailer and suffered from malnutrition. He was the brother of cowboy star Kermit Maynard.

# Melanie Mayron

**Born:** October 20, 1952; Philadelphia, PA

**Years Active in the Industry:** by decade

| 10s | 20s | 30s | 40s | 50s | 60s | 70s | 80s | 90s |
|-----|-----|-----|-----|-----|-----|-----|-----|-----|
|     |     |     |     |     |     |     |     |     |

Melanie Mayron trained at the American Academy of Dramatic Arts, then studied with Sandra Seacat and Lohn Lehne. She debuted in a touring production of *Godspell* which ran for three years, and gained a small supporting role in Paul Mazursky's *Harry and Tonto* (1974). Since then she has divided her time between stage, screen, and TV work. For her performance in *Girlfriends* (1978), she won the Best Actress Award at the 1979 Locarno Film Festival; also in 1979, she made her New York stage debut, in *The Goodbye People*. In the late '80s she teamed up with Catlin Adams to write and produce films; their work has included the film *Sticky Fingers* (1988) and the TV movies *Tunes for a Small Harmonica* and *The Pretend Game*. She is best-known as a co-star of the TV series *thirtysomething,* for which she won an Emmy in 1989. **Selected Works:** *Missing* (1982), *My Blue Heaven* (1990), *Playing for Time* (1980), *The Babysitter's Club* (1995)

# Paul Mazursky (Irwin Mazursky)

**Born:** April 25, 1930; Brooklyn, NY

**Years Active in the Industry:** by decade

| 10ˢ | 20ˢ | 30ˢ | 40ˢ | 50ˢ | 60ˢ | 70ˢ | 80ˢ | 90ˢ |
|---|---|---|---|---|---|---|---|---|

Paul Mazursky began acting professionally while still in college. He later studied method acting with Lee Strasberg, going on to appear on stage and in TV plays. In the late '50s he had some success as a stand-up comedian, teaming up with Herb Hartig in the act "Igor and H." He moved to Los Angeles in 1959, taking film courses and performing. In 1963 he began writing regularly for TV sitcoms such as *The Danny Thomas Show*. Mazursky broke into films as the screenwriter of *I Love You, Alice B. Toklas* (1968); so upset with the way his script was handled, he set out to make his own films. His first effort was the hit *Bob & Carol & Ted & Alice* (1969), about two couples who attempt to swap partners; the film was successful enough to pave the way to a career as a filmmaker. He has also made some film appearances as an actor, including *Punchline* (1988), *Love Affair* (1994), and *Miami Rhapsody* (1995). His most successful film has been *An Unmarried Woman* (1978), with Jill Clayburgh, which he directed, produced, and wrote. **Selected Works:** *Blackboard Jungle* (1955), *Enemies, a Love Story* (1989), *Harry and Tonto* (1974)

# Jim McBride

**Born:** September 16, 1941; New York, NY

**Years Active in the Industry:** by decade

| 10ˢ | 20ˢ | 30ˢ | 40ˢ | 50ˢ | 60ˢ | 70ˢ | 80ˢ | 90ˢ |
|---|---|---|---|---|---|---|---|---|

One of the most active and least heralded of the Manhattan-based experimental filmmakers of the 1960s, director/writer Jim McBride won several awards for his first feature, *David Holzman's Diary* (1967). He didn't have to dig around much for story material: the film was all about an independent moviemaker's day-to-day existence. In most of his subsequent films, McBride acted as well as directed—but neither outlet for his talents brought much food on the table. Compelled to teach school and drive cabs to survive for several years, McBride made a comeback as an actor in the 1979 *Last Embrace*, directed by another experimental filmmaker who graduated to the mainstream, Jonathan Demme. Back on his feet again, Jim McBride wielded the megaphone for such lucrative big-budget

features as *The Big Easy* (1987) and *Great Balls of Fire* (1987)—but not before one last stab at cinema verite with his 1983 remake of Jean-Luc Goddard's *Breathless*. **Selected Works:** *Wrong Man* (1993), *Blood Ties* (1993)

# Mercedes McCambridge (Carlotta Mercedes Agnes McCambridge)

**Born:** March 17, 1918; Joliet, IL

**Years Active in the Industry:** by decade

| 10ˢ | 20ˢ | 30ˢ | 40ˢ | 50ˢ | 60ˢ | 70ˢ | 80ˢ | 90ˢ |
|---|---|---|---|---|---|---|---|---|

While still a college student, Mercedes McCambridge began performing on radio, and soon became one of the busiest and most respected radio actresses of her time. In the late '40s she appeared successfully in several Broadway productions, leading to an invitation from Hollywood. For her screen debut in *All the King's Men* (1949), she won a Best Supporting Actress Oscar. Despite her early success, she went on to appear in films only intermittently, usually in intense, volatile roles. For her work in *Giant* (1956), she received a second Oscar nomination. A long bout with alcoholism forced her to put her career on hold for several years in the '60s; she eventually triumphed over her problem. McCambridge was never seen onscreen in what was perhaps her best-known performance: that of the demon's voice in the huge hit *The Exorcist* (1975). From 1950-62 she was married to writer-director Fletcher Markle. In 1987, her son shot his wife and daughters and then killed himself. McCambridge authored two autobiographies, *The Two of Us* (1960) and *A Quality of Mercy* (1981). **Selected Works:** *Farewell to Arms* (1957)

# Leo McCarey

**Born:** October 3, 1898; Los Angeles, CA
**Died:** 1969

**Years Active in the Industry:** by decade

| 10ˢ | 20ˢ | 30ˢ | 40ˢ | 50ˢ | 60ˢ | 70ˢ | 80ˢ | 90ˢ |
|---|---|---|---|---|---|---|---|---|

Los Angeles-born Leo McCarey was, along with Frank Capra, one of the most popular and successful comedy directors of the pre-World War II era. Unlike Capra, however, McCarey's success endured well after World War II, and like Capra, his work is still influencing filmmakers in the 1990s. Originally an attorney, McCarey entered films by a circuitous route shortly after starting his own practice, beginning as an assistant to Todd Browning. During the 1920's, he went to work for Hal Roach Studios as a gag writer and director and, within two years, was a vice president. It was while at Roach that McCarey teamed Stan Laurel and Oliver Hardy together for the first time, thus creating one of the most enduring comedy teams of all time. As a director, he imposed a frantically-paced, breakneck speed to comedy which quickly became his trademark in the 1930s. A triple-threat as writer and producer as well as director, McCarey made some of the most inspired comedies of the decade, including *The Milky Way, Ruggles of Red Gap,* and *The Awful Truth,* collecting an armload of Academy Awards as a director, writer, and producer in the process. His work also had a serious side—McCarey was a devout Catholic and deeply concerned with social issues— which came out in films such as *Make Way for Tomorrow* (1937), a groundbreaking film about the displaced elderly. During the 1940s, his work became more serious—McCarey was concerned with the battles that had yet to be fought for human dignity, after World War II was won—but this only seemed to make his work more popular. His share in the profits of *Going My Way* (1944), starring Bing Crosby and Barry Fitzgerald, gave McCarey the highest reported income in the U.S. for the year 1944, and its follow-up, *The Bells of St. Mary's,* which was made by McCarey's own production company, was equally successful. After the war, McCarey's vision darkened, and the public reacted negatively. *My Son John,* an overblown anti-Communist diatribe, failed at the box office, but five years later he was back on track, as co-author, producer, and director of *An Affair to Remember,* a romantic comedy that became the basis for the 1993 hit *Sleepless In Seattle* and, thru the latter's success, found a whole new audience 36 years after it was made. McCarey was unable to put his newfound success, after nearly a decade of inactivity, to good use— like Frank Capra, with whom he was frequently compared, McCarey's most serious movies found relatively little reward at the box office, but he kept trying, and his last movie, *Satan Never Sleeps,* returned to anti-communism as a theme and failed. **Selected Works:** *Love Affair* (1939)

# Andrew McCarthy

**Born:** November 29, 1962; Westfield, NJ

**Years Active in the Industry:** by decade

| 10ˢ | 20ˢ | 30ˢ | 40ˢ | 50ˢ | 60ˢ | 70ˢ | 80ˢ | 90ˢ |
|-----|-----|-----|-----|-----|-----|-----|-----|-----|

Andrew McCarthy was still not yet twenty when he began appearing in productions at New York's Circle-in-the-Square theatre. He enjoyed what many consider one of the most enviable screen debuts of any 21-year-old actor in film history: as the bedmate of Jacqueline Bisset in 1983's *Class.* Because of his age and choice of roles, McCarthy was regarded as a member of the Hollywood "Brat Pack;" accordingly, his busiest movie year was 1985 (*Heaven Help Us, St. Elmo's Fire* and *Less Than Zero*). Taking a break from his romantic-lead responsibilities, Andrew McCarthy exhibited an unexpected flair for low comedy when he was teamed with nerdish Jonathan Silverman in the dumb-and-dumber *Weekend at Bernies'* films of the early 1990s. **Selected Works:** *Year of the Gun* (1991)

# Tim McCoy (Timothy John Fitzgerald McCoy)

**Born:** April 10, 1891; Saginaw, MI
**Died:** 1978

**Years Active in the Industry:** by decade

| 10ˢ | 20ˢ | 30ˢ | 40ˢ | 50ˢ | 60ˢ | 70ˢ | 80ˢ | 90ˢ |
|-----|-----|-----|-----|-----|-----|-----|-----|-----|

An authentic cowboy from the age of 15, Timothy McCoy moved to a large Wyoming ranch next to a Sioux Indian reservation after some college studies; he became an authority on Indian languages, customs, and folk history, and mastered Indian sign language. He served in World War I, and was then appointed Indian Agent for his territory. In 1922, he was employed as a technical advisor and co-ordinator of Indian extras for the film *The Covered Wagon* (1923); McCoy may also have done some trick riding for the film. He later he resigned his government post, having been offered a key supporting role in the western *The Thundering Herd* (1925). MGM signed him to a film contract in 1925; he was to star in westerns and action movies based on historical anecdotes of the American frontier. By the early '30s he was among the most popular western stars; he always appeared dresed in black, with an oversized white Stetson hat and a pearl-handled gun. McCoy interrupted his screen career in 1935 to travel with the Ringling Brothers circus. In 1938 he started his own Wild West show, but it was unsuccessful. He returned to the screen in 1940, and for two years he co-starred in the low-budget *Rough Rider* western series; the series ended when Buck Jones, another of its stars, died in a fire. He served in World War II (in which he was awarded the Bronze Star), then retired to his ranch; from 1949, however, he worked on TV and in occasional film cameo roles. He won an Emmy for his TV program *The Tim McCoy Show.* Until 1976 McCoy continued working 300 days a year as the headliner of Tommy Scott's Country Music Circus. In 1974 he was inducted into the Cowboy Hall of Fame. He authored an autobiography (assisted by his son Ronald), *Tim McCoy Remembers the West* (1977).

# Joel McCrea (Joel Albert McCrea)

**Born:** November 5, 1905; South Pasadena, CA
**Died:** October 20, 1990; Woodland Hills, CA

**Years Active in the Industry:** by decade

| 10ˢ | 20ˢ | 30ˢ | 40ˢ | 50ˢ | 60ˢ | 70ˢ | 80ˢ | 90ˢ |
|-----|-----|-----|-----|-----|-----|-----|-----|-----|

American actor Joel McCrea came from a California family with roots reaching back to the pioneer days. As a youth, McCrea satiated his fascination with movies by appearing as an extra in a serial starring Ruth Roland. By 1920, high schooler McCrea was a movie stunt double, and by the time he attended USC, he was regularly appearing at the Pasadena Playhouse. McCrea's big Hollywood break came with a part in the 1929 talkie *Jazz Age;* he matriculated into one of the most popular action stars of the 1930s, making lasting friendships with such luminaries as director Cecil B. DeMille and comedian Will Rogers. It was Rogers who instilled in McCrea a strong business sense, as well as a love of ranching; before the 1940s had ended, McCrea was a multi-millionaire, as much from his land holdings and ranching activities as from his film work. Concentrating almost exclusively on westerns after appearing in *The Virginian* (1946), McCrea became one of that genre's biggest box-office attractions. He extended his western fame to an early-1950s radio series, *Tales of the Texas Rangers,* and a weekly 1959 TV oater, *Wichita Town,* in which McCrea costarred with his son Jody. In the late 1960s, McCrea increased his wealth by selling 1200 acres of his Moorpark (California) ranch to an oil company, on the proviso that no drilling would take place within sight of the actor's home. By the time he retired in the early 1970s, McCrea could take pride in having earned an enduring reputation not only as one of Hollywood's shrewdest businessmen, but as one of the few honest-to-goodness gentlemen in the motion picture industry. **Selected Works:** *Dead End* (1937), *Foreign Correspondent* (1940), *More the Merrier* (1943), *Sullivan's Travels* (1941), *These Three* (1936)

# Hattie McDaniel

**Born:** June 10, 1895; Wichita, KS
**Died:** 1952

**Years Active in the Industry:** by decade

| 10ˢ | 20ˢ | 30ˢ | 40ˢ | 50ˢ | 60ˢ | 70ˢ | 80ˢ | 90ˢ |
|-----|-----|-----|-----|-----|-----|-----|-----|-----|
|     |     |     |     |     |     |     |     |     |

Although her movie career consisted almost entirely of playing stereotypic maids and other servants, Hattie McDaniel was in fact the first black woman to sing on the radio and the first black performer to win an Academy Award, for her portrayal of Mammy

in *Gone with the Wind* (1939). Before coming to Hollywood, she had been a blues singer and had toured as Queenie in *Show Boat,* later playing the same role in the 1936 Irene Dunne version of the film. Her considerable film credits include *Blonde Venus* (1932) with Marlene Dietrich, *I'm No Angel* (1933) with Mae West, *Nothing Sacred* (1937) with Carole Lombard and Fredric March, *The Shopworn Angel* (1938) with Margaret Sullavan, *They Died with Their Boots On* (1941), James Thurber's story *The Male Animal* (1942), *Thank Your Lucky Stars* (1943), *Since You Went Away* (1944), and *Mr. Blandings Builds*

*His Dream House* (1948). She starred in the *Beulah* series on radio and was scheduled to take over the role from Ethel Waters for the television series, which would have reunited her with *GWTW* costar Butterfly McQueen, when she became ill and was replaced by Louise Beavers. **Selected Works:** *Alice Adams* (1935), *Great Lie* (1941), *Song of the South* (1946)

# Dylan McDermott

**Born:** October 26, 1962; Waterbury, CT

**Years Active in the Industry:** by decade

| 10ˢ | 20ˢ | 30ˢ | 40ˢ | 50ˢ | 60ˢ | 70ˢ | 80ˢ | 90ˢ |
|-----|-----|-----|-----|-----|-----|-----|-----|-----|
|     |     |     |     |     |     |     |     |     |

The son of playwright Eve Ensler, Dylan McDermott prepared for an acting career by attending New York's Neighborhood Playhouse. He acted on stage (notably Neil Simon's *Biloxi Blues*) before appearing as platoon leader Sgt. Franz in his first film, 1987's *Hamburger Hill.* McDermott later appeared as Julia Roberts' husband in the 1989 film version of Richard Harling's *Steel Magnolias.* One of McDermott's showiest roles was as the doomed-from-the-start partner of CIA agent Clint Eastwood in *In the Line of Fire* (1993). **Selected Works:** *Fear Inside* (1992), *Into the Badlands* (1992), *Miracle on 34th Street* (1994)

# Mary McDonnell

**Born:** 1953; Wilkes Barre, PA

**Years Active in the Industry:** by decade

| 10ˢ | 20ˢ | 30ˢ | 40ˢ | 50ˢ | 60ˢ | 70ˢ | 80ˢ | 90ˢ |
|-----|-----|-----|-----|-----|-----|-----|-----|-----|
|     |     |     |     |     |     |     |     |     |

Actress Mary McDonnell was born in Wilkes-Barre, Pennsylvania, raised in Ithaca, New York; she graduated from the State University of New York at Fredonia. After a few seasons in regional repertory, McDonnell established herself on Broadway with such

successful 1980s plays as *The Heidi Chronicles.* Her debut film was 1984's *Garbo Talks;* three years later, she was showered with critical adulation for her portrayal of Elma Radnor in director John Sayles' *Matewan.* McDonnell won a Best Supporting Actress Oscar nomination for her 1990 performance as Stands with a Fist, a white woman raised by the Lakota Sioux, in Kevin Costner's *Dances with Wolves.* One year later, she starred in the PBS "American Playhouse" dramatization of Willa Cather's *O Pioneers!,* and her film career has continued with roles in *Passion Fish* (1992) and *Blue Chips* (1994). McDonnell also appeared on the Elliot Gould TV sitcom *E/R* (not to be confused with the NBC drama of the same name). **Selected Works:** *Grand Canyon* (1991), *Sneakers* (1992)

# Frances McDormand

**Born:** 1958; IL

**Years Active in the Industry:** by decade

| 10s | 20s | 30s | 40s | 50s | 60s | 70s | 80s | 90s |
|-----|-----|-----|-----|-----|-----|-----|-----|-----|

Frances McDormand studied at Yale Drama School, then appeared in a number of serious, literary plays around the country. She debuted onscreen in the Coen brothers' first film, *Blood Simple* (1984), playing a dimwitted adulteress; the film gained much attention, but its cast was largely forgotten. She became intimate with filmmaker Joel Coen, and went on to share an apartment with him. She got little film work over the next four years, meanwhile earning a Tony nomination for her portrayal of Stella in a New York stage revival of Tennessee Williams's *A Streetcar Named Desire;* she also had a recurring role in the TV series *Hill Street Blues,* and starred in the short-lived series *Leg Work.* She got a big break when she landed a costarring role as a redneck sheriff's abused wife in *Mississippi Burning* (1988), for which she received a Best Supporting Actress Oscar nomination. She has gone on to average one film a year, displaying great versatility; however, she still has low name-recognition with the public. **Selected Works:** *Crazy in Love* (1992), *Darkman* (1990), *Hidden Agenda* (1990)

# Roddy McDowall (Roderick Andrew Anthony Jude McDowall)

**Born:** September 17, 1928; London, England

**Years Active in the Industry:** by decade

| 10s | 20s | 30s | 40s | 50s | 60s | 70s | 80s | 90s |
|-----|-----|-----|-----|-----|-----|-----|-----|-----|

British actor Roddy McDowall's father was an officer in the English merchant marine, and his mother was a would-be actress. When it came time to choose a life's calling, McDowall bowed to his mother's influence. After winning an acting prize in a school play, he was able to secure film work in Britain, beginning at age ten with 1938's *Scruffy.* He appeared in 16 roles of varying sizes and importance before he and his family were evacuated to the U.S. during the 1940 Battle of Britain. McDowall arrival in Hollywood coincided with the wishes of 20th Century-Fox executive Darryl F. Zanuck to create a "new Freddie Bartholomew." He tested for the

juvenile lead in Fox's *How Green Was My Valley* (1941), winning both the role and a long contract. McDowall's first adult acting assignment was as Malcolm in Orson Welles' 1948 film version of *MacBeth;* shortly afterward, he formed a production company with *MacBeth* co-star Dan O'Herlihy. McDowall left films for the most part in the 1950s, preferring TV and stage work; among his Broadway credits were *No Time for Sergeants, Compulsion,* (in which he co-starred with fellow former child star Dean Stockwell) and Lerner and Loewe's *Camelot* (as Mordred). McDowall won a 1960 Tony Award for his appearance in the short-lived production *The Fighting Cock.* The actor spent the better part of the early 1960s playing Ptolemy in the mammoth production *Cleopatra,* co-starring with longtime friend Elizabeth Taylor. An accomplished photographer, McDowall was honored by having his photos of Taylor and other celebrities frequently published in the leading magazines of the era. He was briefly an advising photographic editor of *Harper's Bazaar,* and in 1966 published the first of several collections of his camerawork, *Double Exposure.* McDowall's most frequent assignments between 1968 and 1975 found him in elaborate simian makeup as Cornelius in the *Planet of the Apes* theatrical films and TV series. Still accepting the occasional guest-star film role and theatrical assignment into the 1990s, McDowall has been most active in the administrative end of show business, serving on the executive boards of the Screen Actors Guild and the Academy of Motion Picture Arts and Sciences. A lifelong movie collector (a hobby which once nearly got him arrested by the FBI!), McDowall has also worked diligently with the National Film Preservation Board. **Selected Works:** *Deadly Game* (1991), *Inconvenient Woman* (1991), *Sands of Time, Part 1* (1992), *Mirror, Mirror 2: Raven Dance* (1994)

# Malcolm McDowell

**Born:** June 15, 1943; Leeds, England

**Years Active in the Industry:** by decade

| 10s | 20s | 30s | 40s | 50s | 60s | 70s | 80s | 90s |
|-----|-----|-----|-----|-----|-----|-----|-----|-----|

When British actor Malcolm McDowell starred as a regional coffee salesman in director Lindsay Anderson's *O Lucky Man,* the role required very little research on the actor's part. McDowell had in fact been a coffee salesman in Yorkshire (his experiences were woven into Anderson's script) before wearying of the job and turning to acting. After training with a rep company in the Isle of Wight, McDowell spent nearly two years in bits and extra roles with the Royal Shakespearean Company; this led to TV work and his first film, 1967's *Poor Cow.* Before McDowell's scene was cut from that film, it had attracted the attention of director Lindsay Anderson, who cast the 25 year old actor as a prep-school rebel in *If...* (1968). Director Stanley Kubrick was likewise impressed by McDowell's ability to project working-class insolence; Kubrick starred the actor as futuristic street gang leader Alex in the controversial *A Clock-*

work Orange (1971). While Alex dished out plenty of violence and brutality, he got back as good as he gave in the scenes wherein he was "cured" of his aggressiveness; at one point, poor McDowell spent several shooting days bound in a straitjacket, his eyes pried open by surgical clamps. McDowell has been able to shed his earlier punkish image in favor of sensitive, introspective roles, such as that of H. G. Wells in *Time After Time* (1979) and Maxfield Perkins in *Cross Creek* (1983); he costarred in both of these films with Mary Steenburgen, who was his wife from 1980 to 1990. **Selected Works:** *Happily Ever After* (1991), *Jezebel's Kiss* (1990), *Player* (1992), *Bopha* (1993), *Star Trek Generations* (1994)

# Darren McGavin

**Born:** May 7, 1922; Galt, CA

**Years Active in the Industry:** by decade

| 10s | 20s | 30s | 40s | 50s | 60s | 70s | 80s | 90s |
|-----|-----|-----|-----|-----|-----|-----|-----|-----|

Darren McGavin dropped out of college after one year and moved to New York, where he trained for the stage at the Neighborhood Playhouse and the Actors Studio. In the mid '40s he began landing small roles in occasional films, but worked primarily onstage. He first made an impression onscreen as a painter in David Lean's *Summertime* and a drug pusher in Otto Preminger's *The Man with the Golden Arm* (both 1955); nevertheless, his subsequent film work tended to occur in intermittent spurts, with long periods off-screen between roles. He is best known as a TV actor; he starred in the TV series *Crime Photographer*, *Mike Hammer*, *Riverboat*, *The Outsider*, and *Kolchak: The Night Stalker*, and also appeared in a number of TV movies. He occasionally directed episodes of his TV shows, and directed and produced the film *Happy Mother's Day, Love George* (1973), whose title was later changed to *Run, Stranger, Run*. **Selected Works:** *Blood & Concrete: A Love Story* (1990), *Child in the Night* (1990), *Christmas Story* (1983), *Diamond Trap* (1991), *Blood and Concrete* (1991)

# Kelly McGillis

**Born:** July 9, 1957; Newport Beach, CA

**Years Active in the Industry:** by decade

| 10s | 20s | 30s | 40s | 50s | 60s | 70s | 80s | 90s |
|-----|-----|-----|-----|-----|-----|-----|-----|-----|

Actress Kelly McGillis claims to have been a lonely, overweight adolescent who found an escape from her misery through acting. She studied at Pacific Conservatory of Performing Arts and Julliard, making an impressive film debut as the erstwhile lady friend/"savior" of drunken poet Tom Conti in 1983's *Reuben, Reuben*. McGillis spent considerable time with an Amish family to prepare for her next important film role as a young Amish widow in 1985's *Witness*; the family wasn't happy in retrospect, claiming that Kelly misrepresented her interest in their lifestyle. The actress's best role since *Witness* has been as the attorney defending rape victim Jodie Foster in *The Accused* (1988); during production, McGillis made public the story of her *own* earlier rape, and became a militant advocate for assault victim's rights. In 1992, McGillis was second-billed in *The Babe* (1992) as Claire Hodgson, the no-nonsense second wife of baseball great Babe Ruth (John Goodman). **Selected Works:** *Grand Isle* (1992)

# Elizabeth McGovern

**Born:** July 18, 1961; Evanston, IL

**Years Active in the Industry:** by decade

| 10s | 20s | 30s | 40s | 50s | 60s | 70s | 80s | 90s |
|-----|-----|-----|-----|-----|-----|-----|-----|-----|

Blue-eyed and moon-faced, Elizabeth McGovern is a radiant lead actress with "girl next door" looks. As a teenager she trained for the stage at San Francisco's American Conservatory Theater and New York's Juilliard School of Dramatic Art. While still a high school student she appeared in a production of Thornton Wilder's *The Skin of Our Teeth;* spotted by agent Joan Scott, she went on to land the role of Timothy Hutton's girlfriend in *Ordinary People* (1980), her screen debut. For her portrayal of millionaire's wife Evelyn Nesbit in Milos Forman's *Ragtime* (1981), her second film, she received a Best Supporting Actress Oscar nomination. However, her subsequent roles failed to sustain her early career momentum, and—although her film work has been steady—she has not gone on to be a major screen star. **Selected Works:** *Handmaid's Tale* (1990), *King of the Hill* (1993), *Shock to the System* (1990), *Women and Men: Stories of Seduction* (1990)

# Dorothy McGuire

**Born:** June 14, 1918; Omaha, NE

**Years Active in the Industry:** by decade

| 10s | 20s | 30s | 40s | 50s | 60s | 70s | 80s | 90s |
|-----|-----|-----|-----|-----|-----|-----|-----|-----|

American actress Dorothy McGuire made her stage debut at age 13 in *A Kiss For Cinderella* in her home town of Omaha, opposite fellow aspiring actor and Omaha native Henry Fonda. McGuire went to Broadway in 1938 to understudy Martha Scott in the role of Emily Webb in *Our Town*, eventually taking over the part; she also underwent an ingenue's ordeal by fire, acting opposite the dissipated John Barrymore in *My Dear Children. Claudia*, produced in 1941, was Dorothy's first starring stage vehicle. On the strength of this play, she was put under contract by film producer David O. Selznick, whose first move was to lend the actress out to 20th Century-Fox to recreate her role as the immature newlywed in the 1943 filmization of *Claudia*. So popular was this film that a followup was made three years later, again starring McGuire, titled *Claudia and David* (1946). In the meantime she had played a far more mature role as the beleagured wife of alcoholic James Dunn in *A Tree Grows in Brooklyn* (1945), then finally made a film for Selznick, portraying an imperiled mute girl in *The Spiral Staircase* (1946). Always a star and never a starlet, Dorothy refused to pose for cheesecake stills, turned down attempts to publicize her private life, and vetoed wearing makeup for her role as an extremely homely woman in *The Enchanted Cottage* (1945), opting (wisely) to convey the homeliness through facial expressions and lighting. The actress was nominated for an Academy Award for her role as Gregory Peck's fiancee in *Gentleman's Agreement* (1947), but Oscars went instead to supporting actress Celeste Holm and to the picture itself. Alone among actresses her age, Dorothy was able to fluctuate from romantic leads in such films as *Three Coins in the Fountain* (1954) to character parts in films like *Friendly Persuasion* (1956), relying neither on actor's affectations in the younger roles nor age makeup in the older ones. At age 46, she was still able to successfully portray the Virgin Mary in *The Greatest Story Ever Told* (1965). Living reclusively with her wealthy husband John Swope, McGuire chose her roles slowly and carefully in the latter part of her career, making quality appearances in such made-for-TV dramas as *Rich Man Poor Man* (1976) and *Little Women* (1979). **Selected Works:** *Caroline?* (1990), *Dark at the Top of the Stairs* (1960), *Mister 880* (1950).

## Frank McHugh (Francis Curran McHugh)

**Born:** May 23, 1898; Homestead, PA
**Died:** September 11, 1981; Greenwich, CT

**Years Active in the Industry:** by decade

| 10s | 20s | 30s | 40s | 50s | 60s | 70s | 80s | 90s |
|-----|-----|-----|-----|-----|-----|-----|-----|-----|

At age ten, Frank McHugh began performing in his parent's stock company, side by side with his siblings Matt and Kitty. By age 17, McHugh was resident juvenile with the Marguerite Bryant stock company. Extensive vaudeville experience followed, and in 1925 McHugh made his first Broadway appearance in *The Fall Guy*, three years later, he made his movie debut in a Vitaphone short. Hired by Warner Bros. for the small role of a motorcycle driver in 1930's *The Dawn Patrol*, McHugh appeared in nearly 70 Warners films over the next decade. He was often cast as the hero's best pal or as drunken comedy relief; his peculiar trademark was a lightly braying laugh. Highlight performances during his Warners tenure included Jimmy Cagney's pessimistic choreographer in

*Footlight Parade* (1933), "rude mechanical" Quince in *A Midsummer Night's Dream* (1935), an erstwhile poet and horserace handicapper in *Three Men on a Horse* (1936) and a friendly pickpocket in *One Way Passage* (1932)—a role he'd repeat word-for-word in *Till We Meet Again*, 1940 remake of *Passage*. He continued showing up in character roles in such films as *Going My Way* (1944) and *A Tiger Walks* (1964) until the late 1960s. McHugh was also a regular on the 1960s TV series *The Bing Crosby Show* and *F Troop*. **Selected Works:** *Four Daughters* (1938), *Last Hurrah* (1958), *Roaring Twenties* (1939).

## Michael McKean

**Born:** October 17, 1947; New York, NY

**Years Active in the Industry:** by decade

| 10s | 20s | 30s | 40s | 50s | 60s | 70s | 80s | 90s |
|-----|-----|-----|-----|-----|-----|-----|-----|-----|

You knew him as Lenny Koznowski, the nasal, nerdish pal of Andrew "Squiggy" Squigman (David L. Lander) on the hit TV series *Laverne and Shirley*. Show-biz insiders knew Michael McKean as an intelligent, versatile actor and writer. Shedding himself of the "Lenny" image after *Laverne and Shirley* folded in 1983, McKean became involved in several ensemble comedy projects with such kindred spirits as Harry Shearer, Rob Reiner and Christopher Guest. In the 1984 "rockumentary" spoof *This Is Spinal Tap*, McKean played the cockney-accented heavy metal musician David St. Hubbins. Apparently McKean enjoyed posing as an Englishman, inasmuch as he has done it so often and so well since *Spinal Tap*, most recently as Brian Benben's snippish boss on the cable TV sitcom *Dream On*. In the early '90s, McKean was one of the stars of another, less memorable TV comedy, *Grand*, and appeared for two seasons on *Saturday Night Live*. He continues to land film roles, usually in comedies, including the successful *The Brady Bunch Movie* (1995). **Selected Works:** *Coneheads* (1993), *Memoirs of an Invisible Man* (1992), *True Identity* (1991).

## Ian McKellen

**Born:** 1939; Burnley, Lancashire, England

**Years Active in the Industry:** by decade

| 10s | 20s | 30s | 40s | 50s | 60s | 70s | 80s | 90s |
|-----|-----|-----|-----|-----|-----|-----|-----|-----|

British actor Ian McKellen began acting in college, and in the early '60s quickly became well-respected on the professional stage. Eventually he was considered one of the best classical actors of modern theater, especially skilled at interpreting Shakespeare; he won tremendous acclaim for his one-man-show *Ian McKellen Acting Shakespeare*. He won a Best Actor Tony Award for his portrayal of Salieri in Broadway's *Amadeus* (1981). He has appeared in only a handful of films, beginning in the late '60s. He has been a leading spokesman for gay rights; as an openly gay man, he was criticized for accepting a knighthood in 1990 after a law was passed forbidding the government from allocating money which might "promote homosexuality." He has lectured at Oxford as a visiting professor of contemporary theater. **Selected Works:** *And the Band Played On* (1993), *Ballad of Little Jo* (1993), *Six Degrees of Separation* (1993)

# Victor McLaglen

**Born:** December 10, 1886; Tunbridge Wells, England
**Died:** 1959

**Years Active in the Industry:** by decade

| 10s | 20s | 30s | 40s | 50s | 60s | 70s | 80s | 90s |
|-----|-----|-----|-----|-----|-----|-----|-----|-----|

A boy soldier during the Boer War, British actor Victor McLaglen later worked as a prizefighter (once losing to Jack Johnson in six rounds) and a vaudeville and circus performer. He served in World War I as a captain with the Irish Fusiliers and as provost marshal of Baghdad. In the early '20s he broke into British films. He soon moved to Hollywood, where he got lead and supporting roles; his basic screen persona was that of a large, brutish, but soft-hearted man of action. He appeared in many John Ford films, often as a military man. McLaglen made the transition to sound successfully, and for his work in Ford's *The Informer* (1935), he won the Best Actor Oscar. He remained a busy screen actor until the late '50s. Five of his brothers were also film actors: Arthur, Clifford, Cyril, Kenneth, and Leopold. He was the father of director Andrew V. McLaglan. **Selected Works:** *Gunga Din* (1939), *Lost Patrol* (1934), *Quiet Man* (1952), *She Wore a Yellow Ribbon* (1949)

# Steve McQueen (Terrence Steven McQueen)

**Born:** March 24, 1930; Slater, MO
**Died:** 1980

**Years Active in the Industry:** by decade

| 10s | 20s | 30s | 40s | 50s | 60s | 70s | 80s | 90s |
|-----|-----|-----|-----|-----|-----|-----|-----|-----|

Abandoned by his father in infancy, Steve McQueen spent part of his youth in reform school. In his teens he drifted from one odd job to another, interrupted by a stint in the Marines which included six weeks in the brig on AWOL charges. He joined New York's Neighborhood Playhouse in 1952 and studied acting with Uta Hagen and Herbert Berghof. Performing in stock and with the Actors Studio, McQueen received his big break when he was chosen to replace Ben Gazzara in Broadway's *A Hatful of Rain* (1955). He debuted onscreen in a bit role in *Somebody Up There Likes Me* (1956), then played his first film lead in the science-fiction cult classic *The Blob* (1958). In 1958 he got the lead role in the TV series *Wanted: Dead or Alive*, which stayed on the air for several

years and made him a well-known actor. His breakthrough role as a screen actor was that of a supercool POW in *The Great Escape* (1963), which established him as a star; a racing enthusiast, McQueen did all of the motorcycle stunts in the movie himself. For his work in *The Sand Pebbles* (1966) he received a Best Actor Oscar nomination. After *Bullitt* (1968), he was a superstar, and for several years he remained at or near the top of the Biggest Box-Office Draws list. He had an onscreen charisma that enabled him to dominate a film without apparent effort; in his best-known roles McQueen was a cool, introverted antihero. After fulfilling a life-long ambition of getting equal billing with Paul Newman—in the film *The Towering Inferno* (1974)—he took an extended leave from films, ultimately appearing onscreen only three more times. He died at age 50 of a heart attack while undergoing surgery for cancer. He married and divorced actresses Neile Adams and Ali McGraw, whom he co-starred with in *The Getaway* (1972). **Selected Works:** *Love with the Proper Stranger* (1963), *Magnificent Seven* (1960), *Papillon* (1973), *Reivers* (1969)

# John McTiernan

**Born:** January 8, 1951; New York, NY

**Years Active in the Industry:** by decade

| 10s | 20s | 30s | 40s | 50s | 60s | 70s | 80s | 90s |
|-----|-----|-----|-----|-----|-----|-----|-----|-----|

During his relatively brief career as a director of mainstream features, John McTiernan has established himself as a master craftsman notable for his almost Hitchcockian ability to create sus-

pense and keep action moving at an exhilarating pace. McTiernan has been involved with theatrical arts for most of his life. His father was an opera singer, and McTiernan made his theatrical debut at age seven playing bit roles in his father's shows. After high school he became involved with summer stock, where he directed, acted, and designed until attended Julliard and New York University, where he studied film. He then became designer and technical director at the Manhattan School of Music. McTiernan went on to make over 200 television commercials before making his feature film debut by directing the fantasy horror movie *Nomads* (1985). He next directed *Predator* (1987), a thriller featuring Arnold Schwarzenegger. McTiernan is most famous for his next film, 1988's blockbuster actioner *Die Hard*. Since then, he has continued making fast-paced, suspenseful films. **Selected Works:** *Hunt for Red October* (1990), *Last Action Hero* (1993), *Medicine Man* (1992)

# Peter Medak

**Born:** December 23, 1937; Budapest, Hungary

**Years Active in the Industry:** by decade

| 10ˢ | 20ˢ | 30ˢ | 40ˢ | 50ˢ | 60ˢ | 70ˢ | 80ˢ | 90ˢ |
|-----|-----|-----|-----|-----|-----|-----|-----|-----|
|     |     |     |     |     |     |     |     |     |

Were it not for the Russian put-down of the Hungarian uprising in 1956, director Peter Medak might well have been one of the leading lights of the New Hungarian Cinema of the 1970s. As it happened, Medak was forced to flee to Britain, where after a lengthy apprenticeship he was allowed to direct TV movies and to work as second-unit director on such films as *Kaleidescope* (1966) and *Funeral in Berlin* (1967). After making his theatrical-film directorial bow in 1968, Medak garnered praise for his handling of the very black comedy *A Day in the Death of Joe Egg* (1972). He followed this with *The Ruling Class* (1972) a rude, irreverent, achingly funny combination of theatrical and cinematic knowhow which skewered every traditional value held near and dear by the British aristocracy (the hero imagines he's Jesus Christ, then switches to Jack the Ripper). In between bread-and-butter assignments like *Zorro the Gay Blade* (1982), Medak has continued pushing the envelope of taste and style with such films as *The Krays*, a 1990 crime story concerning London's notorious identical-twin gang bosses (whom Medak knew personally), and *Romeo Is Bleeding* (1994), a horrifying and sometimes darkly hilarious study of modern-day gang activity. **Selected Works:** *Let Him Have It* (1991), *Nabokov on Kafka* (1990), *Pontiac Moon* (1994)

# Donald Meek

**Born:** July 14, 1880; Glasgow, Scotland
**Died:** November 18, 1946

**Years Active in the Industry:** by decade

| 10ˢ | 20ˢ | 30ˢ | 40ˢ | 50ˢ | 60ˢ | 70ˢ | 80ˢ | 90ˢ |
|-----|-----|-----|-----|-----|-----|-----|-----|-----|
|     |     |     |     |     |     |     |     |     |

For nearly two decades in Hollywood, Scottish-born actor Donald Meek lived up to his name by portraying a series of tremulous, shaky-voiced sycophants and milquetoasts—though he was equally effective (if not more so) as nail-hard businessmen, autocratic schoolmasters, stern judges, compassionate doctors, small-town Babbitts, and at least one Nazi spy. An actor since the age of eight, Meek joined an acrobatic troupe, which brought him to America in his teens. At 18 Meek joined the American military and was sent to fight in the Spanish-American War. He contracted yellow fever, which caused him to lose his hair—and in so doing, secured his future as a character actor. Meek made his film bow in 1928; in the early talkie era, he starred with John Hamilton in a series of New York-filmed short subjects based on the works of mystery writer S. S. Van Dyne. Relocating to Hollywood in 1933, Meek immediately found steady work in supporting roles. So popular did Meek become within the next five years that director Frank Capra, who'd never worked with the actor before, insisted that the gratuitous role of Mr. Poppins be specially written for Meek in the film version of *You Can't Take It With You* (1938) (oddly, this first association with Capra would be the last). Meek died in 1946, while working in director William Wellman's *Magic Town;* his completed footage remained in the film, though he was certainly conspicuous by his absence during most of the proceedings. **Selected Works:** *Captain Blood* (1935), *Informer* (1935), *Tortilla Flat* (1942), *Young Mr. Lincoln* (1939), *Dr. Ehrlich's Magic Bullet* (1940)

# Georges Méliès (Marie Georges Jean Méliès)

**Born:** December 8, 1861; Paris, France
**Died:** 1938

**Years Active in the Industry:** by decade

| 10ˢ | 20ˢ | 30ˢ | 40ˢ | 50ˢ | 60ˢ | 70ˢ | 80ˢ | 90ˢ |
|-----|-----|-----|-----|-----|-----|-----|-----|-----|
|     |     |     |     |     |     |     |     |     |

Georges Méliès was one of the true pioneers of cinema, best known for his discovery that the camera could be used to create fantastic special effects. He was also one of the first to use film to tell stories rather than chronicle mundane events. ,Born the son of a prominent French bootmaker, Méliès showed special talent for artwork and puppetry as a youth. After serving as a corporal in the French infantry, Méliès defied his father—who wanted him to enter the family business—and enrolled in the Ecole des Beaux Arts. While living in London during 1884, Méliès began his lifelong fascination with stage magic and illusion. He was so enthralled that he soon became a magician and began performing in Paris. When his father died, Méliès and his brother began managing the family business until 1888, when he bought the Theatre Robert-Houdin. There he soon gained renown for his flamboyant and technically innovative magic shows. In 1895 Méliès attended the premiere exhibition of the Lumiere brothers' cinematographe. He was thrilled by the possibilities of their moving pictures and immediately offered to buy their machine. They refused to sell, so he bought a Bioscope in London and began showing Edison Kinetoscope shorts during performances. He then built his own movie camera and began making his own movies under the heading Star Film. While filming a scene in the Parisian streets, Méliès' camera temporarily jammed. After fixing it, he resumed filming and soon discovered that people prior to the jam had simply disappeared! Thus began his fascination with special effects possibilities. Between 1896-1897, he made 131 one minute films. In 1897, he built Europe's first movie studio, where he began to film stories based on literature and stage. He made his most famous film, *A Trip to the Moon*, in 1902. During the early part of the century, Méliès' films were internationally popular, but by 1905 his career was on the wane; more sophisticated audiences began getting bored by his weak stories that only functioned as an excuse to present a stream of special effects. Méliès stopped making films in 1911. Four years later, he was forced to sell his estate, and convert his studio to a variety theater where he resumed performing his stage illusion. He went bankrupt in 1923. His films lay forgotten until 1931, when he was awarded a Legion of Honor medal. One year later, he was given a rent-free apartment where he lived out the rest of his life.

# Chris Menges

**Born:** September 15, 1940; Kingston, England

**Years Active in the Industry:** by decade

| 10ˢ | 20ˢ | 30ˢ | 40ˢ | 50ˢ | 60ˢ | 70ˢ | 80ˢ | 90ˢ |
|-----|-----|-----|-----|-----|-----|-----|-----|-----|
|     |     |     |     |     |     |     |     |     |

British-born Chris Menges worked his way up from the editing room to documentary cameraman, earning the respect of his peers through his willingness to film in perilous locations under near-impossible circumstances. This may be why Menges evinced no fear of formidable director Lindsay Anderson when he was hired in 1968 as camera operator on Anderson's *If....* By 1970, Menges was a full director of photography, and during the next two decades amassed such impressive credits as *Black Beauty* (1971), *The Empire Strikes Back* (1980), *The Killing Fields* (1984) and *The Mission* (1986); for the last two films, Menges won Academy Awards. Menges became a director with 1988's *A World Apart*, which kept in line with the sociopolitical themes explored in *Killing Fields* and *Mission* by exposing the horrors of South African apartheid as seen through the eyes of an activist's teenaged daughter. Menges' subsequent directorial assignment, 1991's *Crisscross*, was likewise politically charged (Vietnam was the "subtext" this time around) but nowhere near as dramatically involving as *A World Apart*. **Selected Works:** *Second Best* (1994)

# Adolphe Menjou

**Born:** February 18, 1890; Pittsburgh, PA
**Died:** 1963

**Years Active in the Industry:** by decade

| 10ˢ | 20ˢ | 30ˢ | 40ˢ | 50ˢ | 60ˢ | 70ˢ | 80ˢ | 90ˢ |
|-----|-----|-----|-----|-----|-----|-----|-----|-----|
|     |     |     |     |     |     |     |     |     |

Debonair and sophisticated, Adolphe Menjou was an impeccably-dressed lead actor with a waxed black mustache. At age 21 he moved to New York with no intention of becoming an actor;

three years later he drifted into films as an extra, then got some larger roles before serving as a captain in the Ambulance Corps for three years in World War I. Back in the U.S. Menjou returned to acting, playing supporting roles in a number of major productions. He became a star after playing the lead role in Charlie Chaplin's *A Woman of Paris* (1923), which established his screen persona: a dapper, suave man of the world. He went on to play this role in more than 100 films, at first as a leading man and later as a character actor. He made the transition to sound easily and received a Best Actor Oscar nomination for his work in *The Front Page* (1931). He gained a reputation as one of the world's best-dressed men, a fact alluded to in the title of his autobiography, *It Took Nine Tailors* (1948). Active in politically conservative causes, in 1944 Menjou became a co-founder of the Motion Picture Alliance for the Preservation of American Ideals; later he was a "friendly" witness in the 1947 hearings of the House Un-American Activities Committee. From 1928-33 he was married to actress Kathryn Carver, and from 1934 on he was married to actress Verree Teasdale. **Selected Works:** *Farewell to Arms* (1932), *Morocco* (1930), *Stage Door* (1937), *Star Is Born* (1937), *You Were Never Lovelier* (1942)

# Ismail Merchant

**Born:** December 25, 1936; Bombay, India

**Years Active in the Industry:** by decade

| 10ˢ | 20ˢ | 30ˢ | 40ˢ | 50ˢ | 60ˢ | 70ˢ | 80ˢ | 90ˢ |
|-----|-----|-----|-----|-----|-----|-----|-----|-----|
|     |     |     |     |     |     |     |     |     |

Educated in Bombay and the U.S., Indian-born Ismail Merchant was destined for a business administration career. Rather than waste away in banking or speculating, lifelong movie buff Merchant put his skills to work in the creative arts. He found the perfect collaborators in the form of German/Indian novelist Ruth Prawer Jhabvala and California-born director James Ivory. The Merchant/Ivory productions written by Jhabvala, among them *Shakespeare Wallah* (1965), *Bombay Talkie* (1969), *Roseland* (1977), *The Europeans* (1979), *A Room with a View* (1984), and *Howard's End* (1992), have set an international standard for superior production values at the least possible cost. These accomplishments are all the more remarkable when one realizes that Merchant and Ivory are almost constantly at each other's throats over artistic and financial matters—and make no effort to hide their squabbles from the public. In addition to his administrative duties, Merchant has occasionally turned director; among his efforts was the Oscar-nominated short *The Creation of a Woman*. Merchant has also carved a niche in the culinary world with his best-selling cookbook, *Ismail Merchant's Indian Cuisine*. **Selected Works:** *In Custody* (1994)

# Burgess Meredith (Oliver Burgess Meredith)

**Born:** November 16, 1908; Cleveland, OH

**Years Active in the Industry:** by decade

| 10s | 20s | 30s | 40s | 50s | 60s | 70s | 80s | 90s |
|-----|-----|-----|-----|-----|-----|-----|-----|-----|

Originally a newspaper reporter, Burgess Meredith came to the screen in 1936, repeating his stage role in *Winterset,* a part written for him by Maxwell Anderson. Meredith has had a long and varied film career, playing everything from George in *Of Mice and Men* (1939) to Sylvester Stallone's trainer in *Rocky* (1976). He received Oscar nominations for *The Day of the Locust* (1975) and *Rocky.* As comfortable with comedy as with drama, Meredith also appeared in *Idiot's Delight* (1939); *Second Chorus* (1940), with Fred Astaire; *Diary of a Chambermaid* (1942), which he also wrote and produced; *The Story of G.I. Joe* (1945); and *Mine Own Executioner* (1947). He also directed *Man on the Eiffel Tower* (1949). On television, he made countless guest appearances in dozens of dramatic and variety productions, including one of the first episodes of *The Twilight Zone,* the touching *Time Enough to Last,* and as host on the first episode of *Your Show of Shows.* He was a regular on *Mr. Novak* (1963-64) and *Search* (1972-73), hosted *Those Amazing Animals* (1981), co-starred with Sally Struthers in *Gloria* (1982-83), and made classic appearances as the Penguin on *Batman* (1966-68). He won an Emmy in 1977 for *Tailgunner Joe* and has done voiceover work for innumerable commercials. He was briefly married to Paulette Goddard in the 1940s. **Selected Works:** *Mr. Corbett's Ghost* (1990), *Oddball Hall* (1991), *State of Grace* (1990), *Grumpy Old Men* (1993), *Night of the Hunter* (1991)

# Una Merkel

**Born:** December 10, 1903; Covington, KY
**Died:** January 1986

**Years Active in the Industry:** by decade

| 10s | 20s | 30s | 40s | 50s | 60s | 70s | 80s | 90s |
|-----|-----|-----|-----|-----|-----|-----|-----|-----|

Although she is best known for her later work, Una Merkel actually started in film in 1920 as Lillian Gish's stand-in for *Way Down East.* After a stage career in the 1920s, she returned to films as Ann Rutledge in D. W. Griffith's *Abraham Lincoln* (1930). The vivacious character actress brightened up dozens of films, playing mostly comic roles interspersed with an occasional dramatic part. Films to watch include *Dangerous Female* (1931); *Private Lives* (1931); *Red-Headed Woman* (1932); *42nd Street* (1933), the film in which she memorably says of Ginger Rogers' character Anytime Annie: "The only time she ever said no she didn't hear the question;" *The Merry Widow* (both 1934 and 1952); *Broadway Melody of 1936* (1935); *Born to Dance* (1936); *Destry Rides Again* (1939), where she and Marlene Dietrich have a frenzied hair-pulling battle over the hapless Mischa Auer; *On Borrowed Time* (1939); *The Bank Dick* (1940); *Road to Zanzibar* (1941); *This Is the Army* (1943); *With a Song in My Heart* (1952); and *The Parent Trap* (1961), among many others. In 1956, she won a Tony Award for *The Ponder Heart* and in 1961 was nominated for an Academy Award for *Summer and Smoke* in the role she had originated on the stage.

# Ethel Merman (Ethel Agnes Zimmerman)

**Born:** January 16, 1908; Astoria, MS
**Died:** 1984; New York, NY

**Years Active in the Industry:** by decade

| 10s | 20s | 30s | 40s | 50s | 60s | 70s | 80s | 90s |
|-----|-----|-----|-----|-----|-----|-----|-----|-----|

22-year-old ex-stenographer and former nightclub singer Ethel Merman achieved overnight superstardom when, in 1930, she first belted out "I Got Rhythm" in the Broadway production of *Girl Crazy.* Merman's subsequent stage hits included *Anything Goes, Red Hot and Blue, Panama Hattie, Annie Get Your Gun, Call Me Madam,* and *Gypsy.* While her Living Legend status was secure on the Great White Way, Ethel was less fortunate in the movies. She was upstaged by Ed Wynn in *Follow the Leader* (1930), by Bing Crosby and Burns and Allen in *We're Not Dressing* (1934), by Eddie Cantor in *Kid Millions* (1934), and—most ignominiously—by the Ritz Brothers in *Straight, Place and Show* (1938). While she was permitted to repeat her stage roles in movie versions of *Anything Goes* (1936) and *Call Me Madam* (1954), she had to endure watching Betty Hutton wail her way through the film adaptations of *Red, Hot and Blue* (1949) and *Annie Get Your Gun* (1950), and withstand the spectacle of a miscast Rosalind Russell misplaying the part of Mama Rose in the 1963 filmization of *Gypsy.* Perhaps Merman's talents were too big and bombastic for the comparatively intimate medium of films; or perhaps she just didn't photograph well enough to suit the Hollywood higher-ups. Merman's best movie work includes the two Irving Berlin catalogues *Alexander's Ragtime Band* (1938) and *There's No Business Like Show Business* (1954), and her character role as Milton Berle's behemoth mother-in-law in *It's a Mad, Mad, Mad, Mad World* (1963). Ethel Merman's final film appearance was a cameo in *Airplane* (1980): she played the unfortunate Lieutenant Hurwitz, who is confined to the psycho ward because he thinks he's Ethel Merman.

# Laurie Metcalf

**Born:** June 16, 1955; Edwardsville, IL

**Years Active in the Industry:** by decade

| 10ˢ | 20ˢ | 30ˢ | 40ˢ | 50ˢ | 60ˢ | 70ˢ | 80ˢ | 90ˢ |
|-----|-----|-----|-----|-----|-----|-----|-----|-----|
|     |     |     |     |     |     |     | ■   |     |

Matriculating from Illinois State University, actress Laurie Metcalf was one of the charter members of Chicago's groundbreaking Steppenwolf Theatre troupe. She moved on to New York in the early 1980s, winning a 1984 Theatre World Award and an Obie for her performance in *Balm in Gilead*. In films since 1985, the flexible Metcalf has been seen in director Susan Seidelman's *Desperately Seeking Susan* (1985) and *Making Mr. Right* (1987), and also in several other highly regarded productions, notably *Uncle Buck* (1989), *JFK* (1991) and *Mistress* (1992). Metcalf is best known to the TV-watching public for her Emmy-winning portrayal of Roseanne Conner's police-officer sister Jackie Harris on the longrunning sitcom *Roseanne*. Despite her hectic schedule, Laurie Metcalf still finds time for an occasional return-to-the-womb appearance at the Steppenwolf Theatre, usually in the company of fellow Steppenwolfians John Malkovich, Gary Sinise, and/or Glenne Headly. **Selected Works:** *Pacific Heights* (1990), *Blink* (1994)

# Nicholas Meyer

**Born:** December 24, 1945; New York, NY

**Years Active in the Industry:** by decade

| 10ˢ | 20ˢ | 30ˢ | 40ˢ | 50ˢ | 60ˢ | 70ˢ | 80ˢ | 90ˢ |
|-----|-----|-----|-----|-----|-----|-----|-----|-----|
|     |     |     |     |     |     | ■   |     |     |

Director/writer Nicholas Meyer began his movie career in Hollywood's equivalent to the mailroom: a studio publicity department. After helping to promote Paramount's late-1960s product, Meyer took a job as a Warner Bros. story editor. He parlayed a lifelong fascination with Sherlock Holmes into his 1974 novel *The Seven Percent Solution*, which he sold to the movies on the condition that he adapt the screenplay. Several scripts and novels later, Meyer made his directorial bow with 1979 *Time After Time*, a Holmesian time-travel adventure which pitted H. G. Wells against Jack the Ripper. Meyer then directed what many consider the best and most basic of the *Star Trek* theatrical-film series, *Star Trek II: The Wrath of Khan* (1982). The following year, Meyer helmed the controversial post-Apocalyptic TV movie *The Day After* (1983). Meyer returned to the *Star Trek* fold with his collaboration on the screenplay for 1986's *Star Trek IV: The Voyage Home*, and his direction and coscripting of 1991's *Star Trek VI: The Undiscovered Country*. **Selected Works:** *Sommersby* (1993)

# Russ Meyer (Russell Albion Meyer)

**Born:** March 21, 1922; Oakland, CA

**Years Active in the Industry:** by decade

| 10ˢ | 20ˢ | 30ˢ | 40ˢ | 50ˢ | 60ˢ | 70ˢ | 80ˢ | 90ˢ |
|-----|-----|-----|-----|-----|-----|-----|-----|-----|
|     |     |     |     | ■   |     |     |     |     |

The product of an extremely unstable home life, American filmmaker Russ Meyer channelled his youthful energies into photography, winning several awards for his amateur films before he was fifteen. Experience under more grueling circumstances came when he worked as a newsreel cameraman in Europe during World War II. As a civilian, Meyer at first specialized in glamour photos of beautiful models, then found that the money came quicker and the work was more plentiful in the world of male-oriented "nudie" magazines; he was among the first and most prolific of the centerfold photographers for Hugh Hefner's *Playboy* magazine. From there, Meyer moved on to nudie films, a field in which he managed to strike a happy medium, titilating the audience while remaining within the boundaries of local censor boards. His first film, 1959's *The Immoral Mr. Teas*, has a plentitude of female flesh, but the storyline—a man subjected to a powerful anesthetic discovers that he can see through the clothes of every woman who walks past him—precluded any physical contact between man and woman. Arguing that nudity in and of itself is not obscene so long as it is kept at arm's length, Meyer was able to circumvent the bluenoses and get his film booked into theatres. Shot silent on a budget of $24,000, *The Immoral Mr. Teas* made over 40 times its cost. When other producers began muscling in on his territory, Meyer decided to move beyond mere voyeurism, and with *Lorna* (1964) added elements of sexual contact (always stopping short of actual fornication) and violence: the director's excesses in terms of blood and carnality reached a peak with his "classics" *Motor Psycho* (1965), *Faster, Pussycat, Kill! Kill!* (1966), and *Harry, Cherry and Raquel* (1969). With the 71-minute *Vixen* (1969), Meyer deliberately courted obscenity charges, reasoning that the best way to keep one's head above water in the sexually liberated movie scene of the late 1960s was to stir up as much publicity as possible. Suddenly the director was making appearances on such conservative TV programs as *The Art Linkletter Show*, defending the artistic merits of *Vixen*—and as a result, the film, put together for a mere $76,000, was a hit to the tune of $6 million. 20th Century-Fox, financially strapped and desperate to cash in on the sudden respectability of X-rated films (via the Oscar win for 1969's *Midnight Cowboy*), signed Meyer to direct his first big-studio picture. *Beyond the Valley of the Dolls* (1970), coscripted by no less than Roger Ebert, was a success, emboldening Meyer to make his chanciest career move yet: *The Seven Minutes* (1971), a sexy but nonetheless "mainstream" all-star film based on a bestselling novel by Irving Wallace. Without his usual lascivious story ingredients to fall back on, Meyer proved to be an inept director, and the film ended up his first failure. Meyer continued making films into the late 1970s—now firmly established as a cultural icon, hosannahed at various respectable film festivals. Despite his body of film work, Russ Meyer's most lasting legacy may be his "protegee" and former wife Edy Williams, the busty perennial starlet who can always be counted on to show a lot of skin at the annual Academy Awards show.

# Bette Midler

**Born:** December 1, 1945; Honolulu, HI

**Years Active in the Industry:** by decade

| 10ˢ | 20ˢ | 30ˢ | 40ˢ | 50ˢ | 60ˢ | 70ˢ | 80ˢ | 90ˢ |
|-----|-----|-----|-----|-----|-----|-----|-----|-----|

Gloriously flamboyant American entertainer Bette Midler was born in Hawaii to the only Jewish family in the neighborhood. After dropping out of a drama course at the University of Hawaii, she took a tiny role in the 1966 film *Hawaii,* playing a seasick boat passenger (though it's hard to see her when viewing the film today). Training for a dancing career in New York, Midler made the casting rounds for several months, finally attaining a chorus role, and then the featured part of Tzeitel, in the long-running Broadway musical *Fiddler on the Roof.* It helps to do something well that no one else does, and Midler found her forte by singing at the Continental Baths, a gay hangout in New York. Most bath house performers were tacky and terrible, but Midler established herself by combining genuine talent with the tackiness expected of her. As "The Divine Miss M," Midler did an act consisting of campy (and dirty) specialty numbers, dead-on imitations of such earlier performers as the Andrews Sisters and Libby Holman, and the most outrageously revealing costumes this side of Bob Mackie. Soon she outgrew the bath houses and went on to nightclub and recording-artist fame, earning a Grammy Award in 1973. After several years of sellout tours, Midler re-entered films as the star of *The Rose,* an "a clef" film based on Janis Joplin. The movie itself was rather too obviously aimed at getting a shelf-full of Academy Award nominations (Midler was even given a "telephone scene", just like the one that earned Luise Rainer her Oscar back in 1936), but *The Rose* made up for its contrivances with a concert finale that was beautifully shot by a battalion of Hollywood's top cinematographers. *The Rose* was a success, but it failed to establish Midler as a dramatic actress; audiences, particularly the gay fans, still preferred the Divine Miss M. *Jinxed* (1982), Midler's next film, lived up to its name with well-publicized production squabbles between Midler, the director, the producers, and a few of the co-stars. Following the failure of *Jinxed,* Midler wasn't seen on screen until she signed a contract with Disney Studios in 1986. Establishing a new screen identity as a character comedienne, Midler sparkled in *Down and Out in Beverly Hills* (1986), and was even better as a loudmouthed kidnap victim in *Ruthless People* (1987). Using her restored film stature, Midler set up her own production company and produced *Beaches* (1988), a "pals through the years" saga that suffered from a saggy ending but also served to introduce Mayim Byalik (later star of TV's *Blossom*), who convincingly played Midler as a child. Once again attempting to establish herself as a tragedian, Midler starred in *Stella* (1990), an unnecessary (and anachronistic) remake of *Stella Dallas. For the Boys* (1992), which seemingly went on forever, offered Midler in tons of old-age makeup as a Martha Raye-style USO star (Raye responded to this "tribute" by suing the studio). Nor were *Scenes from a Mall* (1991), mismatching Midler with Woody Allen, and *Hocus Pocus,* a silly

"witchcraft" fantasy, truly worthy of her talents. Though her film career has waned a bit, Midler still performs live in concert to turn-away crowds. And in late 1993, Midler scored an enormous success in a superb TV adaptation of the Broadway musical *Gypsy.* In private life, Midler is the antithesis of her public persona: a woman of recognized taste both in decorating her home and in choosing her wardrobe, and also a most devoted wife (to commodities broker Martin von Haselberg) and mother.

# Toshiro Mifune

**Born:** April 1, 1920; Tsingtao, China

**Years Active in the Industry:** by decade

| 10ˢ | 20ˢ | 30ˢ | 40ˢ | 50ˢ | 60ˢ | 70ˢ | 80ˢ | 90ˢ |
|-----|-----|-----|-----|-----|-----|-----|-----|-----|

Born in China to Japanese parents, Toshiro Mifune became Japan's top male star. After serving with the Japanese army in World War II, he won a studio talent contest and debuted onscreen in 1946. Early in his career he began working with legendary director Akira Kurosawa; he became world-famous after their second film together, the classic *Rashomon* (1950). He went on to a busy and spectacularly successful film career, displaying versatility in roles ranging from drama to ironic comedy; he became the best-known Japanese actor in the world. He won the Venice Film Festival Best Actor Award for *Yojimbo* (1961) and again for *Red Beard* (1965). Mifune formed his own production company in 1963, and went on to direct the film *The Legacy of the Five Hundred Thousand* (1964); he has also produced several films. From the mid-'60s he frequently appeared in Hollywood productions. He was prominently featured in the English-language TV mini-series *Shogun* (1980). **Selected Works:** *Hidden Fortress* (1958), *High and Low* (1962), *Life of Oharu* (1952), *Seven Samurai* (1954), *Throne of Blood* (1957)

# Nikita Mikhalkov (Nikita Sergeyevich Mikhalkov-Konchalovsky)

**Born:** October 21, 1945; Moscow, Russia

**Years Active in the Industry:** by decade

| 10ˢ | 20ˢ | 30ˢ | 40ˢ | 50ˢ | 60ˢ | 70ˢ | 80ˢ | 90ˢ |
|-----|-----|-----|-----|-----|-----|-----|-----|-----|

Born to a family of celebrated painters and poets, Muscovite Nikita Mikhalkov studied to become an actor while still a child, making his stage bow at the age of 16. After several years of success as a leading man, Mikhalkov enrolled in the State Film School (VGIK), studying the rudiments of directing under the great Mikhail Romm. He then returned to acting for four years, finally unveiling his first theatrical-release directorial assignment, *A Slave of Love*, in 1974. An avowed idolator of playwright Anton Chekhov, Mikhalkov adapted Chekhov's very first play *Platonov* into the autumnal dramatic film *An Unfinished Piece for Mechanical Piano* (1977). Mikhalkov won several awards for this effort, and would do so again for his subsequent films *Oblomov* (1980) and the Italian-produced *Oci Ciornie* (*Dark Eyes*, 1987). In 1995, a breathless Mikhalkov, in the company of his beaming young daughter, accepted the Best Foreign Picture Oscar for his *Burnt by the Sun* (1994). Mikhalkov is the younger brother of director Andrei Mikhalkov-Konchalovsky; Nikita has yet to follow Andrei to Hollywood. **Selected Works:** *Close to Eden* (1990)

# Alyssa Milano

**Born:** December 19, 1972; Brooklyn, NY

**Years Active in the Industry:** by decade

| 10s | 20s | 30s | 40s | 50s | 60s | 70s | 80s | 90s |
|-----|-----|-----|-----|-----|-----|-----|-----|-----|
|     |     |     |     |     |     |     | ■   |     |

Child actress and model Alysa Milano rose to fan-magazine fame in the role of Samantha Micelli on the TV series *Who's the Boss* (1984). During the run of this series, Milano made her TV-movie bow opposite no less than Sir John Gielgud in 1986's *The Canterville Ghost*. Like many former child stars, Milano has done her utmost to break her earlier image by appearing in adult roles calling for heavy breathing and come-hither glances: perhaps her most spectacular appearance along these lines was in the role of the estimable Amy Fisher in the the 1992 TV movie *Casualties of Love: The Long Island Lolita Story*. According to those who keep tabs on such things, Milano has lined up roles in "three or four very adult movies." **Selected Works:** *Little Sister* (1992), *Where the Day Takes You* (1992)

# Sylvia Miles

**Born:** September 9, 1932; New York, NY

**Years Active in the Industry:** by decade

| 10s | 20s | 30s | 40s | 50s | 60s | 70s | 80s | 90s |
|-----|-----|-----|-----|-----|-----|-----|-----|-----|
|     |     |     |     |     | ■   | ■   | ■   | ■   |

American actress Sylvia Miles was one of several performers of the 1960s to parlay a vulgar, sex-obsessed screen personality into a successful career. Miles started out at the Actors Studio, then moved on to Broadway, playing fairly conservative roles.

The first foretaste of things to come was Miles's role as The Thief in the off-Broadway production of *The Balcony,* in which she allowed a man dressed as a judge to whip her—but only after she forced him to lick her foot! Though this kind of material is kid's stuff today, it packed quite a wallop in 1960, and established Miles as, at best, a "peculiar" personality. In 1969 Miles was nominated for an Oscar for her brief role in *Midnight Cowboy,* in which she outhustles would-be hustler Jon Voigt following an athletic and sometimes amusing sex scene. Her second Oscar nomination was for *Farewell My Lovely* (1975), in which she played a boozer with something to hide from detective Phillip Marlowe (Robert Mitchum). The story most often told about Miles concerns the time she responded to a bad review from critic John Simon by dumping a greasy plate of food on his head. Less often told is the story of how Miles came awfully close to being a regular on *The Dick Van Dyke Show*. In the 1959 *Van Dyke* pilot, then titled *Head of the Family*, Miles played comedy writer Sally Rogers—the role ultimately played by another outspoken actress, Rose Marie. **Selected Works:** *Wall Street* (1987)

# Lewis Milestone (Lewis Milstein)

**Born:** September 30, 1895; Chisinau, Ukraine, Russia
**Died:** September 25, 1980; Los Angeles, CA

**Years Active in the Industry:** by decade

| 10s | 20s | 30s | 40s | 50s | 60s | 70s | 80s | 90s |
|-----|-----|-----|-----|-----|-----|-----|-----|-----|
|     | ■   | ■   | ■   | ■   | ■   |     |     |     |

Lewis Milestone (born Lewis Milstein in the Ukraine) came to the U.S. as a teenager, and while in the Army during World War I was an assistant director on training films. In Hollywood, he began working as an editor, and after writing and assistant directing in the early 1920s, he helmed his first feature for producer Howard Hughes, *Seven Sinners* (1925). Milestone's comedy *Two Arabian Knights* (1927) was widely admired, but the director didn't hit his stride until 1930 with *All Quiet on the Western Front*, his landmark adaptation of Erich Maria Remarque's war novel. In the '30s Milestone scored major achievements in several genres, including comedy (*The Front Page* [1931]), musical (*Hallelujah, I'm a Bum* [1933]), and espionage (*The General Died at Dawn* [1936]); he capped the decade with his classic drama *Of Mice And Men* (1939), adapted from John Steinbeck's novella. Notable among his work of the 1940s and '50s are the war films *Edge of Darkness* (1943), *The Purple Heart* (1944), *A Walk in the Sun* (1946), and *Pork Chop Hill* (1959); *The Strange Love Of Martha Ivers* (1946), a stylish noir; and the Steinbeck adaptation *The Red Pony* (1949). Milestone began directing for television in the mid-'50s, and his film output quickly dropped off; after presiding over the Rat Pack in *Ocean's 11* (1960) and Marlon Brando in *Mutiny on the Bounty* (1962), his only other '60s credits are two films he started but which were completed and signed by others, *PT 109* (1963) and *The Dirty Game.*

# John Milius (John Frederick Milius)

**Born:** April 11, 1944; St. Louis, MO

**Years Active in the Industry:** by decade

| 10s | 20s | 30s | 40s | 50s | 60s | 70s | 80s | 90s |
|-----|-----|-----|-----|-----|-----|-----|-----|-----|
|     |     |     |     |     |     |     |     |     |

American director John Milius is regarded by some Holly-woodites as the living embodiment of the word "macho;" with this in mind, it is understandable that Milius would want to manifest his rugged view of the world in films after being rejected by the Marines for medical reasons. Winning a National Student Film Festival award in 1967 for *I'm So Bored,* a short subject filmed while the director was attending University of Southern California, Milius moved into studio work under the guidance of low-budget king Roger Corman and producer Lawrence Gordon. Milius' first major writing job was *Evel Knievel* (1969), a two-fisted biopic of the famed stunt driver. Other projects in the same gutsy vein followed: *The Life and Times of Judge Roy Bean* (1972) (more introspective than most of Milius' work), *Jeremiah Johnson* (1972), and *Magnum Force* (1973). Milius' first directorial effort, *Dillinger* (1973), gave evidence of Roger Corman's penny-pinching influence, but the film's combination of stylistic bloodletting and strong male bonding was pure Milius. In *The Wind and the Lion* (1975), the director's first big-budget project, Milius took a minor incident in the history of American foreign relations and expanded it into a world-rattling *mano y mano* showdown between a proud Moroccan shiek and President Theodore Roosevelt. Milius shared an Oscar nomination with Francis Ford Coppola for the screenplay of *Apocalypse Now* (1979), though it's hard to tell from viewing that much-reshaped project who contributed what. While he continued working into the 1990s, *Red Dawn,* released in 1984, may well stand as Milius' best and most typical production: the film speculated that America's only line of defense against enemy invasion would be a legion of volatile, undisciplined, raging-hormone teenaged misfits. **Selected Works:** *Hunt for Red October* (1990), *Geronimo: An American Legend* (1993), *Clear and Present Danger* (1994)

# Ray Milland

**Born:** January 3, 1905; Neath, Glamorganshire, Wales
**Died:** March 10, 1986; Torrance, CA

**Years Active in the Industry:** by decade

| 10s | 20s | 30s | 40s | 50s | 60s | 70s | 80s | 90s |
|-----|-----|-----|-----|-----|-----|-----|-----|-----|
|     |     |     |     |     |     |     |     |     |

Welsh actor Ray Milland spent the 1930s and early 1940s playing light romantic leads in such films as *Next Time We Love* (1936); *Three Smart Girls* (1936); *Easy Living* (1937), in which he is especially charming opposite Jean Arthur in an early Preston Sturges script; *Everything Happens at Night* (1939); *The Doctor Takes a Wife* (1940); and the major in Billy Wilder's *The Major and the Minor* opposite Ginger Rogers. Others worth watching are *Reap*

*the Wild Wind* (1942); *Forever and a Day* (1943), and *Lady in the Dark* (1944). He made *The Uninvited* in 1944 and won an Oscar for his intense and realistic portrait of an alcoholic in *The Lost Weekend* (1945). Unfortunately, it was one of his last good films or performances. With the exception of *Dial M for Murder* (1954), *X, The Man With X-Ray Eyes* (1953), *Love Story* (1970), and *Escape to Witch Mountain* (1975), his later career was made up of mediocre parts in mostly bad films. One of the worst and most laughable was the horror film *The Thing with Two Heads* (1972), which paired him with football player Rosie Grier as the two-headed monster. Milland was also an uninspired director in *A Man Alone* (1955), *Lisbon* (1956), *The Safecracker* (1958), and *Panic in Year Zero* (1962). **Selected Works:** *Beau Geste* (1939), *It Happens Every Spring* (1949), *Kitty* (1945), *Star Spangled Rhythm* (1942)

# Richard Miller

**Born:** December 25, 1928; New York, NY

**Years Active in the Industry:** by decade

| 10s | 20s | 30s | 40s | 50s | 60s | 70s | 80s | 90s |
|-----|-----|-----|-----|-----|-----|-----|-----|-----|
|     |     |     |     |     |     |     |     |     |

Large and muscular at an early age, American actor Dick Miller entered the Navy during World War II while still a teenager, distinguishing himself as a boxer. He attended CCNY, Columbia University and New York University, supporting himself with semi-pro football jobs, radio DJ gigs and as a psychological assistant at Bellevue. At age 22, he was host of a Manhattan-based TV chat show, *Midnight Snack.* Stage and movie work followed, and Miller joined the stock company/entourage of low-budget auteur Roger Corman. His first great Corman role was as the hyperthyroid salesman in *Not in this Earth* (1956); a handful of rock-and-roll quickies followed before Miller received his first sci-fi lead in *War of the Satellites* (1958). In Corman's *Bucket of Blood* (1959), Miller originated the role of Walter Paisley, the nebbishy sociopath who "creates" avant-garde sculpture by murdering his subjects and dipping them in plaster. He was then cast in the immortal *Little Shop of Horrors* (1960); Miller not only makes a terrific entrance by buying a bouquet of flowers and then eating them, but also narrates the picture. Miller stayed with Corman into the 1970s, at which time the director was in charge of New World Pictures. Seldom making a liveable income in films, Miller remained an unknown entity so far as the "big" studios were concerned—but his teenaged fans were legion, and he was besieged on the streets and in public places for autographs. When the adolescent science-fiction fans of the 1950s became the directors of the 1980s, Miller began receiving some of the best roles of his career. In Joe Dante's *Gremlins* (1984), Miller was paired with his *Little Shop* costar Jackie Joseph, as a rural couple whose house is bulldozed by a group of hostile gremlins. Miller and Joseph returned in the sequel *Gremlins 2: The New Batch* (1989), in which the actor heroically helped squash the gremlins' invasion of New York. Miller's most Pirandellian role was as the "decency league" activist in *Matinee* (1993) who is actually an actor in the employ of William Castle-like showman John Goodman. Directed again by longtime Miller fan Dante, *Matinee* contains a wonderful "in" joke wherein Miller is identified as a fraud via his photograph in a *Famous Monsters of Filmland*-type fanzine—the very sort of publication which canonized Miller throughout the 1970s. **Selected Works:** *After Hours* (1985), *Unlawful Entry* (1992), *Batman: Mask of the Phantasm* (1993)

*Daisies*, actress Penelope Ann Miller was born in California and raised in Texas. After a year of attending Menlo College, Miller dropped out to train with acting coach Herbert Berghof. Her first role of note was as ditsy ingenue Daisy in the Neil Simon Broadway comedy *Biloxi Blues*, a role she would later recreate in the film version. For her role in *Our Town* she was nominated for a Tony award in 1989. In 1987, the blonde, saucer-eyed actress made her film debut in the wacked-out comedy *Adventures in Babysitting*, after which she costarred with popular leading men ranging from Pee-Wee Herman (*Big Top Pee-Wee* [1988]) to Al Pacino (*Carlito's Way* [1993]). Some of Miller's best known film roles have included that of Marlon Brando's enigmatic daughter in *The Freshman* (1990), a brief turn as silent film actress Edna Purviance in *Chaplin* (1992), and the svelte 1930s pulp heroine Margot Lane in *The Shadow* (1994). **Selected Works:** *Awakenings* (1990), *Gun in Betty Lou's Handbag* (1992), *Kindergarten Cop* (1990), *Other People's Money* (1991)

# George Miller (George Trumbull Miller)

**Born:** March 3, 1945; Brisbane, Queensland, Australia

**Years Active in the Industry:** by decade

| 10s | 20s | 30s | 40s | 50s | 60s | 70s | 80s | 90s |
|-----|-----|-----|-----|-----|-----|-----|-----|-----|
|     |     |     |     |     |     |     | ■   | ■   |

Scottish-born film director George T. Miller has spent much of his career characterized as "the other George Miller." This is because Miller, a veteran of Australian television, did not make his first theatrical feature until 1982—three years after the release of *Mad Max*, which was the inaugural effort of another Aussie-based director named George Miller. Miller attempted for a while to differentiate himself by including the middle initial "T" in his billing. The success of his first film *The Man from Snowy River* (1982) stirred up so much publicity over the fact that Australia boasted *two* talented George Millers that Miller decided to allow the "confusion" to stand, figuring that his true fans would be able to separate the two Georges. *Snowy River* would remain the "other" George Miller's biggest hit; subsequent films like *The Neverending Story II* (1988) and TV projects like *Anzacs* (1984) had their moments, but failed to generate the same excitement as Miller's first effort. **Selected Works:** *Lorenzo's Oil* (1992), *Over the Hill* (1993), *Andre* (1994)

# Penelope Ann Miller

**Born:** January 13, 1964; Santa Monica, CA

**Years Active in the Industry:** by decade

| 10s | 20s | 30s | 40s | 50s | 60s | 70s | 80s | 90s |
|-----|-----|-----|-----|-----|-----|-----|-----|-----|
|     |     |     |     |     |     |     | ■   | ■   |

The daughter of Mark Miller, an actor best known for his starring role on the mid-1960s TV sitcom *Please Don't Eat the*

# Hayley Mills

**Born:** April 18, 1946; London, England

**Years Active in the Industry:** by decade

| 10s | 20s | 30s | 40s | 50s | 60s | 70s | 80s | 90s |
|-----|-----|-----|-----|-----|-----|-----|-----|-----|
|     |     |     |     |     | ■   | ■   | ■   | ■   |

The daughter of actor John Mills and novelist-playwright Mary Hayley Bell, and the sister of actress Juliet Mills, Hayley Mills debuted onscreen at age 13 in her father's film *Tiger Bay* (1959); for her performance, she received much critical praise and won an acting award at the Berlin Film Festival. As a result, Walt Disney signed her to a five-year contract; she went on to play sweet, innocent adolescents in a number of Disney films, her first being *Pollyanna* (1960), for which she received a special Oscar. She changed her wholesome image with a nude scene in *The Family Way* (1967) and with a widely publicized love affair with producer-director Roy Boulting, who was 33 years older than she. Mills and Boulting were married from 1971-76. She has a son by actor Leigh Lawson. Her film roles have been infrequent since 1975. **Selected Works:** *Whistle Down the Wind* (1962), *Back Home* (1990)

# Sir John Mills

**Born:** February 22, 1908; Felixstowe, E. Suffolk, England
**Died:** 1992

**Years Active in the Industry:** by decade

| 10s | 20s | 30s | 40s | 50s | 60s | 70s | 80s | 90s |
|-----|-----|-----|-----|-----|-----|-----|-----|-----|
|     | ■   | ■   | ■   | ■   | ■   | ■   | ■   | ■   |

British actor John Mills began his performing career in 1929, working in a London revue as a song-and-dance chorus

boy; in 1930 he began working on the legitimate stage, and he debuted onscreen in 1932. His progress was slow but steady, and, by the early '40s, he was one of Britain's leading movie stars; he tended to play reserved, stoic characters. Mills remained popular as a leading man through the early '50s, before moving into character roles. He sustained a steady and sometimes busy screen career through the '80s. For his portrayal of a mute village idiot in David Lean's *Ryan's Daughter* (1970), he won a Best Supporting Actor Oscar. He directed and produced the film *Sky West and Crooked* (1966). From 1931-40 he was married to actress Aileen Raymond, and was the father of actresses Hayley and Juliet Mills. He was knighted in 1977. **Selected Works:** *Goodbye, Mr. Chips* (1939), *Great Expectations* (1946), *Hobson's Choice* (1953), *In Which We Serve* (1943), *Tunes of Glory* (1960)

# Yvette Mimieux

**Born:** January 8, 1939; Los Angeles, CA

**Years Active in the Industry:** by decade

| 10ˢ | 20ˢ | 30ˢ | 40ˢ | 50ˢ | 60ˢ | 70ˢ | 80ˢ | 90ˢ |
|-----|-----|-----|-----|-----|-----|-----|-----|-----|
|     |     |     |     |     |     |     |     |     |

Born to a French father and Mexican mother, actress Yvette Mimieux grew up within shouting distance of Hollywood Boulevard. The blonde, well-proportioned Mimieux was a beauty contest winner and model when signed to an MGM contract in 1959. With her second film appearance as ethereal 800th century girl Weena in *The Time Machine* (1960), Mimieux achieved stardom; with her next film, *Where the Boys Are* (1960), she proved capable of heavy dramatics via a discreetly handled "gang rape" sequence. An appearance as a terminally ill girl on the 1964 *Dr. Kildare* episode "Tyger Tyger" drew a great deal of press attention for Mimieux, principally because she spent most of her early scenes in a bikini. The actress's subsequent roles showed promise, but she generally found herself playing second fiddle to the leading man; in Disney's *Monkeys Go Home* (1966), she was upstaged by a chimpanzee. Tired of adhering to the whims of others, Mimieux took to writing her own screenplays: in the 1974 TV movie *Hit Lady*, she is undeniably impressive as a scantily clad professional assassin. Since her 1972 marriage to director Stanley Donen, Mimieux has curtailed her film appearances to devote her time to her husband, her poetry, her dance and music lessons, and her many lucrative business endeavors.

# Sal Mineo (Salvatore Mineo)

**Born:** January 10, 1939; Bronx, NY
**Died:** 1976

**Years Active in the Industry:** by decade

| 10ˢ | 20ˢ | 30ˢ | 40ˢ | 50ˢ | 60ˢ | 70ˢ | 80ˢ | 90ˢ |
|-----|-----|-----|-----|-----|-----|-----|-----|-----|
|     |     |     |     |     |     |     |     |     |

Short and intense Sal Mineo was a sad-eyed juvenile and adult actor with black curls. At age eight his misbehavior caused him to be kicked out of a parochial school; he went on to attend dancing classes and two years later was cast in Broadway's *The Rose Tattoo*, moving from there to a prominent adolescent role in *The King and I* with Yul Brynner. Mineo debuted onscreen in 1955 and for the next decade he was a busy screen actor, first in juvenile roles and then in youthful leads; his characters were often troubled. For his work at age 16 in *Rebel Without a Cause* (1955), his third feature, he received a Best Supporting Actor Oscar nomination; he was nominated in the same category for *Exodus* (1960). His film work began to dry up after the mid-'60s and Mineo turned to TV and the stage. He directed the play *Fortune and Men's Eyes* on the West Coast and on Broadway. He was stabbed to death on the street in 1976. **Selected Works:** *Giant* (1956), *Longest Day* (1962), *Somebody Up There Likes Me* (1956)

# Liza Minnelli (Liza May Minnelli)

**Born:** March 12, 1946; Los Angeles, CA

**Years Active in the Industry:** by decade

| 10ˢ | 20ˢ | 30ˢ | 40ˢ | 50ˢ | 60ˢ | 70ˢ | 80ˢ | 90ˢ |
|-----|-----|-----|-----|-----|-----|-----|-----|-----|
|     |     |     |     |     |     |     |     |     |

Liza Minnelli grew up on the front lines of entertainment; her mother was the great singer/actress Judy Garland and her father the director/designer Vincente Minnelli. Minnelli made her first film appearance, uncredited, as Garland's daughter (with co-star Van Johnson) in the last few seconds of *In the Good Old Summertime* (1948). When Garland shared a 1964 concert engagement at the London Palladium with her 18-year-old daughter, Minnelli's performing career was kickstarted. A year later, Minnelli had won the Tony Award for *Flora, the Red Menace*—the youngest performer ever to do so—and by 1974 had won an Oscar as well, for her performance as Sally Bowles in Bob Fosse's dramatic musical *Cabaret*. Several of her TV specials, particularly "Liza with a Z," received critical acclaim. Despite her auspicious beginnings in show business, her film career after *Cabaret* has been less than notable, with the possible exception of *Arthur* (1981) with Dudley Moore and Sir John Gielgud. Married three times, first to cabaret artist Peter Allen, then to Jack Haley, Jr., then to artist Mark Gero, for a time she was also linked romantically with Desi Arnaz, Jr., and Peter Sellers. Her concert appearances continue to sell out, at which she often performs the music of John Kander and Fred Ebb, who wrote the score for *Cabaret*. **Selected Works:** *Sterile Cuckoo* (1969), *Tell Me That You Love Me, Junie Moon* (1970)

# Vincente Minnelli

**Born:** February 28, 1910; Chicago, IL
**Died:** July 25, 1986; Beverly Hills, CA

**Years Active in the Industry:** by decade

| 10ˢ | 20ˢ | 30ˢ | 40ˢ | 50ˢ | 60ˢ | 70ˢ | 80ˢ | 90ˢ |
|-----|-----|-----|-----|-----|-----|-----|-----|-----|
|     |     |     |     |     |     |     |     |     |

By the late 1920s, Vincente Minnelli was a costume designer and assistant director for stage shows in Chicago theaters. He then became a costume and set designer at the Paramount Theater in

New York, and by 1933 was made art director at Radio City Music Hall. After directing several Broadway musicals, he came to Hollywood and MGM in 1940, where he handled some of Judy Garland's numbers in Busby Berkeley's musicals *Strike Up The Band* and *Babes on Broadway*. He began directing features in 1942 with the all-black musical *Cabin in the Sky,* and the fol-

lowing year helmed the classic musical *Meet Me in St. Louis* starring Garland. They married in 1945, after making *The Clock,* a stylish romantic drama; their daughter Liza Minnelli was born in 1946. Minnelli's films of the late '40s include the memorable musicals *Yolanda and the Thief* (1945), *Ziegfeld Follies* (1946), and *The Pirate* (1948); he also continued to branch out, with his drama *Undercurrent* (1946) and his colorful Flaubert adaptation *Madam Bovary* (1949). The 1950s saw most of Minnelli's major films, most notably the musicals *An American In Paris* (1951) with Gene Kelly; *The Band Wagon* (1953) with Fred Astaire; and *Gigi* (1958) with Leslie Caron. He also scored with his Spencer Tracy comedies *Father of the Bride* (1950) and *Father's Little Dividend* (19511) and with several high-voltage dramas: his Hollywood expose *The Bad and the Beautiful* (1952); his Van Gogh biopic *Lust for Life* (1956); and his James Jones adaptation *Some Came Running* (1958). Minnelli's career in the '60s and '70s marked a decline, but his notable later efforts include his Judy Holliday musical *Bells Are Ringing* (1960); his *Bad and the Beautiful* follow-up, *Two Weeks in Another Town* (1962); and his last films, the Barbra Streisand musical *On A Clear Day You Can See Forever* (1970) and the studio-mangled *A Matter of Time* (1976) with his daughter, Liza Minnelli. **Selected Works:** *Bad & the Beautiful* (1952), *The Story of Three Loves* (1953), *The Courtship of Eddie's Father* (1963), *The Sandpiper* (1965)

# Miou-Miou (Sylvette Hery)

**Born:** February 22, 1950; Paris, France

**Years Active in the Industry:** by decade

| 10ˢ | 20ˢ | 30ˢ | 40ˢ | 50ˢ | 60ˢ | 70ˢ | 80ˢ | 90ˢ |
|-----|-----|-----|-----|-----|-----|-----|-----|-----|
|     |     |     |     |     |     |     |     |     |

French actress Miou-Miou has successfully pulled off the considerable trick of combining intoxicating sensuality with down-to-earth humor. After spending the better part of her childhood helping her greengrocer mother, Miou-Miou took on a few more rent-paying jobs before joining nightclub comic Coluche and improv actor Patrick Dewaere in a coffee-theatre revue troupe. In 1971, she launched her still-prospering movie career with *La Cavale*. Miou-Miou's most fondly regarded screen appearances have included her supporting appearance as a street gang moll in *Going Places* (1974), her star turn in director Diane Kurys' *Entre Nouse* (1983), and her adroit portrayal of a sexy "professional reader" in *La Lectrice* (1988). **Selected Works:** *Jonah Who Will Be 25 in the Year 2000* (1976), *May Fools* (1990), *Germinal* (1993)

# Carmen Miranda (Maria da Cuhna)

**Born:** February 9, 1909; Lisbon, Portugal
**Died:** August 5, 1955

**Years Active in the Industry:** by decade

| 10ˢ | 20ˢ | 30ˢ | 40ˢ | 50ˢ | 60ˢ | 70ˢ | 80ˢ | 90ˢ |
|-----|-----|-----|-----|-----|-----|-----|-----|-----|
|     |     |     |     |     |     |     |     |     |

Moviedom's "Brazilian Bombshell" was actually born in Portugal, but as a child Carmen Miranda moved with her large and prosperous family to Rio de Janeiro. That she became a popular musical comedy star is all the more remarkable when one realizes that Miranda was born with deformed feet and had to wear special "lifts" for her performances. Miranda was a well-established and much beloved Brazilian radio, stage, and film personality when, at age 34, she was brought to America by the Schubert Brothers to appear in the 1939 Broadway revue *The Streets of Paris* (which also served as the "legit" debut of former burlesque comics Abbott and Costello). She was signed to a long-term 20th Century-Fox contract in 1940, which proved a wise move when World War II dried up the European movie market, leaving South America as practically the only foreign outlet for Hollywood films. A flamboyant exponent of the "good neighbor" policy, Miranda sang and danced her way through a series of garish Fox musicals, the most outrageous of which was *The Gang's All Here* (1943), in which she sang "The Lady in the Tutti Frutti Hat" while adorned with a seemingly gargantuan piece of fruit-laden headgear. When the demand for South-of-the-Border musicals petered out during the postwar era, Miranda began limiting her screen performances, spending more of her professional time with successful nightclub engagements. Off-screen, Miranda was a talented sketch artist and costume designer; she was also very active in charitable work, seeing to it that a generous percentage of her earnings were sent to the destitute in South America. After completing a strenuous dance number for a 1955 episode of TV's *The Jimmy Durante Show*, Miranda suffered a fatal heart attack; her death touched off widespread mourning throughout all of Latin America. The actress' memory is kept alive by the Carmen Miranda Museum in Rio De Janeiro.

# Helen Mirren

**Born:** July 26, 1945; London, England

**Years Active in the Industry:** by decade

| 10s | 20s | 30s | 40s | 50s | 60s | 70s | 80s | 90s |
|-----|-----|-----|-----|-----|-----|-----|-----|-----|

British actress Helen Mirren is descended from White Russian nobility; even so, her dad was obliged to make ends meet as a civil servant. Though her parents wanted her to be a teacher, Mirren gravitated to acting, making her Old Vic debut at age 19 in *Antony and Cleopatra*. This led to a long stint with the Royal Shakespeare Company, beginning in 1967. Though the roles were small, Mirren is eminently recognizable in the film versions of the Royal Shakespeare's *Herostratus* (1967) and *A Midsummer Night's Dream* (1968). Mirren hit her stride in the 1970s, a time in which the measure of an actress's talents often included her willingness to appear in the nude. For all of her excellent stage notices, movie producers seemed obsessed with undressing the amply endowed Mirren in such tripe as 1980's *Caligula*. Once this phase of her career ended, Mirren continued racking up impressive film and stage credits, nearly always selected on their artistic rather than box office qualities. Perhaps few day-to-day moviegoers saw Mirren in such films as *The Mosquito Coast* (1988), *Pascal's Island* (1988), and *The Cook, The Thief, His Wife and Her Lover* (1989), but she was more interested in the role at hand than in building up a following. On television, Mirren has been seen in *Cousin Bette*, a 1972 entry on PBS' "Masterpiece Theatre," and in the briefly popular 1990s TV weekly "Prime Suspect." **Selected Works:** *Comfort of Strangers* (1991), *Long Good Friday* (1979), *Where Angels Fear to Tread* (1991), *Madness of King George* (1994), *Prime Suspect 3* (1994).

# Cameron Mitchell

**Born:** November 18, 1918; Dallastown, PA
**Died:** July 6, 1994; Pacific Palisades, CA

**Years Active in the Industry:** by decade

| 10s | 20s | 30s | 40s | 50s | 60s | 70s | 80s | 90s |
|-----|-----|-----|-----|-----|-----|-----|-----|-----|

The son of a Pennsylvania minister, actor Cameron Mitchell first appeared on Broadway in 1934, in the Lunts' modern-dress version of *Taming of the Shrew*. He served as a bombardier during World War II, and for a brief period entertained thoughts of becoming a professional baseball player (he allegedly held an unsigned contract with the Detroit Tigers until the day he died). Mitchell was signed to an MGM contract in 1945, but stardom would elude him until he appeared as Happy in the original 1949 Broadway production of *Death of the Salesman*. He recreated this role for the 1951 film version, just before signing a long-term contract with 20th Century-Fox. Throughout the 1950s, Mitchell alternated between likeable characters (the unpretentious business executive in *How to Marry a Millionaire* [1952]) and hissable ones (Jigger Craigin in *Carousel* [1956]); his best performance, in the opinion of fans and critics alike, was as drug-addicted boxer Barney Ross in the 1957 biopic *Monkey on My Back*. Beginning in the 1960s, Mitchell adroitly sidestepped the IRS by appearing in dozens of Spanish and Italian films, only a few of which were released in the U.S. He also starred in three TV series: *The Beachcomber* (1961), *The High Chapparal* (1969-71), and *Swiss Family Robinson* (1976). Mitchell spent the better part of the 1970s and 1980s squandering his talents in such howlers as *The Toolbox Murders*, though there were occasional bright moments, notably his performance as a neurotic mob boss in 1982's *My Favorite Year*. A note for trivia buffs: Cameron Mitchell also appeared in the first CinemaScope film, *The Robe* (1953). Mitchell was the voice of Jesus in the Crucifixion scene. **Selected Works:** *Love Me or Leave Me* (1955), *My Favorite Year* (1982), *They Were Expendable* (1945)

# Thomas Mitchell

**Born:** July 11, 1892; Elizabeth, NJ
**Died:** 1962

**Years Active in the Industry:** by decade

| 10s | 20s | 30s | 40s | 50s | 60s | 70s | 80s | 90s |
|-----|-----|-----|-----|-----|-----|-----|-----|-----|

Unforgettable, top-ranking, dazzlingly versatile character actor Thomas Mitchell worked as a reporter before becoming a stage actor, and acted exclusively onstage (save one silent film) until he made his talkie debut in 1934, when he was in his early 40s. He wrote a number of plays, some of which eventually were adapted to the screen; his play *Little Accident*, co-written with Floyd Dell, was adapted to the screen in 1934, 1939, and 1944. He also collaborated on the screenplay *All of Me* (1934). Mitchell was twice nominated for a Best Supporting Actor Oscar, and he won for his portrayal of the drunken Doc Boone in John Ford's *Stagecoach* (1939). **Selected Works:** *Gone with the Wind* (1939), *High Noon, Part 1* (1952), *Hurricane* (1937), *Sullivans* (1944), *Swiss Family Robinson* (1940), *It's a Wonderful Life* (1946)

# Robert Mitchum (Robert Charles Durman Mitchum)

**Born:** August 6, 1917; Bridgeport, CT

**Years Active in the Industry:** by decade

| 10ˢ | 20ˢ | 30ˢ | 40ˢ | 50ˢ | 60ˢ | 70ˢ | 80ˢ | 90ˢ |
|-----|-----|-----|-----|-----|-----|-----|-----|-----|
|     |     |     |     |     |     |     |     |     |

Lead actor with tired-looking eyes and a low-key manner, Robert Mitchum traveled around the country working in a variety of odd jobs, then settled down after he married his high school sweetheart and had a child. While working for Lockheed Aircraft in 1942, Mitchum joined the Long Beach Theater Guild and was soon actively involved in the Guild's productions. In 1943 he debuted on-screen in a number of *Hopalong Cassidy* westerns, and played supporting roles in a variety of other films; altogether, he appeared in 18 films that year. At first he wasn't considered much of an actor; because of his rugged good looks and casual attitude; he was thought to be just another "beefcake" screen presence. His breakthrough film was *The Story of G.I. Joe* (1945), for which he received a Best Supporting Actor nomination; this film brought him into the limelight. Shortly thereafter Mitchum was drafted and spent eight months in the Army. After being discharged he resumed his film career as a star, gaining popularity as a strong, insouciant leading man. In 1948 he was convicted for possession of marijuana; to the surprise of many, this incident didn't damage his film career. He has gone on to make films into '80s, and in 1991 appeared briefly in *Cape Fear*, a remake of the 1961 thriller in which he starred. His heavily-lidded eyes, considered his sexiest trademark, are attributed by him to a combination of chronic insomnia and a boxing injury that caused astigmatism. **Selected Works:** *Crossfire* (1947), *Farewell, My Lovely* (1975), *Longest Day* (1962), *Sundowners* (1960), *Heaven Knows, Mr. Allison* (1957), *The Night of the Hunter* (1955)

# Tom Mix (Thomas Mix)

**Born:** January 6, 1880; Mix Run, PA
**Died:** 1940

**Years Active in the Industry:** by decade

| 10ˢ | 20ˢ | 30ˢ | 40ˢ | 50ˢ | 60ˢ | 70ˢ | 80ˢ | 90ˢ |
|-----|-----|-----|-----|-----|-----|-----|-----|-----|
|     |     |     |     |     |     |     |     |     |

The most legendary cowboy hero in cinema history, Tom Mix served in the U.S. Artillery as a career sargeant, but never saw any action and was officially listed as a deserter in 1902; he also served briefly as a Texas Ranger. A skilled horseman from childhood, in 1906 he joined the famous Miller Brothers 101 Ranch Wild West Show; in 1909 he won the national riding and rodeo championship. He was hired to round up cattle for the film *Ranch Life in the Great Southwest* (1910), and in the course of production Mix was assigned a supporting role in the film. The film's producers, Selig Polyscope, retained him as an actor, and from 1911-17 he appeared in a variety of roles in over 100 one- and two-reelers, often producing and/or directing his films. Over the years his Selig films improved in quality and became more lengthy, and their high quota of daredevil stunts made them very popular with young audiences; he did his own stunts, and often was injured during production. Selig went out of business in 1917 and Mix was signed by Fox, which starred him in the westerns that established him as the premier cowboy star; almost entirely due to Mix's worldwide success, Fox became a major studio. His films at Fox were action-packed, carefully packaged, attentive to detail, and directed and filmed by top talent. As opposed to the slower and more authentic style of films made by other cowboy stars such as William S. Hart, Mix's films were fast-paced and exciting, and he wore fancy clothes and performed stunts that defied reality. He directed only a few of these films, but he was instrumental in establishing the formula that dominated westerns from then on. In the late '20s and early '30s he quit films for three years to tour with the Ringling Brothers Circus (along with his famous horse, Tony). From 1932-35 he starred in several talkie westerns, then retired from the screen. He went on to perform across North and Central America in The Tom Mix Circus. He married a total of five times, and lived in grandiose style, owning mansions and custom-made cars. In 1940 he died in a car crash.

# Kenji Mizoguchi

**Born:** May 16, 1898; Tokyo, Japan
**Died:** August 24, 1956; Kyoto, Japan

**Years Active in the Industry:** by decade

| 10ˢ | 20ˢ | 30ˢ | 40ˢ | 50ˢ | 60ˢ | 70ˢ | 80ˢ | 90ˢ |
|-----|-----|-----|-----|-----|-----|-----|-----|-----|
|     |     |     |     |     |     |     |     |     |

An actor in Japanese films of the late teens, Kenji Mizoguchi became an assistant director and in 1922 helmed his first film, *Resurrection of Love*. Quickly recognized as a major filmmaker in his own country, Mizoguchi's reputation in the west rests on several of his films from the 1940s—most notably his samurai epic *The 47 Ronin, Parts I and II* (1947) and *Utamaro and His Five Women* (1946), his biopic of the 18th-century artist—and on his series of masterpieces from the '50s, including *The Life of Oharu* (1952), *Ugetsu Monogatari* (aka *Ugetsu* [1953]), *A Geisha* (1953) *Sansho the Bailiff* (1954), *Chikamatsu Monogatari* (aka *Crucified Lovers* [1954]), *Princess Yang Kwei Fei* (1955), and *Street of*

*Shame* (1956). Mizoguchi's abiding concern was with the role of women in Japanese society through the centuries; he showed himself to be a remarkable director of actresses (and actors), as well as a nuanced and subtle technician who could invest reality, lyricism, and poetry to his compositions and camerawork.

# Matthew Modine

**Born:** March 22, 1959; Loma Linda, CA

**Years Active in the Industry:** by decade

| 10ˢ | 20ˢ | 30ˢ | 40ˢ | 50ˢ | 60ˢ | 70ˢ | 80ˢ | 90ˢ |
|-----|-----|-----|-----|-----|-----|-----|-----|-----|
|     |     |     |     |     |     |     |     |     |

The son of a drive-in theater manager, Matthew Modine moved around often during his early years. After high school, he moved to New York; there he studied acting with Stella Adler. Modine went on to appear in a number of plays, as well as TV commercials. He debuted onscreen with a small part in *Baby It's You* (1983), which won him a role in Robert Altman's *Streamers* (1983); the entire cast of that film won the Best Actor award at the Venice Film Festival (Modine also appeared in Altman's *Short Cuts* in 1993). *Vision Quest* (1985), a coming-of-ager in which he played a high school wrestler in love with an older woman, gained him recognition with movie audiences. From there he has gone on to a consistent film career, working with such directors as Stanley Kubrick, Jonathan Demme, and John Schlesinger; meanwhile, he has continued performing occasionally on stage. In 1993 he starred in HBO's *And the Band Played On*, based on Randy Shilts' 1987 chronicle of the AIDS epidemic. **Selected Works:** *Birdy* (1984), *And the Band Played On* (1993), *Wind* (1992), *Browning Version* (1994), *Bye Bye, Love* (1995)

# Alfred Molina

**Born:** May 24, 1953; London, England

**Years Active in the Industry:** by decade

| 10ˢ | 20ˢ | 30ˢ | 40ˢ | 50ˢ | 60ˢ | 70ˢ | 80ˢ | 90ˢ |
|-----|-----|-----|-----|-----|-----|-----|-----|-----|
|     |     |     |     |     |     |     |     |     |

Briton Alfred Molina began as one half of a street-corner comedy team, then "went legit" in 1977 as a member of the Royal Shakespeare Company. His film career is bookended by two memorable untrustworthy portrayals. Molina was the devious native guide in *Raiders of the Lost Ark* (1981) who bids an imperiled Harrison Ford a cheery "Adios, Amigo" before he is skewered by an ancient booby trap; and more recently, he was the villain in *Maverick* (1994), again done in by his own perfidy. The range of Andrew Molina's talents is broad enough to accomodate such roles as the homosexual lover (and eventual murderer) of playright Joe Orton in *Prick Up Your Ears* (1987), the tyrannical Iranian husband of American Sally Field in *Not Without My Daughter* (1991), and the kindly, easily led bumbler in *Enchanted April* (1992).

# Marilyn Monroe (Norma Jean Mortenson)

**Born:** June 1, 1926; Los Angeles, CA
**Died:** August 5, 1962; Los Angeles, CA

**Years Active in the Industry:** by decade

| 10ˢ | 20ˢ | 30ˢ | 40ˢ | 50ˢ | 60ˢ | 70ˢ | 80ˢ | 90ˢ |
|-----|-----|-----|-----|-----|-----|-----|-----|-----|
|     |     |     |     |     |     |     |     |     |

Blond sex goddess Marilyn Monroe was born Norma Jean Mortenson, soon changed to Norma Jean Baker. More than any other star, Monroe become synonymous with "Hollywood;" her

pictures have become modern icons of glamour. Born illegitimate to a mentally disturbed mother, she spent much of her youth in foster homes, where she was often neglected and abused. At nine she entered an orphanage and at 11 she moved in with a friend of her mother's. Monroe quit high school at 16 to marry Jim Dougherty, a 21-year-old with whom she had little in common; a year later she attempted suicide. While her husband served in World War II, she got a job in a defense plant, where she was discovered by an Army photographer; she modeled for GI pin-ups and gained some popularity, leading to more modeling work with other photographers. She got a divorce and began working for a modeling agency in 1946, meanwhile improving her social skills at a charm school; her photo appeared on several magazine covers and caught the eye of film producer Howard Hughes, who offered her a screen test. Before the test, she was signed by 20th Century-Fox, and changed her name soon after. Monroe received plenty of publicity, along with acting, singing, and dancing lessons, but nevertheless she appeared in no films. She finally debuted onscreen in a bit part in *Scudda-Hoo! Scudda-Hay!* (1948), but her brief appearance was almost entirely edited out of the film. After another bit role she was dropped by Fox. After continued acting classes, Columbia signed her in 1948 to play the lead in the low-budget musical *Ladies of the Chorus,* her first major film. Soon thereafter she was dropped by Columbia. Out of work, she posed for nude photographs (receiving $50), which later became famous but at first were used as part of a best-selling calendar. She managed to land small roles in several films, usually cast as a dumb blonde; Fox then re-signed her. Again there was a well organized publicity campaign, and gradually she landed better roles. She first attracted attention in supporting roles in *The Asphalt Jungle* and *All About Eve* (both 1950), but it was with *Gentlemen Prefer Blondes* (1953) that she became a major star; soon she was the screen's newest "sex goddess" and Fox's biggest box-office attraction. In January of 1954 she married legendary baseball player Joe DiMaggio; nine months later they were divorced. After several other major films, she left Fox and moved to New York, announcing the formation of her own company, Marilyn Monroe Productions, and explaining to a skeptical and mocking press that she wanted to play serious roles. She took acting classes at the Actors' Studio, studying with Lee and Paula Strasberg, and hung out with New York's intellectuals; there she met esteemed playwright Arthur Miller (who years later wrote a play based on the relationship, *After the Fall*), and the two of them were married in June of 1956 after she converted to Judaism. In December of 1955 Fox offered her a very lucrative contract and she accepted. Critics began to recognize her as a singularly talented actress and screen comedienne. Over the next several years her mental health deteriorated; she was frequently ill and depressed, and began to rely on pills to keep her going. She divorced Miller in January of 1961, a week before the opening of what was to be her last film, *The Misfits* (1961), with Clark Gable; it also turned out to be Gable's last film. A month later she entered a hospital for psychiatric care. In 1962 she began working on the film *Something's Got to Give*, but she was fired from the production after missing work too often. A month after she was fired, in August of 1962, she was found dead at home, having overdosed on barbiturates; it has never been determined whether her death was accidental or a suicide, and some have speculated that foul play was involved (due in part to her romantic entanglements with President John F. Kennedy and Attorney General Robert Kennedy). In death she became an international icon of almost mythical proportions, and has been the subject of many biographies and dramatic productions. **Selected Works:** *Bus Stop* (1956), *Seven Year Itch* (1955), *Some Like It Hot* (1959)

# Ricardo Montalban (Ricardo Gonzalo
Pedro Montalban y Merino)

**Born:** November 25, 1920; Mexico City, Mexico

**Years Active in the Industry:** by decade

| 10ˢ | 20ˢ | 30ˢ | 40ˢ | 50ˢ | 60ˢ | 70ˢ | 80ˢ | 90ˢ |
|-----|-----|-----|-----|-----|-----|-----|-----|-----|

Born in Mexico, Ricardo Montalban spent some of his youth in America and began his acting career in bit roles on Broadway. He debuted in Mexican films in 1941; after appearing in a number of productions he was signed in 1947 by MGM, which put him to work in "Latin lover" roles. After some time he managed to break out of this screen persona in non-romantic dramatic parts. Later Montalban began to perform on TV in a wide range of roles; he acted in many TV dramas, and was a semi-regular on *The Loretta Young Show* (Young was his sister-in-law). He remained sporadically busy in films, and also appeared in several Broadway plays; throughout his career he has continued to work onstage. He played the title role in a dramatic reading of Shaw's *Don Juan in Hell* which toured the U.S., costarring Agnes Moorehead and Paul Henreid. His greatest popularity came from his starring role on the TV series

*Fantasy Island* and his appearances on *The Colbys*, although he continues to make occasional films. For his work in the TV movie *How the West Was Won, Part II* (1978), he won an Emmy. His brother is actor Carlos Montalban, best known to the public as a character in a long-running series of coffee commercials. He authored an autobiography, *Reflections: A Life in Two Worlds* (1980). **Selected Works:** *Battleground* (1949), *Sayonara* (1957), *Star Trek 2: The Wrath of Khan* (1982)

# Yves Montand (Ivo Livi)

**Born:** October 13, 1921; Monsummano Alto, Florence, Italy
**Died:** November 8, 1991; Senlis, France

**Years Active in the Industry:** by decade

| 10ˢ | 20ˢ | 30ˢ | 40ˢ | 50ˢ | 60ˢ | 70ˢ | 80ˢ | 90ˢ |
|-----|-----|-----|-----|-----|-----|-----|-----|-----|

Italian-born, French-speaking actor/singer/composer Yves Montand sprang to fame after being discovered by the French singer Edith Piaf. Montand garnered acclaim for his starring role in

Henri Clouzot's suspense film *The Wages of Fear* (1952), starred opposite Marilyn Monroe in *Let's Make Love* (1960) and Barbra Streisand in *On a Clear Day You Can See Forever* (1969), and appeared as the villainous uncle in *Jean de Florette* (1986) and *Manon of the Spring* (1986). Other films include *Is Paris Burning?* (1966) and *Z* (1969), along with many French films over the years. Montand was married to Oscar-winning actress Simone Signoret, with whom he shared strong and controversial political convictions. **Selected Works:** *Confession* (1970)

# George Montgomery (George
Montgomery Letz)

**Born:** August 29, 1916; Brady, MT

**Years Active in the Industry:** by decade

| 10ˢ | 20ˢ | 30ˢ | 40ˢ | 50ˢ | 60ˢ | 70ˢ | 80ˢ | 90ˢ |
|-----|-----|-----|-----|-----|-----|-----|-----|-----|

Rugged, handsome, stalwart, taciturn leading man George Montgomery began appearing under his given name in low-budget films as an extra, stuntman, and bit player in 1935. He changed his name in 1940 when he began getting lead roles, going on to a busy screen career primarily in westerns and action films. For a time

Montgomery was very popular, receiving much publicity for his offscreen romances with such stars as Ginger Rogers, Hedy Lamarr, and Dinah Shore; he and Shore were married from 1943-62. Service in World War II interrupted his career, and after the war he was assigned mostly to minor productions. He starred in the late '50s TV series *Cimarron City*. In the early '60s Montgomery directed, produced, and wrote several low-budget action films shot in the Philippines. He was rarely onscreen after 1970.

# Demi Moore (Demi Guynes)

**Born:** November 11, 1962; Roswell, NM

**Years Active in the Industry:** by decade

| 10s | 20s | 30s | 40s | 50s | 60s | 70s | 80s | 90s |
|-----|-----|-----|-----|-----|-----|-----|-----|-----|
|     |     |     |     |     |     |     | ■   | ■   |

Demi Moore is a brunette leading lady with a husky voice. At age 15 she moved to Los Angeles, finding work as a model and occasionally landing roles on TV shows. In her late teens she became part of the cast of the TV soap opera *General Hospital,* where she remained for three years. She debuted onscreen in *Choices* (1981), going on to make several more films before getting her first lead role, in the teen-oriented romantic comedy *No Small Affair* (1984). After becoming a familiar screen presence over several years with roles in other popular fare such as *St. Elmo's Fire* (1985), *One Crazy Summer* (1986), and *About Last Night...* (1986), she starred in her first big hit, *Ghost* (1991). Her tearful, touching performance (as well as a steamy love scene involving Patrick Swayze and lots of wet clay) established her as a star and made her one of the highest paid, most in-demand actresses in Hollywood; her subsequent performances in *Indecent Proposal* (1993) and *Disclosure* (1994) as well as her nude *Vanity Fair* cover photos have capitalized on her undeniable sex appeal. Moore has also done some work onstage, and for her off-Broadway performance in *The Early Girl* she won a Theater World Award in 1987. She is married to actor Bruce Willis and has three daughters. **Selected Works:** *Few Good Men* (1992), *Mortal Thoughts* (1991), *Scarlet Letter* (1995), *Now and Then* (1995)

# Dudley Moore

**Born:** April 19, 1935; London, England

**Years Active in the Industry:** by decade

| 10s | 20s | 30s | 40s | 50s | 60s | 70s | 80s | 90s |
|-----|-----|-----|-----|-----|-----|-----|-----|-----|
|     |     |     |     |     | ■   | ■   | ■   | ■   |

A talented musician from an early age, British actor Dudley Moore went to Oxford University on a scholarship and earned a music degree in 1958. Skilled in jazz and comedy, his performances in university revues and cabaret brought him into contact with three other performers: Jonathan Miller, Alan Bennett, and Pe-

ter Cook. They developed a satirical show called *Beyond the Fringe* which became the hit of the 1960 Edinburgh Festival. Later they performed in the show for long runs in the West End and on Broadway. Moore and Cook later formed a comedy team and starred in a long-running BBC TV show, *Not Only ... But Also*. He debuted onscreen in *The Wrong Box* (1966), going on to make a handful of films over the next six years. After five years without film work, he appeared in his first Hollywood production, *Foul Play* (1978), with Goldie Hawn; his work brought him to the attention of director Blake Edwards, who cast him as the co-star of the hit comedy *10* (1979). After this film, the diminutive actor became an unlikely thinking-woman's sex symbol, going on to star in the very successful *Arthur* (1981), for which he received a Best Actor Oscar nomination. He has continued to sustain a fairly busy screen career, primarily as a romantic leading man in broad comedies. Moore has been married to actresses Suzy Kendall and Tuesday Weld, and once maintained a long-term relationship with the statuesque actress Susan Anton. **Selected Works:** *Blame It on the Bellboy* (1992), *Pickle* (1993), *Micki and Maude* (1984)

# Mary Tyler Moore

**Born:** December 29, 1937; Brooklyn, NY

**Years Active in the Industry:** by decade

| 10s | 20s | 30s | 40s | 50s | 60s | 70s | 80s | 90s |
|-----|-----|-----|-----|-----|-----|-----|-----|-----|
|     |     |     |     |     | ■   | ■   | ■   | ■   |

New York-born actress/dancer Mary Tyler Moore has starred in the definitive television comedies of both the 1960s and the 1970s: *The Dick Van Dyke Show* (1961-66) and *The Mary Tyler Moore Show* (1970-77). For her performances as Laura Petrie and Mary Richards, she won five Emmy Awards, in 1965, 1966, 1973, 1974, and 1976. Moore got her television start in commercials and then as the disembodied voice and legs of Sam, the answering service lady, on *Richard Diamond, Private Detective* (1957-1960). Three unsuccessful shows and a series of TV specials followed her more notable series: *Mary* (1978), *Mary* (1985-86), and the *Mary Tyler Moore Hour* (1979). Her dramatic career took off in 1981, when she was nominated for an Academy Award for her portrayal of the repressed mother in *Ordinary People* (1980). She made a success on Broadway in *Whose Life is it Anyway?*, appeared in the highly acclaimed *Finnegan, Begin Again* with Robert Preston on HBO and won a CableACE Award in 1993 for her performance as an evil orphanage director in *Stolen Babies*. A well-known diabetic, Moore has represented the Juvenile Diabetes Foundation. **Selected Works:** *Last Best Year* (1990)

# Roger Moore

**Born:** October 14, 1927; London, England

**Years Active in the Industry:** by decade

| 10s | 20s | 30s | 40s | 50s | 60s | 70s | 80s | 90s |
|-----|-----|-----|-----|-----|-----|-----|-----|-----|
|     |     | ■   | ■   | ■   | ■   | ■   | ■   | ■   |

The only child of a London policeman, Roger Moore grew up fat and miserable, ridiculed for his obesity by friends and family alike. Thinning out to the point of emaciation in his teen years, Moore began developing an interest in painting. While hanging out with London's "bohemian" art crowd, Moore picked up pocket money by working as a film extra, which led him to puruse acting seriously by attending the Royal Academy of Dramatic Art. He began his film, radio and stage career just after World War II (his early credits are often confused with American actor Roger Moore, a minor Columbia contractee of the 1940s), and also performed with a military entertainment unit. Signed on the basis of his good looks to an MGM contract in 1954, Moore began making appearances in American films, none of which amounted to much dramatically; his biggest success of the 1950s was as star of the British-filmed TV series *Ivanhoe*. Signed by Warner Bros. Television for the 1959 adventure weekly *The Alaskans*, Moore became the latest of a long line of James Garner surrogates on *Maverick*, appearing during the 1960-61 season as cousin Beau. After a few years in European films, Moore was chosen to play Simon Templar in the TV-series version of Leslie Charteris' *The Saint* (an earlier attempt at a *Saint* series with David Niven had fallen through). Moore remained with the series from 1963-67, occasionally directing a few episodes (he was never completely comfortable as an actor pure and simple, forever claiming that he was merely getting by on his face and physique). After another British TV series, 1971's *The Persuaders*, Moore was selected to replace Sean Connery in the James Bond films. His initial Bond effort was 1973's *Live and Let Die*, but the consensus (in which the actor heartily concurred) was that Moore didn't truly "grow" into character until 1977's *Spy Who Loved Me*. Few of Moore's non-Bond movie appearances of the 1970s and 1980s were notably successful, save for an amusing part as a Jewish mama's boy who *thinks* he's Bond in Burt Reynolds' *Cannonball Run* (1981). Moore's last 007 film was 1985's *A View to a Kill*. In 1991, Moore was made a special representative of UNICEF, an organization with which he'd been active since the 1960s. **Selected Works:** *Bed and Breakfast* (1992)

## Terry Moore (Helen Koford)

**Born:** January 7, 1929; Los Angeles, CA

**Years Active in the Industry:** by decade

| 10$^s$ | 20$^s$ | 30$^s$ | 40$^s$ | 50$^s$ | 60$^s$ | 70$^s$ | 80$^s$ | 90$^s$ |
|---|---|---|---|---|---|---|---|---|

Terry Moore was born Helen Koford; during her screen career she was billed as Helen Koford, Judy Ford, Jan Ford, and (from 1949) Terry Moore. She debuted onscreen at age 11 in 1940 and went on to play adolescent roles in a number of films. As an adult actress, the well-endowed Moore fell into the late-'40s/early-'50s "sexpot" mold, and was fairly busy onscreen until 1960; after that her screen work was infrequent, though she ultimately appeared in more than a half-dozen additional films. She claimed she was secretly wed to billionaire Howard Hughes in 1949, and that

they were never divorced; for years she sued Hughes' estate for part of his will, and finally was given an undisclosed sum in an out-of-court settlement. She wrote a book detailing her secret life with Hughes from 1947-56, *The Beauty and the Billionaire*, in 1984; she claimed she bore him a stillborn baby in 1952. She has had a number of other widely-publicized offscreen affairs and marriages as well. For her work in *Come Back, Little Sheba* (1952) she received a Best Supporting Actress Oscar nomination. She co-produced the film *Beverly Hills Brat* (1989), in which she also appeared. **Selected Works:** *Gaslight* (1944), *Peyton Place* (1957), *Marilyn and Me* (1991)

## Agnes Moorehead

**Born:** December 6, 1906; Clinton, MA
**Died:** 1974

**Years Active in the Industry:** by decade

| 10$^s$ | 20$^s$ | 30$^s$ | 40$^s$ | 50$^s$ | 60$^s$ | 70$^s$ | 80$^s$ | 90$^s$ |
|---|---|---|---|---|---|---|---|---|

At age three Agnes Moorehead first appeared onstage, and at 11 she made her professional debut in the ballet and chorus of the St. Louis Opera. As a teenager she regularly sang on local radio. She earned a Ph.D. in literature and studied theater at the American Academy of Dramatic Arts. She began playing small roles on Broadway in 1928; shortly thereafter she shifted her focus to radio acting, becoming a regular on the radio shows *March of Time*, *Cavalcade of America*, and a soap opera series. She toured in vaudeville from 1933-36 with Phil Baker. In 1940 she joined Orson Welles's Mercury Theater Company, giving a great boost to her career. Moorehead debuted onscreen as Kane's mother in Welles's film *Citizen Kane* (1941). Her second film was Welles's *The Magnificent Ambersons* (1942), for which she received a Best Supporting Actress Oscar nomination; ultimately she was nominated for an Oscars five times, never winning. In films, she tended to play authoritarian, neurotic, puritanical, or soured women, but also played a wide range of other roles, and was last onscreen in 1972. In the '50s she toured the U.S. with a stellar cast giving dramatic readings of Shaw's *Don Juan in Hell*. In 1954 she began touring in *The Fabulous Redhead*, a one-woman show she eventually took to over 200 cities across the world. She was also active on TV; later audiences remember her best as the witch Endora, Elizabeth Montgomery's mother, in the '60s TV sitcom *Bewitched*. Moorehead's last professional engagement was in the Broadway musical *Gigi*. She died of lung cancer in 1974. She was married to actors John Griffith Lee (1930-52) and Robert Gist (1953-58). **Selected Works:** *Johnny Belinda* (1948), *Mrs. Parkington* (1944), *Seventh Cross* (1944), *Since You Went Away* (1944), *Caged* (1950)

## Rick Moranis

**Born:** April 18, 1954; Toronto, Ontario, Canada

**Years Active in the Industry:** by decade

| 10ˢ | 20ˢ | 30ˢ | 40ˢ | 50ˢ | 60ˢ | 70ˢ | 80ˢ | 90ˢ |
|-----|-----|-----|-----|-----|-----|-----|-----|-----|
|     |     |     |     |     |     |     | ▓   | ▓   |

Funny man Rick Moranis began his professional career hosting a comedy show on radio, and went on to perform in Toronto night clubs, cabarets, and TV. He came to prominence on the sketch-comedy TV series *SCTV*; during the long run of that show he and Dave Thomas created the McKenzie Brothers, beer-drinking Canadians who hosted their own short TV show, and in 1983 the McKenzies were brought to the big screen film in Moranis's screen debut *Strange Brew*, which he co-directed and co-wrote. He has gone on to a busy screen career, often playing goofy nerdy types. He has appeared in several blockbusters, including *Ghostbusters* (1984) and *Parenthood* (1989); his first lead role in a box-office smash came with *Honey, I Shrunk the Kids* (1989), and he brought cartoon sidekick Barney Rubble to life in *The Flintstones* (1994). **Selected Works:** *Honey, I Blew up the Kid* (1992), *Little Shop of Horrors* (1986), *My Blue Heaven* (1990)

# Jeanne Moreau

**Born:** January 23, 1928; Paris, France

**Years Active in the Industry:** by decade

| 10ˢ | 20ˢ | 30ˢ | 40ˢ | 50ˢ | 60ˢ | 70ˢ | 80ˢ | 90ˢ |
|-----|-----|-----|-----|-----|-----|-----|-----|-----|
|     |     |     | ▓   | ▓   | ▓   | ▓   | ▓   | ▓   |

After training at the Paris Conservatory, French actress Jeanne Moreau did extensive stage work and some bits in films. Not considered "pretty enough" for movie stardom—principally

because she disdained the makeup table—Jeanne was fortunate enough to make the acquaintance of a director who found her unadorned beauty ideal for the screen—Louis Malle, who directed the actress in her first film success, the "new wave" murder mystery *Frantic* (1957). So far as Moreau is concerned, *Frantic* constitutes her true film debut. She remained Malles' favorite actress and off-screen lover for the next several years; their 1958 collaboration *The Lovers* was steamy enough to be banned in certain parts of the U.S., leading certain American gossip columnists to tag Moreau as "the new Bardot." Her first international success was as the enigmatic, free-spirited heroine of Francois Truffault's *Jules et Jim* (1962); for the same di-

rector, she starred as an icy murderess in the popular Hitchcock derivation *The Bride Wore Black* (1967). Still regally beautiful in her 40s, Moreau began accepting the worldly, Colette-style character roles that she seems to enjoy far more than her sensual leading-lady assignments. Linked romantically with dozens of high-profile males over the years, Moreau was for a brief period married to *Exorcist* director William Friedkin, though she was far too independent and strong-willed to settle for being a mere "Hollywood Wife." Averaging two to three film and/or television appearances per year, Moreau has also directed a brace of self-reflective features, *Lumiere* (1976) and *The Adolescent* (1979). Though she both looks and admits her age, Jeanne Moreau still possesses one of the classic screen faces and remains one of filmdom's most luminescent actresses. **Selected Works:** *Map of the Human Heart* (1993), *Until the End of the World* (1991), *La Femme Nikita* (1990), *Viva Maria* (1965), *Summer House* (1993)

# Frank Morgan (Francis Phillip Wupperman)

**Born:** June 1, 1890; New York, NY
**Died:** September 18, 1949

**Years Active in the Industry:** by decade

| 10ˢ | 20ˢ | 30ˢ | 40ˢ | 50ˢ | 60ˢ | 70ˢ | 80ˢ | 90ˢ |
|-----|-----|-----|-----|-----|-----|-----|-----|-----|
| ▓   | ▓   | ▓   | ▓   |     |     |     |     |     |

Years before he played The Wizard (and four other roles) in *The Wizard of Oz* (1939), Frank Morgan had a long career in silent film and was nominated for a Best Actor Oscar for *The Affairs of Cellini* (1934). Although adept at flustered and bewildered comic roles, Morgan was also an excellent dramatic actor; he was an ever-present figure in many of MGM's classiest films of the period. Highlights of his career include: *Hallelujah, I'm a Bum* (1931), *When Ladies Meet* (1933), *Bombshell* (1933), *Cat and the Fiddle* (1934), *The Good Fairy* (1935), *Naughty Marietta* (1935), *Dimples* (1936), *The Last of Mrs. Cheyney* (1937), *Saratoga* (1937), *Rosalie* (1937), *Boom Town* (1940), *Broadway Melody of 1940* (1940), and *The Three Musketeers* (1948). He was especially effective in *The Shop Around the Corner* (1940), *The Mortal Storm* (1940), *The Human Comedy* (1943) and *Summer Holiday* (1948), the musical remake of Thornton Wilder's *Ah, Wilderness*. Morgan died while filming *Annie Get Your Gun,* in which he would have played Buffalo Bill. The most famous anecdote about Morgan is that while rehearsing for *The Wizard of Oz*, he went looking for a coat to help him feel like Prof. Marvel; the one he found in a second-hand shop turned out to have originally belonged to *Wizard* author L. Frank Baum. **Selected Works:** *Great Ziegfeld* (1936), *Tortilla Flat* (1942), *Laughter* (1930)

# Harry Morgan

**Born:** April 10, 1915; Detroit, MI

**Years Active in the Industry:** by decade

| 10s | 20s | 30s | 40s | 50s | 60s | 70s | 80s | 90s |
|-----|-----|-----|-----|-----|-----|-----|-----|-----|

Harry Morgan is one of the most prolific and versatile actors in television history. He has starred or co-starred in eleven different TV series and is best known for his roles as Col. Sherman Potter on *M*A*S*H* from 1975-83 and as Officer Bill Gannon on Jack Webb's second version of *Dragnet* (1967-70). Originally using the name Henry Morgan, the slight actor made his film debut in 1942 in *To the Shores of Tripoli.* He is most recognizable in *Dragonwyck* (1946), *The Glenn Miller Story* (1953), *Inherit the Wind* (1960), and *Support Your Local Sheriff* (1969). But television has always been Morgan's forte; he's worked continuously on TV since the 1950s. He has played a wide variety of roles in his television and film appearances, displaying an acting brilliance that is not often acknowledged. Series include: *December Bride* (1954-58), *Pete and Gladys* (1960-62), *The Richard Boone Show* (1964), *Kentucky Jones* (1964-65), *The D.A.* (1971), *Hec Ramsey* (1972-74), *Aftermash* (1983-84), *Blacke's Magic* (1986), and *You Can't Take It With You* (1987). Morgan won an Emmy Award in 1980 for his performance in *M*A*S*H.* **Selected Works:** *Not As a Stranger* (1955), *Ox-Bow Incident* (1943), *Shootist* (1976), *Well* (1951), *Against Her Will: An Incident in Baltimore* (1992)

# Pat Morita (Noriyuki Morita)

**Born:** June 28, 1936; Berkeley, CA

**Years Active in the Industry:** by decade

| 10s | 20s | 30s | 40s | 50s | 60s | 70s | 80s | 90s |
|-----|-----|-----|-----|-----|-----|-----|-----|-----|

Billed in his nightclub days as "the Hip Nip," actor/comedian Pat Morita learned to make people laugh as a defense mechanism against the bigotry greeting Japanese-Americans during and after World War II. Morita's first important club engagement was at the Copa in 1964, the result of an error: the manager had thought "Pat Morita" was an Italian comedian like "Pat Cooper." In his first film, *Thoroughly Modern Millie* (1967), Morita was compelled to wear "Comic Jap" glasses and costuming in his role as one of Bea Lillie's henchmen—something he's seldom had to lower himself to do since. Morita's career moved smoothly if not spectacularly until 1974, when he was hired to play malt-shop owner Arnold on the high-rated sitcom *Happy Days.* He spoke "pidgin English" again, but this time around Morita's character had an innate dignity and humanity that transcended the stereotype. He left *Happy Days* in 1976 for a series of his own, *Mr. T and Tina,* which is widely regarded by media historians as one of the worst situation-comedies in history. He was far better served as star of the detective series *Ohara* in 1987, which survived two seasons and several format changes. Billing himself under his own name, Noriyuki Morita, the actor enjoyed his biggest commercial success as Mr. Miyagi, the

black-belt karate champ and parttime janitor in *The Karate Kid* (1982). Morita would play Miyagi in three sequels over the next twelve years; in the most recent one, *The Next Karate Kid* (1994), he taught the rudiments of Japanese self-defense to a teenaged girl. Morita is so firmly entrenched as a film actor in the 1990s that it was hard to remember those hilarious days back in the 1960s when "the Hip Nip" fractured audiences with jokes rather than karate chops. **Selected Works:** *Auntie Lee's Meat Pies* (1992), *Hiroshima: Out of the Ashes* (1990), *Honeymoon in Vegas* (1992)

# Robert Morley

**Born:** May 25, 1908; Semley, Wiltshire, England
**Died:** June 3, 1992; Reading, England

**Years Active in the Industry:** by decade

| 10s | 20s | 30s | 40s | 50s | 60s | 70s | 80s | 90s |
|-----|-----|-----|-----|-----|-----|-----|-----|-----|

A charming, rotund, portly, double-chinned character actor of British and American stage and screen, Robert Morley tended to be cast in jovial or pompous comedic roles. He was educated in England, Germany, France, and Italy, intending to go into diplomacy. He switched to acting and studied theater at London's Royal Academy of Dramatic Art. Morley debuted on the London stage in 1929, and on Broadway in 1938 when he reprised his London performance in the title role of *Oscar Wilde.* Also in 1938, he debuted onscreen in the Hollywood film *Marie Antoinette,* portraying the feeble-minded Louis XVI opposite Norma Shearer; for that performance he received a Best Supporting Actor Oscar nomination. He went on to play supporting roles in many films on both sides of the Atlantic. He was also a playwright; one of his plays, *Edward My Son* (written with Noel Langley), became a film in 1949. He was frequently seen as a witty, erudite guest on TV talk shows, and he was the TV commercial spokesman for British Airways. **Selected Works:** *African Queen* (1951), *Major Barbara* (1941), *Those Magnificent Men in Their Flying Machines* (1965), *Topkapi* (1964), *Little Dorrit* (1989)

# Ennio Morricone

**Born:** October 11, 1928; Rome, Italy

**Years Active in the Industry:** by decade

| 10s | 20s | 30s | 40s | 50s | 60s | 70s | 80s | 90s |
|-----|-----|-----|-----|-----|-----|-----|-----|-----|

Ennio Morricone is one of the most prolific composers in international cinema. He is known for his versatility and has scored over 350 films ranging from dramas, light farces, spaghetti westerns, thrillers, and epic spectacles. Occasionally Morricone works under the stage name Leo Nichols. He received his musical education at the Accademia di Santa Cecilia, Rome, and began writing movie music in the early '60s. Morricone's most recognizable tune is the haunting theme from Sergio Leone's classic western, *A Fistful of Dollars* (1964); he went on to score many more of Leone's films. Other directors he has worked for include Bertolucci, De Palma, and Polanski. **Selected Works:** *Bugsy* (1991), *Cinema Paradiso* (1988), *Days of Heaven* (1978), *Untouchables* (1987), *Love Affair* (1994)

# Paul Morrissey

**Born:** 1939; New York, NY

**Years Active in the Industry:** by decade

| 10s | 20s | 30s | 40s | 50s | 60s | 70s | 80s | 90s |
|-----|-----|-----|-----|-----|-----|-----|-----|-----|

Paul Morrissey began making underground short films in the early 1960s, and soon became a production assistant for Andy Warhol. He was the cameraman on several Warhol films, including *Lonesome Cowboys;* the two co-directed the transvestite comedy *Women in Revolt* and *L'Amour* (1973). With Warhol as producer, Morrissey made several outstanding films starring Joe Dallesandro, most notably his early comedies *Flesh* (1968), *Trash* (1970), and *Heat* (1972), and the stylish horror films *Andy Warhol's Frankenstein* (aka *Flesh For Frankenstein* [1974]) and *Andy Warhol's Dracula* (aka *Blood For Dracula* [1974]). Morrissey's major works on his own include his offbeat tales of teenage hustlers (*Forty Deuce* [1982]) and drug pushers (*Mixed Blood* [1984]), the historical drama *Beethoven's Nephew* (1985), and the comedy *Spike of Bensonhurst* (1988).

# Rob Morrow

**Born:** July 21, 1962; Westchester County, NY

**Years Active in the Industry:** by decade

| 10s | 20s | 30s | 40s | 50s | 60s | 70s | 80s | 90s |
|-----|-----|-----|-----|-----|-----|-----|-----|-----|

Supporting himself as a waiter and balloon messenger in his earliest acting days, Morrow made his prime time network TV debut in 1988 as Marco on the weekly dramatic series *Tattinger's*. A year later, he was up for the lead in a planned series called *The Antagonists*, but he opted instead for a tailor-made role in the shortlived stage play *The Substance of Fire*. Though warned by his agent that this move would cost him any future TV work, Morrow went on to achieve fame in 1990 as Dr. Joel Fleischman, the misplaced general practitioner of Cicely, Alaska, on CBS' *Northern Exposure*. Two years into the series, Morrow threatened to quit if he wasn't given a substantial pay hike; but when September rolled around, Morrow was back as Dr. Fleischman. Morrow left *Northern Exposure* for good in 1994 (the series was obviously on its last legs anyway), but not before appearing as cigar-chomping,

Boston-accented, fiercely moralistic federal attorney Richard Goodwin in *Quiz Show*, the 1994 film re-enactment of the 1958 TV game-show cheating scandal.

# Joe Morton

**Born:** October 18, 1948; New York, NY

**Years Active in the Industry:** by decade

| 10s | 20s | 30s | 40s | 50s | 60s | 70s | 80s | 90s |
|-----|-----|-----|-----|-----|-----|-----|-----|-----|

Joe Morton is an African American supporting actor known for his serious, intellectual demeanor on film, and is typically cast as a doctor, lawyer, scientist, or elected official. In addition to feature film, Morton has also appeared on stage and TV. He began on the stage and made his debut in 1968's *Hair*. Morton became well-known for his subsequent work in Broadway musicals and earned a Tony nomination for his role in *A Raisin in the Sun*. Morton has also appeared on several TV series. He made a critically acclaimed feature film debut in *The Brother from Another Planet* (1984), but he is best known as the scientist who researched cyborg components in *Terminator 2: Judgement Day* (1991). **Selected Works:** *Forever Young* (1992), *Legacy of Lies* (1992), *Of Mice and Men* (1992), *Speed* (1994)

# Zero Mostel (Samuel Joel Mostel)

**Born:** February 28, 1915; Brooklyn, NY
**Died:** 1977

**Years Active in the Industry:** by decade

| 10s | 20s | 30s | 40s | 50s | 60s | 70s | 80s | 90s |
|-----|-----|-----|-----|-----|-----|-----|-----|-----|

Before he turned to performing, Zero Mostel intended to be a painter, but by his late 20s he had begun appearing in nightclubs and on radio. A few Hollywood films followed: *DuBarry Was A Lady* (1943), *Panic in the Streets* (1950), and *The Enforcer* (1951), among other early '50s films. Unfortunately, his career was amputated when he became a victim of Hollywood's McCarthy-era blacklisting, and he would not work again until the end of the decade. His talent was rewarded when he won three Tony Awards for his Broadway appear-

ances in *Rhinoceros*, *A Funny Thing Happened on the Way to the Forum*, which he repeated for the screen in 1966, and *Fiddler on the Roof*. He followed *Forum* with one of the classic comedy performances of all time, producer Max Bialystock in Mel Brooks' *The Producers* (1968). Almost all of Mostel's performances are worth watching, but especially *The Angel Levine* (1970), *The Hot Rock* (1972), and his poignant, heart-rending performance as a blacklisted TV comic in *The Front* (1976). Mostel's final appearance was in the Academy Award-winning documentary *Best Boy* (1979). His son is actor Josh Mostel. **Selected Works:** *Model and the Marriage Broker* (1951)

# Alan Mowbray

**Born:** August 18, 1896; London, England
**Died:** March 26, 1969; Hollywood, CA

**Years Active in the Industry:** by decade

| 10s | 20s | 30s | 40s | 50s | 60s | 70s | 80s | 90s |
|-----|-----|-----|-----|-----|-----|-----|-----|-----|
|     |     |     |     |     |     |     |     |     |

Born to a non-theatrical British family, Alan Mowbray was in his later years vague concerning the exact date that he took to the stage. In some accounts, he was touring the provinces before joining the British Navy in World War I; in others, he turned to acting *after* the war, purportedly because he was broke and had no discernable "practical" skills. No matter when he began, Mowbray climbed relatively quickly to Broadway and London stardom, spending several seasons on the road with the Theatre Guild; his favorite stage parts were those conceived by Bernard Shaw and Noel Coward. Turning to films in the early talkie era, Mobray received good notices for his portrayal of George Washington in 1931's *Alexander Hamilton* (a characterization he'd repeat along more comic lines for the 1945 musical *Where Do We Go From Here?*). He also had the distinction of appearing with *three* of the screen's Sherlock Holmeses: Clive Brook (*Sherlock Holmes* [1932]), Reginald Owen (*A Study in Scarlet* [1933], in which Mowbray played Lestrade) and Basil Rathbone (*Terror by Night* [1946]). John Ford fans will remember Mobray's brace of appearances as alcoholic ham actors in *My Darling Clementine* (1946) and *Wagonmaster* (1950). Lovers of films comedies might recall Mowbray's turns as the long-suffering butler in the first two *Topper* films and as The Devil Himself (as he was billed) in the 1942 Hal Roach "streamliner" *The Devil With Hitler*. And there was one bonafide romantic lead (in Technicolor yet), opposite Miriam Hopkins in *Becky Sharp* (1935). Otherwise, Mowbray was shown to best advantage in his many "pompous blowhard" roles, and in his frequent appearances as the "surprise" killer in murder mysteries (*Charlie Chan in London*, *The Case Against Mrs. Ames*, *Abbott and Costello Meet the Killer: Boris Karloff*, and so many others). In his off hours, Mowbray was a member of several acting fraternities, and also of the Royal Geographic Society. One of Alan Mowbray's favorite roles was as the softhearted con-man protagonist in the TV series *Colonel Humphrey Flack*, which ran on the Dumont net-

work in 1953, then as a syndicated series in 1958. **Selected Works:** *King and I* (1956), *My Man Godfrey* (1936), *Merrily We Live* (1938)

# Dermot Mulroney

**Born:** October 31, 1963; Alexandria, VA

**Years Active in the Industry:** by decade

| 10s | 20s | 30s | 40s | 50s | 60s | 70s | 80s | 90s |
|-----|-----|-----|-----|-----|-----|-----|-----|-----|
|     |     |     |     |     |     |     | ■   | ■   |

American actor Dermot Mulroney is decidedly in tune with the 1990s: his film characters are often eccentric, unpredictable, and total strangers to personal hygiene. Curiously, when called upon to appear as a scruffy street kid in *Where the Day Takes You* (1992), Mulroney seemed a bit too squeaky-clean. An alumnus of Northwestern University, he first made moviegoers' acquaintance in 1988 with *Sunset* and as part of the Brat Pack western *Young Guns*. In the acclaimed *Longtime Companion* (1990), Mulroney played a collar-and-tie type who was still essentially an outsider due to the character's homosexuality and vulnerability to AIDS. Much of Mulroney's subsequent work has gone largely unseen, including the dismal *Bad Girls* (1994). **Selected Works:** *Bright Angel* (1991), *Point of No Return* (1993), *Samantha* (1992), *The Thing Called Love* (1993)

# Paul Muni (Muni Weisenfreund)

**Born:** September 22, 1895; Lemberg, Austria (Lvov, Russia)
**Died:** 1967

**Years Active in the Industry:** by decade

| 10s | 20s | 30s | 40s | 50s | 60s | 70s | 80s | 90s |
|-----|-----|-----|-----|-----|-----|-----|-----|-----|
|     | ■   |     |     |     |     |     |     |     |

Paul Muni was an intense dramatic stage and film actor who got his start as a child actor in the Yiddish theater. After he appeared on Broadway, he was signed to a movie contract. Muni be-

came famous for *Scarface* (1932) and *I Am a Fugitive from a Chain Gang* (1932) before making a succession of highly acclaimed dramatic biographical films that include *The Good Earth* (1937), *Juarez* (1939), and *Angel on My Shoulder* (1946). Muni only made 22 films in 30 years, but he was nominated five times for an Academy

Award, for *The Valiant* (1929), *I Am a Fugitive from a Chain Gang*, *The Life of Emile Zola* (1937), and *The Last Angry Man* (1959), winning in 1936 for *The Story of Louis Pasteur*. In 1956, he won a Tony for *Inherit the Wind*. Failing eyesight ended his career in 1959.

# F.W. Murnau (Friedrich Wilhelm Plumpe)

**Born:** December 28, 1888; Bielefeld, Germany
**Died:** March 11, 1931; Southern CA

**Years Active in the Industry:** by decade

| 10s | 20s | 30s | 40s | 50s | 60s | 70s | 80s | 90s |
|-----|-----|-----|-----|-----|-----|-----|-----|-----|

To this day German filmmaker F. W. Murnau remains one of the most influential directors of cinema. After studying art and literature history at the University of Heidelberg, he became a student of director Max Reinhardt until serving in World War I as a combat pilot. During a flight, he accidentally strayed into Switzerland and stayed there till the war's end. He made his directorial debut in 1919 back in Germany; although he made several films over the next three years, most of them have been lost. Murnau first gained international renown with *Nosferatu the Vampire* in 1922. Unlike others, Murnau filmed this still chilling masterpiece on location. His next film, *The Last Laugh* (1924), utilized unique camera techniques that later became the basis for mise-en-scene. He continued making German films, notable for their pessimism and pervading sense of doom, until he moved to Hollywood in 1926 to work for Fox studios. His first American film, *Sunrise: A Story of Two Humans* (1927), is considered to be the apex of German silent cinema, and was internationally acclaimed. He made two more films at Fox, and then teamed up with famed documentarist Robert Flaherty. Together they made *Tabu* (1931), which was shot in the South Seas. Their artistic visions for the work differed dramatically, and eventually Murnau bought up Flaherty's share and finished it himself. The film became a box-office hit, but the week before it opened, Murnau was killed in an auto accident. He was only 42.

# Audie Murphy

**Born:** June 20, 1924; Kingston, TX
**Died:** 1971

**Years Active in the Industry:** by decade

| 10s | 20s | 30s | 40s | 50s | 60s | 70s | 80s | 90s |
|-----|-----|-----|-----|-----|-----|-----|-----|-----|

Brought up in poverty, Audie Murphy became famous for receiving more decorations than any other GI in World War II (24, including the Congressional Medal of Honor). Handsome in a boyish, baby-faced way, he was invited to Hollywood and debuted on-screen in a bit part in *Beyond Glory* (1948); he soon began playing leads as the heroes of low-budget westerns. He played himself in the biopic *To Hell and Back* (1955), based on his 1949 memoir of the same name, which described his wartime experiences. He had a steady screen career through the mid-'60s, then ran into serious business problems; he declared bankruptcy in 1968. In 1970, Murphy severely beat a man during a barroom fight; he was later cleared of attempted murder charges for the incident. He produced the film *A Time for Dying* (1971), in which he portrayed Jesse James. Murphy died in a plane crash at age 46. He was married from 1949-50 to actress Wanda Hendrix, with whom he appeared in *Sierra* (1950). **Selected Works:** *Red Badge of Courage* (1951)

# Eddie Murphy

**Born:** April 3, 1961; Hempstead, NY

**Years Active in the Industry:** by decade

| 10s | 20s | 30s | 40s | 50s | 60s | 70s | 80s | 90s |
|-----|-----|-----|-----|-----|-----|-----|-----|-----|

Eddie Murphy discovered in his mid-teens that he could make people laugh, and began doing stand-up comedy for $25-$50 a night in Long Island clubs. At 17 he appeared at Manhattan's

Comic Strip Club, got a new manager, and went on to tour clubs along the east coast. In 1980 he was signed as a part-time performer on the TV sketch-comedy series *Saturday Night Live;* the series had its all-time worst year, and quickly Murphy rose to dominate the show as its only true new star, known especially for the characters he portrayed, including Buckwheat ("Oh Tay!), Gumby, ("I'm Gumby, dammit!), Velvet Jones, and Mr. Robinson (of Mr. Robinson's Neighborhood). He was soon signed to his debut film, *48 Hrs.* (1982), which became a smash hit. He went on to make a couple of concert films and starred in the blockbuster, including *Beverly Hills Cop* (1984); he even launched a singing career, and for while he was the hottest property in Hollywood (with the biggest entourage). In the mid-'80s his appeal waned (especially after the abysmal *Harlem Nights* [1989], which he starred in, directed, wrote, and produced), and several of his films were unsuccessful. A string of comeback movies in the '90s, however, have fared moderately, including *Boomerang* (1992) and *The Distinguished Gentleman* (1992), although his third turn as renegade cop Axel Foley in *Beverly Hills Cop 3* (1994) was a flop. **Selected Works:** *Trading Places* (1983)

# George Murphy

**Born:** July 4, 1902; New Haven, CT
**Died:** May 3, 1992; Palm Beach FL

**Years Active in the Industry:** by decade

| 10s | 20s | 30s | 40s | 50s | 60s | 70s | 80s | 90s |
|-----|-----|-----|-----|-----|-----|-----|-----|-----|
|     |     |  █  |  █  |     |     |     |     |     |

Actor George Murphy was the son of an Olympic track coach. He tried the Navy at age 15, but soon returned home to complete his high school and college education. He never finished college, choosing instead to pursue a dancing career. In 1927, Murphy and his partner-wife Julie Johnson made it to Broadway; by the early 1930s Mrs. Murphy had retired and George had become a star solo dancer. He made his screen bow in support of Eddie Cantor, Ethel Merman, and Ann Sothern in *Kid Millions* (1934). Never a major star, Murphy was an agreeable presence in several big-budget musicals of the 1930s and 1940s, and later essayed straight dramatic parts in such films as *Border Incident* (1949) and *Battleground* (1949). He also crossed paths with two of his future fellow Republican politicos, dancing with Shirley Temple in *Little Miss Broadway* (1938) and playing the father of Ronald Reagan (nine years Murphy's junior!) in *This Is the Army* (1943). Like Reagan, Murphy was a Democrat until becoming involved in intra-Hollywood politics. Changing to Republicanism in 1939, Murphy worked to cement relationships between local government and the movie industry, and in 1945 he served the first of two terms as President of the Screen Actors Guild (Reagan was, of course, one of his successors). After his last film, an odd MGM second feature about mob mentality titled *Talk About a Stranger* (1952), Murphy retired from show business to devote his full time to political and business activities. He was instrumental in getting Desilu Studios, the TV factory created by Desi Arnaz and Lucille Ball, off the ground in the late 1950s, serving for several years on its board of directors. Murphy became one of the first actors to throw his hat into the political arena in 1964 when he was elected to the U.S. Senate. Despite throat surgery which prevented him from speaking above a hoarse whisper, Murphy remained active in Republican circles into the 1970s, helping smooth the path to several elections of increasing importance for his old pal Ronald Reagan. **Selected Works:** *Tom, Dick, & Harry* (1941)

# Bill Murray

**Born:** September 21, 1950; Chicago, IL

**Years Active in the Industry:** by decade

| 10s | 20s | 30s | 40s | 50s | 60s | 70s | 80s | 90s |
|-----|-----|-----|-----|-----|-----|-----|-----|-----|
|     |     |     |     |     |     |  █  |     |     |

After a brief stint as a pre-med student, Bill Murray joined Chicago's famed improvisational troupe Second City, where his brother Brian Doyle-Murray already worked. He went on to work

with his brother as a duo on the *National Lampoon Radio Hour* and then in the off-Broadway revue *The National Lampoon Show*. He also provided the voice of Johnny Storm (the Human Torch) on the Marvel Comics radio show *The Fantastic Four*. After Chevy Chase left the ensemble cast of the hot TV sketch-comedy series *Saturday Night Live*, Murray was hired to replace him, first appearing in late 1976. The show appealed strongly to the demographically powerful audience of teens and twenty-somethings, and established a number of stars; by the time Murray left in 1980 he was a famous comedic performer. Having appeared in a couple of minor films, he starred in the low-budget comedy *Meatballs* (1979), which became a surprise hit; he went on to appear in two more hits, *Caddyshack* (1980) and *Stripes* (1981), after which he was much in demand in Hollywood. He also starred in the remake of *The Razor's Edge* (1984), then co-starred in the blockbuster comedy *Ghostbusters* (1984), which in terms of box office receipts became the most successful comedy ever. He has sustained a successful career since; he co-directed one of his films, *Quick Change* (1990), and appeared in the clever *Groundhog Day* (1993) and peculiar *Ed Wood* (1994). **Selected Works:** *Little Shop of Horrors* (1986), *Mad Dog and Glory* (1993), *What About Bob?* (1991)

# Mike Myers

**Born:** May 25, 1963; Scarborough, Canada

**Years Active in the Industry:** by decade

| 10s | 20s | 30s | 40s | 50s | 60s | 70s | 80s | 90s |
|-----|-----|-----|-----|-----|-----|-----|-----|-----|
|     |     |     |     |     |     |     |     |  █  |

Emmy-winning comic actor Mike Myers seemed destined by fate to link up with *Saturday Night Live*; when he made his TV debut as a commercial actor at age eight, his costar (playing his mother) was pre-*SNL* Gilda Radner. Working steadily in his native Canada, Myers was a member of Toronto's Second City troupe, the star of his own TV series *Mullarkey and Myers* at age twenty, and the "veejay" of an all-night Canadian music video show in 1987. In all of these career stepping stones, Myers continued testing out the comic characterizations that would win him fame in his *SNL* days. His most popular character (which he'd been doing at parties since high school) was spacey teenage coach potato Wayne Campbell, who with equally airheaded best friend Garth Algar (Dana Carvey) hosted the Aurora, Illinois, cable-access series *Wayne's World*. This *SNL* skit begat a popular

*Wayne's World, Part 2* (1993)

like-titled film in 1992, and a less popular 1993 sequel. Despite the tepid response to *Wayne's World II*, it would seem that Mike Myers as Wayne is more readily accept-able to film fans than Mike Myers as Anyone Else, if the disappoint-ing 1993 comedy *So I Married an Axe Mur-derer* is any indication. **Selected     Works:**

# Conrad Nagel

**Born:** March 16, 1897; Keokuk, IA
**Died:** 1970

**Years Active in the Industry:** by decade

| 10s | 20s | 30s | 40s | 50s | 60s | 70s | 80s | 90s |
|-----|-----|-----|-----|-----|-----|-----|-----|-----|
|     |     |     |     |     |     |     |     |     |

In 1914 Nagel began acting professionally onstage. He broke into films in 1918 and soon became one of the top (and most suave) matinee idols of the silent screen. After an extremely busy career in silents, he starred in one of the first talkies, *Glorious Betsy* (1928); his voice and performance were impressive, and he was thereafter much in demand for sound films. He directed one film, *Love Takes Flight* (1937). Nagel remained intermittently busy as a screen actor until 1940, after which he appeared in only a handful of additional films. He starred on both radio and Broadway in the '40s. He was a co-founder of the Academy of Motion Picture Arts and served for a time as its president, and he was involved in the creation of the Academy Awards. Until his death he was president of the Associated Actors and Artists of America. In 1947 he was awarded a special Oscar for his work on the Motion Picture Relief Fund. He hosted the TV drama anthology series "The Silver Theater" (having long hosted its earlier radio incarnation) and was the MC of the TV quiz show "Celebrity Time."

# J. Carrol Naish (Joseph Patrick Carrol Naish)

**Born:** January 21, 1897; New York, NY
**Died:** January 24, 1973; La Jolla, CA

**Years Active in the Industry:** by decade

| 10s | 20s | 30s | 40s | 50s | 60s | 70s | 80s | 90s |
|-----|-----|-----|-----|-----|-----|-----|-----|-----|
|     |     |     |     |     |     |     |     |     |

Though descended from a highly respected family of Irish politicians and civil servants, actor J. Carroll Naish played every sort of nationality *except* Irish during his long career. Naish joined the Navy at age sixteen, and spent the next decade travelling all over the world, absorbing the languages, dialects and customs of several nations. Drifting from job to job while stranded in California, Naish began picking up extra work in Hollywood films. The acting bug took hold, and Naish made his stage debut in a 1926 touring company of *The Shanghai Gesture*. Within five years he was a well-established member of the theatrical community (the legendary actress Mrs. Leslie Carter was the godmother of Naish's daughter). Naish thrived during the early days of talking pictures thanks to his expertise in a limitless variety of foreign dialects. At various times he was seen as Chinese, Japanese, a Frenchman, a South Seas Islander, Portuguese, an Italian, a German, and a Native American (he played Sitting Bull in the 1954 film of the same name). Many of his assignments were villainous in nature (he was a gangster boss in virtually every Paramount "B" of the late 1930s), though his two Oscar nominations were for sympathetic roles: the tragic Italian POW in *Sahara* (1943) and the indigent Mexican father of a deceased war hero in *A Medal For Benny* (1954). Naish continued to flourish on radio and television, at one point playing both a priest and a rabbi on the same anthology series. He starred in both the radio and TV versions of the melting-pot sitcom "Life with Luigi," essayed the title role in 39 episodes of "The New Adventures of Charlie Chan" (1957), and played a comedy Indian on the 1960 sitcom "Guestward Ho." Illness forced him to retire in 1969, but J. Carroll Naish was cajoled back before the cameras by quickie producer Al Adamson for the 1970 ultracheapie *Dracula vs. Frankenstein;* even weighed down by bad false teeth, coke-bottle glasses and a wheelchair, Naish managed to act the rest of the cast right off the screen. **Selected Works:** *Captain Blood* (1935), *Charge of the Light Brigade* (1936), *Fugitive* (1948), *Humoresque* (1946), *Southerner* (1945)

# Charles Napier

**Born:** 1930

**Years Active in the Industry:** by decade

| 10ˢ | 20ˢ | 30ˢ | 40ˢ | 50ˢ | 60ˢ | 70ˢ | 80ˢ | 90ˢ |
|-----|-----|-----|-----|-----|-----|-----|-----|-----|
|     |     |     |     |     |     |     |     |     |

Towering blonde American character actor Charles Napier has the distinction of being one of the few actors to transcend a career start in "nudies" and sustain a successful mainstream career. Napier, clothed and otherwise, was first seen in such Russ Meyer gropey-feeley epics as *Cherry, Harry and Raquel* (1969) and *Beyond the Valley of the Dolls* (1970). Graduating from this exuberant tawdriness, Napier became a dependable film and TV villain. Even when he wasn't totally nasty, he was at least dishonest, as witness his comically bigamous truck driver in *Handle With Care* (1977) Not only were Napier's characters mean, they were often foolhardy; look what happeded to him when he double-crossed Sylvester Stallone in *Rambo* (1984). Some of Napier's more recent credits include *The Blues Brothers* (1980), *Married to the Mob* (1990), *Ernest Goes to Jail* (1991) and the-Oscar winning *Silence of the Lambs* (1991) (as Lt. Boyle). TV also served Napier well, allowing him recurring roles on such series as "The Oregon Trail" and "Outlaws," and at least one bonafide heroic title role in the TV movie *Big Bob Johnson's Fantastic Speed Circus* (1978), in which he played a barnstorming aerialist. He was also a most imposing Adam in the 1969 "Star Trek" episode "The Way to Eden." In 1994, a most atypical Charles Napier could be seen as the incorruptible judge in *Philadelphia*, compassionately trying a homosexual-discrimination case with nary a sneer or scowl on his weatherbeaten countenance. **Selected Works:** *Grifters* (1990), *Miami Blues* (1990), *Skeeter* (1994)

# Mildred Natwick

**Born:** June 19, 1908; Baltimore, MD
**Died:** 1992

**Years Active in the Industry:** by decade

| 10ˢ | 20ˢ | 30ˢ | 40ˢ | 50ˢ | 60ˢ | 70ˢ | 80ˢ | 90ˢ |
|-----|-----|-----|-----|-----|-----|-----|-----|-----|
|     |     |     |     |     |     |     |     |     |

Fresh out of Bryn Mawr college, American actress Mildred Natwick started the road to stage success in amateur shows in her native Baltimore. By 1932 Natwick was on Broadway in *Carrie Nation;* establishing what would become her standard operating procedure, the actress played a character much older than herself. In 1940, Natwick was introduced to movie audiences as the cockney "lady of the evening" in John Ford's *The Long Voyage Home* (1940)—the first of several assignments for Ford, which included *Three Godfathers* (1948), *She Wore a Yellow Ribbon* (1948) and *The Quiet Man* (1952). Seldom starring in a film role, Natwick nonetheless made the most of what she was given, as in her one-scene part as an advocate of birth control who inadvertently pitches her program to the parents of 12 children in *Cheaper By the Dozen* (1950). And it was Natwick who, as skulking sorceress Grizelda in Danny Kaye's *The Court Jester* (1956), inaugurates the side-splitting "The pellet with the poison's in the vessel with the pestle" rou-

tine. A frequent visitor to TV, Natwick briefly settled down on the tube in the mystery series "The Snoop Sisters," which costarred Helen Hayes. In films until 1988, Natwick was honored with a long-overdue Oscar nomination for her work as Jane Fonda's martyr mama in 1967's *Barefoot in the Park*. **Selected Works:** *Dangerous Liaisons* (1988), *Enchanted Cottage* (1945)

# Patricia Neal

**Born:** January 20, 1926; Packard, KY

**Years Active in the Industry:** by decade

| 10ˢ | 20ˢ | 30ˢ | 40ˢ | 50ˢ | 60ˢ | 70ˢ | 80ˢ | 90ˢ |
|-----|-----|-----|-----|-----|-----|-----|-----|-----|
|     |     |     |     |     |     |     |     |     |

A leading lady of American plays and film, Neal studied drama in college and worked as a model before debuting on Broadway in *The Voice of the Turtle* (1946). Her performance in the play *Another Part of the Forest* got the attention of Hollywood, and she made her screen debut in the light farce *John Loves Mary* (1949); that same year she was impressive in *The Fountainhead* opposite Gary Cooper, whom she later said was the great love of her life. As she continued performing in routine movies, her affair with Cooper became well-publicized, and when it came to an end she suffered a nervous breakdown. After marrying British writer Roald Dahl in 1953 she disappeared from the screen for several years, returning in 1957's *A Face in the Crowd,* after which she was more selective in choosing her film roles. For her performance in *Hud* (1963) she won the Best Actress Oscar. In 1965 she suffered a massive series of strokes that left her confined to a wheelchair, semi-paralyzed and nearly unable to speak; she made a remarkable recovery over several years, returning to the screen in *The Subject Was Roses* (1968), for which she received another Best Actress Oscar nomination. Also in 1968, she was presented by President Johnson with the Heart of the Year Award. She underwent two other tragedies: One of her children was hit by a cab as a baby and underwent eight brain operations, and another died of measles at age 13. Later in life, after divorcing Dahl acrimoniously, she underwent a much-publicized conversion to "Born Again" Christianity and published an autobiography, *As I Am*. **Selected Works:** *Breakfast at Tiffany's* (1961), *Caroline?* (1990), *Hasty Heart* (1949)

# Liam Neeson

**Born:** June 7, 1952; Ballymena, Northern Ireland

**Years Active in the Industry:** by decade

| 10ˢ | 20ˢ | 30ˢ | 40ˢ | 50ˢ | 60ˢ | 70ˢ | 80ˢ | 90ˢ |
|-----|-----|-----|-----|-----|-----|-----|-----|-----|
|     |     |     |     |     |     |     |     |     |

Irish actor Liam Neeson held down several blue-collar jobs—truck driver, forklift operator, assistant architect—to sustain him after he gave up professional boxing at age 17. In 1976, he responded to an ad placed by Belfast's Lyric Player's Theatre for a "tall

guy" to appear in the play *In the Risen*; at 6'4", Neeson certainly filled the billed. While working with the Lyric, Neeson was spotted by director John Boorman, who cast the actor in the sword 'n' sorcery film *Excalibur* (1981). It would be nine more years before Neeson received his first starring film role, as the reclusive, mutilated hero of *Darkman* (1990). In 1993, Neeson was Oscar-nominated for his multitextured portrayal of manufacturer and erstwhile humanitarian Oskar Schindler in Steven Spielberg's *Schindler's List*. Two years later, Neeson returned to the swashbuckling milieu of *Excalibur* with his star performance in *Rob Roy*. Liam Neeson is married (after a long live-in courtship) to actress Natasha Richardson. **Selected Works:** *Ethan Frome* (1992), *Husbands and Wives* (1992), *Shining Through* (1992), *Under Suspicion* (1992), *Nell* (1994)

# Jean Negulesco

**Born:** February 26, 1900; Craiova, Romania
**Died:** July 18, 1993; Marbella, Spain

**Years Active in the Industry:** by decade

| 10ˢ | 20ˢ | 30ˢ | 40ˢ | 50ˢ | 60ˢ | 70ˢ | 80ˢ | 90ˢ |
|-----|-----|-----|-----|-----|-----|-----|-----|-----|
|     |     |     |     |     |     |     |     |     |

Jean Negulesco ran away to Vienna, Austria in 1915, and by 1919 had established himself as a painter in Bucharest, Romania. He later worked as a stage decorator in Paris. He came to New York for an exhibition of his paintings in 1927 and stayed. He entered the movie industry in 1934 as an assistant producer and later became a second unit director on pictures such as *Captain Blood* and *A Farewell To Arms*. He spent much of the middle and late 1930s as an associate director and screenwriter (including the original story for the Laurel and Hardy musical comedy *Swiss Miss*). He made two-reel shorts at Warner Bros., and was given his abortive feature directorial debut in 1941's *Singapore Woman*, from which he was removed but retained credit as director. In the early days of 1942, he took over direction (including the denouement) of *Across The Pacific* from John Huston when Huston was called up for military service. *The Mask of Dimetrios* (1944) was Negulesco's formal debut, and proved successful as an offbeat thriller based on an Eric Ambler mystery novel. He later made *Johnny Belinda* (1948), a groundbreaking drama about a deaf-mute girl who is the victim of rape, which won Jane Wyman an Oscar as Best Actress, and the fact-based prisoner-of-war drama *Three Came Home* (1950), starring Claudette Colbert. During the 1950s, Negulesco moved com-

fortably into slicker entertainment, including the comedy *How To Marry A Millionaire* (1953), the first film shot in CinemaScope, and *Three Coins In the Fountain* (1954), as well as Fred Astaire's first wide-screen feature, *Daddy Long Legs* (1954). He retired from filmmaking after many years of declining work in features, and was one of the most honored of Hollywood's elder statesmen for the last two decades of his life. Although never a noted director, Negulesco, in his early prime, showed unusual sensitivity in his choice of subjects and actors.

# Sam Neill (Nigel Neill)

**Born:** 1948; Northern Ireland

**Years Active in the Industry:** by decade

| 10ˢ | 20ˢ | 30ˢ | 40ˢ | 50ˢ | 60ˢ | 70ˢ | 80ˢ | 90ˢ |
|-----|-----|-----|-----|-----|-----|-----|-----|-----|
|     |     |     |     |     |     |     |     |     |

Raised in New Zealand from the age of seven, he began acting while in college, and then joined New Zealand's National Film Unit as an actor; there he ended up directing a number of shorts and documentary subjects. After

moving to Australia in the '70s he began to find work as an actor in that country's growing film industry, and debuted onscreen in *Ashes* (1975). Neill became internationally known after his co-starring role in *My Brilliant Career* (1979), then in 1980 began making films in Hollywood and England. He has alternated leads with supporting roles. In 1983 he starred in the BBC TV show "Reilly—Ace of Spies" (later shown on PBS in America). He was one of the stars of *Jurassic Park* (1993), the most successful movie ever. Neill can also be seen in *The Piano* (1993), *Sirens* (1994), and *In the Mouth of Madness* (1994). **Selected Works:** *Cry in the Dark* (1988), *Hunt for Red October* (1990), *Country Life* (1995), *Dead Calm* (1989)

# Kate Nelligan (Patricia Colleen Nelligan)

**Born:** March 16, 1951; London, Ontario, Canada

**Years Active in the Industry:** by decade

| 10ˢ | 20ˢ | 30ˢ | 40ˢ | 50ˢ | 60ˢ | 70ˢ | 80ˢ | 90ˢ |
|-----|-----|-----|-----|-----|-----|-----|-----|-----|
|     |     |     |     |     |     |     |     |     |

Three-time Tony Award nominee Kate Nelligan has pursued a successful acting career in three separate English-speaking nations. While attending the University of Toronto, the Canadian-born Nelligan transferred to London, England's Central School of Speech and Drama. It was in Bristol that she first appeared on stage professionally with the Old Vic in 1973; one year later, she returned to London for her stage bow there. In 1975, Nelligan made her screen debut in *The Romantic Englishwoman*, but most American filmgoers saw her first as Lucy in the Frank Langella version of *Dracula* (1979). Several appearances in British made-for-TV movies followed in the early 1980s; most of these popped up on U.S. TV screens courtesy of the burgeoning Arts & Entertainment cable network. In 1980 she made her first Canadian film, *Mr. Patman*. Kate Nelligan's most recent movie appearances have been in such American projects as *Frankie and Johnny* (1990), *The Prince of Tides* (1991), and *Shadows and Fog* (1992). **Selected Works:** *Love and Hate* (1990), *Wolf* (1994), *How to Make an American Quilt* (1995)

# Craig T. Nelson

**Born:** April 4, 1946; Spokane, WA

**Years Active in the Industry:** by decade

| 10s | 20s | 30s | 40s | 50s | 60s | 70s | 80s | 90s |
|-----|-----|-----|-----|-----|-----|-----|-----|-----|
|     |     |     |     |     |     |     |     |     |

Solidly built American actor Craig T. Nelson started out as a comedy writer and performer, doing radio and nightspot gigs in the Los Angeles area. Success was not immediately forthcoming, and Nelson took a four-year sabbatical from show business, moving with his family to a remote cabin in Northern California. In 1979, he made his first film, *...And Justice For All*, written by his onetime partner Barry Levinson. While film stardom eluded him (a case can be made for his nominal-hero assignment in *Poltergeist* [1982]), Nelson did quite well on television, making a good impression on a shortlived 1984 military drama, *Call to Glory*. Since February of 1989, Craig T. Nelson has starred as college athletics instuctor Hayden Fox on the top-ranked ABC sitcom *Coach*. **Selected Works:** *Josephine Baker Story* (1990), *Killing Fields* (1984), *Poltergeist* (1982)

# Judd Nelson

**Born:** November 28, 1959; Portland, ME

**Years Active in the Industry:** by decade

| 10s | 20s | 30s | 40s | 50s | 60s | 70s | 80s | 90s |
|-----|-----|-----|-----|-----|-----|-----|-----|-----|
|     |     |     |     |     |     |     |     |     |

Even by the unexacting standard of Hollywood's 1980s "brat pack," actor Judd Nelson seemed wildly undisciplined and self-indulgent on screen. One tends to conclude that Nelson (a former philosophy student and the son of a Maine politician) has played his screen characters as written: he was, after all, very well trained by famed drama coach Stella Adler, and came up from the exacting ranks of summer stock. Among his earliest screen assignments—all in his watershed year of 1985—including the dope-smoking detentionee in *The Breakfast Club*, Kevin Costner's para-

chute-jumping fraternity pal in *Fandango*, and Ally Sheedy's philandering live-in boyfriend in *St. Elmo's Fire*. Always seeming to be on the verge of punching someone out, Nelson was well cast as a mercurial killer in 1989's *Relentless*. Like many brat-packers, Judd Nelson has appeared in fewer and fewer films in the 1990s. In Tommy Chong's *Far Out Man* (1990), Nelson appears ingratiatingly as himself. **Selected Works:** *Hiroshima: Out of the Ashes* (1990), *New Jack City* (1991), *Primary Motive* (1992), *Blindfold: Acts of Obsession* (1994)

# Mike Newell

**Born:** 1942; England

**Years Active in the Industry:** by decade

| 10s | 20s | 30s | 40s | 50s | 60s | 70s | 80s | 90s |
|-----|-----|-----|-----|-----|-----|-----|-----|-----|
|     |     |     |     |     |     |     |     |     |

A former stage director, Briton Mike Newell has always brought a touch of high theatrics to his films, but never so much as to make them seem stagebound. Newell's breakthrough film *Dance with a Stranger* (1985), a style-conscious retelling of the notorious Ruth Ellis murder case (she was the last woman executed in England), brought full stardom to British actress Miranda Richardson, while the director's *Enchanted April* (1992), also with Richardson, ended up a surprise moneymaker in the US. Sometimes Newell's larger-than-life approach comes a cropper, as witness the fuzzy-headed allegory *Amazing Grace and Chuck* (1987) and the confusing fantasy overtones in *Into the West* (1993). In 1994, Mike Newell made up for past missteps with *Four Weddings and A Funeral*, which outgrossed *Enchanted April* (and practically everything else) at the box office and was nominated for an Academy Award. **Selected Works:** *Common Ground, Part 1* (1990), *Common Ground, Part 2* (1990)

# Paul Newman

**Born:** January 26, 1925; Cleveland, OH

**Years Active in the Industry:** by decade

| 10s | 20s | 30s | 40s | 50s | 60s | 70s | 80s | 90s |
|-----|-----|-----|-----|-----|-----|-----|-----|-----|
|     |     |     |     |     |     |     |     |     |

After serving as a radioman in the Pacific during World War II, Newman enrolled in college and, while there, began acting in

plays. He went on to act in stock in Wisconsin and Illinois, then enrolled at the Yale Drama School. After landing a part on the TV series "The Aldrich Family," he quit Yale, and went on to appear in numerous TV shows. In 1952, Newman joined the Actors Studio in New York and debuted on Broadway in *Picnic,* a successful 1953 performance that attracted Hollywood's attention. Warner Brothers signed him to a film contract, and he debuted onscreen in *The Silver Chalice* (1955), a disastrously bad epic. He overcame this unfortunate debut and soon rose to stardom. For his work in *The Long Hot Summer* (1958) he won the Cannes Film Festival Best Actor Award, meanwhile receiving a Best Actor Oscar nomination for *Cat on a Hot Tin Roof* (1959). In 1958 he married actress Joanne Woodward. He has shown good judgment in his selection of films throughout his career, and, for the most part, he has appeared in superior productions. After numerous Oscar nominations he finally won a Best Actor Oscar for his work in *The Color of Money* (1986); the previous year he had been awarded a special Oscar "in recognition of his many memorable and compelling screen performances and for his personal integrity and dedication to his craft." He made his directorial debut with *Rachel, Rachel* (1968), starring Joanne Woodward; the film was nominated for a Best Picture Oscar and Newman won the New York Critics Circle Best Director award. He went on to frequently produce or co-produce and occasionally direct films, and co-wrote one film, *Harry and Son* (1984). Newman can also be seen in *The Hudsucker Proxy* (1994) and *Nobody's Fool* (1994), for which he was nominated for a Best Actor Oscar. Newman co-owns First Artists, a production company whose other owners include Sidney Poitier and Barbra Streisand. He and Woodward have been among Hollywood's most politically active couples, and have campaigned for numerous liberal causes and political candidates. President Jimmy Carter appointed Newman as a U.S. delegate to the U.N. Conference on Nuclear Disarmament. He has also contributed enormous amounts of money to a wide variety of charities and social causes, including the anti-drug Scott Newman foundation, which he founded following the 1978 death of his son (from his first marriage). "Newman's Own," a line of food products bearing his name, contributes all its proceeds to charity. **Selected Works:** *Absence of Malice* (1981), *Butch Cassidy and the Sundance Kid* (1969), *Cool Hand Luke* (1967), *Hustler* (1961), *Verdict* (1982)

# Julie Newmar

**Born:** August 16, 1935; Los Angeles, CA

**Years Active in the Industry:** by decade

| 10s | 20s | 30s | 40s | 50s | 60s | 70s | 80s | 90s |
|-----|-----|-----|-----|-----|-----|-----|-----|-----|
|     |     |     |     | ■   | ■   | ■   | ■   | ■   |

American actress Julie Newmar's father was a college instructor and her mother was a former Ziegfeld dancer. This odd mix may explain why Julie complemented her dancing and acting career with offscreen intellectual pursuits. A lifelong student of ballet, Newmar was accepted as a dancer by the Los Angeles Opera Comany at age 15, and before her UCLA enrollment was under way she'd left college to try her luck in films. A stint as a gold-painted exotic dancer in *Serpent of the Nile* (1954) was usually conveniently ignored by Newmar's biographers, who preferred to list *Seven Brides for Seven Brothers* (1954) as her screen debut. From here it was on to Broadway for a featured dance in the musical *Can-Can,* then to the sizable but nonspeaking role of Stupefyin' Jones in *Li'l Abner.* It was for Newmar's performance as a Swedish sexpot in the genteel farce *The Marriage-Go-Round* that the actress attained true stardom - and also won a Tony Award. Recreating her stage roles for the film versions of *Li'l Abner* (1959) and *Marriage-Go-Round* (1961), Newmar spent the next few years dividing her time between stage work and TV guest spots (she played the Devil in the 1963 "Twilight Zone" episode "Of Late I Think of Cliffordville"). In 1964, Newmar was cast as a beautiful robot on the TV sitcom "My Living Doll," a series that languished opposite "Bonanza" and barely got through the season. According to Newmar, she accepted her best-remembered TV role, that of Catwoman on the weekly series "Batman," on the advice of her brother, a Harvard fellow in Physics who, along with his classmates, was a rabid "Batman" fan. Newmar played Catwoman for two seasons, but contractual committments kept her from appearing in the 1966 feature film version of *Batman,* wherein her role was taken over by Lee Meriweather. For diverse reasons, Newmar wasn't back as Catwoman for the final "Batman" season, so Eartha Kitt essayed the role. Newmar's film career peaked with *MacKenna's Gold* (1968) and *The Maltese Bippy* (1969), after which she was consigned to such deathless projects as *Hysterical* (1983), *Nudity Required* (1990) and *Ghosts Can't Do It* (1991). In the mid 1980s, Julie Newmar began making the personal-appearance rounds thanks to the publicity attending the 20th anniversary of the "Batman" series, and in 1992 Julie was again an interview subject as a byproduct of Michelle Pfeiffer's unforgettable Catwoman stint in the 1992 feature film *Batman Returns.*

# Robert Newton

**Born:** June 1, 1905; Shaftesbury, Dorest, England
**Died:** March 25, 1956; Beverly Hills, CA

**Years Active in the Industry:** by decade

| 10s | 20s | 30s | 40s | 50s | 60s | 70s | 80s | 90s |
|-----|-----|-----|-----|-----|-----|-----|-----|-----|
|     |     | ■   | ■   | ■   |     |     |     |     |

Professionally, British actor Robert Newton was two people: The wry, sensitive, often subtle performer seen in such plays as

Noel Coward's *Private Lives* and such films as *This Happy Breed* (1944), and the eye-rolling, chop-licking ham in such roles as Bill Sykes in *Oliver Twist* (1948) and Long John Silver (arr! arr!) in *Treasure Island* (1950). Born into a gifted family—his mother was a writer, his father and his siblings painters—Newton made his professional debut when he was 15 with the British Repertory Company. Before he was 25, Newton had toured the world as an actor and stage manager, making his Broadway bow when he replaced Laurence Olivier in *Private Lives*. There was little of Olivier (except perhaps the older Olivier) in most of Newton's movie roles; despite his wide actor's range, he seemed happiest tearing a passion to tatters in such films as *Jamaica Inn* (1939), *Blackbeard the Pirate* (1952) and *The Beachcomber* (1954). Ripe though his acting could be, it was clear Newton knew his audience. From 1947 through 1951 he was one of Britain's top ten moneymaking film stars, so who were the critics to tell him what to do? Newton's final film role was the dogged Inspector Fix in the blockbuster *Around the World in 80 Days* (1956). If it seems as though his part fades out towards the end of the film, the explanation is both simple and tragic. A heavy drinker, Newton had promised *Around the World* producer Mike Todd that he'd remain cold sober for the filming—but *only* for the filming. When Todd decided he was disatisfied with Inspector Fix's final scenes a few weeks after principal photography wrapped up, he called upon Newton for retakes, only to find the actor so besotted with alcohol that he barely knew his own name. Less than one month after completing *Around the World in 80 Days,* Robert Newton died of a heart attack in the arms of his wife. **Selected Works:** *Henry V* (1944), *Odd Man Out* (1947), *High and the Mighty* (1954)

# The Nicholas Brothers

**Years Active in the Industry:** by decade

| 10s | 20s | 30s | 40s | 50s | 60s | 70s | 80s | 90s |
|-----|-----|-----|-----|-----|-----|-----|-----|-----|

Fayard (b. 1917) and Harold (b. 1924) Nicholas, a sophisticated dance team, featured an intricate, highly acrobatic, smooth style. The children of vaudeville musicians, they began dancing onstage in their early youth. Harold began teaching Fayard dance steps as soon as the latter was old enough to walk. They made their professional debut as a team in 1931, and a year later appeared at the legendary Cotton Club, where they remained as regulars for many years. They went on to perform on Broadway in such shows as *Ziegfeld Follies of 1936* and *Babes in Arms* (1937); they also toured in clubs and theaters around the country and appeared in Europe in such shows as *Blackbirds of 1936.* Debuting onscreen in 1932, the brothers appeared in a number of films through the late '40s and gained renown for their jumps, backflips, and splits; later they quit movies, but frequently appeared on TV. Late in their lives, both brothers made solo dramatic appearances on stage and screen. Harold married and divorced actress Dorothy Dandridge. **Selected Works:** *Pirate* (1948)

# Dudley Nichols

**Born:** April 6, 1895; Wapakoneta, OH
**Died:** 1960

**Years Active in the Industry:** by decade

| 10s | 20s | 30s | 40s | 50s | 60s | 70s | 80s | 90s |
|-----|-----|-----|-----|-----|-----|-----|-----|-----|

An Oscar-winning screenwriter and sometime director, Dudley Nichols started out as a reporter for the *New York World* and ventured to Hollywood in 1929 when the film capital began drawing in writers to work with the new medium of talking pictures. He began an early association with John Ford in *Men Without Women* (1930), and subsequently wrote or co-authored the screenplays for some of Ford's best-known films, including *The Lost Patrol, Judge Priest, The Informer* (which earned Oscars for writer and director), *Stagecoach, The Long Voyage Home,* and *The Fugitive.* Nichols' other screenwriting credits include Howard Hawks' *Bringing Up Baby* and *Air Force;* the scripts for Jean Renoir's two best English-language films, *Swamp Water* and *This Land Is Mine;* Fritz Lang's *Man Hunt* and *Scarlet Street;* and Leo McCarey's *The Bells of St. Mary's.* At its best, Nichols' screenwriting displays startling elements of lyricism and poetry—*Swamp Water,* for example, has long, haunting passages amid its complex character development that sings of the mystery and wonder of its rural, swampland setting, and was so effective as a script that it was remade a decade later as *Lure of the Wilderness.* Conversely, *The Bells of St. Mary's,* despite its relatively light touch and gentle humor, raises serious philosophical and spiritual questions that give the movie much more substance than meets the eye. And *Air Force,* despite the restrictions of its wartime setting, manages to avoid most wartime cliches (although it did create a few) and is highlighted by a scene in which a dying pilot takes his plane up one last time, completely in his imagination. *Man Hunt* is a wartime thriller of extraordinary menace and unease, completely unlike the heroic vehicle that one would have expected. And Nichols could also delve into the dark side of the human spirit with equal effectiveness—*The Informer* does just that, while wrestling with decidedly Christian themes of betrayal and morality. And *Scarlet Street* is so utterly bleak and amoral, that it is scary to watch, even 50 years later. Nichols also directed a handful of features: *Government Girl, Sister Kenny,* and *Morning Becomes Electra,* all of which received favorable critical notices but failed financially.

# Mike Nichols (Michael Igor Peschkowsky)

**Born:** November 6, 1931; Berlin, Germany

**Years Active in the Industry:** by decade

| 10s | 20s | 30s | 40s | 50s | 60s | 70s | 80s | 90s |
|-----|-----|-----|-----|-----|-----|-----|-----|-----|

Born in Berlin, Germany, Mike Nichols came to the United States at age seven when his family fled the Nazis. His father died when he was 12, but Nichols managed to complete his education by working various jobs. He studied acting with Lee Strasberg in New York, but returned to Chicago and formed an improvisational troupe with Barbara Harris, Alan Arkin, and Elaine May that earned a three-year booking at the Compass Club in Chicago. He and May then formed a team and ended up on Broadway for an extended run in *An Evening with Nichols and May*. After they split up, Nichols decided to try his hand at directing and scored a hit his first time out with Neil Simon's *Barefoot in the Park;* he had six more consecutive successes, and Hollywood beckoned, first with a film version of *Who's Afraid of Virginia Woolf?* (1966) and with *The Graduate* (1967). The former was an unexpected success, while the latter went on to become one of the biggest hit films of the 1960s, as well as earning him a Best Director Oscar. Nichols' track record earned him an \$11 million budget for a film version of Joseph Heller's *Catch-22* (1970). His next movie, the more modestly budgeted *Carnal Knowledge* (1971), was one of the most controversial and uncompromising films of its era, taking a harsh up-close look at male sexuality, which brought it to the center of obscenity cases and made a star of Jack Nicholson. Nichols pursued lighter fare for the next several years, such as *The Day of the Dolphin* (1973) and *The Fortune* (1975), none of which elicited either the excitement or the box office response of his early films. He returned to form somewhat with topical dramas: *Silkwood* (1983), *Heartburn* (1986), and *Biloxi Blues* (1988) were respectable efforts, but it wasn't until *Working Girl* (1988) that Nichols had another real hit, and received another Oscar nomination. His drama *Regarding Henry* (1991), starring Harrison Ford as a man who reshapes his life after a tragedy, was also a major success, and put Nichols back in the front rank of directors. Nichols' more recent films include *The Remains of the Day* (1993), as co-executive producer, and *Wolf* (1994). **Selected Works:** *Postcards from the Edge* (1990)

# Jack Nicholson

**Born:** April 22, 1937; Neptune, NJ

**Years Active in the Industry:** by decade

| 10ˢ | 20ˢ | 30ˢ | 40ˢ | 50ˢ | 60ˢ | 70ˢ | 80ˢ | 90ˢ |
|-----|-----|-----|-----|-----|-----|-----|-----|-----|
|     |     |     |     |     |     |     |     |     |

A charismatic, charming, one-of-a-kind Hollywood star with raised eyebrows, a sly grin, and a sarcastic manner; it took him well over a decade of steady film work before he became a star. He was raised by his maternal grandmother, whom he believed to be his mother, and two "sisters," one of whom was in fact his mother. At the age of 17 he went to California to visit his aunt (whom he thought was his sister); a chance encounter led him to a job as an office boy in MGM's cartoon department. He studied acting with a group called the Players Ring Theater, going on to perform on stage and in TV soap operas. He debuted onscreen in the lead role of Roger Corman's low-budget *The Cry Baby Killer* (1958), and went on to appear in numerous cheap, quickly-filmed horror, motorcycle, and action films made by

Corman and other directors working outside mainstream Hollywood. He soon began producing and writing some of these films, in collaboration with Monte Hellman, another Corman protege; to reduce expenses, several of their films were made in the Philippines. After Rip Torn was fired from the cast of *Easy Rider* (1969), Nicholson got his big break by being asked to fill the role (that of a lawyer who drops out and becomes a biker); the film was a huge success, and for his performance he received the first of several Oscar nominations. From then on Nicholson began establishing himself as one of the screen's most noteworthy performers, winning Oscar nominations for his work in Bob Rafelson's *Five Easy Pieces* (1970), Hal Ashby's *The Last Detail* (1973), and Roman Polanski's *Chinatown* (1974). (For the latter film he received a New York Film Critics Award.) Nicholson has tended to play outsiders and drifters who stay out of "the system." He finally won a Best Actor Oscar for his performance as a sane mental hospital patient in Milos Forman's *One Flew Over the Cuckoo's Nest* (1975). He also won a Best Supporting Actor Oscar for his portrayal of a retired astronaut in *Terms of Endearment* (1983). In 1971, he directed his first film, *Drive, He Said* (he had co-directed several others); in 1978, his second, *Goin' South;* and in 1990, his third, *The Two Jakes*, a sequel to *Chinatown*. An extremely versatile actor, he has played everything from the Joker (in *Batman*, [1989]) to a homicidal maniac (in Stanley Kubrick's *The Shining*, [1979]) to the Devil himself (in *The Witches of Eastwick*, [1987]). Nicholson can also be seen in *A Few Good Men* (1992), *Hoffa* (1992), and *Wolf* (1994). For over a decade, he was romantically involved with actress Anjelica Huston, with whom he appeared in *Prizzi's Honor* (1985). **Selected Works:** *Broadcast News* (1987), *Carnal Knowledge* (1971), *King of Marvin Gardens* (1972), *Reds* (1981), *The Crossing Guard* (1995)

# Leslie Nielsen

**Born:** February 11, 1926; Regina, Saskatchewan, Canada

**Years Active in the Industry:** by decade

| 10ˢ | 20ˢ | 30ˢ | 40ˢ | 50ˢ | 60ˢ | 70ˢ | 80ˢ | 90ˢ |
|-----|-----|-----|-----|-----|-----|-----|-----|-----|
|     |     |     |     |     |     |     |     |     |

Nielsen worked as a radio announcer and disc jockey before acting on stage and TV in the early '50s. His big-screen debut came in *Ransom* (1956), after which he sustained a steady, if unexciting,

film career. He also starred in the TV series "Bracken's World" and "The Bold Ones." His career gained new life after he appeared in the disaster movie satire *Airplane* (1979), in which his droll, dead-pan style was very effective amidst broad comedy. This led to a starring role in the satirical TV series "Police Squad," which spawned three more *Airplane*-like films: *The Naked Gun* (1988), *The Naked Gun 2 1/2* (1991), and *The Naked Gun 33 1/3* (1994). **Selected Works:** *Forbidden Planet* (1956)

# Leonard Nimoy

**Born:** March 26, 1931; Boston, MA

**Years Active in the Industry:** by decade

| 10ˢ | 20ˢ | 30ˢ | 40ˢ | 50ˢ | 60ˢ | 70ˢ | 80ˢ | 90ˢ |
|-----|-----|-----|-----|-----|-----|-----|-----|-----|
|     |     |     |     |     |     |     |     |     |

After getting his B.A. and Master's Degree in Drama, serving in the military, and holding several odd jobs, Nimoy trained at the Pasadena Playhouse and debuted onscreen in 1951. He went on to

play supporting roles in numerous films and TV shows, meanwhile working as an acting teacher. He is best known as Mr. Spock, the pointy-eared Vulcan on the science-fiction TV series "Star Trek" (1966-69) and its six big-screen episodes; he directed two of the films, *Star Trek III: The Search for Spock* (1984) and *Star Trek IV: The Voyage Home* (1986). He has also directed several other films, including the hit comedy *Three Men and a Baby* (1987). In 1977 he starred on Broadway in *Equus;* later he was acclaimed for his work in the one-man stage show *Vincent,* in which he portrayed Vincent Van Gogh. He is the author of several collections of poetry, three books on photography, and an autobiography, *I Am Not Spock* (1975). He also costarred in the TV series "Mission: Impossible." **Selected Works:** *Never Forget* (1991), *Star Trek 6: The Undiscovered Country* (1991)

# David Niven (James David Graham Niven)

**Born:** March 1, 1910; Kirriemuir, Scotland
**Died:** July 29, 1983; Vaud, Switzerland

**Years Active in the Industry:** by decade

| 10ˢ | 20ˢ | 30ˢ | 40ˢ | 50ˢ | 60ˢ | 70ˢ | 80ˢ | 90ˢ |
|-----|-----|-----|-----|-----|-----|-----|-----|-----|
|     |     |     |     |     |     |     |     |     |

The son a well-to-do British Army captain who died at Gallipoli in 1915, Niven was shipped off to a succession of boarding schools by his stepfather, who didn't care much for the boy.

Young David hated the experience and was a poor student, but his late father's reputation enabled the boy to enter Royal Military College; later he earned a second lieutenant rank in the Highland Light Infantry. Rakishly handsome and naturally charming, Lt. Niven met several society higher-ups while stationed in Malta, and through their auspices made several important contacts while attending parties. Though he later claimed to have been nothing more than a wastrel-like "professional guest" at this stage of his life, the truth is that Niven was excellent company, a superb raconteur, and a loyal friend, and he paid back every one of his social obligations by giving lavish parties of his own once he'd become famous. Niven also insisted that he fell into acting without any prior interest; actually he'd done amateur theatricals in college, and had built up a fascination with drama via his platonic friendship with actress Ann Todd. Society hostess Elsa Maxwell was the person who encouraged Niven (then weaving his way through several dead-end jobs) to parlay his good looks and pleasant personality into a film career; he became a Hollywood extra in 1935, and ultimately came to the attention of producer Samuel Goldwyn, who was then building up a stable of attractive young contract players. Having made his speaking debut in *Without Regret* (1935), Niven learned rather quickly (with the help of his friends and coworkers) to successfully get through a movie scene, and after several secondary roles for Goldwyn he was loaned out for a lead role in the 20th Century Fox second feature *Thank You, Jeeves* (1936). The actor formed lasting friendships with several members of Hollywood's British community (notably Errol Flynn, with whom he lived briefly) and was quite popular with the American-born contingent as well—especially the ladies. Though he worked steadily in the 1930s, it was usually in support of bigger stars; he was seldom permitted to carry a film by himself, except for such modest programmers as *Dinner at the Ritz* (1937) and *Raffles* (1939). Anxious to do something more substantial than act during World War II, Niven re-entered the British service as a Lieutenant Colonel, where he served nobly if not spectacularly. (His batman, or valet, during the war was Pvt. Peter Ustinov, himself an actor of no mean talent.) Married by the end of the war, Niven went back to films but found that he still wasn't getting important assignments; despite ten years experience, he was considered too "lightweight" to be a major name. His life momentarily shattered by the accidental death of his wife, Niven's spirit was restored by his second marriage to Swedish model Hjordis Tersmeden, who remained Mrs. Niven until the actor's death. Once again, Niven took a self-deprecating attitude towards his domestic life, claiming to be a poor husband and worse father, but again the facts are otherwise; despite the time spent away from his family, they cherished his concern and affection for them. After his Goldwyn contract ended in 1949, Niven marked time with inconsequential movies before alligning with Dick Powell, Charles Boyer, and Ida Lupino to form Four-Star, a television production firm. Niven finally was able to choose strong dramatic roles for himself, becoming one of TV's first and most prolific stars—though his public still preferred Niven as a light comedian. The actor's film career also took an upswing in the 1950s with starring performances in the controversial *The Moon Is Blue* (1953)—a harmless concoction which was denied a Production Code seal because the word "virgin" was bandied about—and the mammoth *Around the World in 80 Days* (1956), in which Niven played his most famous role, erudite 19th century globetrotter Phileas Fogg. When Laurence Olivier dropped out of the 1958 film *Separate Tables,* Niven stepped in to play an elderly, disgraced British military man. Though he was as usual flippant about the part, telling interviewer Tony Thomas that "they gave me very good lines and then cut to Deborah Kerr while I was saying them," Niven won an Academy Award for this performance. The actor continued his career as a high-priced "A list" actor into the 1960s, returning to television in a stylish "caper" series *The Rogues* in 1964. He returned to his hobby of writing in the early 1970s (an earlier novel, *Round the Ragged Rocks,* wasn't a best seller but gave him pleasure while working on it), producing two breezy autobiographies, *The Moon's a Balloon* and *Bring on the Empty Horse.* Writing alone and without help of a "ghost" (as opposed to many celebrity "authors"), Niven was able to entertainingly transfer his charm and wit to the printed page (even if he seldom let the facts impede his storytelling). In 1982, Niven discovered he was suffering from a neurological illness commonly known as Lou Gehrig's Disease, which would prove fatal within a year. Courageously keeping up a front with his friends and his public, Niven continued making media appearances, though it was obvious that he was deteriorating. While, appearing in his last film, *Trail of the Pink Panther* (1982), Niven's speech became so slurred due to his illness that his lines were dubbed by impressionist Rich Little. Waving away all artificial life-support systems, Niven died with dignity in his Switzerland home. While he left a relatively small legacy of worthwhile films, and despite his own public attitude that his life had been something of an elborate fraud, Niven left behind countless friends and family members who adored him; indeed, journalists sent out to "dig up dirt"

following the actor's death came back amazed (and perhaps secretly pleased) that not one person could find anything bad to say about David Niven. **Selected Works:** *Bachelor Mother* (1939), *Bishop's Wife* (1947), *Dodsworth* (1936), *Guns of Navarone* (1961), *Wuthering Heights* (1939)

# Philippe Noiret

**Born:** October 1, 1930; Lille, France

**Years Active in the Industry:** by decade

| 10s | 20s | 30s | 40s | 50s | 60s | 70s | 80s | 90s |
|-----|-----|-----|-----|-----|-----|-----|-----|-----|

There is very little that cherubic French actor Philippe Noiret cannot do well. Since receiving his training at the Centre Dramatique de l'Ouest, Noiret has been a nightclub entertainer, stage star, comedian, tragedian, and international film celebrity. He appeared in a handful of films in the late 1940s, but Noiret truly emerged as a movie actor of note with 1960's *Zazie Dans le Metro*, in which he played the heroine's uncle, an outspoken transvestite. For his portrayal of a clueless husband in *Therese* (1962), Noiret won a Venice Festival Prize; and for his performance in 1975's *Le Vieux Fusil* (*The Old Gun*), he won France's Cesar Award. Noiret is most closely associated with director Bernard Tavernier, who has often referred to the versatile Noiret as "my autobiographical actor". American filmgoers are most familiar with Philippe Noiret as the philosophical Italian projectionist in the Oscar-winning *Cinema Paradiso* (1988). **Selected Works:** *Clockmaker* (1976), *Life and Nothing But* (1989), *Three Brothers* (1980)

# Lloyd Nolan

**Born:** August 11, 1902; San Francisco, CA
**Died:** September 27, 1985; Los Angeles, CA

**Years Active in the Industry:** by decade

| 10s | 20s | 30s | 40s | 50s | 60s | 70s | 80s | 90s |
|-----|-----|-----|-----|-----|-----|-----|-----|-----|

The son of a San Francisco shoe factory owner, American actor Lloyd Nolan made it clear early on that he had no intention of entering the family business. Nolan developed an interest in acting while in college, at the expense of his education—it took him five years to get through Santa Clara College, and he flunked out of Stanford, all because of time spent in amateur theatricals. Attempting a "joe job" on a freighter, Nolan gave it up when the freighter burned to the waterline. In 1927, he began studying at the Pasadena Playhouse, living on the inheritance left him by his father. Stock company work followed, and in 1933 Nolan scored a Broadway hit as vengeful small-town dentist Biff Grimes in *One Sunday Afternoon* (a role played in three film versions by Gary Cooper, James Cagney, and Dennis Morgan, respectively—but never, worse luck, by Nolan). Nolan's first film was *Stolen Harmony* (1935); his breezy urban manner and Gaelic charm saved the actor from being confined to the bad guy parts he played so well, and by 1940 Nolan was, if not a star, certainly one of Hollywood's most versatile second-echelon leading men. As film historian William K. Everson has pointed out, the secret to Nolan's success was his integrity—the audience *respected* his characters, even when he was the most cold-blooded of villains. The closest Nolan got to film stardom was a series of B detective films made at 20th Century-Fox from 1940 to 1942, in which he played private eye Michael Shayne—a "hard-boiled dick" character long before Humphrey Bogart popularized this type as Sam Spade. Nolan was willing to tackle any sort of acting, from movies to stage to radio, and ultimately television, where he starred as detective Martin Kane in 1951; later TV stints would include a season as an IRS investigator in the syndicated "Special Agent 7" (1958), and three years as grumpy-growley Dr. Chegley on the Diahann Carroll sitcom "Julia" (1969-71). In 1953, Nolan originated the role of the paranoid Captain Queeg in the Broadway play *The Caine Mutiny Court Martial,* wherein he'd emerge from a pleasant backstage nap to play some of the most gut-wrenching "character deterioration" scenes ever written. Never your typical Hollywood celebrity, Nolan publicly acknowledged that he and his wife had an autistic son, proudly proclaiming each bit of intellectual or social progress the boy would make—this at a time when many image-conscious movie star-parents barely admitted even having children, normal or otherwise. Well liked by his peers, Nolan was famous (in an affectionate manner) for having a photographic memory for lines but an appallingly bad attention span in real life; at times he was unable to give directions to his own home, and when he did so the directions might be three different things to three different people. A thorough professional to the last, Nolan continued acting in sizeable roles into the 1980s; he was terrific as Maureen O'Sullivan's irascible stage-star husband in Woody Allen's *Husbands and Wives* (1986). Lloyd Nolan's last performance was as an aging soap opera star on an episode of the TV series "Murder She Wrote;" star Angela Lansbury, fiercely protective of an old friend and grand trouper, saw to it that Nolan's twilight-years reliance upon cue cards was cleverly written into the plotline of the episode. **Selected Works:** *Hannah and Her Sisters* (1986), *Peyton Place* (1957), *Tree Grows in Brooklyn* (1945)

# Nick Nolte

**Born:** February 8, 1941; Omaha, NE

**Years Active in the Industry:** by decade

| 10ˢ | 20ˢ | 30ˢ | 40ˢ | 50ˢ | 60ˢ | 70ˢ | 80ˢ | 90ˢ |
|-----|-----|-----|-----|-----|-----|-----|-----|-----|

Laconic, earthy, rugged leading man with a powerful build and an underlying intensity, Nolte attended five colleges (all on football scholarships) in four years. While at Phoenix City College in 1960, he joined the Actors' Inner Circle of Phoenix. He went on to perform in some 160 roles over the next eight years, some of them in summer stock in Colorado. In 1968 he joined Minneapolis's Old Log Theater, then worked with the La Mama experimental theater

troupe in New York before settling in Los Angeles. He began to find work in TV, getting his big break as a co-star of the hit mini-series *Rich Man, Poor Man* in 1976-77. Although he had appeared in two films (in one of which he had the lead), his first important screen role was in *The Deep* (1977) opposite Jacqueline Bisset. He continued to work in major films, but his real breakthrough was the smash hit *48 Hours* (1982) with Eddie Murphy; this film firmly established his star status, and since its release he has been much in demand. In 1994, Nolte could be seen in three pictures, including *Blue Chips*, as basketball coach Pete Bell; *I Love Trouble*, a romantic comedy featuring Nolte and Julia Roberts as reporters at rival Chicago newspapers; and *Jefferson In Paris*, a Merchant-Ivory vehicle in which Nolte plays Thomas Jefferson. For his work in Barbra Streisand's *The Prince of Tides* (1991) he received a Best Actor Oscar nomination. **Selected Works:** *Another 48 Hrs.* (1990), *Cape Fear* (1991), *Lorenzo's Oil* (1992), *North Dallas Forty* (1979), *Under Fire* (1983)

# Alex North

**Born:** December 4, 1910; Chester, PA
**Died:** September 8, 1991; Pacific Palisades, CA

**Years Active in the Industry:** by decade

| 10ˢ | 20ˢ | 30ˢ | 40ˢ | 50ˢ | 60ˢ | 70ˢ | 80ˢ | 90ˢ |
|-----|-----|-----|-----|-----|-----|-----|-----|-----|

American composer Alex North hardly needed films to enhance his reputation. A graduate of Julliard and the pupil of such musical heavyweights as Ernst Toch and Aaron Copland, North was responsible for the incidental music in several major Broadway productions of the 1940s, notably *Death of a Salesman*. He also composed for the ballet, for symphony orchestra, and even for Benny Goodman. North's earliest film work consisted of the scores for documentary films, an activity he engaged in from 1937 through the early 1950s. His first feature-film score was for 20th Century-Fox's *The 13th Letter;* he followed this with a steady parade of scores for such memorable pictures as *Viva Zapata* (1952), *The Rose Tattoo* (1955), *The Bad Seed* (1956), *Spartacus* (1960), *Who's Afraid of Virginia Woolf* (1967), *Under the Volcano* (1984) and *Prizzi's Honor* (1985). His most popular composition, "Unchained Melody" (for the 1955 prison picture *Unchanged*), received a whole new lease on life in 1990 thanks to the runaway hit film *Ghost*. Yet despite so impressive a resume, Alex North never received an Oscar in any of his 15 nominations. Finally, in 1986, the Academy threw him that guilt-absolving bone, the "Lifetime Achievement Award." Perhaps Alex North's most ambitious film score was the one nobody heard—he was engaged by Stanley Kubrick to write the music for *2001: A Space Odyssey,* only to have Kubrick rudely pull the rug from under him by substituting such classical pieces as "Thus Spake Zarathustra" and "The Blue Danube Waltz." With teeth clenched, Alex North wrote a terse article describing his frustration for Jerome Agel's 1969 compendium *The Making of Kubrick's 2001.* **Selected Works:** *Bite the Bullet* (1975), *Streetcar Named Desire* (1951), *Viva Zapata!* (1952)

## Sheree North (Dawn Bethel)

**Born:** January 17, 1933; Hollywood, CA

**Years Active in the Industry:** by decade

| 10ˢ | 20ˢ | 30ˢ | 40ˢ | 50ˢ | 60ˢ | 70ˢ | 80ˢ | 90ˢ |
|-----|-----|-----|-----|-----|-----|-----|-----|-----|
|     |     |     |     |     |     |     |     |     |

North began dancing professionally at age 10 and, during her teens, modeled and danced in clubs and for film loops; meanwhile, she got married at 15 and soon had a child. She got bit roles in a couple of films, and in 1953 gained Hollywood's attention with a wild dance performance in the Broadway musical *Hazel Flagg.* North reprised her role in the play's screen version, *Living It Up* (1954), with Martin and Lewis. Soon thereafter she was signed to a film contract by Fox, which tried to make her into a '50s-style platinum blond "sexpot" and potential replacement for Marilyn Monroe; the studio mounted a big publicity campaign and starred her in several light productions. She proved herself to be a skilled comedian and dancer and a reasonably good actress. However, within a few years other actresses usurped her "dumb blond" roles, and after 1958 she disappeared from the screen for almost a decade. She went on to perform in stock, on the road, and on TV. Gradually, she developed a reputation as a serious actress, an unprecedented transformation of performing personas for an actress of her generation. In the late '60s she began appearing regularly in films in character roles, and she sustained a busy screen and TV career through the '90s. **Selected Works:** *Defenseless* (1991), *Shootist* (1976)

## Kim Novak (Marilyn Pauline Novak)

**Born:** February 13, 1933; Chicago, IL

**Years Active in the Industry:** by decade

| 10ˢ | 20ˢ | 30ˢ | 40ˢ | 50ˢ | 60ˢ | 70ˢ | 80ˢ | 90ˢ |
|-----|-----|-----|-----|-----|-----|-----|-----|-----|
|     |     |     |     |     |     |     |     |     |

A cool, aloof, earthy, sensual blond movie star and sex symbol of the '50s and '60s, Novak had a number of early odd jobs, including touring the country as a refrigerator pitch-lady called "Miss Deepfreeze." She broke into films in 1954, playing a bit role

in *The French Line* with Jayne Mansfield. Signed to a contract by Columbia, Novak was groomed for stardom by Columbia chief Harry Cohn, who hoped she might replace the difficult Rita Hayworth as the studio's most attractive actress. Although inexperienced, she soon became a popular star, and by 1956 she was the nation's top box-office attraction; she may have been the last "sex goddess" manufactured by the old Hollywood studio system. Novak gained publicity for her supposed romantic liaisons with such celebrities as Frank Sinatra, Cary Grant, and Aly Khan; in 1958 she was given a sports car by Dominican dictator Rafael Trujillo, an event discussed in the U.S. Congress. She gradually became a skilled actress, but in the early '60s her popularity waned. From 1965-66 she was married to actor Richard Johnson, with whom she had appeared in *The Amorous Adventures of Moll Flanders* (1965). Following a second marriage in 1976, Novak retired from the screen in the late '70s to raise horses and breed llamas in Oregon and California. In the late '80s she began appearing again in occasional films and TV productions. **Selected Works:** *Pal Joey* (1957), *Picnic* (1955), *Vertigo* (1958)

## Phillip Noyce

**Born:** April 29, 1950; Griffith, New South Wales, Australia

**Years Active in the Industry:** by decade

| 10ˢ | 20ˢ | 30ˢ | 40ˢ | 50ˢ | 60ˢ | 70ˢ | 80ˢ | 90ˢ |
|-----|-----|-----|-----|-----|-----|-----|-----|-----|
|     |     |     |     |     |     |     |     |     |

Australian Phillip Noyce was "movie crazy" from an early age, experimenting with an 8mm camera as a teen and producing an independent short, *Better to Reign in Hell,* before graduating from high school. He entered the University of Sydney's law school, quit to play amateur rugby, then re-enrolled in the University's fine arts department. Noyce continued turning out short documentaries on the more offbeat aspects of Australian life and also ran the University's film society before being accepted at the fledgling Australian Film and Television School in 1972. Two years later, he won the Sydney Film Festival's Rouben Mamoulien award for his documentary *Castor and Pollux.* With *God Knows Why, But It Works,* a 1975 docudrama about medical care among the Aborigines, Noyce became a professional filmmaker. His first feature, 1977's *Backroads* (which he also produced and wrote), expanded on certain race-relations themes explored in *God Knows Why etc.* *Newsfront* (1978), a paean to pioneering Australian newsreel cameramen, was Noyce's final nonfiction project. The director's first international success was the minimalist melodrama *Dead Calm* (1989), which, despite an idiotic slasher-movie ending, was potent enough to gain Noyce entry into Hollywood. His first American film, an adaptation of Tom Clancy's technothriller *Patriot Games* (1992), showed he knew how to take charge of a big-budget, big-star project. Alas, Noyce's next effort, *Sliver* (1993) was a misfire Sharon Stone vehicle plagued by in-production indecision and a surprising lack of genuine suspense. **Selected Works:** *Blind Fury* (1990), *Clear and Present Danger* (1994)

# Sven Nykvist

**Born:** December 3, 1922; Moheda, Sweden

**Years Active in the Industry:** by decade

| 10s | 20s | 30s | 40s | 50s | 60s | 70s | 80s | 90s |
|-----|-----|-----|-----|-----|-----|-----|-----|-----|

Swedish-born cinematographer Sven Nykvist is best known as the photographer of most of Ingmar Bergman's best known movies of the 1960s. Born to a missionary couple who spent most of their time in Africa, Nykvist was raised in the strictly religious household of relatives who severely limited his film attendance, but developed a fascination with the medium nonetheless, and started as an assistant cameraman in 1941. He became a cinematographer in 1945, and worked on a multitude of films over the next 15 years, most of which were not shown outside of Sweden. He first worked with Ingmar Bergman on *Sawdust And Tinsel* (aka *The Naked Night*) in 1953, when the director's usual cinematographer Gunnar Fischer was unavailable, and, after a rough start, the two developed a good working relationship. However, it was not until seven years later, with *The Virgin Spring,* that Nykvist became Bergman's permanent cinematographer—the two developed a close working relationship, with Nykvist capturing every visual nuance of Bergman's work like an extra set of the director's eyes. Nykvist won Academy Awards for his work on *Cries and Whispers* (1973) and *Fanny and Alexander* (1982). With Bergman's withdrawal from directing, Nykvist has also worked on films by numerous other directors, and won Oscar nominations for Philip Kaufman's *The Unbearable Lightness of Being* (1989) and his own *The Ox* (1991). **Selected Works:** *Crimes and Misdemeanors* (1989), *Sleepless in Seattle* (1993), *Only You* (1994)

# Edmond O'Brien

**Born:** September 10, 1915; Bronx, NY
**Died:** May 8, 1985; Inglewood, CA

**Years Active in the Industry:** by decade

| 10ˢ | 20ˢ | 30ˢ | 40ˢ | 50ˢ | 60ˢ | 70ˢ | 80ˢ | 90ˢ |
|-----|-----|-----|-----|-----|-----|-----|-----|-----|
|     |     |     | ███ | ███ | ███ | ███ |     |     |

Reportedly a neighbor of Harry Houdini while growing up in the Bronx, American actor Edmond O'Brien decided to emulate Houdini by becoming a magician himself. The demonstrative skills gleaned from this experience enabled O'Brien to move into acting while attending high school. After majoring in drama at Columbia University, he made his first Broadway appearance at age 21 in *Daughters of Atrus*. O'Brien's mature features and deep, commanding voice allowed him to play characters far older than himself, and it looked as though he was going to become one of Broadway's premiere character actors. Yet when he was signed for film work by RKO in 1939, the studio somehow thought he was potential leading man material—perhaps as a result of his powerful stage performance as young Marc Antony in Orson Welles' modern dress version of *Julius Caesar*. As Gringoire the poet in *The Hunchback of Notre Dame* (1939), O'Brien was a bit callow and overemphatic, but he *did* manage to walk off with the heroine (Maureen O'Hara) at the end of the film. O'Brien's subsequent film roles weren't quite as substantial, though he was shown to excellent comic advantage in the Moss Hart all-serviceman play *Winged Victory,* in a role he repeated in the 1944 film version while simultaneously serving in World War II (he was billed as "Sergeant Edmond O'Brien"). Older and stockier when he returned to Hollywood after the war, O'Brien was able to secure meaty leading parts in such "films noir" as *The Killers* (1946), *The Web* (1947) and *White Heat* (1949). In the classic melodrama *D.O.A.* (1950), O'Brien enjoyed one of the great moments in "noir" history when, as a man dying of poison, he staggered into a police station at the start of the film and gasped "I want to report a murder...mine." As one of many top-rank stars of 1954's *The Barefoot*

*Contessa,* O'Brien breathed so much credibility into the stock part of a Hollywood press agent that he won an Academy Award. On radio, the actor originated the title role in the long-running insurance-investigator series "Yours Truly, Johnny Dollar" in 1950. On TV, O'Brien played a Broadway star turned private eye in the 1959 syndicated weekly "Johnny Midnight," though the producers refused to cast him unless he went on a crash vegetarian diet. Plagued by sporadic illnesses throughout his life, O'Brien suffered a heart seizure in 1961 while on location in the Arabian desert to play the Lowell Thomas counterpart in *Lawrence of Arabia,* compelling the studio to replace him with Arthur Kennedy. O'Brien recovered sufficiently in 1962 to take the lead in a TV lawyer series, "Sam Benedict;" another TV stint took place three years later in "The Long Hot Summer." The actor's career prospered for the next decade, but by 1975 illness had begun to encroach upon his ability to perform; he didn't yet know it, but he was in the first stages of Alzheimer's Disease. Edmond O'Brien dropped out of sight completely during the next decade, suffering the ignominity of having his "death" reported by tabloids several times during this period. The real thing mercifully claimed the tragically enfeebled O'Brien in 1985. **Selected Works:** *Double Life* (1947), *Man Who Shot Liberty Valance* (1962), *Seven Days in May* (1964)

# Margaret O'Brien (Angela Maxine O'Brien)

**Born:** January 15, 1937; Los Angeles, CA

**Years Active in the Industry:** by decade

| 10ˢ | 20ˢ | 30ˢ | 40ˢ | 50ˢ | 60ˢ | 70ˢ | 80ˢ | 90ˢ |
|-----|-----|-----|-----|-----|-----|-----|-----|-----|
|     |     | ███ |     |     |     |     |     |     |

Thanks to the strenuous efforts of her mother, a former dancer, American child actress Margaret O'Brien won her first film role at age four in the Mickey Rooney-Judy Garland musical *Babes on Broadway* (1941). MGM was so impressed by the child's expressiveness and emotional range that she was given the title role in the wartime morale-booster *Journey For Margaret* (1942). She was so camera-savvy by the time she appeared in *Dr. Gillespie's Criminal Case* (1943) that the film's star Lionel Barrymore declared that had this been the Middle Ages, O'Brien would have been burned at the stake! Some of her coworkers may secretly have wished that fate on O'Brien, since she reportedly flaunted her celebrity on the set, ostensibly at the encouragement of her parents. Famed for her crying scenes, O'Brien really let the faucets flow in her best film, *Meet Me in St. Louis* (1944), in which her character also predated Wednesday Addams by two decades with a marked fascination for death and funerals. In 1944, O'Brien was given a special Academy Award, principally for work in *Meet Me In St. Louis.* As she grew, her charm faded; by 1951's *Her First Romance,* she was just one of a multitude of Hollywood teen ingenues. A comeback attempt in the 1956 film *Glory* was servicable, but the film was badly handled by its distributor RKO Radio and failed to re-establish the actress. A more fruitful role awaited her in a 1958 TV musical version of *Little Women,* in which O'Brien played Beth, the same role she'd essayed in the 1949 film version. In 1960, O'Brien had a strong supporting part in the period picture *Heller in Pink Tights* (1960), ironically playing a onetime child actress whose stage mother is trying to keep her in "kid" roles. In between summer theatre productions, O'Brien would resurface every so often in another TV show, reviewers would welcome her back, and then she'd be forgotten until the next part. The actress gained a great deal of weight in the late 1960s, turning this debility into an asset when she appeared in a "Marcus Welby MD" TV episode (starring her *Journey for Margaret* costar Robert Young) in which she played a woman susceptible to quack diet doctors. A bit thinner, and with eyes as wide and expressive as ever, O'Brien has recently appeared in a handful of episodes of "Murder She Wrote," that evergreen refuge for MGM luminaries of the past. **Selected Works:** *Madame Curie* (1943)

# Pat O'Brien (William Joseph Patrick O'Brien, Jr.)

**Born:** November 11, 1899; Milwaukee, WI
**Died:** October 15, 1983; Santa Monica, CA

**Years Active in the Industry:** by decade

| 10s | 20s | 30s | 40s | 50s | 60s | 70s | 80s | 90s |
|-----|-----|-----|-----|-----|-----|-----|-----|-----|
|     |     |     |     |     |     |     |     |     |

American actor Pat O'Brien could never remember just *why* he wanted to go on stage; it just sort of happened naturally, just as his college football activities at Marquette University and his enlistment in the Navy for World War I. In the company of college chum Spencer Tracy, O'Brien moved to New York in the early twenties, where, while studying at Sargent's Academy, they were cast as robots in the theatrical production *RUR.* O'Brien spent several years with numerous stock companies, forming lasting friendships with such future Hollywood notables as Frank McHugh, James Gleason and Percy Kilbride. He also met his wife, actress Eloise Taylor, with whom he remained for the next five

decades. In 1930, O'Brien was brought to Hollywood to play ace reporter Hildy Johnson in *The Front Page* (1931); this came about because the director mistakenly believed O'Brien had played the role on Broadway, when in fact he'd played managing editor Walter Burns in a Chicago stock-company version. This misunderstanding was forgotten when O'Brien scored a success in *Front Page,* which led to a long term contract with Warner Bros. Casual film fans who believe that O'Brien played nothing but priests and football coaches might be surprised at the range of roles during his first five years at Warners. Still, the performances for which Pat O'Brien is best remembered are Father Jerry in *Angels with Dirty Faces* (1938), in which he begs condemned killer Jimmy Cagney to "turn yellow" during the Last Walk so Cagney won't be a hero to the neighborhood kids, and, of course, the title role in *Knute Rockne, All American* (1940), wherein he exhorted his flagging team to "win just one for the Gipper." Too old to serve in World War II, O'Brien tirelessly did his bit with several hazardous USO tours in the thick of the action. Following the war, O'Brien continued to play leads in a good series of RKO films, but he'd put on weight and lost a few hairs in the years since his Warner Bros. heyday, thus was more effectively cast in character roles like Dean Stockwell's vaudeville dad in *The Boy With Green Hair* (1949). Then, inexplicably, the roles dried up. O'Brien always believed that he was the victim of a blacklist—not for being a Communist, but for being such a *right* winger that he was frozen out by Hollywood's liberal contingent. The diminishing box office for his films and an overall slump in the movie industry may also have played a part in O'Brien's fall from grace, but the fact was he found the going rough in the '50s. Fortunately, he had an aggresive agent and several loyal friends—notably Spencer Tracy, who refused to star in MGM's *The People Against O'Hara* unless the studio set aside a big part for O'Brien. Television and summer stock kept O'Brien busy throughout most of the 1950s, with a brief comeback to stardom via a good part in Billy Wilder's *Some Like It Hot* (1959) and a weekly TV sitcom, "Harrigan and Son" (1960). O'Brien also worked up a well-received nightclub act, in which he described himself as "an Irish Myron Cohen" (Cohen was a popular Jewish dialect comedian of the era). Unlike his close friend James Cagney, O'Brien never stopped working, touring with his wife Eloise in straw hat productions of *Never too Late* and *On Golden Pond.* His performances proved that this was no pathetic oldster clinging desperately to the past, but a vibrant, up-to-date talent who could still deliver the goods. Nor was Pat O'Brien falsely modest. In answer to an interviewer's query if he felt that he'd been underrated by Hollywood, the seventy-plus O'Brien mustered all his Irish pugnacity and snapped "I'm damn good and I know it." As did everyone who saw Pat O'Brien's feisty final film performances in *The End* (1978) and *Ragtime* (1981). **Selected Works:** *Last Hurrah* (1958), *Secret Command* (1944)

# Carroll O'Connor

**Born:** August 2, 1925; Bronx, NY

**Years Active in the Industry:** by decade

| 10ˢ | 20ˢ | 30ˢ | 40ˢ | 50ˢ | 60ˢ | 70ˢ | 80ˢ | 90ˢ |
|-----|-----|-----|-----|-----|-----|-----|-----|-----|

In the tradition of fellow Irish-American Eugene O'Neill, the young Carroll O'Connor satiated his wanderlust by heading off to sea. O'Connor served with the Merchant Marine, then attended the University College of Dublin, making his professional acting debut with that Irish city's Gate Theatre. He made his Broadway bow in 1958 and his first film, *A Fever in the Blood*, three years later. O'-Connor's doughy face was seen and his sandpaper voice was heard in dozens of movie and TV roles in the early 1960s, some sympathetic (the truck driver who has a date with destiny—and Kirk Douglas—in 1961's *Lonely are the Brave*), some villainous, and some nearly invisible (he was all but removed from the final release print of the gargantuan *Cleopatra* [1963]). O'Connor may well have continued in this character-actor vein had not Mickey Rooney turned down the role of Archie Bunker on the proposed Norman Lear sitcom *Those Were the Days*. Lear and his partner Bud Yorkin recalled O'Connor's portrayal of a bullnecked army general in *What Did You Do In the War, Daddy?* (1966) and decided that he'd be perfect in the role of "lovable bigot" Archie. After two misfire pilot films, *Those Were the Days* premiered in January of 1971—under the new title *All in the Family*. An overnight sensation after twenty years in the business, O'Connor became a major star on the strength of *Family*, earning him top billing in such televised specials as *Of Thee I Sing* (1972) and such TV movies as *The Last Hurrah* (1977), winning him four Emmy awards, and even allowing him to headline a Las Vegas nightclub act. As his popularity grew, O'Connor used his clout to increase his salary and his control over *All in the Family*; by the time the series ended in 1979, he was listed as one of the head writers. *All in the Family* begat *Archie Bunker's Place* in 1979, which remained on the air until 1983. Following his 12-year stint as Archie Bunker, O'Connor starred in and directed several Broadway plays, none of which were notably successful. After a delicate heart bypass surgery in 1989, Carroll O'Connor, looking absolutely none the worse for wear, launched a third popular TV series, the weekly hour long drama *In the Heat of the Night* (1988-93). Costarring in this series as a deputy was O'Connor's son Hugh, whose 1994 death from a drug overdose brought forth an overwhelming flood of public sympathy and support for the devasted O'Connor.

# Donald O'Connor

**Born:** August 28, 1925; Chicago, IL

**Years Active in the Industry:** by decade

| 10ˢ | 20ˢ | 30ˢ | 40ˢ | 50ˢ | 60ˢ | 70ˢ | 80ˢ | 90ˢ |
|-----|-----|-----|-----|-----|-----|-----|-----|-----|

The son of a stage acrobat, American actor/dancer/singer Donald O'Connor was hoofing away as a child in his family's vaudeville act. He was discovered for films in 1938's *Sing, You Sinners,* spending the next few years in movies usually playing

"the star as a child"—that is, cast as the younger version of the film's leading man for prologue and flashback sequences. A 1941 Universal contract led to a string of peppy medium-budget musicals with such pure-forties titles as *Get Hep to Love* (1941) and *Are You With It?* (1949); O'Connor's most frequent costar was another teenage vaudeville vet, Peggy Ryan. In 1950, O'Connor was cast in the non-dancing role of a hapless army private who can't convince anyone that a mule can talk in *Francis* (1950). The film was a major moneymaker, leading Universal to inaugurate a *Francis* series starring O'Connor, Francis the Mule, and Francis' voice, Chill Wills. O'Connor bailed out before the final film in the series, *Francis in the Haunted House* (1956), complaining that the mule was getting more fan mail than he was. During the *Francis* epics, O'-Connor was loaned to MGM for what is regarded as his finest film role, happy-go-lucky Cosmo Brown in *Singin' in the Rain* (1952). If he'd never made another film, O'Connor would be a musical-comedy immortal solely on the basis of his *Rain* setpiece, the athletically uproarious *Make 'Em Laugh* (1952). When the sort of musicals in which he specialized went into a Hollywood eclipse, O'Connor concentrated on TV and nightclubs, save for a few less than satisfying cinematic assignments such as *The Buster Keaton Story* (1957) and the Italian-made curiosity *The Wonders of Alladin* (1961). When O'Connor returned to films for 1965's *That Funny Feeling* it was in support of the musical flavor-of-the-decade Bobby Darin. In 1967, O'Connor tried his hand at a syndicated talk-variety program, where he proved excellent as usual at performing but ill at ease as an interviewer. The 1970s were a maelstrom of summer theatre appearances, club dates and an on-and-off liquor problem for O'Connor; when he resurfaced briefly in 1981's *Ragtime*, movie audiences breathed a sigh of satisfaction that an old friend was back and seemingly as fit as ever. Donald O'Connor's most recent film appearance was a cameo at the beginning of Barry Levinson's *Toys* (1992), wherein he supplied a much-needed chunk of solid entertainment value to an otherwise ponderous project. **Selected Works:** *Beau Geste* (1939)

# Chris O'Donnell

**Born:** 1970; Chicago, IL

**Years Active in the Industry:** by decade

| 10ˢ | 20ˢ | 30ˢ | 40ˢ | 50ˢ | 60ˢ | 70ˢ | 80ˢ | 90ˢ |
|-----|-----|-----|-----|-----|-----|-----|-----|-----|

Winnetka native Chris O'Donnell was planning to study for a career in finance when he was spotted by a talent agent, who was so taken by the young man's natural star quality that he advised him *not* to take acting lessons. After a handful of movie roles, O'-Donnell made the quantum leap to A-list performer in the 1992 film *Scent of a Woman,* in which he played the high school-age companion and general factotum to tenacious blind retired military officer Al Pacino. "Hunk hearthrob" status came O'Donnell's way with his appearance as D'Artagnan in the 1993 filmization of *The Three Musketeers* and 1994's *Circle of Friends*, in which he played an innocent young Irish lad dealing with burgeoning hormones

and Catholic values in the 1950s. With 1995's *Batman Forever,* Chris O'Donnell's star ascended into blockbuster heaven with his high-octane performance as Robin, the Boy Wonder **Selected Works:** *Fried Green Tomatoes* (1991), *Blue Sky* (1994)

# Rosie O'Donnell

**Born:** 1962; Commack, NY

**Years Active in the Industry:** by decade

| 10ˢ | 20ˢ | 30ˢ | 40ˢ | 50ˢ | 60ˢ | 70ˢ | 80ˢ | 90ˢ |
|-----|-----|-----|-----|-----|-----|-----|-----|-----|
|     |     |     |     |     |     |     | ▓   |     |

It is all too facile to dismiss comic actress Rosie O'Donnell as a Roseanne wannabe, simply because of her very slight physical and stylistic resemblance to the former Mrs. Arnold. All too facile, and all too unfair, since O'Donnell is a highly individual talent on her own—you don't win the *Star Search* competition five times by being an imitation of someone else. Since her network TV bow on *Gimme a Break* in 1986, O'Donnell has seldom been unemployed, and has been a frequent and hilarious visitor on the crowded talk-show circuit. Seemingly in every other comedy film produced between 1992 and 1994, Rosie O'Donnell has sparkled in *A League of Their Own* (1992) as an outspoken female ballplayer, in *Sleepless in Seattle* (1993) as Meg Ryan's sentimental best pal, and in *The Flintstones* (1993) as the one and only Betty Rubble (high-decibel giggle and all). It is hardly Rosie O'Donnell's fault that her star turn as a phony dominatrix in *Exit to Eden* (1994) sank without a trace; after all, the market for S&M slapstick comedies has always proven rather limited. **Selected Works:** *Another Stakeout* (1993), *Now and Then* (1995)

# Catherine O'Hara

**Born:** March 4, 1954; Toronto, Ontario, Canada

**Years Active in the Industry:** by decade

| 10ˢ | 20ˢ | 30ˢ | 40ˢ | 50ˢ | 60ˢ | 70ˢ | 80ˢ | 90ˢ |
|-----|-----|-----|-----|-----|-----|-----|-----|-----|
|     |     |     |     |     |     | ▓   |     |     |

Canadian comic actress and writer Catherine O'Hara first came to the attention of American audiences with the 1977 premiere of the satirical series *Second City Television.* For the next several seasons, audiences were convulsed by her portrayal of such me-oriented "celebrities" as Lola Heatherton and Lorna Minnelli. Before leaving the series in the early 1980s, she would share an Emmy with the rest of the *SCTV* writing/ performing staff. In films since 1980, O'Hara has frequently found herself shunted away in negligible roles that have required only a fraction of her talents. Catherine O'Hara's best screen assignment was as Mac-Cauley Culkin's self-involved, but ultimately superprotective mother in the two moneyspinning *Home Alone* flicks of the 1990s. **Selected Works:** *After Hours* (1985), *Betsy's Wedding* (1990), *Little Vegas* (1990)

# Maureen O'Hara (Maureen FitzSimons)

**Born:** August 17, 1920; Millwall, Ireland

**Years Active in the Industry:** by decade

| 10ˢ | 20ˢ | 30ˢ | 40ˢ | 50ˢ | 60ˢ | 70ˢ | 80ˢ | 90ˢ |
|-----|-----|-----|-----|-----|-----|-----|-----|-----|
|     |     | ▓   |     |     |     |     |     |     |

Born in Millwall, Ireland, near Dublin, O'Hara was trained at the Abbey School and appeared on radio as a young girl, before making her stage debut with the Abbey Players in the mid 1930s.

She went to London in 1938, and made her first important screen appearance that same year in the Charles Laughton/Erich Pommer produced drama *Jamaica Inn* (1939), directed by Alfred Hitchcock. She was brought to Hollywood with Laughton's help and co-starred with him in the celebrated costume drama *The Hunchback of Notre Dame,* which established O'Hara as a major new leading lady. Although she appeared in dramas such as *How Green Was My Valley* with Walter Pidgeon, *The Fallen Sparrow* opposite John Garfield, and *This Land Is Mine* with Laughton, it was in Hollywood's swashbucklers that O'Hara became most popular and familiar. Beginning with *The Black Swan* opposite Tyrone Power in 1942, she always seemed to be fighting (or romancing) pirates, especially once Technicolor became standard for such films—her red hair photographed exceptionally well, and with her good looks, she exuded a sexuality that made her one of the most popular actresses of the late 1940s and early 1950s. O'Hara was also a good sport, willing to play scenes that demanded a lot of her physically for the good of the picture, which directors and producers appreciated. The *Spanish Main, Sinbad The Sailor,* and *Against All Flags* (the latter starring Errol Flynn) were among her most popular action films of the 1940s, but during this period, O'Hara also starred as young Natalie Wood's beautiful, strong-willed mother in the classic holiday fantasy *Miracle On 34th Street* and as John Wayne's estranged wife in the John Ford cavalry drama *Rio Grande.* O'Hara became John Wayne's most popular leading lady, most notably in Ford's *The Quiet Man,* but her career was interrupted during the late 1950s when she filed suit against the scandal magazine *Confidential.* Wayne and Ford stood by her, and she also got to do the occasional offbeat project such as the satire *Our Man In Havana* (based on a Graham Greene novel), starring Alec Guinness. During the 1960s, she moved into more distinctly maternal roles, playing the mother of Hayley Mills in Disney's extremely popular *The Parent Trap.* She also starred with John Wayne in the comedy western *McLintock!* and with James Stewart in the *The Rare Breed,* both directed by Andrew V. McLaglen. Following her last film with John Wayne, *Big Jake,* and a 1973 television adaptation of John Steinbeck's *The Red Pony,* O'Hara went into retirement. She returned to the screen in 1991 to play John Candy's overbearing mother in the comedy *Only The Lonely.* **Selected Works:** *Sitting Pretty* (1948)

# Dennis O'Keefe (Edward Flanagan)

**Born:** March 29, 1908; Fort Madison, IA
**Died:** 1968

### Years Active in the Industry: by decade

| 10s | 20s | 30s | 40s | 50s | 60s | 70s | 80s | 90s |
|-----|-----|-----|-----|-----|-----|-----|-----|-----|

O'Keefe was a lithe, brash, charming, tall, rugged lead actor. The son of vaudevillians, he began appearing onstage in his parents' act while still a toddler. By age 16 he was writing scripts for "Our Gang" comedy shorts. He attended some college and did more work on vaudeville before entering films in the early '30s, appearing in bit roles in more than 50 films under the name Bud Flanagan. His work in a small role in the film *Saratoga* (1937) impressed Clark Gable, who recommended that he be cast in leads. MGM agreed, so he changed his name to Dennis O'Keefe and went on to play leads in numerous films, beginning with *Bad Man of Brimstone* (1938). Besides many light action-oriented films, he also appeared in numerous '40s comedies, and later specialized in tough-guy parts. Later in his career he directed a film or two and also wrote mystery stories. In the late '50s O'Keefe starred in the short-lived TV series "The Dennis O'Keefe Show." He was in two films in the '60s. He died at 60 of lung cancer. His widow is actress Steffi Duna. **Selected Works:** *Broadway Bill* (1934), *Hangmen Also Die* (1943)

# Ryan O'Neal (Patrick Ryan O'Neal)

**Born:** April 20, 1941; Los Angeles, CA

### Years Active in the Industry: by decade

| 10s | 20s | 30s | 40s | 50s | 60s | 70s | 80s | 90s |
|-----|-----|-----|-----|-----|-----|-----|-----|-----|

The son of screenwriter-novelist Charles O'Neal and actress Patricia Callaghan O'Neal, he grew up in California and several foreign countries. His occasionally troubled youth included a 51-day stay in jail for assault and battery, the result of a brawl at a New Year's party. He worked as a lifeguard and amateur boxer, and was a Golden Gloves competitor. At 17 he began working as a stuntman on a German TV series in Munich. Back in the U.S. he began getting roles in TV shows, and was a regular on the series "Empire." He became well-known as a regular on the long-running hit "Peyton Place." He appeared in two films before being selected as the lead of *Love Story* (1970), a huge hit which established him as a star; he received a Best Actor Oscar nomination for his performance. In the early '70s he appeared in several other major films, but by decade's end his popularity had waned and he started working in low-quality films. By the late '80s he had almost no movie career to speak of. He married and divorced actresses Joanna Moore and Leigh Taylor-Young, and later had a long live-in relationship with actress Farrah Fawcett, with whom he had a son. He also costarred with Fawcett in the short-lived TV series "Good Sports." He is the father of actor Griffin O'Neal and actress Tatum O'Neal. He costarred with Tatum in *Paper Moon* (1973). He is the brother of actor Kevin O'Neal. **Selected Works:** *Barry Lyndon* (1975), *Man Upstairs* (1993)

# Tatum O'Neal

**Born:** November 5, 1963; Los Angeles, CA

### Years Active in the Industry: by decade

| 10s | 20s | 30s | 40s | 50s | 60s | 70s | 80s | 90s |
|-----|-----|-----|-----|-----|-----|-----|-----|-----|

The youngest-ever recipient of the Academy Award, American actress Tatum O'Neal is the daughter of actors Ryan O'Neal and Joanna Moore. When her father was cast as the confidence trickster protagonist of *Paper Moon* (1973), O'Neal was awarded the part of Addie Pray, the con-man's "ward" and partner in crime. For this remarkable debut, O'Neal won the Oscar for Best Supporting Actress—which enabled her to demand profit percentage points on her next film, *Bad News Bears* (1976). Playing the only female member of a misfit junior-league baseball team (she was doubled by two young baseball champs), O'Neal's highlight scene in *Bears* was the one in which she all but promised her body to a pre-teen punk to get him to join the ball club. Mid-1970s audiences were oddly attuned to films in which children swore and swilled beer, so *Bad News Bears* was O'Neal's second box office hit in a row. *Nickelodeon* (1976) followed, wherein O'Neal played a 12-year-old silent-film scenarist, a character based on Anita Loos. This film, in which she was reunited with her *Paper Moon* costar/father Ryan O'Neal and director Peter Bogdanovich, may have represented the actress' best work, but few filmgoers saw it. By 1980, O'Neal was old enough to appear as a summer-camp girl determined to lose her virginity in *Little Darlings,* but her acting skills paled beside those of her costar, Kristy McNichol. As O'Neal got older, the roles became less interesting and her acting less natural and appealing. Also, her divalike on-set attitude while still a child discouraged producers from bankrolling her as an adult actress. Though she hasn't acted much in the last few years, O'Neal has managed to keep her name in the public eye through her marriage (recently dissolved) with the terror of the tennis courts, John McEnroe.

# Maureen O'Sullivan

**Born:** May 17, 1911; Boyle, Ireland

**Years Active in the Industry:** by decade

| 10s | 20s | 30s | 40s | 50s | 60s | 70s | 80s | 90s |
|-----|-----|-----|-----|-----|-----|-----|-----|-----|

Raised in Ireland and educated at a London convent and a French finishing school, O'Sullivan was discovered in her early teens at Dublin's International Horse Show by director Frank Borzage. He signed her to a contract with Fox, and she soon arrived in Hollywood. She debuted onscreen in 1930 and appeared in many films over the next dozen years, tending to play supporting roles in major productions and leads in B-movies. She is best remembered for playing Jane in six "Tarzan" movies with Johnny Weissmuller. In 1936 O'Sullivan married director John Farrow, and in 1942 she retired from the screen to raise her children. After 1948 she began appearing again in occasional films. In the '50s she hosted "Irish Heritage," a syndicated TV show, and was briefly a regular on the "Today" show. In the '60s she appeared in several Broadway productions. She is the mother of actresses Mia and Tisa Farrow; she appeared with Mia Farrow in the film *Hannah and Her Sisters* (1986). **Selected Works:** *Anna Karenina* (1935), *Barretts of Wimpole Street* (1934), *David Copperfield* (1935), *Peggy Sue Got Married* (1986), *Thin Man* (1934)

# Peter O'Toole

**Born:** August 2, 1932; Wicklow, Ireland

**Years Active in the Industry:** by decade

| 10s | 20s | 30s | 40s | 50s | 60s | 70s | 80s | 90s |
|-----|-----|-----|-----|-----|-----|-----|-----|-----|

Blond, blue-eyed, flamboyant, sexy Irish-born leading man with a virile physique and sensitive, poetic-looking face, O'Toole is especially talented at portraying thoughtful, uncertain heroes. He quit school in Leeds, England, at the age of 14, then worked his

way up from messenger and copy boy to cub reporter for the *Yorkshire Evening Post.* O'Toole debuted in an amateur stage production at age 17, then served two years with the Royal Navy. He studied (on a scholarship) at the Royal Academy of Dramatic Art. His professional acting career commenced with the Bristol Old Vic company from 1955-58 and also on British television. He won great acclaim for his work in the play *The Long, the Short and the Tall* in 1959. O'Toole debuted onscreen in *Kidnapped* (1960), going on to play secondary roles until 1962, when he became famous in the title role of David Lean's epic *Lawrence of Arabia;* for his performance he received a Best Actor Oscar nomination, the first of seven nominations altogether. There followed the films *Becket* (1964) and *Lord Jim* (1965), by which time he was firmly established as a screen star. O'Toole was one of the biggest box-office attractions in the late '60s and early '70s. He has also excelled in eccentric, comedic roles. For his work in *My Favorite Year* (1982) he received his most recent Best Actor Oscar nomination. O'Toole's career has been negatively affected by occasional problems with alcohol. His weirdly manic performance in a 1980 stage production of *Macbeth* was attributed to such problems, and was probably the low point in his career. **Selected Works:** *Dark Angel* (1991), *Last Emperor* (1987), *Lion in Winter* (1968), *Ruling Class* (1972), *Stunt Man* (1980)

# Jack Oakie (Lewis Delaney Offield)

**Born:** November 12, 1903; Sedalia, MO
**Died:** January 23, 1978; Northridge, CA

**Years Active in the Industry:** by decade

| 10s | 20s | 30s | 40s | 50s | 60s | 70s | 80s | 90s |
|-----|-----|-----|-----|-----|-----|-----|-----|-----|

The parents of American actor Jack Oakie had hopes that their son would enter the business world, but a spell as telephone clerk in a brokerage house convinced Oakie to look elsewhere for a career. After appearing at an amateur show staged by Wall Street executives for the Cardiac Society, Oakie was encouraged by the show's director to give acting his full attention. Oakie's professional debut was in the chorus of the 1922 George M. Cohan musical *Little Nellie Kelly.* Several Broadway productions later, Oakie travelled westward to try his luck in films, the first of which was *Finders Keepers.* Transferring without a hitch to talkies, Oakie found himself much in demand, usually playing a dimwitted braggart (with one of the best "double takes" in the business) who somehow made good and got the girl before fadeout time. An over-sized ego and a poor business sense scuttled Oakie's starring career by the late 1930s; he discovered upon return from a trip to Europe that many people in Hollywood had forgotten. The experience humbled the bombastic comedian and convinced him take a new approach to his career. After his unforgettable Mussolini take-off in Chaplin's *The Great Dictator* (1940), Oakie entered a new movie phase as second lead and character actor, which sustained him through many a musical comedy of the 1940s. And when called upon to do so, he could still carry a picture with finesse, as witness the 1945 fantasy *That's the Spirit.* Stage and TV work took up much of his time in the 1950s and 1960s, with occasional choice character parts in such films as *The Rat Race* (1960) and *Lover Come Back* (1962). Unpredictable in his likes and dislikes, Oakie was the sort of fellow who brusquely shooed away autograph seekers, but who also visited ailing comedian Stan Laurel, a man Oakie barely knew, to brighten up Stan's hospital stay at a time when some of Laurel's "close" pals didn't want to show up. Just before his death, Jack Oakie committed his memories to a sometimes fanciful but always entertaining biography, *Jack Oakie's Double Takes,* which was published posthumously by Jack's widow, actress Victoria Horne. **Selected Works:** *It Happened Tomorrow* (1944)

## Merle Oberon (Estelle Merle O'Brien Thompson)

**Born:** February 19, 1911; Calcutta, India
**Died:** November 23, 1979; Los Angeles, CA

**Years Active in the Industry:** by decade

| 10ˢ | 20ˢ | 30ˢ | 40ˢ | 50ˢ | 60ˢ | 70ˢ | 80ˢ | 90ˢ |
|-----|-----|-----|-----|-----|-----|-----|-----|-----|

The daughter of British and Ceylonese parents, actress Merle Oberon was raised in India. In 1928 she travelled to England to become a cabaret singer under the name Queenie O'Brien (years later her stepston Vincent Korda would write a "roman a clef" titled *Queenie*). Oberon adopted the name Estelle Thompson when she entered films in 1930, but by the time she made her first cinematic impression in the small role of Anne Boleyn in *The Private Life of Henry VIII* (1933), she was billed as Merle Oberon. *Henry VIII* producer Alexander Korda decided to prepare Oberon for major stardom, a business interest that eventually turned personal, resulting in marriage. Before her allignment with Korda, Oberon had enjoyed the attentions of numerous handsome actors (including, it is rumored, David Niven). Realizing that Oberon could only go so far in the British film industry, Korda sold part of the actress' contract to Sam Goldwyn, an American producer who could assemble better and more expensive vehicles than the popular but economical Korda product. From 1935 through 1939, Goldwyn showcased Oberon in such opulent productions as *The Dark Angel* (1935), *The Cowboy and the Lady* (1938), and *Wuthering Heights* (1939), while Korda invested in Technicolor to show off Oberon's charms in such froth as *Over the Moon* (1937) and *The Divorce of Lady X* (1938). She

was slated to play in Charles Laughton's ambitious *I Claudius,* but was injured in an auto accident in 1937 and the production was shelved. (Portions of the completed scenes have made the rounds for years as part of a BBC special on *Claudius* titled *The Epic That Never Was.*) Oberon continued her Hollywood career after the breakup of her marriage to Korda. Her second husband was cinematographer Lucien Ballard, who photographed her to fullest effect in such 1940s projects as *The Lodger* (1944) and *Berlin Express* (1948). In the 1950s, Oberon's career lost its way amidst several second-rate European productions; she also surprisingly showed up as host of an American TV adventure anthology, "Assignment Foreign Legion" (1957). She retired to marry Italian industrialist Bruno Pagliai in 1957, re-emerging professionally only for a cameo in *The Oscar* (1966) and a stellar supporting role in *Hotel* (1967), which earned her favorable reviews, most of them concentrating on her ageless beauty. A resident of Mexico at the time of her 1973 divorce from her third husband, Oberon financed her own comeback film, *Interval* (1973), a lugubrious tale of an older woman falling for a younger man. Her costar in this film was Robert Wolders, a wealthy, handsome young man who'd been linked romantically with several older actresses. Oberon eventually married Wolders, who loved her deeply and took compassionate care of the ailing actress until her death in 1979. **Selected Works:** *These Three* (1936)

## Gary Oldman

**Born:** March 21, 1958; South London, England

**Years Active in the Industry:** by decade

| 10ˢ | 20ˢ | 30ˢ | 40ˢ | 50ˢ | 60ˢ | 70ˢ | 80ˢ | 90ˢ |
|-----|-----|-----|-----|-----|-----|-----|-----|-----|

As a youth Oldman performed with the Greenwich Young People's Theater, then won a scholarship to drama school and toured in repertory. In 1980, he joined the prestigious Citizens Theater in Glasgow. Establishing his reputation as a fine young stage actor, Oldman appeared in several outstanding performances in London's West End, including *Rat in the Skull* and *Serious Money* at the Royal Court theater. For his performance in *The Pope's Wedding* he won both the Best Actor and Best Newcomer Awards in 1985; that same year he made some dramatic appearances on British TV, including his role as an artist in "Honest, Decent and True." Oldman debuted onscreen as real-life punk rocker Sid Vicious (of the Sex Pistols) in

Alex Cox's *Sid and Nancy* (1986), for which he won the *London Evening Standard*'s Best Newcomer Award. He went on from there to appear in one or more films in each of the subsequent years, including *State of Grace* (1990); *JFK* (1991); *Bram Stoker's Dracula* (1992), in which he had the title role; *Romeo Is Bleeding* (1993); *True Romance* (1993); and *The Professional* (1994), in which he played a sadistic drug enforcement agent. He's divorced from actress Uma Thurman, his second wife. **Selected Works:** *Immortal Beloved* (1994), *The Scarlet Letter* (1995)

# Lena Olin

**Born:** 1955; Stockholm, Sweden

**Years Active in the Industry:** by decade

| 10$^s$ | 20$^s$ | 30$^s$ | 40$^s$ | 50$^s$ | 60$^s$ | 70$^s$ | 80$^s$ | 90$^s$ |
|---|---|---|---|---|---|---|---|---|
|  |  |  |  |  |  |  | ■ | ■ |

Lithe, intense Swedish leading lady of Hollywood and international films, Olin's parents were both actors. Her father Stig starred in several early Ingmar Bergman films. She has long been a member of the Royal Dramatic Theater in Sweden, where she has made outstanding appearances in work ranging from Shakespeare and Strindberg to contemporary plays. While still in drama school, Olin made her Swedish film debut in *Karleken* (1980). Two of her next three films were made by Bergman: *Fanny and Alexander* (1983) and *After the Rehearsal* (1984); her part in the latter was created for her by Bergman. She also did a four-hour Swedish TV film, *Hebriana*. Her English-language film debut was in *The Unbearable Lightness of Being* (1988). For her second English-language role, that of a survivor of a Nazi death camp in Paul Mazursky's *Enemies, A Love Story* (1989), Olin received a New York Film Critics award and an Oscar nomination. She is the only Swedish actress to have made an impact in Hollywood since Ingrid Bergman. **Selected Works:** *Havana* (1990)

# Sir Laurence Olivier

**Born:** March 22, 1907; Dorking, Surrey, England
**Died:** July 11, 1989; Steyning, West Sussex, England

**Years Active in the Industry:** by decade

| 10$^s$ | 20$^s$ | 30$^s$ | 40$^s$ | 50$^s$ | 60$^s$ | 70$^s$ | 80$^s$ | 90$^s$ |
|---|---|---|---|---|---|---|---|---|
|  | ■ |  |  |  |  |  |  |  |

Although best known for his acting, Laurence Olivier became recognized as a formidable directorial talent in 1944 with his adaptation of Shakespeare's *Henry V*, which received multiple Oscar nominations and earned Olivier a special Academy Award. His ability to tell and structure a story was most impressive, displaying a spellbinding technique, and the film's public acceptance was even more striking—*Henry V* was the first Shakespeare adaptation of the talking-film era to make money. Olivier's *Hamlet* was simi-

larly successful, and his *Richard III* was the greatest of the trilogy, a tour-de-force of acting and screencraft. He directed only one film subsequent to this, *The Prince And The Showgirl*, which Olivier made in association with co-star Marilyn Monroe. **Selected Works:** *The Entertainer* (1960), *Marathon Man* (1976), *Sleuth* (1972), *Spartacus* (1960), *Wuthering Heights* (1939)

# Edward James Olmos

**Born:** 1947; Los Angeles, CA

**Years Active in the Industry:** by decade

| 10$^s$ | 20$^s$ | 30$^s$ | 40$^s$ | 50$^s$ | 60$^s$ | 70$^s$ | 80$^s$ | 90$^s$ |
|---|---|---|---|---|---|---|---|---|
|  |  |  |  |  |  |  | ■ | ■ |

A fine Hispanic-American actor, Olmos tried to have a singing career with a band after his college days. In the early '70s he began to land bit parts in TV series such as "Kojak" and "Hawaii Five-O;" he also appeared in a supporting role (billed as Eddie Olmos) in the film *Aloha, Bobby and Rose* (1975). He came to prominence as an actor in the play *Zoot Suit;* for his performance he received the Los Angeles Drama Critics Award, then (after the play moved to Broadway) a Theater World award and a Tony nomination. He also appeared in the movie version, released in 1981. He became better known in the early '80s as Lt. Castillo in the TV cop show *Miami Vice*, winning an Emmy for his work in 1985. After a series of supporting roles in movies of the '80s, he won the lead role in *Stand and Deliver* (1988), playing a tough high-school math teacher in the barrios of East L.A.; he received a Best Actor Oscar nomination. **Selected Works:** *American Me* (1992), *Blade Runner* (1982)

# Miroslav Ondrícek

**Born:** 1933; Czechoslovakia

**Years Active in the Industry:** by decade

| 10$^s$ | 20$^s$ | 30$^s$ | 40$^s$ | 50$^s$ | 60$^s$ | 70$^s$ | 80$^s$ | 90$^s$ |
|---|---|---|---|---|---|---|---|---|
|  |  |  |  |  | ■ |  |  |  |

Czech cinematographer Miroslav Ondricek polished his skills with the state-owned Documentary Film Studios. His first non-documentary work was with Czech director Milos Forman, notably *Loves of a Blonde* (1965), *Intimate Lighting* (1965) and *The*

*Fireman's Ball* (1966). When Forman set up shop in the U.S. after the 1968 Russian invasion of Czechoslovakia, Ondricek followed suit, working with Forman on such American films as *Hair* (1979), *Ragtime* (1981), *Amadeus* (1984) and *Valmont* (1989). Miroslav Ondricek has also worked harmoniously with such directors as Lindsay Anderson (*O Lucky Man* [1971]), George Roy Hill (*The World According to Garp* [1982]) and Penny Marshall (*Awakenings* [1990]). **Selected Works:** *A League of Their Own* (1992)

# Marcel Ophuls

**Born:** November 21, 1927; Frankfurt, Germany

**Years Active in the Industry:** by decade

| 10s | 20s | 30s | 40s | 50s | 60s | 70s | 80s | 90s |
|-----|-----|-----|-----|-----|-----|-----|-----|-----|
|     |     |     |     |     |     |     |     |     |

German director Marcel Ophuls, the son of famed director Max Ophuls, has continued his father's legacy of films centering on oppression and prejudice. Recognized for his hard-hitting documentaries, Ophuls is best known for his internationally-acclaimed, award-winning film *The Sorrow and the Pity* (1970), a provocative French film that chronicled events in Nazi occupied France. It also examined the ways in which some locals in the town of Clemont-Ferrand collaborated with the Germans at that time, which led it to be banned from French TV until 1981, as it was considered too disturbing. The German born Ophuls came to the U.S. with his exiled father where he attended high school in Hollywood. He then went on to study at Occidental College, Los Angeles; the University of California, Berkely; and at the Sorbonne in Paris. In 1951, while still in France, he became an assistant for filmmakers Julien Duvivier, John Huston, and Anatole Litvak. He also began working in German and French television. In 1962, he made an unremarkable directorial debut with the anthology film, *Love at Twenty*. Following the success of *The Sorrow and the Pity,* Ophuls continued to produce historical documentaries on a wide variety of social issues. Beyond directing, he also acted and wrote magazine articles for periodicals such as *American Film*. In addition, he served on the board of the French Filmmakers Society. He has also lectured at American universities. In 1988 he made *Hotel Terminus: The Life and Times of Klaus Barbie,* which won that year's Oscar for best documentary and the International Critics Prize at Cannes. **Selected Works:** *Memory of Justice* (1976)

# Max Ophuls

**Born:** May 6, 1902; Saarbrucken, Germany
**Died:** March 26, 1957; Hamburg, Germany

**Years Active in the Industry:** by decade

| 10s | 20s | 30s | 40s | 50s | 60s | 70s | 80s | 90s |
|-----|-----|-----|-----|-----|-----|-----|-----|-----|
|     |     |     |     |     |     |     |     |     |

Filmmaker Max Ophuls was known for his costume dramas, romances and melodramas. He made films in France, the Nether-

lands, and the U.S. during the 1930s, '40s, and '50s. At the time, his films were not well recieved by critics, but in the '60s he began to be considered a true artist in his own right. He began his career in his native Germany during the 1920s as a stage director. After the Nazis rose to power, he left for France and has stayed there, except for a brief stay in America during the 1940s and '50s. Despite his constant roving, Ophuls' work is very consistent with his use of complex, but fluid, camera movement and his tendency to set stories during Vienna at the end of the 19th-century. **Selected Works:** *Ronde* (1950)

# Jerry Orbach

**Born:** October 20, 1935; Bronx, NY

**Years Active in the Industry:** by decade

| 10s | 20s | 30s | 40s | 50s | 60s | 70s | 80s | 90s |
|-----|-----|-----|-----|-----|-----|-----|-----|-----|
|     |     |     |     |     |     |     |     |     |

New York native and Northwestern University alumnus Jerry Orbach has often commented, without false modesty, that he is fortunate indeed to have been a steadily working actor since the age of 20. After training with Herbert Berghof and Lee Strasberg, the lanky, deep-voiced Orbach received his first off-Broadway job as an understudy in the popular 1955 revival of *The Threepenny Opera*, eventually playing the lead role of MacHeath. During the *Threepenny* run, Orbach made his first film appearance in the Manhattan-filmed low budgeter *Cop Killer* (1958). In 1960, Orbach created the role of flamboyant interlocutor El Gallo in the off-Broadway smash *The Fantasticks*. That musical is still running, but Orbach has since starred in such Broadway productions as *Carnival* (1961), *Promises Promises* (1966), *Chicago* (1975) and *42nd Street* (1983). By day, Orbach made early-1960s appearances in several New York-based TV series, notably *The Shari Lewis Show*. At first, Orbach's film assignments were infrequent, but starting with 1985's *Brewster's Millions*, the actor managed to show up in at least one movie per year. His more fondly remembered screen roles include the part of Jennifer Grey's father in *Dirty Dancing* (1987), the voice of the Chevalieresque candellabra in the Disney cartoon feature *Beauty and the Beast* (1990), and Billy Crystal's easily amused agent in *Mr. Saturday Night* (1992). On TV, Jerry Orbach has starred in the 1985 *Murder She Wrote* spinoff *The Law and Harry McGraw*, and was one of the many revolving-door regulars on the 1990s cop series *Law and Order*. **Selected Works:** *Crimes and Misdemeanors* (1989), *Last Exit to Brooklyn* (1990), *Prince of the City* (1981)

# Julia Ormond

**Born:** 1965; England

**Years Active in the Industry:** by decade

| 10s | 20s | 30s | 40s | 50s | 60s | 70s | 80s | 90s |
|-----|-----|-----|-----|-----|-----|-----|-----|-----|
|     |     |     |     |     |     |     |     |     |

British actress Julia Ormond had several solid years of stage work to her credit—not to mention the starring role in the made-for-cable Catherine the Great biography *Young Catherine* (1991)—when, at 27, she was costarred in the expensive HBO biopic *Stalin* (1992). Most of the publicity guns were aimed at Robert Duvall's heavily accented portrayal of the Soviet dictator, but at least one observer singled out Ormond's performance as the long-suffering Mrs. Stalin as one of the highlights of the picture. That observer was director Ed Zwick, then preparing his own big-budget theatrical feature *Legends of the Fall* (1994). Thanks to her excellent showing in the formidable company of *Fall* costars Brad Pitt, Aidan Quinn, and Henry Thomas, Ormond found herself, on the verge of 30, the actress *du jour* in Hollywood. Before 1995 was over, the graceful, silken-haired Ormond had played Guinevere opposite Sean Connery's King Arthur in *First Knight* and had been cast in the title role of the 1995 remake of *Sabrina*. When asked by *Premiere* magazine what her future plans were, Julia Ormond replied "Along with Godzilla and the rest of the acting community, I'd like to direct."

# Reginald Owen

**Born:** August 5, 1887; Hartfordshire, England
**Died:** November 5, 1972; Los Angeles, CA

**Years Active in the Industry:** by decade

| 10ˢ | 20ˢ | 30ˢ | 40ˢ | 50ˢ | 60ˢ | 70ˢ | 80ˢ | 90ˢ |
|-----|-----|-----|-----|-----|-----|-----|-----|-----|
|     |     |     |     |     |     |     |     |     |

British actor Reginald Owen was a graduate of Sir Herbert Beerbohm Tree's Academy of Dramatic Arts. He made his stage bow in 1905, remaining a highly-regarded leading man in London for nearly two decades before traversing the Atlantic to make his Broadway premiere in *The Swan*. His film career commenced with *The Letter* (1929), and for the next forty years Owen was one of Hollywood's favorite Englishmen, playing everything from elegant aristocrats to seedy villains. Modern viewers are treated to Owen at his hammy best each Christmas when local TV stations run MGM's 1938 version of *The Christmas Carol*. As Ebeneezer Scrooge, Owen was a last-minute replacement for an ailing Lionel Barrymore, but no one in the audience felt the loss as they watched Owen go through his lovably cantankerous paces. Reginald Owen's film career flourished into the 1960s and 1970s. He was particularly amusing and appropriately bombastic as Admiral Boom, the cannon-happy eccentric neighbor in Disney's *Mary Poppins* (1964). **Selected Works:** *Great Ziegfeld* (1936), *Pirate* (1948), *Random Harvest* (1942), *Tale of Two Cities* (1935), *Woman of the Year* (1942)

# Frank Oz (Frank Oznowicz)

**Born:** 1944; England

**Years Active in the Industry:** by decade

| 10ˢ | 20ˢ | 30ˢ | 40ˢ | 50ˢ | 60ˢ | 70ˢ | 80ˢ | 90ˢ |
|-----|-----|-----|-----|-----|-----|-----|-----|-----|
|     |     |     |     |     |     |     |     |     |

Born in Hereford, England, Frank Oz graduated from California's Oakland City College during 1962 and joined Jim Henson's fledgling Muppets as a puppeteer the following year. He was part of the first-season cast of "Saturday Night Live" as the Mighty Favag and also appeared in *The Blues Brothers,* starring John Belushi and Dan Aykroyd. After the Muppet Show (1976-81) went on the air, Oz assumed the post of vice-president of the Henson organization, and was responsible for the portrayals of Miss Piggy, Fozzie Bear, and Animal, among other characters. He earned three Emmy Awards on the show. He later served as creative consultant

for *The Great Muppet Caper* (1980), directed by Henson. Oz ascended to the director's chair with *The Dark Crystal* (1981), and continued in this role for *The Muppets Take Manhattan* (1984). Two years later, with Henson in the director's chair, Oz was one of the voices in *Labyrinth* (1986). Moving outside of the Henson orbit, Oz directed the screen version of the musical *Little Shop of Horrors* (1986), *Dirty Rotten Scoundrels* (1988), and *What About Bob?* (1991), and served as the voice of Yoda in the *The Empire Strikes Back* and *Return of the Jedi*. **Selected Works:** *Housesitter* (1992)

# Yasujiro Ozu

**Born:** December 15, 1903; Tokyo, Japan
**Died:** December 11, 1963

**Years Active in the Industry:** by decade

| 10ˢ | 20ˢ | 30ˢ | 40ˢ | 50ˢ | 60ˢ | 70ˢ | 80ˢ | 90ˢ |
|-----|-----|-----|-----|-----|-----|-----|-----|-----|
|     |     |     |     |     |     |     |     |     |

The most respected of all Japanese filmmakers, Yasujiro Ozu began his directorial career at the age of 24. In contrast to such celebrated filmmakers as Kurosawa and Inagaki, whose best-known work usually dwells on historical subjects of great importance, and approaches them in ways that are especially accessible to western viewers, Ozu's films tend toward more seemingly mundane material—the lives of Japanese families—which he handles like a poet. His work possesses a gentle, subtle dramatic and visual lyricism that western audiences only belatedly began to grasp. Ozu's most popular movie in America was probably *Floating Weeds,* a story about the aging leader of a struggling theatrical troupe and the intertwining relationships in his life that nearly destroy his family.

# P

## G.W. Pabst (Georg Wilhelm Pabst)

**Born:** August 27, 1885; Raudnitz, Bohemia
**Died:** May 29, 1967; Vienna Austria

**Years Active in the Industry:** by decade

| 10s | 20s | 30s | 40s | 50s | 60s | 70s | 80s | 90s |
|-----|-----|-----|-----|-----|-----|-----|-----|-----|

Born in Bohemia to Viennese parents, director G. W. Pabst made only one American film in his career, yet became the darling of U.S. critics and movie historians for a handful of brilliant silent works. Pabst studied at Vienna's Academy of Decorate Arts, then embarked on a theatrical career in 1906. He worked as a stage director in Europe and briefly in New York with a German-language company until World War I. In France, when hostilities broke out, he was required to be a "guest of the state" until the Armistice. During this period, he continued as a director of French-language plays. Back in Vienna in the early 1920s, Pabst was one of the vanguards of the experimental theatre movement. This led to an interest in the less-confining vistas of film. Establishing himself as a movie director in 1923, Pabst made his mark by turning out productions of pessimistic realism, intermixed with unstressed impressionism. He directed Garbo in *A Joyless Street* (1925), then helmed the pioneering Freudian drama *Secrets of a Soul* (1926). Pabst helped create the "Louise Brooks mystique" by casting the expatriate American actress in two of his most elaborate (and most heavily censored) sociological sex dramas, *Pandora's Box* (1928) and *Diary of a Lost Girl* (1929). Whenever speaking of Pabst in later years, Brooks was quick to note that the effectiveness of her highly-disciplined performances was almost entirely due to Pabst's ability to precisely envision the film's final cut—camera angles, titles, closeups—before he even started shooting. Despite his meticulous pre-planning, Pabst's results invariably seemed fresh and spontaneous, adding to the underlying realism of his work. The director launched his talkie career with three of his finest films: *Westfront 1918*, an antiwar picture; *The Threepenny Opera,* the definitive version of that Brecht/Weill musical (filmed in two languages, both versions starring legendary Brechtian actress Lotte Lenya); and *Kameradschaft,* a German/French co-production that preached a doctrine of solidarity between nations. With this last film in particular, Pabst was out of step with the edicts of the burgeoning Nazi party. He fled Germany the day Hitler took over, summing up his animosity towards Der Fuhrer nearly a quarter-century later with the fevered "bunker" drama *The Last Ten Days* (1956). In Hollywood in 1934, after two French-made projects, Including *Don Quixote* (1933), with opera star Feodor Chaliapin, Pabst directed *A Modern Hero* (1934), an indifferent soap opera starring Richard Barthelmess. Back in France at the outbreak of World War II, Pabst announced his intention to emigrate to Switzerland, then surprised his followers by moving to Germany, where he made two films for the government he professed to despise. Pabst's true feelings concerning Nazism could be seen in his postwar *The Trial* (1948), a prize-winning attack against anti-Semitism. Pabst continued making films in Germany, Austria, and Italy until his retirement in 1956.

## Al Pacino (Alberto Pacino)

**Born:** April 25, 1940; New York, NY

**Years Active in the Industry:** by decade

| 10s | 20s | 30s | 40s | 50s | 60s | 70s | 80s | 90s |
|-----|-----|-----|-----|-----|-----|-----|-----|-----|

Pacino attended the famed High School of Performing Arts in Manhattan but dropped out when he was 17. He spent several years in various odd jobs. When he had saved enough money, he enrolled at Herbert Berghof's acting school, where he was tutored by Charles Laughton. He appeared in small roles in off-off-Broadway productions. He was admitted to Lee Strasberg's Actors Studio in 1966. In 1968, Pacino portrayed a drunken psychotic in the off-Broadway play *The Indian Wants the Bronx,* for which he won an Obie Award. This led to a role as a drug addict in the Broadway play *Does a Tiger Wear a Necktie?,* for which he won a Tony Award in 1969. That same

year, he debuted onscreen in a small role in *Me Natalie*. He had an important role as a drug addict in his second film, *Panic in Needle Park* (1971). It gained the attention of filmmaker Francis Ford Coppola, who cast him in a key costarring role in *The Godfather* (1972), for which he received a Best Supporting Actor Oscar nomination. He was also nominated for an Oscar three years later for his performance in *Dog Day Afternoon* (1975). Now established as a major star, he went on to an intermittently busy screen career in a variety of brooding, intense roles; he ultimately received six more Oscar nominations, and won the Best Actor Oscar for *Scent of a Woman* (1992). He also went on to do additional stage work, and won another Tony for his performance in the 1977 Broadway play *The Basic Training of Pavlo Hummel.* **Selected Works:** *Dick Tracy* (1990), *Glengarry Glen Ross* (1992), *Serpico* (1973), *A Day to Remember* (1995), *Heat* (1995)

# Joanna Pacula

**Born:** January 1, 1957; Tomazsow Lubelski, Poland

**Years Active in the Industry:** by decade

| 10s | 20s | 30s | 40s | 50s | 60s | 70s | 80s | 90s |
|-----|-----|-----|-----|-----|-----|-----|-----|-----|
|     |     |     |     |     |     |     | ■   | ■   |

Polish-born lead actress of Polish and American films, Pacula is an exotic beauty with innate simplicity. She studied acting at the Academy of Theatrical Arts in Warsaw, then debuted onscreen with a small role in Krzysztof Zanussi's *Bawry Ochronne* (1976), shown in the West in 1979 as *Camouflage*. Soon she landed larger roles in films and TV, making a big impression in the Polish TV serial *Jan Serce* (1981). When martial law was declared in Poland in December 1981, she was vacationing in Paris. She remained there and became romantically involved with exiled Polish director Roman Polanski, who got her some work as a model. Shortly thereafter, Pacula moved to the United States, where she was featured in *Vogue*. Polanski recommended her for the female lead in *Gorky Park* (1983); even though she spoke no English, she got the part, leading to top billing in her next film, the kibbutz-situated love story *Not Quite Jerusalem* (1985). From there she sustained a consistent Hollywood career. **Selected Works:** *Black Ice* (1992), *Eyes of the Beholder* (1992), *Tombstone* (1993)

# Geraldine Page

**Born:** November 22, 1924; Kirksville, MO
**Died:** June 13, 1987; NY

**Years Active in the Industry:** by decade

| 10s | 20s | 30s | 40s | 50s | 60s | 70s | 80s | 90s |
|-----|-----|-----|-----|-----|-----|-----|-----|-----|
|     |     |     |     |     | ■   | ■   | ■   |     |

Excellent performer of American stage, films, and television, Page is a leading exponent of "Method" acting, known for her unconventional performances. She began acting in stock at age 17. In 1952, she broke through with an impressive off-Broadway performance in *Summer and Smoke*, for which she received the New York Drama Critics award. Though she went on to much success, her work on stage and screen has been sparse due to her choosiness in accepting parts. For her work in the play *Sweet Bird of Youth* Page received another New York Drama Critics award. She won Emmy awards for her work in the TV plays *A Christmas Memory* and *Thanksgiving Visitor*. First onscreen in 1947, she did not begin to appear in many movies until the '60s. She has been nominated for four Best Actress Oscars and three Best Supporting Actress Oscars, finally winning the Best Actress Oscar for *Trip to Bountiful* (1985). She was married to actor Rip Torn. **Selected Works:** *Interiors* (1978), *You're a Big Boy Now* (1966), *Hondo* (1953)

# Alan Pakula

**Born:** April 7, 1928; New York, NY

**Years Active in the Industry:** by decade

| 10s | 20s | 30s | 40s | 50s | 60s | 70s | 80s | 90s |
|-----|-----|-----|-----|-----|-----|-----|-----|-----|
|     |     |     |     |     | ■   | ■   | ■   |     |

During the 1970s, filmmaker Alan Pakula was one of the most sought after directors in Hollywood. Upon graduating from the Yale Drama School, Pakula began working as an assistant in

the cartoon department at Warners in 1949. One year later, he began apprenticing at MGM and worked as a production assistant for Paramount the following year. He produced his first film, *Fear Strikes Out*, in 1957. During the early '60s, he and director Robert Mulligan formed their own production company where they created the highly acclaimed *To Kill a Mockingbird* (1962). Pakula did not make his own directorial debut until 1969 with *The Sterile Cuckoo*, a sensitive, often strange, love story. His reputation grew when he directed the critical and box office hit *Klute* (1971), but his career didn't really explode until he directed the blockbuster chronicle of the Watergate investigation, *All* the President's Men (1976). **Selected Works:** Presumed Inno-cent (1990), Sophie's Choice (1982), Pelican Brief (1993)

# George Pal

**Born:** February 1, 1908; Cegled, Hungary
**Died:** May 12, 1980; California

**Years Active in the Industry:** by decade

| 10ˢ | 20ˢ | 30ˢ | 40ˢ | 50ˢ | 60ˢ | 70ˢ | 80ˢ | 90ˢ |
|-----|-----|-----|-----|-----|-----|-----|-----|-----|
|     |     |     |     |     |     |     |     |     |

Trained as an architect at the Budapest Academy of the Arts, Hungarian filmmaker George Pal had trouble securing work in his chosen profession in the late 1920s; to keep food on the table, he designed "art" subtitles for silent films. At the Berlin studios of UFA in 1931, Pal began designing sets, then cultivated an interest in stop-motion animation. Moving to Holland in 1933, Pal pro-duced a group of animated puppet shorts for Phillips Radio of Hol-land. Reportedly, Pal's European career was cut short when he had the temerity to produce an anti-fascist allegorical short. Pal arrived in the U.S. in 1939 to lecture at Columbia University, where he was approached by representatives of Paramount Pictures, who were interested in releasing a series of Pal-produced animated one-reel-ers. Beginning in 1940, Pal was responsible for the Puppettoons series (also known as Madcap Marionettes), a lucrative property that won the producer a special Oscar in 1943. Seen today, the Puppetoons remain dazzling technical achievements, even though their storylines range from skimpy to bewildering. The best of the Puppetoons include John Henry and the Inky-Poo, Tubby the Tuba, and the "Jasper and the Scarecrow" series. After filming a special animated sequence for the 1947 feature film Variety Girl, Pal and Paramount parted company. He became an independent producer with the 1950 Jimmy Durante comedy The Great Rupert, in which Durante costarred with an animated squirrel. Pal's next project, the slow-moving but visually exciting science-fiction en-deavor Destination Moon (1950), won an Academy Award for best special effects. Back at Paramount in 1951, Pal inherited two un-produced sci-fi properties from Cecil B. DeMille. The resultant films, When Worlds Collide (1951) and War of the Worlds (1951), added two more special-effects Oscars to Pal's mantle. Curiously, his first non-fantasy Paramount production, Houdini (1953), was utterly unconvincing in recreating Houdini's legendary illusions. Pal's remaining Paramount productions were equally disappoint-ing, but he made up for his past missteps with his first directorial assignment (which he also produced), MGM's Tom Thumb. This imaginative musical comedy not only won Pal his fourth Oscar, but also happily revived his "Puppetoon" concept, now smoother and more convincing than ever. Oscar number five was bestowed upon the special effects for Pal's The Time Machine (1960), which falters in the dramatic scenes but excells in its vision of the future. The cheapjack Atlantis the Lost Continent (1961) was next, followed by the Cinerama "special" The Wonderful World of the Brothers

Grimm (1962), which had as its main attractions a screenful of Pupppetoon elves and a fire-breathing dragon. Many of Pal's fans consider 1964's Seven Faces of Dr. Lao his finest work. Unfortu-nately Lao was a bit too rareified to succeed at the box office, and it would be a decade before Pal would direct his next—and last—film. Doc Savage: The Man of Bronze (1975), a serviceable adven-ture romp, was weakened by post-production efforts to "camp" the material (e.g. adding an animated gleam to the hero's eye). The failure of Doc Savage prevented Pal from raising the necessary funds for his proposed series of science-fiction films in the late 1970s. As one fan has noted, Pal may have been too nice a guy to survive in the sharktank Hollywood of the era. Nonetheless, the George Pal legend has endured long after his death in 1980. Devo-tees are referred to two recent retrospective films, the semi-docu-mentary Fantasy World of George Pal (1986) and the compilation feature The Puppetoon Movie (1987).

# Jack Palance (Walter Jack Palahnuik)

**Born:** February 18, 1920; Lattimer Mines, PA

**Years Active in the Industry:** by decade

| 10ˢ | 20ˢ | 30ˢ | 40ˢ | 50ˢ | 60ˢ | 70ˢ | 80ˢ | 90ˢ |
|-----|-----|-----|-----|-----|-----|-----|-----|-----|
|     |     |     |     |     |     |     |     |     |

Born Walter Jack Palahnuik, Palance is the son of a coal miner. He worked in the mines, as a professional boxer, and, in World War II, he piloted bombers, one of which crashed. The se-

vere burns he received led to extensive facial surgery, resulting in his gaunt, characteristic face. Palance worked on stage for several years, then moved to Holly-wood. In his early film roles he was almost al-ways cast in sinister, villainous roles, but in some of his later films he revealed a more vul-nerable side. For his performances in both Sudden Fear (1952) and Shane (1953) he received Best Supporting Actor Oscar nomina-tions. Beginning in the late '50s he appeared in numerous foreign (especially Italian) films. He starred in the TV series "The Greatest Show on Earth" and "Bronk," as well as numerous TV dramas, no-tably Rod Serling's Requiem For A Heavyweight. In the early '90s he won over a new generation of viewers with his performances in City Slickers and its sequel. For the former, he received a Best Supporting Actor Oscar. **Selected Works:** Bagdad Cafe (1988), Panic in the Streets (1950), Swan Princess (1994)

# Michael Palin

**Born:** May 5, 1943; Sheffield, England

**Years Active in the Industry:** by decade

| 10s | 20s | 30s | 40s | 50s | 60s | 70s | 80s | 90s |
|-----|-----|-----|-----|-----|-----|-----|-----|-----|
|     |     |     |     |     |     | ■ | ■ | ■ |

Palin earned a degree in history from Oxford, where he joined its Experimental Theater Club and debuted onstage in London in 1964. He worked as a comedy writer-performer with such British TV programs as "Do Not Adjust Your Set" (1967-69) and "Complete and Utter History of Britain" (1969). In 1969, he joined the surrealistic comedy troupe that wrote and performed the BBC-TV show "Monty Python's Flying Circus," which stayed on the air through 1974 and was a hit in syndication in America. The troupe made several movies, then stopped working together in the early '80s. Palin has appeared in a number of major films as a supporting actor. For his portrayal of a stuttering crook in *A Fish Called Wanda* (1988) he won the British Film Academy Best Supporting Actor Award. Palin received a lot of recognition for his travel book and TV series "Pole to Pole."

# Eugene Pallette

**Born:** July 8, 1889; Winfield, KS
**Died:** September 3, 1954; Los Angeles, CA

**Years Active in the Industry:** by decade

| 10s | 20s | 30s | 40s | 50s | 60s | 70s | 80s | 90s |
|-----|-----|-----|-----|-----|-----|-----|-----|-----|
| ■ | ■ | ■ | ■ |     |     |     |     |     |

Believe it or not, barrel-bellied, frog-voiced American actor Eugene Pallette was once upon a time a slim romantic lead. Having previously worked as a streetcar conductor and a jockey, Pallette became a touring stock company performer, entering films as an extra in 1910 and working his way to lead roles in less than a month. His most famous pre-1920 performance was as the dashing leading man in the French sequences of the four-part D.W. Griffith epic *Intolerance* (1916). However, upon returning from World War I service Pallette found that younger, handsomer men had taken his place. He still enjoyed good supporting parts such as one of the Three Musketeers in the 1921 Douglas Fairbanks film of the same name, but his bland features consigned him to bits until he decided to make himself conspicuous by gaining weight. Eventually clocking in at 300 pounds, Pallette was suddenly much in demand as a character actor. In 1927, he signed with Hal Roach Studios, where work as a comedy foil was plentiful. Among his two-reel appearances was the role of the insurance man in the Laurel and Hardy classic *Battle of the Century* (1927). Talkies catapulted Pallette back to prominence. His distinctive deep croaking voice made the actor a natural for detective, promoter, con man, and "boss" roles. In films like *My Man Godfrey* (1936), *The Ghost Goes West* (1937), and *The Lady Eve* (1941), Pallette became a comedy fixture in the recurring stereotype of the self-made million-

aire who can't get anyone to listen to him until he throws a childish fit. Eugene Pallette made his last film, *Silver River*, in 1948, when illness compelled him to retire. **Selected Works:** *Mark of Zorro* (1940), *Mr. Smith Goes to Washington* (1939), *Topper* (1937)

# Chazz Palminteri

**Born:** May 15, 1951; Bronx, NY

**Years Active in the Industry:** by decade

| 10s | 20s | 30s | 40s | 50s | 60s | 70s | 80s | 90s |
|-----|-----|-----|-----|-----|-----|-----|-----|-----|
|     |     |     |     |     |     |     |     | ■ |

Actor Chazz Palminteri made his professional New York debut in the off-Broadway production *On the Right Track*, which moved on Broadway soon after its premiere. The versatile actor was born in the Bronx, attended Bronx College, and one of his most celebrated Broadway appearances was in *A Bronx Tale*. Chazz Palminteri is best known to moviegoers for his Oscar-nominated performance as the gangster-turned-Broadway impresario in Woody Allen's *Bullets Over Broadway* (1994). **Selected Works:** *Jade* (1995), *The Usual Suspects* (1995)

# Franklin Pangborn

**Born:** January 23, 1893; Newark, NJ
**Died:** July 20, 1958; Santa Monica, CA

**Years Active in the Industry:** by decade

| 10s | 20s | 30s | 40s | 50s | 60s | 70s | 80s | 90s |
|-----|-----|-----|-----|-----|-----|-----|-----|-----|
|     | ■ | ■ | ■ | ■ |     |     |     |     |

American actor Franklin Pangborn spent most of his theatrical days playing straight dramatic roles, but Hollywood saw things differently. From his debut film *Exit Smiling* (1926) to his final appearance in *The Story of Mankind* (1957), Pangborn was relegated to almost nothing but comedy roles. With his prissy voice and floor-walker demeanor, Pangborn was the perfect desk clerk, hotel manager, dressmaker, society secretary, or all-around busybody in well over 100 films. Except for a few supporting appearances in features and a series of Mack Sennett short subjects in the early 1930s, most of Pangborn's pre-1936 appearances were in bits or minor roles, but a brief turn as a snotty society scavenger-hunt scorekeeper in *My Man Godfrey* (1936) cemented his reputation as a surefire laugh-getter. The actor was a particular favorite of W. C. Fields, who saw to it that Pangborn was prominently cast in Fields' *The Bank Dick* (1940) (as hapless bank examiner J. Pinkerton Snoopington) and *Never Give a Sucker An Even Break* (1941). Occasionally, Pangborn longed for more dramatic roles, so to satisfy himself artistically he'd play non-comic parts for Edward Everett Horton's Los Angeles-based Majestic Theatre; Pangborn's appearance in Preston Sturges' *Hail the Conquering Hero* (1942) likewise permitted him a few straight, serious moments. When jobs became scarce in films for highly specialized character actors in the 1950s, Pangborn thrived on television, guesting on a number of comedy shows, including an appearance as a giggling serial-killer in a "Red Skelton Show" comedy sketch. One year before his death, Pangborn eased quietly into TV-trivia books by appearing as guest star (and guest announcer) on Jack Paar's very first "Tonight Show." **Selected Works:** *Stage Door* (1937), *A Star Is Born* (1937), *Sullivan's Travels* (1941)

# Anna Paquin

**Born:** 1982

**Years Active in the Industry:** by decade

| 10ˢ | 20ˢ | 30ˢ | 40ˢ | 50ˢ | 60ˢ | 70ˢ | 80ˢ | 90ˢ |
|---|---|---|---|---|---|---|---|---|
| | | | | | | | | ■ |

New Zealander Anna Paquin made her stage bow in the coveted role of a skunk in a grade school play. After attracting attention for her work in a TV commercial, Paquin was selected from some 5,000 applicants to portray Holly Hunter's precocious daughter in director Jane Campion's dour period piece *The Piano*. The film was completed in 1992 when Paquin was nine. She kept busy for the next year or so in a series of American TV ads for a computer company, portraying an androgynous "young DaVinci" type. In 1994, an amazed 11-year-old Paquin rushed on the stage of the Dorothy Chandler Pavillion to accept the best supporting actress award for her performance in *The Piano*—a "hard R" film that she would not be permitted to see without parental accompaniment for another seven years.

# Michael Pare

**Born:** October 9, 1958; Brooklyn, NY

**Years Active in the Industry:** by decade

| 10ˢ | 20ˢ | 30ˢ | 40ˢ | 50ˢ | 60ˢ | 70ˢ | 80ˢ | 90ˢ |
|---|---|---|---|---|---|---|---|---|
| | | | | | | | ■ | ■ |

An American leading man with hooded eyes and curled lip, Pare worked as a *sous-chef* at Cafe Europa on New York's Upper West Side after training at the New York Culinary Institute. While there he was spotted by a modeling agent and soon began to model. Later he spent two years studying acting with Uta Hagen

and Marvin Nelson, and was hired to play the lead in a TV series, "The Greatest American Hero." The series fell through (though it was later produced without him), but he managed to get the lead in a TV movie, *Crazy Times,* which led to the role of the rock icon Eddie in the film *Eddie and the Cruisers* (1983). Filmmaker Walter Hill spotted him in that part and cast him in Hill's next film, *Streets of Fire* (1984). After that film did very poorly at the box office, his career faltered and he made a string of silly B-movies. He has yet to break back into major films. **Selected Works:** *Into the Sun* (1992), *Killing Streets* (1991), *Moon 44* (1990)

# Alan Parker

**Born:** February 14, 1944; Islington, London, England

**Years Active in the Industry:** by decade

| 10ˢ | 20ˢ | 30ˢ | 40ˢ | 50ˢ | 60ˢ | 70ˢ | 80ˢ | 90ˢ |
|---|---|---|---|---|---|---|---|---|
| | | | | | ■ | ■ | ■ | ■ |

An advertising gofer turned writer and director, Alan Parker began in film through his association with producer David Puttnam, another advertising man with cinematic aspirations, who hired Parker to write the screenplay for the pre-teen romance *Melody* (1966). After a stint in television commercials and making short films for the BBC, Parker made his first film, *Bugsy Malone,* in 1976. He joined the front ranks of young filmmakers two years later with the fact-based thriller *Midnight Express,* and followed it two years later with the mega-hit *Fame,* which was a box office hit and spawned a long-running television series. Parker's next movie, *Shoot The Moon* (1981), was a relative failure despite several superb performances, owing to its unpleasant subject matter—the agonizing breakup of a marriage. A year later, Parker made a spectacular achievement in a more difficult category of film with *Pink Floyd—The Wall,* a film adaptation of a Pink Floyd concept album that received critical approval and attracted a substantial audience. His film *Birdy* (1985), about a Vietnam veteran who experiences flight fantasies, won an award at the Cannes Film Festival, and his *Mississippi Burning* (1988) struck a responsive chord with the public and critics alike in recreating the investigation of the murders of three civil rights workers in Mississippi in the mid-1960s. Parker's 1991 *The Commitments,* about an Irish rock band and its travails, was another hit. Stylistically, Parker's movies have all been marked by striking, even daring visual conceits, which run the risk of becoming self-indulgent and occasionally (as in *Fame* and *Shoot The Moon*) voyeuristic. **Selected Works:** *Come See the Paradise* (1990)

# Eleanor Parker

**Born:** June 26, 1922; Cedarville, OH

**Years Active in the Industry:** by decade

| 10ˢ | 20ˢ | 30ˢ | 40ˢ | 50ˢ | 60ˢ | 70ˢ | 80ˢ | 90ˢ |
|---|---|---|---|---|---|---|---|---|
| | | | ■ | ■ | ■ | ■ | | |

Ohioan Eleanor Parker hesitated but little in choosing a career; she was still in her teens when she began appearing in professional stage productions in Cleveland and at California's Pasadena Playhouse. Signed at Warner Bros. in 1941, the red-haired actress was given the slow buildup in such "B"s as *The Mysterious Doctor* before graduating to leads in prestige pictures like *Pride of the Marines* (1945). As the sluttish Mildred in the 1946 remake of *Of Human Bondage*, Parker was not nearly as effective as Bette Davis in the 1934 version, but she learned from this comparative failure and matured into a versatile actress, equally adept at comedy and heavy dramatics. She was Oscar-nominated for *Caged* (1950), in which she plays an utterly deglamourized prison inmate; *Detective Story* (1951), wherein, as Kirk Douglas' wife, she agonizingly harbors the secret of a past abortion; and *Interrupted Melody* (1955), in which she portrays polio-stricken opera diva Marjorie Lawrence. Though she tended towards down-to-earth portrayals, Parker could be flamboyantly sexy if required, via her performance as Mel Ferrer's tempestuous lover in *Scaramouche*. Still regally beautiful into the 1960s and 1970s, Parker was always worth watching no matter if the role was thankless (the Countess in *Sound of Music* [1965]) or "Baby Jane"-style horrific (the terrorized, elderly cripple in *Eye of the Cat* [1969]). **Selected Works:** *An American Dream* (1966), *The Man With the Golden Arm* (1955), *The King and Four Queens* (1956), *Madison Avenue* (1962)

# Mary-Louise Parker

**Born:** August 2, 1964; Jackson, SC

**Years Active in the Industry:** by decade

| 10s | 20s | 30s | 40s | 50s | 60s | 70s | 80s | 90s |
|-----|-----|-----|-----|-----|-----|-----|-----|-----|
|     |     |     |     |     |     |     |     |     |

A graduate of the North Carolina School of the Arts and winner of the Theatre World award for her performance in the Broadway production of *Prelude to a Kiss*, Mary Louise Parker has developed into the Mae Marsh of the 1990s: the eternal victim. However, unlike silent star Marsh, Parker's characters usually enjoy a satisfying "worm has turned" moment—one of her first major film roles was as the abused wife in *Fried Green Tomatoes* (1991) who finally reduces her husband to hash—literally. A more self-reliant Parker was seen in the 1990 AIDS-related TV movie *Longtime Companion*, as the supportive "earth mother" to a group of urban homosexual men. Still, there's a foredoomed quality in Mary-Louise Parker's performances that can't be easily shaken—the minute we lay eyes on her in the 1994 "girl buddy" film *Boys on the Side*, we *know* she won't survive to the fade-out. **Selected Works:** *Grand Canyon* (1991), *The Client* (1994), *Bullets over Broadway* (1994)

# Sarah Jessica Parker

**Born:** March 25, 1965; Nelsonville, OH

**Years Active in the Industry:** by decade

| 10s | 20s | 30s | 40s | 50s | 60s | 70s | 80s | 90s |
|-----|-----|-----|-----|-----|-----|-----|-----|-----|
|     |     |     |     |     |     |     |     |     |

Ohio-born actress Sarah Jessica Parker came from a family of ten. She was but one of several siblings engaged in show business careers. At age 12, Parker made her Broadway debut with Clare Bloom in *The Innocents*. She followed this with a small role in the long-running musical *Annie;* before this engagement ended, she had taken over the title role. Though she made her film debut in 1979's *Rich Kids,* the next phase of her career was mostly confined to series television, with regular roles in "Square Pegs" (typecast as a tall, gawky teen), "A Year in the Life," and "Equal Justice." Her film assignments have included *Footloose* (1983), *Girls Just Want to Have Fun* (1985), *LA Story* (1988), *Honeymoon in Vegas* (1993), *Hocus Pocus* (1993), and *Ed Wood* (1994). Off-camera, Parker has been extremely active in the campaign to further AIDS research. She has also kept her name in print via several high-profile Hollywood boyfriends.

# Estelle Parsons

**Born:** November 20, 1927; Lynn, MA

**Years Active in the Industry:** by decade

| 10s | 20s | 30s | 40s | 50s | 60s | 70s | 80s | 90s |
|-----|-----|-----|-----|-----|-----|-----|-----|-----|
|     |     |     |     |     |     |     |     |     |

Parsons attended law school and was involved in local politics before joining the staff of the "Today" show. She moved from production assistant to writer and feature producer. In the late '50s she began appearing onstage in satirical revues and plays, working in stock and on and off Broadway. She began appearing in character roles onscreen in 1963. For her work in *Bonnie and Clyde* (1967) she won a Best Supporting Actress Oscar, then was again nominated in the same category for *Rachel, Rachel* (1968). She went on to give a number of memorable screen performances (though she did almost no film work in the late '70s and '80s), and also acted on stage and television. In 1983 she starred in the feminist one-woman show *Adulto Orgasmo Escapes From the Zoo.* She has also taught acting for many years. In the '80s and '90s she was a semi-regular on the hit TV sitcom "Roseanne." **Selected Works:** *Dick Tracy* (1990), *I Never Sang for My Father* (1970), *Private Matter* (1992)

# Dolly Parton (Dolly Rebecca Parton)

**Born:** January 19, 1946; Sevierville, TN

**Years Active in the Industry:** by decade

| 10s | 20s | 30s | 40s | 50s | 60s | 70s | 80s | 90s |
|-----|-----|-----|-----|-----|-----|-----|-----|-----|

Born into relative poverty, Parton was singing and playing gospel music on Knoxville radio by the age of eleven. Upon graduating from high school, she moved to Nashville to launch a career as a country singer. In 1967, she joined Porter Wagoner's Wagon Masters Band. For the next seven years she performed with this group at the Grand Old Opry, in tours and on records. Parton became a solo artist in 1974, very quickly gaining immense popularity as a singer-songwriter. Nationally known as a media celebrity by the late '70s, she appeared frequently on TV specials and talk shows. She debuted onscreen in the film *9 to 5* (1980), for which she received an Oscar nomination as the composer of the title song. Starring or costarring in a handful of other films through the '90s, Parton often composed music for her films. She heads Dolly Parton Enterprises, a $100 million media empire. In 1986 her company opened Dollywood, a theme park celebrating her Smokey Mountain upbringing in Tennessee. **Selected Works:** *Steel Magnolias* (1989), *Straight Talk* (1992), *Beverly Hillbillies* (1993)

# Adrian Pasdar

**Born:** 1965; Pittsfield, MA

**Years Active in the Industry:** by decade

| 10s | 20s | 30s | 40s | 50s | 60s | 70s | 80s | 90s |
|-----|-----|-----|-----|-----|-----|-----|-----|-----|

Pasdar studied English literature in college and played college football until he suffered a serious car accident. While recuperating from the injuries he moved home to Philadelphia and interned as a technician (building sets) at the People's Light Theater Company. He injured his thumb at work, and the disabilities payment financed a trip to New York. There he attended the Lee Strasberg Theater Institute. After finishing at the Institute he auditioned for the film *Top Gun* (1986). Director Tony Scott was so impressed with Pasdar that he added a part into the movie for him. The success of *Top Gun* (in which his part was small) led to a supporting role for him in *Sugarbabies* (1986). Eventually he got his first lead, as a cowboy in love with (and bitten by) a vampire, in *Near Dark* (1987). After making a few more films he went on to appear in a string of theater productions, notably Tennessee Williams's *The Glass Menagerie*, and in two TV movies, the avant-garde *Big Time* (1989) for "American Playhouse" on PBS, and *The Lost Capone*, in which he played the straight-living brother of Al Capone. He spent some time in Paris, where he wrote a screenplay that was later optioned, then returned to Hollywood to continue making films. **Selected Works:** *Grand Isle* (1992), *Carlito's Way* (1993)

# Pier Paolo Pasolini

**Born:** March 5, 1922; Bologna, Italy
**Died:** 1975

**Years Active in the Industry:** by decade

| 10s | 20s | 30s | 40s | 50s | 60s | 70s | 80s | 90s |
|-----|-----|-----|-----|-----|-----|-----|-----|-----|

By the age of 19, Pasolini was a published poet, and over the next decade he established himself as a novelist and essayist. In 1954 he entered films as a screenwriter on Mario Soldati's *La Donna del Fiume*, then went on to collaborate on several other prestigious screenplays. He made his directorial debut in 1961 with *Accattone!* Based on his novel *Una Vita Violenta/A Violent Life*, it depicted the grim life of a pimp in a slum section of Rome. Much of his work showed compassion for the social underclass, informed by a combination of Marxism and mysticism. In 1962 he was arrested on charges that he had insulted the church in his film *Rogopag* (1962), which satirized cinema Biblical epics. As a result, he went on to make his best-known film, *The Gospel According to St. Matthew* (1964), casting his own mother in the role of the Virgin Mary and non-actors in most of the other roles. His later films often returned to literary masterpieces for their basis. He often contended with the church and Italian authorities over the sex, violence, and anti-establishment "blasphemy" of his films. Two of his films, *The Canterbury Tales* (1972) and *Solo—The 120 Days of Sodom* (1975), were declared obscene and their Italian release was delayed by months. In late 1975 he was murdered by a 17-year-old, who bludgeoned him and then ran over his body with his own sports car. **Selected Works:** *Decameron* (1970), *Mamma Roma* (1962)

# Mandy Patinkin

**Born:** November 30, 1952; Chicago, IL

**Years Active in the Industry:** by decade

| 10s | 20s | 30s | 40s | 50s | 60s | 70s | 80s | 90s |
|-----|-----|-----|-----|-----|-----|-----|-----|-----|

Patinkin studied drama and music at the prestigious Juilliard School in New York, then worked a great deal in regional theater; he also appeared at Joseph Papp's Public Theater in the New York Shakespeare Festival. He later worked on Broadway, where he won the Tony Award for Best Actor in a Musical for his portrayal of Che Guevara in *Evita*. Known for his wonderful singing voice, he has gained a reputation as an interpreter of Stephen Sondheim; he had the title role in the hit Sondheim musical *Sunday in the Park with George* opposite Bernadette Peters. He debuted onscreen in a small role in *The Big Fix* (1978), since which he has had an occasional film career in mostly unsuccessful productions. He won a 1995 Emmy for his work in TV's "Chicago Hope" **Selected Works:** *Dick Tracy* (1990), *Princess Bride* (1987), *Ragtime* (1981), *The Music of Chance* (1993)

# Jason Patric (Jason Miller, Jr.)

**Born:** 1966; Queens, NY

**Years Active in the Industry:** by decade

| 10ˢ | 20ˢ | 30ˢ | 40ˢ | 50ˢ | 60ˢ | 70ˢ | 80ˢ | 90ˢ |
|-----|-----|-----|-----|-----|-----|-----|-----|-----|
|     |     |     |     |     |     |     | ■   | ■   |

The son of actor/playwright Jason Miller—and grandson of TV legend Jackie Gleason—Jason Patric's first starring movie role was as teenager-cum-vampire Michael in *The Lost Boys* (1987). Seldom betraying the emotional makeup of his characters by resorting to facial expressions, Patric has allowed his characters' actions to speak for them. Frequently those actions have been villainous, especially when Patric essays such roles as the violence-prone, doped-up narc in *Rush* (1992). He has also played a few heroic roles, notably the "voice of conscience" Cavalry officer in 1992's *Geronimo: An American Legend.* Jason Patric is the older brother of actor Joshua Miller, who is best known for his performance in 1986's *The River's Edge.* **Selected Works:** *After Dark, My Sweet* (1990), *The Journey of August King* (1995)

# Will Patton

**Born:** June 14, 1954; Charleston, SC

**Years Active in the Industry:** by decade

| 10ˢ | 20ˢ | 30ˢ | 40ˢ | 50ˢ | 60ˢ | 70ˢ | 80ˢ | 90ˢ |
|-----|-----|-----|-----|-----|-----|-----|-----|-----|
|     |     |     |     |     |     |     | ■   | ■   |

After attending the North Carolina School of the Arts, Patton moved to New York and studied with Lee Strasberg at the Actors Studio and Joseph Chaikin at the Open Theater. Soon he was getting parts on and off Broadway in a number of plays. For his performance in *Tourists and Refugees,* he won a Best Actor Obie; he won another for his work in Sam Shepard's *Fool For Love.* He was also a member of the Winter Project, an experimental theater group in New York. He landed parts in the TV soap operas "Search for Tomorrow" and "Ryan's Hope" and appeared in the short underground film *Minus Zero* (1979). In the early '80s he began to get parts in independent New York-made films, beginning with *The Third Person* (1981). His first Hollywood film was *Desperately Seeking Susan* (1985), after which he made a number of other big-budget films. **Selected Works:** *Murder on the Bayou* (1991), *Rapture* (1991), *The Client* (1994)

# Bill Paxton

**Born:** 1955; Fort Worth, TX

**Years Active in the Industry:** by decade

| 10ˢ | 20ˢ | 30ˢ | 40ˢ | 50ˢ | 60ˢ | 70ˢ | 80ˢ | 90ˢ |
|-----|-----|-----|-----|-----|-----|-----|-----|-----|
|     |     |     |     |     |     | ■   | ■   | ■   |

Bill Paxton is a supporting actor who has appeared in many contemporary films. With his special talent for becoming totally involved in a story, he is often not recognized for his good work. His tall, rangy body and boyish looks gets him parts in many action films. He began his film career in 1974 as a set dresser for New World Pictures. After appearing as an extra in *Crazy Mama* (1975), Paxton headed to New York to study acting. By the early eighties, he was working in low-budget movies and television. In addition, he also became an independent filmmaker specializing in off-beat shorts that he wrote, produced, directed, and occasionally starred in. One film, the cult classic *Fish Heads,* was shown on TV's "Saturday Night Live." Paxton gradually began getting small roles in bigger-budget films, but it was not until John Hughes' *Weird Science* (1985) that he got his first major supporting role. Paxton continues to appear steadily in a variety of mainstream and little-known films. **Selected Works:** *Aliens* (1986), *Indian Summer* (1993), *Tombstone* (1993), *True Lies* (1994)

# John Payne

**Born:** May 23, 1912; Roanoke, VA
**Died:** December 1989

**Years Active in the Industry:** by decade

| 10ˢ | 20ˢ | 30ˢ | 40ˢ | 50ˢ | 60ˢ | 70ˢ | 80ˢ | 90ˢ |
|-----|-----|-----|-----|-----|-----|-----|-----|-----|
|     |     | ■   | ■   | ■   |     |     |     |     |

The son of an opera soprana, he studied drama at Columbia and voice at Juilliard. He began his career as a singer, then did some acting in stock. He moved to Hollywood in 1935, playing leads in a number of Fox musicals by the '40s, often opposite Alice Faye or Betty Grable. Frequently appearing bare-chested, he was very popular with female fans, and for a time he was the top male pin-up. In the '50s, still muscular but no longer boyish, he switched to medium-budget Westerns and action movies. In 1957 he retired from the screen to star in the TV series "The Restless Gun" and appeared in only two more films. He directed one of his last films, *They Ran for Their Lives* (1968). He finished his career in a 1973 Broadway revival of the musical *Good News,* appearing opposite Alice Faye. He became wealthy with shrewd real estate investments in southern California. From 1937-43 he was married to actress Anne Shirley; their daughter is actress Julie Payne. From 1944-50 he was married to actress Gloria DeHaven. **Selected Works:** *Dodsworth* (1936), *The Razor's Edge* (1946), *Miracle on 34th Street* (1947)

# Gregory Peck (Eldred Gregory Peck)

**Born:** April 5, 1916; La Jolla, CA

**Years Active in the Industry:** by decade

| 10ˢ | 20ˢ | 30ˢ | 40ˢ | 50ˢ | 60ˢ | 70ˢ | 80ˢ | 90ˢ |
|-----|-----|-----|-----|-----|-----|-----|-----|-----|
|     |     |     |     |     |     |     |     |     |

Tall, dark, and handsome Hollywood leading man Gregory Peck projects strength, kindness, conviction, intelligence, morality, and honesty. As a pre-med student he became interested in acting.

After enrolling at the Neighborhood Playhouse in New York he debuted memorably on Broadway in *The Morning Star* in 1942. He appeared in one more play and then moved to Hollywood. With many stars absent due to World War II, Peck soon became a major star, barred from service due to a spinal injury. He debuted on-screen in *Days of Glory* (1943). For the next several decades he appeared in films of every genre, nearly always playing steady, upstanding, likable characters, though at times he has been criticized for being wooden. With the studio system crumbling in the late '40s and early '50s, he was one of the first actors to work only in the movies he chose and to secure financially rewarding leads for himself. After four Oscar nominations he finally won the fifth time around, for his portrayal of a liberal Southern lawyer in *To Kill a Mockingbird* (1962). He produced two films, *The Trial of the Catonsville Nine* (1972) and *The Dove* (1974). In the '70s there were rumors that his career was over, but after he appeared in the lead of the smash hit *The Omen* (1976) he came back strongly. Although Peck made only three films in the '80s, in the early '90s he appeared quickly in three more. He is known for being liberal politically (one source calls him "the liberal conscience of American cinema"), and has been active in many causes, whether political, charitable, or related to the film industry. He served from 1967-69 as the chairman of the Board of Trustees of the American Film Institute; from 1967-70 he was president of the Academy of Motion Picture Arts and Sciences. He has been awarded the Medal of Freedom Award and the Academy's Jean Hersholt Humanitarian Award and is also the author of an autobiography, *An Actor's Life* (1978). **Selected Works:** *Big Country* (1958), *Gentleman's Agreement* (1947), *Roman Holiday* (1953), *Spellbound* (1945), *Yearling* (1946)

# Sam Peckinpah

**Born:** February 21, 1925; Fresno, CA
**Died:** December 28, 1984; Inglewood, CA

**Years Active in the Industry:** by decade

| 10ˢ | 20ˢ | 30ˢ | 40ˢ | 50ˢ | 60ˢ | 70ˢ | 80ˢ | 90ˢ |
|-----|-----|-----|-----|-----|-----|-----|-----|-----|
|     |     |     |     |     |     |     |     |     |

As might be deduced from his film output, American director Sam Peckinpah's life was chock-full of unexpected bursts of violence and long stretches of "macho" solitude. A troublesome youth, Peckinpah compromised his high school football performances with an insatiable thirst for liquor. He finished his education in military school, hoping to impose some discipline upon himself, then served in the Marines in World War II. His first wife was Marie Selland, a drama student at Fresno State College who encouraged Peckinpah to enroll in drama classes. Upon graduation, Peckinpah went to work in the props department at Los Angeles TV station KLAC, where at one point he was a staffer on "The Liberace Show." Peckinpah then became an assistant of director Don Siegel, who allowed the young man to coscript *Invasion of the Body Snatchers* (1956) and also play a small part in that science fiction cult classic. Through the kindnesses of Siegel, Peckinpah moved on to write and direct for such TV westerns as *The Rifleman* and *Tombstone Territory*, ultimately creating his own series, 1960's "The Westerner," which despite a loyal following succumbed to bad ratings after 13 weeks. Peckinpah made efforts to work in the Hollywood mainstream, but his brutal, iconoclastic viewpoint closed many doors to him; he would later claim to have offered a script to the Disney studios, only to be rejected with the statement "Too many shootings, not enough animals." Few saw Peckinpah's first feature-film directorial job, *The Deadly Companions* (1961), but his second film, *Ride the High Country* (1962) enjoyed a wave of critical adulation, mostly for its magnificent camerawork and its teaming of Western legends Joel McCrea and Randolph Scott. *Major Dundee* (1965), Peckinpah's next film, was severely cut by the studio and thus became something of *cause celebre* among French film cultists. With *The Wild Bunch* (1969), Peckinpah was firmly established as the foremost violent-action director of his period. The bloodletting in *Wild Bunch*, much of it caressingly filmed in slow motion, repelled many viewers, but thrilled many more, and soon virtually every Western and action film was emulating Peckinpah's technique and gift of imbuing moral ambiguity in the standard "good guy-bad guy" setup. After *Ballad of Cable Hogue* (1970), another film allegedly ruined by studio interference, Peckinpah was back in form with *Straw Dogs* (1971), a "revenge for a rape" opus that could be taken as both a celebration and a condemnation of random violence. Taking a breather with the low-key *Junior Bonner* (1970), Peckinpah put Steve McQueen and Ali McGraw through their paces in *The Getaway* (1972), which received as much notoriety for the hot-and-cold romance between the stars as for its well-calculated mayhem. Shortly afterward, Peckinpah seemed to lose his touch; perhaps it was the liquor, perhaps the corporate intrigues of his many Hollywood enemies, but whatever the case, Peckinpah's *Bring Me the Head of Alfredo Garcia* (1974), *The Killer Elite* (1975) and *Cross of Iron* (1976) were major letdowns. By 1978, Peckinpah's financial status was so precarious that he was forced to take a commissioned job, *Convoy* (1978), a silly contrivance based on a then-popular song. Sam Peckinpah's last film was *The Osterman Week-end* (1983), in which the director seemed to be deliberately distancing himself from his material. Shortly after completing this film, Peckinpah died - officially of a heart attack, but more likely of living too hard and absorbing too much.

# Mario Van Peebles

**Born:** January 15, 1957; Mexico City, Mexico

**Years Active in the Industry:** by decade

| 10s | 20s | 30s | 40s | 50s | 60s | 70s | 80s | 90s |
|-----|-----|-----|-----|-----|-----|-----|-----|-----|
|     |     |     |     |     |     |     | ■   |     |

The son of African American director/writer Melvin Van Peebles, Mario Van Peebles made his acting bow in a small role in his dad's *Sweet Sweetback's Baadasssss Song* (1971). At the time, Van Peebles had no burning desire to become a performer, choosing instead to study economics at Columbia University. He wavered between a financial and an acting career before becoming a full-time actor with the 1984 film *Cotton Club*. In 1988, Van Peebles starred in a conformist TV comedy adventure series, *Sonny Spoon*, playing a glib private eye with a predilection for elaborate disguises; this brief series afforded him his first opportunity to direct. Three years later he made his film directing debut with *New Jack City*, a film widely praised by some as being a truthful, no-nonsense dissection of ghetto life, and widely derided by others as merely a slick outgrowth of the "blaxploitation" flicks of the 1970s. Van Peebles reserved a juicy role for himself in *New Jack City*, as he would in his subsequent *Posse* (1993), a somewhat narcissistic revisionist Western about a Utopian all-black community. Van Peebles' next directorial endeavor was *Panthers* (1995), a fanciful recounting of the Black Panther Movement that came under fire from several of the real-life activists depicted in the film. **Selected Works:** *Highlander: The Final Dimension* (1995), *Blue Bayou* (1990), *Triumph of the Heart: The Ricky Bell Story* (1991), *Panther* (1995)

# Melvin Van Peebles (Melvin Peebles)

**Born:** 1932; Chicago, IL

**Years Active in the Industry:** by decade

| 10s | 20s | 30s | 40s | 50s | 60s | 70s | 80s | 90s |
|-----|-----|-----|-----|-----|-----|-----|-----|-----|
|     |     |     |     |     |     | ■   |     |     |

In the '50s Van Peebles became interested in film and went to Hollywood, where he had no luck. He moved to Holland and acted with the Dutch National Theater, then went to France; he couldn't break into French cinema, so he decided to become a novelist in the hope of directing a screen version of one of his books. He wrote and published five novels, one of which became the basis for the film *Story of a Three-Day Pass* (1967), his directorial debut. The film was well-received. His third film, *Sweet Sweetback's Baadasssss Song* (1971), was one of the first independent productions by a black filmmaker that found a national audience. He went on to work on and off Broadway and on TV as well as in films. In 1985 he became the only black trader on the floor of the American Stock Exchange. He is the father of actor Mario Van Peebles. **Selected Works:** *Boomerang* (1992), *Posse* (1993), *Sophisticated Gents* (1981), *True Identity* (1991), *Erotic Tales* (1994)

# Arthur Penn

**Born:** September 27, 1922; Philadelphia, PA

**Years Active in the Industry:** by decade

| 10s | 20s | 30s | 40s | 50s | 60s | 70s | 80s | 90s |
|-----|-----|-----|-----|-----|-----|-----|-----|-----|
|     |     |     |     |     | ■   |     |     |     |

Arthur Penn was initially trained in his father's profession as a watchmaker, but gravitated to theater while still in high school. During his infantry service in World War II, he formed a theatrical company at Fort Jackson, South Carolina. After leaving the service he attended the Actors Studio in Los Angeles, studying under Michael Chekhov. He went into television in 1951 as an NBC employee, serving as floor manager of the *Colgate Comedy Hour*. Within two years, he'd begun writing dramas for television and directing *Philco Playhouse* and, later on, *Playhouse 90*. His feature film debut came in 1957 with *The Left-Handed Gun,* a highly mannered psychological interpretation of the story of Billy The Kid starring Paul Newman, which was removed from Penn's control. It failed in the United States but was well received in Europe. He began directing for the stage soon after and found success on Broadway with *Two For the See Saw* and *The Miracle Worker,* followed by *Toys In the Attic* and *All The Way Home,* all major hits on stage within a period of only three years. It was *The Miracle Worker* (1961) that brought Penn back into movies, with a bravura screen adaptation of the play that remains undiminished in its power over 30 years later, and earned Oscars for stars Ann Bancroft and Patty Duke, and a nomination as Best Director for Penn. His career moved between stage and screen for the next several years, with two failures in *Mickey One* (1965) and *The Chase* (1966). But in 1967, Penn surprised the public and the critics alike with one of the most popular and influential films of the decade, *Bonnie and Clyde,* starring Faye Dunaway and Warren Beatty. One of the most successful crime films ever made, this movie, with its mix of rich characterizations and graphic violence, coupled with surprisingly frank sexuality for its time, took the public by storm, and, for the next decade or so, anyone doing movies about criminals of the early twentieth century felt compelled to emulate its style and look—most failed, although a few, such as John Milius's *Dillinger,* starring Warren Oates, had something to offer all their own. Penn followed this triumph with a most unusual feature, *Alice's Restaurant* (1969)—probably the only serious American feature based entirely on a popular song. Although not a major hit, this whimsical, gently lyrical and satirical movie became a major cult favorite, and may be the finest American film ever to attempt to look at the anti-war movement and the people around it. Penn's *Little Big Man* (1970), a revisionist look at the conquest of the west, fit in nicely with the anti-Vietnam sensibilities of its period, and has held up remarkably well as a reasonably honest look at a troubled past, with Dustin Hoffman turning in one of the best performances of his career. Penn's subsequent movies have seen his fortunes decline, as success eluded him through the 1970s and 1980s (1981's *Four Friends* is a particularly galling picture). Apart from the offbeat comedy Penn and Teller *Get Killed,* his most recent public appearance has been as the designated replacement for David Lean on the latter's unfinished project *Nostromo.* Lean's death before the project had gotten sufficiently far along led to its cancellation rather than Penn's picking up the film as his own. **Selected Works:** *Penn & Teller Get Killed* (1990)

# Christopher Penn

**Born:** 1967; Los Angeles, CA

**Years Active in the Industry:** by decade

| 10ˢ | 20ˢ | 30ˢ | 40ˢ | 50ˢ | 60ˢ | 70ˢ | 80ˢ | 90ˢ |
|---|---|---|---|---|---|---|---|---|
| | | | | | | | | |

Christopher Penn is the son of director Leo Penn and the younger brother of actor Sean Penn. Like brother Sean, Christopher made his movie "debut" in the 8-mm films shot by childhood chum Charlie Sheen. Thus far, Penn has not exhibited his older brother's peculiar gift for running afoul of the Law. Among Christopher Penn's Hollywood film credits are *Footloose* (1984), *Pale Rider* (1986) and *Short Cuts* (1994). **Selected Works:** *Reservoir Dogs* (1992), *True Romance* (1993), *Beethoven's 2nd* (1993)

# Sean Penn

**Born:** August 17, 1960; Santa Monica, CA

**Years Active in the Industry:** by decade

| 10ˢ | 20ˢ | 30ˢ | 40ˢ | 50ˢ | 60ˢ | 70ˢ | 80ˢ | 90ˢ |
|---|---|---|---|---|---|---|---|---|
| | | | | | | | | |

An intense, stocky leading actor with a boxer-like face and commanding screen presence, Penn is the son of director Leo Penn and actress Eileen Ryan, and brother of actor Christopher Penn. He was drawn to acting from an early age. After high school he joined the Los Angeles Group Repertory Theater, but worked in small roles in only a few plays while helping out backstage. He

also directed a one-act play. Penn went on to take acting lessons and later debuted before the cameras in an episode of the TV series "Barnaby Jones." He landed several other small roles, then moved to New York and began to get work on Broadway. He debuted onscreen as Timothy Hutton's roommate in *Taps* (1981), then became a star with his performance as an over-aged, spaced-out high school student in the popular comedy *Fast Times At Ridgemont High* (1982). He continued to appear in films at the rate of about one per year, and soon developed a reputation as one of the premier actors of his generation, known for portraying dubious characters, outsiders, and rebels. He also continued to appear regularly onstage in New York and Los Angeles. He wrote, directed, and starred in the film *Indian Runners* (1991). His off-screen exploits brought much publicity, and he became known as a "bad boy." Penn's most infamous act occurred when he punched out a photographer, having repeatedly expressed his dislike of having his privacy intruded upon. He was briefly married to pop-singer/actress Madonna (with whom he appeared in the flop *Shanghai Surprise,* 1986), and their marriage was an event notoriously surrounded by press people in helicopters swooping over the crowd in search of photographs. Their divorce was a controversial episode in which Madonna claimed that Penn had abused her and, one night, left her tied to a chair. In the '90s his off-screen activities quieted down significantly. **Selected Works:** *State of Grace* (1990), *Carlito's Way* (1993), *The Crossing Guard* (1995), *Dead Man Walking* (1995)

# George Peppard

**Born:** October 1, 1928; Detroit, MI
**Died:** May 8, 1994; Los Angeles, CA

**Years Active in the Industry:** by decade

| 10ˢ | 20ˢ | 30ˢ | 40ˢ | 50ˢ | 60ˢ | 70ˢ | 80ˢ | 90ˢ |
|---|---|---|---|---|---|---|---|---|
| | | | | | | | | |

The son of a light-opera singer, Peppard performed on radio and in stock, then trained at the Actors Studio in New York before moving on to Broadway and television. In 1957 he debuted onscreen, making his biggest impression as the costar of *Breakfast At Tiffany's* (1961), after which it seemed he might be headed for stardom. However, he went on to mostly mediocre roles, often with a tough-guy slant, and never became a major leading man. He starred in the TV series "Banacek," "Doctors' Hospital," and "The A-Team," and between TV engagements he sustained a fairly busy film career. He produced and directed *Five Days From Home* (1978). From 1966-72 he was married to actress Elizabeth Ashley. **Selected Works:** *How the West Was Won* (1963), *Night of the Fox* (1990), *Chinatown Murders: Man Against the Mob* (1992)

# Rosie Perez

**Born:** September 6, 1964; Brooklyn, NY

**Years Active in the Industry:** by decade

| 10ˢ | 20ˢ | 30ˢ | 40ˢ | 50ˢ | 60ˢ | 70ˢ | 80ˢ | 90ˢ |
|-----|-----|-----|-----|-----|-----|-----|-----|-----|
|     |     |     |     |     |     |     |     |     |

Brooklyn-born actress/choreographer Rosie Perez attended Los Angeles City College before making the cattle-call rounds for dancing jobs. She worked a few seasons with the TV variety series *Soul Train*, then went on to perform at the LA club Funky Reggae. Here she was spotted by director Spike Lee, who cast her in a choice role in his 1989 film *Do The Right Thing*. She can also be seen dancing to the title tune under the opening credits. As a choreographer, Perez has staged shows for Diana Ross and Bobby Brown, and was Emmy-nominated for her work on the Fox comedy/variety series *In Living Color* (1990-94). She has been shown to best advantage on screen in explosive supporting roles, such as the *Jeopardy*-obsessed girlfriend of Woody Harrelson in *White Men Can't Jump* (1992) and the hilariously covetous wife of lottery winner Nicholas Cage in *It Could Happen to You* (1994). On a more somber note, Perez was excellent as the troubled plane-crash survivor in *Fearless* (1993).

# Anthony Perkins

**Born:** April 4, 1932; New York, NY
**Died:** September 12, 1992; Los Angeles, CA

**Years Active in the Industry:** by decade

| 10ˢ | 20ˢ | 30ˢ | 40ˢ | 50ˢ | 60ˢ | 70ˢ | 80ˢ | 90ˢ |
|-----|-----|-----|-----|-----|-----|-----|-----|-----|
|     |     |     |     |     |     |     |     |     |

Perkins, the son of actor Osgood Perkins, began acting in summer stock when he was 15. Six years later he debuted on-screen in *The Actress* (1953), playing Jean Simmons's boyfriend. He went on to appear on Broadway and in TV dramas, not returning to the screen untill his appearance in *Friendly Persuasions* (1956),

for which he received a Best Supporting Actor Oscar nomination. At first Perkins tended to play awkward, anxious, gawky, neurotic adolescents and young men; this trend culminated in his most famous screen role, that of the "mama's boy" murderer Norman Bates in Alfred Hitchcock's classic *Psycho* (1960). That film's great success made him internationally famous, and he went on to major roles in a number of American and international films in the '60s. However, he remained forever identified in the audience's mind with Norman Bates, and his career never quite took off the way it ought to have after the success of *Psycho*. In 1973 he married photographer Berinthia Berenson, the sister of actress Marisa Berenson. In the '80s and early '90s he returned to the character of Norman Bates in three *Psycho* sequels, one of which he directed. **Selected Works:** *Catch-22* (1970), *Goodbye Again* (1961), *On the Beach* (1959)

# Elizabeth Perkins

**Born:** November 18, 1960; Queens, NY

**Years Active in the Industry:** by decade

| 10ˢ | 20ˢ | 30ˢ | 40ˢ | 50ˢ | 60ˢ | 70ˢ | 80ˢ | 90ˢ |
|-----|-----|-----|-----|-----|-----|-----|-----|-----|
|     |     |     |     |     |     |     |     |     |

Born in New York and raised in Vermont, actress Elizabeth Perkins headed for Chicago after high school, where she was trained at the Goodman School of Drama. In a busy three-year period (1984-87), Perkins costarred in the touring company of Neil Simon's *Brighton Beach Memoirs*, married Chicago-based actor Terry Kinney (they have since split), was featured on Broadway, and made her film debut in *About Last Night...* (1986). The actress went on to play Tom Hanks' vis-a-vis in *Big* (1988), the terminal cancer patient with whom William Hurt begins a relationship in *The Doctor* (1992), and the "She" to Kevin Bacon's "He" in *He Said, She Said* (1991). The biggest box-office hit with which Elizabeth Perkins has been associated was 1994's *The Flintstones*, in which she portrayed the long-suffering Wilma. **Selected Works:** *Avalon* (1990), *Miracle on 34th Street* (1994), *Moonlight and Valentino* (1995)

# Frank Perry

**Born:** August 21, 1930; New York, NY
**Died:** August 29, 1995

**Years Active in the Industry:** by decade

| 10ˢ | 20ˢ | 30ˢ | 40ˢ | 50ˢ | 60ˢ | 70ˢ | 80ˢ | 90ˢ |
|-----|-----|-----|-----|-----|-----|-----|-----|-----|
|     |     |     |     |     |     |     |     |     |

American director Frank Perry went to work for the Westport Country Playhouse as a teenager, albeit in the capacity of parking lot attendant. Perry eventually worked his way up to producer at the Playhouse, beginning a show business career that would extend into the 1990s, interrupted only by Korean War service. After putting in time as a TV documentary producer, Perry directed the 1962 film *David and Lisa,* a location-shot drama about two emotionally disturbed teenagers in a mental institution. Thanks to the attractiveness of stars Keir Dullea and Janet Margolin, *David and Lisa* developed a following among teens and young adults, making Perry quite bankable in Hollywood. Perry's second film, the low-budget *Ladybug Ladybug* (1962), was a study of how a false nuclear attack announcement would effect otherwise normal people—a disturbingly prescient premise, given the subsequent Cuban Missile Crisis. *The Swimmer* (1968), based on a John Cheever story, was a somewhat surrealistic drama that followed a wealthy suburbanite (Burt Lancaster), who witnesses his life deteriorating as he travels from swimming pool to swimming pool in his exclusive Connecticut neighborhood. Many of Perry's works were similarly concentrated character studies, notably *Diary of a Mad Housewife* (1970) and *Play it as It Lays* (1972). Somehow or other, Perry's work has since devolved from sensitivy to sensationalism, notably with his campy interpretations of the notorious *Mommie Dearest* (1981) and the phlegmatic "sinning clergy" epic *Monsignor* (1982). For many years, Frank Perry worked in collaboration with his wife, the late writer/producer Eleanor Perry. They separated in 1970 and went off to their own individual projects.

# Luke Perry

**Born:** Fredericktown, OH

**Years Active in the Industry:** by decade

| 10ˢ | 20ˢ | 30ˢ | 40ˢ | 50ˢ | 60ˢ | 70ˢ | 80ˢ | 90ˢ |
|-----|-----|-----|-----|-----|-----|-----|-----|-----|
|     |     |     |     |     |     |     |     |     |

Ohioan Luke Perry did well enough on the high school baseball team, but he was a somewhat lackadaisical student, with no real aim in life except for a vague desire to become an actor someday. That desire solidified into reality when Perry headed for Los Angeles in 1984, took acting lessons, and sought out auditions while supporting himself with construction and asphalting jobs. Eventually he landed the role of Ned Bates on the TV daytime drama *Loving.* In 1990, Perry was cast in the Fox Network's *Beverly Hills 90210* in the supporting role of Dylan McKay. Audience response to Perry was so overwhelming that, by the time *90210* swung into its second season, he was not only one of the series leading characters, but a full-fledged teen idol. From all accounts, Perry handled his "hunk heartthrob" status with class and diplomacy; this latter quality served him well during the well-publicized brouhaha over costar Shannen

Doherty. At the beginning of every season, Perry has intimated that he might leave *Beverly Hills 90210* for the greener pastures of theatrical films: judging by the indifferent response to his film appearances in *Buffy the Vampire Slayer* (1992) and *8 Seconds* (1994), Perry may well be a *90210* regular for awhile longer. **Selected Works:** *Terminal Bliss* (1991)

# Joe Pesci

**Born:** February 9, 1943; Newark, NJ

**Years Active in the Industry:** by decade

| 10ˢ | 20ˢ | 30ˢ | 40ˢ | 50ˢ | 60ˢ | 70ˢ | 80ˢ | 90ˢ |
|-----|-----|-----|-----|-----|-----|-----|-----|-----|
|     |     |     |     |     |     |     |     |     |

By the age of five he was performing onstage, and at 10 Pesci became a regular on the TV variety show "Startime Kids." Later he became a nightclub singer under the name Joe Ritchie and

recorded a few records in the mid '60s. He subsequently found work as a guitarist with Joey Dee and the Starlighters, then formed a vaudeville-style nightclub comedy act with Frank Vincent. While still in New Jersey Pesci appeared in the low-budget film *The Death Collector* (1975), shot in New Jersey. This prompted him to go to Hollywood to seek an acting career, but he had no luck and eventually returned to the East Coast. Ready to give up on acting, he was invited to audition for the role of Jake LaMotta's brother in Martin Scorsese's *Raging Bull* (1980). He got the part, for which he received a Best Supporting Actor Oscar nomination and won awards from the New York Film Critics and the National Society of Film Critics. He went on to sustain a busy screen career, often playing tough gangsters. He also starred in the short-lived TV series "Half Nelson." For his work in Scorsese's *Goodfellas* (1990) he won the Best Supporting Actor Oscar. **Selected Works:** *Home Alone* (1990), *JFK* (1991), *My Cousin Vinny* (1992), *Bronx Tale* (1993), *Casino* (1995)

# Bernadette Peters (Bernadette Lazzara)

**Born:** February 28, 1948; Ozone Park, NY

**Years Active in the Industry:** by decade

| 10ˢ | 20ˢ | 30ˢ | 40ˢ | 50ˢ | 60ˢ | 70ˢ | 80ˢ | 90ˢ |
|-----|-----|-----|-----|-----|-----|-----|-----|-----|
|     |     |     |     |     |     |     |     |     |

American actress Bernadette Peters was a five-year-old performer on Horn and Hardart's kiddie-talent radio program, and by age 11 was appearing on Broadway in *Most Happy Fella*. Bernadette achieved national fame in 1968 with her campy performance as Ruby, the 1930s-style chorus girl protagonist of the off-Broadway musical pastiche *Dames at Sea*. The role demonstrated only one aspect of her talents, but nonetheless threatened to typecast her as a squeaky-voiced dumb blonde. Bernadette scuttled that stereotype herself as leading lady in the 1969 Joel Grey musical *George M*. The following year she played Mabel Normand opposite Robert Preston's Mack Sennett in the musical comedy *Mack and Mabel*, which, though a failure, has become a staple of community theatres. (The amateur Mabels have an ongoing tendency to imitate Bernadette Peters.) In 1976, Bernadette costarred with Richard Crenna on *All's Fair*, a Norman Lear TV sitcom that showed neither star to best advantage. Reluctant to leave her native New York City, Bernadette has nonetheless occasionally travelled to Hollywood for an off-and-on movie career. Hilarious as a babaloo-ing cabaret entertainer in *Silent Movie* (1976), the actress was even better as the long-suffering wife of goony Steve Martin in *The Jerk* (1977). She was reunited with Martin in *Pennies From Heaven* (1981), an uneven but fascinating attempt to juxtapose the fanatasies of 1930s popular music with the grim realities of Depression life. Offscreen, Bernadette's relationship with Martin was intensely romantic for several years. Feeling unfulfilled in Hollywood, Bernadette Peters returned to Broadway in the mid 1980s, reclaiming her *Dames at Sea* prominence tenfold in such musicals as *Sunday in the Park With George, Song and Dance,* and *Into the Woods,* nearly unrecognizable in the latter in her heavy makeup as the wizened witch of "Hansel and Gretel" fame. **Selected Works:** *Alice* (1990), *Impromptu* (1990)

# William Petersen

**Born:** 1953; Chicago, IL

**Years Active in the Industry:** by decade

| 10s | 20s | 30s | 40s | 50s | 60s | 70s | 80s | 90s |
|-----|-----|-----|-----|-----|-----|-----|-----|-----|
|     |     |     |     |     |     |     |     |     |

Athletic leading man William L. Petersen began acting in his home town of Chicago, where he was a regular with the Remains Theatre. His first significant success was in the role of author/murderer Jack Henry Abbott in a stage adaptation of Abbott's *The Belly of the Beast*. This assignment led to his film debut as a scuzzy narcotics cop in *To Live and Die in LA* (1985). In 1987, Petersen starred in his first made-for-TV film, an enjoyable baseball yarn titled *Long Gone*, in which he appeared with fellow Chicagoan Virginia Madsen. **Selected Works:** *Keep the Change* (1992), *Young Guns, Part 2* (1990)

# Lori Petty

**Born:** 196?; Chattanooga, TN

**Years Active in the Industry:** by decade

| 10s | 20s | 30s | 40s | 50s | 60s | 70s | 80s | 90s |
|-----|-----|-----|-----|-----|-----|-----|-----|-----|
|     |     |     |     |     |     |     |     |     |

Actress Lori Petty started making a name for herself in television, brightening such short-lived series as *The Thorns* (1988) and *Booker* (1990). Her film career began with bland leading-lady parts in films like *Point Break* (1991). Contractually shunted to fourth billing in *A League of Their Own*, Petty virtually walked away with the latter portions of the picture as the envious younger sister of female ballplayer Geena Davis. Petty was finally afforded a movie vehicle of her own in 1995—the ill-conceived comic book derivation *Tank Girl*. **Selected Works:** *Cadillac Man* (1990)

# Michelle Pfeiffer

**Born:** April 29, 1959; Orange County, CA

**Years Active in the Industry:** by decade

| 10s | 20s | 30s | 40s | 50s | 60s | 70s | 80s | 90s |
|-----|-----|-----|-----|-----|-----|-----|-----|-----|
|     |     |     |     |     |     |     |     |     |

In her late teens Pfeiffer won the Miss Orange County beauty contest and then the title of Miss Los Angeles, after which she auditioned for commercials and modeling assignments and attended acting school. She debuted before the cameras in a one-line role on the TV series "Fantasy Island," going on to a string of bit parts on TV. She debuted onscreen in a small part in *Falling in Love Again* (1980), then had small roles in two more films before she got her big break in the role of Stephanie in the film version of the rock musical *Grease 2*

(1982). This led to her portrayal of Al Pacino's wife in Brian De Palma's *Scarface* (1983), which gained her much attention and set her on the road to stardom. Her first starring role was in the comedy thriller *Into the Night* (1984) with Jeff Goldblum. For her work in *Dangerous Liaisons* (1988) she received a Best Supporting Actress Oscar nomination, and for her portrayal of a nightclub singer in *The Fabulous Baker Boys* (1989) she received a Best Actress Oscar nomination. She married and divorced actor Peter Horton. **Selected Works:** *Batman Returns* (1992), *Married to the Mob* (1988), *Russia House* (1990), *Age of Innocence* (1993), *Wolf* (1994), *Dangerous Minds* (1995)

# Lou Diamond Phillips

**Born:** 1962; Philippines

**Years Active in the Industry:** by decade

| 10ˢ | 20ˢ | 30ˢ | 40ˢ | 50ˢ | 60ˢ | 70ˢ | 80ˢ | 90ˢ |
|-----|-----|-----|-----|-----|-----|-----|-----|-----|
|     |     |     |     |     |     |     | ■   | ■   |

Mixed-blood and Filipino-born, Phillips was raised in Arlington, Texas, where he began acting at age 10. After receiving his college degree in theater, he studied film technique with Adam Roarke at the Film Actor's Lab in Dallas. Between 1983 and 1986 he worked at the Lab as an assistant director and instructor. Concurrently, he performed in several plays in Dallas and Fort Worth, including *Doctor Faustus* and *Hamlet.* From 1983-87 Phillips appeared in several small, independent, Texas-made films, beginning with *Angel Alley;* one of these, *Trespasses* (1987), he co-wrote, while he associate-produced another, *Dakota* (1988). His big break came when director Luis Valdez was casting the Hollywood biopic *La Bamba* (1987), which focused on early rock 'n' roller Richie Valens. Someone suggested Phillips for the role of Valens' brother, but after he auditioned he was selected by Valdez to play the lead. With his performance as a barrio boy in *Stand and Deliver* (1988) he further established himself as a leading Hispanic star and representative of the Hispanic community. After playing an American Indian in the youth Western *Young Guns* (1988), he found himself fascinated with Indian culture and became a Cherokee blood brother. He wrote one of his films, *Ambition* (1991). **Selected Works:** *Extreme Justice* (1993), *Young Guns, Part 2* (1990), *Sioux City* (1994)

# River Phoenix

**Born:** August 23, 1971; Madras, OR
**Died:** October 31, 1993; Los Angeles, CA

**Years Active in the Industry:** by decade

| 10ˢ | 20ˢ | 30ˢ | 40ˢ | 50ˢ | 60ˢ | 70ˢ | 80ˢ | 90ˢ |
|-----|-----|-----|-----|-----|-----|-----|-----|-----|
|     |     |     |     |     |     |     | ■   | ■   |

Born into a "hippie" family, Phoenix spent his childhood moving from place to place, and lived for a time in South and Central America. As an adolescent he debuted before the camera in an episode of the daytime TV series "Fantasy," after which he appeared in the series "Family Ties," got parts in a couple of mini-series, and finally landed a regular role in the short-lived TV series "Seven Brides for Seven Brothers." He debuted onscreen in Joe Dante's *Explorers* (1985) but first made a big impression in his second film, Rob Reiner's sleeper hit *Stand By Me* (1986). He soon gained a reputation as a precociously talented actor with a singular ability to reach inside himself. He made the transition to adult roles as a young hustler in Gus Van Sant's *My Own Private Idaho* (1991). His brother Leaf has also acted onscreen. Phoenix died of an overdose of cocaine and amphetamines in October, 1993. **Se-**

**lected Works:** *Dog-fight* (1991), *I Love You to Death* (1990), *Indiana Jones and the Last Crusade* (1989), *Running on Empty* (1988)

# Mary Pickford (Gladys Smith)

**Born:** April 8, 1893; Toronto, Ontario, Canada
**Died:** 1979

**Years Active in the Industry:** by decade

| 10ˢ | 20ˢ | 30ˢ | 40ˢ | 50ˢ | 60ˢ | 70ˢ | 80ˢ | 90ˢ |
|-----|-----|-----|-----|-----|-----|-----|-----|-----|
|     |     |     |     |     |     |     |     |     |

Born Gladys Smith, Pickford was put to work as a child actress by her mother after her father died. She went on to tour with various road companies, billed as "Baby Gladys." At 14 she burst into producer David Belasco's office and persuaded him to cast her in the starring role of his Broadway play *The Warrens of Virginia.* Belasco changed her name to Mary Pickford. At 16 she similarly charmed filmmaker D.W. Griffith, becoming his principal leading lady. By 1910 she had appeared in a great many films. Unbilled, she came to be known as "Little Mary" or "The Girl with the Golden Hair." Through the decade her star status grew, and by 1916 she was earning $10,000 a week; in 1917 she got a contract for $350,000 per movie. She was the nation's biggest box-office draw for many years, beloved for her childlike aura; she came to be known as "America's Sweetheart." As late as 1920, when she was 27, Pickford portrayed a 12-year-old onscreen; although she tried to move into other roles, the public demanded to see her as a child. She was very powerful in Hollywood, having formed her own company in 1916; she had veto power over her scripts, costars, and directors. In 1919 she formed a partnership with Charlie Chaplin, D.W. Griffith, and Douglas Fairbanks, creating the United Artists Corporation. From 1911-19 she was married to actor Owen Moore. In 1920 she married Fairbanks, and they came to represent the ultimate "fairy tale" couple of Hollywood. Through the '20s she continued playing her standard roles, sustaining much of her popularity. In 1928 she cut off her trademark curls and in 1929 appeared in her first talkie, *Coquette,* wearing her shingled hairstyle and playing a modern swinger; she won a Best Actress Oscar, but the film was unpopular. She costarred with Fairbanks in the disastrous *The Taming of the Shrew* (1929), following which she appeared in only two more films. She later appeared frequently on radio. In 1936 she divorced Fairbanks, marrying actor Charles "Buddy" Rogers in 1937. Also in 1936, she was named first vice president of United Artists. In 1953, she and Chaplin (the sole survivors of the original four) sold United Artists. Having bought many of her early silent films with the intention of having them burned after her death, she had a change of heart and donated most of them to the American Film Institute. In 1975 she received a special Oscar in recognition of her entire career. Pickford was the sister of actors Jack and Lottie Pickford. She authored an autobiography, *Sunshine and Shadow* (1955). **Selected Works:** *My Best Girl* (1927)

# Sir Walter Pidgeon

**Born:** September 23, 1898; New Brunswick, Canada
**Died:** September 25, 1984

**Years Active in the Industry:** by decade

| 10s | 20s | 30s | 40s | 50s | 60s | 70s | 80s | 90s |
|-----|-----|-----|-----|-----|-----|-----|-----|-----|

Pidgeon spent 17 months in the hospital after sustaining injuries in World War I, then he moved to New York to forge an acting career. After some work on stage he began appearing in films in 1925, and was quite busy in supporting roles through the end of the silent era. In early musicals he was frequently called upon to sing, but through the '30s he remained a second-string actor. In the '40s Pidgeon enjoyed stardom as the result of several excellent roles and a string of eight film appearances with Greer Garson. For two of the latter, *Mrs. Miniver* (1942) and *Madame Curie* (1943), he received Best Actor Oscar nominations. He moved into character roles in the '50s, meanwhile performing in the Broadway shows *The Happiest Millionaire* and *Take Me Along*. He spent five years as president of the Screen Actors Guild in the '50s. **Selected Works:** *Bad & the Beautiful* (1952), *Funny Girl* (1968), *How Green Was My Valley* (1941)

# Jada Pinkett

**Born:** 1971; Baltimore, MD

**Years Active in the Industry:** by decade

| 10s | 20s | 30s | 40s | 50s | 60s | 70s | 80s | 90s |
|-----|-----|-----|-----|-----|-----|-----|-----|-----|

Jada Pinkett once claimed that she wanted to either be an actress or a lawyer; both professions would have offered her an opportunity to perform before crowds. Acting won out, and Jada trained at the Baltimore School of the Arts and the North Carolina School of the Arts. In 1991 she was cast as saucy and sassy college freshman Lena James on the Bill Cosby-produced sitcom *A Different World*. Tiny in stature (barely five feet) but a giant-talent wise, Jada Pinkett became one of the most in-demand black leading ladies in Hollywood, with roles in *Menace II Society* (1993), *The Inkwell* (1994), *Jason's Lyric* (1994), and *A Low Down Dirty Shame* (1994).

# Harold Pinter

**Born:** October 10, 1930; Hackney, East London

**Years Active in the Industry:** by decade

| 10s | 20s | 30s | 40s | 50s | 60s | 70s | 80s | 90s |
|-----|-----|-----|-----|-----|-----|-----|-----|-----|

It is difficult to determine what was in the psychological makeup of Briton Harold Pinter that resulted in a playwrighting style distinguished by tension-filled pregnant pauses. Possibly this minimal use of wordage stemmed from Pinter's own communication problems with his Portuguese-born Jewish father. In the 1950s, Pinter attended RADA and hoped to be an actor under the Anglo-Saxon professional name David Baron. Instead he turned to writing, penning his first play, *The Room*, for the Bristol University drama department. After a lukewarm response to his first professionally produced play *The Birthday Party* (1958), Pinter rose to fame with the 1960 stage production *The Caretaker*. With 1963's *The Servant*, Pinter made his bow as a screenwriter, and also essayed his first film role (he has since acted in other films, most recently 1985's *Turtle Diary*, but hasn't declared any intention of making this his life's work). While many of his films (*The Caretaker*, *The Birthday Party*, the Oscar-nominated *Betrayal*) are adapted from his own plays, just as many have been screen originals. Pinter's film scripts aren't quite as enigmatic or confusing as his plays, in fact many have been models of clarity and succintness, notably his Oscar-nominated adaptation of John Fowles' complex *The French Lieutenant's Woman* (1981). For a man who isn't overly fond of excess verbiage, Pinter has had considerable success on BBC radio, but here again it's what's *not* said in Pinter's plays that's most important. In 1974, Harold Pinter ventured into film directing with *Butley*, an over-the-top comedy by Peter Gray that's as far removed from the usual Pinter style as a Marx Brothers film. **Selected Works:** *Go-Between* (1971), *Handmaid's Tale* (1990), *Remains of the Day* (1993)

# Brad Pitt (William Bradley Pitt)

**Born:** December 18, 1963; Shawnee, OK

**Years Active in the Industry:** by decade

| 10s | 20s | 30s | 40s | 50s | 60s | 70s | 80s | 90s |
|-----|-----|-----|-----|-----|-----|-----|-----|-----|

Brad Pitt may look and sound like a "Generation X" slacker, but he has worked hard for most of his adult life. Pitt studied journalism at the University of Missouri, then launched his performing career with such unprepossessing jobs as a chicken-costumed restaurant mascot. After attracting attention as a magazine-ad model for Levi's, Pitt made his TV debut in *Dallas* and his film bow in *Cutting Class* (1989). His first film role of note was as the hitchiker in *Thelma and Louise* (1991). Since that time, Pitt has exhibited a range above and beyond his "Hey dude" demeanor in such films as *A River Runs Through It* (1993), *True Romance* (1993), *Interview*

with the Vampire (1994), and *Legends of the Fall* (1994). **Selected Works:** *Johnny Suede* (1992), *Kalifornia* (1993), *Seven* (1995), *Twelve Monkeys* (1995)

# ZaSu Pitts

**Born:** January 3, 1900; Parsons, KS
**Died:** 1963

### Years Active in the Industry: by decade

| 10s | 20s | 30s | 40s | 50s | 60s | 70s | 80s | 90s |
|-----|-----|-----|-----|-----|-----|-----|-----|-----|
|     |     |     |     |     |     |     |     |     |

At 19 she was cast in supporting roles in two Mary Pickford films, bringing her to the public's attention. Pitts went on to play leads and supporting roles in over 100 films. Although in silents she had shown herself to be a skilled tragedienne, in the sound era she appeared almost exclusively in comedic roles, usually playing scatterbrained characters. In 1931-33 she costarred with Thelma Todd in 17 comedy shorts. In her feature film starring roles, she often appeared opposite Slim Summerville. Pitts' trademark was zany bewilderment, marked by her sighing "Oh me, oh my;" she brought this to TV in a regular role on the '50s series "Oh! Susanna" (later called "The Gale Storm Show"). Her last film was released in 1963, the year of her death from cancer. **Selected Works:** *Life with Father* (1947), *Ruggles of Red Gap* (1935)

# Donald Pleasence

**Born:** October 5, 1919; Nottinghamshire, England
**Died:** February 2, 1995; St. Paul de Vence, France

### Years Active in the Industry: by decade

| 10s | 20s | 30s | 40s | 50s | 60s | 70s | 80s | 90s |
|-----|-----|-----|-----|-----|-----|-----|-----|-----|
|     |     |     |     |     |     |     |     |     |

Balding, deceptively bland-looking British actor Donald Pleasence was first seen on the London stage in a 1939 production of *Wuthering Heights*. He then served in the RAF, spending the last years of the war incarcerated in a German POW camp. Pleasence first came to New York in the company of Laurence Olivier in 1950, appearing in *Caesar and Cleopatra*. While he was in films from 1954 on, Pleasence's British fame in the 1950s rested upon his TV

work, notably his recurring role as Prince John in the "Robin Hood" series. He also costarred in televised productions of *The Millionairess, Man In A Moon,* and *Call Me Daddy.* In 1958 Pleasence was voted British television actor of the year. After producing and hosting a 1960 TV series titled "Armchair Mystery Theatre," Pleasence created the stage role for which he was best remembered—Davies, the menacing tramp in Harold Pinter's *The Caretaker.* The actor recreated the part throughout his career, appearing as Davies for the last time in 1991. Pleasence was fortunate enough to be associated with the international film success *The Great Escape* (1963), which led to a wealth of American offers. Four years later, the actor portrayed arch criminal Ernst Blofeld in the James Bond film *You Only Live Twice*—the first time that the secretive Blofeld's scarred face was seen on-screen in the Bond series. Firmly established as a villain, Pleasence gradually eased into horror films like *Halloween* (1978), *The Devonsville Terror* (1979) and *Buried Alive* (1990); commenting upon this phase of his career, Pleasence remarked "I only appear in odd films." One of his few "mainstream" appearances during this period was virtually invisible. Pleasence is seen and prominently billed as a rabbi in Carl Reiner's *Oh, God* (1978), but the role was deemed dispensable and all the actor's lines were cut. Pleasence continued working (17 pictures alone between 1987 and 1989) until undergoing heart surgery just before Christmas of 1994; he died of an undisclosed ailment two months later. Married four times, Donald Pleasence was the father of six daughters, among them actress Angela Pleasence. **Selected Works:** *Hearts of the West* (1975), *Sons and Lovers* (1960)

# Joan Plowright

**Born:** October 28, 1929; Brigg, England

### Years Active in the Industry: by decade

| 10s | 20s | 30s | 40s | 50s | 60s | 70s | 80s | 90s |
|-----|-----|-----|-----|-----|-----|-----|-----|-----|
|     |     |     |     |     |     |     |     |     |

Trained at the Old Vic, British actress Joan Plowright made her regional stage debut in 1951 and her London stage bow in 1954. In 1956 she joined the English Stage Company, where she essayed her most popular role up to that time, Margery Pincher in Wycherly's *The Country Wife.* That same year she appeared in her first film, *Moby Dick* (1956). In the original 1958 stage production of John Osborne's *The Entertainer*, Ms. Plowright costarred with Sir Laurence Olivier, whom she would marry in 1961, a union that lasted until Olivier's death in 1989. Joan appeared on-screen with her husband in the film versions of *The Entertainer* (1960) and *The Three Sisters* (1970), the latter film also directed by Olivier. During the same period, Plowright and Olivier were mainstays of London's National Theatre. In 1961, Ms. Plowright won a Tony award for her Broadway appearance in *A Taste of Honey.* Her stage work was briefly curtailed in the mid-to-late 1960s, allowing her time to raise her family. From 1982 on, Joan began appearing in films with increasing regularity, demonstrating at least two traits she'd evidently picked up from Olivier—a propensity for elaborate foreign accents (the hero's Jewish mother in *Avalon* [1990], the heroine's Yugoslavian mom in *I Love You to Death* [1990]) and a willingness to take assignments purely for the money (Mrs. Wilson in *Dennis the Menace* [1993]). While an Oscar win is long overdue, Ms. Plowright was at least nominated for her work in 1992's *Enchanted April*. Perhaps Joan Plowright's most endearing portrayal in recent years was as the high school teacher in *The Last Action Hero* who runs a clip from Laurence Olivier's *Hamlet* (1948) for her class, introducing Olivier as "the fellow who did all those Polaroid commercials." **Selected Works:** *Stalin* (1992), *Summer House* (1993), *The Scarlet Letter* (1995)

# Amanda Plummer

**Born:** March 23, 1957; New York, NY

**Years Active in the Industry:** by decade

| 10ˢ | 20ˢ | 30ˢ | 40ˢ | 50ˢ | 60ˢ | 70ˢ | 80ˢ | 90ˢ |
|-----|-----|-----|-----|-----|-----|-----|-----|-----|
|     |     |     |     |     |     |     |     |     |

The daughter of Canadian actor Christopher Plummer and American actress Tammy Grimes, Amanda Plummer adhered to family tradition by taking to the stage. After several well-received Broadway appearances, Plummer won the Tony and the Drama Desk award for her performance as a schizophrenic nun in the 1982 stage production of *Agnes of God*. One year earlier, she'd made her film bow as one-half of the title role in the critically acclaimed western *Cattle Annie and Little Britches*. While Plummer has nearly always gleaned excellent reviews for her film work, many of her movie roles are of the wildly eccentric variety—meaning that half the audience will be enthralled while the other half will recoil. Gifted with a thrilling, highly individualistic stage voice, Plummer made one of her most vivid screen impressions in the non-speaking role of "reluctant martyr" Ellen James in *The World According to Garp* (1982). **Selected Works:** *So I Married an Axe Murderer* (1993), *Fisher King* (1991), *Pulp Fiction* (1994)

# Christopher Plummer (Arthur Christopher Orme Plummer)

**Born:** December 13, 1927; Toronto, Ontario, Canada

**Years Active in the Industry:** by decade

| 10ˢ | 20ˢ | 30ˢ | 40ˢ | 50ˢ | 60ˢ | 70ˢ | 80ˢ | 90ˢ |
|-----|-----|-----|-----|-----|-----|-----|-----|-----|
|     |     |     |     |     |     |     |     |     |

From his 1950 debut onward, Christopher Plummer has been regarded as one of the most brilliant Canadian actors of his generation. His portrayal of Hamlet was a major ratings coup when telecast over the CBC in the early 1960s. Since his first Broadway appearance in 1954 (among his New York stage credits are *JB*, *Royal Hunt of the Sun* and *The Good Doctor*), efforts have been made to convert Plummer into an American matinee idol, most of these attempts resisted by Plummer himself. His first two films,

*Stage Struck* (1957) and *Wind Across the Everglades* (1958), set no new box office records. He was shown to better advantage in such live network-TV presentations as *The Prisoner of Zenda* and *A Doll's House*. In 1965, Plummer was cast as Baron von Trapp in *The Sound of Music* (1965)—an assignment he despised, referring to the musical blockbuster as *The Sound of Mucus*. Nonetheless, and as Plummer has ruefully noted on many occasions, this one film did more to make the actor bankable in Hollywood than any previous effort. Among Plummer's notable later film appearances were 1976's *Murder by Decree* (as Sherlock Holmes), 1980's *Somewhere in Time*, 1991's *Star Trek VI: The Undiscovered Country* and 1994's *Wolf*. He hasn't yet won an Oscar, but Plummer was honored with a Tony Award for the musical *Cyrano* and an Emmy for the TV miniseries *The Moneychangers*. Christopher Plummer and his first wife Tammy Grimes are the parents of actress Amanda Plummer. **Selected Works:** *Malcolm X* (1992), *Man Who Would Be King* (1975), *Twelve Monkeys* (1995)

# Sidney Poitier

**Born:** February 20, 1927; Miami, FL

**Years Active in the Industry:** by decade

| 10ˢ | 20ˢ | 30ˢ | 40ˢ | 50ˢ | 60ˢ | 70ˢ | 80ˢ | 90ˢ |
|-----|-----|-----|-----|-----|-----|-----|-----|-----|
|     |     |     |     |     |     |     |     |     |

Handsome black actor and director Poitier is considered the actor most responsible for the emergence of black actors into mainstream films. Raised in poverty in the Bahamas, he dropped out of school at age 13 and later moved to Miami. After a series of menial jobs and a stint in the Army, he tried to join the American Negro Theater but was laughed off the stage in his audition; for the next six months he tried (successfully) to lose his Bahamian accent, then went back and auditioned again, this time gaining entrance. He debuted on Broad-

way in 1946, in the all-black production of *Lysistrata*. Besides an appearance in an Army documentary, his first screen role came in *No Way Out* (1950). Poitier's rise in the world of acting was so swift as to be almost miraculous. He soon became Hollywood's number one black actor; by the '60s he was established as a charismatic star whose appeal extended across the race line and whose talents allowed him to play a wide variety of roles. For his work in *The Defiant Ones* (1958) he received a Best Actor Oscar nomination, then won the Best Actor Oscar for *Lilies of the Field* (1963), becoming the first black performer to win in that category. In 1972 he began directing his own films. He married actress Joanna Shimkus in 1976. **Selected Works:** *Cry, the Beloved Country* (1951), *Guess Who's Coming to Dinner* (1967), *In the Heat of the Night* (1967), *Lilies of the Field* (1963), *Raisin in the Sun* (1961)

# Roman Polanski

**Born:** August 18, 1933; Paris, France

**Years Active in the Industry:** by decade

| 10ˢ | 20ˢ | 30ˢ | 40ˢ | 50ˢ | 60ˢ | 70ˢ | 80ˢ | 90ˢ |
|-----|-----|-----|-----|-----|-----|-----|-----|-----|
|     |     |     |     |     | ■   | ■   | ■   | ■   |

Born in Paris to Polish-Jewish parents, Polanski and his family returned to Krakow when he was three. When he was eight, his parents were taken to a Nazi concentration camp, where his mother died. He managed to escape the Krakow ghetto, then wandered the Polish countryside and lived with a succession of Catholic families; exposed to many horrors along the way, he was also used for target practice by German soldiers. When the war wound down he became fascinated with films and went to a movie every day. At age 12 he was reunited with his father, who sent him to technical school; this was his first formal education. He began acting on children's radio shows, and from age 14 to 20 he acted in many stage productions. He went on to attend the Polish film school from 1954-59, where he acted in films and directed several documentary shorts; one of these, *Two Men and a Wardrobe*, won five international awards. After spending two years in Paris, he returned to Poland, became a major filmmaker, and won a number of awards. From the mid '60s all his films have been in English; at the same time he took up residence in Hollywood. He was married to actress Sharon Tate, who was murdered in the infamous Manson killings of August, 1969. He left Hollywood and moved back to Europe. In March of 1977 he was charged with drugging and raping a 13-year-old girl; he denied the charges, then entered a partial guilty plea. Free on bail, he fled from the U.S. and escaped prosecution. He has continued making films through the '90s, though his work is intermittent. **Selected Works:** *Chinatown* (1974), *Knife in the Water* (1962), *Repulsion* (1965), *Rosemary's Baby* (1968), *Death and the Maiden* (1994)

# Sydney Pollack

**Born:** July 1, 1934; Lafayette, IN

**Years Active in the Industry:** by decade

| 10ˢ | 20ˢ | 30ˢ | 40ˢ | 50ˢ | 60ˢ | 70ˢ | 80ˢ | 90ˢ |
|-----|-----|-----|-----|-----|-----|-----|-----|-----|
|     |     |     |     |     | ■   | ■   | ■   | ■   |

Sydney Pollack was the son of first generation Russian-Jewish Americans. After graduating from high school in 1952, he went to New York and became a student at the Neighborhood Playhouse, a celebrated Greenwich Village school, where he studied under Sanford Meisner. He served two years in the army before returning to the Neighborhood Playhouse in 1958 as a teacher, and began appearing as an actor in live television dramas. His appearance in a John Frankenheimer-directed television production led him to a job as dialogue coach in the filmmaker's 1961 crime drama *The Young Savages*. He quickly moved into television directing on programs such as "The Defenders," "The Naked City," "The Fugitive," "Dr. Kildare," and "Ben Casey" during the early and mid 1960s, and in 1965 made his feature film debut in the director's chair with *The Slender Thread*. Pollack established himself as a competent, if unexceptional, director in such works as *This Property Is Condemned*, and one sequence of the Frank Perry-directed drama *The Swimmer* (based on a work of John Cheever). However, his real breakthrough came in 1969 with the downbeat period drama *They Shoot Horses, Don't They?*, a brutal Depression-era piece set against the backdrop of a dance marathon contest, starring Jane Fonda and Gig Young. Young won the Oscar for Best Supporting Actor while Pollack and Fonda were nominated for Best Director and Best Actress, respectively. (Fonda was said to have lost only because of the controversy surrounding her anti-Vietnam War activities.) Pollack again proved his skill at handling period drama four years later with *The Way We Were*, a romantic drama starring Barbra Streisand and Robert Redford that became one of the most popular serious movies of the decade. During the mid 1970s, Pollack also delved into the action genre with *The Yakuza*, about a kidnapping committed by Japanese gangsters. He achieved much greater success with *Three Days of the Condor*, a post-Watergate suspense thriller starring Robert Redford, Cliff Robertson, and Faye Dunaway that proved an enduring favorite among genre fans as well as a hit with general audiences. *The Electric Horseman* (1979) united his two top leads, Jane Fonda and Robert Redford, in a predictable but very successful update of the '30s screwball comedy, while *Absence of Malice* (1981), starring Paul Newman and Sally Field, took a much more serious tone in dealing with a story of an innocent man whose career is ruined by an ambitious reporter. *Tootsie* (1982) saw Pollack return to comedy in top form, with the story of an out-of-work actor (Dustin Hoffman) who achieves success by masquerading as a woman. *Out Of Africa* (1985), with Robert Redford, was one of a dwindling number of serious romantic dramas aimed at middle-class, middle-brow, middle-aged audiences that scored big at the box office, but *Havana* (1990), also starring Redford, was a notorious failure. Pollack was back on top in 1993 with the thriller *The Firm*. Although a competent filmmaker, Pollack has never shown a defining style. Nevertheless, he has made some of the most successful dramas and non-teen comedies of the last two decade, as well as two unabashed classics of their respective decades, *They Shoot Horses* and *Tootsie.* **Selected Works:** *Husbands and Wives* (1992), *Jeremiah Johnson* (1972), *Presumed Innocent* (1990), *Searching for Bobby Fischer* (1993), *Sabrina* (1995)

# Natalie Portman

**Born:** Long Island, NY

**Years Active in the Industry:** by decade

| 10s | 20s | 30s | 40s | 50s | 60s | 70s | 80s | 90s |
|-----|-----|-----|-----|-----|-----|-----|-----|-----|

New York-born Natalie Portman was sitting in a pizza parlor when she was spotted by an agent and hired on the spot as a child model. At age 13, Portman received her first feature film role in the R-rated *The Professional* (1994). The script required that young Portman fall in love with her next-door neighbor, who repays the compliment by training her to be a professional assassin. Portman allowed that making her first film in the toughest sections of Spanish Harlem was frightening—but not quite so frightening, she claimed, as going back to school once shooting wrapped.

# Dick Powell (Richard E. Powell)

**Born:** November 14, 1904; Mountain View, AR
**Died:** 1963

**Years Active in the Industry:** by decade

| 10s | 20s | 30s | 40s | 50s | 60s | 70s | 80s | 90s |
|-----|-----|-----|-----|-----|-----|-----|-----|-----|

Curly-haired actor, director, and producer, Powell worked as a vocalist and instrumentalist for bands (he had several hit records), and occasionally was an M.C. He debuted onscreen in 1932, at first as a crooner in '30s Warner Bros. backstage musicals, often opposite Ruby Keeler. After playing choir-boy-type leads for a decade, he made a surprising switch to dramatic roles in the 1940s, showing special skill as tough heroes or private eyes such as Philip Marlowe. Powell's last big-screen appearance was in *Susan Slept Here* (1954), in which he once again sang; he went on to appear frequently on TV. His career took another turn in the early '50s when he began producing and directing films; he was also a founder and president of Four Star Television, a prosperous TV production company. His second wife was actress Joan Blondell, with whom he appeared in *Model Wife* (1941) and *I Want a Divorce* (1940); his widow is actress June Allyson. In John Schlesinger's *The Day of the Locust* (1975) he was portrayed by his son, Dick Powell, Jr. **Selected Works:** *42nd Street* (1933), *Bad & the Beautiful* (1952), *Gold Diggers of 1933* (1933)

# Michael Powell

**Born:** September 30, 1905; Bekesbourne, Kent, England
**Died:** February 19, 1990; Avening, Gloucestershire, England

**Years Active in the Industry:** by decade

| 10s | 20s | 30s | 40s | 50s | 60s | 70s | 80s | 90s |
|-----|-----|-----|-----|-----|-----|-----|-----|-----|

A one time studio gofer, stills photographer, and comic actor, Michael Powell became one of the most celebrated and controversial directors ever to come out of England. Born in Canterbury, Powell became enamored of films while still a teenager and, after a start in the mid 1920s and a stint as stills photographer and co-scenarist with Alfred Hitchcock in the early sound era, Powell broke into directing in low-budget British thrillers and comedies. In 1937, after directing and writing his first notable movie, *The Edge of the World,* he moved to London Films where he began his two-decade association with Emeric Pressburger, a gifted young author and screenwriter. Their partnership began shortly after they left London Films (where they collaborated on *The Spy In Black,* and Powell co-directed *The Thief of Baghdad*), with the wartime thrillers *Contraband* and *Forty-Ninth Parallel*—the latter attracted much attention around the world (including an Oscar nomination for Best Picture and an Academy Award for best original story), and resulted in the creation of The Archers, an independent production company through which they went on jointly to write, produce, and direct *The Life and Death of Colonel Blimp, A Canterbury Tale, I Know Where I'm Going,* and *Stairway To Heaven* during World War II. These films, with their idiosyncratic humor and point of view alienated many British critics but delighted audiences on both sides of the Atlantic. After the war, Powell and Pressburger made a series of movies that emblazoned their names around the world: *Black Narcissus,* a story of nuns who are nearly destroyed by their own passions while trying to found a convent in the Himalayas; *The Red Shoes,* a phenomenally successful film about the life and death of a ballet dancer, whose multi-year run in America and multi-million dollar success made possible such pictures as *An American In Paris;* and *The Tales of Hoffmann,* an opera/ballet amalgam of unprecedented stylistic flare and daring. The early 1950s saw a decline in their fortunes, and the partnership dissolved in 1956. Powell continued to make movies of a fiercely personal nature until 1960, when the critical reaction to *Peeping Tom*—now considered a classic, about a man who mixes voyeurism, cinema, and murder—ended his career in England. He worked for American and European television during the 1960s and 1970s, and late in that decade was rediscovered with the help of Francis Coppola and Martin Scorsese, each of whom regarded Powell as one of the most important influences on his own work. Museum retrospectives, restorations, and reopenings of his classic films followed, along with a multi-volume autobiography that he completed prior to his death. **Selected Works:** *Invaders* (1941)

# William Powell (William Horatio Powell)

**Born:** July 29, 1892; Pittsburgh, PA
**Died:** March 5, 1984; Palm Springs, CA

**Years Active in the Industry:** by decade

| 10s | 20s | 30s | 40s | 50s | 60s | 70s | 80s | 90s |
|-----|-----|-----|-----|-----|-----|-----|-----|-----|

A villain in Hollywood silents, in the sound era he was a suave, sophisticated, gentlemanly leading man of romantic comedies and light-hearted detective stories. Powell debuted on Broadway in 1912. In the early '20s he began appearing in silents; his first screen role was in *Sherlock Holmes* (1922), in which he played the detective's arch-enemy, Professor Moriarty. Altogether Powell appeared in 34 silents. In the early sound era he appeared in a string of light mysteries, playing sleuth Philo Vance in work adapted from the stories of S.S. Van Dine. His career took off after he appeared in the low-budget surprise hit, *The Thin Man* (1934), in which he and Myrna Loy played the wealthy, cocktail-swilling husband-and-wife detective team Nick and Nora Charles. He received a Best Actor Oscar nomination for his performance; the film led to six sequels and seven additional films with Loy. He also received Oscar nominations for his work in *My Man Godfrey* (1936) and *Life with Father* (1947). In 1936 he was among the top-ten box office attractions, in part due to his appearance that year as Florenz Ziegfeld in *The Great Ziegfeld;* he played Ziegfeld again in *Ziegfeld Follies* (1946). He was engaged to actress Jean Harlow at the time of her death, and was married from 1931-33 to actress Carole Lombard, with whom he appeared in *Man of the World* (1931) and *My Man Godfrey.* From 1940 on he was married to actress Diana Lewis. **Selected Works:** *Last Command* (1928), *Libeled Lady* (1936), *Mister Roberts* (1955), *One Way Passage* (1932)

# Tyrone Power (Tyrone Edmund Power, Jr.)

**Born:** May 5, 1914; Cincinnati, OH
**Died:** 1958

### Years Active in the Industry: by decade

| 10s | 20s | 30s | 40s | 50s | 60s | 70s | 80s | 90s |
|-----|-----|-----|-----|-----|-----|-----|-----|-----|
|     |     |     |     |     |     |     |     |     |

The son of a stage and screen actor, Power began performing onstage in his teens, then got bit roles in a few films. In 1937 his studio showcased him as a star, and from 1938-40 he was

among the top-ten box office stars, playing romantic leads. Service in World War II interrupted his career; when he returned he was unable to recapture his former popularity, though he still remained active and well-liked by the public. He was effective in every genre of films, including swashbucklers, Westerns, period dramas, modern comedies, contemporary dramas, musical dramas, and war films. He later worked frequently in theater. He died of a heart attack at age 45. From 1939-48 he was

married to actress Annabella, and from 1949-55 he was married to actress Linda Christian. His daughter Romina and his son Tyrone have both appeared in films. **Selected Works:** *Mark of Zorro* (1940), *Razor's Edge* (1946), *Witness for the Prosecution* (1957), *Mississippi Gambler* (1953), *Rains Came* (1939)

# Otto Preminger (Otto Ludwig Preminger)

**Born:** December 5, 1906; Vienna, Austria
**Died:** April 23, 1986; New York, NY

### Years Active in the Industry: by decade

| 10s | 20s | 30s | 40s | 50s | 60s | 70s | 80s | 90s |
|-----|-----|-----|-----|-----|-----|-----|-----|-----|
|     |     |     |     |     |     |     |     |     |

Originally a law student, Preminger got his first acting experience with Max Reinhardt's theater company while studying for his degree. He entered the theater as a producer and director, came to America as a theatrical director in 1935, and was hired by 20th Century-Fox. After leaving the studio for Broadway at the end of the 1930s, he returned in the early 1940s, specializing in Nazi roles despite his Jewish faith. Preminger got back into the director's chair with the movie *Margin For Error,* an adaptation of a play that Preminger had directed on Broadway. *Laura,* based on the hit novel and play by Vera Caspary, was to have been directed by Rouben Mamoulian, but he was fired soon after production began, and Preminger finished the film—which went on to become a huge hit—as director. Preminger's most important subsequent movie at Fox was *Forever Amber,* which failed at the box office but enhanced his reputation nonetheless. In the early 1950s, Preminger became an independent producer/director, and immediately began making a name for himself through a series of successful challenges to the restrictive production code, which forbade the use of various controversial subjects on screen. His sophisticated comedy *The Moon Is Blue* broke through the barrier with regard to sexual subjects, with its relatively frank treatment of such matters as virginity and pregnancy, while *The Man With The Golden Arm* was the first major Hollywood film to deal with the subject of drug addiction. Preminger's *Carmen Jones* proved a critically successful venture into musicals, which led directly to Samuel Goldwyn's choosing Preminger to direct his screen adaptation of George and Ira Gershwin's opera *Porgy and Bess.* Preminger's box office record was rather scattershot during this era and included the notorious disaster *Saint Joan* and the huge hit *Anatomy of a Murder.* Preminger's early-1960s movies grew in size and pretentiousness, and included such epic-length releases as *Advise And Consent, The Cardinal,* and *In Harm's Way,* but by the middle of the decade, he had receded in ambition and success, with *Bunny Lake Is Missing, Skidoo,* and *Tell Me That You Love Me Junie Moon.* The 1970s saw the release of the failed thrillers *Rosebud* and *The Human Factor.* He died in 1986, several years after the onset of Alzheimer's Disease brought an end to his career. Always a flamboyant personality, Preminger was one of the more visible and better known director/producers of his era, and became known to an entire generation of children with his portrayal of the villainous Mr. Freeze on the "Batman" television series. **Selected Works:** *Exodus* (1960), *Stalag 17* (1953), *Pied Piper* (1942)

# Elvis Presley (Elvis Aron Presley)

**Born:** March 8, 1935; Tupelo, MS
**Died:** August 16, 1977; Memphis, TN

**Years Active in the Industry:** by decade

| 10s | 20s | 30s | 40s | 50s | 60s | 70s | 80s | 90s |
|---|---|---|---|---|---|---|---|---|
| | | | | | | | | |

One of the all-time great rock 'n' rollers and an unprecedented, phenomenal show-business success, Elvis also starred in 31 consecutive box-office successes; he was among the top ten box-office attractions in 1957 and from 1961-66. When he was 13 he moved to Memphis with his family, going on to work as an usher in a movie theater and as a truck driver. He toured locally as a singer billed "The Hillbilly Cat" and recorded several singles for a local label; in 1955 he was signed by RCA and became an instant hit, racking up one hit single after another. Onstage he gyrated his midsection seductively, leading him to aquire the nickname "Elvis the Pelvis;" his concert appearances inspired hysteria among his young female fans, and he was considered by many to be a negative moral influence. However, he maintained his clean-cut, "mama's boy" image and soon had fans of every generation. He began appearing in films in 1956, debuting in *Love Me Tender*. Never successful among critics, his films were designed around his casual, good-ol'-boy character, successful flirtations with his pretty female costars, and numerous musical numbers; each made money, altogether grossing more than $150 million. After he served a stint in the army, his singing career declined in the early '60s, when the Beatles and other new groups dominated the airwaves; he continued making successful films until 1969 (his last was *Change of Habit* with Mary Tyler Moore, who played a nun). He also appeared in two concert documentaries, *That's the Way It Is* (1970) and *Elvis On Tour* (1972). In the early '70s, after a decade of few personal appearances, he began doing live entertainment again, and his drawing power was as strong as ever. However, he began neglecting his health and gained large amounts of weight. He died of a prescription-drug-induced heart attack in 1977, after which his cult of personality grew to enormous proportions; he is perhaps more popular in death than he was during his life.

# Priscilla Presley

**Born:** May 24, 1945; Brooklyn, NY

**Years Active in the Industry:** by decade

| 10s | 20s | 30s | 40s | 50s | 60s | 70s | 80s | 90s |
|---|---|---|---|---|---|---|---|---|
| | | | | | | | | |

Priscilla Beaulieu was the 14-year-old daughter of an American air force officer when, in 1959, she first met army sergeant Elvis Presley. It was love at first sight, but the ever-gentlemanly Elvis courted Priscilla for a respectable eight years, waiting until she came of age before escorting her to the altar. Presley tried to make the marriage work, but a combination of drugs, liquor and too many female hangers-on virtually foredoomed the union. Still respectful of Priscilla, Elvis saw to it that she and their daughter Lisa Marie were generously provided for in the divorce settlement. After Elvis' death, Priscilla invested very wisely and launched her own performing career, cohosting the 1980 television "reality" show "Those Amazing Animals" and costarring for five years (1983-88) on the nighttime TV serial "Dallas." At age 43 (but looking at least 15 years younger), Priscilla made her cinematic bow as Leslie Nielsen's leading lady in the adventure spoof *Naked Gun: From the Files of Police Squad* (1988); she repeated the role, with ever-increasing comic expertise, in two *Naked Gun* sequels, the last released in 1994. That same year, Priscilla Presley became the world's most famous (and undoubtedly most surprised) mother-in-law when her daughter Lisa Marie wed rock-legend Michael Jackson. **Selected Works:** *Naked Gun 2 1/2: The Smell of Fear* (1991), *Naked Gun 33 1/3: The Final Insult* (1994)

# Kelly Preston

**Born:** October 13, 1962; Honolulu, HI

**Years Active in the Industry:** by decade

| 10s | 20s | 30s | 40s | 50s | 60s | 70s | 80s | 90s |
|---|---|---|---|---|---|---|---|---|
| | | | | | | | | |

Actress Kelly Preston was first seen on a national basis in the last-billed role of a general's daughter on the weekly 1983 TV drama *For Love and Honor*. She established herself as an agreeable comedienne in such films as *Mischief* (1985) and *Secret Admirer* (1985), then became lost in the turgid melodramatics of *52 Pick-Up* (1986). Her big movie break was supposed to have been her costarring stint with Arnold Schwarzenegger and Danny DeVito in *Twins* (1988), but the role was too nondescript to engender any enthusiasm. Nonetheless, Preston has perservered, delivering great performances in such offbeat fare as the 1993 made-for-cable movie *The American Clock*. Kelly Preston is the wife of film star John Travolta, whom she met on the set of the direct-to-video *The Experts* (1989). **Selected Works:** *Only You* (1992), *Perfect Bride* (1991)

# Robert Preston (Robert Preston Meservey)

**Born:** June 8, 1918; Newton Highlands, MA
**Died:** March 21, 1987; Santa Barbara, CA

**Years Active in the Industry:** by decade

| 10s | 20s | 30s | 40s | 50s | 60s | 70s | 80s | 90s |
|-----|-----|-----|-----|-----|-----|-----|-----|-----|
|     |     |     |     |     |     |     |     |     |

A vital, virile, exciting Broadway performer, Preston was once called, "the best American actor—with a voice like golden thunder," by Richard Burton. He decided to become an actor at age 15. After studying acting at the Pasadena Playhouse, he became a steady, dependable performer in Hollywood films from the late '30s. Preston became well-known after Cecil B. DeMille cast him as Barbara Stanwyck's gambler husband in *Union Pacific* (1939). He was almost strictly a second-lead actor for 20 years, finally breaking through to lead roles after becoming a star on Broadway. For his Broadway performance (his first in a musical) as ebulliant con-artist Henry Hill in *The Music Man* he won a Tony Award; he repeated the role in the screen version (1962) and it became the work for which he is best-known. Another outstanding performance was as Julie Andrews' gay friend Toddie in Blake Edwards's *Victor/Victoria* (1982); for his performance he received a Best Supporting Actor Oscar nomination. **Selected Works:** *Beau Geste* (1939), *How the West Was Won* (1963), *Dark at the Top of the Stairs* (1960)

# Vincent Price

**Born:** May 27, 1911; St. Louis, MO
**Died:** October 25, 1993; Los Angeles, CA

**Years Active in the Industry:** by decade

| 10s | 20s | 30s | 40s | 50s | 60s | 70s | 80s | 90s |
|-----|-----|-----|-----|-----|-----|-----|-----|-----|
|     |     |     |     |     |     |     |     |     |

Lisping, sinister-looking character and lead actor of stage, films, radio, and TV, Price is best known for his work in horror movies. Born into the upper class, he received a degree from Yale (in English and art history) and then tried unsuccessfully to make it as a

stage actor in New York; afterwards he went to England, getting a master's degree and debuting onstage in a small part in *Chicago* with John Gielgud in 1935. Later that year he won the lead role in a West End production of *Victoria Regina,* going on to star in the same play opposite Helen Hayes on Broadway. By the time he began appearing in Universal films in 1938 he was already an established stage star. He debuted onscreen in *Service de Luxe* (1938). At first playing romantic leads (often in costume dramas), Price soon fell into playing character roles, shining especially as treacherous or effete villains. He also continued to appear in plays, including *Don Juan in Hell* and *Outward Bound.* From the '50s he starred in numerous horror films including *House of Wax* (1953), *The Fly* (1958), and a series of Poe adaptations made by Roger Corman in the '60s; it was in the horror genre that he hit his stride as an actor, and it is this work with which he is most identified. He was an art collector and connoisseur, often lecturing on art; for several years he was the Sears-Roebuck company's art-buying consultant. Price was the author of a number of books, most of them concerning art or cooking. His first wife was actress Edith Barrett. His third was actress Coral Browne, to whom he was married until her death. **Selected Works:** *Edward Scissorhands* (1990), *Laura* (1944), *Once upon a Midnight Scary* (1990), *Song of Bernadette* (1943), *Ten Commandments* (1956)

# Jason Priestley

**Born:** Vancouver, BC

**Years Active in the Industry:** by decade

| 10s | 20s | 30s | 40s | 50s | 60s | 70s | 80s | 90s |
|-----|-----|-----|-----|-----|-----|-----|-----|-----|
|     |     |     |     |     |     |     |     |     |

The son of a Canadian actress, Jason Priestley began his own career as a child actor in TV commercials, then dropped out of acting in his teens to concentrate on high school sports. Back in the professional swim after graduation, Priestley began accepting one-shot roles on such Canada-based TV series as *21 Jump Street.* The young actor's first American TV assignment was the regular role of teen orphan Todd Mahaffey on the 1989 sitcom *Sister Kate.* Producer Aaron Spelling's daughter Tori spotted Priestley on *Sister Kate* and suggested that her father audition him for a role in the upcoming Fox series *Beverly Hills 90210.* Priestley was cast as Brandon Walsh, twin brother of the estimable Brenda (Shannen Doherty). Like many of his young series costars, Priestley has already begun laying the groundwork for life after *90210.* Though his first movie starring role in Penny Marshall's *Calendar Girl* (1993) came and went without fanfare, he has enjoyed some success as a *90210* director. Unlike other teen idols who rue the day when the fan mail will cease, Priestley claims he is happy that his idoldom seems to be on a downward slide: "It's like having a big cancerous *lesion* on your shoulder. "Because people are *fickle*, man." **Selected Works:** *Tombstone* (1993), *Coldblooded* (1995)

# Jurgen Prochnow

**Born:** 1941; Berlin, Germany

**Years Active in the Industry:** by decade

| 10s | 20s | 30s | 40s | 50s | 60s | 70s | 80s | 90s |
|-----|-----|-----|-----|-----|-----|-----|-----|-----|
|     |     |     |     |     |     |     |     |     |

An actor since the age of 14, Berlin-born Jurgen Prochnow was firmly established on stage and TV when he was featured in his first film, *Zoff*, in 1971. Prochnow has been able to harness his well-modulated voice, versatile facial features and athletic frame to portray both the most admirable of heroes and the most despicable of villains. In the latter category, Prochnow all but entreated hisses and tossed tomatoes with his portrayal of the sadistic South African secret police captain in 1989's *A Dry White Season*. It was in the role of a more compassionate captain that Jurgen Prochnow achieved international fame—he appeared as the stern but humanistic submarine commander in the 1981 Oscar-winning *Das Boot*. **Selected Works:** *Fourth War* (1990), *Robin Hood* (1991), *In the Mouth of Madness* (1994)

# Robert J. Prosky

**Born:** December 13, 1930; Philadelphia, PA

**Years Active in the Industry:** by decade

| 10ˢ | 20ˢ | 30ˢ | 40ˢ | 50ˢ | 60ˢ | 70ˢ | 80ˢ | 90ˢ |
|-----|-----|-----|-----|-----|-----|-----|-----|-----|
|     |     |     |     |     |     |     | ■   | ■   |

A holder of an economics degree from Philadelphia's Temple University, Philly-born actor Robert Prosky kicked off his career by winning a televised talent contest. With his sharp-edged voice and mashed-potato features, Prosky rose to prominence as a character actor, spending 23 years with Washington, D.C.'s prestigious Arena Stage. In 1983, he was cast in the original Broadway production of *Glengarry Glen Ross*, winning a Tony award for his performance; he later received excellent notices for his performance as an ageing Soviet bureaucrat in *A Walk in the Woods*. Prosky's first film role was as the backstabbing mob boss in 1981's *Thief*. Since that time, he has graced several films in a variety of roles—few more likeable than the wistful, washed-up horror show host in *Gremlins 2* (1988), and the enigmatic projectionist in *The Last Action Hero* (1993). Among Robert Prosky's many TV assignments was the regular role of Sgt. Stan Jablonski, who in 1984 took over the morning roll call from the late Sgt. Phil Esterhaus (Michael Conrad) in *Hill Street Blues*. **Selected Works:** *Broadcast News* (1987), *Far and Away* (1992), *Hoffa* (1992), *Mrs. Doubtfire* (1993)

# Jonathan Pryce

**Born:** 1947; Hollywell, North Wales

**Years Active in the Industry:** by decade

| 10ˢ | 20ˢ | 30ˢ | 40ˢ | 50ˢ | 60ˢ | 70ˢ | 80ˢ | 90ˢ |
|-----|-----|-----|-----|-----|-----|-----|-----|-----|
|     |     |     |     |     |     |     | ■   | ■   |

At first he studied art, but switched to acting after winning a scholarship to the Royal Academy of Dramatic Arts; he graduated in 1972, then joined the Liverpool Everyman Theater. Later he worked with the Royal Shakespeare Company. Pryce was very suc-cessful in the 1975 play *Comedians* in Nottingham and London; he won a Tony after the play moved to Broadway. He then debuted on-screen in 1976, but was rarely onscreen before the '80s. He went on to become a versatile and offbeat lead and supporting actor in numerous films, some made in Hollywood. He was the subject of controversy in 1990 when he was cast to repeat his role as a Eurasian pimp in the Broadway version of *Miss Saigon;* Actors Equity demanded that an Asian actor play the role, but later backed down. **Selected Works:** *Glengarry Glen Ross* (1992), *Age of Innocence* (1993)

# Richard Pryor

**Born:** December 1, 1940; Peoria, IL

**Years Active in the Industry:** by decade

| 10ˢ | 20ˢ | 30ˢ | 40ˢ | 50ˢ | 60ˢ | 70ˢ | 80ˢ | 90ˢ |
|-----|-----|-----|-----|-----|-----|-----|-----|-----|
|     |     |     |     |     | ■   | ■   | ■   | ■   |

African-American comedian Richard Pryor grew up bombarded by mixed messages. Pryor's grandmother owned a string of brothels, his mother was a prostitute, and his father was a pimp; still, they raised him to be honest, polite, and religious. Living in one of the worst slums in Peoria, Illinois, Pryor found that he could best defend himself by getting gang members to laugh at him instead of pummelling him. This led to his reputation as a disruptive class clown, though at least one understanding teacher allowed Pryor one minute per week to "cut up" so long as he behaved himself the rest of the time. At 14, he became involved in amateur dramatics at Peoria's Carver Community Center, which polished his stage presence. In 1963, Pryor headed to New York to seek work as a standup comic; after small gigs in the black nightclub circuit, he was advised to pattern himself after Bill Cosby—that is, to be what white audiences perceived as "nonthreatening." For the next five years, the young comic flourished in clubs and on TV variety shows, making his film bow in *The Busy Body* (1967). But Pryor was frustrated that his black pride and anger at the white power structure was being suppressed. One night, sometime between the years 1969 and 1971, he "lost it" while performing a gig in Las Vegas; he either walked offstage without a word or he obscenely proclaimed that he was sick of it. In the next few years, Pryor found himself banned from many nightclubs, allegedly due to offending the mob-connected powers-that-be, and lost many of his so-called "friends" who'd been sponging off him. Broke, Pryor went "underground" in Berkeley, California in the early 1970s; and when he re-emerged as a performer he was a road-company Cosby no more. His act, replete with colorful epithets, painfully accurate "character studies" of street types, and hilarious (and, to some, frightening) hostility over black-white inequities, struck just the right note with audiences of the "committed" 1970s. Record company executives, concerned that Pryor's humor would appeal only to blacks, were amazed at how well his first post-Berkeley album, *The Nigger's Crazy!*, sold with young white consumers. But Hollywood wasn't quite attuned to Pryor. He was supposed to write and star in a Mel

Brooks-directed western comedy about a black sheriff, but when *Blazing Saddles* was finally filmed in 1974, Pryor was listed as one of five writers, and the star was the less controversial Cleavon Little. When Pryor did appear on-screen in *The Bingo Long Travelling All-Stars and Motor Kings* (1976) and *Silver Streak* (1977), it was as a supporting actor. But Pryor's popularity built momentum, and by the end of the 1970s he was the highest-paid starring comedian in films, with long-range contracts ensuring him work well into the next decade. His comedy albums—and later, comedy videocassettes—sold out as quickly as they were recorded. The only entertainment arena still too timid for Pryor was network television—his 1977 NBC variety series has become legendary for the staggering amount of network interference and censorship imposed upon it (It wasn't just symbolic that the opening gag on the series was supposed to suggest that Pryor had been castrated.) In the early 1980s, Richard Pryor was on top of the entertainment world. Then came a near-fatal catastrophe when Pryor, while freebasing cocaine, set himself afire. Upon recovery, he was able to joke about his brush with death, but otherwise he seemed to change; his comedy became more introspective, more rambling, more tiresome. The deterioration began with a thinly-disguised film autobiography, *Jo Jo Dancer, Your Life is Calling* (1986), which Pryor directed as well as starred in. The films declined in popularity, the audiences grew more hostile at the concerts, and Pryor himself seemed to be physically deteriorating. By 1990 it was painfully obvious that Richard Pryor was a very sick man, though every effort was made by his industry friends and supporters to celebrate his past accomplishments and buoy his spirits. Whatever Richard Pryor's future holds, one thing is undeniable: without Pryor's trailblazing efforts, the in-your-face humor of such African-American comedians as Eddie Murphy and Martin Lawrence would probably not have enjoyed so wide and ethnically varied an audience. **Selected Works:** *California Suite* (1978)

# Bill Pullman

**Born:** 1954; Delphi, NY

**Years Active in the Industry:** by decade

| 10ˢ | 20ˢ | 30ˢ | 40ˢ | 50ˢ | 60ˢ | 70ˢ | 80ˢ | 90ˢ |
|-----|-----|-----|-----|-----|-----|-----|-----|-----|
|     |     |     |     |     |     |     |  ■  |     |

An alumnus of State University of New York and the University of Massachussetts, American actor Bill Pullman excelled in both wacky comedy and intense drama during his stage years, working with such repertory companies as the Folger Theatre Groupe and the Los Angeles Theatre Center. In films, Pullman could be relied upon to almost invariably lose the girl, as witness his brace of 1993 films, *Sleepless in Seattle* and *Sommersby*. He almost lost his screen wife Geena Davis to Tom Hanks in *A League of Their Own* (1992), but this gratuitous plot point was eliminated from the script. Only since 1994 has Pullman won the heroine's

hand with any regularity. The summer of 1995 found Bill Pullman with back-to-back leading roles in two of the season's biggest box-office successes: *While You Were Sleeping* and *Casper: The Movie.* **Selected Works:** *Accidental Tourist* (1988), *Singles* (1992), *Last Seduction* (1994)

# David Puttnam

**Born:** 1941; London, England

**Years Active in the Industry:** by decade

| 10ˢ | 20ˢ | 30ˢ | 40ˢ | 50ˢ | 60ˢ | 70ˢ | 80ˢ | 90ˢ |
|-----|-----|-----|-----|-----|-----|-----|-----|-----|
|     |     |     |     |     |     |  ■  |     |     |

Producer David Puttnam valued artistry and the moral accountability of film characters over box-office returns. Born of a working-class family in England, he got his start as an advertising photographer in London during the 1960s. He then moved to movie production and made a few little-known films before he and director Alan Parker scored big with *Bugsy Malone* (1976). He and Parker then went on to make the Academy Award winning *Midnight Express* (1978). Amidst all the acclaim for that gripping true story of an American placed in a Turkish prison after drugs are found on him in customs, Puttnam publicly apologized for any exploitative affects the film had on audiences, thus earning him the reputation as a "responsible renegade." During his career, he had an eye for talented new directors and facilitated the debuts or breakthroughs of filmmakers such as Ridley Scott, Roland Joffe, and Bill Forsyth. He became chief of production for Columbia Pictures in 1986. There he promised to focus on cost-effective productions with an emphasis on artistry and also promised to bring in international filmmakers to diversify the type of films Columbia put out. Many of the films he produced there dealt with sensitive areas of society and politics. Puttnam avoided exploitation films and became aggressively dogmatic in his criticism of films such as *Rambo* because he felt the film's message morally irresponsible. He also showed little respect for the intelligence and moral fortitude of his audiences; eventually his ethical arrogance began to grate on those he worked with, and Puttnam was persuaded to leave Columbia—with a $3 million golden parachute to soften the blow. His productions there were never released. Finally Puttnam went back to England where he continued to make films. **Selected Works:** *Chariots of Fire* (1981), *Killing Fields* (1984), *Memphis Belle* (1990)

# Dennis Quaid

**Born:** April 9, 1954; Houston, TX

**Years Active in the Industry:** by decade

| 10ˢ | 20ˢ | 30ˢ | 40ˢ | 50ˢ | 60ˢ | 70ˢ | 80ˢ | 90ˢ |
|---|---|---|---|---|---|---|---|---|
|  |  |  |  |  |  | ■ | ■ | ■ |

The brother of actor Randy Quaid (who began making films when Dennis was in his late teens), Dennis took up drama in high school. At age 20 he dropped out of college and moved to Los Angeles in search of an acting career. For a year he was unable to get an agent, but by lobbying producers he landed a role as a small-town youth in *September 30, 1975* (1977). For the next six years he appeared in youth-oriented films, making an impression in *Breaking Away* (1979) but otherwise remaining unknown. His break came when he was cast as real-life astronaut Gordo Cooper in *The Right Stuff* (1983), after which he was in demand for substantial Hollywood productions; his work in *The Big Easy* (1987) established him as a sexy romantic lead. He appeared with his brother Randy in *The Long Riders* (1980). He married and divorced actress P.J. Soles, and is married to actress Meg Ryan, with whom he has appeared in three films. **Selected Works:** *Come See the Paradise* (1990), *Postcards from the Edge* (1990), *Undercover Blues* (1993), *Wyatt Earp* (1994)

# Randy Quaid

**Born:** October 1, 1950; Houston, TX

**Years Active in the Industry:** by decade

| 10ˢ | 20ˢ | 30ˢ | 40ˢ | 50ˢ | 60ˢ | 70ˢ | 80ˢ | 90ˢ |
|---|---|---|---|---|---|---|---|---|
|  |  |  |  |  |  | ■ | ■ | ■ |

Six-foot four-inch, beefy character actor with rubbery, homely face, Quaid's first professional show-business work was as the "straight man" half of a comedy duo with actor Trey Wilson in Houston. While a third-year college drama student he was cast by Peter Bogdanovich in a supporting role in *The Last Picture Show* (1971), then went on to have small roles in Bogdanovich's next two movies. He made a big impression as a naive sailor alongside Jack Nicholson in *The Last Detail* (1973), for which he received a Best Supporting Actor Oscar nomination. By the mid '70s, he worked in films frequently, usually typecast as a dim-witted fool or redneck. In the mid '80s he was (for one season) in the regular cast of the weekly sketch-comedy series "Saturday Night Live," on which he demonstrated his considerable comedic talent and often impersonated President Ronald Reagan. More recently he has gotten straight dramatic roles, a transition marked by his off-Broadway stage debut in *True West* in 1983. He has also worked frequently in TV movies, portraying Lenny in *Of Mice and Men* (1981) and Lyndon Johnson in *LBJ: The Early Days* (1987); for his portrayal of Mitch in the TV version of *A Streetcar Named Desire* (1984) he won an Emmy. He is the brother of actor Dennis Quaid, with whom he appeared in *The Long Riders* (1980). **Selected Works:** *Bound for Glory* (1976), *Days of Thunder* (1990), *Midnight Express* (1978), *Paper Moon* (1973), *Paper* (1994)

# Sir Anthony Quayle (John Anthony Quayle)

**Born:** September 7, 1913; Ainsdale, England
**Died:** October 20, 1989; London, England

**Years Active in the Industry:** by decade

| 10s | 20s | 30s | 40s | 50s | 60s | 70s | 80s | 90s |
|-----|-----|-----|-----|-----|-----|-----|-----|-----|
|     |     |     |     |     |     |     |     |     |

Quayle trained for the theater at the Royal Academy of Dramatic Art, meanwhile debuting onstage at age 18. In 1932 he joined the Old Vic company, and four years later he debuted on Broadway. After World War II service with the Royal Artillery he frequently directed plays, and from 1948-56 he managed the Shakespeare Memorial Theater Company of Stratford-on-Avon. On the basis of a few small screen roles, his film career took off in the mid '50s; he generally appeared in supporting roles but also had a few leads. For his portrayal of Cardinal Wolsey in *Anne of the Thousand Days* (1969) Quayle received a Best Supporting Actor Oscar nomination. He also did much work on TV. He was the author of two novels, *Eight Hours from England* and *On Such a Night*. In 1985 he was knighted. He was married to actress Dorothy Hyson. **Selected Works:** *Guns of Navarone* (1961), *Lawrence of Arabia* (1962), *Wrong Man* (1956)

# Aidan Quinn

**Born:** March 8, 1959; Chicago, IL

**Years Active in the Industry:** by decade

| 10s | 20s | 30s | 40s | 50s | 60s | 70s | 80s | 90s |
|-----|-----|-----|-----|-----|-----|-----|-----|-----|
|     |     |     |     |     |     |     |     |     |

Born in Chicago to Irish parents, Quinn spent much of his youth in Ireland, where he first became interested in acting. At age 19 he returned to Chicago and became involved in several local the-

ater groups. His onstage debut came in a production of *The Man in 60,* after which he appeared in many plays, including *Hamlet* in Chicago's Wisdom Bridge Theater. Quinn then moved to New York, where he first appeared off-Broadway in Sam Shepard's *Fool For Love.* Following several other acclaimed performances, he landed his first big-screen role, as a low-class biker in *Reckless* (1984), which costarred Daryl Hannah. His second film, the highly-successful comedy *Desperately Seeking Susan* (1985), made him familiar to an international audience; he gained further exposure in the role of an AIDS victim in the TV movie *An Early Frost* (1985), for which he received an Emmy. Since then, he has appeared steadily in high-quality feature films, usually in challenging supporting roles. **Selected Works:** *Avalon* (1990), *Benny and Joon* (1993), *Handmaid's Tale* (1990), *Mary Shelley's Frankenstein* (1994), *The Stars Fell on Henrietta* (1995)

# Anthony Quinn

**Born:** April 21, 1916; Chihuahua, Mexico

**Years Active in the Industry:** by decade

| 10s | 20s | 30s | 40s | 50s | 60s | 70s | 80s | 90s |
|-----|-----|-----|-----|-----|-----|-----|-----|-----|
|     |     |     |     |     |     |     |     |     |

Irish-Mexican star who later specialized in roles as an earthy, virile, full-blooded man, Quinn was born in Mexico but raised in the U.S. He worked briefly on the stage before debuting onscreen in 1936. Through the '40s his career remained stagnant as he played mostly bit and supporting parts, usually as a foreign bad guy or a blood-thirsty Indian; his marriage to Cecil B. Demille's daughter in 1937 didn't inspire his father-in-law to help him out. Following some time acting on Broadway (where he portrayed Stanley Kowalski in *A Streetcar Named Desire*), Quinn's career picked up substantially in the '50s; he began playing leading roles which underscored his earthiness and somewhat brutish masculinity. He won Best Supporting Actor Oscars for both *Viva Zapata* (1952) and *Lust for Life* (1956), in the latter of which he portrayed French painter Paul Gauguin. He was also nominated for a Best Actor Oscar for *Wild is the Wind* (1957). Much of his work in the '50s was produced in Europe, notably Fellini's *La Strada* (1954). He directed *Buccaneer* (1958) but the film was a failure. He went from success to success, appearing in the '60s in such films as *Zorba The Greek* (1964), for which he received a Best Actor Oscar nomination. He starred in the TV series "The Man in the City" in the early '70s. He is the author of an autobiography, *The Original Sin* (1972). **Selected Works:** *Guns of Navarone* (1961), *Jungle Fever* (1991), *Lawrence of Arabia* (1962), *Ox-Bow Incident* (1943), *Viva Zapata!* (1952)

Gilda Radner

John Ritter

Tim Roth
Dame Margaret Rutherford

Winona Ryder

## Gilda Radner

**Born:** 1946; Detroit, MI
**Died:** 1989

**Years Active in the Industry:** by decade

| 10ˢ | 20ˢ | 30ˢ | 40ˢ | 50ˢ | 60ˢ | 70ˢ | 80ˢ | 90ˢ |
|-----|-----|-----|-----|-----|-----|-----|-----|-----|
|     |     |     |     |     |     | ■   | ■   |     |

Comedienne-actress Radner began her career with the Second City improvisation troupe in Toronto; her fellow members included John Belushi, with whom she starred on radio in the "National Lampoon Radio Hour" and *The National Lampoon Show.* In 1975 she was the first cast member named for the new sketch-comedy series "Saturday Night Live," thus becoming one of the original "Not Ready for Prime-Time Players;" she quickly became popular for the characters she created on the show. In 1979 she starred on Broadway in *Gilda Live,* which was filmed and theatrically released in 1980. From 1980-82 she was married to "Saturday Night Live" musician (later bandleader) G.E. Smith. In 1984 she married actor-filmmaker Gene Wilder, and costarred with him in several of his films. She died from ovarian cancer at age 42. She authored an autobiography, *It's Always Something* (1989).

## Bob Rafelson

**Born:** February 21, 1933; New York, NY

**Years Active in the Industry:** by decade

| 10ˢ | 20ˢ | 30ˢ | 40ˢ | 50ˢ | 60ˢ | 70ˢ | 80ˢ | 90ˢ |
|-----|-----|-----|-----|-----|-----|-----|-----|-----|
|     |     |     |     |     | ■   | ■   | ■   |     |

The nephew of famed playwright Samson Rafelson, American director Bob Rafelson decided to forego the expensive education planned for him and take up cross-country vagabondage instead. He worked in a rodeo at 15, became an ocean-liner deckhand two years later, and a jazz drummer a year after that. He entered but then dropped out of Dartmouth College, after which he worked as a deejay on an Armed Forces radio outlet. As a writer, Rafelson toiled in numerous New York-based TV shows, then travelled westward to try his luck in Hollywood. His breezy, patchwork writing style was perfectly suited to the Beatles-like TV sitcom *The Monkees* (1966-67), wherein Rafelson worked as writer, director, and coproducer (with Bert Schneider). In concert with then-partner Jack Nicholson, Rafelson penned the script for the surrealistic Monkees feature film *Head* (1968), which he also directed. The film was suitable impetus to the Columbia Pictures higher ups to bankroll another Rafelson-Nicholson collaboration. *Five Easy Pieces* (1971), was an intensely personal and somewhat autobiographical study of a young man (Nicholson) whose alienation with the status quo causes him to chuck the security of his musical career and his wealthy family for a life of drifting. The critics loved *Five Easy Pieces,* but were less enthusiastic about the 1972 Rafelson/Nicholson concoction, *King of Marvin Gardens*, in which Nicholson played the establishment figure, while fellow 1970s icon Bruce Dern played the dreamer. *Stay Hungry* (1976) was a story of bodybuilding juxtaposed with the changes in the New South, boasting an early leading role for Arnold Schwarzenegger—and the first-ever nude scene for costar Sally Field. Critics of *Stay Hungry* called Rafelson on the carpet for his credit-grabbing attempts to become an "auteur" director, even though these same critics had applauded Rafelson's auterism in his earlier productions. With *The Postman Always Rings Twice* (1981)—again with Nicholson as star—Rafelson lost much of his critical support for having the audacity to turn out a purely commercial product. Actually, Rafelson was hardly the "conformist" he seemed to be, and had lost as many projects as he'd directed due to his violent temper. It's simply that his improvisational style had gotten slicker as he gained more experience. Bob Rafelson's most recent film was *Mountains of the Moon* (1990) a lavish but still distinctly Rafelsonesque period piece about a 19th century "anti-establishment" rugged individualist, explorer Sir Richard Burton. **Selected Works:** *Erotic Tales* (1994)

# George Raft

**Born:** September 26, 1895; New York, NY
**Died:** 1980

**Years Active in the Industry:** by decade

| 10s | 20s | 30s | 40s | 50s | 60s | 70s | 80s | 90s |
|-----|-----|-----|-----|-----|-----|-----|-----|-----|
|     |     |     |     |     |     |     |     |     |

Raft spent his childhood in the tough Hell's Kitchen area of New York, then left home at 13. He went on to be a prizefighter, ballroom dancer, and taxi-driver, meanwhile maintaining close contacts with New York's gangster underworld. He eventually made it to Broadway, then went to Hollywood in the late '20s. At first considered a Valentino-like romantic lead, Raft soon discovered his forte in gangster roles. He was the actor most responsible for creating the '30s cinema image of gangster-as-hero, particularly after his portrayal of coin-flipping Guido Rinaldo in *Scarface* (1932). He was highly successful for almost two decades, but then bad casting diminished his popularity. By the early '50s he was acting in European films in a vain attempt to regain critical respect, but he was unsuccessful. He starred in the mid-'50s TV series "I Am the Law," a failure that seriously hurt his financial status. In 1959 a Havana casino he owned was closed by the Castro government, further damaging his revenues; meanwhile, he owed a great deal to the U.S. government in back taxes. In the mid '60s he was denied entry into England (where he managed a high-class gambling club) due to his underworld associations. Most of his film appearances after 1960 were cameos. He was portrayed by Ray Danton in the biopic *The George Raft Story* (1961). **Selected Works:** *Some Like It Hot* (1959)

# Sam Raimi

**Born:** October 23, 1959; Royal Oak, MI

**Years Active in the Industry:** by decade

| 10s | 20s | 30s | 40s | 50s | 60s | 70s | 80s | 90s |
|-----|-----|-----|-----|-----|-----|-----|-----|-----|
|     |     |     |     |     |     |     |     |     |

Like most children of the 1960s, Sam Raimi grew up acting out his fantasies with the benefit of an 8-millimeter movie camera. The film gauge grew to "35" when Raimi, with the aid of friends and relatives, raised $500,000 to film a horror feature, *The Evil Dead* (1983). Not your average sliced-up-teenager epic, *Evil Dead* was a marvelously wicked assault on the senses, belying its tiny budget with several extremely clever (if nausea-inducing) setpieces. Raimi switched to slapstick comedy with *Crimewave* (1985), a wild Detroit-based crime caper coscripted by Raimi's fellow devotees of the bizarre, Joel and Ethan Coen. *Evil Dead II* (1985) suffered from the same fate as most sequels, but Raimi was back in form with *Darkman* (1990), a comic-book inspired fantasy/adventure representing the director's biggest production budget to date. Also expensively mounted was *Army of Darkness* (1993), a time-travel swashbuckler that gave evidence of extensive post-production tinkering (notably its skimpy 80-minute run-

ning time). Though it was hard to tell, *Army* was actually a sequel to the first two *Evil Dead* flicks. Seen only as an actor in recent years (*Body Bags* [1993] and *Hudsucker Proxy* [1994]), Sam Raimi will no doubt direct again, hopefully with more stylistic consistency than he showed in *Army of Darkness*. **Selected Works:** *Hard Target* (1993), *Indian Summer* (1993), *Timecop* (1994)

# Claude Rains

**Born:** November 10, 1889; London, England
**Died:** 1967

**Years Active in the Industry:** by decade

| 10s | 20s | 30s | 40s | 50s | 60s | 70s | 80s | 90s |
|-----|-----|-----|-----|-----|-----|-----|-----|-----|
|     |     |     |     |     |     |     |     |     |

Suave, controlled, charming, character actor with a unique, quietly commanding voice and an incisive intelligence, Rains played villainous, kindly, or cynical roles with equal effectiveness. First appearing on the London stage at age 11, he toured the U.S. in 1914 and became a main performer for the Theater Guild in 1926. He finally broke into films in 1933, when he was in his mid 40s. Rains' big-screen debut was in the title role of *The Invisible Man* (1933), in which his face appeared only briefly. He went on to a long string of character roles, nominated for Oscars four times: *Mr. Smith Goes to Washington* (1939), *Casablanca* (1943), *Mr. Skeffington* (1944), and *Notorious* (1946). His first of five marriages was to actress Isabel Jeans. He was the father of actress Jessica Rains. **Selected Works:** *Adventures of Robin Hood* (1938), *Juarez* (1939), *Lawrence of Arabia* (1962), *Sea Hawk* (1940), *King's Row* (1942)

# Harold Ramis

**Born:** November 21, 1944; Chicago, IL

**Years Active in the Industry:** by decade

| 10s | 20s | 30s | 40s | 50s | 60s | 70s | 80s | 90s |
|-----|-----|-----|-----|-----|-----|-----|-----|-----|
|     |     |     |     |     |     |     |     |     |

After college Ramis spent two years as an associate editor of *Playboy*, primarily screening jokes received from readers. In 1970 he began writing for the celebrated Second City improvisational comedy troupe of Chicago, remaining there three years. He

next moved to New York, where he worked as a writer and performer for the "National Lampoon Radio Hour" and the theater revue *The National Lampoon Show.* From there he joined the cast of the TV sketch-comedy series "SCTV." He broke into movies as the co-writer of the blockbuster comedy *Animal House* (1978). Since then he has acted in, written, and/or directed numerous films, including the wildly successful *Ghostbusters* (1984). He debuted onscreen in *Stripes* (1981), which he also co-wrote. **Selected Works:** *Groundhog Day* (1993), *Rover Dangerfield* (1991), *Untamed Heart* (1993)

# Tony Randall (Leonard Rosenberg)

**Born:** February 26, 1920; Tulsa, OK

**Years Active in the Industry:** by decade

| 10ˢ | 20ˢ | 30ˢ | 40ˢ | 50ˢ | 60ˢ | 70ˢ | 80ˢ | 90ˢ |
|-----|-----|-----|-----|-----|-----|-----|-----|-----|

Randall moved to New York at age 19 and studied theater with Sanford Meisner and at the Neighborhood Playhouse. His stage debut was in *The Circle of Chalk* (1941). From 1942-46 he served with the U.S. Army, following which he acted on radio and TV. He began appearing onscreen in 1957 and was a fairly busy film actor through the mid '60s. He is best known for his work on TV, particularly for his portrayal of fastidious Felix Unger on the sitcom "The Odd Couple." He also starred or costarred in the series "One Man's Family," "Mr. Peepers," "The Tony Randall Show," and "Love, Sidney." He frequently appears on TV talk shows, where he is witty, erudite, and urbane. In 1991 he created the National Actors Theater, a repertory company; its purpose is to bring star-filled classic plays to broad-based audiences at low prices. **Selected Works:** *King of Comedy* (1982), *Lover Come Back* (1961), *Pillow Talk* (1959)

# Basil Rathbone (Philip St. John Basil Rathbone)

**Born:** June 13, 1892; Johannesburg, South Africa
**Died:** 1967

**Years Active in the Industry:** by decade

| 10ˢ | 20ˢ | 30ˢ | 40ˢ | 50ˢ | 60ˢ | 70ˢ | 80ˢ | 90ˢ |
|-----|-----|-----|-----|-----|-----|-----|-----|-----|

Rathbone was born in South Africa but educated in England, where in 1911 he debuted onstage. He went on to perform in both England and the U.S. in numerous classical roles, including much Shakespeare. He entered films in the early '20s and moved to Hollywood in 1924. At first cast often in romantic leads, in the early sound era Rathbone became the screen's finest villain, characterised by his distinguished voice, polished manner, and gaunt, saturnine, cerebral persona. In the '40s he became even more popular as cinema's most prolific portrayer of Sherlock Holmes, appearing in that guise in 14 films. Throughout his career he frequently returned to the stage, notably in the '50s drama *J.B.* For his work in *Romeo and Juliet* (1936) and *If I Were King* (1938) he received nominations for Best Supporting Actor Oscars. He was married to actress-screenwriter Ouida Bergere. **Selected Works:** *Adventures of Robin Hood* (1938), *Anna Karenina* (1935), *David Copperfield* (1935), *A Tale of Two Cities* (1935)

# Nicholas Ray (Raymond Nicholas Kienzle)

**Born:** August 7, 1911; Galesville, WI
**Died:** 1979

**Years Active in the Industry:** by decade

| 10ˢ | 20ˢ | 30ˢ | 40ˢ | 50ˢ | 60ˢ | 70ˢ | 80ˢ | 90ˢ |
|-----|-----|-----|-----|-----|-----|-----|-----|-----|

Wisconsin-born Nicholas Ray was originally an architecture student—and studied with no less a figure than Frank Lloyd Wright—before becoming interested in the stage. He originally became an actor and joined John Houseman's Phoenix Theater Company in the 1930s, and worked for Houseman during the latter's tenure as a head of programming for the Office of War Information during World War II in New York. He came to films first as an assistant to his one-time stage colleague Elia Kazan, and began directing with Houseman's blessing on the RKO production of *They Live By Night* (1948). This story of youth corrupted by the social forces around them was played with infinitely more sincerity and depth than the typical delinquency drama of the period. At the time the critics largely ignored the movie—it took several years for it to begin building a cult audience, during which time Ray also made *Knock On Any Door* (1949), an urban delinquency drama, and several successful films with Humphrey Bogart, John Wayne, and Robert Ryan, among other leading men, establishing his commercial credentials. In 1955, after doing *Johnny Guitar*—a compelling psychological western—for Republic, Ray inherited *Rebel Without A Cause,* a project that had been kicking around Warner Bros. for several years, and, with the fortuitous casting of James Dean in the lead role, created one of the most popular and enduring movies of the 1950s. In the process, Ray also achieved special popularity, not only among the more film conscious youth of the 1960s, who embraced the movie as a foretelling of their own stories to one degree or another, but also among film students of that period, for whom Ray became a role model and de facto mentor. Ironically, Ray's own career began sliding downhill with the end of the 1950s, as Hollywood cut back its production schedule, and an unfortunate detour by this most intimate and dramatic of directors into the field of blockbuster spectacle—*King of Kings* (which works reasonably well scene-for-scene) and *55 Days at Peking*—marked the end of Ray's commercial film career. Health problems took their toll in the later years, although in his final years, Ray found himself the object of reverence by an entire generation of film students and filmmakers, including Wim Wenders.

## Satyajit Ray

**Born:** May 2, 1921; Calcutta, India
**Died:** April 23, 1992; Calcutta, India

**Years Active in the Industry:** by decade

| 10s | 20s | 30s | 40s | 50s | 60s | 70s | 80s | 90s |
|-----|-----|-----|-----|-----|-----|-----|-----|-----|
|     |     |     |     | ■   | ■   | ■   |     |     |

An Indian director who was, for many years, India's premier filmmaker, Ray was at times referred to as the "Indian Ingmar Bergman," due to the fact that his films focused on relationships and the beauty to be found in the lives of ordinary men and women. Ray is best-known for his first three films, referred to as the "Apu" trilogy: *Pather Panchali* (1955), *Aparajito* (1956), and *The World of Apu* (1959), focusing on life in a Bengali village. All of Ray's films were in the Bengali language until *Satranj ke Kilhari (The Chess Players)* (1977), which was produced in both Hindi and English versions. While Ray's leisurely-paced films are often reminiscent of British cinema, they have been heralded for their simplicity, beauty, and authenticity. **Selected Works:** *Distant Thunder* (1973), *Stranger* (1992), *Broken Journey* (1994)

## Martha Raye (Margaret Teresa Yvonne O'Reed)

**Born:** August 27, 1914; Butte, MT
**Died:** October 19, 1994

**Years Active in the Industry:** by decade

| 10s | 20s | 30s | 40s | 50s | 60s | 70s | 80s | 90s |
|-----|-----|-----|-----|-----|-----|-----|-----|-----|
|     | ■   | ■   | ■   | ■   | ■   | ■   |     |     |

A comedic actress with a notably wide, elastic mouth, Raye first appeared in her parents' vaudeville act at age three. At 13 she was a speciality singer with a band, and she gained much experience onstage and in nightclubs during her teens. She broke into films in 1934, at first appearing in short subjects. She went on to play zany comedic roles in many films, mostly minor productions. She took several years off from the screen in the early '40s to entertain troops in World War II; later in her life she did the same during the Korean War and the Vietnam War. After a prominent role in Chaplin's *Monsieur Verdoux* (1947), her screen work became infrequent. She continued performing in nightclubs and burlesque shows, and in the mid '50s she hosted "The Martha Raye Show" on TV. Her later work on Broadway included major roles in *Hello Dolly* and *No No Nanette*. In 1969 she received a special Academy Award

for her work as an entertainer of Vietnam War troops. In the '70s she costarred on the TV series *McMillan and Wife*. In the '80s, she had a supporting role on the series "Alice." For many years she was featured in commercials for a denture toothpaste, and most of her considerable wealth derived from that source. Confined to a wheelchair, she was the subject of some controversy over the intentions of a young fan who married her and took care of her. In 1991 she sued the producers of the film *For the Boys,* claiming that it was based on her own life; she lost the suit. She was married six times. **Selected Works:** *Hellzapoppin'* (1941)

## Stephen Rea

**Born:** 1946; Belfast, Northern Ireland

**Years Active in the Industry:** by decade

| 10s | 20s | 30s | 40s | 50s | 60s | 70s | 80s | 90s |
|-----|-----|-----|-----|-----|-----|-----|-----|-----|
|     |     |     |     |     |     | ■   | ■   | ■   |

Actor Stephen Rea was brought up in a blue-collar, Protestant family in Northern Ireland and attended the Abbey Theatre School. He went on to co-create the Field Day Theatre with playwright Brian (*Philadelphia Here I Come*) Friel. In 1982, Rea and director Neil Jordan made their joint film debut with *Danny Boy* (aka *Angel*). Rea has remained closely associated with Jordan ever since, with choice roles in the director's *The Company of Wolves* (1984), *Interview with a Vampire* (1994), and, most famously, *The Crying Game* (1993), which earned Rea an Oscar nomination for his portrayal of a reluctant IRA gunman. **Selected Works:** *Life Is Sweet* (1991), *Angie* (1994), *Princess Caraboo* (1994)

## Ronald Reagan

**Born:** February 6, 1911; Tampico, IL

**Years Active in the Industry:** by decade

| 10s | 20s | 30s | 40s | 50s | 60s | 70s | 80s | 90s |
|-----|-----|-----|-----|-----|-----|-----|-----|-----|
|     |     | ■   | ■   | ■   | ■   |     |     |     |

Reagan's first show-biz job was as a sportscaster for a Des Moines, Iowa, radio station, from which he went on to be the Chicago Cubs' play-by-play announcer. In the mid '30s he went to Hollywood, signing with Warner Brothers in 1937. He debuted onscreen in *Love is On the Air* (1937). He went on to play straightforward, somewhat unexciting romantic leads and second leads in 50 films, most of which were B movies. His most memorable films were *King's Row* (1941), *Knute Rockne—All-American* (1940), and *The Hasty Heart* (1950). In World War II, Reagan served as a non-combative captain with the Army Air Corps, mainly producing training films. From 1947-52 he was president of the Screen Actors Guild, serving again in 1959. He freelanced among studios in the '50s, but his screen work was drying up. His career was revived by TV; he hosted the "Death Valley Days" Western anthology series for three years, then hosted "General Electric Theater" for eight years, often appearing in the program's dramas. Meanwhile, he was being drawn into political activity; having been known as a liberal for much of his adult life, he emerged in 1962 as a champion of conservatism. After campaigning for Republican presidential candidate Barry Goldwater in 1964 he launched his own political career, and in 1966 was elected Governor of California; during his eight years in that office he became increasingly influential in the Republican party. In 1976 he ran against President Gerald Ford in the Republican presidential primary but lost. He won that primary in 1980 and was elected president of the United States in 1980, winning re-election in 1984. His two marriages were to actresses Jane Wyman and Nancy Davis. **Selected Works:** *Dark Victory* (1939), *Louisa* (1950)

# Robert Redford (Charles Robert Redford, Jr.)

**Born:** August 18, 1937; Santa Monica, CA

**Years Active in the Industry:** by decade

| 10ˢ | 20ˢ | 30ˢ | 40ˢ | 50ˢ | 60ˢ | 70ˢ | 80ˢ | 90ˢ |
|-----|-----|-----|-----|-----|-----|-----|-----|-----|
|     |     |     |     |     |     |     |     |     |

Extraordinarily handsome star of American films with a dazzling smile and gorgeous features, Redford was the "golden boy" of American films in the early '70s. He attended college on a baseball scholarship, but soon dropped out and went to Europe, where he pursued his desire to be a painter. After returning to the U.S., he enrolled in an art college and at the same time trained for the stage at the American Academy of Dramatic Arts. In 1959, Redford debuted on Broadway in a minor role in *Tall Story*, then gradually landed bigger parts; by 1963 he was starring in the hit *Barefoot in the Park*. Meanwhile, he appeared on a number of TV shows and had an isolated film appearance in 1962. He began his screen career in earnest in 1965, playing standard

leads in routine films. He became a full-fledged superstar after costarring in the hit *Butch Cassidy and the Sundance Kid* (1969) with long-established star Paul Newman. By 1974 he was the top screen actor in America, and soon founded his own production company. His directorial debut came with *Ordinary People* (1980), for which he won the Best Director Oscar. In the '80s he was more selective in his choice of screen roles, and his appearances became more intermittent; meanwhile, he worked behind the camera in an increasing number of films. Known for his support for liberal and environmental causes, in 1980 he established the Sundance Institute in Utah, which provides practical workshops, development resources, and support to promising independent filmmakers. He co-founded Resource Management, a forum whose aim is to persuade land developers and environmentalists to cooperate. **Selected Works:** *All the President's Men* (1976), *Out of Africa* (1985), *A River Runs Through It* (1992), *Sting* (1973), *Quiz Show* (1994)

# Lynn Redgrave

**Born:** March 8, 1943; London, England

**Years Active in the Industry:** by decade

| 10ˢ | 20ˢ | 30ˢ | 40ˢ | 50ˢ | 60ˢ | 70ˢ | 80ˢ | 90ˢ |
|-----|-----|-----|-----|-----|-----|-----|-----|-----|
|     |     |     |     |     |     |     |     |     |

The daughter of actor Sir Michael Redgrave and actress Rachel Kempson, and sister of actresses Corin and Vanessa Redgrave, she attended the Central School of Music and Drama in London. In 1962, Redgrave made her professional stage debut, then debuted onscreen the next year in *Tom Jones*. Her third film, *Georgy Girl* (1966), made her a star; she won the New York Film Critics Best Actress Award (in a tie) and was nominated for a Best Actress Oscar. She went on to play numerous leads on stage and screen in both Britain and America. She moved to the U.S. in 1974, appearing often on TV talk shows and game shows and hosting the sydicated talk show "Not For Women Only." She went on to star in three short-lived TV series, "House Calls," "Teachers Only," and "Chicken Soup," and also became a TV-ad spokeswoman for a diet program. In 1990 she and her sister Vanessa costarred in a London production of Chekov's *Three Sisters,* then in 1991 they appeared together in a TV remake of the film *Whatever Happened to Baby Jane?* She starred on Broadway in the one-woman show *Shakespeare for My Father.* She is married to John Clark, an actor, producer, and director. She has written one book, *This is Living: An Inspirational Guide to Freedom* (1988).

# Sir Michael Redgrave

**Born:** March 20, 1908; Bristol, England
**Died:** March 21, 1985; Denham, England

**Years Active in the Industry:** by decade

| 10ˢ | 20ˢ | 30ˢ | 40ˢ | 50ˢ | 60ˢ | 70ˢ | 80ˢ | 90ˢ |
|-----|-----|-----|-----|-----|-----|-----|-----|-----|
|     |     |     |     |     |     |     |     |     |

The son of British actor Roy Redgrave, Michael Redgrave attended Clifton College and Cambridge University. While teaching high school, Redgrave became involved with amateur theatricals. A professional by 1934, Redgrave made his London debut in *Love's Labours Lost* in 1936, and that same year appeared in his first film, Hitchcock's *The Secret Agent* (1936). It was thanks to his leading role in another Hitchcock effort, *The Lady Vanishes* (1938), that Redgrave achieved stardom. He was excellent in several starring vehicles of the 1940s, and at his very best in his 20-minute turn as a paranoid ventriloquist in *Dead of Night* (1946). An attempt to become a Hollywood star via *Mourning Becomes Electra* (1947) was scuttled due to the film's poor box office take, though Redgrave did earn an Oscar nomination for his performance. After starring in *The Dam Busters*, Britain's most popular 1955 movie release, Redgrave settled into film character roles, continuing all the while to headline on stage. He also wrote and directed several theatrical productions throughout his career, and was the author of four books: the instructional *The Actor's Ways and Means*, the novel *The Mountebank's Tale*, and two autobiographies. In 1959, Redgrave was knighted for his achievements in his chosen field. Long married to actress Rachel Kempson, Michael Redgrave was the father of actors Vanessa, Corin and Lynn Redgrave, and the grandfather of actresses Jemma Redgrave and Natasha and Joely Richardson. **Selected Works:** *The Browning Version* (1951), *The Captive Heart* (1947), *The Importance of Being Earnest* (1952), *The Stars Look Down* (1939), *Oh! What a Lovely War* (1969)

# Vanessa Redgrave

**Born:** January 30, 1937; London, England

**Years Active in the Industry:** by decade

| 10s | 20s | 30s | 40s | 50s | 60s | 70s | 80s | 90s |
|-----|-----|-----|-----|-----|-----|-----|-----|-----|

Star of the British stage and international films, this daughter of actors Sir Michael Redgrave and Rachel Kempson, and sister of actors Corin and Lynn Redgrave, studied acting at the Central School of Music and Dance in London. In 1957 she debuted onstage, then made her screen debut in *Behind the Mask* (1958), which starred her father (whose character's daughter she portrayed). In the early '60s she worked onstage with the Royal Shakespeare Company, steadily building her reputation. She didn't

return to the screen until 1966, after which she became one of the more popular British actresses of the late '60s and early '70s. Redgrave also became a controversial public figure, supporting left-wing causes and, several times, unsuccessfully running for a seat in Parliament as a candidate of the Workers' Revolutionary Party. In 1978 she caused much controversy at the Academy Awards ceremony, where (in front of the cameras, playing to a vast world-wide audience) she stressed her support for Palestinians; previously she had produced a documentary titled *The Palestinian* (1977). In 1967 she divorced director Tony Richardson on the grounds of adultery and in 1969 she gave birth to a son by actor Franco Nero, with whom she had appeared in *Camelot* (1967). She has received four Best Actress Oscar nominations; for her work in *Julia* (1977) she won the Best Supporting Actress Oscar. She is the mother of actresses Joely and Natasha Richardson. **Selected Works:** *Howard's End* (1992), *A Man for All Seasons* (1966), *Morgan* (1966), *Blow-Up* (1966), *Mary, Queen of Scots* (1971)

# Sir Carol Reed

**Born:** December 30, 1906; London, England
**Died:** April 25, 1976

**Years Active in the Industry:** by decade

| 10s | 20s | 30s | 40s | 50s | 60s | 70s | 80s | 90s |
|-----|-----|-----|-----|-----|-----|-----|-----|-----|

Carol Reed was, according to his family's plans, supposed to have become a farmer upon graduation from school. However, he was more interested in theater and made a career as an actor from the mid 1920s, and later as a stage manager and assistant to author Edgar Wallace. He moved into film as a dialogue director to filmmaker Basil Dean, and became a director himself in 1935, specializing in modestly budgeted dramas. He joined the British Army's documentary film unit during World War II, making training films, and in 1944 directed the feature *The Way Ahead,* one of the most popular and enduring military dramas of the war. However, it was with the end of hostilities that Reed came into his own as a director with the dark psychological drama *Odd Man Out* (1946), about the last hours of a dying IRA gunman. *The Fallen Idol* (1947), a story of a boy desperately trying to hide the guilt of his friend, a butler suspected of killing his wife, followed soon after. *The Third Man* (1949) made Reed's career internationally, its tale of corruption and decay in postwar Vienna sparked by the superb performances of Orson Welles, Joseph Cotten, Alida Valli, and Trevor Howard. Unfortunately, the retrenchment of the British film industry that began at the outset of the 1950s seemed to cost Reed several opportunities, and his next widely-seen works were such high-profile, large-scale films as *Trapeze* (1956) and the disastrous blockbuster *Mutiny On the Bounty* (1962). He made a commercial recovery with the musical *Oliver!* (1968), but suitable projects were hard to find, and Reed's later films lack any of the tautness, style, and care of his 1940s work. **Selected Works:** *The Stars Look Down* (1939)

# Donna Reed (Donna Belle Mullenger)

**Born:** January 27, 1921; Denison, IA
**Died:** January 1986

**Years Active in the Industry:** by decade

| 10s | 20s | 30s | 40s | 50s | 60s | 70s | 80s | 90s |
|-----|-----|-----|-----|-----|-----|-----|-----|-----|
|     |     |     | ■   | ■   | ■   |     |     |     |

Reed was elected beauty queen of her high school and Campus Queen of her college. The latter honor resulted in her photo making the L.A. papers, and as a result she was invited to take a screen test with MGM, which signed her in 1941. She played supporting roles in a number of minor films (at first being billed as "Donna Adams"), then in the mid '40s she began getting leads; with rare exceptions, she portrayed sincere, wholesome types and loving wives and girlfriends. She went against type playing a prostitute in *From Here to Eternity* (1953), for which she won a Best Supporting Actress Oscar. Rarely getting rewarding roles, she retired from the screen in 1958 to star in the TV series "The Donna Reed Show," which was a great success and remained on the air through 1966. After 1960 she appeared in only one more film. In the mid '80s she emerged from retirement to star in "Dallas;" Bel Geddes returned to the show in 1985, and Reed won a $1 million settlement for a breach of contract suit against the show's producers. She died of cancer several months later. **Selected Works:** *Human Comedy* (1943), *It's a Wonderful Life* (1946), *They Were Expendable* (1945)

# Oliver Reed

**Born:** February 13, 1938; Wimbledon, England

**Years Active in the Industry:** by decade

| 10s | 20s | 30s | 40s | 50s | 60s | 70s | 80s | 90s |
|-----|-----|-----|-----|-----|-----|-----|-----|-----|
|     |     |     |     |     | ■   | ■   | ■   | ■   |

At age 17 Reed dropped out of school and ran away from home, going on to support himself in a variety of odd jobs. He served in the military with the Medical Corps, then began getting extra and bit parts in British films. His first lead came in the cheap horror film *The Curse of the Werewolf* (1961), produced by Hammer Studios. He went on to specialize in ill-tempered, sometimes cruel roles, but gradually developed into a versatile leading man in sympathetic roles. Although he remained very busy as a screen ac-

tor, he was plagued by alcoholism and a weight problem, and by the 1980s he was appearing in low-quality films and was no longer taken seriously as a major actor. He married and divorced actress Kate Byrne. **Selected Works:** *Oliver!* (1968), *Three Musketeers* (1974), *Ghost in Monte Carlo* (1990)

# Pamela Reed

**Born:** April 2, 1949; Tacoma, WA

**Years Active in the Industry:** by decade

| 10s | 20s | 30s | 40s | 50s | 60s | 70s | 80s | 90s |
|-----|-----|-----|-----|-----|-----|-----|-----|-----|
|     |     |     |     |     |     | ■   | ■   | ■   |

Actress Pamela Reed was born in Washington and raised in Maryland; she returned to the Northwest to work on the Trans-Alaska Pipeline—and, incidentally, to earn her drama degree from the University of Washington. A relatively late bloomer, Reed was pushing 30 when she began making the casting rounds in New York and LA. She has held down regular roles on three weekly TV series: *The Andros Targets* (1977), *Tanner 88* (1988), and *Grand* (1990). Reed made her movie bow in the role of Belle Starr in the 1980 revisionist Western *The Long Riders*. Her most famous film role was as LAPD officer Arnold Schwarzenegger's partner in *Kindergarten Cop* (1990); for the purposes of the plot, her character was a former schoolteacher. **Selected Works:** *Kindergarten Cop* (1990), *Melvin and Howard* (1980), *The Right Stuff* (1983)

# Christopher Reeve

**Born:** September 25, 1952; New York, NY

**Years Active in the Industry:** by decade

| 10s | 20s | 30s | 40s | 50s | 60s | 70s | 80s | 90s |
|-----|-----|-----|-----|-----|-----|-----|-----|-----|
|     |     |     |     |     |     | ■   | ■   | ■   |

Reeve began performing as a child, studying piano and voice, singing with a madrigal group, working as an assistant conductor of an orchestra, and debuting onstage at age nine with a

small Princeton theater company. After college he studied drama at Juilliard and with John Houseman; as part of his master's degree course he performed at London's Old Vic and the Comedie Francaise. After returning to New York, he landed a role in the TV soap opera "Love of Life," which led to his Broadway debut in 1976 in *A Matter of Gravity*, which ran for seven months and starred Katherine Hepburn. He debuted onscreen in an unmemorable role in *Gray Lady Down* (1978). After several top names turned down the title role for the proposed film *Superman* (1978), he got the part, which he played with charm, humor, and irony after participating in a fitness program to beef up his physique; the film made him famous and led to three sequels. Refusing to be typecast, he made an effort to find diverse roles in films, and appeared on Broadway as a gay amputee in Lanford Wilson's *Fifth of July* in 1980, then was on Broadway again in *The Marriage of Figaro* in 1985; on the London stage he appeared with Vanessa Redgrave in *The Aspern Papers*. Other than the four Superman films, his screen work has been only occasional. Reeves suffered a paralyzing injury in 1995 while competing in an equestrian event. **Selected Works:** *Mortal Sins* (1992), *Remains of the Day* (1993), *Speechless* (1994)

# Keanu Reeves

**Born:** 1965; Beirut, Lebanon

**Years Active in the Industry:** by decade

| 10ˢ | 20ˢ | 30ˢ | 40ˢ | 50ˢ | 60ˢ | 70ˢ | 80ˢ | 90ˢ |
|-----|-----|-----|-----|-----|-----|-----|-----|-----|
|     |     |     |     |     |     |     |     |     |

Good-looking, half-Hawaiian leading man with somewhat Asian features, Reeves is one of the busiest young actors of his generation. While growing up, he lived in Lebanon, Australia, New York, and Toronto, where he settled. He studied acting at Toronto's High School for the Performing Arts, later participating in the Second City Workshop. At 16 he made a TV commercial for Coca-Cola and won a role in a Toronto TV show, "Hanging In." He went on to appear on the Toronto stage and spent a season in summer stock in Pennsylvania. He debuted onscreen in the Canadian feature *Flying* (1986), but first came to prominence in the American market in *River's Edge* (1987). He went on to make 11 films in the next four years, and he has worked with directors such as Lawrence Kasdan and Francis Ford Coppola. **Selected Works:** *Dangerous Liaisons* (1988), *Much Ado About Nothing* (1993), *My Own Private Idaho* (1991), *Little Buddha* (1994), *Speed* (1994) *A Walk in the Clouds* (1995), *Bill & Ted's Excellent Adventure* (1989), *Bill & Ted's Bogus Journey* (1991)

# Carl Reiner

**Born:** March 20, 1922; Bronx, NY

**Years Active in the Industry:** by decade

| 10ˢ | 20ˢ | 30ˢ | 40ˢ | 50ˢ | 60ˢ | 70ˢ | 80ˢ | 90ˢ |
|-----|-----|-----|-----|-----|-----|-----|-----|-----|
|     |     |     |     |     |     |     |     |     |

Carl Reiner joined the WPA Dramatic Workshop while in his late teens. Later, Reiner worked with actor Maurice Evans's GI troupe in the South Pacific during World War II. At war's end he worked onstage with several road companies and performed on Broadway. In the '50s he costarred with Sid Caesar in the TV

sketch-comedy series "Your Show of Shows." Out of work in the early '60s, he tried to design a TV series for himself but his pilot was rejected; he redesigned the show and it became the successful sitcom "The Dick Van Dyke Show." Between 1956-67 he won eleven Emmy Awards as a performer, producer, and writer. In 1958 he published the semi-autobiographical novel *Enter Laughing,* later adapting it to the stage (1963) and the screen (1967). He also had a great deal of success as a recording comedian, teaming up with Mel Brooks on a series of records spotlighting Brooks' character, "the 2,000-year-old man." He began appearing in films as an actor in the late 1950s, then in the late '60s he began directing for the big screen. He became very successful in the late '70s and '80s as a director of comedies, particularly in collaboration with Steve Martin. He is the father of actor-filmmaker Rob Reiner. **Selected Works:** *Sibling Rivalry* (1990)

# Rob Reiner

**Born:** March 6, 1945; New York, NY

**Years Active in the Industry:** by decade

| 10ˢ | 20ˢ | 30ˢ | 40ˢ | 50ˢ | 60ˢ | 70ˢ | 80ˢ | 90ˢ |
|-----|-----|-----|-----|-----|-----|-----|-----|-----|
|     |     |     |     |     |     |     |     |     |

The son of the multi-talented Carl Reiner, Reiner spent his teenage summers working on his father's sets and in local theater. He studied drama in college, then began working in improvisational comedy. He broke into TV through writing scripts for such shows as "The Smothers Brothers' Comedy Hour" and making occasional guest appearances; he also appeared in his father's first two movies. His big break came when he was cast to play Michael "Meathead" Stivic in the sitcom "All in the Family," which became a long-running hit and made him nationally known; for his work in that show, he received two Emmys. He continued working as a writer, notably for the TV movie *More Than Friends,* in which he co-starred with his wife (later divorced), actress-director Penny Marshall. In the mid '80s he began directing movies, beginning with the pseudo-documentary *This Is Spinal Tap* (1984) about a second-rate heavy metal rock band; that film became a cult hit, and its modest success helped him get the backing for his second feature, the romantic comedy *The Sure Thing* (1985). From there he went on to direct a string of successful films, while also occasionally acting in films. His other credits as a director include *Stand By Me, The Princess Bride, When Harry Met Sally, Misery,* and *A Few Good Men.* **Selected Works:** *Postcards from the Edge* (1990),

*Sleepless in Seattle* (1993), *Bullets over Broadway* (1994), *The American President* (1995)

# Judge Reinhold

**Born:** 1956; Wilmington, DE

**Years Active in the Industry:** by decade

| 10s | 20s | 30s | 40s | 50s | 60s | 70s | 80s | 90s |
|-----|-----|-----|-----|-----|-----|-----|-----|-----|
|     |     |     |     |     |     |     | ■   |     |

Reinhold became interested in acting while in high school and took a drama course in college. He went on to join the Burt Reynolds Dinner Theater in Florida, then moved to California and was signed to a contract with Paramount Television. His work in TV was unmemorable but helped him land small parts in his first two films, *Running Scared* (1980) and *Stripes* (1981). His first major role was as a high school student in the hit comedy *Fast Times at Ridgemont High* (1982), and he greatly increased his public familiarity after portraying a rookie policeman in the huge hit *Beverly Hills Cop* (1984) with Eddie Murphy. His first lead role was in *Roadhouse 66* (1984). He went on to play light comedic roles in a number of films, most of them unsuccessful. **Selected Works:** *Baby on Board* (1992), *Black Magic* (1992), *The Santa Clause* (1994)

# Ivan Reitman

**Born:** 1946; Czechoslovakia

**Years Active in the Industry:** by decade

| 10s | 20s | 30s | 40s | 50s | 60s | 70s | 80s | 90s |
|-----|-----|-----|-----|-----|-----|-----|-----|-----|
|     |     |     |     |     |     | ■   |     |     |

Czechkoslovakian-descended filmmaker Ivan Reitman, raised in Canada, started out making short films in the 1960s, and became a director/producer in the 1970s in Canada. As a producer, he was responsible for several early David Cronenberg features, but it wasn't until *National Lampoon's Animal House* (1977), that Reitman was noticed by Hollywood, and the spectacular success of *Meatballs* (1979)—the highest grossing movie ever made in Canada up to that time—gave him all the credibility he needed as a director. *Stripes* (1982) only enhanced his reputation, and the megahit *Ghostbusters* (1984) and its sequel established Reitman as one of the "money directors" of his generation. Misfires like *Stop! Or My Mom Will Shoot* (1992) alternate with blockbusters like *Beethoven* (1991) and *Dave* (1993). **Selected Works:** *Dave* (1993), *Kindergarten Cop* (1990), *Junior* (1994)

# James Remar

**Born:** December 31, 1953; Boston, MA

**Years Active in the Industry:** by decade

| 10s | 20s | 30s | 40s | 50s | 60s | 70s | 80s | 90s |
|-----|-----|-----|-----|-----|-----|-----|-----|-----|
|     |     |     |     |     |     |     | ■   |     |

Supporting and character actor James Remar has become the epitome of contemporary Hollywood villains. With his rugged, brooding looks, Remar has played a variety of psychopaths and thugs on stage, screen, and television. As a young man, he dropped out of high school to tour in a rock band before studying acting at New York's Neighborhood Playhouse with Sanford Meisner. (He later went back and earned his high school diploma.) He made his film debut playing a street punk in *On the Yard* (1978), but he was not really noticed until he played Ajax in Walter Hill's *The Warriors* (1979). He went on to play in three more of Hill's films, and made his Broadway debut in 1979 playing a Nazi in *Bent*. In 1980, Remar played in the *Windwalker,* a native American drama filmed entirely in Crow and Cheyenne. During filming the Cheyenne's gave him the honorary title "Standing 20." He continued making films through the mid '80s when his drug problem forced him to lose the male lead in *Aliens* (1986), and he was forced to stop working. By 1989, Remar had staged a comeback, again playing criminals and killers. **Selected Works:** *48 Hours* (1982), *Drugstore Cowboy* (1989), *Boys on the Side* (1995)

# Lee Remick

**Born:** December 14, 1935; Quincy, MA
**Died:** July 2, 1991; Brentwood, CA

**Years Active in the Industry:** by decade

| 10s | 20s | 30s | 40s | 50s | 60s | 70s | 80s | 90s |
|-----|-----|-----|-----|-----|-----|-----|-----|-----|
|     |     |     |     |     | ■   |     |     |     |

Lee Remick began her career as a dancer, then after acting onstage and TV she debuted onscreen in *A Face in the Crowd* (1957). Remick went on to a series of strong screen performances which established her as a major leading lady; for her work in *Days of Wine and Roses* (1962) she received a Best Actress Oscar nomination. She sustained a fairly busy screen career into the late '70s, meanwhile also working often on the stage and TV. From 1957-68 Remick was married to TV director-producer William Colleran. In 1970 she married director William Rory "Kip" Gowens, with whom she moved to England. In the '80s she rarely appeared onscreen but increased her work in TV movies and mini-series. In 1988 she formed a production company in partnership with James Garner and Peter Duchow. Remick died from cancer at age 55. **Selected Works:** *Anatomy of a Murder* (1959), *Days of Wine & Roses* (1962), *Wild River* (1960)

# Jean Renoir

**Born:** September 15, 1894; Montmartre, France
**Died:** February 12, 1979; Hollywood, CA

**Years Active in the Industry:** by decade

| 10s | 20s | 30s | 40s | 50s | 60s | 70s | 80s | 90s |
|-----|-----|-----|-----|-----|-----|-----|-----|-----|
|     |     | ■   |     |     |     |     |     |     |

The son of the painter Auguste Renoir, Jean Renoir became one of France's most important and respected filmmakers during the middle of the 20th century. A philosophy and math student, Renoir became a cavalryman but was invalided out of the army before World War I. He later joined the infantry—injured in that service, and became a pilot. He later married a model and aspiring actress and, following the death of his father and the acquisition of his inheritance, set up his own production company in order to produce movies for his wife. Renoir learned from these early experiences financing movies and watching other films, and became a director in 1924. He later took directing assignments from other producers as a means of supporting himself, augmented by an occasional acting role. With the coming of sound, Renoir's career was quickly made with a series of profitable films, including *Le Chienne* (1931), a savage and dark drama about a man's self-destruction, which was later remade by Fritz Lang as *Scarlet Street.* Renoir's subsequent films, including *The Lower Depths* (1936) and *Grand Illusion* (1937), were among the finest made in France before the war, and were well-acknowledged at the time of their release. The latter became an international hit. However, *His Rules of the Game* (1939), with its strong criticism of French society, struck a raw nerve with critics and the public alike on the eve of World War II, and was quickly withdrawn from distribution and subsequently re-edited. Renoir served in the film unit of the French army at the outbreak of World War II, but was fortunate enough to get to Lisbon and then America after the fall of France. Renoir was later put under contract at 20th Century-Fox, where he made the rural drama *Swamp Water* (1941), a beautiful, lyrical, and poetic story of injustice and vengeance. At RKO, he made the patriotic drama—possibly the best the studio ever produced—*This Land Is Mine* (1943), and returned to rural American subjects for *The Southerner* (1945), released by United Artists. *Diary of a Chambermaid* (1946) was another independent production, while *Woman On the Beach* (1947), a dark romantic drama, was done for RKO. Renoir's first post-American film (and his first in color) was financed by a Beverly Hills florist, but was shot in India—*The River* (1951), based on a story by Rumer Godden, told the story of the coming of age of three young women in India, and received tremendous international acclaim but relatively little public attention. Now it is one of his most popular films. His next films, *The Golden Coach* (1952) and *French Can-Can* (1955), marked Renoir's return to Europe and France, respectively, and to profitable filmmaking. The early 1960's saw the restoration and re-release—to belated acclaim as a masterpiece—of *Rules of the Game.* His later films were less successful and more modestly produced, and made extensive use of television techniques, the most popular of which was *The Little Theater of Jean Renoir* (1969), which was originally made for television. Throughout his career, Renoir's style embraced a multitude of genres, and its permutations make it almost impossible to characterize. However, his social realism was usually on target, as *Le Chienne* showed to his advantage and *Rules of the Game* presented so disturbingly to the French public. **Selected Works:** *Toni* (1934), *Ways of Love* (1950)

# Alain Resnais

**Born:** June 3, 1922; Vannes, France

**Years Active in the Industry:** by decade

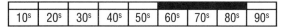

| 10s | 20s | 30s | 40s | 50s | 60s | 70s | 80s | 90s |
|-----|-----|-----|-----|-----|-----|-----|-----|-----|
|     |     |     |     |     |     |     |     |     |

French director Alain Resnais was an "auteur" at age 14, making brief films with his own 8mm camera. He studied the performing end of the business under drama instructor Rene Simon, then took directing courses at the newly formed Institut des Hautes Etudes Cinematographie from 1943 through 1945. He made his first professional appearance in 1945 as a member of an Allied Occupation entertainment troupe called Les Arlequins; one year later, he went back to directing, initially turning out 16mm shorts, then graduating to 35mm documentaries and dramas. In 1948, Resnais attracted critical attention with his short subject *Van Gogh,* the vanguard of a brief series of documentaries scrutinizing the works of such artists as Gaugin and Picasso. Eleven years later, Resnais burst upon the film-festival and art-house scene with his first feature, *Hiroshima Mon Amour* (1959), which juxtaposed a modern love story with scenes of the atomic-bomb-induced carnage at Hiroshima. (Resnais had earlier toyed with this technique in his famous 1955 short subject *Night and Fog,* a study of the Nazi concentration camp system.) The film's ambiguity and lack of linear structure confused many, while others hailed *Hiroshima* as a brilliant exercise in "personal" cinema. Resnais stirred up further controversy with his next feature, *Last Year at Marienbad* (1961), a Proustian tale of love lost and found that won the 1961 Venice grand prize. (Not that everyone was enamored by this often impenetrable exercise; cartoonist Al Capp denigrated the film as "The world's longest wallpaper commercial.") The director's next award-winner was 1966's *La Guerre est Finie,* which eschewed his dreamlike style in favor of a more conventional narrative. Over the next two decades, Resnais would turn out the occasional "commercial" film in order to finance his more personal, esoteric projects. Most of Resnais' films are variations of the *Hiroshima Mon Amour* conceit of wavering between the tactile experiences of the present and the haunting memories of the past; perhaps his most characteristic effort is 1968's *Je t'aime, je t'aime,* in which the hero is trapped in a malfunctioning time machine. Alain Resnais' most recent film was the little-seen 1989 project *I Want to Go Home,* which starred American screenwriter Adolph Green. **Selected Works:** *Mon Oncle D'Amerique* (1980), *Muriel* (1963), *Stavisky* (1974)

# Burt Reynolds (Burton Leon Reynolds, Jr.)

**Born:** February 11, 1936; Waycross, GA

**Years Active in the Industry:** by decade

| 10s | 20s | 30s | 40s | 50s | 60s | 70s | 80s | 90s |
|-----|-----|-----|-----|-----|-----|-----|-----|-----|
|     |     |     |     |     |     |     |     |     |

Charming, easy-going, handsome, witty lead actor and former mega-star, Reynolds attended college on a football scholarship, becoming an all-star Southern conference halfback. After a knee injury and a debilitating car accident he switched from athletics to college drama. In 1955 he dropped out of college and went to New York, looking for work onstage; all he got were occasional TV bit parts, and for two years he had to support himself as a dishwasher and bouncer. In 1957 he appeared in a New York City Center revival of *Mister Roberts,* and shortly thereafter was signed to a TV contract. He went on to regular roles in the TV series "Riverboat," "Gunsmoke," "Hawk," and "Dan August." He appeared in numerous films in the '60s, but failed to make much of an impression. In the early '70s his popularity began to increase, in part due to his witty appearances on TV talk shows. His breakthrough film was *Deliverance* (1972), which established him as both a star and a serious actor. He became a major sex symbol when he was featured as the first nude male centerfold in the April 1972 *Cosmopolitan.* He went on to become the biggest box-office attraction in America for several years. However, by the mid '80s his heyday was over, and he ceased to be a successful film star. Switching to TV, he starred in the popular sitcom "Evening Shade," for which he won an Emmy. He has also directed several films, and in 1979 he established the Burt Reynolds Dinner Theater in Florida. From 1963-66 he was married to actress Judy Carne, who later accused him of having been an abusive husband. He has been romantically linked with actresses Dinah Shore and Sally Field, and tennis star Chris Evert. He was married from 1988-93 to actress Loni Anderson; their marriage ended in one of the most widely-publicized acrimonious divorces in Hollywood history, which caused Reynolds' popularity to decrease considerably. **Selected Works:** *Starting Over* (1979), *The Man from Left Field* (1994), *B. L. Stryker: Night Train* (1990)

# Debbie Reynolds (Mary Frances Reynolds)

**Born:** April 1, 1932; El Paso, TX

**Years Active in the Industry:** by decade

| 10ˢ | 20ˢ | 30ˢ | 40ˢ | 50ˢ | 60ˢ | 70ˢ | 80ˢ | 90ˢ |
|-----|-----|-----|-----|-----|-----|-----|-----|-----|
|     |     |     |     |     |     |     |     |     |

In the late 1940s Debbie Reynolds won the Miss Burbank beauty contest, leading to a film contract with Warner Bros. However, she appeared in only one movie, *June Bride* (1948). She

changed studios and in 1950 began a busy screen career, usually playing enthusiastic, wholesome, "girl next door" leads. From 1955-59 Reynolds was married to singer Eddie Fisher; when Fisher left her for Elizabeth Taylor, Reynolds's popularity peaked as she received a wave of public sympathy. She remarried in 1960 and continued to

be fairly busy onscreen until 1971, after which her film work was minimal. For her work in *The Unsinkable Molly Brown* (1964) she received a Best Actress Oscar nomination. In the '70s she starred on Broadway in the hit revival of *Irene,* from which she went on to the extravagant revue *The Debbie Reynolds Show.* She divorced her husband in 1975, after his business failed, and she was held responsible for $2 million of his debts. She remarried in 1984. In the mid '80s she released two aerobic-exercise videos. In 1993 she opened a Las Vegas club, where she performs and displays her extensive collection of Hollywood memorabilia. She authored an autobiography, *Debbie: My Life* (1988) and is the mother of actress-novelist Carrie Fisher and TV director Todd Fisher. **Selected Works:** *How the West Was Won* (1963), *Singin' in the Rain* (1952), *The Pleasure of His Company* (1961)

# Christina Ricci

**Born:** 1981

**Years Active in the Industry:** by decade

| 10ˢ | 20ˢ | 30ˢ | 40ˢ | 50ˢ | 60ˢ | 70ˢ | 80ˢ | 90ˢ |
|-----|-----|-----|-----|-----|-----|-----|-----|-----|
|     |     |     |     |     |     |     |     |     |

Juvenile actress Christina Ricci made her film debut as Cher's youngest daughter in 1990's *Mermaids.* She truly came into her own as the dour, demonic Wednesday in 1991's *The Addams*

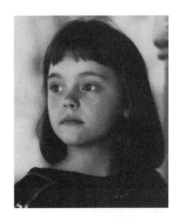

*Family,* a role she repeated with equal effectiveness in 1993's *Addams Family Values.* In 1995, she was costarred with everyone's favorite Friendly Ghost in *Casper: The Movie.* **Selected Works:** *Addams Family Values* (1993), *Gold Diggers: The Secret of Bear Mountain* (1995), *Now and Then* (1995)

# Joely Richardson

**Born:** 1965; London, England

**Years Active in the Industry:** by decade

| 10ˢ | 20ˢ | 30ˢ | 40ˢ | 50ˢ | 60ˢ | 70ˢ | 80ˢ | 90ˢ |
|-----|-----|-----|-----|-----|-----|-----|-----|-----|
|     |     |     |     |     |     |     |     |     |

British actress Joely Richardson is the daughter of actress Vanessa Redgrave and director Tony Richardson. She is also the granddaughter of actors Michael Redgrave and Rachel Kempson, niece of actors Corin and Lynn Redgrave, and sister of actress

Natasha Richardson. Richardson's film credits range from the art-house favorite *Drowning By Numbers* (1987)—in which she is one of three murderesses, all named Cissy Colpitts—to the abortive musical *I'll Do Anything* (1993). **Selected Works:** *King Ralph* (1991), *Shining Through* (1992), *Heading Home* (1990)

# Miranda Richardson

**Born:** 1958; Lancashire, England

**Years Active in the Industry:** by decade

| 10ˢ | 20ˢ | 30ˢ | 40ˢ | 50ˢ | 60ˢ | 70ˢ | 80ˢ | 90ˢ |
|-----|-----|-----|-----|-----|-----|-----|-----|-----|
|     |     |     |     |     |     |     | ■   | ■   |

Blonde British actress Miranda Richardson dropped out of school at age 17 to study at the Old Vic in Bristol. A professional before she was twenty, Richardson toured in repertory and appeared on TV before making her film bow at age 27 in *Dance with a Stranger* (1985), in which she played the real-life Ruth Ellis, the last woman to be executed for murder in Britain. The film was warmly received by critics but withered at the box office; several more British-financed productions followed before Miranda was cast in her first Hollywood-financed picture, Spielberg's *Empire of the Sun* (1987). She gained an American following with her appearances in *Enchanted April* (1991) and *The Crying Game* (1993), and was Oscar-nominated for her performance as Jeremy Irons' long-suffering wife in 1993's *Damage*. In 1994, Miranda Richardson was teamed with American actor Willem Dafoe in *Tom & Viv,* the story of the turbulent relationship between poet T. S. Eliot and his wife; the film earned Richardson her second Oscar nomination. **Selected Works:** *The Bachelor* (1993), *Tom and Viv* (1994)

# Natasha Richardson

**Born:** May 11, 1963; London, England

**Years Active in the Industry:** by decade

| 10ˢ | 20ˢ | 30ˢ | 40ˢ | 50ˢ | 60ˢ | 70ˢ | 80ˢ | 90ˢ |
|-----|-----|-----|-----|-----|-----|-----|-----|-----|
|     |     |     |     |     |     |     | ■   | ■   |

The daughter of British actress Vanessa Redgrave and director Tony Richardson, Natasha Richardson was named not for the constant companion of Boris Badenov but for the heroine in

Tolstoy's *War and Peace.* Richardson made her film bow at age four, playing one of her own mother's bridesmaids in *Charge of the Light Brigade* (1968), which was directed by her father. Trained at the Central School for Speech and Drama, Richardson did her first professional stage work at the Leeds Playhouse in 1983, then went on to specialize in Shakespeare (like virtually everyone else of Redgrave lineage) at the Old Vic. In the company of her mother Vanessa and her aunt Lynn, Natasha made an excellent impression in a 1985 staging of Chekhov's *Three Sisters;* the following year, she won the London Theatre Critics Award for Most Promising Newcomer. The honor was a trifle belated, as Richardson had been acting on stage for three years and costarring in films since 1984's *Every Picture Tells a Story.* Her film roles have ranged from passive (*Patty Hearst* [1989]) to aggressive (*King Ralph* [1991]), but always distinctive. Among Richardson's most memorable assignments have been the 1990 film *The Handmaid's Tale,* her 1993 performance in a PBS restaging of *Suddenly Last Summer,* and a Broadway appearance that same year in a revival of O'Neill's *Anna Christie.* **Selected Works:** *The Comfort of Strangers* (1991), *Hostages* (1993), *Nell* (1994)

# Sir Ralph Richardson (Ralph David Richardson)

**Born:** December 19, 1902; Cheltenham, England
**Died:** October 10, 1983; London, England

**Years Active in the Industry:** by decade

| 10ˢ | 20ˢ | 30ˢ | 40ˢ | 50ˢ | 60ˢ | 70ˢ | 80ˢ | 90ˢ |
|-----|-----|-----|-----|-----|-----|-----|-----|-----|
|     | ■   | ■   | ■   | ■   | ■   | ■   | ■   |     |

Illustrious, but not very handsome character actor of the British stage and screen, Richardson vastly preferred theater to movies, but made films (he claimed) to make money in his "spare time." He began his acting career in the 1920s, when a small legacy gave him the freedom to quit his office job; he toured for a while, then joined the Birmingham Rep. Working with the Old Vic in the '30s and '40s, he became one of the premier character players of the British stage playing many Shakespearean roles. Richardson debuted onscreen in *The Ghoul* (1933), going on to frequently play well-bred, modest intellectual characters, commoners, and eccentrics; he lacked the good looks to be a romantic lead. He has done much work on Broadway. He won the British Best Actor Award for his work in *Breaking the Sound Barrier* (1952). For his performances in *The Heiress* (1949) and *Greystoke: The Legend of Tarzan* (1984) he received Best Supporting Actor Oscar nominations, the latter posthumously. He was married to actress Meriel Forbes and was knighted in 1947. **Selected Works:** *Four Feathers* (1939), *Long Day's Journey into Night* (1962), *Man Who Could Work Miracles* (1937), *O Lucky Man* (1973), *Richard III* (1955)

# Robert Richardson

**Born:** 19??

**Years Active in the Industry:** by decade

| 10s | 20s | 30s | 40s | 50s | 60s | 70s | 80s | 90s |
|-----|-----|-----|-----|-----|-----|-----|-----|-----|

The great talent of American cinematographer Robert Richardson is his ability to dramatically harness the photographic styles and techniques of days gone by. This is well exemplified by his work in John Sayles' *Eight Men Out*, where, through the use of tinted filters and soft-edged frames, Richardson recreated the ambience of 1919 by coming up with images reminiscent of a hand-colored postcard. Undoubtedly, Richardson's best work has been in the films of director Oliver Stone. In *Born on the Fourth of July* (1989), *JFK* (1991) and *Natural Born Killers* (1994), Robert Richardson used a vast array of film stock and lenses to recreate the "look" of such evocative cinematic tangibles as 8-millimeter home movies, grainy 1960s newsfilm, and cheap 1970s color videotape. **Selected Works:** *City of Hope* (1991), *Few Good Men* (1992), *Platoon* (1986)

# Tony Richardson (Cecil Antonio Richardson)

**Born:** June 5, 1928; Shipley, Yorkshire, England
**Died:** November 14, 1991; Los Angeles, CA

**Years Active in the Industry:** by decade

| 10s | 20s | 30s | 40s | 50s | 60s | 70s | 80s | 90s |
|-----|-----|-----|-----|-----|-----|-----|-----|-----|

A graduate of Oxford, Tony Richardson rose from head of the university's dramatic society to the pinnacle of the British film industry during the early 1960s, scoring several theatrical successes as a director along the way, most notably *Look Back In Anger,* by John Osborne, with whom Richardson would enjoy a long professional relationship. The play became Richardson's feature-film debut, and established him as the first of a new wave of directors who would take over British cinema during the early and mid 1960s—his subsequent movies, including *The Loneliness of the Long Distance Runner* (1962) and, more notably, *Tom Jones* (1963), established him as that rarity among British filmmakers up to that time. He was considered a successful iconoclast, challenging his audience and dazzling them as well with his creative camera work and inventiveness. Unfortunately, Richardson's 1968 reworking of *The Charge of the Light Brigade* fell flat at the box office, and the commercial/artistic spell was broken. He made several more films, including *Ned Kelly* (1969), *Joseph Andrews* (1977), *The Border* (1982), and *Hotel New Hampshire* (1984)—the latter a major disaster for everyone involved—but none of them caught the public's taste and all seemed to echo finer films from the early 1960s. His daughter Natasha Richardson, ironically enough, achieved stardom on her own during Richardson's final years, when his career—apart from a recut reissue of *Tom Jones*—was in near complete eclipse. **Selected Works:** *A Taste of Honey* (1961), *Women and Men: Stories of Seduction* (1990), *Blue Sky* (1994)

# Alan Rickman

**Born:** 1946; Hammersmith, London, England

**Years Active in the Industry:** by decade

| 10s | 20s | 30s | 40s | 50s | 60s | 70s | 80s | 90s |
|-----|-----|-----|-----|-----|-----|-----|-----|-----|

Originally a graphic designer in London, Rickman decided to become a professional actor at age 26. He studied acting at the Royal Academy of Dramatic Arts. Working with the Birmingham Repertory Theater Company, he appeared in several stage productions, then moved on to the National Theater and finally the Royal Shakespeare Company; there he received much acclaim, particularly for his performance in the play *Les Liaisons Dangereuses*. He reprised the role on Broadway and received a Tony nomination in 1987. Meanwhile, he appeared in BBC TV productions, including *Therese Raquin* (1981) and *Smiley's People* (1982). Also, in 1981 he directed the play *Desperately Yours* in New York. After a decade of such work he was offered the role of the "bad guy" in the enormously successful movie *Die Hard* with Bruce Willis. From there he became a busy performer in Hollywood productions and also appeared in the British film *Truly, Madly, Deeply* (1990). **Selected Works:** *Bob Roberts* (1992), *Quigley Down Under* (1990), *Sense and Sensibility* (1995)

# Leni Riefenstahl (Helene Berta Amalie Riefenstahl)

**Born:** August 22, 1902; Berlin, Germany

**Years Active in the Industry:** by decade

| 10s | 20s | 30s | 40s | 50s | 60s | 70s | 80s | 90s |
|-----|-----|-----|-----|-----|-----|-----|-----|-----|

German actress/ filmmaker Leni Riefenstahl began her performing career as a dancer in 1920, studying with famed instructor Mary Wigman. In 1926, she was cast by director Dr. Arnold Fanck in the first of her many "mountain films" (a genre peculiar to Germany that had been popularized by Fanck), *Peaks of Destiny* (1926). The best known and most popular of her athletic starring vehicles was 1929's *The White Hell of Pitz Palu*. Having learned the whys and wherefores of directing and photography from Dr. Fanck, Riefenstahl expressed a desire to direct a film herself. The result was *The Blue Light* (1931), a true "auteur" effort: starring

Riefenstahl, directed, edited and cowritten by Riefenstahl, and released through the newly formed Leni Riefenstahl Studio-Film. *The Blue Light* impressed many people, including Adolf Hitler, who, upon gaining power in 1933, appointed Riefenstahl "film expert" to the National Socialist Party. Her first effort on behalf of the Nazis was the cheaply produced 1933 documentary *Victory of the Faith*. The following year, with the full cooperation of Hitler and with 30 cameras and 120 assistants at her disposal, Riefenstahl made a film of the fourth Nuremberg rally, *Triumph of the Will* (1934). Observed objectively, the film is an artistic triumph. Still, it is blatant propaganda on behalf of the Third Reich, and as such has engendered controversy ever since its release. The debate still rages as to whether Riefenstahl was merely recording events that had been staged by the Party (as she has claimed), or whether she alone was responsible for the film's persuasive visual dynamics and production design. Her next project was even more impressive: *Olympia* (1936), a filmed record of the 1936 Berlin Olympics. Though attacked by latter-day critics as being "fascistic" in its celebration of the muscular male physique, *Olympia* is virtually bereft of proselytizing. To be sure, there are plenty of shots of Hitler and his minions (no one knows to this day if the film was Nazi-sponsored or independently produced), but just as much screen time is alotted to the decidedly non-Aryan athlete Jesse Owens. Many of Riefenstahl's innovations and techniques in *Olympia*—the slow-motion shots of the athletes, the telephoto lens used for closeups of the events, the ground-level shots, the overhead panoramas taken from blimps—have been utilized by sports documentaries and broadcasts ever since. *Olympia* would be the last of Riefenstahl's 1930s films: she turned down as many assignments as she received from the Nazis, and attempted unsuccessfully to launch two large-scale historical epics. Her last feature film, three years in the making, was *Tiefland* (1943) a magnificently photographed return to the mountain-film genre. She returned to acting in this film as a Spanish dancer, and also utilized gypsy concentration camp inmates as extras (she would later claim she had no idea what fate was in store for these unfortunate souls). When Germany fell to the allies in 1945, Riefenstahl was arrested and her films confiscated. She spent three years in various allied prison camps, then underwent several more years of persecution on the grounds that she had been a top-ranking Nazi official. In fact, she had never joined the Party (though she was quite vocal in her support of Hitler), and in 1952 she was finally exonerated of all charges. Still, she never made another film in Germany, even though several of the more rabidly pro-Nazi directors—notably Viet Harlan, who'd helmed the viciously anti-semitic *Jud Suss*—continued making movies without any difficulty. In 1956, Riefenstahl travelled to Africa to begin work on *Black Cargo*, a documentary on the modern slave trade made on behalf of the London Anti-Slave Society; this project came to an end when she was seriously injured in a car accident in Kenya. She returned to Africa in 1961 to photograph the fascinating rituals of the Mesakin Nuba tribe. Though this odyssey resulted in an attractive coffee-table book of photographs, Riefenstahl never assembled her film footage into a feature. She was honored with numerous international film awards in the 1970s, though the ceremonies were often interrupted by the protests of Holocaust victims.

In recent interviews, Riefenstahl has allowed that the end result of Nazism was horrendous, but she refuses to apologize for her work; she is fond of quoting a pro-Hitler comment allegedly made by Winston Churchill in the mid-1930s, then argues that if Churchill could not foresee the horrors to come, how could she? Those interviewers expecting to meet an embittered, defensive old woman are often amazed at Riefenstahl's youthful vigor, softspokenness, courtesy and sense of humor. In her nineties, Riefenstahl has become an enthusiastic scuba diver, hoping to assemble the underwater films that she has lensed into one last documentary feature. In 1991, she published her autobiography, *Leni Riefenstahl: A Memoir*, and in 1993, she was the subject of a lively British documentary, *The Wonderful, Horrible Life of Leni Riefenstahl*.

# Peter Riegert

**Born:** April 11, 1947; New York, NY

**Years Active in the Industry:** by decade

| 10s | 20s | 30s | 40s | 50s | 60s | 70s | 80s | 90s |
|-----|-----|-----|-----|-----|-----|-----|-----|-----|
|     |     |     |     |     |     | ■   | ■   | ■   |

University of Buffalo graduate, former Bella Abzug campaign worker, and onetime schoolteacher Peter Riegert finessed an early flair for comedy into appearing with an improv troupe called the War Babies. This led to Riegert's Broadway bow in 1975, then to his being hired by the National Lampoon people for several projects, the first of which was *Animal House* (1978), in which the actor portrayed Donald "Boon" Schoenstein. He went on to play such roles as the feckless corporate-flunky good guy in *Local Hero* (1983) and the unhitched pickle vendor whom Amy Irving would never marry in a million years but does anyway in *Crossing Delancey* (1989). Usually bypassed by the gossip columnists (which he doesn't seem to mind at all), Riegert raised journalistic eyebrows when he was cast opposite his onetime lady friend Bette Midler in the 1993 TV version of *Gypsy*. **Selected Works:** *The Object of Beauty* (1991), *Mask* (1994), *Coldblooded* (1995)

# Diana Rigg

**Born:** July 20, 1938; Doncaster, England

**Years Active in the Industry:** by decade

| 10s | 20s | 30s | 40s | 50s | 60s | 70s | 80s | 90s |
|-----|-----|-----|-----|-----|-----|-----|-----|-----|
|     |     |     |     |     | ■   | ■   | ■   | ■   |

Look up "statuesque" in the dictionary and you just might find a picture of British actress Diana Rigg. Born in a Yorkshire industrial town, Rigg was two years old when her father, a railroad constructionist, moved the family to India. Six years later, she was back in Yorkshire, suffering through the discipline and rigors of private school until one of her teachers introduced her to the world of the theatre. After graduation, Rigg was accepted by the Royal Academy of Dramatic Art; she went on to the Royal Shakespeare Company, where her deeply distinctive voice, flaming red hair, and towering height (5'8") assured her such dynamic roles as Viola in *Twelfth Night* and Cordelia in *King Lear*. Though never lacking in prestige, the Royal Shakespeare paid starvation wages, compelling Rigg to moonlight in the more lucrative world of movies and TV. In 1965, she was selected to replace Honor Blackman on the popular tongue-in-cheek TV-adventure series "The Avengers," and for the next two years captivated little boys of all ages with her energetic portrayal of coolheaded, leather-clad karate expert Mrs. Emma Peel. Film stardom followed in short order with plum roles in *The Assassination Bureau* (1968) and the James Bond flick *On Her Majesty's Secret Service* (1969). Though she was always welcome in films and television (she headlined a brief American sitcom, "Diana," in 1973), Rigg preferred to think of herself as a "theatre animal," and continued to star in the classics on stage, still frequently accepting a miniscule salary in order to satisfy her muse. In the last decade, Rigg published the hilarious book *No Turn Unstoned,* in which she gathered together the worst reviews ever received by the world's best actors (including her own bad notices); in the early 1990s, she replaced Vincent Price as the host of PBS' "Mystery" anthology. **Selected Works:** *Hospital* (1971)

# Molly Ringwald

**Born:** February 14, 1969; Sacramento, CA

**Years Active in the Industry:** by decade

| 10s | 20s | 30s | 40s | 50s | 60s | 70s | 80s | 90s |
|-----|-----|-----|-----|-----|-----|-----|-----|-----|
|     |     |     |     |     |     |     | ■   |     |

At age four she sang with her father's Great Pacific Jazz Band, debuting onstage the next year and recording her own jazz album (*I Wanna Be Loved By You*) when she was six. Ringwald became a regular on the TV show "The New Mickey Mouse Show," which led to a supporting role in a West Coast production of *Annie* and a continuing role in the TV series "The Facts of Life." She debuted onscreen in Paul Mazursky's *Tempest* (1982), for which she won a Golden Globe award. Writer-director John Hughes saw her in the film and wrote *Sixteen Candles* (1984) for her, which became her fourth film and first leading role and led to two more films with Hughes; the second of these, the high school Cinderella story *Pretty in Pink* (1986), was a huge hit. However, her career since then has been surprisingly unsuccessful, although she did give a good performance in Stephen King's *The Stand*. **Selected Works:** *Betsy's Wedding* (1990), *Women and Men: Stories of Seduction* (1990), *Stand* (1994)

# Robert Riskin

**Born:** 1897; New York, NY
**Died:** 1955; California

**Years Active in the Industry:** by decade

| 10s | 20s | 30s | 40s | 50s | 60s | 70s | 80s | 90s |
|-----|-----|-----|-----|-----|-----|-----|-----|-----|
|     | ■   |     |     |     |     |     |     |     |

Screenwriter Robert Riskin entered the film business as a teenager, at a time (1914) when anyone with a glimmer of talent was allowed to work on what were then called scenarios. During the 1920's, Robertson kept busy on Broadway, penning such popular plays as *Illicit* and *Bless You Sister*. On the Columbia Pictures payroll in 1931, Riskin found himself adapting many of his own works for the screen—including *Bless You Sister*, which ended up as the Frank Capra production *The Miracle Woman*. Riskin and Capra liked each other's work, and, as a result, Riskin contributed the wisecracking dialogue for Capra's *Platinum Blonde* (1931). Future Riskin/Capra collaborations included *American Madness* (1932), *Lady for a Day* (1933), *It Happened One Night* (1934) (which won Riskin an Oscar), *Broadway Bill* (1934), *Mr. Deeds Goes To Town* (1936), *Lost Horizon* (1937) and *You Can't Take It With You* (1938). Free of their Columbia contracts in 1941, Riskin and Capra formed their own production company to put together *Meet John Doe*. In later years, Capra would sometimes comment that he'd often have to tone down Riskin's Manhattan-bred cynicism; it's also likely that Riskin may have bristled at Capra's tendency to take all the credit for his collaborators' contributions. In 1937, Riskin ventured into directing for the first and last time with the Grace Moore musical *When You're In Love* (1937). In 1942, he married actress Fay Wray, who later put her own career on hold to nurse Riskin through a debilitating (and eventually fatal) neurological illness.

# Michael Ritchie

**Born:** November 28, 1938; Waukesha, WI

**Years Active in the Industry:** by decade

| 10s | 20s | 30s | 40s | 50s | 60s | 70s | 80s | 90s |
|-----|-----|-----|-----|-----|-----|-----|-----|-----|
|     |     |     |     |     | ■   |     |     |     |

The son of a psychology professor, American director Michael Ritchie began directing collegiate plays while attending Harvard. At the tender age of 22, Ritchie was thrust into the limelight for his direction of the Arthur Kopit play *Oh Dad, Poor Dad, Mama's Hung You in the Closet and I'm Feeling So Sad*. He moved to television as director and associate producer for the 1964 historical anthology "Profiles in Courage." After several years of episodic television, Ritchie directed his first theatrical feature, *Downhill Racer* (1969), ostensibly a Robert Redford vehicle about skiing, but actually a soured glance at the pitfalls of the American success ethic. Redford worked again with Ritchie on *The Candidate* (1972), one of the best movie exposes of political gamesmanship. Ritchie then directed *Smile* (1975), a perceptively satirical view of the beauty pageant scene. *Smile* didn't click at the box office, but, on its strength, Ritchie was hired to direct *The Bad News Bears* (1978). While it might appear that Ritchie was engaged to skewer little-league baseball in *Bad News Bears* because of his previous dissections of American institutions, the director himself insisted he was hired for *Bears* because he'd shown in *Smile* that he could direct little kids to "talk dirty." *Bad News Bears* led to two sequels, one of them produced by Ritchie, but neither within shouting distance of the original's quality. Most subsequent Ritchie films were pure-entertainment vehicles with little to indicate that the director had a point of view beyond that of the scriptwriters—these films include *The Island* (1979), *The Survivors* (1983), the Eddie Murphy extravaganza *The Golden Child* (1986), and the two Chevy Chase *Fletch* films. **Selected Works:** *Diggstown* (1992), *Positively True Adventures of the Alleged Texas Cheerleader-Murdering Mom* (1993), *The Scout* (1994)

# Martin Ritt

**Born:** March 2, 1920; New York, NY
**Died:** December 8, 1990; Santa Monica, CA

**Years Active in the Industry:** by decade

| 10s | 20s | 30s | 40s | 50s | 60s | 70s | 80s | 90s |
|-----|-----|-----|-----|-----|-----|-----|-----|-----|

American film director Martin Ritt started out as a Broadway actor. Ritt's stage role as Gleason in *Winged Victory* brought him to Hollywood for the film version, for which the studio publicity billed him, along with the rest of the male cast, by the rank he held in the Army (Private First Class Martin Ritt). A victim of the Hollywood blacklist, Ritt's career came to a standstill in the early 1950s. He reemerged, not as an actor, but as a director for the 1956 film *Edge of the City*. A favorite of actor Paul Newman, Ritt directed Newman in *The Long Hot Summer* (1958), *Paris Blues* (1961), *Hemingway's Adventures of a Young Man* (1962), *Hud* (1963), *The Outrage* (1964) and *Hombre* (1967). Other Ritt-directed films of note were *Pete 'n' Tillie* (1972), *Cross Creek* (1984), *Murphy's Romance* (1985), and, his last film, *Stanley and Iris* (1990). If there doesn't seem to be a central throughline in these films it was because Ritt steadfastly refused to be typecast as a director. One project that brought him immense satisfaction was *The Front* (1976), a comedy-drama of the blacklist years in which Ritt worked with fellow blacklistees Martin Balsam, Zero Mostel, Joshua Shelley, Herschel Bernardi, Lloyd Gough, and screenwriter Walter Bernstein. In 1985, Ritt made a surprising but delightful return to acting in the role of an excitable baseball manager in the otherwise disposable *The Slugger's Wife* (1985). **Selected Works:** *Norma Rae* (1979), *Sounder* (1972), *Spy Who Came in from the Cold* (1965)

# John Ritter (Jonathan Ritter)

**Born:** September 17, 1948; Hollywood, CA

**Years Active in the Industry:** by decade

| 10s | 20s | 30s | 40s | 50s | 60s | 70s | 80s | 90s |
|-----|-----|-----|-----|-----|-----|-----|-----|-----|

The son of country-and-western star Tex Ritter, he majored in drama in college, going on to stage work which included a production at the Edinburgh Festival. Soon he began landing roles in

TV movies, for which he received both Emmy and Golden Globe nominations. Ritter's film debut came in Disney's *The Barefoot Executive* (1971), after which he went on to a spotty and generally unsuccessful movie career. He became famous in the late '70s as the result of his costarring role in the hit TV sitcom *Three's Company*, which established his reputation for playing overenergetic, somewhat foolish comedic characters. His career dried up in the mid '80s, but was greatly furthered by his work in the blockbuster film *Problem Child* (1990) and its sequel (1992). **Selected Works:** *Noises Off* (1992), *Dreamer of Oz: The L. Frank Baum Story* (1990)

# Tex Ritter (Woodward Maurice Ritter)

**Born:** January 12, 1905; near Murvaul, TX
**Died:** 1974

**Years Active in the Industry:** by decade

| 10s | 20s | 30s | 40s | 50s | 60s | 70s | 80s | 90s |
|-----|-----|-----|-----|-----|-----|-----|-----|-----|

As a college student, Tex Ritter began studying cowboy ballads and southwest folklore, and later dropped out of law school to launch a stage and radio folk-singing career. He debuted on Broadway in 1930; his first screen appearance was in *Song of the Gringo* (1936). Almost immediately, he rivalled Gene Autry in popularity (as a singing cowboy) among movie fans; from 1937-41 and 1944-45 he was on the top-ten Western stars list, and ultimately he appeared in 85 films. He was often referred to as "America's most beloved cowboy." In the latter half of the '40s he stopped making films, instead touring with White Flash, his horse, in live shows; he also continued his successful recording career. He went on to provide the title songs of five Westerns, narrate a sixth, and appear on TV's "Zane Grey Theater." Ritter sang the Academy-award winning, "Do Not Forsake Me, Oh My Darlin'," featured in *High Noon* (1952). He moved to Nashville and became a weekly fixture at the Grand Ole Opry. He also founded a restaurant franchise, "Tex Ritter's Chuck Wagons." In 1966 he had a prominent role in the film *The Girl from Tobacco Row* and was featured in cameos as himself in two others. In 1970 he ran in the Republican primary for U.S. Senator in Tennessee, but lost. He was the only entertainer to be elected to both the Cowboy Hall of Fame and the Country Music Hall of Fame. He was married to actress Dorothy Fay; their son is actor John Ritter.

# Thelma Ritter

**Born:** February 14, 1905; Brooklyn, NY
**Died:** February 5, 1968; Queens, NY

**Years Active in the Industry:** by decade

| 10s | 20s | 30s | 40s | 50s | 60s | 70s | 80s | 90s |
|-----|-----|-----|-----|-----|-----|-----|-----|-----|

At the tender age of eight, Thelma Ritter was regaling the students and faculty of Brooklyn's Public School 77 with her recitals of such monologues as "Mr. Brown Gets His Haircut" and "The Story of Cremona." After appearing in high school plays and stock companies, Ritter was trained at the American Academy of Dramatic Arts. Throughout the Depression years, she and her actor husband Joe Moran did everything short of robbing banks to support themselves; when vaudeville and stage assignments dried up, they entered slogan and jingle contests. Moran forsook performing to become an actor's agent in the mid-1930s, while Ritter also briefly gave up acting to raise a family. She started working professionally again in 1940 as a radio performer. In 1946, director George Seaton, an old friend of Ritter, offered her a bit role in the upcoming New York-lensed *Miracle on 34th Street*. Ritter's single scene as a weary Yuletide shopper went over so well that 20th Century-Fox head Darryl F. Zanuck insisted that the actress' role be expanded. After Ritter garnered good notices for her unbilled *Miracle* role, Joseph L. Mankiewicz wrote a part specifically for her in his 1948 film *A Letter to Three Wives* (1949). She was afforded screen billing for the first time in 1949's *City Across the River*. During the first few years of her 20th Century-Fox contract, Ritter was Oscar-nominated for her performance as Bette Davis' acerbic maid in *All About Eve*, and for her portrayal of upwardly mobile John Lund's just-folks mother in *The Mating Season* (1951). In all, the actress would receive five nominations—the other three were for *With a Song in My Heart* (1952), *Pickup on South Street* (1953) and *Pillow Talk* (1959)—though she never won the gold statuette. Ritter finally received star billing in the comedy/drama *The Model and the Marriage Broker* (1952), in which she assuages her own loneliness by finding suitable mates for others. After a showcase part as James Stewart's nurse in Hitchcock's *Rear Window* (1954), Ritter made do with standard film supporting parts and starring roles on TV. In 1957, Ritter appeared as waterfront barfly Marthy in the Broadway musical *New Girl in Town*, a bowdlerization of Eugene O'Neill's *Anna Christie*. Ritter interrupted her still-thriving screen career in 1965 for another Broadway appearance in James Kirkwood's *UTBU*. Shortly after a 1968 guest appearance on TV's *The Jerry Lewis Show*, Ritter suffered a heart attack which would ultimately prove fatal; the actress' last screen appearance, like her first, was a cameo role in a George Seaton-directed comedy, *What's So Bad About Feeling Good?* (1968). **Selected Works:** *Birdman of Alcatraz* (1962), *Titanic* (1953)

# Ritz Brothers [Al, Jimmy, Harry]

**Years Active in the Industry:** by decade

| 10s | 20s | 30s | 40s | 50s | 60s | 70s | 80s | 90s |
|-----|-----|-----|-----|-----|-----|-----|-----|-----|
|     |     | ■   |     |     |     |     |     |     |

"Subtle they're not. New they're not. But funny." This 1961 newspaper review of the Ritz Brothers succinctly summed up their appeal for their millions of fans—and also was (except for the final sentence) a fair assessment of their *lack* of appeal for their millions of nonfans. The sons of Austrian-born haberdasher Max Joachim, the brothers grew up in New Jersey and Brooklyn, deciding individually to pursue show business careers. Al, the oldest, took the plunge first, winning numerous dance contests and doing extra work for a Long Island movie studio; Jimmy and Harry followed suit, securing solo stage bookings as singer/dancers. After all three Joachim brothers graduated from high school, they decided to team up as a song-and-comedy act, adopting the stage name "Ritz," reportedly having spotted their new cognomen on a laundry truck. With fourth brother George as their agent, the Ritz Brothers worked their way up from nightclubs and vaudeville to several featured spots in the lavish Broadway revues of legendary showman George White. The boys' act, which substantially remained the same throughout the years, consisted of the threesome indulging in precision dancing, tongue-twisting lampoons of popular stories and song hits, and plenty of knockabout comedy. While all three brothers had healthy egos, they had no qualms about building several of their routines around the superior talents of Harry Ritz, as witness their famous bit "The Man in the Middle is the Funny One." In 1934, the Ritz boys made their screen debut in the two-reel comedy *Hotel Anchovy*, which led to their being signed by 20th Century-Fox as a specialty act for that studio's big budget musicals. *Sing Baby Sing* (1936) was the first feature film to costar the Ritzes, and, after several comedy-relief appearances, the brothers were allowed to carry a film all by themselves—1937's *Life Begins in College*. Though they had an intensely loyal fan following, the Ritz Brothers soon wore out their welcome with most moviegoers, and by 1938 Fox had demoted them to B pictures. The brothers clashed with the studio over their treatment, exhibiting some of the most eccentric displays of temperament that Hollywood has ever seen: At one point, Al Ritz refused to do a barefoot hillbilly dance unless the costume department outfitted him with rubber feet. Hostilities ceased temporarily when the Ritzes were cast in their best-ever picture, *The Three Musketeers* (1939), which, despite their foolery and a bunch of forgettable songs, was a surprisingly faithful rendition of the Dumas novel. With lush production values and first-rate Ritz material, *Three Musketeers* should have kept the boys happy at Fox; unfortunately, after two more films of diminishing quality, the studio and the Brothers terminated their association. While the Brothers remained an S.R.O. attraction in nightclubs, the remainder of their movie career was devoted to cheaply assembled musicals at Universal, the last of which, *Never a Dull Moment*, was released in 1943. Throughout the 1940s and 1950s, the Ritz Brothers continued knocking 'em dead on the supper club and resort circuit, scoring additional success as TV guest stars. The Ritzes were appearing at New Orleans' Roosevelt Hotel in December of 1965 when Al Ritz died of a heart attack. Harry and Jimmy kept the act going as best they could after that, though by the end of the 1960s the remaining Ritzes settled for semi-retirement, surfacing occasionally as talk show guests and game show contestants. When comedian-director Mel Brooks, riding the crest of his popularity in the mid 1970s, began telling the world that the Brothers were his idols, Harry and Jimmy briefly returned to the limelight; both Ritzes made guest appearances in *Blazing Stew-*

ardesses (1975) and *Won Ton Ton, The Dog Who Saved Hollywood* (1976), while Harry made a handful of solo TV and movie appearances. Harry and Jimmy retired permanently in the 1980s, proud of the fact that, in spite of loud and abrasive arguments among the brothers and the attempts of studio executives to break up the trio with separate contracts, the Ritz Brothers weathered seven decades as one of show business' most professionally harmonious comedy teams.

# Hal Roach

**Born:** January 14, 1892; Elmira, NY
**Died:** November 2, 1992; Los Angeles, CA

**Years Active in the Industry:** by decade

| 10ˢ | 20ˢ | 30ˢ | 40ˢ | 50ˢ | 60ˢ | 70ˢ | 80ˢ | 90ˢ |
|-----|-----|-----|-----|-----|-----|-----|-----|-----|

American producer/director Hal Roach was overtaken by wanderlust early in life. Leaving his upstate New York home in his teens, Roach was an Alaskan gold prospector and mule skinner before he reached the age of twenty. In 1912, he spotted an ad placed by Hollywood's Universal Pictures offering a dollar a day for genuine cowboys to act as western technical advisers. Roach spent the next year making the rounds as an extra, in the company of his new friend Harold Lloyd. As the result of a small inheritance, Roach bought an office in Los Angeles' Bradbury Mansion in 1914, set up a small film production unit, and hired Lloyd as his star comedian. Roach's initial "Willie Work" one-reelers found no buyers, and, when the funds ran out, Lloyd left briefly for Keystone while Roach signed on as a director with the Chaplin unit at Essanay. Teaming with Dan Lintchicum, Roach re-entered the production end with his new Rolin Phunphilm Company; Lloyd returned to the fold, this time as a Chaplin rip-off character named Lonesome Luke. Throughout 1916 and 1917, Roach released his "Luke" comedies through Pathe; the films were popular not only because of the seemingly bottomless reserve of sight gags, but also because Roach insisted upon emphasizing strong story values as well as slapstick. In 1917, Lloyd dropped his "Luke" makeup in favor of his now-famous "glasses" character. While both Lloyd and Roach would later take credit for hitting upon the innovation of allowing a comedian to play "himself" rather than a heavily made-up buffoon, the important end result was that Lloyd became the most popular comic working in films. To ensure a consistency of product, Roach set up a preview system for the Lloyd comedies, screening them before test audiences and re-editing them for full comic impact before their general release. Roach began adding to his comic roster in 1919, building comedies around such stars as Snub Pollard, Stan Laurel, and black youngster "Sunshine" Sammy Morrison. He also gave a free creative hand to such writers and directors as Charlie Chase, Alf Goulding, and Fred Newmeyer, who controlled the output while Roach concentrated on administrative duties. Chancing to see a couple of kids arguing over a block of wood in

1922, Roach decided that a series of comedies built around the joys and problems of real-life children would clean up at the box office. The result was "Our Gang," one of the longest-lasting short subjects series of all time (1922-44). Writer/director Charlie Chase became Roach's top comedian after Lloyd left in 1924, turning out a successful yearly manifest of sophisticated domestic comedies; many of these were directed by Leo McCarey, who became Roach's supervising director. According to many contemporaries, it was McCarey and not Roach who first fully realized the potential of teaming comedian/gagman/director Stan Laurel with supporting actor Oliver Hardy in late 1926—culminating in the most successful series of two-reelers ever made at the Roach Studio. Unlike other independents, Roach was not intimidated in the least by the coming of sound in 1929. A sweetheart deal with RCA Victor and Western Electric enabled Roach to turn out the most technically proficient talkie shorts on the market, enhanced by the lilting background music scores (another innovation) written by LeRoy Shield and Marvin Hatley. With Laurel and Hardy, Our Gang, and Charlie Chase going full blast in the early 1930s, Roach developed several new series: The Boy Friends, The Taxi Boys, Thelma Todd/ZaSu Pitts and Thelma Todd/Patsy Kelly. Committed to the short subject form, Roach declared that he wanted to make 20-minute films with the production gloss usually associated with feature films. But the diminishing shorts market in the mid 1930s forced Roach to rethink his policy and concentrate on feature films. He'd been making features sporadically since the Harold Lloyd days in 1922. His two most successful productions, Lloyd's *Grandma's Boy* (1922) and Laurel and Hardy's *The Devil's Brother* (1933), were both feature-length, and there was also a brief series of silent multi-reelers starring Rex the Wonder Horse. In 1935, Roach began curtailing his two-reel activity by phasing out the Laurel and Hardy shorts. A year later, Charlie Chase was let go, and, in 1938, the last-ever Roach short subject, Our Gang's *Hide and Shriek,* was issued through MGM. Roach's subsequent feature output included his always popular Laurel and Hardy and the three *Topper* films. In 1938, Roach switched distribution from MGM to United Artists, turning out such feature successes as *There Goes My Heart* (1938), *Captain Fury* (1939), and the pioneering special-effects extravaganza *One Million BC* (1940). As a result of a lawsuit with director Lewis Milestone, Roach agreed to produce Milestone's *Of Mice and Men* (1939), perhaps the studio's best non-comic effort. In 1941, Roach came up with the concept of "Streamliners"—45-minute films especially designed for double bills. While some of these were successful (notably a series of service comedies starring Joe Sawyer and William Tracy), many were on a par with the notorious *The Devil With Hitler* (1943). In the last two years of World War II, Hal Roach received a Colonel's commission and turned his studio over to the government for the purpose of making training films—Ronald Reagan spent most of his military service as an actor at "Fort Roach." In the late 1940s, Roach found it difficult to regain his footing in theatrical films. Undaunted, he switched to turning out TV films; he was the first major Hollywood producer to do so. Among the 1950s series filmed at the Roach lot were *My Little Margie, Amos 'n' Andy, Topper, Racket Squad,* and *The Abbott and Costello Show*. Though seldom making a false career move, Roach was nearly scuttled by an ill-advised association with Benito Mussolini in the 1930s. Two decades later, he made his most injurious error by turning his operation over to Hal Roach Jr., who entered into a partnership with a "businessman" of dubious character—a move which bankrupted the studio. Though his sound stages were demolished in 1963, Hal Roach remained active into the 1980s, overseeing theatrical, TV, and home-movie distribution of his films and participating in the formative years of cable television and computer colorization. Roach received an honorary Oscar at the age of 92; he lived long enough to be honored again at the Academy Awards telecast of 1992—looking at least thirty years younger than his actual age of 100.

# Jason Robards, Jr.

**Born:** July 22, 1992; Chicago, IL

**Years Active in the Industry:** by decade

| 10ˢ | 20ˢ | 30ˢ | 40ˢ | 50ˢ | 60ˢ | 70ˢ | 80ˢ | 90ˢ |
|-----|-----|-----|-----|-----|-----|-----|-----|-----|
|     |     |     |     |     |     |     |     |     |

One of the finest older actors in Hollywood, Robards has a rich deep voice and authoritative aura; he is often called upon to play distinguished citizens. The son of stage and screen actor Jason Robards, Sr., he moved to New York in search of a stage career after serving seven years in the Navy. (He was present at the attack on Pearl Harbor in 1941, and later received the Navy Cross.) He found work in unprestigious plays as well as in radio soap operas and live TV dramas, meanwhile driving a cab and teaching school to support himself. Relegated to obscurity for a decade, in 1956 he rose to prominence in the Circle in the Square production of O'Neill's *The Iceman Cometh.* In 1957 he appeared on Broadway in *Long Day's Journey Into Night,* for which he won a New York Drama Critics Award; after that success he remained a busy and popular Broadway performer. He debuted onscreen in *The Journey* (1959) and maintained a TV and screen career while continuing to work on the stage. During the '60s he tended to appear in two or three movies a year. In 1972 he was in a serious car crash, and upon arriving at the hospital he had no heartbeat. However, he made a complete recovery and was back on Broadway two years later. He won Best Supporting Actor Oscars for his work in *All The President's Men* (1976) and *Julia* (1977), and was nominated for the same award for *Melvin and Howard* (1979), in which he played reclusive billionaire Howard Hughes. Also, between 1960 and 1974 he was nominated for six Tony Awards. In 1978 he directed himself in another production of *A Long Day's Journey Into Night,* which opened Brooklyn's Opera House. He appeared with his father on Broadway in *The Disenchanted* (1958). He was married to actress Lauren Bacall. Always more enthusiastic about the stage than movies, he has referred to films as "piece work" whose main function is to help him pay his alimony; he affects a laid-back disregard about the demands of working in movies. **Selected Works:** *Philadelphia* (1993), *The Paper* (1994), *The Trial* (1994), *Parenthood* (1989)

# Tim Robbins

**Born:** October 16, 1958; West Covina, CA

**Years Active in the Industry:** by decade

| 10ˢ | 20ˢ | 30ˢ | 40ˢ | 50ˢ | 60ˢ | 70ˢ | 80ˢ | 90ˢ |
|-----|-----|-----|-----|-----|-----|-----|-----|-----|
|     |     |     |     |     |     |     | ■ | ■ |

The son of a noted Greenwich Village folksinger, Robbins grew up in New York and began acting while in high school. As a teenager he worked in an off-Broadway theater as a lighting technician, meanwhile acting in street theater around New York. He went on to study theater in college, first in New York and then California. After college he studied with French actor George Bigot of the Theatre Du Soleil. Shortly thereafter, he and a group of friends formed the Actors' Gang, which quickly became one of the top theater companies in Los Angeles; while with the Actors' Gang, he acted, wrote, directed, and helped with the financing. At the same time he got some work in TV movies and had guest spots on the TV series "St. Elsewhere" and "Hill Street Blues." At 26 he debuted onscreen in *Toy Soldiers* (1984); along with lesser appearances, he went on to successful performances in Rob Reiner's *The Sure Thing* (1985) and the huge hit *Top Gun* (1986), which greatly increased his familiarity with the public. His breakthrough role, however, was as dim-witted baseball pitcher Nuke Laloosh in *Bull Durham* (1988); while filming that movie he became romantically involved with costar Susan Sarandon, with whom he has sustained a long-term live-in relationship. He went on to make an enormous impression in the lead role of Robert Altman's dark Hollywood yarn *The Player* (1992), for which he won the Cannes Film Festival Best Actor award. He also directed, wrote, and starred in the impressive *Bob Roberts* (1992), whose numerous parodic songs he co-wrote and performed. **Selected Works:** *Jacob's Ladder* (1990), *Jungle Fever* (1991), *The Hudsucker Proxy* (1994), *The Shawshank Redemption* (1994), *Dead Man Walking* (1995)

# Eric Roberts (Eric Anthony Roberts)

**Born:** April 18, 1956; Biloxi, MS

**Years Active in the Industry:** by decade

| 10ˢ | 20ˢ | 30ˢ | 40ˢ | 50ˢ | 60ˢ | 70ˢ | 80ˢ | 90ˢ |
|-----|-----|-----|-----|-----|-----|-----|-----|-----|
|     |     |     |     |     |     |     | ■ | ■ |

His parents were involved in the founding and running of an actors/writers workshop in Georgia, and Roberts first appeared onstage at the age of five. When he was 17 he moved to London and studied theater at the Royal Academy of Dramatic Arts, then went on to the American Academy of Dramatic Arts. His professional stage debut was in *Rebel Women,* after which he did much stage work, at one point taking over the lead role from John Malkovich in the Broadway play *Burn This.* Roberts also found work on TV. His screen debut was in *King of the Gypsies* (1978), and he has sustained a fairly busy screen career since the early '80s. However, he has had few successful films and remains far from being a star. For his work in *Runaway Train* (1985) he received a Best Supporting Actor Oscar nomination. His sister is actress Julia Roberts. **Selected Works:** *Descending Angel* (1990), *Final Analysis* (1992), *Lost Capone* (1990)

# Julia Roberts

**Born:** October 28, 1967; Atlanta, GA

**Years Active in the Industry:** by decade

| 10s | 20s | 30s | 40s | 50s | 60s | 70s | 80s | 90s |
|-----|-----|-----|-----|-----|-----|-----|-----|-----|
|     |     |     |     |     |     |     |     |     |

Her parents ran theater workshops in Georgia and Atlantic City, and her brother, actor Eric Roberts, appeared in his first film when she was not yet a teenager. After graduating from high school, Roberts moved to New York to pursue an acting career; eventually she got an agent and made the rounds of auditions without much success. In 1986 she appeared in a small role in her brother's film *Blood Red,* but it went unreleased (until 1990, when it no longer mattered to her career). She struck success in 1988, appearing in the film *Satisfaction* and a TV movie before costarring in *Mystic Pizza,* a performance which brought her to the attention of casting directors. Roberts' next film was an ensemble piece with an all-star cast, *Steel Magnolias* (1989), and her stellar screen company greatly enhanced her own career status, while also earning her a Best Supporting Actress Oscar nomination. Her next film, *Pretty Woman* (a Cinderella story in which she played a high-class prostitute who becomes romantically involved with Richard Gere), was the most successful movie of 1990 and made her a superstar; for some time afterwards she was considered "the most powerful woman in Hollywood." After appearing in three 1991 releases she went into near-seclusion for two years before making her next film, *The Pelican Brief* (1993). She was also seen in 1994's *I Love Trouble,* with Nick Nolte, and 1995's *Something to Talk About.* She was engaged to actor Kiefer Sutherland and was married for a short time to alternative country singer Lyle Lovett. **Selected Works:** *Flatliners* (1990), *Hook* (1991), *Mary Reilly* (1995)

# Rachel Roberts

**Born:** September 20, 1927; Llanelly, Wales
**Died:** 1980

**Years Active in the Industry:** by decade

| 10s | 20s | 30s | 40s | 50s | 60s | 70s | 80s | 90s |
|-----|-----|-----|-----|-----|-----|-----|-----|-----|
|     |     |     |     |     |     |     |     |     |

She studied theater at the Royal Academy of Dramatic Arts, then began her professional career in 1951. Roberts focused primarily on the stage, but appeared in about two dozen movies from 1953-80; she was often cast as a blowsy, sensual housewife. For her work in *This Sporting Life* (1963) she received a Best Actress Oscar nomination and won the British Film Academy Best Actress award. She also won British Film Academy awards for her work in *Saturday Night and Sunday Morning* (1960) and *Yanks* (1979). In the mid '70s, Roberts moved to Los Angeles, going on to costar as the housekeeper Mrs. McClellan on the TV sitcom "The Tony Randall Show." From 1955-61 she was married to actor Alan Dobie; from 1962-71 she was married to actor Rex Harrison, with whom she appeared in *A Flea in Her Ear* (1968). She died at 53 from barbiturate poisoning; her death was ruled a suicide. **Selected Works:** *Murder on the Orient Express* (1974), *O Lucky Man* (1973)

# Cliff Robertson (Clifford Parker Robertson III)

**Born:** September 9, 1925; La Jolla, CA

**Years Active in the Industry:** by decade

| 10s | 20s | 30s | 40s | 50s | 60s | 70s | 80s | 90s |
|-----|-----|-----|-----|-----|-----|-----|-----|-----|
|     |     |     |     |     |     |     |     |     |

The scion of a prosperous California ranching family, actor Cliff Robertson took up drama in high school simply because it was the only "legal" way to cut classes. After wartime service, Robertson entered Ohio's Antioch College, beginning his professional career as a radio announcer. His first extensive stage work consisted of two years with the touring company of *Mister Roberts.* He made it to Broadway in 1952 in a play directed by Joshua Logan, and in 1955 made his film debut in the Logan-directed movie version of *Picnic.* As Joan Crawford's schizophrenic boyfriend in *Autumn Leaves* (1955), Robertson achieved the critical acceptance that would enable him to seek out choice film roles. In 1963, Robertson became the first American actor to portray a living American president when he was selected to play John F. Kennedy in *PT 109;* one year later, he showed up as a paranoid Nixon type in *The Best Man.* Equally busy on television, Robertson was universally applauded for his grueling performance as an alcoholic in the 1958 TV staging of *Days of Wine and Roses,* and in 1965 won an Emmy for a guest appearance on the dramatic anthology *Bob Hope Chrysler Theatre.* Having lost the film version of *Wine and Roses* to Jack Lemmon, Robertson made certain that he'd star in the filmization of his 1961 TV drama *The Two Worlds of Charly Gordon* by buying up the story rights. The result was the 1968 film *Charly,* in which Robertson played a retarded adult turned into a genius by a scientific experiment—for which he won an Academy Award. In 1977, Robertson made headlines when he was one of the whistle-blowers in the embezzlement scandal involving Columbia executive David Begelman—a fact that did more harm to Robertson's career than Begelman's. While Robertson has continued to act into the 1990s, to many couch potatoes of the 1960s he will always be remembered for his guest-starring stints on *Batman* as the cowardly outlaw "Shame;" costarring in these *Batman* episodes was Robertson's wife, actress Dina Merrill. **Selected Works:** *Three Days of the Condor* (1975), *Wild Hearts Can't Be Broken* (1991), *Wind* (1992)

# Paul Robeson

**Born:** April 9, 1898; Princeton, NJ
**Died:** 1976

### Years Active in the Industry: by decade

| 10ˢ | 20ˢ | 30ˢ | 40ˢ | 50ˢ | 60ˢ | 70ˢ | 80ˢ | 90ˢ |
|-----|-----|-----|-----|-----|-----|-----|-----|-----|

His father was a Presbyterian minister who had escaped from slavery in his youth; his mother was a schoolteacher. An outstanding athlete, Robeson attended Rutgers on a scholarship and lettered in baseball, basketball, track, and football; later he played pro football while attending law school. Meanwhile, he performed in an amateur stage production at the Harlem YMCA. His acting was very successful and well received; playwright Eugene O'Neill requested that he star in his plays *All God's Chillun Got Wings* and *The Emperor Jones.* Thus he gave up law for the theater, and soon gained much critical praise. Robeson began singing in recitals and appearing in films, soon becoming known as one of the most talented performers of his generation; his fame spread to Europe, where he frequently performed onstage and in concerts. He became especially identified with the song "Ole Man River," made famous by his vibrant baritone rendition. In 1934 he visited the Soviet Union, returning several times in subsequent years. Seeking remedies to American civil rights abuses and racism, he became an exponent of leftist politics. In the early '40s he performed on Broadway and in a national tour in *Othello.* Robeson quit making movies after appearing in *Tales of Manhattan* (1942), in which ridiculous portrayal of rural blacks made him disgusted with Hollywood stereotypes; he denounced the film and never acted onscreen again. He became increasingly controversial for his political views. In 1946 he denied under oath that he had been a member of the Communist party, but refused to repeat his denial in a later inquiry. In 1950 his passport was revoked by the State Department. In 1952 he was awarded the Stalin Peace Prize, but not until 1958 was he permitted to leave the country to receive it. Although publicity about his political views led to a great reduction in his income, he continued touring Europe until the early '60s, when illness obliged him to return to the U.S. He was the subject of a documentary, *Paul Robeson: Portrait of an Artist* (1979). **Selected Works:** *Show Boat* (1936)

# Edward G. Robinson (Emmanuel
Goldenberg)

**Born:** December 12, 1893; Bucharest, Romania
**Died:** 1973

### Years Active in the Industry: by decade

| 10ˢ | 20ˢ | 30ˢ | 40ˢ | 50ˢ | 60ˢ | 70ˢ | 80ˢ | 90ˢ |
|-----|-----|-----|-----|-----|-----|-----|-----|-----|

Robinson was a stocky, forceful, zesty star of Hollywood films who is best known for his roles as gangsters in the '30s. A "little giant" of the screen with a pug-dog face, drawling nasal voice, and a snarling expression, he is considered the quintessential tough-guy actor. He emigrated with his family to the U.S. when he was ten. After planning to be a rabbi or a lawyer, he decided on an acting career while a student at City College, where he was elected to the Elizabethan Society. Robinson attended the American Academy of Dramatic Arts on a scholarship, then in 1913 began appearing in summer stock after changing his name to Edward G. (for Goldenberg) Robinson. In 1915 he debuted on Broadway, becoming a noted stage character actor over the next fifteen years; he co-wrote one of the plays he appeared in, *The Kibitzer* (1929). He appeared in one silent film, *The Bright Shawl* (1923), but not until the sound era did he begin working regularly in films, the first being *The Hole in the Wall* (1929) with Claudette Colbert. It was his eighth sound film, *Little Caesar* (1931), that brought him to the attention of American audiences; portraying gangster boss Rico Bandello, he established a prototype for a number of gangster roles he performed in the following years. After being typecast as a gangster he gradually expanded the scope of his roles, and in the '40s gave memorable performances as "good guys" in a number of psychological dramas; he has played federal agents, scientists, Biblical characters, business men, bank clerks, and other roles. During the '50s he experienced a number of personal problems. He was falsely linked to Communist organizations and called before the House Un-American Activities Commission, eventually being cleared of all suspicion. Having owned one of the world's largest private art collections, he was forced to sell it in 1956 as part of his divorce settlement with his wife of 29 years, actress Gladys Lloyd. His only son frequently got into trouble with the law and attempted suicide several times. However, Robinson continued his career, which now included work on TV. He remained a busy actor until shortly before his death from cancer in 1973; his final film was *Soylent Green* (1973). Two months after his death he was given an honorary Oscar "for his outstanding contribution to motion pictures," having been notified of the honor before he died. He was the author of a posthumously published autobiography, *All My Yesterdays* (1973). **Selected Works:** *Double Indemnity* (1944), *Key Largo* (1948), *Sea Wolf* (1941)

# Mark Robson

**Born:** December 4, 1913; Montreal, Canada
**Died:** 1978

**Years Active in the Industry:** by decade

| 10s | 20s | 30s | 40s | 50s | 60s | 70s | 80s | 90s |
|-----|-----|-----|-----|-----|-----|-----|-----|-----|

Canadian-born Mark Robson began his career in the movie industry in the prop department at 20th Century-Fox, and subsequently joined RKO, where he moved through various departments before settling into editing. He worked with Robert Wise on the editing of Orson Welles' *Citizen Kane,* and then, with Wise, was swept up in the turmoil surrounding Welles' ouster from the studio, and landed a spot as an editor working for Val Lewton's B-movie unit at RKO. Robson (later joined by Wise) succeeded Jacques Tourneur as Lewton's director for his low budget horror movies—today regarded as some of the finest pictures ever made by the studio—including *The Ghost Ship* and *The Seventh Victim.* RKO's instability finally led to Robson's exit in 1948. He was fortunate to find a berth with independent producer Stanley Kramer, who was about to embark on an ambitious program of film production—among the movies that Robson got to direct were *Champion* (1949), one of the most celebrated boxing movies of its era, and *Home of the Brave* (1949). Robson also went to work for Samuel Goldwyn and directed the underrated, seldom seen dark drama *Edge of Doom* (1950) and the Korean War drama *I Want You* (1951). He reached his commercial peak soon after, with films such as *The Bridges At Toko-Ri* (1955); *The Harder They Fall* (1956), (Humphrey Bogart's final film); and *Peyton Place* (1957), which moved Robson into big-budget, high-profile movies. *The Prize* (1963), *Von Ryan's Express* (1965), and *Valley of the Dolls* (1967) were among his most successful films of the 1960s. He seemed to lose his commercial touch after that, although he made a brief comeback—at least to box office success—in the 1970s in a production partnership with Robert Wise, with the movie *Earthquake* (1974), a critical and artistic disaster that cleaned up at the box office. **Selected Works:** *The Inn of the Sixth Happiness* (1958), *Trial* (1993)

# Nicolas Roeg

**Born:** August 15, 1928; London, England

**Years Active in the Industry:** by decade

| 10s | 20s | 30s | 40s | 50s | 60s | 70s | 80s | 90s |
|-----|-----|-----|-----|-----|-----|-----|-----|-----|

London-born Nicolas Roeg served in the military as a projectionist, and joined the movie industry immediately after World War II as a gofer and apprentice editor. He joined MGM's British studios in 1950, and eventually moved up to become a cinematographer in 1959, working on a multitude of movies of all types, from second unit work on *Lawrence of Arabia* (1962) to primary photography on the rock 'n' roll exploitation films *Just For Fun* (1963), *Everyday's A Holiday* (1964), and *The System* (1966). He moved into the director's chair on *Performance* (1970), which he co-directed, and made a major impression with the low-keyed, eerily compelling drama *Walkabout* (1971). By the mid 1970s, Roeg was one of England's most rspected directors, responsible for the unsettling thriller *Don't Look Now* (1972), and the science-fiction drama *The Man Who Fell To Earth* (1973). His most popular film to date, however, is probably *The Witches* (1990). **Selected Works:** *Company Business* (1991), *Without You I'm Nothing* (1990)

# Ginger Rogers (Virginia Katherine McMath)

**Born:** July 16, 1911; Independence, MO
**Died:** April 25, 1995

**Years Active in the Industry:** by decade

| 10s | 20s | 30s | 40s | 50s | 60s | 70s | 80s | 90s |
|-----|-----|-----|-----|-----|-----|-----|-----|-----|

This daughter of a divorced "stage mother" was groomed for a show business career, taking dancing and singing lessons from early youth. At five, Rogers appeared in a few regional commercials, and a year later she went to Hollywood with her mother, who became a screenwriter for Fox; later they moved to New York. Although she was offered a film contract to become a child actress, her mother decided she wasn't ready for a career. At 14 she first performed professionally, filling in for a week as a dancer in Eddie Foy's vaudeville show. After winning a Charleston contest at 15 she began singing and dancing on the vaudeville circuit; from 1928-31 she was married to Jack Pepper, and for a year she appeared in a dual act with him before going back to soloing, now with the Eddie Lowry band in Chicago and the Paul Ash orchestra in New York. In the late '20s Rogers also appeared in a number of short films. Her big break came in 1929, when she landed the second female lead in the Broadway musical *Top Speed,* from which she went on to the musical *Girl Crazy.* Meanwhile, she began her film career, playing leads and second leads in minor films shot on the East Coast. She moved to Hollywood in 1931 and became a busy screen actress, often playing wisecracking blondes. In the mid '30s she was assigned to be Fred Astaire's dancing partner and female lead, and she became extremely popular in the series of films she made with him. She also showed great versatility as a straight actress; for her work in *Kitty Foyle* (1940) she won a Best Actress Oscar. In 1945 she was the highest-paid performer in Hollywood and had the eighth highest individual income in the U.S. In the '50s she continued making a film a year (until 1957), but began devoting much more of her time to stage work. She had a successful Broadway comeback in 1965, when she starred in the musical *Hello Dolly!* In 1969 she starred in the London production of *Mame.* Her husbands included actors Lew Ayres, Jacques Bergerac, and William Marshall. Rogers authored an autobiography, *Ginger: My Story* (1991), in which she said she'd had romances with George Gershwin, Cary Grant, Jimmy Stewart, Rudy Vallee, Mervyn LeRoy, and Howard Hughes. **Selected Works:** *42nd Street* (1933), *Gay Divorcee* (1934), *Gold Diggers of 1933* (1933), *Stage Door* (1937), *Top Hat* (1935)

## Mimi Rogers

**Born:** January 27, 1956; Coral Gables, FL

**Years Active in the Industry:** by decade

| 10$^s$ | 20$^s$ | 30$^s$ | 40$^s$ | 50$^s$ | 60$^s$ | 70$^s$ | 80$^s$ | 90$^s$ |
|---|---|---|---|---|---|---|---|---|

Mimi Rogers spent her youth moving around with her family to various parts of the U.S. and England; she settled in Los Angeles. Graduating from high school at age 14, she became involved with community work and working with drug addicts, Vietnam vets, and the mentally retarded. She didn't begin acting until her early 20s. Rogers debuted onscreen in *Blue Skies Again* (1983) as the manager of a girl who wants to join a baseball team. She didn't make another film for three years, meanwhile working extensively on TV; she had regular roles on the TV series "Paper Dolls" and "The Rousers," made guest appearances on a number of shows, and appeared in a few TV movies. She began making her reputation as a screen actress with her portrayal of a Manhattan heiress in Ridley Scott's *Someone to Watch Over Me* (1987), her fourth film. Most of her films have been unsuccessful, and she has yet to attain star status. For three years she was married to actor Tom Cruise. **Selected Works:** *The Doors* (1991), *Fourth Story* (1990), *The Rapture* (1991)

## Roy Rogers (Leonard Slye)

**Born:** November 5, 1911; Cincinnati, OH

**Years Active in the Industry:** by decade

| 10$^s$ | 20$^s$ | 30$^s$ | 40$^s$ | 50$^s$ | 60$^s$ | 70$^s$ | 80$^s$ | 90$^s$ |
|---|---|---|---|---|---|---|---|---|

Rogers moved to California as a migratory fruit picker in 1929. He formed a singing duo with a cousin, later changing his name to Dick Weston and forming a singing group, the Sons of the Pioneers; the group became successful, and appeared on Los Angeles radio and later in films. In 1935 he began appearing in bit roles in Westerns onscreen; by the early '40s Rogers had succeeded Gene Autry as "King of the Cowboys." His success was aided by the fact that Autry went to war and Rogers didn't; he also copied Autry's singing cowboy formula and wore clothes that went one better than Autry's ostentatiously fancy duds. Through the early '50s he starred in dozens of Westerns, often accompanied by his horse, Trigger (billed "the smartest horse in the movies"), and his sidekick, Gabby Hayes; his female lead was often Dale Evans, whom he married in 1947. From 1951-57 he starred in the TV series "The Roy Rogers Show." Meanwhile, he formed a chain of enterprises in the '50s; eventually this combination (a TV production company, Western products distributor/manufacturers, real estate interests, cattle, thoroughbred horses, rodeo shows, and a restaurant chain) was worth over $100 million.

## Will Rogers

**Born:** November 4, 1879; Cologah, OK
**Died:** 1935

**Years Active in the Industry:** by decade

| 10$^s$ | 20$^s$ | 30$^s$ | 40$^s$ | 50$^s$ | 60$^s$ | 70$^s$ | 80$^s$ | 90$^s$ |
|---|---|---|---|---|---|---|---|---|

As a boy, Rogers became an expert rider and rope-twirler; he first performed in a Johannesburg Wild West Show during the Boer War. In the U.S. he worked in fairs and vaudeville, gradually developing an act that included humor. He began appearing in musical comedy in 1912; five years later he starred with the Ziegfeld Follies. Beginning in 1918 Rogers appeared in many feature and short films, but his appeal in the silent medium was limited; when he tried to produce and direct his own films, he lost a good deal of his own money. However, once the sound era began, he quickly became one of the nation's most popular performers—his folksy wit and down-home philosophy making him an ambassador of rural America and spokesman for the common folk. Rogers also worked on radio and wrote newspaper columns. He turned down an offer to run for Governor of Oklahoma, but served as Mayor of Beverly Hills and campaigned actively (via his very influential columns) for Franklin D. Roosevelt in 1932. He died in an airplane crash with aviator Wiley Post in 1935. He was portrayed in three films by his lookalike son, Will Rogers Jr.—one was the biopic *The Will Rogers Story* (1952). He was also the central subject of the Broadway musical *The Will Rogers Follies*, in which he was portrayed by Keith Carradine and Mac Davis. **Selected Works:** *State Fair* (1933)

## Eric Rohmer

**Born:** April 4, 1920; Nancy, France

**Years Active in the Industry:** by decade

| 10$^s$ | 20$^s$ | 30$^s$ | 40$^s$ | 50$^s$ | 60$^s$ | 70$^s$ | 80$^s$ | 90$^s$ |
|---|---|---|---|---|---|---|---|---|

Long before he ever saw the inside of a movie studio, French filmmaker Eric Rohmer taught literature in high school; in 1946, he put his literary expertise to practical use by authoring the novel *Elizabeth*. Moving into film criticism in 1950, Rohmer was co-founder of *La Gazette Du Cinema*, and in 1957 became editor in chief of the highly influential *Cahiers du Cinema*. That same year, he and fellow critic Claude Chabrol wrote *Hitchcock*, one of the earliest and best of the many career studies of "The Master." Having previously directed a few independent short subjects, Rohmer became a fulltime filmmaker in 1959 with the feature-length *Le Signe du Lion* (1959). He then directed many educational and commercial films for French television before revitalizing his feature career in 1963. Chabrol's first important body of work was his "Six Moral Tales," a sextet of films offering variations on the basic theme of making difficult moral decisions: *La Boulangerie de Monceau* (1963), *La Carriere de Suzanne* (1963), *My Night at Maud's* (1967, released 1969), *La Collectioneuse* (1967), *La Genoue de Claire* (*Claire's Knee*) (1970) and *L'Amour l'apres-midi* (*Chloe in the Afternoon*) (1973). A second cycle of Rohmer-directed films, "Comedies et Proverbes" (*Parables*), was launched with 1980's *La Femme de l'aviateur*, unlike the somewhat cloistered "Moral Tales," which seldom concentrated on more than two or three main characters, *Parables* dealt with entire social groups. Rohmer's third series, "Tales of the Four Seasons," was inaugurated with 1990's *Comte de Printemps*; within its self-imposed seasonal limits, this cycle expanded upon notions previously explored in the "Moral Tales." Though Rohmer is an intensely private person, preferring to let his work speak for him (his scripts are *extremely* verbose), he has occasionally come out of his shell to accept his many film awards: the Max Ophuls award for *My Night at Maud's*, the Louis Dellac and Melies awards for *Claire's Knee*, the Cannes Festival Special Jury Prize for *Marquise of O* (1976), and the Berlin Festival's Silver Bear award for *Pauline at the Beach* (1983). **Selected Works:** *Summer* (1990), *Tale of Springtime* (1991), *The Tale of Winter* (1994)

# Owen Roizman

**Born:** September 22, 1936; Brooklyn, NY

**Years Active in the Industry:** by decade

| 10s | 20s | 30s | 40s | 50s | 60s | 70s | 80s | 90s |
|-----|-----|-----|-----|-----|-----|-----|-----|-----|
|     |     |     |     |     |     |     |     |     |

The patriarchal system which once ruled the American Society of Cinematographers, dictating that practically the only way to join the union was to be born into it, was not an altogether bad thing whenever it resulted in an Owen Roizman. The son of a newsreel cameraman, Roizman spent the 1960s working on TV commercials, then made as auspicious a feature-film debut as has ever been witnessed. It was Roizman who lensed the street-smart, thrill-a-minute *The French Connection* (1971), earning an Oscar in the process. The contributions made by Roizman for *French Connection* could fill a cinematography textbook in itself: using a handheld Ariflex for the New York street scenes (tracking shots were ac-

complished not with a heavy dolly but with a lightweight wheelchair), rigging actual interiors to look as though they were being illuminated by "natural light," underexposing certain dramatic scenes to give them a harsh, grey look, and so on. Roizman replicated many of his *French Connection* effects, notably the famous Brooklyn car chase, in the runaway-subway meller *The Taking of Pelham One Two Three* (1973). More sedate but no less effective was Roizman's work on comedies (*Play It Again, Sam*, *The Heartbreak Kid*), Westerns (*Return of a Man Called Horse*), satires (*Network*) and musicals (*Sgt. Pepper's Lonely Hearts Club Band*). In recent collaboration with production designer Ken Adam, Roizman faithfully rendered the gloomy hilarity of Charles Addams' *New Yorker* cartoons in 1991's *The Addams Family* (1991)—one of several "comeback" features for Roizman, who'd taken a sabbatical from filmmaking in the 1980s to operate his own TV-ad production firm. **Selected Works:** *The Exorcist* (1973), *Grand Canyon* (1991), *Tootsie* (1982)

# Cesar Romero

**Born:** February 15, 1907; New York, NY
**Died:** January 1, 1994; Beverly Hills, CA

**Years Active in the Industry:** by decade

| 10s | 20s | 30s | 40s | 50s | 60s | 70s | 80s | 90s |
|-----|-----|-----|-----|-----|-----|-----|-----|-----|
|     |     |     |     |     |     |     |     |     |

Born in New York City to parents of Cuban extraction, American actor Cesar Romero studied for his craft at Collegiate and Riverdale Country schools. After a brief career as a ballroom dancer, the tall, sleekly handsome Romero made his Broadway debut in the 1927 production *Lady Do*. He received several Hollywood offers after his appearance in the Preston Sturges play *Strictly Dishonorable*, but didn't step before the cameras until 1933 for his first film *The Shadow Laughs* (later biographies would claim that Romero's movie bow was in *The Thin Man* [1934], in which he was typecast as a callow gigolo). Long associated with 20th Century-Fox, Romero occasionally cashed in on his heritage to play Latin Lover types, but was more at home with characters of indeterminate nationalities, usually playing breezily comic second leads (whenever Romero received third billing, chances were he wasn't going to get the girl). Cheerfully plunging into the Hollywood social scene, Romero became one of the community's most eligible bachelors; while linked romantically with many top female stars, he chose never to marry, insisting to his dying day that he had no regrets over his confirmed bachelorhood. While he played a variety of film roles, Romero is best remembered as "The Cisco Kid" in a brief series of Fox programmers filmed between 1939 and 1940, though in truth his was a surprisingly humorless, sullen Cisco, with little of the rogueish charm that Duncan Renaldo brought to the role on television. The actor's favorite movie role, and indeed one of his best performances, was as Cortez in the 1947 20th Century-Fox spectacular *The Captain From Castile*. When his Fox contract ended in 1950, Romero was wealthy enough to retire, but the acting bug had never left his system; he continued to star throughout the 1950s in cheap B pictures, always giving his best no matter how seedy his surroundings. In 1953 Romero starred in a 39-week TV espionage series "Passport to Danger," which he cheerfully admitted to taking on because of a fat profits-percentage deal. TV fans of the 1960s most closely associate Romero with the role of the white-faced "Joker" on the "Batman" series. While Romero was willing to shed his inhibitions in this villainous characterization, he refused to shave his trademark moustache, compelling the makeup folks to slap the clown white over the 'stache as well (you can still see the outline in the close-ups). As elegant and affluent-looking as ever, Romero signed on for the recurring role of Peter Stavros in the late-1980s nighttime soap opera "Falcon Crest." In the early 1990s, he showed up as host of a series of classic 1940s romantic films on cable's American Movie Classics. Romero died of a blood clot on New Year's Day, 1994, at the age of 86.

# George Romero (George Andrew Romero)

**Born:** February 4, 1940; Bronx, NY

**Years Active in the Industry:** by decade

| 10s | 20s | 30s | 40s | 50s | 60s | 70s | 80s | 90s |
|-----|-----|-----|-----|-----|-----|-----|-----|-----|

American director George A. Romero was making films from the age of 14—with an 8mm camera, like most teen movie enthusiasts. Matriculating into the industrial-film business in Philadelphia, Romero accrued enough capital to make his first feature-length film, a graphically gruesome zombie picture titled *Night of the Living Dead* (1968). Barely making back its cost on its first release, *Night* received some welcome, if adverse, publicity when *Reader's Digest* devoted an article to the film. The magazine was appalled at the scenes of cannibalism and similar horrors, going so far as to insist that a movement be started to have the picture banned! Naturally, this made *Night of the Living Dead* more popular than ever, much more so than if *Reader's Digest* had simply ignored it. The profits of *Living Dead* enabled Romero to finance several more low-budget scare pictures before he broke into the "mainstream" with *Dawn of the Dead*, a semi-comic sequel to his first film. *Day of the Dead* (1985), the third of the "Dead" trilogy, was more elaborate than his earlier films, but also more disappointing. Still, Romero could point with pride to such productions as *Martin* (1978), *Creepshow* (1980) and his weekly TV terror anthology "Tales From the Darkside" (1984-86) which belied its tiny budget with excellent scripting, first rate actors (Barnard Hughes, Fritz Weaver, Jerry Stiller, Eddie Bracken, et al.) and bone-chilling makeup effects. Though remaining in the realm of B pictures by choice, Romero has exerted considerable influence on a whole school of higher-budget horror directors, notably John Carpenter, Wes Craven, and especially Brian De Palma. **Selected Works:** *Dark Half* (1991), *Silence of the Lambs* (1991), *Two Evil Eyes* (1990)

# Michael Rooker

**Born:** 1956; Jasper, AL

**Years Active in the Industry:** by decade

| 10s | 20s | 30s | 40s | 50s | 60s | 70s | 80s | 90s |
|-----|-----|-----|-----|-----|-----|-----|-----|-----|

Raised in Chicago by his divorced mother, Michael Rooker lived a hand-to-mouth, welfare check-to-welfare check existence until his teens. Rooker successfully auditioned for the Goodman School, and upon graduation appeared in Chicago-area stage productions. He made a spectacular film debut in the sociopathic title role of *Henry: Portrait of a Serial Killer*, filmed in 1986 but not given a general release until four years later. *Henry* established Rooker as a gifted purveyor of "don't screw with *me*" roles, such as chief "Black Sox" conspirator Chick Gandil in *Eight Men Out* (1988). Michael Rooker's more rugged film assignments of the 1990s include *Cliffhanger* (1993) and *Tombstone* (1994). **Selected Works:** *JFK* (1991), *Mississippi Burning* (1988), *Sea of Love* (1989)

# Mickey Rooney (Joe Yule, Jr.)

**Born:** September 23, 1920; Brooklyn, NY

**Years Active in the Industry:** by decade

| 10s | 20s | 30s | 40s | 50s | 60s | 70s | 80s | 90s |
|-----|-----|-----|-----|-----|-----|-----|-----|-----|

Rooney, a short, energetic, versatile American screen actor was a former juvenile star in the late '20s and early '30s. His parents were vaudevillians who first incorporated him into their act when he was 15 months old. Within a few years he was on stage singing, dancing, mimicking, and telling jokes, becoming an important part of the family act. He debuted on-screen at age six in the silent short *Not to Be Trusted* (1926), playing a cigar-smoking midget. His next film was the feature-length *Orchids and Ermine* (1927). Over the next six years he starred in over 50 two-reel comedies as "Mickey McGuire," a name he legally adopted; the series was based on a popular comic strip, "Toonerville Folks." In 1932 he changed his name to "Mickey Rooney" when he began to appear in small roles in feature films. He was signed by MGM in 1934 and gave one of the most memorable juvenile performances in film history by portraying Puck in *A Midsummer Night's Dream* (1935). A turning point in his career came with his appearance as Andy Hardy, the wise-cracking son of a small-town judge, in the B movie *A Family Affair* (1937). The movie proved to be such a success that it led to a string of 15 more "Andy Hardy" pictures over the next twenty years, and the character became the one with which Rooney is most identified; the films were sentimental light comedies that celebrated small-town domestic contentment and the simple pleasures. Rooney went on to a memorable performance in *Boys Town* (1938) and to several high-energy musicals with Judy Garland. Added to his Andy Hardy work, these performances caused his popularity to skyrocket, and by 1939 he was America's biggest box-office attraction. He was awarded a special Oscar (along with Deanna Durbin) in 1938 for "significant contribution in bringing to the screen the spirit and personification of youth, and as a juvenile player setting a high standard of ability and achievement." His popularity peaked in the early '40s with his appearances in such films as *The Human Comedy* (1943) and *National Velvet* (1944), the latter with a young Elizabeth Taylor. However, he was called to serve in World War II, and, after his discharge, his drawing power as a star decreased drastically, never to be recovered; he was only acceptable as a juvenile, not a man. In the late '40s he formed his own production company, but it was a financial disaster and he went broke. To pay off his debts he was obliged to take a number of low-quality roles. By the mid 1950s, though, he had begun a new stage as an adult character actor, starring in a number of good films including *Baby Face Nelson* (1957), in which he had the title role. He filed for bankruptcy in 1962; none of his $12 million career earnings was left. He continued to perform into the '90s, appearing on stage, screen, TV, and in nightclubs. He debuted on Broadway in *Sugar Babies* in 1979. During the course of his career he received two Best Actor Oscar nominations and two Best Supporting Actor Oscar nominations, the last of which was for his work in 1979's *The Black Stallion*. He also won an Emmy for the TV movie *Bill*. In the early '80s he underwent a well-publicized conversion to "Born Again" Christianity. In 1983 he was awarded a special Lifetime Achievement Oscar "in recognition of his 60 years of versatility in a variety of memorable film performances." He is the author of an autobiography, *i.e.* (1965). His eight wives included actresses Ava Gardner and Martha Vickers. **Selected Works:** *Breakfast at Tiffany's* (1961), *Bridges at Toko-Ri* (1955), *Bold and the Brave* (1956)

# Roseanne

**Born:** Salt Lake City, UT

### Years Active in the Industry: by decade

| 10s | 20s | 30s | 40s | 50s | 60s | 70s | 80s | 90s |
|-----|-----|-----|-----|-----|-----|-----|-----|-----|
|     |     |     |     |     |     |     | ■   | ■   |

Born Jewish in predominantly Mormon Salt Lake City, young Roseanne Barr—aka Roseanne Arnold, aka Roseanne—was never quite certain where she stood spiritually. Her father, a Mormon convert, sold crucifixes door to door, while her mother vacillated between Judaism and Mormonism on what seemed to be an hourly ba-

sis. Though many of her relatives refute the charge, Roseanne insists she was sexually abused as a child, a memory which she suppressed until adulthood. She also claims to have suffered from multiple-personality syndrome, though again her relatives have challenged this statement. Other experiences from Roseanne's formative years are more easily verifiable. Nearly killed in an auto accident at age 16, she vowed to be more aggressive in demanding what she wanted out of life—which resulted in her mother having Roseanne committed to a mental institution. At age 18, Roseanne had an out-of-wedlock baby, and was forced by her family to give the child up for adoption. Finally breaking free of her family's oppressive influence, Roseanne joined a hippielike commune in Colorado, then married hotel desk clerk Bill Pentland. After enduring three poverty-stricken years as a wife and mother, Roseanne went on the road with a comedy act based on her life experiences. The path to success was pock-marked with fleapit nightclubs and hostile audiences, but she stuck it out, finally grabbing the brass ring as a guest on Johnny Carson's *Tonight Show* in 1985. This appearance led to a five-month stint as the opening act for singer Julio Inglesias, an HBO special, and ultimately her own top-rated sitcom, *Roseanne*, which began its marathon run in the fall of 1988. Widely praised for its fundamental realism, *Roseanne* has won several Emmies—though the actress herself was, for various reasons, frozen out of the awards ceremony for several years. Evidently operating on the theory that any publicity is good publicity, Roseanne has sometimes comported herself like a trailer-park hausfrau who's just won the lottery. She has made loud, obscene public complaints about everything that peeves her, from her *Roseanne* production staff to the fact that a network news broadcast had inadvertently mispelled her name. She once accused a mildly remonstrative TV critic of being a homosexual—this after Roseanne had earned the praise of gay activist groups for including openly lesbian characters on her series. At a San Diego Padres game in 1990, she climaxed a screeching rendition of "The Star Spangled Banner" by grabbing her crotch and spitting, then walked off the field amidst a chorus of boos. And, in concert with second husband Tom Arnold, she has committed such social outrages as affixing obscene messages to the cars of the *Seinfeld* cast in the Paramount parking lot. No matter how questionable her off-screen behavior, Roseanne's TV popularity has remained unabated, though she has thus far been unable to carry over this success into a movie career; nor was she able to turn husband Tom Arnold into a sitcom star on his own. On the plus side, she has set several new standards for the sitcom genre, and has helped open career doors for a multitude of "working class" comediennes, notably Brett Butler, Ellen Degeneres and Margaret Cho. Those who believed that Roseanne would mellow after undergoing plastic surgery, dumping husband Tom Arnold, remarrying, and carrying her fourth child, were nonplussed to discover in 1995 that she was at it again in the pages of *The New Yorker* magazine, suggesting (among other things) that more wives should murder their husbands.

# Diana Ross (Diane Ross)

**Born:** March 26, 1944; Detroit, MI

**Years Active in the Industry:** by decade

| 10s | 20s | 30s | 40s | 50s | 60s | 70s | 80s | 90s |
|---|---|---|---|---|---|---|---|---|
|  |  |  |  |  | ■ | ■ | ■ | ■ |

Having sung in church as a girl, Ross formed the singing group the Supremes as a teenager with childhood friends Mary Wilson and Florence Ballard. After a string of hits in the '60s, she left the trio and became a solo singer; she also began looking for film work. She was chosen to play singer Billie Holiday in the biopic *Lady Sings the Blues* (1972) opposite Billy Dee Williams. Despite industry predictions that she wouldn't be up to the role, she gave a stunning performance and received a Best Actress Oscar nomination. However, her second film, *Mahagony* (1975), also featuring Williams, was a bomb. Ross went on to appear in *The Wiz* (1978), in which she played Dorothy in an all-black version of *The Wizard of Oz*. She starred in the TV movie *Out of Darkness* (1994).

# Herbert Ross

**Born:** May 13, 1927; New York, NY
**Died:** 1934

**Years Active in the Industry:** by decade

| 10s | 20s | 30s | 40s | 50s | 60s | 70s | 80s | 90s |
|---|---|---|---|---|---|---|---|---|
|  |  |  |  |  | ■ | ■ | ■ | ■ |

American director/choreographer Herbert Ross divided his time between Broadway and the American Ballet Theatre in the 1950s and 1960s. Ross also choreographed numerous live television programs, and handled the dance sequences of such films as *Carmen Jones* (1954), *Inside Daisy Clover* (1963) and *Dr. Doolittle* (1967). His first screen directorial job was *Goodbye Mr. Chips,* an overblown 1969 remake of a well-regarded 1939 MGM feature. Ross' subsequent cinema reputation rested on his ability to transfer popular stage plays to the screen, as witness *The Owl and The Pussycat* (1970), *The Sunshine Boys* (1975) and *California Suite* (1978). While he was expert in cinematizing the plays of Neil Simon, Ross was critcally lambasted for his conformist approach to Woody Allen's *Play it Again Sam* (1972), though this film was one of Allen's biggest moneymakers. Ross also directed a brace of Neil Simon screenplays, *The Goodbye Girl* (1977) (which won an Oscar for star Richard Dreyfuss) and *Max Dugan Returns* (1982). Considered by some detractors to be merely a conduit for the works of more talented writers, Ross countered his critics with such remarkable personal-expression pieces as *The Turning Point* (1978), a story of the ballet world which became an unexpected box-office smash, and *Pennies From Heaven* (1981), a courageous if not wholly successful juxtaposition of wish-dream fantasy and tragic reality. Ross has worked with everyone from Raquel Welch to Barbra Streisand, so he is unimpressed by the excesses of "star mystique." He was roundly criticized by the costars of *Steel Magnolias* (1989) for his rough treatment of then-supporting actress Julia Roberts, but the fact is that Roberts gave a far better performance for Ross than she would for many of her pre-approved directors once she achieved superstardom. In private life, Ross has had two high-pro-

file marriages—his first wife was ballet dancer Nora Kaye, who produced many of her husband's films until her death in 1987 and his second wife was Lee Radziwill, the sister of Jackie Kennedy. **Selected Works:** *My Blue Heaven* (1990), *Soapdish* (1991), *True Colors* (1991), *Undercover Blues* (1993), *Boys on the Side* (1995)

# Katharine Ross

**Born:** January 29, 1942; Los Angeles, CA

**Years Active in the Industry:** by decade

| 10s | 20s | 30s | 40s | 50s | 60s | 70s | 80s | 90s |
|---|---|---|---|---|---|---|---|---|
|  |  |  |  |  | ■ | ■ | ■ | ■ |

Actress Katharine Ross was trained at the San Francisco Workshop, barely completing her apprenticeship before landing leading roles on television. She made her TV debut as a spoiled teenager implicated in a fatal auto accident in "Are There Any More Out There Like You?", a 1963 installment of the NBC anthology "Kraft Suspense Theatre." Ross was Oscar nominated for her second film role as Dustin Hoffman's *amour* in *The Graduate* (1967). After successfully teaming with Paul Newman and Robert Redford in *Butch Cassidy and the Sundance Kid,* she became mired in a series of steadily worsening films. She staged a comeback as Francesca in the 1985 nighttime TV serial "The Colbys." At that time, Ross was married to her fifth husband, actor Sam Elliot. Together, Ross and Elliot scripted and starred in an above-average western TV movie, *Conagher* (1991).

# Isabella Rossellini

**Born:** June 18, 1952; Rome, Italy

**Years Active in the Industry:** by decade

| 10s | 20s | 30s | 40s | 50s | 60s | 70s | 80s | 90s |
|---|---|---|---|---|---|---|---|---|
|  |  |  |  |  |  |  | ■ | ■ |

The daughter of director Roberto Rossellini and actress Ingrid Bergman, Rossellini moved to New York when she was 19. While in New York she attended college, taught Italian, translated for the Italian News Bureau, and spent three years as a correspondent for Italian TV. Later, she became a highly paid TV and magazine model for a cosmetics company. She appeared in a couple of Italian movies and in an Italian TV sitcom, then in 1985 started her screen career in earnest with her appearance in *White Nights* (1985).

She became very well known after her costarring role in David Lynch's controversial *Blue Velvet* (1986). (Rossellini and Lynch were romantically involved for a number of years.) She has tended to choose demanding, intriguing roles. She was married to director Martin Scorsese from 1979-83 and is currently engaged to actor Gary Oldman. **Selected Works:** *Wild at Heart* (1990), *Fearless* (1993), *Immortal Beloved* (1994)

# Roberto Rossellini

**Born:** May 8, 1906; Rome, Italy
**Died:** June 4, 1977

**Years Active in the Industry:** by decade

| 10s | 20s | 30s | 40s | 50s | 60s | 70s | 80s | 90s |
|-----|-----|-----|-----|-----|-----|-----|-----|-----|

An Italian director, Rossellini was a leader of the "neo-realist" movement in Italian films directly after World War II. His masterpiece, *Open City* (1946), deals with the Italian underground resistance to the Nazis. It is filmed in newsreel-like styler with no attempt to glamorize the proceedings. In his next film, *Paisan* (1946), Rossellini was able to extract beautiful performances from a cast of non-professionals. Rossellini invented a number of lens, lighting, and camera devices, which he used to great effect in his films. Rossellini's life was not without controversy. His earliest films were commissioned by Mussollini. He was called a "scoundrel" by Indian Prime Minister Nehrup Rossellini and gained a measure of notoriety when he broke up Ingrid Bergman's marriage to her first husband and left his own wife for Bergman. Their professional collaborations were less than satisfying. In particular, their first, *Stromboli* (1950). He is the father of Isabella Rossellini. **Selected Works:** *Amore* (1948), *Europa '51* (1952), *Flowers of St. Francis* (1950), *General Della Rovere* (1959), *Ways of Love* (1950)

# Nino Rota

**Born:** December 31, 1911; Milan, Italy
**Died:** April 10, 1979

**Years Active in the Industry:** by decade

| 10s | 20s | 30s | 40s | 50s | 60s | 70s | 80s | 90s |
|-----|-----|-----|-----|-----|-----|-----|-----|-----|

Italian composer Nino Rota's first oratorio was performed in 1921, when he was a veteran at age 11. Refining his skills at the Milan Conservatory, the Santa Cecilia Academy of Italy, and the Curtis Institute of the United States, Rota continued turning out symphonies, operas and ballets throughout his long career, and also spent nearly four decades as director of the Bari Conservatory. His best known operas include *Torquemada* (1942), *The Florentine Straw Hat* (1946) and *Alladin and His Magic Lamp* (1968), all bearing the influence of his many years as a film composer. Rota's

first movie work was for Italy's "white telephone" romances and musicals of the 1930s. It an earthier vein, Rota composed for several of the neorealist directors of the postwar era. His longest professional association (25 years!) was with director Federico Fellini, who once described the relationship thusly: "It is a harmonious collaboration that I haven't felt like changing. His music is a kind of frama that is very true for my story and images." Rota's better-known Fellini scores were for *La Strada* (1954), *Il Bidone* (1955), *Nights of Cabiria* (1956), and, perhaps best of all, *La Dolce Vita* (1961). One of Rota's many stage compositions was for a late-1950s ballet version of *La Strada*. When director Francis Ford Coppola wanted an authentic Italian "feel" for the music of the *Godfather*, he knew exactly who to contact: Nino Rota, who won his first-ever Oscar for the now-classic *Godfather* score (alas, he was later disqualified because he'd lifted his themes from one of his own earlier film scores). Outside of *Godfather*, Nino Rota's most popular film composition was the love theme from Zefferelli's *Romeo and Juliet* (1968). **Selected Works:** *Godfather, Part 2* (1974), *Godfather, Part 3* (1990), *Hundred and One Nights* (1995)

# Joe Roth

**Born:** June 13, 1948; New York, NY

**Years Active in the Industry:** by decade

| 10s | 20s | 30s | 40s | 50s | 60s | 70s | 80s | 90s |
|-----|-----|-----|-----|-----|-----|-----|-----|-----|

A onetime communications major at Boston University, producer/director Joe Roth worked as a production assistant with several San Francisco-based film companies. Utilizing several of the improvisational comics who had worked with him at Los Angeles' Pitchel Players (he ran lights while they got laughs), Roth produced an inexpensive "TV of the future" spoof called *Tunnelvision*. The film did well on its first release in 1976, and even better in later years by virtue of its stars-in-the-making cast, which included Chevy Chase, Betty Thomas, Howard Hesseman and Ron Silver. After several years' worth of low-budget but high-grossing films like *Bachelor Party* (1984) and *Moving Violations* (1986), Roth made his directing bow with *Streets of Gold* (1986). Forming Morgan Creek productions with partner Jim Robinson, Roth continued his winning box-office record with such films as *Young Guns* (1988) and *Dead Ringers* (1989). In 1989, Roth made his last film as director, *Coupe de Ville*. That same year, he became chairman of 20th Century-Fox's theatrical film division, toting up more hits (*White Men Can't Jump*, *Die Hard 2*, *Sleeping with the Enemy*) than misses (*Barton Fink*). His last months at Fox were marred with disappointments like *Toys* (1992) and *Hoffa* (1992), but Roth had gained a strong reputation for having the uncanny knack for attracting and mollifying some of the biggest and most difficult talents in Hollywood; one magazine characterized him as "filmmaker friendly." From Fox, Roth moved to Disney's Caravan Pictures unit, raking in the bucks with productions like *Angels in the Outfield* (1994). In September of 1994, Joe Roth replaced Jeffrey

Katzenberg as Disney CEO, and in so doing became the first director ever to hold that position in a major studio; he proved his worthiness for that position almost instantly with the smash Yuletide release *The Santa Clause* (1994). **Selected Works:** *Pacific Heights* (1990), *Three Musketeers* (1993), *I Love Trouble* (1994), *Low Down Dirty Shame* (1994), *Houseguest* (1995)

# Tim Roth

**Born:** May 14, 1961; London

**Years Active in the Industry:** by decade

| 10ˢ | 20ˢ | 30ˢ | 40ˢ | 50ˢ | 60ˢ | 70ˢ | 80ˢ | 90ˢ |
|-----|-----|-----|-----|-----|-----|-----|-----|-----|
|     |     |     |     |     |     |     | ■   | ■   |

Londoner Tim Roth's father was a journalist and his mother a landscape painter. Initially enrolling in art school in hopes of becoming a sculptor, the blonde, cherub-faced Roth decided instead to try acting. His first appearance was in a production of Jean Genet's *The Screens*. On stage, screen, and television, Roth has made his greatest impression as emotionally troubled villains, including 1983's *The Hit*, 1992's *Reservoir Dogs* and 1994's *Pulp Fiction*. Roth was more sympathetic, but no less troubled, in his portrayals of Vincent Van Gogh in *Vincent and Theo* (1990) and Guildenstern in *Rosencrantz and Guildenstern Are Dead* (1990). **Selected Works:** *The Cook, the Thief, His Wife and Her Lover* (1990), *Four Rooms* (1995), *Little Odessa,* (1994)

# Richard Roundtree

**Born:** September 7, 1942; New Rochelle, NY

**Years Active in the Industry:** by decade

| 10ˢ | 20ˢ | 30ˢ | 40ˢ | 50ˢ | 60ˢ | 70ˢ | 80ˢ | 90ˢ |
|-----|-----|-----|-----|-----|-----|-----|-----|-----|
|     |     |     |     |     |     | ■   | ■   | ■   |

Leading man Roundtree is best known for his performance as "Shaft" in '70s movies and on TV. In high school he was voted most popular, best dressed, and best looking senior. Roundtree attended college on a football scholarship, but gave up athletics for acting. He briefly toured as a model with the Ebony Fashion Fair and enrolled in the Negro Ensemble Company's workshop program in 1967. Several years later he auditioned for a black detective film to be directed by Gordon Parks, Sr.; the film was *Shaft* (1971), and he got the title role. It was an enormous success (it is credited with having helped save MGM from bankruptcy) and led to two sequels, *Shaft's Big Score* (1972) and *Shaft in Africa* (1973), as well as a short-lived TV series. He soon appeared on the covers of *Newsweek, Ebony,* and *Jet* magazines, and became a hero, the epitome of "cool," to countless children and teens. This success led to a string of solid film roles, but by the late '70s his popularity had waned, and in the '80s and '90s he made unmemorable films. **Selected Works:** *Body of Influence* (1993), *Christmas in Connecticut* (1992)

# Mickey Rourke

**Born:** September 1955; Schenectady, NY

**Years Active in the Industry:** by decade

| 10ˢ | 20ˢ | 30ˢ | 40ˢ | 50ˢ | 60ˢ | 70ˢ | 80ˢ | 90ˢ |
|-----|-----|-----|-----|-----|-----|-----|-----|-----|
|     |     |     |     |     |     |     | ■   | ■   |

Little is known of Rourke's beginnings other than his tenure at the Actors Studio. Rourke appeared in small roles in *1941* (1979) and *Heaven's Gate* (1980) before being noticed in *Body Heat* (1981) and *Diner* (1982). He followed these with admirable work in *Rumble Fish* (1983) and *The Pope of Greenwich Village* (1984). Rourke then gave a bravura performance as fanatically determined police captain Stanley White in *Year of the Dragon* (1985). When the film was slammed by critics, Rourke defended director Michael Cimino and refused critics interviews. He immediately gained a reputation as a difficult perfectionist, agreeing only to work with directors and projects that met with his high standards of acting. His 1987 performances in *Angel Heart, A Prayer For The Dying,* and *Barfly* attest to this, but starring roles in the infamous *9 1/2 Weeks* (1986) and *Wild Orchid* (1990) have given him a "Eurotrash" taint. Since then the film career of this disillusioned actor with the potential of DeNiro has had a downward spiral. He wrote, produced, and starred in *Homeboy* (1988) a film about a near brain-dead prize fighter. It was given no theatrical release and went straight to home video. The masochistic connection between this film and his "new career" as a boxer is undeniable. He has since appeared sporadically in small films. **Selected Works:** *Desperate Hours* (1990), *White Sands* (1992)

# Philippe Rousselot

**Born:** 1945; Meurthe-et-Moselle, France

**Years Active in the Industry:** by decade

| 10ˢ | 20ˢ | 30ˢ | 40ˢ | 50ˢ | 60ˢ | 70ˢ | 80ˢ | 90ˢ |
|-----|-----|-----|-----|-----|-----|-----|-----|-----|
|     |     |     |     |     |     |     | ■   | ■   |

French cinematographer Philippe Rousselot began as an assistant to Nestor Almendaros on the Eric Rohmer-directed films of the late 1960s and early 1970s. On his own, Rousselot lensed several of the nostalgic films of director Diane Kurys (*Peppermint Soda*, *Cocktail Molotov*). For his versatile Eastmancolor camerawork (including an incredible subway chase) in Jean-Jacques Benaix's *Diva*, Rosselot won the first of his Cesar awards; his second was for the realistically stylish *Therese* (1986). Philippe Rousselot's accomplishments on the international scene have included the British *The Emerald Forest* (1984) and *Hope and Glory* (1987), and the American *Henry and June* (1991), *Sommersby* (1993) and *Interview with the Vampire* (1994). **Selected Works:** *Bear* (1989), *River Runs through It* (1992), *Queen Margot* (1994)

# Gena Rowlands

**Born:** June 19, 1934; Cambria, WI

**Years Active in the Industry:** by decade

| 10s | 20s | 30s | 40s | 50s | 60s | 70s | 80s | 90s |
|-----|-----|-----|-----|-----|-----|-----|-----|-----|
|     |     |     |     |     |     |     |     |     |

An alumnus of the American Academy of Dramatic Art, Wisconsin-born actress Gene Rowlands entered the Broadway talent pool in 1952; she also did plenty of Manhattan-based television during this period, including a recurring role on the forgotten filmed syndicated series *Top Secret USA*. From 1955 through 1957, the blonde, frosty-eyed actress costarred with Edward G. Robinson in the original Broadway production of *Middle of the Night*. She made her first film, *The High Cost of Loving*, in 1958, the same year that she married actor/director John Cassavetes. The excellent response to her performance as the deaf-mute wife of a detective on the 1961 TV series *87th Precinct* sparked a grass-roots campaign to have Rowlands appear on the series on a weekly basis, but her film commitments were such that she couldn't be confined to any one part for very long. Always a capable leading lady, Rowlands blossomed into full stardom in the films directed by her husband John Cassavetes. She was Oscar-nominated for her work in Cassavetes' *A Woman Under the Influence* (1974) and *Gloria* (1980); she has also won Emmies for her appearances in the made-for-TV movies *The Betty Ford Story* (1987) and *Face of a Stranger* (1991). After her husband's death in 1989, Rowlands took a two-year sabbatical from films, returning to play Holly Hunter's mother—and Richard Dreyfuss' mother-in-law—in *Once Around* (1991). One of Gena Rowlands' more recent film appearances has been as the "steel magnolia" wife of Robert Duvall and mother of Julia Roberts in *Something to Talk About* (1995). **Selected Works:** *Crazy in Love* (1992), *Early Frost* (1985)

# Miklos Rozsa

**Born:** April 18, 1907; Budapest, Hungary
**Died:** July 27, 1995; Los Angeles, CA

**Years Active in the Industry:** by decade

| 10s | 20s | 30s | 40s | 50s | 60s | 70s | 80s | 90s |
|-----|-----|-----|-----|-----|-----|-----|-----|-----|
|     |     |     |     |     |     |     |     |     |

Hungarian-born musician/composer Miklos Rozsa studied in Leipzig under Hermann Grabner and Theodor Kroyer. He composed his first orchestral work in 1929, then moved to Paris two years later to further his education. In London from 1935, Rozsa went to work for movie mogul and fellow Hungarian expatriate Alexander Korda: his first film score was written for Korda's *Knight without Armour* (1937). Moving with Korda to Hollywood, Rozsa made his American bow with his music for the popular *That Hamilton Woman* (1941). During the 1940s, Rozsa was a prime contributor to the "film noir" genre. One of his most effective scores was for the stylish murder melodrama *A Double Life* (1948); the film must have had special meaning for the composer, in that he lifted its title for his 1982 autobiography. Nominated for 16 Academy Awards, Rozsa won the prize for *A Double Life*, *Spellbound* (1945) and the 1959 version of *Ben-Hur*. Rozsa's final film work was the deliberately "retro" score for the Steve Martin private eye spoof *Dead Men Don't Wear Plaid* (1982). **Selected Works:** *Double Indemnity* (1944), *The Lost Weekend* (1945), *Quo Vadis* (1951)

# Saul Rubinek

**Born:** 1948; Munich, Germany

**Years Active in the Industry:** by decade

| 10s | 20s | 30s | 40s | 50s | 60s | 70s | 80s | 90s |
|-----|-----|-----|-----|-----|-----|-----|-----|-----|
|     |     |     |     |     |     |     |     |     |

Born in a German refugee camp, actor Saul Rubinek was raised in Canada, where he began his career. After several years of activity with the Toronto Free Theater, the versatile Rubinek headed for New York, where he worked in repertory and on Broadway. Rubinek's performance as the best friend of religious cult member Nick Mancuso in the little-seen *Ticket to Heaven* (1981) was a critical coup for the actor, though most mainstream filmgoers ignored the film. A reliable presence in such meaty supporting roles as the Ned Buntline-ish dime novelist in *The Unforgiven* (1994), Rubinek was equally believable in the starring role of a neurotic, love-hungry Jewish New Yorker in *Soup for One* (1982). TV credits for Rubinek include the 1989 *Diner*-style series *Men*, and the made-for-cable Randy Shilts biopic *And the Band Played On* (1993). **Selected Works:** *True Romance* (1993), *Undercover Blues* (1993), *Wall Street* (1987)

# Alan Rudolph

**Born:** December 18, 1943; Los Angeles, CA

**Years Active in the Industry:** by decade

| 10s | 20s | 30s | 40s | 50s | 60s | 70s | 80s | 90s |
|-----|-----|-----|-----|-----|-----|-----|-----|-----|
|     |     |     |     |     |     |     |     |     |

American director Alan Rudolph was the son of Oscar Rudolph, a one-time actor who later directed such low budget films as *Twist Around the Clock* and such economical TV fare as "The

Lone Ranger." While studying accounting at UCLA, the younger Rudolph dropped out to work in minor production capacities in the Hollywood studio system. As an assistant to director Robert Altman, Rudolph worked on such major Altman projects as *The Long Goodbye* (1973) and *Nashville* (1975), ultimately getting a chance to direct his own film for Altman's production company, *Welcome to LA* (1977). (Rudolph had actually made his directorial bow in 1972, but chose to stay with Altman for the experience.) Rudolph frequently seemed to *be* Altman, with his fascination with tiny budgets, favorite cast members, quirky intra-personal character relationships, surrealistic set-piece sequences, and improvisational (if not hallucinatory) plotlines. Even when attempting to make a "mainstream" film like *Made in Heaven* (1987), Rudolph still appeared to be operating from another planet. Still, he deserves his faithful fan following if for nothing else than his masterpiece, the breathtakingly inventive *Choose Me* (1984). **Selected Works:** *Equinox* (1993), *Mortal Thoughts* (1991), *The Player* (1992), *Mrs. Parker and The Roundtable* (1994)

# Mercedes Ruehl

**Born:** 1954; Silver Springs, Maryland

**Years Active in the Industry:** by decade

| 10s | 20s | 30s | 40s | 50s | 60s | 70s | 80s | 90s |
|-----|-----|-----|-----|-----|-----|-----|-----|-----|
|     |     |     |     |     |     |     |     |     |

American actress Mercedes Ruehl was the daughter of a much-travelled FBI agent, who finally settled in Silver Spring, Maryland. After attending Catholic College in New Rochelle, Ruehl began her career in regional theatre, taking odd jobs during the many dry spells between engagements. For several years, it looked as though she'd be a permanent employee of the Baltimore Gas and Electric Company. In the late 1970s, Ruehl began chalking up New York stage successes, notably *I'm Not Rappaport*. She won an Obie for the off-Broadway *The Wedding of Betty and Boo* and a Tony for *Lost in Yonkers*. In films since 1979's *The Warriors,* Ruehl worked steadily but in relative anonymity until winning the Best Supporting Actress award for *The Fisher King* (1992). Ruehl wasn't able to fill houses as star of the lukewarm film version of *Lost in Yonkers* (1993), though she still is a most welcome supporting presence in such films as *The Last Action Hero* (1993). **Selected Works:** *Big* (1988), *Married to the Mob* (1988)

# Charlie Ruggles

**Born:** February 8, 1888; Los Angeles, CA
**Died:** December 23, 1970

**Years Active in the Industry:** by decade

| 10s | 20s | 30s | 40s | 50s | 60s | 70s | 80s | 90s |
|-----|-----|-----|-----|-----|-----|-----|-----|-----|
|     |     |     |     |     |     |     |     |     |

Whimsical, expressive comic actor Charles Ruggles was the son of a Los Angeles wholesale druggist. Intending to become a doctor, Ruggles was sidetracked into theatre, making his debut in a 1905 San Francisco stock company production of *Nathan Hale*. Because of his medium height and flexible facial and vocal expressions, Ruggles was able to play everything from teenagers to grandpas during his formative years in stock. In 1914, the actor first set foot on a Broadway stage in *Help Wanted*. One year later, he appeared in his first film, a now-lost adaptation of Ibsen's *Peer Gynt*. Though there would be a smattering of subsequent silent film appearances, Ruggles' heart remained in his stage work—he starred in such long-running productions as *The Passing Show of 1918* (1918), *The Demi-Virgin* (1921), *Battling Butler* (1923), and his biggest stage success, *Queen High* (1930). While appearing in the Rodgers and Hart musical *Spring is Here* (1929), Ruggles made his talking picture bow in *Gentleman of the Press* (1929), portraying the first in what would turn out to be a long line of drunken reporters. In 1932, Ruggles was teamed with Mary Boland in *If I Had A Million*. The two farceurs worked so well together that they would subsequently costar in such memorable film comedies as *Six of a Kind* (1934), *Ruggles of Red Gap* (1935), *Early to Bed* (1936), and *Boy Trouble* (1939). By the late 1930s, Ruggles was securely established as one of Hollywood's favorite befuddled comedy-relief players, though in such films as *Exclusive* (1937) and *The Parson of Panamint* (1941) he proved equally expert at straight dramatics. In 1949, Ruggles began a 12-year movie moratorium, returning to the stage and distinguishing himself in television. He headlined two early TV series, "The Ruggles" and "The World of Mr. Sweeney," and lent his vocal skills (*sans* screen credit) to the "Aesop and Son" component of the classic cartoon weeklies "Rocky and His Friends" (1959-61) and "The Bullwinkle Show" (1961-62). He returned to films in 1961, recreating his award-winning Broadway role in *The Pleasure of His Company*. Ruggles' best-remembered TV work of the 1960s included his recurring role as Mrs. Drysdale's rakish father in the popular sitcom "The Beverly Hillbillies." With the Disney film *Follow Me Boys* (1966) and the 1967 TV staging of Rodgers and Hammerstein's *Carousel,* Ruggles quietly brought his six-decade acting career to a close. A few years before his death in December of 1970, Ruggles was asked by a reporter what his future plans were. With the wry smile, twinkling eyes, and self-effacing humor that characterized his best screen work, Charlie Ruggles answered, "Forest Lawn, I guess. After you've played everything I have, there ain't no more." **Selected Works:** *One Hour with You* (1932)

# Sig Rumann

**Born:** 1884; Hamburg, Germany
**Died:** February 14, 1967

**Years Active in the Industry:** by decade

| 10s | 20s | 30s | 40s | 50s | 60s | 70s | 80s | 90s |
|-----|-----|-----|-----|-----|-----|-----|-----|-----|
|     |     |     |     |     |     |     |     |     |

Born in Germany, actor Sig Rumann studied electro-technology in college before returning to his native Hamburg to study acting. He worked his way up from bits to full leads in such theatrical centers as Stettin and Kiel before serving in World War I. Rumann came to New York in 1924 to appear in German-language plays. He was discovered simultaneously by comedian George Jessel, playwright George S. Kaufman, and critic Alexander Woollcott. He began chalking up an impressive list of stage roles, notably Baron Preysig in the 1930 Broadway production of *Grand Hotel* (in the role played by Wallace Beery in the 1932 film version). Rumann launched his film career at the advent of talkies, hitting his stride in the mid 1930s. During his years in Hollywood, he whittled down his stage name from Siegfried Rumann to plain Sig Ruman. The personification of Prussian pomposity, Rumann was a memorable foil for the Marx Brothers in *A Night at the Opera* (1935), *A Day at the Races* (1937), and *A Night in Casablanca* (1946). He also was a favorite of director Ernst Lubitsch, appearing in *Ninotchka* (1939) as a bombastic Soviet emissary and in *To Be or Not to Be* (1942) as the unforgettable "Concentration Camp Ehrardt." With the coming of World War II, Ruman found himself much in demand as thick-headed, sometimes sadistic Nazis. Oddly, in *The Hitler Gang* (1944), Rumann was cast in a comparatively sympathetic role, as the ailing and senile Von Hindenburg. After the war, Rumann was "adopted" by Lubitsch admirer Billy Wilder, who cast the actor in such roles as the deceptively good-natured Sgt. Schultz in *Stalag 17* (1953) and a marinet doctor in *The Fortune Cookie* (1966); Wilder also used Rumann's voice to dub over the guttural intonations of German actor Hubert von Meyerinck in *One, Two, Three* (1961). In delicate health during his last two decades, Rumann occasionally accepted unbilled roles, such as the kindly pawnbroker in *O. Henry's Full House* (1952). During one of his heartier periods, he had a recurring part on the 1952 TV sitcom *Life with Luigi*. Rumann's last film appearance was as a shoe-pounding Russian UN delegate in Jerry Lewis' *Way Way Out* (1967). **Selected Works:** *Only Angels Have Wings* (1939), *Dr. Ehrlich's Magic Bullet* (1940), *It Happened Tomorrow* (1944)

# Jane Russell (Ernestine Jane Geraldine Russell)

**Born:** June 21, 1921; Bemidji, MN

**Years Active in the Industry:** by decade

| 10s | 20s | 30s | 40s | 50s | 60s | 70s | 80s | 90s |
|-----|-----|-----|-----|-----|-----|-----|-----|-----|
|     |     |     |     |     |     |     |     |     |

Voluptuous sex symbol and star of Hollywood films, TV, and nightclubs, Russell was the daughter of an actress. She worked as a receptionist and model, and studied theater at Max Reinhardt's Theatrical Workshop and with Maria Ouspenskaya. Endowed with a 38-inch bust, she won the lead role in Howard Hughes's *The Outlaw* (1941) after Hughes conducted a nationwide search for a busty actress. The film caused a storm of controversy due primarily to the amount of cleavage shown by Russell on-screen, and after brief releases in 1941 and 1943 it was not officially released until 1950. The controversy brought her much publicity, often in the form of off-color, sophomoric jokes. However,

she surpassed her mindless "bombshell" image and went on to perform with versatility in a number of films during the subsequent three decades, including comedies with Bob Hope and musicals with Marilyn Monroe. She often played cynical "tough broads." She starred in the Broadway musical *Company* in 1971. TV viewers will remember her for a series of bra commercials in the '70s.

# Ken Russell (Henry Kenneth Alfred Russell)

**Born:** July 3, 1927; Southampton, England

**Years Active in the Industry:** by decade

| 10s | 20s | 30s | 40s | 50s | 60s | 70s | 80s | 90s |
|-----|-----|-----|-----|-----|-----|-----|-----|-----|
|     |     |     |     |     |     |     |     |     |

British director Ken Russell started out in training for a naval career, but after wartime RAF and merchant navy service he switched goals and went into ballet. Supplementing his dancing income as an actor and still photographer, Russell put together a handful of amateur films in the 1950s, then was hired as a staff director by the BBC. During the first half of the 1960s, Russell made a name for himself (a name not always spoken in reverence) by directing a series of iconoclastic TV dramatizations of the lives of famous composers and dancers. If he felt that the facts were getting in the way of his story, he'd make up his own—frequently bordering on the libelous; if he had any respect for the famous persons whose lives he probed, it was secondary to his fascination with revealing all warts and open wounds. A film director since 1963, Russell burst into the international consciousness with 1969's *Women in Love,* a hothouse version of D.H. Lawrence's novel. No director who staged a scene in a mainstream 1969 movie in which two men wrestled in the nude could escape notice, and thus Russell became more of a "star" than his actors. While some viewers had their sensibilities shaken by *Women in Love,* others had their sensibilities run through the blender with Russell's next film, *The Music Lovers.* Predicated on the notion that Peter Tschaikovsky and his wife were homosexual and nymphomaniac respectively, the film's much discussed "highlight" is the scene in which Nina Tschaikovsky (Glenda Jackson) allows the inmates in the cellar of an insane asylum to reach up and play with her privates. This was kid's stuff compared to Russell's *The Devils* (1971), an ultraviolent and perversely anachronistic adaptation of Aldous Huxley's *The Devils of Loudin.* Russell returned to his musical theatre roots with *The Boy Friend* (1971), a bloated version of Sandy Wilson's intimate 1920s pastiche, then went back to biography with the insanely innacurate *Lisztomania* (1974) and *Valentino* (1975). The latter film not only suggested that Rudolph Valentino (Rudolph Nuryev) performed totally nude in his silent films, but also offered us the spectacle of Huntz Hall as producer Jesse Lasky. At this point, even some of the most devoted fans of Russell's outrageous (but undeniably brilliant) visual sense were fed up with his "shock for shock's sake" approach and his all-consuming narcissism. As outrageousness in filmmaking became the industry norm in the 1980s, Russell's reputation began to fade. He was back in his old form with 1991's *Whore,* which told us several times over that life on the streets is Hell—then for good measure, told us a few more times. Backed by a childishly slavering ad campaign, *Whore* brought Ken Russell into the spotlight again, but now his act, once so revolutionary and energetic, seemed tired and played out. **Selected Works:** *Altered States* (1980), *Women and Men: Stories of Seduction* (1990), *Erotic Tales* (1994)

# Kurt Russell

**Born:** March 17, 1951; Springfield, MA

**Years Active in the Industry:** by decade

| 10s | 20s | 30s | 40s | 50s | 60s | 70s | 80s | 90s |
|-----|-----|-----|-----|-----|-----|-----|-----|-----|
|     |     |     |     |     | ■ | ■ | ■ | ■ |

The son of baseball player turned actor Bing Russell, he debuted onscreen at age nine in *The Absent-Minded Professor* (1960), then went on to have a busy acting career as a juvenile in

Disney movies as well as a number of TV shows. He appeared with his father in *The Computer Wore Tennis Shoes* (1969). Russell looked upon acting as a part-time job and intended to become a baseball player, but was sidelined by a shoulder injury. Having become known as one of Disney's stock juvenile actors, he re-emerged as an adult leading man in a 1979 TV movie in which he portrayed superstar Elvis Presley. In the '80s he completely changed his screen image, largely due to his against-type performances in three John Carpenter films, *Escape from New York* (1981), *The Thing* (1982), and *Big Trouble in Little China* (1986). While filming *Swing Shift* (1984) he met actress Goldie Hawn, and the two of them established a long-term live-in relationship; he also appeared with Hawn in *Overboard* (1987). **Selected Works:** *Backdraft* (1991), *Silkwood* (1983), *Unlawful Entry* (1992), *Tombstone* (1993), *Stargate* (1994)

# Rosalind Russell

**Born:** June 4, 1908; Waterbury, CT
**Died:** 1976

**Years Active in the Industry:** by decade

| 10s | 20s | 30s | 40s | 50s | 60s | 70s | 80s | 90s |
|-----|-----|-----|-----|-----|-----|-----|-----|-----|
|     |     | ■ | ■ | ■ | ■ |     |     |     |

A witty and stylish lead actress of stage and screen, Russell tended to play successful career women who were skilled in repartee. She trained at the American Academy of Dramatic Arts, then began her stage career in her early '20s. She debuted onscreen in 1934 and immediately had a very busy film career. At first appearing in routine films, in the '40s she began to specialize in light, sophisticated comedies, for which she had a unique talent. In the '50s her career briefly declined and she went to Broadway, where she starred in three successful productions. One of these was *Auntie Mame,* later made into a film in which she reprised her stage role (1958). She went on to appear in a handful of films before she was struck by crippling arthritis. Known for her charity work, in 1972 she received the Jean Hersholt Humanitarian Award, a special Oscar. Russell received four Academy Award nominations during her career. She was married to producer Frederick Brisson. She authored an autobiography, *Life is a Banquet.* **Selected Works:** *Citadel* (1938), *Picnic* (1955), *Mourning Becomes Electra* (1947), *My Sister Eileen* (1942), *Night Must Fall* (1937)

# Theresa Russell (Theresa Paup)

**Born:** March 20, 1957; San Diego, CA

**Years Active in the Industry:** by decade

| 10s | 20s | 30s | 40s | 50s | 60s | 70s | 80s | 90s |
|-----|-----|-----|-----|-----|-----|-----|-----|-----|
|     |     |     |     |     |     | ■ | ■ | ■ |

A model at age 12, Theresa Russell left school a few years later to study acting at the Lee Strasberg Institute. Her film debut was as Robert Mitchum's love-hungry daughter in *The Last Tycoon* (1976). Her most memorable screen roles have included the self-destructive alcoholic Sophie in the 1984 remake of *Razor's Edge* (the role played by Anne Baxter in the 1946 version), and the ethereal "Marilyn Monroe" counterpart in the Sartre-like *Insignificance* (1982). Theresa married the director of the latter film, Nicholas Roeg, thirty years her senior. Like Roeg, Russell has evinced a preference for rarefied art-house efforts rather than "audience pictures," though she certainly has not wanted for publicity: her most controversial role was the burned-out title character in *Whore* (1991), an otherwise worthless film directed by Ken Russell (no relation). **Selected Works:** *Impulse* (1990), *Kafka* (1991), *Bad Timing: A Sensual Obsession* (1980)

# Dame Margaret Rutherford

**Born:** May 11, 1892; London, England
**Died:** 1972

**Years Active in the Industry:** by decade

| 10s | 20s | 30s | 40s | 50s | 60s | 70s | 80s | 90s |
|-----|-----|-----|-----|-----|-----|-----|-----|-----|
|     |     | ■ | ■ | ■ | ■ |     |     |     |

Rutherford was a bulky, eccentric comedic supporting player of British films and plays. Following a number of years spent as a speech and piano teacher, she trained at the Old Vic and debuted onstage in 1925, when she was in her 30s; it was 1933 before she appeared in London. Rutherford began appearing in films in 1936 and went on to have a sporadically busy screen career through the late '60s, meanwhile continuing her illustrious stage career. She is best remembered as Miss Marple, the little old lady detective of Agatha Christie novels, in four films made in the '60s. For her work in *The V.I.P.s* (1963) she won a Best Supporting Actress Oscar. In 1967 Rutherford became a Dame of the British Empire. She was married to actor Stringer Davis, with whom she appeared in several films; one of their adopted children was writer Gordon Langley Hall, who underwent a sex-change operation in 1968 and later wrote a biography of Rutherford under the name "Dawn Langley Hall." She wrote an autobiography, *Margaret Rutherford* (1972). **Selected Works:** *Blithe Spirit* (1945), *I'm All Right Jack* (1959), *Importance of Being Earnest* (1952), *Passport to Pimlico* (1949), *V.I.P.'s* (1963)

# Meg Ryan

**Born:** November 19, 1961; Fairfield, CT

**Years Active in the Industry:** by decade

| 10ˢ | 20ˢ | 30ˢ | 40ˢ | 50ˢ | 60ˢ | 70ˢ | 80ˢ | 90ˢ |
|-----|-----|-----|-----|-----|-----|-----|-----|-----|
|     |     |     |     |     |     |     |     |     |

Pretty, blond-haired, blue-eyed leading lady with an effervescent personality, Ryan is the daughter of a casting agent. She debuted onscreen in a small role as Candice Bergin's daughter in

*Rich and Famous* (1981), but she intended to become a journalist. While studying journalism in night school, she got a lucky break and landed a part on the TV soap opera "As The World Turns;" her character became popular and she remained on the show for two years. After some time traveling, she returned to college, was in the cast of a short-lived TV series, and had some more small roles in two films between 1981-86. Ryan's screen career really began to develop when she landed an important supporting role in the blockbuster *Top Gun* (1986); this led to the female lead in Steven Spielberg's *Inner Space* (1987). While filming that movie she met actor Dennis Quaid, whom she later married; the two of them went on to appear together again in two other films. With her lead role in Rob Reiner's hit *When Harry Met Sally* (1989) she established herself as a star. After appearing in another successful romantic comedy, *Sleepless*

*in Seattle* (1993), Ryan chose a tougher role as an alcoholic wife and mother in 1994's *When a Man Loves a Woman*. **Selected Works:** *Flesh and Bone* (1993), *I.Q.* (1994), *Restoration* (1995), *French Kiss* (1995)

# Mark Rydell

**Born:** March 23, 1934; New York, NY

**Years Active in the Industry:** by decade

| 10ˢ | 20ˢ | 30ˢ | 40ˢ | 50ˢ | 60ˢ | 70ˢ | 80ˢ | 90ˢ |
|-----|-----|-----|-----|-----|-----|-----|-----|-----|
|     |     |     |     |     |     |     |     |     |

After attending the Juilliard School of Music, Rydell trained for the stage at New York's Neighborhood Playhouse, then joined the Actors Studio. In the '50s he appeared in several Broadway productions and also worked as a jazz pianist. He also had a prominent role on the TV soap opera "As The World Turns" for six years. He debuted onscreen in *Crime in the Streets* (1956) but appeared in no other films until 1973. Rydell changed course in mid-career, going to Hollywood to work as a TV director. His big-screen directorial debut was *The Fox* (1968), following which he directed a number of other films through the '90s. For *On Golden Pond* (1981) he received a Best Director Oscar nomination. He and director Sidney Pollack formed Sanford, a production company. **Selected Works:** *For the Boys* (1991), *Havana* (1990)

# Winona Ryder (Winona Laura Horowitz)

**Born:** October 29, 1971; Winona, MN

**Years Active in the Industry:** by decade

| 10ˢ | 20ˢ | 30ˢ | 40ˢ | 50ˢ | 60ˢ | 70ˢ | 80ˢ | 90ˢ |
|-----|-----|-----|-----|-----|-----|-----|-----|-----|
|     |     |     |     |     |     |     |     |     |

Ryder was brought up by unconventional, intellectual, quasi-hippie parents, and as a child she spent time with countercultural figures such as Allen Ginsberg and Timothy Leary (who is

her godfather). As a child she lived in the "hippie capital" Haight-Ashbury and in a commune before settling in Petaluma, California. Because she was unhappy in junior high school, her parents sent her to the well-known American Conservatory Theater School in San Francisco; there she was spotted by a talent agent and given a screen test, after which she made her screen debut at age 15 in *Lucas* (1986). Her first role in a hit movie came in *Beetlejuice* (1988), though it was her lead role in the black comedy *Heathers* (1989) that established her as a rising star. She received an Academy nomination as Best Supporting Actress for her work in the *Age of Innocence* (1993) and was oscar-nominated for a very memorable performance as Jo in 1994's *Little Women*. **Selected Works:** *Bram Stoker's Dracula* (1992), *Edward Scissorhands* (1990), *Night on Earth* (1991), *Age of Innocence* (1993), *How to Make an American Quilt* (1995)

# S

## Eva Marie Saint

**Born:** July 4, 1924; Newark, NJ

**Years Active in the Industry:** by decade

| 10s | 20s | 30s | 40s | 50s | 60s | 70s | 80s | 90s |
|-----|-----|-----|-----|-----|-----|-----|-----|-----|
|     |     |     |     | ■   | ■   | ■   | ■   | ■   |

After studying briefly at Bowling Green State University, New Jersey-born actress Eva Marie Saint entered the hectic world of live television. With a coolness and maturity that belied her youthfulness, Saint made an excellent impression in her first important stage appearance, 1953's *A Trip to Bountiful*. The euphoria attending her winning the Drama Critics Award was doubled by her 1954 Oscar win for her costarring stint (with Marlon Brando) in *On the Waterfront*. The following year, the blonde, graceful actress appeared with Paul Newman in a TV musical version of *Our Town* (wherein "stage manager" Frank Sinatra introduced the song hit "Love and Marriage"). Saint continued starring in films with everyone from Bob Hope (*That Certain Feeling* [1956]) to Cary Grant (in the Hitchcock classic *North By Northwest* [1959]). A string of mediocre films in the 1970s prompted Saint to seek out more satisfying roles on television before returning to the stage in 1983. More recently, Saint won an Emmy for her performance in the 1989 dramatic special *People Like Us*. **Selected Works:** *Exodus* (1960), *Voyage of Terror: The Achille Lauro Affair* (1990), *When Hell Was in Session* (1982), *Hatful of Rain* (1957)

## George Sanders

**Born:** July 3, 1906; St. Petersburg, Russia
**Died:** 1972

**Years Active in the Industry:** by decade

| 10s | 20s | 30s | 40s | 50s | 60s | 70s | 80s | 90s |
|-----|-----|-----|-----|-----|-----|-----|-----|-----|
|     |     | ■   | ■   | ■   | ■   | ■   |     |     |

Sanders was an England-reared half-Slavic leading man who almost always played suave, snobbish, world-weary cynics. Long thought to have been raised by British parents living in Russia, he was, according to his sister, the son of an illegitimate Russian posing as an Englishman. During the Russian Revolution his family returned to England. After college he went into the textile business and then the tobacco business. Then he decided to pursue an acting career. In the early '30s he debuted onstage and was in British films by mid-decade. In 1936, shortly after beginning his screen career, Sanders moved to Hollywood and began making films there; he soon became a star, playing both sympathetic leading men and suave cads, though he tended more often to portray villains. While often appearing as Nazis during World War II, he was also the lead in two film series, "The Saint" (five movies, 1939-41) and "The Falcon" (four movies, 1941-42). For his performance as a nasty drama critic in *All About Eve* (1950) he received a Best Supporting Actor Oscar nomination. In the '60s he appeared primarily in European films. His last film was *The Kremlin Letter* (1970). While staying in a Barcelona hotel in 1972 he committed suicide with an overdose of sleeping pills; the suicide note cited boredom with his life as a motivating impulse. His wives included actresses Zsa Zsa Gabor and Benita Hume. He authored an autobiography, *Memoirs of a Professional Cad* (1960). His brother was actor Tom Conway, who took over the "Falcon" series after Sanders quit. **Selected Works:** *Foreign Correspondent* (1940), *The Ghost and Mrs. Muir* (1947), *The Man Who Could Work Miracles* (1937), *The Picture of Dorian Gray* (1945), *Rebecca* (1940)

## Adam Sandler

**Born:** 1966; Brooklyn, NY

**Years Active in the Industry:** by decade

| 10s | 20s | 30s | 40s | 50s | 60s | 70s | 80s | 90s |
|-----|-----|-----|-----|-----|-----|-----|-----|-----|
|     |     |     |     |     |     |     |     | ■   |

One of several children of an electrical engineer and his wife, comedian Adam Sandler was born in Brooklyn and raised in New Hampshire. An incorrigible class clown, Sandler apparently never entertained any career goal other than making people laugh. In 1990, Sandler was hired as a writer on NBC's *Saturday Night Live*; one year later he'd become an on-camera regular, creating such calculatedly moronic characters as Opera Man and Canteen Boy. After apprenticing with supporting parts in such film comedies as *Coneheads*, *Airheads* and *Mixed Nuts* (all filmed between 1993 and 1994), Sandler was given his first starring movie, 1994's *Billy Madison*, in which he played a twentyish slacker forced to go back to grade school in order to claim an inheritance. **Selected Works:** *Shakes the Clown* (1992)

# Julian Sands

**Born:** 1958; Otley, West Yorkshire, England

**Years Active in the Industry:** by decade

| 10s | 20s | 30s | 40s | 50s | 60s | 70s | 80s | 90s |
|-----|-----|-----|-----|-----|-----|-----|-----|-----|
|     |     |     |     |     |     |     | ■   | ■   |

Interested in acting from the age of six, Sands trained at the Central School of Speech and Drama in London. He went on to form a company that performed in small fringe establishments and schools. He studied with Derek Jarman, who offered him his first screen role in the short *Broken English*. Sands got some work in television and a one-line part in the film *Privates on Parade* (1982). His first significant screen role was a supporting part in Roland Joffe's *The Killing Fields* (1984), following which he gave up theater for full-time work in the movies. He has gone on to a busy screen career, playing everything from psychologist Carl Jung to a schizophrenic to a drug addict. **Selected Works:** *Grand Isle* (1992), *Impromptu* (1990), *A Room with a View* (1986), *Warlock* (1991), *Leaving Las Vegas* (1995)

# Laura San Giacomo

**Born:** 1962; Orange, NJ

**Years Active in the Industry:** by decade

| 10s | 20s | 30s | 40s | 50s | 60s | 70s | 80s | 90s |
|-----|-----|-----|-----|-----|-----|-----|-----|-----|
|     |     |     |     |     |     |     | ■   | ■   |

Carnegie-Mellon graduate Laura San Giacomo made a spectacular screen debut as the promiscuous Cynthia Bishop (who has an affair with her own brother-in-law) in Steven Soderbergh's *sex, lies, and videotape* (1989). From here, she was supposed to have starred in a film based on the life of legendary Mexican artist Frida Kahlo, but protesters nixed this project because the actress was not of Mexican derivation. All things considered, Laura's supporting role as Julia Roberts' wiselipped best friend in *Pretty Woman* (1990) probably did more for her Hollywood career than the Kahlo biopic would have done. More recently, San Giacomo

starred in the Stephen King TV miniseries *The Stand*. **Selected Works:** *Once Around* (1991), *Quigley Down Under* (1990), *Where the Day Takes You* (1992)

# Mia Sara

**Born:** 1968; Brooklyn, NY

**Years Active in the Industry:** by decade

| 10s | 20s | 30s | 40s | 50s | 60s | 70s | 80s | 90s |
|-----|-----|-----|-----|-----|-----|-----|-----|-----|
|     |     |     |     |     |     |     | ■   | ■   |

American actress Mia Sara started out in TV commercials and in a brief recurring role on the daytime soaper *All My Children*. Her first film, lensed in England, was 1985's *Legend*, in which she played a fairytale ingenue opposite Tom Cruise. Few of her later films are worthy of mention, though she was effectively cast as Matthew Broderick's girlfriend and prankish co-conspirator in *Ferris Bueller's Day Off* (1986). Banking on her slight resemblance to actress Merle Oberon, Sara adequately filled the role of the Oberon counterpart in the 1987 TV movie *Queenie*. **Selected Works:** *A Climate for Killing* (1991), *A Stranger Among Us* (1992), *Blindsided* (1992), *Timecop* (1994)

# Susan Sarandon (Susan Tomaling)

**Born:** October 4, 1946; New York, NY

**Years Active in the Industry:** by decade

| 10s | 20s | 30s | 40s | 50s | 60s | 70s | 80s | 90s |
|-----|-----|-----|-----|-----|-----|-----|-----|-----|
|     |     |     |     |     |     | ■   | ■   | ■   |

Born Susan Tomaling, Sarandon attended college but did not study acting or take lessons elsewhere. Her career began when she landed a regular role on the TV soap opera "A World Apart."

She debuted onscreen in *Joe* (1970), then made only one more film before 1974, when she began appearing onscreen regularly; she first made an impression in the comedy *The Front Page* (1974). She costarred in the midnight-movie classic *The Rocky Horror Picture Show* (1975), which has given her something of a cult status among that film's fans. She was married to actor Chris Sarandon; their divorce resulted in a nervous breakdown for her in 1976. Although she has always maintained a fairly steady film career, her work took on new life in the late 1980s with a string of successes that began with *The Witches of Eastwick* (1987). For her work in *Atlantic City* (1980) she received a Best Actress Oscar nomination; later she earned the same nomination for her work in *Thelma and Louise* (1991). While filming *Bull Durham* (1988) she met actor Tim Robbins, with whom she has established a long-term live-in relationship; she appeared in a cameo as a TV news anchor in Robbins's *Bob Roberts* (1992), and also appeared briefly in *The Player* (1992), in which he starred. Sarandon garnered another Best Actress Oscar nomination for her performance in *The Client.* (1994) **Selected Works:** *Lorenzo's Oil* (1992), *Little Women* (1994), *Dead Man Walking* (1995)

# John Savage

**Born:** 1949; Old Bethpage, NY

**Years Active in the Industry:** by decade

| 10s | 20s | 30s | 40s | 50s | 60s | 70s | 80s | 90s |
|-----|-----|-----|-----|-----|-----|-----|-----|-----|
|     |     |     |     |     |     | ■   | ■   | ■   |

Savage was active in New York theater and organized a childrens theater group that performed in public housing. He performed both on and off-Broadway; for his work in *One Flew Over the Cuckoo's Nest* in L.A. and Chicago he won a Drama Circle Award. His film career began with a role in *Love Is a Carousel* (1970) and continued through 1975, after which he took a four-year break from movies while continuing to act frequently on TV. Savage returned to the big screen in 1979 with *The Deer Hunter,* after which he appeared in numerous films. His movies tended to do more for the careers of his costars than for his own. Most of the films he made in the '80s and '90s were commercially unsuccessful. **Selected Works:** *Bad Company* (1972), *Do the Right Thing* (1989), *The Godfather, Part 3* (1990), *Hunting* (1992), *Primary Motive* (1992)

# Telly Savalas (Aristotle Savalas)

**Born:** January 21, 1925; Garden City, NY
**Died:** February 22, 1994; Los Angeles, CA

**Years Active in the Industry:** by decade

| 10s | 20s | 30s | 40s | 50s | 60s | 70s | 80s | 90s |
|-----|-----|-----|-----|-----|-----|-----|-----|-----|
|     |     |     |     |     | ■   | ■   | ■   |     |

American actor Telly Savalas was born into a transplanted Greek family in Garden City, New York. After dropping out of Columbia University, Savalas served in World War II, from which he was discharged with a Purple Heart disability. Though not a performer himself, Savalas was active in show business with the Information Services of the State Department, which led to a news director post at the ABC network. An attempt in the mid 1950s to start a stage career as a producer came to grief when Savalas ran a summer theater into bankruptcy. Subsequent to this debacle, Savalas

was often called upon to help producers locate foreign-speaking actors for the various live TV dramatic series of the era. In 1959, Savalas attended an audition for the CBS anthology series "Armstrong Circle Theatre," intending to prompt an actor friend who was up for a role. Instead, the casting director took Savalas' sinister demeanor (and bald head) into account and cast him in a character part, which led to other TV assignments. The 1960 television anthology "Witness," though not a ratings success, brought the novice actor a great deal of acclaim for his portrayal of racketeer Lucky Luciano, gaining attention from audiences, producers, and even a few of Luciano's old associates (who liked the show). More TV and movie roles of a slimy-villain nature followed, and then Savalas was cast as Burt Lancaster's fellow Alcatraz inmate in *The Birdman of Alcatraz* (1962)—a performance that earned an Oscar nomination. Many in the industry felt that Savalas had what it took to be a leading man; Imogene Coca, with whom Savalas worked on an episode of Coca's TV series "Grindl," announced publicly that the actor was one of the funniest men she'd ever met (this from an actress who once costarred with Sid Caesar). Still, producers continued to use Savalas as a supporting bad guy. Even in *The Greatest Story Ever Told* (1965), Savalas incurred audience hisses as Pontius Pilate. In 1973 Savalas starred as police lieutenant Theo Kojak in *The Marcus-Nelson Murders,* a TV movie based on a real-life homicide. The actor's fully rounded interpretation of the sarcastic, incorruptible, lollipop-sucking New York detective earned him a full time TV job as the star of the CBS series "Kojak." Now a genuine, 14-carat celebrity, Savalas assumed a great deal of creative control on "Kojak," which included full script approval, choice of directors, and the insistence upon casting Savalas' brother George (professionally named "Demosthenes") in the role of Detective Stavros. "Kojak" lasted until 1978, during which time Savalas became a fixture of TV variety shows, where he frequently demonstrated his questionable singing talents. After the series, the actor embarked on a globe-trotting existence involving numerous forgettable European films and a sumptuous bon vivant lifestyle (which included the squiring of several attractive and much-younger ladies). Savalas periodically revived the character of Kojak in a few 1980s TV movies and a shortlived monthly "Kojak" series in 1989, but for the most part he was seen on the tube as spokesman for a high-priced credit card company. In the early 1990s, Savalas contracted cancer, ultimately succumbing to the disease (after a noble and highly public battle against it) at the age of 72. **Selected Works:** *Dirty Dozen* (1967)

# Nancy Savoca

**Born:** Bronx, NY

**Years Active in the Industry:** by decade

| 10s | 20s | 30s | 40s | 50s | 60s | 70s | 80s | 90s |
|-----|-----|-----|-----|-----|-----|-----|-----|-----|
|     |     |     |     |     |     |     | ■   | ■   |

Of Sicilian and Argentinian heritage, American director Nancy Savoca spent the better part of the eighties raising funds for her debut film, *True Love* (1989). Drawing from the lives of her parents, Savoca fashioned a story of a multi-cultural marriage; the director's attention to detail and keen sense of ethnic ambience were key factors in her winning a United States Film Festival prize. Savoca's next film *Dogfight* (1991) utilized the moment-by-moment approach first seen in *True Love* to chronicle the last day of "freedom" of a Vietnam-bound Marine. The director's most recent film was 1993's *Household Saints*, wherein Italian-American bachelor Vincent D'Onofrio woos and wins the spinsterish girl (Tracey Ullmann) he has "won" in a pinochle game. Like the rest of Savoca's films, *Household Saints* was coscripted by Savoca and her husband Richard Guay.

# John Saxon (Carmen Orrico)

**Born:** August 5, 1935; Brooklyn, NY

**Years Active in the Industry:** by decade

| 10ˢ | 20ˢ | 30ˢ | 40ˢ | 50ˢ | 60ˢ | 70ˢ | 80ˢ | 90ˢ |
|-----|-----|-----|-----|-----|-----|-----|-----|-----|
|     |     |     |     | ■ | ■ | ■ | ■ | ■ |

Actor John Saxon was a handsome Hollywood leading man from the mid 1950s through the early '60s. Prior to making his film debut in *Running Wild* (1955), Saxon, born Carmine Eric in Brooklyn, New York, worked as a model. He became fleetingly popular with teens after appearing in *The Reluctant Debutante* opposite Sandra Dee in 1958. By the early '60s, his bright star had waned, and he appeared in minor productions abroad and in the U.S. He then went on to star in TV series such as "The Doctors" and "The Bold Ones." Occasionally, Saxon also works in the theater. **Selected Works:** *Blackmail* (1991), *The Electric Horseman* (1979), *Payoff* (1991)

# John Sayles

**Born:** 1950; Schenectady, NY

**Years Active in the Industry:** by decade

| 10ˢ | 20ˢ | 30ˢ | 40ˢ | 50ˢ | 60ˢ | 70ˢ | 80ˢ | 90ˢ |
|-----|-----|-----|-----|-----|-----|-----|-----|-----|
|     |     |     |     |     |     |     | ■ | ■ |

While holding down odd jobs, he began to publish fiction in his 20s; his second novel, *Union Dues* (1977), was nominated for a National Book Award and a National Book Critics Circle Award. He also acted and directed in summer stock and adapted a novel into a screenplay; this work was sent to Hollywood, leading to a job offer from Roger Corman's New World Pictures. Sayles wrote a number of scripts for New World, then in 1980 he invested $50,000 in his first independent film, *The Return of the Secaucus Seven,* which he wrote, directed, edited, and acted in; the film earned over $2 million. From there, he went on to a successful career as a filmmaker, often appearing in supporting roles in his own films or those of others. **Selected Works:** *City of Hope* (1991), *Passion Fish* (1992), *The Secret of Roan Inish* (1994)

# Greta Scacchi

**Born:** 1960; Milan, Italy

**Years Active in the Industry:** by decade

| 10ˢ | 20ˢ | 30ˢ | 40ˢ | 50ˢ | 60ˢ | 70ˢ | 80ˢ | 90ˢ |
|-----|-----|-----|-----|-----|-----|-----|-----|-----|
|     |     |     |     |     |     |     | ■ | ■ |

Actress Greta Scacchi has found international success playing sexy but smart women in film. The daughter of an Italian father and an English mother, the Milan-born Scacchi was educated in Australia before debuting in a German film. (As she didn't speak German, she learned her lines phonetically.) In 1983, she starred in her first major feature, *Heat and Dust,* for which she won critical acclaim. She is best recognized for the natural sexuality and intelligence she exudes on the screen. Scacchi continued to work steadily through the '80s in good and bad films, but she was often dismissed by critics as a two-dimensional actress and has yet to become a major star. However, Sacchi rallied back with an outstanding performance in Altman's 1992 film *The Player.* **Selected Works:** *Fires Within* (1991), *Presumed Innocent* (1990), *Shattered* (1991), *The Browning Version* (1994), *Country Life* (1995)

# Roy Scheider

**Born:** November 10, 1935; Orange, NJ

**Years Active in the Industry:** by decade

| 10ˢ | 20ˢ | 30ˢ | 40ˢ | 50ˢ | 60ˢ | 70ˢ | 80ˢ | 90ˢ |
|-----|-----|-----|-----|-----|-----|-----|-----|-----|
|     |     |     |     |     |     | ■ | ■ | ■ |

Thin, ordinary-looking leading man, Scheider's prominent nose got its shape when it was broken in a high school Golden Gloves boxing match. He studied drama in college, then in 1961 debuted onstage professionally in the New York Shakespeare Festival production of *Romeo and Juliet.* For several years he worked in repertory, primarily playing classical roles. Scheider appeared in one film in the mid '60s, *The Curse of the Living Corpse* (1964), but his film career didn't really get off the ground till the early '70s, when he appeared in two hit films, *Klute* (1971) and *The French Connection* (1971). For his work in the latter he was nominated for a Best Supporting Actor Oscar. He co-starred in *Jaws* (1975), one of the biggest box-office successes in film history. By the mid '70s he was a familiar, intriguing, and versatile leading man. For his work in *All That Jazz* (1979) he received a Best Actor Oscar nomination and a Golden Palm award at the Cannes Film Festival; in that film he also showed his talents as a singer and dancer. In the early '90s he starred in the science-fiction TV series "Sea Quest." **Selected Works:** *Marathon Man* (1976), *Naked Lunch* (1991), *Somebody Has to Shoot the Picture* (1990)

# Maximilian Schell

**Born:** December 8, 1930; Vienna, Austria

**Years Active in the Industry:** by decade

| 10s | 20s | 30s | 40s | 50s | 60s | 70s | 80s | 90s |
|-----|-----|-----|-----|-----|-----|-----|-----|-----|
|     |     |     |     | ■   | ■   | ■   | ■   | ■   |

Schell's father was a Swiss poet-playwright, his mother, an Austrian actress. By his late teens, his sister, Maria, had established herself as a screen actress. He was raised in Austria and Switzerland, and educated at the universities of Zurich, Basel, and Munich. In 1952 Schell began his professional career onstage, then debuted onscreen in 1955. Appearing in the Broadway play *Interlock,* he attracted Hollywood's attention, leading to his first American film, *The Young Lions* (1958). Throughout the next decade he had leads and supporting roles in mostly minor films of several nations; he won the Best Supporting Actor Oscar for his work in *Judgment at Nuremberg* (1961), but was generally dissatisfied with his work. In 1968 Schell produced a film, *Das Schloss;* then in 1970 he directed *First Love.* He went on to produce, direct, write, and/or act in numerous films, meanwhile working in the same capacity onstage. For his work in *The Man In The Glass Booth* (1975) and *Julia* (1977) he received Best Actor and Best Supporting Actor Oscar nominations, respectively. *The Pedestrian* (1974), a film he produced, directed, wrote, and starred in, received a Best Foreign Film Oscar nomination; another of his films, *Marlene* (1984), about Marlene Dietrich, received a Best Documentary Oscar nomination. **Selected Works:** *A Far Off Place* (1993), *Miss Rose White* (1992), *Stalin* (1992), *Judgement at Nuremburg* (1961)

# Fred Schepisi

**Born:** December 26, 1936; Melbourne, Australia

**Years Active in the Industry:** by decade

| 10s | 20s | 30s | 40s | 50s | 60s | 70s | 80s | 90s |
|-----|-----|-----|-----|-----|-----|-----|-----|-----|
|     |     |     |     |     |     | ■   | ■   | ■   |

The son of an Australia car salesman, Fred Schepisi half-heartedly pursued a life as a priest, but bolted the seminary by the age of 15. Schepisi then shifted his interest to the world of TV advertising. After directing several commercials, he moved into documentary filmmaking, winning an Australian Film Institute award in the process. Schepisi then set up his own highly respected production company, The Film House. He was 36 years old before he had the time and financial backing to direct his first fictional feature, the semi-autobiographical *The Devil's Playground* (1976). With his race-conscious *The Chant of Jimmy Blacksmith* (1978), Schepisi gained international renown; he used his new industry clout to leave Australia behind for a Hollywood career, briefly returning to his native country for the wrenchingly true story of trial-by-headline, *A Cry in the Dark* (1988). Schepisi's American-produced output has included *Iceman* (1984), *The Russia House* (1989), *Six Degrees of Separation* (1993), and the long-delayed *Mister Baseball* (1993).

# Joseph Schildkraut

**Born:** March 22, 1895; Vienna, Austria
**Died:** 1964

**Years Active in the Industry:** by decade

| 10s | 20s | 30s | 40s | 50s | 60s | 70s | 80s | 90s |
|-----|-----|-----|-----|-----|-----|-----|-----|-----|
| ■   | ■   | ■   | ■   | ■   |     |     |     |     |

The son of esteemed actor Rudolph Schildkraut, he trained for the stage under Albert Basserman—his father's rival. Accompanying his father on tour, he went to the U.S. in 1910 and remained till 1913; there he enrolled at the American Academy of Dramatic Arts. Back in Germany, Schildkraut joined his father in the Berlin stage company of Max Reinhardt and quickly rose to stardom. He moved to the U.S. in 1920; within a year he was a major matinee idol on Broadway. Meanwhile, having appeared in a small number of German films, he began playing suave leading men in American silents; by the mid 1930s he had moved into character roles, often villainous. He remained a busy screen actor (between stage roles) until 1948, when he took a decade off from movies; he returned to the screen to reprise his stage role in the film version of *The Diary of Anne Frank* (1959), following which he appeared in only two more movies. For his portrayal of Captain Dreyfus in *The Life of Emile Zola* (1937), he won a Best Supporting Actor Oscar. He authored an autobiography, *My Father and I* (1959). **Selected Works:** *Viva Villa!* (1934), *Rains Came* (1939)

# John Schlesinger

**Born:** February 16, 1926; London, England

**Years Active in the Industry:** by decade

| 10s | 20s | 30s | 40s | 50s | 60s | 70s | 80s | 90s |
|-----|-----|-----|-----|-----|-----|-----|-----|-----|
|     |     |     |     | ■   | ■   | ■   | ■   | ■   |

British film director John Schlesinger spent the World War II years entertaining his army buddies with a magic act, then

moved on to acting at Oxford University. Establishing himself as a character actor in films and TV in the 1950s, Schlesinger could be seen in such movies as *Pursuit of the Graf Spee* (1958) and such TV weeklies as "Colonel March of Scotland Yard" (1954). He switched gears in 1957 when he was taken on as a director by BBC television. American audiences first noted the name "John Schlesinger" in a behind-the-camera capacity as co-director of the interview sequences on the 26-week documentary *Winston Churchill: The Valiant Years* (1961). Winning first prize at the 1961 Venice Film Festival for a 5-reel documentary about Waterloo Station, Schlesinger moved into feature film work. Seen today, Schlesinger's *A Kind of Loving* (1963) and *Billy Liar* (1964) seem to be warmups for his first major success, *Darling* (1965); all three films skewer the fallacies of the British social structure by demonstrating how every one, no matter what their station in life, was deep down a desperate opportunist. A multi-award winner for *Darling,* Schlesinger was promoted to more expensive films with *Far From the Madding Crowd* (1967), an epic dramatization of the Thomas Hardy novel. Then Schlesinger took on the American-made *Midnight Cowboy* (1969), the first X-rated picture to win the Academy Award (though it probably would earn a soft "R" today). The director transferred his British-film preoccupation with the falsehoods of the success ethic to the streets of New York, relating the sad tale of small-time hustler Joe Buck (Jon Voigt) and his friendship with smaller-time promoter Ratso Rizzo (Dustin Hoffman). Schlesinger won an Oscar for his efforts, enabling him to work with impunity in both Hollywood and England. Some of his later films have been more self-indulgent and less heartfelt than his earlier works, notably the Hollywood-as-Hell *Day of the Locust* (1973) and the standard-issue thriller *Marathon Man* (1976) (which, in a fascinating study of contrasts, teamed Dustin Hoffman with Laurence Olivier). In the last decade, Schlesinger has evinced a tendency to put commercialism before personal expression, as witness the slickly ultra-violent *Goodfellas* (1991) and the opulent but draggy *The Age of Innocence* (1993). On the other hand, Schlesinger has in recent years given us *Mme. Sousatzka* (1988), a determinedly "small" film featuring Shirley MacLaine in one of her best performances as a demanding piano instructor. **Selected Works:** *Pacific Heights* (1990), *Sunday, Bloody Sunday* (1971), *Question of Attribution* (1992), *Cold Comfort Farm* (1995)

# Volker Schlondorff

**Born:** March 31, 1939; Wiesbaden, Germany

**Years Active in the Industry:** by decade

| 10s | 20s | 30s | 40s | 50s | 60s | 70s | 80s | 90s |
|-----|-----|-----|-----|-----|-----|-----|-----|-----|
|     |     |     |     |     | ■   | ■   | ■   | ■   |

German filmmaker Volker Schlondorff was educated at Paris' Lycee Henry IV and the Sorbonne; he majored in political science (a hardly surprising revelation considering the subject matter of later films) and economics. While still in Paris, Schlondorff studied directing at the highly regarded IDHEC film school. He worked in France for four years as an assistant director, then made his directorial bow with 1966's *Young Torless* (1966). Set in an exclusive boys school, the film was designed as a parable concerning the unprotested rise of Nazism; it won the critics prize at the Cannes Festival, and its box office success helped open career doors for many other "New German Cinema" directors, among them Rainer Werner Fassbinder and Wim Wenders. Schlondorff formed a partnership in the late 1960s with a consortium of German TV stations, which underwrote many of his subsequent projects. In 1979, Schlondorff's *The Tin Drum*, an allegorical tale of a young boy who refuses to grow up mentally *or* physically as a reaction to the horrors of war, won still another Cannes prize, as well as the "best foreign picture" Oscar. The director made his American debut with the 1985 TV filmization of *Death of a Salesman*, which starred Dustin Hoffman. 1990's *The Handmaid's Tale*, a horror fantasy combining the themes of eugenics and feminism, was his most recent international success. Schlondorff often works in collaboration with his wife, actress/writer/director Margarethe Von Trotta. **Selected Works:** *Murder on the Bayou* (1991), *Voyager* (1991)

# Romy Schneider (Rosemarie Albach-Retty)

**Born:** September 23, 1938; Vienna, Austria
**Died:** 1982

**Years Active in the Industry:** by decade

| 10s | 20s | 30s | 40s | 50s | 60s | 70s | 80s | 90s |
|-----|-----|-----|-----|-----|-----|-----|-----|-----|
|     |     |     | ■   | ■   | ■   | ■   |     |     |

Schneider was born Rosemarie Albach-Retty. The daughter of actors Wolf Albach-Retty and Magda Schneider, she was the teen-age heroine of the "Sissi" series—corny films about the Austro-Hungarian royal family. The films were very popular in the German-speaking world, making her a star. For a time she was derisively referred to as "Shirley Templehof," in reference to her juvenile roles in saccharine films. In the early '60s Schneider began landing mature roles, largely due to her work with directors Visconti and Orson Welles; the latter directed her in *The Trial* (1962), while the former launched her to international fame by directing her in an episode of *Boccaccio '70* (1961). Fluent in German, English, Italian, and French, she went on to be an extremely busy leading lady in international productions. She died of a heart attack at age 43. **Selected Works:** *Death Watch* (1981)

# Ernest B. Schoedsack

**Born:** June 8, 1893; Council Bluffs, IA
**Died:** 1979; California

**Years Active in the Industry:** by decade

| 10s | 20s | 30s | 40s | 50s | 60s | 70s | 80s | 90s |
|-----|-----|-----|-----|-----|-----|-----|-----|-----|

Six-foot-six Iowa-native Ernest Schoedsack was fascinated with the mechanics of film photography long before taking his first movie job with the Keystone Studios in 1914. During World War I, he worked as a Signal Corps cameraman, and after the Armistice he labored mightily on behalf of Polish war relief, helping thousand of Poles escape the Russian occupied territories. While in the Ukraine in 1920 he met Captain Merian Cooper, who, like Schoedsack, was a fervent anti-Bolshevik—and also an aspiring film director. The men renewed their friendship after the hostilities, collaborating on a brace of documentary films, *Grass* (1926) and *Chang* (1927). Still in partnership with Cooper, Schoedsack co-directed the fictional adventure film *The Four Feathers* (1929), then, after another documentary, the Cooper-Schoedsack team helmed RKO's *The Most Dangerous Game* (1932), which featured *Four Feathers* leading-lady Fay Wray. Concurrently with *Game,* Schoedsack and O'Brien launched their most ambitious project to date: the matchless fantasy classic *King Kong* (1933) ( also with Wray). Ruth Rose, Schoedsack's wife and an adventure lover in her own right, collaborated on the *Kong* screenplay. When Merian Cooper assumed leadership of RKO Radio, he took Schoedsack with him as a contract director. Some of Schoedsack's projects were sedate little domestic comedies like *Long Lost Father* (1934), while others were along the spectacular lines of *The Last Days of Pompeii* (1936). At Paramount, Schoedsack returned to the live action/miniature combo that had served him well on *Kong* for his first Technicolor production, *Dr. Cyclops* (1940). Still on the cutting edge of technological advances in the 1950s, Schoedsack directed the in-your-face prologue of the 1952 box-office hit *This is Cinerama.*

# Paul Schrader

**Born:** July 22, 1946; Grand Rapids, MI

**Years Active in the Industry:** by decade

| 10s | 20s | 30s | 40s | 50s | 60s | 70s | 80s | 90s |
|-----|-----|-----|-----|-----|-----|-----|-----|-----|

In contrast to the steamy eroticism of his film work, American writer/director Paul Schrader grew up in a straight-laced religious household—so much so that he was not allowed to see his first film until he was 18. Schrader had been slated by his parents for a divinical career; instead he took up filmmaking during a summer course at Columbia University. Following the lead of writers-cum-filmmakers Francois Truffault and Peter Bogdanovich, Schrader started his career writing film criticism for numerous mainstream and "underground" publications, displaying a preference for the cerebral works of foreign film directors. His Hollywood entree was a cowriter's credit on 1975's *The Yazuka,* but Schrader truly came into his own with his script for Martin Scorcese's *Taxi Driver* (1976), a hellish look at New York's subculture which Schrader wrote while confined to a hospital bed. Long plagued by private demons who manifested themselves whenever he was drunk, Schrader sobered up long enough to concentrate those demons onto the printed page, turning *Taxi Driver*'s leading character Travis Bickel into one of the most fascinating sociopaths in screen history. Schrader's first directorial job was *Blue Collar* (1978), a cynical labor-relations drama which was idiotically advertised as a comedy due to Richard Pryor's presence in the cast. With *American Gigolo* (1979), Schrader established himself as one of the foremost Hollywood purveyors of kinky sex scenes. This talent was further developed in *Cat People* (1982), a murky, heat-oppressed remake of the 1942 Val Lewton horror classic, which starred Schrader's then-current girlfriend Nastassia Kinski. The director's work veered far afield from box-office considerations with 1982's *Mishima: A Life in Four Chapters,* the story of the life and death of a cult-figure Japanese novelist; and *The Mosquito Coast* (1986), in which star Harrison Ford proved capable of playing an obsessed, anti-social heel. Not quite as bankable in the 1990s as he'd been a decade earlier, Schrader has nonetheless preserved his own integrity, preferring the esoteric excesses of *Light Sleeper* (1992) (one of the few films in the politically correct era to feature a cocaine-dealing protagonist) to the temptations of safer, more commercial projects. **Selected Works:** *Havana* (1990), *Raging Bull* (1980), *The Comfort of Strangers* (1991)

# Barbet Schroeder

**Born:** April 26, 1941; Teheran, Iran

**Years Active in the Industry:** by decade

| 10s | 20s | 30s | 40s | 50s | 60s | 70s | 80s | 90s |
|-----|-----|-----|-----|-----|-----|-----|-----|-----|

Barbet Schroeder's German geologist father was on assignment in Iran when Barbet was born. After a globetrotting childhood, Schroeder was educated at the Sorbonne; then, like half the under-30 population of France (or so it seemed), he became a movie critic. Brief jobs as a jazz-concert producer and news photographer followed before Schroeder went to work as an assistant for one of his role models, French director Jean-Luc Godard. In 1964, the 22-year-old Schroeder set up his own film production company, Les Films du Losange. Among the many prominent pictures produced by Schroeder include director Eric Rohmer's "Moral Tales" *La Collectioneuse* (1966), *My Night at Maud's* (1969) and *Claire's Knee* (1970). Schroeder himself turned director with 1969's *More,* gaining critical attention with several unorthodox documentaries. With the American film *Barfly* (1987), Schroeder established himself as a prime purveyor of "slice of life" drama—albeit entertaining enough to please the crowd. Oscar-nominated for his take-no-sides direction of *Reversal of Fortune* (1990), the story of the controversial Claus von Bulow case, Schroeder has since helmed the tense—and successful—"cat and mouse" thriller *Single White Female* (1992)

# Joel Schumacher

**Born:** August 29, 1942; New York, NY

**Years Active in the Industry:** by decade

| 10s | 20s | 30s | 40s | 50s | 60s | 70s | 80s | 90s |
|-----|-----|-----|-----|-----|-----|-----|-----|-----|

American screenwriter/director Joel Schumacher was raised in New York City by his Scandanavian mother after his Knoxville-born father died when Schumacher was four. He later moved to Miami with his mother and became involved with the drug culture. In 1965, Schumacher graduated from the Parson School of Design. While he made piles of money in the clothes-design business (he worked for Revlon for many years), Schumacher's habit caught up with him, and he ended up throwing away his fortune on drugs. Going cold turkey, Schumacher began looking up the showbiz friends he'd made during his moneyed days and was able to obtain a costumer's job for the 1972 feature *Play It As It Lays*. Turning to screenwriting in 1976 with *Sparkle*, Schumacher found himself associated with a hit via his script for the black-oriented comedy *Car Wash* (1976). With 1978's *The Incredible Shrinking Woman*, Schumacher kicked off his directing career. The bulk of his work was deliberately geared to the "youth" market, notably *D.C. Cab* (1981) and *St. Elmo's Fire* (1985). *Flatliners* (1990) brought him in contact with up-and-coming star Julia Roberts, with whom Schumacher became enamored, a fact that clouded his critical judgement—resulting in the lesser Roberts vehicle *Dying Young* (1991). Schumacher has remained a saleable directorial commodity into the 1990s with such fingers-on-the-pulse films as *Falling Down* (1993), *The Client* (1994), and *Batman Forever* (1995).

# Arnold Schwarzenegger

**Born:** July 30, 1947; Graz, Austria

**Years Active in the Industry:** by decade

| 10s | 20s | 30s | 40s | 50s | 60s | 70s | 80s | 90s |
|-----|-----|-----|-----|-----|-----|-----|-----|-----|

While his police-chief father wanted him to become a soccer player, Austrian-born actor Arnold Schwarzenegger opted for a bodybuilding career. He won several European contests and international titles (including Mr. Olympia), then came to the U.S. for body-building exhibitions, billing himself immodestly but fairly accurately as "The Austrian Oak." Though his thick Austrian ac-

cent and slow speech patterns led some to believe that the Austrian Oak was shy a few leaves, in fact Schwarzenegger was a highly intelligent, highly motivated young man; after graduating from the University of Wisconsin with a degree in business and economics, he invested his contest earnings in real estate and a mail-order bodybuilding equipment company. A millionaire before the age of 22, Schwarzenegger decided to try acting. Producers were impressed by his physique but not the mouthful of a last name, so it was as "Arnold Strong" that he made his film bow in the low-budget spoof *Hercules in New York* (1970) (with a dubbed voice). He reverted to his own name for the 1976 film *Stay Hungry*, then achieved stardom as "himself" in the 1977 documentary *Pumping Iron*. In *The Villain* (1979), a cartoon-like western parody, Arnold played "Handsome Stranger," exhibiting a gift for under-stated comedy that would more or less go unexploited for many years thereafter. With *Conan the Barbarian* (1982) and its sequel *Conan the Destroyer* (1984), the actor established himself as an action star, though his acting was backtracking into two-dimensionality (understandably, given the nature of the Conan role). As the murderous android title character in *The Terminator* (1984), Schwarzenegger became a bonafide box-office draw, and also established his trademark of coining repeatable catchphrases in his films: "I'll be back" in *Terminator*, "Consider this a divorce" in *Total Recall* (1990), and so on. As Danny DeVito's unlikely pacifistic sibling in *Twins* (1988), Schwarzenegger received the praise of critics who noted his "unsuspected" comic expertise (quite forgetting *The Villain*). In *Kindergarten Cop* (1991), Schwarzenegger played a hard-bitten police detective who found his true life's calling as a schoolteacher (his character was a cop only because it was expected of him by his policeman father, which could have paralleled his own life). *Terminator 2: Judgment Day* (1991), wherein Schwarzenegger exercised his star prerogative and insisted that the Terminator become a good guy, was the most expensive film ever made up to its time—and one of the biggest moneymakers. The actor's subsequent action films were equally as costly; sometimes the expenditures paid off, while other times the result was immensely disappointing—for the the box-office disappointment *Last Action Hero* (1992), Schwarzenegger refreshingly took full responsibility, rather than blaming the failure on his production crew or studio as other "superstars" have been known to do. A rock-ribbed Republican despite his marriage to JFK's niece Maria Shriver, in 1990, George Bush appointed Schwarzenegger chairman of the President's Council of Physical Fitness and Sports, a job he took as seriously and with as much dedication as any of his films. A much-publicized investment in the showbiz eatery Planet Hollywood has increased the coffers in Schwarzenegger's already bulging bank account. In the last few years, Arnold Schwarzenegger has added directing to his many accomplishments, piloting a few episodes of the cable-TV series "Tales From the Crypt" as well as a 1992 remake of the 1945 film *Christmas in Connecticut*. In addition, Arnold bounced back from the disastrous *Last Action Hero* with 1994's *True Lies*, which, despite its mile-wide streak of misogyny and its gaping plot and logic holes, was one of the major hits of that summer's movie season. **Selected Works:** *Junior* (1994)

# Anabella Sciorra

**Born:** 1964; Connecticut

**Years Active in the Industry:** by decade

| 10ˢ | 20ˢ | 30ˢ | 40ˢ | 50ˢ | 60ˢ | 70ˢ | 80ˢ | 90ˢ |
|---|---|---|---|---|---|---|---|---|
|  |  |  |  |  |  |  |  | ■ |

At age 13, Sciorra enrolled at New York's HB studio, going on to the American Academy of Dramatic Arts. She acquired much stage experience in small productions. After answering an ad in *Backstage* magazine, she auditioned and landed her first screen role, the lead in the low-budget *True Love* (1989). The following year Sciorra appeared in three films (and a TV mini-series) and her screen career was underway. Her first big hit was *The Hand that Rocks the Cradle* (1992). She has not yet established a solid film persona or achieved much name-recognition; instead of stardom she seems to be headed for a career as a character actress. **Selected Works:** *Cadillac Man* (1990), *Jungle Fever* (1991), *Prison Stories: Women on the Inside* (1991), *Reversal of Fortune* (1990), *The Addiction* (1995)

# Paul Scofield

**Born:** January 21, 1922; Hurst Pierpoint, England

**Years Active in the Industry:** by decade

| 10ˢ | 20ˢ | 30ˢ | 40ˢ | 50ˢ | 60ˢ | 70ˢ | 80ˢ | 90ˢ |
|---|---|---|---|---|---|---|---|---|
|  |  |  |  | ■ |  |  |  |  |

A professional since age 14, British actor Paul Scofield is widely regarded as one of the finest (if not *the* finest) interpreters of Shakespeare of the 20th century. His first role of note was as The

Bastard in a Birmingham Repertory staging of Shakespeare's *King John*. Scofield's *Hamlet* has already entered the realm of theatrical legend, though he has been equally celebrated for his interpretations of *Henry V, Pericles*, and *King Lear* (a somewhat clumsily directed *King Lear* starring Scofield was filmed in 1971). In 1955, Scofield played Hamlet in the Soviet Union, the first English actor to be invited to do so since the 1917 revolution. While his rough facial features prevented him from becoming a movie matinee idol along the lines of Olivier, Scofield has always been welcome in his extremely infrequent film appearances. His first picture was 20th Century-Fox' *That Lady,* in which he potrayed King Philip II of Spain. In 1966, Scofield gained international film stardom—and won an Academy Award—for recreat-

ing his Tony-winning Broadway portrayal of Sir Thomas More in *A Man for All Seasons*. At age 72, Scofield was once again Oscar-nominated, this time for his performance as American poet Mark Van Doren in director Robert Redford's *Quiz Show* (1994). **Selected Works:** *The Train* (1965), *Hamlet* (1990)

# Ettore Scola

**Born:** 1931; Trevico, Italy

**Years Active in the Industry:** by decade

| 10ˢ | 20ˢ | 30ˢ | 40ˢ | 50ˢ | 60ˢ | 70ˢ | 80ˢ | 90ˢ |
|---|---|---|---|---|---|---|---|---|
|  |  |  |  |  | ■ |  |  |  |

Italian filmmaker Ettore Scola studied law before he entered journalism, writing comedy material for various publications. This line of work led to his writing for the movies, enjoying a particularly fruitful partnership with fellow scenarist Ruggero Maccari. Their best known collaborations include *The Easy Life* (1962), *The Magnificent Cuckold* (1963) and *Made in Italy* (1965). The team remained intact even after Scola turned to directing with *Let's Talk About Women* (1964). In "clown plays Hamlet" tradition, Scola gradually veered away from pure comedies into sociopolitical dramas like *We All Loved Each Other Very Much* (1974) and *A Special Day* (1977). The latter film caused quite a stir because of Scola's casting of the virile Italian film star Marcello Mastrioanni as a homosexual (it was on the occasion of the American release of *A Special Day* that Mastrioanni and Sophia Loren made their notorious "dirty word" appearance on PBS's *Dick Cavett Show*). The political content of his work increasing with each passing year, Scola has remained a prime mover and shaker in the Italian film industry. **Selected Works:** *Passione D'Amore* (1982), *Mario, Maria and Mario* (1994)

# Martin Scorsese

**Born:** November 17, 1942; Flushing, NY

**Years Active in the Industry:** by decade

| 10ˢ | 20ˢ | 30ˢ | 40ˢ | 50ˢ | 60ˢ | 70ˢ | 80ˢ | 90ˢ |
|---|---|---|---|---|---|---|---|---|
|  |  |  |  |  | ■ |  |  |  |

One of the most respected American filmmakers of his generation, Martin Scorsese was a movie buff from childhood. Born in Queens, New York, and raised on Manhattan's Lower East Side, Scorsese attended New York University, where he earned a graduate degree and learned the fundamentals of filmmaking. He made several acclaimed short films in the early 1960s; his first feature was *Who's That Knocking at My Door?* in 1968. Scorsese was the supervising editor on Woodstock, and spent a short time working for CBS News before making his second feature, *Boxcar Bertha,* in 1972. *Mean Streets* marked Scorsese's major studio debut, and the first of the major urban dramas with which he has largely made his name. *Taxi Driver* was Scorsese's first hit, and since then he has

always attracted serious attention—if not always large audiences—for his pictures. *New York, New York* (1977) was considered a lapse, but *Raging Bull* (1980) marked a return to success, and his documentary *The Last Waltz* (1978) is regarded as one of the finest rock music features ever made. His recent *Cape Fear* (1991) was a loving remake of a classic thriller that succeeded far better than the original in box office terms, and his 1993 hit *The Age of Innocence,* a period romance based on a literary classic, marked the beginning of a major new phase in Scorsese's career. **Selected Works:** *Alice Doesn't Live Here Anymore* (1974), *Goodfellas* (1990), *Amazing Stories: The Movie 4* (1991), *Quiz Show* (1994), *Casino* (1995)

# Campbell Scott

**Born:** July 19, 1962; New York, NY

**Years Active in the Industry:** by decade

| 10$^s$ | 20$^s$ | 30$^s$ | 40$^s$ | 50$^s$ | 60$^s$ | 70$^s$ | 80$^s$ | 90$^s$ |
|---|---|---|---|---|---|---|---|---|

Campbell Scott is the son of actors George C. Scott and Colleen Dewhurst. Though he obviously inherited some of their talent, he curiously resembles neither one of his famous parents—which has perhaps enabled him to seek out the romantic-lead roles that eluded his parents in their formative years. For one so young, Scott has been associated with several projects linked with the Grim Reaper: the PBS AIDS-related drama *Longtime Companion* (1991), the Civil War-based TV movie *Perfect Tribute* (1991) (which climaxes on the bloody grounds of Gettysburg), and the self-explanatory *Dead Again* (1991) and *Dying Young* (1992). One of most curious film assignments for the handsome, lithe Scott was as the plain and portly humorist Robert Benchley in *Mrs. Parker and the Vicious Circle* (1994). **Selected Works:** *Sheltering Sky* (1990), *Singles* (1992)

# George C. Scott (George Campbell Scott)

**Born:** October 18, 1927; Wise, VA

**Years Active in the Industry:** by decade

| 10$^s$ | 20$^s$ | 30$^s$ | 40$^s$ | 50$^s$ | 60$^s$ | 70$^s$ | 80$^s$ | 90$^s$ |
|---|---|---|---|---|---|---|---|---|

An impressive, magnetic, aggressive leading man, Scott graduated from college and spent four years in the Marines, then

became a teacher and aspiring writer. He began acting in campus productions, then gradually worked his way up in summer stock, off-Broadway, Broadway, TV, and films. He debuted onscreen in 1959. After starring in the title role of *Patton* (1970) he declared that he would not accept an Academy Award, and that the Oscars were "a meaningless, self-serving meat parade;" nevertheless, to the Academy's embarrassment, he won the Best Actor Oscar, refusing to accept it. Later he won an Emmy for his work in the TV production of Arthur Miller's *The Price,* but did not accept that award either. He has also directed some of his movies, beginning with *Rage* (1972). He married and divorced actress Colleen Dewhurst, with whom he fathered a son, actor Campbell Scott. He is married to actress Trish Van Devere. **Selected Works:** *Anatomy of a Murder* (1959), *Hospital* (1971), *Hustler* (1961), *Petulia* (1968), *Angels* (1995)

# Lizabeth Scott (Emma Matzo)

**Born:** September 29, 1922; Scranton, PA

**Years Active in the Industry:** by decade

| 10$^s$ | 20$^s$ | 30$^s$ | 40$^s$ | 50$^s$ | 60$^s$ | 70$^s$ | 80$^s$ | 90$^s$ |
|---|---|---|---|---|---|---|---|---|

Born into the Czech ghetto in Scranton, Pennsylvania, she attended the Alvienne School of Drama in New York and began her career in stock. Scott's first break came when she was cast as Tallulah Bankhead's understudy in Broadway's *The Skin of Our Teeth* (1942); meanwhile, she also worked as a fashion model. Starmaker Hal Wallis spotted her, and she did well in a screen test, leading to her film debut in 1945. She went on to play alluring leads in a number of films throughout the next decade, hyped by her studio as another Lauren Bacall or Veronica Lake. There was speculation that Scott would marry Wallis, but this never occurred, and he dropped her option in 1957, effectively ending her movie career. In 1955 she sued *Confidential* magazine over its allegations concerning her sexual preferences. She has appeared in one additional film, *Pulp* (1972), with Michael Caine; she also provided the voiceovers for a series of cat food commercials.

# Randolph Scott (Randolph Crane)

**Born:** January 23, 1903; Orange County, VA
**Died:** March 2, 1987; Los Angeles, CA

**Years Active in the Industry:** by decade

| 10ˢ | 20ˢ | 30ˢ | 40ˢ | 50ˢ | 60ˢ | 70ˢ | 80ˢ | 90ˢ |
|---|---|---|---|---|---|---|---|---|

Born Randolph Crane, this virile, weathered, prototypical cowboy star with a gallant manner and slight Southern accent lied about his age at 14 and enlisted for service in World War I. After returning home he got a degree in engineering, then joined the Pasadena Community Playhouse. While golfing, Scott met millionaire filmmaker Howard Hughes, who helped him enter films as a bit player. In the mid '30s he began landing better roles, both as a romantic lead and as a costar. Later he became a Western star, and from the late '40s to the '50s he starred exclusively in big-budget color Westerns (39 altogether). From 1950-53 he was one of the top ten box-office attractions. Later in the '50s he played the aging cowboy hero in a series of B-Westerns directed by Budd Boetticher for Ranown, an independent production company. He retired from the screen in the early '60s. Having invested in oil wells, real estate, and securities, he was worth between $50-$100 million. **Selected Works:** *My Favorite Wife* (1940)

# Ridley Scott

**Born:** 1939; South Shields, Northumberland, England

**Years Active in the Industry:** by decade

| 10ˢ | 20ˢ | 30ˢ | 40ˢ | 50ˢ | 60ˢ | 70ˢ | 80ˢ | 90ˢ |
|---|---|---|---|---|---|---|---|---|

An art student in college, Briton Ridley Scott became a set designer for the British Broadcasting Company in the early 1960s. Scott was promoting to directing such popular BBC series as the long-running police adventure *Z Cars*. Setting up his own firm, Ridley Scott Associates, Scott was on the ground floor of some of the most inventive European TV commercials of the 1970s. He moved on to the Big Screen with his direction of 1977's *The Duellists*, a visually striking (if dramatically confused) Napoleonic-war film which copped an award at the Cannes Film Festival. With 1979's ultra-stylish *Alien*, Scott became the shining knight of horror devotees. The director found himself at the center of an artistic *cause celebre* due to his expensive 1982 sci-fier *Blade Runner*. The studio decided that the final product was too complex and downbeat for a general audience, thus a voiceover narrator was added and a

more positive ending tacked on. The results sparked an outcry from film purists, but it wasn't until the early 1990s that Scott's own cut of *Blade Runner* would resurface in theatrical revival and on videocassette. In the non-fantasy field, Scott's best work was 1991's *Thelma & Louise*, wherein the plot holes and inconsistencies are smoothed over by the star performances of Susan Sarandon and Geena Davis. *Thelma & Louise* seemed to herald an unending procession of hits for Scott. But then came the costly and unsuccessful *1492: Conquest of Paradise* (1992). Ridley Scott is the brother of director Tony Scott, best known for such escapist action fare as *Top Gun* (1986). **Selected Works:** *Black Rain* (1990)

# Tony Scott

**Born:** July 21, 1944; Newcastle, England

**Years Active in the Industry:** by decade

| 10ˢ | 20ˢ | 30ˢ | 40ˢ | 50ˢ | 60ˢ | 70ˢ | 80ˢ | 90ˢ |
|---|---|---|---|---|---|---|---|---|

The younger brother of British filmmaker Ridley Scott, Tony Scott attended London's Royal College of Art, then entered the film industry as a TV and commercial director. His first feature film was *The Hunger* (1983), a horror picture that offered us the spectacle of a love scene between ageing roue David Bowie and female vampire Catherine Deneuve—*and* a few lesbian couplings of Deneuve and Susan Sarandon (no other film can make this claim!) Scott became "box office" after the success of *Top Gun* (1986), a dramatically empty but visually fascinating tale of student pilots. For a time thereafter, the director had problems shaking the *Top Gun* association, even going so far as to open his 1987 crime melodrama *Revenge* with a gratuitous airborne chase. After a brief dry period, Scott made a strong return with *True Romance* (1993), an acceptable filmization of a gore-laden Quentin Tarantino script; and in 1995, with uncredited script assistance by Tarantino, Scott scored another success with his nuclear-sub thriller *Crimson Tide*. **Selected Works:** *Days of Thunder* (1990), *The Last Boy Scout* (1991)

# Steven Seagal

**Born:** 1950; Detroit, MI

**Years Active in the Industry:** by decade

| 10ˢ | 20ˢ | 30ˢ | 40ˢ | 50ˢ | 60ˢ | 70ˢ | 80ˢ | 90ˢ |
|---|---|---|---|---|---|---|---|---|

At age 17 he moved to Japan, where he studied the martial arts while working as an English teacher; eventually Seagal earned black belts in aikido, karate, judo, and kendo. He became the first non-Asian to open his own martial arts school in Japan and choreographed fight scenes for the movies. Later he entered the security business, setting up "safe houses" and directing special security operations. He has also been a bounty hunter, and has hinted that

he has worked for the CIA. Seagal moved to Los Angeles when he was in his 30s, setting up a martial arts academy; he also served as a personal bodyguard for celebrities, including his future wife and co-star Kelly Le Brock (they were later divorced). He served as bodyguard to super-agent Michael Ovitz, who provided Seagal with valuable Hollywood contacts. Suspecting that there was a demand for his martial arts skills in films, he and Andrew Davis reworked a routine cop picture script and co-produced *Above the Law* (1988), Seagall's screen debut; Davis directed the film, which peformed well at the box office. Seagal went on to appear in a string of highly successful action-adventure films in which he demonstrated his martial arts skills. **Selected Works:** *Out for Justice* (1991), *Under Siege* (1992), *Under Siege 2: Dark Territory* (1995)

## John Seale

**Born:** Warwick, Queensland, Australia

**Years Active in the Industry:** by decade

| 10ˢ | 20ˢ | 30ˢ | 40ˢ | 50ˢ | 60ˢ | 70ˢ | 80ˢ | 90ˢ |
|-----|-----|-----|-----|-----|-----|-----|-----|-----|
|     |     |     |     |     |     |     |     |     |

Australian cinematographer John Seale's first credits as camera operator include several films directed by fellow countryman Peter Weir. When Weir moved to America, he invited Seale to join him; after handling the second unit photography of the director's *Year of Living Dangerously* (1982), Seale was Oscar-nominated for his work as director of photography for Weir's *Witness* (1985). He earned his second Oscar nomination for his vivid color camerawork on director Barry Levinson's *Rain Main* (1988). Seale made the inevitable crossover from photographer to director with the 1991 murder tale *Til There Was You*, which was summed up by one commentator with a terse "pretty scenery can't save this one." **Selected Works:** *Doctor* (1991), *The Firm* (1993), *Lorenzo's Oil* (1992)

## Jean Seberg

**Born:** November 13, 1938; Marshalltown, IA
**Died:** September 8, 1979

**Years Active in the Industry:** by decade

| 10ˢ | 20ˢ | 30ˢ | 40ˢ | 50ˢ | 60ˢ | 70ˢ | 80ˢ | 90ˢ |
|-----|-----|-----|-----|-----|-----|-----|-----|-----|
|     |     |     |     |     |     |     |     |     |

At 17 she was selected (from thousands of candidates) by filmmaker Otto Preminger to play the title role in his *Saint Joan* (1957); the considerable publicity attending the film made her famous, although the movie itself flopped critically and commercially. However, she continued getting screen roles, then ran into great luck when she was cast in Jean-Luc Godard's directorial debut *Breathless* (1960); with the film's success she became popular in France and soon was in much demand among French filmmakers. She maintained a busy international screen career through the mid '70s. Offscreen, Seberg was politically active as a supporter of the Black Panther movement, which resulted in her harrassment by the FBI; at one point, the FBI planted a false story that the baby she was carrying had been fathered by a member of the Black Panther. After the child miscarried she sufferred a nervous breakdown. In 1979, at age 40, she died from an overdose of barbiturates; it was assumed that she'd committed suicide. She authored a memoir, *Blue Jeans.* Her husbands included filmmaker Francois Moreuil, novelist Romain Gary, and director Dennis Berry. **Selected Works:** *Airport* (1970), *The Mouse That Roared* (1960), *Lilith* (1964), *Paint Your Wagon* (1969)

## Kyra Sedgwick

**Born:** 1965; New York, NY

**Years Active in the Industry:** by decade

| 10ˢ | 20ˢ | 30ˢ | 40ˢ | 50ˢ | 60ˢ | 70ˢ | 80ˢ | 90ˢ |
|-----|-----|-----|-----|-----|-----|-----|-----|-----|
|     |     |     |     |     |     |     |     |     |

USC graduate Kyra Sedgwick had comparatively little trouble scaling the theatrical heights; if we are to believe her official biography, she was sixteen when she made her off-Broadway bow in *Time Was.* She won a Theatre World Award for the 1988 revival of *Ah, Wilderness* and earned critical plaudits for her performance of a Jewish career woman in search of her past in the 1992 *Hallmark Hall of Fame* TV drama *Miss Rose White.* Sedgwick's other film and TV assignments include the wife of a chain-gang fugitive in *The Man Who Broke 1000 Chains* (1987), paraplegic Vietnam vet Ron Kovic's high school sweetheart in *Born on the Fourth of July* (1989), one of four awkward "guardian angels" in *Heart and Souls* (1993), and the crotch-kicking sister of infidelity victim Julia Roberts in *Something to Talk About* (1995). Sedgwick has been married for years to actor Kevin Bacon. **Selected Works:** *Mr. & Mrs. Bridge* (1991), *Singles* (1992), *Women and Men 2* (1991),

## Susan Seidelman

**Born:** December 11, 1952; Abington, PA

**Years Active in the Industry:** by decade

| 10ˢ | 20ˢ | 30ˢ | 40ˢ | 50ˢ | 60ˢ | 70ˢ | 80ˢ | 90ˢ |
|-----|-----|-----|-----|-----|-----|-----|-----|-----|
|     |     |     |     |     |     |     |     |     |

American filmmaker Susan Seidelman majored in art and fashion design at Drexel University. She worked at an independent

TV station in Philadelphia before enrolling at NYU's film school. Her feminist-oriented student films, made between 1976 and 1977, won several awards and plenty of industry attention. Seidelman's first feature, the independently produced *Smithereens* (1983), made very little headway in mainstream theaters, but was a hit on the festival circuit. On the strength of *Desperately Seeking Susan* (1985), Seidelman was lauded as one of Hollywood's few "bankable" female directors; the film's success was probably due more to the supporting performance of Madonna than to its director. Seidelman's next two films, *Making Mr Right* (1987) and *Cookie* (1989), failed to match the standard set by *Desperately Seeking Susan*. In 1989's *She-Devil*, Seidelman attempted to do for Roseanne Barr what she had done for Madonna— that is, transform Roseanne into a viable film personality. But *She Devil* did nothing for anyone, least of all Susan Seidelman, whose much-vaunted bankability was injured to the point that she hasn't directed a feature film since. **Selected Works:** *Erotic Tales* (1994)

# George B. Seitz

**Born:** January 3, 1888; Boston, MA
**Died:** 1944

**Years Active in the Industry:** by decade

| 10ˢ | 20ˢ | 30ˢ | 40ˢ | 50ˢ | 60ˢ | 70ˢ | 80ˢ | 90ˢ |
|-----|-----|-----|-----|-----|-----|-----|-----|-----|

A one-time illustrator turned stage actor and playwright, George Brackett Seitz began in movies as an actor and screenwriter in 1913. Soon after, he revolutionized screen story-telling with his screenplay for the serial *Perils of Pauline*, and he subsequently directed and starred in several silent serials, a genre that he dominated through the mid 1920s. He turned to features and directed several classics, including *Vanishing American* (1925), one of the earliest Hollywood films to deal with the plight of Native Americans; the 1936 version of *Last of the Mohicans*, starring Randolph Scott; as well as numerous entries in the Andy Hardy series at MGM.

# Tom Selleck

**Born:** January 29, 1945; Detroit, MI

**Years Active in the Industry:** by decade

| 10ˢ | 20ˢ | 30ˢ | 40ˢ | 50ˢ | 60ˢ | 70ˢ | 80ˢ | 90ˢ |
|-----|-----|-----|-----|-----|-----|-----|-----|-----|

Leading man and sex symbol, Selleck has a gentle, humorous manner. He attended college on an athletic scholarship, majoring in business. A drama coach suggested he become an actor; soon he began making the rounds of auditions. He won a part in the disastrous film *Myra Breckinridge* (1970), his screen debut, then appeared in small roles in a handful of films during the '70s. Meanwhile, Selleck was signed to a seven-year contract with Fox, leading to a great many TV roles, including appearances as a re-

curring character on the TV series "The Rockford Files." Eventually he was chosen as the lead for the TV series "Magnum P.I.;" the show became a hit, staying on the air from 1980-88, and he became a star and sex symbol, winning an Emmy, a Golden Globe award, and a star on Hollywood Boulevard. He suffered a serious career setback in 1981, when he was chosen to star in the Lucas-Spielberg blockbuster *Raiders of the Lost Ark,* but couldn't get released from his TV responsibilities. Beginning in 1983 he tried to break back into films, finally landing a major hit in a co-starring role in *Three Men and a Baby* (1987); although he appeared in a dozen films after 1983 he never firmly established himself as a screen star. He has also been active as a TV producer. He is married to English dancer Jillie Mack. **Selected Works:** *Mr. Baseball* (1992), *Quigley Down Under* (1990), *Broken Trust* (1995)

# Peter Sellers (Richard Henry Sellers)

**Born:** September 8, 1925; Southsea, England
**Died:** 1980

**Years Active in the Industry:** by decade

| 10ˢ | 20ˢ | 30ˢ | 40ˢ | 50ˢ | 60ˢ | 70ˢ | 80ˢ | 90ˢ |
|-----|-----|-----|-----|-----|-----|-----|-----|-----|

Born Richard Henry Sellers, this son of comedians began appearing onstage with his parents while still a child. At 13 he won a talent contest, then was a camp entertainer with the Royal Air Force, which he joined at 17. In 1949 Sellers began appearing on the BBC Radio comedy series "The Goon Show" with Harry Secombe and Spike Milligan; he also appeared with them in his screen debut, *Penny Points to Paradise* (1951). He worked on British TV and made short films in the early '50s. He began to be noticed as a film actor after his performance in *The Ladykillers* (1955) with Alec Guinness. Sellers' popularity in America greatly increased after he played three different roles in the popular comedy *The Mouse that Roared* (1959); the same year he appeared in *I'm All Right, Jack* (1959), which became a huge hit in England and for which he won the British Film Academy Award for Best Actor. He is perhaps best known for his portrayal of the bumbling French detective Inspector Clouseau in a series of films beginning with *The Pink Panther* (1963). He further increased his reputation for versatility by playing three roles in Stanley Kubrick's classic *Dr. Strangelove* (1963), by which time he had firmly established himself as an international star. For one of his last roles (and the one of which he was proudest), as the TV-addled Chauncey Gardener in *Being There* (1979), he received a Best Actor Oscar nomination. Sellers was known as a workaholic who pushed himself to the limit despite heart attacks; he died of one in 1980. His four marriages included one to actress Britt Ekland. **Selected Works:** *World of Henry Orient* (1964), *Dr. Strangelove - or - How I Learned to Stop Worrying and Love the Bomb* (1964)

# David Selznick (David Oliver Selznick)

**Born:** May 10, 1902; Pittsburgh, PA
**Died:** June 22, 1965; Hollywood, CA

**Years Active in the Industry:** by decade

| 10s | 20s | 30s | 40s | 50s | 60s | 70s | 80s | 90s |
|-----|-----|-----|-----|-----|-----|-----|-----|-----|
|     |     |     |     |     |     |     |     |     |

It doesn't *really* say "The Man Who Made *Gone With the Wind*" on the tombstone of David O. Selznick, but he was quite right in predicting that this phrase would serve as his epitaph. One of two sons of silent-movie producer Lewis J. Selznick (brother Myron would become an actor's agent), David had already decided on a film career before he ever set foot in Columbia University. His hopes of entering movies on an executive level were dashed when his father lost his fortune in the late 1920s, but Selznick was bright and brimming with self-confidence and was able to wangle a $100-per-week job as an MGM script reader. Promoted to assistant of MGM producer Harry Rapf, Selznick decided to accept a lower-paying job at Paramount, feeling that he had a better chance to grow professionally at that studio. He quickly earned a reputation for arrogance and outspokenness, which he tempered with a keen acumen for successful moviemaking. While still at Paramount, Selznick courted Irene Mayer, the daughter of MGM head man Louis B. Mayer, who was dead set against his daughter marrying someone from the "enemy" camp but eventually had to acquiesce to his daughter's wishes. Though the Mayer-Selznick marriage was doomed by Selznick's workaholism and rampant infidelity, he remained friends with Irene even after their 1948 divorce, continually soliciting her advice in business and personal matters (Irene would become a successful Broadway producer). Selznick left Paramount in 1931 for RKO Radio Studios, where among many other accomplishments he discovered Katharine Hepburn and gave the go-ahead for the mortgage-lifting *King Kong*. He was back at MGM in 1933 as vice-president and head of his own autonomous unit, turning out first-rate productions like *Viva Villa* (1934), *David Copperfield* (1934), and *Tale of Two Cities* (1935). Resentful of accusations that he'd gotten his MGM job through his marriage to Mayer's daughter, and eager to have even tighter control over his films, Selznick bolted MGM in 1936 to set up his own company, Selznick International. He moved into the old Thomas Ince studios and purchased the Pathe lot then owned by RKO. There he continued his practice of filming famous literary works such as *The Garden of Allah* (1936), *Little Lord Fauntleroy* (1937) and *Tom Sawyer* (1938),

adding box-office clout to these properties by lensing most of them in Technicolor. He also scored with two "originals," *Nothing Sacred* (1937) and *A Star is Born* (1937). From 1936 onward, Selznick was heavily involved in the production of what was to be his masterpiece, a mammoth adaptation of Margaret Mitchell's bestseller *Gone with the Wind* (during this period, Selznick's habit of sending long, detailed memos to his staff reached gargantuan dimensions). Three directors and 15 scriptwriters later, *Gone with the Wind* opened to unanimous critical and public approval in December of 1939; it was the year's biggest moneymaker (indeed the biggest moneymaker of all time until *The Sound of Music* came along) and won Selznick his first Best Picture Academy Award. In 1940, Selznick won his second Oscar for *Rebecca*, which also represented the Hollywood debut of British director Alfred Hitchcock. After *Rebecca*, Selznick's production schedule slowed down, with releases fewer and farther between; he kept his operation going financially by loaning out his large stable of talent (including Hitchcock, Joseph Cotten and Ingrid Bergman) to other studios. His "comeback" picture, 1944's *Since You Went Away*, was another hit, as was his 1946 western extravaganza *Duel in the Sun*. With *Duel*, Selznick began suffering from the curse of *Gone with the Wind*. Whenever production would come to a creative standstill, Selznick would "solve" the problem by saying "Here's how we did it in *Gone with the Wind*." This philosophy proved disastrous for Selznick's final independent production, the 1957 remake of *A Farewell to Arms* (an outgrowth of his recent involvement in such European coproductions as *The Third Man* [1949]), which bloated Ernest Hemingway's intimate love story into "epic" proportions, thereby scuttling its chances to earn back its cost. After *Farewell*, Selznick involuntarily retired from active filmmaking, though he continued exerting meticulous control over the career of his second wife, actress Jennifer Jones, whom he'd signed to a contract in 1943 and married six years later. While he was well off financially and still a highly respected Hollywood figure in the 1960s, David O. Selznick's efforts to return to moviemaking after *A Farewell to Arms* were futile; he died, tired and ill but still hoping, at the age of 63.

# Dean Semler

**Born:** Australia

**Years Active in the Industry:** by decade

| 10s | 20s | 30s | 40s | 50s | 60s | 70s | 80s | 90s |
|-----|-----|-----|-----|-----|-----|-----|-----|-----|
|     |     |     |     |     |     |     |     |     |

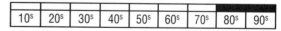

Australian cinematographer Dean Semler worked the "reality" side of the street in newsreels and documentaries before moving into fictional features in 1976. Semler's first movie of note was *Mad Max 2: The Road Warrior* (1981), in which he convincingly conveyed a parched, dusty post-apocalyptic world. *Mad Max 2* proved to be Semler's ticket to Hollywood, where he received an Oscar nomination for his deft blending of actual western landscapes with optical effects and glass shots in Kevin Costner's *Dances With Wolves* (1990). More recently, Semler has manned the cameras for Costner's *Waterworld* (1995), an obscenely expensive effort that many observers have labelled "*Mad Max* on water". **Selected Works:** *City Slickers* (1991), *The Last Action Hero* (1993), *Power of One* (1992), *Young Guns, Part 2* (1990), *The Three Musketeers* (1993)

# Mack Sennett (Mikall Sinnott)

**Born:** January 17, 1884; Danville, Quebec, Canada
**Died:** November 5, 1960; Woodland Hills, CA

**Years Active in the Industry:** by decade

| 10ˢ | 20ˢ | 30ˢ | 40ˢ | 50ˢ | 60ˢ | 70ˢ | 80ˢ | 90ˢ |
|-----|-----|-----|-----|-----|-----|-----|-----|-----|
|     |     |     |     |     |     |     |     |     |

While not the first producer of Hollywood comedies, Canadian-born Mack Sennett was one of the best organized and most successful—a man who truly deserved the appellation "King of Comedy." Growing up in Canada, Sennett had dreams of becoming an opera singer, but economic considerations forced him into such blue collar jobs as iron worker, boilermaker and assistant plumber when his Irish immigrant family moved to the US. In 1902, Sennett made the chance acquaintance of a fellow Canadian, musical comedy star Marie Dressler. The actress was unimpressed by Sennett's minimal talents, but she did write Sennett a letter of introduction to Broadway impresario David Belasco. Belasco was equally underwhelmed by Sennett, but the young aspiring actor persisted and managed to get a few chorus-boy jobs (which, in the early 20th century, required no real talent other than height). In 1908, Sennett went to work as a film actor at New York's Biograph Studios. He was fascinated by the studio's star director D.W. Griffith and latched himself onto the older man, learning everything he could about staging, camera placement, and editing. Griffith responded to Sennett's enthusiasm by allowing the young man to direct several films on his own. But where Griffith specialized in drama, Sennett leaned towards comedy productions, usually ending in wild slapstick chases (a technique which Sennett admitted to stealing from the popular French farce films of the period). Gradually, Sennett concentrated his plots on the skills of three close friends from the Biograph stock company: Fred Mace, Ford Sterling and Mabel Normand. He also was obsessed with the notion of using comedy policeman in his chase finales. Leaving Biograph in 1912, Sennett set up his own studio, with principal financing from ex-book-

ies Adam Kessel and Charles O. Bauman; Sennett later claimed that he owed Kessel and Bauman money, and convinced them it would be to their advantage to invest in movies rather than beat him up for a bad debt. Sennett's new Keystone studio was constructed in Edendale, California, where he began grinding out one-reel comedies starring Sterling, Mace, and Normand, with whom the producer had fallen in love. Taking advantage of Normand's physical attributes, and noting that a front-page picture of a pretty girl invariably sold newspapers, Sennett assembled several leggy starlets who were known unofficially as the Bathing Beauties. He also persisted in ending his films with a bunch of policemen falling over themselves—these were now called the Keystone Kops, and for many years each new Sennett star (Chester Conklin, Fatty Arbuckle, Hank Mann, Slim Summerville) was required to do Kop duty to prove his worth. No such requirement was made of Charlie Chaplin, whom Sennett spotted in a stage revue in 1913. Chaplin made 35 films during his year with Sennett, including *Tillie's Punctured Romance,* the first feature-length comedy; *Tillie* also starred Marie Dressler, who'd given Sennett his first break way back when. Chaplin left Sennett when the producer refused to meet his salary demands, a route subsequently taken by such Sennett stars as Mack Swain and Fatty Arbuckle. In 1915, Sennett expanded his operation and aligned himself with Thomas Ince and D.W. Griffith to form the Triangle Studios. During this period, Sennett began signing Broadway stars like Eddie Foy and Weber and Fields, with variable results. He also helped launch the career of a 17-year-old ingenue named Gloria Swanson. 1917 was a year of both highs and lows for Sennett—he pulled out of Triangle, which required him to leave his "Keystone" label behind but led to the establishment of an even more successful Mack Sennett Studios. He also underwent an acrimonious breakup with erstwhile girlfriend Mabel Normand, though he would insist for the rest of his life that she was the only girl he ever loved (Sennett never married, claiming "My work is my wife"). In the late teens and early twenties, Sennett stepped up production on feature films, and kept his two-reel schedule afloat with such popular stars as Ben Turpin and Billy Bevan. While his comedies of the 1920s were slicker and funnier than those of the teens, he still adhered to the principles of violent slapstick and zany chase finales. Normand briefly returned to the fold, though her relationship with "the old man" was now strictly business, and the resultant films not the best for either star or producer. Sennett's biggest discovery in the 1920s was Harry Langdon, whose fey screen image was carefully nurtured by such Sennett gagmen as Frank Capra and Harry Edwards. Even though his was still a money-spinning operation, Sennett was no longer the leader in the comedy scene—Chaplin, Keaton, and Lloyd were heading the comedy-feature pack, while Hal Roach was rapidly approaching and sometimes surpassing Sennett's dominance in the two-reel market. Sennett had just installed several elaborate new sound stages in the San Fernando Valley (a studio site later occupied by Republic, then by CBS Television) when the 1929 stock-market crash wiped out most of his assets. He switched distribution from the failing Pathe exchanges to the low-budget Educational Studios Operation, which resulted in fewer theaters running the Sennett product. In the first years of the talkies, Sennett's biggest (and virtually only) star was Andy Clyde, who made nearly two dozen shorts per year; some were directed by Sennett himself, who, freed from administrative duties by Educational, returned to his first love of calling the shots on the set. In 1931, Sennett signed singer Bing Crosby for a group of six short subjects, all of them hits. A subsequent quartet of two-reelers starring Sennett's friend and golfing partner W. C. Fields were less profitable, though in later years the Fields films were acknowledged as comedy classics. Much of the Sennett product of the period was shot in a process called Natural Color, while some shorts bore titles like *Hello Television;* these moves were meant to indicate that Sennett was keeping abreast of changing comedy tastes, an illusion dispelled by the bulk of the studio's retrogressive two-reelers. After completing a season of shorts for Paramount release, Sennett produced and directed a 1933 feature film, *Hypnotized,* starring blackface comedians Moran and Mack. The film was a bomb, and Sennett was forced to close down his studio for good. He worked briefly as a director at Educational Studios until finally retiring in 1935. In 1937, Sennett was honored with a special Academy Award, but only an honorary "associate producer" post at 20th Century-Fox resulted from the publicity. Several times during the next 20 years, Sennett would find himself with an unexpected financial windfall, only to lose it all through bad investments and income tax. Still, he remained active in Hollywood social circles, and occasionally appeared in films that nostalgically tried to evoke the good ol' days (*Hollywood Cavalcade, Down Memory Lane, Abbott and Costello Meet the Keystone Kops*). During his last decade, Sennett wrote his highly suspect autobiography, was feted at the Cannes Film Festival, was toasted by the TV series *This is Your Life,* and was frequently called upon by interviewers for his opinions on the new crop of comedians and the bikinied Bathing Beauties of the era. Fourteen years after his 1960 death at the Motion Picture Country Home, Mack Sennett's life was heavily fictionalized in the short-lived Broadway musical *Mack and Mabel;* in 1993, Dan Aykroyd was cast as Sennett in Robert Downey Jr.'s. lavish biopic *Chaplin.*

# Jane Seymour

**Born:** February 15, 1951; Hillingdon, England

**Years Active in the Industry:** by decade

| 10ˢ | 20ˢ | 30ˢ | 40ˢ | 50ˢ | 60ˢ | 70ˢ | 80ˢ | 90ˢ |
|---|---|---|---|---|---|---|---|---|
| | | | | | | | | |

The raven-haired daughter of a prosperous British gynecologist, Jane Seymour made her stage debut at 13 as a member of the London Festival Ballet, after training at the Arts Educational School. Five years later, she switched to acting, making her screen bow as part of a huge ensemble in *Oh, What A Lovely War!* (1968). She entered the fan-mag files with her portrayal of the enigmatic Domino in the 1973 James Bond epic *Live and Let Die,* following

this with a barely dressed ingenue turn in *Sinbad and the Eye of the Tiger* (1974). While her subsequent film appearances were well received (as was her engagement in the 1980 Broadway production of *Amadeus*), Seymour's larger fame rested on her prolific TV work, notably on such miniseries as "East of Eden" and "War and Remembrance." In 1988, she won an Emmy for her portrayal of Maria Callas in the TV miniseries "Onassis." Evidently the fiery temperament of Callas was not all that much a stretch for Seymour; in a 1989 *TV Guide* poll, the actress' mercurial deportment earned her a "Bad Guy" award from a cross-section of producers, directors, writers, and crew members. Since 1993, Seymour has starred in the popular TV Western series "Dr. Quinn, Medicine Woman." **Selected Works:** *Are You Lonesome Tonight* (1992), *Oh! What a Lovely War* (1969)

# Omar Sharif

**Born:** April 10, 1932; Alexandria, Egypt

**Years Active in the Industry:** by decade

| 10ˢ | 20ˢ | 30ˢ | 40ˢ | 50ˢ | 60ˢ | 70ˢ | 80ˢ | 90ˢ |
|---|---|---|---|---|---|---|---|---|
| | | | | | | | | |

Born into a wealthy Lebanese-Egyptian family, Omar Sharif was a math and physics major at Cairo's Victory College. He worked briefly in his father's lumber business before pursuing an

acting career. Entering movies in 1953 as Omar El-Sharif, the young actor's popularity zoomed when he married popular Egyptian star Faten Hamama (the marriage ended in 1974). Well established in his native country, Sharif made his English-language film debut (with one of the longest and most impressive "delayed entrances" ever filmed) as Sherif Ali Ibn El Karish in David Lean's *Lawrence of Arabia* (1962). Sharif's next film for Lean, *Doctor Zhivago* (1965), launched the "superstar" phase of the actor's career. When he was cast as Nicky Arnstein opposite Barbra Streisand's Fanny Brice in *Funny Girl* (1968), Sharif's films were banned in his native Egypt because he made love to a Jewish woman on screen. As Sharif's starring career began its slow downward slide in the mid-1970s, he began devoting more and more of his time to his one great passion in life: bridge. Today Sharif is best known in cardplaying circles as that famous bridge expert who happens to show up in movies from time to time.

# Ray Sharkey

**Born:** November 14, 1952; Brooklyn, NY
**Died:** June 12, 1993; Los Angeles, CA

**Years Active in the Industry:** by decade

| 10s | 20s | 30s | 40s | 50s | 60s | 70s | 80s | 90s |
|-----|-----|-----|-----|-----|-----|-----|-----|-----|
|     |     |     |     |     |     | ■ | ■ | ■ |

Trained at HB Studio, rough-edged American actor Ray Sharkey quickly graduated to movies and television. Sharkey's first film was *The Lords of Flatbush* (1974), a street-gang drama that also featured early appearances by Henry Winkler and Sylvester Stallone. The actor's breakthrough film was 1980's *The Idolmaker,* in which he played rock 'n' roll entrepreneur Bob Marcucci; that same year, he was Phil in the low-budget but highly praised *Willie and Phil.* Sharkey's best known role was as Atlantic City gangster Sonny Steelgrave on the TV series "Wiseguy" (1987-90). Shortly after finishing work on the 1992 Burt Reynolds vehicle *Cop and A Half,* Sharkey made public the fact that he had contracted AIDS through indiscriminate drug use; he died less than one year later. **Selected Works:** *Chrome Soldiers* (1992), *Relentless 2: Dead On* (1991), *Round Trip to Heaven* (1992), *Zebrahead* (1992)

# William Shatner

**Born:** March 22, 1931; Montreal, Quebec, Canada

**Years Active in the Industry:** by decade

| 10s | 20s | 30s | 40s | 50s | 60s | 70s | 80s | 90s |
|-----|-----|-----|-----|-----|-----|-----|-----|-----|
|     |     |     |     | ■ | ■ | ■ | ■ | ■ |

Shatner attended college in his native Montreal, appearing in many student productions. He went on to perform with the Stratford (Ontario, Canada) Shakespeare Festivals, playing a number of Shakespearean roles. After moving to New York he worked in live-TV dramas and on Broadway. He debuted onscreen as Alexei in *The Brothers Karamazov* (1958). Shatner's film work after that was sporadic, though he continued to work on TV, notably in several episodes of *The Twilight Zone* (he was the panic-stricken airline passenger who sees a monster on the wing). For three years beginning in 1966 he played Captain James T. Kirk on the sci-fi TV series "Star Trek;" the show became a cult hit and led to a string of movies beginning with *Star Trek—The Motion Picture* (1979). He has also starred in three other TV series, "Barnaby Coast," "T.J. Hooker," and "Rescue 911," but his identification with Captain Kirk is without a doubt the hallmark of his career. He directed one of the Star Trek films, *Star Trek V: The Final Frontier* (1989), which is considered by many to be the weakest of the Star Trek series. He also breeds horses and is active in conservation and environmental causes. He has written several science-fiction novels known as the "Tek" series; in the mid '90s these were made into a syndicated TV series, in which he co-starred. **Selected Works:** *Star Trek 4: The Voyage Home* (1986), *Star Trek 6: The Undiscovered Country* (1991), *Star Trek Generations* (1994)

# Helen Shaver

**Born:** February 24, 1952; St. Thomas, Ontario, Canada

**Years Active in the Industry:** by decade

| 10s | 20s | 30s | 40s | 50s | 60s | 70s | 80s | 90s |
|-----|-----|-----|-----|-----|-----|-----|-----|-----|
|     |     |     |     |     |     | ■ | ■ | ■ |

Classically trained at the Banff School of Fine Arts and celebrated in her native country for her brilliant stage interpretations of Shaw and Ibsen, Canadian actress Helen Shaver made her American debut in, of all things, a TV sitcom, 1980's *United States.* Neither this nor her second series *Jessica Novak* (1981) were successful, but she remained in demand in films and theatre productions in both the U.S. and Canada. The best of Shaver's many movie roles include fortyish Ann McDonald in *In Praise of Older Woman* (filmed in 1978, when she was 25), and Paul Newman's ever-patient lady friend in *The Color of Money* (1986). Additionally, Shaver was showcased in several made-for-TV movies, among them *Lovey: A Circle of Children 2* (1978) and *This Park is Mine* (1985). **Selected Works:** *Innocent Victim* (1990), *Trial and Error* (1992), *Zebrahead* (1992), *Dr. Bethune* (1993), *Survive the Night* (1992)

# Robert Shaw

**Born:** August 9, 1927; Westhoughton, England
**Died:** 1978

**Years Active in the Industry:** by decade

| 10s | 20s | 30s | 40s | 50s | 60s | 70s | 80s | 90s |
|-----|-----|-----|-----|-----|-----|-----|-----|-----|
|     |     |     |     | ■ | ■ | ■ |     |     |

When he was 12, his alcoholic father committed suicide, after which he was raised in Scotland and then Cornwall. Drawn to acting and writing from his youth, Shaw trained at the Royal Academy of Dramatic Art. In 1949 he debuted onstage at the Shakespeare Memorial Theater at Stratford-on-Avon. From 1951 he appeared in British and (later) American films as a character actor, frequently playing heavies. He became better known internationally after appearing in the James Bond movie *From Russia with Love* (1963), and he received a Best Supporting Actor Oscar nomination for his portrayal of Henry VIII in *A Man for All Seasons.* (1966). In the mid '70s he suddenly became a highly paid star after his appearances in several blockbuster movies, including *The Sting* (1973), *Jaws* (1975), and *The Deep* (1977). He wrote a play and several novels, including *The Man in the Glass Booth* (1967), which he adapted into a play; it was successful in both London and New York, and in 1975 was made into a film. His novel *The Hiding Place* (1959) was the source material for the screen comedy *Situation Hopeless—But Not Serious* (1965). He died of a heart attack at age 51. His second wife (of three) was actress Mary Ure.

# Wally Shawn

**Born:** November 12, 1943; New York, NY

**Years Active in the Industry:** by decade

| 10s | 20s | 30s | 40s | 50s | 60s | 70s | 80s | 90s |
|-----|-----|-----|-----|-----|-----|-----|-----|-----|

Nondescript-looking but multitalented Wallace Shawn was the son of erudite *New Yorker* editor William Shawn. Growing up around the stage luminaries and literary giants of Manhattan, it was perhaps natural that the younger Shawn would seek out a career as either a playwright or actor. As it turned out, he did both. After his education at Harvard and Oxford and a Fulbright-financed teaching stint in India, Shawn launched his theatrical career, first as a playwright. His 1975 play *Our Late Night* won an Obie award. His first film was *Manhattan* (1979), directed by kindred spirit Woody Allen, with whom Shawn would work again in *Radio Days* (1987) and *Shadows and Fog* (1992). In 1981, Wallace Shawn cowrote and costarred in *My Dinner with Andre*, a film that truly lives up to its title; the bulk of this sometimes maddening, often inspired film is a dinner conversation between Shawn and his director friend Andre Gregory. Though it would never be a big-timer at the box office, *My Dinner With Andre* was well enough received for Shawn to become a bankable movie character actor. Much of Shawn's subsequent work has been in colorful cameo roles in such films as *The Princess Bride* (1987) and *Mom and Dad Save the World* (1992). **Selected Works:** *All That Jazz* (1979), *Atlantic City* (1981), *Cemetery Club* (1993), *Micki and Maude* (1984), *Vanya on 42nd Street* (1994)

# Norma Shearer (Edith Norma Shearer)

**Born:** August 10, 1903; Montreal, Canada
**Died:** 1983

**Years Active in the Industry:** by decade

| 10s | 20s | 30s | 40s | 50s | 60s | 70s | 80s | 90s |
|-----|-----|-----|-----|-----|-----|-----|-----|-----|

The winner of a beauty contest at 14, she was born into a wealthy family that lost everything in the 1910s. Her mother brought her to New York in the hope that show business might provide the family with money. Shearer failed an audition with Florence Ziegfeld but found some work as a model. She began appearing in bit roles in New York-shot films in 1920; in one of these, *The Stealers* (1920), she was spotted by talent scout Irving Thalberg, who couldn't track her down until 1923. Signed to a long-term screen contract in 1925, she began playing leads in numerous films. Meanwhile, Thalberg rose to a position of authority at MGM; she married him in 1927 and started getting the best roles the studio had to offer, leading her to stardom. Shearer got her pick of directors and scripts, and made sure to vary her work so she would avoid being typecast. She received five Oscar nominations, winning for *The Divorcee* (1930). Soon she was billed by MGM as "the First Lady of the Screen." Thalberg died at age 37 in 1936, after which Shearer showed bad judgment in her choice of films; she turned down the leads in *Gone with the Wind* and *Mrs. Miniver* and

instead appeared in two consecutive flops, *We Were Dancing* and *Her Cardboard Lover* (both 1942). After that she retired from the screen, meanwhile marrying a ski instructor 20 years her junior. **Selected Works:** *Barretts of Wimpole Street* (1934), *Romeo and Juliet* (1936), *Smilin' Through* (1932)

# Ally Sheedy (Alexandra Sheedy)

**Born:** 1962; New York, NY

**Years Active in the Industry:** by decade

| 10s | 20s | 30s | 40s | 50s | 60s | 70s | 80s | 90s |
|-----|-----|-----|-----|-----|-----|-----|-----|-----|

Brown-eyed chestnut-haired actress Ally Sheedy has been involved with the acting craft for most of her life. The daughter of a literary agent mother, she began making TV commercials and appearing on stage at age 15. Three years earlier, she published a children's book, *She Was Nice to Mice*. She has also been published in periodicals such as *The New York Times*. After high school, the New York-born Sheedy headed west to the University of California where, in addition to her studies, she also appeared in television films. At age 21, she began her feature-film career playing adolescent girls in films such as *Bad Boys* and *War Games* (both 1983). She joined the notorious "Brat Pack" in 1985 after appearing in John Hughes' *The Breakfast Club*. That film was a box-office success, but her subsequent films have not done as well, and by the late '80s her future as a major star in film looked uncertain. **Selected Works:** *Betsy's Wedding* (1990), *Fear* (1990), *Only the Lonely* (1991), *Twice in a Lifetime* (1985)

# Charlie Sheen (Carlos Estevez)

**Born:** September 3, 1965; New York, NY

**Years Active in the Industry:** by decade

| 10s | 20s | 30s | 40s | 50s | 60s | 70s | 80s | 90s |
|-----|-----|-----|-----|-----|-----|-----|-----|-----|

From the get-go, actor Charlie Sheen has been as much a rebel and iconoclast as his famous father Martin Sheen. Sheen made his first film appearance at age 9, as an extra in his dad's TV movie *The Execution of Private Slovik*. Never quite happy at Santa Monica High School, Sheen evinced interest only in the school's baseball team, but was kicked off after skipping too many practices. He also played ball at the Mickey Owens Baseball Camp, at one point boasting a pitching speed of 85 miles per hour. Reportedly, he was seriously scouted by the major leagues, but Sheen chose acting over baseball. Technically, he'd been a filmmaker since childhood, lensing 8-mm epics starring his brothers and other future-star siblings like Rob and Chad Lowe and Sean and Christopher Penn. Sheen's first "adult" film appearance was in 1984's *Red Dawn*; his breakthrough picture was *Platoon*, one of four films he made in 1986. Two years later, he combined the two abiding loves of his life by portraying baseball players in a brace of films, *Eight Men Out* and *Major League*. Not at all concerned with protecting any sort of screen image, Sheen has gleefully poked fun at his frequent "macho" roles in the two *Hot Shots* films of the early 1990s. It is perhaps just as well that Sheen is able to laugh at himself; this quality has helped him ride out several brushes with the law and potential scandals in his life, notably his tenuous association with "Hollywood Madam" Heidi Fleiss. In addition to his acting accomplishments, Charlie Sheen has also expressed himself artistically with a volume of bizarre poetry, which, though unpublished, has shown up in book form on Hollywood's *sub rosa* circuit. **Selected Works:** *Hot Shots! Part Deux* (1993), *Men at Work* (1990), *Wall Street* (1987), *The Three Musketeers* (1993)

played Robert Kennedy in *The Missiles of October*. He may have remained mainly a TV actor and occasional screen presence if not for a chance airport encounter with film-maker Francis Ford Coppola, who was searching desperately for the lead actor for his new project; Sheen got the part in what turned out to be the highly acclaimed *Apocalypse Now* (1979). During the grueling filming of that movie (in the Philippines) he suffered a near-fatal heart attack, which made him re-orient his life and tackle a serious drinking problem. His success in that film led to steady screen work in the 1980s, usually in supporting roles. He became an outspoken proponent of liberal causes, particularly as an advocate of the homeless. He is the father of actors Charlie Sheen and Emilio, Ramon, and Renee Estevez. **Selected Works:** *Gandhi* (1982), *Gettysburg* (1992), *Wall Street* (1987), *The American President* (1995)

# Martin Sheen (Ramon Estevez)

**Born:** August 3, 1940; Dayton, OH

**Years Active in the Industry:** by decade

| 10ˢ | 20ˢ | 30ˢ | 40ˢ | 50ˢ | 60ˢ | 70ˢ | 80ˢ | 90ˢ |
|---|---|---|---|---|---|---|---|---|
| | | | | | | | | |

Born Ramon Estevez, the son of a Spanish father and Irish mother, Sheen dropped out of high school in his senior year to commit himself to acting. After borrowing money he moved to New York in 1959, where he supported himself in a string of odd jobs. He joined the Actors Co-op, whose members contributed the money to rent a loft and do showcase performances for agents; another member was Barbra Streisand. After losing a job he became a prop-man for the off-off-Broadway Living Theater, working alongside Al Pacino, who had a similar job. Eventually, he began landing roles in the company's productions. His career began to progress in 1963, when he made his TV debut on the series "East Side, West Side;" later he became a regular on the soap opera "As the World Turns." In 1964 he debuted on Broadway; later that year he had his first major success as the lead in the Broadway play *The Subject Was Roses* (he also appeared in the 1968 film version). He debuted onscreen as a punk who terrorizes the passengers on a subway train in *The Incident* (1967). In 1970 he moved to Hollywood, making notable appearances in *Catch-22* (1970) and *Badlands* (1973), in which he starred as real-life murderer Charles Starkweather. However, it was on TV that he really began to make his mark, starring in a string of TV movies such as *The Execution of Private Slovik* (1974); he also

# Ron Shelton

**Born:** September 15, 1945; Whittier, CA

**Years Active in the Industry:** by decade

| 10ˢ | 20ˢ | 30ˢ | 40ˢ | 50ˢ | 60ˢ | 70ˢ | 80ˢ | 90ˢ |
|---|---|---|---|---|---|---|---|---|
| | | | | | | | | |

Californian Ron Shelton toyed with a sculpting career before answering the clarion call of the sports world. A basketball star in college, Shelton spent five years as a baseball player in the Baltimore Orioles' farm system. He closed out his diamond career with the Rochester Red Wings at age 25. After a series of "joe jobs," Shelton decided he needed a bit more education to survive, and went on to earn an MFA degree at Arizona State. Still drifting from one dead-end job to another, Shelton began writing screenplays, his favorite being a semi-autobiographical work about a minor league catcher titled *A Player to Be Named Later*. Failing to make a sale, Shelton signed on as a rewrite man and second-unit director for director Roger Spottiswoode's *Under Fire* (1983). Impressed by the results, Spottiswoode gave Shelton another second-unit assignment in the 1985 football comedy *The Best of Times*, allowing Shelton to direct the climactic gridiron sequences himself. Through the auspices of Spottiswoode, Shelton was finally able to sell *A Player to Be Named Later*, which, under the title *Bull Durham*, was directed by Shelton on a tiny budget in 1988. The film was a surprise box-office hit, making a major star out of Kevin Costner and earning Shelton a best-screenplay Oscar nomination. Shelton's next project was *Blaze* (1990), a near-lampoon account of the romance between Louisiana governor Earl Long (Paul Newman) and stripper Blaze Starr (Lola Davidovitch). The film failed to connect with the public, but Shelton's next effort was an unadulterated hit: *White Men Can't Jump* (1992), an uproarious, profanity-laden study of "street basketball" that scored with black and white audiences alike. In 1994, ex-baseballer Shelton came full circle with *Cobb*, the much awaited biopic of controversial baseball legend Ty Cobb (Tommy Lee Jones); alas, by concentrating only on Cobb's vitriolic final years (and only peripherally on his baseball activities), the film proved a letdown to both Cobb's and Shelton's fans, ending up a box-office loser.

# Sam Shepard (Samuel Shepard Rogers)

**Born:** 1943; Fort Sheridan, IL

**Years Active in the Industry:** by decade

| 10s | 20s | 30s | 40s | 50s | 60s | 70s | 80s | 90s |
|-----|-----|-----|-----|-----|-----|-----|-----|-----|
|     |     |     |     |     |     |     |     |     |

A tall, handsome actor, writer, and director, Shepard was born Samuel Shepard Rogers. An "army brat" who later lived on a farm as a boy, in his late teens he moved to New York to pursue a career as a playwright. When he was only 20 his first two plays were staged in New York. He went on to write more than 40 plays, winning numerous awards, including ten Obies; in 1978 his play *Buried Child* won the Pulitzer Prize. Beginning with *Me and My Brother* (1967) he has also written or contributed to a number of screen plays. He has acted and directed for the stage, played drums in his band The Holy Modal Rounders (who toured in 1975's Rolling Thunder Revue with Bob Dylan and a host of other stars), and collaborated with punk singer/songwriter/poet Patty Smith. His first dramatic screen role was in Terrence Malick's *Days of Heaven* (1978), after which he acted in a number of films, notably *The Right Stuff* (1983). He received a Best Supporting Actor Oscar nomination for his role as pilot Chuck Yeager. Shepard's screen persona has been part cowboy, part drifter, always with a languid, laidback attitude. He has directed two films, *Far North* (1988) and *Silent Tongue* (1993). He is in a long-term live-in relationship with actress Jessica Lange, with whom he has had children; the two of them appeared together in a number of films beginning with *Frances* (1982). **Selected Works:** *Defenseless* (1991), *Thunderheart* (1992), *Voyager* (1991), *The Pelican Brief* (1993), *Safe Passage* (1994)

# Cybill Shepherd

**Born:** February 18, 1950; Memphis, TN

**Years Active in the Industry:** by decade

| 10s | 20s | 30s | 40s | 50s | 60s | 70s | 80s | 90s |
|-----|-----|-----|-----|-----|-----|-----|-----|-----|
|     |     |     |     |     |     |     |     |     |

American actress Cybill Shepherd's pre-acting career included a runner-up stint in the Miss Teenage America pageant and seemingly thousands of modeling gigs, most prominently for Cover Girl makeup. She was spotted adorning a magazine cover by film director Peter Bogdanovich, who selected her to play a small town heartbreaker in his prestigious 1971 film *The Last Picture Show.* Shepherd was praised for her cinematic debut, though the reviews devoted more space to her diving-board striptease than her delivery of lines. Except for a part as Charles Grodin's dream girl in *The Heartbreak Kid* (1972), Shepherd did most of her subsequent early film work for Bogdanovich, once her lover as well as her mentor. Reviewers were barely tolerant of her performance in *Daisy Miller* (1974)—and with the next Bogdanovich-directed appearance in *At Long Last Love* (1975) the gloves were off. Stories still circulate in the Hollywood Hills of how Shepherd's singing and dancing in this musical blunderbuss was hissed and booed off the screen. But she recovered, at least professionally, and did quite well for herself in Martin Scorsese's *Taxi Driver* (1975). The "Peter Bogdanovich's Girlfriend" onus took years to suppress; it was still being bandied about when she appeared in her first (short-lived) TV series "The Yellow Rose" (1983). But with her starring role in the popular detective/comedy weekly "Moonlighting" (1985), Shepherd made up for lost time and attained star status without any association with her onetime "Svengali." Shepherd and costar Bruce Willis played the reluctant partners in a failing detective agency, but the plotlines were secondary to the banter and witticisms between the stars—not to mention the winks at the audience and "in" jokes that let the folks at home know that the *characters* knew that they were just acting on TV. An instant success, "Moonlighting" was plagued with production problems almost from the outset. Shepherd and Willis made no secret of their distaste for one another, and both behaved rather boorishly to those around them. Possibly in repayment for her years of humiliation, Shepherd gained a reputation for being all but impossible to work with, and also as a person with a vengeful streak (nor was Willis, a former bartender whose sudden fame had inflated his ego to Hindenberg proportions, blameless in the "Moonlighting" wars). Firings and tantrums were almost everyday occurences on the set, and this, plus the problem of turning out a quality script each week, caused the series to fall woefully behind in schedule. Soon it became a media event if "Moonlighting" ran something other than a repeat. In 1987, Shepherd became pregnant with twins, which forced a speedup in production and some wildly convoluted (and often tasteless) scripts to accomodate the actress' condition. Power struggles continued between Shepherd and producer Glenn Caron (and the people that replaced Caron), while audiences gave up caring; "Moonlighting" was cancelled in 1989. Since that time, Shepherd has signed a fat endorsement contract with L'Oreal cosmetics, while continuing to appear in films and TV movies of variable quality (including *Texasville,* the best-forgotten sequel to *The Last Picture Show*). Besides becoming a favored and most entertaining guest on the talk-show circuit, Shepherd is currently involved in another TV series titled *Cybill.* **Selected Works:** *Alice* (1990), *Memphis* (1991), *Which Way Home* (1990)

# Ann Sheridan

**Born:** February 21, 1915; Denton, TX
**Died:** 1967

**Years Active in the Industry:** by decade

| 10s | 20s | 30s | 40s | 50s | 60s | 70s | 80s | 90s |
|-----|-----|-----|-----|-----|-----|-----|-----|-----|

Ann Sheridan was born Clara Lou Sheridan, the name under which she was billed in 1934 and part of 1935. At 18 she won a "Search for Beauty" contest, and was rewarded with a bit part in a film by that name (1934). Signed to a contract, she appeared in small roles in more than 20 films throughout the next two years. She changed her first name and, in 1936, switched studios to Warner Bros., which launched a publicity campaign hyping her as the sexy "Oomph Girl." Sheridan went on to a very busy career in better roles, usually cast as a wise, practical girl; her work in *King's Row* (1942) best demonstrated her acting ability and opened the door to a wider variety of parts. She remained popular and busy through the early '50s, when available roles began drying up for her; by the mid '50s her screen career was over. She later starred in the TV soap opera "Another World" and on "live" TV dramatic shows, and also worked in stock. At the time of her death from cancer she was starring in the TV series "Pistols 'n' Petticoats." She was married three times: to actors Edward Norris, George Brent, and Scott McKay. **Selected Works:** *Angels with Dirty Faces* (1938), *The Man Who Came to Dinner* (1941)

# Jim Sheridan

**Born:** 1949; Dublin, Ireland

**Years Active in the Industry:** by decade

| 10s | 20s | 30s | 40s | 50s | 60s | 70s | 80s | 90s |
|-----|-----|-----|-----|-----|-----|-----|-----|-----|

Irish filmmaker Jim Sheridan emulated his stage-director father by working in Dublin-based children's theater, then with the "alternate theater" Project Art Centre, an organization Sheridan co-founded. He left the  Centre over a dispute concerning a gay-themed production, then moved to New York, where he briefly enrolled in the NYU film school and served as artistic director of the Irish Arts Center. With his movie directorial debut, the Oscar-nominated *My Left Foot* (1989), Sheridan inaugurated a harmonious working relationship with Irish actor Daniel Day-Lewis, which has yielded such excellent projects as *In the Name of the Father* (1993). Thus far, Sheridan's most ambitious film project has been *Into the West* (1992), a

child's-eye-view affair that juggles reality with fantasy with dizzying expertise. **Selected Works:** *Into the Past* (1990)

# Brooke Shields

**Born:** May 31, 1965; New York, NY

**Years Active in the Industry:** by decade

| 10s | 20s | 30s | 40s | 50s | 60s | 70s | 80s | 90s |
|-----|-----|-----|-----|-----|-----|-----|-----|-----|

Managed by an energetic mother who is an ex-actress, Shields began modeling as an infant; for her appearances in Ivory soap ads she was declared "the most beautiful baby in America." Throughout her youth she was a busy and highly paid model before making her screen debut at age 11 in the forgettable *Alice Sweet Alice* (1977). She became internationally famous the following year when she played a child prostitute in Louis Malle's controversial *Pretty Baby* (1978). Between 1978 and 1983 she appeared in a number of films, including the successful *Blue Lagoon* (1980) and *Endless Love* (1983). In the mid '80s Shields took time off from acting to attend Princeton University, at which her BA thesis was titled "From Innocence to Experience in the work of Louis Malle." She began making films again in 1989, having little success in landing good roles or good projects. She is the author of an autobiography, *On Your Own*. She is the granddaughter of tennis star-actor Frank Shields and is presently dating tennis star Andre Agassi. **Selected Works:** *Backstreet Dreams* (1990), *Diamond Trap* (1991)

# Talia Shire

**Born:** 1946; Jamaica, New York

**Years Active in the Industry:** by decade

| 10s | 20s | 30s | 40s | 50s | 60s | 70s | 80s | 90s |
|-----|-----|-----|-----|-----|-----|-----|-----|-----|

Born Talia Coppola, Shire attended the Yale School of Drama and landed roles in several Roger Corman films. The sister of filmmaker Francis Ford Coppola, she benefited from her family connection when she was cast in Coppola's classic *The Godfather* (1972), launching her screen career in earnest. After receiving a Best Supporting Actress Oscar nomination for *The Godfather Part II* (1974), she was cast by Sylvester Stallone to play the girlfriend of Stallone's eponymous hero in the hit *Rocky* (1976), for which she won the New York Film Critics Award and received a Best Actress Oscar nomination. She went on to appear sporadically in a number of films, but her career has revolved around the eight films emerging from *The Godfather* and *Rocky*. Divorced from composer David Shire, she is married to producer Jack Schwartzman; the two of them have produced films together, forming the TaliaFilm production company. She directed the film *One Night Stand* (1994). **Selected Works:** *Bed and Breakfast* (1992), *For Richer, For*

*Poorer* (1992), *The Godfather 1902-1959: The Complete Epic* (1981), *Mark Twain and Me* (1991), *Rocky 2* (1979)

# Martin Short

**Born:** 1950; Hamilton, Ontario, Canada

**Years Active in the Industry:** by decade

| 10ˢ | 20ˢ | 30ˢ | 40ˢ | 50ˢ | 60ˢ | 70ˢ | 80ˢ | 90ˢ |
|-----|-----|-----|-----|-----|-----|-----|-----|-----|
|     |     |     |     |     |     |     | ■   |     |

A small, wiry, rubber-faced comic actor of stage, screen, and TV, Short met Eugene Levy and Dave Thomas in college; the three of them were later cast as members of the "SCTV" sketch-comedy TV series. He worked for five years in stage, cabaret, and revue productions, which included a stint in the rock musical *Godspell,* then became part of the SCTV troupe, with which he gained wide exposure. He also appeared in TV movies and the series "The Associates." For a year in the mid '80s he was a cast member of the weekly sketch-comedy series "Saturday Night Live," which gave him the visibility and contacts necessary for a film career. He debuted onscreen in *Three Amigos* (1986) with Chevy Chase and Steve Martin, both of whom had also become famous on "Saturday Night Live." He has sustained a busy career as a screen comic/actor, meanwhile also appearing in a musical on Broadway. **Selected Works:** *Father of the Bride* (1991)

# Elisabeth Shue

**Born:** 1963; South Orange, NJ

**Years Active in the Industry:** by decade

| 10ˢ | 20ˢ | 30ˢ | 40ˢ | 50ˢ | 60ˢ | 70ˢ | 80ˢ | 90ˢ |
|-----|-----|-----|-----|-----|-----|-----|-----|-----|
|     |     |     |     |     |     |     | ■   |     |

American actress Elisabeth Shue was first seen on a national basis as Jackie Sarnac, teenaged daughter of Air Force colonel Raynor Sarnac, on the 1984 TV series *Call to Glory*. She spent the next few years concentrating on "best girl" film roles: girlfriend to Ralph Macchio in *The Karate Kid* (1984), to Tom Cruise in *Cocktail* (1988), and to Michael J. Fox in the second and third *Back to the Future* flicks. She was also Sally Field's daughter-I-never-knew in *Soapdish* (1991). We eagerly await another film assignment for Elisabeth Shue that will match her marvelous interpretation of resourceful teenager Chris Parker in 1987's *Adventures in Babysitting*. She is the sister of TV actor Andrew Shue, who plays Billy on the popular series *Melrose Place*. **Selected Works:** *Back to the Future, Part 3* (1990), *Heart and Souls* (1993), *The Marrying Man* (1991), *Leaving Las Vegas* (1995)

# George Sidney

**Born:** October 4, 1916; Long Island City, NY
**Died:** 1945

**Years Active in the Industry:** by decade

| 10ˢ | 20ˢ | 30ˢ | 40ˢ | 50ˢ | 60ˢ | 70ˢ | 80ˢ | 90ˢ |
|-----|-----|-----|-----|-----|-----|-----|-----|-----|
|     |     | ■   | ■   | ■   | ■   |     |     |     |

American director George Sidney was the nephew of the Jewish comic actor of the same name. After working as a child actor, Sidney received a messenger-boy position at MGM in 1933, through the auspices of another relative, Louis K. Sidney. Before long, the teenager was working as a film editor; he moved up to assistant director in 1935, and one year later was given an opportunity to direct a "Pete Smith Specialty" one-reel short. Sidney's extreme youth prompted MGM to hype the novice director as a "boy wonder," listing his age at 16 (a pretense Sidney himself would maintain for years afterward). He remained busy in the MGM short subjects department, even handling a few "Our Gang" shorts—an experience which he'd later claim would condition him to hate all kids. After winning Oscars for two of the Pete Smith shorts, Sidney was promoted to "B" feature films. Under the aegis of producer Arthur Freed, Sidney became a top director of musical comedies; he also proved adept at such larger than life swashbucklers as *Scaramouche* (1953). After directing the disastrous Esther Williams vehicle *Jupiter's Darling* in 1955, Sidney decided it was high time to leave MGM. He became an independent producer for Columbia in the late 1950s, and at the same time became an executive of the fledgling Hanna-Barbera cartoon firm. Bill Hanna and Joe Barbera were old friends from the MGM days, who had contributed the "dancing mouse" sequence for Sidney's *Anchors Aweigh;* Sidney repaid the favor by helping to finance their new studio, and also smoothing the path for Hanna-Barbera's valuable distribution deal with Screen Gems, Columbia's TV division. After the success of 1963's *Bye Bye Birdie,* Sidney remained with musicals to the end of the 1960s as both producer and director. His last film was 1968's *Half a Sixpence.*

# Sylvia Sidney (Sophia Kosow)

**Born:** August 8, 1910; Bronx, NY

**Years Active in the Industry:** by decade

| 10ˢ | 20ˢ | 30ˢ | 40ˢ | 50ˢ | 60ˢ | 70ˢ | 80ˢ | 90ˢ |
|-----|-----|-----|-----|-----|-----|-----|-----|-----|
|     |     | ■   |     |     |     |     | ■   |     |

Born Sophie Kosow, Sidney was an intense, vulnerable, waif-like leading lady with a heart-shaped face, trembling lips, and sad eyes. The daughter of Jewish immigrants from Russia, she made her professional acting debut at age 16 in Washington after training at the Theater Guild School. The following year she made her first New York appearance and quickly began to land lead roles on Broadway. She debuted onscreen as a witness in a courtroom drama, *Through Different Eyes* (1929). In 1931 she was signed by Paramount and moved to Hollywood. In almost all of her roles she was typecast as a downtrodden, poor but proud girl of the lower classes—a Depression-era heroine. Although she occasionally got parts that didn't conform to this type, her casting was so consistent that she had tired of film work by the late '40s and began devoting herself increasingly to the stage; she has since done a great deal of theater work, mostly in stock and on the road. After three more screen roles in the '50s, Sidney retired from the screen altogether; seventeen years later she made one more film, *Summer Wishes, Winter Dreams* (1973), for which she received a Best Supporting Actress Oscar nomination, the first Oscar nomination of her career. In 1985 she portrayed a dying woman in the TV movie *Finnigan, Begin Again.* Her first husband was publisher Bennett Cerf and her second was actor Luther Adler. **Selected Works:** *Dead End* (1937), *Early Frost* (1985), *Fury* (1936), *Trail of the Lonesome Pine* (1936)

# Don Siegel (Donald Siegel)

**Born:** October 26, 1912; Chicago, IL
**Died:** April 29, 1991; Nipomo, CA

**Years Active in the Industry:** by decade

| 10s | 20s | 30s | 40s | 50s | 60s | 70s | 80s | 90s |
|-----|-----|-----|-----|-----|-----|-----|-----|-----|
|     |     |     |  ■  |  ■  |  ■  |  ■  |     |     |

Coming out of a musical family and trained as a stage actor, Don Siegel became one of the most respected directors of action films in Hollywood. He came to pictures as a film librarian and advanced through the editing department at Warner Bros., where he frequently directed transition and linking footage in the early 1940s, and directed two Oscar-winning short films during this same period. Siegel became a feature-film director in 1946 with an offbeat mystery called *The Verdict,* starring Sydney Greenstreet and Peter Lorre. His second film, the much-underrated *Night Unto Night,* proved so difficult a subject—as a psychological drama about a dying man (Ronald Reagan) and a suicidal woman (Viveca Lindfors, who was then Siegel's wife)—that its release was delayed for over two years. During the early 1950s, Siegel made his reputation as an efficient, reliable, often inspired maker of action and crime films, of which the most notable were *Riot In Cell Block H* and *Private Hell 36* (both 1954). His ability to transform difficult or lackluster script material into original, memorable, often startling motion pictures was established with 1955's *Invasion Of the Body Snatchers,* one of the most unsettling, popular, and profitable science fiction films of the 1950s. Siegel thrived for the next 15 years in relative obscurity to the public (although he made one of Elvis Presley's finest films, *Flaming Star*), until the late 1960s, when he began his association with Clint Eastwood. His Eastwood vehicles included *Two Mules For Sister Sara, The Beguiled* (both 1970), and the phenomenally popular and controversial police thriller *Dirty Harry* (1971). The actor and future director was just rising to fame after his success in Sergio Leone's spaghetti westerns, and Siegel's recognition rose commensurately with Eastwood's popularity. He became something of a mentor to Eastwood and appeared in a cameo role in Eastwood's directorial debut, *Play Misty For Me* (1971). His 1970s films included John Wayne's final movie, *The Shootist* (1976), and the much-underrated Cold War thriller *Telefon* (1977).

# Simone Signoret (Simone Kaminker)

**Born:** March 25, 1921; Wiesbaden, Germany
**Died:** September 30, 1985; Normandy, France

**Years Active in the Industry:** by decade

| 10s | 20s | 30s | 40s | 50s | 60s | 70s | 80s | 90s |
|-----|-----|-----|-----|-----|-----|-----|-----|-----|
|     |     |     |  ■  |  ■  |  ■  |  ■  |  ■  |     |

Born Simone Kaminker, Signoret was raised in Paris. In her early 20s she began appearing in bit roles onscreen, and by 1946 she was playing leads. For the first decade of her career she spe-

cialized in playing tarts or lovesick women, later maturing into more matronly roles. She began working in more international productions, and by the late '50s she was a leading screen personality around the world. For her work in *Room at the Top* (1958) she won the Best Actress Oscar, and was nominated for another for *Ship of Fools* (1965). Signoret continued averaging a film a year through the early '80s. From 1948-49 she was married to director Yves Allegret. From 1951 she was married to actor-politician Yves Montand, with whom she costarred in several films. She authored two volumes of memoirs and a novel. **Selected Works:** *Diabolique* (1955), *Ronde* (1950), *Confession* (1970)

# Joan Micklin Silver

**Born:** May 24, 1935; Omaha, NE

**Years Active in the Industry:** by decade

| 10s | 20s | 30s | 40s | 50s | 60s | 70s | 80s | 90s |
|-----|-----|-----|-----|-----|-----|-----|-----|-----|
|     |     |     |     |     |     |  ■  |  ■  |  ■  |

American director Joan Micklin Silver was educated at Sarah Lawrence College, then moved to New York for a job directing schoolroom films for the Learning Corporation of America and the Encyclopedia Brittanica. In 1972, she attained her first important screenplay credit with one of the earliest films to deal with Vietnam veterans, *Limbo.* While doing research for an educational short about immigrants, Silver read a story about a young Jewish newlywed titled "Yekl;" this would develop into her first feature film, *Hester Street* (1975), which, though minimally budgeted, became a favorite with audiences weaned on the mega-bucks *Jaws.* A year later, Silver scored with a half-hour Public Television adaptation of Fitzgerald's *Bernice Bobs Her Hair,* which, like *Hester*

*Street*, was a breathtakingly accurate recreation of a bygone chapter of American history—and again, one created on a shoestring budget. Joan's experiences writing for *The Village Voice* would be manifested in her first feature film, *Between the Lines* (1977), the saga of an "alternative" newspaper with a remarkable young cast of stars-to-be, including John Heard, Jeff Goldblum, Jill Eikenberry, Bruno Kirby, Lane Smith, and Marilu Henner. Silvers' most distinctive skill was the ability to weave scriptwriting contrivances into a semi-documentary style; she did this admirably with the larger-budget film *Crossing Delancey* (1988), an update of the "arranged marriage" conceit of *Hester Street*. In recent years, Silver has switched to a lighter style with *Loverboy* (1989), a low-key comedy about a pizza delivery boy's many *amours* with lonely older women, and *Big Girls Don't Cry...They Get Even* (1992), which took a "laughing through the tears" approach to the subject of teenagers from broken homes. **Selected Works:** *Prison Stories: Women on the Inside* (1991), *A Private Matter* (1992)

# Joel Silver

**Born:** July 14, 1952; South Orange, NJ

**Years Active in the Industry:** by decade

| 10s | 20s | 30s | 40s | 50s | 60s | 70s | 80s | 90s |
|-----|-----|-----|-----|-----|-----|-----|-----|-----|
|     |     |     |     |     |     |     | ■ | ■ |

A movie buff practically since infancy, American producer Joel Silver attended the film school at New York University. After graduation Silver quickly worked his way up to an assistant producer post under Universal's Lawrence Gordon; after considerable success with a series of popular pictures, including a handful of Burt Reynolds vehicles, Silver was appointed president of Lawrence Gordon Productions. As head of his own Silver Pictures in 1980, Silver began inauspiciously with the mishmosh Olivia Newton-John vehicle *Xanadu* before finding his niche with the stylized violent action of 1984's *Streets of Fire*. Intense and demanding, Silver drove his staff, cast and crews mercilessly, but such prize properties as the *Lethal Weapon* and *Die Hard* series made the effort worthwhile. Silver was able to maintain his industry standing on the basis of these successes, permitting him to ride out his many failures, including *Jumpin' Jack Flash* (1985), *Ford Fairlane* (1990), and the potentially career-busting *Hudson Hawk* (1991). Silver more or less played himself (loud clothes and all) in the on-camera role of an explosive cartoon director in 1988's *Who Framed Roger Rabbit?* (1988). **Selected Works:** *Die Hard 2: Die Harder* (1990), *The Last Boy Scout* (1991), *Lethal Weapon, Part 3* (1992), *Ricochet* (1991), *Demolition Man* (1993)

# Ron Silver

**Born:** 1946; New York, NY

**Years Active in the Industry:** by decade

| 10s | 20s | 30s | 40s | 50s | 60s | 70s | 80s | 90s |
|-----|-----|-----|-----|-----|-----|-----|-----|-----|
|     |     |     |     |     |     |     | ■ | ■ |

Silver was born Ron Zimelman. After studying languages at college and getting a master's degree in Chinese history at Taiwan's College of Chinese Culture, he changed directions and enrolled in acting classes with Herbert Berghof in New York. He also studied with Uta Hagen and at the Actors Studio with Lee Strasberg. Besides a part in *Semi-Tough* (1971), which led nowhere, his first big break came as a cast member of the hit satirical stage show *El Grande De Coca-Cola* in 1976; after that success he moved to California and got a part on the TV sitcom "Rhoda." From then on Silver remained steadily employed in TV and theater; his screen career was renewed in the early '80s (he appeared in no fewer than five 1985 releases), and by the late '80s he was landing lead roles in major productions. He is known as a highly charged, aggressive, electrifying stage actor; for his performance in David Mamet's Broadway play *Speed-The-Plow* he won the Tony and Drama Desk awards. **Selected Works:** *Enemies, a Love Story* (1989), *Mr. Saturday Night* (1992), *Reversal of Fortune* (1990), *Silkwood* (1983), *Timecop* (1994)

# Jonathan Silverman

**Born:** 1966; Beverly Hills, CA

**Years Active in the Industry:** by decade

| 10s | 20s | 30s | 40s | 50s | 60s | 70s | 80s | 90s |
|-----|-----|-----|-----|-----|-----|-----|-----|-----|
|     |     |     |     |     |     |     | ■ | ■ |

Jonathan Silverman was discovered while acting in a play at Beverly Hills High School. The gangly, chipmunk-faced Silverman was thrust into stardom when he replaced Matthew Broderick in the role of Neil Simon's teenaged alter ego Eugene Jerome in Simon's Broadway play *Brighton Beach Memoirs*. The young actor recreated this role for the 1986 film version, then continued the Eugene Jerome saga in Simon's followup plays *Biloxi Blues* and *Broadway Bound*. The actor is also well known for his role as dimwitted Andrew McCarthy's dim-witted-er cohort in the two *Weekend at Bernie's* films. Silverman's first TV stint was as the husband of Laurie Hendler on the 1980s sitcom *Gimme a Break*; in 1995, Silverman headlined his own weekly comedy series, *The Single Guy*. **Selected Works:** *Age Isn't Everything* (1991), *Class Action* (1991), *Death Becomes Her* (1992), *For Richer, for Poorer* (1992), *Little Sister* (1992)

# Phil Silvers

**Born:** May 11, 1912; Brooklyn, NY
**Died:** 1985

**Years Active in the Industry:** by decade

| 10s | 20s | 30s | 40s | 50s | 60s | 70s | 80s | 90s |
|-----|-----|-----|-----|-----|-----|-----|-----|-----|
|     |     | ■ | ■ |     |     |     |     |     |

From age 13 he sang in vaudeville, and a few years later was featured in some musical two-reelers. In 1934 Silvers joined Minsky's burlesque troop as a comedian. He began appearing in feature films as comic relief in 1940 and was quite busy onscreen through 1945, usually playing the hero's friend; after 1945 his film work was much less frequent, but he continued appearing onscreen through the early '80s. In 1951 he starred on Broadway in the musical comedy *Top Banana,* later reprising his role in the play's screen version (1954). In the late '50s Silvers was extremely popular as Sgt. Bilko on the TV sitcom "You'll Never Get Rich" (later re-titled "The Phil Silvers Show"), for which he won an Emmy Award. He authored an autobiography, *The Laugh Is On Me* (1973). **Selected Works:** *Tom, Dick, & Harry* (1941), *Thousand and One Nights* (1945)

# Alastair Sim

**Born:** October 9, 1900; Edinburgh, Scotland
**Died:** August 19, 1976; London, England

**Years Active in the Industry:** by decade

| 10ˢ | 20ˢ | 30ˢ | 40ˢ | 50ˢ | 60ˢ | 70ˢ | 80ˢ | 90ˢ |
|-----|-----|-----|-----|-----|-----|-----|-----|-----|
|     |     |     |     |     |     |     |     |     |

Droll, moon-faced Scottish actor Alastair Sim was for the first decade of his adult life a professor of elocution. A late bloomer, Sim made his stage debut at age 30; in 1935 he broke into British films, appearing in no fewer than five pictures during his first year. In many of his early films, Sim portrayed slow-witted, regional types, notably the buffoonish sergeant in the Inspector Hornleigh mysteries of the late 1930s. He achieved movie stardom during the 1940s, frequently portraying dithering eccentrics who weren't quite as distracted or disorganized as they seemed: the undercover detective in *Cottage to Let* (1943), the inquisitive Inspector Cockrill in *Green for Danger* (1946), the befuddled birdwatcher in *Hue and Cry* (1947). Among his most fondly remembered roles of the 1950s were the taciturn moralist forced to break the law in order to qualify for an inheritance in *Laughter in Paradise* (1952); the enigmatic "voice of conscience" in *An Inspector Calls* (1954); the mild-mannered professional assassin in *The Green Man* (1956); his "drag" appearances as the snooty headmistress in the *St. Trinians* farces; and, of course, the title role in *Scrooge* (1951), his finest hour-and-a-half. Seemingly growing funnier with each passing year, the 72-year-old Sim all but stole the show as a doddering cleric in the outrageous *The Ruling Class* (1972). Throughout his four-decade film career, Sim retained his ties to the theatre, directing and starring in several of the works of playright James Bridie and, by popular request, making frequent appearances as Captain Hook in Barrie's *Peter Pan*; Sim made his last stage appearance in 1975, the year before his death.

# Jean Simmons

**Born:** January 31, 1929; London, England

**Years Active in the Industry:** by decade

| 10ˢ | 20ˢ | 30ˢ | 40ˢ | 50ˢ | 60ˢ | 70ˢ | 80ˢ | 90ˢ |
|-----|-----|-----|-----|-----|-----|-----|-----|-----|
|     |     |     |     |     |     |     |     |     |

At age 14 she was chosen from among a group of dance students to appear in the film *Give Us the Moon* (1944), then appeared in three more films that year. Simmons was becoming a recognizable screen presence after her portrayal of Estelle in *Great Expectations* (1946); two years later she was chosen by Laurence Olivier to play opposite him as Ophelia in *Hamlet* (1948), which established her as a star when she was still a teenager. For that role, she won the Venice Film Festival's Best Actress Prize and a Best Supporting Actress Oscar nomination. In 1950 she married actor Stewart Granger, with whom she moved to Hollywood; there she worked for Fox after freeing herself from a contract with Howard Hughes. In 1960 she divorced Granger and married director Richard Brooks, who directed her in *Elmer Gantry* (1960). For her work in *The Happy Ending* (1969) she received a Best Actress Oscar nomination. Simmons went into semi-retirement from the screen after 1971, but still occasionally appeared in films; she went on to do some work on TV and toured for two years with the play *A Little Night Music.* **Selected Works:** *Big Country* (1958), *Black Narcissus* (1947), *Guys and Dolls* (1955), *Spartacus* (1960), *How to Make an American Quilt* (1995)

# Neil Simon (Marvin Neil Simon)

**Born:** July 4, 1927; Bronx, NY

**Years Active in the Industry:** by decade

| 10ˢ | 20ˢ | 30ˢ | 40ˢ | 50ˢ | 60ˢ | 70ˢ | 80ˢ | 90ˢ |
|-----|-----|-----|-----|-----|-----|-----|-----|-----|
|     |     |     |     |     |     |     |     |     |

As the most financially successful playwright in history, Bronx-born Neil Simon hardly needs TV and movies to enhance his reputation—though at least one-third of his output has been

geared exclusively to non-theatrical projects. Upon graduating from New York University, Simon began penning comedy material for nightclubs and revues, then signed on as a staff writer for TV comedian Sid Caesar. During his years with Caesar, and his later tenure on Phil Silvers' military sitcom "You'll Never Get Rich" (1955-59), Simon became skilled in the art of allowing jokes to flow naturally from the situation and the characters, rather than merely inserting gags arbitrarily for quick, cheap laughs. After an ignoble Broadway debut as librettist for the short-lived musical *The Adventures of Marco Polo* (1959), Simon scored a hit with his play *Come Blow Your Horn* (1961), which later became a successful Frank Sinatra film vehicle. Simon's first script written directly for the screen was *After the Fox* (1966), an uneven "international" comedy suffering from too many cooks (including star Peter Sellers and director Vittorio de Sica). Simon's next movie original, *The Out of Towners* (1969), was far more successful both financially and artistically. While his stage plays of the 1970s and 1980s were almost invariably hits, Simon's film scripts of the same period fluctuated wildly in quality. There are few if any faults in *The Heartbreak Kid* (1972), *The Goodbye Girl* (1977), and *Seems Like Old Times* (1979). Conversely, Simon's movie-genre spoofs *Murder by Death* (1975) and *The Cheap Detective* (1978), while frequently uproarious, are little more than elongated Sid Caesar sketches. And *The Slugger's Wife* (1983) is not only Simon's weakest screenplay, but also one of the worst big-budget pictures ever made. However, in the final analysis, Simon has hit the mark far more often than not—in addition to his Pulitzer Prize for the 1991 play *Lost in Yonkers*, his scripts for *The Odd Couple* (1968), *The Goodbye Girl* (1977), and *California Suite* (1978) have been honored with Academy Awards. As he entered the 1990s, Simon suffered one major cinematic setback with 1991's *The Marrying Man*, then—as always—regained lost ground with still another Broadway smash, 1993's *Laughter on the 23rd Floor*. **Selected Works:** *Sunshine Boys* (1975)

# Simone Simon

**Born:** April 23, 1911; Bethune, France

**Years Active in the Industry:** by decade

| 10s | 20s | 30s | 40s | 50s | 60s | 70s | 80s | 90s |
|-----|-----|-----|-----|-----|-----|-----|-----|-----|
|     |     | ██  | ██  | ██  |     |     |     |     |

Born in Bethune, France, Simon grew up in Marseille and went to Paris in 1930. She worked for a time as a designer and model before making her screen debut in 1931 in a comedy by Marc Allegret, who made his own debut as a feature filmmaker that same year. Simon displayed an innocent, girl/woman sensuality that anticipated Brigitte Bardot (ironically, also a discovery of Allegret) by several decades, and it wasn't long before she was discovered by the American movie industry. In 1935 she was signed by Fox studios in Hollywood. However, soon after arriving things began to go wrong for her with an abortive attempt to cast her in *Message To Garcia* with Wallace Beery, during the filming of which she was hospitalized. *Girls' Dormitory* (1936) became her first American film, but despite the fact that she enjoyed working on it, she didn't get along with her director. After making a handful of subsequent movies, she returned to France in 1938—but not before she found herself caught in a minor scandal involving her friend, the late composer George Gershwin. It was Jean Renoir who rescued Simon's career, casting her as the beautiful but predatory female lead in *La Bete humaine* (1938). That film brought her an invitation from director/producer William Dieterle for the role of Belle in *The Devil and Daniel Webster*. That movie brought her to the attention of producer Val Lewton, who offered her the leading role in the horror B-movie *Cat People* (1942). The role of the tormented Irena in

*Cat People* proved to be the high point of Simon's film career, embedding her in the memory of millions of viewers, and she briefly reprised the role in *Curse of the Cat People*. However, none of her other Hollywood roles took, and she soon found herself confined to B-movies. She returned to Europe after World War II and continued making movies, of which the most notable was Max Ophuls' *La Ronde* (1952).

# O.J. Simpson

**Born:** July 9, 1947; San Francisco, CA

**Years Active in the Industry:** by decade

| 10s | 20s | 30s | 40s | 50s | 60s | 70s | 80s | 90s |
|-----|-----|-----|-----|-----|-----|-----|-----|-----|
|     |     |     |     |     |     | ██  | ██  |     |

African American sports personality O.J. Simpson was forced as a child to wear leg braces because of a severe case of rickets. That he mended well is evidenced by his athletic record: USC football star; 1968 Heisman Trophy winner; record-setting 2000 yards gained during the 1973 season with the Buffalo Bills; installment in the pro football Hall of Fame in 1985. Like many pro footballers, O.J. had yearnings to act, but swore that he'd remain an athlete until his team made it to the Super Bowl. The team didn't, but O.J. did...act, that is, and quite well, in such TV projects as *Roots* and such films as *The Towering Inferno* (1974) and the riotous *Naked Gun* trilogy. He also showed up from time to time in the announcing booth on ABC's *Monday Night Football*, and was the "high-flying" star of a series of Hertz Rent-a-Car TV ads. In the spring of 1994, Simpson, who'd previously starred in several failed television pilots like *Cocaine and Blue Eyes*, had just completed several episodes of the syndicated TV series *Frogmen*, when he was arrested and accused of the murder of his ex-wife Nicole Simpson and her friend Ronald Goldman. **Selected Works:** *Naked Gun 2 1/2: The Smell of Fear* (1991)

# Frank Sinatra (Francis Albert Sinatra)

**Born:** December 12, 1917; Hoboken, NJ

**Years Active in the Industry:** by decade

| 10s | 20s | 30s | 40s | 50s | 60s | 70s | 80s | 90s |
|-----|-----|-----|-----|-----|-----|-----|-----|-----|
|     |     |     | ██  | ██  | ██  | ██  | ██  |     |

After working for a newspaper, Frank Sinatra organized "The Hoboken Four," a singing group. He got his first break when he won first prize on radio's "Major Bowes Amateur Hour." He went on to perform in nightclubs and on radio, then landed the job of vocalist with the Harry James band, later switching to the Tommy Dorsey band. In the early '40s he became a solo artist; soon he was the "dream-date" idol of millions of American girls and, for several years, was enormously popular on stage, radio, records, in night-

clubs, and in light musical films. His first screen acting role came in *Higher and Higher* (1943). He suffered a career setback in 1952 when his vocal cords hemorrhaged and he was dropped by MCA, the giant talent agency. Having established a shaky screen career, he fought back and landed the role of Maggio in *From Here to Eternity* (1953) after begging Columbia for the part and agreeing to take it for a mere $8,000; for his performance he won the Best Supporting Actor Oscar. Having regained his screen career, he appeared in several more movies, then received another Oscar nomination for his portrayal of a drug addict in *The Man with the Golden Arm* (1955). Soon he was back on top as a performer, earning the nickname "The Chairman of the Board." He continued to do frequent film work through the '80s and went on to have hit records as late as the early '90s. His four wives included actresses Ava Gardner and Mia Farrow. He is the father of actor-singers Frank and Nancy Sinatra. **Selected Works:** *Guys and Dolls* (1955), *Manchurian Candidate* (1962), *On the Town* (1949), *Pal Joey* (1957), *Von Ryan's Express* (1965)

# Lori Singer

**Born:** November 6, 1962; Corpus Christi, TX

**Years Active in the Industry:** by decade

| 10$^s$ | 20$^s$ | 30$^s$ | 40$^s$ | 50$^s$ | 60$^s$ | 70$^s$ | 80$^s$ | 90$^s$ |
|---|---|---|---|---|---|---|---|---|
| | | | | | | | | |

Lori Singer rose to fame on *Fame*, and that's not double talk. Her first role of significance was teenage cellist Julie Miller on the 1982 TV-series version of the 1981 film *Fame*. When the series moved from network to syndication in 1983, Singer decided not to go along for the ride; a few months later, she made her big-screen bow as the rebellious daughter of puritanical minister John Lithgow in *Footloose* (1984). Other films to Singer's credit include the true-life espionager *The Falcon and the Snowman* (1985) (in which she played traitorous Timothy Hutton's girlfriend), *The Man With One Red Shoe* (1985) (as Tom Hank's vis-a-vis), the rural romantic triangle drama *Summer Heat* (1987), and the brain-dead witchcraft effort *Warlock* (1991). **Selected Works:** *Equinox* (1993), *Storm and Sorrow* (1990), *Warlock* (1991), *Short Cuts* (1993)

# John Singleton

**Born:** January 6, 1968; Los Angeles, CA

**Years Active in the Industry:** by decade

| 10$^s$ | 20$^s$ | 30$^s$ | 40$^s$ | 50$^s$ | 60$^s$ | 70$^s$ | 80$^s$ | 90$^s$ |
|---|---|---|---|---|---|---|---|---|
| | | | | | | | | |

In its own way, the movie directorial debut of 23-year-old African American John Singleton caused as much excitement as the similar debut 50 years earlier of the 25-year-old Orson Welles.

Fresh from winning the Jack Nicholson award at the USC film school, Singleton directed *Boyz N the Hood*, an intimate portrait of life and death in south-central LA. Singleton was not only Oscar-nominated for *Boyz*, but was also the youngest director to ever be so honored. Perhaps this was due to the fact that, for all its up-to-date grittiness, *Boyz* was rather conservatively directed, with Singleton avoiding the wild camera angles, MTV pacing and ragged editing so common to the works of many of his contemporaries. Singleton has since directed two more films, neither of which has matched the critical and financial success of *Boyz*—1993's *Poetic Justice*, a surrealistic probe of street violence distinguished by the performance of Janet Jackson and the poetry of Maya Angelou, and 1994's *Higher Learning*, a sledge-hammer study of racial polarization in America's colleges.

# Gary Sinise

**Born:** 1955; Chicago, IL

**Years Active in the Industry:** by decade

| 10$^s$ | 20$^s$ | 30$^s$ | 40$^s$ | 50$^s$ | 60$^s$ | 70$^s$ | 80$^s$ | 90$^s$ |
|---|---|---|---|---|---|---|---|---|
| | | | | | | | | |

Gary Sinise has most recently won critical acclaim for his supporting role as a crippled war veteran (thanks to special effects wizardry) who becomes Tom Hanks' best friend and business partner in *Forrest Gump* (1994). An excellent supporting actor on the screen, Sinise is also a successful theater actor, director, and co-founder of Chicago's esteemed Steppenwolf Theater where he worked as artistic director for plays such as *The Miss Firecracker Contest*, *Tracers*, and *Waiting for the Parade*. He next directed a 1987 episode of the television show "Crime Story" before making his directorial debut in the feature drama *Miles from Home* (1988). He made his feature-film acting debut in *A Midnight Clear* (1992). In that year he also directed and starred in a moving and faithful version of Steinbeck's *Of Mice and Men* with fellow Steppenwolf

actor John Malkovich. In 1993, Sinise let his sinister side show by playing a mentally unbalanced veteran in *Jack the Bear* (1993). **Selected Works:** *True West* (1986), *Apollo 13* (1995)

# Robert Siodmak

**Born:** August 8, 1900; Memphis, TN
**Died:** 1973

**Years Active in the Industry:** by decade

| 10s | 20s | 30s | 40s | 50s | 60s | 70s | 80s | 90s |
|-----|-----|-----|-----|-----|-----|-----|-----|-----|

Born in Memphis, Tennessee, where his German banker father and his wife were traveling, Robert Siodmak—the older brother of Curt Siodmak—was raised and educated in Germany and became an actor after graduating from the University of Marburg. His lack of success on stage forced him into business, but in 1926 he entered the movie business as a translator of inter-titles on American films. Siodmak became an editor in 1926 and three years later, on *Menshen am Sontag* (*People on Sunday*), he made his directorial debut in asociation with Edgar G. Ulmer, with future director Fred Zinnemann as the co-cinematographer, and Curt Siodmak and Billy Wilder as screenwriters. He was established as a director in Germany, but the rise of the Nazi Party forced him into exile in Paris, where he continued making movies. He barely made it out of France ahead of the German occupation in 1940. After arriving in Hollywood, Siodmak was put to work in B-movies such as *West Point Widow*. In 1943, he directed *Son of Dracula*, the best of the later Universal horror films, and its success moved him up to better pictures—the results were immediately evident in dark drama like *Phantom Lady, Uncle Harry, The Spiral Staircase* (usually considered Siodmak's best film), and *The Killers*, a landmark example of film noir, which played a key role in the early careers of both Burt Lancaster (who was later directed by Siodmak in several more pictures) and Ava Gardner, and moved Siodmak solidly into A-features. Siodmak also directed the strange psychological chiller *The Dark Mirror*, about identical twins (played by Olivia de Havilland), one of whom is a psychopathic murderer, which today is a very highly regarded film noir. Siodmak's American films are, in the observation of Andrew Sarris, even more Germanic than his German films and filled with dark, atmospheric touches. All possess a seriously unsettling quality on repeated viewing. Ironically, his last American movie, *The Crimson Pirate*, starring Lancaster, was a costume satire with element of slapstick, and it worked as well as his thrillers did. Siodmak left America after 1953 to resume his career in Europe, returning first to France and then to Germany. Among the relative handful of his later pictures to get wide exposure in the United States were *Escape From East Berlin* and *Custer of the West*, the latter starring Robert Shaw as the late U.S. Cavalry colonel—it had interesting moments, especially the action scenes, but as a joint U.S./Spanish co-production, lacked the cohesion needed for a good historical western.

# Richard "Red" Skelton (Richard Bernard Skelton)

**Born:** July 18, 1913; Vincennes, IN

**Years Active in the Industry:** by decade

| 10s | 20s | 30s | 40s | 50s | 60s | 70s | 80s | 90s |
|-----|-----|-----|-----|-----|-----|-----|-----|-----|

His father, a circus clown, died before Skelton was born; his mother raised him alone, in dire poverty. By age seven he was singing for change on the streets, and at 10 he quit school to join a medicine show. He spent the rest of his youth entertaining in circuses, burlesque, vaudeville, and on show boats. Throughout the early '30s he appeared as a small-time comic in one-night stands, but then a doughnut-dunking routine he'd developed gained popularity and led to an engagement at New York's Paramount Theater. He soon became popular on radio, and then debuted onscreen in 1938. He went on to become a popular comedy star in many films of the '40s and '50s, and then became enormously popular as a TV entertainer. He was famous for his pantomiming and his comic characters, who included Freddie the Freeloader and Clem Kadiddlehopper. He also wrote music, including the theme song for the film *Made in Paris* (1966). He was rarely onscreen after the mid '50s, and infrequently on TV after the late '60s. He continued to perform in clubs and comedy concerts, and in 1990, at the age of 80, he starred in a nostalgia act at Carnegie Hall. **Selected Works:** *Those Magnificent Men in Their Flying Machines* (1965), *Ziegfeld Follies* (1946), *Flight Command* (1940)

# Tom Skerritt

**Born:** August 25, 1933; Detroit, MI

**Years Active in the Industry:** by decade

| 10s | 20s | 30s | 40s | 50s | 60s | 70s | 80s | 90s |
|-----|-----|-----|-----|-----|-----|-----|-----|-----|

Tom Skerritt is probably the best-known actor whose name is never remembered. A rugged "outdoors" type, Skerritt briefly attended Wayne State University and UCLA before making his film bow at age 19 in *War Hunt* (1962). His subsequent film and TV roles were sizeable, but so adept was Skerritt at immersing himself in his character that he seemed to have no tangible, recurrent personality of his own. Billed second as "Duke" in the original *M\*A\*S\*H\** (1970), Skerritt did his usual finely-honed job, but audiences of the time preferred the demonstrative, mannered acting technique of Elliot Gould, Donald Sutherland and Robert Duvall; significantly, Skerritt's character was not carried over into the even more unsubtle *M\*A\*S\*H* TV series. Finally, in 1980, Skerritt began to attain a following with his authoritative performance in *Alien*. Since that time, there's been no stopping him. He posed in a popular series of "Guess?" Jeans ads, appeared as a 1987-88 regular on "Cheers," starred in 1992's *A River Runs Through It* (directed by his long-ago *War Hunt* costar Robert Redford), and won a 1994 Emmy for his work on the TV series "Picket Fences." **Selected Works:** *Getting up and Going Home* (1992), *Poison Ivy* (1992), *Steel Magnolias* (1989), *Knight Moves* (1993), *Thieves Like Us* (1974)

# Ione Skye

**Born:** September 4, 1971; London, England

**Years Active in the Industry:** by decade

| 10s | 20s | 30s | 40s | 50s | 60s | 70s | 80s | 90s |
|-----|-----|-----|-----|-----|-----|-----|-----|-----|
|     |     |     |     |     |     |     | ■   | ■   |

The daughter of 1960s rock singer Donovan and younger sister of British actor Donovan Leitch, actress Ione Skye was born in London and raised in Los Angeles by her mother. By age 16, Skye had begun a modelling career, which led to her first film appearance as a neurotic American high schooler in *The River's Edge* (1987). Arguably, her best film was *Carmilla* (1989), based on Sheridan La Fanu's notorious novel about female vampirism. Most of Skye's films have done well with critics but have been ignored by audiences; an exception to this pattern was the well-crafted teen comedy *Say Anything...* (1989). Skye was recently seen in a cute cameo bit in the 1992 raunchfest *Wayne's World* and in a leading role as an Arthurian "ladye faire" in the expensive weekly TV flop *Covington Cross* (1992). **Selected Works:** *Gas Food Lodging* (1992), *Mindwalk* (1991)

# Christian Slater

**Born:** 1969; New York, NY

**Years Active in the Industry:** by decade

| 10s | 20s | 30s | 40s | 50s | 60s | 70s | 80s | 90s |
|-----|-----|-----|-----|-----|-----|-----|-----|-----|
|     |     |     |     |     |     |     | ■   | ■   |

Slater was born Christian Hawkins. The son of a stage actor and a casting director, he began acting professionally at age seven after his mother got him a role in the TV soap opera "One Life To Live." At age nine he appeared on Broadway in *The Music Man*

with Dick Van Dyke, then went on to Broadway productions of *Macbeth* and *David Copperfield*. After more work on stage and some on TV, he debuted on-screen at age 15 in *The Legend of Billie Jean* (1985), but didn't make a strong impression until his second film, *The Name of the Rose* (1986). His breakthrough role was as a sociopathic, murderous teen in *Heathers* (1989), in which his performance style strongly emulated Jack Nicholson's. He went on from there to become a very busy screen actor, appearing in six films released in 1991 alone. **Selected Works:** *Pump up the Volume* (1990), *Robin Hood: Prince of Thieves* (1991), *True Romance* (1993), *Untamed Heart* (1993), *Broken Arrow* (1995)

# Helen Slater

**Born:** December 15, 1963; New York, NY

**Years Active in the Industry:** by decade

| 10s | 20s | 30s | 40s | 50s | 60s | 70s | 80s | 90s |
|-----|-----|-----|-----|-----|-----|-----|-----|-----|
|     |     |     |     |     |     |     | ■   | ■   |

American actress Helen Slater was trained at New York's High School for the Performing Arts. In 1984 she was signed for the leading role in *Supergirl*, perhaps hoping that this modest special-effects fest would do for her what *Superman* did for another unknown, Christopher Reeve. Alas, *Supergirl* was a failure, not so much due to Slater's spunky but antiseptic performance as to an uninvolving script and lackluster direction. Since *Supergirl*, Slater has been seen to best advantage in supporting parts, notably the sweet-tempered kidnapper in *Ruthless People* (1986) and cattle-drive novice Bonnie Rayburn in *City Slickers* (1991). In 1990, Slater played cub reporter Anne McKenna on the three-week TV series *Capital News*.

# Dame Maggie Smith

**Born:** December 28, 1934; Ilford, Essex, England

**Years Active in the Industry:** by decade

| 10s | 20s | 30s | 40s | 50s | 60s | 70s | 80s | 90s |
|-----|-----|-----|-----|-----|-----|-----|-----|-----|
|     |     |     |     |     | ■   | ■   | ■   | ■   |

She trained for the stage at the Oxford (University) Playhouse School. In 1952 Smith made her London debut in a stage revue, and in 1956 she first appeared on Broadway when she was featured in the annual *New Faces*. She went on to a busy and acclaimed stage career on both sides of the Atlantic. Since the late '50s she has been intermittently busy onscreen. Smith has received five Oscar nominations, winning Best Actress for *The Prime of Miss Jean Brodie* (1969) and Best Supporting Actress for *California Suite* (1978). From 1967-75 she was married to actor Robert Stephens. In 1975 she married screenwriter Beverley Cross. **Selected Works:** *A Room with a View* (1986), *Sister Act* (1992), *Oh! What a Lovely War* (1969), *Othello* (1965), *Ricard III* (1995)

# William Smith

**Born:** April 24, 1933; Columbia, MO

**Years Active in the Industry:** by decade

| 10ˢ | 20ˢ | 30ˢ | 40ˢ | 50ˢ | 60ˢ | 70ˢ | 80ˢ | 90ˢ |
|-----|-----|-----|-----|-----|-----|-----|-----|-----|
|     |     |     |     |     |     |     |     |     |

Lanky, cleft-chinned William Smith was regularly employed on television in the 1950s, 1960s and 1970s, never quite a star but always in there pitching. At first billing himself as Bill Smith to avoid confusion with another actor, Smith was a regular in such TV series as *The Asphalt Jungle* (1961), *Laredo* (1966) and *Hawaii Five-O* (from the 1979 season onward). He also became a familiar presence in the many motorcycle pictures being ground out by American International and other such concerns. In 1976, Smith was cast as the unspeakable Falconetti in the TV miniseries *Rich Man, Poor Man*, an assignment that would assure him larger roles and better billing in all future endeavors. He even began showing up in top-of-the-bill pictures like *Any Which Way You Can* (1980), in which Smith and star Clint Eastwood participated in a display of friendly-enemy fisticuffs straight out of *The Quiet Man*. William Smith was finally awarded top billing on a TV series when he headlined the 1985 Western *Wildside*, playing veteran "shootist" Brodie Hollister. **Selected Works:** *Spirit of the Eagle* (1990), *Where the Day Takes You* (1992)

# Jimmy Smits

**Born:** July 9, 1955; Brooklyn, NY

**Years Active in the Industry:** by decade

| 10ˢ | 20ˢ | 30ˢ | 40ˢ | 50ˢ | 60ˢ | 70ˢ | 80ˢ | 90ˢ |
|-----|-----|-----|-----|-----|-----|-----|-----|-----|
|     |     |     |     |     |     |     |     |     |

Bitten by the acting bug while in high school, Jimmy Smits earned a BA from Brooklyn College and an MFA from Cornell. His excellent work in off-Broadway productions led to his being cast in several movie and TV projects, notably the two-hour pilot for *Miami Vice* (1984). In 1986, Smits was signed to play tyro attorney Victor Sifuentes on the weekly NBC series *LA Law*, a role which would win him a fervent fan following as well as an Emmy. He eventually left the series to pursue a theatrical film career, but by

1994 was back on the small screen in such cable-TV production as *The Cisco Kid* and *Solomon and Sheba*. While filming the latter production in Morocco, Smits was asked by the producers of the TV series *NYPD Blue* to replace *another* actor with movie aspirations, David Caruso. In the fall of 1994, Smits made his *NYPD Blue* bow in the role of detective Bobby Simone, almost immediately reclaiming the viewers who'd sworn to desert the series when Caruso left. Following this personal triumph, Smits starred in 1995's *Mi Familia*, a critically acclaimed film of barrio life. **Selected Works:** *Fires Within* (1991), *Switch* (1991)

# Wesley Snipes

**Born:** July 31, 1962; Orlando, FL

**Years Active in the Industry:** by decade

| 10ˢ | 20ˢ | 30ˢ | 40ˢ | 50ˢ | 60ˢ | 70ˢ | 80ˢ | 90ˢ |
|-----|-----|-----|-----|-----|-----|-----|-----|-----|
|     |     |     |     |     |     |     |     |     |

Snipes attended the celebrated High School for the Performing Arts in Manhattan until his family moved to Florida; he again took up acting in college. He went on to appear in several

Broadway productions, debuting onscreen in 1986. But it was his appearance in Michael Jackson's music video "Bad" that led to his breakthrough screen role in *New Jack City* (1991). For his work in the cable-produced movie *Vietnam War Stories* (1989) he won the Best Actor ACE award. His status as a star was confirmed by his lead role in Spike Lee's *Jungle Fever* (1991). Later, he made a number of high-tech action films, becoming one of the few black stars to specialize in this genre for general audiences. **Selected Works:** *Rising Sun* (1993), *Waterdance* (1991), *White Men Can't Jump* (1992), *To Wong Foo, Thanks for Everything, Julie Newmar* (1995), *Money Train* (1995)

# Steven Soderbergh

**Born:** 1963; Atlanta, GA

**Years Active in the Industry:** by decade

| 10s | 20s | 30s | 40s | 50s | 60s | 70s | 80s | 90s |
|-----|-----|-----|-----|-----|-----|-----|-----|-----|
|     |     |     |     |     |     |     | ■   | ■   |

Born in Georgia, director Steven Soderbergh grew up in Louisiana, where his father was College of Education dean at Louisiana State University. While still in high school, Soderbergh enrolled in the University's film animation class, producing short 16-mm films with second-hand equipment. One desultory trip to Hollywood later, young Soderbergh was back in Baton Rouge, where he found work at a video production company which turned out TV commercials and music videos. Soderbergh's feature-length concert video starring the rock group Yes was nominated for a Grammy, but the director failed to capitalize on the success, due to an unfortunate preoccupation with liquor. It was a clean-and-sober Soderbergh who filmed the short subject *Winston*, a study in sexual gamesmanship which he would expand into his first feature film, *sex, lies and videotape* (1989). With this multi-award-winning film (produced on a sliver-thin $1.2 million budget) Soderbergh became the fair-haired boy of the foreign film festival circuit, becoming the youngest-ever recipient of the Cannes' Palm d'Or prize. Little of what Steven Soderbergh has done since has been as widely celebrated as *sex, lies and videotape*, though he has come close with his 1991 semi-biopic *Kafka* (filmed on Franz Kafka's home turf in Prague) and his contribution (along with fellow new-age directors Jonathan Kaplan, Phil Joanou, and Alfonso Cuaron) to the videotaped private-eye anthology *Fallen Angels* (1993). **Selected Works:** *King of the Hill* (1993)

# Gale Sondergaard (Edith Holm Sondergaard)

**Born:** February 15, 1899; Litchfield, MN
**Died:** August 14, 1985; Woodland Hills, CA

**Years Active in the Industry:** by decade

| 10s | 20s | 30s | 40s | 50s | 60s | 70s | 80s | 90s |
|-----|-----|-----|-----|-----|-----|-----|-----|-----|
|     |     | ■   | ■   | ■   | ■   | ■   | ■   |     |

Sloe-eyed character actress whose icy persona lent itself to the portrayal of villainous women, Sondergaard took up acting after college, paying her dues with several years in stock and then reaching Broadway in the late '20s. In 1930 she married director Herbert Biberman, whom she followed to Hollywood in the mid 1930s. Reluctantly, she accepted a role in *Anthony Adverse* (1936), her screen debut; for her work she won the Best Supporting Actress Oscar (the first ever awarded). For the next decade-plus she specialized in playing evil women, though occasionally her characters were warm-hearted. In the late '40s she became yet another victim of the Red Scare witch hunts—her husband was one of the "Hollywood Ten" sentenced to prison terms following appearances before the House Un-American Activities Committee, and neither he nor she could get any more work. Sondergaard returned to acting in 1965 with *Woman,* an off-Broadway one-woman show. Her first film appearance in 20 years was in *Slaves* (1969)—the last film her husband ever directed. After *Slaves* she appeared in two more movies throughout the next fifteen years. **Selected Works:** *Juarez* (1939), *Letter* (1940), *Life of Emile Zola* (1937), *Mark of Zorro* (1940), *Anna and the King of Siam* (1946)

# Barry Sonnenfeld

**Born:** 1953; New York, NY

**Years Active in the Industry:** by decade

| 10s | 20s | 30s | 40s | 50s | 60s | 70s | 80s | 90s |
|-----|-----|-----|-----|-----|-----|-----|-----|-----|
|     |     |     |     |     |     |     | ■   | ■   |

Cinematographer Barry Sonnenfeld learned the basics of photography as a darkroom lab tecnician. While at the New York University film department (he'd previously attained an NYU poly sci degree), Sonnenfeld lensed the 1982 documentary *In Our Water,* which caught the attention of the Academy Awards judges. In collaboration with NYU classmates Joel and Ethan Coen, Sonnefeld handled the photography on such Coen-directed efforts as *Blood Simple* (1984) and *Raising Arizona* (1985). After several years' work on the films of A-list directors like Rob Reiner, Danny De Vito and Penny Marshall, Sonnenfeld was at last given a directorial assignment of his own—1991's *The Addams Family.* He responded to this daunting professional boost by fainting dead away during the first day's shooting. When *Addams Family* proved a hit, the resuscitated Sonnenfeld was immediately assigned the director's position on the sequel, *Addams Family Values* (1993). **Selected Works:** *Big* (1988), *Miller's Crossing* (1990), *Misery* (1990), *When Harry Met Sally* (1989), *Get Shorty* (1995)

# Ann Sothern

**Born:** January 22, 1912; Valley City, ND

**Years Active in the Industry:** by decade

| 10s | 20s | 30s | 40s | 50s | 60s | 70s | 80s | 90s |
|-----|-----|-----|-----|-----|-----|-----|-----|-----|
|     |     | ■   | ■   | ■   | ■   | ■   | ■   |     |

Born Harriet Lake, the name under which she was billed until 1933, Sothern debuted onscreen in 1929 in a bit part, and went on to play small roles in several other films before leaving Hollywood for Broadway. She soon began landing leads, bringing another invitation from Hollywood. She signed a screen contract and changed her name, then began a very busy film career as the light-hearted heroine of B-movies. In 1939, Sothern switched studios and achieved greater popularity as the star of the "Maisie" comedy-adventure series; she appeared as the energetic, scatterbrained Maisie in ten films during the next eight years. She also appeared in musicals, in which her good voice and comedic talents were displayed. Never a major screen star, she became most popular after switching to TV; she starred in the TV series "Private Secretary" and "The Ann Sothern Show." She went on to tour with stage musicals, then returned to the screen in occasional character roles after 1964. For her work in *The Whales of August* (1987), her most recent film to date, she received a Best Supporting Actress Oscar nomination. From 1936-42 she was married to actor Roger Pryor and from 1943-49 she was married to actor Robert Sterling. Her daughter is actress Tisha Sterling, with whom she appeared in *Crazy Mama* (1975) and *The Whales of August* (1987); in the latter, Sterling played Sothern's character as a young woman. **Selected Works:** *The Best Man* (1964), *A Letter to Three Wives* (1949)

# Sissy Spacek (Mary Elizabeth Spacek)

**Born:** December 25, 1949; Quitman, TX

**Years Active in the Industry:** by decade

| 10s | 20s | 30s | 40s | 50s | 60s | 70s | 80s | 90s |
|-----|-----|-----|-----|-----|-----|-----|-----|-----|

Spacek originally wanted to be a country-rock singer, and, after winning a singer/songwriter contest, she moved in with her cousin Rip Torn and his wife Geraldine Page in New York hoping to break into the record industry. Meanwhile, she enrolled at the Actors Studio and also studied with Lee Strasberg for eight months. While in New York she would sing and play in Washington Square or at The Bitter End, where she got $10 a night. After doing some work as a model (and appearing as an extra in one of Andy Warhol's films, *Trash* [1970]), she moved to Hollywood. She did some TV work and then debuted onscreen in *Prime Cut* (1972). She first made an impression in her third film, *Badlands* (1973), with Martin Sheen, in which, at the age of 24, she played a 15-year-old country girl. She went three years without making a film before landing the title role in Brian De Palma's horror flick *Carrie* (1976), in which she once again played a teenager. After three more films she firmly established herself as a major actress with the lead role of singer Loretta Lynn in *Coal Miner's Daughter* (1979), in which her character is introduced as a 13-year-old; for her performance she won the Best Actress Oscar. In the '80s she selected her roles carefully, and at one point went four years between films. She starred on Broadway in *'night, Mother,* then appeared in that play's screen version (1986). After winning her Oscar she went on to receive three more nominations. **Selected Works:** *Crimes of the Heart* (1986), *JFK* (1991), *Missing* (1982), *Three Women* (1977), *The Grass Harp* (1995)

# Kevin Spacey

**Born:** 1959; South Orange, NJ

**Years Active in the Industry:** by decade

| 10s | 20s | 30s | 40s | 50s | 60s | 70s | 80s | 90s |
|-----|-----|-----|-----|-----|-----|-----|-----|-----|

A product of Los Angeles' Valley College and the Julliard school, actor Kevin Spacey performed in comedy clubs and repertory theatres before making his off-Broadway bow in a 1981 production of *Henry IV, Part 2*. He hit Broadway one year later, and in 1986 won a Tony award for his performance in *Lost in Yonkers*. After playing deranged criminal Mel Proffitt on the TV series *Wiseguy*, Spacey made a name for himself in films in eccentric, sometimes "certifiable" characterizations. Kevin Spacey was well cast as Henry Miller's oddball roomate in *Henry and June* (1990), as a leechlike Florida real estate salesman in *Glengarry Glen Ross* (1991), and as Dennis Leary's victim in crime in *The Ref* (1993). **Selected Works:** *Glengarry Glen Ross* (1992), *Henry and June* (1990), *Working Girl* (1988), *The Usual Suspects* (1995), *Seven* (1995)

# James Spader

**Born:** February 7, 1960; Boston, MA

**Years Active in the Industry:** by decade

| 10s | 20s | 30s | 40s | 50s | 60s | 70s | 80s | 90s |
|-----|-----|-----|-----|-----|-----|-----|-----|-----|

The descendent of a long line of teachers and professors, Bostonian James Spader interrupted his formal education to study acting at the Michael Chekhov school. In the fallow periods between such acting assignments as the 1981 film *Endless Love* and the 1983 TV series *Family Tree*, Spader kept alive with a dizzying variety of "civilian" jobs, including yoga teacher. After 1985, his movie assignments increased in frequency. The apotheosis of Spader's many small-time creep and spoiled-brat roles was his award-winning performance as the enigmatic video freak in *sex, lies, and videotape* (1989). Having played so many nasty yuppies in the past (few nastier than the slimy lawyer in 1987's *Wall Street*), it must have been refreshing for Spader to play a reasonably nice, albeit emotionally scrambled, young urban professional in *White Palace* (1990). Thus far the biggest moneymaker with which Spader has been associated is the sci-fi spectacular *Stargate* (1994), in which he portrays a likeably nerdish Egyptologist who is given a chance to prove his historical theories first-hand. When asked about his movie career, James Spader has allowed that he enjoys working in all his films—as long as he doesn't have to see any of them. **Selected Works:** *Storyville* (1992), *Music of Chance* (1993), *Dream Lover* (1994), *Wolf* (1994)

# Vincent Spano

**Born:** 1962; Brooklyn, NY

**Years Active in the Industry:** by decade

| 10s | 20s | 30s | 40s | 50s | 60s | 70s | 80s | 90s |
|-----|-----|-----|-----|-----|-----|-----|-----|-----|

Dark-haired, brown-eyed, Spano is a versatile young actor whose career has experienced several bumps on the road to stardom. He began his professional career at age 14 in the 1977 production of *The Shadow Box* at the Long Wharf Theater. He then appeared on Broadway until winning a small part in *The Double McGuffin* (1979). This led to television roles and resumption of his schooling with the occasional film appearance. He didn't get a real break until he costarred as the Irish-Catholic boy "The Sheik" in 1983's *Baby It's You* with Rosanna Arquette. This role won him critical praise, and his star appeared to be rising. Unfortunately it was not so, and he didn't find great success in subsequent roles until he played in *Good Morning Babylon* (1987). Since then he has continued to work steadily in the hopes that he will at last, become a star. **Selected Works:** *Afterburn* (1992), *Alive* (1993), *City of Hope* (1991), *Indian Summer* (1993), *Oscar* (1991)

# Penelope Spheeris

**Born:** 1945; New Orleans, LA

**Years Active in the Industry:** by decade

| 10ˢ | 20ˢ | 30ˢ | 40ˢ | 50ˢ | 60ˢ | 70ˢ | 80ˢ | 90ˢ |
|-----|-----|-----|-----|-----|-----|-----|-----|-----|
|     |     |     |     |     |     |     |  ■  |  ■  |

For a person whose 1990s bankability rested upon her comedy films, writer/director Penelope Spheeris endured a private life that cannot by any stretch of the imagination be labelled amusing. Spheeris' father, an Olympic wrestler and strongman who ran a travelling carnival, was murdered in a knife brawl. Her mother was an alcoholic who married nine times. And the father of Spheeris' own daughter Anna died from a drug overdose. Virtually on her own from childhood, Spheeris strove heroically to rise above her squalid surroundings and, upon graduating from high school, was voted most likely to succeed. Majoring in film at UCLA, Spheeris launched her career by producing short subjects for satirist Albert Brooks, many of which were highlights of "Saturday Night Live's" first season. When Brooks stepped up to feature films with *Real Life* (1978), Spheeris stayed on as his producer. Her first "auteur" feature project was *The Decline of Western Civilization* (1981), a punk-rock documentary that she wrote, produced, and directed. After several years' work in documentaries of a doggedly non-comic (and unappealing) nature, Spheeris returned to laughmaking with *Wayne's World,* which became one of 1992's biggest hits. Spheeris would remain a comedy director, though her subsequent features varied wildly in quality. 1993's *The Beverly Hillbillies* opened strong, but was killed by word-of-mouth (deservedly so, since the film was an overwritten stinker with little or no relation to the original), while 1994's *The Little Rascals* managed to convey much of the sweetness and innocence of the old Hal Roach two-reelers of the 1930s—albeit with the requisite 1990's feminist slant. **Selected Works:** *Prison Stories: Women on the Inside* (1991)

# Steven Spielberg

**Born:** December 18, 1947; Cincinnati, OH

**Years Active in the Industry:** by decade

| 10ˢ | 20ˢ | 30ˢ | 40ˢ | 50ˢ | 60ˢ | 70ˢ | 80ˢ | 90ˢ |
|-----|-----|-----|-----|-----|-----|-----|-----|-----|
|     |     |     |     |     |     |  ■  |  ■  |  ■  |

The maker of a half-dozen of the highest-grossing movies of all time, Steven Spielberg is arguably the most successful director/producer in Hollywood history. Born in Cincinnati, he was a

movie buff from an early age and made his own movies as a boy. He studied at California State College, and made his debut with a short entitled *Amblin'.* As a director for television, his thriller *Duel* achieved a unique distinction at the time by earning a subsequent theatrical release in Europe, where it was very successful. Spielberg's first box-office blockbuster was *Jaws,* which was one of the top-grossing movies of the 1970s. He followed this with the megahits *Close Encounters of the Third Kind* (1977), *Raiders of the Lost Ark* (1981), and *E.T.: The Extra-Terrestrial* (1982). He has emerged as a major producer as well. Spielberg's movies—with the exception of his most serious dramas, such as *The Color Purple* (1985), in which the appeal is more general—seem uniquely suited to appeal to the baby-boomer generation in pacing and subject matter, and, coupled with the meticulous care that he usually takes in his work, are frequently dazzling to his critics as well. His *Jurassic Park* became the highest-grossing movie of all time late in 1993 and his film *Schindler's List* (1993) won much praise from the critics, as well as several awards. Spielberg once again made headlines with the announcement that he had formed a new company, Dreamworks SKG, along with partners Jeffrey Katzenberg and David Geffen. **Selected Works:** *Arachnophobia* (1990), *Back to the Future, Part 1* (1985), *Back to the Future, Part 3* (1990), *Gremlins 2: The New Batch* (1990), *Who Framed Roger Rabbit?* (1988)

# Dante Spinotti

**Born:** 1941; Tolmezzo, Italy

**Years Active in the Industry:** by decade

| 10ˢ | 20ˢ | 30ˢ | 40ˢ | 50ˢ | 60ˢ | 70ˢ | 80ˢ | 90ˢ |
|-----|-----|-----|-----|-----|-----|-----|-----|-----|
|     |     |     |     |     |     |     |  ■  |  ■  |

A superb stylist, Italian cinematographer Dante Spinotti was a prime factor in the artistic success of such 1980s critical favorites as Fabrio Carpi's *Basileus Quartet* (1982) and Lina Wertmuller's *Sotto...Sotto* (1984). Spinotti's first American film, *Choke*

*Canyon,* is distinguished by its excellent use of the widescreen format and its heartstopping aerial photography. Throughout the late 1980s and early 1990s, Spinotti has alternated between American and Italian productions with finesse. In 1991 alone, Dante Spinotti aimed his lenses at *Hudson Hawk, True Colors* and *Frankie and Johnny;* although the dramatic value of these films is questionable, they cannot in any way be faulted photographically. **Selected Works:** *The Comfort of Strangers* (1991), *Last of the Mohicans* (1992), *Blink* (1994), *The Quick and the Dead* (1995), *Nell* (1994)

# Roger Spottiswoode

**Born:** 1945; Canada

**Years Active in the Industry:** by decade

| 10ˢ | 20ˢ | 30ˢ | 40ˢ | 50ˢ | 60ˢ | 70ˢ | 80ˢ | 90ˢ |
|-----|-----|-----|-----|-----|-----|-----|-----|-----|
|     |     |     |     |     |     | ■   |     |     |

Filmmaker Roger Spottiswoode is a highly competent director of mainstream films. The Canadian-born son of Raymond Spottiswoode, an ex-producer and technical planning officer with the National Film Board of Canada, young Spottiswoode was raised in Britain where he worked as a TV and documentary editor until he edited three Sam Peckinpah films *Straw Dogs* (1971), *The Getaway* (1972), and *Pat Garrett* (1973). He continued editing other features and did television work until 1980 when he made his directorial debut with *Terror Train,* a typical slasher movie featuring Jamie Lee Curtis. In 1981, he was one of three directors to work on *The Pursuit of D.B. Cooper,* and in 1982 he co-wrote *48 Hrs.* As a director, Spottiswoode came into his own with the 1983 political thriller *Under Fire,* which is one of the few films he was involved with from start to finish. The film earned him international recognition. Since then his career has been rather spotty with films ranging from good (*Shoot to Kill* [1988]) to awful (*Stop or My Mom Will Shoot* [1992]). Much of the problem seems to be that Spottiswoode has become a hired gun for the studios who often have him take over productions already begun, as in *Air America* (1990), or make him work with weak scripts, as in *Turner and Hooch* (1989). **Selected Works:** *And the Band Played On* (1993)

# Robert Stack (Robert Langford Modini)

**Born:** January 13, 1919; Los Angeles, CA

**Years Active in the Industry:** by decade

| 10ˢ | 20ˢ | 30ˢ | 40ˢ | 50ˢ | 60ˢ | 70ˢ | 80ˢ | 90ˢ |
|-----|-----|-----|-----|-----|-----|-----|-----|-----|
|     |     | ■   |     |     |     |     |     |     |

American actor Stack broke into films at age 20 in *First Love* (1939), for which he received much publicity as "the first boy to kiss Deanna Durbin." For several years he played youthful romantic leads in a number of films, then was offscreen for five years during and after World War II, when he served in the Navy. He returned to a busy career in 1948. During the '50s he had several

challenging screen roles that allowed him to display his talents as an actor. For his work in *Written on the Wind* (1957) he received a Best Supporting Actor Oscar nomination. He is best known for his portrayal of crime-fighting G-man Eliot Ness in the TV series "The Untouchables," for which he won an Emmy in 1960. He later starred in the series "The Name of the Game," "Most Wanted," and "Strike Force," and served as the narrator for the popular docudrama series "Unsolved Mysteries." He authored an autobiography, *Straight Shooting* (1980). His screen career since 1960 has been intermittent. **Selected Works:** *Joe Versus the Volcano* (1990), *To Be or Not to Be* (1942), *High and the Mighty* (1954), *Return of Eliot Ness* (1991)

# Sylvester Stallone

**Born:** July 6, 1946; New York, NY

**Years Active in the Industry:** by decade

| 10ˢ | 20ˢ | 30ˢ | 40ˢ | 50ˢ | 60ˢ | 70ˢ | 80ˢ | 90ˢ |
|-----|-----|-----|-----|-----|-----|-----|-----|-----|
|     |     |     |     |     |     | ■   |     |     |

Powerfully-built Italian-American actor, writer, and director, Stallone was born into a poor one-parent home. He grew up in the Hell's Kitchen neighborhood of Manhattan, then spent several

years with foster families in Maryland and Philadelphia; he was expelled from 14 schools in 11 years. Already muscular, he attended the American College in Switzerland on an athletics scholarship, then briefly studied drama at the University of Miami, where his instructors tried to discourage him from pursuing an acting career. He moved to New York, where he supported himself in a string of odd jobs while looking for roles. He debuted onscreen in the low-budget soft-core porn film *A Party at Kitty and Stud's Place* (1968), and three years later got a bit part in Woody Allen's *Bananas* (1971). He debuted off-Broadway in the nude drama *Score,* then landed a substantial role in the film *The Lords of Flatbush* (1974), which led to decent roles in several more films after he moved to Los Angeles. However, thinking his career would dead-end unless he made his own luck, Stallone decided to write a script with a starring role for himself, and three days later it was finished. He managed to sell the script to producers Irwin Winkler and Robert Chartoff, accepting a small sum but insisting that he be given the lead role and a share in the profits. The film was *Rocky* (1976), and it became one of the most surprising successes in film history, doing great business and earning a number of Oscars, including Best Picture and Best Director. He went on to become one of the screen's biggest stars, often writing and directing his films; he made four sequels to *Rocky* and three "Rambo" films—action-adventure tales set in the Far East and featuring enormous firepower (beginning with *First Blood* [1982]). Audiences have been unwilling to accept him in other roles, and a number of his other films have been bombs. He has complained about being typecast as a dumb muscleman, and claims to be an intellectual; he has written novelizations and TV scripts under the pseudonym Q. Moonblood, and has appeared in several comedies, none of which was successful. **Selected Works:** *Cliffhanger* (1993), *Demolition Man* (1993), *The Specialist* (1994), *Assassins* (1995)

# Terence Stamp

**Born:** July 22, 1939; Stepney, East London

**Years Active in the Industry:** by decade

| 10s | 20s | 30s | 40s | 50s | 60s | 70s | 80s | 90s |
|-----|-----|-----|-----|-----|-----|-----|-----|-----|
|     |     |     |     |     |     |     |     |     |

Intense, soulful-eyed British actor Terence Stamp made his mark on the consciousness of moviegoers with his film debut as the martyred hero of *Billy Budd* (1962). While some regard this role as unplayable (certainly enough "name" actors turned it down), Stamp acquitted himself so well that he was nominated for an Oscar. He switched from victim to aggressor in *The Collector* (1965), playing an addled butterfly fancier who kidnaps Samantha Eggar in hopes of adding her to his collection. Movie roles of fluctuating quality followed, then Stamp renounced filmmaking in 1969, disillusioned by an unhappy romance and the hollowness of fame. After several years of self-imposed exile in England, a leaner, sharper-featured Stamp returned to movies in villainous roles, notably the indomitable Zod in *Superman: The Movie* (1978) and *Superman 2* (1981). He broadened his skills in 1988 by writing a candid and witty autobiography, *Coming Attractions*, and in 1991 with his first directorial assignment, *Stranger in the House* (1992). In 1994, Stamp could be seen in the wildly uncharacteristic role of a barnstorming professional drag queen in *The Adventures of Priscilla, Queen of the Desert*. **Selected Works:** *Meetings with Remarkable Men* (1979), *Wall Street* (1987), *Alien Nation* (1988)

# Lionel Stander

**Born:** January 11, 1908; New York, NY
**Died:** November 30, 1994

**Years Active in the Industry:** by decade

| 10s | 20s | 30s | 40s | 50s | 60s | 70s | 80s | 90s |
|-----|-----|-----|-----|-----|-----|-----|-----|-----|
|     |     |     |     |     |     |     |     |     |

Lionel Stander began his acting career in stage plays at age 19. Five years later he began appearing in film shorts, and he made his feature film debut in 1935. Aside from a break during World War

II, he remained a busy screen actor until the late '40s, specializing in eccentric, somewhat threatening character roles. In the early '50s he became yet another victim of the McCarthy Era when he was blacklisted after being called before the House Un-American Activities Committee. He continued to act for a while in summer stock, then had a stint as a Wall Street broker. He returned to films in the mid '60s; a few years later he costarred in several "spaghetti Westerns" which won him new popularity. His screen career continued into the late '70s, after which his film work was minimal. He was a regular on the TV series "Hart to Hart" from 1979-84. **Selected Works:** *Mr. Deeds Goes to Town* (1936), *A Star Is Born* (1937), *Scoundrel* (1935)

# Harry Dean Stanton

**Born:** 1926; West Irvine, KY

**Years Active in the Industry:** by decade

| 10s | 20s | 30s | 40s | 50s | 60s | 70s | 80s | 90s |
|-----|-----|-----|-----|-----|-----|-----|-----|-----|
|     |     |     |     |     |     |     |     |     |

Lean, leathery character actor with hollowed cheeks and deep-set eyes, Stanton studied acting in college on the G.I. Bill after serving in the Navy during World War II. Then he spent four years at the Pasadena Playhouse and toured in several shows. He moved to Los Angeles and began to find small roles in films and TV; for the first fifteen years of his career he was billed as "Dean Stanton." Gradually, he began to be typecast in the roles of losers, eccentrics, outcasts, and criminals; by the end of the '60s he was a recognizable character actor, even if his name was not widely known. He is one of the busiest screen actors of his generation, but not until the '80s did he begin to land really great roles. His first lead was in a part written for him in *Paris, Texas* (1984). **Selected Works:** *Cool Hand Luke* (1967), *Hostages* (1993), *The Last Temptation of Christ* (1988), *Wild at Heart* (1990), *Never Talk to Strangers* (1995)

# Barbara Stanwyck (Ruby Stevens)

**Born:** July 16, 1907; Brooklyn, NY
**Died:** January 20, 1990; Santa Monica, CA

**Years Active in the Industry:** by decade

| 10s | 20s | 30s | 40s | 50s | 60s | 70s | 80s | 90s |
|-----|-----|-----|-----|-----|-----|-----|-----|-----|
|     |     |     |     |     |     |     |     |     |

Stanwyck was orphaned at the age of four and raised by her older sister and various relatives. After quitting school in her early teens she began dancing in speakeasies; at age 15 she became a

Ziegfeld chorus girl. Gradually, she began getting parts in plays, ultimately landing the lead role in the Broadway play *The Noose,* which ran for nine months in 1926. In 1927 she debuted onscreen in the silent *Broadway Nights,* filmed in New York. After more work on Broadway she married comedian Frank Fay, whom she followed to Hollywood after he

was signed to a contract at Warners. Soon she too had signed film contracts and quickly became a star in the successful Frank Capra production *Ladies of Leisure* (1930). Admired by directors for her professionalism, unspoiled nature, and love for her work, by the late '30s she was a popular leading lady; many Hollywood insiders have commented on her fine qualities as an off-screen personality. She received her first Oscar nomination for *Stella Dallas* (1937), and went on to receive three more nominations without ever winning. Her career peak came in the early '40s with such films as *The Lady Eve* (1941) and *Double Indemnity* (1944). In 1944 the IRS named her as the highest-paid woman in America. Equally skilled at comedy and drama, she is best known for her portrayal of aggressive, pragmatic, tough women. In the '50s her career diminished and she tended to work in poor films, and she retired from the big screen in the '60s. However, she starred in the TV series "The Barbara Stanwyck Show" and "The Big Valley," which introduced her to a new generation of viewers. She won an Emmy for each show. She went on to star in the mini-series "The Thorn Birds" (1983), for which she won a third Emmy. She also starred in the TV series "The Colbys." In 1981 Stanwyck received an honorary Oscar as "an artist of impeccable grace and beauty, a dedicated actress and one of the great ladies of Hollywood," for "superlative creativity and unique contribution to the art of screen acting." She was married to actor Robert Taylor for 13 years, and appeared with him in *This is My Affair* (1937) and, her final film, *The Night Walker* (1965). Her brother was actor Byron Stevens. **Selected Works:** *Ball of Fire* (1941), *Executive Suite* (1954), *Meet John Doe* (1941), *Sorry, Wrong Number* (1948), *Titanic* (1953)

# Maureen Stapleton

**Born:** June 21, 1925; Troy, NY

**Years Active in the Industry:** by decade

| 10ˢ | 20ˢ | 30ˢ | 40ˢ | 50ˢ | 60ˢ | 70ˢ | 80ˢ | 90ˢ |
|-----|-----|-----|-----|-----|-----|-----|-----|-----|
|     |     |     |     |     |     |     |     |     |

Upon graduating from high school, Maureen Stapleton moved to Manhattan, where she worked as a waitress and model while taking night classes at the Herbert Berghof Acting School. In 1946 she debuted on Broadway; five years later she was a great success in Broadway's *The Rose Tattoo.* During the '50s she starred in numerous Broadway productions, including several more works by Tennessee Williams. She debuted onscreen in *Lonelyhearts* (1959), for which she received a Best Supporting Actress Oscar nomination. Stapleton went on to a sporadic screen career, marked by intermittently busy bursts; she was especially active onscreen from 1984-88. She received three more Oscar nominations, winning the Best Supporting Actress Oscar for her portrayal of Emma Goldman in *Reds* (1981). She has done much work on TV, and won an Emmy for her performance in the TV movie *Among the Paths to Eden* (1968). Throughout her career Stapleton has remained primarily a stage actress, often playing earthy, frowzy, unkempt women. She was married to playwright David Rayfiel. Her sister is actress Jean Stapleton. **Selected Works:** *Airport* (1970), *Cocoon* (1985), *Interiors* (1978), *Miss Rose White* (1992), *Plaza Suite* (1971)

# Charles Starrett

**Born:** March 28, 1903; Athol, MA
**Died:** March 22, 1986; Borrego Springs, CA

**Years Active in the Industry:** by decade

| 10ˢ | 20ˢ | 30ˢ | 40ˢ | 50ˢ | 60ˢ | 70ˢ | 80ˢ | 90ˢ |
|-----|-----|-----|-----|-----|-----|-----|-----|-----|
|     |     |     |     |     |     |     |     |     |

While on the Dartmouth College football team, Charles Starrett was hired for an extra role in a 1926 film titled *The Quarterback.* Starrett honed his performing skills in vaudeville and stock, eventually obtaining leading-man roles on Broadway. His first film was 1930's *Fast and Loose;* three years later, Starrett was one of several movie performers who put his career on the line by helping to organize the Screen Actors Guild. After several years of relatively colorless romantic leads, Starrett switched to Westerns, signing with Columbia Pictures in 1936 and remaining there until the 1950s; the actor's latter-day trade ads proudly proclaimed "Twenty years with the same brand." One of the most popular of all cowboy stars, Starrett was best known for his portrayal of the Durango Kid, a Lone Ranger-like masked avenger. **Selected Works:** *Royal Family of Broadway* (1930)

# Barbara Steele

**Born:** December 29, 1938; Trenton Wirrall, England

**Years Active in the Industry:** by decade

| 10ˢ | 20ˢ | 30ˢ | 40ˢ | 50ˢ | 60ˢ | 70ˢ | 80ˢ | 90ˢ |
|-----|-----|-----|-----|-----|-----|-----|-----|-----|
|     |     |     |     |     |     |     |     |     |

Exotic, voluptuous, nostril-flaring British actress Barbara Steele originally aspired to be a painter. At 20, she was sidetracked into acting, and within a year she made her film bow in a one-line bit as a student in *Bachelor of Hearts* (1958). Most of her roles were nondescript until she moved to Italy and launched her horror-film cycle with her performance as a resuscitated witch in *Black Sunday* (1961). Throughout the next fifteen years, Steele thrived as an internationally popular "scream queen," undergoing the usual ordeals of being whipped, strangled, dismembered and set ablaze, but also dishing it out as well as taking it—especially in the role of a demonic woman's prison warden in *Caged Heat* (1974). Steele attracted the attention of the movie cognoscenti when she answered an open call posted by director Federico Fellini, who promptly cast her in a flashy role in *8 1/2* (1963); fourteen years later, she appeared as Violet in director Louis Malle's controversial *Pretty Baby* (1977). For many years, Steele was the wife of screenwriter James Poe, who wrote a good part for her in *They Shoot Horses, Don't They?* (1969), only to see the role whittled into oblivion by director Sydney Pollack. Steele remained close to Poe even after their divorce, retiring from the screen when Poe died in 1980. **Selected Works:** *Dolce Vita* (1960)

# Bob Steele

**Born:** January 23, 1906; Pendleton, OR
**Died:** 1988

**Years Active in the Industry:** by decade

| 10s | 20s | 30s | 40s | 50s | 60s | 70s | 80s | 90s |
|-----|-----|-----|-----|-----|-----|-----|-----|-----|
|     |     | ███ | ███ |     |     |     |     |     |

Born Robert Bradbury, he began appearing (at age 14) in semi-documentary nature shorts directed by his father, prolific silent director Robert North Bradbury; he later appeared in juvenile parts in some Westerns his father directed. In 1927 he began starring in cowboy films, maintaining his career in screen Westerns through the early '40s; he was one of the "Three Mesquiteers" in the series of that name. He also played straight dramatic roles, including the part of Curly in *Of Mice and Men* (1940). After the mid '40s he played character roles, appearing in films every few years until the early '70s. He was a regular on the '60s TV sitcom "F Troop."

# Mary Steenburgen

**Born:** February 8, 1953; Newport, AR

**Years Active in the Industry:** by decade

| 10s | 20s | 30s | 40s | 50s | 60s | 70s | 80s | 90s |
|-----|-----|-----|-----|-----|-----|-----|-----|-----|
|     |     |     |     |     |     | ███ | ███ | ███ |

Curly-haired, sandy-voiced actress Mary Steenburgen was the daughter of a railroad employee. Pursuing drama in college, Steenburgen headed to New York in 1972, where she worked with an improvisational troupe. She was spotted by Jack Nicholson, who cast Steenburgen as his feisty "in name only" frontier wife in 1976's *Goin' South*. Two years later, she won a best supporting actress Oscar for her performance as Melvin Dummar's inamorata in

*Melvin and Howard* (1979). Able to convey a wide age and character range, Steenburgen has been effectively cast as prim authoress Marjorie Rawlins in *Cross Creek* (1979), a free spirited Frisco girl in *Time After Time* (1979), the corsetted matriarch of a turn-of-the-century household in *Ragtime* (1981), a long-suffering suburban housewife in *Parenthood* (1989), and a Marcia Clark-like attorney in *Philadelphia* (1993). She also portrayed the Jules Verne-loving Western schoolmarm Clara in *Back to the Future, Part 3* (1990), a role she perpetuated (via voiceover) on the 1990 *Back to the Future* TV cartoon series. In 1987, she was executive producer of *End of the Line*, in which she also appeared. Steenburgen is one of many show-biz luminaries who has ardently campaigned for (and been a frequent White House guest of) Bill and Hillary Clinton. Formerly married for several years to actor Malcolm McDowell, Steenburgen has more recently been romantically linked to former *Cheers* star Ted Danson. **Selected Works:** *The Whales of August* (1987), *The Grass Harp* (1995)

# Rod Steiger (Rodney Stephen Steiger)

**Born:** April 14, 1925; West Hampton, NY

**Years Active in the Industry:** by decade

| 10s | 20s | 30s | 40s | 50s | 60s | 70s | 80s | 90s |
|-----|-----|-----|-----|-----|-----|-----|-----|-----|
|     |     |     | ███ | ███ | ███ | ███ | ███ | ███ |

At 16 Rod Steiger quit school to serve in World War II and spent the entire war on a destroyer in the Pacific. Then he stayed on with the Navy as a clerk. Steiger began acting with an amateur group, an experience which persuaded him to apply his GI Bill scholarship toward drama studies. He enrolled at the Dramatic Workshop of the New School for Social Research, where he remained for two years; later he trained at the New York Theater Wing and the Actors Studio. He appeared in one movie but did most of his early work on the stage and TV; he first attracted wide recognition for his work in the title role of the TV production *Marty*. In 1954 he began his screen career in earnest, playing Marlon Brando's brother in *On the Waterfront,* for which he received a Best Supporting Actor Oscar nomination. He was nominated twice more, and won the Best Actor Oscar for *In the Heat of the Night* (1967). He has sustained a very busy screen career despite a tendency to appear in unpopular films and genuine box-office disasters. From 1959-69 he was married to actress Claire Bloom. **Selected Works:** *The Ballad of the Sad Cafe* (1991), *Doctor Zhivago* (1965), *The Pawnbroker* (1965), *Passion in Paradise* (1994), *The Specialist* (1994)

# Max Steiner (Maximilian Raoul Steiner)

**Born:** May 10, 1888; Vienna, Austria
**Died:** December 28, 1971; Los Angeles, CA

**Years Active in the Industry:** by decade

| 10ˢ | 20ˢ | 30ˢ | 40ˢ | 50ˢ | 60ˢ | 70ˢ | 80ˢ | 90ˢ |
|-----|-----|-----|-----|-----|-----|-----|-----|-----|

Austrian-born film composer Max Steiner was the grandson of the musical impresario who discovered Strauss and brought Offenbach to Vienna. Growing up with a rich heritage of opera and symphony all about him, Steiner developed into a musical prodigy; at the age of thirteen he graduated from the Imperial Academy of Music, completing the course in one year and winning the Gold Medal of the Emperor. Already a composer at 14 and conductor at 16, Steiner moved from Austria to England in 1905, remaining there to conduct at His Majesty's Theatre until 1914. With the outbreak of the war, Steiner emigrated to America, where he kept busy with Broadway musicals and operettas. One of his most beneficial American jobs was to compose the music to be conducted during screenings of the silent film *The Bondman* (1915); he became a friend of William Fox, the film's producer, giving Steiner early entree into the Hollywood that would so gainfully employ him in later years. In 1929, he was brought to fledgling RKO Radio Studios to orchestrate the film adaptation of Ziegfeld's *Rio Rita* (1929). Always confident in his talents, Steiner was realistic enough to understand that he was hired by RKO because he cost a tenth of what someone like Stowkowski would charge. While at RKO, Steiner developed his theory that music should be a function of the dramatic content of a film, and not merely background filling. His scores for such films as *Symphony of Six Million* (1932), *The Informer* (1935), and, especially, *King Kong* (1933) are carefully integrated works, commenting upon the visual images, augmenting the action, and heightening the dramatic impact. While Steiner's detractors would characterize his spell-it-out technique as "Mickey Mousing" (in reference to the music heard in animated cartoons), producers, directors, and stars came to rely upon Steiner to make a good film better, and a great film superb. After 111 pictures at RKO, Steiner was hired by David O. Selznick, who assigned the composer to write the score for *Gone with the Wind* (1939). Virtually 75 percent of this 221-minute epic required music of some sort, and Steiner rose to the occasion with what many consider his finest work. One concept refined in *Gone with the Wind* was to give each important character his or her own separate musical motif—quite an undertaking when one realizes how many speaking parts there were in the film. Around that time Steiner began working at Warner Bros, where he penned the studio's famous "opening logo" fanfare and also provided evocative scores for such classics as *Now Voyager* (1941), *Casablanca* (1942) and *Mildred Pierce* (1945). A proud, vain man, Steiner frequently found himself the butt of good-natured practical jokes from his fellow composers, but at Oscar time it was usually Steiner who had the last laugh. Steiner remained active until 1965, contributing scores to *The Caine Mutiny* (1954), *The Searchers* (1955), *A Summer Place* (1959) and many other films. It was only at the very end of his career, with such retrogressive scores as *Youngblood Hawke* (1964), that Max Steiner's once-revolutionary technique began to sound old hat. **Selected Works:** *Charge of the Light Brigade* (1936), *Dark Victory* (1939), *Johnny Belinda* (1948), *Since You Went Away* (1944), *Treasure of the Sierra Madre* (1948)

# Daniel Stern

**Born:** 1957; Bethesda, MD

**Years Active in the Industry:** by decade

| 10ˢ | 20ˢ | 30ˢ | 40ˢ | 50ˢ | 60ˢ | 70ˢ | 80ˢ | 90ˢ |
|-----|-----|-----|-----|-----|-----|-----|-----|-----|

Stern is a tall, lanky, beak-nosed comic actor with a nasal voice. After acting on the New York stage he made a big impression in his second film, *Breaking Away* (1979). His best theater role came in 1980 when he portrayed Lee in Sam Shepard's *True West*. He had a steady screen career throughout the '80s, usually in small or supporting roles. He became well-known after his co-starring roles in the hit comedies *Home Alone* (1990) and *City Slickers* (1991). He provided the voice-over narration for the TV series "The Wonder Years," beginning in 1988, and he also directed several episodes, as well as the film *Rookie of the Year* (1993). **Selected Works:** *Diner* (1982), *Hannah and Her Sisters* (1986), *Home Alone 2: Lost in New York* (1992), *City Slickers 2: The Legend of Curly's Gold* (1994), *Bushwhacked* (1995)

# Fisher Stevens

**Born:** 1963; Chicago, IL

**Years Active in the Industry:** by decade

| 10ˢ | 20ˢ | 30ˢ | 40ˢ | 50ˢ | 60ˢ | 70ˢ | 80ˢ | 90ˢ |
|-----|-----|-----|-----|-----|-----|-----|-----|-----|

Youthful character actor Fisher Stevens was first seen on Broadway at age 19 in Harvey Fierstein's *Torch Song Trilogy*; he followed this with a plum role in Neil Simon's *Brighton Beach Memoirs*. Stevens' film resume includes *The Flamingo Kid* (1984), *The Boss' Wife* (1986), *Reversal of Fortune* (1990) and *The Marrying Man* (1991). During what may turn out to be the most highly publicized period in his life, Stevens was the significant other of actress Michelle Pfeiffer. Stevens is familiar to most filmgoers for his role as malaprop-laden Indian technical whiz Ben Jabituya in the two *Short Circuit* films of the late 1980s. **Selected Works:** *Mystery Date* (1991), *When the Party's Over* (1993), *Only You* (1994)

# George Stevens

**Born:** December 18, 1904; Oakland, CA
**Died:** March 8, 1975; Lancaster, CA

**Years Active in the Industry:** by decade

| 10s | 20s | 30s | 40s | 50s | 60s | 70s | 80s | 90s |
|-----|-----|-----|-----|-----|-----|-----|-----|-----|

American producer/director/cinematographer George Stevens made his professional acting debut at age five in the company of his actor parents. Developing an interest in photography as a hobby, Stevens became an assistant movie cameraman at the age of 17. From 1927 through 1930, he was principal cameraman at Hal Roach Studios, shooting such classic two-reelers as Laurel and Hardy's *Two Tars* (1928) and *Below Zero* (1930), as well as a handful of feature films, including the 1927 Western *No Man's Law.* Stevens was elevated to director in 1930 for Roach's *Boy Friends* series. Dismissed from Roach during an economy drive in 1931, Stevens moved to Universal and then to RKO to direct comedy shorts (he later professed to hate two-reel comedies, though he enjoyed the company of the comedians with whom he worked, especially Laurel and Hardy). RKO promoted Stevens to features in 1934; after several medium-budget projects, he was assigned the "A" feature *Alice Adams* (1935) over the protests of the film's star, Katharine Hepburn. When *Alice Adams* proved successful, Hepburn's attitude toward Stevens did a "360," and she insisted that he direct her starring vehicle *Quality Street* (1936). Another Stevens triumph from this period was the Astaire/Rogers confection *Swing Time* (1936), in which the director's father Landers Stevens played an important supporting role. Producing as well as directing from 1938's *Vivacious Lady* onward, Stevens turned out a string of critical and financial successes: *Gunga Din* (1939) for RKO, *Woman of the Year* (1942) for MGM, and *Penny Serenade* (1941), *Talk of the Town* (1942) and *The More the Merrier* (1943), all for Columbia. Stevens' directorial style displayed the same acute sense of visual dynamics that had distinguished his earlier work as a cameraman; the director refined and improved upon that style through sweat and persistence. Once he reached the "A" list, Stevens became one of the most meticulous and painstaking directors in the business, commencing production only after extensive research, filming take after take until perfection was achieved, and then spending as much as a full year editing the finished product. During World War II, Stevens was made an officer in the Signal Corps, filming vivid color footage of such historical milestones as the D-Day maneuvers and the liberation of the death camps; much of this footage was incorporated into the 1984 documentary *George Stevens: A Filmaker's Journey*, assembled by George Stevens Jr. After the war, Stevens produced and directed his final RKO assignment, *I Remember Mama* (1948), then moved to Paramount for what many consider his crowning achievement—1951's *A Place in the Sun,* a brilliant filmization of the Theodore Dreiser novel *An American Tragedy.* While much of the film's content is dated, Stevens succeeded in transferring a bulky and verbose novel to the screen in purely visual terms; he also thrilled the bobbysoxer fans of Montgomery Clift and Elizabeth Taylor by shooting their love scenes in huge, provocatively lit closeups. *A Place in the Sun* won Stevens his first Oscar for best directing in 1951. Fifteen years later, he threatened legal action against NBC should the network edit out any portion of *Place in the Sun* for telecasting purposes, and he

was backed up in his suit by the California Legislature. The more time and effort Stevens expended on his individual projects, the fewer he produced. His output between 1953 and 1959 consisted of *Shane* (1953); *Giant* (1956), in which he put the awkward Cinemascope screen to superb artistic use, winning his second Oscar in the process; and *The Diary of Anne Frank* (1959). From 1960 through 1965, Stevens labored on a mammoth filmization of the life of Christ, *The Greatest Story Ever Told* (1965). The film was a failure for several reasons, not least of which was Stevens' curious insistence upon using big-name stars in every role (this is the movie in which John Wayne, as the centurion at the Crucifixion, proclaims "Trew-ly this man wuz the son of Gawd"). *Greatest Story* lost Stevens his hard-earned autonomy; for his last film, *The Only Game in Town* (1970), he was little more than a glorified hired hand to stars Elizabeth Taylor and Warren Beatty. While George Stevens' reputation was tarnished by the disappointments of his last years, critics and fans alike have taken a "forgive and forget" stance since his death in 1975, preferring to cite his huge manifest of hits rather than his final faltering misses.

# Inger Stevens

**Born:** October 18, 1934; Stockholm, Sweden
**Died:** 1970

**Years Active in the Industry:** by decade

| 10s | 20s | 30s | 40s | 50s | 60s | 70s | 80s | 90s |
|-----|-----|-----|-----|-----|-----|-----|-----|-----|

After her parents divorced, she moved with her father to the U.S. when she was 13; when her father remarried she ran away from home. At age 16, Stevens broke into show business in a Kansas City burlesque show. She moved to New York at age 18, working in the garment center and as a chorus girl while studying theater at the Actors Studio and making the rounds of Broadway agents. She appeared in several TV commercials, leading to roles in TV dramas. In 1956 she debuted on Broadway, then made her first film in 1957. She went on to appear in a dozen or so films during the next decade-plus. Stevens achieved some popularity as the star of the '60s TV series "The Farmer's Daughter." Her private life was unhappy. Her first marriage lasted four months, and she went on to failed romances with actor/singer Bing Crosby and with a famous married star; the latter affair led to a suicide attempt in 1959 that left her blind for two weeks. At age 36 she died from an overdose of barbiturates. It was later revealed that she had been secretly married since 1961 to black musician Isaac (Ike) Jones.

# James Stewart

**Born:** May 20, 1908; Indiana, PA

**Years Active in the Industry:** by decade

| 10s | 20s | 30s | 40s | 50s | 60s | 70s | 80s | 90s |
|-----|-----|-----|-----|-----|-----|-----|-----|-----|

Drawling, gawky, gentle leading man with a shy, small-town, persona, Stewart was an amateur magician from boyhood, appearing in Princeton Triangle Club shows while in college.

There he studied architecture, and, after graduating, he was persuaded by classmate Joshua Logan to join the University Players in Falmouth, Massachusetts; the group included fledgling actors Henry Fonda and Margaret Sullavan. Fonda was Stewart's roommate as the two of them broke into Broadway in 1932, and then again when they went to Hollywood in 1935. He benefited from his association with Sullavan, who insisted that he be given roles in her films. By the late '30s Stewart was a favorite among directors for his "regular guy" appeal, a leading man who didn't always have the aura of stardom. He won a New York Film Critics Best Actor award for his work in *Mr. Smith Goes to Washington* (1939), for which he also received the first of five Best Actor Oscar nominations; he won that award once, for *The Philadelphia Story* (1940). During World War II, Stewart was a bomber pilot, flying twenty missions over Germany and rising from private to full colonel; he didn't fully retire from the service until 1968, by which time he was an Air Force Brigadier General and the highest-ranking entertainer in the U.S. military. After the war he generally stopped playing the shy, absent-minded characters of so many of his early films, and branched out into a variety of starring roles that included the leads in four Hitchcock films. In the '50s he was one of the first actors to negotiate for percentages of his films' profits, a move that made him very wealthy after he appeared in a number of box-office hits. He continued starring in films into the early '70s, when he also returned to Broadway in the play *Harvey*. **Selected Works:** *Anatomy of a Murder* (1959), *It's a Wonderful Life* (1946), *Rear Window* (1954), *The Spirit of St. Louis* (1957), *Vertigo* (1958)

# Patrick Stewart

**Born:** July 13, 1940; Mirfield, Yorkshire, England

**Years Active in the Industry:** by decade

| 10s | 20s | 30s | 40s | 50s | 60s | 70s | 80s | 90s |
|-----|-----|-----|-----|-----|-----|-----|-----|-----|
|     |     |     |     |     |     |     |     |     |

The product of a home life that cannot by any stretch of the imagination be called happy, young British-born Patrick Stewart sought to escape his miserable existence via writing and acting. After first pursuing a career as a journalist, Stewart was trained as

an actor at the Bristol Old Vic Theatre School, making his stage bow in a 1959 production of *Treasure Island*. He was profitably employed in stage and film character roles at the time he was chosen to portray Captain Jean-Luc Picard in the 1987 syndicated series *Star Trek: The Next Generation*. Industry wags spent the first year of the series' run making stupid jokes about Stewart's hairlessness, the humor usually on the level of "to baldly go where no man has gone before." For his part, Stewart was so certain that he would be fired from the series that he didn't unpack his luggage for six weeks. But Stewart and the new *Star Trek* clicked, and continued clicking for eight seasons. The actor has extended his Picard characterization into the 1995 film *Star Trek Generations*, during the filming of which he allegedly conducted a feud with his costar and previous *Enterprise* commander William Shatner. While Patrick Stewart is appreciative and grateful of his hard-earned star status, he bristles whenever the subject of his baldness is broached—he refuses to regard his lack of hair as "sexy," a la Yul Brynner, and has stated that he'd much prefer being judged on his considerable acting ability rather than his appearance. **Selected Works:** *L.A. Story* (1991), *Jeffrey* (1995)

# Ben Stiller

**Born:** New York, NY

**Years Active in the Industry:** by decade

| 10s | 20s | 30s | 40s | 50s | 60s | 70s | 80s | 90s |
|-----|-----|-----|-----|-----|-----|-----|-----|-----|
|     |     |     |     |     |     |     |     |     |

The son of comic actors Jerry Stiller and Anne Meara, Ben Stiller was a filmmaker at age 10, making wish-fulfillment 8 mm epics in which he surreptitiously got even with the schoolyard bullies who tormented him. After attending UCLA, Stiller continued making short comedy films, which led to a 1988 stint as a regular on *Saturday Night Live*, and, eventually, his own MTV series. He also appeared on the NBC sitcom *A Different World*, as well as a brief starring series on the Fox Network. Ben Stiller's directorial feature debut came by way of *Reality Bites* (1994).

# Whit Stillman

**Born:** 1951; New York, NY

**Years Active in the Industry:** by decade

| 10s | 20s | 30s | 40s | 50s | 60s | 70s | 80s | 90s |
|-----|-----|-----|-----|-----|-----|-----|-----|-----|
|     |     |     |     |     |     |     |     |     |

Young Manhattan-based director Whit Stillman's fame rests on a single auteur effort, which happened to be his very first film. 1990's *Metropolitan* was a remarkable Eric Rohmer-like character piece about the fading debutante scene in New York. Stillman's visual style needed work, but he exhibited a marvelous fly-on-the-wall ear for the way Privileged Youth talks and interracts. Whit Stillman earned an Oscar nomination for the screenplay of *Metro-*

*politan*, quite a coup for what was essentially a non-mainstream independent project. **Selected Works:** *Barcelona* (1994)

# Sting (Gordon Matthew Sumner)

**Born:** October 2, 1951; Newcastle-upon-Tyne, England

**Years Active in the Industry:** by decade

| 10ˢ | 20ˢ | 30ˢ | 40ˢ | 50ˢ | 60ˢ | 70ˢ | 80ˢ | 90ˢ |
|-----|-----|-----|-----|-----|-----|-----|-----|-----|
|     |     |     |     |     |     |     |     |     |

British rock artist/actor Sting came into the world as Gordon Sumner, earning his more famous soubriquet thanks to his predilection for wearing bee-like striped shirts. At 17, Sting toured the world as a musical performer on the Princess Cruise luxury-vacation line. He attended Warwick University, then made ends meet as a teacher, income tax clerk, and construction worker before achieving fame as lead singer of the rock group The Police. Following the 1977 release of the Police's inaugural recording *Fall Out,* Sting was approached by the producers of the James Bond film *For Your Eyes Only* to costar as the megalomaniac villain. He refused, choosing instead to make his film bow in the more characteristic role of a teen punk in *Quadrophenia* (1979). One of his more impressive film appearances was as the enigmatic antihero of the pitch-black comedy *Brimstone and Treacle* (1982). While filmmaking remains a lucrative sideline for Sting—his feature films include *Dune* (1984), *The Bride* (1985), and *Bring on the Night* (1986)—he continues to invest most of his energy into music, winning seven Grammies for his recording work.

# Dean Stockwell

**Born:** March 5, 1936; North Hollywood, CA

**Years Active in the Industry:** by decade

| 10ˢ | 20ˢ | 30ˢ | 40ˢ | 50ˢ | 60ˢ | 70ˢ | 80ˢ | 90ˢ |
|-----|-----|-----|-----|-----|-----|-----|-----|-----|
|     |     |     |     |     |     |     |     |     |

The son of Broadway artists, he and his younger brother (Guy Stockwell) debuted onstage at the age of seven in Broadway's *The Innocent Voyage.* He debuted onscreen at age nine in the MGM Gene Kelly musical *Anchors Aweigh* (1945). As a child, Stockwell was a "pretty boy" with curly hair, popular among directors for his natural demeanor and ability to avoid being too cute. Between 1945-51 he appeared in more than a dozen films, but didn't like his work; later he said that he'd resented being exploited and treated "like a piece of meat." He dropped out of films from 1951-57, then returned as a sensitive and intense leading man, though his film work was sporadic; he often went as long as three years between roles. He enjoyed a renaissance as an actor in the '80s, appearing in twenty films between 1984-90; he was particularly effective as a way-out oddball in David Lynch's *Blue Velvet* (1986). He became better known to a new generation of viewers as the result of his con-

tinuing role on the TV series "Quantum Leap." In 1982 he and rock star Neil Young co-wrote and co-directed the anti-nuclear comedy *Human Highway.* For his portrayal of a comedic mafioso in *Married to the Mob* (1988) he received a Best Supporting Actor Oscar nomination. **Selected Works:** *Long Day's Journey into Night* (1962), *Son of the Morning Star* (1991), *Tucker: The Man & His Dream* (1988), *Compulsion* (1959), *Sons and Lovers* (1960)

# Eric Stoltz

**Born:** 1961; Whittier, CA

**Years Active in the Industry:** by decade

| 10ˢ | 20ˢ | 30ˢ | 40ˢ | 50ˢ | 60ˢ | 70ˢ | 80ˢ | 90ˢ |
|-----|-----|-----|-----|-----|-----|-----|-----|-----|
|     |     |     |     |     |     |     |     |     |

A pale, slim, red-haired actor, Stoltz was born in California but spent some of his youth in America Samoa. He began acting while in high school, then briefly studied theater arts in college; he

dropped out of school to study with the top acting coaches, including Stella Adler, William Taylor, and Peggy Feury. Later he played a season with an American rep company in Edinburgh. After returning to the States, Stoltz landed small roles in TV series before debuting onscreen as a supporting actor in the popular comedy *Fast Times At Ridgemont High* (1982).

He made several minor films before landing his first major screen role, that of Cher's disfigured son in Peter Bogdanovich's *Mask* (1986); the role required him to act while wearing a great deal of prosthetic make-up. He went on to both lead and supporting roles in a number of films. Meanwhile, after a successful off-Broadway career, he made his Broadway debut in 1988 in the revival of Thornton Wilder's *Our Town,* for which he received Tony and Drama Desk nominations. **Selected Works:** *Bodies, Rest & Motion* (1993), *Waterdance* (1991), *Naked in New York* (1994), *Pulp Fiction* (1994), *Little Women* (1994), *Killing Zoe* (1994)

# George E. Stone

**Born:** May 23, 1903; Lodz, Poland
**Died:** May 26, 1967; California

**Years Active in the Industry:** by decade

| 10ˢ | 20ˢ | 30ˢ | 40ˢ | 50ˢ | 60ˢ | 70ˢ | 80ˢ | 90ˢ |
|-----|-----|-----|-----|-----|-----|-----|-----|-----|
|     |     |     |     |     |     |     |     |     |

Probably no one came by the label "Runyonesque" more honestly than Polish-born actor George E. Stone; a close friend of writer Damon Runyon, Stone was seemingly put on this earth to play characters named Society Max and Toothpick Charlie, and to mouth such colloquialisms as "It is known far and wide" and "More than somewhat." Starting his career as a Broadway "hoofer," the diminuitive Stone made his film bow as The Sewer Rat in the 1927 silent *Seventh Heaven*. His most prolific film years were 1929-1936, during which period he showed up in dozens of Warner Bros. "urban" films and backstage musicals, and also appeared as the doomed Earle Williams in the 1931 version of *The Front Page*. He was so closely associated with gangster parts by 1936 that Warners felt obligated to commission a magazine article showing Stone being transformed, via makeup, into an un-gangsterish Spaniard for *Anthony Adverse* (1936). For producer Hal Roach, Stone played three of his oddest film roles: a self-pitying serial killer in *The Housekeeper's Daughter* (1938), an amorous Indian brave in *Road Show* (1940), and Japanese envoy "Suki Yaki" in *The Devil With Hitler* (1942). Stone's most popular role of the 1940s was as The Runt in Columbia's *Boston Blackie* series. In the late 1940s, Stone was forced to severely curtail his acting assignments due to failing eyesight. Though he was totally blind by the mid-1950s, Stone's show business friends, aware of the actor's precarious financial state, saw to it that he got TV and film work, even if it meant that his costars had to literally lead him by the hand around the set. No one was kinder to George E. Stone than the cast and crew of the *Perry Mason* TV series, in which Stone was given prominent billing as the Court Clerk, a part that required nothing more of him than sitting silently at a desk and occasionally holding a Bible before a witness. **Selected Works:** *42nd Street* (1933), *Little Caesar* (1930), *Viva Villa!* (1934)

# Lewis Stone

**Born:** November 15, 1879; Worcester, MA
**Died:** 1953

**Years Active in the Industry:** by decade

| 10ˢ | 20ˢ | 30ˢ | 40ˢ | 50ˢ | 60ˢ | 70ˢ | 80ˢ | 90ˢ |
|-----|-----|-----|-----|-----|-----|-----|-----|-----|
|     |     |     |     |     |     |     |     |     |

He was an established matinee idol in his mid 30s when he broke into films in 1915. After a career interruption caused by service in the cavalry in World War I, he returned to films as a popular leading man. Throughout the '20s he was very busy onscreen playing dignified, well-mannered romantic heroes. For his work in *The Patriot* (1928) he received a Best Actor Oscar nomination. Stone's career remained very busy through the mid '30s, and then continued at a slower pace through the early '50s; in the early sound era, when he was in his 50s, he played mature leads for some time before moving into character roles. Stone is best remembered as Judge Hardy, Andy's father in the "Andy Hardy" series of films with Mickey Rooney; typically, later in his career he played Judge Hardy-like senior citizens. Ultimately, he appeared in over 200

films, almost all of them at MGM. **Selected Works:** *David Copperfield* (1935), *Grand Hotel* (1932), *Queen Christina* (1933), *Big House* (1930), *Madame X* (1929)

# Oliver Stone

**Born:** September 15, 1946; New York, NY

**Years Active in the Industry:** by decade

| 10ˢ | 20ˢ | 30ˢ | 40ˢ | 50ˢ | 60ˢ | 70ˢ | 80ˢ | 90ˢ |
|-----|-----|-----|-----|-----|-----|-----|-----|-----|
|     |     |     |     |     |     |     |     |     |

Few modern filmmakers have been as heavily scrutinized and analyzed as American writer/director Oliver Stone. To hear the critics and pundits tell it, Stone has used the arena of cinema solely to purge his own personal demons. Stone's father was an embittered stockbroker, thus the director made the embittered *Wall Street* (1987); Stone's dad died around the same time as the Kennedy assassination, therefore Stone felt compelled to make *JFK* (1991); Stone was disillusioned by three tours of duty in Vietnam, therefore he got even by making *Platoon* (1986) and *Born on the Fourth of July* (1988). The *reductio ad absurdum* of this would be that Stone made *The Doors* (1991) and *Natural Born Killers* (1994), because he'd been, respectively, a drugged-out rock star and a serial murderer. Levity aside, the fact is that Stone, who made his directorial debut in 1974, has indeed put a lot of himself into his filmmaking—and this emotional involvement had resulted in some of the most compelling cinema seen in the past two decades. However, at base, Stone is an entertainer in the Frank Capra tradition. He knows how to persuasively construct a tale with clear-cut good guys and bad guys, and how to get the audience to accept theories and speculations at face value by bombarding the senses with so much persuasive imagery that one can't help but be pulled over to Stone's point of view—at least, until one thinks it over after seeing the film. Also like Capra, Stone tends not to let facts get in the way of a good story. Such relatively accurate films as *Salvador* (1985) aside, the director has been playing fast and loose with truth and chronology ever since his Oscar-winning *Platoon*, which conveyed the Hell of Vietnam by sending one platoon through more spectacular battle sequences than any single soldier ever *really* went through (this is confirmed even by those Vietnam vets who enjoyed the film). To make loss-of-innocence points in *Born on the Fourth of July*, Stone shows a group of intelligent high school kids in the late

1960s wondering just where in the world Vietnam was (one of them even mispronounces the country). In *The Doors,* he suggests that Jim Morrison was never able to get through a concert without being dragged offstage by oppressive police officials, and in *JFK,* Stone tries to legitimize the long-discredited "conspiracy" case of Jim Garrison by juggling so many facts and fallacies that, in the end, it appears that everyone was in on the plot to kill Kennedy except Caroline and John-John. Nonetheless, Stone is a dynamic filmmaker, and his movies are true works of art, even if not exactly mirrors of reality. With *Natural Born Killers* (1994), his most recent film, Stone suggests that America is a land of lame-brains so seduced by the "celebrity" ethic that they're willing to laud homicidal maniacs as folk heroes. While *Natural Born Killers* was praised to the heavens by critics, it did betray Oliver Stone's one major moviemaking fault—he evidently assumes that the audiences *are* lamebrains who won't understand any plot point unless it is repeated three times over. **Selected Works:** *Dave* (1993), *Midnight Express* (1978), *Nixon* (1995).

# Sharon Stone

**Born:** 1958; Meadville, PA

**Years Active in the Industry:** by decade

| 10ˢ | 20ˢ | 30ˢ | 40ˢ | 50ˢ | 60ˢ | 70ˢ | 80ˢ | 90ˢ |
|---|---|---|---|---|---|---|---|---|
| | | | | | | | ■ | ■ |

Brought up in a small town, Stone won several local beauty contests as a teenager. She dropped out of college at age 19 to work as an Eileen Ford model, moving to Italy to do her photo shoots. She returned to New York in the late '70s to pursue an acting career. At an extras audition she was hand-picked by Woody Allen to appear as the "pretty girl on train" (as she was listed in the credits) in *Stardust Memories* (1980). She went on to land blonde-bombshell roles in a series of mediocre films throughout most of the '80s. Her big break came when she was cast in a supporting role opposite Arnold Schwarzenegger in the blockbuster *Total Recall* (1990), directed by Paul Verhoeven. Verhoeven was impressed with her performance and cast her in the lead female role in his next film, *Basic Instinct* (1992), in which she played a bisexual author and sexual adventurer. That film's massive success launched her into stardom. **Selected Works:** *Diary of a Hitman* (1991), *He Said, She Said* (1991), *Sliver* (1993), *The Specialist* (1994), *Casino* (1995).

# Vittorio Storaro

**Born:** 1940; Rome, Italy

**Years Active in the Industry:** by decade

| 10ˢ | 20ˢ | 30ˢ | 40ˢ | 50ˢ | 60ˢ | 70ˢ | 80ˢ | 90ˢ |
|---|---|---|---|---|---|---|---|---|
| | | | | | ■ | ■ | ■ | ■ |

Italian cinematographer Vittorio Storaro attended Duca D'Aosta Technical Photographic Institute, the Italian Cinemagraphic Training Center, and Centro Sperimental di Cinematografia. In 1969

he manned the cameras for his first film, *Delitto al Circolo del Tennis.* Among the many directors who have benefited from the knowhow of Storaro and his faithful Italian camera crew have been Michael Apted (*Agatha* [1979]), Richard Donner (*Ladyhawke* [1983]), and especially Bernardo Bertolucci (*Last Tango in Paris* [1972], *1900* [1976], *The Sheltering Sky* [1990]). He won an Oscar for his photography on Bertolucci's *The Last Emperor* (1987), and additional Oscars for his work on the films of two other frequent collaborators, Warren Beatty (*Reds* [1981]) and Francis Ford Coppola (*Apocalypse Now* [1979]). Coppola was in fact such an admirer of Storaro's work that he signed Storaro for *Apocalypse Now* before he'd even cast the film. Frequent visitors to Disneyworld will be familiar with Vittorio Storaro through his "consultant" credit for the Michael Jackson 3-D extravaganza *Captain EO.*

# Madeleine Stowe

**Born:** August 18, 1958; Los Angeles, CA

**Years Active in the Industry:** by decade

| 10ˢ | 20ˢ | 30ˢ | 40ˢ | 50ˢ | 60ˢ | 70ˢ | 80ˢ | 90ˢ |
|---|---|---|---|---|---|---|---|---|
| | | | | | | | ■ | ■ |

Madeleine Stowe's father was a California-based civil engineer and her mother was a Costa Rican emigre. Stowe attended University of Southern California, but cut classes to watch plays. Her

"career" as a waitress came to an end when she was fired for being "too spacey." She was anything but spacey when it came to pursuing an acting career in the California theatre circuit. Fortunately, Stowe attracted the attention of Richard Dreyfuss' agent—not for her stage work, but because the agent spotted her watching one of Dreyfuss' stage appearances. This serendipitous turn of events enabled Stowe to attain a bit part on the TV series "Baretta," which led to more substantial roles on other programs. While working on the mid 1980s miniseries "The Gangster Chronicles," Stowe met her husband, future "Dream On" star Brian Benben. Stowe's screen career has not exactly been a string of hits—did anyone *really* see *Worth Winning* (1989), *Closet Land* (1990), and *Blink* (1994)?—but she has usually been able to garner excellent reviews and positive audience response, so that when she is in a bonafide hit like *The Last of the Mohicans* (1992), reviewers will be inclined to credit Stowe for at least some of the film's success. **Selected Works:** *The Two Jakes* (1990), *Unlawful Entry* (1992), *Short Cuts* (1993), *Twelve Monkeys* (1995), *China Moon* (1991).

# David Strathairn

**Born:** 1949; San Francisco, CA

**Years Active in the Industry:** by decade

| 10ˢ | 20ˢ | 30ˢ | 40ˢ | 50ˢ | 60ˢ | 70ˢ | 80ˢ | 90ˢ |
|-----|-----|-----|-----|-----|-----|-----|-----|-----|
|     |     |     |     |     |     |     |     |     |

California-born actor David Strathairn stretched his intellect at Williams College and enhanced his physical dexterity at the Ringling Brothers Clown College. Strathairn's entree into films came by way of his Williams schoolmate John Sayles, who directed the actor in their joint movie debut *The Trial of the Secaucus Seven* (1979). Remaining a member in good standing of the Sayles stock company, Strathairn went on to appear in such Sayles-directed efforts as *Brother From Another Planet* (1984), *Matewan* (1986), *Eight Men Out* (1988) and *City of Hope* (1991). The actor also received prominent supporting roles in non-Sayles films, and was featured as bookstore owner Moss Goodman on the TV "dramedy" series *Days and Nights of Molly Dodd*. The tall, soft-spoken David Strathairn hit a winning streak during the years 1992-94, with costarring assignments in *A League of Their Own* (1992), *Sneakers* (1993), *The River Wild* (1994) and several other important releases. **Selected Works:** *Lost in Yonkers* (1993), *O Pioneers!* (1991), *Passion Fish* (1992), *Losing Isaiah* (1995)

# Meryl Streep (Mary Louise Streep)

**Born:** June 22, 1949; Summit, NJ

**Years Active in the Industry:** by decade

| 10ˢ | 20ˢ | 30ˢ | 40ˢ | 50ˢ | 60ˢ | 70ˢ | 80ˢ | 90ˢ |
|-----|-----|-----|-----|-----|-----|-----|-----|-----|
|     |     |     |     |     |     |     |     |     |

Born Mary Louise Streep, this blond, radiant, expressive leading lady with patrician good looks and quiet intensity is considered among the finest actresses of her generation. She began taking voice lessons for opera at age 12, and while in high school she became interested in acting and starred in several productions. She majored in drama at Vassar, studied costume design and playwriting for a term at Dartmouth, then did her graduate work at the Yale University School of Drama. Streep appeared in more than forty plays in three years with the Yale Repertory Theater. After moving to New York she appeared in several Broadway plays, notably Tennessee Williams's *27 Wagons Full of Cotton,* for which she received a Tony Award nomination. In 1976 she joined the New York Shakespeare Festival. She debuted onscreen in *Julia* (1977) and almost instantly was considered an up-and-coming star. For her second film, *The Deer Hunter* (1978), she received a Best Supporting Actress Oscar nomination and won the National Society of Film Critics Award for Best Actress; the same year she won an Emmy for her work in the TV mini-series "Holocaust." By 1994 Streep had received nine Oscar nominations; she won the Best Actress Oscar for *Sophie's Choice* (1982) and the Best Supporting Actress Oscar for *Kramer vs. Kramer* (1979). She won the highly coveted role as the lead actress in the filming of Robert James Waller's bestselling novel *The Bridges of Madison County* (1995). She is married to sculptor Donald Gummer. **Selected Works:** *A Cry in the Dark* (1988), *The French Lieutenant's Woman* (1981), *Out of Africa* (1985), *Postcards from the Edge* (1990), *Silkwood* (1983)

# Barbra Streisand (Barbara Joan Streisand)

**Born:** April 24, 1942; New York, NY

**Years Active in the Industry:** by decade

| 10ˢ | 20ˢ | 30ˢ | 40ˢ | 50ˢ | 60ˢ | 70ˢ | 80ˢ | 90ˢ |
|-----|-----|-----|-----|-----|-----|-----|-----|-----|
|     |     |     |     |     |     |     |     |     |

Superstar performer of stage, TV, films, and recordings, with a prominent nose and cat-like eyes set close together, Streisand harbored show business ambitions from childhood. In 1960, when she was 18, Streisand won a talent contest at The Lion, a Greenwich Village nightclub; she went on to gain some recognition on the nightclub circuit and appeared in an off-Broadway revue. In 1962 she made her Broadway debut in a supporting role in *I Can Get It For You Wholesale;* the musical wasn't very successful, but she stole the show with her singing and comedic skills, leading to a New York Critics Award and instant stardom. The star of the show was Elliot Gould, whom she married in 1963 (they were divorced in 1971). She went on to become extremely popular in supper clubs and TV guest appearances, particularly a TV appearance with Judy Garland that gained the attention of the nation. She topped her own success in a stunning performance as the lead in the hit Broadway musical *Funny Girl* (1964); she repeated her portrayal of real-life entertainer Fanny Brice in the musical's film version (1968), her big screen debut, for which she won a Best Actress Oscar. Meanwhile, CBS signed her to a multi-million dollar recording contract and she starred in a number of elaborate TV specials. In 1970 she was presented with a special Tony award as Broadway's "Actress of the Decade." She went on to become a successsful screen actress in an up-and-down career that included starring roles in musicals, comedies, and dramas. Later, she often produced or co-produced her films. In 1983 she directed, co-wrote, and starred in *Yentl,* then went on to direct and star in *The Prince of Tides* (1991). By 1990 she had won five Emmys and seven Grammys, plus the Best Song Oscar for her composition

"Evergreen" from her remake of *A Star Is Born* (1976). She is considered one of the most powerful and independent women in show business. **Selected Works:** *The Way We Were* (1973)

# Woodrow "Woody" Strode
(Woodrow Strode)

**Born:** 1914; Los Angeles, CA

**Years Active in the Industry:** by decade

| 10ˢ | 20ˢ | 30ˢ | 40ˢ | 50ˢ | 60ˢ | 70ˢ | 80ˢ | 90ˢ |
|-----|-----|-----|-----|-----|-----|-----|-----|-----|

Strode was a star in the Canadian Football League and later a professional wrestler; aside from a film appearance in 1941, he didn't begin his screen career until 1951, when he was in his mid 30s. He went on to play black musclemen in numerous films. His presence was often more decorative than dramatically necessary, and sometimes he was required to do little more than bare his chest and flex his muscles. His first significant role was in John Ford's *Sergeant Rutledge* (1960), in which he portrayed a soldier on trial for rape and murder. This began a new phase in his career, and he began landing more impressive parts. **Selected Works:** *The Man Who Shot Liberty Valance* (1962), *Posse* (1993), *Spartacus* (1960), *Storyville* (1992), *The Ten Commandments* (1956)

# John Sturges (John Eliot Sturges)

**Born:** January 3, 1910; Oak Park, IL
**Died:** August 18, 1992; San Luis Obispo, CA

**Years Active in the Industry:** by decade

| 10ˢ | 20ˢ | 30ˢ | 40ˢ | 50ˢ | 60ˢ | 70ˢ | 80ˢ | 90ˢ |
|-----|-----|-----|-----|-----|-----|-----|-----|-----|

One of Hollywood's top action directors of the late 1950s and 1960s, John Sturges, for a time, was a name associated almost exclusively with large-scale action-adventure films. A one-time assistant in RKO's blueprint department, Sturges spent most of his early career in the studio's art department and editing room (an especially productive department, where directors Robert Wise and Mark Robson also got their starts), before joining David O. Selznick as a production assistant and later as an editor. He be-

came a director in the U.S. Army Air Force, making documentary and training films, including *Thunderbolt,* in collaboration with veteran director William Wyler. He returned to Hollywood as a director and, for a time, made successful if fairly undistinguished films (mostly action or suspense) until 1954, when he took on *Bad Day At Black Rock.* Sturges, who had shown a knack for working with the increasingly difficult Spencer Tracy (in *The People Against O'Hara*), coaxed a great performance out of the legendary star (and some of the best work ever by Lee Marvin, Robert Ryan, and Anne Francis, among others) and transformed the film from a routine suspense vehicle into a powerful thriller, dealing with the then increasingly topical subject of racism and violence. Sturges received his only Academy Award nomination for *Bad Day At Black Rock,* and his career was made, as he became sought out by Hollywood's top producers. *Gunfight At the O.K. Corral* (1957), which he directed for producer Hal Wallis, was another hit. He was also responsible for *The Old Man and the Sea* (1958) and *The Last Train From Gun Hill* (1959), starring Spencer Tracy and Kirk Douglas. Sturges then became his own producer, beginning with *The Magnificent Seven* (1960), a large-scale Western action vehicle adapted from Akira Kurosawa's *The Seven Samurai* (1954). It turned most of its featured players (including Steve McQueen, Charles Bronson, and James Coburn) into stars and was popular enough to generate four sequels as well as a major hit musical theme by Elmer Bernstein. *The Great Escape* (1963), a fact-based all-star World War II thriller, was the high water mark of Sturges' career. It became an enormous theatrical hit and a subsequent favorite on home video and laserdisc (where there are two rival editions out—one featuring Sturges's own recollections about the movie). His next movie, *The Satan Bug* (1965), based on a popular best-seller, seemed to be a deliberate attempt to get away from big, all-star vehicles. It failed and quickly ended up on television, while *The Hallelujah Trail* (1965) proved an awkward, unpopular Western satire despite its big-name cast. His subsequent movies, including *Ice Station Zebra* (1968) and *Joe Kidd* (1972), were popular but never on the scale of Sturges's early 1960s work. And his *Hour of the Gun* (1967), a more personal, deeply psychological reinterpretation of events surrounding the gunfight at the O.K. Corral, was a failure at the box office. *Marooned* (1969), which he inherited as a project from Frank Capra, was initially a failure, until the story of an Apollo spacecraft trapped in orbit suddenly took on new relevancy in the wake of the Apollo 13 explosion; it became a hit soon after. *The Eagle Has Landed* (1976), a return to *Great Escape*-style action and scale dealing with an attempt by the Germans to kidnap Winston Churchill during World War II, was successful, but also marked his retirement. In 1991, Sturges came out of retirement to participate in the making of a special laserdisc edition of *The Great Escape* for Voyager Company. Although not highly regarded as a stylist, Sturges had a way of working with actors and designing scenes that elicited strong emotional response from audiences—especially men—that made his pictures extremely compelling. He probably rated Academy Award consideration for *The Magnificent Seven* and *The Great Escape.* Curiously, he seemed to understand the special appeal that his films had for male audiences seeking escapist entertainment, and several of his films, including *The*

*Great Escape* and *Ice Station Zebra,* don't feature a single female cast member. However, he never descended into cheap entertainment in catering to his audience. And one actress, Anne Francis, did some of her best work in two of his movies, *Bad Day At Black Rock* and *The Satan Bug.*

# Preston Sturges (Edmund Preston Biden)

**Born:** August 29, 1898; Chicago, IL
**Died:** August 6, 1959; New York, NY

**Years Active in the Industry:** by decade

| 10s | 20s | 30s | 40s | 50s | 60s | 70s | 80s | 90s |
|-----|-----|-----|-----|-----|-----|-----|-----|-----|

One of Hollywood's genuinely legendary directors, for a time during the early 1940s Preston Sturges redefined the boundaries and meaning of screen comedy. The son of a socially prominent couple, Sturges had a cosmopolitan upbringing throughout Europe and America, and served in the Air Corps during World War I. He worked for a time in his mother's cosmetics company, before moving into other fields, including inventing. He began writing plays in the late 1920s, creating one major hit, *Strictly Dishonorable.* He got some experience writing dialogue for the screen and became a scriptwriter in 1933. By the middle of the decade he had developed a reputation at Paramount Pictures for his witty, sophisticated, but unpretentious writing, most notably in *The Good Fairy* and *Easy Living.* He also learned a lot about filmmaking during this period, and in 1940 convinced the studio to allow him to direct his first picture, *The Great McGinty,* a political satire (always considered a risky category of film) that astonished everybody by becoming a major hit—Sturges was subsequently allowed to direct *Christmas In July* (1940), *The Lady Eve* (1941), *Sullivan's Travels* (1941), *The Palm Beach Story* (1942), *The Miracle of Morgan's Creek* (1944), and *Hail The Conquering Hero* (1944), all of which were solid commercial and critical successes. These movies today seem even more extraordinary for what they achieved—through its pacing and sheer bravado, *Morgan's Creek* somehow made it past the censors with its story about an out-of-wedlock pregnancy, while *Sullivan's Travels* (considered by many as his best film) managed to satirize Hollywood itself, on numerous levels. He got Hollywood to laugh at itself and Americans to laugh at their own sentimentality and cultural sacred cows, and his success was such that many

screenwriters began to move into directing. However, Sturges' own career faltered, over a dispute with studio management and the failure of an ill-advised "serious" historical drama, *The Great Moment* (1944). He left Paramount in 1944 and tried to recoup his career in collaboration with screen legend Harold Lloyd in *Mad Wednesday* (1950), which failed. Sturges then directed the successful, sophisticated comedy *Unfaithfully Yours* (1948) and faded out of Hollywood after making *The Beautiful Blonde From Bashful Bend* (1949), a Western satire that was a shadow of his former work. A difficult partnership with Howard Hughes ended disastrously, and Sturges retreated to Europe, where he made one movie, *The French, They Are A Funny Race,* four years before his death. A superb writer and dazzling stylist in his prime, Sturges' reputation looms larger today than it did during his lifetime, even more amazing when one considers that his reputation rests principally on a half-dozen pictures made during a four year period. **Selected Works:** *Star Spangled Rhythm* (1942)

# Margaret Sullavan (Margaret Brooke)

**Born:** May 16, 1911; Norfolk, VA
**Died:** 1960

**Years Active in the Industry:** by decade

| 10s | 20s | 30s | 40s | 50s | 60s | 70s | 80s | 90s |
|-----|-----|-----|-----|-----|-----|-----|-----|-----|

Having studied dance and drama since childhood, Sullavan debuted onstage at age 17 with the now-celebrated University Players, a troupe which included several other future stars, including Jimmy Stewart and Henry Fonda. Three years later she made it to Broadway, and in 1933 she signed a lucrative film contract. For most of the next decade she was busy as a lead actress, but she had frequent disputes with her studio; easily angered and disdainful of Hollywood, she occasionally went back to Broadway. In films she tended to be cast in melodramatic tear-jerkers, although she also proved her talents in straight dramas and sophisticated comedies. For her work in *Three Comrades* (1938) she won the New York film critics best actress award. For her work in Broadway's *The Voice of the Turtle* (1943) she won the Drama Critics Award. She retired from the screen in 1943, returning in only one additional film, *No Sad Songs for Me* (1950). In the late '40s she began to lose her hearing, and eventually she was nearly deaf; nevertheless, she continued a successful stage career. Her four husbands included actor Henry Fonda, director William Wyler, and producer-agent Leland Hayward. At 49 she took an overdose of barbiturates and died; her death was ruled a suicide. Her daughter, Brooke Hayward, wrote a memoir of the tragic years leading to Sullavan's death called *Haywire.*

# Barry Sullivan (Patrick Barry)

**Born:** August 29, 1912; New York, NY
**Died:** Sherman Oaks, CA

**Years Active in the Industry:** by decade

| 10ˢ | 20ˢ | 30ˢ | 40ˢ | 50ˢ | 60ˢ | 70ˢ | 80ˢ | 90ˢ |
|---|---|---|---|---|---|---|---|---|

Actor Barry Sullivan was a theater usher and department store employee at the time he made his first Broadway appearance in 1936. His "official" film debut was in the 1943 Western *Woman of the Town*, though in fact Sullivan had previously appeared in a handful of 2-reel comedies produced by the Manhattan-based Educational Studios in the late 1930s. A bit too raffish to be a standard leading man, Sullivan was better served in tough, aggressive roles, notably the title character in 1947's *The Gangster* and the boorish Tom Buchanan in the 1949 version of *The Great Gatsby*. One of his better film assignments of the 1950's was as the Howard Hawks-style movie director in *The Bad and the Beautiful* (1952). Sullivan continued appearing in movie roles of varying importance until 1978. A frequent visitor to television, Barry Sullivan starred as Sheriff Pat Garrett in the 1960s Western series *The Tall Man*, and was seen as the hateful patriarch Marcus Hubbard in a 1972 PBS production of Lillian Hellman's *Another Part of the Forest*. **Selected Works:** *The Bad & the Beautiful* (1952), *American Dream* (1966)

# Donald Sutherland

**Born:** July 17, 1934; St. John, New Brunswick, Canada

**Years Active in the Industry:** by decade

| 10ˢ | 20ˢ | 30ˢ | 40ˢ | 50ˢ | 60ˢ | 70ˢ | 80ˢ | 90ˢ |
|---|---|---|---|---|---|---|---|---|

A tall lanky leading man with unconventional looks, a slow style of delivering lines, and a relaxed, laconic persona, Sutherland worked as a disc jockey at a Nova Scotia radio station when he was

only fourteen. He began acting in student plays while in college; after an acclaimed performance in James Thurber's *The Male Animal*, he gave up his engineering major and began devoting himself to theater. After graduating, he moved to England in 1956 and enrolled at the London Academy of Music and Dramatic Art, going on to make several appearances on the London stage during a year with the Perth Repertory Theater. He also found roles in several BBC TV shows, including "The Saint" and "The Avengers." Soon he debuted onscreen in a dual role in the Italian horror film *The Castle of the Living Dead,* produced by Warren Kiefer, after whom Sutherland named his first son. He went on to

play supporting roles in a handful of films before landing his first really notable part in Robert Aldrich's *The Dirty Dozen* (1967) (his oversized ears were part of the reason he got the part). This led to a great deal of screen work throughout the next two years, and ultimately to his breakthrough role as Hawkeye Pierce in Robert Altman's extremely successful Korean War comedy *M*A*S*H* (1969), after which he was an established star. Meanwhile, he was a political activist and Vietnam War protester; his second wife Shirley was arrested in 1970 for giving hand grenades to the Black Panthers. When he appeared with the politically active actress Jane Fonda in *Klute* (1971), the two of them were already in love, having collaborated in the anti-Vietnam troop show "F.T.A." (Free The Army), the film of which he co-scripted, co-produced, and co-directed. After *M*A*S*H* he became an unusually busy screen actor, appearing in one to four films per year. Although never a superstar, he has remained a successful and well-respected screen actor. He is the father of actor Kiefer Sutherland. **Selected Works:** *Ordinary People* (1980), *Six Degrees of Separation* (1993), *Disclosure* (1994), *Outbreak* (1995), *The Oldest Living Confederate Widow Tells All* (1994)

# Kiefer Sutherland

**Born:** 1966; London, England

**Years Active in the Industry:** by decade

| 10ˢ | 20ˢ | 30ˢ | 40ˢ | 50ˢ | 60ˢ | 70ˢ | 80ˢ | 90ˢ |
|---|---|---|---|---|---|---|---|---|

The son of actors Donald Sutherland and Shirley Douglas, Kiefer Sutherland wanted to be an actor from childhood, and in his early teens he participated in local theater workshops. Living in Canada, at 17 he won the lead in *The Bad Boy* (1984), a Canadian production for which he received a Canadian Academy Award nomination. He moved to New York, where he rejected an offer to work in a soap opera and then spent a year unemployed; he then moved to Los Angeles, where he soon landed a part in an episode of the TV series "Amazing Stories." He went on to become a busy screen actor, primarily in supporting and costarring roles. For a time he was engaged to actress Julia Roberts, with whom he appeared in *Flatliners* (1990). **Selected Works:** *Article 99* (1992), *A Few Good Men* (1992), *The Vanishing [USA]* (1993), *Young Guns, Part 2* (1990), *The Three Musketeers* (1993)

# Gloria Swanson

**Born:** March 27, 1897; Chicago, IL
**Died:** April 4, 1983

**Years Active in the Industry:** by decade

| 10ˢ | 20ˢ | 30ˢ | 40ˢ | 50ˢ | 60ˢ | 70ˢ | 80ˢ | 90ˢ |
|---|---|---|---|---|---|---|---|---|

Swanson was born Gloria Swenson. An "army brat," she had attended more than a dozen schools by her early teens. Finally settling in Chicago, at age 16 she was hired as an extra at Essanay Studios, where she met actor Wallace Beery; three years later, in 1916, she and Beery were married and moved to Hollywood. Beery signed with Mack Sennett's Keystone company on the condition that Swanson also be given a contract. She started out in a series of romantic comedies, then starred in melodramatic tearjerkers. In 1919 she joined Cecil B. DeMille's team and soon rose to major stardom in euphemism-laden bedroom farces. By the mid 1920s, now specializing in drama, she was a reigning Queen of Hollywood, expertly handling the film world's publicity machine to increase her own glamour. Meanwhile, she divorced Beery in 1919, married and divorced again, then married a marquis. In 1927 she began producing her own films; a year later she was nearly bankrupted by the costs of Erich von Stroheim's production of *Queen Kelly* (1928). She proved herself capable of both speaking and singing well in the sound era, but her talkies were mostly unsuccessful and she retired from the screen in 1934. Throughout the next four decades she appeared in five additional films, the most important of which was *Sunset Boulevard* (1950), for which she received her third Best Actress Oscar nomination. Later, she occasionally appeared on TV talk shows, often promoting health food. In 1971 she starred on Broadway in *Butterflies Are Free*. Altogether, she was married six times. **Selected Works:** *Sadie Thompson* (1928)

However, an old knee injury from his football days made him worry that his dancing days were numbered, and he turned to acting; having danced in a Broadway musical, he landed the role of Danny in the hit Broadway rock musical *Grease*. He moved to Los Angeles and debuted onscreen in a small role in the forgettable *Skatetown U.S.A.* (1979). Four years went by before his next screen role, during which he played teens and tough guys in guest spots on TV series, and notably portrayed a soldier dying of leukemia in an episode of "M*A*S*H." Finally, he got a role in Francis Ford Coppola's youth ensemble film *The Outsiders* (1983), a big break that unfortunately resulted in only a string of appearances in mediocre films. He became well-known as the result of his work in the TV mini-series "North and South" (1985) and its sequel (1986). He became an overnight superstar after his dancing-acting role in the sleeper hit *Dirty Dancing* (1987), a low-budget teen-oriented film that did astoundingly well at the box office; he wrote and performed one of the film's songs, which went on to become a hit. He went on to a few disappointing films before scoring big again in the supernatural romance *Ghost* (1990), another unexpected hit which grossed over $200 million. He is the brother of actor Don Swayze. **Selected Works:** *City of Joy* (1992), *Point Break* (1991), *Three Wishes* (1995), *To Wong Foo, Thanks for Everything, Julie Newmar* (1995)

# Patrick Swayze

**Born:** August 18, 1954; Houston, TX

**Years Active in the Industry:** by decade

| 10$^s$ | 20$^s$ | 30$^s$ | 40$^s$ | 50$^s$ | 60$^s$ | 70$^s$ | 80$^s$ | 90$^s$ |
|---|---|---|---|---|---|---|---|---|
| | | | | | | | | |

A football star in high school, he attended college on a gymnastics scholarship. In his youth, Swayze had a reputation as a heavy-drinking, motorcycle-riding troublemaker. The son of a  dancer-choreographer, he studied dance from an early age and, as a young man, worked with the Harkness and Joffrey Ballet companies—two of the most respected in America. He was also a principal dancer in the Eliot Feld company. His professional debut came as Prince Charming in a traveling company of *Disney On Parade*.

# D.B. Sweeney (Daniel Bernard Sweeney)

**Born:** 1961; Shoreham, Long Island, NY

**Years Active in the Industry:** by decade

| 10$^s$ | 20$^s$ | 30$^s$ | 40$^s$ | 50$^s$ | 60$^s$ | 70$^s$ | 80$^s$ | 90$^s$ |
|---|---|---|---|---|---|---|---|---|
| | | | | | | | | |

Empire State native D.B. Sweeney attended both Tulane and New York University. Though he had trouble getting sizeable roles in student productions, upon his graduation he was immediately cast in the Broadway revival of *Caine Mutiny Court Martial*. He went on to guest-star stints on such TV series as *The Edge of Night* and *Spencer for Hire* before entering movies, where he scored with the critics for his portrayal of an idealistic, gung-ho Vietnam enlistee in Francis Ford Coppola's *Gardens of Stone* (1987). While he has accrued several noteworthy screen assignments (including the starring role of a nasty hockey player in 1992's *The Cutting Edge*), D.B. Sweeney is best remembered for his even-keel portrayal of the tragic Shoeless Joe Jackson in *Eight Men Out* (1988); if he looked like a "natural" on the ballfield, it was because Sweeney had once actually played minor-league baseball with the Kenosha Twins, hanging up his spikes after a knee injury. **Selected Works:** *A Day in October* (1992), *Lonesome Dove* (1989), *Memphis Belle* (1990), *Miss Rose White* (1992), *Roommates* (1995)

Lyle Talbot

Lily Tomlin

Jean Louis Trintignant

Rip Torn

Cicely Tyson

## Lyle Talbot (Lysle Henderson)

**Born:** 1902; Pittsburgh, PA

**Years Active in the Industry:** by decade

| 10s | 20s | 30s | 40s | 50s | 60s | 70s | 80s | 90s |
|-----|-----|-----|-----|-----|-----|-----|-----|-----|

Talbot began his career as a magician, touring in his late teens in tent shows with his parents. Later he began acting, traveling a great deal with stock and rep companies; eventually he founded his own Memphis-based company, the Talbot Players. He debuted onscreen in 1932 and immediately began a very busy film career as a leading man in B movies and a frequent heavy in both B's and A's; he was often cast as underworld types. Meanwhile, he continued performing on Broadway and later did much work on TV; he was a regular on the TV series "The Adventures of Ozzie and Harriet" and "The Bob Cummings Show." He retired from films in 1960. **Selected Works:** *Sunrise at Campobello* (1960)

## Akim Tamiroff

**Born:** October 29, 1899; Baku, Russia
**Died:** 1972

**Years Active in the Industry:** by decade

| 10s | 20s | 30s | 40s | 50s | 60s | 70s | 80s | 90s |
|-----|-----|-----|-----|-----|-----|-----|-----|-----|

Akim Tamiroff trained for the stage at the Moscow Art Theater drama school; in 1923 he toured the U.S. with an acting troupe and decided to stay. After establishing himself as an actor with the New York Theater Guild, he launched a busy screen career in 1932; a flamboyant, charismatic actor, he played some character leads but primarily had supporting roles, often as suspicious, Slavic-accented foreigners. He was steadily employed in Hollywood until 1949, after which he appeared mostly in British and European films. In 1959 he played the lead role in the Broadway adaptation of *Rashomon*. For his work in *The General Died at Dawn* (1936) and *For Whom the Bell Tolls* (1943) he received Best Supporting Actor Oscar nominations. **Selected Works:** *Anastasia* (1956), *Great McGinty* (1940), *Miracle of Morgan's Creek* (1944), *Topkapi* (1964), *Tortilla Flat* (1942)

## Jessica Tandy

**Born:** June 7, 1909; London, England
**Died:** September 11, 1994

**Years Active in the Industry:** by decade

| 10s | 20s | 30s | 40s | 50s | 60s | 70s | 80s | 90s |
|-----|-----|-----|-----|-----|-----|-----|-----|-----|

After studying acting at the Ben Greet Academy of Acting, she debuted on the British stage at 16, then debuted in New York at 21. She debuted onscreen in *The Indiscretions of Eve* (1932), then appeared in only one more film during the '30s. Meanwhile, she became a star of the stage, giving her most celebrated performance as Blanche Dubois in the original cast of Tennessee Williams's *A Streetcar Named Desire* (1947), for which she won a Best Actress Tony. She returned to films in the mid '40s, but her screen work was sporadic until the '80s, when she cornered the market on "old lady" roles and appeared in almost a dozen films; at age 81 she won the Best Actress Oscar for her performance in *Driving Miss Daisy* (1989). She married and divorced actor Jack Hawkins, then in 1942 married actor Hume Cronyn, with whom she often teamed up on Broadway. They also appeared together in several films, notably *Cocoon* (1985). In 1978 she won another Tony award for her work in *The Gin Game*. **Selected Works:** *Birds* (1963), *Fried Green Tomatoes* (1991), *World According to Garp* (1982), *Nobody's Fool* (1994)

# Quentin Tarantino

**Born:** 1963; Knoxville, TN

**Years Active in the Industry:** by decade

| 10s | 20s | 30s | 40s | 50s | 60s | 70s | 80s | 90s |
|-----|-----|-----|-----|-----|-----|-----|-----|-----|
|     |     |     |     |     |     |     |     | ■   |

Director/screenwriter/actor Quentin Tarantino was the most distinctive and volatile talent to emerge in American film in the early '90s. Unlike the previous generation of American filmmakers,

Tarantino didn't learn his craft in film school—he learned it from videos. Consequently, he developed an audacious fusion of pop culture and independent art-house cinema; his films were thrillers that were distinguished as much by their clever, twisting dialogue as their outbursts of extreme violence. Tarantino initially began his career as an actor (his biggest role was an Elvis impersonator on an episode of "The Golden Girls"), taking classes while he was working at Video Archives in Manhattan Beach, California. During his time at Video Archives, he began writing screenplays, completing his first, *True Romance*, in 1987. With his co-worker Roger Avary (who would later also become a director), Tarantino tried to get financial backing to film the script. After years of negotiations, he decided to sell the script, which wound up in the hands of director Tony Scott. During this time, Tarantino wrote the screenplay for *Natural Born Killers*. Again, he was unable to come up with enough investors to make a movie and gave the script to his partner Rand Vossler. Tarantino used the money he made from *True Romance* to begin preproduction on *Reservoir Dogs*, a film about a failed heist. *Reservoir Dogs* received financial backing from LIVE Entertainment after Harvey Keitel agreed to star in the movie. Word-of-mouth on *Reservoir Dogs* began to build at the 1992 Sundance film festival, which led to scores of glowing reviews, making the film a cult hit. While many critics and fans were praising Tarantino, he developed a sizable amount of detractors. Claiming he ripped off entire

scenes from obscure foreign thrillers, the critics only added to the buzz about Tarantino. During 1993, he wrote and directed his next feature, *Pulp Fiction,* which featured three interweaving crime story lines; Tony Scott's big-budget production of *True Romance* was also released in 1993. The following year, Tarantino was elevated from a cult figure to a major celebrity. In May, *Pulp Fiction* won the Palme d'or at Cannes Film Festival, beginning the flood of good reviews for the picture. Before *Pulp Fiction* was released in October, Oliver Stone's bombastic version of *Natural Born Killers* hit the theaters in August; Tarantino distanced himself from the film and was only credited for writing the basic story. *Pulp Fiction* soon eclipsed *Natural Born Killers* in both acclaim and popularity. Made for $8 million, the film eventually grossed over $100 million and topped many critics' top ten lists. *Pulp Fiction* earned seven Academy Award nominations, including Best Picture, Best Director, Best Original Screenplay (Tarantino and Avary), Best Actor (John Travolta), Best Supporting Actor (Samuel L. Jackson), and Best Supporting Actress (Uma Thurman). After the film became a hit, Tarantino was everywhere, from talk-shows to a cameo in the low-budget *Sleep With Me.* At the beginning of 1995, he prepared to shoot a segment of the anthology film *Four Rooms,* starring himself and *Pulp Fiction* alumni Bruce Willis. In the meantime, he directed an episode of the NBC TV hit, "ER," appeared in Margaret Cho's sitcom "All-American Girl," and had a starring role in the comedy *Destiny Turns On The Radio.* **Selected Works:** *Desperado* (1995), *Four Rooms* (1995), *From Dusk Till Dawn* (1995)

# Jacques Tati (Jacques Tatischeff)

**Born:** October 9, 1908; Le Pecq, France
**Died:** November 5, 1982

**Years Active in the Industry:** by decade

| 10s | 20s | 30s | 40s | 50s | 60s | 70s | 80s | 90s |
|-----|-----|-----|-----|-----|-----|-----|-----|-----|
|     |     |     | ■   |     |     |     |     |     |

After a stint as a professional rugby player, in his mid 20s Jacques Tatischuff began performing in cabarets and music halls; his act consisted of pantomiming the top sports figures of the day, and was so successful that several of his routines were made into short films. After World War II, he played small dramatic roles in two films, then directed a short comedy featuring himself, *L'Ecole des Facteurs* (1947); the film's producer decided to expand it into a feature, *Jour de Fete* (1949), which was recognized as a milestone in the development of French cinema and won the Venice Film Festival Best Screenplay award. Four years passed before his next film, *Mr. Hulot's Holiday* (1953), also considered a masterpiece; the delay was due to the difficulties of raising money for the film, as well as Tati's meticulous, time-consuming preproduction preparations. Throughout his subsequent career he had great difficulties getting financing for his projects, and in a three-decade career, he made only six features. In each of his major films he played Mr. Hulot, a tall, gawky, pipe-smoking, gently foolish eccentric; Hulot is now considered one of the all-time greatest screen inventions. **Selected Works:** *Monsieur Hulot's Holiday* (1953), *My Uncle* (1958)

# Bertrand Tavernier

**Born:** April 25, 1941; Lyons, France

**Years Active in the Industry:** by decade

| 10s | 20s | 30s | 40s | 50s | 60s | 70s | 80s | 90s |
|-----|-----|-----|-----|-----|-----|-----|-----|-----|
|     |     |     |     |     |     |     |     |     |

Like many French directors of the 1960s, Bernard Tavernier got his professional start as a movie critic for such auteur-conscious magazines as *Positif* and *Cahier du Cinema*. After working as a film industry press agent, Tavernier directed his first movie, *L'Horloger de St. Paul* (*The Clockmaker*) in 1974; the film won him the Prix Louis Delluc. One year later, Tavernier won two French Cesar Awards for *Que la fete Commence* (*Let Joy Reign Supreme*). Tavernier's most frequent star was Philipe Noiret, whom he regarded as his cinematic alter ego—though the director refuses to label his films as autobiographical. Some observers have detected a strain of feminist sympathies in Tavernier's works, citing the strongly pro-female stance in *A Week's Vacation* (1981) and other films; in truth, Tavernier has depicted *all* of the principal characters in his films with warmth and empathy, be they male or female (he does, however, exhibit a preference for "bourgeois" characters who are not insulated from life's problems by wealth and position). The director's biggest international success was *Round Midnight* (1986), a richly atmospheric tale of a burned-out American jazz musician in the Parisian nightclub circuit of the 1950s. Bernard Tavernier was for many years married to writer Colo O'Hagan, who continued to successfully collaborate with Tavernier even after their divorce. **Selected Works:** *Life and Nothing But* (1989), *Fresh Bait* (1995)

# Paolo Taviani

**Born:** November 8, 1931; San Miniato, Pisa, Italy

**Years Active in the Industry:** by decade

| 10s | 20s | 30s | 40s | 50s | 60s | 70s | 80s | 90s |
|-----|-----|-----|-----|-----|-----|-----|-----|-----|
|     |     |     |     |     |     |     |     |     |

Italian filmmaker Paolo Taviani and his brother Vittorio, known for their politically charged re-workings of historical events, began their long, fruitful collaboration while still in school. Their earliest films were documentaries, and their liberal political tendencies are already apparent in their first finished short *San Miniato, July 1944* (1954), a chronicle of a Nazi massacre in their hometown done in collaboration with Cesare Zavattini. The notorious resistance fighter Valentino Orsini was a friend and also had a tremendous effect on their work. The brothers gained notoriety in 1967 with the groundbreaking *Subversives,* a film that combined actual footage of a Communist leader's funeral with the story of

four people for whom the death marks a major turning point in their political futures. With their feature films, the brothers Taviani share every aspect of filmmaking from writing and design, to directing. When they began in features, they adopted conventions of Neo-Realism by using non-pro actors, natural lighting, location shoots, natural sound, and working class scenarios. Later, they branched off in search of their own style of blurring the lines between traditional documentary and fictional features by presenting subjective views of actual facts to create a metaphorical look at history. A good example of their vision and style can be seen in *La notte di San Lorenzo* (1984), a remake of their first film. The film reflects the Taviani's commitment to retelling history in a manner apropos to contemporary needs in order to prevent a repetition of its tragedies. **Selected Works:** *Fiorile* (1993), *Night Sun* (1990)

# Elizabeth Taylor

**Born:** February 27, 1932; London, England

**Years Active in the Industry:** by decade

| 10s | 20s | 30s | 40s | 50s | 60s | 70s | 80s | 90s |
|-----|-----|-----|-----|-----|-----|-----|-----|-----|
|     |     |     |     |     |     |     |     |     |

Elizabeth Taylor took ballet lessons from early childhood. Her parents, Americans living in London, moved to Los Angeles in 1939. A beautiful child, she attracted the attention of Hollywood  scouts, who soon cast her in her screen debut, *There's One Born Every Minute* (1942). She signed a long-term contract with MGM and became a popular child and juvenile star; her physical maturity was rapid, and soon she moved into romantic leads, now touted as one of the most beautiful women in the world. Meanwhile, her romantic life was turbulent; at 17 she dated Howard Hughes, then married hotelier Nick Hilton; a few months later they split up. She went on to marry actor Michael Wilding, showman Mike Todd, singer Eddie Fisher, actor Richard Burton (twice), Senator John Warner, and Larry Fortensky. She converted to Judaism before marrying Todd; he died in a plane crash a year after their marriage. Except for Todd and her latest marriage to Fortensky, all of her unions have ended in divorce. She remained busy onscreen through the '70s, after which her film work was infrequent. Taylor has been nominated several times for Oscars; she won the Best Actress Oscar for her work in *Butterfield 8* (1960) and *Who's Afraid of Virginia Woolf?* (1966). In the '80s she launched a successful line of perfumes; meanwhile, she raised millions of dollars for AIDS research. **Selected Works:** *Cat on a Hot Tin Roof* (1958), *Father of the Bride* (1950), *Giant* (1956), *National Velvet* (1944), *A Place in the Sun* (1951)

# Lili Taylor

**Born:** 1966; Chicago, IL

**Years Active in the Industry:** by decade

| 10s | 20s | 30s | 40s | 50s | 60s | 70s | 80s | 90s |
|-----|-----|-----|-----|-----|-----|-----|-----|-----|

Lili Taylor is one of the most versatile character actresses working in films today. While the more glamorous stars go through their paces, Taylor is the girl with whom most of the audience identifies. She starred in *Mystic Pizza* (1988) as one of three overly amorous pizzeria girls (the other two were Julia Roberts and Annabeth Gish). In *Say Anything...* (1989), Taylor played an obsessive, suicidal highschooler; in *Bright Angel* (1991), she was cast as the drifter sister of a jailbird; and in *Dogfight* (1991) she was the obligatory "ugly duckling" transformed by her reluctant date River Phoenix. Taylor has proven to be a willing and able ensemble player in the works of several stellar directors: Oliver Stone's *Born on the Fourth of July* (1989), Nancy Savoca's *Household Saints* (1993), and Robert Altman's *Short Cuts* (1994) **Selected Works:** *Rudy* (1993), *The Addiction* (1995)

# Robert Taylor (Spangler Arlington Brugh)

**Born:** August 5, 1911; Filley, NE
**Died:** 1969

**Years Active in the Industry:** by decade

| 10s | 20s | 30s | 40s | 50s | 60s | 70s | 80s | 90s |
|-----|-----|-----|-----|-----|-----|-----|-----|-----|

Taylor appeared in a student play at a California college and was spotted by a scout, who offered him a screen test, leading to a long-term contract with MGM. He debuted onscreen in 1934 and soon was both very busy and popular; billed as "the Man With the Perfect Profile," he was Clark Gable's main contender as the screen's top romantic star. At first considered just another glamour boy, Taylor gradually developed into a solid, mature actor with an excellent reputation among directors; he was known for his no-nonsense attitude toward acting and willingness to work hard. During World War II he served as a flight instructor with the Navy's Air Transport; meanwhile, he directed 17 Navy training films. He was married from 1939-51 to actress Barbara Stanwyck, and from 1954 to actress Ursula Thiess. He died from lung cancer at 57. **Selected Works:** *Camille* (1936), *Quo Vadis* (1951), *Three Comrades* (1938), *Waterloo Bridge* (1940), *Flight Command* (1940)

# Rod Taylor (Robert Taylor)

**Born:** January 11, 1929; Sydney, Australia

**Years Active in the Industry:** by decade

| 10s | 20s | 30s | 40s | 50s | 60s | 70s | 80s | 90s |
|-----|-----|-----|-----|-----|-----|-----|-----|-----|

Just as British-born James Stewart found it necessary to change his name to Stewart Granger upon embarking on an acting career, so too was Australian Robert Taylor compelled to choose another cognomen upon entering show business. He tried Rodney Taylor at first, then shortened it to the more "macho" Rod Taylor. A trained painter, Taylor switched to acting in his early twenties, toting up Australian stage credits before making his first Aussie film, *The Stuart Exposition*, in 1951. A villainous stint as Israel Hand in the 1954 Australian/U.S. production *Long John Silver* gave evidence that Taylor might be able to handle leading roles. However, he was still among the supporting ranks in his first American film, *The Virgin Queen* (1955). Signed to a nonexclusive contract by MGM in 1957, Taylor was cast in predominantly American roles, and accordingly managed to submerge his Australian accent in favor of a neutral "mid-Atlantic" cadence; even when playing an Englishman in 1960's *The Time Machine*, he spoke with barely a trace of a discernable accent. His film career peaked in the early to mid 1960s; during the same period he starred in the TV series *Hong Kong* (1961), the first of several weekly television stints (other series included *Bearcats*, *The Oregon Trail*, *Masquerade* and *Outlaws*). He was so long associated with Hollywood that, upon returning to Australia to appear in the 1977 film *The Picture Show Man*, Taylor was cast as an American. Gaining a bit of avoirdupois in recent years, Rod Taylor has retained his rugged, robust features and has thrived in character roles as ageing, but still virile, outdoorsmen. **Selected Works:** *The Birds* (1963), *Separate Tables* (1958)

# Shirley Temple

**Born:** April 23, 1928; Santa Monica, CA

**Years Active in the Industry:** by decade

| 10s | 20s | 30s | 40s | 50s | 60s | 70s | 80s | 90s |
|-----|-----|-----|-----|-----|-----|-----|-----|-----|

At age three Temple began taking dancing lessons. In 1932 she was selected to appear in a series of one-reel films, "Baby Burlesks," in which she would imitate leading ladies in parodies of popular films; she also began playing bit roles in features. In 1934 she attracted attention in a song-and-dance number she performed in the film *Stand Up and Cheer;* this led to a screen contract for child lead-roles, and, within months, she was enormously popular. At the end of her first year as a star, she received a special Academy Award "in grateful recognition of her outstanding contribution to screen entertainment during the year 1934." By 1938 she was the top box-office attraction, and a whole industry had developed around her: Shirley Temple dolls, coloring books, clothes, etc.

However, as she approached adolescence her popularity quickly waned. She continued appearing in films through the '40s, then retired from the screen at age 21. In 1958 she attempted a comeback as hostess of the TV show "The Shirley Temple Storybook," but it was soon cancelled; she fared no better with the 1960 series "The Shirley Temple Show." In the late '60s she entered politics, running unsuccessfully for the Republican congressional seat of San Mateo, California. In 1968 she was appointed as a U.S. representative to the United Nations. From 1974-76 she was U.S. ambassador to Ghana, then became U.S. Chief of protocol. In 1989 she became ambassador to Czechoslovakia. She was married from 1945-49 to actor John Agar; in 1960 she married TV executive Charles Black and was henceforth known as Shirley Temple Black. She authored an autobiography, *Child Star* (1988). **Selected Works:** *Since You Went Away* (1944)

# Irving Thalberg

**Born:** May 30, 1899; Brooklyn, NY
**Died:** September 14, 1936; Los Angeles, CA

### Years Active in the Industry: by decade

| 10ˢ | 20ˢ | 30ˢ | 40ˢ | 50ˢ | 60ˢ | 70ˢ | 80ˢ | 90ˢ |
|-----|-----|-----|-----|-----|-----|-----|-----|-----|
|     |     |     |     |     |     |     |     |     |

A sickly child, Irving Thalberg was brought through his many illnesses by his strong-willed mother. Forced to leave high school because of rheumatic fever, Thalberg read voraciously during his convalescence, mentally warehousing story ideas and standards of quality that would serve him well in his filmmaking years. After several dead-end secretarial jobs, Thalberg met Carl Laemmle, the head of Universal Pictures, who was impressed by the young man's concentration skills and capacity for hard work. As Laemmle's secretary, Thalberg expressed several solid theories as to how to improve efficiency on the rambling Universal lot in California. When Laemmle went on an extended vacation, he put the 21-year-old Thalberg in charge of the studio, where the frail young man proved a born leader and decision-maker. Eventually outgrowing Universal, and seeking a larger salary and wider-ranging responsibilities, Thalberg accepted a vice-president post at the newly formed MGM in 1924. While Louis B. Mayer handled the financial end of MGM, Thalberg took over the creative end, turning out a steady stream of movie hits. One of his most famous policies, which on the surface seemed the height of budgetary folly, was to allow MGM's producers and directors to shoot limitless retakes of scenes that hadn't played right in the projection room or before preview audiences. While industry wags referred to MGM as "Retake Valley," this perfection-at-all-costs policy resulted in excellent box-office returns. Tagged "the Boy Wonder," Thalberg commanded great respect throughout Hollywood, not only because of his near-infallible gift for moviemaking but also because he was a polite, respectful boss, willing to listen to anyone's input so long as it was for the general good of the studio. Additionally, and despite his assuredness at his job, there was a pronounced streak of modesty in Thalberg; he refused to allow his name to appear in the credits of his films, arguing that "Credit you give yourself isn't worth having." However, not everyone was enchanted by the Boy Wonder—disciples of Erich Von Stroheim, who was fired twice by Thalberg, singled the young producer out for some particularly vicious invective; Broadway writers like George S. Kaufman despaired at being kept waiting in the busy Thalberg's outer office for hours and days on end; and actor Edward G. Robinson deeply resented Thalberg's intention to "mold" Robinson's career, rather than allowing the actor his creative freedom. But the yea-sayers outweighed the nay-sayers, and Thalberg continued riding high until a heart attack in 1932 forced him to take several months off. During that period, Louis Mayer, who'd always been jealous of Thalberg's accomplishments, maneuvered things so that Thalberg's powers would be severely reduced upon his return. By 1936, Thalberg was on the verge of bolting MGM and setting up his own independent production company, in the manner of David O. Selznick. Such a move never took place; Thalberg died of pneumonia at the age of 37. He left behind a widow, actress Norma Shearer, and a legend that persists to this day. In 1937, the Academy of Motion Picture Arts and Sciences created the Irving G. Thalberg Memorial Award, to honor high-quality production achievements; and that same year, Irving Thalberg's name appeared on screen for the first time, at the beginning of MGM's *The Good Earth*.

# Henry Thomas

**Born:** September 9, 1971; San Antonio, TX

### Years Active in the Industry: by decade

| 10ˢ | 20ˢ | 30ˢ | 40ˢ | 50ˢ | 60ˢ | 70ˢ | 80ˢ | 90ˢ |
|-----|-----|-----|-----|-----|-----|-----|-----|-----|
|     |     |     |     |     |     |     | ██  |     |

The only son of a San Antonio hydraulic machinist, actor Henry Thomas was escorted by his mother to an open audition for the location-filmed *Raggedy Man* (1981). Though he had no performing experience whatsoever, 9-year-old Thomas was selected to play Sissy Spacek's son. He next appeared in the TV movie *The Steeler and the Pittsburgh Kid* (1981), based on a popular Coca Cola commercial of the era. Thomas went from professional child actor to merchandising icon with his next role—Elliot, the boy with a "secret friend," in the super-blockbuster *ET* (1982). Thomas wasn't able to sustain his new-found stardom thanks to a series of substandard films, but there were occasional high points during his awkward teens, notably the role of an 18th-century paramour in *Valmont* (1989). In 1993, the now-fully-grown Thomas came full circle with another "alien encounter" film, *Fire in the Sky.* Thomas' return to stardom seemed to be a "given" during the 1994-95 season with the choice role of young frontiersman Samuel Ludlow in *Legends of the Fall* (1994) and a starring part as an accused child molester in the made-for-TV *Indictment: The McMartin Trial* (1995). In his spare time, Thomas performed with a Celtic folk-rock band called the Rain Dogs. **Selected Works:** *Taste for Killing* (1992)

# Emma Thompson

**Born:** 1959; London, England

**Years Active in the Industry:** by decade

| 10s | 20s | 30s | 40s | 50s | 60s | 70s | 80s | 90s |
|-----|-----|-----|-----|-----|-----|-----|-----|-----|
|     |     |     |     |     |     |     |     |     |

British actress Emma Thompson is the daughter of actors Eric Thompson (creator of of the hit British TV series "The Magic Roundabout") and Phyllida Law. While studying English Literature at Cambridge University, Thompson became one of the few women allowed to perform in Cambridge's Footlights Theatrical Troupe; eventually she staged the Footlights' first all-female revue. Though well versed in the Classics, Thompson aspired to become a stand-up comic. She appeared in the British TV revue series "Al Fresco" with prominent comedians Robbie Coltrane, Hugh Laurie, and Stephen Fry, and also starred in the sitcoms "Up For Grabs" and "Tutti Frutti." In 1988 she was given the opportunity to create and star in her own TV series, "Thompson," which curiously turned out to be a humorless disaster (which Thompson will readily admit). On the dramatic scene, Thompson did plenty of Shakespeare on stage and appeared in the mid 1980s "Masterpiece Theatre" miniseries "Fortunes of War" with her husband, actor/director Kenneth Branagh. A film actress of astonishing range, Thompson has costarred with Branagh in *Henry V* (1989); *Dead Again* (1991), in two roles—one convincingly American; *Peter's Friends* (1992), which featured her mother Phyllida Law; and *Much Ado About Nothing* (1993). She has also been co-pacetically teamed with Anthony Hopkins in *Howard's End* (1992) and *Remains of the Day* (1993). **Selected Works:** *Impromptu* (1990), *In the Name of the Father* (1993), *Carrington* (1995), *Sense and Sensibility* (1995)

# Lea Thompson

**Born:** May 31, 1961; Rochester, MN

**Years Active in the Industry:** by decade

| 10s | 20s | 30s | 40s | 50s | 60s | 70s | 80s | 90s |
|-----|-----|-----|-----|-----|-----|-----|-----|-----|
|     |     |     |     |     |     |     |     |     |

A small, delicate-looking, perky actress, Thompson studied dance as a child, and was dancing professionally by age 14; she won scholarships to the Pennsylvania Ballet, American Ballet, and the San Francisco Ballet. However, she felt she was too short to become a prima ballerina and gave up dance in favor of acting. After moving to New York she appeared in some 20 Burger King TV commercials, then debuted onscreen in *Jaws 3-D* (1983). Shortly thereafter she got her first important role, opposite Tom Cruise in the hit *All the Right Moves* (1983). She is best known for her multiple roles in the three *Back to the Future* movies; aside from those highly successful movies, she has not gone on to appear in any hit productions. She also appeared in the TV movies *Nightbreaker* (1989), *Montana* (1990), and the PBS playhouse co-production *The Wizard of Loneliness* (1988). **Selected Works:** *Article 99* (1990), *Dennis the Menace* (1993), *Beverly Hillbillies* (1993)

# The Three Stooges

**Years Active in the Industry:** by decade

| 10s | 20s | 30s | 40s | 50s | 60s | 70s | 80s | 90s |
|-----|-----|-----|-----|-----|-----|-----|-----|-----|
|     |     |     |     |     |     |     |     |     |

The dictionary definition of "stooge" is "foil for a comedian or the butt of his jokes." When the American comedy team known as The Three Stooges came together in 1925, they were doing stooging for stage and vaudeville comedian Ted Healy. The team consisted of Healy's lifelong friend Moe Howard, who'd unsuccessfully pursued a dramatic acting career in his youth; Moe's brother Shemp, who'd previously teamed with his sibling in a fifth-rate blackface act; and Larry Fine, fresh from a vaudeville turn in which he played the violin while doing a Russian dance. Healy preferred his stooges short, stupid-looking and adorned with bizarre hairstyles—Moe, Shemp and Larry fit the first two qualifications naturally, meeting the third requirement by having Moe wear a bowl haircut, Shemp an unkempt mop of hair split down the middle, and Larry a frizzy Einstein-like hairdo. Ted Healy and his Stooges hit Broadway in the late 1920s in Earl Carroll's *Vanities,* and when Healy made his first film, *Soup to Nuts* (1930), the Stooges appeared (with a fourth member, Fred Sanborn), as "the Racketeers." Shemp disliked Healy and dropped out of the act to become a solo. He was replaced by younger brother Jerry, who'd been doing a comedy "orchestra" act. Casting about for a distinctive haircut for Jerry, Healy decided to shave his new stooge's hair to the bone; thereafter, Jerry was known as Curly. Continuing to work with Healy in films and on stage until 1934, Moe Howard decided to strike out with Larry and Curly in a separate act. As "Howard, Fine and Howard," the threesome signed with Columbia Pictures' short subject unit in 1934 as "The Three Stooges." They'd stay with Columbia to make 190 slapstick comedies until 1957. Moe took over Ted Healy's role as the abusive "boss" off the group, hitting and poking his partners at the slightest provocation;

Curly was the patsy of the trio, famed for his squeals, grunts, "Nyuk nyuks," "Woo woos," and sociopathic behavior; Larry was the nebbish middleman, whose only line seemed to be "I'm sorry, Mo, it was an accident." The Three Stooges' contract at Columbia called for eight two-reelers a year, to be filmed within 40 weeks; the rest of the time, the Stooges were permitted to make all the personal appearances they wanted. As it turned out, the Stooges made more money on tour than they did with Columbia's tight-wad $60,000 per year contract. In 1946, when Curly suffered a severe stroke that rendered him a virtual invalid, Curly was replaced by the man he'd replaced back in 1933, older brother Shemp. Though purists prefer the Stooge shorts with Curly, Shemp was in fact a more talented comedian, given to zany adlibs and nonsequiturs. Shemp worked with the team during the 1950s, a time in which Columbia cut back budgets and began relying heavily on stock footage from earlier two-reelers. Shemp died suddenly in 1955, compelling the studio to film that year's remaining manifest of Stooges shorts with Moe and Larry alone; Shemp appeared only in stock footage, replaced in the newly-shot scenes by actor Joe Palma, who kept his back to the camera. Columbia replaced Shemp in 1956 with Joe Besser, who was at the time starring in his own two-reelers for the studio. Besser's "fat sissy" characterization didn't mesh well with the rougher antics of Larry and Moe, but he gave a welcome energy boost to the team's otherwise mediocre final 16 two-reelers. The Stooges were let go by Columbia in late 1957, though enough film had been shot to continue releasing shorts until 1959. Besser left the team because of his wife's illness, to be replaced by burlesque comic Joe DeRita. A derivative performer whose style resembled that of Lou Costello, DeRita was made over into a reincarnation of Curly Howard; he shaved his head and changed his name to "Curly Joe." The act wasn't doing so well by 1958, and there was talk of breaking up the team when Columbia's Screen Gems TV subsidiary released the old Stooge shorts to television. Eagerly devoured by millions of kiddie viewers, the Three Stooges became the hottest TV commodity of 1959, thrusting the team back into the limelight. Full-fledged (and high-priced) stars again, the Stooges supplemented their personal appearances with a new string of low-budget feature films. As always, the Stooge humor was a matter of taste, but even nonfans enjoyed such nonsensical outings as *The Three Stooges Meet Hercules* (1963) and *The Outlaws is Coming* (1965). In 1965, the team provided voices and live-action vignettes for a series of 156 Three Stooges cartoons, but by this time the initial euphoria had worn off; within a few years the Stooges were unemployable again. Some of the kids who'd enjoyed the Stooge comedies in the 1950s grew up to become film historians and cultists, and the early 1970s found the Three Stooges being exalted as comic geniuses (an assessment disputed by many, including the Stooges). However, this time there would be no reteaming—Larry Fine suffered a debilitating stroke in 1970; Moe retired, but made the rounds on lecture tours and talk show appearances (though he made it clear he'd take any and all film work); and Curly Joe tried unsuccessfully to form a "new Three Stooges" act on his own. Both Moe and Larry died in 1975, putting an end to a 50-year era. But Three Stooges fans can take heart because Jeffrey Scott, Moe Howard's grandson, is for-

mulating plans for a big-budget Stooge feature film, with three young hip new guys as Curly, Larry, and Moe.

# Uma Thurman

**Born:** 1970; Boston, MA

**Years Active in the Industry:** by decade

| 10s | 20s | 30s | 40s | 50s | 60s | 70s | 80s | 90s |
|---|---|---|---|---|---|---|---|---|
|  |  |  |  |  |  |  | ■ |  |

The daughter of a professor, Thurman spent her youth on the campus of Amherst College. From age 12-14 she lived with her family in India. Back in the States, she attended boarding school; deciding to become an actress, she then went to the Professional Children's School in Manhattan. She started modeling at age 16, and shortly thereafter made her screen debut in the independent 16-mm thriller *Kiss Daddy Good Night* (1987). Her first big-budget film was *Johnny Be Good* (1988) opposite Anthony Michael Hall, but her breakthrough role was in her next film, *Dangerous Liaisons* (1988), in which she played a virgin corrupted by John Malkovich's character. She was married to actor Gary Oldman. **Selected Works:** *Final Analysis* (1992), *Henry and June* (1990), *Jennifer 8* (1992), *Mad Dog and Glory* (1993), *Pulp Fiction* (1994)

# Gene Tierney

**Born:** November 20, 1920; Brooklyn, NY
**Died:** November 6, 1991; Houston, TX

**Years Active in the Industry:** by decade

| 10s | 20s | 30s | 40s | 50s | 60s | 70s | 80s | 90s |
|---|---|---|---|---|---|---|---|---|
|  |  |  | ■ |  |  |  |  |  |

Born into great wealth, Tierney expressed an interest in acting as a child; her father promptly established Belle-Tier, a corporation to promote her. In 1939 she debuted on Broadway, going on to play supporting roles in several plays. Movie mogul Darryl F. Zanuck spotted her and signed her to a screen contract. She began appearing in films in 1940, remaining busy onscreen through the mid '50s. She generally played leads in routine films, though there were enough high-quality productions in her career to establish

her as an important actress. For her work in *Leave Her to Heaven* (1945) she received a Best Actress Oscar nomination. From 1941-52 she was married to designer Oleg Cassini; their first daughter was born mentally retarded due to the German measles Tierney had contracted during her pregnancy. In the '50s Tierney became romantically involved with Aly Khan, but their marriage plans were opposed by the Aga Khan. When the relationship ended, Tierney suffered a nervous breakdown, and, during the next several years, she twice spent lengthy periods in mental institutions. In 1960 she married an oilman and returned to acting in occasional roles. She authored an autobiography, *Self Portrait* (1979), in which she revealed that her nervous breakdown was only one stage of protracted mental illness, which included delusions. **Selected Works:** *The Ghost and Mrs. Muir* (1947), *Heaven Can Wait* (1943), *Laura* (1944), *The Razor's Edge* (1946)

## Jennifer Tilly

**Born:** 1962; British Columbia, Canada

**Years Active in the Industry:** by decade

| 10s | 20s | 30s | 40s | 50s | 60s | 70s | 80s | 90s |
|-----|-----|-----|-----|-----|-----|-----|-----|-----|
|     |     |     |     |     |     |     |  ■  |  ■  |

Beginning her own career in the early 1980s, Jennifer Tilly appeared as a regular on the now-you-see-it-now-you-don't 1984 sitcom *Shaping Up*. Many of her earlier films were on a par with the 1985 *Police Academy* clone *Moving Violations*. Recently, Jennifer Tilly was seen as a willing and libidinous hostage in 1994's *The Getaway*, the role played by Sally Struthers in the original 1969 version of the same property. She was nominated for a Best Supporting Actress Oscar for *Bullets Over Broadway* (1994). She is the younger sister of actress Meg Tilly. **Selected Works:** *The Fabulous Baker Boys*

(1989), *Made in America* (1993), *Shadow of the Wolf* (1992), *Heads* (1994)

## Meg Tilly

**Born:** February 14, 1960; California

**Years Active in the Industry:** by decade

| 10s | 20s | 30s | 40s | 50s | 60s | 70s | 80s | 90s |
|-----|-----|-----|-----|-----|-----|-----|-----|-----|
|     |     |     |     |     |     |     |  ■  |  ■  |

Ethereal-looking lead actress with pale skin and almond-shaped eyes, Tilly began training for the ballet at age 14, but a dance-related back injury made her change her focus to acting. Raised in Canada, she moved to New York at age 16; there she landed small roles, including parts in an episode of the TV series "Hill Street Blues" and in the movie *Fame* (1980), her screen debut. She moved to Los Angeles in 1982, and within six months had landed the female lead in the film *Tex* (1982) opposite Matt Dillon. Although never a major star, she established her reputation as an actress with her portrayal of a disturbed young nun in *Agnes of God* (1985), for which she received a Best Supporting Actress Oscar nomination. **Selected Works:** *Leaving Normal* (1992), *Two Jakes* (1990), *The Big Chill* (1983), *Body Snatchers* (1994), *Sleep with Me* (1994)

## Dimitri Tiomkin

**Born:** May 10, 1899; St. Petersburg, Russia
**Died:** November 11, 1979; London, England

**Years Active in the Industry:** by decade

| 10s | 20s | 30s | 40s | 50s | 60s | 70s | 80s | 90s |
|-----|-----|-----|-----|-----|-----|-----|-----|-----|
|     |     |  ■  |  ■  |  ■  |  ■  |     |     |     |

It was once considered cute by Hollywood wits to poke fun at Russian-born composer Dimitri Tiomkin's borscht-flavored accent. How amusing it was to hear him yell out "Switt lyand of lyaberty!" while orchestrating "The Star Spangled Banner" for Frank Capra's *Mr. Smith Goes To Washington* (1939). A graduate of the St. Petersburg Academy (where he studied under the famed composer Glazunov) and a holder of both a law and music degree, Tiomkin exhibited a fondness for native American music early in his career; while a touring concert pianist, it was Tiomkin who was most instrumental in introducing the works of Gershwin to Europe. Tiomkin left Russia for the U.S. in 1925, becoming an American citizen twelve years later and making his conducting debut with the LA Philharmonic in 1938. Most of his first compositions for American consumption were live ballets (his wife was choreographer Albertina Raasch); he didn't start working in films until 1933. With *Lost Horizon* (1937), Tiomkin began a long association with director Frank Capra, which unfortunately ended in bitterness due to artistic clashes on the set of *It's a Wonderful Life* (1946). Though juke-box acceptance was probably never a priority with Tiomkin, he was responsible for several top-ten hit songs, all of which originated in his film scores: "Do Not Forsake Me" from *High Noon* (1952), the whistled main theme from *The High and the Mighty* (1954), the credit music from *Friendly Persuasion* (1956), and "Green Leaves of Summer" from *The Alamo* (1960), among others. The winner of five Academy Awards (among many other international honors), Tiomkin remained active in films until 1970, the year that he produced, directed and orchestrated the U.S./Soviet coproduction *Tschiakovsky*. **Selected Works:** *55 Days at Peking* (1962), *Champion* (1949), *Guns of Navarone* (1961), *Old Man and the Sea* (1958)

# Gregg Toland

**Born:** May 29, 1904; Charleston, IL
**Died:** September 28, 1948; Hollywood, CA

**Years Active in the Industry:** by decade

| 10s | 20s | 30s | 40s | 50s | 60s | 70s | 80s | 90s |
|-----|-----|-----|-----|-----|-----|-----|-----|-----|

American cinematographer Gregg Toland started in the film business as a studio office boy, eventually becoming assistant cameraman to George Barnes at the Sam Goldwyn studio. Before he was thirty, Toland had graduated to Goldwyn's principal cinematographer, building up a small but loyal staff that he'd later take with him from studio to studio. Around 1934, the "Toland touch" began to assert itself, a style distinguished by innovative lighting techniques and crystal-clear deep focus. Goldwyn made a great deal of money loaning the valuable Toland out to other studios; for Goldwyn himself, Toland contributed one excellent film after another, reaching a high point with 1939's *Wuthering Heights,* for which the cinematographer won an Oscar. Toland also worked extensively with director John Ford, notably in *Grapes of Wrath* (1940). A wartime propaganda short directed by Ford and shot by Toland, *December 7th* (1942), is still being cannibalized for TV documentaries into the '90s. Toland's most celebrated achievement was Orson Welles' *Citizen Kane* (1941). Reversing the usual hiring procedure, Toland offered his services to Welles, hoping that this ambitious young filmmaker would allow him to experiment to his heart's content. Welles responded by giving Toland a completely free hand, and the results were breathtaking. Many of the innovations in *Kane* that have been attributed to Welles were actually Toland's, notably the famous "passing through glass" shot at Susan Alexander's tawdry nightclub (one can find a similar effect in Goldwyn's *Dead End*, a film shot by Toland in 1937). After the war, Toland devoted himself to Goldwyn's lavish but more conventionally lensed productions, notably *The Best Years of Our Lives* (1946). Gregg Toland died of heart disease at the age of 44, shortly after he and his crew had celebrated their 15th year together. Toland's last film, *Enchantment* (1948), was released posthumously. **Selected Works:** *Intermezzo: A Love Story* (1939), *Miserables* (1935), *Long Voyage Home* (1940)

# Sidney Toler

**Born:** April 28, 1874; Warrensburg, MO
**Died:** February 12, 1947

**Years Active in the Industry:** by decade

| 10s | 20s | 30s | 40s | 50s | 60s | 70s | 80s | 90s |
|-----|-----|-----|-----|-----|-----|-----|-----|-----|

After graduating from the University of Kansas, Missouri-born Sidney Toler took to the stage. Among his theatrical credits were such plays as *Canary Dutch* and *Lulu Belle,* as well as a drama he wrote himself, *Belle of Richmond*. At age 55, Toler headed to Hollywood to give those newfangled talking pictures a try, making his cinematic bow in *Madame X* (1929). For the next decade, Toler showed up in numerous meaty supporting roles, generally playing such abrasive characters as detectives, sea captains, and stage managers. One of his showier roles was as Daniel Webster in 1936's *The Gorgeous Hussy*. In 1938, Toler was selected to replace the late Warner Oland in 20th Century-Fox's *Charlie Chan* series. Like his predecessor Oland, Toler preferred to use a minimum of makeup in his Oriental characterization, merely narrowing his eyes and adopting a Pidgin-English vocal cadence. Except for the occasional sidetrip in such films as *White Savage* (1943) and *It's in the Bag* (1945), Toler specialized in Charlie Chan for the rest of his life, moving his base of operations from 20th Century-Fox to Monogram in 1942; in all, he made 22 appearances as the Honolulu-based sleuth, more than any other cinematic Chan. Upon his death in 1947, Toler was replaced in the *Charlie Chan* series by Roland Winters. **Selected Works:** *If I Were King* (1938)

# Marisa Tomei

**Born:** December 4, 1964; Brooklyn, NY

**Years Active in the Industry:** by decade

| 10s | 20s | 30s | 40s | 50s | 60s | 70s | 80s | 90s |
|-----|-----|-----|-----|-----|-----|-----|-----|-----|

Actress Marisa Tomei was one year into her college education at Boston University when she was tapped for a costarring role on the CBS daytime drama "As the World Turns." She made her film debut in 1984 in *The Flamingo Kid,* and three years later was featured as Maggie Lawton, Lisa Bonet's college roommate, on TV's "A Different World" (she didn't finish *that* term, either). In 1992, Tomei costarred as Joe Pesci's potty-mouthed girl friend in *My Cousin Vinny,* a performance that won her a Best Supporting Actress Oscar.

Later that year, she turned up briefly as a snippy Mabel Normand in director Richard Attenborough's mammoth biopic *Chaplin*. In 1993, Marisa Tomei was seen in her first starring film, *Untamed Heart*. **Selected Works:** *Only You* (1994), *The Perez Family* (1994)

# Lily Tomlin (Mary Jean Tomlin)

**Born:** September 1, 1939; Detroit, MI

**Years Active in the Industry:** by decade

| 10s | 20s | 30s | 40s | 50s | 60s | 70s | 80s | 90s |
|-----|-----|-----|-----|-----|-----|-----|-----|-----|
|     |     |     |     |     |     | ■   | ■   | ■   |

Tomlin dropped out of college to perform in local cabaret and study mime with Paul Curtis, then moved to New York in 1966; while appearing on the coffee-house circuit she gained exposure on the short-lived TV program "The Garry Moore Show" in 1967. She got her big break when she was signed for the cast of "Rowan & Martin's Laugh-In" in 1969; the show became a hit and she became famous, introducing American audiences to her characters Ernestine the telephone operator and Edith Ann the precocious five-year-old. Tomlin went on to make TV specials, comedy albums, and live appearances. She debuted onscreen in Robert Altman's celebrated *Nashville* (1975), for which she won a New York Critics Circle Award and received a Best Supporting Actress Oscar nomination. Her subsequent film career was highly uneven, and she never established herself as a major screen actress. However, her one-woman stage show *The Search for Signs of Intelligent Life in the Universe* was a great success both critically and commercially. She produced one of her films, *The Incredible Shrinking Woman* (1981). **Selected Works:** *And the Band Played On* (1993), *Late Show* (1977)

# Franchot Tone (Stanislas Pascal Franchot Tone)

**Born:** February 27, 1905; Niagara Falls, NY
**Died:** September 18, 1968

**Years Active in the Industry:** by decade

| 10s | 20s | 30s | 40s | 50s | 60s | 70s | 80s | 90s |
|-----|-----|-----|-----|-----|-----|-----|-----|-----|
|     |     | ■   | ■   | ■   | ■   |     |     |     |

He began acting while a college student, then became president of his school's Dramatic Club. In 1927 Tone began his professional stage career in stock, then soon made it to Broadway. He began appearing in films in 1932, going on to a busy screen career in which he was typecast as a debonair, tuxedo-wearing playboy or successful man-about-town. For his work in *Mutiny on the Bounty* (1935) he received a Best Actor Oscar nomination. In the early '50s he gave up films to return to the stage; after appearing in an off-Broadway production of *Uncle Vanya* he returned to film in the play's screen version (1958), which he co-produced, co-directed, and starred in. He appeared in a handful of films in the '60s; mean-

while, onstage he got good reviews for his performance in the New York revival of *Strange Interlude*. In the mid '60s he costarred in the TV series "Ben Casey." He was married four times; his wives included actresses Joan Crawford, Jean Wallace, Barbara Payton, and Dolores Dorn-Heft. In the early '50s he and actor Tom Neal got into a dispute over the affections of Payton, and Neal beat Tone badly enough to put him in the hospital. **Selected Works:** *Lives of a Bengal Lancer* (1935), *Three Comrades* (1938), *The King Steps Out* (1936)

# Rip Torn (Elmore Rual Torn, Jr.)

**Born:** February 6, 1931; Temple, TX

**Years Active in the Industry:** by decade

| 10s | 20s | 30s | 40s | 50s | 60s | 70s | 80s | 90s |
|-----|-----|-----|-----|-----|-----|-----|-----|-----|
|     |     |     |     | ■   | ■   | ■   | ■   | ■   |

Torn decided to act profesionally to earn enough money to become a rancher; he hitched to Hollywood and took menial jobs before landing some small roles on TV and in films (he debuted onscreen in 1956). Torn moved to New York, where he studied under Lee Strasberg at the Actors Studio and took dancing lessons with Martha Graham. He began landing meatier screen roles in the early '60s, making a strong impression as Finley Jr. in *Sweet Bird of Youth* (1962). For his work in *Cross Creek* (1983) he received a Best Supporting Actor Oscar nomination. He is known as an explosive, unpredictable man, and has often been cast as surly, violent, unbalanced characters; he has also shown talent in comedy, though, leading to his costarring role in the '90s TV series "The Larry Sanders Show." He directed *The Telephone* (1988). He married and divorced actress Geraldine Page, with whom he appeared in *Sweet Bird of Youth* and *Nasty Habits* (1976). **Selected Works:** *Beautiful Dreamers* (1992), *Dead Ahead: The Exxon Valdez Disaster* (1992), *Defending Your Life* (1991), *T Bone N Weasel* (1992), *Where the Rivers Flow North* (1994)

# Jacques Tourneur

**Born:** November 12, 1904; Paris, France
**Died:** December 19, 1977; Bergerac, France

**Years Active in the Industry:** by decade

| 10s | 20s | 30s | 40s | 50s | 60s | 70s | 80s | 90s |
|-----|-----|-----|-----|-----|-----|-----|-----|-----|
|     |     |     | ■   | ■   | ■   |     |     |     |

A resident of the United States from the age of ten, Jacques Tourneur became one of America's leading directors of horror and film noir, after a long apprenticeship. The son of the celebrated director Maurice Tourneur, he went to work at MGM as an office boy and subsequently became a script clerk on his father's movies, and returned to France as his father's editor in 1928. Tourneur made his debut as a director in France in 1931, but found, upon returning to Hollywood four years later, that there was no work for him in this capacity. He worked for David O. Selznick as a second-unit director on *A Tale of Two Cities*, in partnership with writer Val Lewton, and eventually moved back into the director's chair in short subjects and very low budget B pictures. In 1942, Lewton put together a low-budget horror production unit at RKO and arranged for Tourneur to direct the first two entries, *Cat People* and *I Walked With a Zombie*, a pair of deeply atmospheric, spine-tingling, yet subtle horror movies (the second one was based on Jane Eyre), both of which became major hits for the studio and established Tourneur's credentials. He was taken away from Lewton and given bigger-budget non-horror projects, and acquitted himself well in those, most notably the classic film noir *Out of the Past* (1947). But Tourneur also had a flair for swashbucklers, as he showed in *The Flame And the Arrow* (1950). He also directed one sword-and-sandal adventure film, *The Giant of Marathon*. Along with the first two Lewton movies, his most famous film is probably *Curse of the Demon* (1957), a chilling horror film whose reputation has grown during the four decades since its release.

# Robert Towne

**Born:** November 23, 1934; Los Angeles, CA

**Years Active in the Industry:** by decade

| 10s | 20s | 30s | 40s | 50s | 60s | 70s | 80s | 90s |
|-----|-----|-----|-----|-----|-----|-----|-----|-----|
|     |     |     |     |     |     |     |     |     |

Robert Towne would prefer his appearance as the stick-like leading actor Edward Wain in the prententious Roger Corman post-apocalyptic effort *The Last Woman on Earth* (1960) be forgotten—in addition to the film's screenplay, which was Towne's first. Despite this inauspicious beginning (and his followup starring appearance in *Creature From the Haunted Sea* [1961]), Towne appreciated the early opportunity afforded him by Corman, and remained with the producer/director to pen the screenplay for *Tomb of Ligeia* (1965) (two more scripts for Corman, *A Time for Killing* and *Captain Nemo and the Underwater City*, were heavily revised by others). From there, Towne could only go up, and this he did as script consultant for Warren Beatty's *Bonnie and Clyde* (1967) and as full screenwriter for *Villa Rides* (1967). After one more acting turn in *Drive, He Said* (1971), Towne made a good living as a screenwriter and troubleshooting script doctor. Towne's output ranged from the salty profanities of *The Last Detail* (1967) to the insightful glances at Nixon-era mores in *Shampoo* (1968) to the misty mysticism of *The Natural* (1984)—and more recently, to the dewy-eyed romanticism of Warren Beatty's 1994 remake of *Love Affair*. In 1974, Towne won a "best screenplay" Academy Award for director Roman Polanski's *Chinatown*. This film contained one of the few totally unhappy endings in the Towne canon—for the most part, he prefers upbeat denouements, to the extent of overhauling the endings for the screen versions of Bernard Malamud's *The Natural* and John Grisham's *The Firm*. In 1981, Robert Towne made his directorial debut with *Personal Best*; more successful was the second

Towne-directed effort, 1988's *Tequila Sunrise*. **Selected Works:** *Days of Thunder* (1990), *The Two Jakes* (1990)

# Robert Townsend

**Born:** February 6, 1957; Chicago, IL

**Years Active in the Industry:** by decade

| 10s | 20s | 30s | 40s | 50s | 60s | 70s | 80s | 90s |
|-----|-----|-----|-----|-----|-----|-----|-----|-----|
|     |     |     |     |     |     |     | ■   | ■   |

Townsend debuted onscreen at age 17 in *Cooley High* (1974), but then stopped acting. In his early 20s he performed stand-up and improvisational comedy with Chicago's Second City troupe, then joined the Experimental Black Actors Guild. He appeared in a half-dozen films in the first half of the '80s, then made his name as the producer, director, co-writer, and star of *Hollywood Shuffle* (1987), a humorous look at the problems encountered by black actors; the film has become a legend for its unconventional financing—half the budget was supplied by credit cards and much of the film was donated. He also directed the Eddie Murphy concert film, *Raw* (1987), the highest-grossing concert film in screen history. He produced, directed, wrote, and starred in *The Five Heartbeats* (1991), and wrote, directed, and starred in *Meteor Man* (1993); both films performed poorly at the box office. He also starred in the short-lived TV sketch-comedy series "Townsend TV." **Selected Works:** *A Soldier's Story* (1984)

# Spencer Tracy

**Born:** April 5, 1900; Milwaukee, WI
**Died:** June 10, 1967

**Years Active in the Industry:** by decade

| 10s | 20s | 30s | 40s | 50s | 60s | 70s | 80s | 90s |
|-----|-----|-----|-----|-----|-----|-----|-----|-----|
|     | ■   | ■   | ■   | ■   | ■   |     |     |     |

Stocky, craggy-faced, unhandsome leading man and character player, Tracy had an unpretentious, humorous, straightforward screen persona. As a teenager he thought he was headed for the

priesthood, but he dropped out of school at age 17 to enlist in the Navy during World War I. In college after the war he was surprisingly successful in a 1921 student play, after which he decided to become an actor; in 1922 he enrolled at New York's American Academy of Dramatic Arts, meanwhile getting a bit role on Broadway (as one of the robots in Karel Capek's *R.U.R.*). Graduating in 1923, he was unable to find acting work and took a series of odd jobs. Finally, he found work in stock, gaining a reputation as a skilled leading man with an unfortunate tendency toward moodiness, rudeness, and a short temperament. In the late '20s he began appearing frequently on Broadway, finally landing a lead role in 1930 in *The Last Mile;* this led to his screen career when director John Ford saw him in the play and cast him as the lead in the gangster film *Up the River* (1930). Signed by Fox, for some time he was typecast as a "tough guy." His break came when he switched to MGM in 1935 and began getting better roles. Soon he was not only popular with the public but well-respected as a versatile, apparently effortless "underplayer" of roles. Laurence Olivier once said, "I've learned more about acting from watching Tracy than in any other way." Throughout his career he received nine Oscar nominations and won the Best Actor Oscar for *Captains Courageous* (1937) and *Boys Town* (1938), becoming the first and only actor to win the Best Actor Oscar in successive years. As he aged, Spencer moved into warm and dignified but cranky fatherly roles. He was married in his early 20s to screen actress Louise Treadwell; a devout Catholic, he never divorced her even though they spent years apart. He had a publicized affair with actress Loretta Young in the early '30s, then, in 1942, began a lifelong intimate relationship with actress Katherine Hepburn, with whom he appeared in nine films, including his last, *Guess Who's Coming to Dinner* (1967). **Selected Works:** *Adam's Rib* (1950), *Father of the Bride* (1950), *Inherit the Wind* (1960), *Judgement at Nuremburg* (1961), *Old Man and the Sea* (1958)

# Nancy Travis

**Born:** 1961; Astoria, NY

**Years Active in the Industry:** by decade

| 10s | 20s | 30s | 40s | 50s | 60s | 70s | 80s | 90s |
|-----|-----|-----|-----|-----|-----|-----|-----|-----|
|     |     |     |     |     |     |     | ■   | ■   |

She got a degree in drama, then joined the Circle In The Square repertory company. Her work in a touring production of Neil Simon's *Brighton Beach Memoirs* led to small roles in a few TV movies, including "High School Narc" and "Malice in Wonderland." She then landed the lead in the mini-series *Harem* (1986). She debuted onscreen as the female lead in the hit comedy *Three Men and a Baby* (1987). She went on to supporting roles in a number of films. She has remained active in the New York theater, appearing on Broadway in *I'm Not Rappaport;* she co-founded the Naked Angels, a successful off-Broadway troupe. **Selected Works:** *Air America* (1990), *Married to the Mob* (1988), *Passed Away* (1992), *So I Married an Axe Murderer* (1993), *Vanishing [USA]* (1993)

# John Travolta

**Born:** February 18, 1954; Englewood, NJ

**Years Active in the Industry:** by decade

| 10s | 20s | 30s | 40s | 50s | 60s | 70s | 80s | 90s |
|-----|-----|-----|-----|-----|-----|-----|-----|-----|
|     |     |     |     |     |     | ■   | ■   | ■   |

A good-looking, well-built Italian-Irish leading man, Travolta has a flashing grin and cleft chin. He dropped out of high school at age 16, then began his acting career in New Jersey summer stock. After some

time spent training as an actor and dancer, he started finding work in commercials and off-Broadway. He moved to Hollywood and got occasional small roles on TV, then joined the national touring company of the rock musical *Grease;* later, he acted in *Grease* on Broadway and also appeared in the Broadway musical *Over Here!* He became well-known after landing a role in the cast of the TV sitcom *Welcome Back, Kotter,* on which he played the dim-witted high school student Vinnie Barbarino; this led to his first important screen role, as a high school student in Brian De Palma's horror film *Carrie* (1976). He briefly enjoyed a period of superstardom after he starred and danced in the blockbuster disco film *Saturday Night Fever* (1977), for which he received a Best Actor Oscar nomination. He continued his success in the screen version of *Grease* (1978). Throughout the '80s, he gave a series of good screen performances, but the films he appeared in tended to be unsuccessful; this chain of bad luck was broken with his co-starring role in the huge hit comedy *Look Who's Talking* (1989). More recently, he enjoyed a very successful comeback in Tarantino's smash hit *Pulp Fiction* (1994). He is the brother of actors Joey and Ellen Travolta. He's married to actress Kelly Preston. **Selected Works:** *Broken Arrow* (1995), *Get Shorty* (1995), *White Man's Burden* (1995)

# Claire Trevor (Claire Wemlinger)

**Born:** March 8, 1909; New York, NY

**Years Active in the Industry:** by decade

| 10s | 20s | 30s | 40s | 50s | 60s | 70s | 80s | 90s |
|-----|-----|-----|-----|-----|-----|-----|-----|-----|
|     |     | ■   | ■   | ■   |     |     |     |     |

After attending Columbia and the American Academy of Dramatic Arts, she began her acting career in the late '20s in stock. By 1932 she was starring on Broadway; that same year she began appearing in Brooklyn-filmed Vitaphone shorts. She debuted onscreen in feature films in 1933 and soon became typecast as a gang moll, a saloon girl, or some other kind of hard-boiled, but warm-hearted floozy. Primarily in B movies, her performances in major productions showed her to be a skilled screen actress; nominated for Oscars three times, she won the Best Supporting Actress Oscar for her work in *Key Largo* (1948). In the '50s she began to appear often on TV; in 1956 she won an Emmy for her performance in *Dodsworth* opposite Fredric March. **Selected Works:** *Dead End* (1937), *Murder, My Sweet* (1944), *Stagecoach* (1939), *High and the Mighty* (1954)

# Jean-Louis Trintignant

**Born:** December 11, 1930; Fiolenc (or Nimes), France

**Years Active in the Industry:** by decade

| 10s | 20s | 30s | 40s | 50s | 60s | 70s | 80s | 90s |
|-----|-----|-----|-----|-----|-----|-----|-----|-----|
|     |     |     |     |     |     |     |     |     |

Internationally popular star of French films, noted for his economy of expression and ambiguous, mysterious screen presence, he moved to Paris to study acting at age 20; Trintignant debuted onstage a year later and went on to a busy stage career. In 1956 he appeared in two films, including the international sensation *And God Created Women* (1956), Brigitte Bardot's debut; an offscreen romance with Bardot increased his sudden fame. However, his new film career was immediately interrupted when he was drafted for military service in Algeria. He returned to films in 1959 and gradually worked his way up to stardom in mostly routine films. In 1966 he became popular with international audiences after he appeared in the highly successful *A Man and a Woman*. For his work in *Z* (1969) he won the Cannes Film Festival Best Actor award. Formerly married to actress Stephane Audron, he is now married to director Nadine Trintignant, who directed several of his films. He made his directorial debut with *Une Journee bien remplie* (1973). **Selected Works:** *Conformist* (1971), *Under Fire* (1983), *Three Colors: Red* (1994)

# Jeanne Tripplehorn

**Born:** 1963; Tulsa, OK

**Years Active in the Industry:** by decade

| 10s | 20s | 30s | 40s | 50s | 60s | 70s | 80s | 90s |
|-----|-----|-----|-----|-----|-----|-----|-----|-----|
|     |     |     |     |     |     |     |     |     |

Launching her performing career in her native Tulsa, Jeanne Tripplehorn spent several years as a local radio and TV host. She had been educated at both the University of Oklahoma and Julliard. In 1991, Tripplehorn was first seen on a nationwide basis in a supporting role in the made-for-TV movie *The Perfect Tribute*, a fictionalized retelling of the events leading up to Lincoln's Gettysburg Address. Most of Tripplehorn's film characterizations have ranged from mildly eccentric to deeply disturbed, thanks in great part to her breakthrough appearance as Michael

Douglas' "rough sex" partner in the erotic chiller *Basic Instinct* (1992). **Selected Works:** *The Firm* (1993), *Waterworld* (1995)

# Fernando Trueba

**Born:** Not Available

**Years Active in the Industry:** by decade

| 10s | 20s | 30s | 40s | 50s | 60s | 70s | 80s | 90s |
|-----|-----|-----|-----|-----|-----|-----|-----|-----|
|     |     |     |     |     |     |     |     |     |

A relatively obscure name on the international scene, Spanish director Fernando Trueba has long been well known in his native country for his preoccupation with eccentric projects, which have ever so delicately skirted good taste. One of Trueba's earliest film was 1980's *Opera Prima*, a comedy about a romance between cousins. 1990's *Twisted Obsession* (1990) did *Opera Prima* one better in probing a slightly unnatural brother-sister relationship. Fernando Trueba's biggest success thus far has been 1992's surprise hit *Belle Epoque* **Selected Works:** *Air America* (1990), *Belle Epoque* (1992)

# François Truffaut

**Born:** February 6, 1932; Paris, France
**Died:** October 21, 1984; Neuilly, France

**Years Active in the Industry:** by decade

| 10s | 20s | 30s | 40s | 50s | 60s | 70s | 80s | 90s |
|-----|-----|-----|-----|-----|-----|-----|-----|-----|
|     |     |     |     |     |     |     |     |     |

By age 15 Francois Truffaut was working in a factory. However, he was already a film fanatic, and in his teens he organized cinema clubs. He went on to join the staff of the prestigious film

magazine *Cahiers du Cinema* at the invitation of its publisher, critic Andre Bazin. Shortly thereafter he was drafted; he deserted, served a prison sentence, and was discharged. Back at *Cahiers* he became a very influential film critic, attacking conventional French cinema and helping to formulate the ideas of the French New Wave. He made a short 16-mm film in 1954, then made another short in 1957; the latter, *Les Mistons*, was acclaimed and opened the door to his first feature film, *The 400 Blows* (1959). He went on to become one of the most influential filmmakers in the world. He died at age 52 of a brain tumor. **Selected Works:** *Day for Night* (1973), *Jules and Jim* (1962), *The Last Metro* (1980), *Story of Adele H.* (1975), *Wild Child* (1970)

# Forrest Tucker

**Born:** February 12, 1919; Plainfield, IN
**Died:** October 25, 1986; Woodland Hills, CA

**Years Active in the Industry:** by decade

| 10ˢ | 20ˢ | 30ˢ | 40ˢ | 50ˢ | 60ˢ | 70ˢ | 80ˢ | 90ˢ |
|-----|-----|-----|-----|-----|-----|-----|-----|-----|

After leaving George Washington University, Forrest Tucker made his stage bow in Burlesque. He spent two years in the Army, then returned to performing. After appearing in his first film, 1940's *The Westerner*, Tucker signed with Columbia, then spent *another* two year hitch in uniform. Most of his postwar films cast Tucker as a bully or outlaw, but his roles took a heroic turn after a good supporting part in Republic's *Sands of Iwo Jima* (1949). After several years as Republic's answer to Gary Cooper, Tucker began appearing in TV and on stage (he starred in the Broadway production *Fair Game for Lovers*), developing a solid after-hours reputation as a champion golfer. Among Tucker's starring TV series were *F Troop* (1965-66), *Dusty's Trail* (1973) and *Ghost Busters* (1975). In his last years, Tucker fell victim to a serious liquor problem, which frequently resulted in bizarre, detached performances on stage and on the set. However, he never let his public down when starring on the straw-hat circuit in his favorite role—Professor Harold Hill in *The Music Man*. **Selected Works:** *Auntie Mame* (1958), *The Yearling* (1946)

# Janine Turner

**Born:** December 6, 1963; Lincoln, NE

**Years Active in the Industry:** by decade

| 10ˢ | 20ˢ | 30ˢ | 40ˢ | 50ˢ | 60ˢ | 70ˢ | 80ˢ | 90ˢ |
|-----|-----|-----|-----|-----|-----|-----|-----|-----|

Actress Janine Turner was trained at New York's Professional Children's School. (She can still do a mean tap-dance if called upon.) Though she endured the usual audition rounds while seeking out acting and modelling work, Turner's break came by way of fortuitous happenstance—at 17, she was spotted while standing in a supermarket checkout line by TV producer Leonard Katzman, who asked her to read for a small part on "Dallas." Two years later she was cast as kleptomaniac espionage agent Laura Templeton on TV's "General Hospital," a role that required her to dye her coffee-brown hair blonde. Turners's film debut was in *Young Doctors in Love* (1982), a spoof of daytime dramas that costarred several other soap regulars. In 1990, Turner was cast as fiesty Alaskan mail pilot Maggie O'Donnell on the quirky prime-time series "Northern Exposure," a role that made her a major star.

She continued to essay the part until the series' demise in 1995. Turner's more recent assignments have included a standard damsel-in-distress turn in the Sylvester Stallone vehicle *Cliffhanger* (1993), and a series of automobile advertisements, each as graceful and classy as Turner herself. **Selected Works:** *Ambulance* (1990), *Steel Magnolias* (1989)

# Kathleen Turner

**Born:** June 19, 1954; Springfield, MO

**Years Active in the Industry:** by decade

| 10ˢ | 20ˢ | 30ˢ | 40ˢ | 50ˢ | 60ˢ | 70ˢ | 80ˢ | 90ˢ |
|-----|-----|-----|-----|-----|-----|-----|-----|-----|

Sexy, bold, classy, statuesque leading lady, Kathleen Turner is adept at both comedy and drama. The daughter of a diplomat, her childhood was spent in places as diverse as Venezuela, Cuba, and Canada; while living in London as a teenager she became interested in theater and decided to become an actress. She studied acting in college and appeared in student plays, then moved to New York, where she did some stage work before landing a continuing role in the TV soap opera "The Doctors," on which she worked for almost two years. Meanwhile, she moved from off-off-Broadway roles to performing for nine months in the Broadway hit *Gemini*. She debuted onscreen as a murderous femme fatale in Lawrence Kasdan's *Body Heat* (1981) opposite William Hurt. However, the film that established her as a star was *Romancing the Stone* (1984), in which she portrayed a romance writer who gets drawn into a real-life adventure alongside Michael Douglas. She went on to an inconsistent career punctuated by occasional hits. For her performance in Francis Ford Coppola's *Peggy Sue Got Married* (1986) she received a Best Actress Oscar nomination. She also continued acting onstage, appearing as Maggie in the Broadway revival of *Cat On a Hot Tin Roof*, for which she received a Tony nomination. **Selected Works:** *Accidental Tourist* (1988), *Prizzi's Honor* (1985), *Moonlight and Valentino* (1995)

# Lana Turner (Julia Jean Mildred Frances Turner)

**Born:** February 8, 1921; Wallace, ID
**Died:** June 29, 1995

**Years Active in the Industry:** by decade

| 10ˢ | 20ˢ | 30ˢ | 40ˢ | 50ˢ | 60ˢ | 70ˢ | 80ˢ | 90ˢ |
|-----|-----|-----|-----|-----|-----|-----|-----|-----|

Turner was discovered as a teenager by an editor of *The Hollywood Reporter* at the Top Hat Cafe, across the street from Hollywood High School; she was wearing a tight sweater and was, for a time, publicized as "the sweater girl." Turner appeared as a starlet in numerous films beginning in 1937. In the '40s she was turned into a star and ended up specializing in melodrama. For her work in *Peyton Place* (1957) she received a Best Actress Oscar

nomination. In 1958, her teenage daughter, Cheryl Crane, stabbed to death underworld hoodlum Johnny Stompanato, Turner's boyfriend; Crane was found not guilty on the grounds that she was protecting her mother. Oddly, the adverse publicity had no negative effect on Turner's career. She went on to appear in a handful of additional films, on stage, and on TV; she was a semi-regular on the TV series "Falcon Crest." Altogether, she was married eight times; her seven husbands included bandleader Artie Shaw, actor Stephen Crane, and actor Lex Barker. She authored an autobiography, *Lana: The Lady, the Legend, the Truth* (1982). **Selected Works:** *The Bad & the Beautiful* (1952), *Imitation of Life* (1959)

# Tina Turner

**Born:** November 26, 1938; Brownsville, TX

**Years Active in the Industry:** by decade

| 10ˢ | 20ˢ | 30ˢ | 40ˢ | 50ˢ | 60ˢ | 70ˢ | 80ˢ | 90ˢ |
|-----|-----|-----|-----|-----|-----|-----|-----|-----|
|     |     |     |     |     |     |     |     |     |

American entertainer Tina Turner first met her future husband-collaborator Ike Turner in 1959, when he was fronting a popular East St. Louis band called the Kings of Rhythm. From 1960 through 1975, the Ike and Tina Turner Revue toted 25 top-ten Rhythm and Blues hits, the most famous of which was that perennial wedding favorite, "Proud Mary." Turner broke loose from what had become an intolerable and abusive relationship in the mid-1970s, making an impressive solo movie debut as the ear-shattering Acid Queen in 1975's *Tommy* (five years earlier, she had been featured in the company of Ike in the Rolling Stones' concert documentary *Gimme Shelter*). As a non-singing film actress, Turner has thus far been confined to a showy villainous turn in 1985's *Mad Max Beyond Thunderdome*. Turner was portrayed (rather along Mother Teresa lines) by Angela Bassett in the 1993 biopic *What's Love Got to Do With It?*, which was based on Turner's own book (written with Kurt Loder) and which costarred Laurence Fishburne as Ike. **Selected Works:** *That Was Rock* (1984)

# John Turturro

**Born:** February 28, 1957; Brooklyn, NY

**Years Active in the Industry:** by decade

| 10ˢ | 20ˢ | 30ˢ | 40ˢ | 50ˢ | 60ˢ | 70ˢ | 80ˢ | 90ˢ |
|-----|-----|-----|-----|-----|-----|-----|-----|-----|
|     |     |     |     |     |     |     |     |     |

Italian-American character actor with a long face, curved nose, and slightly crooked mouth, he was a movie fanatic from an early age; after graduating from college he won a scholarship to study acting at Yale. He went on to work in regional theater and off-Broadway; for his starring role in *Danny and the Deep Blue Sea* he won an Obie Award. In 1984 he debuted on Broadway in *Death of a Salesman;* also in 1984, he debuted onscreen in *Exterminator II*. After a number of film roles, most of them small, he began to establish himself as a major supporting actor in two 1987 releases, *The Sicilian* (scripted by Gore Vidal) and *Five Corners*. His credits also include performances in three Spike Lee films. In 1990 he was named by *Rolling Stone* magazine as the "hot actor" of 1990. For his lead performance in the Coen Brothers' *Barton Fink* (1991), he won the Cannes Film Festival Best Actor award. His brother is actor Nicholas Turturro, best known as James Martinez of TV's "NYPD Blue." They appeared together as brothers in Spike Lee's *Mo' Better Blues* (1990) and also appeared together in Lee's *Jungle Fever* (1991). He wrote, directed, and starred in *Mac* (1992). **Selected Works:** *Miller's Crossing* (1990), *Fearless* (1993), *Quiz Show* (1994), *Clockers* (1995), *Unstrung Heroes* (1995)

# Tom Tyler

**Born:** August 9, 1903; Port Henry, NY
**Died:** 1954

**Years Active in the Industry:** by decade

| 10ˢ | 20ˢ | 30ˢ | 40ˢ | 50ˢ | 60ˢ | 70ˢ | 80ˢ | 90ˢ |
|-----|-----|-----|-----|-----|-----|-----|-----|-----|
|     |     |     |     |     |     |     |     |     |

Athletically inclined, Tyler entered films at age 21 as a stuntman and extra. He went on to play supporting roles in several late silents, then signed a contract to star in Westerns. He soon became a popular screen cowboy, often accompanied by sidekick Frankie Darro; he survived the transition to sound, going on to star in a number of serials in the early '30s. He remained popular through the early '40s and occasionally played supporting roles in major films. In 1943 he was struck by a crippling rheumatic condition; although he appeared in a handful of additional films throughout the next decade, his career was effectively ended as he was relegated to minor roles. By the early '50s he was broke. He died of a heart attack at age 50. **Selected Works:** *The Grapes of Wrath* (1940), *Stagecoach* (1939), *The Talk of the Town* (1942), *They Were Expendable* (1945), *Westerner* (1940)

# Cicely Tyson

**Born:** December 19, 1933; New York, NY

**Years Active in the Industry:** by decade

| 10s | 20s | 30s | 40s | 50s | 60s | 70s | 80s | 90s |
|-----|-----|-----|-----|-----|-----|-----|-----|-----|
|     |     |     |     |     |     |     |     |     |

The daughter of Caribbean immigrants, she grew up in Harlem. After working for a while as a typist she took up modeling in her late teens, becoming very successful. Tyson made her acting debut in a Harlem YMCA production of *Dark of the Moon,* then be-gan working in a string of off-Broadway productions; for her work in the play *The Blacks* in 1961 she won The Vernon Rice Award. She became well-known as the result of playing George C. Scott's secretary in the TV series "East Side, West Side" in the mid '60s; she also began getting frequent guest roles on other TV series. Having first appeared in films in the late '50s, she began making more frequent film appearances in the mid '60s; with her performance in *Sounder* (1972) she became a star, receiving a Best Actress Oscar nomination. She was widely praised for her performance in the title role of the TV movie *The Autobiography of Miss Jane Pittman* (1974), for which she won a "Best Actress in a Special" Emmy; with that triumph she became a household name and appeared on numerous magazine covers. However, during the rest of her career she has had a hard time finding good roles, and her talents are often wasted in second-rate productions. **Selected Works:** *Duplicates* (1992), *Fried Green Tomatoes* (1991), *Heat Wave* (1990), *The Kid Who Loved Christmas* (1990), *The Oldest Living Confederate Widow Tells All* (1994)

Tracey Ullman

Liv Ullmann

Edgar G. Ulmer

S. Pete Ustinov

# U

## Tracey Ullman

**Born:** December 29, 1959; London, England

**Years Active in the Industry:** by decade

| 10ˢ | 20ˢ | 30ˢ | 40ˢ | 50ˢ | 60ˢ | 70ˢ | 80ˢ | 90ˢ |
|-----|-----|-----|-----|-----|-----|-----|-----|-----|
|  |  |  |  |  |  |  | ■ | ■ |

An irrepressible "Jill of All Trades," British actress Tracey Ullman is master of all of them. Winning an arts scholarship at age 12, Ullman worked as a professional dancer with a German ballet company before channelling her energies into musical comedy. For her work in the West End production *Four in a Million,* Ullman was honored with the London Theatre Critics' award as Most Promising New Actress of 1981. Two years later, she was presented with a British Academy Award for her efforts on BBC Television. While still in her early twenties, she headlined her own British comedy/variety TV series, "Three of a Kind," and climbed the pop-music charts with her singles "You Broke My Heart in Seventeen Places" and "They Don't Know." After an inauspicious film debut in 1983's *Give My Regards to Broad Street,* Ullman ascended to film stardom in such productions as *Plenty* (1985), *Jumpin' Jack Flash* (1986), *I Love You to Death* (1990), *Death Becomes Her* (1992) and *I'll Do Anything* (1994). In 1987, she launched her American TV career with the Fox Network's weekly "The Tracey Ullman Show," a superb showcase for her many offbeat characterizations, including mixed-up teen Francesca, selfish yuppie Sara Downey, repressed spinster Kay, and Goodallesque anthropologist Ceci Beckwith. "The Tracy Ullman Show" not only won the Fox Network its first Emmy nomination, but also spawned the popular cartoon series "The Simpsons," which first took shape as a series of between-the-acts animated vignettes. **Selected Works:** *Happily Ever After* (1991), *Robin Hood: Men in Tights* (1993), *Household Saints* (1993), *Bullets over Broadway* (1994)

## Liv Ullmann

**Born:** December 16, 1939; Tokyo, Japan

**Years Active in the Industry:** by decade

| 10ˢ | 20ˢ | 30ˢ | 40ˢ | 50ˢ | 60ˢ | 70ˢ | 80ˢ | 90ˢ |
|-----|-----|-----|-----|-----|-----|-----|-----|-----|
|  |  |  |  |  | ■ | ■ | ■ | ■ |

Although Norwegian, she didn't live in Norway until her teens; there she joined a provincial theater group in the mid '50s and soon became an esteemed actress of the Oslo stage and Norwegian films. For years Ullmann was director Ingmar Bergman's primary actress; as the result of her work in Bergman's films, she was internationally known by the early '70s. She and Bergman lived together for five years and had a daughter. She has also starred in international productions, on Broadway, and on the European stage. For her work in *The Emigrants* (1971) and *Face to Face* (1976) she received Best Actress Oscar nominations. She co-wrote and directed the film *Sofie* (1993). She also authored an autobiography, *Changing* (1977). **Selected Works:** *Autumn Sonata* (1978), *Cries and Whispers* (1972), *The Passion of Anna* (1970), *Persona* (1966), *Scenes from a Marriage* (1973), *Shame* (1968)

## Edgar G. Ulmer

**Born:** September 17, 1904; Vienna, Austria
**Died:** September 30, 1972; Woodland Hills, CA

**Years Active in the Industry:** by decade

| 10ˢ | 20ˢ | 30ˢ | 40ˢ | 50ˢ | 60ˢ | 70ˢ | 80ˢ | 90ˢ |
|-----|-----|-----|-----|-----|-----|-----|-----|-----|
|  | ■ | ■ | ■ | ■ | ■ |  |  |  |

The most highly regarded B movie director of the mid 20th century, Edgar George Ulmer was one of the very few filmmakers in his field who chose B status over A status. Born in Vienna, Austria, he worked as a stage actor and set designer while studying architecture and philosophy, and later joined the company of the legendary theatrical producer Max Reinhardt. He came to Broadway in the 1920s after coming to America with a Reinhardt production, and became briefly involved with Universal Pictures. On his return to Germany he became an assistant to filmmaker F.W. Murnau, and made one more trip to Hollywood at the end of the 1920s, before returning to Germany in 1929 to co-direct *Menschen am Sonntag* with Robert Siodmak. Ulmer returned to Hollywood as an art director, and by 1933 had moved up to the film director's chair, with *Damaged Lives* and *Mr. Broadway.* However, *The Black Cat* (1933) was his only notable big studio picture—a bizarre, harrowing, and extremely effective horror thriller starring Bela Lugosi and Boris Karloff, this movie seemed to herald the arrival of a major new talent in the genre. But when Ulmer was ordered to direct a Shirley Temple film at Fox on loan-out, he balked, was fired, and gave up any desire to work for a major studio—from that day forward, he chose his films on the basis of the degree of independence that they allowed him. Working for various small studios, Ulmer became Poverty Row's acknowledged master at making something out of nothing, mostly in the field of ethnic films—he directed numerous Yiddish films, features for the black theater circuits, and even one low-budget Western, and infused them all with a passion and vibrancy that belied their miniscule budgets and shooting schedules. During the early 1940s, he hooked up with Producers Releasing Corporation, the lowest of Hollywood's low-budget outfits, where he proceeded to create a series of legendary films: *Bluebeard* (1944), an ultra-cheap but incredibly good looking, graceful, and suspenseful thriller starring John Carradine; *Strange Illusion* (1945), a harrowing and piercing modern dress adaptation of *Hamlet;* and *Detour* (1945), a cross-country thriller, shot in four days for under $20,000, that is still shown widely on television, revived regularly in theaters, and studied in film courses around the world. After the demise of PRC, Ulmer worked for independent producers in America and Europe and continued creating superb films, including *Carnegie Hall* (1947), *The Man From Planet X* (1951), *L'Atlantide* (*Journey Beneath The Desert*) (1961), and *Beyond The Time Barrier* (1960).

# Sir Peter Ustinov

**Born:** April 16, 1921; London, England

**Years Active in the Industry:** by decade

| 10s | 20s | 30s | 40s | 50s | 60s | 70s | 80s | 90s |
|-----|-----|-----|-----|-----|-----|-----|-----|-----|
|     |     |     | ■   | ■   | ■   | ■   | ■   | ■   |

Hirsute, puckish "renaissance man" Peter Ustinov was born in England to parents of Russian lineage. Trained at the London Theatre Studio, Ustinov was on stage from the age of 17, performing sketches written by himself in the 1939 revue *Late Joys.* In 1940, the year that his first play *Fishing for Shadows* was staged, the 19-year-old Ustinov appeared in his first film. Just before entering the British army, Ustinov penned his first screenplay, *The True Glory* (1945). 1946's *School for Secrets* was the first of several films starring, written and directed by Ustinov; others include *Vice Versa* (1946), *Private Angelo* (1949), *Romanoff and Juliet* (1961) (adapted from his own stage play) and *Lady L* (1965). Perhaps Ustinov's most ambitious film directorial project was *Billy Budd* (1962), a laudable if not completely successful attempt to transfer the allegorical style of Herman Melville to the screen. As an actor in films directed by others, Ustinov has sparkled in parts requiring what can best be described as "justifiable ham"—he was Oscar-nominated for his riveting performance as the addled Nero in 1951's *Quo Vadis* and has won the Best Supporting Actor prize for *Spartacus* (1961) and *Topkapi* (1964). Never one to turn down a good television assignment, Ustinov has appeared on American TV in such guises as King George and Dr. Samuel Johnson, winning the first of his three Emmy Awards for the latter characterization; he is also a frequent talk-show guest, regaling audiences with his droll wit and his mastery over several dialects. While he has never starred on-camera in a weekly TV series, his voice could be heard essaying virtually all the roles on the 1981 syndicated cartoon series *Dr. Snuggles.* The closest he has come to repeating himself was with his frequent theatrical-film and TV-movie appearances as Agatha Christie's Belgian detective Hercule Poirot in the late 1970s and early 1980s. The author of several plays (the most popular of which included *Love of Four Colonels* and *Photo Finish*) and books (including two autobiographies), Peter Ustinov was still going strong into the 1990s, making a long-overdue return to Hollywood in the 1992 film *Lorenzo's Oil.* **Selected Works:** *Sundowners* (1960)

# Roger Vadim (Roger Vadim Plemiannikov)

**Born:** January 26, 1928; Paris, France

**Years Active in the Industry:** by decade

| 10s | 20s | 30s | 40s | 50s | 60s | 70s | 80s | 90s |
|-----|-----|-----|-----|-----|-----|-----|-----|-----|
|     |     |     |     |     |     |     |     |     |

Originally a stage actor, and also a part-time journalist and screenwriter, Roger Vadim came to film as an assistant to movie director Marc Allegret, and subsequently married Allegret's most well known discovery, Brigitte Bardot, whom he also starred with in numerous films of the 1950s. Vadim became internationally known for his 1956 debut film *And God Created Woman,* which trod new ground in eroticism during the 1950s, and also starred Bardot. His later films luxuriated in their lushness and decadence, a process that continued with Vadim's subsequent marriage to Jane Fonda, who also became one of his most renowned leading ladies. However, since the late 1960s, with the general opening up of American films to more overtly sexual content, Vadim's popularity and success outside of Europe have fallen off markedly, and an American remake of *And God Created Woman* (1988) provoked yawns as much as curiosity from critics and the public alike. Vadim and Fonda have since divorced.

# Rudolph Valentino (Rudolfo Guglielmi)

**Born:** May 6, 1895; Castellaneta, Italy
**Died:** August 23, 1926

**Years Active in the Industry:** by decade

| 10s | 20s | 30s | 40s | 50s | 60s | 70s | 80s | 90s |
|-----|-----|-----|-----|-----|-----|-----|-----|-----|
|     |     |     |     |     |     |     |     |     |

Valentino moved to New York in 1913, where he had several odd jobs and occasionally got in trouble with the law on suspicions of petty theft and blackmail. He became a taxi dancer and began showing off his prowess with various partners in dance halls and nightclubs. Eventually, he replaced Clifton Webb as the partner of

Bonnie Glass, a popular dancer. He later joined the cast of a touring musical that folded in Utah; he continued on his own to San Francisco, where he resumed his dancing career. In 1917 he moved to Hollywood and began getting extra and bit parts in films, usually as an exotic dancer or swarthy villain. In 1919 he married actress Jean Acker, but the marriage was never consummated and they divorced after two years. In 1921 he got his big break—screenwriter June Mathis insisted that he be given the lead in *The Four Horsemen of the Apocalypse;* the film was a huge hit and Valentino was launched into stardom, reaffirmed by several more blockbusters. Handsome, well-built, graceful, and sensual, he had unprecedented popularity among women, to whom he represented mysterious, taboo sexuality, and passion. For several years he remained on top, but his popularity waned when his second wife, Natasha Rambova, took over his career and made his screen persona become more and more effeminate; a backlash arose against his powdered, bejeweled image. However, his films continued to be successful. In 1926, at age 31, he died suddenly from complications arising from a perforated ulcer; his death was an occasion of enormous public mourning, and a cult following of Valentino arose afterwards. He was portrayed by Anthony Dexter in a 1951 film biography, and then by Rudolf Nureyev in another in 1977.

# Lee Van Cleef

**Born:** January 9, 1925; Somerville, NJ
**Died:** December 14, 1989; Oxnard, CA

**Years Active in the Industry:** by decade

| 10s | 20s | 30s | 40s | 50s | 60s | 70s | 80s | 90s |
|-----|-----|-----|-----|-----|-----|-----|-----|-----|
|     |     |     |     |     |     |     |     |     |

Following a wartime navy hitch, New Jersey-born Lee Van Cleef supported himself as an accountant. Like his fellow accountant-turned-actor Jack Elam, Van Cleef was advised by his clients that he had just the right Satanic facial features to thrive as a movie villain. With such rare exceptions as *The Beast from 20,000 Fathoms* (1954), Van Cleef spent most of his early screen career on the wrong side of the law, menacing everyone from Gary Cooper (*High Noon*) to the Bowery Boys (*Private Eyes*) with his cold, shark-eyed stare. In the 1960s, Van Cleef left Hollywood to appear in European "spaghetti Westerns," first as a secondary actor; he was, for example, the "Bad" in Clint Eastwood's *The Good, the Bad and the Ugly* (1966). Within a few years, Van Cleef was starring in blood-spattered actioners that bore such titles as *Day of Anger* (1967), *El Condor* (1970) and *Mean Frank and Crazy Tony* (1973). For many years, the actor was one of the international film scene's biggest box-office draws. Returning to Hollywood in the late 1970s, Lee Van Cleef starred in a very short-lived martial-arts TV series *The Master* (1984), the pilot episodes of which have been rabbeted together into an ersatz feature film for videocassette rental. **Selected Works:** *High Noon* (1952), *The Man Who Shot Liberty Valance* (1962), *Young Lions* (1958), *Gunfight at the O.K. Corral* (1957)

# Jean-Claude Van Damme

**Born:** 1961; Brussels, Belgium

**Years Active in the Industry:** by decade

| 10s | 20s | 30s | 40s | 50s | 60s | 70s | 80s | 90s |
|-----|-----|-----|-----|-----|-----|-----|-----|-----|
|     |     |     |     |     |     |     |     |     |

Belgian-born film star Jean Claude Van Damme *can* be called an actor, though it's more accurate to describe him as a bodybuilder and kickboxer. It evidently wasn't in the genes; Van

Damme's father was an accountant and flower salesman. Taking up the study of shotokan karate at the age of 10, Van Damme went on to win the middleweight championship of the European Professional Karate Association, where he thrilled one and all with his 360-degree leap-kick. Cashing in on his fame, the 18-year-old Van Damme launched the California Gym in Brussels. When he finally flew to LA, he had $7,000 to his

name and spoke only French and Flemish. At first he took many odd jobs, the least prepossessing of which was a carpet layer. Van Damme's first film was a bit in Chuck Norris' *Missing in Action* (1984). Groomed for stardom by Cannon Films' Menachem Golem, Van Damme became a big box-office commodity via such epics as *No Retreat, No Surrender* (1986); *Predator* (1987); *Bloodsport* (1988); *Cyborg* (1988); *Kickboxer* (1989), which he co-wrote; *Lionheart* (1990); and *Universal Soldier* (1991). Fully cognizant of his own histrionic limitations, Jean Claude Van Damme has not yet tried to branch out into comedy or "sensitive" roles as has Arnold Schwarzenegger; when starring in the popular futuristic actioner *Time Cop* (1994), Van Damme wisely left the acting to villain Ron Silver. **Selected Works:** *Death Warrant* (1990), *Double Impact* (1991), *Hard Target* (1993), *Nowhere to Run* (1993), *Sudden Death* (1995)

# Mamie Van Doren (Joan Lucille Olander)

**Born:** February 6, 1933; Rowena, SD

**Years Active in the Industry:** by decade

| 10s | 20s | 30s | 40s | 50s | 60s | 70s | 80s | 90s |
|-----|-----|-----|-----|-----|-----|-----|-----|-----|
|     |     |     |     |     |     |     |     |     |

1950s "sex bomb" Mamie Van Doren *could* act, but reviewers seldom got any farther than commenting on her torpedo bras and skin-tight capri pants. She made her professional bow as a band singer, acting in stock companies before signing a contract with Universal Pictures in 1953. There would be a few A pictures in her future, notably the Clark Gable-Doris Day comedy *Teacher's Pet* (1958), but Van Doren's career was mainly devoted to tawdry exploitation programmers and drive-in quickies. She became the resident Marilyn Monroe-type for fast-buck producer Albert Zugsmith in the late 1950s and early 1960s, starring in such Oscar-calibre hits as *The Beat Generation* (1958), *The Big Operator* (1959), *The Private Lives of Adam and Eve* (1960), and her signature film, *Sex Kittens Go To College* (1960). She also showed up in the "musical j.d." epic *Born Reckless* (singing five songs) and as a neurotic striptease artist in director Tommy Noonan's tickle-and-tease farce *Three Nuts in Search of a Bolt* (1964). Disappearing from films in the 1970s, Van Doren continued popping up at important Hollywood social functions and awards presentations, as *zaftig* and exhibitionist as ever, much to the delight of her ever-growing fan club. In 1987 Mamie Van Doren wrote her memoirs, *Playing the Field,* in which she claims she slept with practically every male star in the entertainment industry.

# Dick Van Dyke

**Born:** December 13, 1925; West Plains, MO

**Years Active in the Industry:** by decade

| 10s | 20s | 30s | 40s | 50s | 60s | 70s | 80s | 90s |
|-----|-----|-----|-----|-----|-----|-----|-----|-----|
|     |     |     |     |     |     |     |     |     |

Dick Van Dyke began his performing career in a two-person nightclub pantomime act billed as "The Merry Mutes." Later he worked on local TV, leading to roles on network shows; he eventually starred on Broadway in the musical *Bye Bye Birdie*, then later appeared in the play's film version (1963), his screen debut. He became well-known as the star of "The Dick Van Dyke Show," a hit sitcom of the early '60s; he won three Emmy Awards for his work on the show. He had a fairly busy screen career in the '60s, but after 1971 his film work was infrequent. He attempted a TV comeback in a number of failed shows before finally landing in a winner in the '90s, "Diagnosis Murder." He is the brother of actor Jerry Van Dyke. **Selected Works:** *Dick Tracy* (1990), *Mary Poppins* (1964)

# W.S. Van Dyke II

**Born:** March 21, 1889; San Diego, CA
**Died:** February 5, 1943; Hollywood, CA

**Years Active in the Industry:** by decade

| 10s | 20s | 30s | 40s | 50s | 60s | 70s | 80s | 90s |
|-----|-----|-----|-----|-----|-----|-----|-----|-----|
|     |     |     |     |     |     |     |     |     |

W. S. "Woody" Van Dyke II inaugurated his career at age three as a stage actor, in the company of his widowed actress-mother. When acting jobs were scarce, young Van Dyke worked as a miner, electrician and (allegedly) a soldier-for-hire in Mexico during the 'teens. In 1916, he was hired as one of several assistants to director D. W. Griffith, working in this capacity on Griffith's mammoth *Intolerance*. After assisting director James Young at Paramount, Van Dyke was allowed to direct his first solo film in 1917. He spent most of the 1920s laboring on quickie Westerns, earning a reputation for speed and efficiency. In 1928, he was brought into MGM's troubled production *White Shadows on the South Seas*, which, under the snail's-pace direction of Robert J. Flaherty (a brilliant documentary maker whose skills at fictional filmmaking was slight), was running way behind schedule. When *White Shadows* opened to critical and audience approval, Van Dyke was elevated to Hollywood's A-list of directors, though even when handed huge budgets and big stars he never altered his rush-it-through directorial technique (the one exception to this was his year-long sojourn on *Trader Horn* [1931]). "One Take Woody" was often derided by his fellow MGM directors, who bemoaned Van Dyke's "carelessness" and "sloppiness." However, Van Dyke's best films—*The*

*Thin Man* (1934), *San Francisco* (1936), *It's a Wonderful World* (1939)—hold up far better than the works of many of his more art-conscious colleagues. A favorite of no-nonsense leading men like Clark Gable and William Powell, Van Dyke was not held in as high esteem by certain actresses accustomed to being fussed over for hours before stepping in front of the cameras; still, he got along quite well with the temparamental Norma Shearer when he took over direction of the troubled Shearer epic *Marie Antoinette* (1938). Working at MGM until 1942, the year before his death, Van Dyke could take pride in the fact that virtually all his films made money for the studio—and virtually none went over budget.

# Gus Van Sant (Gus Van Sant, Jr.)

**Born:** 1953; Louisville, KY

**Years Active in the Industry:** by decade

| 10s | 20s | 30s | 40s | 50s | 60s | 70s | 80s | 90s |
|-----|-----|-----|-----|-----|-----|-----|-----|-----|
|     |     |     |     |     |     |     | ■   | ■   |

Starting out conventionally enough as a TV commercial producer, Kentucky-born Gus Van Sant learned the rudiments of independent filmmaking under the tutelage of Roger Corman. Van Sant's first directorial effort (which he also edited, produced and wrote) was *Mala Noche* (1985), a cheap ($25,000) but powerful study of a starcrossed gay romance that won the Los Angeles Critics Award for best independent film. Distribution problems with *Mala Noche* kept Van Sant out of the public view for nearly four years—but when he re-emerged, it was with another multi-award-winner, *Drugstore Cowboy* (1989), an alternately repellant and fascinating study of young lowlifes who steal and hustle to survive. Appearing in the cast of *Drugstore Cowboy* is self-destructive beat poet William Burroughs, whom Van Sant has cited as his mentor (oddly, when time came to film Burroughs' *Naked Lunch*, David Cronenberg was director). The gay subthemes in *Drugstore Cowboy* were brought to the forefront in Van Sant's *My Own Private Idaho* (1991), the story of a homosexual hustler (played by the late River Phoenix), which, like *Cowboy*, was lensed in Van Sant's adopted home town of Portland Oregon. Unfortunately, Van Sant's next project broke his winning streak—*Even Cowgirls Get the Blues*, an all-star, no-brains adaptation of Tom Robbins' outdated lesbian-oriented novel that barely received a theatrical release.

# Agnés Varda

**Born:** May 30, 1928; Brussels, Belgium

**Years Active in the Industry:** by decade

| 10s | 20s | 30s | 40s | 50s | 60s | 70s | 80s | 90s |
|-----|-----|-----|-----|-----|-----|-----|-----|-----|
|     |     |     |     | ■   |     |     |     |     |

A French director, Vards's chief interests are in human relationships and levels of awareness. *Cleo from 5 to 7* (1962) deals with a woman's enhanced perceptions during the period in which she awaits a potentially negative medical prognosis. *Le Bonheur* (1965) follows the actions and emotions of a man who fantasizes that he can set up housekeeping with both his wife and his mistress and that they will understand and accept him. And *One Sings, the Other Doesn't* (1977) examines the lives of two women from a feminist standpoint. Varda has also directed several short films that reflect her somewhat left-of-center orientation, including documentaries on Vietnam and on the Black Panthers. **Selected Works:** *Hundred and One Nights* (1995)

# Conrad Veidt (Hans Walter Konrad Veidt)

**Born:** January 22, 1893; Potsdam, Germany
**Died:** April 3, 1943; Hollywood, CA

**Years Active in the Industry:** by decade

| 10ˢ | 20ˢ | 30ˢ | 40ˢ | 50ˢ | 60ˢ | 70ˢ | 80ˢ | 90ˢ |
|-----|-----|-----|-----|-----|-----|-----|-----|-----|

He studied theater with Max Reinhardt, debuting onstage in 1913 at Reinhardt's Deutsches Theater in Berlin. Veidt entered films in 1917 and soon became a prominent actor in German cinema, specializing in demonic, demented, or tormented character roles. By the mid '20s he was world-famous, leading to an invitation from Hollywood, where he appeared in several films. With the advent of sound films, he returned to Germany in 1929. After the Nazi victory in 1933 he went into exile with his Jewish wife in England. Throughout the '30s he appeared in British and French films, then he went to Hollywood in 1940 and appeared in a number of American films. He died of a heart attack at age 50. **Selected Works:** *Casablanca* (1942), *The Men in Her Life* (1941), *Thief of Bagdad* (1940)

# Paul Verhoeven

**Born:** July 18, 1938; Amsterdam, Holland

**Years Active in the Industry:** by decade

| 10ˢ | 20ˢ | 30ˢ | 40ˢ | 50ˢ | 60ˢ | 70ˢ | 80ˢ | 90ˢ |
|-----|-----|-----|-----|-----|-----|-----|-----|-----|

Dutch film director Paul Verhoeven held a PhD in mathematics and physics, but it was as a filmmaker that he worked for the Royal Dutch Navy, then for television in his native land. Starting out with documentaries, Verhoeven moved into fictional filmmaking with a popular Dutch TV series before making his first theatrical feature, *Business is Business* (1971). 1973's *Turkish Delight* (*The Shelter of Your Arms*), was the director's first international success, and also the earliest example of his expertise in cinematic eroticism. Verhoeven's *Soldier of Orange* (1977), a grim coming-of-age story set in World War II, became a staple of the more esoteric moviehouses when it was released in the U.S. in 1979—later enjoying a whole new life amongst young intellectuals on videocassette. With his then-favorite actor Rutger Hauer, Verhoeven fur-

thered his reputation with *Spetters* (1980), an adroit head-on collision of adolescent fantasies, graphic violence and hot-blooded sex. Verhoeven added suspense to his repertoire with *The Fourth Man* (1984), a quasi-detective story with a gay writer as protagonist and a "mystery woman" as antagonist (the film was made in 1979, but unreleased in the U.S. for five years). The director's first English-language film was *Flesh and Blood* (1985), a raunchy 16th century adventure film deceptively retitled *The Sword and the Rose* on videocassette. Verhoeven's first boxoffice bonanza was *Robocop* (1986), a master blend of special effects, brutality and nail-biting tension (since dissipated by two non-Verhoeven *Robocop* sequels of lesser quality). *Total Recall* (1990), starring Arnold Schwarzenegger, was an eye-popping exercise in "virtual reality"—*before* that computer-generated pastime fell into popular usage—that managed to sustain its spectacular fantasy trappings while still doing homage to the existentialism of its Philip K. Dick source novel. Sharon Stone, a supporting actress in *Total Recall*, starred in Verhoeven's most notorious film, *Basic Instinct* (1992). Utilizing much of the premise of his earlier *The Fourth Man*, Verhoeven managed to combine many of his past subthemes—political duplicity, urban decay, the gay scene, appalling violence, kinky sex, the abnormality lurking within normality—into an extraordinary film that offended as many people as it entertained. *And* Verhoeven managed to turn Sharon Stone, a veteran of 18 films, into an "overnight star" simply by asking her to cross her legs. Verhoeven's latest film *Showgirls* (1995) promises to be just as controversial as the rest of his oeuvre.

# King Vidor (King Wallis Vidor)

**Born:** February 8, 1894; Galveston, TX
**Died:** November 1, 1982

**Years Active in the Industry:** by decade

| 10ˢ | 20ˢ | 30ˢ | 40ˢ | 50ˢ | 60ˢ | 70ˢ | 80ˢ | 90ˢ |
|-----|-----|-----|-----|-----|-----|-----|-----|-----|

King Vidor was the son of a wealthy lumber manufacturer who became interested in movies as a young boy and took a job at a local movie theater—he took this early opportunity to watch the same movies over and over and turned it to his advantage, learning much from what he saw. After working as an amateur photographer, he began shooting newsreel material on his own and selling it to different clients. He broke into Hollywood slowly, after his

marriage in 1915, and after working as a day laborer, clerk, and extra, while trying to write scripts at the same time. Vidor made his directorial debut at Universal in two-reel shorts before moving to feature films in 1919. Soon after, he formed his own production company and made a number of small features before joining MGM in the mid 1920s, where he made his most celebrated silent films, *The Big Parade* (1925) and *The Crowd* (1928). With the coming of sound, Vidor proved especially adept at using the new medium, as exhibited in his 1929 musical *Hallelujah,* which worked better than most musicals of the era simply because Vidor refused to let the presence of sound restrict his visuals or the mobility and editing of his shots. He made one major socially conscience film, *Our Daily Bread* (1934), which is widely celebrated today for its stylistic eloquence as well as its message, but was equally successful with more overtly commercial films such as *Street Scene* and *The Champ* (both 1931), of which the latter was one of the most popular melodramas of its era (and was remade in the 1980s). Vidor's output from the early 1930s is somewhat uneven, owing to the number of outsized productions with which he was involved as one of several directors, most notably *The Wizard of Oz, Gone With the Wind,* and *Duel In the Sun,* all of which were as much producers' movies as directors' movies. But among even the lesser of them, such as *Comrade X* (an awkward attempt to replicate Ninotchka), there is a flair and verve that overcomes the difficulties of the participants with their material, and several of them, such as *Northwest Passage,* have aged extremely well. His adaptation of *The Fountainhead* (1949) is a delightfully audacious filming of a seemingly unfilmable book, and has improved with age, while other late era movies, such as his 1956 international production of *War And Peace,* have not aged nearly so well. **Selected Works:** *The Citadel* (1938), *Hallelujah!* (1929)

# Jean Vigo (Jean Bonaventure de Vigo)

**Born:** April 26, 1905; Paris, France
**Died:** October 26, 1934; Paris, France

**Years Active in the Industry:** by decade

| 10s | 20s | 30s | 40s | 50s | 60s | 70s | 80s | 90s |
|-----|-----|-----|-----|-----|-----|-----|-----|-----|
|     |     |     |     |     |     |     |     |     |

As the son of notorious French anarchist Eugene Bonaventure de Vigo (aka Miguel Alemreyda), young Jean Vigo and his family were obliged to stay on the move, usually under assumed names. After his father was found dead in his prison cell in 1917, Vigo attended boarding school under the name Jean Sales. A tuberculosis victim, Vigo moved to Nice to recuperate in 1929. While on the mend, he directed his first film, the surrealist *A propos de Nice* (1930). His next project was the 11-minute *Taris,* a documentary about France's reigning swimming champion. *Zero de conduite* (1932), Vigo's third film (at 45 minutes it was not quite a short but not exactly a feature), combined the absurd qualities of his first picture with the straight-on realities of the second. The naturalistic central setting of a dismal, restrictive boys' school is undercut with the absurdity of a pint-sized instructor, a World War I-style pillow fight, and a wish-fulfillment climactic scene in which the schoolboys pelt their adult tormentors with fruit (echoes of this film persisted in the later works of Jean Luc Godard, Lindsay Anderson and Francois Truffaut). *Zero de conduite* was perceived by the French authorities as an unpatriotic attack on the Establishment, and as such was banned until 1945. Vigo's fourth film, *L'Atlante* (1935), is regarded as his masterpiece. The film superbly blends realism (an unhappily married couple chugging up and down the Seine in a barge) with poetic flights of surrealism. Sadly, *L'Atlante,* like *Zero de conduite,* fell victim to the censors; its producers savagely cut the picture into incomprehensibility, arguing (as before) that its attack on the bourgeoisie was "anti-France." Penniless, Jean Vigo died of leukemia at the age of 29. His legacy has been kept alive by his filmmaking disciples, by the annual Jean Vigo Prize, and by the recently restored version of his "chef d'ouevre" *L'Atlante.*

# Luchino Visconti (Count Don Luchino Visconti Di Modrone)

**Born:** November 2, 1906; Milan, Italy
**Died:** March 17, 1976; Rome, Italy

**Years Active in the Industry:** by decade

| 10s | 20s | 30s | 40s | 50s | 60s | 70s | 80s | 90s |
|-----|-----|-----|-----|-----|-----|-----|-----|-----|
|     |     |     |     |     |     |     |     |     |

Italian director who heralded his country's celebrated neorealist movement with his first film, *Ossessione* (1942), Visconti's preoccupation seems to have been with the moral disintegration of families. *Ossessione* is an Italian version of James M. Cain's *The Postman Always Rings Twice,* about a woman who murders her husband. *Bellissima* (1951) examines a stage mother hell-bent on exploiting her daughter and *Rocco and His Brothers* (1960) chronicles a rural family who seek a better life in the city. Visconti's segment in *Boccaccio '70* (1962) is a study of casual adultery, and his last (and perhaps best) film, *The Innocent* (1976), illustrates the consequences of an aristocrat's having neglected his wife. Aristocrats and their trials are another recurring feature of Visconti's films; he came from an extremely well-to-do family, and, like many sympathizers with communism, maintained a lavish lifestyle. One of his aristocracy-oriented films, *The Leopard* (1963) featured Burt Lancaster and is considered a masterpiece. (A second film with Lancaster, *Conversation Piece* [1975] was less successful.) Visconti worked effectively and repeatedly with Anna Magnani, Silvano Mangano, Claudia Cardinale, Marcello Mastroianni, Alain Delon, Dirk Bogarde, and Helmut Berger (although Visconti's worst film , *Ludwig: The Mad King of Bavaria* (1973), features Berger. Visconti managed to film successfully both Camus (*The Stranger* [1967]) and Thomas Mann (*Death in Venice,* [1971]). He wrote the screenplays for many of his films. **Selected Works:** *Terra Trema* (1948)

# Jon Voight

**Born:** December 29, 1938; Yonkers, NY

**Years Active in the Industry:** by decade

| 10s | 20s | 30s | 40s | 50s | 60s | 70s | 80s | 90s |
|-----|-----|-----|-----|-----|-----|-----|-----|-----|
|     |     |     |     |     | ■   | ■   | ■   | ■   |

Voight acted in student plays in high school and college, then trained for the stage at New York's Neighborhood Playhouse. He landed a part in the Broadway musical *The Sound of Music,* then did more work off-Broadway and in stock; he also did some work on TV. He debuted onscreen in 1967; two years later he was launched to sudden stardom when he portrayed a cowboy prostitute in the hit *Midnight Cowboy* (1969), for which he received a Best Actor Oscar nomination. Voight never became a screen superstar, but he did go on to appear in a number of fine movies. His screen work since the mid '80s has been minimal. For his work in *Coming Home* (1978) he won a Best Actor Oscar and the Cannes Film Festival Best Actor award; he received another Best Actor Oscar nomination for *Runaway Train* (1985). **Selected Works:** *Catch-22* (1970), *Deliverance* (1972), *Last of His Tribe* (1992), *Chernobyl: The Final Warning* (1991), *The Convict Cowboy* (1995)

# Erich Von Stroheim

**Born:** September 22, 1885; Vienna, Austria
**Died:** May 12, 1957; Maurepas, France

**Years Active in the Industry:** by decade

| 10s | 20s | 30s | 40s | 50s | 60s | 70s | 80s | 90s |
|-----|-----|-----|-----|-----|-----|-----|-----|-----|
| ■   | ■   | ■   | ■   |     |     |     |     |     |

Back in the 1920s and 1930s, it was fashionable for Hollywood hacks and professional joke writers to deride the accomplishments of Austrian-born director Erich von Stroheim, dismissing him as a posturing phony who hid his inadequacies as a director with a mania for pointless detail. It is ironic that these same scoffers often accepted as a gospel the one truly "phony" aspect of von Stroheim's personality—his family background. Stroheim insisted that his full name was Erich Hans Carl Maria Stroheim von Nordenwall, that he was descended from Vienesse nobility, and that he'd been an officer in the Austrian cavalry. In fact, von Stroheim was the son of a Jewish straw hat manufacturer;

he had indeed been in the army, though never as an officer. But that dueling scar over his left eye was quite real, as was his expertise in all things military; equally real was his deep abiding love for moviemaking, which he inherited from his first boss in Hollywood, director D. W. Griffith. Stroheim played bits in Griffith's *Birth of a Nation* (1915) and *Intolerance* (1916), essayed more substantial roles in such Griffith-produced films as *Old Heidelberg* (1916), and functioned as a military technical advisor when the occasion demanded. With America's entry into World War I, demand for von Stroheim's services as a movie-heavy increased tenfold. Not only did he look the part of the "Hideous Hun," but he extended the role into his offscreen activities, deliberately provoking the angered reactions of anti-German passersby by wearing a full Prussian uniform when dining in restaurants. It was all a carefully crafted campaign of self-promotion, of course; the actor was able to build up a successful screen career as "The Man You Love To Hate" (a tag attached by an anonymous studio publicist), and once the war was over, von Stroheim had entered the household-word category. A prolific writer, von Stroheim begged Universal studio head Carl Laemmle to allow him to direct an adaptation of his own novel "The Pinnacle." Legend has it that Laemmle rejected the title because he thought it sounded too much like "pinochle;" but he also took von Stroheim up on his request, and the result was the 1919 feature film *Blind Husbands.* It was the first of von Stroheim's sex-triangle melodramas which luxuriated in the debauchery and depravity of the European upper classes—and it was a hit. The quality of von Stroheim's second film, *The Devil's Passkey* (1919), can't be determined since it no longer exists, but his third Universal directorial assignment, *Foolish Wives* (1921) is readily available to historian and casual viewer alike. It was on the set of *Foolish Wives* that von Stroheim inagurated his painstaking attention to detail, demanding that all costumes, uniforms, props, gestures, facial expressions and even lovemaking techniques be absolutely authentic to the Monte Carlo "milieu" of the picture. He also supervised construction of a full-scale replica of Monte Carlo itself, which pushed the budget well past $1 million. At first aghast, producer Laemmle used the expenditure to his advantage, publicizing *Foolish Wives* as "the million dollar picture." While the film seems buried in decor and detail when seen today, audiences in 1921 ate it up, and von Stroheim had another box-office smash to his name. But the rough cut ran nearly six hours, obliging Universal to cut the picture by nearly 12 reels—the first of many instances wherein a studio would slice a von Stroheim project to but a fraction of its intended length. Rather than curb his excesses, von Stroheim became even more profligate with his next picture, 1923's *Merry Go Round,* which prompted Universal's new general manager Irving Thalberg to fire the director. On the strength of his past reputation, von Stroheim was able to secure a job at Goldwyn studios for his next project, a faithful adaptation of Frank Norris' "naturalistc" novel *McTeague*. This time the finished product ran 42 reels (roughly 8 hours)—which sat not at all well with the new executive regime of Goldwyn, now merged into Metro-Goldwyn-Mayer and under the guidance of von Stroheim's old nemesis Irving Thalberg. Under protest, von Stroheim cut *McTeague* to 24 reels, then allowed his director friend Rex Ingram to prepare an 18-reel version. Thalberg eventually released the film in a 10-reel abridgement titled *Greed,* which, despite some abrupt transitions and clumsy "bridging" subtitles, remains von Stroheim's masterpiece. While *Greed* was not the financial disaster that MGM claimed it was (it actually posted a profit), the brouhaha over its length and cost permanently damaged von Stroheim's reputation as a bankable director. While von Stroheim's next MGM project, *The Merry Widow* (1926), was his most financially successful film, Thalberg decided that the detail-obsessed director was not worth the trouble and fired him again. With the financing of independent producer Pat Powers, von Stroheim directed 1928's *The Wedding March* and its (now lost) sequel, *The Honeymoon.* The film remains one of von Stroheim's best (it even includes a rare sympathetic performance from the star/director), but it failed to attract paying customers. Stroheim's last silent was *Queen Kelly* (1929) starring Gloria Swanson, who poured a lot of her own money into the production. When Swanson realized that the film's plot, involving an American girl who inherits a string of European brothels, would bring down the wrath of every censor in the nation, she pulled out of the project, screaming "There's a madman in charge!" A hastily completed version of *Queen Kelly* was released in Europe, but it failed to re-establish von Stroheim. Upon the arrival of talkies, von Stroheim had little difficulty securing work as an actor, but directorial assignments were not forthcoming. When he was given one last opportunity at Fox Studios to direct the 1932 melodrama *Walking Down Broadway,* the film was yanked from his hands, completed by others, and released *sans* any director credit as *Hello Sister.* For the rest of his career, von Stroheim was confined to acting in other director's pictures. On rare occasions, his film roles would be more than worthwhile, such as his compassionate German prison-camp commander in Renoir's *Grande Illusion* (1937), his perceptive portrayal of General Rommel in Billy Wilder's *Five Graves to Cairo* (1943), and, best of all, his enigmatic butler Max von Mayerling in Wilder's *Sunset Boulevard* (1950). In the mid 1930s, von Stroheim contributed to several screenplays at MGM, often without credit. And

in the early 1950s, he starred in the pilot for a TV series about a disguise-prone detective, *The Man of Many Skins.* Shortly before his death in 1957, the nearly impoverished Erich von Stroheim was awarded the French Legion of Honor—characteristically taking the opportunity to rail against the Hollywood that had long since rejected him. **Selected Works:** *Grand Illusion* (1937)

# Max Von Sydow (Carl Adolf Von Sydow)

**Born:** April 10, 1929; Lund, Sweden

**Years Active in the Industry:** by decade

| 10s | 20s | 30s | 40s | 50s | 60s | 70s | 80s | 90s |
|-----|-----|-----|-----|-----|-----|-----|-----|-----|

Towering, cadaverous, Swedish leading actor Max Von Sydow trained for his craft at the Royal Dramatic Theatre School in Stockholm. His stage and film career began almost simultaneously; he made his first picture, *Only a Mother* (1949), at age 20. With *The Seventh Seal,* Von Sydow began his long and fruitful association with director Ingmar Bergman. Contrary to popular opinion, the actor played as many contemporary characters as he did ethereal and historical types, but common to all his roles was the theme of inward struggle against society's travails. Though renowned in art-film circles, Von Sydow was virtually unknown to the average American filmgoer in 1964, which is one of the reasons that director George Stevens cast the actor as Jesus in his multimillion-dollar epic *The Greatest Story Ever Told* (1965). Unlike other actors, such as H.B. Warner and Jeffrey Hunter, Von Sydow did not find his career in the doldrums after his portrayal of Jesus. In fact, he has gone out of his way to remove the "stigma" of the son of God by playing as many villainous or unpleasant characters as possible, including Ming the Merciless in 1980's *Flash Gordon.* In Woody Allen's *Hannah and Her Sisters* (1984), Von Sydow portrays a self-centered professor who delivers a long harangue *against* Jesus and Christianity; and in 1993, the actor was Satan Himself in *Needful Things* (1993). Von Sydow has alternated between bread-and-butter film assignments (notably *The Exorcist* [1974], in which he reportedly was so appalled by the scatalogical dialogue assigned to the "possessed" Linda Blair that he forgot his own lines) and roles which are more rewarding artistically than financially. In 1989, Max Von Sydow received his first Oscar nomination for *Pele the Conqueror.* **Selected Works:** *Best Intentions* (1992), *Until the End of the World* (1991), *Virgin Spring* (1959), *Emigrants* (1972)

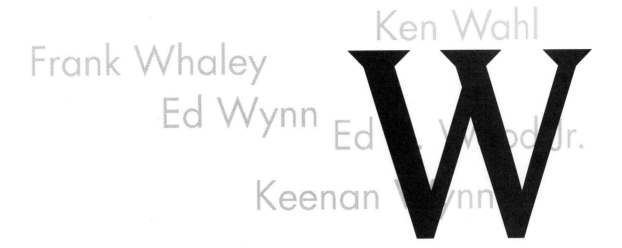

Ken Wahl

Frank Whaley

Ed Wynn    Ed Wood Jr.

Keenan Wynn

# Ken Wahl

**Born:** 1957; Chicago, IL

**Years Active in the Industry:** by decade

| 10s | 20s | 30s | 40s | 50s | 60s | 70s | 80s | 90s |
|-----|-----|-----|-----|-----|-----|-----|-----|-----|
|     |     |     |     |     |     |     |     |     |

Broad-shouldered American actor Ken Wahl has proven time and again that he's more than just a mass of muscle. After a handful of supporting roles, Wahl entered cult-film Valhalla with his starring role as a Bronx-Italian highschooler in *The Wanderers* (1979). Arguably, his best screen role was as the "see no evil" partner of conscience-stricken cop Paul Newman in *Fort Apache, the Bronx* (1981). His many film appearances aside, Wahl's popularity rests with his three-year performance as underground cop Vinnie Teranova in *Wiseguys* (1987-90), which was impressive enough to make viewers forget Wahl's earlier series-TV stint in the unlamented adventure series *Double Dare* (1985).

# Tom Waits

**Born:** December 7, 1949; Pomona, CA

**Years Active in the Industry:** by decade

| 10s | 20s | 30s | 40s | 50s | 60s | 70s | 80s | 90s |
|-----|-----|-----|-----|-----|-----|-----|-----|-----|
|     |     |     |     |     |     |     |     |     |

Gravel-voiced, versatile singer/song writer Tom Waits has composed and played music in a variety of films ranging from Coppola's *One from the Heart* (1982) to Jean-Luc Godard's *First Name: Carmen* (1983). He has also acted in a number of off-beat independent productions. On or off camera Waits is a colorful, quirky character noted for his surreal humor. Many of Wait's songs reflected his interest in the movies either with direct references or sly musical suggestions. During the late 1970s he became more directly involved in film, composing songs and even playing piano

onscreen in *Paradise Alley* (1979). In the early eighties Waits teamed up with Coppola, first with the Greek Choir-like narration for *One from the Heart* and then as an actor in several of his films. In the first, Waits was given a one-line role as a bar owner in *The Outsiders* (1983). He next gave Waits a bigger part as Benny in *Rumblefish* (1983). Coppola then dressed the rangy singer in a tuxedo and cast him as the MC in *The Cotton Club* (1984). Though he was often offered roles to play nutcases and psychos in commercial films, Waits has preferred to working in independent productions such as *Down by Law* (1986). He entered mainstream film with 1987's offbeat drama *Ironweed*. He played himself in the concert film *Big Time* (1988), in which he performs his stage musical Frank's *"Wild Years"* and plays the roles of a bored box-office manager, usher, and a lighting grip. He also appeared in *Bram Stoker's Dracula* (1992). **Selected Works:** *At Play in the Fields of the Lord* (1991), *Queens Logic* (1991), *Fisher King* (1991), *Short Cuts* (1993)

# Andrzej Wajda

**Born:** March 6, 1926; Suwalki, Poland

**Years Active in the Industry:** by decade

| 10s | 20s | 30s | 40s | 50s | 60s | 70s | 80s | 90s |
|-----|-----|-----|-----|-----|-----|-----|-----|-----|
|     |     |     |     |     |     |     |     |     |

The son of a Polish cavalry officer who was killed early in World War II, director Andrzej Wajda was a teenager when he fought in the Resistance movement against the Nazis. After the war, Wajda studied to be a painter before entering the Lodz film school. On the heels of his apprenticeship to director Alexander Ford, Wajda was given the opportunity to direct a film on his own. With *A Generation* (1954), Wajda poured out all his bitterness and disillusionment regarding blind patriotism and wartime heroics, using as his alter ego a young, James Dean-style antihero played by Zbigniew Cybulski. The Wajda/Cybulski team went on to make two more films of ever-increasing brilliance, which further developed the anti-war theme of *A Generation: Kanal* (1957) and *Ashes and Diamonds* (1958). While perfectly capable of turning out mainstream commercial pictures (often dismissed as "trivial" by his critics), Wajda was more interested in works of allegory and symbolism, with certain symbolic devices (such as setting fire to a glass of liquor, representing the flame of youthful idealism that was extinguished by the war) popping up again and again in his films. In 1967, Wajda's friend and colleague Zbignew Cybulski was killed in an auto accident, whereupon the director articulated his grief with what is considered his most personal film, *Everything for Sale* (1968). Wajda's later devotion to Poland's burgeoning Solidarity movement was manifested in *Man of Marble* (1979) and *Man of Iron* (1981), with Solidarity leader Lech Walesa appearing as himself in the latter film. The director's involvement in this movement would prompt the Polish government to force Wajda's production company out of business. After several years' exile in France, Wajda returned to his politically liberated homeland in 1989. In the early 1990s, Andrzej Wajda was elected a senator and also appointed artistic director of Warsaw's Teatr Powschensky. **Selected Works:** *Danton* (1982), *Korczak* (1990), *Conductor* (1993), *Landscape After the Battle* (1970), *Nastazja* (1994)

# Christopher Walken (Ronald Walken)

**Born:** March 31, 1943; Astoria, NY

**Years Active in the Industry:** by decade

| 10ˢ | 20ˢ | 30ˢ | 40ˢ | 50ˢ | 60ˢ | 70ˢ | 80ˢ | 90ˢ |
|-----|-----|-----|-----|-----|-----|-----|-----|-----|
|     |     |     |     |     |     |     |     |     |

Walken debuted on Broadway at age 16 in Elia Kazan's production of Archibald Macleish's *J.B.* After graduating from college he returned to the New York stage, where he appeared in several

musicals. Having acted under the name "Ronald Walken," he changed his name to "Christopher" when he began getting lead roles. He went on to win much acclaim in Shakespearean roles before breaking into films in 1969. While never abandoning the stage, he went on to become a well-known, popular screen actor, particularly after his first major role, that of a Vietnam soldier in *The Deer Hunter* (1978), for which he won a Best Supporting Actor Oscar. **Selected Works:** *Batman Returns* (1992), *The Comfort of Strangers* (1991), *King of New York* (1990), *Sarah, Plain & Tall* (1991), *Pulp Fiction* (1994)

# Robert Walker

**Born:** October 14, 1919; Salt Lake City, UT
**Died:** August 28, 1951; Brentwood, CA

**Years Active in the Industry:** by decade

| 10ˢ | 20ˢ | 30ˢ | 40ˢ | 50ˢ | 60ˢ | 70ˢ | 80ˢ | 90ˢ |
|-----|-----|-----|-----|-----|-----|-----|-----|-----|
|     |     |     |     |     |     |     |     |     |

In his late teens he showed acting talent in college productions, leading him to enroll at New York's Academy of Dramatic Arts in 1938. In 1939 he married fellow student Phyllis Isley, later to become actress Jennifer Jones; they went to Hollywood, but neither of them could get more than bit roles onscreen. They returned to New York, where Walker landed a regular role on a radio series. In 1942 they returned to Hollywood, and both soon became successful screen actors. Walker landed boy-next-door leads in several films. In 1945 he and Jones divorced. He was also troubled by alcoholism, and during the next few years he had several nervous breakdowns. In 1948 he married the daughter of director John Ford, but six weeks later the marriage ended. Shortly thereafter he was arrested for drunken driving, and a nervous breakdown led to his institutionalization for nearly a year. He returned to film work and won raves for his portrayal of a charming psychopath in Hitchcock's *Strangers on a Train* (1951). He died suddenly in 1951 after doctors had given him sedatives. He was the father of actors Robert Walker Jr. and Michael Walker. **Selected Works:** *Madame Curie* (1943), *Since You Went Away* (1944), *Thirty Seconds over Tokyo* (1944)

# Eli Wallach

**Born:** December 7, 1915; Brooklyn, NY

**Years Active in the Industry:** by decade

| 10ˢ | 20ˢ | 30ˢ | 40ˢ | 50ˢ | 60ˢ | 70ˢ | 80ˢ | 90ˢ |
|-----|-----|-----|-----|-----|-----|-----|-----|-----|
|     |     |     |     |     |     |     |     |     |

He first acted at age 15 in a boy's club play, going on to train for the stage at New York's Neighborhood Playhouse. After World War II service, Wallach made his Broadway debut in 1945; throughout the next decade he became a highly respected "Method" actor known for his great versatility. He debuted onscreen in a major role in Elia Kazan's *Baby Doll* (1956). With occasional breaks, he has had a busy screen career since 1960; at first, he tended to play mean heavies. In the '80s he did much work in TV movies and made-for-cable movies. He is married to actress Anne Jackson, with whom he has frequently performed. **Selected Works:** *Article 99* (1992), *The Godfather, Part 3* (1990), *Legacy of Lies* (1992), *The Magnificent Seven* (1960), *Night and the City* (1992)

# J.T. Walsh

**Born:** San Francisco, CA

**Years Active in the Industry:** by decade

| 10s | 20s | 30s | 40s | 50s | 60s | 70s | 80s | 90s |
|-----|-----|-----|-----|-----|-----|-----|-----|-----|
|     |     |     |     |     |     |     | ■   | ■   |

Actor J.T. Walsh has played in many films, usually as a scheming executive or petty anal-retentive authority. He was born in San Francisco, but raised in Newport, Rhode Island and Europe. Until joining an off-Broadway theater company at age 30, Walsh worked in sales. He soon racked up substantial stage credits, and was nominated for a Tony for his work in Mamet's *Glengarry Glen Ross*. In 1987, Walsh broke into films in two Barry Levinson vehicles, *Tin Men* and *Good Morning, Vietnam,* in which he had small roles. Still, these roles led to larger supporting roles in other mainstream films such as *Crazy People* (1990) and *Blue Chips* (1994). Walsh continues to work steadily in films. **Selected Works:** *Backdraft* (1991), *Few Good Men* (1992), *Grifters* (1990), *Client* (1994), *Last Seduction* (1994)

## M. Emmet Walsh (Michael Emmet Walsh)

**Born:** March 22, 1935; Ogdensburg, NY

**Years Active in the Industry:** by decade

| 10s | 20s | 30s | 40s | 50s | 60s | 70s | 80s | 90s |
|-----|-----|-----|-----|-----|-----|-----|-----|-----|
|     |     |     |     |     |     | ■   | ■   | ■   |

Rotund character actor M. Emmet Walsh has become one of the most prolific supporting players in contemporary Hollywood. He is usually cast as the slimy characters from society's dregs. He didn't begin his acting career until the late 1960s when he began playing character parts on television shows like *Little House on the Prairie* and *The Rockford Files*. By the 1980's Walsh was well-known in the industry for his "seedy" characters that worked as well in comedy as they did in serious drama. His most memorable role was as a co-star in the Coen's *Blood Simple* in which he played a souless amoral detective. He has also played in cult favorites such as 1987's *Raising Arizona*. In *Clean and Sober* (1988) Walsh got to show his versatility by playing a kindly recovering alcoholic who helps lead Michael Keaton through his own addiction. **Selected Works:** *Blade Runner* (1982), *Narrow Margin* (1990), *Silkwood* (1983), *White Sands* (1992), *Music of Chance* (1993)

## Raoul Walsh

**Born:** March 11, 1887; New York, NY
**Died:** 1980

**Years Active in the Industry:** by decade

| 10s | 20s | 30s | 40s | 50s | 60s | 70s | 80s | 90s |
|-----|-----|-----|-----|-----|-----|-----|-----|-----|
|     | ■   | ■   | ■   | ■   | ■   |     |     |     |

One of Hollywood's most prolific and respected action directors, Raoul Walsh was also one of the longest-lived figures in film, with a career that spanned almost a half-century. After running away

from home as a boy and working in a variety of capacities, including as a cowboy in the West, Walsh drifted into stage acting in New York and later into motion pictures as an actor. He became an assistant director to D.W. Griffith and, in 1914, made his first movie. By the mid 1920s, Walsh had a reputation for direct, straightforward, no frills narrative, and his style was particularly suited to action films and outdoor dramas, although his biggest film of that decade was the fantasy epic *The Thief of Bagdad,* produced by and starring Douglas Fairbanks Sr., which continues to be shown seven decades later. His work in the 1930s, mostly for 20th Century-Fox, embraced comedy and drama in equal measure, but it was with Warner Bros., beginning at the end of the 1930s, that Walsh came into his own, directing such classics as *The Roaring Twenties* (1939), *They Drive By Night* (1940), *High Sierra* (1941), *Desperate Journey* (1942), and *Northern Pursuit* (1943), starring James Cagney, Humphrey Bogart, and Errol Flynn. Despite his reputation as an action director, Walsh's movies were usually much more sophisticated than was typical for the genre—he revelled in psychological themes, and he loved offbeat characterizations and unusual narrative structures, attributes best reflected in the dark Western drama *Pursued* (1947), starring Robert Mitchum, and the crime film *White Heat* (1949), with James Cagney. He also served as unofficial co-director on one of Humphrey Bogart's most interesting later movies, *The Enforcer* (1951). His later movies showed a slackening of style, and he never did seem as effective working in color as he did in black-and-white. Walsh lost an eye while working on *In Old Arizona* in 1929, and his deteriorating sight in the other eye led to his retirement in 1964.

## Tracey Walter

**Born:** November 25, 1942; Jersey City, NJ

**Years Active in the Industry:** by decade

| 10s | 20s | 30s | 40s | 50s | 60s | 70s | 80s | 90s |
|-----|-----|-----|-----|-----|-----|-----|-----|-----|
|     |     |     |     |     |     |     | ■   | ■   |

The memorable but fleeting appearance of American actor Tracey Walter as "Bob the Goon" in *Batman* was typical of Walter's career. In the grand tradition of such Hollywood character actors as Percy Helton, Dick Wessel and Louis Jean Heydt, Walter is in the "who *is* that?" category—familiar yet anonymous—and has developed a cult following amongst cinema buffs. The stage-trained Walters can be seen in such films as *Repo Man* (1984) *City Slickers* (1991), *Pacific Heights* (1992), and *Philadelphia* (1993). As far back as the 1984 critic's-darling sitcom *Best of the West*, Walter played Frog, the knuckle-dragging henchman of villain Leonard Frey. **Selected Works:** *Delusion* (1991), *Liquid Dreams* (1992), *Silence of the Lambs* (1991), *Young Guns, Part 2* (1990), *Not of This World* (1991)

# Julie Walters

**Born:** February 22, 1950; Birmingham, England

**Years Active in the Industry:** by decade

| 10ˢ | 20ˢ | 30ˢ | 40ˢ | 50ˢ | 60ˢ | 70ˢ | 80ˢ | 90ˢ |
|---|---|---|---|---|---|---|---|---|
| | | | | | | | | |

An alumnus of Manchester Polytech, British-born Julie Walters abandoned a nursing career in favor of acting—a fact that would be recounted time and time again in her early interviews. Walters appeared as an actress, singer, dancer or combination thereof in a variety of British stage presentations. She won a Tony award for her "modern Eliza Doolittle" characterization in the London and Broadway play *Educating Rita* and was nominated for an Oscar after costarring in the 1983 version. Walter's next film triumph was 1987's *Personal Services*, in which she played a strictly-business character based on real-life "madam" Cynthia Payne. Walter's first American film role was as a Buffalo, New York housewife-turned-tapdancer in 1991's *Stepping Out*. **Selected Works:** *Summer House* (1993), *Just Like a Woman* (1995)

# Wayne Wang

**Born:** January 12, 1949; Hong Kong

**Years Active in the Industry:** by decade

| 10ˢ | 20ˢ | 30ˢ | 40ˢ | 50ˢ | 60ˢ | 70ˢ | 80ˢ | 90ˢ |
|---|---|---|---|---|---|---|---|---|
| | | | | | | | | |

Director Wayne Wang grew up in a Hong Kong household that worshipped at the altar of Hollywood—he himself was named for movie star John Wayne. After attending California's College of  Arts and Sciences, Wang returned to Hong Kong hoping to become a film "auteur." However, at that time, his native country's film industry was geared more to chop-socky than to the cinema of personal statement. After TV work, Wang handled direction of the Hong Kong-based scenes of the American film *Golden Needles* (1975),

then codirected a melodrama shot in San Francisco, *A Man, A Woman and A Killer* (1975). Realizing that the mainstream would continue to stifle his creativity, Wang sought out funding from various arts foundations, then produced, directed, edited and cowrote the Chinatown culture-clash drama *Chan is Missing* (1981) on a beggarly $22,000 budget. Some felt that the critical adulation heaped upon *Chan is Missing* grew solely out of respect for Wang's ability to do so much with so little; in fact, the film is a brilliant work, fully deserving its vaunted reputation. Upon attaining fame, Wang discovered that he was most effective marching to his own beat; an attempt at "popular" moviemaking, *Slam Dance* (1987), failed to make the turnstyles click. Wang's best (and best-received) projects include *Dim Sum: A Little Bit of Heart* (1988), *Eat a Bowl of Tea* (1989) and *The Joy Luck Club* (1993). Wayne Wang is married to actress Cora Miao, who often appears in her husband's films. **Selected Works:** *Strangers* (1991), *Smoke* (1995), *Blue in the Face* (1995)

# Fred Ward

**Born:** 1943; San Diego, CA

**Years Active in the Industry:** by decade

| 10ˢ | 20ˢ | 30ˢ | 40ˢ | 50ˢ | 60ˢ | 70ˢ | 80ˢ | 90ˢ |
|---|---|---|---|---|---|---|---|---|
| | | | | | | | | |

After service with the U.S. Air Force Fred Ward studied acting in New York and Rome, where he worked in mime, dubbed Italian movies, and appeared in two Roberto Rossellini films. Back in America he did much experimental stage work and also had roles on TV. He debuted onscreen in America in 1978, then appeared in several films during the next few years; his screen career took off in 1983, when he appeared in *The Right Stuff*, *Silkwood*, and *Uncommon Valor*. He went on to become a busy screen actor in supporting roles and some leads, but he has yet to appear in a major hit. **Selected Works:** *Cast a Deadly Spell* (1991), *Henry and June* (1990), *Miami Blues* (1990), *The Player* (1992), *Thunderheart* (1992)

# Rachel Ward

**Born:** 1957; Oxfordshire, England

**Years Active in the Industry:** by decade

| 10ˢ | 20ˢ | 30ˢ | 40ˢ | 50ˢ | 60ˢ | 70ˢ | 80ˢ | 90ˢ |
|---|---|---|---|---|---|---|---|---|
| | | | | | | | | |

Former model, and daughter of the Earl of Dudley, actress Rachel Ward has appeared in several mainstream films and on television primarily during the 1980s. She attended Byram Art School in London before leaving at 16 to become a top fashion model who made many television commercials. In 1983 Ward, with her thick dark hair, husky voice, and large eyes, was voted one of the ten most beautiful women in the U.S. Although she had appeared in two slasher movies, she made her official feature film debut in *Sharky's Machine* in 1981. More films followed, but she did-n't become really well-known until she starred opposite Richard Chamberlain in the popular television mini-series "The Thorn Birds." Ward disappeared from pictures for three years as she played wife to husband Bryan Brown, whom she met on the "Thorn Birds" set, and studied acting. She then reappeared in 1987, play-ing opposite her husband in *The Good Wife*. Though she has con-tinued to work sporadically in films, she has yet to achieve true stardom. **Selected Works:** *After Dark, My Sweet* (1990), *Black Magic* (1992), *Double Jeopardy* (1992), *Wide Sargasso Sea* (1992), *And the Sea Will Tell, Part 1* (1991)

# Jack Warden

**Born:** September 18, 1920; Newark, NJ

### Years Active in the Industry: by decade

| 10s | 20s | 30s | 40s | 50s | 60s | 70s | 80s | 90s |
|-----|-----|-----|-----|-----|-----|-----|-----|-----|
|     |     |     |     | ■   | ■   | ■   | ■   | ■   |

Gruff-mannered and gravelly-voiced character actor Jack Warden has had success working on stage, screen, and television. Before becoming an actor, Warden served as a paratrooper during World War II. After briefly working in Dallas repertory, he began a distinguished career on Broadway. He has also made many guest appearances on television. Warden has been working in feature films since the early '50s when he was usually cast as a tough guy, and most frequently as a military man. During his long career, Warden has been nominated for two Academy Awards for best sup-porting actor: first in *Shampoo* (1975) and then in *Heaven Can Wait* (1978). **Selected Works:** *Judgment* (1990), *Night and the City* (1992), *Verdict* (1982), *Bullets over Broadway* (1994), *Things to Do in Denver When You're Dead* (1995)

# Andy Warhol (Andrew Warhola)

**Born:** August 8, 1927; Cleveland, OH
**Died:** February 22, 1987; New York, NY

### Years Active in the Industry: by decade

| 10s | 20s | 30s | 40s | 50s | 60s | 70s | 80s | 90s |
|-----|-----|-----|-----|-----|-----|-----|-----|-----|
|     |     |     |     |     | ■   |     |     |     |

American pop artist Andy Warhol became himself a pop icon, symbolizing the wild decadence of 'the beautiful people" of the 1970s. He studied at the Carnegie Institute of Technology and then designed advertisements for women's shoes. After gaining notoriety for his pop-art renditions of things such as Campbell soup cans and silk screens of Marilyn Monroe, Warhol began making experimental films during the early '60s. Most of his early works were little more than passive chronicles of almost nothing. For example, in the film *Sleep*, he simply recorded a man sleeping for eight hours. Such endeavors were heralded as groundbreaking by other experimental filmmakers, but the public and most critics

generally regarded them as wastes of film, and their time. Still, Warhol continued making these plotless films until he eventually began adding crude soundtracks and sketchy scripts. Many of these films are filled with his 'players': the beautiful people, the 'freaks,' and the wealthy dilettantes that constantly surrounded the artist and his film "factory." His films can be considered a form of cinema verite, a voyeur's delight of strange people doing equally strange things. Some of the "players" Warhol turned into under-ground superstars include Candy Darling, Viva, Holly Woodlawn, and Ingrid Superstar. These stars simply played versions of them-selves leaving the viewer to decide if they are in fact real people or simply fantastical figures. Many of his films are centered on sex and death. The sex in his films is often explicit and transcends tra-ditional gender boundaries. In 1968, Warhol was mortally wounded by a disgruntled "factory" reject. While healing, he began to withdraw from filmmaking, closed the 'factory,' and turned over the reins to other filmmakers such as Paul Morrissey, who helped make subsequent films more commercially accessible. Morrissey was behind Warhol's best known films *Frankenstein* and *Dracula,* both of which he made while in Rome in 1974. Though he stopped making films, Warhol did continue his voyeurism of the strange lives of his illustrious friends via the Polaroid camera he carried with him until he died in 1987.

# Jack L. Warner

**Born:** August 2, 1892; London, Ontario, Canada
**Died:** 1978

### Years Active in the Industry: by decade

| 10s | 20s | 30s | 40s | 50s | 60s | 70s | 80s | 90s |
|-----|-----|-----|-----|-----|-----|-----|-----|-----|
|     | ■   | ■   |     |     |     |     |     |     |

One of the longest lived of the legendary Hollywood moguls, Canadian-born Jack Warner (of Polish-Jewish extraction) was the youngest of the four Warner brothers (there were 12 chil-dren in all) to venture into the movie business in 1905. In 1912 they went into actual film production, and the studio called Warner Bros. was established in the mid 1920s; its initial success was as-sured two years later with *The Jazz Singer,* the first talking picture. The studio developed a reputation during the 1930s as the most "street smart" of the Hollywood organizations, with its gangster films—sparked by a new young discovery named James Cagney and, later, Humphrey Bogart—and dazzling (yet surprisingly gritty) musicals, most notably *42nd Street* (1933) and its various follow-ups, driven by the choreography of Busby Berkeley. Warner Bros. was also responsible for several more ambitious films, in-cluding the controversial social drama *I am a Fugitive from a Chain Gang* (1932) and the Shakespearean adaptation *A Midsummer Night's Dream* (1934). By the middle and late 1930s, it had a star roster, the envy of other studios, that included Errol Flynn, Bogart, Cagney, Bette Davis, Paul Muni, John Garfield, a powerhouse pro-ducer in the guise of Hal Wallis, and a directorial staff—led by

Michael Curtiz and John Huston—capable of handling virtually any type of film well. Even the studio's B-level stars, such as Ronald Reagan, were among the best of their kind and superior to the leading men of several of the other studios. Warner kept his share in the studio long after the others sold out their interests, and was still making good deals well into the 1950s, most notably when he secured the film rights—in partnership with CBS, which had financed the play—for *My Fair Lady* (1960) As late as 1972, he was active as an independent producer, bringing the musical *1776* to the screen, ironically the same year that he also produced *Dirty Little Billy,* an all-but-forgotten account of Billy the Kid's life and career.

# Lesley Ann Warren

**Born:** August 16, 1946; New York, NY

**Years Active in the Industry:** by decade

| 10s | 20s | 30s | 40s | 50s | 60s | 70s | 80s | 90s |
|-----|-----|-----|-----|-----|-----|-----|-----|-----|
|     |     |     |     |     |     |     |     |     |

Lesley Ann Warren trained for the stage at the Lee Strasberg Studio, having made her Broadway debut at age 16 in 1963. Warner played the title role in a TV version of Rogers and Hammerstein's *Cinderella;* spotted by a Disney scout, she appeared in a couple of family films in the late '60s. In 1972 she began appearing in mainstream films, and has had a sporadic screen career since However, she has tended to appear in unpopular films. For her work in *Victor/Victoria* (1982) she received a Best Supporting Actress Oscar nomination. She was a regular on the TV series "Mission: Impossible" for a season, and appeared in many TV movies in the '70s and '80s. **Selected Works:** *Life Stinks* (1991)

# Denzel Washington

**Born:** December 28, 1954; Mt. Vernon, NY

**Years Active in the Industry:** by decade

| 10s | 20s | 30s | 40s | 50s | 60s | 70s | 80s | 90s |
|-----|-----|-----|-----|-----|-----|-----|-----|-----|
|     |     |     |     |     |     |     |     |     |

Denzel Washington is a distinguished actor known for his intelligence and versatility. After earning a BA in Journalism from Fordham University, he studied acting at the esteemed American Conservatory Theater School in San Francisco. He gained national popularity in 1982 as a regular on the television series "St. Elsewhere" before breaking into feature films later that year in *Carbon Copy,* in which he played the black illegitimate son of a white man. Many of Washington's films have centered around racism, and his next film *A Soldier's Story* (1984) was no exception. He appeared in another film before landing the role that made him a star as South African anti-apartheid activist Steve Biko in Attenborough's *Cry Freedom.* His portrayal of Biko was so realistic and powerful

that he was nominated for an Oscar for Best Supporting Actor. Two years later, he won an Oscar for his portrayal of a brave and embittered runaway slave in *Glory.* Since then he has steadily appeared in a wide variety of films ranging from comedies (*Heart Condition* [1990]) to thrillers (*Ricochet* [1991]). Not all of these films were successful. In 1990 he played a talented, but self-centered jazz musician in Spike Lee's *Mo' Better Blues.* In 1992, he again worked with Lee for his most challenging and controversial role as the lead in *Malcolm X.* He later received an Oscar nomination for his portrayal. **Selected Works:** *Mississippi Masala* (1992), *The Pelican Brief* (1993), *Philadelphia* (1993), *Virtuosity* (1995), *Devil in a Blue Dress* (1995)

# John Waters

**Born:** 1946; Baltimore, MD

**Years Active in the Industry:** by decade

| 10s | 20s | 30s | 40s | 50s | 60s | 70s | 80s | 90s |
|-----|-----|-----|-----|-----|-----|-----|-----|-----|
|     |     |     |     |     |     |     |     |     |

A product of a very straight middle-class household in Baltimore, John Waters is best known for his outrageous independent films, which frequently challenge the sensibilities of audiences

with their stories about trans-sexuals, transvestites, castration, and other risque material. Waters attended New York University but had an uneasy relationship with the school authorities. He began his career as an underground filmmaker in New York, making shorts featuring such performers as the transvestite star Divine, whom he had known for years. His first real underground hit was *Mondo Trasho,* which he followed up with *Pink Flamingos* and *Polyester.* In the late 1980s, Waters released his first mainstream film, *Hairspray,* which became an unexpected hit with its parody of early 1960s sexual and social morays. His 1990 film, *Cry Baby,* was also extremely well received by general audiences and critics alike. **Selected Works:** *Serial Mom* (1994)

# Sam Waterston

**Born:** November 15, 1940; Cambridge, MA

**Years Active in the Industry:** by decade

| 10s | 20s | 30s | 40s | 50s | 60s | 70s | 80s | 90s |
|-----|-----|-----|-----|-----|-----|-----|-----|-----|

Educated at Yale and the Sorbonne, Sam Waterston is far more than the "general purpose actor" he was pegged to be by one well-known film historian. A leading man on the New York stage, Waterston has been in films as a character actor since 1967's *Fitzwilly.* Non-New York audiences were made acutely aware of the depth and breadth of Waterston's talents when, in 1972, he starred as Benedick in the CBS TV adaptation of Joseph Papp's staging of *Much Ado About Nothing.* He proved to be the best of the screen's Nick Carraways when he was cast in that expository role in the 1974 version of *The Great Gatsby;* subsequent films ranged from the midnight-movie favorite *Rancho Deluxe* (1975) to the unmitigated disaster *Heaven's Gate* (1979). In the early 1980s, Waterston was "adopted" by Woody Allen, joining the director's ever-increasing unofficial stock company for such films as *Hannah and Her Sisters* (1985) and *September* (1989). Waterston was nominated for an Academy Award for his powerful portrayal of a conscience-stricken American journalist in *The Killing Fields* (1984). Sam Waterston's TV credits include the title roles in the miniseries *Oppenheimer* and *Gore Vidal's Lincoln,* and starring assignments on the TV series *I'll Fly Away* and *Law and Order.* **Selected Works:** *Crimes and Misdemeanors* (1989), *Interiors* (1978), *Mindwalk* (1991), *The Man in the Moon* (1991)

# David Watkin

**Born:** March 23, 1925; Margate, England

**Years Active in the Industry:** by decade

| 10s | 20s | 30s | 40s | 50s | 60s | 70s | 80s | 90s |
|-----|-----|-----|-----|-----|-----|-----|-----|-----|

The number of British cinematographers who started out as studio messenger boys would probably fill the Albert Hall. One such cinematographer was David Watkin, who went from gopher to documentary cameraman in 1955. His work on dramatic films have demonstrated a rare versatility; Watkin was equally adept at the "mod" silliness of *Help* (1965) and *The Knack* (1966) as he was at the sweaty asylum agonies of *Marat/Sade* (1967). Some of his best work has been concentrated on period films, taking full advantage of the extreme color contrasts (from purple pageantry to murky mud) of days gone by: *The Devils* (1971), *The Three Musketeers* (1973), *The Four Musketeers* (1974), *Robin and Marian* (1976), *Yentl* (1983), *Hamlet* (1990), and many others. David Watkin won an Academy

Award for his lush, lavish work on the Oscar-winning *Out of Africa* (1985). **Selected Works:** *Chariots of Fire* (1981), *Moonstruck* (1987), *This Boy's Life* (1993), *Used People* (1992), *Bopha* (1993)

# Franz Waxman (Franz Wachsmann)

**Born:** December 24, 1906; Konigshntte, Germany (Chorzow)
**Died:** 1967

**Years Active in the Industry:** by decade

| 10s | 20s | 30s | 40s | 50s | 60s | 70s | 80s | 90s |
|-----|-----|-----|-----|-----|-----|-----|-----|-----|

Franz Waxman was among Hollywood's most talented composers of musical scores, best known for his suspenseful scores of many Hitchcock films. He was born Franz Wachsmann in 1906 in what is now Chrozow, Poland, and began playing piano as a child. At age 17, he enrolled in the Dresden Music Academy and later in the Berlin Music Conservatory, working nights playing piano in nightclubs and cafes. After a brief stint in the UFA, Waxman began scoring German films until 1934 when he was beaten up in Berlin by an anti-Semitic street gang. This caused him to move first to Paris, and then to the U.S. where he began scoring films in Hollywood. He founded the Los Angeles Music Festival in 1947. In 1950, he won his first Oscar for the music of *Sunset Boulevard.* He won another in 1951 for *A Place in the Sun,* and was nominated several times after that. **Selected Works:** *Humoresque* (1946), *The Nun's Story* (1959), *Objective, Burma!* (1945), *Rebecca* (1940), *Suspicion* (1941), *Young in Heart* (1938)

# Damon Wayans

**Born:** 1960; New York, NY

**Years Active in the Industry:** by decade

| 10s | 20s | 30s | 40s | 50s | 60s | 70s | 80s | 90s |
|-----|-----|-----|-----|-----|-----|-----|-----|-----|

Like his older brother Keenen Ivory Wayans, African American performer Damon Wayans matriculated from standup comedy to series television to movies. He was a regular on TV's *Saturday Night Live* and—along with virtually eveyone else in the Wayans family—*In Living Color.* Exhibiting a fondness for the outrageous, Wayans attracted both adulation and condemnation for his many *In Living Color* characterizations, notably the dour Homey the Clown and the excessively effeminate cohost of the "Men on Film" skits. Damon's first film was 1984's *Beverly Hills Cop 2;* he has since functioned as costar (with brother Marlon), coproducer, cowriter and director of *Mo' Money* (1992), and has been heard but not seen as the voice of a troublesome baby in *Look Who's Talking 2* (1992). It boggles the mind to contemplate the notion of Damon Wayans playing a role once essayed by Charlton Heston, but that's just what happened when Wayans starred in 1995's *Major Payne,* a remake of Heston's *The Private War of Major Benson* (1955). **Selected Works:** *The Last Boy Scout* (1991)

# Keenen Ivory Wayans

**Born:** June 8, 1958; New York, NY

**Years Active in the Industry:** by decade

| 10ˢ | 20ˢ | 30ˢ | 40ˢ | 50ˢ | 60ˢ | 70ˢ | 80ˢ | 90ˢ |
|-----|-----|-----|-----|-----|-----|-----|-----|-----|
|     |     |     |     |     |     |     | ■ | ■ |

African American "renaissance" man Keenen Ivory Wayans is but one member of a large and excessively talented performing family. His siblings include Damon, Kim, Shawn, and Marlon, all of whom have worked with Keenen in some capacity during his brief but spectacular career. A graduate of the Tuskegee Institute, Wayans' entree into the comedy world was as a standup performer, then as a scenarist for *Hollywood Shuffle* (1987) and *Eddie Murphy Raw* (1987). Wayan's big-screen breakthrough was *I'm Gonna Git You Sucka* (1988), a rollicking parody of 1970s blaxploitation flicks which he wrote, directed, and acted in. In 1988, Wayans produced and starred in the Fox Network's iconoclastic, influential, cutting-edge comedy/variety series *In Living Color,* which proved not only a boost for Wayans and his entire family, but also solidified the stardom of white comedian Jim Carrey. Keenen Ivory Wayans' projects of the early 1990s haven't maintained the quality or profitability of his earlier work, though he remains a powerhouse performing presence. **Selected Works:** *The Five Heartbeats* (1991)

# John Wayne (Marion Michael Morrison)

**Born:** May 26, 1907; Encino, CA
**Died:** 1979

**Years Active in the Industry:** by decade

| 10ˢ | 20ˢ | 30ˢ | 40ˢ | 50ˢ | 60ˢ | 70ˢ | 80ˢ | 90ˢ |
|-----|-----|-----|-----|-----|-----|-----|-----|-----|
|     | ■ | ■ | ■ | ■ | ■ | ■ |     |     |

Arguably the most popular—and certainly the busiest—movie leading man in Hollywood history, John Wayne entered the film business while working as a laborer on the Fox lot during summer vacations from USC, which he attended on a football scholarship. He met and was befriended by John Ford, a young director who was beginning to make a name for himself in action films, comedies, and dramas. Wayne was cast in small roles in Ford's late 1920s films, occasionally under the name Duke Morrison. It was Ford who recommended Wayne to director Raoul Walsh for the male lead in the 1930 west-

ern epic *The Big Trail*—although it was a failure at the box office, the movie showed Wayne's potential as a leading man, and during the next nine years, be busied himself in a multitude of B Westerns and serials, most notably *Shadow of the Eagle* and *The Three Musketeers* series, in between occasional bit parts in larger features such as Warner Bros.' *Baby Face,* starring Barbara Stanwyck. But it was in action roles that Wayne excelled, exuding a warm and imposing manliness on screen that audiences—both men and women—could respond to. In 1939, Ford cast Wayne as the Ringo Kid in the western adventure *Stagecoach,* a brilliant western of modest scale but tremendous power (and incalculable importance to the genre), and the actor finally showed what he could do. Wayne nearly stole a picture filled with Oscar-caliber performances, and his career was made. He starred in most of Ford's subsequent major films, whether Westerns (*Fort Apache* [1948], *She Wore A Yellow Ribbon* [1949], *Rio Grande* [1950], *The Searchers* [1956]), war pictures (*They Were Expendable* [1945]), or serious dramas (*The Quiet Man* [1952], in which Wayne also directed some of the action sequences). He also starred in numerous movies for other directors, including several extremely popular World War II thrillers (*Flying Tigers* [1942], *Back To Bataan* [1945], *Fighting Seabees* [1944], *Sands of Iwo Jima* [1949]), costume actioners (*Reap The Wild Wind* [1942], *Wake of the Red Witch*[1949]), and Westerns *(Red River* [1948]). His box-office popularity rose steadily through the 1940s, and by the beginning of the 1950s he'd also begun producing movies through his company Wayne-Fellowes, later Batjac, in association with his sons Michael and Patrick (who also became an actor). Most of these films were extremely successful and included *Angel And The Badman* (1947), *Island In The Sky* (1953), *The High and the Mighty* (1954), and *Hondo* (1953). The 1958 Western *Rio Bravo,* directed by Howard Hawks, proved so popular that it was remade by Hawks and Wayne twice, once as *El Dorado* and later as *Rio Lobo.* At the end of the 1950s, Wayne began taking on bigger films, most notably *The Alamo* (1960), which he produced and directed as well as starred in. It was well received but had to be cut to sustain any box-office success (the film was restored to full-length in 1992). During the early 1960s, concerned over the growing liberal slant in American politics, Wayne emerged as a spokesman for conservative causes, especially support for America's role in Vietnam, which put him at odds with a new generation of journalists and film critics. Coupled with his advancing age, and a seeming tendency to overact, he became a target for liberals and leftists. However, his movies remained popular. *McLintock!,* which, despite well articulated statements against racism and the mistreatment of Native Americans, and in support of environmentalism, seemed to confirm the left's worst fears, but also earned over $10 million and made the list of top-grossing films of 1963-64. Virtually all of his subsequent movies, including the pro-Vietnam War drama *The Green Berets* (1968), were very popular with audiences, but not with critics. Further controversy erupted with the release of *The Cowboys,* which outraged liberals with its seeming justification of violence as a solution to lawlessness, but it was successful enough to generate a short-lived television series. Amid all of the shouting and agonizing over his politics, Wayne won an Oscar for his role as marshal Rooster Cogburn in *True Grit,* a part that he later reprised in a sea sequel. Wayne weathered the Vietnam War, but, by then, time had become his enemy. His action films saw him working alongside increasingly younger costars, and the decline in popularity of the Western ended up putting him into awkward contemporary action films like *Mc Q* (1974). Following his final film, *The Shootist* (1976)—possibly his best western since *The Searchers*—the news that Wayne was stricken with cancer wiped the slate clean, and his support for the Panama Canal Treaty at the end of the 1970s belatedly made him a hero for the left. Wayne finished his life honored by the film community, the United States Congress, and the American people as no actor before or since. He remains among the most popular actors of his generation, as evidenced by the fact that *McLintock!* jumped into the top-20 selling videocassette releases when it was released by MPI Home Video during the spring of 1993, almost 30 years after it was made. **Selected Works:** *How the West Was Won* (1963), *The Long Voyage Home* (1940), *The Longest Day* (1962), *The Man Who Shot Liberty Valance* (1962)

# Sigourney Weaver (Susan Weaver)

**Born:** October 8, 1949; New York, NY

**Years Active in the Industry:** by decade

| 10s | 20s | 30s | 40s | 50s | 60s | 70s | 80s | 90s |
|-----|-----|-----|-----|-----|-----|-----|-----|-----|
|     |     |     |     |     |     |     |     |     |

Weaver took her screen name from a line in the novel *The Great Gatsby*. The daughter of NBC president Pat Weaver and actress Elizabeth Inglis, and niece of comedic actor Doodles Weaver, she attended the Yale School of Drama. She was a struggling actress throughout most of the '70s; told she was too tall (5' 11") for leads in major productions, she appeared in artsy off-off-Broadway productions, then landed a role in the TV soap opera "Somerset" and got a bit role in Woody Allen's *Annie Hall* (1977). While appearing off-Broadway she was spotted by scouts for the sci-fi horror film *Alien* (1979); she was given the lead role, and the film's success established her as a familiar American screen actress if not quite a star. She has since sustained a fairly busy film career, meanwhile continuing to work in such stage productions as Broadway's *Hurlyburly* opposite William Hurt. She is married to stage director Jim Simpson. **Selected Works:** *Aliens* (1986), *Dave* (1993), *Gorillas in the Mist* (1988), *Working Girl* (1988), *Death and the Maiden* (1994)

# Chloe Webb

**Born:** 195?; New York, NY

**Years Active in the Industry:** by decade

| 10s | 20s | 30s | 40s | 50s | 60s | 70s | 80s | 90s |
|-----|-----|-----|-----|-----|-----|-----|-----|-----|
|     |     |     |     |     |     |     |     |     |

A go-getter from an early age, actress Chloe Webb attended the Boston Conservatory of Drama and Music at the age 16. Harnessing her gift for mimicry and satire, Webb helped write several sessions of the popular New York review *Forbidden Broadway*; she appeared prominently in these irreverent productions, as well as many other major stage presentations on both coasts. Webb's film debut was as self-destructive Nancy Spungen in *Sid and Nancy* (1988), costarring with Gary Oldman (as punk-rocker Sid Vicious). Webb has continued essaying offbeat performances in offbeat films like *Belly of an Architect* (1992), and has been equally effective in such "normal" efforts as *Twins* (1988), *Ghostbusters 2* (1989) (unbilled as a highly suspect alien-abduction victim), and *Heart Condition* (1990). **Selected Works:** *Queens Logic* (1991)

# Clifton Webb (Webb Parmallee Hollenbeck)

**Born:** November 19, 1891; Indianapolis, IN
**Died:** 1966

**Years Active in the Industry:** by decade

| 10s | 20s | 30s | 40s | 50s | 60s | 70s | 80s | 90s |
|-----|-----|-----|-----|-----|-----|-----|-----|-----|
|     |     |     |     |     |     |     |     |     |

From early childhood Clifton Webb took dancing and acting lessons, and by age 10 he had done much performing. He quit school at age 13, and four years later he sang with the Boston Opera Company. At 19 Webb began focusing on dance work, quickly becoming a leading ballroom dancer around New York; his frequent partner was popular dancer Bonnie Glass, who later partnered with the young Rudolph Valentino. In his mid 20s he began getting roles in musical comedies, and in his 30s he played straight dramatic roles in London, on Broadway, and in a few silent films. He continued working exclusively as a stage actor until 1944, when director Otto Preminger cast him as the fastidious, smooth villain in *Laura* (1944); for his work he received a Best Supporting Actor Oscar nomination. He was again nominated for an Oscar for his third sound film, *The Razor's Edge* (1946). He became typecast as a pedantic, irritable bachelor, a role he perfected as Mr. Belvedere, the pompous babysitter in *Sitting Pretty* (1948)—for which he was nominated for a Best Actor Oscar—and its several sequels. He remained fairly busy onscreen through the late '50s. **Selected Works:** *Titanic* (1953), *Three Coins in the Fountain* (1954), *Boy on a Dolphin* (1957), *Holiday for Lovers* (1962)

# Jack Webb

**Born:** April 2, 1920; Santa Monica, CA
**Died:** 1982

**Years Active in the Industry:** by decade

| 10s | 20s | 30s | 40s | 50s | 60s | 70s | 80s | 90s |
|-----|-----|-----|-----|-----|-----|-----|-----|-----|
|     |     |     |     |     |     |     |     |     |

Following World War II, California native Jack Webb planned to renew the art studies that he'd abandoned for the military. Instead, he turned to acting, appearing on various San Francisco-based radio programs. He briefly hosted his own satirical comedy series before finding his true metier in detective melodramas. In collaboration with future Oscar-winning screenwriter Richard L. Breen (who remained a Webb associate until his death in 1967), Webb concocted a "hard boiled" private eye show titled *Pat Novak For Hire*. The popularity he gained from this effort enabled Webb to secure small film roles—one of these was as a police lab technician in the 1948 film noir *He Walked By Night* (1948). Intrigued by the police procedure he'd learned while preparing for the role, Webb immersed himself in the subject until he felt ready to launch what many observers still consider the first realistic radio cop show—*Dragnet*, which premiered June 3, 1949. Webb carried over his terse characterization of LA police sergeant Joe Friday into the *Dragnet* TV series (which he also directed) beginning in 1952. Armed with a bottomless reserve of police terminology and a colorful repertoire of catchphrases, the laconic, ferret-faced Webb became one of the most successful—and most widely imitated—TV personalities of the 1950s; almost always in the Top Ten, *Dragnet*, produced by Webb's own Mark VII Productions, ran until 1959. Webb's newfound industry clout permitted him to direct for the Big Screen as well—his 1950s movie credits (outside of such pre-star efforts as *The Men*, *Sunset Boulevard* and *Halls of Montezuma*) include the 1954 feature version of *Dragnet*, 1955's *Pete Kelly's Blues* (based on another of Webb's radio series), 1957's *The DI*, and 1959's *30*. In addition, Webb's Mark VII produced such TV series as *Noah's Ark*, *The DA's Man*, and the video version of *Pete Kelly's Blues*. Webb kicked off the 1960s with a rare attempt at directing comedy, *The Last Time I Saw Archie* (1961). From 1962 through 1964, he was in charge of Warner Bros.' television division, an assignment which came to an end as a result of several failed TV ventures. A 1966 TV-movie version of *Dragnet* kicked off Webb's second career. He went on to star in a successful weekly *Dragnet* revival, which ran from 1967 through 1970, while his Mark VII outfit was responsible for a score of TV series, the most successful of which were *Emergency* and *Adam 12*. Regarded as something of a relic by the "hipper" viewers, Jack Webb nonetheless remained profitably active in television until the late 1970s; he might have continued into the 1980s had not his drinking and smoking habits accelerated his death at the age of 62. Married three times, Jack Webb's first wife was singing star Julie London, whom he'd first met when he was 21 and she was 15.

# Peter Weir (Peter Lindsay Weir)

**Born:** August 21, 1944; Sydney, Australia

**Years Active in the Industry:** by decade

| 10s | 20s | 30s | 40s | 50s | 60s | 70s | 80s | 90s |
|-----|-----|-----|-----|-----|-----|-----|-----|-----|
|     |     |     |     |     |     |     |     |     |

The son of an Australian real estate agent, writer/director Peter Weir made a stab at entering his dad's business, but opted instead to wander aimlessly around Europe. Upon returning to Australia, Weir secured a  job with the Commonwealth Film Unit, learning his craft in documentaries and educational films. His first directorial effort, *Three to Go* (1970), came and went without fanfare, but he managed to get international bookings for his 1975 feature *The Cars That Ate Paris*, which, despite its distributor-grafted title, was not a horror film but a black comedy about the impoverished citizens of a small town (Paris, Texas) who arrange auto accidents so they can strip the cars and sell the spare parts. *Picnic at Hanging Rock,* a haunting 1975 period piece about the disappearance of a schoolteacher and her three young charges, was the film that brought Weir to the attention of movie theorists and festival organizers. With *The Last Wave* (1977), Weir demonstrated how the "haves" in society insist upon imposing a separate set of laws of values on the "have-nots;" it was a theme he'd revisit in *Gallipoli* (1981), in which blue-blooded British military officers callously send "disposable" lowborn Aussie troops on a foredoomed mission. *Gallipoli* star Mel Gibson also appeared in Weir's first big financial success, *The Year of Living Dangerously* (1982), a romantic drama set against the toppling of Indonesia's Sukarno regime in 1965. The film's central theme was manifested in the clash of cultures between the Indonesians and the interloping White Europeans. In his subsequent American films, the director perpetuates the "culture clash" throughline as seen through the eyes of an urban cop in an Amish farm community (*Witness* [1982]), a bullheaded inventor who journeys into the Central American jungles (*The Mosquito Coast* [1986]), an unorthodox literary professor in a hidebound boy's school (*Dead Poets Society* [1988]), and an illegal alien anxious to marry his way into American citizenship (*Green Card* [1989]). Peter Weir's film, *Fearless,* contains still another "outside looking in" protagonist—the survivor (Jeff Bridges) of an airline disaster who can't fathom why he has been spared while so many others have perished.

# Johnny Weissmuller (Peter John Weissmuller)

**Born:** June 2, 1904; Windber, PA
**Died:** Janurary 20, 1984; Acapulco, Mexico

**Years Active in the Industry:** by decade

| 10ˢ | 20ˢ | 30ˢ | 40ˢ | 50ˢ | 60ˢ | 70ˢ | 80ˢ | 90ˢ |
|-----|-----|-----|-----|-----|-----|-----|-----|-----|

He won five gold medals as a swimmer at the 1924 and 1928 Olympics, setting many free-style records. Weissmuller appeared in several sports shorts, then was hired by MGM to play Tarzan onscreen. Beginning in 1932, he starred in 12 "Tarzan" adventures, meanwhile doing almost no other film work. In the late '40s he quit "Tarzan" and began starring in a new series, "Jungle Jim," while occasionally appearing in other films through the mid '50s, after which he retired from acting. He was married six times. His stormy marriage to actress Lupe Velez (1933-38) received much coverage in scandal sheets. He authored an autobiography, *Water, World and Weissmuller* (1967).

# Raquel Welch (Raquel Tejada)

**Born:** September 5, 1940; Chicago, IL

**Years Active in the Industry:** by decade

| 10ˢ | 20ˢ | 30ˢ | 40ˢ | 50ˢ | 60ˢ | 70ˢ | 80ˢ | 90ˢ |
|-----|-----|-----|-----|-----|-----|-----|-----|-----|

Welch began entering and winning beauty contests at age 14. She married her high school boyfriend, James Welch, at 18; they had two children, then separated in 1961. She went on to study at the drama department of San Diego State College and perform with local repertory groups. After earning enough money to get a nose job, she went to Hollywood in 1963, where she got bit roles in two films. She and press agent Patrick Curtis formed Curtwell Enterprises to promote her as an actress and voluptuous sex symbol; she and Curtis subsequently married. She got a screen contract and appeared in a couple of TV shows, then went on an unbelievably successful publicity tour through Europe; having appeared in no important films, she became famous and soon was the biggest sex-goddess of the '60s. She soon had a busy screen career, becoming one of the highest-paid actresses in the world. In 1971 she and Curtis were divorced. She had trouble being accepted as a serious actress and her popularity waned, so she rarely appeared onscreen after 1977. However, she continued to appear occasionally in TV movies, and later endorsed fitness products and appeared in successful exercise videos. She is the mother of actress Tahnee Welch. **Selected Works:** *Tainted Blood* (1993), *Three Musketeers* (1974)

# Tuesday Weld (Susan Ker Weld)

**Born:** August 27, 1943; New York, NY

**Years Active in the Industry:** by decade

| 10ˢ | 20ˢ | 30ˢ | 40ˢ | 50ˢ | 60ˢ | 70ˢ | 80ˢ | 90ˢ |
|-----|-----|-----|-----|-----|-----|-----|-----|-----|

She began working as a child model at age three and, later, also as a TV performer; she was the sole source of income for her widowed mother and two siblings. At age nine Weld had her first nervous breakdown, a year later she began drinking heavily, and a year later she attempted suicide. She debuted onscreen at age 13 in *Rock Rock Rock* (1956), and throughout her teens and early 20s she played "sex kitten" types in numerous films. She often appeared in low-budget "exploitation" films and melodramas, and her liberated lifestyle drew much scorn from moralists and gossip columnists. Meanwhile, she went through an extended period of depression and seclusion. In the mid '60s her waning career was somewhat rejuvenated when she developed a cult following; her fans saw her as a talented actress who had been stuck in terrible films. She began getting better roles, though she took five years off from movies in the '70s. Tuesday Weld film festivals continue to be held in Manhattan and elsewhere. From 1980-85 she was married to actor Dudley Moore. **Selected Works:** *Falling Down* (1993), *Looking for Mr. Goodbar* (1977), *Pretty Poison* (1968), *Thief* (1981)

# Peter Weller

**Born:** June 24, 1947; Stevens Point, WI

**Years Active in the Industry:** by decade

| 10ˢ | 20ˢ | 30ˢ | 40ˢ | 50ˢ | 60ˢ | 70ˢ | 80ˢ | 90ˢ |
|-----|-----|-----|-----|-----|-----|-----|-----|-----|

Though he is best remembered for the humanity he brought to the title character of *Robocop* (1987), actor Peter Weller is a versatile actor who has played in a wide variety of films as both lead and supporting actor. Prior to coming to films, Weller had a distinguished theatrical career. Before that he studied with famed acting coach Uta Hagen. He made his screen debut as a determined lawman in *Butch and Sundance: The Early Years* (1979). He played romantic leads in his next two films before starring in W.D. Richter's 1984 cult favorite *The Adventures of Buckaroo Banzai*. His role in this sci-fi satire eventually lead to *Robocop*, where he was chosen by the director for his "expressive lips." The film was quite successful, and Weller went on to play in a series of minor thrillers and one sequel to *Robocop* before playing an aspiring writer whacked out on drugs in David Cronenberg's disturbing noir fantasy *Naked Lunch* (1991). As bizarre as the film was, it gave Weller an opportunity to stretch and show his ability as a serious dramatic actor. Though the film was not a commercial success, he did garner much critical praise for his role. **Selected Works:** *Cat Chaser* (1990), *Fifty-Fifty* (1993), *Road to Ruin* (1991), *Robocop 2* (1990), *Women and Men: Stories of Seduction* (1990)

# Orson Welles (George Orson Welles)

**Born:** May 6, 1915; Kenosha, WI
**Died:** October 9, 1985

**Years Active in the Industry:** by decade

| 10ˢ | 20ˢ | 30ˢ | 40ˢ | 50ˢ | 60ˢ | 70ˢ | 80ˢ | 90ˢ |
|-----|-----|-----|-----|-----|-----|-----|-----|-----|
|     |     |     |     |     |     |     |     |     |

The most well known filmmaker to the public this side of Alfred Hitchcock, Orson Welles was the classic example of the genius that burns bright early in life and flickers and fades later on.

The prodigy son of an inventor and a musician, Welles was well versed in literature at an early age—especially Shakespeare—and, through the unusual circumstances of his life (both of his parents had died by the time he was 12, leaving him with an inheritance and not a lot of family obligations), he found himself free to indulge his many interests, which included theater. He was educated in private school and travelled the world, even wangling stage work with Dublin's Gate Players while still a teenager. He found it tougher to get onto the Broadway stage, and travelled the world some more, before returning to get a job with Katharine Cornell, with help from such notables as Alexander Woollcott and Thornton Wilder. He later became associated with John Houseman, and together, the two of them set the New York theater afire during the 1930s with their work for the Federal Theatre Project, which led to the founding of the Mercury Theater. The Mercury Theater's 1938 "War of the Worlds" broadcast made history when thousands of listeners mistakenly believed aliens had landed on Earth. The Mercury Players later graduated to radio and, in 1940, Hollywood beckoned. Welles and company went west to RKO, and it was there that he began his short-lived reign over the film world. Working as director, producer, co-author and star, he made *Citizen Kane* (1941), the most discussed—if not the greatest—movie ever made in America. It made striking use of techniques that had been largely forgotten or overlooked by other American filmmakers. Welles was greatly assisted on the movie by veteran cinematographer Gregg Toland. *Kane* attracted more attention than viewers, especially outside the major cities, and a boycott of advertising and coverage by the newspapers belonging to William Randolph Hearst—who had served as a major model for the central figure of Charles Foster Kane—ensured that it racked up a modest loss. His second film, *The Magnificent Ambersons,* ran into major budget and production problems, which brought down the studio management that had hired Welles—coupled with the director's having over-extended himself, the situation between Welles and RKO deteriorated. Faced with a major loss on a picture that was considered unreleasable, RKO gained control of the film and ordered it recut without Welles' consent or input, and the result is considered a flawed masterpiece. However, it was a loss for

RKO, and soon after Welles' Mercury Players were evicted from RKO, word quickly passed around the film community of Welles's difficulty in following shooting schedules and budgets. His career never fully recovered, and although he directed other films in Hollywood, including *The Stranger* (1946), *Macbeth* (1948), and *A Touch of Evil* (1958), he was never again given full control of his movies. However, European producers were more forgiving, and with some effort and help from a few well-placed friends, Welles was able to make such pictures as *Othello* (1952), *Chimes At Midnight* (1967), and *The Trial* (1963). He also remained highly visible as a personality—he discovered in the mid 1940s that for $100,000 a shot, he could make money as an actor to help finance his films and his fairly expensive lifetsyle, which resulted in Welles' appearances in *The Third Man* (1949), *The Roots of Heaven* (1958), and *Catch-22* (1970), among other pictures. He also made appearances on television, did voice-overs and recordings, and occasional commercials. Despite his lack of commercial success, he remains one of the most well-known, discussed, and important directors in the history of motion pictures. **Selected Works:** *A Man for All Seasons* (1966), *Compulsion* (1959), *The Long Hot Summer* (1958), *Crack in the Mirror* (1960)

# William Wellman

**Born:** February 19, 1896; Brookline, MA
**Died:** December 9, 1975; Los Angeles, CA

**Years Active in the Industry:** by decade

| 10ˢ | 20ˢ | 30ˢ | 40ˢ | 50ˢ | 60ˢ | 70ˢ | 80ˢ | 90ˢ |
|-----|-----|-----|-----|-----|-----|-----|-----|-----|
|     |     |     |     |     |     |     |     |     |

A trouble-prone youngster, Massachussetts-born director William Wellman gravitated towards contact sports like professional hockey and barroom brawling. When World War I broke out in Europe, Wellman decided not to sit it out in "neutral" America; he joined the French Foreign Legion as an ambulance driver, then became a pilot in the Lafayette Flying Corps (not the Lafayette Escadrille, as has often been reported). During the war, Wellman earned the soubriquet of "Wild Bill," not so much for his daring in the air as for his earthbound predeliction for drinking and fisticuffs. (In later years, Wellman attributed his nickname to his frequent tiltings with such authority figures as military officers and movie executives; but Wellman seldom let facts get in the way of a good story.) Decorated many times over for his wartime valor, Wellman tried to settle down to a "normal" civilian life, but before long was a barnstorming pilot in a travelling air circus. A chance meeting with Douglas Fairbanks led to an entree into motion pictures, first as a bit actor and then as a propman, assistant director, and finally in 1923 as director of Fox studios' *Buck Jones* Westerns. Signed to a seven-year contract with Paramount in 1927, Wellman drew upon his wartime experiences for the blockbuster *Wings* (1927), which went on to win the first-ever Best Picture Academy Award. Halfway through his Paramount contract, Wellman moved to Warner Bros., where among several other noteworthy talkies he directed the pacesetting Jimmy Cagney gangster picture *The Public Enemy*

(1931). It was Wellman who, upon learning that the innoccuous Edward Woods had been cast as the lead in *Public Enemy* and Cagney had been given a thankless supporting role, insisted that Woods and Cagney exchange parts—and the rest is history. (Wellman also claimed to have been the first director to recognize the potential of Gary Cooper by giving him a pivotal role in *Wings* [1927], but unlike the Cagney story, this legend does not hold up in the light of Cooper's earlier, more sizeable role in Henry King's *The Winning of Barbara Worth* [1926].) Wellman continued to turn out first-rate work like *Call of the Wild* (1935), *Nothing Sacred* (1937), *A Star is Born* (1937), *Beau Geste* (1939), *The Ox-Bow Incident* (1943), and *Buffalo Bill* (1944). In 1945, producer Lester Cowan begged Wellman to direct *The Story of GI Joe,* but Wild Bill refused on the basis that it wouldn't be appropriate for an ex-flying ace to direct a film about the infantry. The director eventually gave in to Cowan, and the result was arguably the best World War II film ever made. Wellman's later infantry picture, *Battleground* (1949), was even more successful financially, though the director himself preferred *GI Joe* because he wasn't saddled with the gratuitous romantic subplot that weakened *Battleground.* Wellman's work in the 1950s included John Wayne's *High and the Mighty* (1954) (Wellman's friendship with Wayne was strong enough to withstand the many times the two men nearly came to blows) and *Track of the Cat* (1954), a fascinating, if not wholly successful attempt to impose a black-and-white "look" upon a Technicolor film. The director's final film was *Lafayette Escadrille* (1958), in which William Wellman Jr. portrayed his own father. Throughout his career, Wellman maintained the reputation of a tough, no-nonsense martinet, capable of chewing out such major stars as Ronald Colman and Spencer Tracy if the circumstances dictated it, but equally capable of intense loyalty towards his favorite coworkers. One such favorite was character actor George Chandler, whom Wellman cast prominently in virtually all his films of the 1930s and 1940s; in the 1950s, Wellman secured several good roles for his hunting guide and drinking buddy, former child star Carl "Alfalfa" Switzer. A popular interview subject in the 1960s and 1970s, Wellman penned two highly entertaining (and highly unreliable) memoirs, *A Short Time for Insanity* and *Growing Old Disgracefully.*

# Wim Wenders

**Born:** August 14, 1945; Dusseldorf, Germany

**Years Active in the Industry:** by decade

| 10s | 20s | 30s | 40s | 50s | 60s | 70s | 80s | 90s |
|-----|-----|-----|-----|-----|-----|-----|-----|-----|
|     |     |     |     |     |     |     |     |     |

Born just after the end of World War II, German film director Wim Wenders grew up "pigging out" on American movies. Wenders wasn't all that interested in the big-budget product, but he developed a fascination with the B product, notably melodramas and Westerns. After studying medicine and philosophy in Germany, Wenders took up art study in Paris (a mecca for viewing American films), then returned to his homeland to attend Munich's Academy of Film and Television. Like many of his French movie-fan brethren, Wenders began his career writing film criticism before directing a few short subjects of his own; in 1970 he and several other young filmmakers formed a production-distribution firm, Filmverlag Der Autoren. *Summer in the City* (1970) was Wenders' first feature film, but it was his 1973 adaptation of Nathaniel Hawthorne's *The Scarlet Letter* that first brought him attention outside Germany. One of the film's accomplishments was making the landscapes of Spain resemble 17th century New England; the other was coaxing a superb performance from Senta Berger as Hester Prynne. At this point, Wenders began his "road movie" cycle, inspired by such American pictures as *Easy Rider* (1970) and *Two Lane Blacktop* (1971). Three films in this genre followed in quick succession: *Alice in the Cities* (1974), *The Wrong Move* (1975) and *Kings of the Road* (1976). For his first English-language picture, *The American Friend* (1977), Wenders cast three of his American movie idols: actor Dennis Hopper (director/star of *Easy Rider*) and "cult" directors Nicholas Ray (*Rebel Without a Cause*) and Samuel Fuller (*The Steel Helmet*). Wenders would later codirect a film with Ray, *Lightning Over Water* (1980). Wenders' American-financed films *Hammett* (1980) and *Paris, Texas* (1983) were remarkable in their evocation of time and place, and the director could certainly have continued copacetically in Hollywood, but seemed to prefer activity in Europe, even though he was always one step ahead of his creditors—especially when running his own studio, Gray City. Wenders' love of on-the-road location filming was manifested even into his films of the 1990s, *Until the End of the World* (1991) (filmed on four continents and designed to be "the ultimate road movie"), and *Faraway So Close* (1993), a marathon experience (originally 164 minutes) wherein an angel wanders about to observe the changing scene in a newly-unified Germany. **Selected Works:** *Wings of Desire* (1988)

# Lina Wertmuller (Arcangela Felice Assunta Wertmuller von Elgg)

**Born:** August 14, 1928; Rome, Italy

**Years Active in the Industry:** by decade

| 10s | 20s | 30s | 40s | 50s | 60s | 70s | 80s | 90s |
|-----|-----|-----|-----|-----|-----|-----|-----|-----|
|     |     |     |     |     |     |     |     |     |

Director Lina Wermuller is best known for her sociosexual Italian-style comedies. Born in Italy of an aristocratic Swiss family, she began her career by performing in children's shows and theater. During the 1960s, she also wrote a variety of shows, musicals, and comedies for televison. Her first job in cinema was working as Fellini's assistant director in 1963's *8½.* She made her directorial debut in 1972 with *I basilischi.* In 1977, after a string of successes in Italy, Wermuller was offered a contract to make English language films in the U.S. with Warner Bros. It was there that she made her most successful films. **Selected Works:** *Love and Anarchy* (1973), *Seduction of Mimi* (1974), *Seven Beauties* (1976), *Ciao Professore* (1994)

# Mae West

**Born:** August 17, 1892; Brooklyn, NY
**Died:** November 23, 1980

## Years Active in the Industry: by decade

| 10s | 20s | 30s | 40s | 50s | 60s | 70s | 80s | 90s |
|-----|-----|-----|-----|-----|-----|-----|-----|-----|
|     |     | ■   |     |     |     |     |     |     |

A seductive, overdressed, endearing, intelligent, buxom, sometimes vulgar blonde actress and sex symbol with drooping eyelids, West featured a come-hither voice, aggressive sexuality, and a genius for comedy. She began working as an entertainer at age five. After a few years in stock she moved into burlesque, where she was billed as "The Baby Vamp." She began working in vaudeville and Broadway revues at age 14; she was the first to do the "shimmy" on stage, and she also appeared as a male impersonator. Between 1907-18 West often re-wrote her material and began thinking of herself as a playwright. In 1926 her first play, *Sex,* which she wrote, produced, and directed on Broadway, caused a scandal and led to her imprisonment on Welfare Island for over a week on obscenity charges. She wrote and directed her second play, *Drag,* in 1927; about homosexuality, the play was a smash hit in Paterson, New Jersey, but she was warned not to bring it to Broadway. Finally, she had a legitimate success on Broadway with *Diamond Lil* in 1928, and, after two more successful stage productions, she was invited to Hollywood. With a reputation as a provocative sexual figure, she was watched carefully by the censors and often clashed with them; still, she managed to inject much sexuality into her films through innuendo and double entendre. For most of her films she wrote her own lines and collaborated on the scripts; her witticisms and catch-phrases soon entered the speech of mainstream America. Having debuted on-screen in 1932 in *Night After Night,* by 1935 she was the highest-paid woman in the United States. Throughout the '30s her films were anticipated as major events, but by the end of the decade she seemed to have reached her limit and her popularity waned; puritanism was on the rise and censorship was severely limiting her career. After making *The Heat's On* (1943), she planned to retire from the screen, and went back to Broadway and on a tour of English theaters. In 1954, when she was 62, she began a nightclub act in which she was surrounded by musclemen; it ran for three years and was a great success. By now a legend and cult figure, she went into retirement. She appeared in two more films in the '70s. She is the author of an autobiography, *Goodness Had Nothing to Do with*

*It* (1959). **Selected Works:** *She Done Him Wrong* (1933), *I'm No Angel* (1933), *Bell of the Nineties* (1934)

# Haskell Wexler

**Born:** 1926; Chicago, IL

## Years Active in the Industry: by decade

| 10s | 20s | 30s | 40s | 50s | 60s | 70s | 80s | 90s |
|-----|-----|-----|-----|-----|-----|-----|-----|-----|
|     |     |     |     |     | ■   |     |     |     |

A Chicago-born amateur filmmaker, Haskell Wexler broke into feature films in 1959 as a cinematographer on the documentary *The Savage Eye* (1960). Wexler photographed the dramas *The Hoodlum Priest* (1961), *Angel Baby* (1961), *The Best Man* (1964), and later distinguished himself as cinematographer on the Mike Nichols drama *Who's Afraid of Virginia Woolf?* (1965). He worked on such high profile feature films as *In The Heat of the Night* (1967) and *The Thomas Crown Affair* (1968), but also produced and directed the documentaries *The Bus* and *Medium Cool* (1969), the latter a very successful and controversial look at the violence and strife surrounding the anti-war movement and the 1968 Democratic National Convention in Chicago. During the 1980s, he also produced and directed the feature film *Latino* (1985), which was highly critical of American policy in Central America. Wexler has won Academy Awards for his work in *Who's Afraid of Virginia Woolf?* and *Bound For Glory* (1976), and also worked on such documentaries as *Gimme Shelter* and *The Stones At the MAX.* **Selected Works:** *Babe* (1992), *One Flew over the Cuckoo's Nest* (1975), *Canadian Bacon* (1994), *Secret of Roan Inish* (1994)

# James Whale

**Born:** July 22, 1896; Dudley, England
**Died:** 1957

## Years Active in the Industry: by decade

| 10s | 20s | 30s | 40s | 50s | 60s | 70s | 80s | 90s |
|-----|-----|-----|-----|-----|-----|-----|-----|-----|
|     |     | ■   |     |     |     |     |     |     |

British-born director James Whale started his professional life as a newspaper cartoonist before turning to acting during his time as a prisoner in World War I. From acting, he turned to set design and then to directing, and went to Hollywood in 1930 for the screen version of his stage hit *Journey's End.* He served as a dialogue director on the World War I aerial drama *Hell's Angels,* but it was as a director of horror movies at Universal that Whale made his mark, with *Frankenstein* (1931), *The Old Dark House* (1932), *The Invisible Man* (1933), and *The Bride of Frankenstein* (1935). Apart from *Frankenstein,* which was a wholly serious horror film, these movies freely mixed chills and black comedy, and caused nearly as much laughter as shock to audiences, who devoured the potent mixture of horror and humor. His graceful adaptation of *Show Boat* (1936) was one of the finest screen musicals of the

1930s, but a change in management at the studio, coupled with Whale's unhappiness at the recutting of his drama *The Road Back* (1937), led to his exit from Universal. He directed other films after leaving Universal, including *The Man In the Iron Mask* (1939), but nothing that he did after *Show Boat* had any of the flair of his earlier movies, and Whale's career declined during the early 1940s. He died in a drowning accident in his pool, under what are widely regarded as mysterious circumstances.

# Frank Whaley

**Born:** 1962; Syracuse, NY

**Years Active in the Industry:** by decade

| 10s | 20s | 30s | 40s | 50s | 60s | 70s | 80s | 90s |
|-----|-----|-----|-----|-----|-----|-----|-----|-----|
|     |     |     |     |     |     |     |     |     |

With the role of Steve Bushak in 1990's *The Freshman*, actor Frank Whaley inaugurated a fruitful film career. Whaley went on to be prominently featured in three 1991 pictures. He played real-life guitarist Robby Krieger in *The Doors*, and two leading roles: the hapless tourist caught up in literary espionage in *Back in the USSR* (1991) and the feckless night watchman with both a runaway heiress and a gang of burglars on his hands in *Career Opportunities* (1991). Whaley has continued averaging two to three film appearances per annum; would that the films themselves were more profitable than the likes of *Swing Kids* (1993) and *A Midnight Clear* (1993). **Selected Works:** *Hoffa* (1992), *JFK* (1991), *Pulp Fiction* (1994)

# Joanne Whalley-Kilmer

**Born:** August 25, 1964; Manchester, England

**Years Active in the Industry:** by decade

| 10s | 20s | 30s | 40s | 50s | 60s | 70s | 80s | 90s |
|-----|-----|-----|-----|-----|-----|-----|-----|-----|
|     |     |     |     |     |     |     |     |     |

Before she was 20, Joanne Whalley was an established stage actress with England's Royal Court Theatre and had appeared in the 1982 film *Pink Floyd: The Wall*. Her first important American film was director Ron Howard's fantasy epic *Willow* (1988); one year later she garnered plenty of critical adulation for her performance as British call girl Christine Keeler in *Scandal* (1989). Since her 1989 marriage to her *Willow* costar Val Kilmer, the actress has billed herself as Joanne Whalley-Kilmer. However, the couple split in 1995, shortly after the birth of her second child. In 1994, Whalley-Kilmer courageously stepped into the forbidding shoes of Vivien Leigh as star of the TV miniseries *Scarlett*, the much-anticipated (and as it turned out, much-maligned) sequel to *Gone With the Wind*. Many of her fans assumed that this represented her TV debut, but in fact Whalley-Kilmer had previously made a good impression as the nurse in the surrealistic BBC series *The Singing Detective*. **Selected Works:** *Shattered* (1991), *Storyville* (1992), *Trial by Jury* (1994), *A Good Man in Africa* (1994)

# Forest Whitaker

**Born:** 1961; Longview, TX

**Years Active in the Industry:** by decade

| 10s | 20s | 30s | 40s | 50s | 60s | 70s | 80s | 90s |
|-----|-----|-----|-----|-----|-----|-----|-----|-----|
|     |     |     |     |     |     |     |     |     |

Whitaker attended college on a football scholarship, then transferred to USC on two more scholarships to study music and theater (he was interested in opera). He landed small roles on TV and in two films, beginning with *Fast Times at Ridgemont High* (1982). He got his big break when he appeared in Oliver Stone's *Platoon* and Martin Scorsese's *The Color of Money* (both 1986). After a few more supporting roles in films, Whitaker got his first lead in Clint Eastwood's *Bird* (1988), in which he played the title role—heroin-addicted jazz great Charlie Parker; for his performance he won the Cannes Film Festival Best Actor award. Although now better-known as an actor, he was unable to greatly capitalize on his success and remained mainly a supporting player in films. He is the brother of actor Damon Whitaker. **Selected Works:** *Article 99* (1992), *Crying Game* (1992), *Good Morning, Vietnam* (1987), *Strapped* (1993), *Waiting to Exhale* (1995)

# Stuart Whitman

**Born:** February 1, 1928; San Francisco, CA

**Years Active in the Industry:** by decade

| 10s | 20s | 30s | 40s | 50s | 60s | 70s | 80s | 90s |
|-----|-----|-----|-----|-----|-----|-----|-----|-----|
|     |     |     |     |     |     |     |     |     |

Stuart Whitman, with a rugged build and sensitive face, rose from bit player to competent lead actor, but never did make it as a popular star in film. The San Francisco-born Whitman served three years with the Army Corps of Engineers where he was a light heavyweight boxer in his spare time. He next went on to study drama at the Los Angeles City College where he joined a Chekhov stage group. He began his film career in the early '50s as a bit player. Although never a star, he did manage to quietly accumulate $100 million dollars through shrewd investments in securities, real estate, cattle, and Thoroughbreds. For his role as a sex offender attempting to change in the 1961 British film *The Mark*, Whitman was nominated for an Oscar. In addition to features, Whitman has also appeared extensively on television. **Selected Works:** *Texas Guns* (1990), *Those Magnificent Men in Their Flying Machines* (1965), *Murder, Inc.* (1960), *American Dream* (1966)

# James Whitmore

**Born:** October 1, 1921; White Plains, NY

**Years Active in the Industry:** by decade

| 10s | 20s | 30s | 40s | 50s | 60s | 70s | 80s | 90s |
|-----|-----|-----|-----|-----|-----|-----|-----|-----|
|     |     |     |     |     |     |     |     |     |

Whitmore attended Yale, where he joined the Yale Drama School Players and co-founded the Yale radio station. After serving in World War II with the Marines, he did some work in stock and then debuted on Broadway in 1947's *Command Decision*. He entered films in 1949, going on to play key supporting roles; occasionally, he also played leads. For his work in *Battleground* (1949), his second film, he received a Best Supporting Actor Oscar nomination. He starred in the early '60s TV series "The Law and Mr. Jones." He won much acclaim for his work in the one-man stage show *Give 'Em Hell, Harry!*, in which he played Harry Truman; he reprised the role in the 1975 screen version, for which he received a Best Actor Oscar nomination. After 1980 his screen appearances were infrequent. He is the father of actor James Whitmore Jr. **Selected Works:** *Asphalt Jungle* (1950), *Kiss Me Kate* (1953), *Oklahoma!* (1955), *Planet of the Apes* (1968), *The Shawshank Redemption* (1994)

# Dame May Whitty

**Born:** June 19, 1865; Liverpool, England
**Died:** May 29, 1948; Beverly Hills, CA

**Years Active in the Industry:** by decade

| 10ˢ | 20ˢ | 30ˢ | 40ˢ | 50ˢ | 60ˢ | 70ˢ | 80ˢ | 90ˢ |
|-----|-----|-----|-----|-----|-----|-----|-----|-----|
|     |     |     |     |     |     |     |     |     |

The daughter of a Liverpool newspaper editor, British actress Dame May Whitty first stepped on a London stage in 1882. Shortly afterward she was engaged by the St. James Theatre, serving mostly in an understudy capacity. From there, Whitty went into a travelling stock company, finally attaining leading roles. She had been one of the leading lights of the British stage for nearly 25 years when she appeared in her first film, *Enoch Arden*, in 1914; caring little for the experience, she made only a smattering of silent films thereafter. In 1918, the 53-year-old May Whitty was made a Dame Commander of the British Empire in recognition of her above-and-beyond activities performing before the troops in World War I. After a string of 1930s Broadway successes, Whitty went to Hollywood for the same reasons that many of her British contemporaries had previously done so—the work was easy and the money fabulous. In keeping with the regality of her name, Whitty was usually cast in high-born roles, sometimes imperious, often warmhearted. In her first talking picture *Night Must Fall* (1937), she is the foolhardy invalid who falls for the charms of homicidal Robert Montgomery, and as consequence winds up literally losing her head. In Hitchcock's *The Lady Vanishes* (1938) she plays the title role, enduring a great deal of physical exertion while never losing her poise and dignity. Whitty was also capable of playing working-class types, such as the dowdy phony psychic in *The Thirteenth Chair* (1937). She was twice nominated for the Oscar, first for *Night Must Fall* in 1937, then for *Mrs. Miniver* in 1942. Despite her advanced age, Whitty became extremely active on the Hollywood social circuit in the 1940s—at least for the benefit of the newsreel photographers. Whitty died at the age of 82, shortly

after completing her scenes for Columbia's *The Sign of the Ram* (1948). She was the wife of London producer Ben Webster, and the mother of actress/playwright Margaret Webster, who wrote a 1969 biography of Whitty, *The Same Only Different*. **Selected Works:** *Gaslight* (1944), *Lassie Come Home* (1943), *Madame Curie* (1943), *Suspicion* (1941), *Constant Nymph* (1943)

# Richard Widmark

**Born:** December 26, 1914; Sunrise, MN

**Years Active in the Industry:** by decade

| 10ˢ | 20ˢ | 30ˢ | 40ˢ | 50ˢ | 60ˢ | 70ˢ | 80ˢ | 90ˢ |
|-----|-----|-----|-----|-----|-----|-----|-----|-----|
|     |     |     |     |     |     |     |     |     |

The son of a travelling salesman, actor Richard Widmark had lived in six different midwestern towns by the time he was a teenager. He entered Illinois' Lake Forest College with plans to  earn a law degree, but gravitated instead to the college's theatre department. He stayed on after graduation as a drama instructor, then headed to New York to find professional work. From 1938 through 1947, Widmark was one of the busiest and most successful actors in radio, appearing in a wide variety of roles from benign to menacing, and starring in the daytime soap opera *Front Page Farrell*. He did so well in radio that he'd later quip "I am the only actor who *left* a mansion and swimming pool to head to Hollywood." Widmark's first stage appearance was in Long Island summer stock; in 1943 he starred in the Broadway production of *Kiss and Tell*, and was subsequently top billed in four other New York productions. When director Henry Hathaway was looking for Broadway-based actors to appear in his New York-lensed melodrama *Kiss of Death* (1947), Widmark won the role of giggling, psychopathic gangster Tommy Udo. The moment Widmark (as Udo) pushed a wheelchair-bound old woman down a staircase, a movie star was born (Widmark always found it amusing that he'd become an audience favorite by playing a homicidal creep; he also noted with only slightly less amusement that after the release of the film, women would stop him on the street and smack his face, yelling "Take *that*, you little squirt!"). The actor signed a 20th Century-Fox contract and moved to Hollywood on the proviso that he not be confined to villainous roles; the first of his many sympathetic, heroic movie parts was in 1949's *Down to the Sea in Ships*. After his Fox contract ended in 1954, Widmark freelanced in such films as *The Cobweb* (1955) and *St. Joan*

(1957), the latter representing one of the few times that the actor was uncomfortably miscast (as the childish Dauphin). In 1957, Widmark formed his own company, Heath Productions; its first effort was *Time Limit*, directed by Widmark's old friend Karl Malden. Widmark spent most of the 1960s making box-office films like *The Alamo* (1960) and *Cheyenne Autumn* (1964), so that he could afford to appear in movies that put forth a political or sociolgical message. These included *Judgment at Nuremberg* (1961) and *The Bedford Incident* (1965). A longtime TV holdout, Widmark made his small-screen debut in *Vanished* (1971), the first two-part TV movie. He later starred in a 1972 series based on his 1968 theatrical film *Madigan*, and in 1989 he was successfully teamed with Faye Dunaway in the made-for-cable *Cold Sassy Tree*. Richard Widmark has been married since 1942 to Jean Hazelwood, a former actress and occasional screenwriter (she wrote the script for her husband's 1961 film *The Secret Ways* [1961]); their daughter Anne is the wife of baseball star Sandy Koufax. **Selected Works:** *Broken Lance* (1954), *How the West Was Won* (1963), *Murder on the Orient Express* (1974), *Panic in the Streets* (1950), *Pickup on South Street* (1953)

# Dianne Wiest

**Born:** March 28, 1948; Kansas City, MO

**Years Active in the Industry:** by decade

| 10s | 20s | 30s | 40s | 50s | 60s | 70s | 80s | 90s |
|-----|-----|-----|-----|-----|-----|-----|-----|-----|
|     |     |     |     |     |     |     |  ■  |  ■  |

Wiest studied for a ballet career, then switched to acting. After touring with the American Shakespeare Company, she moved to New York and then to Washington, D.C., where she was a member of the Arena Stage Theater; with Arena she toured the Soviet Union. She went on to work with other regional groups and with the New York Shakespeare Festival; she played Desdemona opposite James Earl Jones in a Broadway production of *Othello*. In the mid '80s Wiest began directing plays, including a successful off-Broadway production of *Not About Heroes*. After a few small roles in films, she became one of film-maker Woody Allen's regular list of actors; she appeared in five Allen films between 1985-94, including *The Purple Rose of Cairo* (1985), in which she played a hooker; *Radio Days* (1987); *September* (1987); *Hannah and Her Sisters* (1986), for which she won the Best Supporting Actress Oscar; and *Bullets Over Broadway* (1994), for which she took home the same award. She was also Oscar-

nominated for her performance as a single mom in Ron Howard's *Parenthood* (1988). She has sustained a fairly steady screen career as a character actress. **Selected Works:** *Edward Scissorhands* (1990), *Little Man Tate* (1991), *The Lost Boys* (1987), *Cookie* (1989)

# Cornel Wilde (Cornelius Louis Wilde)

**Born:** October 18, 1918; New York, NY
**Died:** October 16, 1989; Los Angeles, CA

**Years Active in the Industry:** by decade

| 10s | 20s | 30s | 40s | 50s | 60s | 70s | 80s | 90s |
|-----|-----|-----|-----|-----|-----|-----|-----|-----|
|     |     |     |  ■  |  ■  |  ■  |  ■  |     |     |

His father was a traveling salesman who did a lot of business in Europe, and Wilde spent much of his youth traveling in Europe with him, where he became fluent in several languages. For several years he studied medicine in college, but he gave it up to pursue acting; he also gave up a spot on the 1936 U.S. Olympic fencing team. He appeared in a number of plays in New York and on the road, playing everything from bit parts to leads. In 1940 he was hired as a fencing instructor and a featured player for the Broadway production of *Hamlet* with Laurence Olivier; some of the rehearsals were in Hollywood, where he landed a film contract. On-screen from 1940, Wilde played small roles as heavies in several films, then switched studios and began getting leads in B movies. His career took off after he played Chopin in *A Song to Remember* (1945), for which he received a Best Actor Oscar nomination. For several years he starred in major productions, then in the '50s he was back in B movies, often playing swashbucklers. In 1955 he formed his own company, Theodora Productions, to produce, direct, and star in his own films; he ultimately made 11 films in that capacity, but earned little critical respect for his work. Divorced from actress Patricia Knight, Wilde married his frequent costar, actress Jean Wallace. **Selected Works:** *The Greatest Show on Earth* (1952), *Leave Her to Heaven* (1946), *A Thousand and One Nights* (1945), *The Big Combo* (1955), *Forever Amber* (1947)

# Billy Wilder (Samuel Wilder)

**Born:** June 22, 1906; Vienna, Austria

**Years Active in the Industry:** by decade

| 10s | 20s | 30s | 40s | 50s | 60s | 70s | 80s | 90s |
|-----|-----|-----|-----|-----|-----|-----|-----|-----|
|     |     |  ■  |  ■  |  ■  |  ■  |  ■  |     |     |

Originally a law student in Vienna, Billy Wilder chose journalism as a career, and entered films as a screenwriter, in association with Robert Siodmak in 1929. He was a successful screenwriter in Germany until Hitler came to power, and Wilder was forced to move to Paris. It was there that he co-directed his first movie. He came to the United States in 1934, and survived despite his lack of ability with the English language, mostly with the help of other expatriate Germans and Austrians. It was in association with

writer/producer Charles Brackett that Wilder began a successful screenwriting career in Hollywood, which led to his work as a director at Paramount beginning in 1942. The work by the pair included the screenplays to *Ninotchka* (1939) and *Ball of Fire* (1941), and their own films included *Five Graves To Cairo* (1943), *The Major and the Minor* (1942), *Double Indemnity* (1944), *The Lost Weekend* (1945), and *Sunset Boulevard* (1950). Wilder later became his own producer and made such classics as *Ace In The Hole, Stalag 17* (1953), *The Seven Year Itch* (1955), *Witness For The Prosecution* (1957), *Some Like It Hot* (1959), *The Apartment* (1960), *The Fortune Cookie* (1966), *One Two Three* (1961), *The Private Life of Sherlock Holmes* (1970), and *The Front Page* (1974). Wilder's movies, whether comedy or drama, are characterized by a knowing cynicism, and many contain a striking sexual tension between their male and female protagonists, which can be played for thrills, laughs, or both. His brother, W. Lee Wilder, who was also a director, excelled at low budget science fiction chillers such as *Killers From Space* and *Phantom From Space*. **Selected Works:** *Sabrina* (1954), *Hold Back the Dawn* (1941)

# Gene Wilder (Jerry Silberman)

**Born:** June 11, 1935; Milwaukee, WI

**Years Active in the Industry:** by decade

| 10ˢ | 20ˢ | 30ˢ | 40ˢ | 50ˢ | 60ˢ | 70ˢ | 80ˢ | 90ˢ |
|-----|-----|-----|-----|-----|-----|-----|-----|-----|

Wilder, the son of a Russian immigrant, was born Jerry Silberman. He took drama classes in college and played some summer stock. After graduating he went to England, where he enrolled at the Old Vic Theater School in Bristol; at that school he won the fencing championship, and ended up teaching fencing for a living after he returned to the U.S. After a couple more odd jobs he debuted off-Broadway in 1961; he went on to join the Actors Studio and began to land important roles on Broadway. He debuted on-screen in a small but notable role in the hit *Bonnie and Clyde* (1967), playing a sheepish undertaker who (along with his wife) is temporarily and comically held hostage in the back of a car by the Barrow gang. For his portrayal of a neurotic misfit in his second film, Mel Brooks's *The Producers* (1968), he received a Best Supporting Actor Oscar nomination. He developed a screen persona as a comically neurotic, jittery, vulnerable, and often embarrassed character. He co-wrote and starred in Brooks's *Young Frankenstein*

(1974), then went on to occasionally write and direct himself in films, beginning with *The Adventures of Sherlock Holmes's Smarter Brother* (1975). He was popular in four comedies in which he co-starred with Richard Pryor. He was married to comedic actress Gilda Radner until her death in 1989; she costarred with him in two of his efforts as a writer-director, *The Woman in Red* (1984) and *Haunted Honeymoon* (1986). **Selected Works:** *Blazing Saddles* (1974), *Silver Streak* (1976), *Hanky Panky* (1982)

# Billy Dee Williams

**Born:** April 6, 1937; New York, NY

**Years Active in the Industry:** by decade

| 10ˢ | 20ˢ | 30ˢ | 40ˢ | 50ˢ | 60ˢ | 70ˢ | 80ˢ | 90ˢ |
|-----|-----|-----|-----|-----|-----|-----|-----|-----|

The screen's first authentic black romantic leading man, Williams is often referred to as "the black Gable." He first appeared onstage as a child actor in *The Firebrand of Florence* (1947) with German actress Lotte Lenya; his mother was an elevator operator at New York's Lyceum Theater, and when she heard of an opening for a child in the play she brought him to the producer, who hired him. He went on to study acting at New York's High School of Music and Art and The National Academy of Fine Arts; for a few months he was taught by Sidney Poitier at Harlem's Actors Workshop. He began working onstage in the mid '50s, then landed his breakthrough role in the play *A Taste of Honey* in 1960. He debuted on-screen as a rebellious ghetto kid in *The Last Angry Man* (1959). However, he did not appear in another film for over a decade. In the '60s he began landing roles on TV, including a continuing role on the soap opera *Another World* and guest spots on TV series. He made a big impression as the costar of the TV movie *Brian's Song* (1970). His breakthrough screen role was as the lover of Billie Holliday (Diana Ross) in the hit *Lady Sings the Blues* (1972), which brought him to stardom and established him as a romantic lead. He went on to appear in a number of movies, few of which fully used his talents; he portrayed Lando Calrissian in the second and third *Star Wars* films, *The Empire Strikes Back* (1980) and *Return of the Jedi* (1983). In the mid '80s he began appearing again frequently on TV, and starred in the short-lived series *Double Dare* in 1985; he was also a regular for a while on *Dynasty*. **Selected Works:** *Jacksons: An American Dream* (1992), *Deadly Ice* (1994)

# Esther Williams

**Born:** August 8, 1923; Los Angeles, CA

**Years Active in the Industry:** by decade

| 10ˢ | 20ˢ | 30ˢ | 40ˢ | 50ˢ | 60ˢ | 70ˢ | 80ˢ | 90ˢ |
|-----|-----|-----|-----|-----|-----|-----|-----|-----|

A champion swimmer in her teens and a part-time model, she was spotted by a Hollywood scout while swimming in Billy Rose's Aquacade. At first a standard starlet, she appeared in two films before beginning her career in earnest in *Bathing Beauty* (1944), which set the standard for her subsequent swimming extravaganzas—musical comedies in color, punctuated by elaborately choreographed underwater swimming scenes. She was promoted as "Hollywood's Mermaid" and "The Queen of the Surf." Her films remained quite successful through the mid '50s. In the late '50s she tried to extend her career in straight dramatic roles, but she was unsuccessful, and in 1961 she retired from acting. She is the widow of actor Fernando Lamas; their son is actor Lorenzo Lamas. **Selected Works:** *Ziegfeld Follies* (1946), *On an Island With You* (1948); *Neptune's Daughter* (1950), *Million Dollar Mermaid* (1953)

# Guinn Williams

**Born:** April 26, 1899; Decatur, TX
**Died:** 1962

**Years Active in the Industry:** by decade

| 10ˢ | 20ˢ | 30ˢ | 40ˢ | 50ˢ | 60ˢ | 70ˢ | 80ˢ | 90ˢ |
|-----|-----|-----|-----|-----|-----|-----|-----|-----|
|     |     |     |     |     |     |     |     |     |

Strapping actor Guinn Williams was best known as Big Boy Williams who played in many of Will Rogers' silent Westerns. A congressman's son, Williams played professional baseball before making his debut in Hollywood in 1919. Initially, he played bit parts at Goldwyn. He then began playing in Westerns for various studios during the early 20s. By the time he teamed up with Rogers, he had become a character actor. Williams was briefly a cowboy star during the '30s, but soon was relegated back to character parts, frequently playing the comically dull-witted cowpoke. Occasionally, he got to play a bad-guy. He made his final film in 1962; he died later that year.

# JoBeth Williams

**Born:** 1953; Houston, TX

**Years Active in the Industry:** by decade

| 10ˢ | 20ˢ | 30ˢ | 40ˢ | 50ˢ | 60ˢ | 70ˢ | 80ˢ | 90ˢ |
|-----|-----|-----|-----|-----|-----|-----|-----|-----|
|     |     |     |     |     |     |     | ■   |     |

She first attracted attention as a student at Brown University, when she was selected as one of *Glamour* magazine's Top Ten College Girls of 1969-70. Williams acted with repertory companies in Rhode Island, Philadelphia, Boston, and Washington, D.C. In the late '70s she worked for two years on the TV soap operas *Somerset* and *The Guiding Light.* Her screen debut was a small role as Dustin Hoffman's girlfriend in *Kramer vs. Kramer* (1979), after which she went on to star in Broadway's *A Coupla White Chicks Sitting Around Talking.* She was soon landing roles in major movies, and has sustained a fairly busy screen career as a supporting actress and occasional lead. She married TV director John Pasquin. **Selected Works:** *Me, Myself & I* (1992), *Poltergeist* (1982), *Switch* (1991), *Victim of Love* (1991), *The Big Chill* (1983)

# John Williams

**Born:** 1903; Chalfont, St. Giles, England
**Died:** 1983

**Years Active in the Industry:** by decade

| 10ˢ | 20ˢ | 30ˢ | 40ˢ | 50ˢ | 60ˢ | 70ˢ | 80ˢ | 90ˢ |
|-----|-----|-----|-----|-----|-----|-----|-----|-----|
|     |     |     | ■   |     |     |     |     |     |

The son of a movie-studio musician, John Williams was trained for the Family Business at UCLA and Julliard. Proficient with several instruments, Williams settled down to a thriving career as a jazz pianist. Billing himself as Johnny Williams to avoid confusion with British character actor John Williams, the young composer worked closely with Henry Mancini on the *Peter Gunn* series, then branched out to compose his own scores for several of the 1960s TV adventure programs produced by Irwin Allen. Williams' first film credit was for the 1960 social drama *I Passed For White*. A composer, arranger and musical supervisor throughout the 1960s, Williams received the first of several Oscars for his orchestrations in *Fiddler on the Roof* (1971), his second movie musical. In the 1970s, Williams' name became conjoined with the twin *wunderkinds* George Lucas and Steven Spielberg. He composed the music for all three of Lucas' *Star Wars* films, and for *all* of Spielberg's films, from *Sugarland Express* onward. Williams' main themes for *Jaws, E.T.* and *Raiders of the Lost Ark* have inspired so many fifth-rate imitations from lesser composers that it's a wonder Williams has never issued a blanket lawsuit to protect himself from defamation. In 1980, John Williams succeeded the late Arthur Fiedler as conductor of the Boston Pops; with becoming modesty, the bearded, avuncular Williams allowed that he'd probably never be able to fully fill Fiedler's shoes—and then, for the next thirteen years, proceeded to do just that. **Selected Works:** *Close Encounters of the Third Kind* (1977), *Schindler's List* (1993), *Jurassic Park* (1993), *JFK* (1991), *Hook* (1991)

# Robin Williams

**Born:** July 21, 1951; Chicago, IL

**Years Active in the Industry:** by decade

| 10ˢ | 20ˢ | 30ˢ | 40ˢ | 50ˢ | 60ˢ | 70ˢ | 80ˢ | 90ˢ |
|-----|-----|-----|-----|-----|-----|-----|-----|-----|
|     |     |     |     |     |     |     | ■   |     |

Williams became interested in comedy by memorizing the records of Jonathan Winters. At age 18 he began working in comic improvisation, for which he has an extraordinary talent; he also studied acting at California's Marin College. After moving to New York he studied drama with John Houseman at the Juilliard School (working as a street mime to pay some of the tuition), then moved back to California and began appearing in comedy clubs. He landed the role of the zany alien Mork on an episode of the TV sitcom *Happy Days,* leading to the starring role in the resulting "spin-off" sitcom, *Mork and Mindy,* which became a hit and made him

famous; meanwhile he continued to work in stand-up comedy, becoming one of the three or four most successful comics in America. He debuted onscreen in the title role of Robert Altman's *Popeye* (1980), after which he tended to appear in one film a year. He had no big successes until *Good Morning, Vietnam* (1987), in which he gave a manic comic performance as real-life U.S. forces disc jockey Adrian Cronauer; the film established him as a screen star and earned him the first of three Oscar nominations. Off-screen, in the '80s he had a serious drug problem, which he was able to overcome. He is active in political causes and co-hosts the annual "Comic Relief" charity telethon. His hit comedy *Mrs. Doubtfire* (1993) was produced by his wife, who is also his manager. **Selected Works:** *Awakenings* (1990), *Dead Poets Society* (1989), *The Fisher King* (1991), *Birds of a Feather* (1995), *Jumanji* (1995)

# Treat Williams (Richard Williams)

**Born:** December 1, 1951; Rowayton, CT

**Years Active in the Industry:** by decade

| 10s | 20s | 30s | 40s | 50s | 60s | 70s | 80s | 90s |
|-----|-----|-----|-----|-----|-----|-----|-----|-----|
|     |     |     |     |     |     |     |     |     |

The muscular-bodied and darkly handsome Treat Williams has been a leading actor of the '70s and early '80s. He was born in Rowayton, Connecticut. As a young man, he began playing in Shakespeare productions with the Fulton reperatory company in Pennsylvania during summer breaks from college. He then went on to understudy for the character of Danny Zuko, the lead in the Broadway musical *Grease*. Williams later played the lead in the play. On screen he made his debut as an attractive, high-voiced detective in Richard Lester's gay bathhouse comedy *The Ritz* (1976). He is perhaps best known for his 1979 role in *Hair*, in which he did a notorious table-top dance. He continued to work in lead roles in a variety of films during the '80s. **Selected Works:** *Final Verdict* (1991), *Max & Helen* (1990), *Prince of the City* (1981), *Water Engine* (1992), *Things to Do in Denver when You're Dead* (1995)

# Bruce Willis

**Born:** March 19, 1955; West Germany

**Years Active in the Industry:** by decade

| 10s | 20s | 30s | 40s | 50s | 60s | 70s | 80s | 90s |
|-----|-----|-----|-----|-----|-----|-----|-----|-----|
|     |     |     |     |     |     |     |     |     |

Born in Germany, Willis grew up in New Jersey from age two. His first work as an entertainer involved playing the harmonica in a band called Loose Goose; also, while attending college he appeared in a student play. He worked for a time as a security guard, then began acting, supporting himself by working in a bar. Acting lessons in the mid '70s led to a small part in an off-Broadway production, after which he struggled in his career, getting occasional work onstage and in TV comercials. In the early '80s he had tiny parts in three films made in New York. After he moved to Los Angeles he got his big break in 1985 when he was cast as David Addison in the TV series "Moonlighting" with Cybil Shepherd; the show became a hit and he became famous, after which Hollywood beckoned. His Hollywood movie debut was as the costar (with Kim Basinger) in the comedy *Blind Date* (1987). He became a screen star after the huge success of his third film, *Die Hard* (1988), an action-adventure flick with large amounts of firepower, in which he played a New York cop in Los Angeles. His career since has been uneven. He is married to actress Demi Moore. **Selected Works:** *Death Becomes Her* (1992), *Mortal Thoughts* (1991), *Pulp Fiction* (1994), *Nobody's Fool* (1994), *Four Rooms* (1995)

# Gordon Willis

**Born:** Queens, NY

**Years Active in the Industry:** by decade

| 10s | 20s | 30s | 40s | 50s | 60s | 70s | 80s | 90s |
|-----|-----|-----|-----|-----|-----|-----|-----|-----|
|     |     |     |     |     |     |     |     |     |

American cinematographer Gordon Willis began as a summer-stock actor, but turned to photography full time after experience as an Air Force cameraman. The slow uphill climb peaked in 1970, when the 39-year-old Willis lensed his first feature film. Among his best known assignments were the three *Godfather* films and several of Woody Allen's projects, notably the documentary-style *Zelig* (1983). As well known for his outspokenness as his photographic brilliance, Willis raised hackles on the set of *The Godfather*, responding to many of director Francis Ford Coppola's instructions by moaning, "Oh, that's dumb!" Perhaps partially due to this abrasiveness, Willis has received only two Oscar nominations, for *Zelig* (1982) and *The Godfather III* (1990). In 1980, Gordon Willis directed his first film, the visually intriguing but otherwise worthless mad-killer melodrama *Windows*. **Selected Works:** *Presumed Innocent* (1990)

# Chill Wills

**Born:** July 18, 1903; Seagoville, TX
**Died:** 1978

**Years Active in the Industry:** by decade

| 10s | 20s | 30s | 40s | 50s | 60s | 70s | 80s | 90s |
|-----|-----|-----|-----|-----|-----|-----|-----|-----|
|  |  | ██ | ██ | ██ | ██ | ██ |  |  |

He began performing in early childhood, going on to appear in tent shows, vaudeville, and stock throughout the Southwest. He formed Chill Wills and the Avalon Boys, a singing group in which he was the leader and bass vocalist, in the '30s. After appearing with the group in several Westerns, beginning with his screen debut, *Bar 20 Rides Again* (1935), he disbanded the group in 1938. For the next fifteen years he was busy onscreen as a character actor, but after 1953 his film work became less frequent. He provided the voice of Francis the Talking Mule in the "Francis" comedy series of films. In the '60s he starred in the TV series "Frontier Circus" and "The Rounders." For his work in *The Alamo* (1960) he received a Best Supporting Actor Oscar nomination. In 1975 he released a singing album—his first. **Selected Works:** *Giant* (1956), *Westerner* (1940), *Yearling* (1946)

# Oprah Winfrey

**Born:** 1954; Kosciusko, MS

**Years Active in the Industry:** by decade

| 10s | 20s | 30s | 40s | 50s | 60s | 70s | 80s | 90s |
|-----|-----|-----|-----|-----|-----|-----|-----|-----|
|  |  |  |  |  |  |  | ██ |  |

At age 17 Winfrey was a part-time radio news announcer. While attending college she was crowned Miss Black Tennessee. She went on to work as a reporter/anchor for Nashville's CBS affiliate and in 1976 became the co-anchor for a Baltimore TV station. From 1977-83 she hosted the local TV show "People Are Talking," leading to an invitation in 1984 to move to Chicago and host "A.M. Chicago;" the show was a hit and within two years it was re-named "The Oprah Winfrey Show." The show went into syndication and became the biggest syndicated afternoon talk show on the air; Winfrey was frequently among the highest-paid people in America. Producer Quincy Jones appeared on her show and decided to cast her as Sofia in the film *The Color Purple* (1985), her screen debut; for her work she received a Best Supporting Actress Oscar nomination. She has gone on to a few more film and TV roles, but has not pursued acting as anything more than a sideline.

# Marie Windsor (Emily Marie Bertelson)

**Born:** December 11, 1922; Marysvale, UT

**Years Active in the Industry:** by decade

| 10s | 20s | 30s | 40s | 50s | 60s | 70s | 80s | 90s |
|-----|-----|-----|-----|-----|-----|-----|-----|-----|
|  |  |  | ██ | ██ | ██ | ██ |  |  |

A Utah girl born and bred, actress Marie Windsor attended Brigham Young University and repsresented her state as "Miss Utah" in the Miss America pageant. She studied acting under Russian stage and screen luminary Maria Ouspenskaya, supporting herself as a telephone operator between performing assignments. After several years of radio appearances and movie bits, Windsor was moved up to feature film roles in 1947's *Song of the Thin Man*. She was groomed to be a leading lady, but her height precluded her costarring with many of Hollywood's sensitive, slightly built leading men. (She later noted with amusement that at least one major male star had a mark on his dressing room door at the 5'6" level; if an actress was any taller than that, she was out.) Perservering, Windsor found steady work in second-lead roles as dance-hall queens, gun molls, floozies and exotic villainesses. She is affectionately remembered by disciples of director Stanley Kubrick for her portrayal of Elisha Cook's coldblooded, castrating wife in *The Killing* (1956). Curtailing her screen work in the late 1980s, Windsor, who is far more agreeable in person than on screen, began devoting the greater portion of her time to her sizeable family. Because of her many appearances in Westerns (she was an expert horsewoman), Windsor has become a welcome and highly sought-after presence on the nostalgia convention circuit. **Selected Works:** *Hearts of the West* (1975), *Narrow Margin* (1952)

# Debra Winger

**Born:** May 16, 1955; Cleveland, OH

**Years Active in the Industry:** by decade

| 10s | 20s | 30s | 40s | 50s | 60s | 70s | 80s | 90s |
|-----|-----|-----|-----|-----|-----|-----|-----|-----|
|  |  |  |  |  |  | ██ | ██ | ██ |

The daughter of a Kosher frozen-food distributor, American actress Debra Winger dropped out of high school at 16 in order to join an Israeli kibbutz. Upon returning to the U.S., she studied criminology and sociology at California State University, but before long she had dropped out and became a tour guide at the Magic Mountain amusement park. A serious accident suffered on the job at age 18 gave Winger time to contemplate her future, and it was then that she settled upon an acting career. Her first taste of fame was as the superpowered younger sister of Lynda Carter in the fantasy TV series "Wonder Woman." But Winger chafed at the impositions placed on her by tight TV filming schedules and retreated to theatrical films, where she made a most inauspicious debut in the award-losing *Slumber Party 57* (1977). Winger became a full-fledged audience favorite for her peppery role opposite John Travolta in *Urban Cowboy* (1980), which led to the most famous of her "working class" roles in *An Officer and a Gentlemen* (1982). Already balking at the Hollywood Game, Winger made no secret of her discomfort in that film's famous nude love scene, nor of her failure to truly connect with costar Richard Gere. The actress' next truly important part was as Shirley MacLaine's foredoomed daughter in *Terms of Endearment* (1983). Winger clashed with MacLaine constantly, insisted that her part be expanded to equal her costar's screen time (resulting in a death scene that goes on for eons), and drove cast and crew bonkers by remaining "in character" 24 hours a day. Withal, her resultant *Terms* performance was so good that it warranted an Oscar nomination. Winger never again had a box-office success to match *Terms of Endearment*, though she remained a darling of the film critics for her work in such little-seen epics as *Mike's Murder* (1984) and *Black Widow* (1986). As the actress' star stature diminished, media scrutiny of her private life increased thanks to her romance with Nebraska governor Robert Kerrey. Winger's roles became fewer and more unorthodox as she continued to seek out acting challenges—never more so than when she popped up in a lengthy unbilled *male* part (complete with goatee) in *Made in Heaven* (1987), which starred her then-husband, Timothy Hutton. Winger has continued to appear in high-profile but low-grossing films into the 1990s, delighting critics and fans in such films as *The Sheltering Sky* (1990) and *Shadowlands* (1993). Winger missed out on appearing in one of the most profitable films of the 1990s when her prima donna behavior caused her to be replaced by Geena Davis in *A League of Their Own* (1993); it was not temperament but personal injuries and a recurring back ailment that prevented Winger from participating in two other major moneymakers, *Peggy Sue Got Married* (1986) and *Bull Durham* (1988). **Selected Works:** *Leap of Faith* (1992), *An Officer and a Gentleman* (1982), *Forget Paris* (1995)

# Henry Winkler

**Born:** October 30, 1945; New York, NY

**Years Active in the Industry:** by decade

| 10s | 20s | 30s | 40s | 50s | 60s | 70s | 80s | 90s |
|-----|-----|-----|-----|-----|-----|-----|-----|-----|
|     |     |     |     |     |     |     |     |     |

A graduate of the Yale School of Drama, American actor Henry Winkler first appeared on Broadway and in films (*Crazy Joe*, *The Lords of Flatbush* [both 1974]) before making the guest-star rounds on TV sitcoms. He worked several times for MTM productions, appearing in such roles as Valerie Harper's date on *Rhoda* and a charming thief undergoing psychoanalysis on *The Bob Newhart Show*. In 1973, Winkler was selected among hundreds of candidates (including ex-Monkee Micky Dolenz) to play the small recurring role of Arthur "Fonzie" Fonzarelli, a leather-jacketed auto mechanic, on the new TV sitcom *Happy Days*. Though the series stars' were ostensibly Ron Howard, Anson Williams and Donny Most, the bulk of the fan mail sent to *Happy Days* during its first season was addressed to "The Fonz." By the time the second season rolled around, Winkler was afforded second billing and a larger slice of screen time on each week's episode. Soon the more impressionable TV fans of America were parroting such Fonzie catchphrases as "Aaaaay" and "Sit on it!," while the nonplussed Winkler, who always regarded himself as a Dustin Hoffmanesque character actor, climbed to teen-idol status, complete with fan magazine interviews, posters and Fonzie dolls. He also enjoyed a substantial salary boost, from $750 per episode to (eventually) $80,000. At first, the offstage Winkler could be as testy and sarcastic as his on-stage persona, but as Fonzie assumed "role model" proportions, the

actor began comporting himself in as polite and agreeable a manner as possible. Accordingly, Fonzie became less of a Marlon Brando-type hoodlum and more of a basically good-hearted, moralistic young fellow who happened to be a motorcycle-racing dropout. By the time *Happy Days* ended in 1983 (by which time Winkler was elevated to top billing), Fonzie was a "drop-in," with a good job as a high school shop teacher and the possibility of a solid marriage. During his *Happy Days* heyday, Winkler was determined to prove he was capable of playing parts above and beyond Fonzie by taking film roles as far removed from his TV character: the troubled Vietnam vet in *Heroes* (1977), the vainglorious actor-turned-wrestler in *The One and Only* (1981), a 1930s-style Scrooge in *An American Christmas Carol* (1982), and the timorous morgue attendant in *Night Shift* (1983). Following the example of his *Happy Days* costar Ron Howard, Winkler also began working his way into the production and direction end of the business. In addition, Winkler used his name value for the benefit of others, remaining active in charitable and political causes. After several years away from the camera, Winkler returned to acting in the 1991 TV-movie *Absolute Strangers*, playing the husband of a woman caught in the middle of a volatile pro-life/pro-choice argument. And in 1993, Henry Winkler starred in the brief TV sitcom *Monty*, portraying a bombastic Limbaugh-type conservative TV personality.

# Mare Winningham

**Born:** 1959; Northridge, CA

**Years Active in the Industry:** by decade

| 10s | 20s | 30s | 40s | 50s | 60s | 70s | 80s | 90s |
|-----|-----|-----|-----|-----|-----|-----|-----|-----|
|     |     |     |     |     |     |     |     |     |

Mare Winningham is a critically acclaimed performer on stage, television, and occasionally feature films. She began her career with a song on TV's notorious "Gong Show." While performing as Maria in a high school production of *The Sound of Music*, Winningham was spotted by a Hollywood agent. Meyer Mishkin got her cast in a short-lived TV Western series *The Young Pioneers* in 1978. This led her to appear in her first TV movie *Special Olympics*. For her role as an independent-minded farmer's daughter in 1980's *Amber Waves*, she won an Emmy. During that year, she also made her feature film debut in the ill-fated *One-Trick Pony*. She fared better in her next film, *Threshold* (1981), where she played the recipient of an artificial heart. Winningham then went on to play a number of supporting roles and the occasional lead in a series of unremarkable films. She continues to fare much better on television, where she has appeared in popular films such as *The Thorn Birds* (1983) and *Helen Keller: The Miracle Continues* (1984). **Selected Works:** *Eye on the Sparrow* (1991), *Crossing to Freedom* (1990), *She Stood Alone* (1991)

# Alex Winter (Alexander Winter)

**Born:** July 17, 1965; London, England

**Years Active in the Industry:** by decade

| 10ˢ | 20ˢ | 30ˢ | 40ˢ | 50ˢ | 60ˢ | 70ˢ | 80ˢ | 90ˢ |
|-----|-----|-----|-----|-----|-----|-----|-----|-----|
|     |     |     |     |     |     |     |  ■  |     |

The son of two modern dancers, he began training as a dancer at age four. His family moved to the U.S., where at the age of seven he began to work with an improvisation group founded by members of the celebrated Second City troupe; this led to work in regional productions and, eventually, to Broadway. As a teenager Winter spent six years on Broadway, debuting in a production of *The King and I.* He went on to study film production, writing and editing at New York University. He debuted onscreen in *Death Wish III* (1985), then waited two years for his next screen role, as a supporting player in the teen vampire flick *The Lost Boys* (1987); the film's success helped him get work in a series of TV commercials and the TV series *The Equalizer.* He scored a big success in his fifth movie, the hit comedy *Bill and Ted's Excellent Adventure* (1989), which greatly increased his recognition as an actor. **Selected Works:** *Bill & Ted's Bogus Journey* (1991), *Freaked* (1993)

# Shelley Winters (Shirley Schrift)

**Born:** August 18, 1922; Saint Louis, MO

**Years Active in the Industry:** by decade

| 10ˢ | 20ˢ | 30ˢ | 40ˢ | 50ˢ | 60ˢ | 70ˢ | 80ˢ | 90ˢ |
|-----|-----|-----|-----|-----|-----|-----|-----|-----|
|     |     |  ■  |  ■  |  ■  |  ■  |  ■  |  ■  |  ■  |

American actress Shelley Winters was the daughter of a tailor's cutter; her mother was a former opera singer. Winters evinced her mom's influence at age four, when she made an impromptu singing appearance at a St. Louis amateur night. When her father moved to Long Island to be closer to the New York garment district, Winters took acting lessons at the New School for Social Research and the Actors Studio. Short stints as a model and a chorus girl led to her Broadway debut in the S. J. Perelman comedy *The Night Before Christmas* in 1940. Winters signed a Columbia Pictures contract in 1943, mostly playing bits except when loaned to United Artists for an important role in *Knickerbocker Holiday* (1944). Realizing she was getting nowhere, Shelley took additional acting instructions and performed in nightclubs. The breakthrough came with her role as a "good time" girl murdered by insane stage star Ronald Colman in *A Double Life* (1947). Her roles became increasingly more prominent during her years at Universal-International, as did her offstage abrasive attitude; the normally mild-mannered James Stewart, Winters' costar in *Winchester 73* (1950), said after filming that the actress should have been spanked. Winters' performance as the pathetic factory girl impregnated and then killed by Montgomery Clift in *A Place in the Sun* (1951) won her an Oscar nomination; unfortunately, for every *Place in the Sun,* her career was blighted by disasters like *Behave Yourself* (1951). Disheartened by bad films and a turbulent marriage, Winters returned to Broadway in *A Hatful of Rain,* in which she received excellent reviews and during which she fell for her future third husband, An-

thony Franciosa. Always battling a weight problem, Winters was plump enough to be convincing as middle-aged Mrs. Van Daan in *The Diary of Anne Frank* (1959), for which Winters finally got her Oscar. In the 1960s, Winters portrayed a brothel madam in two films, *The Balcony* (1963) and *A House is Not a Home* (1964), roles that would have killed her career ten years earlier but which now established her in the press as an actress willing to take any professional risk for the sake of her art. Unfortunately, many of her performances in subsequent films like *Wild in the Streets* (1968) and *Bloody Mama* (1970) became more shrill than compelling, somewhat lessening her standing as a performer of stature. During this period, Winters made some fairly outrageous appearances on talk shows, where she came off as the censor's nightmare; she also made certain her point of view wouldn't be ignored, as in the moment when she poured her drink over Oliver Reed's head after Reed made a sexist remark on "The Tonight Show." Appearances in popular films like *The Poseidon Adventure* (1972) and well-received theatre appearances, like her 1974 tour in *Effect of Gamma Rays on Man-in-the-Moon Marigolds,* helped counteract such disappointments in Winters career as her appearance in the musical comedy *Minnie's Boys* (as the Marx Brothers' mother) and the movie loser *Flap* (1970). Treated generously by director Paul Mazursky in above-average films like *Blume in Love* (1974) and *Next Stop Greenwich Village* (1977), Winters has in recent years managed some excellent performances, though she still leans towards hamminess when the script is weak. Winters has added writing to her many achievements in the last two decades, penning a pair of tell-all autobiographies which delineate a private life every bit as rambunctious as some of Winter's screen performances. **Selected Works:** *Alfie* (1966), *Executive Suite* (1954), *The Night of the Hunter* (1955) *A Patch of Blue* (1965), *Stepping Out* (1991), *Searching for Bobby Fischer* (1993)

# Robert Wise

**Born:** September 10, 1914; Winchester, IN

**Years Active in the Industry:** by decade

| 10ˢ | 20ˢ | 30ˢ | 40ˢ | 50ˢ | 60ˢ | 70ˢ | 80ˢ | 90ˢ |
|-----|-----|-----|-----|-----|-----|-----|-----|-----|
|     |     |  ■  |  ■  |  ■  |  ■  |  ■  |  ■  |  ■  |

One of the most successful directors of the 1960s, when he became an efficient maker of epic-length pictures, Robert Wise is one of Hollywood's few popularly recognized filmmakers. He joined RKO in the 1930s as a cutter and eventually became one of the studio's top editors, working in this capacity on classics such as *The Devil and Daniel Webster* (1941), *Citizen Kane* (1941), and *The Magnificent Ambersons* (1942). He became a director with help from producer Val Lewton, who assigned Wise to finish *Curse of the Cat People* (1944), a B movie that had fallen behind schedule, and the resulting picture proved extremely haunting and enduring. Wise later directed *The Body Snatcher* (1945) for Lewton, but after the producer left RKO, he found himself locked into B movies. His 1948 psychological western *Blood On The Moon,* starring Robert Mitchum, and the acclaimed boxing drama *The*

*Set-Up* (1949) were the only two important pictures that Wise got to do during his last four years at the studio. Wise left RKO at the end of the 1940s and went to 20th Century-Fox, where his most important film, among a string of popular releases, was the visionary pacifist science fiction drama *The Day The Earth Stood Still*. He also formed a short-lived production company with his former RKO colleague Mark Robson, producing the acclaimed fact-based crime drama *Captive City* (1952). During the mid 1950s, Wise's film rapidly rose in importance and visibility, including *Executive Suite* (1954), *I Want To Live* (1958), and *Odds Against Tomorrow* (1959), all of which embraced important topical and sociological subjects amid their compelling performances. However, Wise's breakthrough as a "money director" came with *West Side Story* (1961), a screen adaptation of the stage hit (co-directed with Jerome Robbins) that earned multiple Oscars and a huge return at the box office. After a return to occult subjects with *The Haunting* (1963), which he also produced, Wise found himself in a position to establish himself as a major producer. Director William Wyler had been chosen by 20th Century-Fox to direct the screen version of the Rodgers and Hammerstein musical *The Sound of Music*, but had balked at the last moment and went to England to film *The Collector*. Wise was suggested as a replacement, and agreed to make the movie, but only if the studio agreed to finance Wise's production of *The Sand Pebbles* (1966), which he had been trying to raise money to make for several years. Fox agreed, and *The Sound of Music* (1965) went on to become one of the biggest box office hits of the decade, acquiring a shelf of Academy Awards in the process. *The Sand Pebbles*, starring Steve McQueen, was too serious a movie for the public to accept in 1966, with its overtones of the Vietnam War and its downbeat ending, although it eventually made money on re-release. Much less successful was *Star* (1968), Wise's epic musical based on the life of Gertrude Lawrence, which was heavily cut after a disastrous first run (and was only recently restored to full-length), and which never recovered its huge costs. After forming a new production company with Mark Robson, Wise returned to the profitable column with the science fiction drama *The Andromeda Strain* (1971), based on Michael Crichton's bestseller. His serious, adult romance *Two People* (1973) ran into problems with the censors and was heavily cut. And *The Hindenburg* came out too late in the 1970s disaster film cycle to attract huge audiences, despite its more-serious-than-usual theme for such a genre film. Wise's fortunes declined following *Audrey Rose* (1977), a sensitively made and effective occult drama; *Star Trek: The Motion Picture* (1980) was marred by major production problems; and *Rooftops*, a 1980s urban musical, was ignored by the public and derided by the critics. However, as a spokesman for the Academy of Motion Picture Arts and Sciences, Wise has remained a very visible and well known director and figure in Hollywood since the 1970s. **Selected Works:** *I Want to Live!* (1958), *Set-Up* (1949)

# Frederick Wiseman

**Born:** January 1, 1930; Boston, MA

**Years Active in the Industry:** by decade

| 10s | 20s | 30s | 40s | 50s | 60s | 70s | 80s | 90s |
|-----|-----|-----|-----|-----|-----|-----|-----|-----|
|     |     |     |     |     |     |     |     |     |

Frederick Wiseman was a prolific documentarian noted for his ability to capture the nuances of life in American institutions such as prisons, hospitals, welfare offices, and high schools. He has steadily produced over 20 films since 1968. All but his first, *Titicut Follies* (1967), have been broadcast on PBS. He started out in 1963 by producing a fictional feature film *The Cool World*, an examination of the lives of Harlem teenagers. In the beginning, Wiseman was a staunch social reformist, and his films were calls for change. *Titicut Follies*, his first documentary, is an expose of life in a prison for the criminally insane in Bridgewater, Massachusetts. It was controversial and left Wiseman with the reputation of being a muckraker. His four subsequent documentaries were all exposes of other tax-supported institutions designed to show the ineffectiveness of the bureaucracy that not only threatens to destroy them, but also dehumanizes the people they were meant to serve. Wiseman toned down his message and began focusing more on American culture to point out the symbolism of daily activities in his film *Primate* (1974). In the eighties, he began examining institutions as they relate to ideology. Unlike other documentaries, Wiseman's work does not progress chronologically; rather, the segments are arranged thematically, like an essay, and are linked via rhetorical devices such as comparison, contrast to create a patterned structure. His films are never narrated, thereby forcing viewers to make connections between the sequences themselves. Wiseman has occasionally returned to fictional films, as with his script for *The Stunt Man* (1980) and the mainstream experimental film *Seraphita's Diary* (1982).

# John Woo

**Born:** 1946; China

**Years Active in the Industry:** by decade

| 10s | 20s | 30s | 40s | 50s | 60s | 70s | 80s | 90s |
|-----|-----|-----|-----|-----|-----|-----|-----|-----|
|     |     |     |     |     |     |     |     |     |

Chinese writer/director John Woo was four years old when his family moved from the Mainland to Hong Kong in 1950. Virtually a lifelong employee of the Hong Kong film industry, Woo made his directing bow with 1977's *Young Dragons,* the first of several "chop-socky" actioners. With *A Better Tomorrow* (1986), his first international success, Woo began tempering his action scenes with stronger plots and characterization. Woo's *The Killer* (1989), in which his favorite actor Chow Yung-Fat delivered a richly textured performance as a sentimental hit man, wound up the highest-grossing Hong Kong film since the heyday of Bruce Lee. American critics have tended to dismiss Woo's films as childish and excessive, suggesting that the director is unaware of how ridiculous his productions seem to non-Oriental viewers. A complete survey of Woo's work would indicate that his operatic orgies of outrageous violence are deliberate stylistic choices, and that any "ridiculous" elements in his films are strictly intentional. Hollywood held John Woo in high enough esteem (due to the profibility of his output) to invite him to direct his first American movie in 1993, the Jean-Claude Van Damme vehicle *Hard Target.* **Selected Works:** *Bullet in the Head* (1990), *Broken Arrow* (1995)

# Ed D. Wood, Jr.

**Born:** October 10, 1924; Poughkeepsie, NY
**Died:** December 10, 1978

**Years Active in the Industry:** by decade

| 10s | 20s | 30s | 40s | 50s | 60s | 70s | 80s | 90s |
|-----|-----|-----|-----|-----|-----|-----|-----|-----|

One of the strangest men to ever occupy the director's chair in Hollywood, Ed D. Wood Jr. was a denizen of the netherside of the film capital. After arriving in Hollywood as an actor, Wood moved around Poverty Row for a few years, picking up odd assignments, and emerged as a writer-director in the mid 1950s in a series of low-budget movies focusing on crime, sexual deviance, transvestism, flying saucers, atomic radiation, and the occult. Wood admitted that the transvestism was autobiographical, but how involved he was with any of the other subjects is an open question. *Glen or Glenda?* (1953) was his most personal film, an ineptly written and directed, but sincere, plea for an understanding of transvestism that presented Bela Lugosi in an incomprehensible featured role and Wood himself (acting under a psedonym) and his wife as the main subjects of the film. Other films, including *The Sinister Urge* (1960), a cautionary tale about the effects of pornography, and *Bride of the Monster* (1956) followed, but Wood's immortality as a filmmaker was established with *Plan Nine From Outer Space* (1956), a bizarre but utterly entertaining story of grave robbers from deep space, featuring ludicrous dialogue, non-existent special effects, and some of the worst acting ever to grace a feature film, all pulled together in an utterly inept but ultimately near-hypnotic manner by Wood. His follow-up film, *Night Of The Ghouls* (1959), remained in the lab for 23 years because Wood couldn't pay the processing bill. During the '60s and '70s he moved on the periphery of Hollywood, supporting himself by grinding out pornographic novels, among other works. He died in 1978, just two years before a loving public rediscovered him and *Plan Nine From Outer Space,* which has since acquired a cult following akin to *The Rocky Horror Picture Show.* He would, no doubt, be pleased, amused, and amazed by the international following and recognition he has achieved in the decades since.

# Elijah Wood

**Born:** January 28, 1981; Cedar Rapids, IA

**Years Active in the Industry:** by decade

| 10s | 20s | 30s | 40s | 50s | 60s | 70s | 80s | 90s |
|-----|-----|-----|-----|-----|-----|-----|-----|-----|

"Move over, Macaulay Culkin!" trumpeted columnists during the 1990s ascent to stardom of American child actor Elijah Wood. This convenient journalistic bracketing ignored the fact that kiddie superstar Culkin and 10-year-old Wood had entirely different screen personalities. While Culkin was a precocious Dennis the Menace type, Wood projected a more down-to-earth, next-door-neighbor image; besides, as the 1993 Culkin/Wood costarring effort *The Good Son* revealed, Wood was actually the more versatile of the two. Making his first public impression with a small role in a Paula Abdul video, young Wood began toting up some impressive big-screen credits in such films as *Back to the Future 2* (1988), *Internal Affairs* (1990), and *Avalon* (1990). When he finally attained leads, it was unfortunately in such box-office disappointments as *Radio Flyer* (1992), *The Adventures of Huck Finn* (1993), and *North* (1994). Though certainly capable of carrying a film all by himself, Wood was shown to better advantage in his costarring stints with Mel Gibson in *Forever Young* (1993) and with Kevin Costner in *The War* (1994). **Selected Works:** *Paradise* (1991)

# Natalie Wood (Natasha Gurdin)

**Born:** July 20, 1938; San Francisco, CA
**Died:** November 29, 1981; off Santa Catalina Island, CA

**Years Active in the Industry:** by decade

| 10s | 20s | 30s | 40s | 50s | 60s | 70s | 80s | 90s |
|-----|-----|-----|-----|-----|-----|-----|-----|-----|

Born Natasha Gurdin, Wood was the daughter of a ballet dancer, and she began taking dance lessons as soon as she could walk. At age five she was among many residents of Santa Clara, California, who appeared as extras in *Happy Land* (1943); she made an impression on the director, Irving Pichel, who cast her three years later in a featured role in *Tomorrow Is Forever* (1946). She went on to a busy screen career as a child star, then made an unusually succesful transition to teenage and ingenue roles. By her late teens she was a beautiful leading lady. She received Oscar nominations for her work in *Rebel Without a Cause* (1955), *Splendor In the Grass* (1961), and *Love With the Proper Stranger* (1963). Her screen work after 1966 was intermittent. From 1957-63 she was married to actor Robert Wagner, whom she remarried in 1972; they costarred in *All the Fine Young Cannibals* (1960). She was the sister of actress Lana Wood and the mother (with producer Richard Gregson) of actress

Natasha Wagner. She died in a drowning accident after disappearing from a yacht in 1981. She was in the process of filming *Brainstorm* when she died. It was released two years later to mixed reviews. **Selected Works:** *Bob & Carol & Ted & Alice* (1969), *The Ghost and Mrs. Muir* (1947), *West Side Story* (1961), *Miracle on 34th Street* (1947)

# Alfre Woodard

**Born:** November 8, 1953; Tulsa, OK

**Years Active in the Industry:** by decade

| 10ˢ | 20ˢ | 30ˢ | 40ˢ | 50ˢ | 60ˢ | 70ˢ | 80ˢ | 90ˢ |
|-----|-----|-----|-----|-----|-----|-----|-----|-----|
|     |     |     |     |     |     |     | ■   | ■   |

She gained acting experience onstage with the Arena Theater in Washington, D.C., and the Mark Taper Forum in Los Angeles. Woodard appeared on TV and made her screen debut in the late '70s. For her work in *Cross Creek* (1983) she received a Best Supporting Actress Oscar nomination, becoming the first black actress nominated in that category since 1967. For her work as a guest star on the TV series *Hill Street Blues* and *L.A. Law* she won two Emmy Awards. Her screen career has been steadily busy since the late '80s, but she has yet to become a widely recognized film personality. She was a regular on the TV series "St. Elsewhere." **Selected Works:** *Grand Canyon* (1991), *Passion Fish* (1992), *Rich in Love* (1993), *Bopha* (1993), *How to Make an American Quilt* (1995)

# James Woods

**Born:** April 18, 1947; Vernal, UT

**Years Active in the Industry:** by decade

| 10ˢ | 20ˢ | 30ˢ | 40ˢ | 50ˢ | 60ˢ | 70ˢ | 80ˢ | 90ˢ |
|-----|-----|-----|-----|-----|-----|-----|-----|-----|
|     |     |     |     |     |     | ■   | ■   | ■   |

An "army brat," he spent his youth in several states and the island of Guam. He won a full scholarship to MIT and earned his degree in political science; while there Woods became interested in acting and appeared in 36 plays at MIT and Harvard, and with Boston's Theater Company. He worked in repertory summer stock at Rhode Island's Providence Playhouse, then debuted on

Broadway in Brendan Behan's *Borstal Boy*. Shortly thereafter he won an Obie and a Clarence Derwent Award (the latter given to the most promising actor of the year) for his work in the lead role of *Saved*. He continued his stage career through the '70s, meanwhile debuting onscreen in Elia Kazan's *The Visitors* (1972). His work in the TV drama *All the Way Home* led to a lead role in the blockbuster mini-series "Holocaust" (1978); ultimately, he has made over 40 TV appearances and has won two Emmy Awards. For his work in *Salvador* (1986) he received a Best Actor Oscar nomination. He was the subject of much gossip for the aftermath of his alleged affair with actress Sean Young, with whom he appeared in *The Boost* (1988); he sued Young for harrassment. **Selected Works:** *Citizen Cohn* (1992), *Onion Field* (1979), *Casino* (1995)

# Joanne Woodward

**Born:** February 27, 1930; Thomasville, GA

**Years Active in the Industry:** by decade

| 10ˢ | 20ˢ | 30ˢ | 40ˢ | 50ˢ | 60ˢ | 70ˢ | 80ˢ | 90ˢ |
|-----|-----|-----|-----|-----|-----|-----|-----|-----|
|     |     |     |     | ■   | ■   | ■   | ■   | ■   |

Woodward began acting in college, then gained experience at a small community theater in South Carolina. She moved to New York and studied at the Neighborhood Playhouse and the Actors Studio. She acted in many TV dramas in the '50s; spotted in them by the head of production at 20th Century-Fox, she was signed to a long-term film contract. She debuted onscreen in *Count Three and Pray* (1955). Her career took off after she won the Best Actress Oscar for her portrayal of a woman with multiple personalities in *The Three Faces of Eve* (1957). She remained a busy screen actress through the mid '70s, after which her film appearances have been infrequent. She is married to actor Paul Newman, with whom she has appeared in several films, including *Mr. and Mrs. Bridge* (1990), for which she received a Best Actress Oscar nomination. Newman has also directed several of her films. For her work in the TV movies *See How She Runs* (1978) and *Do You Remember Love?* (1985) she won Emmy Awards. For her work in *The Effect of Gamma Rays On Man-In-The-Moon Marigolds* (1972), which Newman directed, she won the Cannes Film Festival Best Actress Award. **Selected Works:** *Mr. & Mrs. Bridge* (1991), *Rachel, Rachel* (1968), *Age of Innocence* (1993), *Philadelphia* (1993)

# Fay Wray

**Born:** September 15, 1907; Alberta, Canada

**Years Active in the Industry:** by decade

| 10s | 20s | 30s | 40s | 50s | 60s | 70s | 80s | 90s |
|-----|-----|-----|-----|-----|-----|-----|-----|-----|

Wray began trying to break into movies before reaching her teens, and appeared in occasional films from age 12 in 1919. In 1928 she rose to instant stardom after starring in Erich von Stroheim's *The Wedding March*. She went on to play leads in many films through the early '40s. She is best known for portraying the frightened girl carried to the top of the Empire State Building in *King Kong* (1933). From the mid '30s she appeared mostly in low-budget action features. From 1928-39 she was married to playwright John Monk Saunders. In 1942 she married screenwriter Robert Riskin and retired from films; after Riskin's death she returned to films in 1953, going on to appear in a number of character roles throughout the next five years. She has written numerous plays and stories. She authored an autobiography, *On the Other Hand* (1989). **Selected Works:** *Viva Villa!* (1934), *Affairs of Cellini* (1934), *The Richest Girl in the World* (1934)

# Robin Wright

**Born:** 1966; Dallas, TX

**Years Active in the Industry:** by decade

| 10s | 20s | 30s | 40s | 50s | 60s | 70s | 80s | 90s |
|-----|-----|-----|-----|-----|-----|-----|-----|-----|

Robin Wright has been a working actress since her teens, costarring as Kelly Capwell on the NBC soap opera *Santa Barbera*. She made an engaging movie debut as the ever-imperiled Princess Buttercup in Rob Reiner's *The Princess Bride* (1986). Robin Wright's finest film hour (actually 150 minutes) was her portrayal of the emotionally scarred best friend—and later wife—of Tom Hanks in the Oscar-winning *Forrest Gump* (1994). She has a long-standing relationship with, and children by, actor Sean Penn. **Selected Works:** *Playboys* (1992), *State of Grace* (1990), *The Crossing Guard* (1995)

# Teresa Wright (Muriel Teresa Wright)

**Born:** October 27, 1918; New York, NY

**Years Active in the Industry:** by decade

| 10s | 20s | 30s | 40s | 50s | 60s | 70s | 80s | 90s |
|-----|-----|-----|-----|-----|-----|-----|-----|-----|

After apprenticing at the Wharf Theater in Provincetown, Massachusetts, she debuted on Broadway in 1938 as the lead's understudy in *Our Town;* the following year her performance in the ingenue part in *Life With Father* caught film mogul Samuel Goldwyn's attention, and he signed her to a screen contract. Wright debuted onscreen in *The Little Foxes* (1941), for which she received a Best Supporting Actress Oscar nomination. The following year she was nominated in both the Best Actress and Best Supporting Actress categories for her third and fourth films, *The Pride of the Yankees* and *Mrs. Miniver,* respectively; she won the Best Supporting Actress Oscar. She remained busy onscreen through 1959, after which she appeared in only a handful of films during the next three decades. From 1942-52 she was married to novelist and screenwriter Niven Busch; later she married, divorced, and remarried playwright Robert Anderson. In the '70s she appeared in TV dramas. Her later stage work included *Mary, Mary* (1962) and the Broadway revival of *Death of a Salesman* (1975). **Selected Works:** *The Best Years of Our Lives* (1946), *Men* (1950), *Shadow of a Doubt* (1943)

# Robert Wuhl

**Born:** 1951; Union Township, NJ

**Years Active in the Industry:** by decade

| 10s | 20s | 30s | 40s | 50s | 60s | 70s | 80s | 90s |
|-----|-----|-----|-----|-----|-----|-----|-----|-----|

Although he has a laid-back Huck Finn demeanor, actor/writer/director Robert Wuhl is one of the hardest-working denizens of Tinseltown. He began as a comedy writer, functioning as story editor on the cult TV series *Police Squad* and winning Emmies for his work (in collaboration with Billy Crystal) on the annual Academy Awards telecast. A film actor since 1980's *Hollywood Knights*, Wuhl is best remembered for his portrayal of the feckless reporter Alexander Knox in *Batman: The Movie* (1988), and for his starring stint in *Mistress* (1992). One of the more noteworthy aspect of Robert Wuhl's career is his ongoing association with baseball—he played the bullpen-chattering minor league coach in *Bull Durham* (1988), and the beleagured biographer of contentious ballplayer Ty Cobb in *Cobb* (1993); and, taking a brief breather from film work, Wuhl wrote the chapter on Roger Maris in author/editor Danny Peary's 1989 compendium *Cult Baseball Players*. **Selected Works:** *The Bodyguard* (1992), *Good Morning, Vietnam* (1987), *Blue Chips* (1994), *Open Season* (1995)

# William Wyler

**Born:** July 1, 1902; Mulhouse, France
**Died:** 1981

**Years Active in the Industry:** by decade

| 10s | 20s | 30s | 40s | 50s | 60s | 70s | 80s | 90s |
|-----|-----|-----|-----|-----|-----|-----|-----|-----|

One of the most honored directors in the history of Hollywood, with three Best Director Oscars, William Wyler was the mainstay of Samuel Goldwyn Productions for over a decade, and continued making important—if not always successful—pictures

right into the dawn of the 1970s. The son of a merchant, he was educated in Switzerland and studied the violin at the National Music Conservatory in Paris. A chance meeting with Carl Laemmle, the head of Universal Pictures, led to his entry into the movie business as a publicity writer. He later became an assistant director, and later helmed a string of Western shorts. By the beginning of the 1930s, he had moved up to full-length action features. **Selected Works:** *Ben-Hur* (1959), *Little Foxes* (1941), *Mrs. Miniver* (1942), *Roman Holiday* (1953), *Wuthering Heights* (1939)

# Jane Wyman

**Born:** January 4, 1914; Saint Joseph, MO

**Years Active in the Industry:** by decade

| 10s | 20s | 30s | 40s | 50s | 60s | 70s | 80s | 90s |
|-----|-----|-----|-----|-----|-----|-----|-----|-----|
|     |     |     |     |     |     |     |     |     |

Born Sarah Jane Fulks, she tried to break into films as a child but was unsuccessful despite encouragement from her mother. A decade later she began her show business career as a radio singer, using the name Jane Durrell. In 1936 she began appearing in films as a chorus girl and bit player. Eventually, she moved into secondary roles and occasional leads, usually playing brassy blondes in comic relief. She broke out of this mold with her performance in *The Lost Weekend* (1945), in which she demonstrated her talents as a serious actress; this led to better roles as a major star. For her work in *The Yearling* (1946) she received a Best Actress Oscar nomination, then won an Oscar for her portrayal of a deaf-mute rape victim in *Johnny Belinda* (1948). She went on to star in many films, demonstrating her vasatility in both comedies and tearjerkers. She was twice more nominated for Oscars, for *The Blue Veil* (1951) and *Magnificent Obsession* (1954). After 1956 her screen work was infrequent. She returned from retirement in the early '80s to play a regular role on the TV series *Falcon Crest*. From 1940-48 she was married to Ronald Reagan; their daughter Maureen Reagan was a singer-actress.

# Ed Wynn (Isaiah Edwin Leopold)

**Born:** November 9, 1886; Philadelphia, PA
**Died:** 1966

**Years Active in the Industry:** by decade

| 10s | 20s | 30s | 40s | 50s | 60s | 70s | 80s | 90s |
|-----|-----|-----|-----|-----|-----|-----|-----|-----|
|     |     |     |     |     |     |     |     |     |

Born Isaiah Edward Leopold, Wynn ran away from home at 15 to work as a utility boy for a stage company, with which he also acted. The company failed and he returned home. Shortly thereafter he moved to New York, soon becoming a vaudeville comic headliner. In 1914 he began appearing with the Ziegfeld Follies, billed as The Perfect Fool; menawhile, he got into a widely publicized feud with another Ziegfeld star, W.C. Fields. After organizing an actors' strike, in 1919 he was boycotted by the Shuberts. At the height of his popularity as a Broadway comic star, he got around the boycott by writing and producing his own shows, which were both critical and popular successes. Having appeared in a few films, in the '30s he increased his popularity on radio as the Texaco Fire Chief. At the end of the '30s several of his business ventures collapsed, including a radio chain; he suffered a nervous breakdown and his career seemed over. He bounced back on Broadway in the '40s. In 1949 he won the first TV Emmy Award as Best Actor in a Series. Out of work in the '50s, when his comedy style had become dated, he was encouraged by his son—actor Keenan Wynn—to launch a new career as a film actor. From 1957-67 he was busy onscreen as a dramatic character actor, and for his work in *The Diary of Anne Frank* (1959) he received a Best Supporting Actor Oscar nomination. He also appeared in TV dramas. **Selected Works:** *The Absent-Minded Professor* (1961), *Mary Poppins* (1964), *That Darn Cat* (1965)

# Keenan Wynn (Francis Xavier Wynn)

**Born:** July 24, 1916; New York, NY
**Died:** October 14, 1986; Brentwood, CA

**Years Active in the Industry:** by decade

| 10s | 20s | 30s | 40s | 50s | 60s | 70s | 80s | 90s |
|-----|-----|-----|-----|-----|-----|-----|-----|-----|
|     |     |     |     |     |     |     |     |     |

Actor Keenan Wynn was the son of legendary comedian Ed Wynn and actress Hilda Keenan, and grandson of stage luminary Frank Keenan. After attending St. John's Military Academy, Wynn obtained his few professional theatrical jobs with a Maine Stock Company. After overcoming the "Ed Wynn's Son" onus (his father arranged his first job, with the understanding that Keenan would be on his own after that), Wynn developed into a fine comic and dramatic actor on his own in several Broadway plays and on radio. He was signed to an MGM contract in 1942, scoring a personal and professional success as the sarcastic sergeant in 1944's *See Here Private Hargrove* (1944). Wynn's new-found popularity as a supporting actor aroused a bit of jealousy from his father Ed, who underwent professional doldrums in the 1940s; father and son grew closer in the 1950s when Ed, launching a second career as a dramatic actor, often turned to his son for moral support and professional advice. Wynn's film career flourished into the 1960s and 1970s, during which time he frequently appeared in such Disney films as *The Absent-Minded Professor* (1960) and *The Love Bug* (1968) as apoplectic villain Alonso Hawk. Wynn also starred in such TV series as *Troubleshooters* and *Dallas*. Encroaching deafness and a drinking problem plagued Wynn in his final years, but he always delivered the goods on-screen. Wynn was the father of writer/director Tracy Keenan Wynn and writer/actor Edmund Keenan (Ned) Wynn. **Selected Works:** *Kiss Me Kate* (1953), *Nashville* (1975), *Since You Went Away* (1944), *Dr. Strangelove - or - How I Learned to Stop Worrying and Love the Bomb* (1964)

# Y

## Peter Yates

**Born:** July 24, 1929; Ewshott, Surrey, England

**Years Active in the Industry:** by decade

| 10s | 20s | 30s | 40s | 50s | 60s | 70s | 80s | 90s |
|-----|-----|-----|-----|-----|-----|-----|-----|-----|
|     |     |     |     |     |     |     |     |     |

British director Peter Yates graduated from his early 1960's low-budget feature debut, the musical-comedy *Summer Holiday* (1963), starring Cliff Richard and the Shadows, to the superb thriller *Robbery* (1967), with Stanley Baker. It was a short jump to the American thriller *Bullitt* (1968), starring Steve McQueen, the definitive cop-thriller of its decade with the first car chase that anyone remembers in movies, through the streets of San Francisco. *John and Mary* (1969), starring Dustin Hoffman and Mia Farrow, was a big date movie at the end of the 1960s, and *The Hot Rock* (1972) was a groundbreaking comedy thriller of its era, while *The Friends of Eddie Coyle* (1973) was a crime drama with one of Robert Mitchum's best performances. Since then, Yates has moved easily between genres, from the black comedy of *Mother, Jugs, and Speed* (1976) to the comic-book style action of *Krull* (1983), pausing along the way for the sensitive period drama of *The Dresser* (1983) and the suspense of *Eyewitness* (1981). **Selected Works:** *Breaking Away* (1979), *Roommates* (1995), *The Run of the Country* (1995)

## Zhang Yimou

**Born:** 1950; Xi'an, Shaanxi Province, China

**Years Active in the Industry:** by decade

| 10s | 20s | 30s | 40s | 50s | 60s | 70s | 80s | 90s |
|-----|-----|-----|-----|-----|-----|-----|-----|-----|
|     |     |     |     |     |     |     |     |     |

There were few opportunities for Zhang Yimou to pursue a film career during China's Cultural Revolution of the late 1960s. Things began breaking for Zhang when the Beijing Film Academy reopened after several years' dormancy in 1978. He began his career as a cinematographer, then in 1988 directed *Red Sorghum*, a tragic tale revolving around an arranged marriage. Zhang Yimou's star was Gong Li, with whom he formed a felicitous working relationship, resulting in such internationally popular films as *Raise the Red Lantern* (1988) and the anti-bureaucracy masterpiece *The Story of Qui Ju* (1992). The director has persisted in making films in a social-protest vein, despite being habitually subjected to disciplinary rebukes from his government. *Ju Dou*, Zhang Yimou's 1990 saga of a woman (Gong Li again) victimized by the patriarchal Chinese establishment, was banned in China, but went on to become the first Chinese film ever to be nominated for an Academy Award. **Selected Works:** *To Live* (1994), *Shanghai Triad* (1995)

## Susannah York (Susannah Yolande Fletcher)

**Born:** January 9, 1941; London, England

**Years Active in the Industry:** by decade

| 10s | 20s | 30s | 40s | 50s | 60s | 70s | 80s | 90s |
|-----|-----|-----|-----|-----|-----|-----|-----|-----|
|     |     |     |     |     |     |     |     |     |

York was raised in a remote Scottish village and graduated from the Royal Academy of Dramatic Art in London. After gaining experience on the provincial stage, in repertory and pantomime, she broke into films in 1960; after a couple of standard ingenue roles she established herself as a star with sex appeal after her work in *Tom Jones* (1963). For her work in *They Shoot Horses, Don't They?* (1969) she received an Oscar nomination, and for her performance in Robert Altman's *Images* (1972) she won the Cannes Film Festival Best Actress award. With occasional breaks she has sustained a steady screen career through the '90s, including playing the role of Superman's mother in three of the *Superman* films. She co-wrote the screenplay for her film *Falling in Love Again* (1980). She is the author of *Lark's Castle* and the successful children's fantasy book *In Search of Unicorns*. She is married to writer-actor Michael Wells. **Selected Works:** *Illusions* (1991), *A Man for All Seasons* (1966), *Tunes of Glory* (1960), *Oh! What a Lovely War* (1969)

# Freddie Young

**Born:** 1902; England

**Years Active in the Industry:** by decade

| 10s | 20s | 30s | 40s | 50s | 60s | 70s | 80s | 90s |
|-----|-----|-----|-----|-----|-----|-----|-----|-----|

British cinematographer Freddie Young was in the film industry from the age of 15, picking up rent and food money with a variety of menial jobs. A lighting cameraman from the 1920s onward, Young hit his stride in the 1930s with such elaborately lensed pictures as *Victoria the Great* (1937) and *Goodbye Mr. Chips* (1939). Following war service, Young became one of a handful of British artisians who were as proficient with Technicolor as with black and white; he even managed to bring the paintings of Van Gogh to vibrant life with the pedestrian hues of Metrocolor in *Lust for Life* (1956). Young was best known in the 1960s for his long association with director David Lean, winning Oscars for his work on Lean's *Lawrence of Arabia* (1962) and *Doctor Zhivago* (1965). While many of his contemporaries urged Young to become a director himself, it wasn't until he turned 82 that Young directed his first film, the made-for-TV *Arthur's Hallowed Ground* (1985).

# Gig Young (Byron Barr)

**Born:** November 4, 1913; St. Cloud, MN
**Died:** 1978; Manhattan, NY

**Years Active in the Industry:** by decade

| 10s | 20s | 30s | 40s | 50s | 60s | 70s | 80s | 90s |
|-----|-----|-----|-----|-----|-----|-----|-----|-----|

After graduating from high school, where he had acted in student plays, he appeared with an amateur theater group. He went on to train for the stage at the Pasadena Playhouse, attending on a scholarship; his work there led to a screen contract. He debuted onscreen in 1940, appearing under his real name in bit roles in a few films. His first featured role was as a character named "Gig Young" in *The Gay Sisters* (1942), and he took the name as his own because there was another Hollywood actor named "Byron Barr;" he was also occasionally billed "Bryant Fleming." He served with the Coast Guard in World War II. When he returned to films he became typecast as a second leading man, often playing fun-loving bachelors or unsuccessful suitors in comedies; occasionally he had a lead role in a B movie. He was nominated three times for Oscars, and won for his work in *They Shoot Horses, Don't They?* (1969). He also did much work on the stage and TV, and was a regular on the series "The Rogues."

From 1956-63 he was married to actress Elizabeth Montgomery, his third wife. In 1978, three weeks after getting married again, he shot his wife and then shot himself. **Selected Works:** *Lovers and Other Strangers* (1970), *Teacher's Pet* (1958), *Come Fill the Cup* (1951)

# Loretta Young (Gretchen Michaela Young)

**Born:** January 6, 1913; Salt Lake City, UT

**Years Active in the Industry:** by decade

| 10s | 20s | 30s | 40s | 50s | 60s | 70s | 80s | 90s |
|-----|-----|-----|-----|-----|-----|-----|-----|-----|

Young's family moved to Hollywood and she began appearing (at age four) as a child extra in movies, as did her sisters (one of whom later became known as actress Sally Blane). At 14 she got a small supporting role in *Naughty But Nice* (1927), leading to a screen contract. She moved quickly from teenage to ingenue to leading lady roles, appearing in many films and successfully making the transition to the sound era. By the mid '30s she was an established star, usually cast in decorative roles in routine programmers. For her work in *The Farmer's Daughter* (1947) she won the Best Actress Oscar, and was nominated again for *Come to the Stable* (1949). After a consistently busy screen career of 25 years, she retired from films in 1953 to host the TV series "The Loretta Young Show," a weekly half-hour teleplay; she appeared in about half of the show's episodes, winning three Emmy Awards. Since the early '60s she has devoted most of her energies to Catholic charities. She has been married twice. In 1930 she made headlines when, at age 17, she eloped with actor Grant Withers. However, the marriage was annulled after a year. She later married producer and writer Thomas Lewis, from whom she eventually separated. She authored the memoir *The Things I Had to Learn* (1961). After NBC unlawfully broadcast her TV shows abroad, she sued the network in 1972 and won $600,000. **Selected Works:** *The Bishop's Wife* (1947), *House of Rothschild* (1934), *Kentucky* (1938), *The Men in Her Life* (1941)

# Robert Young

**Born:** February 22, 1907; Chicago, IL

**Years Active in the Industry:** by decade

| 10s | 20s | 30s | 40s | 50s | 60s | 70s | 80s | 90s |
|-----|-----|-----|-----|-----|-----|-----|-----|-----|

Chicago-born Robert Young carried his inbred "never give up" work ethic into his training at the Pasadena Playhouse. After a few movie-extra roles, he was signed by MGM to play a bit part as Helen Hayes' son in 1931's *Sin of Madelon Claudet*. At the request of MGM head Irving Thalberg, Young's role was expanded during shooting, thus the young actor was launched on the road to stardom (his first-released film was the Charlie Chan epic *Black Camel*

[1931], which he made while on loan to Fox Studios). Young appeared in as many as nine films per year in the 1930s, usually showing up in "bon vivant" roles. Alfred Hitchcock sensed a darker side to Young's ebullient nature, and accordingly cast the actor as a likeable American who turns out to be a sang-froid spy in 1936's *The Secret Agent*. Some of Young's best film work was in the 1940s, with such roles as the facially disfigured war veteran in *The Enchanted Cottage* (1945) and the no-good philanderer in *They Won't Believe Me* (1947). In 1949, Young launched the radio sitcom *Father Knows Best*, starring as insurance salesman/paterfamilias Jim Anderson (it was his third weekly radio series). The series' title was originally ironic in that Anderson was perhaps one of the most stupidly stubborn of radio dads. By the time *Father Knows Best* became a TV series in 1954, Young had refined his Jim Anderson characterization into the soul of sagacity. Young became a millionaire thanks to his part-ownership of *Father Knows Best*, which, despite a shaky beginning, ran successfully until 1960 (less popular was his 1961 TV "dramedy" *Window On Main Street*, which barely lasted a full season). Outwardly charming and a seemingly "perfect" husband (married to the same woman since 1933), Young tended to be a bit distant in real life, seldom mingling with the rest of the *Father* cast. The main reason for his aloofness was that Young was an alcoholic and didn't want his coworkers or fans to know. He didn't make his affliction public until well into his second successful series, *Marcus Welby MD* (1968-73); since then he has overcome his drinking problem and has been an active advocate of Alcoholics Anonymous. Young's most recent TV work has included one-shot revivals of *Father Knows Best* and *Marcus Welby*, and the well-received 1986 TV-movie *Mercy or Murder*, in which Young essayed the role of a real-life pensioner who killed his wife rather than allow her to endure a painful, lingering illness. **Selected Works:** *Crossfire* (1947), *Northwest Passage (Book 1 - Rogers' Rangers)* (1940), *Three Comrades* (1938), *House of Rothschild* (1934), *Sitting Pretty* (1948)

# Robert M. Young (Robert Milton Young)

**Born:** 1924; New York, NY

**Years Active in the Industry:** by decade

| 10s | 20s | 30s | 40s | 50s | 60s | 70s | 80s | 90s |
|-----|-----|-----|-----|-----|-----|-----|-----|-----|

New York-born Robert M. Young began his directorial career in association with Michael Roemer in 1962, with the Italian-made documentary *The Inferno*. Their second film together, *Nothing But a Man* (1965), became an acclaimed drama dealing with race relations in the United States as few feature films were willing to attempt, telling the tale of a black man (Ivan Dixon) with dreams beyond the station that society is willing to permit, and the price that he pays for them. Young didn't make his next movie as a director, *Alambrista!*, until a dozen years later, but has always worked in serious films, often at the expense of popular acceptance. His adaptation of the stage prison drama *Short Eyes* (1978) proved

critically successful, and *One Trick Pony* (1980)—perhaps Young's most obvious attempt at a "commercial" film—attracted a lot of attention as a vehicle for Paul Simon as an actor, although it ultimately failed due to Simon's limitations in that role. The violent, feminist-oriented drama, *Extremities* (1986), helped establish Farrah Fawcett as a serious actress, but received considerable criticism, mostly owing to its theatrical origins, which didn't allow the work to translate well to the screen. *Dominick and Eugene* (1988) is his most successful film, a serious drama about the love between a young physician (Ray Liotta) and his child-like twin (Tom Hulce). **Selected Works:** *Alive and Kicking* (1991)

# Sean Young

**Born:** November 20, 1959; Louisville, KY

**Years Active in the Industry:** by decade

| 10s | 20s | 30s | 40s | 50s | 60s | 70s | 80s | 90s |
|-----|-----|-----|-----|-----|-----|-----|-----|-----|

Sean Young worked as a model in New York, then was signed by the powerful ICM agency. At age 20, Young debuted on-screen in *Jane Austen in Manhattan* (1980), then attracted much attention for her third film, *Blade Runner* (1982), in which she portrayed a sympathetic android. After her appearance in *No Way Out* (1987), which included a steamy sex scene with Kevin Costner in the back of a limo, she was heralded as a major star, but subsequently failed to live up to her potential. She has been the center of off-screen controversy and has a reputation for being "difficult," though many who work with her have said her reputation is unfair. She had a well-publicized dispute with director Tim Burton after he dropped her from the cast of *Batman;* and, most notoriously, she was sued for harrassment by actor James Woods after the two of them worked together on the movie *The Boost* (1988). Regardless, she has remained a busy screen actress. **Selected Works:** *Blue Ice* (1993), *A Kiss Before Dying* (1991), *Sketch Artist* (1992), *Wall Street* (1987), *Hold Me, Thrill Me, Kiss Me* (1993), *Cousins* (1989)

# Terence Young

**Born:** June 20, 1915; Shanghai, China
**Died:** 1994

**Years Active in the Industry:** by decade

| 10s | 20s | 30s | 40s | 50s | 60s | 70s | 80s | 90s |
|-----|-----|-----|-----|-----|-----|-----|-----|-----|
|     |     |     |     |     |     |     |     |     |

British filmmaker Terence Young, who was born in Shanghai, began working in the movie business as a screenwriter specializing in comedy at the age of 21 (in 1936). Shortly thereafter, he served in the military during World War II. He co-directed one documentary, *Men of Arnhem* (1944), during the war, and reportedly was one of Laurence Olivier's early choices to direct *Henry V.* But it wasn't until 1948 that he got to make his first movie, *Corridor of Mirrors.* He quickly became an expert at making thrillers, although he occasionally worked in other areas, including the award-winning dance film *Black Tights* (1960). In 1962 he suddenly emerged as a major filmmaker when he was chosen to direct *Dr. No,* the first James Bond movie. Its success, and that of the follow-up film, *From Russia With Love* (1963), established the series and the hero (as well as Sean Connery), but Young pulled out of *Goldfinger* (1964) during pre-production when the producers refused to cut him in for a percentage of the profits. He was back for *Thunderball* (1965), which was the biggest-grossing Bond movie up to that time. His work on *The Amorous Adventures of Moll Flanders* (1965) was lively, but the film failed to find the same audience as Tony Richardson's *Tom Jones,* on which it had been modeled. However, his chilling adaptation of the stage thriller *Wait Until Dark* (1967) was a hit. Young's career from this point on went into gradual decline, as he became involved in difficult international productions, big-budget flops (*Mayerling*), or politically disreputable films such as *Inchon* (1982) (financed by the Unification Church). He made his last movie, the thriller *The Jigsaw Man,* in 1984.

# Billy Zane

**Born:** February 24, 1966; Chicago, IL

**Years Active in the Industry:** by decade

| 10ˢ | 20ˢ | 30ˢ | 40ˢ | 50ˢ | 60ˢ | 70ˢ | 80ˢ | 90ˢ |
|-----|-----|-----|-----|-----|-----|-----|-----|-----|
|     |     |     |     |     |     |     |  ■  |  ■  |

Actor Billy Zane kicked off his stage career in his home town of Chicago. Able to harness his spoiled-brat countenance and quirky gestures to invoke either sympathy or repulsion, Zane has been seen principally in secondary roles in such films as *Back to the Future II* (1988), *Memphis Belle* (1990), and *Posse* (1992). His most flamboyant role was as the young drifter who—obvious to everyone but the hero and heroine—is *not what he seems* in the Australian thriller *Dead Calm* (1989). Billy Zane is the older brother of film and TV actress Lisa Zane. **Selected Works:** *Lake Consequence* (1992), *Poetic Justice* (1993), *Tombstone* (1993), *Orlando* (1993), *Tales from the Crypt Presents: Demon Knight* (1995)

# Darryl F. Zanuck

**Born:** September 5, 1902; Wahoo, NE
**Died:** 1979

**Years Active in the Industry:** by decade

| 10ˢ | 20ˢ | 30ˢ | 40ˢ | 50ˢ | 60ˢ | 70ˢ | 80ˢ | 90ˢ |
|-----|-----|-----|-----|-----|-----|-----|-----|-----|
|     |     |  ■  |  ■  |  ■  |  ■  |     |     |     |

One of the most successful and respected movie moguls of Hollywood's Golden Age, Darryl F. Zanuck was also one of the few major players of his age who was not born in Europe. Hailing from Wahoo, Nebraska, Zanuck first entered the movie business as a child extra in 1908. After service in World War I (he lied about his age to join the Nebraska National Guard) and a period spent as a bantamweight boxer, he turned to writing, amid scratching out a living as a store clerk and waterfront laborer. With some modest success in magazines, he began sending stories into the movie studios. Zanuck joined Warner Bros. as a staff writer in 1923 and distinguished himself with his unusual plots. By 1928, he had been elevated to studio manager and became chief of production the following year, and was largely responsible for the shape of the studio's output during the late 1920s and early 1930s, including such notable scripts as *The Public Enemy* (1931) and *I Am a Fugitive From a Chain Gang* (1932), as well as the celebrated transitional talkie *Noah's Ark* (1929), which Zanuck produced personally. He left Warner Bros. in 1933 to form a new studio, 20th Century Pictures, with Joseph Schenck, which began an ambitious production schedule. Fate took a hand the following year when 20th Century—which was profitable, but had no studio facilities of its own—merged with William Fox's near-bankrupt Fox Studios to form 20th Century-Fox, with Zanuck as chief of production. He immediately set the newly expanded company on an ambitious production schedule, which included not only the exploitation of existing stars such as Shirley Temple, but the establishment of new leading men such as Tyrone Power in big-budget films. In the process, he also brought over many of his most trusted hands from Warner Bros., including publicist (and later producer) Milton Sperling, who was Jack Warner's son-in-law. Zanuck had a special knack for understanding the public taste, and visualizing the right actor in the right role, such as casting Basil Rathbone—previously known for his villain parts—as Sherlock Holmes (although he stopped making the Holmes films after two films, thus giving Universal Pictures an opening to produce another dozen Holmes films with Rathbone and his co-star Nigel Bruce). He also had blindspots where certain performers and film properties were concerned. Following an argument with Zanuck, actor-director Otto Preminger was barred from work on the Fox lot until Zanuck went off to military service. Preminger then returned, first as an actor and then as director of the movie version of his own Broadway hit *Margin For Error*. Preminger later produced and directed *Laura,* despite Zanuck's misgivings about the project and his dislike of the fey Clifton Webb in the key role of Waldo Lydecker. One of the few production chiefs who actually had experience making movies, Zanuck was overall a highly respected figure, who took an active and productive role in the making of many of Fox's biggest films. In the early 1950s, with the arrival of television as competition, he moved Fox to adapt CinemaScope, the first of the wide-screen formats, to keep movies competitive—although it didn't fit every production (*Daddy Long Legs* and *The Man In The Grey Flannel Suit* were especially awkward). Also, the decision to shoot its films in widescreen caused Fox to lose such productions as *On The Waterfront.* The company's films remained competitive, and the presence of stars such as Marilyn Monroe kept Fox among the top Hollywood studios until the end of the 1950s. Zanuck left Fox at the end of the 1950s to embark on a career as an independent producer, and made his most celebrated film, *The Longest Day* (1962), a sprawling all-star dramatization of the Normandy landings on D-Day. He returned to Fox soon after, amid the crisis caused by the enormous cost overruns surrounding *Cleopatra* (1963), and saw several more years of success at the head of the company (with his own son Richard as chief of production) until the dawn of the 1970s, when business reverses resulted in his being forced out of power. Richard Zanuck has since emerged as a major independent producer.

# Franco Zeffirelli

**Born:** February 12, 1923; Florence, Italy

**Years Active in the Industry:** by decade

| 10s | 20s | 30s | 40s | 50s | 60s | 70s | 80s | 90s |
|-----|-----|-----|-----|-----|-----|-----|-----|-----|
|     |     |     |     |     |     |     |     |     |

Italian director Franco Zeffirelli started out as an actor in the stage productions of *Luchino Visconti,* then worked as an assistant on several Visconti-directed films. After World War II, Zeffirelli launched a career designing, costuming, and directing operas, a field of entertainment to which he'd return periodically throughout his life and which led to his first directorial credit, the Swiss-Produced filmization of *La Boheme* (1965). Zeffirelli's reputation in the 1960s rested on his boisterous, non-traditional movie versions of Shakespeare. He directed Richard Burton and Elizabeth Taylor in a lusty adaptation of *Taming of the Shrew* (1967), then became an icon for the Youth Movement by casting 17-year-old Leonard Whiting and 15-year-old Olivia Hussey in *Romeo and Juliet* (1968). Zeffirelli's eye for visual richness served him well in the opulent *Brother Sun/Sister Moon* (1973), a romanticized account of Francis of Assisi. Some of Zeffirelli's later American films were unworthy of his talents, though he made the most of the emotional possibilities of *The Champ* (1979) and actually helped Brooke Shield pass as an actress in the otherwise lachrymose *Endless Love* (1981). The director found himself in the center of a controversy upon finishing the expensive Euro-American TV miniseries "Jesus of Nazareth;" certain religious activists, upset that the ads promised a "human" look at Jesus, forced several sponsors to withdraw their advertising from the telecast. (The "scandal" proved groundless, since Zeffirelli's Jesus was one of the most reverently accurate ever seen in films.) In recent years, Zeffirelli has been rep-resented by his televised stagings of operas, many of which have shown up on American public television. And in 1990, Franco Zeffirelli returned to Shakespeare for an all-star film version of *Hamlet,* wherein the "surprise" was not so much Mel Gibson's superb rendition of the title role as the fact that this was the first movie *Hamlet* that looked like it was actually taking place in 12th century Denmark.

# Robert Zemeckis

**Born:** May 14, 1951; Chicago, IL

**Years Active in the Industry:** by decade

| 10s | 20s | 30s | 40s | 50s | 60s | 70s | 80s | 90s |
|-----|-----|-----|-----|-----|-----|-----|-----|-----|
|     |     |     |     |     |     | ■   | ■   | ■   |

American director Robert Zemeckis studied filmaking at Northwestern University, then moved on to a job with the film-editing  department at WMAQ-TV, the NBC flagship station in Chicago. After commercial work, Zemeckis and his friend and collaborator Bob Gale became assistants to Stephen Spielberg. It was Spielberg who lined up Zemeckis' first directing job, the 1977 nostalgic comedy *I Wanna Hold Your Hand;* despite the film's low budget, it demonstrated Zemeckis' ability to combine credible live-action sequences with elaborate special effects devices. Spielberg then had Zemeckis and Gale work on the screenplay of *1941* (1979), which, despite its disappointing box-office returns, convinced Spielberg that his proteges were valuable commodities. Again under Spielberg's aegis, Zemeckis directed his first real financial success, *Romancing the Stone* (1981), a wild adventure yarn that somehow never loses sight of its sense of humor. The director then took on *Back to the Future* (1984) and its two sequels, once again proving it was possible to meld live actors with special effects without the seams showing. In concert with Spielberg and cartoon producer Richard Williams, Zemeckis directed *Who Framed Roger Rabbit?* (1988), a groundbreaking combo of cartoon animation and "real" action, which matriculated into one of the 1980s' biggest moneymakers. By the early 1990s, Zemeckis was recognized as a director of great technical skill but little personal viewpoint. All this changed upon the 1994 release of *Forrest Gump,* which, beyond its top-heavy special effects, was a heartfelt human drama about a mildly retarded young man (Tom Hanks) who climbs the peaks of professional and personal success by refusing to see anything but the being the top moneyspinner of the summer of 1994—and one of the biggest-grossing movies of all time. Plus, it helped Zemeckis snag a Best Director Oscar, not to mention several other awards. **Selected Works:** *Back to the Future, Part 3* (1990), *Trespass* (1992)

# Mai Zetterling

**Born:** May 24, 1925; Vasteras, Sweden
**Died:** March 17, 1994; London, England

**Years Active in the Industry:** by decade

| 10s | 20s | 30s | 40s | 50s | 60s | 70s | 80s | 90s |
|-----|-----|-----|-----|-----|-----|-----|-----|-----|

Swedish-born Mai Zetterling found acting an escape from an impoverished childhood, and after training at Stockholm's Royal Dramatic Theater School she made her debut on stage and screen at the age of 16. Her movie career took over when she was cast as the teenage girl victimized by a sadistic teacher in *Torment* (1944), a picture directed by Alf Sjoberg that was scripted by Ingmar Bergman, which became a major success among critics all over the world. She went to England in 1946 to star in the drama *Frieda,* about the plight of a European immigrant living in England during the postwar period. She was signed by the Rank Organisation, which tried to turn her into a major star. Unfortunately, she came to England at a time when the film industry was in a period of upheaval and retrenchment, and her films—which included *Quartet* (1948) and *The Bad Lord Byron* (1949)—never really succeeded. After the failure of *The Romantic Age,* she began setting her sights elsewhere from Rank. The early 1960s saw Zetterling appear opposite Peter Sellers in what was probably the most interesting of his late British successes, *Any Number Can Play.* By that time, she was concentrating on directing as well as acting, having made the documentary *The War Game,* which won a prize at the 1963 Venice Film Festival. Her feature films *Loving Couples* and *Night Games* (the latter based on her own novel) established Zetterling as one of the most respected woman filmmakers of her generation, and the fact that her work frequently dealt with issues of special interest to women put her at the forefront of the feminist movement. She continued making occasional appearances as an actress into the 1990s, most notably an extremely popular turn as the grandmother in the Jim Henson-directed fantasy *The Witches* (1990). **Selected Works:** *Hidden Agenda* (1990)

# Howard Zieff

**Born:** 1943; Chicago, IL

**Years Active in the Industry:** by decade

| 10s | 20s | 30s | 40s | 50s | 60s | 70s | 80s | 90s |
|-----|-----|-----|-----|-----|-----|-----|-----|-----|

While still a very young man, Los Angeles Art Center alumnus Howard Zieff became a leading figure of the TV commercial

world. It was a 21-year-old Zieff who directed the 1964 Alka-Seltzer commercial that popularized the song "No Matter What Shape (Your Stomach's In)." Better still, it was Zieff who called the shots on the deathless "spicy meatball" ad for (again) Alka-Seltzer. So dynamic a talent could not be confined to the one-minute form forever, and in 1975 Zieff made his feature film bow with the "succes d'estime" *Hearts of the West* (1975). While *Hearts* did little at the box office, Zieff was luckier with his subsequent star-vehicle hits *House Calls* (1978), *The Main Event* (1979), and *Private Benjamin* (1981). Howard Zieff's most personal project, and one of his best, was the serio-comic 1991 sleeper *My Girl.*

# Fred Zinnemann

**Born:** April 29, 1907; Vienna, Austria

**Years Active in the Industry:** by decade

| 10s | 20s | 30s | 40s | 50s | 60s | 70s | 80s | 90s |
|-----|-----|-----|-----|-----|-----|-----|-----|-----|

Austrian-born director Fred Zinnemann had dreamed of a career as a violinist, then switched gears to study law at the University of Vienna. However, a growing fascination with American silent

films compelled Zinnemann to refocus his ambition a second time. After working as an assistant cameraman in Europe, Zinnemann went to Hollywood, where he took extra work and a handful of assistant-editor jobs. In 1935 he co-directed (with Paul Strand) the Mexican-based documentary *Redes;* this led to his signing with the MGM short subjects department. Zinneman's 1938 MGM one-reeler *That Mothers Might Live* won an Oscar, though it would be another three years before he was given his first feature assignment, the "B" detective yarn *Kid Glove Killer* (1942). He worked on projects of moderate importance throughout the war years, but his breakthrough was 1948's *The Search,* a displaced-persons drama shot on location in Europe. Thanks to the subject matter and the naturalistic performance of Montgomery Clift (in his first film role), *The Search* established Zinneman as a specialist in "realism." *The Men* (1950), which served to introduce Marlon Brando, was in the same semi-documentary vein as *The Search.* However, with the highly successful *High Noon* (1952) Zinnemann began putting realism on the back burner in favor of commercial considerations. Critic Andrew Sarris complained in 1968 that such subsequent Zinnemann films as *From Here to Eternity* (1953), *Oklahoma* (1955), *The Nun's Story* (1959), and *A*

*Man for All Seasons* (1966) betrayed the promise of the director's earliest works and that they "most vividly reveal the superficiality of Zinnemann's commitment." This opinion seems to be more a negative reaction to the commercial success of these films rather than their inherent aesthetic value. Sarris is more on target when he suggests that Zinnemann's style tends to be aloof and emotionless; perhaps in agreement with this critique, Zinnemann surprised the industry with a small "personal" project in 1982, *Five Days One Summer*. The film, Zinneman's last to date, was both unsatisfying and unpopular. A more suitable valedictory project would have been Fred Zinnemann's next-to-last assignment, *Julia* (1977), which cannot be accused of emotional detachment. **Selected Works:** *High Noon* (1952), *Sundowners* (1960), *Day of the Jackal* (1973), *A Hatful of Rain* (1957)

# William (Vilmos) Zsigmond

**Born:** June 16, 1930; Czeged, Hungary

**Years Active in the Industry:** by decade

| 10ˢ | 20ˢ | 30ˢ | 40ˢ | 50ˢ | 60ˢ | 70ˢ | 80ˢ | 90ˢ |
|-----|-----|-----|-----|-----|-----|-----|-----|-----|
|     |     |     |     |     | ■   | ■   | ■   | ■   |

Hungarian-born cinematographer Vilmos Zsigmond, who graduated from the Budapest Film School, emigrated to the United States following the brutal Russian repression of the 1956 Hungarian uprising. He moved up from still photographer and laboratory technician to cinematographer during the next seven years, making his debut with the Arch Hall Jr. exploitation film *The Sadist* (1963). Throughout the next few years, he worked in low budget movies, including *The Time Travellers* (1966) and *The Monitors* (1969), before moving up to serious major pictures in 1971 with James Goldstone's *Red Sky At Morning,* produced by Hal Wallis at Universal. That same year Zsigmond photographed Robert Altman's *McCabe and Mrs. Miller,* a high-profile failure that was widely reviewed and taken very seriously by critics despite its lack of box-office success, and Peter Fonda's *The Hired Hand.* His next notable appearance behind the camera was in John Boorman's *Deliverance* (1972), which became a huge hit, widely acclaimed for all of its production details. Altman's *The Long Goodbye* (1973) and Steven Spielberg's theatrical debut, *The Sugarland Express* (1974), followed. And in 1977, Zsigmond served as photographer of *Close Encounters of the Third Kind,* Spielberg's enormous science fiction hit, for which Zsigmond earned an Oscar. His work since then, in pictures such as *The Last Waltz, The Deer Hunter, Heaven's Gate, The River,* and *The Witches of Eastwick,* has kept him among the most visible of cinematographers. He has also directed one movie, *The Long Shadow* (1992), a joint Israeli-Hungarian production. **Selected Works:** *The Two Jakes* (1990), *Maverick* (1994)

# David Zucker

**Born:** 1947; Milwaukee, WI

**Years Active in the Industry:** by decade

| 10ˢ | 20ˢ | 30ˢ | 40ˢ | 50ˢ | 60ˢ | 70ˢ | 80ˢ | 90ˢ |
|-----|-----|-----|-----|-----|-----|-----|-----|-----|
|     |     |     |     |     |     | ■   | ■   | ■   |

The Wisconsin-born and educated David Zucker, with his brother Jerry and Jim Abrahams, worked with the improvisational Kentucky Fried Theater in Madison, Wisconsin, before coming to movies in 1977 with *Kentucky Fried Movie*, a dazzlingly funny satire of movies, television, and popular culture. Written and produced by the trio, *Kentucky Fried Movie* became an unexpected success. They followed this up three years later with the monster hit *Airplane!*, a brutally funny take-off of disaster movies that not only brought an end to that genre, but made the trio into one of the hottest teams in screen comedy. *Top Secret!* (1984) wasn't nearly as successful, although it did make a profit. However, *Ruthless People* (1986) was a hit. During the early '80s, the Zuckers were responsible for a short-lived cop show parody called "Police Squad," starring Leslie Nielsen, a one-time dramatic film actor who had emerged as a comedy star in *Airplane!*. *The Naked Gun: From the Files of Police Squad* (1988) was borne from the "Police Squad" parody and proved a monster hit; this was followed by *Naked Gun 2 1/2: The Smell of Fear* (1991) and *Naked Gun 33 1/3: The Final Insult* (1994).

# Jerry Zucker

**Born:** March 11, 1950; Milwaukee, WI

**Years Active in the Industry:** by decade

| 10ˢ | 20ˢ | 30ˢ | 40ˢ | 50ˢ | 60ˢ | 70ˢ | 80ˢ | 90ˢ |
|-----|-----|-----|-----|-----|-----|-----|-----|-----|
|     |     |     |     |     |     | ■   | ■   | ■   |

Milwaukee-born filmmaker Jerry Zucker attended Shorewood High school with his older brother David. It was there, in student variety shows, that the Zuckers began displaying the lampoonish *Mad Magazine* style  humor that would distinguish their later work. While attending the University of Wisconsin in Madison, the Zuckers and longtime family friend Jim Abrahams founded the Kentucky Fried Theatre comedy troupe, which by 1978 had gained enough industry prestige to bankroll the zany sketch film *Kentucky Fried Movie* (1978), directed by John Landis. The film set the future Zucker standard—wild parodies of movie genres played out by an utterly straight-faced cast, looney non-sequitur jokes and running gags filling each frame, hilarious celebrity cameos, and outrageous (and endearingly childish) visual puns. On the strength of *Kentucky Fried Movie*'s $20 million take, the Zucker/Abrahams team put together their first mainstream feature for Paramount—1980's *Airplane!*, a scattershot satire of the 1957 airline meller *Zero Hour.* The Zucker boys and Abrahams agreed to this project only on the provision that the three men be allowed to co-direct the film themselves, a triumvirate that held strong throughout the rest of the '80s. The Zucker/Abrahams style would always be hit and miss, but adherents preferred to cherish those hits. The success of *Airplane!* enabled Zucker/Abrams to produce a limited 1982 summer-replacement series "Police Squad," starring *Airplane* cast member Leslie Nielsen as diligent but supremely incompetent police lieutenant Frank Dreben (the casting of heretofore "serious" actors like Nielsen, Lloyd Bridges and Robert Stack as pompous buffoons was another Zucker/Abrahams trademark). Fans of "Police Squad" consider the series the best ever, but the ABC network was nervous with the project, complaining that it didn't have a laughtrack to let the audience know what was funny and that the joke-a-minute style required the audience to actually have an attention span. Zucker/Abrahams' next project, *Top Secret!* (1984), though a box-office disappointment, hilariously maintained the *Airplane*/*Police Squad* trend of "inside" jokes referring to the writer/directors' hometown of Milwaukee. (The East German national anthem was sung to the tune of the anthem for Shorewood High School.) The Zucker/Abrahams team was back on target with its *Naked Gun* and *Hot Shots* theatrical films, though there was a marked attrition rate in the inevitable sequels. In 1990, Zucker astounded his fans (and non-fans) with his sensitive solo direction of *Ghost,* a romantic fantasy that became one of the top-grossing films of the year and won an Oscar for supporting actress Whoopi Goldberg. Jerry Zucker has since fluctuated between his satirical films and more serious works; the only "consistent" aspect of these films is the supporting-cast presence of Jerry and David's mom, Charlotte Zucker. **Selected Works:** *Naked Gun 2 1/2: The Smell of Fear* (1991)

# Daphne Zuniga

**Born:** 1963; Berkeley, CA

**Years Active in the Industry:** by decade

| 10s | 20s | 30s | 40s | 50s | 60s | 70s | 80s | 90s |
|-----|-----|-----|-----|-----|-----|-----|-----|-----|
|     |     |     |     |     |     |     | ■   |     |

Actress Daphne Zuniga achieved nationwide fame through her weekly appearances on Fox's *Melrose Place* in 1994—but despite her comparative unfamiliarity, she was certainly no overnight success. The daughter of a Guatemala-born philosophy professor, Zuniga attended UCLA while dad was teaching at California State. Stardom beckoned when she was cast as John Cusack's recalcitrant travelling companion in *The Sure Thing* (1985). For reasons that defy explanation, this engaging performance did *not* immediately elevate her to the top ranks, and Zuniga would have to mark time in unmemorable films like *Last Rites* (1988) and *Prey of the Chameleon* (1991) before *Melrose Place* secured her popularity.

# Edward Zwick

**Born:** October 8, 1952; Winnetka, IL

**Years Active in the Industry:** by decade

| 10s | 20s | 30s | 40s | 50s | 60s | 70s | 80s | 90s |
|-----|-----|-----|-----|-----|-----|-----|-----|-----|
|     |     |     |     |     |     |     | ■   |     |

Filmmaker/journalist Edward Zwick was trained in the cinematic arts at the AFI in Los Angeles. In collaboration with Marshall Herkowitz, Zwick produced, wrote and directed the popular 1980s weekly TV drama *thirtysomething*. He made his TV-movie directorial bow with *Special Bulletin* (1983), a chilling speculation of what might happen if terrorists got hold of a nuclear device in the U.S.; in the classic *War of the Worlds* fashion, the film was convincingly staged as an ongoing series of news bulletins. Zwick's first theatrical film was *About Last Night...* (1986), a surprisingly softpedalled filmization of the stage play *Sexual Perversity in Chicago.* Zwick's best film to date has been *Glory* (1989), an expansive tale of a black Army regiment during the Civil War.

# Genre Index

## ACTION

Robert Aldrich
Irwin Allen
Maria Conchita Alonso
Dana Andrews
Alfonso Arau
Pedro Armendariz Sr.
John G. Avildsen
John Badham
Carroll Baker
Alec Baldwin
Stephen Baldwin
William Baldwin
George Bancroft
Paul Bartel
Billy Barty
Kim Basinger
Ned Beatty
Noah Beery Sr.
James Belushi
Tom Berenger
Patrick Bergin
Corbin Bernsen
Luc Besson
Charles Bickford
Michael Biehn
Kathryn Bigelow
Robert Blake
Humphrey Bogart
Ward Bond
Ernest Borgnine
Peter Boyle
Klaus-Maria Brandauer
Marlon Brando
Beau Bridges
Lloyd Bridges
Charles Bronson
Pierce Brosnan
Bryan Brown
Johnny Mack Brown
Yul Brynner
Edgar Buchanan

Horst Buchholz
Sandra Bullock
Gary Busey
James Caan
Bruce Cabot
Michael Caine
James Cameron
Yakima Canutt
Kate Capshaw
Jack Cardiff
John Carpenter
David Carradine
Keith Carradine
Tia Carrere
Chevy Chase
Rae Dawn Chong
Lee J. Cobb
James Coburn
Dabney Coleman
Sean Connery
Merian C. Cooper
Francis Ford Coppola
Kevin Costner
Ronny Cox
Broderick Crawford
Donald Crisp
Bob Cummings
Willem Dafoe
Timothy Dalton
Robert Davi
Jan DeBont
Jonathan Demme
Brian Dennehy
Bruce Dern
Laura Dern
Caleb Deschanel
Andy Devine
Danny DeVito
Kevin Dillon
Edward Dmytryk
Roger Donaldson
Robert Donat

Brian Donlevy
Richard D. Donner
Kirk Douglas
Charles Durning
Robert Duvall
George Dzundza
Clint Eastwood
Jack Elam
Danny Elfman
Sam Elliott
Emilio Estevez
Corey Feldman
Abel Ferrara
Laurence Fishburne
Paul Fix
Errol Flynn
Henry Fonda
Peter Fonda
Glenn Ford
John A. Ford
Wallace Ford
Robert Forster
Edward Fox
James Fox
John Frankenheimer
Samuel Fuller
Mel Gibson
Scott Glenn
Louis Gossett Jr.
Stewart Granger
Pamela Grier
Gene Hackman
Corey Haim
Anthony Michael Hall
Mark Hamill
Harry Hamlin
Renny Harlin
Richard A. Harris
Henry Hathaway
Rutger Hauer
Wings Hauser
Jack Hawkins

Howard Hawks
Sessue Hayakawa
Sterling Hayden
George "Gabby" Hayes
Louis Hayward
Mariel Hemingway
Lance Henriksen
Charlton Heston
Walter Hill
Dustin Hoffman
Paul Hogan
William Holden
Tim Holt
Dennis Hopper
John C. Howard
Trevor Howard
Rock Hudson
John Huston
Walter Huston
Peter Hyams
Ice-T
Rex Ingram
Samuel L. Jackson
Richard Jaeckel
Dean Jagger
Norman Jewison
Roland Joffe
Buck Jones
James Earl Jones
Jeffrey Jones
Tommy Lee Jones
Victor Jory
Jonathan Kaplan
Stacy Keach
Brian Keith
David Keith
Arthur Kennedy
George Kennedy
Val Kilmer
Yaphet Kotto
Akira Kurosawa
Alan Ladd

Christopher Lambert
Burt Lancaster
John Landis
Bruce Lee
Sergio Leone
Frank Lloyd
Sondra Locke
Robert Loggia
Jon Lovitz
Dolph Lundgren
Ralph Macchio
Barton MacLane
Michael Madsen
Virginia Madsen
John Mahoney
Karl Malden
Anthony Mann
Michael Mann
Dean Martin
Lee Marvin
James Mason
Raymond Massey
Tim Matheson
Ken Maynard
Jim McBride
Timothy McCoy
Joel D. McCrea
Dylan McDermott
Darren McGavin
Steve McQueen
John McTiernan
Chris Menges
Nicholas Meyer
Toshiro Mifune
Alyssa Milano
Lewis Milestone
John Milius
George T. Miller
John Mills
Cameron Mitchell
Thomas Mitchell
Robert Mitchum
Tom Mix
Ricardo Montalban
George Montgomery
Roger Moore
Terry Moore
Harry Hays Morgan
Joe Morton
Dermot Mulroney
Audie Murphy
Eddie Murphy
Bill Murray
J. Carrol Naish
Charles Napier
Craig T. Nelson
Robert Newton
Dudley Nichols
Phillip Noyce
Carroll O'Connor
Peter O'Toole
Edward James Olmos

Jack Palance
Michael Pare
Adrian Pasdar
Bill Paxton
John Howard Payne
Gregory Peck
Sam Peckinpah
Arthur Penn
Christopher Penn
Sean Penn
George Peppard
Sidney Poitier
Robert Preston
Jurgen Prochnow
Richard Pryor
Randy Quaid
Anthony Quayle
Anthony Quinn
Harold Ramis
Oliver Reed
Pamela Reed
Judge Reinhold
Ivan Reitman
James Remar
Burt Reynolds
Robert Richardson
Michael Ritchie
Cliff Robertson
Michael Rooker
Joe Roth
Richard Roundtree
Kurt Russell
John Savage
Telly Savalas
John Saxon
Joseph Schildkraut
Arnold Schwarzenegger
Tony Scott
Steven Seagal
John Seale
Tom Selleck
Dean Semler
Charlie Sheen
Martin Sheen
Donald Siegel
Jonathan Silverman
O.J. Simpson
Tom Skerritt
William Smith
Wesley Snipes
Vincent Spano
Steven Spielberg
Roger Spottiswoode
Robert Stack
Sylvester Stallone
Harry Dean Stanton
Charles Starrett
Bob Steele
Rod Steiger
Dean Stockwell
Oliver Stone
Sharon Stone

John Sturges
Barry Sullivan
Kiefer Sutherland
Patrick Swayze
D.B. Sweeney
Quentin Tarantino
Rod Taylor
Rip Torn
Jacques Tourneur
Forrest Tucker
John Turturro
Tom Tyler
Lee vanCleef
Jean-Claude vanDamme
Marion vanPeebles
Jon Voight
Ken Wahl
Robert Walker
Eli Wallach
M. Emmet Walsh
Raoul A. Walsh
Fred Ward
Jack Warden
Damon Wayans
Keenen Ivory Wayans
John Wayne
Jack Webb
Johnny Weissmuller
Haskell Wexler
Frank Whaley
Stuart Whitman
James Jr. Whitmore
Richard Widmark
Cornel Wilde
Billy Dee Williams
Guinn "Big Boy" Williams
Bruce Willis
Chill Wills
Marie Windsor
Mare Winningham
John Woo
James Woods
Peter Yates
Terence Young
Billy Zane
Robert Zemeckis
Howard Zieff

## ADVENTURE

Murray   Abraham
Isabelle Adjani
Percy Adlon
Anouk Aimee
Chantal Akerman
Edward Albert
Jane Alexander
Irwin Allen
Karen Allen
Nancy Allen
Maria Conchita Alonso
John A. Alonzo

Robert Altman
Judith Anderson
Lindsay Anderson
Dana Andrews
Jean-Jacques Annaud
Michelangelo Antonioni
Alfonso Arau
Anne Archer
Pedro Armendariz Sr.
Gillian Armstrong
Rosanna Arquette
Peggy Ashcroft
Armand Assante
Richard Attenborough
Rene Auberjonois
Jean-Pierre Aumont
Gene Autry
Charles Aznavour
Jim Backus
Stephen Baldwin
Martin Balsam
Anne Bancroft
George Bancroft
Tallulah Bankhead
Ellen Barkin
John Barrymore
Freddie Bartholomew
Billy Barty
Richard Basehart
Alan Bates
Jean-Paul Belmondo
William Bendix
Annette Bening
Robby Benson
Bruce Beresford
Candice Bergen
Patrick Bergin
Ingmar Bergman
Ingrid Bergman
Charles Bickford
Theodore Bikel
Karen Black
Mel Blanc
Claire Bloom
Ralf D. Bode
Dirk Bogarde
Beulah Bondi
Helena Bonham-Carter
John Boorman
Ernest Borgnine
Frank Borzage
Klaus-Maria Brandauer
Eileen Brennan
Martin Brest
Beau Bridges
James Bridges
Lloyd Bridges
Charles Bronson
Bryan Brown
Nigel Bruce
Yul Brynner
Horst Buchholz

Ellen Burstyn
Richard Burton
Steve Buscemi
Gary Busey
Red Buttons
Gabriel Byrne
James Caan
James Cagney
Michael Caine
James Cameron
John Candy
Dyan Cannon
Yakima Canutt
Kate Capshaw
Jack Cardiff
David Carradine
Keith Carradine
Tia Carrere
John Cassavetes
Stockard Channing
Geraldine Chaplin
Maury Chaykin
Julianne Christie
Michael Cimino
James Coburn
Jean Cocteau
Joan Collins
Ronald Colman
Chris Columbus
Sean Connery
Hans Conried
Gary Cooper
Gladys Cooper
Jackie Cooper
Merian C. Cooper
Francis Ford Coppola
Roger Corman
Kevin Costner
Joseph Cotten
Tom Courtenay
Ronny Cox
Peter Coyote
Larry "Buster" Crabbe
Donald Crisp
Tom Cruise
Tim Curry
Tony Curtis
Vincent Philip D'Onofrio
Timothy Dalton
Rodney Dangerfield
Henry Daniell
Jeff Daniels
Tony Danza
Brad Davis
Judy Davis
Bruce Davison
Daniel Day-Lewis
Alain Delon
Dolores DelRio
Dom DeLuise
William Demarest
Cecil Blount DeMille

Jonathan Demme
Rebecca DeMornay
Gerard Depardieu
Bruce Dern
Caleb Deschanel
William S. Dieterle
Marlene Dietrich
Matt Dillon
Melinda Dillon
Walt Disney
Richard Dix
Edward Dmytryk
Roger Donaldson
Robert Donat
Stanley Donen
Brian Donlevy
Richard D. Donner
Kirk Douglas
Michael Douglas
Lesley-Anne Down
Robert Downey Jr.
Richard Dreyfuss
Faye Dunaway
Robert Duvall
George Dzundza
Clint Eastwood
Buddy Ebsen
Barbara Eden
Jack Elam
Denholm Elliott
Rupert Everett
Douglas Fairbanks Jr.
Douglas Fairbanks Sr.
Frances Farmer
Marty Feldman
Federico Fellini
Jose Luis Ferrer
Mel Ferrer
Betty Field
Peter Finch
Albert Finney
Dave Fleischer
Victor Fleming
Errol Flynn
Henry Fonda
Peter Fonda
John A. Ford
Milos Forman
Frederic Forrest
Robert Forster
Jodie Foster
Meg Foster
Edward Fox
James Fox
John Frankenheimer
Morgan Freeman
Samuel Fuller
Jean Gabin
Clark Gable
Vincent Gardenia
Ava Gardner
John David Garfield

James Garner
Leo Genn
Edward "Hoot" Gibson
Mel Gibson
John Gielgud
John Gilbert
Annabeth Gish
Scott Glenn
Jeff Goldblum
Louis Gossett Jr.
Stewart Granger
Sydney Greenstreet
Jennifer Grey
Joel Grey
Pamela Grier
Melanie Griffith
Gene Hackman
Alan Hale Sr.
Anthony Michael Hall
Mark Hamill
Harry Hamlin
William Hanna
Cedric Hardwicke
Renny Harlin
Mark Harmon
Ed Harris
Richard A. Harris
Rex Harrison
William S. Hart
Laurence Harvey
Henry Hathaway
Rutger Hauer
Wings Hauser
Ethan Hawke
Jack Hawkins
Howard Hawks
Sessue Hayakawa
Sterling Hayden
Helen Hayes
Louis Hayward
Susan Hayward
Rita Hayworth
John Heard
Dan Hedaya
Mariel Hemingway
Lance Henriksen
Jim Henson
Audrey Hepburn
Werner Herzog
Charlton Heston
Walter Hill
Wendy Hiller
Paul Hogan
Oscar Homolka
Dennis Hopper
Bob Hoskins
John Houseman
John C. Howard
Trevor Howard
James Wong Howe
C. Thomas Howell
Rock Hudson

John J. Hughes
Helen Hunt
Linda Hunt
Isabelle Huppert
John Hurt
John Huston
Walter Huston
Lauren Hutton
Timothy Hutton
Wilfrid Hyde-White
Rex Ingram
Amy Irving
James Ivory
Richard Jaeckel
Dean Jagger
Henry Jaglom
Ruth Prawer Jhabvala
Don Johnson
Chuck Jones
James Earl Jones
Jeffrey Jones
Shirley T. Jones
Tommy Lee Jones
Curt Jurgens
Madeline Kahn
Jonathan Kaplan
Harvey Keitel
Brian Keith
David Keith
Sally Kellerman
Grace Kelly
Arthur Kennedy
George Kennedy
Deborah Kerr
Nicole Kidman
Henry King
Ben Kingsley
Nastassja Kinski
Bruno Kirby
Sally Kirkland
Robert Klein
Kevin Kline
Shirley Knight
Alexander Korda
Jeroen Krabbe
Alan Ladd
Veronica Lake
Christopher Lambert
Burt Lancaster
Elsa Lanchester
Martin Landau
Diane Lane
Frank Langella
John Larroquette
Charles Laughton
Cloris Leachman
David Lean
Bruce Lee
Christopher Lee
Jason Scott Lee
John Leguizamo
Janet Leigh

Jennifer Jason Leigh
Claude Lelouch
Sergio Leone
Richard Lester
Christopher Lloyd
Kenneth Loach
Sondra Locke
Herbert Lom
Lyle Lovett
George Lucas
Dolph Lundgren
Kelly Lynch
Ali MacGraw
Anna Magnani
John Malkovich
Anthony Mann
Michael Mann
Jean Marais
Fredric March
Herbert Marshall
Giulietta Masina
James Mason
Raymond Massey
Mary Elizabeth Mastrantonio
Samantha Mathis
Walter Matthau
Victor Mature
Melanie Mayron
Mercedes McCambridge
Andrew McCarthy
Timothy McCoy
Dylan McDermott
Mary McDonnell
Roddy McDowall
Malcolm McDowell
Darren McGavin
Kelly McGillis
Dorothy McGuire
Victor McLaglen
Steve McQueen
John McTiernan
Chris Menges
Ismail Merchant
Burgess Meredith
Nicholas Meyer
Russ Meyer
Toshiro Mifune
John Milius
Ray Milland
Dick Miller
George T. Miller
Hayley Mills
John Mills
Yvette Mimieux
Sal Mineo
Miou-Miou
Helen Mirren
Cameron Mitchell
Thomas Mitchell
Robert Mitchum
Tom Mix
Kenji Mizoguchi

Matthew Modine
Ricardo Montalban
Yves Montand
George Montgomery
Roger Moore
Agnes Moorehead
Rick Moranis
Robert Morley
Eddie Murphy
Charles Napier
Patricia Neal
Liam Neeson
Mike Newell
Paul Newman
Julie Newmar
Robert Newton
Dudley Nichols
Jack Nicholson
David Niven
Philippe Noiret
Lloyd Nolan
Nick Nolte
Phillip Noyce
Edmond O'Brien
Margaret O'Brien
Pat O'Brien
Carroll O'Connor
Catherine O'Hara
Maureen O'Hara
Ryan O'Neal
Tatum O'Neal
Peter O'Toole
Merle Oberon
Frank Oz
Yasujiro Ozu
Al Pacino
Geraldine Page
George Pal
Jack Palance
Michael Pare
Adrian Pasdar
Mandy Patinkin
Bill Paxton
John Howard Payne
Gregory Peck
Sam Peckinpah
George Peppard
Frank Perry
Bernadette Peters
William L. Petersen
Lori Petty
Lou Diamond Phillips
River Phoenix
Donald Pleasence
Amanda Plummer
Christopher Plummer
Sidney Poitier
Sydney Pollack
Michael Powell
Tyrone Power
Elvis Presley
Robert Preston

Dennis Quaid
Anthony Quayle
Anthony Quinn
Claude Rains
Harold Ramis
Basil Rathbone
Nicholas Ray
Robert Redford
Carol Reed
Oliver Reed
Christopher Reeve
Keanu Reeves
Rob Reiner
Jean Renoir
Ralph Richardson
Tony Richardson
Alan L. Rickman
Diana Rigg
Martin Ritt
Jason Robards Jr.
Cliff Robertson
Paul Robeson
Mark Robson
Nicolas Roeg
Roy Rogers
Cesar Romero
Mickey Rooney
Richard Roundtree
Gena Rowlands
Sig Rumann
Jane Russell
Kurt Russell
George Sanders
Mia Sara
Susan Sarandon
John Savage
Telly Savalas
John Saxon
Maximilian Schell
John Schlesinger
Ernest Schoedsack
Joel Schumacher
Arnold Schwarzenegger
George Campbell Scott
Randolph Scott
Ridley Scott
Tony Scott
John Seale
Jean Seberg
Kyra Sedgwick
Tom Selleck
Dean Semler
Jane Seymour
Omar Sharif
Ray Sharkey
Helen Shaver
Robert J. Shaw
Brooke Shields
Talia Shire
Martin Short
Elisabeth Shue
Donald Siegel

Simone Signoret
Jean Simmons
Tom Skerritt
Christian Slater
Maggie Smith
William Smith
Vincent Spano
Steven Spielberg
Roger Spottiswoode
Robert Stack
Sylvester Stallone
Terence Stamp
Harry Dean Stanton
Bob Steele
Rod Steiger
Daniel Stern
Inger Stevens
James Stewart
Patrick Stewart
Ben Stiller
Dean Stockwell
Sharon Stone
Woodrow "Woody" Strode
Barry Sullivan
Patrick Swayze
Akim Tamiroff
Robert Taylor
Rod Taylor
Shirley Temple
Lea Thompson
Gene Tierney
Rip Torn
Jacques Tourneur
Robert Towne
Fernando Trueba
Francois Truffaut
Tom Tyler
Cicely Tyson
Edgar G. Ulmer
Peter Ustinov
Roger Vadim
Rudolph Valentino
Lee vanCleef
Jean-Claude vanDamme
Dick vanDyke
Marion vanPeebles
Melvin vanPeebles
Conrad Veidt
Max vonSydow
Ken Wahl
Tom Waits
Eli Wallach
Raoul A. Walsh
Tracey Walter
Wayne Wang
Fred Ward
Sam Waterston
John Wayne
Sigourney Weaver
Peter Weir
Johnny Weissmuller
Raquel Welch

Peter Weller
Orson Welles
William Augustus Wellman
Wim Wenders
James Whale
Stuart Whitman
James Whitmore Jr.
Richard Widmark
Cornel Wilde
Billy Dee Williams
John Williams
Treat Williams
Henry Winkler
Alex Winter
Robert Wise
Elijah Wood
Joanne Woodward
Fay Wray
Keenan Wynn
Peter Yates
Susannah York
Robert Malcolm Young
Terence Young
Robert Zemeckis
Mai Zetterling
Fred Zinnemann
Vilmos (William) Zsigmond

## CARTOONS

Joseph Barbera
Bob Clampett
Walt Disney
Dave Fleischer
Fritz Freleng
William Hanna
Chuck Jones

## CHILDRENS

Joseph Barbera
Mel Blanc
Anna Chlumsky
Bob Clampett
Tim Conway
Bill Cosby
Macaulay "Mack" Culkin
Walt Disney
Shelley Duvall
Dave Fleischer
Fritz Freleng
William Hanna
Jim Henson
Pee Wee Herman
Chuck Jones
Peter Medak
Hayley Mills
Frank Oz
Ed Wynn

## COMEDY

Bud Abbott

Walter Abel
Jim Abrahams
Percy Adlon
Danny Aiello
Alan Alda
Jason Alexander
Gracie Allen
Karen Allen
Woody Allen
Kirstie Alley
Pedro Almodovar
John A. Alonzo
Don Ameche
Julie Andrews
Ann-Margret
Eve Arden
Alan Arkin
Edward Arnold
Rosanna Arquette
Jean Arthur
Hal Ashby
Mary Astor
Rene Auberjonois
Mischa Auer
Dan Aykroyd
Lew Ayres
Jim Backus
John Bailey
Fay Bainter
Lucille Ball
Anne Bancroft
Binnie Barnes
John Barrymore
Paul Bartel
Billy Barty
Kathy Bates
Ned Beatty
Ralph Bellamy
James Belushi
John Belushi
William Bendix
Roberto Benigni
Richard Benjamin
Constance Bennett
Joan Sterndale Bennett
Jack Benny
Robby Benson
Bruce Beresford
Andrew Bergman
Milton Berle
Sandra Bernhard
Corbin Bernsen
Halle Berry
Joan Blondell
Eric Blore
Ann Blyth
Ralf D. Bode
Peter Bogdanovich
Philip Bosco
Peter Boyle
Eddie Bracken
Alice Brady

Eileen Brennan
Martin Brest
Marshall Brickman
Jeff Bridges
Matthew Broderick
Albert Brooks
James L. Brooks
Mel Brooks
Edward S. Brophy
Jack Buchanan
Billie Burke
George Burns
Tim Burton
Steve Buscemi
David Butler
Charles Butterworth
Spring Byington
Sid Caesar
John Candy
Eddie Cantor
Frank Capra
Art Carney
Jim Carrey
Madeleine Carroll
Jack Carson
Dana Carvey
Phoebe Cates
Charles Chaplin
Geraldine Chaplin
Charlie Chase
Chevy Chase
Maury Chaykin
Maurice Chevalier
Thomas Chong
Rene Clair
Jill Clayburgh
John Cleese
Charles Coburn
Joel Coen
Claudette Colbert
Dabney Coleman
Joan Collins
Ray Collins
Robbie Coltrane
Chris Columbus
Betty Comden
Joyce Compton
Walter Connolly
Hans Conried
Tom Conti
Tim Conway
Jackie Coogan
Martha Coolidge
Jackie Cooper
Bud Cort
Bill Cosby
Jerome Cowan
Alex Cox
Courteney Cox
Jeanne Crain
Frank Craven
Broderick Crawford

Hume Cronyn
Bing Crosby
Jon Cryer
Billy Crystal
Macaulay "Mack" Culkin
Bob Cummings
Tim Curry
Jamie Lee Curtis
Tony Curtis
Joan Cusack
John Cusack
Beverly D'Angelo
Vincent D'Onofrio
Rodney Dangerfield
Bebe Daniels
Jeff Daniels
Ted Danson
Joseph Dante
Tony Danza
Jane Darwell
Marion Davies
Geena Davis
Ossie Davis
Sammy Davis Jr.
Doris Day
Rosemary DeCamp
Sandra Dee
Dom DeLuise
William Demarest
Patrick Dempsey
Sandy Dennis
Reginald Denny
Vittorio DeSica
Danny DeVito
Carlo DiPalma
Divine
Stanley Donen
Melvyn Douglas
Robert Downey Jr.
Marie Dressler
Richard Dreyfuss
John Duigan
Olympia Dukakis
Douglas Dumbrille
Margaret Dumont
James Dunn
Griffin Dunne
Jimmy Durante
Deanna Durbin
Shelley Duvall
Allan Dwan
Buddy Ebsen
Barbara Eden
Anthony Edwards
Blake Edwards
Danny Elfman
Hector Elizondo
Nora Ephron
Leon Errol
Stuart Erwin
Emilio Estevez
Edith Evans

Tom Ewell
Peter Falk
Glenda Farrell
Mia Farrow
Frank Faylen
Corey Feldman
Marty Feldman
Federico Fellini
Stepin Fetchit
Sally Field
W.C. Fields
Harvey Fierstein
Carrie Fisher
Wallace Ford
Milos Forman
Douglas V. Fowley
Michael J. Fox
Brendan Fraser
William Frawley
Stephen Frears
Lowell Ganz
Vincent Gardenia
Reginald Gardiner
William Gargan
James Garner
Teri Garr
Vittorio Gassman
Mitzi Gaynor
Billy Gilbert
Terry Gilliam
Jackie C. Gleason
James Gleason
Crispin Glover
Paulette Goddard
Whoopi Goldberg
Jeff Goldblum
Valeria Golino
John Goodman
Frances Goodrich
Ruth Gordon
Elliott Gould
Betty Grable
Cary Grant
Lee Grant
Richard E. Grant
Spalding Gray
Peter Greenaway
Raymond Griffith
Charles Grodin
Alec Guinness
Steve Guttenberg
Edmund Gwenn
Albert Hackett
Corey Haim
Anthony Michael Hall
Tom Hanks
Daryl Hannah
Oliver Hardy
Jean Harlow
Jessica Harper
Woody Harrelson
Rex Harrison

June Havoc
Goldie Hawn
Glenne Headly
Amy Heckerling
Buck Henry
Katharine Hepburn
Pee Wee Herman
George Roy Hill
Arthur Hiller
Samuel S. Hinds
Dustin Hoffman
Paul Hogan
William Holden
Judy Holliday
Lauren Holly
Celeste Holm
Bob Hope
Edward Everett Horton
Ronald Howard
C. Thomas Howell
John J. Hughes
Thomas Hulce
Marsha Hunt
Holly Hunter
Mary Beth Hurt
Angelica Huston
Betty Hutton
Jim Hutton
Wilfrid Hyde-White
Judith Ivey
Henry Jaglom
Jim Jarmusch
Allen Jenkins
Norman Jewison
Nunnally Johnson
Van Johnson
Jeffrey Jones
Shirley T. Jones
Madeline Kahn
Carol Kane
Garson Kanin
Lawrence Kasdan
Julie Kavner
Danny Kaye
Buster Keaton Jr.
Diane Keaton
Michael Keaton
Cecil Kellaway
Sally Kellerman
Edgar Kennedy
Guy Kibbee
Bruno Kirby
Robert Klein
Kevin Kline
Ernie Kovacs
Swoosie Kurtz
Diane Ladd
Christine Lahti
Arthur Lake
Dorothy Lamour
Elsa Lanchester
John Landis

Harry Langdon
Frank Langella
John Larroquette
Stan Laurel
Peter Lawford
Cloris Leachman
Dennis Leary
Spike Lee
Janet Leigh
Mike Leigh
Mitchell Leisen
Jack Lemmon
Mervin LeRoy
Richard Lester
Barry Levinson
Jerry Lewis
Richard Linklater
Christopher Lloyd
Emily Ann Lloyd
Harold Lloyd
Gina Lollobrigida
Carole Lombard
Shelley Long
Sophia Loren
Jon Lovitz
Robert Lowe
Ernst Lubitsch
William Lundigan
Ralph Macchio
Alexander MacKendrick
Shirley MacLaine
Fred MacMurray
Ann Magnuson
Marjorie Main
Babaloo Mandel
Joseph Leo Mankiewicz
Jayne Mansfield
Richard "Cheech" Marin
Garry Marshall
George E. Marshall
Penny Marshall
Dean Martin
Steve Martin
Marx Brothers
Marsha Mason
Mary Stuart Masterson
Marcello Mastroianni
Tim Matheson
Walter Matthau
Elaine May
Melanie Mayron
Paul Mazursky
Jim McBride
Leo McCarey
Frances McDormand
Roddy McDowall
Frank McHugh
Michael McKean
Donald Meek
Adolphe Menjou
Burgess Meredith
Una Merkel

Bette Midler
Nikita Mikhalkov
Alyssa Milano
Lewis Milestone
Dick Miller
Penelope Ann Miller
Hayley Mills
Vincente Minnelli
Miou-Miou
Alfred Molina
Marilyn Monroe
Dudley Moore
Mary Tyler Moore
Terry Moore
Rick Moranis
Frank Morgan
Harry Morgan
Noriyuki "Pat" Morita
Robert Morley
Paul Morrissey
Rob Morrow
Zero Mostel
Alan Mowbray
Dermot Mulroney
Eddie Murphy
George Murphy
Bill Murray
Mike Myers
Mildred Natwick
Judd Nelson
Julie Newmar
Mike Nichols
Leslie Nielsen
David Niven
Philippe Noiret
Pat O'Brien
Donald O'Connor
Rosie O'Donnell
Catherine O'Hara
Dennis O'Keefe
Ryan O'Neal
Tatum O'Neal
Maureen O'Sullivan
Jack Oakie
Jerry Orbach
Reginald Owen
Frank Oz
Michael Palin
Eugene Pallette
Chazz Palminteri
Franklin Pangborn
Mary-Louise Parker
Sarah Jessica Parker
Estelle Parsons
Dolly Parton
Rosie Perez
Elizabeth Perkins
Joe Pesci
Bernadette Peters
Walter Pidgeon
ZaSu Pitts
Oliver Platt

Joan Plowright
Amanda Plummer
Roman Polanski
Dick Powell
William H. Powell
Otto Preminger
Priscilla Presley
Richard Eddie Pryor
Bill Pullman
Randy Quaid
Gilda Radner
Harold Ramis
Tony Randall
Martha Raye
Ronald Reagan
Lynn Redgrave
Donna Reed
Pamela Reed
Carl Reiner
Rob Reiner
Judge Reinhold
Ivan Reitman
Burt Reynolds
Debbie Reynolds
Christina Ricci
Joely Richardson
Allen L. Rickman
Peter Riegert
Molly Ringwald
Michael Ritchie
John Ritter
Thelma Ritter
Ritz Brothers
Hal Roach
Tim Robbins
Ginger Rogers
Will Rogers
Eric Rohmer
Cesar Romero
Mickey Rooney
Herbert Ross
Joe Roth
Saul Rubinek
Alan Rudolph
Mercedes Ruehl
Charles Ruggles
Sig Rumann
Rosalind Russell
Margaret Rutherford
Meg Ryan
Winona Ryder
Adam Sandler
Nancy Savoca
Joel Schumacher
Ettore Scola
Susan Seidelman
George Brackett Seitz
Peter Sellers
Mack Sennett
Wallace Shawn
Ally Sheedy
Charlie Sheen

Cybill Shepherd
Ann Sheridan
Pauly Shore
Martin Short
Elisabeth Shue
George Sidney
Joan Micklin Silver
Ron Silver
Jonathan Silverman
Phil Silvers
Alastair Sim
Neil Simon
John Singleton
Red Skelton
Ione Skye
Helen Slater
Maggie Smith
Barry Sonnenfeld
Ann Sothern
Penelope Spheeris
Lionel Stander
Maureen Stapleton
Mary Steenburgen
Daniel Stern
Fisher Stevens
Ben Stiller
Preston Sturges
Kristy Swanson
Jacques Tati
Lili Taylor
Shirley Temple
Lea Thompson
Three Stooges
Jennifer Tilly
Marisa Tomei
Lily Tomlin
Franchot Tone
Robert Townsend
Nancy Travis
Fernando Trueba
Janine Turner
Tracey Ullman
Edgar G. Ulmer
Peter Ustinov
Roger Vadim
Mamie vanDoren
Dick vanDyke
Melvin vanPeebles
Gus vanSant Jr.
Jean Vigo
Reynaldo Villalobos
Julie Walters
Wayne Wang
Jack Warden
Andy Warhol
John Waters
Damon Wayans
Keenen Ivory Wayans
Chloe Webb
Clifton Webb
Tuesday Weld
Lina Wertmuller

Mae West
Dianne Wiest
Billy Wilder
Gene Wilder
Esther Williams
JoBeth Williams
Robin Williams
Gordon Willis
Henry Winkler
Alex Winter
Shelley Winters
Elijah Wood
Alfred Woodard
Robert Wuhl
Jane Wyman
Ed Wynn
Keenan Wynn
Frederick A. Young
Robert Young
Robert Zemeckis
Howard Zieff
David Zucker
Jerry Zucker
Daphne Zuniga
Edward Zwick

## CRIME

Danny Aiello
Gregg Araki
Anne Archer
Robert Armstrong
Patricia Arquette
Armand Assante
Lionel Atwill
Lew Ayres
John Bailey
Willaim Baldwin
Martin Balsam
George Bancroft
Ellen Barkin
Ethel Barrymore
Angela Bassett
Jennifer Beals
Ed Begley Sr.
Roberto Benigni
Humphrey Bogart
Philip Bosco
Lara Flynn Boyle
Lorraine Bracco
Jeff Bridges
Edward S. Brophy
Pierce Brosnan
Tod Browning
Raymond Burr
Marcel Carne
John Cassavetes
William Castle
Claude Chabrol
Lon Chaney
Michael Chapman
Ruth Chatterton

Joan Chen
Michael Cimino
Lee J. Cobb
Robbie Coltrane
Jackie Coogan
Elisha Cook Jr.
Jerome Cowan
Richard Crenna
Michael Crichton
Jon Cryer
Robert Davi
Ossie Davis
Laraine Day
Dana Delaney
Alain Delon
Robert DeNiro
Brian Dennehy
Brian DePalma
Matt Dillon
Lesley-Anne Down
Douglas Dumbrille
Mildred Dunnock
Ann Dvorak
Joe Eszterhas
Jeff Fahey
Peter Falk
Glenda Farrell
Rainer Werner Fassbinder
Farrah Fawcett
Abel Ferrara
Ralph Fiennes
Laurence Fishburne
Robert Florey
Bill Forsyth
Douglas V. Fowley
Morgan Freeman
William Friedkin
Edward Furlong
Jean Gabin
John David Garfield
William Gargan
Tony Goldwyn
Ruth Gordon
Conrad L. Hall
Renny Harlin
Hal Hartley
June Havoc
George "Gabby" Hayes
Gregory Hines
Lauren Holly
Thomas Hulce
Marsha Hunt
Peter Hyams
Ice Cube
Samuel L. Jackson
Allen Jenkins
Don Johnson
Buck Jones
Neil Jordan
Philip Clarke Kaufman
Harvey Keitel
Margot Kidder

Val Kilmer
Klaus Kinski
Jack Klugman
Yaphet Laughlin Kotto
Diane Ladd
Fritz Lang
Anthony LaPaglia
Jack LaRue
Marc Lawrence
Dennis Leary
Margaret Lindsay
Kenneth Loach
Robert Loggia
Peter Lorre
Lyle Lovett
Sidney Lumet
Ida Lupino
Kyle MacLachlan
Karl Malden
David Mamet
Jayne Mansfield
Joe Mantegna
Victor Mature
Alyssa Milano
Penelope Ann Miller
Joe Morton
J. Carrol Naish
Charles Napier
Judd Nelson
Lloyd Nolan
Sheree North
Edmond O'Brien
Dennis O'Keefe
Edward James Olmos
Jerry Orbach
Al Pacino
Chazz Palminteri
Christopher Penn
Sean Penn
Joe Pesci
Lou Diamond Phillips
Jada Pinkett
Priscilla Presley
Jason Priestley
Jurgen Prochnow
George Raft
Stephen Rea
James Remar
Lee Remick
Burt Reynolds
Eric Roberts
Edward G. Robinson Jr.
Michael Rooker
Tim Roth
Mickey Rourke
Paul Schrader
Lizabeth Scott
Steven Seagal
George Brackett Seitz
Ray Sharkey
Ann Sheridan
Sylvia Sidney

Lori Singer
Robert Siodmak
Jimmy Smits
Wesley Snipes
Lionel Stander
Barbara Stanwyck
George E. Stone
Lyle Talbot
Quentin Tarantino
Robert Townsend
Nancy Travis
Claire Trevor
Mamie vanDoren
Ken Wahl
J.T. Walsh
Denzel Washington
Tuesday Weld
William Augustus Wellman
Forest Whitaker
Treat Williams
Bruce Willis
John Woo
James Woods
Sean Young
Mai Zetterling

## CULT FILM

Divine
Tobe Hooper
Philip Clarke Kaufman
David Lynch
Paul Morrissey
Bob Rafelson
Andy Warhol
John Waters
Ed D. Wood Jr.

## DRAMA

Walter Abel
Murray  Abraham
Isabelle Adjani
Percy Adlon
Danny Aiello
Anouk Aimee
Chantal Akerman
Edward Albert
Robert Aldrich
Jane Alexander
Karen Allen
Nestor Almendros
John A. Alonzo
Robert Altman
Judith Anderson
Lindsay Anderson
Dana Andrews
Ann-Margret
Jean-Jacques Annaud
Michelangelo Antonioni
Michael Apted

Denys Arcand
Anne Archer
Pedro Armendariz Sr.
Gillian Armstrong
Robert Armstrong
Patricia Arquette
Rosanna Arquette
Dorothy Arzner
Hal Ashby
Peggy Ashcroft
Armand Assante
Mary Astor
Richard Attenborough
Lionel Atwill
Rene Auberjonois
Jean-Pierre Aumont
John G. Avildsen
Lew Ayres
Charles Aznavour
Lauren Bacall
Kevin Bacon
John Badham
John Bailey
Fay Bainter
Carroll Baker
Kathy Baker
Alec Baldwin
Bill Baldwin
Stephen Baldwin
Martin Balsam
Anne Bancroft
George Bancroft
Tallulah Bankhead
Theda Bara
Brigitte Bardot
Ellen Barkin
Ethel Barrymore
John Barrymore
Lionel Barrymore
Richard Barthelmess
Freddie Bartholomew
Richard Basehart
Kim Basinger
Angela Bassett
Alan Bates
Kathy Bates
Anne Baxter
Ned Beatty
Warren Beatty
Bonnie Bedelia
Ed Begley Sr.
Ralph Bellamy
Jean-Paul Belmondo
William Bendix
Annette Bening
Constance Bennett
Joan Sterndale Bennett
Robby Benson
Tom Berenger
Bruce Beresford
Candice Bergen
Patrick Bergin

Ingmar Bergman
Ingrid Bergman
Corbin Bernsen
Bernardo Bertolucci
Luc Besson
Charles Bickford
Michael Biehn
Kathryn Bigelow
Theodore Bikel
Jacqueline Bisset
Karen Black
Linda Blair
Robert Blake
Claire Bloom
Ann Blyth
Ralf D. Bode
Dirk Bogarde
Humphrey Bogart
Peter Bogdanovich
Eric Bogosian
Ward Bond
Beulah Bondi
Helena Bonham-Carter
John Boorman
Frank Borzage
Philip Bosco
Clara Bow
Charles Boyer
Lara Flynn Boyle
Peter Boyle
Lorraine Bracco
Sonia Braga
Kenneth Branagh
Klaus-Maria Brandauer
Marlon Brando
Walter Brennan
George Brent
Robert Bresson
Beau Bridges
James Bridges
Jeff Bridges
Lloyd Bridges
Matthew Broderick
Peter Brook
Louise Brooks
Pierce Brosnan
Tod Browning
Horst Buchholz
Genevieve Bujold
Sandra Bullock
Luis Bunuel
Raymond Burr
Ellen Burstyn
Richard Burton
Steve Buscemi
Gary Busey
Red Buttons
Gabriel Byrne
James Caan
Bruce Cabot
Nicolas Cage
James Cagney

Michael Caine
Jane Campion
Dyan Cannon
Frank Capra
Kate Capshaw
Marcel Carne
Keith Carradine
Madeleine Carroll
John Cassavetes
Claude Chabrol
Lon Chaney
Geraldine Chaplin
Michael Chapman
Ruth Chatterton
Paddy Chayefsky
Maury Chaykin
Joan Chen
Cher
Rae Dawn Chong
Julianne Christie
Michael Cimino
Jill Clayburgh
Montgomery Clift
Glenn Close
Henri-Georges Clouzot
Lee J. Cobb
Jean Cocteau
Ethan Coen
Claudette Colbert
Dabney Coleman
Joan Collins
Ray Collins
Joyce Compton
Jennifer Connelly
William Conrad
Tom Conti
Elisha Jr. Cook
Gary Cooper
Gladys Cooper
Francis Ford Coppola
Roger Corman
Constantin Costa-Gavras
Kevin Costner
Joseph Cotten
Tom Courtenay
Courteney Cox
Ronny Cox
Peter Coyote
Jeanne Crain
Frank Craven
Broderick Crawford
Joan Crawford
Richard Crenna
Donald Crisp
John Cromwell
Hume Cronyn
Tom Cruise
George Cukor
Jamie Lee Curtis
Tony Curtis
Michael Curtiz
Vincent Philip D'Onofrio

Willem Dafoe
Timothy Dalton
Dorothy Dandridge
Henry Daniell
Jeff Daniels
Blythe Danner
Ted Danson
Linda Darnell
Jane Darwell
Jules Dassin
Lolita Davidovich
Bette Davis
Brad Davis
Judy Davis
Ossie Davis
Sammy Davis Jr.
Bruce Davison
Laraine Day
Daniel Day-Lewis
Rosemary DeCamp
Dana Delaney
Alain Delon
Julie Delpy
Dolores DelRio
Cecil Blount DeMille
Jonathan Demme
Rebecca DeMornay
Catherine Deneuve
Robert DeNiro
Brian Dennehy
Sandy Dennis
Brian DePalma
Gerard Depardieu
Johnny Depp
Bruce Dern
Laura Dern
Caleb Deschanel
Vittorio DeSica
Leonardo DiCaprio
Angie Dickinson
William S. Dieterle
Marlene Dietrich
Kevin Dillon
Matt Dillon
Melinda Dillon
Richard Dix
Edward Dmytryk
Shannen Doherty
Roger Donaldson
Robert Donat
Brian Donlevy
Kirk Douglas
Melvyn Douglas
Michael Douglas
Brad Dourif
Lesley-Anne Down
Carl Theodor Dreyer
Richard Dreyfuss
David Duchovny
John Duigan
Olympia Dukakis
Douglas Dumbrille

Faye Dunaway
James Dunn
Griffin Dunne
Irene Dunne
Mildred Dunnock
Charles Durning
Robert Duvall
Ann Dvorak
Allan Dwan
George Dzundza
Sergei Mikhailovich Eisenstein
Hector Elizondo
Denholm Elliott
Sam Elliott
Cary Elwes
Emilio Estevez
Edith Evans
Rupert Everett
Jeff Fahey
Douglas Fairbanks Jr.
Douglas Fairbanks Sr.
Frances Farmer
Glenda Farrell
Mia Farrow
Rainer Werner Fassbinder
Farrah Fawcett
Frank Faylen
Federico Fellini
Sherilyn Fenn
Abel Ferrara
Jose Luis Ferrer
Mel G. Ferrer
Stepin Fetchit
Betty Field
Sally Field
Ralph Fiennes
Harvey Fierstein
Michael Figgis
Peter Finch
Albert Finney
Linda Fiorentino
Laurence Fishburne
Geraldine Fitzgerald
Victor Fleming
Robert Florey
Bridget Fonda
Henry Fonda
Jane Fonda
Joan Fontaine
Glenn Ford
John A. Ford
Wallace Ford
Milos Forman
Frederic Forrest
Jodie Foster
Meg Foster
James Fox
John Frankenheimer
Brendan Fraser
Stephen Frears
Morgan Freeman
Samuel Fuller

Jean Gabin
Clark Gable
Peter Gallagher
Abel Gance
Greta Garbo
Vincent Gardenia
Ava Gardner
John David Garfield
William Gargan
Greer Garson
Leo Genn
Richard Gere
John Gielgud
John Gilbert
Lillian Gish
Robin Givens
Scott Glenn
John Glover
Jean-Luc Godard
Jeff Goldblum
Tony Goldwyn
John Goodman
Ruth Gordon
Louis Gossett Jr.
Edmund Goulding
Gloria Grahame
Stewart Granger
Hugh Grant
Lee Grant
Richard E. Grant
Rupert Graves
Spalding Gray
Peter Greenaway
Sydney Greenstreet
Jennifer Grey
Joel Grey
D.W. Griffith
Melanie Griffith
Raymond Griffith
Alec Guinness
Edmund Gwenn
Lukas Haas
Taylor Hackford
Gene Hackman
Alan Hale Sr.
Conrad L. Hall
Mark Hamill
Linda Hamilton
Harry Hamlin
Daryl Hannah
Ann Harding
Cedric Hardwicke
Jean Harlow
Mark Harmon
Tess Harper
Ed Harris
Richard A. Harris
Rex Harrison
Laurence Harvey
Henry Hathaway
Rutger Hauer
Ethan Hawke

Jack Hawkins
Howard Hawks
Nigel Hawthorne
Sessue Hayakawa
Sterling Hayden
Helen Hayes
Louis Hayward
Susan Hayward
Rita Hayworth
Glenne Headly
John Heard
Dan Hedaya
Mariel Hemingway
Katharine Hepburn
Barbara Hershey
Werner Herzog
Charlton Heston
George Roy Hill
Wendy Hiller
Samuel S. Hinds
Alfred Hitchcock
Dustin Hoffman
Hal Holbrook
William Holden
Agnieszka Holland
Oscar Homolka
Anthony Hopkins
Miriam Hopkins
Dennis Hopper
Bob Hoskins
John Houseman
John C. Howard
Leslie Howard
Trevor Howard
James Wong Howe
C. Thomas Howell
Rock Hudson
Thomas Hulce
Helen Hunt
Linda Hunt
Marsha Hunt
Holly Hunter
Kim Hunter
Isabelle Huppert
John Hurt
Mary Beth Hurt
William Hurt
Angelica Huston
John Huston
Walter Huston
Lauren Hutton
Timothy Hutton
Wilfrid Hyde-White
Ice Cube
Rex Ingram
Jeremy Irons
Amy Irving
Judith Ivey
James Ivory
Glenda Jackson
Samuel L. Jackson
Irene Jacob

Dean Jagger
Emil Jannings
Derek Jarman
Jim Jarmusch
Maurice Jarre
Norman Jewison
Ruth Prawer Jhabvala
Roland Joffe
Don Johnson
Nunnally Johnson
Van Johnson
James Earl Jones
Shirley T. Jones
Tommy Lee Jones
Raul Julia
Curt Jurgens
Chen Kaige
Jonathan Kaplan
Lawrence Kasdan
Philip Clarke Kaufman
Elia "Gadge" Kazan
Stacy Keach
Diane Keaton
Harvey Keitel
David Keith
Sally Kellerman
Grace Kelly
Arthur Kennedy
George Kennedy
Deborah Kerr
Margot Kidder
Nicole Kidman
Krzysztof Kieslowski
Val Kilmer
Henry King
Ben Kingsley
Nastassja Kinski
Bruno Kirby
Sally Kirkland
Jack Klugman
Shirley Knight
Alexander Knox
Alexander Korda
Yaphet Kotto
Jeroen Krabbe
Stanley Kramer
Kris Kristofferson
Stanley Kubrick
Akira Kurosawa
Swoosie Kurtz
Diane Kurys
Alan Ladd
Diane Ladd
Christine Lahti
Veronica Lake
Hedy Lamarr
Christopher Lambert
Burt Lancaster
Diane Lane
Fritz Lang
Jessica Lange
Angela Lansbury

Charles Laughton
Cloris Leachman
David Lean
Jason Scott Lee
Spike Lee
John Leguizamo
Janet Leigh
Jennifer Jason Leigh
Mike Leigh
Vivien Leigh
Claude Lelouch
Robert Sean Leonard
Mervin LeRoy
Juliette Lewis
Viveca Lindfors
Margaret Lindsay
Richard Linklater
Ray Liotta
John Lithgow
Anatole Litvak
Emily Ann Lloyd
Frank Lloyd
Kenneth Loach
Sondra Locke
Heather Locklear
Robert Loggia
Gina Lollobrigida
Herbert Lom
John Lone
Sophia Loren
Peter Lorre
Joseph Losey
Lyle Lovett
Robert Lowe
Myrna Loy
Sidney Lumet
William Lundigan
Ida Lupino
John Lurie
David Lynch
Kelly Lynch
Adrian Lyne
Ralph Macchio
Andie MacDowell
Ali MacGraw
Kyle MacLachlan
Barton MacLane
Amy Madigan
Michael Madsen
Virginia Madsen
Anna Magnani
John Mahoney
Karl Malden
John Malkovich
Louis Malle
David Mamet
Rouben Mamoulian
Joseph Leo Mankiewicz
Anthony Mann
Michael Mann
Joe Mantegna
Jean Marais

Fredric March
Herbert Marshall
Giulietta Masina
James Mason
Marsha Mason
Raymond Massey
Mary Stuart Masterson
Marcello Mastroianni
Richard Masur
Samantha Mathis
Marlee Matlin
Victor Mature
Melanie Mayron
Jim McBride
Mercedes McCambridge
Andrew McCarthy
Joel D. McCrea
Dylan McDermott
Mary McDonnell
Frances McDormand
Roddy McDowall
Malcolm McDowell
Darren McGavin
Kelly McGillis
Elizabeth McGovern
Dorothy McGuire
Frank McHugh
Ian McKellan
Victor McLaglen
Steve McQueen
Peter Medak
Chris Menges
Ismail Merchant
Burgess Meredith
Toshiro Mifune
Nikita Mikhalkov
Sylvia Miles
Lewis Milestone
Ray Milland
Dick Miller
George T. Miller
John Mills
Yvette Mimieux
Sal Mineo
Liza Minnelli
Miou-Miou
Helen Mirren
Cameron Mitchell
Thomas Mitchell
Robert Mitchum
Kenji Mizoguchi
Matthew Modine
Alfred Molina
Yves Montand
Terry Moore
Agnes Moorehead
Jeanne Moreau
Harry Hays Morgan
Robert Morley
Paul Morrissey
Joe Morton
Dermot Mulroney

Paul Muni
F.W. Murnau
Conrad Nagel
J. Carrol Naish
Patricia Neal
Liam Neeson
Jean Negulesco
Sam Neill
Kate Nelligan
Craig T. Nelson
Judd Nelson
Mike Newell
Paul Newman
Robert Newton
Dudley Nichols
Mike Nichols
Jack Nicholson
Leslie Nielsen
Philippe Noiret
Lloyd Nolan
Nick Nolte
Sheree North
Kim Novak
Phillip Noyce
Sven Nykvist
Merle Oberon
Edmond O'Brien
Margaret O'Brien
Pat O'Brien
Carroll O'Connor
Chris O'Donnell
Maureen O'Hara
Dennis O'Keefe
Gary Oldman
Lena Olin
Laurence Olivier
Edward James Olmos
Ryan O'Neal
Tatum O'Neal
Maureen O'Sullivan
Peter O'Toole
Max Ophuls
Jerry Orbach
Julia Ormond
Reginald Owen
Yasujiro Ozu
G.W. Pabst
Al Pacino
Geraldine Page
Alan J. Pakula
Jack Palance
Alan Parker
Eleanor Parker
Mary-Louise Parker
Sarah Jessica Parker
Estelle Parsons
Adrian Pasdar
Pier Paolo Pasolini
Mandy Patinkin
Jason Patric
Will Patton
John Payne

Gregory Peck
Arthur Penn
Christopher Penn
Sean Penn
George Peppard
Rosie Perez
Anthony Perkins
Frank Perry
Luke Perry
Joe Pesci
Bernadette Peters
William L. Petersen
Lori Petty
Michelle Pfeiffer
Lou Diamond Phillips
River Phoenix
Mary Pickford
Walter Pidgeon
Jada Pinkett
Harold Pinter
Brad Pitt
Donald Pleasence
Joan Plowright
Amanda Plummer
Christopher Plummer
Sidney Poitier
Roman Polanski
Sydney Pollack
Michael Powell
Tyrone Power
Otto Preminger
Robert Preston
Jason Priestley
Jurgen Prochnow
Robert J. Prosky
Jonathan Pryce
Bill Pullman
Dennis Quaid
Randy Quaid
Anthony Quayle
Aidan Quinn
Anthony Quinn
Bob Rafelson
George Raft
Claude Rains
Nicholas Ray
Satyajit Ray
Stephen Rea
Ronald Reagan
Robert Redford
Lynn Redgrave
Michael Redgrave
Vanessa Redgrave
Carol Reed
Donna Reed
Oliver Reed
Pamela Reed
Keanu Reeves
James Remar
Lee Remick
Jean Renoir
Alain Resnais

Joely Richardson
Miranda Richardson
Natasha Richardson
Ralph Richardson
Robert Richardson
Tony Richardson
Alan Rickman
Robert Riskin
Martin Ritt
Thelma Ritter
Jason Robards Sr.
Eric Roberts
Julia Roberts
Rachel Roberts
Cliff Robertson
Paul Robeson
Edward G. Robinson Jr.
Mark Robson
Nicolas Roeg
Mimi Rogers
Eric Rohmer
Michael Rooker
Mickey Rooney
Herbert Ross
Katharine Ross
Isabella Rossellini
Roberto Rossellini
Tim Roth
Mickey Rourke
Gena Rowlands
Saul Rubinek
Alan Rudolph
Ken Russell
Kurt Russell
Theresa Russell
Mark Rydell
Winona Ryder
Eva Marie Saint
George Sanders
Julian Sands
Laura SanGiacomo
Mia Sara
Susan Sarandon
John Savage
Telly Savalas
Nancy Savoca
John Saxon
John Sayles
Greta Scacchi
Roy G. Scheider
Maximilian Schell
Fred Schepisi
Joseph Schildkraut
John Schlesinger
Volker Schlondorff
Romy Schneider
Paul Schrader
Barbet Schroeder
Joel Schumacher
Annabella Sciorra
Paul Scofield
Martin Scorsese

Campbell Scott
George Campbell Scott
Lizabeth Scott
John Seale
Jean Seberg
Kyra Sedgwick
George Brackett Seitz
Tom Selleck
Jane Seymour
Omar Sharif
Ray Sharkey
Helen Shaver
Robert J. Shaw
Norma Shearer
Ally Sheedy
Martin Sheen
Ron Shelton
Sam Shepard
Cybill Shepherd
Ann Sheridan
Jim Sheridan
Talia Shire
Sylvia Sidney
Donald Siegel
Simone Signoret
Joan Micklin Silver
Ron Silver
Jean Simmons
Simone Simon
O.J. Simpson
Lori Singer
John Singleton
Gary Sinise
Robert Siodmak
Tom Skerritt
Ione Skye
Christian Slater
Wesley Snipes
Steven Soderbergh
Gale Sondergaard
Sissy Spacek
Kevin Spacey
James Spader
Vincent Spano
Roger Spottiswoode
Robert Stack
Terence Stamp
Harry Dean Stanton
Barbara Stanwyck
Maureen Stapleton
Mary Steenburgen
Rod Steiger
George Stevens Sr.
Inger Stevens
James Stewart
Dean Stockwell
Eric Stoltz
Lewis S. Stone
Oliver Stone
Sharon Stone
Vittorio Storaro
Madeleine Stowe

David Strathairn
Meryl Streep
John Sturges
Margaret Sullavan
Barry Sullivan
Donald Sutherland
Kiefer Sutherland
Patrick Swayze
D.B. Sweeney
Lyle Talbot
Akim Tamiroff
Jessica Tandy
Quentin Tarantino
Bertrand Tavernier
Paolo Taviani
Elizabeth Taylor
Lili Taylor
Robert Taylor
Rod Taylor
Shirley Temple
Henry Thomas
Emma Thompson
Uma Thurman
Gene Tierney
Meg Tilly
Gregg Toland
Franchot Tone
Rip Torn
Jacques Tourneur
Robert Towne
Spencer Tracy
Nancy Travis
John Travolta
Claire Trevor
Jean-Louis Trintignant
Jeanne Tripplehorn
Francois Truffaut
Janine Turner
Lana Turner
John Turturro
Cicely Tyson
Liv Ullmann
Edgar G. Ulmer
Peter Ustinov
Roger Vadim
Rudolph Valentino
Mamie vanDoren
Woodbridge S. vanDyke II
Melvin vanPeebles
Gus vanSant Jr.
Agnes Varda
Conrad Veidt
Paul Verhoeven
King Vidor
Luchino Visconti
Jon Voight
Erich vonStroheim
Max vonSydow
Tom Waits
Andrzej Wajda
Christopher Walken
Robert Walker

Eli Wallach
J.T. Walsh
M. Emmet Walsh
Raoul A. Walsh
Tracey Walter
Julie Walters
Wayne Wang
Fred Ward
Rachel Ward
Jack Warden
Andy Warhol
Lesley Ann Warren
Denzel Washington
Sam Waterston
Chloe Webb
Jack Webb
Peter Weir
Raquel Welch
Tuesday Weld
Peter Weller
Orson Welles
William Augustus Wellman
Wim Wenders
Lina Wertmuller
Haskell Wexler
James Whale
Frank Whaley
Joanne Whalley-Kilmer
Forest Whitaker
Stuart Whitman
James Whitmore Jr.
May Whitty
Richard Widmark
Dianne Wiest
Cornel Wilde
Billy Dee Williams
JoBeth Williams
John Williams
Treat Williams
Gordon Willis
Marie Windsor
Oprah Winfrey
Debra Winger
Henry Winkler
Mare Winningham
Shelley Winters
Robert Wise
Ed D. Wood Jr.
Elijah Wood
Natalie Wood
Alfred Woodard
James Woods
Joanne Woodward
Fay Wray
Robin Wright
Teresa Wright
Robert Wuhl
William Wyler
Keenan Wynn
Peter Yates
Zhang Yimou
Susannah York

Loretta Young
Robert Young
Robert Malcolm Young
Sean Young
Terence Young
Billy Zane
Franco Zeffirelli
Mai Zetterling
Fred Zinnemann
Vilmos Zsigmond
Daphne Zuniga
Edward Zwick

## FANTASY

Tim Burton
Jean Cocteau
Danny Elfman
Peter Medak
Georges Melies
Nicholas Meyer
Rick Moranis
George Pal
Christopher Reeve
Alain Resnais
Steven Spielberg

## FILM NOIR

Dana Andrews
Lauren Bacall
Joan Bennett
Humphrey Bogart
Joseph Cotten
Joan Crawford
Kirk Douglas
Sam Fuller
John Garfield
Gloria Grahame
Sydney Greenstreet
Rita Hayworth
Elia Kazan
Alan Ladd
Veronica Lake
Burt Lancaster
Fritz Lang
Joseph Losey
Ida Lupino
Fred MacMurray
Victor Mature
Robert Mitchum
Dick Powell
Otto Preminger
Nicholas Ray
Edward G. Robinson
Robert Siodmak
Barbara Stanwyck
Gene Tierney
Lana Turner
Orson Welles
Richard Widmark

## HISTORICAL

Helena Bonham-Carter
Kenneth Branagh
Peter Brook
Daniel Day-Lewis
Julie Delpy
Ralph Fiennes
John Gielgud
Rupert Graves
Cedric Hardwicke
James Ivory
Derek Jarman
Roland Joffe
Chen Kaige
Akira Kurosawa
Ian McKellan
Georges Melies
Julia Ormond
Vanessa Redgrave
Paul Scofield
Jim Sheridan
Paolo Taviani
Liv Ullmann
Luchino Visconti
Zhang Yimou

## HORROR

Linda Blair
John Carpenter
John Carradine
William Castle
Lon Chaney
Lon Chaney Jr.
Larry Cohen
Wes Craven
David Cronenberg
Peter Cushing
Joseph Dante
Brad Dourif
Robert Englund
Freddie Francis
Edward Furlong
Tobe Hooper
Kim Hunter
Boris Karloff
John Landis
Christopher Lee
Bela Lugosi
Vincent Price
Sam M. Raimi
Christina Ricci
George A. Romero
Barbara Steele
Alex Winter
Ed D. Wood Jr.

## MUSICALS

Don Ameche
Eve Arden
Fred Astaire

Mischa Auer
Busby Berkeley
Ruben Blades
Eric Blore
Ann Blyth
Ray Bolger
David Bowie
Eddie Bracken
Jack Buchanan
David Butler
Charles Butterworth
Eddie Cantor
Cyd Charisse
Maurice Chevalier
Phil Collins
Jeanne Crain
Bing Crosby
Bebe Daniels
Marion Davies
Doris Day
Jimmy Durante
Deanna Durbin
Nelson Eddy
Leon Errol
Alice Faye
Stepin Fetchit
Bob Fosse
Reginald Gardiner
Judy Garland
Mitzi Gaynor
Billy Gilbert
Betty Grable
Taylor Hackford
June Havoc
Edward Everett Horton
Betty Hutton
Al Jolson
Danny Kaye
Gene Kelly
Kris Kristofferson
Dorothy Lamour
Mario Lanza
Jeanette MacDonald
Gordon MacRae
George E. Marshall
Dean Martin
Ethel Merman
Carmen Miranda
Zero Mostel
George Murphy
Nicholas Brothers
Donald O'Connor
Jack Oakie
Franklin Pangborn
Alan Parker
Dolly Parton
Dick Powell
Elvis Presley
Martha Raye
Debbie Reynolds
Ritz Brothers
George Sidney

Phil Silvers
Frank Sinatra
Red Skelton
Sting
Tina Turner
Esther Williams

## MYSTERY

Lionel Atwill
Edward S. Brophy
Tod Browning
Nigel Bruce
Raymond Burr
William Castle
Joan Chen
Henri-Georges Clouzot
William Conrad
Peter Falk
Michael Figgis
Robert Florey
William Gargan
Leo Genn
Louis Hayward
Alfred Hitchcock
Jack Klugman
Jack LaRue
Margaret Lindsay
Peter Lorre
Bela Lugosi
Sidney Lumet
William Lundigan
Kyle MacLachlan
Ann Magnuson
David Mamet
Lloyd Nolan
Basil Rathbone
Mimi Rogers
Rosalind Russell
George Sanders
Alastair Sim
Robert Siodmak
Steven Soderbergh
Gale Sondergaard
George E. Stone
Meg Tilly
Sidney Toler
Jeanne Tripplehorn
Rachel Ward
Wim Wenders

## POLITICAL

Bernardo Bertolucci
Constantin Costa-Gavras
Agnieszka Holland
Krzysztof Kieslowski
Ian McKellan
Jim Sheridan
Andrzej Wajda
Haskell Wexler
Zhang Yimou

## ROMANCE

Walter Abel
Chantal Akerman
Alan Alda
Kirstie Alley
Nestor Almendros
Don Ameche
Julie Andrews
Ann-Margret
Michelangelo Antonioni
Eve Arden
Edward Arnold
Tom Arnold
Jean Arthur
Dorothy Arzner
Hal Ashby
Mary Astor
Mischa Auer
Lauren Bacall
Fay Bainter
Kathy Baker
Antonio Banderas
Theda Bara
Brigitte Bardot
Binnie Barnes
Ethel Barrymore
Lionel Barrymore
Richard Barthelmess
Kim Basinger
Kathy Bates
Jennifer Beals
Warren Beatty
Ralph Bellamy
Richard Benjamin
Constance Bennett
Andrew Bergman
Ingmar Bergman
Ingrid Bergman
Halle Berry
Jacqueline Bisset
Joan Blondell
Eric Blore
Ann Blyth
Peter Bogdanovich
Beulah Bondi
Helena Bonham-Carter
Frank Borzage
Clara Bow
Charles Boyer
Alice Brady
Kenneth Branagh
George Brent
Robert Bresson
Marshall Brickman
Matthew Broderick
Albert Brooks
James L. Brooks
Louise Brooks
Billie Burke
Richard Burton
Tim Burton
Spring Byington

Nicolas Cage
Frank Capra
Marcel Carne
Madeleine Carroll
Jack Carson
Phoebe Cates
Ruth Chatterton
Paddy Chayefsky
Maurice Chevalier
Julianne Christie
Rene Clair
Jill Clayburgh
Montgomery Clift
Glenn Close
Charles Coburn
Claudette Colbert
Ray Collins
Ronald Colman
Betty Comden
Joyce Compton
Jennifer Connelly
Walter Connolly
Hans Conried
Tom Conti
Martha Coolidge
Gary Cooper
Gladys Cooper
Bud Cort
Frank Craven
Joan Crawford
John Cromwell
Tom Cruise
George Cukor
Bob Cummings
Michael Curtiz
Joan Cusack
John Cusack
Beverly D'Angelo
Dorothy Dandridge
Blythe Danner
Ted Danson
Jane Darwell
Lolita Davidovich
Marion Davies
Bette Davis
Geena Davis
Doris Day
Laraine Day
Rosemary DeCamp
Sandra Dee
Olivia DeHavilland
Julie Delpy
Cecil Blount DeMille
Patrick Dempsey
Catherine Deneuve
Reginald Denny
Gerard Depardieu
Johnny Depp
Bo Derek
Vittorio DeSica
I.A.L. Diamond
William S. Dieterle

Marlene Dietrich
Carlo DiPalma
Stanley Donen
Melvyn Douglas
Marie Dressler
John Duigan
Olympia Dukakis
James Dunn
Griffin Dunne
Irene Dunne
Allan Dwan
Nelson Eddy
Blake Edwards
Cary Elwes
Nora Ephron
Stuart Erwin
Tom Ewell
Frances Farmer
Mia Farrow
Rainer Werner Fassbinder
Frank Faylen
Sally Field
Linda Fiorentino
Carrie Fisher
Geraldine Fitzgerald
Victor Fleming
Bridget Fonda
Jane Fonda
Joan Fontaine
Harrison Ford
Stephen Frears
Clark Gable
Peter Gallagher
Lowell Ganz
Greta Garbo
Ava Gardner
Greer Garson
Vittorio Gassman
Janet Gaynor
Richard Gere
John Gilbert
Lillian Gish
James Gleason
Crispin Glover
Jean-Luc Godard
Paulette Goddard
Frances Goodrich
Edmund Goulding
Cary Grant
Hugh Grant
Rupert Graves
D.W. Griffith
Raymond Griffith
Charles Grodin
Steve Guttenberg
Edmund Gwenn
Albert Hackett
Taylor Hackford
Alan Hale Sr.
Linda Hamilton
Tom Hanks
Daryl Hannah

Ann Harding
Jean Harlow
Woody Harrelson
Goldie Hawn
Helen Hayes
Susan Hayward
Rita Hayworth
Glenne Headly
Amy Heckerling
Audrey Hepburn
Katharine Hepburn
George Roy Hill
Arthur Hiller
Samuel S. Hinds
Judy Holliday
Celeste Holm
Oscar Homolka
Anthony Hopkins
Miriam Hopkins
Edward Everett Horton
Leslie Howard
James Wong Howe
Holly Hunter
Ross Hunter
Isabelle Huppert
William Hurt
Angelica Huston
Jim Hutton
Jeremy Irons
Amy Irving
Judith Ivey
Glenda Jackson
Van Johnson
Neil Jordan
Carol Kane
Garson Kanin
Lawrence Kasdan
Julie Kavner
Diane Keaton
Cecil Kellaway
Deborah Kerr
Guy Kibbee
Nicole Kidman
Henry King
Ben Kingsley
Nastassja Kinski
Alexander Korda
Swoosie Kurtz
Diane Kurys
Christine Lahti
Arthur Lake
Hedy Lamarr
Charles Lane
Jessica Lange
Angela Lansbury
Peter Lawford
David Lean
Jason Scott Lee
Mitchell Leisen
Claude Lelouch
Jack Lemmon
Robert Sean Leonard

Mervin LeRoy
Barry Levinson
Juliette Lewis
Viveca Lindfors
Anatole Litvak
Frank Lloyd
Gina Lollobrigida
Carole Lombard
John Lone
Shelley Long
Sophia Loren
Robert Lowe
Myrna Loy
Ernst Lubitsch
Ida Lupino
Adrian Lyne
Jeanette MacDonald
Andie MacDowell
Ali MacGraw
Shirley MacLaine
Fred MacMurray
Marjorie Main
Louis Malle
Rouben Mamoulian
Babaloo Mandel
Joseph Leo Mankiewicz
Jean Marais
Fredric March
Garry Marshall
Herbert Marshall
Steve Martin
Giulietta Masina
Mary Stuart Masterson
Marcello Mastroianni
Elaine May
Ken Maynard
Paul Mazursky
Hattie R. McDaniel
Kelly McGillis
Elizabeth McGovern
Dorothy McGuire
Frank McHugh
Adolphe Menjou
Una Merkel
Nikita Mikhalkov
Ray Milland
Vincente Minnelli
Matthew Modine
Alfred Molina
Marilyn Monroe
Demi Moore
Dudley Moore
Agnes Moorehead
Jeanne Moreau
Frank Morgan
Alan Mowbray
F.W. Murnau
Mike Myers
Conrad Nagel
Mildred Natwick
Patricia Neal
Jean Negulesco

Kate Nelligan
Julie Newmar
Mike Nichols
Kim Novak
Sven Nykvist
Merle Oberon
Chris O'Donnell
Gary Oldman
Lena Olin
Laurence Olivier
Max Ophuls
Maureen O'Sullivan
Reginald Owen
Yasujiro Ozu
Eugene Pallette
Chazz Palminteri
Franklin Pangborn
Eleanor Parker
Mary-Louise Parker
Estelle Parsons
Elizabeth Perkins
Luke Perry
Michelle Pfeiffer
Mary Pickford
Walter Pidgeon
Harold Pinter
Brad Pitt
ZaSu Pitts
Sydney Pollack
William H. Powell
Tyrone Power
Jason Priestley
Bill Pullman
Claude Rains
Nicholas Ray
Satyajit Ray
Lynn Redgrave
Donna Reed
Carl Reiner
Alain Resnais
Joely Richardson
Miranda Richardson
Tony Richardson
Peter Riegert
Molly Ringwald
Martin Ritt
John Ritter
Thelma Ritter
Tim Robbins
Julia Roberts
Ginger Rogers
Eric Rohmer
Herbert Ross
Isabella Rossellini
Alan Rudolph
Mercedes Ruehl
Charles Ruggles
Jane Russell
Rosalind Russell
Margaret Rutherford
Meg Ryan
Mark Rydell

Winona Ryder
Greta Scacchi
Fred Schepisi
Joseph Schildkraut
Romy Schneider
Barbet Schroeder
Annabella Sciorra
Ettore Scola
Martin Scorsese
Campbell Scott
Kyra Sedgwick
Susan Seidelman
David O. Selznick
Jane Seymour
Wallace Shawn
Norma Shearer
Craig Sheffer
Ron Shelton
Cybill Shepherd
Martin Short
George Sidney
Simone Signoret
Joan Micklin Silver
Phil Silvers
Jean Simmons
Neil Simon
John Singleton
Red Skelton
Ione Skye
Helen Slater
Ann Sothern
James Spader
Barbara Stanwyck
Maureen Stapleton
Mary Steenburgen
Fisher Stevens
George Stevens Sr.
Eric Stoltz
Lewis S. Stone
Meryl Streep
Barbra Streisand
Margaret Sullavan
Jessica Tandy
Elizabeth Taylor
Lili Taylor
Robert Taylor
Emma Thompson
Uma Thurman
Gene Tierney
Jennifer Tilly
Gregg Toland
Marisa Tomei
Franchot Tone
Robert Towne
Spencer Tracy
John Travolta
Jean-Louis Trintignant
Jeanne Tripplehorn
Fernando Trueba
Francois Truffaut
Janine Turner
Kathleen Turner

Lana Turner
Rudolph Valentino
Woodbridge S. vanDyke II
Agnes Varda
Paul Verhoeven
King Vidor
Luchino Visconti
Erich vonStroheim
Julie Walters
Damon Wayans
Chloe Webb
Johnny Weissmuller Jr.
Lina Wertmuller
Mae West
May Whitty
Dianne Wiest
Billy Wilder
Gene Wilder
Gordon Willis
Debra Winger
Natalie Wood
Joanne Woodward
Fay Wray
Robin Wright
Teresa Wright
Robert Wuhl
William Wyler
Jane Wyman
Gig Young
Loretta Young
Robert Young
Franco Zeffirelli
Howard Zieff

## SATIRE

Jim Abrahams
Woody Allen
Robert Altman
Albert Brooks
James L. Brooks
Mel Brooks
Tim Burton
Dana Carvey
John Cleese
Alex Cox
Divine
Terry Gilliam
Buck Henry
Jeffrey Jones
Madeline Kahn
Mike Leigh
Jerry Lewis
Steve Martin
Marx Brothers
Paul Mazursky
Michael McKean
Paul Morrissey
Bill Murray
Michael Palin
Carl Reiner
Peter Riegert

Tim Robbins
Peter Sellers
Preston Sturges
Jacques Tati
John Waters
Mae West
Alex Winter
David Zucker
Jerry Zucker

## SCI-FI

Irwin Allen
James Cameron
Larry "Buster" Crabbe
David Cronenberg
Joseph Dante
Linda Hamilton
George Lucas
Leonard Nimoy
George Pal
William Shatner
Patrick Stewart
Sigourney Weaver

## SEX & SEXUALITY

Woody Allen
Pedro Almodovar
Antonio Banderas
Brigitte Bardot
Paul Bartel
Sandra Bernhard
Bernardo Bertolucci
Sonia Braga
Kenneth Branagh
Martha Coolidge
Bo Derek
Divine
Amanda Donohoe
David Duchovny
Cary Elwes
Harvey Fierstein
Stephen Frears
Robin Givens
Valeria Golino
Hugh Grant
Peter Greenaway
Mary Beth Hurt
Derek Jarman
Diane Kurys
Vivien Leigh
Ray Liotta
Adrian Lyne
Garry Marshall
Jim McBride
Russ Meyer
Kenji Mizoguchi
Eddie Murphy
Pier Paolo Pasolini
Bob Rafelson
Lynn Redgrave
Natasha Richardson

Ken Russell
Julian Sands
Laura SanGiacomo
Nancy Savoca
Paul Schrader
Susan Seidelman
Jennifer Tilly
Kathleen Turner
Gus vanSant Jr.
Paul Verhoeven
Andy Warhol
John Waters

## SLAPSTICK

Bud Abbott
Dan Aykroyd
Charles Chaplin
Thomas Chong
Tim Conway
Rodney Dangerfield
Marty Feldman
W.C. Fields
Lowell Ganz
Oliver Hardy
Buster Keaton Jr.
Stan Laurel
Jerry Lewis
Harold Lloyd
Babaloo Mandel
Marx Brothers
Harold Ramis
Ivan Reitman
Hal Roach
Peter Sellers
Pauly Shore
Jonathan Silverman
Neil Simon
Jacques Tati

## SUSPENSE

Isabelle Adjani
Robert Aldrich
Judith Anderson
Michael Apted
Peggy Ashcroft
Lionel Atwill
Lauren Bacall
Kevin Bacon
Carroll Baker
Drew Barrymore
Richard Basehart
Alan Bates
Bonnie Bedelia
Ed Begley Sr.
Annette Bening
Joan Bennett
Tom Berenger
Bernardo Bertolucci
Linda Blair
John Boorman
Lara Flynn Boyle

Marlon Brando
Marshall Brickman
James Bridges
Tod Browning
Nigel Bruce
Genevieve Bujold
Luis Bunuel
Gabriel Byrne
John Carradine
Jim Carrey
Claude Chabrol
Michael Chapman
Joan Chen
Cher
Rae Dawn Chong
Henri-Georges Clouzot
Larry Cohen
Jennifer Connelly
William Conrad
Elisha Cook Jr.
Roger Corman
Constantin Costa-Gavras
Joseph Cotten
Peter Coyote
Wes Craven
Richard Crenna
Michael Crichton
Hume Cronyn
Tim Curry
Jamie Lee Curtis
Peter Cushing
Willem Dafoe
Henry Daniell
Linda Darnell
Jules Dassin
Lolita Davidovich
Bette Davis
Bruce Davison
Catherine Deneuve
Robert DeNiro
Sandy Dennis
Brian DePalma
Laura Dern
Leonardo DiCaprio
Angie Dickinson
Shannen Doherty
Amanda Donohue
Brad Dourif
Carl Theodor Dreyer
Mildred Dunnock
Hector Elizondo
Robert Englund
Rupert Everett
Sherilyn Fenn
Jose Luis Ferrer
Melchor G. Ferrer
Michael Figgis
Albert Finney
Geraldine Fitzgerald
Frederic Forrest
Freddie Francis
William Friedkin

Teri Garr
Richard Gere
John Glover
Gloria Grahame
Lee Grant
Richard E. Grant
Peter Greenaway
Sydney Greenstreet
Joel Grey
Lukas Haas
Conrad L. Hall
Tess Harper
Ed Harris
Laurence Harvey
John Heard
Barbara Hershey
Wendy Hiller
Alfred Hitchcock
Hal Holbrook
Tobe Hooper
Anthony Hopkins
John Houseman
Kim Hunter
John Hurt
Lauren Hutton
Timothy Hutton
Jeremy Irons
James Ivory
Ruth Prawer Jhabvala
Raul Julia
Boris Karloff
Philip Clarke Kaufman
Elia "Gadge" Kazan
Stacy Keach
Grace Kelly
Klaus Kinski
Jack Klugman
Shirley Knight
Alexander Knox
Stanley Kramer
Stanley Kubrick
Diane Kurys
Martin Landau
Fritz Lang
Jessica Lange
Charles Laughton
Christopher Lee
Viveca Lindfors
John Lithgow
Heather Locklear
Herbert Lom
John Lone
Joseph Losey
Bela Lugosi
Sidney Lumet
David Lynch
Kyle MacLachlan
Amy Madigan
Virginia Madsen
Ann Magnuson
John Mahoney
David Mamet

Marsha Mason
Richard Masur
Mercedes McCambridge
Elizabeth McGovern
Laurie Metcalf
Sylvia Miles
Yvette Mimieux
Helen Mirren
Sam Neill
Kate Nelligan
Craig T. Nelson
Mike Newell
Sheree North
Sven Nykvist
Gary Oldman
Geraldine Page
Alan J. Pakula
Eleanor Parker
Jason Patric
Will Patton
Anthony Perkins
Jada Pinkett
Harold Pinter
Donald Pleasence
Joan Plowright
Christopher Plummer
Roman Polanski
Kelly Preston
Vincent Price
Robert J. Prosky
Jonathan Pryce
Aidan Quinn
Basil Rathbone
Stephen Rea
Vanessa Redgrave
Lee Remick
Miranda Richardson
Natasha Richardson
Jason Robards Jr.
Eric Roberts
Rachel Roberts
Mark Robson
Mimi Rogers
George A. Romero
Katharine Ross
Isabella Rossellini
Tim Roth
Mickey Rourke
Saul Rubinek
Theresa Russell
Eva Marie Saint
George Sanders
Laura SanGiacomo
Mia Sara
Greta Scacchi
Roy G. Scheider
Fred Schepisi
John Schlesinger
Volker Schlondorff
Romy Schneider
Paul Schrader
Annabella Sciorra

Paul Scofield
Martin Scorsese
George Campbell Scott
Lizabeth Scott
Helen Shaver
Robert J. Shaw
Martin Sheen
Sam Shepard
Sylvia Sidney
Ron Silver
O.J. Simpson
Lori Singer
Robert Siodmak
Steven Soderbergh
Gale Sondergaard
Barry Sonnenfeld
Sissy Spacek
Kevin Spacey
James Spader
Barbara Steele
Madeleine Stowe
Meryl Streep
Donald Sutherland
Bertrand Tavernier
Paolo Taviani
Henry Thomas
Meg Tilly
Sidney Toler
Jean-Louis Trintignant
Cicely Tyson
Liv Ullmann
Max vonSydow
Christopher Walken
Tracey Walter
Rachel Ward
Denzel Washington
Jack Webb
Peter Weir
Orson Welles
Frank Whaley
Joanne Whalley-Kilmer
May Whitty
JoBeth Williams
Oprah Winfrey
Shelley Winters
Robert Wise
Ed D. Wood Jr.
Robin Wright
Teresa Wright
William Wyler
Robert Malcolm Young
Sean Young
Fred Zinnemann

**THRILLER**

Nancy Allen
Gregg Araki
Kathy Baker
Drew Barrymore
Luc Besson
Michael Biehn

Kathryn Bigelow
Lorraine Bracco
John Carpenter
Larry Cohen
Wes Craven
Michael Crichton
David Cronenberg
John R. Dahl
Jan DeBont
Rebecca DeMornay
Michael Douglas
Robert Englund
Jeff Fahey
Michael Figgis
Linda Fiorentino
Freddie Francis
William Friedkin
Tony Goldwyn
Mark Harmon
Jessica Harper
Tess Harper
Lance Henriksen
Hal Holbrook
Tobe Hooper
Whitney Houston
Ice-T
Boris Karloff
Joseph Losey
Dolph Lundgren
Michael Madsen
Frances McDormand
John McTiernan
Sam Neill
Alan J. Pakula
Jason Patric
Will Patton
Bill Paxton
Anthony Perkins
Michael Redgrave

Nicolas Roeg
Mimi Rogers
George A. Romero
Theresa Russell
Julian Sands
Roy G. Scheider
Ernest Boaumont Schoedsack
Ridley Scott
Sam Shepard
Henry Thomas
Meg Tilly
Jeanne Tripplehorn
Jon Voight
Christopher Walken
J.T. Walsh
Peter Weller
Joanne Whalley-Kilmer
Billy Zane
Daphne Zuniga

## TRAGEDY

Robert Bresson
Julie Delpy
Emil Jannings
Vivien Leigh
John Malkovich
Kenji Mizoguchi
Campbell Scott
Gary Sinise
Margaret Sullavan

## WAR

Dirk Bogarde
Peter Brook
Tom Courtenay
Kevin Dillon
Abel Gance

Leo Genn
Lukas Haas
Leslie Howard
Curt Jurgens
Alexander Knox
Anatole Litvak
Emily Ann Lloyd
George Lucas
Lee Marvin
Lena Olin
Laurence Olivier
Marcel Ophuls
Michael Powell
Otto Preminger
Michael Redgrave
Roberto Rossellini
Maximilian Schell
Volker Schlondorff
D.B. Sweeney
Andrzej Wajda
Clifton Webb

## WESTERN

Gene Autry
Anne Baxter
Noah Beery Sr.
Robert Blake
Ward Bond
William Boyd
Walter Brennan
Johnny Mack Brown
Edgar Buchanan
Bruce Cabot
Yakima Canutt
Lon Chaney Jr.
Larry "Buster" Crabbe
Andy Devine
Richard Dix

Clint Eastwood
Jack Elam
Sam Elliott
Paul Fix
Glenn Ford
Douglas V. Fowley
Edward "Hoot" Gibson
William S. Hart
George "Gabby" Hayes
Tim Holt
Buck Jones
Victor Jory
Sergio Leone
Barton MacLane
George E. Marshall
Ken Maynard
Timothy McCoy
Joel D. McCrea
Tom Mix
George Montgomery
Audie Murphy
Sam Peckinpah
Tex Ritter
Roy Rogers
Randolph Scott
Charles Starrett
Bob Steele
Woodrow "Woody" Strode
John Sturges
Forrest Tucker
Tom Tyler
Lee vanCleef
Robert Walker
John Wayne
Guinn "Big Boy" Williams
Chill Wills
Marie Windsor

# Birthdate &  Astrological Index

## ARIES

### March 21
W.S. Van Dyke II (1889)
Russ Meyer (1922)
Peter Brook (1925)
Timothy Dalton (1944)
Gary Oldman (1958)
Matthew Broderick (1962)

### March 22
Joseph Schildkraut (1895)
Lawrence Olivier (1907)
Karl Malden (1912)
William Shatner (1931)
M. Emmet Walsh (1935)
Matthew Modine (1959)

### March 23
Joan Crawford (1908)
Akira Kurosawa (1910)
David H. Watkin (1925)
Mark Rydell (1934)
Amanda Plummer (1957)

### March 24
Steve McQueen (1930)
Lara Flynn Boyle (1970)

### March 25
Ed Begley Sr. (1901)
Binnie Barnes (1905)
David Lean (1908)
Simone Signoret (1921)
Bonnie Bedelia (1952)
Sarah Jessica Parker (1965)

### March 26
Sterling Hayden (1916)
Leonard Nimoy (1931)
Alan Arkin (1934)
James Caan (1939)
Diana Ross (1944)
Jennifer Grey (1960)

### March 27
Edward S. Brophy (1895)
Gloria Swanson (1897)

### March 28
Charles Starrett (1903)
Dirk Bogarde (1921)
Freddie Bartholomew (1924)
Dianne Wiest (1948)

### March 29
Dennis O'Keefe (1908)
Bud Cort (1950)
Christopher Lambert (1957)

### March 30
Warren Beatty (1938)

### March 31
Shirley T. Jones (1934)
Volker Schlondorff (1939)
Christopher Walken (1943)

### April 1
Lon Chaney (1883)
Toshiro Mifune (1920)
Debbie Reynolds (1932)
Ali MacGraw (1938)

### April 2
Jack Buchanan (1890)
Buddy Ebsen (1908)
Alec Guinness (1914)
Jack Webb (1920)
Linda Hunt (1945)
Pamela Reed (1949)
Dana Carvey (1955)

### April 3
Allan Dwan (1885)
Leslie Howard (1893)
Doris Day (1922)
Marlon Brando (1924)
Marsha Mason (1942)
Alec Baldwin (1958)
Eddie Murphy (1961)

### April 4
Samuel S. Hinds (1875)
Eric Rohmer (1920)
Elmer Bernstein (1922)
Anthony Perkins (1932)
Craig T. Nelson (1946)
Christine Lahti (1950)
Robert Downey Jr. (1965)

### April 5
Spencer Tracy (1900)
Melvyn Douglas (1901)
Bette Davis (1908)
Gregory Peck (1916)
Roger Corman (1926)
Nigel Hawthorne (1929)
Peter Greenaway (1942)

### April 6
Walter Huston (1884)

### Dudley Nichols (1895)
Billy Dee Williams (1937)

### April 7
James Garner (1928)
Alan J. Pakula (1928)
Francis Ford Coppola (1939)

### April 8
Walter Connolly (1887)
Mary Pickford (1893)
Patricia Arquette (1968)

### April 9
Paul Robeson (1898)
Allen Jenkins (1900)
Ward Bond (1903)
Jean-Paul Belmondo (1933)
Dennis Quaid (1954)

### April 10
Timothy McCoy (1891)
Harry Hays Morgan (1915)
Max Von Sydow (1929)
Omar Sharif (1932)

### April 11
Joel Grey (1932)
John Milius (1944)
Peter Riegert (1947)

### April 12
Andy Garcia Jr. (1956)
Shannen Doherty (1971)

### April 13
Stanley Donen (1924)
Edward Fox (1937)

## April 14

John C. Howard (1913)
Rod Steiger (1925)
Julianne Christie (1940)
Anthony Michael Hall (1968)

## April 15

Hans Conried (1917)

## April 16

Charles Chaplin (1889)
Peter Ustinov (1921)
Henry Mancini (1924)
Jon Cryer (1965)
Lukas Haas (1976)

## April 17

Arthur Lake (1905)
William Holden (1918)
Lindsay Anderson (1923)
Carlo DiPalma (1925)

## April 18

Miklos Rozsa (1907)
Hayley Mills (1946)
James Woods (1947)
Eric Roberts (1956)

## April 19

Jayne Mansfield (1933)
Dudley Moore (1935)
Tim Curry (1946)

# TAURUS

## April 20

Harold Lloyd (1894)
Bruce Cabot (1904)
Larry Cohen (1938)
Ryan O'Neal (1941)
Jessica Lange (1949)

## April 21

Anthony Quinn (1916)
Elaine May (1932)
Charles Grodin (1935)
Tony Danza (1950)

## April 22

Edward Albert (1908)
Jack Nicholson (1937)

## April 23

Frank Borzage (1893)
Simone Simon (1911)
Shirley Temple (1928)
Sandra Dee (1942)

## April 24

William Castle (1914)
William Smith (1933)
Shirley MacLaine (1934)
Barbra Streisand (1942)
Eric Bogosian (1953)

## April 25

Paul Mazursky (1930)
Al Pacino (1940)
Bertrand Tavernier (1941)

## April 26

Edgar Kennedy (1890)
Guinn "Big Boy" Williams (1899)
Jean Vigo (1905)
Barbet Schroeder (1941)

## April 27

Jack Klugman (1922)
Anouk Aimee (1932)
Sandy Dennis (1937)

## April 28

Sidney Toler (1874)
Lionel Barrymore (1878)
Ann-Margret (1941)

## April 29

Fred Zinnemann (1907)
Tom Ewell (1909)
Celeste Holm (1919)
Phillip Noyce (1950)
Daniel Day-Lewis (1957)
Michelle Pfeiffer (1959)

## April 30

Eve Arden (1912)
Cloris Leachman (1926)
Jill Clayburgh (1944)

## May 1

Glenn Ford (1916)

## May 2

Bing Crosby (1901)
Satyajit Ray (1921)
Theodore Bikel (1924)

## May 3

Beulah Bondi (1892)
Jack LaRue (1900)
Mary Astor (1906)
Betty Comden (1916)

## May 4

Alice Faye (1912)
Audrey Hepburn (1929)

## May 5

Tyrone Power (1914)
Michael Palin (1943)
Richard E. Grant (1957)
Annette Bening (1958)

## May 6

Rudolph Valentino (1895)
Max Ophuls (1902)
Stewart Granger (1913)
Orson Welles (1915)
Ross Hunter (1916)

## May 7

George "Gabby" Hayes (1885)
Gary Cooper (1901)
Val Lewton (1904)
Darren McGavin (1922)
Anne Baxter (1923)
Ruth Prawer Jhabvala (1927)
Amy Heckerling (1954)

## May 8

Roberto Rossellini (1906)
Bob Clampett (1913)
David Keith (1954)

## May 9

Richard Barthelmess (1895)
Pedro Armendariz Sr. (1912)
Albert Finney (1936)
Glenda Jackson (1936)
James L. Brooks (1940)
Candice Bergen (1946)

## May 10

Max Steiner (1888)
Fred Astaire (1899)
Dmitri Tiomkin (1899)
Anatole Litvak (1902)
David Oliver Selznick (1902)
Jim Abrahams (1944)
Meg Foster (1948)

## May 11

Margaret Rutherford (1892)
Phil Silvers (1912)
Natasha Richardson (1963)

## May 12

Wilfrid Hyde-White (1903)
Emilio Estevez (1962)

## May 13

Herbert Ross (1927)
Harvey Keitel (1947)

## May 14

Laszlo (Leslie) Kovacs (1933)
George Lucas (1944)
Robert Zemeckis (1951)
Tim Roth (1961)

## May 15

Joseph Cotten (1905)
James Mason (1909)
David Cronenberg (1943)
Chazz Palminteri (1951)
James Belushi (1954)

## May 16

Kenji Mizoguchi (1898)
Henry Fonda (1905)
Margaret Sullavan (1911)
Pierce Brosnan (1952)
Debra Winger (1955)
Janet Jackson (1966)

## May 17

Jean Gabin (1904)
Maureen O'Sullivan (1911)
Dennis Hopper (1936)

## May 18

Frank Capra (1897)

## May 19

James Fox (1939)
Nora Ephron (1941)

# GEMINI

## May 20

James Stewart (1908)
Cher (1946)

**May 21**
Raymond Burr (1917)
Charles Aznavour (1924)

**May 22**
Richard Benjamin (1938)

**May 23**
Douglas Fairbanks Sr. (1883)
James Gleason (1886)
Herbert Marshall (1890)
Frank McHugh (1898)
George E. Stone (1903)
John Howard Payne (1912)
Joan Collins (1933)

**May 24**
Mai Zetterling (1925)
Joan Micklin Silver (1935)
Thomas Chong (1938)
Priscilla Presley (1945)
Alfred Molina (1953)

**May 25**
Robert Morley (1908)
Jeanne Crain (1925)
Mike Myers (1963)

**May 26**
John Wayne (1907)
Peter Cushing (1913)
Helena Bonham-Carter (1966)

**May 27**
Vincent Price (1911)
Christopher Lee (1922)
Louis Gossett Jr. (1936)

**May 28**
Carroll Baker (1935)
Sondra Locke (1947)

**May 29**
Bob Hope (1903)
Gregg Toland (1904)
Rupert Everett (1959)

**May 30**
Howard Hawks (1896)
Irving G. Thalberg (1899)
Stepin Fetchit (1902)
Mel Blanc (1908)
Douglas V. Fowley (1911)
Agnes Varda (1928)

**May 31**
Don Ameche (1908)
Denholm Elliott (1922)
Clint Eastwood (1930)
Jim Hutton (1933)
Rainer Werner Fassbinder (1945)
Tom Berenger (1950)
Lea Thompson (1961)
Brooke Shields (1965)

**June 1**
Frank Morgan (1890)
Robert Newton (1905)
Marilyn Monroe (1926)
Percy Adlon (1935)
Morgan Freeman (1937)
Karen Black (1942)

**June 2**
Johnny Weissmuller Jr. (1904)
Sally Kellerman (1937)
Stacy Keach (1941)
Barry Levinson (1942)

**June 3**
Paulette Goddard (1911)
Alain Resnais (1922)
Tony Curtis (1925)

**June 4**
Rosalind Russell (1908)
Bruce Dern (1936)

**June 5**
William Boyd (1895)
Tony Richardson (1928)
Spalding Gray (1941)

**June 6**
Walter Abel (1898)
Peter Lorre (1904)
Robert Englund (1949)
Harvey Fierstein (1954)
Sandra Bernhard (1955)

**June 7**
Al Jolson (1886)
Jessica Tandy (1909)
James Ivory (1928)
Liam Neeson (1952)

**June 8**
Ernest B. Schoedsack (1893)
Robert Preston (1918)

Kathy Baker (1950)
Griffin Dunne (1955)
Keenen Ivory Wayans (1958)

**June 9**
George Axelrod (1922)
Michael J. Fox (1961)
Johnny Depp (1963)

**June 10**
Sessue Hayakawa (1890)
Hattie R. McDaniel (1895)
Judy Garland (1922)

**June 11**
Gene Wilder (1935)

**June 12**
Irwin Allen (1916)
John A. Alonzo (1934)

**June 13**
Basil Rathbone (1892)
Joe Roth (1948)
Tim Allen (1953)

**June 14**
Dorothy McGuire (1919)
Will Patton (1954)

**June 15**
Harry Langdon (1884)
Malcolm McDowell (1943)
Helen Hunt (1963)
Courteney Cox (1964)
Ice Cube (1969)

**June 16**
Stan Laurel (1890)
Vilmos (William) Zsigmond
　(1930)

**June 17**
Ralph Bellamy (1904)
Dean Martin (1917)
Kenneth Loach (1936)

**June 18**
Jeanette MacDonald (1901)
Carol Kane (1952)
Isabella Rossellini (1952)

**June 19**
May Whitty (1865)
Charles Coburn (1877)
Mildred Natwick (1908)
Gena Rowlands (1934)
Kathleen Turner (1954)

**June 20**
Errol Flynn (1909)
Terence Young (1915)
Susan Hayward (1919)
Audie Murphy (1924)
Olympia Dukakis (1931)
Martin Landau (1931)
Danny Aiello (1933)
John Mahoney (1940)
Stephen Frears (1941)
John Goodman (1952)

**June 21**
Jane Russell (1921)
Judy Holliday (1923)
Maureen Stapleton (1925)
Sammy Davis Jr. (1964)
Juliette Lewis (1973)

# CANCER

**June 22**
Billy Wilder (1906)
Kris Kristofferson (1936)
Klaus-Maria Brandauer (1944)
Meryl Streep (1949)

**June 23**
Bob Foss (1927)
Bryan Brown (1947)

**June 24**
Henry King (1888)
Claude Chabrol (1930)
Peter Weller (1947)
Nancy Allen (1950)

**June 25**
Sidney Lumet (1924)
Denys Arcand (1941)

**June 26**
Eleanor Parker (1922)
John Cusack (1966)

**June 27**
I.A.L. Diamond (1920)
Isabelle Adjani (1955)

**June 28**

Mel Brooks (1926)
Noriyuki "Pat" Morita (1936)
Bruce Davison (1946)
Kathy Bates (1948)

**June 29**

Nelson Eddy (1901)
Bernard Herrmann (1911)
Gary Busey (1944)

**June 30**

Glenda Farrell (1904)
Anthony Mann (1906)
Rupert Graves (1963)

**July 1**

Charles Laughton (1899)
William Wyler (1902)
Olivia DeHavilland (1916)
Sydney Pollack (1934)
Rene Auberjonois (1940)
Genevieve Bujold (1942)
Dan Aykroyd (1950)

**July 3**

Leon Errol (1881)
George Sanders (1906)
Ken Russell (1927)
Tom Cruise (1962)

**July 4**

Louis B. Mayer (1885)
George Murphy (1902)
Eva Marie Saint (1924)
Neil Simon (1927)
Gina Lollobrigida (1928)

**July 5**

Jean Cocteau (1889)
Shirley Knight (1937)

**July 6**

Janet Leigh (1926)
Ned Beatty (1937)
Sylvester Stallone (1946)

**July 7**

George Cukor (1899)
Vittorio DeSica (1902)
Shelley Duvall (1949)

**July 8**

Eugene Pallette (1889)

**July 9**

Marty Feldman (1934)
Kevin Bacon (1958)

Bob Cummings (1908)
Brian Dennehy (1939)
O.J. Simpson (1947)
Angelica Huston (1951)
Jimmy Smits (1955)
Tom Hanks (1956)
Kelly McGillis (1957)

**July 10**

John Gilbert (1892)

**July 11**

Thomas Mitchell (1892)
Yul Brynner (1920)

**July 12**

Tod Browning (1882)
Milton Berle (1908)
Bill Cosby (1937)

**July 13**

Harrison Ford (1842)
Patrick Stewart (1940)
Robert Forster (1941)
Richard "Cheech" Marin (1946)

**July 14**

Donald Meek (1880)
Dave Fleischer (1894)
William Hanna (1910)
Ingmar Bergman (1918)
Joel Silver (1952)

**July 15**

William S. Dieterle (1893)

**July 16**

Barbara Stanwyck (1907)
Ginger Rogers (1911)
Ruben Blades (1948)
Corey Feldman (1971)

**July 17**

James Cagney (1904)
William Gargan (1905)
Donald Sutherland (1934)
Alex Winter (1965)

**July 18**

Richard Dix (1894)

Chill Wills (1903)
Hume Cronyn (1911)
Red Skelton (1913)
Paul Verhoeven (1938)
Elizabeth McGovern (1961)

**July 19**

George Dzundza (1945)
Anthony Edwards (1962)
Campbell Scott (1962)

**July 20**

Theda Bara (1890)
Diana Rigg (1938)
Natalie Wood (1938)

**July 21**

Ken Maynard (1895)
Norman Jewison (1921)
Tony Scott (1944)
Robin Williams (1951)
Rob Morrow (1962)

**July 22**

James Whale (1896)
Jason Robards Jr. (1922)
Terence Stamp (1939)
Paul Schrader (1946)
Albert Brooks (1947)
Danny Glover (1947)
Willem Dafoe (1955)
John Leguizamo (1965)

# LEO

**July 23**

Emil Jannings (1884)
Woody Harrelson (1961)

**July 24**

Keenan Wynn (1916)
Peter Yates (1929)

**July 25**

Walter Brennan (1894)

**July 26**

Charles Butterworth (1896)
Gracie Allen (1902)
Blake Edwards (1922)
Stanley Kubrick (1928)
Peter Hyams (1943)
Helen Mirren (1945)
Mick Jagger (1946)

**July 27**

Donald Crisp (1880)

**July 29**

William H. Powell (1892)

**July 30**

Peter Bogdanovich (1939)
Arnold Schwarzenegger (1947)
Laurence Fishburne (1961)

**July 31**

Geraldine Chaplin (1944)
Michael Biehn (1956)
Wesley Snipes (1962)

**August 1**

Dom DeLuise (1933)

**August 2**

Jack L. Warner (1892)
Myrna Loy (1905)
Ann Dvorak (1912)
Carroll O'Connor (1925)
Peter O'Toole (1932)
Wes Craven (1939)
Mary-Louise Parker (1964)
Edward Furlong (1977)

**August 3**

Dolores DelRio (1905)
Martin Sheen (1940)

**August 5**

Reginald Owen (1887)
John Huston (1906)
Robert Taylor (1911)
Michael Ballhaus (1935)
John Saxon (1935)

**August 6**

Billie Burke (1885)
Edward "Hoot" Gibson (1892)
Lucille Ball (1911)
Robert Mitchum (1917)
Andy Warhol (1931)
Paul Bartel (1938)

**August 7**

Ann Harding (1901)
Nicholas Ray (1911)
John Glover (1944)
David Duchovny (1960)

**August 8**

Robert Siodmak (1900)
Sylvia Sidney (1910)
Esther Williams (1923)
Dustin Hoffman (1937)
Martin Brest (1951)
Keith Carradine (1951)

**August 9**

Tom Tyler (1903)
Leo Genn (1905)
Robert Aldrich (1918)
Robert J. Shaw (1927)
Sam Elliott (1944)
Melanie Griffith (1957)
Whitney Houston (1963)

**August 10**

Norma Shearer (1903)
John Bailey (1942)
Rosanna Arquette (1959)

**August 11**

Lloyd Nolan (1902)

**August 12**

Cecil Blount DeMille (1881)
Oscar Homolka (1898)
Samuel Fuller (1911)
William Goldman (1931)

**August 13**

Alfred Hitchcock (1899)

**August 14**

John Gielgud (1904)
Lina Wertmuller (1928)
Wim Wenders (1945)
James Horner (1953)
Halle Berry (1968)

**August 15**

Ethel Barrymore (1879)
Wendy Hiller (1912)
Nicolas Roeg (1928)

**August 16**

Ann Blyth (1928)
Julie Newmar (1935)
Bruce Beresford (1940)
Lesley Ann Warren (1946)
James Cameron (1954)
Madonna (1958)
Timothy Hutton (1960)

**August 17**

Samuel Goldwyn (1882)
Mae West (1892)
Maureen O'Hara (1920)
Robert DeNiro (1943)
Martha Coolidge (1946)
Sean Penn (1960)

**August 18**

Alan Mowbray (1896)
Marcel Carne (1909)
Shelley Winters (1922)
Roman Polanski (1933)
Robert Redford (1937)
Patrick Swayze (1954)
Madeleine Stowe (1958)

**August 19**

Peter Gallagher (1955)
Kevin Dillon (1965)

**August 20**

Van Johnson (1916)

**August 21**

Fritz Freleng (1906)
Frank Perry (1930)
Peter Weir (1944)

**August 22**

Cecil Kellaway (1893)
Leni Riefenstahl (1902)
Julius J. Epstein (1909)
Philip G. Epstein (1909)
Barbara Eden (1934)

# VIRGO

**August 23**

Gene Kelly (1912)
Ronny Cox (1938)
River Phoenix (1971)

**August 24**

Frank Craven (1875)
Steve Guttenberg (1958)
Marlee Matlin (1965)

**August 25**

Clara Bow (1905)
Melchor G. Ferrer (1917)
Sean Connery (1930)
Tom Skerritt (1933)

John Badham (1939)
Marshall Brickman (1941)
Anne Archer (1947)
Joanne Whalley-Kilmer (1964)

**August 26**

Macaulay "Mack" Culkin (1980)

**August 27**

G.W. Pabst (1885)
Martha Raye (1914)
Tuesday Weld (1943)
Pee Wee Herman (1952)

**August 28**

Charles Boyer (1899)
James Wong Howe (1899)
Donald O'Connor (1925)

**August 29**

Preston Sturges (1898)
Barry Sullivan (1912)
Ingrid Bergman (1915)
George Montgomery (1916)
Richard Attenborough (1923)
Elliott Gould (1938)
William Friedkin (1939)
Joel Schumacher (1942)
Shelley Long (1949)
Rebecca De Mornay (1961)

**August 30**

Raymond Massey (1896)
Joan Blondell (1906)
Fred MacMurray (1908)
John Landis (1950)

**August 31**

Fredric March (1897)
Richard Basehart (1914)
James Coburn (1928)
Lowell Ganz (1948)
Richard Gere (1948)

**September 1**

Johnny Mack Brown (1904)
Jack Hawkins (1910)
Vittorio Gassman (1922)
Lily Tomlin (1939)

**September 2**

Mark Harmon (1951)

**September 3**

Alan Ladd (1913)

Eileen Brennan (1935)
Charlie Sheen (1965)

**September 4**

Edward Dmytryk (1908)
Mitzi Gaynor (1930)
Judith Ivey (1951)
Ione Skye (1971)

**September 5**

Darryl Zanuck (1902)
Raquel Welch (1940)
Werner Herzog (1942)
Michael Keaton (1952)

**September 6**

Swoosie Kurtz (1944)
Rosie Perez (1964)

**September 7**

Elia "Gadge" Kazan (1909)
Anthony Quayle (1913)
Peter Lawford (1923)
Richard Roundtree (1942)
Julie Kavner (1951)
Corbin Bernsen (1954)

**September 8**

Sid Caesar (1922)
Peter Sellers (1925)

**September 9**

Arthur Freed (1894)
Cliff Robertson (1925)
Sylvia Miles (1932)
Henry Thomas (1971)

**September 10**

Robert Wise (1914)
Edmond O'Brien (1915)
Amy Irving (1953)
Chris Columbus (1958)

**September 11**

Brian DePalma (1940)
Amy Madigan (1951)
Virginia Madsen (1963)

**September 12**

Maurice Chevalier (1888)
Billy Gilbert (1894)

**September 13**

Claudette Colbert (1907)

Maurice Jarre (1924)
Jacqueline Bisset (1944)

**September 14**

Robert Florey (1900)

**September 15**

Jean Renoir (1894)
Fay Wray (1907)
Jackie Cooper (1922)
Chris Menges (1940)
Ron Shelton (1945)
Tommy Lee Jones (1946)
Oliver Stone (1946)

**September 16**

Alexander Korda (1893)
Lauren Bacall (1924)
Peter Falk (1927)
Jim McBride (1941)

**September 17**

Edgar G. Ulmer (1904)
Roddy McDowall (1928)
Anne Bancroft (1931)
John Ritter (1948)

**September 18**

Greta Garbo (1905)
Jack Cardiff (1914)
Jack Warden (1920)
Robert Blake (1933)

**September 19**

Margaret Lindsay (1910)
Frances Farmer (1913)

**September 20**

Rachel Roberts (1927)
Sophia Loren (1934)

**September 21**

Chuck Jones (1912)
Caleb Deschanel (1941)
Bill Murray (1950)
Ethan Coen (1957)

**September 22**

Erich VonStroheim (1885)
Paul Muni (1895)
John Houseman (1902)
Owen Roizman (1936)

# LIBRA

**September 23**

Walter Pidgeon (1898)
Mickey Rooney (1920)
Romy Schneider (1938)
Jason Alexander (1959)

**September 24**

Jim Henson (1936)

**September 25**

Robert Bresson (1907)
Michael Douglas (1944)
Pedro Almodovar (1951)
Mark Hamill (1952)
Christopher Reeve (1952)
Heather Locklear (1961)

**September 26**

Edmund Gwenn (1875)
George Raft (1895)
Philip Bosco (1930)
Mary Beth Hurt (1948)
Linda Hamilton (1957)

**September 27**

William Conrad (1920)
Arthur Penn (1922)

**September 28**

Peter Finch (1916)
Marcello Mastroianni (1924)
Brigitte Bardot (1934)
Jeffrey Jones (1947)

**September 29**

Gene Autry (1907)
Greer Garson (1908)
Michelangelo Antonioni (1912)
Stanley Kramer (1913)
Trevor Howard (1916)
Lizabeth Scott (1922)
Robert R. Benton (1932)
Madeline Kahn (1942)

**September 30**

George Bancroft (1882)
Lewis Milestone (1895)
Michael Powell (1905)
Deborah Kerr (1921)
Robert Duvall (1929)
Angie Dickinson (1931)

**October 1**

Walter Matthau (1920)

James Whitmore Jr. (1921)
Laurence Harvey (1928)
George Peppard (1928)
Philippe Noiret (1930)
Richard A. Harris (1932)
Julie Andrews (1935)
Jean-Jacques Annaud (1943)
Randy Quaid (1950)

**October 2**

Bud Abbott (1895)
Sting (1951)

**October 3**

Leo McCarey (1898)

**October 4**

Buster Keaton Jr. (1895)
George Sidney (1916)
Charlton Heston (1924)
Susan Sarandon (1946)
Armand Assante (1949)

**October 5**

John Alton (1901)
Donald Pleasence (1919)
Karen Allen (1951)

**October 6**

Jerome Cowan (1897)
Mitchell Leisen (1898)
Janet Gaynor (1906)
Carole Lombard (1908)

**October 7**

Andy Devine (1905)

**October 8**

Rouben Mamoulian (1898)
Klaus Kinski (1926)
Chevy Chase (1943)
Sigourney Weaver (1949)
Edward Zwick (1952)

**October 9**

Alastair Sim (1900)
Jacques Tati (1908)
Michael Pare (1958)

**October 10**

Helen Hayes (1900)
Richard Jaeckel (1926)
Harold Pinter (1930)
Jessica Harper (1949)

**October 11**

Ennio Morricone (1928)
Joan Cusack (1962)

**October 13**

Douglas Dumbrille (1890)
Laraine Day (1917)
Yves Montand (1921)
Melinda Dillon (1939)
Kelly Preston (1962)

**October 14**

Lillian Gish (1896)
Robert Walker (1919)
Roger Moore (1928)

**October 15**

Jane Darwell (1879)
Mervin LeRoy (1900)
Billy Barty (1924)
Penny Marshall (1943)

**October 16**

Linda Darnell (1923)
Angela Lansbury (1925)
Tim Robbins (1958)

**October 17**

Spring Byington (1893)
Jean Arthur (1905)
Marsha Hunt (1917)
Rita Hayworth (1919)
Montgomery Clift (1920)
Michael McKean (1947)
Margot Kidder (1948)

**October 18**

Miriam Hopkins (1902)
Cornel Wilde (1918)
George C. Scott (1927)
Peter Boyle (1933)
Inger Stevens (1934)
Joe Morton (1948)

**October 19**

Divine (1945)
John Lithgow (1945)

**October 20**

Margaret Dumont (1889)
Charlie Chase (1893)
Jerry Orbach (1935)
Melanie Mayron (1952)

**October 21**

Nikita Mikhalkov (1945)
Carrie Fisher (1956)

**October 22**

Constance Bennett (1905)
Joan Fontaine (1917)
Christopher Lloyd (1938)
Jan DeBont (1943)
Catherine Deneuve (1943)
Jeff Goldblum (1952)
Valeria Golino (1966)

# SCORPIO

**October 23**

Philip Clarke Kaufman (1936)
Sam M. Raimi (1959)

**October 24**

Merian C. Cooper (1893)
F. Murray Abraham (1939)
Michael Crichton (1942)
Kevin Kline (1947)

**October 25**

Abel Gance (1889)

**October 26**

Donald Siegel (1912)
Jackie Coogan (1914)
Bob Hoskins (1942)
Cary Elwes (1962)

**October 27**

Jack Carson (1910)
Teresa Wright (1918)
John Cleese (1939)
Roberto Benigni (1952)

**October 28**

Elsa Lanchester (1902)
Joan Plowright (1929)
Jane Alexander (1939)
Lauren Holly (1966)
Julia Roberts (1967)

**October 29**

Bela Lugosi (1884)
Akim Tamiroff (1899)
Richard Dreyfuss (1947)
Winona Rina Ryder (1971)

**October 30**

Ruth Gordon (1896)
Nestor Almendros (1930)
Louis Malle (1932)
Claude Lelouch (1937)
Henry Winkler (1945)
Harry Hamlin (1951)

**October 31**

Lee Grant (1927)
Sally Kirkland (1944)
John Candy (1950)
Dermot Mulroney (1963)

**November 1**

Lyle Lovett (1957)

**November 2**

Alice Brady (1892)
James Dunn (1901)
Luchino Visconti (1906)
Burt Lancaster (1913)

**November 3**

Charles Bronson (1920)
John Barry (1933)
Dolph Lundgren (1959)

**November 4**

Will Rogers (1879)
Stanley Cortez (1908)
Gig Young (1913)
Art Carney (1918)
Martin Balsam (1919)
Ralph Macchio (1962)

**November 5**

Joel D. McCrea (1905)
Roy Rogers (1911)
Vivien Leigh (1913)
Jonathan Kaplan (1947)
Tatum O'Neal (1963)

**November 6**

Mike Nichols (1931)
Sally Field (1946)
Brad Davis (1949)
Lori Singer (1962)
Ethan Hawke (1971)

**November 7**

Herman J. Mankiewicz (1897)
Dean Jagger (1903)

**November 8**

Katharine Hepburn (1909)
June Havoc (1916)
Paolo Taviani (1931)
Alain Delon (1935)
Alfred Woodard (1953)

**November 9**

Marie Dressler (1869)
Ed Wynn (1886)
Hedy Lamarr (1914)
Dorothy Dandridge (1923)

**November 10**

Claude Rains (1889)
Richard Burton (1925)
Roy Scheider (1935)

**November 11**

Rene Clair (1898)
Pat O'Brien (1899)
Demi Moore (1962)

**November 12**

Jack Oakie (1903)
Jacques Tourneur (1904)
Kim Hunter (1922)
Grace Kelly (1929)
Wallace Shawn (1943)

**November 13**

Jack Elam (1916)
Garry Marshall (1934)
Jean Seberg (1938)
Joe Mantegna (1947)
Whoopi Goldberg (1955)

**November 14**

Dick Powell (1904)
Louise Brooks (1906)
Rosemary DeCamp (1914)
Veronica Lake (1919)
Brian Keith (1921)
Ray Sharkey (1952)

**November 15**

Lewis S. Stone (1879)
Yaphet Laughlin Kotto (1937)
Sam Waterston (1940)
Roger Donaldson (1945)

**November 16**

Burgess Meredith (1909)

**November 17**

Rock Hudson (1925)
Martin Scorsese (1942)
Lauren Hutton (1943)
Danny DeVito (1944)
Roland Joffe (1945)
Mary Elizabeth Mastrantonio (1958)

**November 18**

Cameron Mitchell (1918)
Elizabeth Perkins (1960)

**November 19**

Clifton Webb (1891)
Meg Ryan (1961)
Jodie Foster (1962)

**November 20**

Robert Armstrong (1890)
Reginald Denny (1891)
Henri-Georges Clouzot (1907)
Gene Tierney (1920)
Estelle Parsons (1927)
Richard Masur (1948)
Bo Derek (1956)
Sean Young (1959)

**November 21**

Marcel Ophuls (1927)
Michael Chapman (1935)
Harold Ramis (1944)
Goldie Hawn (1945)

# SAGITTARIUS

**November 22**

Rodney Dangerfield (1921)
Arthur Hiller (1923)
Geraldine Page (1924)
Terry Gilliam (1940)
Tom Conti (1941)
Jamie Lee Curtis (1958)
Mariel Hemingway (1961)

**November 23**

Boris Karloff (1887)
Victor Jory (1902)
Robert Towne (1934)

**November 24**

Garson Kanin (1912)
Geraldine Fitzgerald (1914)

## November 25

Ricardo Montalban (1920)
Tracey Walter (1942)
John Larroquette (1947)

## November 26

Tina Turner (1938)

## November 27

Bruce Lee (1940)
Robin Givens (1964)

## November 28

Gloria Grahame (1925)
Michael Ritchie (1938)
Agnieszka Holland (1948)
Judd Nelson (1959)

## November 29

Busby Berkeley (1895)
Yakima Canutt (1895)
Diane Ladd (1939)
Joel Coen (1954)
Andrew McCarthy (1962)

## November 30

Richard Anthony Crenna Jr.
(1926)
David Mamet (1947)
Mandy Patinkin (1952)

## December 1

Woody Allen (1935)
Richard Pryor (1940)
Bette Midler (1945)
Treat Williams (1951)

## December 3

Sven Nykvist (1922)
Jean-Luc Godard (1930)
Taylor Hackford (1944)
Diane Kurys (1948)

## December 4

Buck Jones (1889)
Alex North (1910)
Mark Robson (1913)
Deanna Durbin (1921)
Horst Buchholz (1933)
Jeff Bridges (1949)
Marisa Tomei (1964)

## December 5

Fritz Lang (1890)

Nunnally Johnson (1897)
Walt Disney (1901)
Otto Preminger (1906)
Jeroen Krabbe (1944)

## December 6

William S. Hart (1870)
Agnes Moorehead (1906)
William Lundigan (1914)
Thomas Hulce (1953)
Janine Turner (1963)

## December 7

Fay Bainter (1891)
Eli Wallach (1915)
Ellen Burstyn (1932)
Tom Waits (1949)
C. Thomas Howell (1966)

## December 8

Georges Melies (1861)
Maximilian Schell (1930)
David Carradine (1936)
Rick Baker (1950)
Kim Basinger (1953)

## December 9

Douglas Fairbanks Jr. (1909)
Lee J. Cobb (1911)
Broderick Crawford (1911)
Kirk Douglas (1916)
John Cassavetes (1929)
Beau Bridges (1941)
John Malkovich (1953)

## December 10

Victor McLaglen (1886)
Ray Collins (1889)
Una Merkel (1903)
Dorothy Lamour (1914)
Kenneth Branagh (1960)

## December 11

Jean Marais (1913)
Marie Windsor (1922)
Jean-Louis Trintignant (1930)
Teri Garr (1944)
Susan Seidelman (1952)

## December 12

Edward G. Robinson Jr. (1893)
Frank Sinatra (1917)

## December 13

Curt Jurgens (1915)
Dick Van Dyke (1925)

Christopher Plummer (1927)
Robert J. Prosky (1930)

## December 14

Lee Remick (1935)

## December 15

Yasujiro Ozu (1903)
Tim Conway (1933)
Don Johnson (1949)
Alex Cox (1954)
Helen Slater (1963)

## December 16

Liv Ullmann (1939)

## December 17

David Butler (1894)
Arthur Kennedy (1914)

## December 18

Gladys Cooper (1888)
George Stevens Sr. (1904)
Jules Dassin (1911)
Betty Grable (1916)
Ossie Davis (1917)
Alan Rudolph (1943)
Steven Spielberg (1947)
Gillian Armstrong (1950)
Ray Liotta (1955)
Brad Pitt (1963)

## December 19

Ralph Richardson (1902)
Cicely Tyson (1933)
Jennifer Beals (1963)
Alyssa Milano (1972)

## December 20

Irene Dunne (1904)
George Roy Hill (1922)

## December 21

John G. Avildsen (1935)
Jane Fonda (1937)

# CAPRICORN

## December 22

Peggy Ashcroft (1907)
Hector Elizondo (1936)
Ralph Fiennes (1962)

## December 23

Eric Blore (1887)
John Cromwell (1888)
Peter Medak (1937)
Frederic Forrest (1938)
Corey Haim (1972)

## December 24

Michael Curtiz (1888)
Ruth Chatterton (1893)
Franz Waxman (1906)
Ava Gardner (1922)
Nicholas Meyer (1945)

## December 25

Barton MacLane (1902)
Dick Miller (1928)
Ismail Merchant (1936)
Sissy Spacek (1949)

## December 26

Elisha Cook Jr. (1906)
Richard Widmark (1914)
Fred Schepisi (1936)

## December 27

Sydney Greenstreet (1879)
Marlene Dietrich (1904)
Gerard Depardieu (1948)

## December 28

F.W. Murnau (1888)
Lew Ayres (1908)
Maggie Smith (1934)
Denzel Washington (1954)

## December 29

George E. Marshall (1891)
Viveca Lindfors (1920)
Mary Tyler Moore (1937)
Barbara Steele (1938)
Jon Voight (1938)
Ted Danson (1947)
Tracey Ullman (1959)

## December 30

Carol Reed (1906)

## December 31

Nino Rota (1911)
Anthony Hopkins (1937)
Ben Kingsley (1943)
Tim Matheson (1947)
James Remar (1953)
Val Kilmer (1959)

**January 1**

Charles Bickford (1889)
Dana Andrews (1909)
Frederick Wiseman (1930)
Frank Langella (1940)
Joanna Pacula (1957)

**January 3**

George Brackett Seitz (1888)
Marion Davies (1897)
Dorothy Arzner (1900)
ZaSu Pitts (1900)
Ray Milland (1908)
John Sturges (1910)
Robert Loggia (1930)
Dabney Coleman (1932)
Mel Gibson (1956)

**January 4**

William Bendix (1906)
Jane Wyman (1914)
Dyan Cannon (1939)
Ann Magnuson (1956)

**January 5**

Jean-Pierre Aumont (1909)
Diane Keaton (1946)

**January 6**

Tom Mix (1880)
Loretta Young (1913)
John Singleton (1968)

**January 7**

Vincent Gardenia (1922)
Terry Moore (1929)
Nicolas Cage (1964)

**January 8**

Jose Luis Ferrer (1912)
Yvette Mimieux (1939)
David Bowie (1947)

**January 9**

Herbert Lom (1917)
Lee Van Cleef (1925)
Susannah York (1941)

**January 10**

Ray Bolger (1904)
Sal Mineo (1939)
Walter Hill (1942)

**January 11**

Lionel Stander (1908)

Rod Taylor (1930)
Alfonso Arau (1932)

**January 12**

Tex Ritter (1905)
Wayne Wang (1949)
Kirstie Alley (1955)

**January 13**

Robert Stack (1919)
Penelope Ann Miller (1964)

**January 14**

Hal Roach (1892)
Bebe Daniels (1901)
Joseph Losey (1909)
Faye Dunaway (1941)
Lawrence Kasdan (1949)

**January 15**

Rex Ingram (1893)
Lloyd Bridges (1913)
Margaret O'Brien (1937)
Mario Van Peebles (1957)

**January 16**

Alexander Knox (1907)
Ethel Merman (1909)
John Carpenter (1948)

**January 17**

Mack Sennett (1884)
James Earl Jones (1931)
Sheree North (1933)
Jim Carrey (1962)

**January 18**

Oliver Hardy (1892)
Cary Grant (1904)
Danny Kaye (1913)
John Boorman (1933)
Kevin Costner (1955)

**January 19**

Richard Lester (1932)
Dolly Parton (1946)

**January 20**

George Burns (1896)
Federico Fellini (1920)
Patricia Neal (1926)
David Lynch (1946)

# AQUARIUS

**January 21**

J. Carrol Naish (1897)
Paul Scofield (1922)
Telly Savalas (1925)
Robby Benson (1956)
Geena Davis (1957)

**January 22**

D.W. Griffith (1875)
Conrad Veidt (1893)
Ann Sothern (1912)
John Hurt (1940)
Jim Jarmusch (1954)
Linda Blair (1959)
Diane Lane (1965)

**January 23**

Raymond Griffith (1890)
Franklin Pangborn (1893)
Humphrey Bogart (1899)
Randolph Scott (1903)
Bob Steele (1906)
Ernie Kovacs (1919)
Sergio Leone (1921)
Jeanne Moreau (1928)
Rutger Hauer (1944)

**January 24**

Ernest Borgnine (1917)
Nastassja Kinski (1959)

**January 25**

Mildred Dunnock (1900)
John Belushi (1949)

**January 26**

Paul Newman (1925)
Roger Vadim (1928)
Scott Glenn (1942)
Henry Jaglom (1943)

**January 27**

Jerome Kern (1885)
Joyce Compton (1907)
Donna Reed (1921)
Mikhail Baryshnikov (1948)
Mimi Rogers (1956)
Bridget Fonda (1964)

**January 28**

Ernst Lubitsch (1892)
Alan Alda (1936)
Elijah Wood (1981)

**January 29**

W.C. Fields (1880)
Victor Mature (1915)
Paddy Chayefsky (1923)
Katharine Ross (1942)
Tom Selleck (1945)

**January 30**

Gene Hackman (1931)
Vanessa Redgrave (1937)

**January 31**

Eddie Cantor (1892)
Tallulah Bankhead (1902)
Mario Lanza (1921)
Jean Simmons (1929)
Derek Jarman (1942)
Phil Collins (1951)

**February 1**

John A. Ford (1895)
Clark Gable (1901)
George Pal (1908)
Stuart Whitman (1928)
Sherilyn Fenn (1965)

**February 2**

Frank Lloyd (1888)
Farrah Fawcett (1947)

**February 3**

Carl Theodor Dreyer (1889)
James Bridges (1936)
Blythe Danner (1944)

**February 4**

Nigel Bruce (1895)
Sergei Mikhailovich Eisenstein
  (1898)
Ida Lupino (1918)
George A. Romero (1940)

**February 5**

John Carradine (1906)
Tim Holt (1918)
Red Buttons (1919)
Michael Mann (1943)
Barbara Hershey (1948)
Jennifer Jason Leigh (1962)

**February 6**

Ronald Reagan (1911)
Rip Torn (1931)
Francois Truffaut (1932)

Mamie Van Doren (1933)
Robert Townsend (1957)

## February 7

Larry "Buster" Crabbe (1908)
Eddie Bracken (1920)
James Spader (1960)

## February 8

Edith Evans (1888)
Charles Ruggles (1888)
King Vidor (1894)
Betty Field (1918)
Lana Turner (1921)
Jack Lemmon (1925)
James Dean (1931)
Nick Nolte (1941)
Robert Klein (1942)
Mary Steenburgen (1953)

## February 9

Brian Donlevy (1889)
Ronald Colman (1891)
Carmen Miranda (1909)
Joe Pesci (1943)
Mia Farrow (1945)

## February 10

Alan Hale Sr. (1892)
Jimmy Durante (1893)
Judith Anderson (1898)
Lon Chaney Jr. (1906)
Jerry Goldsmith (1929)
Michael Apted (1941)
Laura Dern (1966)

## February 11

Joseph Leo Mankiewicz (1909)
Leslie Nielsen (1926)
Burt Reynolds (1936)

## February 12

Wallace Ford (1898)
Forrest Tucker (1919)
Franco Zeffirelli (1923)
Constantin Costa-Gavras (1933)

## February 13

Kim Novak (1933)
Oliver Reed (1938)
Stockard Channing (1944)

## February 14

John Barrymore (1882)
Jack Benny (1894)

Stuart Erwin (1902)
Thelma Ritter (1905)
Alan Parker (1944)
Gregory Hines (1946)
Meg Tilly (1960)
Molly Ringwald (1969)

## February 15

Gale Sondergaard (1899)
Cesar Romero (1907)
Claire Bloom (1931)
Jane Seymour (1951)

## February 16

Robert J. Flaherty (1884)
Albert Hackett (1900)
John Schlesinger (1926)

## February 17

Marc Lawrence (1910)
Hal Holbrook (1925)

## February 18

Edward Arnold (1890)
Adolphe Menjou (1890)
Jack Palance (1920)
George Kennedy (1925)
Milos Forman (1932)
John J. Hughes (1950)
Cybill Shepherd (1950)
John Travolta (1954)
Matt Dillon (1964)

## February 19

Cedric Hardwicke (1883)
William Augustus Wellman (1896)
Merle Oberon (1911)
Lee Marvin (1924)
John Frankenheimer (1930)
Alan Bates (1934)
Jeff Daniels (1955)

# PISCES

## February 20

Robert Altman (1925)
Sidney Poitier (1927)

## February 21

Ann Sheridan (1915)
Sam Peckinpah (1925)
Bob Rafelson (1933)

## February 22

Luis Bunuel (1900)
Robert Young (1907)
John Mills (1908)
Giulietta Masina (1921)
Jonathan Demme (1944)
Miou-Miou (1950)
Julie Walters (1950)
Kyle MacLachlan (1959)
Drew Barrymore (1975)

## February 23

Victor Fleming (1883)
Peter Fonda (1939)

## February 24

Marjorie Main (1890)
Helen Shaver (1952)
Billy Zane (1966)

## February 25

Jim Backus (1913)
Tom Courtenay (1937)
Neil Jordan (1950)

## February 26

William Frawley (1887)
Jean Negulesco (1900)
Madeleine Carroll (1906)
Jackie C. Gleason (1916)
Tony Randall (1920)
Betty Hutton (1921)

## February 27

William Demarest (1892)
Reginald Gardiner (1903)
Franchot Tone (1905)
Joan Sterndale Bennett (1910)
Joanne Woodward (1930)
Elizabeth Taylor (1932)

## February 28

Vincente Minnelli (1910)
Zero Mostel (1915)
Charles Durning (1923)
Michael Figgis (1948)
Bernadette Peters (1948)
John Turturro (1957)
Robert Sean Leonard (1969)

## March 1

Lionel Atwill (1885)
David Niven (1910)
Ronald Howard (1954)

## March 2

Martin Ritt (1920)

## March 3

Jean Harlow (1911)
George T. Miller (1945)

## March 4

John David Garfield (1913)
Catherine O'Hara (1954)

## March 5

Henry Daniell (1894)
Rex Harrison (1908)
Pier Paolo Pasolini (1922)
Dean Stockwell (1936)

## March 6

Guy Kibbee (1882)
Andrzej Wajda (1926)
Rob Reiner (1945)

## March 7

Anna Magnani (1908)
John Heard (1946)

## March 8

Claire Trevor (1909)
Cyd Charisse (1922)
Elvis Presley (1935)
Lynn Redgrave (1943)
Aidan Quinn (1959)

## March 9

Linda Fiorentino (1960)

## March 11

Raoul A. Walsh (1887)
Jerry Zucker (1950)

## March 12

Gordon MacRae (1921)
Georges Delerue (1925)
Liza Minnelli (1946)

## March 13

Henry Hathaway (1898)
Paul Fix (1901)
Glenne Headly (1955)

## March 14

Michael Caine (1933)
Billy Crystal (1947)

## March 15

George Brent (1904)

## March 16

Conrad Nagel (1897)
Jerry Lewis (1926)
Bernardo Bertolucci (1940)
Kate Nelligan (1951)
Isabelle Huppert (1955)

## March 17

Mercedes McCambridge (1918)
Kurt Russell (1951)
Lesley-Anne Down (1954)
Robert Lowe (1964)

## March 18

Edward Everett Horton (1886)

Robert Donat (1905)
Brad Dourif (1950)
Luc Besson (1959)

## March 19

Louis Hayward (1909)
Glenn Close (1947)
Bruce Willis (1955)

## March 20

Edmund Goulding (1891)
Edgar Buchanan (1903)
Michael Redgrave (1908)
Carl Reiner (1922)
William Hurt (1950)
Spike Lee (1956)
Theresa Russell (1957)
Holly Hunter (1958)